THIRD EDITION

Active Directory Cookbook™

Laura E. Hunter and Robbie Allen

O'REILLY®

Beijing · Cambridge · Farnham · Köln · Sebastopol · Taipei · Tokyo

Active Directory Cookbook[TM]**, Third Edition**
by Laura E. Hunter and Robbie Allen

Copyright © 2009 O'Reilly Media. All rights reserved.
Printed in the United States of America.

Published by O'Reilly Media, Inc., 1005 Gravenstein Highway North, Sebastopol, CA 95472.

O'Reilly books may be purchased for educational, business, or sales promotional use. Online editions are also available for most titles (*http://safari.oreilly.com*). For more information, contact our corporate/institutional sales department: (800) 998-9938 or *corporate@oreilly.com*.

Editors: John Osborn and Laurel R.T. Ruma	**Indexer:** Ellen Troutman Zaig
Production Editor: Loranah Dimant	**Cover Designer:** Karen Montgomery
Copyeditor: Colleen Gorman	**Interior Designer:** David Futato
Proofreader: Sada Preisch	**Illustrator:** Jessamyn Read

Printing History:

September 2003:	First Edition.
June 2006:	Second Edition.
December 2008:	Third Edition.

ISBN: 978-0-596-52110-3

[M]

1228942399

Table of Contents

Preface xvii

1. **Getting Started** 1
   1.1 Approach to the Book   1
   1.2 Where to Find the Tools   3
   1.3 Getting Familiar with LDIF   5
   1.4 Programming Notes   7
   1.5 Replaceable Text   10
   1.6 Where to Find More Information   11

2. **Forests, Domains, and Trusts** 15
   2.1 Creating a Forest   21
   2.2 Removing a Forest   22
   2.3 Creating a Domain   24
   2.4 Removing a Domain   25
   2.5 Removing an Orphaned Domain   27
   2.6 Finding the Domains in a Forest   28
   2.7 Finding the NetBIOS Name of a Domain   30
   2.8 Renaming a Domain   32
   2.9 Raising the Domain Mode to Windows 2000 Native Mode   33
   2.10 Viewing and Raising the Functional Level of a Windows Server 2003 or 2008 Domain   36
   2.11 Raising the Functional Level of a Windows Server 2003 or 2008 Forest   39
   2.12 Using AdPrep to Prepare a Domain or Forest for Windows Server 2003 or 2008   42
   2.13 Determining Whether AdPrep Has Completed   44
   2.14 Checking If a Windows Domain Controller Can Be Upgraded to Windows Server 2003 or 2008   47
   2.15 Creating an External Trust   48
   2.16 Creating a Transitive Trust Between Two AD Forests   50
   2.17 Creating a Shortcut Trust Between Two AD Domains   52

    2.18 Creating a Trust to a Kerberos Realm   53
    2.19 Viewing the Trusts for a Domain   55
    2.20 Verifying a Trust   58
    2.21 Resetting a Trust   60
    2.22 Removing a Trust   62
    2.23 Enabling SID Filtering for a Trust   64
    2.24 Enabling Quarantine for a Trust   66
    2.25 Managing Selective Authentication for a Trust   66
    2.26 Finding Duplicate SIDs in a Domain   69
    2.27 Adding Additional Fields to Active Directory Users and Computers   70

3. Domain Controllers, Global Catalogs, and FSMOs **73**
    3.1 Promoting a Domain Controller   76
    3.2 Promoting a Read-Only Domain Controller   77
    3.3 Performing a Two-Stage RODC Installation   78
    3.4 Modifying the Password Replication Policy   80
    3.5 Promoting a Windows Server 2003 Domain Controller from Media   82
    3.6 Promoting a Windows Server 2008 Domain Controller from Media   84
    3.7 Demoting a Domain Controller   86
    3.8 Automating the Promotion or Demotion of a Domain Controller   87
    3.9 Troubleshooting Domain Controller Promotion or Demotion Problems   88
    3.10 Verifying the Promotion of a Domain Controller   89
    3.11 Removing an Unsuccessfully Demoted Domain Controller   90
    3.12 Renaming a Domain Controller   93
    3.13 Finding the Domain Controllers for a Domain   95
    3.14 Finding the Closest Domain Controller   96
    3.15 Finding a Domain Controller's Site   98
    3.16 Moving a Domain Controller to a Different Site   101
    3.17 Finding the Services a Domain Controller Is Advertising   104
    3.18 Restoring a Deleted Domain Controller   105
    3.19 Resetting the TCP/IP Stack on a Domain Controller   106
    3.20 Configuring a Domain Controller to Use an External Time Source   107
    3.21 Finding the Number of Logon Attempts Made Against a Domain Controller   110
    3.22 Enabling the /3GB Switch to Increase the LSASS Cache   110
    3.23 Cleaning Up Distributed Link Tracking Objects   112
    3.24 Enabling and Disabling the Global Catalog   113
    3.25 Determining Whether Global Catalog Promotion Is Complete   115
    3.26 Finding the Global Catalog Servers in a Forest   117
    3.27 Finding the Domain Controllers or Global Catalog Servers in a Site   119

3.28   Finding Domain Controllers and Global Catalogs via DNS   121

3.29   Changing the Preference for a Domain Controller   122

3.30   Disabling the Global Catalog Requirement During
a Domain Login   124

3.31   Disabling the Global Catalog Requirement for Windows Server
2003 or Windows Server 2008   125

3.32   Finding the FSMO Role Holders   126

3.33   Transferring a FSMO Role   129

3.34   Seizing a FSMO Role   131

3.35   Finding the PDC Emulator FSMO Role Owner via DNS   132

3.36   Finding the PDC Emulator FSMO Role Owner via WINS   133

4.   Searching and Manipulating Objects **135**

4.1   Viewing the RootDSE   136

4.2   Viewing the Attributes of an Object   140

4.3   Counting Objects in Active Directory   145

4.4   Using LDAP Controls   147

4.5   Using a Fast or Concurrent Bind   150

4.6   Connecting to an Object GUID   152

4.7   Connecting to a Well-Known GUID   153

4.8   Searching for Objects in a Domain   155

4.9   Searching the Global Catalog   158

4.10   Searching for a Large Number of Objects   161

4.11   Searching with an Attribute-Scoped Query   164

4.12   Searching with a Bitwise Filter   166

4.13   Creating an Object   170

4.14   Modifying an Object   173

4.15   Modifying a Bit Flag Attribute   177

4.16   Dynamically Linking an Auxiliary Class   180

4.17   Creating a Dynamic Object   182

4.18   Refreshing a Dynamic Object   184

4.19   Modifying the Default TTL Settings for Dynamic Objects   186

4.20   Moving an Object to a Different OU or Container   188

4.21   Moving an Object to a Different Domain   191

4.22   Referencing an External Domain   193

4.23   Renaming an Object   195

4.24   Deleting an Object   197

4.25   Deleting a Container That Has Child Objects   200

4.26   Viewing the Created and Last Modified Timestamp of an Object   202

4.27   Modifying the Default LDAP Query Policy   203

4.28   Exporting Objects to an LDIF File   206

4.29   Importing Objects Using an LDIF File   207

4.30   Exporting Objects to a CSV File   208

    4.31 Importing Objects Using a CSV File   209

5. Organizational Units **211**
    5.1 Creating an OU   212
    5.2 Enumerating the OUs in a Domain   214
    5.3 Finding an OU   216
    5.4 Enumerating the Objects in an OU   218
    5.5 Deleting the Objects in an OU   221
    5.6 Deleting an OU   222
    5.7 Moving the Objects in an OU to a Different OU   223
    5.8 Moving an OU   226
    5.9 Renaming an OU   227
    5.10 Modifying an OU   229
    5.11 Determining Approximately How Many Child Objects
           an OU Has   231
    5.12 Delegating Control of an OU   233
    5.13 Assigning or Removing a Manager for an OU   234
    5.14 Linking a GPO to an OU   235
    5.15 Protecting an OU Against Accidental Deletion   238

6. Users **241**
    6.1 Modifying the Default Display Name Used When Creating Users
         in ADUC   244
    6.2 Creating a User   245
    6.3 Creating a Large Number of Users   248
    6.4 Creating an inetOrgPerson User   250
    6.5 Converting a user Object to an inetOrgPerson Object
         (or Vice Versa)   253
    6.6 Modifying an Attribute for Several Users at Once   255
    6.7 Deleting a User   256
    6.8 Setting a User's Profile Attributes   258
    6.9 Moving a User   260
    6.10 Redirecting Users to an Alternative OU   261
    6.11 Renaming a User   263
    6.12 Copying a User   265
    6.13 Finding Locked-Out Users   267
    6.14 Unlocking a User   268
    6.15 Troubleshooting Account Lockout Problems   270
    6.16 Viewing the Domain-Wide Account Lockout and Password Policies 271
    6.17 Applying a Fine-Grained Password Policy to a User Object   275
    6.18 Viewing the Fine-Grained Password Policy That Is in Effect for a
         User Account   276
    6.19 Enabling and Disabling a User   278

6.20 Finding Disabled Users   279
6.21 Viewing a User's Group Membership   281
6.22 Removing All Group Memberships from a User   284
6.23 Changing a User's Primary Group   285
6.24 Copying a User's Group Membership to Another User   287
6.25 Setting a User's Password   290
6.26 Preventing a User from Changing a Password   291
6.27 Requiring a User to Change a Password at Next Logon   293
6.28 Preventing a User's Password from Expiring   294
6.29 Finding Users Whose Passwords Are About to Expire   296
6.30 Viewing the RODCs That Have Cached a User's Password   297
6.31 Setting a User's Account Options (userAccountControl)   299
6.32 Setting a User's Account to Expire   302
6.33 Determining a User's Last Logon Time   303
6.34 Finding Users Who Have Not Logged On Recently   306
6.35 Viewing and Modifying a User's Permitted Logon Hours   307
6.36 Viewing a User's Managed Objects   309
6.37 Creating a UPN Suffix for a Forest   311
6.38 Restoring a Deleted User   312
6.39 Protecting a User Against Accidental Deletion   313

7. Groups 315
7.1   Creating a Group   316
7.2   Viewing the Permissions of a Group   319
7.3   Viewing the Direct Members of a Group   322
7.4   Viewing the Nested Members of a Group   324
7.5   Adding and Removing Members of a Group   326
7.6   Moving a Group Within a Domain   328
7.7   Moving a Group to Another Domain   330
7.8   Changing the Scope or Type of a Group   332
7.9   Modifying Group Attributes   334
7.10 Creating a Dynamic Group   337
7.11 Delegating Control for Managing Membership of a Group   339
7.12 Resolving a Primary Group ID   342
7.13 Enabling Universal Group Membership Caching   344
7.14 Restoring a Deleted Group   347
7.15 Protecting a Group Against Accidental Deletion   348
7.16 Applying a Fine-Grained Password Policy to a Group Object   349

8. Computer Objects 351
8.1   The Anatomy of a computer Object   351
8.2   Creating a Computer   352
8.3   Creating a Computer for a Specific User or Group   354

8.4   Deleting a Computer   360

8.5   Joining a Computer to a Domain   361

8.6   Moving a Computer Within the Same Domain   364

8.7   Moving a Computer to a New Domain   365

8.8   Renaming a Computer   367

8.9   Adding or Removing a Computer Account from a Group   370

8.10 Testing the Secure Channel for a Computer   371

8.11 Resetting a Computer Account   372

8.12 Finding Inactive or Unused Computers   374

8.13 Changing the Maximum Number of Computers a User Can Join to the Domain   375

8.14 Modifying the Attributes of a computer Object   377

8.15 Finding Computers with a Particular OS   379

8.16 Binding to the Default Container for Computers   382

8.17 Changing the Default Container for Computers   385

8.18 Listing All the Computer Accounts in a Domain   387

8.19 Identifying a Computer Role   388

8.20 Protecting a Computer Against Accidental Deletion   390

8.21 Viewing the RODCs That Have Cached a Computer's Password   391

9.   Group Policy Objects **393**

9.1   Finding the GPOs in a Domain   396

9.2   Creating a GPO   397

9.3   Copying a GPO   399

9.4   Deleting a GPO   402

9.5   Viewing the Settings of a GPO   403

9.6   Modifying the Settings of a GPO   406

9.7   Importing Settings into a GPO   407

9.8   Creating a Migration Table   410

9.9   Creating Custom Group Policy Settings   412

9.10 Assigning Logon/Logoff and Startup/Shutdown Scripts in a GPO   415

9.11 Installing Applications with a GPO   416

9.12 Disabling the User or Computer Settings in a GPO   417

9.13 Listing the Links for a GPO   419

9.14 Creating a GPO Link to an OU   422

9.15 Blocking Inheritance of GPOs on an OU   424

9.16 Enforcing the Settings of a GPO Link   426

9.17 Applying a Security Filter to a GPO   428

9.18 Delegating Administration of GPOs   431

9.19 Importing a Security Template   433

9.20 Creating a WMI Filter   434

9.21 Applying a WMI Filter to a GPO   436

9.22 Configuring Loopback Processing for a GPO   438

9.23 Backing Up a GPO 439
9.24 Restoring a GPO 442
9.25 Simulating the RSoP 445
9.26 Viewing the RSoP 446
9.27 Refreshing GPO Settings on a Computer 447
9.28 Restoring a Default GPO 448
9.29 Creating a Fine-Grained Password Policy 449
9.30 Editing a Fine-Grained Password Policy 452
9.31 Viewing the Effective PSO for a User 454

10. Schema **457**
10.1 Registering the Active Directory Schema MMC Snap-in 459
10.2 Enabling Schema Updates 460
10.3 Generating an OID to Use for a New Class or Attribute 462
10.4 Extending the Schema 463
10.5 Preparing the Schema for an Active Directory Upgrade 464
10.6 Documenting Schema Extensions 465
10.7 Adding a New Attribute 466
10.8 Viewing an Attribute 470
10.9 Adding a New Class 473
10.10 Viewing a Class 475
10.11 Indexing an Attribute 476
10.12 Modifying the Attributes That Are Copied When Duplicating a User 479
10.13 Adding Custom Information to ADUC 481
10.14 Modifying the Attributes Included with ANR 483
10.15 Modifying the Set of Attributes Stored on a Global Catalog 486
10.16 Finding Nonreplicated and Constructed Attributes 489
10.17 Finding the Linked Attributes 492
10.18 Finding the Structural, Auxiliary, Abstract, and 88 Classes 494
10.19 Finding the Mandatory and Optional Attributes of a Class . 497
10.20 Modifying the Default Security of a Class 499
10.21 Managing the Confidentiality Bit 501
10.22 Adding an Attribute to the Read-Only Filtered Attribute Set (RO-
       FAS) 503
10.23 Deactivating Classes and Attributes 505
10.24 Redefining Classes and Attributes 507
10.25 Reloading the Schema Cache 507
10.26 Managing the Schema Master FSMO 509

11. Site Topology **513**
11.1 Creating a Site 517
11.2 Listing Sites in a Forest 519
11.3 Renaming a Site 521

11.4 Deleting a Site   522
11.5 Delegating Control of a Site   523
11.6 Configuring Universal Group Caching for a Site   526
11.7 Creating a Subnet   528
11.8 Listing the Subnets   530
11.9 Finding Missing Subnets   531
11.10 Deleting a Subnet   534
11.11 Changing a Subnet's Site Assignment   535
11.12 Creating a Site Link   537
11.13 Finding the Site Links for a Site   539
11.14 Modifying the Sites That Are Part of a Site Link   541
11.15 Modifying the Cost for a Site Link   543
11.16 Enabling Change Notification for a Site Link   545
11.17 Modifying Replication Schedules   547
11.18 Disabling Site Link Transitivity or Site Link Schedules   549
11.19 Creating a Site Link Bridge   551
11.20 Finding the Bridgehead Servers for a Site   553
11.21 Setting a Preferred Bridgehead Server for a Site   554
11.22 Listing the Servers   556
11.23 Moving a Domain Controller to a Different Site   558
11.24 Configuring a Domain Controller to Cover Multiple Sites   560
11.25 Viewing the Site Coverage for a Domain Controller   561
11.26 Disabling Automatic Site Coverage for a Domain Controller   562
11.27 Finding the Site for a Client   563
11.28 Forcing a Host into a Particular Site   564
11.29 Creating a Connection Object   565
11.30 Listing the connection Objects for a Server   566
11.31 Load-Balancing connection Objects   568
11.32 Finding the ISTG for a Site   568
11.33 Transferring the ISTG to Another Server   570
11.34 Triggering the KCC   572
11.35 Determining Whether the KCC Is Completing Successfully   573
11.36 Disabling the KCC for a Site   574
11.37 Changing the Interval at Which the KCC Runs   577

12. Replication 579
12.1 Determining Whether Two Domain Controllers Are in Sync   579
12.2 Viewing the Replication Status of Several Domain Controllers   582
12.3 Viewing Unreplicated Changes Between Two
        Domain Controllers   583
12.4 Forcing Replication from One Domain Controller to Another   586
12.5 Enabling and Disabling Replication   588
12.6 Changing the Intra-Site Replication Interval   589

　12.7　Changing the Intra-Site Notification Delay　　590
　12.8　Changing the Inter-Site Replication Interval　　593
　12.9　Disabling Inter-Site Compression of Replication Traffic　　595
　12.10　Checking for Potential Replication Problems　　597
　12.11　Enabling Enhanced Logging of Replication Events　　597
　12.12　Enabling Strict or Loose Replication Consistency　　597
　12.13　Finding Conflict Objects　　599
　12.14　Finding Orphaned Objects　　602
　12.15　Listing the Replication Partners for a DC　　604
　12.16　Viewing Object Metadata　　605

13.　DNS and DHCP **609**
　13.1　Creating a Forward Lookup Zone　　611
　13.2　Creating a Reverse Lookup Zone　　613
　13.3　Viewing a Server's Zones　　614
　13.4　Converting a Zone to an AD-Integrated Zone　　617
　13.5　Moving AD-Integrated Zones into an Application Partition　　618
　13.6　Configuring Zone Transfers　　620
　13.7　Configuring Forwarding　　622
　13.8　Delegating Control of an Active Directory Integrated Zone　　625
　13.9　Creating and Deleting Resource Records　　627
　13.10　Querying Resource Records　　630
　13.11　Modifying the DNS Server Configuration　　631
　13.12　Scavenging Old Resource Records　　633
　13.13　Clearing the DNS Cache　　635
　13.14　Verifying That a Domain Controller Can Register Its Resource
　　　　Records　　637
　13.15　Enabling DNS Server Debug Logging　　639
　13.16　Registering a Domain Controller's Resource Records　　642
　13.17　Deregistering a Domain Controller's Resource Records　　642
　13.18　Preventing a Domain Controller from Dynamically Registering All
　　　　Resource Records　　643
　13.19　Preventing a Domain Controller from Dynamically Registering
　　　　Certain Resource Records　　645
　13.20　Allowing Computers to Use a Different Domain Suffix Than Their
　　　　AD Domain　　649
　13.21　Authorizing a DHCP Server　　651
　13.22　Locating Unauthorized DHCP Servers　　654
　13.23　Restricting DHCP Administrators　　655

14.　Security and Authentication **659**
　14.1　Enabling SSL/TLS　　660
　14.2　Encrypting LDAP Traffic with SSL, TLS, or Signing　　662

14.3 Disabling LDAP Signing or Encryption   664
14.4 Enabling Anonymous LDAP Access   665
14.5 Restricting Anonymous Access to Active Directory   667
14.6 Using the Delegation of Control Wizard   669
14.7 Customizing the Delegation of Control Wizard   671
14.8 Revoking Delegated Permissions   673
14.9 Viewing the ACL for an Object   674
14.10 Customizing the ACL Editor   676
14.11 Viewing the Effective Permissions on an Object   677
14.12 Configuring Permission Inheritance   678
14.13 Changing the ACL of an Object   680
14.14 Changing the Default ACL for an Object Class in the Schema   681
14.15 Comparing the ACL of an Object to the Default Defined in the
      Schema   682
14.16 Resetting an Object's ACL to the Default Defined
      in the Schema   683
14.17 Preventing the LM Hash of a Password from Being Stored   684
14.18 Enabling Strong Domain Authentication   685
14.19 Enabling List Object Access Mode   686
14.20 Modifying the ACL on Administrator Accounts   688
14.21 Viewing and Purging Your Kerberos Tickets   689
14.22 Forcing Kerberos to Use TCP   691
14.23 Modifying Kerberos Settings   692
14.24 Viewing Access Tokens   693

15. Logging, Monitoring, and Quotas 695
15.1 Enabling Extended dcpromo Logging   697
15.2 Enabling Diagnostics Logging   698
15.3 Enabling NetLogon Logging   700
15.4 Enabling GPO Client Logging   701
15.5 Enabling Kerberos Logging   704
15.6 Viewing DNS Server Performance Statistics   705
15.7 Monitoring the File Replication Service   708
15.8 Monitoring the Windows Time Service   709
15.9 Enabling Inefficient and Expensive LDAP Query Logging   710
15.10 Using the STATS Control to View LDAP Query Statistics   712
15.11 Monitoring the Performance of AD   715
15.12 Using Perfmon Trace Logs to Monitor AD   717
15.13 Creating an Administrative Alert   720
15.14 Emailing an Administrator on a Performance Alert   721
15.15 Enabling Auditing of Directory Access   723
15.16 Enabling Auditing of Registry Keys   726
15.17 Creating a Quota   727

15.18 Finding the Quotas Assigned to a Security Principal   729
15.19 Changing How Tombstone Objects Count Against
       Quota Usage   730
15.20 Setting the Default Quota for All Security Principals
       in a Partition   732
15.21 Finding the Quota Usage for a Security Principal   734

16. Backup, Recovery, DIT Maintenance, and Deleted Objects **737**
16.1   Backing Up Active Directory in Windows 2000 and Windows
      Server 2003   740
16.2   Backing Up Active Directory in Windows Server 2008   742
16.3   Creating an Active Directory Snapshot   742
16.4   Mounting an Active Directory Snapshot   743
16.5   Accessing Active Directory Snapshot Data   744
16.6   Restarting a Domain Controller in Directory Services Restore
      Mode   746
16.7   Resetting the Directory Service Restore Mode Administrator
      Password   747
16.8   Performing a Nonauthoritative Restore   749
16.9   Performing an Authoritative Restore of an Object or Subtree   750
16.10 Performing a Complete Authoritative Restore   752
16.11 Checking the DIT File's Integrity   753
16.12 Moving the DIT Files   754
16.13 Repairing or Recovering the DIT   755
16.14 Performing an Online Defrag Manually   757
16.15 Performing a Database Recovery   759
16.16 Creating a Reserve File   760
16.17 Determining How Much Whitespace Is in the DIT   761
16.18 Performing an Offline Defrag to Reclaim Space   762
16.19 Changing the Garbage Collection Interval   764
16.20 Logging the Number of Expired Tombstone Objects   766
16.21 Determining the Size of the Active Directory Database   767
16.22 Searching for Deleted Objects   769
16.23 Undeleting a Single Object   771
16.24 Undeleting a Container Object   773
16.25 Modifying the Tombstone Lifetime for a Domain   774

17. Application Partitions **777**
17.1   Creating and Deleting an Application Partition   779
17.2   Finding the Application Partitions in a Forest   780
17.3   Adding or Removing a Replica Server for an Application Partition 782
17.4   Finding the Replica Servers for an Application Partition   786
17.5   Finding the Application Partitions Hosted by a Server   787

17.6   Verifying Application Partitions Are Instantiated
      on a Server Correctly   790

17.7   Setting the Replication Notification Delay for an Application
      Partition   792

17.8   Setting the Reference Domain for an Application Partition   794

17.9   Delegating Control of Managing an Application Partition   796

**18.   Active Directory Application Mode and Active Directory Lightweight Directory
Service** **801**

18.1   Installing ADAM/AD LDS   803

18.2   Creating a New ADAM/AD LDS Instance   804

18.3   Creating a New Replica of an ADAM/AD LDS
      Configuration Set   806

18.4   Stopping and Starting an ADAM/AD LDS Instance   808

18.5   Changing the Ports Used by an ADAM/AD LDS Instance   810

18.6   Listing the ADAM Instances Installed on a Computer   810

18.7   Extending the ADAM/AD LDS Schema   812

18.8   Managing ADAM/AD LDS Application Partitions   813

18.9   Managing ADAM/AD LDS Organizational Units   815

18.10   Managing ADAM Users   817

18.11   Changing the Password for an ADAM or AD LDS User   819

18.12   Enabling and Disabling an ADAM User   821

18.13   Creating ADAM or AD LDS Groups   823

18.14   Managing ADAM or AD LDS Group Memberships   825

18.15   Viewing and Modifying ADAM Object Attributes   827

18.16   Importing Data into an ADAM or AD LDS Instance   829

18.17   Configuring Intra-site Replication   831

18.18   Forcing ADAM/AD LDS Replication   831

18.19   Managing AD LDS Replication Authentication   832

18.20   Managing ADAM/AD LDS Permissions   834

18.21   Enabling Auditing of AD LDS Access   836

19.   Active Directory Federation Services **839**

19.1   Installing AD FS Prerequisites for Windows Server 2003 R2   840

19.2   Installing AD FS Prerequisites for Windows Server 2008   842

19.3   Installing the Federation Service in Windows Server 2003 R2   844

19.4   Installing the Federation Service on Windows Server 2008   846

19.5   Configuring an Active Directory Account Store   847

19.6   Configuring an ADAM or AD LDS Account Store   848

19.7   Creating Organizational Claims   849

19.8   Creating an Account Partner   851

19.9   Configuring a Resource Partner   853

19.10   Configuring an Application   854

19.11 Configuring a Forest Trust   856
19.12 Configuring an Alternate UPN Suffix   857
19.13 Configuring the AD FS Web Agent   859
19.14 Enabling Logging for the AD FS Web Agent   861

20. **Microsoft Exchange Server 2007 and Exchange Server 2003** 863
20.1   Exchange Server and Active Directory   863
20.2   Exchange Server 2007 Architecture   864
20.3   Exchange Administration Tools   864
20.4   Preparing Active Directory for Exchange   868
20.5   Installing the First Exchange Server in an Organization   873
20.6   Creating Unattended Installation Files for Exchange Server   879
20.7   Installing Exchange Management Tools   881
20.8   Stopping and Starting Exchange Server   884
20.9   Mail-Enabling a User   888
20.10 Mail-Disabling a User   894
20.11 Mailbox-Enabling a User   898
20.12 Deleting a User's Mailbox   902
20.13 Moving a Mailbox   905
20.14 Viewing Mailbox Sizes and Message Counts   910
20.15 Configuring Mailbox Limits   913
20.16 Creating an Address List   917
20.17 Creating a Storage Group   921
20.18 Creating a Mailbox Store   925
20.19 Installing Anti-Spam Agents on the Hub Transport Servers   928
20.20 Enabling Message Tracking   929
20.21 Summary   933

21. **Microsoft Identity Lifecycle Manager** 935
21.1   Creating the HR Database MA   952
21.2   Creating an Active Directory MA   954
21.3   Setting Up a Metaverse Object Deletion Rule   956
21.4   Setting Up Simple Import Attribute Flow—HR Database MA   957
21.5   Setting Up a Simple Export Attribute Flow to AD   959
21.6   Defining an Advanced Import Attribute Flow—HR Database MA   960
21.7   Implementing an Advanced Attribute Flow Rules Extension—HR
       Database MA   962
21.8   Setting Up Advanced Export Attribute Flow in Active Directory   965
21.9   Configuring a Run Profile to Do an Initial Load of Data from the
       HR Database MA   967
21.10 Loading Initial HR Database Data into ILM Using
       a Run Profile   968

21.11 Configuring a Run Profile to Load the Container
      Structure from AD   969
21.12 Loading the Initial AD Container Structure into ILM Using a Run
      Profile   971
21.13 Setting Up the HR Database MA to Project Objects
      to the Metaverse   972
21.14 Writing a Rules Extension to Provision User Objects   973
21.15 Creating a Run Profile for Provisioning   976
21.16 Executing the Provisioning Rule   978
21.17 Creating a Run Profile to Export Objects from the ADMA to Active
      Directory   979
21.18 Exporting Objects to AD Using an Export Run Profile   980
21.19 Testing Provisioning and Deprovisioning of User Accounts in AD 982
21.20 Creating a Run Profile Script   984
21.21 Creating a Controlling Script   985
21.22 Enabling Directory Synchronization from AD
      to the HR Database   990
21.23 Configuring a Run Profile to Load the telephoneNumber from AD 992
21.24 Loading telephoneNumber Changes from AD into ILM Using a
      Delta Import and Delta Synchronization Run Profile   994
21.25 Exporting telephoneNumber Data to the HR Database   996
21.26 Using the HR Database MA Export Run Profile to Export the
      Telephone Number to the HR Database   997
21.27 Searching Data in the Connector Space   998
21.28 Searching Data in the Metaverse   999
21.29 Deleting Data in the Connector Space and Metaverse   1000
21.30 Extending Object Types to Include a New Attribute   1002
21.31 Previewing Changes to the ILM Configuration   1002
21.32 Committing Changes to Individual Identities Using
      the Commit Preview Feature   1005
21.33 Passing Data Between Rules Extensions Using Transaction
      Properties   1006
21.34 Using a Single Rules Extension to Affect Multiple Attribute Flows 1007
21.35 Flowing a Null Value to a Data Source   1008
21.36 Contributing a UTCCodedTime Attribute in Active Directory   1010
21.37 Importing and Decoding the accountExpires Attribute   1011
21.38 Exporting and Encoding the accountExpires Attribute   1013

Index 1017

Preface

In 1998, when Robbie first became involved with the Microsoft Windows 2000 Joint Development Program (JDP), there was very little data available on Active Directory (AD). In the following months and even after the initial release of Windows 2000, there were very few books or white papers to help early adopters of Active Directory get started. And some of the information that had been published was often inaccurate or misleading. Many early adopters had to learn by trial and error. As time passed, more and more informative books were published, which helped fill the information gap.

By the end of the second year of its release, there was an explosion of information on Active Directory. Not only were there more than 50 books published, but Microsoft also cleaned up their documentation on MSDN (*http://msdn.microsoft.com*) and their AD website (*http://www.microsoft.com/ad*). Now those sites have numerous white papers, many of which could serve as mini booklets. Other websites have popped up as well that contain a great deal of information on Active Directory. With Windows Server 2003 and Windows Server 2008, Microsoft has taken their level of documentation a step higher. Extensive information on Active Directory is available directly from any Windows Server 2003 or 2008 computer in the form of the Help and Support Center (available from the Start Menu). So with all this data available on Active Directory in the form of published books, white papers, websites, and even from within the operating system, why would you want to purchase this one?

In the summer of 2002, Robbie was thumbing through Tom Christiansen and Nathan Torkington's *Perl Cookbook* from O'Reilly, looking for help with an automation script that he was writing for Active Directory. It just so happened that there was a recipe that addressed the specific task he was trying to perform. In Cookbook parlance, a recipe provides instructions on how to solve a particular problem. We thought that since Active Directory is such a task-oriented environment, the Cookbook approach might be a very good format. After a little research, Robbie found there were books (often multiple) on nearly every facet of Active Directory, including introductory books, design guides, books that focused on migration, programming books, and reference books. The one type of book that he didn't see was a task-oriented "how to" book, which is exactly what the Cookbook format provides. With this was born the first edition of *Active Directory Cookbook*, covering Active Directory tasks in Windows 2000 and Windows Server 2003 Active Directory.

In 2005, Laura E. Hunter revised the already popular *Active Directory Cookbook* to include an updated range of automation options, including the use of command-line tools and scripts that had been created by active members of the Directory Services community in the years since AD was first introduced.

Based on our experience, hours of research, and nearly a decade of hanging out on Active Directory newsgroups and mailing lists, we've compiled more than 500 recipes that should answer the majority of "How do I do X?" questions one could pose about Active Directory. And just as in the Perl community, where the *Perl Cookbook* was a great addition that sells well even today, we believe *Active Directory Cookbook*, Third Edition, will also be a great addition to any Active Directory library.

Who Should Read This Book?

As with many of the books in the Cookbook series, *Active Directory Cookbook*, Third Edition, can be useful to anyone who wants to deploy, administer, or automate Active Directory. This book can serve as a great reference for those who have to work with Active Directory on a day-to-day basis. For those without much programming background, the command-line, VBScript, and PowerShell solutions are straightforward and provide an easy way to automate repetitive administrative tasks for any administrator.

The companion to this book, *Active Directory*, Fourth Edition, by Brian Desmond et al. (O'Reilly), is a great choice for those wanting a thorough description of the core concepts behind Active Directory, how to design an Active Directory infrastructure, and how to automate that infrastructure using Active Directory Service Interfaces (ADSI) and Windows Management Instrumentation (WMI). *Active Directory*, Fourth Edition, does not necessarily detail the steps needed to accomplish every possible task within Active Directory; that is more the intended purpose of this book. These two books, along with the supplemental information referenced within each, should be sufficient to answer most questions you have about Active Directory.

What's in This Book?

This book consists of 21 chapters. Here is a brief overview of each chapter:

Chapter 1, *Getting Started*
> Sets the stage for the book by covering where you can find the tools used in the book, VBScript and PowerShell issues to consider, and where to find additional information.

Chapter 2, *Forests, Domains, and Trusts*
> Covers how to create and remove forests and domains, update the domain mode or functional levels, create different types of trusts, and other administrative trust tasks.

Chapter 3, *Domain Controllers, Global Catalogs, and FSMOs*
> Covers promoting and demoting domain controllers, finding domain controllers, enabling the global catalog, and finding and managing Flexible Single Master Operations (FSMO) roles. This will include coverage of the new Read-Only Domain Controller (RODC) that was introduced with Windows Server 2008.

Chapter 4, *Searching and Manipulating Objects*
> Covers the basics of searching Active Directory: creating, modifying, and deleting objects, using LDAP controls, and importing and exporting data using LDAP Data Interchange Format (LDIF) and comma-separated variable (CSV) files.

Chapter 5, *Organizational Units*
> Covers creating, moving, and deleting Organizational Units, and managing the objects contained within them.

Chapter 6, *Users*
> Covers all aspects of managing user objects, including creating, renaming, moving, resetting passwords, unlocking, modifying the profile attributes, and locating users that have certain criteria (e.g., password is about to expire). This chapter includes coverage of the new Fine-Grained Password Policy feature that was introduced in Windows Server 2008.

Chapter 7, *Groups*
> Covers how to create groups, modify group scope and type, and manage membership.

Chapter 8, *Computer Objects*
> Covers creating computers, joining computers to a domain, resetting computers, and locating computers that match certain criteria (e.g., have been inactive for a number of weeks).

Chapter 9, *Group Policy Objects*
> Covers how to create, modify, link, copy, import, back up, restore, and delete GPOs using the Group Policy Management Console and scripting interface, including new Group Policy features that were introduced in Windows Server 2008.

Chapter 10, *Schema*
> Covers basic schema administration tasks, such as generating object identifiers (OIDs) and schemaIDGUIDs, how to use LDIF to extend the schema, and how to locate attributes or classes that match certain criteria (e.g., all attributes that are indexed).

Chapter 11, *Site Topology*
> Covers how to manage sites, subnets, site links, and connection objects.

Chapter 12, *Replication*

Covers how to trigger and disable the Knowledge Consistency Checker (KCC), how to query metadata, force replication, and determine what changes have yet to replicate between domain controllers.

Chapter 13, *DNS and DHCP*

Covers creating zones and resource records, modifying DNS server configuration, querying DNS, and customizing the resource records a domain controller dynamically registers.

Chapter 14, *Security and Authentication*

Covers how to delegate control, view and modify permissions, view effective permissions, and manage Kerberos tickets.

Chapter 15, *Logging, Monitoring, and Quotas*

Covers how to enable auditing, diagnostics, DNS, NetLogon, and Kerberos and GPO logging; obtain LDAP query statistics; and manage quotas.

Chapter 16, *Backup, Recovery, DIT Maintenance, and Deleted Objects*

Covers how to back up Active Directory, perform authoritative and nonauthoritative restores, check DIT file integrity, perform online and offline defrags, and search for deleted objects.

Chapter 17, *Application Partitions*

Covers creating and managing application partitions.

Chapter 18, *Active Directory Application Mode and Active Directory Lightweight Directory Service*

Covers the new Active Directory Application Mode (ADAM) functionality that's available with R2.

Chapter 19, *Active Directory Federation Services*

Covers the new Active Directory Federation Services (AD FS) that are included with Windows Server 2003 R2.

Chapter 20, *Microsoft Exchange Server 2007 and Exchange Server 2003*

Covers common administrative tasks for Exchange Server 2003.

Chapter 21, *Microsoft Identity Lifecycle Manager*

Provides an introduction to Microsoft's Identity Integration Server (MIIS), a service that can be used to synchronize multiple directories or enforce data integrity within a single or multiple stores.

Conventions Used in This Book

The following typographical conventions are used in this book:

Constant width

> Indicates classes, attributes, cmdlets, methods, objects, command-line elements, computer output, and code examples.

Constant width italic

> Indicates placeholders (for which you substitute an actual name) in examples and in registry keys.

Constant width bold

> Indicates user input.

Italic

> Introduces new terms and example URLs, commands, file extensions, filenames, directory or folder names, and UNC pathnames.

> Indicates a tip, suggestion, or general note. For example, we'll tell you if you need to use a particular version or if an operation requires certain privileges.

> Indicates a warning or caution. For example, we'll tell you if Active Directory does not behave as you'd expect or if a particular operation has a negative impact on performance.

Using Code Examples

This book is here to help you get your job done. In general, you may use the code in this book in your programs and documentation. You do not need to contact us for permission unless you're reproducing a significant portion of the code. For example, writing a program that uses several chunks of code from this book does not require permission. Selling or distributing a CD-ROM of examples from O'Reilly books *does* require permission. Answering a question by citing this book and quoting example code does not require permission. Incorporating a significant amount of example code from this book into your product's documentation *does* require permission.

We appreciate, but do not require, attribution. An attribution usually includes the title, author, publisher, and ISBN. For example: *Active Directory Cookbook*, Third Edition, by Laura E. Hunter and Robbie Allen. Copyright 2009 O'Reilly Media, Inc., 978-0-596-52110-3.

If you feel your use of code examples falls outside fair use or the permission given above, feel free to contact us at *permissions@oreilly.com*.

Safari® Books Online

When you see a Safari® Books Online icon on the cover of your favorite technology book, that means the book is available online through the O'Reilly Network Safari Bookshelf.

Safari offers a solution that's better than e-books. It's a virtual library that lets you easily search thousands of top tech books, cut and paste code samples, download chapters, and find quick answers when you need the most accurate, current information. Try it for free at *http://safari.oreilly.com*.

We'd Like Your Feedback!

We at O'Reilly have tested and verified the information in this book to the best of our ability, but mistakes and oversights do occur. Please let us know about errors you may find, as well as your suggestions for future editions, by writing to:

O'Reilly Media, Inc.
1005 Gravenstein Highway North
Sebastopol, CA 95472
800-998-9938 (in the U.S. or Canada)
707-829-0515 (international or local)
707-829-0104 (fax)

We have a web page for the book where we list errata, examples, or any additional information. You can access this page at:

http://www.oreilly.com/catalog/9780596521103

To comment or ask technical questions about this book, send email to:

bookquestions@oreilly.com

For more information about our books, conferences, software, Resource Centers, and the O'Reilly Network, see our website at:

http://www.oreilly.com

Acknowledgments

Robbie Allen, from the First Edition

The people at O'Reilly were a joy to work with. I would like to thank Robert Denn for helping me get this book off the ground. I am especially grateful for Andy Oram's insightful and thought-provoking feedback.

I was very fortunate to have an all-star group of technical reviewers. If there was ever a need to assemble a panel of the top Active Directory experts, you would be hard-pressed to find a more knowledgeable group of guys. Here they are in alphabetical order.

Rick Kingslan is a senior systems engineer and Microsoft Windows Server MVP. If you've ever posted a question to an Active Directory newsgroup or discussion forum, odds are Rick participated in the thread. His uncanny ability to provide useful feedback on just about any Active Directory problem helped ensure I covered all the angles with each recipe.

Gil Kirkpatrick is the executive vice president and CTO of NetPro (*http://www.netpro .com*). Gil is also the author of *Active Directory Programming* from MacMillan. His extensive knowledge of the underpinnings of Active Directory helped clarify several issues I did not address adequately the first time through.

Tony Murray is the maintainer of the website and mailing list, which is one of the premier Active Directory discussion forums. The myriad of questions posed to the list served as inspiration for this book. Tony's comments and suggestions throughout the book helped tremendously.

Todd Myrick has a unique perspective on Active Directory from his experience inside the government. Todd contributed several outside-the-box ideas to the book that only a creative person, such as he, could have done.

joe Richards is the creator of the *http://www.joeware.net* website, which contains many must-have Active Directory tools, such as AdFind, Unlock, and many more. joe is one of the most experienced Active Directory administrators and programmers I've met. He's had to do most of the tasks in this book at one point or another, so his contributions were significant.

Kevin Sullivan is the project manager for Enterprise Directory Management at Aelita. Kevin has as much experience with Active Directory as anyone you'll find. He is a frequent contributor to Active Directory discussion forums, and he provided numerous suggestions and clarifications throughout the book.

Last, but certainly not least, I would like to thank my wife, Janet. Her love, support, and bright smile are constant reminders of how lucky I am. Did I mention she cooks, too?!

Laura E. Hunter, from the Second Edition

Like Robbie, I find that the O'Reilly staff always manages to make the writing and reviewing process a smooth one, and this project was no exception. I'd like to thank Robbie himself for tapping me to update this wonderful book to the second edition. The original incarnation of *Active Directory Cookbook* remains one of the most well-read books on my AD bookshelf, so undertaking this project with Robbie was quite exciting.

I'd also like to thank Robbie for assembling yet another team of amazing technical reviewers, a number of whom have made a return engagement from reviewing the first edition of the book: Robert Buike, Rick Kingslan, Al Mulnick, Tony Murray, and joe Richards.

Throughout the writing and editing process, my technical reviewers have helped me, challenged me, encouraged me, kept me honest, and occasionally even made me laugh out loud (which is quite a blessing when you're plugging away at an extensive project such as this one). I can't imagine completing this project without their advice, assistance, and input.

In addition to my technical reviewers, I would like to thank Brian Puhl of Microsoft for his assistance with the AD FS chapter, Gil Kirkpatrick of NetPro and Steven Plank of Microsoft for their outstanding work on the MIIS content, and Dean Wells of MSE Technology for being a generally outstanding resource for all things Active Directory. (He's not half bad at karaoke, either.)

Finally, many thanks are due to my family for tolerating the continuous game of "Where's Laura?" during the weeks that I hid away in my office to complete this project, as well as my extended family within the Microsoft MVP program: Mark Arnold, Suzanna Moran (my running buddy from 3,000 miles away), Rafael Munoz, Sean O'Driscoll, Susan Leiter, Thomas Lee, Jimmy Andersson, Don Wells, Gary Wilson, Stuart Kwan, and Candice Pedersen.

Laura E. Hunter, from the Third Edition

I am simply thrilled to make a return engagement on the third edition of my all-time favorite book project, *Active Directory Cookbook*. A project as extensive as this one is never undertaken alone, and the staff at O'Reilly have once again stepped up to the plate to assist in every way.

Again as with the second edition, I have been blessed with fantastic technical reviewers who have made this as much a labor of love as I have: joe Richards of Hewlett-Packard and *http://www.joeware.net* fame (who has now tech-reviewed every single edition of this book), and Michael B. Smith of Smith Consulting. This book also would not have been possible without the valued contributions of Brad Turner of Ensynch for his Identity Lifecycle Manager expertise, and William Lefkowicz for his update of the Exchange chapter. Additionally, I am immensely grateful for the time and assistance of various brilliant members of the Directory Services community, including (but certainly not limited to) Dean Wells, Ulf B. Simon-Weidner, Gil Kirkpatrick, Brian Desmond, Jorge de Almeida-Pinto, Brian Puhl, Nathan Muggli, Stuart Kwan and Matt Steele. I must also particularly note the assistance of Brandon Shell, PowerShell MVP, for his unending attempts to get me to "drink the Powershell Kool-Aid" throughout my work on this latest edition of *Active Directory Cookbook*.

And as always, much thanks and love are due to my friends and family for their unflagging support (and amused tolerance) of my workaholic tendencies: in particular my mother, Carol; father, Charles; and my wonderful husband, Mark Arnold.

## CHAPTER 1

Getting Started

1.1 Approach to the Book

If you are familiar with the O'Reilly Cookbook format, which can be seen in other popular books such as the *Perl Cookbook, Java Cookbook*, and *DNS and BIND Cookbook*, then the layout of this book will be familiar to you. The book is composed of 21 chapters, each containing 10 to 30 recipes for performing a specific Active Directory task. Within each recipe are four sections: "Problem," "Solution," "Discussion," and "See Also." The "Problem" section briefly describes the task that the recipe focuses on. The "Solution" section contains step-by-step instructions on how to accomplish the task. The "Discussion" section contains detailed information about the problem or solution. The "See Also" section contains references to additional sources of information that can be useful if you still need more information after reading the discussion. The "See Also" section may reference other recipes, MS Knowledge Base (*http://support.microsoft.com*) articles, or documentation from the Microsoft Developers Network (MSDN; *http://msdn.microsoft.com*).

At Least Three Ways to Do It!

When we first began developing the content for the book, we struggled with how to capture the fact that you can do things multiple ways with Active Directory. You may be familiar with the famous computer science motto: TIMTOWTDI, or There Is More Than One Way To Do It. With Active Directory, there are often At Least Three Ways To Do It! You can perform a task with a graphical user interface (GUI), such as ADSI Edit, LDP, or the Active Directory Users and Computers snap-in; you can use a command-line interface (CLI), such as the *ds* utilities (i.e., *dsadd, dsmod, dsrm, dsquery, dsget*), *nltest, netdom*, or *ldifde*, or freeware tools such as *adfind* and *admod* from *http://www.joeware.net*; and, finally, you can perform the same task using a scripting language, such as VBScript, Perl, or PowerShell. Since people prefer different methods, and no single method is necessarily better than another, we decided to write solutions to the recipes using one of each. That means instead of just a single solution per recipe, we include up to three solutions using GUI, CLI, and programmatic examples; in some cases you'll find more than one option for a given solution, as in the case where there is more than one command-line utility to perform a particular task. However, in cases where one of the methods cannot be used or would be too difficult to use to accomplish a given recipe, only the applicable methods are covered.

 Windows Server 2008 introduces the Server Core installation option, which is a limited Windows installation footprint that includes limited GUI functionality and no local access to the .NET Framework (and, by extension, PowerShell). A Server Core computer can be configured as an Active Directory domain controller. A Server Core DC can be managed locally using command-line tools and scripting languages such as VBScript, or it can be managed remotely using GUI tools and PowerShell.

We also took this approach with the programmatic solutions; we use VBScript for the programming language, primarily because it is widely used among Windows administrators and is the most straightforward from a code perspective when using Active Directory Service Interface (ADSI) and Windows Script Host (WSH). For those familiar with other languages, such as Visual Basic, Perl, and JScript, it is very easy to convert code from VBScript.

The downside to using VBScript is that it does not have all of the facilities necessary to accomplish some complicated tasks. Therefore, we use Perl in a few recipes that require a complicated programmatic solution. For those of you who wish that all of the solutions were written with Perl instead of VBScript, you can go to *http://www.rallenhome .com/books/adcookbook2/code.html* to download the code.

A special note regarding PowerShell coverage in this text: *PowerShell* is a new command-line and scripting language introduced by Microsoft. PowerShell's claim to fame is its use of a predictable *Verb-Noun* syntax that can be leveraged regardless of the technology that it is managing: `Get-Object`, `Get-ChildItem`, `Get-Mailbox`, etc. This predictable syntax is driven by the use of *cmdlets* (pronounced "command-lets") that can be created by individuals and software vendors alike. The first Microsoft product to rely on PowerShell was Exchange 2007, which includes a rich set of cmdlets to perform Exchange management tasks. In fact, there are certain tasks in Exchange 2007 that can *only* be performed using PowerShell!

The challenge that Active Directory administrators face with PowerShell lies in the fact that, as of the release of Windows Server 2008, a set of PowerShell cmdlets has not been produced by Microsoft to support Active Directory administration tasks. AD administrators still have the ability to leverage PowerShell in other ways, most notably through the use of cmdlets that have been created by third-party vendors or members of the Directory Services community. Many of these third-party cmdlets are freely available for download from the Internet; as we reference these third-party cmdlets throughout the text, we will also reference their source. The downside is that, since these cmdlets are provided by third-party vendors or individual contributors, there are currently significant "gaps" in what can be done with these cmdlets.

If you are familiar with .NET programming, it is possible to use PowerShell to interface with Active Directory by using native .NET classes and methods, such as the `DirectoryEntry` and `DirectorySearcher` classes within `System.DirectoryServices`. We have chosen to focus on tasks in this book that can be accomplished relatively easily using these native .NET classes and methods; readers who are looking for more in-depth coverage of these topics should consult *The .NET Developer's Guide to Directory Services Programming* referenced in the Recipe 1.6 section at the end of this chapter. PowerShell can also access the Active Directory Scripting Interface (ADSI) in a similar manner to VBScript; in these cases, PowerShell syntax will largely resemble the VBScript syntax to perform the same task. Additionally, you will find several references to third-party PowerShell cmdlets such as those released by Quest (*http://www.quest .com*) and SDM Software (*http://www.sdmsoftware.com*).

Windows 2000, Windows Server 2003, R2, and Windows Server 2008

Another challenge with writing this book is that there are now multiple versions of Active Directory deployed on most corporate networks. The initial version released with Windows 2000 was followed by Windows Server 2003 and an incremental update to Windows Server 2003 R2, and recently Microsoft released Windows Server 2008, which provides a lot of updates and new features. We've decided to go with the approach of making everything work under the most recent version of Active Directory first, and earlier versions of Windows second. In fact, the majority of the solutions will work unchanged with Windows 2000, 2003, and R2. For the recipes or solutions that are specific to a particular version, we include a note mentioning the version it is targeted for. In particular, since the Windows 2000 operating system is nearing the end of its supported lifecycle, the majority of our focus will be on Windows Server 2003 and later. Most GUI and programmatic solutions will work unchanged with all three versions, but Microsoft introduced several new CLIs with Windows Server 2003 and R2, most of which cannot be run on the Windows 2000 operating system. Typically, you can still use these newer tools on a Windows XP or later computer to manage Windows 2000 Active Directory.

1.2 Where to Find the Tools

For the GUI and CLI solutions to mean much to you, you need access to the tools that are used in the examples. The Windows 2000 Server Resource Kit and Windows Server 2003 Resource Kit are invaluable sources of information, along with providing numerous tools that aid administrators in daily tasks. More information on the Resource Kits can be found at *http://technet.microsoft.com/en-us/windowsserver/bb633748.aspx*. The Windows 2000 Support Tools package, which in Windows Server 2003 is called the Windows Support Tools package, contains many essential tools for people that work with Active Directory. The Microsoft installer (MSI) for the Windows Support Tools can be found on a Windows 2000 Server, Windows Server 2003, or Windows Server 2003 R2 CD in the *\support\tools* directory. You can also use the Tool Finder feature available on the ActiveDir website, located at *http://www.activedir.org/TF/Default .aspx*. In Windows Server 2008, the notion of Resource Kit and Support Tool utilities has been abandoned in favor of including only fully supported utilities packaged with the Active Directory binaries. Almost all of the Support Tools from Windows Server 2003 are included within the Windows Server 2008 standard distribution.

You'll also find a number of references to third-party command-line tools such as *adfind, admod, oldcmp, findexpacc*, and *memberof*. These tools were developed by Microsoft Directory Services MVP joe Richards, and he has made them available for free download from his website at *http://www.joeware.net/freetools*. While these tools are not native to the Windows operating system, they have become an invaluable addition to many Active Directory system administrators' toolkits, and we include them here to showcase their capabilities.

Once you have the tools at your disposal, there are a couple other issues to be aware of while trying to apply the solutions in your environment, which we'll now describe.

Running Tools with Alternate Credentials

A best practice for managing Active Directory is to create separate administrator accounts that you grant elevated privileges, instead of letting administrators use their normal user account that they use to access other Network Operating System (NOS) resources. This is beneficial because an administrator who wants to use elevated privileges has to log on with his administrative account explicitly instead of having the rights implicitly, which could lead to accidental changes in Active Directory. Assuming you employ this method, then you must provide alternate credentials when using tools to administer Active Directory unless you log on to a machine, such as a domain controller, with the administrative credentials.

There are several options for specifying alternate credentials. Many GUI and CLI tools have an option to specify a user and password to authenticate with. If the tool you want to use does not have that option, you can use the runas command instead. The following command would run the enumprop command from the Resource Kit under the credentials of the administrator account in the *adatum.com* domain:

```
> runas /user:administrator@adatum.com
/netonly "enumprop "LDAP://dc1/dc=adatum,dc=com""
```

You can also open up a Windows command prompt using alternate credentials, which will allow you to run commands using these elevated credentials until you close the command prompt window. To open a command prompt using the runas command, simply type runas /user:administrator@adatum.com cmd.

To run a Microsoft Management Console (MMC) console with alternate credentials, simply use mmc as the command to run from runas:

```
> runas /user:administrator@adatum.com /netonly "mmc"
```

This will create an empty MMC console from which you can add consoles for any snap-ins that have been installed on the local computer.

 The /netonly switch is necessary if the user you are authenticating with does not have local logon rights on the machine you are running the command from, such as a user ID from a nontrusted domain.

There is another option for running MMC snap-ins with alternate credentials. Click on the Start menu and browse to the tool you want to open, hold down the Shift key, and then right-click on the tool. If you select Run As, you will be prompted to enter credentials to run the tool under.

Targeting Specific Domain Controllers

Another issue to be aware of when following the instructions in the recipes is whether you need to target a specific domain controller. In the solutions in this book, we typically do not target a specific domain controller. When you don't specify a domain controller, you are using a *serverless bind* and there is no guarantee as to precisely which server you will be hitting. Depending on your environment and the task you need to do, you may want to target a specific domain controller so that you know where the query or change will be taking place. Also, serverless binding can work only if the DNS for the Active Directory forest is configured properly and your client can query it. If you have a standalone Active Directory environment that has no ties to your corporate DNS, you may need to target a specific domain controller for the tools to work.

1.3 Getting Familiar with LDIF

Even with the new utilities available with Windows Server 2003 and Windows Server 2008, native support for modifying data within Active Directory using a command-line tool is relatively weak. The *dsmod* tool can modify attributes on a limited set of object classes, but it does not allow you to modify every object type.

One reason for the lack of native command-line tools to do this is that the command line is not well suited for manipulating numerous attributes of an object simultaneously. If you want to specify more than just one or two values that need to be modified, a single command could get quite long. It would be easier to use a GUI editor, such as ADSI Edit, to do the task instead.

The LDAP Data Interchange Format (LDIF) was designed to address this issue. Defined in RFC 2849 (*http://www.rfc-editor.org*), LDIF allows you to represent directory additions, modifications, and deletions in a text-based file, which you can import into a directory using an LDIF-capable tool.

The *ldifde* utility has been available since Windows 2000, and it allows you to import and export Active Directory content in LDIF format. LDIF files are composed of blocks of entries. An entry can add, modify, or delete an object. The first line of an entry is the distinguished name. The second line contains a `changetype`, which can be `add`, `modify`, or `delete`. If it is an object addition, the rest of the entry contains the attributes that should be initially set on the object (one per line). For object deletions, you do not need to specify any other attributes. And for object modifications, you need to specify at least three more lines. The first should contain the type of modification you want to perform on the object. This can be `add` (to set a previously unset attribute or to add a new value to a multivalued attribute), `replace` (to replace an existing value), or `delete` (to remove a value). The modification type should be followed by a colon and the attribute you want to perform the modification on. The next line should contain the name of the attribute followed by a colon, and the value for the attribute. For example, to replace the last name attribute with the value Smith, you'd use the following LDIF:

```
dn: cn=jsmith,cn=users,dc=adatum,dc=com
changetype: modify
replace: sn
sn: Smith
-
```

Modification entries must be followed by a line that only contains a hyphen (-). You can put additional modification actions following the hyphen, each separated by another hyphen. Here is a complete LDIF example that adds a `jsmith` user object and then modifies the `givenName` and `sn` attributes for that object:

```
dn: cn=jsmith,cn=users,dc=adatum,dc=com
changetype: add
objectClass: user
samaccountname: jsmith
sn: JSmith

dn: cn=jsmith,cn=users,dc=adatum,dc=com
changetype: modify
add: givenName
givenName: Jim
-
replace: sn
sn: Smith
-
```

See Recipes 4.28 and 4.29 for more details on how to use the *ldifde* utility to import and export LDIF files.

1.4 Programming Notes

In the VBScript solutions, our intention was to provide the answer in as few lines of code as necessary. Since this book is not a pure programming book, we did not want to provide a detailed explanation of how to use ADSI or WMI. If you are looking for that, we recommend *Active Directory*, Fourth Edition, by Brian Desmond et al. (O'Reilly).

The intent of the VBScript code is to provide you the basics for how a task can be automated and let you run with it. Most examples only take some minor tweaking to make them do something useful for you.

Just as with the GUI and CLI solutions, there are some important issues to be aware of when looking at the VBScript solutions.

Serverless Binds

We mentioned earlier that in the GUI and CLI examples we do not provide instructions for targeting a specific domain controller to perform a task. Instead, we rely on serverless binds in most cases. The same applies to the scripted solutions. A serverless bind for the RootDSE looks like the following in VBScript:

```
set objRootDSE = GetObject("LDAP://RootDSE")
```

That code will query the RootDSE for a domain controller in the domain of the currently logged-on user. You can target a specific domain instead by simply specifying the domain name in the ADsPath:

```
set objRootDSE = GetObject("LDAP://apac.adatum.com/RootDSE")
```

And similarly, you can target a specific domain controller by including the server name in the ADsPath:

```
set objRootDSE = GetObject("LDAP://dc1/RootDSE")
```

So depending on how your environment is set up and what forest you want to query, you may or may not need to specify a domain or server name in the code.

Running Scripts Using Alternate Credentials

Just as you might need to run the GUI and CLI tools with alternate credentials, you may also need to run your scripts and programs with alternate credentials. One way is to use the runas method described earlier when invoking the script. A better option would be to use the Scheduled Tasks service to run the script under credentials you specify when creating the task. And yet another option is to hardcode the credentials in the script. Obviously, this is not very appealing in some scenarios because credentials can change over time, and as a security best practice you do not want the username and password contained in a script to be easily viewable by others. Nevertheless, it is a necessary evil, especially when developing against multiple forests, and we'll describe how it can be done with ADSI and ADO. As an alternative, you can configure a script to prompt you for the username and password during the actual running of the script.

With ADSI, you can use the `IADsOpenDSObject::OpenDSObject` method to specify alternate credentials. You can quickly turn any ADSI-based example in this book into one that authenticates as a particular user.

For example, a solution to print out the description of a domain might look like:

```
set objDomain = GetObject("LDAP://dc=apac,dc=adatum,dc=com")
WScript.Echo "Description: " & objDomain.Get("description")
```

Using `OpenDSObject`, it takes only one additional statement to make the same code authenticate as the administrator in the domain:

```
set objLDAP = GetObject("LDAP:")
set objDomain = objLDAP.OpenDSObject( _
    "LDAP://dc=apac,dc=adatum,dc=com", _
    "administrator@apac.adatum.com", _
    "MyPassword", _
    0)
WScript.Echo "Description: " & objDomain.Get("description")
```

It is just as easy to authenticate in ADO code as well. Take the following example, which queries all **computer** objects in the *apac.adatum.com* domain:

```
strBase = "<LDAP://dc=apac,dc=adatum,dc=com>;"
strFilter = "(&(objectclass=computer)(objectcategory=computer));"
strAttrs = "cn;"
strScope = "subtree"

set objConn = CreateObject("ADODB.Connection")
objConn.Provider = "ADsDSOObject"
objConn.Open "Active Directory Provider"
set objRS = objConn.Execute(strBase & strFilter & strAttrs & strScope)
objRS.MoveFirst
while Not objRS.EOF
    Wscript.Echo objRS.Fields(0).Value
    objRS.MoveNext
wend
```

Now, by adding two lines (in bold), we can authenticate with the administrator account:

```
strBaseDN = "<LDAP://dc=apac,dc=adatum,dc=com>;"
strFilter = "(&(objectclass=computer)(objectcategory=computer));"
strAttrs  = "cn;"
strScope  = "subtree"

set objConn = CreateObject("ADODB.Connection")
objConn.Provider = "ADsDSOObject"
objConn.Properties("User ID") = "administrator@apac.adatum.com"
objConn.Properties("Password") = "MyPassword"
objConn.Open "Active Directory Provider"
set objRS = objConn.Execute(strBaseDN & strFilter & strAttrs & strScope)
objRS.MoveFirst
```

```
while Not objRS.EOF
    Wscript.Echo objRS.Fields(0).Value
    objRS.MoveNext
wend
```

To authenticate with ADO, you need to set the `User ID` and `Password` properties of the ADO connection object. We used the UPN of the administrator for the user ID. With ADSI and ADO, you can use a UPN, NT 4.0 style account name (e.g., APAC\Administrator), or distinguished name for the user ID.

Defining Variables and Error Checking

An important part of any script is error checking. Error checking allows your programs to gracefully identify any issues that arise during execution and take the appropriate action. Another best practice is to define variables before you use them and clean them up after you are done with them. In this book, most of the programmatic solutions do not include any error checking, predefined variables, or variable cleanup. Admittedly, this is not setting a good example, but if we included extensive error checking and variable management, it would have made this book considerably longer with little added value to the reader. The goal is to provide you with a code snippet that shows you how to accomplish a task, not provide robust scripts that include all the trimmings.

Error checking with VBScript is pretty straightforward. At the beginning of the script include the following declaration:

```
On Error Resume Next
```

This tells the script interpreter to continue even if errors occur. Without that declaration, anytime an error is encountered the script will abort. When you use `On Error Resume Next`, you need to use the `Err` object to check for errors after any step where a fatal error could occur. The following example shows how to use the `Err` object:

```
On Error Resume Next
set objDomain = GetObject("LDAP://dc=adatum,dc=com")

If Err.Number <> 0 then
    Wscript.Echo "An error occured getting the domain object: " & Err.
Description
    Wscript.Quit
end if
```

Two important properties of the `Err` object are `Number`, which if nonzero signifies an error, and `Description`, which will contain the error message.

As far as variable management goes, it is always a good practice to include the following at the beginning of every script:

```
Option Explicit
```

When this is used, every variable in the script must be declared or an exception will be generated when you attempt to run the script. Variables are declared in VBScript using the `Dim` keyword. After you are done with a variable, it is a good practice to set it to

`Nothing` so you release any resources bound to the variable, and don't accidentally re-use the variable with its previous value. The following code shows a complete example for printing the display name for a domain with error checking and variable management included:

```
Option Explicit
On Error Resume Next

Dim objDomain
set objDomain = GetObject("LDAP://cn=users,dc=adatum,dc=com")

if Err.Number <> 0 then
   Wscript.Echo "An error occurred getting the domain object: " & Err.Description
   Wscript.Quit
end if

Dim strDescr
strDescr = objDomain.Get("description")
if Err.Number <> 0 then
   Wscript.Echo "An error occurred getting the description: " & Err.Description
   Wscript.Quit
end if

WScript.Echo "Description: " & strDescr

objDomain = Nothing
strDescr = Nothing
```

1.5 Replaceable Text

This book is filled with examples. Every recipe consists of one or more examples that show how to accomplish a task. Most CLI- and VBScript-based solutions use parameters that are based on the domain, forest, OU, user, etc., that is being added, modified, queried, and so on. Instead of using fictitious names, in most cases we use replaceable text. This text should be easily recognizable because it is in italics and surrounded by angle brackets (<>). Instead of describing what each replaceable element represents every time we use it, we've included a list of some of the commonly used ones here:

<DomainDN>
   Distinguished name of domain (e.g., *dc=amer,dc=adatum,dc=com*)

<ForestRootDN>
   Distinguished name of the forest root domain (e.g., *dc=adatum,dc=com*)

<DomainDNSName>
   Fully qualified DNS name of domain (e.g., *amer.adatum.com*)

<ForestDNSName>
   Fully qualified DNS name of forest root domain (e.g., *adatum.com*)

<DomainControllerName>
> Single-label or fully qualified DNS hostname of domain controller (e.g., *dc01.adatum.com*)

<UserDN>
> Distinguished name of user (e.g., *cn=administrator,cn=users,dc=adatum,dc=com*)

<GroupDN>
> Distinguished name of group (e.g., *cn=DomainAdmins,cn=users,dc=adatum, dc=com*)

<ComputerName>
> Single-label DNS hostname of computer (e.g., *adatum-xp*)

1.6 Where to Find More Information

While it is our hope that this book provides you with enough information to perform most of the tasks you need to do to maintain your Active Directory environment, it is not realistic to think every possible task has been covered. In fact, working on this book has made us realize just how much Active Directory administrators need to know.

Now that Active Directory has been around for a number of years, a significant user base has been built, which has led to other great resources of information. This section contains some of the useful sources of information that we use on a regular basis.

Command-Line Tools

If you have any questions about the complete syntax or usage information for any of the command-line tools we use, you should first take a look at the help information for the tools. The vast majority of CLI tools provide syntax information by simply passing /? as a parameter. For example:

```
> dsquery /?
```

Microsoft Knowledge Base

The Microsoft Support website is a great source of information and is home of the Microsoft Knowledge Base (MS KB) articles. Throughout the book, we include references to pertinent MS KB articles where you can find more information on the topic. You can find the complete text for a KB article by searching on the KB number at the following website: *http://support.microsoft.com/default.aspx*. You can also append the KB article number to the end of this URL to go directly to the article: *http://support .microsoft.com/kb/<ArticleNumber>*.

Microsoft Developers Network

MSDN contains a ton of information on Active Directory and the programmatic interfaces to Active Directory, such as ADSI and LDAP. We sometimes reference MSDN pages in recipes. Unfortunately, there is no easy way to reference the exact page we're talking about unless we provided the URL or navigation to the page, which would more than likely change by the time the book was printed. Instead we provide the title of the page, which you can use to search on via the following site: *http://msdn.microsoft.com/library*.

Websites

Microsoft Active Directory Home Page (http://www.microsoft.com/ad)
   This site is the starting point for Active Directory information provided by Microsoft. It contains links to white papers, case studies, and tools.

Microsoft PowerShell Home Page (http://www.microsoft.com/PowerShell)
   This site is the starting point for PowerShell information provided by Microsoft. This will be an interesting site to keep an eye on as new and updated PowerShell support is released by the various Microsoft product groups.

Microsoft Webcasts (http://support.microsoft.com/default.aspx?scid=fh;EN-US;pwebcst)
   Webcasts are on-demand audio/video technical presentations that cover a wide range of Microsoft products. There are several Active Directory-related webcasts that cover such topics as disaster recovery, upgrading to Windows Server 2003 Active Directory, and Active Directory tools.

DirTeam Blogs (http://blogs.dirteam.com)
   The DirTeam collection of blogs features content from very active members of the Directory Services MVP community.

Code for this book
   Code for this book can be found at *http://techtasks.com/code/viewbook/2*.

joe Richards' Home Page (http://www.joeware.net)
   This is the home of the *joeware* utilities that you'll see referenced throughout this book; you can always download the latest version of *adfind, admod*, etc., from joe's site, as well as browse FAQs and forums discussing each of the utilities.

Petri.co.il by Daniel Petri (http://www.petri.co.il/ad.htm)
   This is another site that's run by a Microsoft MVP that contains a number of valuable links and tutorials.

Ask the Directory Services Team (http://blogs.technet.com/askds)
   This site features regularly updated content from members of the Directory Services support organization within Microsoft.

ActiveDir Home Page (http://www.activedir.org)
> This is the home page for the ActiveDir Active Directory mailing list. It includes links to active Directory Services blogs, as well as articles, tutorials, and links to third-party tools.

Directory Programming (http://www.directoryprogramming.net)
> Just as the ActiveDir list is crucial for AD administrators, this site is extremely valuable for AD developers. It also includes user forums where participants can post questions about AD programming topics.

Newsgroups

microsoft.public.windows.server.active_directory
> This is a very active newsgroup where several top-notch Active Directory experts answer questions posed by users.

microsoft.public.windows.server.dns
> This is another good resource if you have a DNS question you've been unable to find an answer for; odds are someone on this newsgroup will have an answer.

microsoft.public.adsi.general
> If you have questions about ADSI, this is another very active newsgroup where you can find answers.

If you have a question about a particular topic, a good starting point is to search the newsgroups using Google's Groups search engine (*http://groups.google.com*). Just like its web search engine, the group search engine is very fast and is an invaluable resource when trying to locate information.

Mailing Lists

ActiveDir (http://www.activedir.org)
> The ActiveDir mailing list is where the most advanced Active Directory questions can get answered. The list owner, Tony Murray, does an excellent job of not allowing topics to get out of hand (as can sometimes happen on large mailing lists). The list is very active and it is rare for a question to go unanswered. Some of Microsoft's Active Directory program managers and developers also participate on the list and are very helpful with the toughest questions. Keeping track of this list is a must-have for any serious Active Directory administrator.

Microsoft Identity Integration Server Users Group (http://tech.groups.yahoo.com/group/MMSUG/)
> Though it still bears the name of the previous edition of the ILM product, MIIS, this community-run mailing list is an active resource for anyone who is active in the Identity and Access Management space.

Microsoft Exchange Yahoo Group (http://tech.groups.yahoo.com/group/exchange2007/)
> This mailing list provides an excellent resource for discussions of all aspects of the Microsoft Exchange product.

Books and Magazines

In addition to the Resource Kit books, the following books are good sources of information:

Active Directory, Fourth Edition, by Brian Desmond et al. (O'Reilly)
> This is a good all-purpose book on Active Directory. A few of the topics the fourth edition covers are new Windows Server 2008 features, designing Active Directory, upgrading from Windows 2000, Active Directory Lightweight Directory Services (AD LDS), Exchange 2007, and Active Directory automation.

The .NET Developer's Guide to Directory Services Programming, by Joe Kaplan and Ryan Dunn (Addison-Wesley)
> Written by two notables in the Directory Services programming community, this book is a practical introduction to programming directory services, using both versions 1.1 and 2.0 of the .NET Framework.

Windows IT Pro (http://windowsitpro.com/)
> This is a general-purpose monthly magazine for system administrators who support Microsoft products. The magazine isn't devoted to Active Directory, but generally there are related topics covered every month.

## CHAPTER 2

Forests, Domains, and Trusts

2.0 Introduction

To the layperson, the title of this chapter may seem like a hodgepodge of unrelated terms. For the seasoned Active Directory administrator, however, these terms represent the most fundamental and, perhaps, most important concepts within Active Directory. In simple terms, a *forest* is a collection of data partitions and domains; a *domain* is a hierarchy of objects that is replicated between one or more domain controllers; a *trust* is an agreement between two domains or forests to allow security principals (i.e., users, groups, and computers) from one domain to access resources in the other domain.

Active Directory domains are named using the Domain Name Service (DNS) namespace. You can group domains that are part of the same contiguous DNS namespace within the same domain tree. For example, the *marketing.adatum.com*, *sales.adatum.com*, and *adatum.com* domains are part of the *adatum.com* domain tree. A single domain tree is sufficient for most implementations, but one example in which multiple domain trees might be necessary is with large conglomerate corporations. Conglomerates are made up of multiple individual companies in which each company typically wants to maintain its own identity and, therefore, its own namespace. If you need to support noncontiguous namespaces within a single forest, you will need to create multiple domain trees. For example, *adatum.com* and *treyresearch.com* can form two separate domain trees within the same forest.

Assuming that each company within the conglomerate wants its Active Directory domain name to be based on its company name, you have two choices for setting up this type of environment. You could either make each company's domain(s) a domain tree within a single forest, or you could implement multiple forests. One of the biggest differences between the two options is that all the domains within the forest trust each other, whereas separate forests, by default, do not have any trust relationships set up between them. Without trust relationships, users from one forest cannot access resources located in the other forest. In our conglomerate scenario, if you want users in each company to be able to access resources within their own domain, as well as the

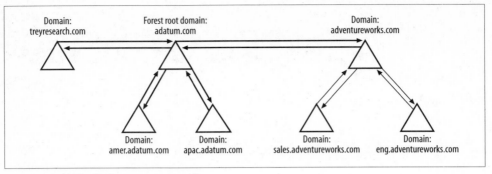

Figure 2-1. Multiple domain trees in a forest

domains belonging to other companies in the organization, using separate domain trees can create an easier approach than separate forests. However, it's important to keep in mind when designing your network that forests form the *security boundary* for Active Directory, as we'll cover in the next section. This is because transitive trusts are established between the root domains of each domain tree within a forest. As a result, every domain within a forest, regardless of which domain tree it is in, is trusted by every other domain. Figure 2-1 illustrates an example with three domain trees in a forest called *adatum.com*.

Each domain increases the support costs of Active Directory due to the need for maintaining additional domain controllers, as well as the time you must spend configuring and maintaining the domain. When designing an Active Directory forest, your goal should be to keep the number of domains that you deploy to an absolute minimum. Since the forest constitutes the security boundary for an Active Directory environment, the minimalist approach toward the number of domains you use in an AD design becomes all the more sensible.

If you implement the alternative approach and create multiple Windows 2000 Active Directory forests, to create the fully trusted model you would have to create individual trusts between the domains in every forest. This can get out of hand pretty quickly if there are numerous domains. Fortunately, with Windows Server 2003 and Windows Server 2008 Active Directory, you can use a trust type called a *cross-forest trust* to create a single transitive trust between two forest root domains. This single trust allows all of the domains in both forests to fully trust each other.

 There are many more issues to consider when deciding how many forests, domains, and domain trees to implement. For a thorough explanation of Active Directory design considerations, we recommend reading Part II of *Active Directory*, Fourth Edition, by Brian Desmond et al. (O'Reilly).

In this chapter, we cover the most common tasks that you would need to do with forests, domains, and trusts. First, we're going to review how each item is represented within Active Directory.

The Anatomy of a Forest

A forest is a logical structure that is a collection of one or more interconnected domains, plus the configuration and schema naming contexts, as well as any application partitions that have been configured. This means that all domains in a forest share a common configuration and schema between them. Forests are considered the security boundary in Active Directory; by this we mean that if you need to definitively restrict access to a resource within a particular domain so that administrators from other domains do not have any access to it whatsoever, you need to implement a separate forest instead of using an additional domain within the current forest. This security concern is due to the transitive trust relationship that exists between all domains in a forest, the writable naming contexts (NCs) that exist on all domain controllers in a forest, and the extensive rights and permissions that are granted to members of the *Administrators* group. In the earliest days of Windows 2000 Active Directory, Microsoft advocated an "empty forest root" design with the intention of protecting the enterprise-wide security principals in the forest root domain from being accessible by domain administrators in the child domains. However, subsequent discoveries have indicated that it is in fact the forest, not the domain, that truly provides security separation between distinct groups of resources and administrators.

Active Directory relies on naming contexts to divide the AD database into separate partitions, each of which contain information that is replicated together as a logical unit. At a minimum, an Active Directory forest consists of three naming contexts: the Domain NC for the forest root domain, the Configuration NC, and the Schema NC. Here is a description of the type of partitions that can be part of a forest:

Configuration NC
> Contains data that is applicable across all domains in a forest, and thus is replicated to all domain controllers in the forest. Some of this data includes the site topology, list of partitions, published services, display specifiers, and extended rights.

Schema NC
> Contains the objects that describe how data can be structured and stored in Active Directory. The `classSchema` objects in the Schema NC represent class definitions for objects. The `attributeSchema` objects describe what data can be stored with classes. The Schema NC is replicated to all domain controllers in a forest.

Domain NC
> A domain is a naming context that holds domain-specific data, including user, group, and computer objects. This forms a collection of objects that is replicated between one or more domain controllers.

Application partitions
> Configurable partitions that can be rooted anywhere in the forest and can be re-plicated to any domain controller in the forest, or to a subset of domain controllers. These are not available with Windows 2000.

The `Partitions` container in the Configuration NC contains the complete list of all partitions associated with a particular forest, e.g., `LDAP://dc=adatum,dc=com/`.

The Anatomy of a Domain

Although forests constitute the security boundary in an Active Directory environment, you can split up your AD infrastructure into separate domains to create smaller administrative or replication boundaries within a large-scale network. In Windows 2000 and Windows Server 2003 Active Directory, domains can also constitute a policy boundary, as certain Group Policy settings such as password policies and account lockout policies can only be applied at the domain level. (Windows Server 2008 introduces the concept of a Fine-Grained Password Policy, which allows administrators to configure multiple password and account lockout policies within a single domain.)

Domains are represented in Active Directory by `domainDNS` objects. The distinguished name (DN) of a `domainDNS` object directly corresponds to the fully qualified DNS name of the domain. For example, the *amer.adatum.com* domain would have a DN of `dc=amer,dc=adatum,dc=com`. Table 2-1 contains a list of some of the interesting attributes that are available on `domainDNS` objects.

Table 2-1. Attributes of domainDNS objects

Attribute	Description
dc	The domain component of the domain distinguished name (e.g., *amer*).
distinguishedName	The DN of the domain (e.g., dc=adatum,dc=com).
fSMORoleOwner	The NTDS Settings object DN of the domain controller on which the schema can be modified. See Recipe 3.32 for more information.
gPLink	List of GPOs that have been applied to the domain. By default it will contain a reference to the Default Domain Policy GPO.
lockoutDuration	A 64-bit integer representing the time an account will be locked out before being automatically unlocked in the absence of any applicable Fine-Grained Password Policies. See Recipe 6.16 for more information.
lockoutObservationWindow	A 64-bit integer representing the time after a failed logon attempt that the failed logon counter for the account will be reset to 0 in the absence of any applicable Fine-Grained Password Policies. See Recipe 6.16 for more information.
lockoutThreshold	Number of failed logon attempts after which an account will be locked in the absence of any applicable Fine-Grained Password Policies. See Recipe 6.16 for more information.

Attribute	Description
maxPwdAge	A 64-bit integer representing the maximum number of days a password can be used before a user must change it, in the absence of any applicable Fine-Grained Password Policies. See Recipe 6.16 for more information.
minPwdAge	A 64-bit integer representing the minimum number of days a password must be used before it can be changed, in the absence of any applicable Fine-Grained Password Policies. See Recipe 6.16 for more information.
minPwdLength	Minimum number of characters allowed in a password in the absence of any applicable Fine-Grained Password Policies. See Recipe 6.16 for more information.
msDS-Behavior-Version	Number that represents the functional level of the domain. This attribute was first introduced in Windows Server 2003. See Recipe 2.10 for more information.
msDS-LogonTimeSyncInterval	Controls how often the lastLogonTimestamp attribute is updated. Defaults to 14 days with a 0–5 day randomization value, which means that lastLogonTimestamp will be updated for a given account every 9 to 14 days to prevent excessive replication of lastLogonTimestamp.
ms-DS-MachineAccountQuota	The number of computer accounts a nonadministrator user account can join to the domain. See Recipe 8.13 for more information.
nTMixedDomain	Number that represents the mode of a domain. See Recipe 2.9 for more information.
pwdHistoryLength	Number of passwords to remember before a user can reuse a previous password in the absence of any applicable Fine-Grained Password Policies. See Recipe 6.16 for more information.
pwdProperties	Bit flag that represents different options that can be configured for passwords used in the domain, including password complexity and storing passwords with reversible encryption. See Recipe 6.16 for more information.
subRefs	Multivalue attribute containing the list of subordinate naming contexts and application partitions, such as DC=ForestDnsZones,DC=adatum,DC=com within the adatum.com domain.
wellKnownObjects	GUIDs for well-known objects, such as the default computer container. See Recipe 8.16 for more information.

In Active Directory, each domain is a naming context and is also represented under the Partitions container in the Configuration NC as a crossRef object, which allows each domain controller in a forest to be aware of every partition in the forest and not just those that are held by one particular DC. In this case, the relative distinguished name (RDN) of the crossRef object is the NetBIOS name of the domain as defined by the netBIOSName attribute of the domain object.

In our previous example of *amer.adatum.com*, the corresponding crossRef object for the domain (assuming the forest name was *adatum.com*) would be located at cn=AMER,cn=Partitions,cn=Configuration,dc=adatum,dc=com.

Table 2-2 contains some interesting attributes of crossRef objects.

All naming contexts and application partitions have `crossRef` objects in the `Partitions` container, not just domain NCs.

Table 2-2. Attributes of crossRef objects

Attribute	Description
cn	Relative distinguished name of the object. If your forest is made up of a contiguous namespace, this value will be the NetBIOS name of the domain.
dnsRoot	Fully qualified DNS name of the domain.
nCName	Distinguished name of the corresponding `domainDNS` object.
netBIOSName	NetBIOS name of the domain. See Recipe 2.7 for more information.
trustParent	Distinguished name of the `crossRef` object representing the parent domain (if applicable).

The Anatomy of a Trust

Microsoft has relied on trust relationships to provide resource access across domain boundaries since the early days of Windows NT. Before Active Directory, all trust relationships were *one-way* and *nontransitive* in nature. A one-way trust relationship, as the name suggests, only enables resource access in a single direction: a single trust relationship will only enable resource access from *DomainA* to *DomainB*, but a separate trust would need to be created to enable access in the other direction. A nontransitive trust relationship means that if you create a trust from *DomainA* to *DomainB* and a second one from *DomainB* to *DomainC, DomainA* does *not* trust *DomainC* by default. This one-way nontransitive trust relationship was the only type that was available in Windows NT. Active Directory improved on this by automatically creating *two-way transitive* trust relationships between every parent and child domain in a domain tree, and between the root domains of all trees in every forest.

Trusts are stored as `trustedDomain` objects within the `System` container of a domain. Table 2-3 lists some of the important attributes of `trustedDomain` objects.

Table 2-3. Attributes of trustedDomain objects

Attribute	Description
cn	Relative distinguished name of the trust. This is the name of the target domain that is trusted. For Windows NT domains, it is the NetBIOS name. For Active Directory domains, it is the DNS name.
trustDirection	Flag that indicates whether the trust is disabled, inbound, outbound, or both inbound and outbound. See Recipes 2.19 and 2.20 for more information.
trustType	Flag that indicates if the trust is to a down-level (NT4), up-level (Windows 2000 or above), or Kerberos (e.g., MIT) domain. See Recipe 2.19 for more information.
trustAttributes	Contain miscellaneous properties that can be enabled for a trust. See Recipe 2.19 for more information.
trustPartner	The name of the trust partner. See Recipe 2.19 for more information.

A trust also has a corresponding user object in the Users container of a domain. This is where the trust password is stored. The RDN of this user object is the same as the cn attribute for the corresponding trustedDomain object with a $ appended.

2.1 Creating a Forest

Problem

You want to create a new forest by creating a new forest root domain.

Solution

Using a graphical user interface

On a Windows 2000 domain controller:

1. Run *dcpromo* from a command line or by clicking on Start→Run.
2. Select "Domain controller for a new domain" and click Next.
3. Select "Create a new domain tree" and click Next.
4. Select "Create a new forest of domain trees" and click Next.
5. Follow the rest of the configuration steps to complete the wizard.

On a Windows Server 2003 domain controller:

1. Run *dcpromo* from a command line or by clicking on Start→Run.
2. Select "Domain controller for a new domain" and click Next.
3. Select "Domain in a new forest" and click Next.
4. Follow the rest of the configuration steps to complete the wizard.

On a Windows Server 2008 domain controller:

1. Open the Server Manager utility. In the lefthand pane, click on Roles.
2. In the righthand pane, click Add role.
3. Click Next. Place a checkmark next to Active Directory Domain Services.
4. Click Next twice and then Install.
5. Click "Close this wizard" and launch the Active Directory Domain Services Installation Wizard (*dcpromo.exe*).
6. Click Next twice to continue. Click the "Create a new domain in a new forest" radio button and click Next.
7. Follow the rest of the configuration steps to complete the wizard.

Using a command-line interface

dcpromo can also be run in unattended mode; this is particularly useful when promoting domain controllers that are running on Server Core. See Recipe 3.8 for more details.

Discussion

The act of creating a forest consists of creating a forest root domain. To do this, you need to use *dcpromo* to promote a Windows 2000 or Windows Server 2003 server to be a domain controller for a new domain. The *dcpromo* program has a wizard interface that requires you to answer several questions about the forest and domain you want to promote the server into. After *dcpromo* finishes, you will be asked to reboot the computer to complete the promotion process.

As you have probably noticed, Windows Server 2008 has changed the nomenclature surrounding Active Directory. What used to simply be called "Active Directory" is now "Active Directory Domain Services," as a number of other server services have been re-branded under the Active Directory umbrella, including Active Directory Certificate Services, Active Directory Rights Management Services, Active Directory Federated Services, and Active Directory Lightweight Directory Services.

When installing a Windows Server 2008 AD DS domain, you must first install the Active Directory Domain Services *role* prior to running *dcpromo*; this is because the necessary binaries to run AD DS are not present until the role is actually installed. If you forget and attempt to run the *dcpromo* utility without first installing the AD DS role, the *dcpromo* utility will check for the existence of the AD DS binaries, and install them in the background prior to launching the *dcpromo* wizard. (This may make *dcpromo* appear temporarily "frozen" as it installs the necessary binaries in the background.)

See Also

Recipe 2.3 for creating a domain, Recipe 3.1 for promoting a domain controller, Recipe 3.8 for automating the promotion of a domain controller, MS KB 238369 (How to Promote and Demote Domain Controllers in Windows 2000), and MS KB 324753 (How to Create an Active Directory Server in Windows Server 2003)

2.2 Removing a Forest

Problem

You want to tear down a forest and decommission any domains contained within it because you no longer need it.

Solution

To remove a forest, you need to demote (using *dcpromo*) all the domain controllers in the forest. When you run *dcpromo* on an existing domain controller, you will be given the option to demote the machine to a member server. After that is completed and depending on how your environment is configured, you may need to remove WINS and DNS entries that were associated with the domain controllers and domains, unless they were automatically removed via WINS deregistration and dynamic DNS (DDNS) during demotion. The following commands can help determine if all entries have been removed:

```
> netsh wins server \\<WINSServerName> show name <DomainNetBiosName> 1b
> netsh wins server \\<WINSServerName> show name <DomainNetBiosName> 1c
> nslookup <DomainControllerDNSName>
> nslookup -type=SRV _ldap._tcp.gc._msdcs.<ForestDNSName>
> nslookup <ForestDNSName>
```

 You should run the first two commands for every domain in the forest if the forest contained more than one.

Discussion

The method described in this solution is the graceful way to tear down a forest. You can also use a brute force method to remove a forest by simply reinstalling the operating system on all domain controllers in the forest. This method is not recommended except in lab or test environments. The brute force method is not a clean way to do it because the domain controllers are unaware the forest is being removed and may generate errors until they are rebuilt. You'll also need to make sure any DNS resource records for the domain controllers are removed from your DNS servers since the domain controllers will not dynamically remove them like they do during the demotion process.

You will also want to remove any trusts that have been established for the forest (see Recipe 2.22 for more details). For more information on how to demote a domain controller, see Recipe 3.7.

 To fully remove an Active Directory forest in Windows Server 2008, you will also need to remove the Active Directory Domain Services role that has been installed on any Windows Server 2008 domain controllers. This will remove the actual system files associated with the AD DS server role. You may also need to remove any associated infrastructure roles from the servers in question, such as the DNS server role or the WINS server role. If you need to forcibly remove a single domain from an AD forest, you can also use the *ntdsutil* command-line utility; see Recipe 2.4 for more information.

See Also

Recipe 2.19 for viewing the trusts for a domain, Recipe 2.22 for removing a trust, and Recipe 3.7 for demoting a domain controller

2.3 Creating a Domain

Problem

You want to create a new domain that may be part of an existing domain tree or the root of a new domain tree.

Solution

Using a graphical user interface

Run *dcpromo* from a command line or Start→Run. (On a Windows Server 2008 server, add the Active Directory Domain Services role prior to running *dcpromo*.)

On a Windows 2000 server, select "Domain controller for a new domain" and then you can select one of the following:

- Create a new domain tree→Place this new domain tree in an existing forest
- Create a new child domain in an existing domain tree

On a Windows Server 2003 server, select "Domain controller for a new domain" and then you can select one of the following:

- Domain in a new forest
- Child domain in an existing domain tree
- Domain tree in an existing forest

On a Windows Server 2008 server, place a checkmark next to "Use advanced mode installation." You can then select one of the following:

- Existing forest
  - — Create a new domain in an existing forest
  - — Create a new domain tree root instead of a new child domain
- Create a new domain in a new forest

Using a command-line interface

dcpromo can also be run in unattended mode. See Recipe 3.8 for more details.

Discussion

The two options *dcpromo* offers to create a new domain allow you a great deal of flexibility in creating an Active Directory infrastructure that maps to your organization's business requirements. You can add a new domain to an existing domain tree, or else create a new domain tree entirely. If you want to create a new domain that is a child domain of a parent domain (i.e., contained within the same contiguous namespace), then you are creating a domain in an existing domain tree. If you are creating the first domain in a forest or a domain that is outside the namespace of the forest root, then you are creating a domain in a new domain tree. For example, if you have already created the *treyresearch.com* domain and then you install the first DC in the *amer.treyresearch.com* domain, then *amer.treyresearch.corp* is a *child domain*. Conversely, if you want to create a domain that is part of the *treyresearch.com* forest but uses an entirely different naming convention (such as *treyresearchasia.com*), then you are creating a new domain tree within an existing forest.

See Also

Recipe 3.1 for promoting a domain controller, Recipe 3.8 for automating the promotion of a domain controller, "Designing the Active Directory Logical Structure" from the *Windows Server 2003 Deployment Guide*, MS KB 238369 (How to Promote and Demote Domain Controllers in Windows 2000), and MS KB 255248 (How to Create a Child Domain in Active Directory and Delegate the DNS Namespace to the Child Domain)

2.4 Removing a Domain

Problem

You want to remove a domain from a forest. You may need to remove a domain during test scenarios or if you are collapsing or reducing the number of domains in a forest.

Solution

Removing a domain consists of demoting each domain controller in the domain, which is accomplished by running *dcpromo* on the domain controllers and following the steps to remove them. For the last domain controller in the domain, be sure to select "This server is the last domain controller in the domain" in the *dcpromo* wizard so that the objects associated with the domain get removed. If you do not select this option for the last domain controller in the domain, take a look at Recipe 2.5 for how to remove an orphaned domain.

If the domain you want to remove has child domains, you must remove these child domains before proceeding.

After all domain controllers have been demoted, depending on how your environment is configured you may need to remove any WINS and DNS entries that were associated with the domain controllers and domain that were automatically removed via WINS deregistration and DDNS during the demotion process. The following commands can help determine if all entries have been removed:

```
> netsh wins server \\<WINSServerName> show name <DomainNetBiosName> 1b
> netsh wins server \\<WINSServerName> show name <DomainNetBiosName> 1c
> nslookup <DomainControllerName>
> nslookup -type=SRV _ldap._tcp.dc._msdcs.<DomainDNSName>
> nslookup <DomainDNSName>
```

You will also want to remove any trusts that have been established for the domain (see Recipe 2.22 for more details). For more information on how to demote a domain controller, see Recipe 3.7.

Discussion

The "brute force" method for removing a forest as described in the section called "Discussion" for Recipe 2.2 is not a good method for removing a domain. Doing so will leave all of the domain controller and server objects, along with the domain object and associated domain naming context hanging around in the forest. If you used that approach, you would eventually see numerous replication and file replication service errors in the event log caused by failed replication events from the nonexistent domain. You would need to remove the metadata associated with the removed domain using *ntdsutil* to correct these errors.

To fully remove an Active Directory forest in Windows Server 2008, you will also need to remove the Active Directory Domain Services role that has been installed on any Windows Server 2008 domain controllers. This will remove the actual system files associated with the AD DS server role. You may also need to remove any associated infrastructure roles from the servers in question, such as the DNS server role or the WINS server role.

See Also

Recipes 2.2, 2.5, 2.19 for viewing the trusts for a domain, Recipe 2.22 for removing a trust, Recipe 3.7 for demoting a domain controller, MS KB 238369 (How to Promote and Demote Domain Controllers in Windows 2000), MS KB 255229 (Dcpromo Demotion of Last Domain Controller in Child Domain Does Not Succeed), and MS KB 332199 (Domain Controllers Do Not Demote Gracefully When You Use the Active Directory Installation Wizard to Force Demotion in Windows Server 2003 and in Windows 2000 Server)

2.5 Removing an Orphaned Domain

Problem

You want to completely remove a domain that was orphaned because the domain was forcibly removed, or the last domain controller in the domain failed or was otherwise decommissioned improperly.

Solution

Using a command-line interface

The following *ntdsutil* commands (in bold) would forcibly remove the *emea.adatum.com* domain from the *adatum.com* forest. Replace *<DomainController-Name>* with the hostname of the Domain Naming Master Flexible Single Master Operation (FSMO; pronounced *fiz-mo*) for the forest:

```
> ntdsutil "meta clean" "s o t" conn "con to server
  <DomainControllerName>" q q
metadata cleanup: "s o t" "list domains"
Found 4 domain(s)
0 - DC=adatum,DC=com
1 - DC=amer,DC=adatum,DC=com
2 - DC=emea,DC=adatum,DC=com
3 - DC=apac,DC=adatum,DC=com
select operation target: sel domain 2
No current site
Domain - DC=emea,DC=adatum,DC=com
No current server
No current Naming Context
select operation target: q
metadata cleanup: remove sel domain
```

You will receive a prompt asking you to confirm the forcible removal of the domain; click Yes. You will then receive a message indicating whether the removal was successful.

Discussion

Removing an orphaned domain consists of removing the domain object for the domain (e.g., dc=emea,dc=adatum,dc=com), all of its child objects, and the associated crossRef object in the Partitions container. You need to target the Domain Naming FSMO when using *ntdsutil* because that server is responsible for creation and removal of domains.

Before you can use *ntdsutil* to remove an orphaned domain, you must first forcibly remove any domain controllers in that domain that were not gracefully demoted. (Forcibly removing individual domain controllers will be discussed in Chapter 3.) You must also remove the DomainDNSZones application partition associated with the orphaned domain, if this was not gracefully removed. (Forcibly removing the `DomainDNSZones` application partition will be discussed in Chapters 13 and 17.)

In the solution, shortcut parameters were used to reduce the amount of typing necessary. If each parameter were typed out fully, the commands would look as follows:

```
> ntdsutil "metadata cleanup" "select operation target" connections
  "connect to server <DomainControllerName>" quit
select operations target: "list domains"
Found 4 domain(s)
0 - DC=adatum,DC=com
1 - DC=amer,DC=adatum,DC=com
2 - DC=emea,DC=adatum,DC=com
3 - DC=apac,DC=adatum,DC=com
select operation target: select domain 2
No current site
Domain - DC=emea,DC=adatum,DC=com
No current server
No current Naming Context
select operation target: quit
metadata cleanup: remove selected domain
```

See Also

Recipe 3.11 for removing an unsuccessfully demoted domain controller; MS KB 230306 (How to Remove Orphaned Domains from Active Directory), MS KB 251307 (How to Remove Orphaned Domains from Active Directory Without Demoting the Domain Controllers), and MS KB 255229 (Dcpromo Demotion of Last Domain Controller in Child Domain Does Not Succeed); Chapter 3 for information on performing a metadata cleanup of individual domain controllers; and Chapters 13 and 17 for information on manually removing the `DomainDNSZones` application partition

2.6 Finding the Domains in a Forest

Problem

You want a list of all domains in an Active Directory forest.

Solution

Using a graphical user interface

Open the Active Directory Domains and Trusts snap-in (*domain.msc*). The list of the domains in the default forest can be browsed in the left pane.

Using a command-line interface

You can retrieve this information using *ntdsutil*, *adfind*, or *dsquery*, as shown here:

```
> ntdsutil "p m" "sel op tar" c "co t s <DomainControllerName>"
q "l d" q q q
```

```
> dsquery * -filter "objectcategory=domainDNS" -scope subtree

> adfind -root -f "objectcategory=domainDNS" -dn
```

 The dsquery and adfind examples will not function correctly in a forest containing multiple domain trees, such as a single forest containing a domain tree named *adatum.com* and *treyresearch.com*. The AdFind syntax can be modified to work in this scenario by replacing the –root switch with the –gcb switch.

Using VBScript

```
' This code gets the list of the domains contained in the
' forest that the user running the script is logged into.

strForestRoot = "<ForestRootDN>" ' i.e., dc=adatum, dc=com
strADsPath = "<LDAP://" & strForestRoot & ">;"
strFilter = "(objectCategory=domainDNS);"
strAttrs = "dnsRoot;"
strScope = "SubTree"

set objConn = CreateObject("ADODB.Connection")
objConn.Provider = "ADsDSOObject"
objConn.Open "Active Directory Provider"
set objRS = objConn.Execute(strADsPath & strFilter & strAttrs & strScope)
objRS.MoveFirst
while Not objRS.EOF
    For Each root in objRS.Fields("dnsRoot").Value
        WScript.Echo(root)
    Next
    objRS.MoveNext
wend
```

Using PowerShell

The following commands assume that the Quest AD cmdlets are installed:

```
connect-QADservice -UseGlobalCatalog
get-QADobject -searchRoot '<ForestRootDN>' -searchScope 'subTree' -ldapFilter
'objectClass=domainDNS'
```

Discussion

Using a graphical user interface

If you want to view the domains for a forest other than the one you are logged into, right-click on "Active Directory Domains and Trusts" in the left pane and select "Connect to Domain Controller." Enter the forest name you want to browse in the Domain field. In the left pane, expand the forest root domain to see any subdomains.

Using a command-line interface

In the *ntdsutil* example, shortcut parameters were used to reduce the amount of typing needed. If each parameter were typed out fully, the command line would look like:

```
> ntdsutil "partition management" "select operation target" connections "connect
to server <DomainControllerName>" quit "List domains" quit quit quit
```

Using VBScript

To find the list of domains for an alternate forest, include the name of the forest as part of the ADsPath used in the first line of code. The following would target the *othercorp.com forest*:

```
set objRootDSE = GetObject("LDAP://othercorp.com/" & "RootDSE")
```

Using PowerShell

In the PowerShell solution, we are relying on the Quest PowerShell Commands for Active Directory. This collection of a dozen or so AD cmdlets is provided free of charge and is downloadable from *http://www.quest.com*. The -UseGlobalCatalog switch is required in multidomain environments so that all domain names will be returned. The get-QADObject syntax in this example returns the following output in a domain containing a forest root and a single child:

```
Name        Type        DN
--------    -------     -----
adatum      domainDNS   DC=adatum,DC=com
amer        domainDNS   DC=amer,DC=adatum,DC=com
```

See Also

Recipe 3.13 for finding the domain controllers for a domain

2.7 Finding the NetBIOS Name of a Domain

Problem

You want to find the NetBIOS name of a domain. Although Microsoft has moved to using DNS for its primary means of name resolution, the NetBIOS name of a domain is still important, especially with down-level clients that are still based on NetBIOS instead of DNS for name resolution.

Solution

Using a graphical user interface

1. Open the Active Directory Domains and Trusts snap-in (*domain.msc*).
2. Right-click the domain you want to view in the left pane and select Properties.

The NetBIOS name will be shown in the "Domain name (pre-Windows 2000)" field.

You can also retrieve this information using LDP, as follows:

1. Open LDP and from the menu, select Connection→Connect.
2. For Server, enter the name of a domain controller (or leave blank to do a serverless bind).
3. For Port, enter 389.
4. Click OK.
5. From the menu select Connection→Bind.
6. Click OK to bind as the currently logged-on user, or else click "Bind with credentials" and enter a username and password.
7. Click OK.
8. From the menu, select Browse→Search.
9. For BaseDN, type the distinguished name of the `Partitions` container (e.g., `cn=partitions,cn=configuration,dc=adatum,dc=com`).
10. For Scope, select Subtree.
11. For Filter, enter:

    `(&(objectcategory=crossref)(dnsRoot=<DomainDNSName>)(netbiosname=*))`

12. Click Run.

Using a command-line interface

To find the NetBIOS name of a Windows domain, use the following command:

```
> dsquery * cn=partitions,cn=configuration, <ForestRootDN> -filter
"(&(objectcategory=crossref)(dnsroot=<DomainDNSName>)(netbiosname=*))" -attr
netbiosname
```

Or you can use the AdFind utility as follows:

```
> adfind -partitions
-f "(&(objectcategory=crossref)(dnsroot=<DomainDNSName>)(netbiosname=*))" cn
netbiosname
```

Using VBScript

```
' This code prints the NetBIOS name for the specified domain
' ------ SCRIPT CONFIGURATION -----
strDomain = "<DomainDNSName>" ' e.g. amer.adatum.com
' ------ END CONFIGURATION --------

set objRootDSE = GetObject("LDAP://" & strDomain & "/RootDSE")
strADsPath = "<LDAP://" & strDomain & "/cn=Partitions," & _
            objRootDSE.Get("configurationNamingContext") & ">;"
strFilter = "(&(objectclass=Crossref)" & _
            "(dnsRoot=" & strDomain & ")(netBIOSName=*));"
strAttrs = "netbiosname;"
```

```
strScope = "Onelevel"
set objConn = CreateObject("ADODB.Connection")
objConn.Provider = "ADsDSOObject"
objConn.Open "Active Directory Provider"
set objRS = objConn.Execute(strADsPath &  strFilter &  strAttrs &  strScope)
objRS.MoveFirst
WScript.Echo "NetBIOS name for " &  strDomain &  " is " &  objRS.Fields(0).Value
```

Using PowerShell

```
$strFilter = "(&(objectclass=Crossref)(dnsRoot=<DomainDNSName>)(netBIOSName=*))"
$objConfig = New-Object System.DirectoryServices.DirectoryEntry("LDAP://<ConfigDN>)"
$objSearcher = New-Object System.DirectoryServices.DirectorySearcher
$objSearcher.SearchRoot = $objConfig
$objSearcher.Filter = ($strFilter)
$colResults = $objSearcher.FindAll()
```

Discussion

Each domain has a `crossRef` object that is used by Active Directory to generate *referrals* to other naming contexts as needed. Referrals are necessary when a client performs a query and the domain controller handling the request does not have the matching object(s) in any naming contexts that it has stored locally. The NetBIOS name of a domain is stored in the domain's `crossRef` object in the `Partitions` container in the Configuration NC. Each `crossRef` object has a `dnsRoot` attribute, which is the fully qualified DNS name of the domain. The `netBIOSName` attribute contains the NetBIOS name for the domain.

2.8 Renaming a Domain

Problem

You want to rename a domain, for example due to organizational changes; legal restrictions; or because of a merger, acquisition, or divestiture. Renaming a domain is a very involved process and should be done only when absolutely necessary. Changing the name of a domain can have an impact on everything from DNS, replication, and GPOs to DFS and Certificate Services. A domain rename also requires rebooting all domain controllers, member servers, and client computers in the domain!

Solution

Under Windows 2000, there is no supported process to rename a domain. There is one workaround for mixed-mode domains in which you revert the domain and any of its child domains back to Windows NT domains. This can be done by demoting all Windows 2000 domain controllers and leaving the Windows NT domain controllers in place, or simply by rebuilding all of the 2000 DCs. You could then reintroduce Windows 2000 domain controllers and use the new domain name when setting up Active

Directory. The process is not very clean and probably won't be suitable for most situations, but you can find out more about it in MS KB 292541.

A domain rename procedure is supported if a forest is running all Windows Server 2003 domain controllers and is at the Windows Server 2003 forest functional level. Microsoft provides a rename tool (*random.exe*) and detailed white paper describing the process at *http://www.microsoft.com/windowsserver2003/downloads/domainrename.mspx*.

Although the domain rename procedure is greatly simplified in Windows Server 2003 and Windows Server 2008, we highly recommend reading the entire white paper before attempting the procedure, as well as attempting the procedure in a test lab before performing it against a production environment.

Discussion

The domain rename process can accommodate very complex changes to your domain model. You can perform the following types of renames:

- Rename a domain to a new name without repositioning it in the domain tree.
- Reposition a domain within a domain tree.
- Create a new domain tree with a renamed domain.

One thing you cannot do with the domain rename procedure is reposition the forest root domain. You can rename the forest root domain, but you cannot change its status as the forest root domain. Another important limitation to note is that you cannot rename any domain in a forest that has had Exchange 2000 or Exchange 2007 installed, though an Exchange Server 2003 is capable of handling domain renames. See the website mentioned in the solution for more information on other limitations. The *random.exe* utility also includes the *gpfixup.exe* utility, which corrects references to Group Policy objects after the domain name changes. When working with Exchange 2003, you can also use the *xdr-fixup* tool to correct Exchange attributes to match the new domain name.

See Also

MS KB 292541 (How to Rename the DNS name of a Windows 2000 Domain) and *http://www.microsoft.com/windowsserver2003/downloads/domainrename.mspx*

2.9 Raising the Domain Mode to Windows 2000 Native Mode

Problem

You want to change the mode of a Windows 2000 Active Directory domain from mixed mode to native mode. You typically want to do this as soon as possible after installing a Windows 2000 domain to take advantage of features that aren't available with mixed-mode domains. (For more information on the features available at the different functional levels, see *http://technet2.microsoft.com/WindowsServer/en/Library/ b3674c9b-fab9-4c1e-a8f6-7871264712711033.mspx.*)

Solution

Using a graphical user interface

1. Open the Active Directory Domains and Trusts snap-in (*domain.msc*).
2. Browse to the domain you want to change in the left pane.
3. Right-click on the domain and select Properties. The current mode will be listed in the Domain Operation Mode box.
4. To change the mode, click the Change Mode button at the bottom.

Using a command-line interface

To change the mode to native mode, create an LDIF file called *change_domain_mode.ldf* with the following contents:

```
dn: <DomainDN>
changetype: modify
replace: ntMixedDomain
ntMixedDomain: 0
-
```

Then run *ldifde* to import the change.

```
> ldifde -i -f change_domain_mode.ldf
```

Alternately, you can use the admod utility to update your domain to native mode using the following syntax:

```
> admod -b dc=adatum,dc=com "ntMixedDomain::0"
```

Using VBScript

```
' This code changes the mode of the specified domain to native
' ------ SCRIPT CONFIGURATION ------
strDomain = "<DomainDNSName>" ' e.g. amer.adatum.com
' ------ END CONFIGURATION ---------

set objDomain = GetObject("LDAP://" &  strDomain)
if objDomain.Get("nTMixedDomain") > 0 Then
   Wscript.Echo "
Changing mode to native ... "
   objDomain.Put "nTMixedDomain", 0
   objDomain.SetInfo
else
   Wscript.Echo "Already a native mode domain"
end if
```

Using PowerShell

You can modify the `nTMixedDomain` attribute using the Quest PowerShell cmdlets or the native ADSI methods, as follows:

```
connect-QADservice -UseGlobalCatalog
set-QADObject -identity '<DomainDN>' -objectAttributes @{ntMixedDomain=0}

$objDom = [ADSI] "LDAP://<DomainDN>"
$objDom.put("ntMixedDomain", "0")
$objDom.SetInfo()
```

Discussion

The mode of a domain restricts the operating systems the domain controllers in the domain can run. In a mixed-mode domain, you can have Windows 2000 (and Windows Server 2003) and Windows NT domain controllers. In a native-mode domain, you can have only Windows 2000 (and Windows Server 2003) domain controllers. There are several important feature differences between mixed and native mode. Mixed mode imposes the following limitations:

- The domain cannot contain Universal security groups.
- Groups in the domain cannot have their scope or type changed.
- The domain cannot have nested groups (aside from global groups in domain local groups).
- Account modifications sent to Windows NT BDCs, including password changes, must go through PDC Emulator for the domain.
- The domain cannot use SID History.

The domain mode can be changed only from mixed to native mode. You cannot change it back from native to mixed mode without restoring your entire Active Directory environment from a previous backup. When a Windows 2000 domain is first created, it starts off in mixed mode even if all the domain controllers are running Windows 2000. The domain mode is stored in the `ntMixedDomain` attribute on the domain object (e.g., `dc=amer,dc=adatum,dc=com`). A value of 0 signifies a native-mode domain and 1 indicates a mixed-mode domain.

Windows Server 2003 and Windows Server 2008 Active Directory have a similar concept called *domain functional levels*. For more information on Windows Server 2003 and 2008 functional levels, see Recipes 2.10 and 2.11.

See Also

Recipe 2.10 for raising the functional level of a Windows Server 2003/2008 domain, Recipe 2.11 for raising the functional level of a Windows Server 2003/2008 forest, MS KB 186153 (Modes Supported by Windows 2000 Domain Controllers)

2.10 Viewing and Raising the Functional Level of a Windows Server 2003 or 2008 Domain

Problem

You want to raise the functional level of a Windows Server 2003 or Windows Server 2008 domain. You should raise the functional level of a domain as soon as possible after installing a new Windows Server 2003 domain or upgrading from Windows 2000 to take advantage of the new features and enhancements.

Solution

Using a graphical user interface

1. Open the Active Directory Domains and Trusts snap-in (*domain.msc*).
2. In the left pane, browse to the domain you want to raise, right-click it, and select Raise Domain Functional Level.
3. From this screen, you can view the current domain functional level. To raise it, select the new functional level and click OK.

After a few seconds you should see a message stating whether the operation was successful.

Using a command-line interface

To retrieve the current functional level using DSQuery, use the following command:

```
> dsquery * <DomainDN> -scope base -attr msDS-Behavior-Version
```

DSQuery will return the following output in a Windows 2000 functional-level domain:

```
> msDS-Behavior-Version
> 0
```

Or you can use the AdFind utility as follows:

```
> adfind -s Base -b <DomainDN> msDS-Behavior-Version
```

AdFind will return the following output in a Windows 2000 functional-level domain:

```
> AdFind V01.37.00cpp Joe Richards (joe@joeware.net) June 2007
>
> Using server: dc1.adatum.com:389
> Directory: Windows Server 2003
>
> dn:dc=adatum,dc=com
>> msDS-Behavior-Version: 0
>
>
> 1 Objects returned
```

To change the functional level to Windows Server 2003, create an LDIF file called *raise_domain_func_level.ldf* with the following contents:

```
dn: <DomainDN>
changetype: modify
replace: msDS-Behavior-Version
msDS-Behavior-Version: 2
-
```

To raise the domain functional level to Windows Server 2008, use a value of '3' for `msDS-Behavior-Version`.

Next, run *ldifde* to import the change:

```
> ldifde -i -f raise_domain_func_level.ldf
```

Alternatively, you can use the admod utility to raise the domain functional level using the following syntax, with the output that follows:

```
> admod -b dc=adatum,dc=com "msDS-Behavior-Version::2"
```

or:

```
> admod -b dc=adatum,dc=com "msDS-Behavior-Version::3"
>
> AdMod V01.10.00cpp Joe Richards (joe@joeware.net) February 2007
>
> DN Count: 1
> Using server: dc1.adatum.com
> Modifying specified objects...
> DN: dc=adatum,dc=com...
>
> The command completed successfully
```

Using VBScript

```
' This code changes the
' functional level of the specified domain to
' the Windows Server 2003 or Windows Server 2008
' domain functional level
' ------ SCRIPT CONFIGURATION ------
strDomain = "<DomainDN>" ' e.g. dc=amer,dc=adatum,dc=com
strDFL = "<DFL Constant>"      ' Set this value to '2' for Windows Server 2003,
                               ' Set this value to '3' for Windows Server 2008
' ------ END CONFIGURATION ---------

set objDomain = GetObject("LDAP://" &  strDomain)
objDomain.GetInfo
if objDomain.Get("msDS-Behavior-Version") < strDFL then
    Wscript.Echo "Changing domain to
requested functional level ... "
    objDomain.Put "msDS-Behavior-Version", strDFL
    objDomain.SetInfo
else
    Wscript.Echo "Domain already at requested functional level "
end if
```

Using PowerShell

```
$domain = [System.DirectoryServices.ActiveDirectory.Domain]::getCurrentDomain()
$domain.RaiseDomainFunctionality('Windows2003Domain') # Or else use
                                                      # 'Windows2008Domain'
```

Discussion

In Windows Server 2003 and Windows Server 2008 Active Directory, functional levels have replaced the domain mode that was used in Windows 2000 to signify what operating systems are allowed to run on the domain controllers in the domain. With Windows Server 2003, there are functional levels for both domains and forests, whereas with Windows 2000, the domain mode only applied to domains. The `msDS-Behavior-Version` attribute of the `domainDNS` object (e.g., `dc=amer,dc=adatum,dc=com`) holds the current domain functional level. Table 2-4 shows the four functional levels, their associated `msDS-Behavior-Version` value, and the operating systems that can be used on domain controllers in each. It is important to note that Windows Server 2008 has dropped *all* support for Windows NT 4.0 BDCs; the minimum domain functional level supported by a Windows Server 2008 domain is Windows 2000 native mode.

Table 2-4. Active Directory domain functional levels

Functional level	msDS-Behavior-Version	Valid operating systems
Windows 2000	0	Windows 2000, Windows NT (when in mixed mode; mixed mode is not available in Windows Server 2008), Windows Server 2003
Windows Server 2003	1	Windows NT 4.0
Interim		Windows Server 2003 (Windows 2000/2003 only; not available in Windows Server 2008)
Windows Server 2003	2	Windows Server 2003
Windows Server 2008	3	Windows Server 2008

When a Windows 2000 domain is at the Windows 2000 functional level, the domain can be in mixed mode or native mode, as described in Recipe 2.9. Various new features of Windows Server 2003 and Windows Server 2008 Active Directory are enabled with each domain functional level. See Chapter 1 of *Active Directory*, Fourth Edition, for more details.

The value contained in `msDS-Behavior-Version` is mirrored in the attribute `domainFunctionality` of the RootDSE. That means you can perform anonymous queries against the RootDSE of a domain to quickly determine what functional level it is currently at.

 One of the benefits of the GUI solution is that if a problem is encountered, you can save and view the output log, which will contain information on any errors that were encountered.

Using PowerShell

While the PowerShell syntax in this recipe drills down to the native .NET classes and methods in the System.DirectoryServices namespace, it is presented here because the syntax is largely self-documenting, and it provides a much shortened alternative to the VBScript method.

See Also

Recipe 2.9 for changing domain mode, Recipe 2.11 for raising the functional level of a Windows Server 2003 forest, Recipe 2.12 for preparing a forest with AdPrep, Chapter 1 of *Active Directory*, Fourth Edition, and MS KB 322692 (How to Raise the Domain Functional Level in Windows Server 2003)

2.11 Raising the Functional Level of a Windows Server 2003 or 2008 Forest

Problem

You want to raise the functional level of a Windows Server 2003 or Windows Server 2008 forest. You should raise the functional level of a forest as soon as possible after installing a new Windows Server 2003/2008 forest or when upgrading from a downlevel forest in order to take advantage of the new features and enhancements available in Windows Server 2003 and Windows Server 2008.

Solution

Using a graphical user interface

1. Open the Active Directory Domains and Trusts snap-in (*domain.msc*).
2. In the left pane, right-click on Active Directory Domains and Trusts and select Raise Forest Functional Level.
3. Select Windows Server 2003 or Windows Server 2008 Functional Level and click OK.

After a few seconds, you should see a message stating whether the operation was successful.

Using a command-line interface

To retrieve the current forest functional level, use the following command:

```
> dsquery * cn=Partitions,cn=Configuration,<ForestRootDN> -scope base -attr msDS
-Behavior-Version
```

```
> adfind -partitions -s base  msDS-Behavior-Version
>
> AdFind V01.37.00cpp Joe Richards (joe@joeware.net) June 2007
>
> Using server: TEST-DC1.test.loc:389
> Directory: Windows Server 2003
> Base DN: CN=Partitions,CN=Configuration,DC=test,DC=loc
>
> dn:CN=Partitions,CN=Configuration,DC=test,DC=loc
> msDS-Behavior-Version: 2
>
>
> 1 Objects returned
```

To change the functional level to Windows Server 2003, create an LDIF file called
raise_forest_func_level.ldf with the following contents:

```
dn: cn=partitions,cn=configuration, <ForestRootDN>
changetype: modify
replace: msDS-Behavior-Version
msDS-Behavior-Version: 2
-
```

To raise the forest functional level to Windows Server 2008, use a value of '3' for msDS-
Behavior-Version.

Next, run *ldifde* to import the change:

```
> ldifde -i -f raise_forest_func_level.ldf
```

Or else you can use the admod utility as follows:

```
> admod -b <ForestDN> "msDS-Behavior-Version::2"
```

or:

```
> admod -b <ForestDN> "msDS-Behavior-Version::3"
```

This will display results similar to the following:

```
> AdMod V01.10.00cpp Joe Richards (joe@joeware.net) February 2007
>
> DN Count: 1
> Using server: dc1.adatum.com
> Modifying specified objects...
> DN: cn=Partitions,cn=Configuration,dc=adatum,dc=com...
>
> The command completed successfully
```

Using VBScript

```
' This code changes the functional level of the forest the
' user running the script is logged into to Windows Server 2003
' or Windows Server 2008.

' ------ SCRIPT CONFIGURATION ------
strFFL = "<FFL Constant>"      ' Set this value to '2' for Windows Server 2003,
                               ' Set this value to '3' for Windows Server 2008
```

```
' ------ END CONFIGURATION ---------

set objRootDSE = GetObject("LDAP://RootDSE")
set objDomain = GetObject("LDAP://cn=partitions," &_
                          objRootDSE.Get("configurationNamingContext") )
if objDomain.Get("msDS-Behavior-Version") < strFFL then
   Wscript.Echo "Attempting to change forest to " & _
                "the requested functional level ... "
   objDomain.Put "msDS-Behavior-Version", strFFL
   objDomain.SetInfo
else
   Wscript.Echo "Forest already at the requested functional level"
end if
```

Using PowerShell

```
$forest = [System.DirectoryServices.ActiveDirectory.Forest]::getCurrentForest()
$forest.RaiseForestFunctionality('Windows2003Forest') # Or use 'Windows2008Forest'
```

Discussion

Windows Server 2003 and Windows Server 2008 forest functional levels are very similar to domain functional levels. In fact, Table 2-4 applies to forest functional levels as well, except that the list of available operating systems applies to all domain controllers in the forest, rather than just a single domain. So even if just one of the domains in the forest is at the Windows 2000 domain functional level, you cannot raise the forest above the Windows 2000 forest functional level. If you attempt to do so you will receive an error that the operation cannot be completed. After you raise the last Windows 2000 domain functional level to Windows Server 2003, you can then raise the forest functional level as well.

You may be wondering why there is a need to differentiate between forest and domain functional levels. The primary reason is new features. Some new features of Windows Server 2003 and Windows Server 2008 Active Directory require that all domain controllers in the forest are running the appropriate operating system. To ensure all domain controllers are running a certain operating system throughout a forest, Microsoft had to apply the functional level concept to forests as well as domains. For more information on the new features that are available with each functional level, see Chapter 1 of *Active Directory*. Just as with the domain functional levels, Windows Server 2008 has dropped *all* support for Windows NT 4.0 BDCs; the minimum forest functional level supported by a Windows Server 2008 domain is Windows 2000 native.

The forest functional level is stored in the msDS-Behavior-Version attribute of the Partitions container in the Configuration NC. For example, in the *adatum.com* forest, it would be stored in cn=partitions,cn=configuration,dc=adatum,dc=com. The value contained in msDS-Behavior-Version is mirrored to the forestFunctionality attribute of the RootDSE, which means you can find the functional level of the forest by querying the RootDSE.

One of the benefits of the GUI solution is that if a problem occurs, you can save and view the output log, which will contain information on any errors that were encountered.

Using PowerShell

While the PowerShell syntax in this recipe drills down to the native .NET classes and methods, it is presented here because the syntax is largely self-documenting, and it provides a much shortened alternative to the VBScript method.

See Also

Recipe 2.9 for changing domain mode, Recipe 2.10 for raising the functional level of a Windows Server 2003/2008 domain, Recipe 2.12 for preparing a forest with AdPrep, Chapter 1 of *Active Directory*, and MS KB 322692 (How to Raise the Domain Functional Level in Windows Server 2003 or Windows Server 2008)

2.12 Using AdPrep to Prepare a Domain or Forest for Windows Server 2003 or 2008

Problem

You want to upgrade your existing Active Directory domain controllers to Windows Server 2003 or Windows Server 2008. Before doing this, you must run the AdPrep tool, which extends the schema and adds several objects in Active Directory that are necessary for new features and enhancements.

Solution

To prepare a Windows 2000 domain or forest for a Windows Server 2003 upgrade, you will first run the following command on the Schema FSMO with the credentials of an account that is in both the *Enterprise Admins* and *Schema Admins* groups:

```
> adprep /forestprep
```

After the updates from **/forestprep** have replicated throughout the forest (see Recipe 2.11), run the following command on the Infrastructure FSMO in each domain with the credentials of an account in the *Domain Admins* group:

```
> adprep /domainprep
```

If the updates from **/forestprep** have not replicated to at least the Infrastructure FSMO servers in each domain, an error will be returned when running **/domainprep**. To debug any problems you encounter, check out the AdPrep logfiles located at *%SystemRoot% \System32\Debug\Adprep\Logs*.

AdPrep can be found in the \i386 directory on the Windows Server 2003 or Windows Server 2008 CD. The tool relies on several files in that directory, so you cannot simply copy that file out to a server and run it. You must either run it from a CD or from a location where the entire directory has been copied.

To prepare to add the first Windows Server 2003 R2 domain controller to an existing domain, you will need to run the version of AdPrep contained on Disc 2 of the R2 media. The R2 preparation also includes a third AdPrep switch that will update permissions on existing Group Policy Objects (GPOs) to allow for updated functionality in the Group Policy Management Console (GPMC):

```
> adprep /domainprep /gpprep
```

The Windows Server 2008 preparation, in addition to `/forestprep`, `/domainprep`, and `/domainprep /gpprep`, also includes `/rodcprep` to allow for the installation of Read-Only Domain Controllers (RODCs), which we will discuss in Chapter 3.

Discussion

The `adprep` command prepares a Windows 2000 forest and domains for Windows Server 2003. Both `/forestprep` and `/domainprep` must be run before you can upgrade any domain controllers to Windows Server 2003 or install new Windows Server 2003 domain controllers.

The `adprep` command serves a similar function to the Exchange 2000 setup `/forestprep` and `/domainprep` commands, which prepare an Active Directory forest and domains for Exchange 2000. The `adprep /forestprep` command extends the schema and modifies some default security descriptors, which is why it must run on the Schema FSMO and under the credentials of someone in both the *Schema Admins* and *Enterprise Admins* groups. In addition, the `adprep /forestprep` and `/domainprep` commands add new objects throughout the forest, many of which are necessary for new features supported in Windows Server 2003 Active Directory.

Although not mandatory, it is helpful to run `/domainprep` from the server hosting the Infrastructure Master FSMO since this is the DC that controls the `/domainprep` process.

If you've installed Exchange 2000 or Services For Unix 2.0 in your forest prior to running AdPrep, there are schema conflicts with the AdPrep schema extensions that you'll need to fix first. MS KB 325379 and 314649 have a detailed list of compatibility issues and resolutions.

Finally, keep in mind that any Windows 2000 or Windows Server 2003 domain being prepared for a 2008 upgrade must be at the Windows 2000 Native domain functional level at minimum, as Windows Server 2008 Active Directory no longer provides support for Windows NT 4.0 BDCs.

See Also

Recipe 2.11, Recipe 2.13 for determining if AdPrep has completed, Chapter 14 of *Active Directory* for information on upgrading to Windows Server 2003, MS KB 331161 (List of Fixes to Use on Windows 2000 Domain Controllers Before You Run the Adprep/ Forestprep Command), MS KB 314649 (Windows Server 2003 Adprep/Forestprep Command Causes Mangled Attributes in Windows 2000 Forests that Contain Exchange 2000 Servers), MS KB 325379 (Upgrade Windows 2000 Domain Controllers to Windows Server 2003), MS KB 309628 (Operations That Are Performed by the adprep.exe Utility When You Add a Windows Server 2003 Domain Controller to a Windows 2000 Domain or Forest), and the Microsoft Technet site for information about the Windows Server 2008 AdPrep process

2.13 Determining Whether AdPrep Has Completed

Problem

You want to determine whether the AdPrep process, described in Recipe 2.12, has successfully prepared a domain or forest for Windows Server 2003 or Windows Server 2008. After AdPrep has completed, you will then be ready to start promoting Windows Server 2003 or Windows Server 2008 domain controllers.

Solution

To determine whether `adprep /forestprep` has completed for a Windows Server 2003 upgrade, check for the existence of the following object where *<ForestRootDN>* is the distinguished name of the forest root domain:

    cn=Windows2003Update,cn=ForestUpdates,cn=Configuration,<ForestRootDN>

To determine whether `adprep /forestprep` has completed for a Windows Server 2008 upgrade, check for the existence of the following object, where *<ForestRootDN>* is the distinguished name of the forest root domain:

    cn=ActiveDirectoryUpdate,cn=ForestUpdates,cn=Configuration,<ForestRootDN>

To determine whether `adprep /domainprep` has completed for a Windows Server 2003 upgrade, check for the existence of the following object where *<DomainDN>* is the distinguished name of the domain:

    cn=Windows2003Update,cn=DomainUpdates,cn=System,<DomainDN>

To determine whether `adprep /domainprep` has completed for a Windows Server 2008 upgrade, check for the existence of the following object where *<DomainDN>* is the distinguished name of the domain:

```
cn=ActiveDirectoryUpdate,cn=DomainUpdates,cn=System,<DomainDN>
```

Discussion

As described in Recipe 2.12, the AdPrep utility is used to prepare an Active Directory forest for the upgrade to Windows Server 2003 or Windows Server 2008. One of the nice features of AdPrep is it stores its progress in Active Directory. For /domainprep, a container with a distinguished name of cn=DomainUpdates,cn=System,<DomainDN> is created that has child object containers cn=Operations and cn=Windows2003Update for Windows Server 2003 domainprep operations. After AdPrep completes a task, such as extending the schema, it creates an object under the cn=Operations container to signify its completion. Each object has a GUID for its name, which represents some internal operation for AdPrep.

After all of the operations have completed successfully, the cn=Windows2003Update object is created to indicate /domainprep has completed for a Windows Server 2003 domainprep (see Figure 2-2).

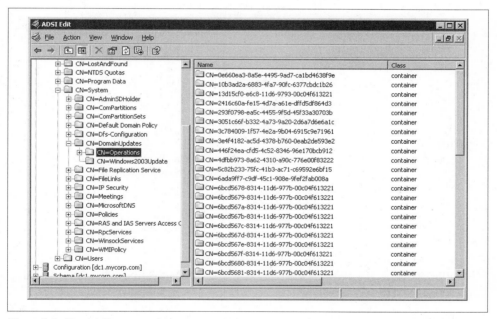

Figure 2-2. DomainPrep containers

For Windows Server 2003 /forestprep, a container with the distinguished name of cn=ForestUpdates,cn=Configuration,<ForestRootDN> is created with child object containers cn=Operations and cn=Windows2003Update.

The same principles apply as for /domainprep: after Windows Server 2003 /forestprep completes, the cn=Windows2003Update object will be created that marks the successful completion of /forestprep, and this object will have its Revision attribute set to 8. Figure 2-3 shows an example of the container structure created by /forestprep for a Windows Server 2003 forestprep.

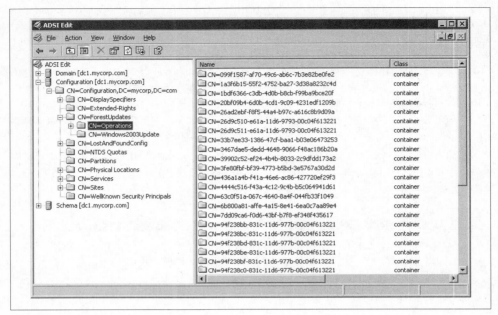

Figure 2-3. ForestPrep containers

For Windows Server 2008 /forestprep, the cn=ActiveDirectoryUpdates object is created with a Revision level of 2. When running domainprep for Windows Server 2008, the cn=ActiveDirectoryUpdate,cn=DomainUpdates,cn=System,<DomainDN> object will have a Revision level of 3.

See Also

Recipe 2.12 for running AdPrep, Chapter 12 for more on verifying Active Directory replication, Chapter 14 of *Active Directory* for upgrading to Windows Server 2003 and beyond, MS KB 324392 (Enhancements to ADPrep.exe in Windows Server 2003 Service Pack 1), MS KB 309628 (Operations That Are Performed by the adprep.exe Utility When You Add a Windows Server 2003 Domain Controller to a Windows 2000 Domain or Forest), and the Microsoft Technet site for information about the Windows Server 2008 AdPrep process

2.14 Checking If a Windows Domain Controller Can Be Upgraded to Windows Server 2003 or 2008

Problem

You want to determine whether a domain controller is ready to be upgraded to Windows Server 2003 or Windows Server 2008.

Solution

Using a graphical user interface

Windows Server 2003

Insert a Windows Server 2003 CD into the Windows 2000 domain controller or map a drive to the files contained on the CD. Run the following command from the \i386 directory:

```
> winnt32 /checkupgradeonly
```

Windows Server 2008

Download and run the Microsoft Assessment and Planning Solution Accelerator from the Microsoft website, which will generate upgrade readiness reports to help your organization prepare for an upgrade to Windows Vista and Windows Server 2008.

Using a command-line interface

To produce a compatibility report from the command line, you first need to create a text file containing the following information:

```
[Unattended]
Win9xUpgrade = Yes

[Win9xUpg]
ReportOnly = Yes
SaveReportTo = "\\server1\upgradereports\"
```

Save this file as *unattend.txt*, and then run the following from the command line:

```
> winnt32 /checkupgradeonly /unattend:c:\unattend.txt
```

Discussion

The /checkupgradeonly switch simulates the initial steps for upgrading a server to Windows Server 2003. It verifies, among other things, that AdPrep has completed and checks any installed applications against a known list of compatible and noncompatible applications with the new operating system.

Windows Server 2008 has eliminated the `/checkupgradeonly` switch in the Windows Server 2008 installation media, instead opting to provide a free inventory and analysis tool in the form of the MS Assessment and Planning (MAP) tools.

See Also

Recipe 2.13 for determining whether AdPrep has completed, MS KB 331161 (List of Fixes to Use on Windows 2000 Domain Controllers Before You Run the Adprep/ Forestprep Command), and the Assessment and Planning Tools Solution Accelerator (*http://technet.microsoft.com/en-us/library/bb977556.aspx*)

2.15 Creating an External Trust

Problem

You want to create a one-way or two-way nontransitive trust from an AD domain to a Windows NT domain, or to a domain within an untrusted Active Directory forest.

Solution

Using a graphical user interface

1. Open the Active Directory Domains and Trusts snap-in (*domain.msc*).
2. In the left pane, right-click the domain you want to add a trust for and select Properties.
3. Click on the Trusts tab.
4. Click the New Trust button.
5. After the New Trust Wizard opens, click Next.
6. Type the NetBIOS name of the NT domain or the DNS name of the AD domain, and click Next.
7. Assuming the domain name was resolvable via its NetBIOS name or FQDN, the next screen will ask for the Direction of Trust. Select Two-way, One-way incoming, or One-way outgoing, and click Next.
8. You will be given the option to create only one side of the trust, or to create both sides of the trust simultaneously. (This assumes you have administrative credentials in both domains.)
9. If you selected Two-way or One-way outgoing, you'll need to select the scope of authentication, which can be either Domain-wide or Selective, and click Next.
10. Enter and retype the trust password and click Next.
11. Click Next twice to finish.

Using a command-line interface

```
> netdom trust TrustingDomainName/d:TrustedDomainName/add
```

For example, to create a trust from the NT4 domain `ADATUM_NT4` to the `AD` domain `ADATUM`, use the following command:

```
> netdom trust ADATUM_NT4 /d:ADATUM /add
        /UserD:ADATUM\administrator /PasswordD:*
        /UserO:ADATUM_NT4\administrator /PasswordO:*
```

You can make the trust bidirectional, i.e., two-way, by adding a `/TwoWay` switch to the example.

Using PowerShell

The following code will create an outbound external trust between the local domain and a remote domain named *treyresearch.net*. This code will need to be mirrored on the opposite side of the trust in order for the trust to be fully functional:

```
$localDom = [System.DirectoryServices.ActiveDirectory.Domain]::getCurrentDomain()
$strRemoteDom = 'treyresearch.net'
$strRemoteUser = 'administrator'
$strRemotePass = 'P@ssw0rd'
$remoteCon = New-Object
System.DirectoryServices.ActiveDirectory.DirectoryContext('Domain',$strRemoteDom,
$strRemoteUser,$strRemotePass)
$remoteDom =
[System.DirectoryServices.ActiveDirectory.Domain]::GetDomain($remoteCon)
$trustDirection = 'Outbound'
$localDom.CreateTrustRelationship($remoteDom, $trustDirection)
```

Discussion

It is common when migrating from a Windows NT environment to Active Directory (or when migrating a single domain within a large, multidomain forest, as in the case of a corporate merger or divestiture) to set up trusts to downlevel master account domains or resource domains, or to create a trust relationship with a single AD domain in a remote, untrusted forest. This allows AD users to access resources in the remote domain without providing alternate credentials. Windows NT does not support transitive trusts and, therefore, your only option when working with Windows NT is to create a nontransitive trust. That means you'll need to set up individual trusts between the NT domain in question and each Active Directory domain that contains users that need to access the resources within the AD domain. In the case of a remote Active Directory forest, you might choose to establish an external trust in order to limit access to and from only the specific domain that you specify, rather than allowing implicit access between all domains on both sides of a transitive trust.

Using PowerShell

The CreateTrustRelationship() method negates the requirement of a manually specified trust password by auto-creating and using its own password under the hood.

See Also

MS KB 306733 (How to Create a Trust Between a Windows 2000 Domain and a
Windows NT 4.0 Domain), MS KB 308195 (How to Establish Trusts with a Windows
NT-Based Domain in Windows 2000), MS KB 309682 (How to Set Up a One-Way
Nontransitive Trust in Windows 2000), MS KB 325874 (How to Establish Trusts with
a Windows NT-Based Domain in Windows Server 2003), and MS KB 816301 (How to
Create an External Trust in Windows Server 2003)

2.16 Creating a Transitive Trust Between Two AD Forests

 This recipe requires at least the Windows Server 2003 forest functional
level in both forests.

Problem

You want to create a transitive trust between two AD forests. This causes all domains
in both forests to trust each other without the need for additional trusts.

Solution

Using a graphical user interface

1. Open the Active Directory Domains and Trusts snap-in (*domain.msc*).
2. In the left pane, right-click the forest root domain and select Properties.
3. Click on the Trusts tab.
4. Click the New Trust button.
5. After the New Trust Wizard opens, click Next.
6. Type the DNS name of the AD forest and click Next.
7. Select Forest trust and click Next.
8. Complete the wizard by stepping through the rest of the configuration screens.

Using a command-line interface

```
> netdom trust <Forest1DNSName> /Domain:<Forest2DNSName> /Twoway /Transitive /ADD
        [/UserD:<Forest2AdminUser> /PasswordD:*]
        [/UserO:<Forest1AdminUser> /PasswordO:*]
```

For example, to create a two-way forest trust from the AD forest *adatum.com* to the AD forest *othercorp.com*, use the following command:

```
> netdom trust adatum.com /Domain:othercorp.com /Twoway /Transitive /ADD
        /UserD:administrator@othercorp.com /PasswordD:*
        /UserO:administrator@adatum.com /PasswordO:*
```

Using PowerShell

The following code will create a two-way transitive trust between the local forest and a remote forest named *treyresearch.net*. This code will need to be mirrored on the opposite side of the trust in order for the trust to be fully functional:

```
$localFor = [System.DirectoryServices.ActiveDirectory.Forest]::getCurrentForest()
$strRemoteFor = 'treyresearch.net'
$strRemoteUser = 'administrator'
$strRemotePass = 'P@ssw0rd'
$remoteCon = New-Object
System.DirectoryServices.ActiveDirectory.DirectoryContext('Forest',
$strRemoteFor,$strRemoteUser,$strRemotePass)
$trustDirection = 'Bidirectional'$localFor.CreateTrustRelationship
($remoteFor, $trustDirection)
```

Discussion

A new type of trust called a *forest trust* was introduced in Windows Server 2003. Under Windows 2000, if you wanted to create a fully trusted environment between two forests, you would have to set up individual external two-way trusts between every domain in both forests. If you have two forests with three domains each and wanted to set up a fully trusted model, you would need nine individual trusts. Figure 2-4 illustrates how this would look.

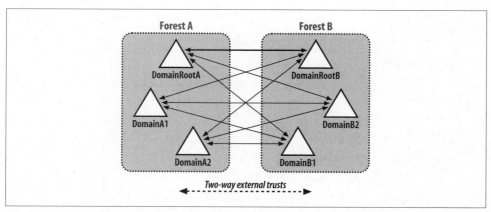

Figure 2-4. Trusts necessary for two Windows 2000 forests to fully trust each other

With a forest trust, you can define a single one-way or two-way transitive trust relationship that extends to all the domains in both forests. You may want to implement a forest trust if you merge or acquire a company and you want all of the new company's Active Directory resources to be accessible for users in your Active Directory environment and vice versa. Figure 2-5 shows a cross-forest trust scenario. To create a forest trust, you need to use accounts from the *Enterprise Admins* group in each forest.

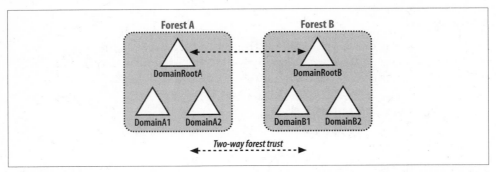

Figure 2-5. *Trust necessary for two Windows Server 2003 or Windows Server 2008 forests to trust each other using a cross-forest trust*

2.17 Creating a Shortcut Trust Between Two AD Domains

Problem

You want to create a shortcut trust between two AD domains that are in the same forest or in two different forests. Shortcut trusts can make the authentication process more efficient between two domains in a forest.

Solution

Using a graphical user interface

1. Open the Active Directory Domains and Trusts snap-in (*domain.msc*).
2. In the left pane, right-click the domain you want to add a trust for, and select Properties.
3. Click on the Trusts tab.
4. Click the New Trust button.
5. After the New Trust Wizard opens, click Next.
6. Type the DNS name of the AD domain and click Next.
7. Assuming the AD domain was resolvable via DNS, the next screen will ask for the Direction of Trust. Select Two-way and click Next.
8. For the Outgoing Trust Properties, select all resources to be authenticated and click Next.

9. Enter and retype the trust password and click Next.

10. Click Next twice.

Using a command-line interface

```
> netdom trust <Domain1DNSName> /Domain:<Domain2DNSName /Twoway /ADD
        [/UserD:<Domain2AdminUser> /PasswordD:*]
        [/UserO:<Domain1AdminUser> /PasswordO:*]
```

To create a shortcut trust from the *emea.adatum.com* domain to the *apac.adatum.com* domain, use the following `netdom` command:

```
> netdom trust emea.adatum.com /Domain:apac.adatum.com /Twoway /ADD
        /UserD:administrator@apac.adatum.com /PasswordD:*
        /UserO:administrator@emea.adatum.com /PasswordO:*
```

Discussion

Consider the forest shown in Figure 2-6. It has five domains in a single domain tree. For authentication requests for Domain 3 to be processed by Domain 5, the request must traverse the path from Domain 3 to Domain 2 to Domain 1 to Domain 4 to Domain 5. If you create a shortcut trust between Domain 3 and Domain 5, the authentication path is just a single hop from Domain 3 to Domain 5. To create a shortcut trust, you must be a member of the *Domain Admins* group in both domains, or a member of the *Enterprise Admins* group.

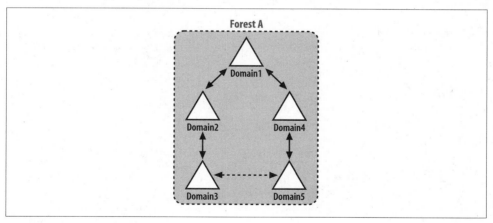

Figure 2-6. Shortcut trust

2.18 Creating a Trust to a Kerberos Realm

Problem

You want to create a trust to a Kerberos realm.

Solution

Using a graphical user interface

1. Open the Active Directory Domains and Trusts snap-in (*domain.msc*).

2. In the left pane, right-click the domain you want to add a trust for and select Properties.

3. Click on the Trusts tab.

4. Click the New Trust button.

5. After the New Trust Wizard opens, click Next.

6. Type the name of the Kerberos realm.

7. Select the radio button beside Realm Trust and click Next.

8. Select either Transitive or Nontransitive and click Next.

9. Select Two-way, One-way incoming, or One-way outgoing and click Next.

10. Enter and retype the trust password and click Next.

11. Click Next and click Finish.

Using a command-line interface

```
> netdom trust <ADDomainDNSName> /Domain:<KerberosRealmDNSName>
        /Realm /ADD /PasswordT:<TrustPassword>
        [/UserO:<ADDomainAdminUser> /PasswordO:*]
```

The `<TrustPassword>` has to match what was set on the Kerberos side. To create a realm trust from the *adatum.com* domain to the Kerberos realm called *kerb.adatum.com*, use the following command:

```
> netdom trust adatum.com /Domain:kerb.adatum.com
        /Realm /ADD /PasswordT:MyKerbRealmPassword
        /UserO:administrator@adatum.com /PasswordO:*
```

Discussion

You can create a Kerberos realm trust between an Active Directory domain and a non-Windows Kerberos v5 realm. A realm trust can be used to allow clients from the non-Windows Kerberos realm to access resources in Active Directory, and vice versa. See Recipe 15.5 for more information on MIT Kerberos interoperability with Active Directory.

See Also

Recipe 15.5, MS KB 260123 (Information on the Transitivity of a Kerberos Realm Trust), and MS KB 266080 (Answers to Frequently Asked Kerberos Questions)

2.19 Viewing the Trusts for a Domain

Problem

You want to view the trusts that have been configured for a domain.

Solution

Using a graphical user interface

1. Open the Active Directory Domains and Trusts snap-in (*domain.msc*).
2. In the left pane, right-click the domain you want to view and select Properties.
3. Click on the Trusts tab.

Using a command-line interface

To enumerate domain trusts using the *netdom* utility, use the following syntax:

```
> netdom query trust /Domain:<DomainDNSName>
```

You can also use *nltest*, available from the Windows Support Tools, as follows:

```
> nltest /domain_trusts /All_Trusts
```

Using VBScript

```
strComputer = "."
Set objWMIService = GetObject("winmgmts:" _
    & "{impersonationLevel=impersonate}!\\" & _
    strComputer &  "\root\MicrosoftActiveDirectory")

Set trustList = objWMIService.ExecQuery _
    ("Select * from Microsoft_DomainTrustStatus")

For each trust in trustList
    Wscript.Echo "Trusted domain: " &  trust.TrustedDomain
    Wscript.Echo "Trust direction: " &  trust.TrustDirection
    Wscript.Echo "(1: inbound, 2: outbound, 3: two-way)"
    Wscript.Echo "Trust type: " &  trust.TrustType
    Wscript.Echo "(1: downlevel, 2: uplevel, 3: realm, 4: DCE)"
    Wscript.Echo "Trust attributes: " &  trust.TrustAttributes
    Wscript.Echo "(1: nontransitive, 2: up-level clients only,"
    Wscript.Echo " 4: tree parent, 8: tree root)"
    Wscript.Echo "Trusted domain controller name: " &  trust.TrustedDCName
Next
```

If the *adatum.com* domain is configured with a two-way external trust with the *barcelona.corp* domain, running this script from *dc1.adatum.com* would produce the following output:

```
Microsoft (R) Windows Script Host Version 5.6
Copyright (C) Microsoft Corporation 1996-2001. All rights reserved.
```

```
Trusted domain: barcelona.corp
Trust direction: 3
(1: inbound, 2: outbound, 3: two-way)
Trust type: 2
(1: downlevel, 2: uplevel, 3: realm, 4: DCE)
Trust attributes: 4
(1: nontransitive, 2: up-level clients only,
4: tree parent, 8: tree root)
Trusted domain controller name: \\dc1.barcelona.corp
```

Using PowerShell

```
$dom = [System.DirectoryServices.ActiveDirectory.Domain]::getCurrentDomain()
$dom.GetAllTrustRelationships() | format-list *
```

If the *adatum.com* domain is configured with a two-way external trust with the *treyresearch.net* domain, running these commands from *adatum.com* would produce the following output:

```
SourceName:      adatum.com
TargetName:      treyresearch.com
TrustType:       External
TrustDirection:  Bidirectional
```

Discussion

Using a graphical user interface

You can view the properties of a particular trust by clicking on a trust and clicking the Properties button.

Using a command-line interface

You can include the /Direct switch with *netdom* if you want to view only direct-trust relationships. If you don't use /Direct, implicit trusts that occur due to transitive trust relationships will also be listed.

The nltest command can take the following additional switches to modify the default behavior of the /domain_trusts switch:

/Primary
    Returns only the domain that the computer account you're running nltest from belongs to

/Forest
    Returns domains that are in the same forest as the primary domain

/Direct_Out
    Returns only those domains that are trusted by the primary domain

/Direct_In
    Returns only those domains that trust the primary domain

/v

   Displays domain SIDs and GUIDs

Using VBScript

The script listed in this recipe uses the TrustMon WMI provider, which is only available in Windows Server 2003 and higher. For Windows 2000 domain controllers, you can use the following script as an alternative:

```
' This code prints the trusts for the specified domain.
' ------ SCRIPT CONFIGURATION ------
strDomain = "<DomainDNSName>" ' e.g. adatum.com
' ------ END CONFIGURATION ---------

' Trust Direction Constants taken from NTSecAPI.h
set objTrustDirectionHash = CreateObject("Scripting.Dictionary")
objTrustDirectionHash.Add "DIRECTION_DISABLED", 0
objTrustDirectionHash.Add "DIRECTION_INBOUND", 1
objTrustDirectionHash.Add "DIRECTION_OUTBOUND", 2
objTrustDirectionHash.Add "DIRECTION_BIDIRECTIONAL", 3

' Trust Type Constants - taken from NTSecAPI.h
set objTrustTypeHash = CreateObject("Scripting.Dictionary")
objTrustTypeHash.Add "TYPE_DOWNLEVEL", 1
objTrustTypeHash.Add "TYPE_UPLEVEL", 2
objTrustTypeHash.Add "TYPE_MIT", 3
objTrustTypeHash.Add "TYPE_DCE", 4

' Trust Attribute Constants - taken from NTSecAPI.h
set objTrustAttrHash = CreateObject("Scripting.Dictionary")
objTrustAttrHash.Add "ATTRIBUTES_NON_TRANSITIVE", 1
objTrustAttrHash.Add "ATTRIBUTES_UPLEVEL_ONLY", 2
objTrustAttrHash.Add "ATTRIBUTES_QUARANTINED_DOMAIN", 4
objTrustAttrHash.Add "ATTRIBUTES_FOREST_TRANSITIVE", 8
objTrustAttrHash.Add "ATTRIBUTES_CROSS_ORGANIZATION", 16
objTrustAttrHash.Add "ATTRIBUTES_WITHIN_FOREST", 32
objTrustAttrHash.Add "ATTRIBUTES_TREAT_AS_EXTERNAL", 64

set objRootDSE = GetObject("LDAP://" & strDomain & "/RootDSE")
set objTrusts = GetObject("LDAP://cn=System," & _
                          objRootDSE.Get("defaultNamingContext") )

objTrusts.Filter = Array("trustedDomain")
Wscript.Echo "Trusts for " & strDomain & ":"

for each objTrust in objTrusts

   for each strFlag In objTrustDirectionHash.Keys
      if objTrustDirectionHash(strFlag) = objTrust.Get("trustDirection") then
         strTrustInfo = strTrustInfo & strFlag & " "
      end If
   next

   for each strFlag In objTrustTypeHash.Keys
```

```
        if objTrustTypeHash(strFlag) = objTrust.Get("trustType") then
            strTrustInfo = strTrustInfo &  strFlag &  " "
        end If
    next

    for each strFlag In objTrustAttrHash.Keys
        if objTrustAttrHash(strFlag) = objTrust.Get("trustAttributes") then
            strTrustInfo = strTrustInfo &  strFlag &  " "
        end If
    next

    WScript.Echo " " &  objTrust.Get("trustPartner") &  " : " &  strTrustInfo
    strTrustInfo = ""
next
```

See Also

Recipe 2.0 for attributes of trustedDomain objects, Recipe 2.20 for another way to query trusts programmatically, MS KB 228477 (How to Determine Trust Relationship Configurations), and MSDN: TRUSTED_DOMAIN_ INFORMATION_EX

2.20 Verifying a Trust

Problem

You want to verify that a trust is working correctly. This is the first diagnostic step to take if users notify you that authentication to a remote domain appears to be failing.

Solution

Using a graphical user interface

For the Windows 2000 version of the Active Directory Domains and Trusts snap-in (*domain.msc*):

1. In the left pane, right-click on the trusting domain and select Properties.
2. Click the Trusts tab.
3. Click the domain that is associated with the trust you want to verify.
4. Click the Edit button.
5. Click the Verify button.

For the Windows Server 2003 and Windows Server 2008 version of the Active Directory Domains and Trusts snap-in:

1. In the left pane, right-click on the trusting domain and select Properties.
2. Click the Trusts tab.
3. Click the domain that is associated with the trust you want to verify.

4. Click the Properties button.

5. Click the Validate button.

Using a command-line interface

```
> netdom trust <TrustingDomain> /Domain:<TrustedDomain> /Verify /verbose
    [/UserO:<TrustingDomainUser> /PasswordO:*]
    [/UserD:<TrustedDomainUser> /PasswordD:*]
```

Using VBScript

```
' The following code lists all of the trusts for the
' specified domain using the Trustmon WMI Provider.
' The Trustmon WMI Provider is supported on Windows Server 2003 and 2008.
' ------ SCRIPT CONFIGURATION ------
strDomain = "<DomainDNSName>" ' e.g. amer.adatum.com
' ------ END CONFIGURATION ---------

set objWMI = GetObject("winmgmts:\\" &  strDomain & _
                       "\root\MicrosoftActiveDirectory")
set objTrusts = objWMI.ExecQuery("Select * from Microsoft_DomainTrustStatus")
for each objTrust in objTrusts
    Wscript.Echo objTrust.TrustedDomain
    Wscript.Echo " TrustedAttributes: " &  objTrust.TrustAttributes
    Wscript.Echo " TrustedDCName: "     &  objTrust.TrustedDCName
    Wscript.Echo " TrustedDirection: "  &  objTrust.TrustDirection
    Wscript.Echo " TrustIsOk: "         &  objTrust.TrustIsOK
    Wscript.Echo " TrustStatus: "       &  objTrust.TrustStatus
    Wscript.Echo " TrustStatusString: " &  objTrust.TrustStatusString
    Wscript.Echo " TrustType: "         &  objTrust.TrustType
    Wscript.Echo ""
next

' This code shows how to search specifically for trusts
' that have failed, which can be accomplished using a WQL query that
' contains the query: TrustIsOk = False
' ------ SCRIPT CONFIGURATION ------
strDomain = "<DomainDNSName>" ' e.g. amer.adatum.com
' ------ END CONFIGURATION ---------

set objWMI = GetObject("winmgmts:\\" &  strDomain & _
                       "\root\MicrosoftActiveDirectory")
set objTrusts = objWMI.ExecQuery("select * " _
                         & " from Microsoft_DomainTrustStatus " _
                         & " where TrustIsOk = False ")
if objTrusts.Count = 0 then
   Wscript.Echo "There are no trust failures"
else
   WScript.Echo "Trust Failures:"
   for each objTrust in objTrusts
      Wscript.Echo " " & objTrust.TrustedDomain & " : " & _
                         objTrust.TrustStatusString
      Wscript.Echo ""
```

```
            next
        end if
```

Using PowerShell

```
get-WMIObject -query "select * from Microsoft_DomainTrustStatus where TrustIsOk =
False" -namespace root/MicrosoftActiveDirectory
```

Discussion

Verifying a trust consists of checking connectivity between the domains and determining if the shared secrets of a trust are synchronized between the two domains.

Using a graphical user interface

The Active Directory Domains and Trusts screens have changed somewhat between Windows 2000 and Windows Server 2003. The Verify button has been renamed Validate.

Using a command-line interface

If you want to verify a Kerberos trust, use the /Kerberos switch with the netdom command.

Using VBScript

The WMI TrustMon Provider is available in Windows Server 2003 and Windows Server 2008. It provides a nice interface for querying and checking the health of trusts. One of the benefits of using WMI to access this kind of data is that you can use WQL, the WMI Query Language, to perform complex queries to find trusts that have certain properties. WQL is a subset of SQL, which is commonly used to query databases. In the second VBScript example, we used WQL to find all trusts that have a problem. You could expand the query to include additional criteria, such as trust direction and trust type.

See Also

MSDN: TrustMon Provider

2.21 Resetting a Trust

Problem

You want to reset a trust password. If you've determined a trust is broken, you need to reset it, which will allow users to authenticate across it again.

Solution

Using a graphical user interface

Follow the same directions as Recipe 2.20. The option to reset the trust will only be presented if the Verify/Validate did not succeed. In Windows Server 2003, if the trust validation process fails, you will be prompted to reset the trust password.

Using a command-line interface

```
> netdom trust <TrustingDomain> /Domain:<TrustedDomain> /Reset /verbose
    [/UserO:<TrustingDomainUser> /PasswordO:*]
    [/UserD:<TrustedDomainUser> /PasswordD:*]
```

Using VBScript

```
' This code resets the specified trust.
' ------ SCRIPT CONFIGURATION ------
' Set to the DNS or NetBIOS name for the Windows 2000,
' Windows NT domain or Kerberos realm you want to reset the trust for.
strTrustName = "<TrustToCheck>"
' Set to the DNS name of the source or trusting domain.
strDomain = "<TrustingDomain>"
' ------ END CONFIGURATION ---------

' Enable SC_RESET during trust enumerations
set objTrustProv = GetObject("winmgmts:\\" & strDomain & _
                 "\root\MicrosoftActiveDirectory:Microsoft_TrustProvider=@")
objTrustProv.TrustCheckLevel = 3 ' Enumerate with SC_RESET
objTrustProv.Put_

' Query the trust and print status information
set objWMI = GetObject("winmgmts:\\" & strDomain & _
                    "\root\MicrosoftActiveDirectory")
set
objTrusts = objWMI.ExecQuery("Select * " _
                    & " from Microsoft_DomainTrustStatus " _
                    & " where TrustedDomain = '" & strTrustName & "'" )
for each objTrust in objTrusts
    Wscript.Echo objTrust.TrustedDomain
    Wscript.Echo " TrustedAttributes: " & objTrust.TrustAttributes
    Wscript.Echo " TrustedDCName: "     & objTrust.TrustedDCName
    Wscript.Echo " TrustedDirection: "  & objTrust.TrustDirection
    Wscript.Echo " TrustIsOk: "         & objTrust.TrustIsOK
    Wscript.Echo " TrustStatus: "       & objTrust.TrustStatus
    Wscript.Echo " TrustStatusString: " & objTrust.TrustStatusString
    Wscript.Echo " TrustType: "         & objTrust.TrustType
    Wscript.Echo ""
next
```

Using PowerShell

```
$localDom = [System.DirectoryServices.ActiveDirectory.Domain]::getCurrentDomain()
$strRemoteDom = 'treyresearch.net'
$remoteCon = New-Object
System.DirectoryServices.ActiveDirectory.DirectoryContext('Domain',$strRemoteDom,
$strRemoteUser,$strRemotePass)
$remoteDom =
[System.DirectoryServices.ActiveDirectory.Domain]::GetDomain($remoteCon)
$localDom.RepairTrustRelationship($remoteDom)
```

Discussion

Resetting a trust synchronizes the shared secrets (i.e., passwords) for the trust. The
PDC Emulators in both domains are used to synchronize the password, so they must
be reachable.

Using a command-line interface

If you are resetting a Kerberos realm trust, you'll need to specify the /PasswordT option
with netdom.

Using PowerShell

To repair a cross-forest trust relationship, you would create objects referencing the local
and remote forests, rather than the local and remote domains. For example:

```
$localFor = [System.DirectoryServices.ActiveDirectory.Forest]::getCurrentForest()
$strRemoteFor = 'treyresearch.net'
$remoteCon = New-Object
System.DirectoryServices.ActiveDirectory.DirectoryContext('Forest',$strRemoteDom,
$strRemoteUser,$strRemotePass)
$remoteFor =
[System.DirectoryServices.ActiveDirectory.Forest]::GetForest($remoteCon)
$localFor.RepairTrustRelationship($remoteFor)
```

See Also

Recipe 2.20 for verifying a trust

2.22 Removing a Trust

Problem

You want to remove a trust. This is commonly done when the remote domain has been
decommissioned or access to it is no longer required.

Solution

Using a graphical user interface

1. Open the Active Directory Domains and Trusts snap-in (*domain.msc*).
2. In the left pane, right-click on the trusting domain and select Properties.
3. Click the Trusts tab.
4. Click on the domain that is associated with the trust you want to remove.
5. Click the Remove button.
6. Click OK.

Using a command-line interface

To remove a trust relationship using the `netdom` utility, use the following syntax:

```
> netdom trust <TrustingDomain> /Domain:<TrustedDomain> /Remove /verbose
   [/UserO:<TrustingDomainUser> /PasswordO:*]
   [/UserD:<TrustedDomainUser> /PasswordD:*]
```

To remove a trust using a combination of AdFind and AdMod, issue the following two commands:

```
> adfind -b cn=<Trusted Domain>,cn=system,<Domain DN> -dsq | admod -rm
> adfind -b cn=<TrustName>$,cn=users,<Domain DN> -dsq | admod -rm
```

> Both of these commands first use AdFind to return the object that needs to be deleted, then use the | operator to send that object to AdMod to perform the actual deletion.

Using VBScript

```
' This code deletes a trust in the specified domain.
' ------ SCRIPT CONFIGURATION ------
' Set to the DNS or NetBIOS name for the Windows 2000,
' Windows NT domain or Kerberos realm trust you want to delete.
strTrustName = "<TrustName>"
' Set to the DNS name of the source or trusting domain
strDomain = "<DomainDNSName>"
' ------ END CONFIGURATION ---------

set objRootDSE = GetObject("LDAP://" &  strDomain &  "/RootDSE")
set objTrust = GetObject("LDAP://cn=System," & _
                         objRootDSE.Get("defaultNamingContext") )
objTrust.Delete "trustedDomain", "cn=" &  strTrustName
set objTrustUser = GetObject("LDAP://cn=Users," & _
                             objRootDSE.Get("defaultNamingContext") )
objTrustUser.Delete "trustedDomain", "cn=" &  strTrustName &  "$"
WScript.Echo "Successfully deleted trust for " &  strTrustName
```

Using PowerShell

The following code will remove an external trust relationship configured between the local domain and the *treyresearch.net* domain. This code needs to be mirrored in the remote domain to fully remove the trust relationship:

```
$localDom = [System.DirectoryServices.ActiveDirectory.Domain]::getCurrentDomain()
$strRemoteDom = 'treyresearch.net'
$strRemoteUser = 'Administrator'
$strRemotePass = 'P@ssw0rd'
$remoteCon = New-Object
System.DirectoryServices.ActiveDirectory.DirectoryContext('Domain',$strRemoteDom,
$strRemoteUser,$strRemotePass)
$remoteDom =
[System.DirectoryServices.ActiveDirectory.Domain]::GetDomain($remoteCon)
$localDom = DeleteTrustRelationship($remoteDom)
```

Discussion

Trusts are stored in Active Directory as two objects: a **trustedDomain** object in the **System** container and a **user** object in the **Users** container. Both of these objects need to be removed when deleting a trust. The GUI and **netdom** solutions take care of that in one step, but in the VBScript and AdMod examples, both objects needed to be explicitly deleted. It is also worth noting that each solution only deleted one side of the trust. If the trust was to a remote AD forest or NT 4.0 domain, you also need to delete the trust in that domain.

2.23 Enabling SID Filtering for a Trust

Problem

You want to enable Security Identifier (SID) filtering for a trust. By enabling SID filtering, you can keep a hacker from spoofing an SID across a trust.

Solution

Using a command-line interface

```
> netdom trust <TrustingDomain> /Domain:<TrustedDomain> /EnableSIDHistory:No
  [/UserO:<TrustingDomainUser> /PasswordO:*]
  [/UserD:<TrustedDomainUser> /PasswordD:*]
```

Using PowerShell

The following PowerShell code retrieves the current SID Filtering setting on an external trust configured between the local domain and the remote *treyresearch.net* domain:

```
$dom = [System.DirectoryServices.Activedirectory.Domain]::getCurrentDomain()
$dom.GetSidFilteringStatus('treyresearch.net')
```

The following code enables SID Filtering on a trust configured between the local domain and the remote *treyresearch.net* domain:

```
$dom = [System.DirectoryServices.Activedirectory.Domain]::getCurrentDomain()
$dom.SetSidFilteringStatus('treyresearch.net', $true)
```

Discussion

A security vulnerability exists with the use of SID history, which is described in detail in MS KB 289243. An administrator in a trusted domain can modify the SID history for a user, which could grant her elevated privileges in the trusting domain. The risk of this exploit is relatively low due to the complexity of forging an SID, but nevertheless, you should be aware of it. To prevent this from happening you can enable SID Filtering for a trust. When SID filtering is enabled, the only SIDs that are used as part of a user's token are from those domains in the trust path of the trusted domain—so if the trusted domain is *adatum.com*, which has a child domain called *emea.adatum.com*, SID filtering would accept SIDs from both the *adatum.com* domain and its child domain *emea*. SIDs that are not a part of the trusted domain's trust path are not included, so an SID from the *barcelona.corp* would be stripped from the user's access token. SID filtering makes things more secure, but prevents the use of SID history and can cause problems with transitive trusts and domain migrations. For example, if we migrated a user from *barcelona.corp* to *adatum.com*, that user's *barcelona.corp* SID history entry would be ignored as long as SID filtering was in place. You would need to update the Access Control Lists (ACLs) on resources in *barcelona.corp* to point to the migrated user's *adatum.com* SID, which would allow the user to access them with SID filtering in place.

SID filtering is enabled by default on all trust relationships created in Windows 2000 Service Pack 4 and later. This can cause unexpected behavior if you create a trust relationship under an earlier Service Pack version, but then delete and re-create the trust under SP4 or later. You can disable SID filtering by running the `netdom` command with the `/EnableSIDHistory:Yes` switch.

Using PowerShell

To target a cross-forest trust instead of an external trust, use the `getCurrentForest()` method to create a forest object and use the same syntax for the `SetSidFilteringStatus()` method.

To disable SID Filtering for a trust, call the `SetSidFilteringStatus()` method with a second parameter of `$false` instead of `$true`. (`$true` and `$false` are constant variables that can be used as Booleans in any method that calls for them; we did not need to manually define the values of `$true` and `$false`.)

See Also

MS KB 289243 (MS02-001: Forged SID Could Result in Elevated Privileges in Windows 2000)

2.24 Enabling Quarantine for a Trust

Problem

You want to enable Quarantine for a trust. By enabling Quarantine, you can greatly restrict the acceptable domain SIDs in a trust relationship.

Solution

Using a command-line interface

```
> netdom trust <TrustingDomain> /Domain:<TrustedDomain> /Quarantine:Yes
  [/UserO:<TrustingDomainUser> /PasswordO:*]
  [/UserD:<TrustedDomainUser> /PasswordD:*]
```

Discussion

A security vulnerability exists with the use of SID history, which is described in detail in MS KB 289243. An administrator in a trusted domain can modify the SID history for a user, which could grant him elevated privileges in the trusting domain. The risk of this exploit is relatively low due to the complexity in forging an SID, but nevertheless, you should be aware of it. You can put in strong restrictions in order to minimize the risk of privilege elevation by enabling Quarantine for a trust. When Quarantine is enabled, the only SIDs that are used as part of a user's token are from those domains in the trusted domain itself. So if the trusted domain is *adatum.com*, which has a child domain called *emea.adatum.com*, Quarantine will only accept SIDs from *adatum.com* itself. Even domain SIDs that are a part of the trusted domain's trust path are not included, so an SID from *emea.adatum.com* would be stripped from the user's access token. Enabling Quarantine for a trust effectively removes the transitivity of a forest trust relationship, restricting the trust relationship to only the domain that you specified when you created the trust. (This causes a forest trust to emulate the default behavior of an external trust instead.)

You can disable Quarantine on a trust relationship by running the `netdom` command again and specifying the `/Quarantine:No` switch.

2.25 Managing Selective Authentication for a Trust

Problem

You want to enable or disable Selective Authentication for a trust. By enabling Selective Authentication, you can control which computers in a trusting domain users in a trusted domain can access. Disabling Selective Authentication will allow users in the trusted domain to authenticate to any computer in the trusting domain.

Solution

Using a graphical user interface

To enable Selective Authentication:

1. Open the Active Directory Domains and Trusts snap-in (*domain.msc*).
2. To enable selective authentication for a forest trust, right-click on the forest root domain and select Properties. To enable selective authentication for an external trust, right-click on the domain you wish to configure and select Properties.
3. On the Trusts tab, right-click on the trust that you wish to administer, and select Properties.
4. On the Authentication tab, click Selective Authentication.
5. Click OK to finish.

To disable Selective Authentication:

1. Open the Active Directory Domains and Trusts snap-in.
2. To enable forest-wide authentication for a forest trust, right-click on the forest root domain and select Properties. To enable domain-wide authentication for an external trust, right-click on the domain you wish to configure and select Properties.
3. On the Trusts tab, right-click on the trust that you wish to administer, and select Properties.
4. In the case of a forest trust, on the Authentication tab click Forest-Wide Authentication. For an external trust, on the Authentication tab click Domain-Wide Authentication.
5. Click OK to finish.

To grant permissions on individual computers in the trusted domain:

1. Open the Active Directory Users and Computers snap-in (*dsa.msc*).
2. Right-click on the computer object that you wish to grant permissions on, and select Properties.
3. On the Security tab, select the user or group that you want to authorize, and select the Allow checkbox next to the Allowed to Authenticate permission.
4. Click OK to finish.

Using a command-line interface

To enable Selective Authentication, use the following syntax:

```
> netdom trust <TrustingDomain> /Domain:<TrustedDomain> /SelectiveAUTH:Yes
  [/UserO:<TrustingDomainUser> /PasswordO:*]
  [/UserD:<TrustedDomainUser> /PasswordD:*]
```

Use the `/SelectiveAUTH:No` switch to enable domain- or forest-wide authentication.

Using PowerShell

To retrieve the current Selective Authentication setting for a trust configured between the local domain and the remote *treyresearch.net* domain, use the following syntax:

```
$dom = [System.DirectoryServices.ActiveDirectory.Domain]::getCurrentDomain()
$dom.GetSelectiveAuthenticationStatus('treyresearch.net')
```

To toggle the Selective Authentication setting for this trust off and on, use the following syntax:

```
$dom.SetSelectiveAuthenticationStatus('treyresearch.net', $true)
$dom.SetSelectiveAuthenticationStatus('treyresearch.net', $false)
```

Discussion

Trust relationships in Windows Server 2003 and Windows Server 2008 forests, by default, allow users in a trusting domain to authenticate to and access shared resources on any computer in the trusted domain. Selective Authentication, also known as the Authentication Firewall, will restrict access to only those computers in the trusted domain that you specifically designate. This level of increased security is particularly useful when you need to grant access to shared resources in your forest, but you need to restrict that access to only a limited set of users in the remote forest.

For users in a trusted Windows Server 2003 or 2008 domain or forest to be able to access resources in a trusting Windows Server 2003 or 2008 domain or forest, where the trust authentication setting has been set to Selective Authentication, each user must be explicitly granted the Allowed to Authenticate permission on the security descriptor of the computer objects (resource computers) that reside in the trusting domain or forest. By default, only members of the *Account Operators, Administrators, Domain Admins, Enterprise Admins*, and *SYSTEM* groups in the trusting domain have the ability to modify this permission.

 Enabling Selective Authentication has the potential to create a huge increase in your AD administrative overhead, and should only be enabled when the security risks justify the administrative implications.

2.26 Finding Duplicate SIDs in a Domain

Problem

You want to find any duplicate SIDs in a domain. Generally, you should never be able to find duplicate SIDs in a domain, but it is possible in some situations, such as when the relative identifier (RID) FSMO role owner has to be seized or you are migrating users from Windows NT domains.

Solution

Using a command-line interface

To find duplicate SIDs, run the following command, replacing *<DomainController-Name>* with a domain controller or domain name:

```
> ntdsutil "sec acc man" "co to se <DomainControllerName" "check dup sid" q q
```

The following message will be returned:

```
Duplicate SID check completed successfully. Check dupsid.log for any duplicates
```

The *dupsid.log* file will be in the directory where you started *ntdsutil*.

If you want to delete any objects that have duplicate SIDs, you can use the following command:

```
> ntdsutil "sec acc man" "co to se <DomainControllerName>" "clean dup sid" q q
```

Like the **check** command, the **clean** command will generate a message like the following upon completion:

```
Duplicate SID cleanup completed successfully. Check dupsid.log for any duplicate
```

Discussion

All security principals in Active Directory have an SID, which is used to uniquely identify the object in the Windows security system. There are two parts of an SID: the domain identifier and the RID. Domain controllers are allocated an RID pool from the RID FSMO for the domain. When a new security principal (user, group, or computer) is created, the domain controller takes an RID from its pool to generate an SID for the account.

In some rare circumstances, such as when the RID master role is seized, overlapping RID pools can be allocated, which can ultimately lead to duplicate SIDs. Having duplicate SIDs is a potentially hazardous problem because a user, group, or computer could gain access to sensitive data they were never intended to have access to.

See Also

MS KB 315062 (How to Find and Clean Up Duplicate Security Identifiers with Ntdsutil in Windows 2000) and MS KB 816099 (How to Find and Clean Up Duplicate Security Identifiers with Ntdsutil in Windows Server 2003)

2.27 Adding Additional Fields to Active Directory Users and Computers

Problem

You want to add to the list of attributes that you can search and sort records by within the ADUC MMC snap-in (*dsa.msc*).

Solution

Using a graphical user interface

In this example, we will add the operating system service-pack-level attributes of computer objects to ADUC to allow you to search and sort by these fields:

1. Open ADSI Edit from the Windows Support Tools.
2. If an entry for the Configuration NC is not already displayed, do the following:
3. Right-click on ADSI Edit in the right pane and click "Connect to...".
4. Under "Select a well-known naming context," select Configuration. Click Advanced if you need to specify alternate credentials, then click OK to create the connection.
5. In the left pane, click on CN=DisplaySpecifiers, then CN=409. Right-click on the container and select Properties.

 If you are using a locale other than US English, specify the appropriate local number in place of CN=409, using the reference listed at *http://www .microsoft.com/globaldev/reference/lcid-all.mspx*.

6. Right-click on cn=computerDisplay and select Properties.
7. Double-click on attributeDisplayNames. Type operatingSystemServicePack, Operating System Service Pack, and click Add.
8. Click Apply, followed by OK.

Using a command-line interface

First create an LDIF file containing the following information, and save it as *modify_display_specifiers.ldif*:

```
dn: cn=computer-display,cn=409,cn=DisplaySpecifiers,
    cn=Configuration, <ForestRootDN>
changetype: modify
add: attributeDisplayNames
attributeDisplayNames: operatingSystemServicePack,Operating System Service Pack
-
```

Then run the following command:

```
> ldifde -v -i -f modify_display_specifiers.ldf
```

You can also modify this information using a combination of AdFind and AdMod, as follows:

```
> adfind -config -rb cn=computer-display,cn=409,cn=DisplaySpecifiers | admod
"attributeDisplayNames:+:operatingSystemServicePack,Operating System Service Pack"
```

Using VBScript

```
' The following script will append a new value to the
' US English display specifiers
'---------- SCRIPT CONFIGURATION ------------------
  Const ADS_PROPERTY_APPEND = 3
  strForestRoot = "<ForestRootDN>" ' i.e., "dc=adatum,dc=com"
' --------- END CONFIGURATION --------------------\

strObjectDN = "cn=computer-display,cn=409,cn=displayspecifiers," & _
              "cn=configuration," &  strForestRoot
set objObject = GetObject("LDAP://" &  strObjectDN)
objObject.PutEx ADS_PROPERTY_APPEND, _
  "attributeDisplayNames", Array("operatingSystemServicePackLevel, " & _
  "Operating System Service Pack Level")
objObject.setInfo

WScript.Echo "Script completed successfully!"
```

Discussion

When working within the Active Directory Users and Computers MMC snap-in, there are a number of default attributes for each type of object that you can use to either search or sort on. Computer objects, for example, allow you to search and sort by the computer name, description, manager, operating system, and pre-Windows 2000 computer name. Once you add a new attribute to the display specifiers, you can access it by opening ADUC, right-clicking on a container, and clicking on Find. Select Computers in the drop-down box next to Find, and click on Advanced. When you click on Field, you'll see the new field that you just added; you can now use it to search for objects within the ADUC snap-in.

Using VBScript

Because the `attributeDisplayNames` attribute is multivalued, we need to use the `PutEx` method to add a value to an existing list of values. If you accidentally use `Put` to update a multivalued attribute, you will overwrite the list of values with the single value you specify in the script.

See Also

Recipe 4.14 for more on modifying an object, MSDN: Attribute-Display-Names [AD Schema], and MSDN: PutEx Method [ADSI]

## CHAPTER 3

Domain Controllers, Global Catalogs, and FSMOs

3.0 Introduction

Domain controllers are servers that host an Active Directory domain and provide authentication and directory services to clients. A domain controller (DC) can only be authoritative (i.e., it can only process authentication requests) for a single domain, but it can store partial read-only copies of objects in other domains in the forest if it is enabled as a global catalog server. All domain controllers in a forest also host a copy of the Configuration and Schema Naming Contexts, which are replicated to all domain controllers in a forest.

In Windows 2000 and Windows Server 2003, Active Directory domain controllers are fully multimaster in nature, meaning that updates to the directory (with a few exceptions, which we'll discuss next) can originate on any domain controller in a forest. However, some tasks are sufficiently sensitive in nature that they cannot be distributed to all DCs, due to the potential of significant issues arising from more than one DC performing the same update simultaneously. For example, if two different domain controllers made conflicting updates to the schema, the impact could be severe and could result in data loss or an unusable directory. For this reason, Active Directory mandates the use of Flexible Single Master Operations (FSMO, pronounced "fiz-mo") roles. For each FSMO role, there is only one domain controller that acts as the role owner and performs the tasks associated with the role. These roles are termed "single master" because only a single DC can hold a role at any one time, but "flexible" because a single physical server can host multiple FSMOs, and a FSMO role can be transferred from one DC to another, largely without repercussion. In each Active Directory forest there are two FSMO roles that are unique across an entire forest, and three FSMO roles that appear within each domain. So in the case of a forest containing three domains, there would be two forest-wide FSMO role-holders and *nine* domain-wide FSMO role-holders, three for each of the three domains. See Recipe 3.32 for more information on FSMO roles.

In Windows Server 2008, Microsoft has introduced the Read-Only Domain Controller, or RODC, to improve security for organizations that need to deploy DCs in branch offices or other remote locations where the physical or logical security of the DC might not be completely assured. An RODC will receive replication updates from writable DCs in the same domain, but no domain controller will replicate from an RODC. See Recipe 3.2 for more information on RODCs.

The Anatomy of a Domain Controller

Each domain controller is represented in Active Directory by several objects; the two main ones are a `computer` object and an `nTDSDSA` object. The `computer` object is necessary because a domain controller needs to be represented as a security principal just like any other type of computer in Active Directory. The default location in a domain for domain controller `computer` objects is the `Domain Controllers` Organizational Unit (OU) at the root of the domain. They can be moved to a different OU, but it is highly recommended that you don't move them unless you know what you are doing and have a good reason for doing so. This is because any DCs that you move outside of the Domain Controller's OU will not receive the same Group Policy Object settings as those within the OU, which can lead to unpredictable behavior on your network. Table 3-1 contains some useful attributes of domain controller `computer` objects.

Table 3-1. Attributes of domain controller computer objects

Attribute	Description
dnsHostName	Fully qualified DNS name of the DC.
msDS-AdditionalDnsHostName	Contains the old DNS name of a renamed DC. This was first introduced in Windows Server 2003.
msDS-AdditionalSamAccountName	Contains the old NetBIOS name of a renamed DC. This was first introduced in Windows Server 2003.
operatingSystem	Textual description of the operating system running on the DC.
operatingSystemHotFix	Currently not being used, but will hopefully be populated with the installed hotfixes at some point.
operatingSystemServicePack	Service pack version installed on the DC.
operatingSystemVersion	Numeric version of the operating system installed on the DC.
sAMAccountName	NetBIOS-style name of the DC.
serverReferenceBL	DN of the DC's `server` object contained under the `Sites` container in the Configuration NC.
servicePrincipalName	List of SPNs supported by the DC.

Domain controllers are also represented by several objects under the `Sites` container in the Configuration NC. The `Sites` container stores objects that are needed to create a site topology, including `site`, `subnet`, `sitelink`, and `server` objects. The site topology is necessary so that domain controllers, DFS file shares, and site-specific Group Policy

Objects can replicate data efficiently around the network. See Chapter 11 for more information on sites and replication.

Each domain controller has an nTDSDSA object that is subordinate to the domain controller's **server** object in the site it is a member of. For example, if the DC1 domain controller were part of the RTP site, its nTDSDSA object would be located here:

```
cn=NTDS Settings,cn=DC1,cn=RTP,cn=sites,cn=configuration,dc=adatum,dc=com
```

Table 3-2 lists some of the interesting attributes that are stored with nTDSDSA objects.

Table 3-2. Attributes of domain controller nTDSDSA objects

Attribute	Description
hasMasterNCs	List of DNs for the naming contexts the DC is authoritative for. This does not include application partitions.
hasPartialReplicaNCs	List of DNs for the naming contexts the DC has a partial read-only copy of.
msDS-HasDomainNCs	The DN of the domain the DC is authoritative for. This is new in Windows Server 2003.
msDS-HasMasterNCs	List of DNs for the naming contexts (domain, configuration, and schema) and application partitions the DC is authoritative for. This is new in Windows Server 2003.
options	If the low-order bit of this attribute is set, the domain controller stores a copy of the global catalog.
invocationID	GUID that is assigned to the Active Directory database itself when the domain controller is first installed. When the DC is first installed, the invocationID value is the same as the objectGUID for the DC itself; however, the invocationID changes whenever a restore operation is performed or when the DC is configured to host an application partition.

RODCs also maintain a number of RODC-specific attributes, primarily relating to the Password Replication Policy (PRP) that is configured for each RODC in an Active Directory forest. As discussed previously, 2000 and 2003 DCs will store an entire copy of the Domain NC on the hard drive of each DC, which creates a significant liability if the physical or logical security of one of these DCs is compromised. By contrast, an RODC will store *most* information from the Domain NC, but by default will not store passwords and other security secrets for any Active Directory user account. (A default RODC will contain only secrets for the local Administrator and the local krbtgt account, both of which are required for the RODC to function.) An Active Directory administrator can configure a Password Replication Policy for a single RODC or for all RODCs in a domain that will specify the following:

- Users and computers whose password secrets are permitted to be cached on a single RODC or on all RODCs in a domain
- Users and computers whose password secrets are *never* permitted to be cached on a single RODC, or on all RODCs in a domain

In order to maintain the above information, each RODC contains a number of attributes relating to the Password Replication Policy. Each RODC will also maintain information pertaining to which user and computer accounts' password secrets have *actually* been cached by a particular RODC, instead of merely being *permitted* to do so.

Table 3-3 lists some of the interesting attributes pertaining to Password Replication Policy that are stored within an RODC's `computer` object.

Table 3-3. Interesting attributes of a Read-Only Domain Controller

Attribute	Description
`msDS-Reveal-OnDemandGroup`	Accounts that are allowed to be cached on the RODC
`msDS-NeverRevealGroup`	Accounts that are not allowed to be cached on the RODC
`msDS-AuthenticatedAtDC`	A forward link indicating a list of RODCs through which a user has successfully authenticated to a full DC
`msDS-AuthenticatedToAccountList`	A backlink indicating a list of accounts that have successfully authenticated to a full DC through the RODC

3.1 Promoting a Domain Controller

Problem

You want to promote a server to a domain controller. You may need to promote a domain controller to initially create a domain in an Active Directory forest, or to add additional domain controllers to a domain for load balancing and fault tolerance.

Solution

On a Windows Server 2003 computer, run *dcpromo.exe* from a command line or via Start→Run and answer the questions according to the forest and domain you want to promote the server into.

On a Windows Server 2008 computer, click Start→Server Manager, and then use the Server Manager MMC to add the Active Directory Domain Services binaries to the server, after which you will be prompted to launch *dcpromo.exe*. (If you launch *dcpromo.exe* prior to adding the AD DS binaries, the *dcpromo.exe* wizard will appear to pause before launching as the binaries are installed in the background.)

Discussion

Promoting a server to a domain controller is the process where the server becomes authoritative for an Active Directory domain. When you run the *dcpromo* program, a wizard interface walks you through a series of screens that collects information about the forest and domain to promote the server into. There are several options for promoting a server to domain controller status:

- Promoting into a new forest (see Recipe 2.1)
- Promoting into a new domain tree or child domain (see Recipe 2.3)
- Promoting into an existing domain

Windows Server 2008 introduces the new Server Manager MMC, which provides a single graphical point of administration for most server administration tasks, such as adding and removing server roles and features. In Windows Server 2008, the Active Directory Domain Services binaries need to be explicitly added to the server before *dcpromo* can be run; this can be done automatically by *dcpromo* or by using the Server Manager console to add the AD DS server role.

Additionally, Windows Server 2008 introduces the *servermanagercmd.exe* command-line tool, which is the equivalent to the Server Manager MMC. To add the Active Directory Domain Services role via the *servermanagercmd* tool, use the following syntax (the name of the role is case-sensitive):

```
servermanagercmd.exe -install ADDS-Domain-Controller
```

You can also automate the promotion process for either operating system by running *dcpromo* during an unattended installation. Windows Server 2008 improves this process by including an "Export Settings" option at the end of the *dcpromo* wizard that allows you to easily create an unattended installation file based on the configuration selections that you made within the wizard. See Recipe 3.8 for more details.

See Also

Recipe 2.1 for creating a new forest, Recipe 2.3 for creating a new domain, and Recipes 3.2 and 3.8

3.2 Promoting a Read-Only Domain Controller

Problem

You want to promote a new RODC in a Windows Server 2008 domain.

 This recipe requires that at least one writable Windows Server 2008 be present in the domain.

Solution

1. First, add the Active Directory Domain Services role using Server Manager. Once the role has been added, run `dcpromo` from a command line or from the Run line on the start menu.

2. Click Next twice to begin the *dcpromo* wizard. After the *dcpromo* wizard starts, select Existing Forest→Add a Domain Controller to an existing domain and click Next.

3. In the Network Credentials screen, enter the name of the domain to which you are adding the DC, and specify valid network credentials for the domain if necessary. Click Next.

4. In the Select a Domain screen, select the domain to which you wish to add the DC and then click Next.

5. In the Select a Site screen, select the site that the new DC should belong to and then click Next.

6. In the Additional Domain Controller Options screen, place a checkmark next to Read-Only Domain Controller. Click Next.

7. On the Location for Database, Log Files, and SYSVOL screen, modify the default location of the Active Directory database files, log files, and SYSVOL share if necessary, or else just click Next.

8. On the Directory Services Restore Mode screen, enter and confirm a recovery password for Active Directory and then click Next.

9. Click Next to begin the promotion; restart the server when prompted.

Discussion

In order to add a Read-Only Domain Controller to an Active Directory domain, the domain must be running at the Windows Server 2003 domain functional mode or better, and there must be at least one writable Windows Server 2008 domain controller available, since a 2008 RODC will only accept replication traffic from a 2008 writable DC.

To further customize the behavior of an RODC installation, you can select the Advanced installation option, which will allow you to install an RODC using IFM media, as well as customizing the Password Replication Policy. The installation of an RODC can also be automated using an *unattend.txt* file as described in a later recipe.

See Also

Recipes 3.3, 3.4, 3.6, and 3.8

3.3 Performing a Two-Stage RODC Installation

Problem

You want to perform a two-stage promotion of an RODC in a Windows Server 2008 domain.

This recipe requires that at least one writable Windows Server 2008 be present in the domain.

Solution

The first stage of the two-stage installation process is performed from a writable Windows Server 2008 domain controller, using the steps listed below.

The server designated to be configured as an RODC must be joined to a workgroup prior to the start of this process; if the computer is joined to the 2008 domain as a member server, these steps will fail. The server must also be configured with the same name that you will specify in the steps below.

1. Open Active Directory Users and Computers.
2. Right-click on the Domain Controllers OU and click "Pre-create Read-Only Domain Controller account...". Click Next twice.
3. The Network Credentials screen appears. Click Next to create the RODC using the credentials of the currently logged-on user, or click the Alternate Credentials radio button and click Set.
4. Click Next. The Computer Name screen appears. Enter the name of the RODC computer account and click Next.
5. The Select a Site screen appears. Select the site that the RODC should reside in and click Next. The Additional Domain Controller Options screen appears. Place a checkmark next to DNS server and/or Global catalog if desired, then click Next.
6. The Delegation of RODC Installation and Administration screen appears. Click Set and enter the name of users or groups who should have local administrator rights to the RODC. Click Next twice.
7. Click Finish.

The second stage of the RODC installation will be completed from the console of the server that is to be configured as an RODC, using the following steps:

1. First, add the Active Directory Domain Services role using Server Manager. Once the role has been added, run `dcpromo` from a command line or from the Run line on the start menu.
2. Click Next twice to begin the *dcpromo* wizard. After the *dcpromo* wizard starts, select Existing Forest→Add a Domain Controller to an existing domain and click Next.

3. In the Network Credentials screen, enter the name of the domain to which you are adding the DC, and specify valid network credentials for the domain if necessary. Click Next.

4. In the Select a Domain screen, select the domain to which you wish to add the DC and then click Next.

5. The *dcpromo* wizard will indicate that it has found a pre-created RODC account matching the name of the computer. Click OK.

6. On the Location for Database, Log Files, and SYSVOL screen, modify the default location of the Active Directory database files, logfiles, and SYSVOL share if necessary, or else just click Next.

7. On the Directory Services Restore Mode screen, enter and confirm a recovery password for Active Directory and then click Next.

8. Click Next to begin the promotion; restart the server when prompted.

Discussion

When deploying RODCs to remote locations, you have the ability to perform a two-stage installation in which you pre-create the RODC's domain controller account from a central location. Once this first stage is completed, an on-site administrator can complete the installation without requiring elevated rights within Active Directory. This *Admin Role Separation* feature allows you to configure one or more users or groups as local administrators of an individual RODC, without granting administrative privileges within the Active Directory domain itself.

When pre-creating the RODC computer account, you can select the Advanced installation option to customize the Password Replication Policy for the RODC prior to deployment.

See Also

Recipe 3.4 and Chapters 6 and 7 for more on managing users and groups.

3.4 Modifying the Password Replication Policy

Problem

You wish to modify the Password Replication Policy on a Read-Only Domain Controller to control which user and computer passwords can and cannot be cached on a particular RODC.

Solution

Using a graphical user interface

1. Open Active Directory Users and Computers.
2. Click View→Advanced Features.
3. Browse to the Domain Controllers OU.
4. Right-click on the RODC's computer account and click Properties.
5. Click on the Password Replication Policy tab.
6. To add a user or group to the Password Replication Policy for this RODC, click Add.
7. To allow the user or users' passwords to be cached on this RODC, click Allow passwords for the account to replicate to this RODC. To prevent the user or users' passwords from being cached on this RODC, click Deny passwords for this account from replicating to this RODC. Click OK.
8. To remove a user or group from the Password Replication Policy from the RODC, highlight the user or group and click Remove. Click Yes to confirm.

Using a command-line interface

To add a user or group to the "Allowed to Cache" list, use the following syntax:

```
admod -b <DN of RODC> msDS-RevealOnDemandGroup:+:<DN of User/Group>
```

To remove a user or group from the "Allowed to Cache" list, use the following syntax:

```
admod -b <DN of RODC> msDS-NeverRevealGroup:-:<DN of User/Group>
```

To add a user or group to the "Denied to Cache" list, use the following syntax:

```
admod -b <DN of RODC> msDS-NeverRevealGroup:+:<DN of User/Group>
```

Using VBScript

To add a user or group to the "Allowed" or "Denied" list, use the following syntax:

```
Const ADS_PROPERTY_APPEND = 3
Set objRODC = GetObject("LDAP://<RODC DN>")
objRODC.PutEx ADS_PROPERTY_DELETE, "msDS-RevealOnDemandGroup",
Array("<DN of User/group>")
```

Discussion

A separate Password Replication Policy can be maintained individually on each Read-Only Domain Controller; this is implemented by the addition of several attributes on each RODC that control which users' passwords can and cannot be cached on the RODC in question. As a best practice it is advisable to manage these attributes using security groups rather than individual users or computers, as this makes for a much more simplified management model. By default, the following domain groups are added to the Password Replication Policy of each RODC in the domain:

- `msDS-NeverRevealGroup`
  — Account Operators
  — Administrators
  — Backup Operators
  — Denied RODC Password Replication Group
  — Server Operators
- `msDS-RevealOnDemandGroup`
  — Allowed RODC Password Replication Group

When Windows evaluates the Password Replication Policy, a "Deny" setting would override an "Allow" setting; for example, if a user is a member of two security groups that are configured with contradictory settings. As with most aspects of Windows security, the "Keep It Simple" principle should be followed whenever possible.

Using VBScript

The `msDS-NeverRevealGroup` and `msDS-RevealOnDemandGroup` attributes are multivalued, which requires the use of the `PutEx` method.

See Also

Chapter 4 for more on searching and updating Active Directory, and Chapters 6 and 7 for more on managing users and groups

3.5 Promoting a Windows Server 2003 Domain Controller from Media

 This recipe requires that the server being promoted is running Windows Server 2003.

Problem

You want to promote a new domain controller using a backup from another domain controller as the initial source of the Active Directory database instead of replicating the entire *NTDS.DIT* file over the network.

Solution

1. You first need to back up the system state of an existing domain controller in the domain the new server will go in. This can be accomplished by running the MS Backup utility found at Start→Programs→Accessories→System Tools→Backup.

2. Once you have a good backup, you then need to restore it to the new server, which can also be done using MS Backup. You should restore the files to an alternate location, not to their original location.

3. Next, run `dcpromo` with the `/adv` switch from a command line or by clicking Start→Run, as follows:

   ```
   dcpromo /adv
   ```

4. After the *dcpromo* wizard starts, select Additional Domain Controller for an existing domain and click Next.

5. Under Copy Domain Information, select "From these restored backup files." Browse to the files that you restored in Step 2, and then click Next.

6. Enter credentials of a user in the *Domain Admins* group in the domain you are promoting the domain controller into and click Next.

7. Choose the folders in which to store the Active Directory database and logfiles and click Next.

8. Choose the folder in which to store SYSVOL and click Next.

9. Enter a Restore Mode password and click Next.

10. Click Next to start the promotion.

Discussion

The ability to promote a domain controller using the System State backup of another domain controller was introduced in Windows Server 2003. With Windows 2000, a new domain controller had to replicate the entire *NTDS.DIT* Active Directory database file over a network connection object by object from an existing domain controller. For organizations with a sizable Active Directory DIT file and/or very poor network connectivity to a remote site, replicating the full contents over the network presented challenges. Under these conditions, the promotion process could take a prohibitively long time to complete. With the "Install from Media" option, the initial domain controller promotion process can be substantially quicker. After you've done the initial installation from media (i.e., backup tape or CD/DVD), the new domain controller will replicate any changes that have been made to the Active Directory database since the backup media was created.

Be sure that the age of the backup files you are using is significantly less than your AD forest's tombstone lifetime. If you install a domain controller using backup files that are older than the tombstone lifetime value, you could run into issues with deleted objects being reinjected into the Active Directory database after their tombstone lifetime has expired. In Windows Server 2003 and Windows Server 2003 R2, the default tombstone lifetime is 60 days, or 180 days for a domain that has been newly installed with Windows Server 2003 Service Pack 1 or Windows Server 2008.

See Also

Recipe 3.6, Chapter 16 for more on backing up Active Directory, Recipe 16.25 for modifying the tombstone lifetime of a domain, MS KB 216993 (Useful Shelf Life of a System-State Backup of Active Directory), and MS KB 311078 (How to Use the Install from Media Feature to Promote Windows Server 2003-based Domain Controllers)

3.6 Promoting a Windows Server 2008 Domain Controller from Media

Problem

You want to promote a new domain controller using a backup from another domain controller as the initial source of the Active Directory database instead of replicating the entire *NTDS.DIT* file over the network.

Solution

1. You first need to create an IFM backup of an existing Windows Server 2008 domain controller in the domain the new server will go in. This can be accomplished using the *ntdsutil* utility.

2. Next, add the Active Directory Domain Services role using Server Manager. Once the role has been added, run **dcpromo** with the **/adv** switch from a command line, or place a checkmark next to Use Advanced Options on the first screen of the *dcpromo* wizard.

3. Click Next twice to begin the *dcpromo* wizard. After the *dcpromo* wizard starts, select Existing Forest→Add a Domain Controller to an existing domain and click Next.

4. In the Network Credentials screen, enter the name of the domain to which you are adding the DC, and specify valid network credentials for the domain if necessary. Click Next.

5. In the Select a Domain screen, select the domain to which you wish to add the DC and then click Next.

6. In the Select a Site screen, select the site that the new DC should belong to and then click Next.

7. In the Additional Domain Controller Options screen, select one or all of the following configuration options for the new DC: DNS Server, Global Catalog, and Read-Only Domain Controller. Click Next.

8. On the Install from Media screen, select the "Replicate data from media at the following location" radio button, and browse to the location of the IFM backup that you created in step 1. Click Next.

9. On the Source Domain Controller screen, select the existing DC that you want this new DC to replicate information from, or select the "Let the wizard choose an appropriate domain controller" radio button. Click Next.

10. On the Location for Database, Log Files, and SYSVOL screen, modify the default location of the Active Directory database files, logfiles, and SYSVOL share if necessary, or else just click Next.

11. On the Directory Services Restore Mode screen, enter and confirm a recovery password for Active Directory and then click Next.

12. Click Next to begin the promotion; restart the server when prompted.

Discussion

The IFM feature in Windows Server 2008 provides a number of flexible options when promoting a 2008 DC from media:

- Creating IFM media for a writable domain controller or an AD LDS instance
- Creating IFM media for a read-only DC
- Creating IFM media for a writable DC, including a copy of the SYSVOL directory
- Creating IFM media for an RODC, including a read-only copy of the SYSVOL directory

See Also

Chapter 16 for more on backing up Active Directory, Recipe 16.25 for modifying the tombstone lifetime of a domain, MS KB 216993 (Useful Shelf Life of a System-State Backup of Active Directory), and MS KB 311078 (How to Use the Install from Media Feature to Promote Windows Server 2003-based Domain Controllers)

3.7 Demoting a Domain Controller

Problem

You want to demote a domain controller from a domain. If you want to decommission a domain controller for whatever reason, you'll need to follow these demotion procedures.

Solution

Using a graphical user interface

1. Run the dcpromo command from a command line or Start→Run.
2. Click Next.
3. If the server is the last domain controller in the domain, check the box beside "This server is the last domain controller in the domain."
4. Click Next.
5. Type and confirm the password for the local Administrator account.
6. Click Next twice to begin the demotion.

Discussion

Before demoting a domain controller, you first need to ensure that all of the FSMO roles have been transferred to other servers; otherwise, they will be transferred to random domain controllers that may not be optimal for your installation. (Managing FSMO role holders is discussed in Recipe 3.32.) Also, if the DC is a global catalog server or running a service such as DNS, WINS, DHCP, etc., ensure that you have sufficient GCs and other infrastructure servers elsewhere in your forest that can handle the increased load.

It is important to demote a domain controller before decommissioning or rebuilding it so that its associated objects in Active Directory are removed, its DNS locator resource records are dynamically removed, and replication with the other domain controllers is not interrupted. If a domain controller does not successfully demote, or if you do not get the chance to demote it because of some type of hardware failure, see Recipe 2.4 for removing a domain from Active Directory, and Recipe 3.7 for instructions on manually removing a domain controller from Active Directory.

See Also

Recipe 2.4, Recipe 3.7, Recipe 3.11 for removing an unsuccessfully demoted domain controller, Recipe 3.24 for disabling the global catalog, Recipe 3.32, Recipe 3.33 for transferring FSMO roles, and MS KB 238369 (How to Promote and Demote Domain Controllers in Windows 2000)

3.8 Automating the Promotion or Demotion of a Domain Controller

Problem

You want to automate the installation or removal of a domain controller. You can make the promotion process part of your standard build process by incorporating the necessary configuration lines in your answer file(s).

Solution

You can automate the promotion of a domain controller by using the unattended process when building the server or by manually running *dcpromo* after the system has been built. Pass an answer file containing the necessary lines to promote the server to *dcpromo* by specifying an /answer switch. Here is an example:

```
> dcpromo /answer:<path_to_answer_file>
```

If you want to run *dcpromo* as part of an unattended setup, you need to add a [GUIRunOnce] section in your unattended setup file that calls the *dcpromo* process.

You can promote a domain controller only after setup has completed and someone logs in for the first time. That is why it is necessary to use a [GUIRunOnce] section, which sets the RunOnce registry key to kick off *dcpromo* on the first user logon, either at the console or via Terminal Services. Here is an example:

```
[GUIRunOnce]
"dcpromo /answer:%systemroot%\system32\$winnt$.inf"
```

The dcpromo answer section starts with [DCInstall]. Here is an example answer file for adding a domain controller to an existing domain in the *adatum.com* forest:

```
[DCINSTALL]
UserName=administrator
Password=AdatumAdminPassword
UserDomain=adatum.com
DatabasePath=%systemroot%\ntds
LogPath=%systemroot%\ntds
SYSVOLPath=%systemroot%\sysvol
SafeModeAdminPassword=DSrestoreModePassword
CriticalReplicationOnly=no
ReplicaOrNewDomain=Replica
ReplicaDomainDNSName=adatum.com
RebootOnSuccess=yes
CreateOrJoin=Join
```

Discussion

For a complete list of Windows Server 2008 unattended installation settings, enter dcpromo /?:Promotion at the command line, or reference Windows Help and Support or the Microsoft Technet site. For a complete list of Windows Server 2003

[DCInstall] settings, see the *ref.chm* help file in *\support\tools\deploy.cab* that can be found on the Windows Server 2003 CD. For Windows 2000, the settings can be found in the *unattend.doc* file in *\support\tools\deploy.cab* on the Windows Server 2003 CD. You'll specify each parameter using the following syntax: `Parameter = Value`. A portion of an unattended installation file that creates a new AD forest might look something like this:

```
[DCInstall]
CreateOrJoin = Create
AllowAnonymousAccess = No
AutoConfigDNS = Yes
```

See Also

MS KB 223757 (Unattended Promotion and Demotion of Windows 2000 Domain Controllers), MS KB 224390 (How to Automate Windows 2000 Setup and Domain Controller Setup), Planning for Unattended Setup in the Windows Server 2003 Help and Support Center, and Appendix of Unattended Installation Parameters in the Windows Server 2008 Technical Library.

3.9 Troubleshooting Domain Controller Promotion or Demotion Problems

Problem

You are having problems promoting or demoting a domain controller and you want to troubleshoot it.

Solution

The best source of information about the status of promotion or demotion problems are the *Dcpromo.log* and *Dcpromoui.log* files contained in the *%SystemRoot%\Debug* folder on the server. The *Dcpromo.log* captures the input entered into *dcpromo* and logs the information that is displayed as *dcpromo* progresses. The *Dcpromoui.log* file is much more detailed and captures discrete actions that occur during *dcpromo* processing, including any user input. A sample *dcpromoui.log* file might look something like this:

```
dcpromoui D38.A65 0000 opening log file C:\WINDOWS\debug\dcpromoui.log
dcpromoui D38.A65 0001 C:\WINDOWS\system32\dcpromo.exe
dcpromoui D38.A65 0002 file timestamp 11/19/2005 07:02:35.000
dcpromoui D38.A65 0003 local time 11/19/2005 07:03:45.406
dcpromoui D38.A65 0004 running Windows NT 5.2 build 3718
(BuildLab:3718.dnsrv.021114-1947) i386
...
dcpromoui D38.A65 00E3 Enter ControlSubclasser::UnhookWindowProc
dcpromoui D38.A65 00E4 exitCode = 0
dcpromoui D38.A65 00E5 closing log
```

Additionally, the Windows Server 2003 and Windows Server 2008 versions of *dcdiag* contain two new tests that can aid in troubleshooting promotion problems. The *dcpromo* test reports anything it finds that could impede the promotion process. The *RegisterInDNS* test checks if the server can register records in DNS. Here is an example of running both commands to test against the *adatum.com* domain:

```
> dcdiag /test:dcpromo /DnsDomain:adatum.com /ReplicaDC /test:RegisterInDNS
```

Discussion

In most cases, the level of detail provided by *Dcpromoui.log* should be sufficient to pinpoint any problems, but you can increase logging if necessary. To enable the highest level of logging available, set the following registry value to `FF0003`: `HKLM\Software\Microsoft\Windows\CurrentVersion\AdminDebug`. You can confirm that this mask took effect by running *dcpromo* again, checking the *Dcpromoui.log*, and searching for "logging mask." For more information on the various logging settings, see MS KB 221254.

If *dcdiag* does not return sufficient information, the Network Monitor (*netmon*) program is very handy for getting a detailed understanding of the network traffic that is being generated and any errors that are being returned. Network Monitor is available as a free download from the Microsoft website. Using Network Monitor, you can identify what other servers a DC is communicating with or if it is timing out when attempting to perform certain queries or updates.

See Also

MS KB 221254 (Registry Settings for Event Detail in the Dcpromoui.log File)

3.10 Verifying the Promotion of a Domain Controller

Problem

You want to verify that a domain controller has been successfully promoted within an Active Directory domain.

Solution

Using a command-line interface

```
> netdiag /test:dns
> netdiag /test:member
> netdiag /test:dsgetdc
> dcdiag  /test:replications
> dcdiag  /s:<DCName> /test:knowsofroleholders
> dcdiag  /s:<DCName> /test:fsmocheck
```

The *netdiag.exe* utility is not available on Windows Server 2008 domain controllers.

Discussion

Once you've installed a domain controller using the *dcpromo* process, there are several steps that you can take to ensure that the promotion process has completed successfully. In Windows 2000 and Windows Server 2003, *dcdiag* and *netdiag* are two utilities that come with the Windows Support tools. In Windows Server 2008, *dcdiag.exe* has been built directly into the AD DS binaries; *netdiag.exe* is no longer supported. Regardless of the version of the server operating system, *dcdiag* and *netdiag* can perform a number of diagnostic tests, including the following:

- Verify that all necessary DNS records have been registered and are present on the DNS server.
- Check the domain membership for the newly promoted computer.
- Confirm that the new DC can communicate with other DCs in the domain.
- Confirm that the new DC is replicating with other DCs.
- Verify that the new DC can communicate with all of the FSMO role holders.

In addition, you can verify a successful domain controller promotion by verifying that it is responding on TCP port 389 and 3268, running *dcdiag/replsum*, confirming that the SYSVOL directory has been shared, as well as checking the Directory Service log in the Event Viewer for any errors or warnings.

See Also

MS KB 839880 (How to Troubleshoot RPC Endpoint Mapper Errors), MS KB 250842 (Troubleshooting Group Policy Application Problems), and MS KB 321708 (How to Use the Network Diagnostics Tool [Netdiag.exe] in Windows 2000)

3.11 Removing an Unsuccessfully Demoted Domain Controller

Problem

You want to manually remove a domain controller from Active Directory if the *dcpromo* process was unsuccessful or you are unable to bring a domain controller back online after a hardware or software failure.

Solution

The first step in the removal process is to run the following `ntdsutil` command, where `<DomainControllerName>` is a domain controller in the same domain as the one you want to forcibly remove.

 The following *ntdsutil* syntax is applicable to Windows 2000 and Windows Server 2003 installations without Service Pack 1 installed. Windows Server 2003 Service Pack 1 and Windows Server 2008 greatly simplify the syntax involved; we will cover the new syntax later.

```
> ntdsutil "meta clean" conn "co to ser <DomainControllerName>"q "s o t" "l d"
Found 2 domain(s)
0 - DC=adatum,DC=com
1 - DC=emea,DC=adatum,DC=com
```

Select the domain of the domain controller you want to remove. In this case, we'll select the *emea.adatum.com* domain:

```
select operation target: sel domain 1
```

Now, list the sites and select the site the domain controller is in (use `1` for `MySite1`):

```
select operation target: list sites
Found 4 site(s)
0 - CN=Default-First-Site-Name,CN=Sites,CN=Configuration,DC=adatum,DC=com
1 - CN=MySite1,CN=Sites,CN=Configuration,DC=adatum,DC=com
2 - CN=MySite2,CN=Sites,CN=Configuration,DC=adatum,DC=com
3 - CN=MySite3,CN=Sites,CN=Configuration,DC=adatum,DC=com
select operation target: sel site 1
```

Next, select the server you want to remove; in this case, we're choosing 0 for DC5:

```
select operation target: list servers for domain in site
Found 2 server(s)
0 - CN=DC5,CN=Servers,CN=MySite1,CN=Sites,CN=Configuration,DC=adatum,DC=com
1 - CN=DC9,CN=Servers,CN=MySite1,CN=Sites,CN=Configuration,DC=adatum,DC=com
select operation target: sel server 0
```

Type `quit` to get back to the `metadata cleanup` menu:

```
select operation target: quit
metadata cleanup:
```

Finally, remove the server:

```
metadata cleanup: remove selected server
```

If successful, a message will state that the removal was complete. However, if you receive an error message, check to see if the server's nTDSDSA object (e.g., CN=NTDSSettings,CN=DC5,CN=Servers,CN=MySite1,CN=Sites,CN=Configuration,DC=adatum,DC=com) is present. If so, *dcpromo* may have already removed it, and it will take time for the change to replicate. If it is still present, try the *ntdsutil* procedure again and if that doesn't work, manually remove that object and the parent object (e.g., CN=DC5) using ADSI Edit or another tool. (Deleting Active Directory objects is discussed in Recipe 4.24.)

In Windows Server 2003 Service Pack 1, the *ntdsutil* syntax for removing metadata from a failed server has been greatly simplified, as follows:

1. Go to the Windows command line and type ntdsutil.
2. From the ntdsutil menu, type metadata cleanup.
3. Type remove selected server cn=*<ServerName>*,cn=Servers,cn=*<SiteName>*, cn=Sites,cn=Configuration,dc=*<ForestRootDomain>* to remove the server metadata associated with *dc1.adatum.com*.

Follow these additional steps to remove all traces of the domain controller:

1. Delete the CNAME record from DNS for *<GUID>*._msdcs.*<RootDomainDNSName>*, where *<GUID>* is the objectGUID for the server's nTDSDSA object as obtained via ADSI Edit or a command-line tool such as AdFind. If scavenging is not enabled, you'll need to manually delete all associated SRV records. Delete any A and PTR records that exist for the server. When using Microsoft DNS, you can use the DNS MMC snap-in to accomplish these tasks.
2. Delete the computer object for the server under OU=DomainControllers,*<DomainDN>*. This can be done using the Active Directory Users and Computers snap-in or the admod utility. (Deleting objects is described in Chapter 4.)
3. Delete the FRS Member object for the computer contained under CN=DomainSystemVolume (SYSVOL share),CN=file replication serv ice,CN=system,*<DomainDN>*. This can be done using the Active Directory Users and Computers snap-in when Advanced Features has been selected from the View menu (so the System container will be displayed), or with the AdMod tool.
4. Delete the server object associated with the failed domain controller in the Active Directory Sites and Services MMC.

Discussion

If the domain controller that you are forcibly removing from Active Directory is the last one in an Active Directory domain, you'll need to manually remove the domain from the forest as well. See Recipe 2.5 for more information on removing orphaned domains.

Here are some additional issues to consider when you forcibly remove a domain controller:

- Seize any FSMO roles the DC may have had to another domain controller. (Managing FSMO roles is discussed later in this chapter.)
- If the DC was a global catalog server, ensure there is another global catalog server configured in the site that can handle the increased workload.

- If the DC was a DNS server, ensure there is another DNS server that can handle the additional name resolution queries, and be sure that your clients are configured to use the correct nameserver.
- If the DC was the RID FSMO master, check to make sure duplicate SIDs have not been issued (see Recipe 2.26).
- Check to see if the DC hosted any application partitions and if so, consider making another server a replica server for those application partitions (see Recipe 16.9).

If the (former) domain controller that you forcibly removed is still active or otherwise returns to your network, you should strongly consider reinstalling the operating system to avoid potential conflicts from the server trying to reinsert itself back into Active Directory. To remove Active Directory from a server without reinstalling the operating system, you can run dcpromo /forceremoval from a command line to forcibly remove Active Directory from a server. See MS KB 332199 for more information.

 The /forceremoval switch is available with Windows Server 2008, Windows Server 2003, and Windows 2000 SP4 or later.

See Also

Recipe 2.5 for removing an orphaned domain, Recipe 2.26, Recipe 3.34 for seizing FSMO roles, Recipe 4.24, Recipe 16.9, MS KB 216498 (How to Remove Data in Active Directory After an Unsuccessful Domain Controller Demotion), and MS KB 332199 (Domain Controllers Do Not Demote Gracefully When You Use the Active Directory Installation Wizard to Force Demotion in Windows Server 2003 and in Windows 2000 Server)

3.12 Renaming a Domain Controller

Problem

You want to rename a domain controller.

Solution

Windows 2000 Active Directory

To rename a domain controller, you must first demote it to a member server. You can then rename it and then promote it back to a domain controller.

Windows Server 2003 Active Directory

Your first step in renaming a Windows Server 2003 domain controller is as follows, where *<NewName>* is a fully qualified domain name (FQDN):

```
> netdom computername <CurrentName> /Add:<NewName>
```

The new name will be automatically replicated throughout Active Directory and DNS. Once you've verified that the new name has replicated (which may take some time depending on your replication topology), you can designate it as the domain controller's primary name as follows, and then reboot the domain controller:

```
> netdom computername <CurrentName> /MakePrimary:<NewName>
```

 See Chapter 12 for information on verifying Active Directory replication.

Once you're satisfied that your clients are accessing the domain controller using its new name, you can remove the old computer name using the following syntax:

```
> netdom computername <NewName> /remove:<OldName>
```

 To use the domain controller rename functionality, you must be running at the Windows Server 2003 or Windows Server 2008 domain functional level.

Discussion

There is no supported means to rename a Windows 2000 domain controller, which is why the only way you can approximate the process is by demoting the server before performing the rename, and then promoting the server to DC status using the new name. Before you demote the domain controller, you should transfer any FSMO roles it holds to other servers in your domain or forest. You can allow *dcpromo* to transfer the roles during the demotion process, but you should check afterward to verify which server(s) the role(s) were transferred to ensure that they are placed appropriately for your environment. Likewise, if the domain controller is a global catalog server, ensure that another global catalog server is available to take its place.

Renaming a domain controller without needing to demote it was introduced in Windows Server 2003. A new option has been added to the *netdom* utility to allow an alternate computer name to be associated with a computer in Active Directory. Once you've added a new name, you can then set that name to be the primary name, thereby renaming the computer.

The old name effectively remains with the domain controller until you remove it, which can be done using the `netdom computername /Remove:<Name>` command. You should reboot the server before removing the old name. The old names are stored in the `msDS-AdditionalDnsHostName` and `msDS-AdditionalSamAccountName` attributes on the domain controller's `computer` object.

If the domain controller has any version of Microsoft Exchange installed on it, renaming the domain controller is unsupported.

See Also

MS KB 195242 (Cannot Change Computer Name of a Domain Controller), MS KB 296592 (How to Rename a Windows 2000 Domain Controller)

3.13 Finding the Domain Controllers for a Domain

Problem

You want to find the domain controllers in a domain.

Solution

Using a graphical user interface

1. Open the Active Directory Users and Computers snap-in (*dsa.msc*).
2. Right-click on the target domain and select Find.
3. In the Find drop-down box, select "Computers."
4. In the Role drop-down box, select "Domain controller."
5. Click Find Now. The list of domain controllers for the domain will be present in the right pane.

Using a command-line interface

```
> adfind -h domain.com -default -s base -asq  msds-masteredby -dn
```

Using VBScript

```
' This code displays the
' domain controllers for the specified domain.
' ------ SCRIPT CONFIGURATION -----
strDomain = "<DomainDNSName>" ' e.g. emea.adatum.com
' ------ END CONFIGURATION --------

set objRootDSE = GetObject("LDAP://" & strDomain & "/RootDSE")
set objDomain = GetObject("LDAP://" & objRootDSE.Get("defaultNamingContext"))
strMasteredBy = objDomain.GetEx("masteredBy")
for each strNTDSDN in strMasteredBy
```

```
    set objNTDS = GetObject("LDAP://" & strNTDSDN)
    set objServer = GetObject(objNTDS.Parent)
    Wscript.echo objServer.Get("dNSHostName")
next
```

Using PowerShell

```
$dom = [System.DirectoryServices.ActiveDirectory.Domain]::getCurrentDomain()
$dom.FindAllDomainControllers()
```

Discussion

There are several ways to get a list of domain controllers for a domain. The GUI solution simply uses the built-in "Find" functionality of the Active Directory Users & Computers MMC. The CLI and VBScript solutions take a slightly different approach by looking at the masteredBy attribute on the domain object (e.g., dc=emea,dc=adatum,dc=com) of the domain. The masteredBy attribute contains a list of distinguished names of the nTDSDSA objects of all the domain controllers for that domain. The server object of the domain controller, which is the parent object of the nTDSDSA object, has a distinguishedName attribute that contains the distinguished name of the server.

And for yet another solution, see Recipe 3.28 to find out how to query DNS to get the list of domain controllers for a domain.

See Also

Recipe 3.28 for finding domain controllers via DNS

3.14 Finding the Closest Domain Controller

Problem

You want to find the closest domain controller for a particular domain.

Solution

Using a command-line interface

The following command finds the closest domain controller in the specified domain (*<DomainDNSName>*); that is, a domain controller that is located in the same site or in the closest site if a local DC is not available. By default, it will return the closest DC for the computer *nltest* is being run from, but you can optionally use the /server option to target a remote host. If you are interested in finding a DC within a particular site regardless of whether it is the closest DC to you, you can also optionally specify the /site option to find a domain controller that belongs to a particular site:

```
> nltest/dsgetdc:<DomainDNSName> [/site:<SiteName>] [/server:<ClientName>]
```

Using VBScript

 The IADsTools functionality is not supported under Windows Vista or Windows Server 2008.

```
' This code finds the closest domain controller in the domain
' that the computer running the script is in.
' ------ SCRIPT CONFIGURATION ------
strDomain = "<DomainDNSName>" ' e.g. emea.adatum.com
' ------ END CONFIGURATION --------

set objIadsTools = CreateObject("IADsTools.DCFunctions")
objIadsTools.DsGetDcName( Cstr(strDomain) )
Wscript.Echo "DC: " & objIadsTools.DCName
Wscript.Echo "DC Site: " & objIadsTools.DCSiteName
Wscript.Echo "Client Site: " & objIadsTools.ClientSiteName
```

Using PowerShell

```
$dom = [System.DirectoryServices.ActiveDirectory.Domain]::getCurrentDomain()
$dom.FindDomainController()
```

Discussion

The DC locator process as described in MS KB 314861, and MS KB 247811 defines how clients find the closest domain controller. The process uses the site topology stored in Active Directory to calculate the site a particular client is in. After the client site has been identified, then it is a matter of finding a domain controller that is either a member of that same site or that is covering for that site.

The Microsoft DsGetDcName Directory Services API method implements the DC Locator process, but unfortunately cannot be used directly from a scripting language, such as VBScript. The IADsTools interface provides a wrapper around DsGetDcName, which is what we used. The nltest /dsgetdc command is also a wrapper around the DsGetDcName method, and is a handy tool when troubleshooting client issues related to finding an optimal domain controller.

Using a command-line interface

You can use *nltest* to return the closest domain controller that is serving a particular function. Some of the available functions include a global catalog server (/GC switch), time server (/TIMESERV switch), KDC (/KDC switch), and PDC (/PDC switch). Run nltest /? from a command line for the complete list.

Using VBScript

Similar to *nltest*, you can specify additional criteria for finding a domain controller by calling the `SetDsGetDcNameFlags` method before calling `DsGetDcName`. `SetDsGetDcNameFlags` accepts a comma-delimited string of the following flags:

```
DS_FORCE_REDISCOVERY
DS_DIRECTORY_SERVICE_REQUIRED
DS_DIRECTORY_SERVICE_PREFERRED
DS_GC_SERVER_REQUIRED
DS_PDC_REQUIRED
DS_IP_REQUIRED
DS_KDC_REQUIRED
DS_TIMESERV_REQUIRED
DS_WRITABLE_REQUIRED
DS_GOOD_TIMESERV_PREFERRED
DS_AVOID_SELF
DS_IS_FLAT_NAME
DS_IS_DNS_NAME
DS_RETURN_DNS_NAME
DS_RETURN_FLAT_NAME
```

Using PowerShell

If you don't specify a site when using the `FindDomainController()` method, the method will return a DC in the site closest to the client running the code.

See Also

For more information on the `IADsTools` interface, see *IadsTools.doc* in the Support Tools, MS KB 247811 (How Domain Controllers Are Located in Windows), MS KB 314861 (How Domain Controllers Are Located in Windows XP), MSDN: DsGetDcName, and MSDN: MicrosoftDNS

3.15 Finding a Domain Controller's Site

Problem

You need to determine the site of which a domain controller is a member.

Solution

Using a graphical user interface

1. Open LDP and from the menu, select Connection→Connect.
2. For Server, enter the name of a domain controller (or leave blank to do a serverless bind).
3. For Port, enter 389.

4. Click OK.

5. From the menu select Connection→Bind.

6. Enter credentials of a domain user.

7. Click OK.

8. From the menu, select Browse→Search.

9. For BaseDN, type the distinguished name of the `Sites` container (for example, `cn=sites,cn=configuration,dc=adatum,dc=com`).

10. For Scope, select Subtree.

11. For Filter, enter:

    `(&(objectcategory=server)(dnsHostName=<DomainControllerName>))`

12. Click Run.

Using a command-line interface

To retrieve the site for a particular DC, use the following command syntax:

```
> nltest /dsgetsite /server:<DomainControllerName>
```

 The `nltest /dsgetsite` command is a wrapper around the `DsGetSiteName` method.

You can also use the AdFind utility as follows:

```
adfind -h <Domain FQDN> -rootdse servername
```

For example, to find the site containing the server *dc1* in the *adatum.com* domain, you would see the following output:

```
> adfind -config -rb cn=sites -f "(&(objectcategory=server)(cn=dc1))"
distinguishedName
> AdFind  V01.37.00cpp Joe Richards (joe@joeware.net) June 2007

> Using server: dc1.adatum.com:389
> Directory: Windows Server 2003
> Base DN: cn=sites,CN=Configuration,DC=adatum,DC=com
>
> dn:CN=dc1,CN=Servers,CN=Raleigh,CN=Sites,CN=Configuration,DC=adatum,DC=com
> distinguishedName: CN=dc1,CN=Servers,CN=Raleigh,CN=Sites,CN=Configuration,
DC=adatum,DC=com
>
> 1 Objects returned
```

You can also specify the FQDN of the DC in question by using (&(objectcategory=server)(dnsHostName=dc1.adatum.com)).

Using VBScript

```
' This code prints the
' site the specified domain controller is in
' ------ SCRIPT CONFIGURATION -----
strDC = "<DomainControllerName>" ' e.g. dc1.adatum.com
' ------ END CONFIGURATION --------

set objRootDSE = GetObject("LDAP://" & strDC & "/RootDSE")
set objNTDS = GetObject("LDAP://" & objRootDSE.Get("
dsServiceName"))
set objSite = GetObject(GetObject(GetObject(objNTDS.
Parent).Parent).Parent)
WScript.Echo objSite.Get("cn")
```

Using PowerShell

```
$dcname = <DomainDNSName>
$context = New-Object
System.DirectoryServices.ActiveDirectory.DirectoryContext('DirectoryServer',
$dcname)
$dc =
[System.DirectoryServices.ActiveDirectory.DomainController]::getDomainController
($context)
$dc.SiteName
```

Discussion

Domain controllers are represented in the site topology by a **server** object and a child nTDSDSA object. Actually, any type of server can conceivably have a **server** object; it is the nTDSDSA object that differentiates domain controllers from other types of servers. You'll often see the nTDSDSA object of a domain controller used to refer to that domain controller elsewhere in Active Directory. For example, the fSMORoleOwner attribute that represents the FSMO owners contains the distinguished name of the nTDSDSA object of the domain controller that is holding the role.

Using VBScript

Since we cannot use the DsGetSiteName method directly in VBScript, we need to take a more indirect approach. By querying the RootDSE of the target server, we can retrieve the dsServiceName attribute.

That attribute contains the DN of the nTDSDSA object for the domain controller, e.g., cn=NTDSSettings,cn=dc1,cn=MySite,cn=Sites,cn=Configuration,dc=adatum,dc=com.

Then, by calling the `Parent` method three consecutive times, we can retrieve the object for `cn=MySite,cn=Sites,cn=Configuration,dc=adatum,dc=com`.

Using PowerShell

The constructor for the `DirectoryContext` object can be used to create any of the following contexts:

- Domain
- Forest
- DirectoryServer
- ConfigurationSet
- ApplicationPartition

The code listing in this recipe will connect to the DC using the credentials of the logged-on user. If you need to connect to a domain controller using alternate credentials, you can do so as follows:

```
$dcname = <DomainDNSName>
$user = "TREYRESEARCH\Administrator"
$pass = "Password"
$context = New-Object
System.DirectoryServices.ActiveDirectory.DirectoryContext('DirectoryServer',
$dcname, $user, $pass)
$dc =
[System.DirectoryServices.ActiveDirectory.DomainController]::getDomainController($context)
```

See Also

MSDN: DsGetSiteName, MSDN: DomainController

3.16 Moving a Domain Controller to a Different Site

Problem

You want to move a domain controller to a different site.

Solution

Using a graphical user interface

1. Open the Active Directory Sites and Services snap-in (*dssite.msc*).
2. In the left pane, expand the site that contains the domain controller.
3. Expand the Servers container.
4. Right-click on the domain controller you want to move and select Move.

5. In the Move Server box, select the site to which the domain controller will be moved and click OK.

Using a command-line interface

When using DSMove, you must specify the DN of the object you want to move. In this case, it needs to be the distinguished name of the **server** object for the domain controller. The value for the -newparent option is the distinguished name of the **Servers** container you want to move the domain controller to:

```
> dsmove "<ServerDN>" -newparent "<NewServersContainerDN>"
```

For example, the following command would move *dc2* from the **Default-First-Site-Name** site to the **Raleigh** site:

```
> dsmove "cn=dc2,cn=servers,cn=Default-First-Site-
Name,cn=sites,cn=configuration,cn=
adatum,dc=com" -newparent
"cn=servers,cn=Raleigh,cn=sites,cn=configuration,cn=adatum,dc=com"
```

You can also move an object using AdMod, as follows:

```
> admod -b cn=<ServerName>,cn=servers,cn=<OldSite>,cn=sites,
cn=configuration,<ForestRootDN> -move cn=servers,cn=<NewSite>,
cn=sites,cn=configuration,<ForestRootDN>
```

Using VBScript

```
' This code moves a domain controller to a different site
' ------ SCRIPT CONFIGURATION ------
strDCName       = "<DomainControllerName>" ' e.g. dc2
strCurrentSite = "<CurrentSiteName>"       ' e.g. Default-First-Site-Name
strNewSite     = "<NewSiteName>"           ' e.g. Raleigh
' ------ END CONFIGURATION ---------

strConfigDN = GetObject("LDAP://RootDSE").Get("configurationNamingContext")
strServerDN = "LDAP://cn=" & strDCName & ",cn=servers,cn=" & _
                      strCurrentSite & ",cn=sites," & strConfigDN
strNewParentDN = "LDAP://cn=servers,cn=" & strNewSite & ",cn=sites," & _
                      strConfigDN

set objCont = GetObject(strNewParentDN)
objCont.MoveHere strServerDN, "cn=" & strDCName
WScript.Echo "Successfully moved " & strDCName & " to " & strNewSite
```

Using PowerShell

```
$dcname = <DomainDNSName>
$newSite = "HQ"
$context = New-Object
System.DirectoryServices.ActiveDirectory.DirectoryContext('DirectoryServer',
$dcname)
$dc =
[System.DirectoryServices.ActiveDirectory.DomainController]::getDomainController
```

```
($context)
$dc.MoveToAnotherSite($newSite)
```

Discussion

When you install a new domain controller, a **server** object and **nTDSDSA** object for the domain controller get added to the site topology. The Knowledge Consistency Checker (KCC) and Intersite Topology Generator (ISTG) use these objects to determine whom the domain controller should replicate with.

A domain controller is assigned to the site that has been mapped to the subnet it is located on. If there is no **subnet** object that has an address range that contains the domain controller's IP address, the **server** object is added to the `Default-First-Site-Name` site. If the domain controller should be in a different site, you'll then need to manually move it. It is a good practice to ensure that a **subnet** object that matches the domain controller's subnet is already in Active Directory before promoting the server into the forest. That way you do not need to worry about moving it after the fact.

 When moving a **server** object, remember that it has to be moved to a **Servers** container within a site, not directly under the site itself.

Using a command-line interface

In the solution provided, you need to know the current site of the domain controller you want to move. If you do not know the site it is currently in, you can use DSQuery to find it. In fact, you can use DSQuery in combination with DSMove in a single command line:

```
> for /F "usebackq" %i in ('dsquery server
    -name"<DomainControllerName>"') do dsmove -newparent "cn=servers,
    cn=Default-First-Site,cn=sites, cn=configuration,<ForestDN>" %i
```

This command is long so we'll break it up into three parts to clarify it. The first part contains the **for** command extension that is built into the *cmd.exe* shell. When the /F "usebackq" syntax is specified, it is typically used to iterate over output from a command and perform certain functions on the output.

```
for /F "usebackq" %i in
```

The next part of the **for** loop contains the data to iterate over. In this case, we use DSQuery to return the distinguished name of the **server** object for *dc2*:

```
('dsquery server -name "<DomainControllerName>"')
```

The last part executes a command for each result returned from DSQuery. In this case, there should only be one result, so this command will only run once:

```
do dsmove -newparent "cn=servers,cn=Default-First-
Site,cn=sites,cn=configuration,<ForestDN>" %i
```

Using VBScript

Just as with the CLI solution, in the VBScript solution you need to specify which site the server is currently in. If you prefer, you can programmatically query for the current site, as shown in Recipe 3.15.

See Also

Recipe 3.15 for finding a domain controller's site and Recipe 4.20 for moving objects to different containers

3.17 Finding the Services a Domain Controller Is Advertising

Problem

You want to find the services that a domain controller is advertising.

Solution

The following command will display the list of services a domain controller is advertising:

```
> dcdiag /v /s:<DomainControllerName> /test:advertising
```

Running this command on a typical domain controller will produce the following output:

```
Starting test: Advertising
      The DC dc1 is advertising itself as a DC and having a DS.
      The DC dc1 is advertising as an LDAP server
      The DC dc1 is advertising as having a writable directory
      The DC dc1 is advertising as a Key Distribution Center
      The DC dc1 is advertising as a time server
      The DS dc1 is advertising as a GC.
```

You can also use *nltest* to get similar information:

```
> nltest /server:<DomainControllerName> /dsgetdc:<DomainName>
```

Running this command on a domain controller in the *adatum.com* domain will produce the following output:

```
        DC: \\dc1.adatum.com
        Address: \\10.0.0.1
       Dom Guid: ac0e4884-cf79-4c9d-8cd9-817e3bfdab54
       Dom Name: adatum.com
    Forest Name: adatum.com
  Dc Site Name: Raleigh
Our Site Name: Raleigh
          Flags: PDC GC DS LDAP KDC TIMESERV GTIMESERV WRITABLE DNS_DC DNS_DOMAIN
DNS_FOREST CLOSE_SITE
```

In the previous example, `GTIMESERV` denotes a DC that is a master time server. `WRITABLE` denotes a DC that holds a writable copy of the Active Directory database. Prior to Windows Server 2008, only NT 4.0 BDCs would not possess this flag; in 2008 Read-Only Domain Controllers will also lack the `WRITABLE` flag.

Discussion

The `dcdiag /test:advertising` command is a wrapper around the `DsGetDcName` method. `DsGetDcName` returns a structure called `DOMAIN_CONTROLLER_INFO` that contains the list of services a domain controller provides. Table 3-4 contains the possible values returned from this call.

Table 3-4. DOMAIN_CONTROLLER_INFO flags

Value	Description
DS_DS_FLAG	Directory server for the domain
DS_GC_FLAG	Global catalog server for the forest
DS_KDC_FLAG	Kerberos Key Distribution Center for the domain
DS_PDC_FLAG	Primary domain controller of the domain
DS_TIMESERV_FLAG	Time server for the domain
DS_WRITABLE_FLAG	Hosts a writable directory service

See Also

MSDN: DsGetDcName and MSDN: DOMAIN_CONTROLLER_INFO

3.18 Restoring a Deleted Domain Controller

Problem

You want to restore the computer account of a domain controller that has been accidentally deleted.

Using a graphical user interface

1. Reboot a domain controller that is currently functioning correctly into Directory Services Restore Mode.
2. Perform a System State restore.
3. Before rebooting the server, perform the steps listed in the following section.

Using a command-line interface

To restore the computer account, use the following sequence of commands in Windows 2000 or Windows Server 2003:

```
> ntdsutil
> authoritative restore> restore subtree <ComputerDN>
> quit
> exit
```

In Windows Server 2008, you must enter the following command before accessing the authoritative restore menu:

```
activate instance ntds
```

Restart the domain controller after running these commands.

Discussion

When you restore a deleted object within Active Directory, you have the option of performing an *authoritative* or a *nonauthoritative* restore. In both cases, any changes that have been made to the AD database subsequent to the time that the backup was taken will be replicated back to the restored DC. With an authoritative restore, the version number of the object(s) being restored is incremented so that the restored objects will "win" in the case of any replication collisions. In a case where you want to restore an object that has been inadvertently deleted, you need to perform an authoritative restore to prevent the deletion from repropagating to the restored domain controller. You can mark an entire restore as authoritative, or any subtree of your AD environment down to a single object (in this case, the computer object for the DC that was deleted).

See Also

Chapter 16 for more on recovering and restoring Active Directory and MS KB 216993 (Useful Shelf Life of a System-State Backup of Active Directory)

3.19 Resetting the TCP/IP Stack on a Domain Controller

Problem

You want to uninstall and reinstall the TCP/IP protocol on a domain controller as part of a disaster recovery or troubleshooting operation.

Solution

Using a command-line interface

```
> netsh ip reset <Log_File_Name>
```

Discussion

Beginning in Windows 2000, the TCP/IP protocol has been installed as the default network protocol for Windows server and client products. In Windows 2000 in particular, uninstalling TCP/IP was a fairly laborious process involving numerous registry changes. This was greatly improved in Windows Server 2003 with the addition of the reset commands within *netsh*. Resetting the TCP/IP stack using *netsh* will remove all configuration information, including the default gateway and any configured DNS and WINS servers. This procedure might be necessary during a disaster recovery situation where you're restoring System State data to a server with a dissimilar hardware configuration, for example, as the restore process might corrupt the TCP/IP stack on the destination computer.

Using a command-line interface

In addition to resetting the TCP/IP stack, you can also reset Winsock using the following command:

```
> netsh winsock reset
```

Use this command with care, though, as resetting Winsock can cause network applications such as antivirus scanners to malfunction and require reinstallation.

See Also

MS KB 317518 (How to Reset "Internet Protocol" [TCP/IP] in Windows Server 2003), MS KB 325356 (How to Remove and Reinstall TCP/IP on a Windows Server 2003 Domain Controller), and MS KB 299451 (How to Remove and Reinstall TCP/IP on a Windows 2000 Domain Controller)

3.20 Configuring a Domain Controller to Use an External Time Source

Problem

You want to set the reliable time source for a domain controller.

Solution

Using the Registry

To configure your Windows Server 2003 or Windows Server 2008 PDC Emulator to sync to an external time provider, set the following Registry keys:

```
[HKLM\System\CurrentControlSet\Services\W32Time\Parameters\]
Type: REG_SZ - "NTP"

[HKLM\System\CurrentControlSet\Services\W32Time\Config\]
AnnounceFlags: REG_DWORD - 10

[HKLM\System\CurrentControlSet\Services\W32Time\TimeProviders\]
NTPServer: REG_DWORD - 1

[HKEY_LOCAL_MACHINE\SYSTEM\CurrentControlSet\Services\W32Time\Parameters\]
NTPServer: REG_SZ -<Peer1>,0x1,<Peer2>,0x1,<Peer3>,0x1
```

 <Peers> in this case refers to a comma-separated list of FQDNs of external time servers. Each DNS name must be followed by ,0x1 for the rest of these settings to take effect.

```
[HKEY_LOCAL_MACHINE\SYSTEM\CurrentControlSet\Services\W32Time\TimeProviders\
NtpClient\]
SpecialPollInterval: REG_DWORD -<TimeBetweenPollsInSeconds>

[HKEY_LOCAL_MACHINE\SYSTEM\CurrentControlSet\Services\W32Time\Config\]
MaxPosPhaseCorrection: REG_DWORD -<MaximumForwardOffsetInSeconds>

[HKEY_LOCAL_MACHINE\SYSTEM\CurrentControlSet\Services\W32Time\Config\]
MaxNegPhaseCorrection: REG_DWORD -<MaximumBackwardOffsetInSeconds>
```

Once you have made these changes to the Registry, stop and restart the W32time service by issuing the following commands:

```
> net stop w32time
> net start w32time
```

Using VBScript

```
' This codes configures a reliable
' time source on a domain controller'
 ------ SCRIPT CONFIGURATION ------
strPDC = "<DomainControllerName>          ' e.g. dc01.adatum.com
strTimeServer = "<TimeServerNameOrIP>" ' e.g. ntp01.adatum.com
' ------ END CONFIGURATION --------

strTimeServerReg = "SYSTEM\CurrentControlSet\Services\W32Time\Parameters"
const HKLM = &H80000002
set objReg = GetObject("winmgmts:\\" & strPDC & "\root\default:StdRegProv")
objReg.GetStringValue HKLM, strTimeServerReg, "ntpserver", strCurrentServer
WScript.Echo "Current Value: " & strCurrentServer
objReg.SetStringValue HKLM, strTimeServerReg, "ntpserver", strTimeServer
objReg.SetStringValue HKLM, strTimeServerReg, "type", "NTP"
strCurrentServer = ""
objReg.GetStringValue HKLM, strTimeServerReg, "ntpserver", strCurrentServer
WScript.Echo "New Value: " & strCurrentServer

' Restart Time Service
```

```
set objService = GetObject("winmgmts://" & strPDC & _
                           "/root/cimv2:Win32_Service='W32Time'")
WScript.Echo "Stopping " & objService.Name
objService.StopService()

Wscript.Sleep 2000 ' Sleep for 2 seconds to give service time to stop

WScript.Echo "Starting " & objService.Name
objService.StartService()
```

Discussion

You need to set a reliable time source on the PDC Emulator FSMO for only the forest root domain. All other domain controllers sync their time either from that server or from a PDC (or designated time server) within their own domain. The list of external time servers is stored in the registry under the W32Time Service registry key: HKLM\SYSTEM\CurrentControlSet\Services\W32Time\Parameters\ntpserver.

If you want a domain controller such as the PDC to use an external time source, you have to set the ntpserver registry value along with the type value. The default value for type on a domain controller is Nt5DS, which means that the domain controller will use the Active Directory domain hierarchy to find a time source. You can override this behavior and have a domain controller contact a non-DC time source by setting type to NTP. In the CLI example, the /setsntp switch automatically sets the type value to NTP. In the VBScript solution, we had to set it in the code.

After setting the time server, the W32Time service should be restarted for the change to take effect. You can check that the server was set properly by running the following command:

```
> net time /querysntp
```

Since the PDC Emulator is the time source for the other domain controllers, you should also make sure that it is advertising the time service, which you can do with the following command:

```
> nltest /server:<DomainControllerName> /dsgetdc:<DomainDNSName> /TIMESERV
```

> To configure the PDC Emulator to use its own internal clock as a time source instead of relying on an external clock, modify the HKLM\SYSTEM \CurrentControlSet\Services\W32Time\Config\AnnounceFlags DWORD value to contain a value of 0x0A.

See Also

MS KB 216734 (How to Configure an Authoritative Time Server in Windows 2000), MS KB 223184 (Registry Entries for the W32Time Service), MS KB 224799 (Basic Operation of the Windows Time Service), MS KB 816042 (How to Configure an

Authoritative Time Server in Windows Server 2003), and MSDN: StdRegProv, and MSDN: Win32_Service

3.21 Finding the Number of Logon Attempts Made Against a Domain Controller

Problem

You want to find the number of logon requests a domain controller has processed.

Solution

The following query returns the number of logon requests processed:

```
> nltest /server:<DomainControllerName> /LOGON_QUERY
```

This will produce output similar to the following:

```
Number of attempted logons: 1054
```

Discussion

The `nltest /LOGON_QUERY` command is a wrapper around the `I_NetLogonControl2` method, and can be useful to determine how many logon requests are being processed by a server. Viewing the results of the command over a period of time and comparing them against another DC in the same domain can also tell you if one domain controller is being used significantly more or less than the others.

See Also

MSDN: I_NetLogonControl2

3.22 Enabling the /3GB Switch to Increase the LSASS Cache

Problem

You have installed more than 1 GB of memory on your 32-bit domain controllers and want to enable the /3GB switch so that the LSASS process can use more memory.

Solution

Using a command-line interface

In Windows Server 2003, run the following command:

```
> bootcfg /raw /"3GB" /ID <BootID>
```

If you do not know the Boot ID of the partition you wish to modify, simply run `bootcfg` from a command prompt without any switches.

In Windows Server 2008, use the following command:

```
> bcdedit /set IncreaseUserVA 3072
```

Alternatively, you can edit the *boot.ini* file on a Windows Server 2003 domain controller to contain the **/3GB** switch:

```
[boot loader]
timeout=30
default=multi(0)disk(0)rdisk(0)partition(2)\WINDOWS
[operating systems]
multi(0)disk(0)rdisk(0)partition(2)\WINDOWS="Windows Server 2003" /3GB
```

Restart the computer.

Note that the *boot.ini* file is not present on Windows Server 2008 computers.

On Windows Server 2003, you can edit the *boot.ini* file by opening the System applet in the Control Panel. Click the Startup and Recovery tab and click the Edit button, or else use the built-in `msconfig` utility.

On Windows 2000, the process involves a few more steps. You need to open an Explorer window, select Tools→Folder Options, and click the View tab. Uncheck "Hide protected operating system files (Recommended)," and check "Show hidden files and folders." Now browse to the root of your operating system partition (e.g., *C:*) and edit the *boot.ini* file with a text editor.

Discussion

When computers are referred to as 32-or 64-bit computers it means they support memory addresses that are 32- or 64-bits long. This is the total available memory (virtual and real) that can be processed by the system. Since the days of Windows NT, Microsoft has split memory allocation in half by giving applications up to 2 GB and the Windows kernel 2 GB of memory to use (32 bits of address space = 2^{32} = 4 GB). In many cases, administrators would rather allocate more memory to applications than to the kernel. For this reason, Microsoft developed the **/3GB** switch to allow applications running on 32-bit versions of Windows to use up to 3 GB of memory, leaving the kernel with 1 GB. This configuration is not necessary for 64-bit versions of Windows.

The **/3GB** switch is supported on Windows 2000 Advanced Server; Windows 2000 Datacenter Server; and Windows Server 2003 Standard, Enterprise, and Datacenter Edition; it should be used only if the computer has more than 1 GB of physical memory. However, if you have more than 16 GB of RAM in a Windows Server 2003 computer, the extra RAM will not be utilized unless you manually remove the /3GB switch from the *boot.ini* file. For a good description of how LSASS uses memory, see MS KB 308356.

See Also

MS KB 99743 (Purpose of the BOOT.INI File in Windows 2000 or Windows NT), MS KB 291988 (A Description of the 4 GB RAM Tuning Feature and the Physical Address Extension Switch), and MS KB 308356 (Memory Usage By the Lsass.exe Process on Windows 2000-Based Domain Controllers)

3.23 Cleaning Up Distributed Link Tracking Objects

Problem

You want to make sure the Distributed Link Tracking (DLT) service is disabled and all DLT objects are removed from Active Directory. The Distributed Link Tracking Server service is used to track links to files on NTFS partitions. If a file that has a shortcut to it is renamed or moved, Windows uses the DLT service to find the file when the shortcut is opened. Most organizations are unaware this service even exists, yet it can populate thousands of objects in Active Directory. Unless you are actively using the functionality of the DLT service, it is recommended that you disable it.

Solution

If you upgrade a Windows 2000 domain controller to Windows Server 2003, the DLT Server service is stopped and set to disabled. A new install of Windows Server 2003 also has the service stopped and set to disabled. But the DLT Server service on Windows 2000 domain controllers is enabled by default. Unless you need it, you should stop the service and disable it on all of your domain controllers.

Next, remove any DLT objects (`linkTrackVolEntry` and `linkTrackOMTEntry`) from Active Directory. Since there can be hundreds of thousands of DLT objects, you will probably want to stagger the deletion of those objects. (This is not so much because of the delete operation itself, but because the scavenging process that occurs afterward can be quite memory-intensive.) The script in MS KB 315229 (*dltpurge.vbs*) can delete DLT objects over a period of time instead of all at once. Here is an example of running the *dltpurge.vbs* script against the *dc1* domain controller in the *adatum.com* domain:

```
> cscript dltpurge.vbs -s dc1 -d dc=adatum,dc=com
```

Once you've run the DLT Purge process and the AD tombstone and garbage collection process has completed, it's also recommended that you perform an offline defragmentation of the Active Directory database if you are low on disk space and need to reduce the size of the AD database file (*NTDS.DIT*).

Discussion

DLT consists of a client and server service. The server service runs on domain controllers and the client service can run on any Windows 2000 or later machine. The server service stores data in Active Directory in the form of `linkTrackVolEntry` and `linkTrackOMTEntry` objects, which are used to track the names and locations of files on NTFS partitions. The `cn=ObjectMoveTable,cn=FileLinks,cn=System,<DomainDN>` container stores `linkTrackOMTEntry` objects containing information about files moved on computers in the domain, while the container `cn=VolumeTable,cn=FileLinks,cn=System,<DomainDN>` stores `linkTrackVolEntry` objects that represent NTFS volumes on computers in the domain.

Over time, the number of DLT objects can grow substantially. Even though those objects do not take up much space (in fact, they will take up more space while waiting to be scavenged post-deletion than they will as active objects within the directory), if you are not actively taking advantage of this service, you should consider disabling it and removing all DLT objects from Active Directory.

See Also

Recipe 16.18 for more on performing an offline defragmentation of the AD database, MS KB 232122 (Performing Offline Defragmentation of the Active Directory Database), MS KB 312403 (Distributed Link Tracking on Windows-Based Domain Controllers), and MS KB 315229 (Text Version of Dltpurge.vbs for Microsoft Knowledge Base Article Q312403)

3.24 Enabling and Disabling the Global Catalog

Problem

You want to enable or disable the global catalog (GC) on a particular server.

Solution

Using a graphical user interface

1. Open the Active Directory Sites and Services snap-in (*dssite.msc*).
2. Browse to the nTDSDSA object (NTDS Settings) underneath the **server** object for the domain controller you want to enable or disable the global catalog for.
3. Right-click on NTDS Settings and select Properties.
4. Under the General tab, check (to enable) or uncheck (to disable) the box beside Global Catalog.
5. Click OK.

Using a command-line interface

In the following command, *<ServerObjectDN>* should be the **server** object DN, not the DN of the nTDSDSA object:

```
> dsmod server "<ServerObjectDN>" -isgc yes|no
```

For example, the following command will enable the global catalog on *dc1* in the Raleigh site:

```
> dsmod server
"cn=DC1,cn=servers,cn=Raleigh,cn=sites,cn=configuration,dc=adatum,dc=com" -isgc
Yes
```

You can also use AdMod with the following syntax and output to disable the GC; to enable it, use options::{{.:CLR:1}}:

```
> adfind -b "cn=NTDS
Settings,cn=dc1,cn=Servers,cn=Raleigh,cn=Sites,cn=Configuration,dc=adatum,dc=com"
options -adcsv | admod options::{{.:SET:1}}
```

 See Chapter 4 for information on safely modifying bitwise operators.

Using VBScript

```
' This code enables or disables the GC for the specified DC
' ------ SCRIPT CONFIGURATION ------
strDC = "<DomainControllerName>"   ' e.g. dc01.adatum.com
strGCEnable = 1                    ' 1 = enable, 0 = disable
' ------ END CONFIGURATION --------

set objRootDSE = GetObject("LDAP://" & strDC & "/RootDSE")
objNTDS = GetObject("LDAP://" & strDC & "/" & _
                    objRootDSE.Get("dSServiceName"))
objNTDS.Put "options", strGCEnable
objNTDS.SetInfo
```

Using PowerShell

```
$dcname = <DomainDNSName>
$context = New-Object
System.DirectoryServices.ActiveDirectory.DirectoryContext('DirectoryServer',$dcname)
$dc =
[System.DirectoryServices.ActiveDirectory.DomainController]::getDomainController
($context)
$dc.EnableGlobalCatalog()
```

Discussion

The first domain controller promoted into a forest is also made a global catalog (GC) server by default. If you want additional servers to have the global catalog, you have to enable it manually. In a single-domain environment, the global catalog server incurs

---

no memory or bandwidth overhead beyond that of a domain controller, so you could conceivably configure each DC in a single-domain forest as a GC without any ill effects. In a multidomain environment, however, each global catalog server will require additional disk space to store a partial replica of other domains in the forest, and will require additional network bandwidth to replicate with other GCs. For more details on DC and GC placement planning, see *Active Directory*.

The global catalog on a domain controller becomes enabled when the low-order bit on the options attribute on the nTDSDSA object under the server object for the domain controller is set to 1, or disabled when it is set to 0. The DN of this object for *dc1* in the Default-First-Site-Name site looks like this:

```
cn=NTDSSettings,cn=DC1,cn=Default-First-Site-
Name,cn=Sites,cn=Configuration,dc=adatum,dc=com
```

After enabling the global catalog, it can take some time before the domain controller can start serving as a global catalog server. The length of time is based on the amount of data that needs to replicate and the type of connectivity between the domain controller's replication partners. This is also dependent on the Global Catalog Partition Occupancy setting, which is set in the HKLM\System\CurrentControlSet\Services\NTDS \Parameters key on the GC itself, which specifies how many directory partitions must be fully replicated to the GC before it is considered ready; this can range from no occupancy requirement whatsoever, to requiring that all partitions be fully synchronized before the GC can begin servicing requests. After replication is complete, you should see Event 1119 in the Directory Services log stating the server is advertising itself as a global catalog. At that point you should also be able to perform LDAP queries against port 3268 on that server. See Recipe 3.25 for more information on how to determine if global catalog promotion is complete.

See Also

Recipe 3.25 for determining if global catalog promotion is complete and MS KB 313994 (How to Create or Move a Global Catalog in Windows Server 2003)

3.25 Determining Whether Global Catalog Promotion Is Complete

Problem

You want to determine whether a domain controller is a global catalog server. After you initially enable the global catalog on a domain controller, it can take some time for all of the read-only naming contexts to replicate to it, depending on the number of domains, the volume of directory data, and the underlying network topology.

Solution

Query the isGlobalCatalogReady attribute on the RootDSE for the domain controller. A TRUE value means the server is a global catalog and a FALSE value indicates it is not.

For more information on how to query the RootDSE, see Recipe 4.1.

You can also check the Directory Services Event Log in the Event Viewer MMC for the presence of Event ID 1119, whose text reads as follows:

```
"This Windows Domain Controller is now a Global Catalog Server"
```

Using the Registry

To confirm that GC promotion has completed, check the value of the following Registry key:

```
> HKLM\System\CurrentControlSet\Services\NTDS\Parameters\
> Global Catalog Promotion Complete: REG_DWORD - "1" if complete, "0" if not.
```

Using a command-line interface

To confirm that a domain controller in the *adatum.com* domain is functioning as a global catalog server, use *nltest* with the following syntax:

```
> nltest /dsgetdc:adatum.com
```

If the DC in question is functioning as a GC, you'll see output similar to the following:

```
> C:\>nltest /dsgetdc:adatum.com
>           DC: \\dc1.adatum.com
>      Address: \\10.0.0.1
>     Dom Guid: ac0e4884-cf79-4c9d-8cd9-817e3bfdab54
>     Dom Name: adatum.com
>  Forest Name: adatum.com
> Dc Site Name: Raleigh
> Our Site Name: Raleigh
>        Flags: PDC GC DS LDAP KDC TIMESERV GTIMESERV WRITABLE DNS_DC DNS_DOMAIN
> DNS_FOREST CLOSE_SITE
> The command completed successfully
```

Using PowerShell

```
$dcname = <DomainDNSName>
$username = <Username>
$pass = <Password>
$context = New-Object
System.DirectoryServices.ActiveDirectory.DirectoryContext('DirectoryServer',$dcname
,$username,$pass)
$dc =
[System.DirectoryServices.ActiveDirectory.DomainController]::getDomainController
($context)
$dc.IsGlobalCatalog()
```

Discussion

Once a server has completed initial replication of the global catalog, the attribute `isGlobalCatalogReady` in the RootDSE will be marked `TRUE`. Another way to determine if a domain controller has been at least flagged to become a global catalog is by checking if the `options` attribute on the `nTDSDSA` object for the server has been set to `1`. (Note that this does not necessarily mean the server is accepting requests as a global catalog.) An additional query to the RootDSE as described in the section called "Solution" or directly to port 3268 (the global catalog port) could also confirm that the appropriate flag has been set.

See Also

Recipe 4.1 for viewing the RootDSE

3.26 Finding the Global Catalog Servers in a Forest

Problem

You want a list of the global catalog servers in a forest.

Solution

Using a graphical user interface

1. Open LDP and from the menu select Connection→Connect.
2. For Server, enter the name of a DC.
3. For Port, enter 389.
4. Click OK.
5. From the menu select Connection→Bind.
6. Enter the credentials of a domain user.
7. Click OK.
8. From the menu select Browse→Search.
9. For BaseDN, type the DN of the Sites container, for example, `cn=sites,cn=configuration,dc=adatum,dc=com`.
10. For Scope, select Subtree.
11. For Filter, enter `(&(objectcategory=ntdsdsa)(options=1))`.
12. Click Run.

Using a command-line interface

To enumerate all GCs in a forest using DSQuery, use the following syntax:

```
> dsquery server -forest -isgc
```

You can also use AdFind as follows:

```
> adfind -sites -f "(&(objectcategory=ntdsdsa)
    (options:AND:=1))" -bit -dn
```

Using VBScript

```
' This code prints the global catalog servers for the specified forest.
' ------ SCRIPT CONFIGURATION -----
strForestName = "<ForestDNSName>" ' e.g. rallencorp.com
' ------ END CONFIGURATION --------

set objRootDSE = GetObject("LDAP://" & strForestName & "/" & "RootDSE")
strADsPath = "<LDAP://" & objRootDSE.Get("configurationNamingContext") & ">;"
strFilter = "(&(objectcategory=ntdsdsa)(options=1));"
strAttrs   = "distinguishedname;"
strScope   = "SubTree"

set objConn = CreateObject("ADODB.Connection")
objConn.Provider = "ADsDSOObject"
objConn.Open "Active Directory Provider"
set objRS = objConn.Execute(strADsPath & strFilter & strAttrs & strScope)
objRS.MoveFirst
while not objRS.EOF
    set objNTDS = GetObject("LDAP://" & objRS.Fields(0).Value)
    set objServer = GetObject( objNTDS.Parent )
    Wscript.Echo objServer.Get("dNSHostName")
    objRS.MoveNext
wend
```

Using PowerShell

To find all global catalogs in the current domain, use the following syntax:

```
$dom = [System.DirectoryServices.ActiveDirectory.Domain]::getCurrentDomain()
$dom.FindAllDomainControllers() | where {$_.IsGlobalCatalog() -eq "TRUE" }
```

To find all global catalogs in the forest, use the following:

```
$for = [System.DirectoryServices.ActiveDirectory.Forest]::getCurrentForest()
$dom.FindAllGlobalCatalogs()
```

Discussion

To find the global catalog servers in a forest, you need to query for NTDS Settings objects that have the low-order bit of the options attribute equal to 1 under the sites container in the Configuration Naming Context. That attribute determines if a domain controller should be a global catalog server, but it does not necessarily mean it is a global catalog server yet. See Recipe 3.25 for more information on how to tell if a server marked as a global catalog is ready to accept requests as one.

Another option for locating global catalogs is DNS, which is described in Recipe 3.28.

Using PowerShell

The PowerShell syntax in this recipe to find all GCs in a specific domain utilizes a PowerShell technique that allows you to "pipe" the results of one query into a second query to further refine the results. In this case, the `System.DirectoryServices.Active Directory.Domain` class contains a `FindAllDomainControllers()` method, but it does not contain a `FindAllGlobalCatalogServers()` method. However, the `DomainControllers` class contains an `IsGlobalCatalog()` method as we've seen in a previous recipe. So the English equivalent of this PowerShell syntax is "Give me all of the DCs in the current domain, such that the `IsGlobalCatalog()` method returns a value of `"True"` for that DC." As you can see, the `Forest` class contains a `FindAllGlobalCatalogs()` method, which obviates the need for a `"where"` clause.

See Also

Recipe 3.25 for determining if global catalog promotion is complete and Recipe 3.28 to locate global catalogs using DNS

3.27 Finding the Domain Controllers or Global Catalog Servers in a Site

Problem

You want a list of the domain controllers or global catalog servers in a specific site.

Solution

Using a graphical user interface

1. Open the Active Directory Sites and Services snap-in (*dssite.msc*).
2. In the right pane, expand the site that contains the domain controller.
3. For the list of domain controllers, expand the `Servers` container.
4. To find the global catalog servers, expand each domain controller, right-click on `NTDS Settings`, and select Properties.
5. Global catalog servers will have the appropriate box checked beside Global Catalog.

Using a command-line interface

The following query finds all domain controllers in the specified site:

```
> adfind -sites-rb cn=<SiteName> -f (objectcategory=ntdsdsa)
```

To find only the global catalog servers in a site, use the same command with the `-bit` filter enabled to perform a bitwise search for a `1` in the `options` attribute:

```
adfind -sites -rb cn=<SiteName> -f
"(&(objectcategory=ntdsdsa)(options:AND:=1))" -bit
```

Using VBScript

```
' This code prints the domain controllers in a site and then
' prints the global catalog servers in the site
' ------ SCRIPT CONFIGURATION -----
strSite = "<SiteName>" ' e.g. Default-First-Site-Name
strForest = "<ForestDNSName>" ' e.g. rallencorp.com
' ------ END CONFIGURATION --------

set objRootDSE = GetObject("LDAP://" & strForest & "/RootDSE")
strADsPath = "<LDAP://cn=servers,cn=" & strSite & ",cn=sites," & _
             objRootDSE.Get("configurationNamingContext") & ">;"
strFilter = "(objectcategory=ntdsdsa);"
strAttrs  = "distinguishedName;"
strScope  = "SubTree"

WScript.Echo "Domain controllers in " & strSite & ":"
set objConn = CreateObject("ADODB.Connection")
objConn.Provider = "ADsDSOObject"
objConn.Open "Active Directory Provider"
set objRS = objConn.Execute(strADsPath & strFilter & strAttrs & strScope)
objRS.MoveFirst
while not objRS.EOF
    Set objNTDS = GetObject("LDAP://" & objRS.Fields(0).Value)
    Set objServer = GetObject( objNTDS.Parent )
    Wscript.Echo " " & objServer.Get("dNSHostName")
    objRS.MoveNext
wend

' Global Catalog filter
strFilter = "(&(objectcategory=ntdsdsa)(options=1));"
WScript.Echo ""
WScript.Echo "
Global Catalogs in " & strSite & ":"
set objRS = objConn.Execute(strADsPath & strFilter & strAttrs & strScope)
objRS.MoveFirst
while not objRS.EOF
    set objNTDS = GetObject("LDAP://" & objRS.Fields(0).Value)
    set objServer = GetObject( objNTDS.Parent )
    Wscript.Echo " " & objServer.Get("dNSHostName")
    objRS.MoveNext
wend
```

Using PowerShell

To find all of the domain controllers in SiteA for the current domain, use the following syntax:

```
$dom = [System.DirectoryServices.ActiveDirectory.Domain]::getCurrentDomain()
$dom.FindAllDomainControllers("SiteA")
```

To find all GCs in SiteA for the current domain, use the following:

```
$dom = [System.DirectoryServices.ActiveDirectory.Domain]::getCurrentDomain()
$dom.FindAllDomainControllers("SiteA") | where {$_.IsGlobalCatalog() -eq "TRUE" }
```

To find all global catalogs in SiteA in the entire forest, use the following:

```
$for = [System.DirectoryServices.ActiveDirectory.Forest]::getCurrentForest()
$dom.FindAllGlobalCatalogs("SiteA")
```

Discussion

Each domain controller has a `server` object within the `Servers` container for the site it is a member of (for example, `cn=DC1,cn=Servers,cn=MySite,cn=site,cn=configuration,dc=adatum,dc=com`). Since other types of servers can have server objects in a site's `Servers` container, domain controllers are differentiated by the `nTDSDSA` object that is a child of the `server` object (e.g., `cn=NTDSSettings,cn=DC1,cn=Servers,cn=MySite,cn=site,cn=configuration,dc=adatum,dc=com`). Querying for this `nTDSDSA` object will return a list of domain controllers in the site. Locating global catalog servers consists of the same query, except where the low-order bit of the `options` attribute of the `nTDSDSA` object is equal to 1. Note that this may not be available if replication has not completed after enabling the GC.

3.28 Finding Domain Controllers and Global Catalogs via DNS

Problem

You want to find domain controllers or global catalogs using DNS lookups.

Solution

Domain controllers and global catalog servers are represented in DNS as SRV records. You can query SRV records using *nslookup* by setting the `type=SRV`, such as the following:

```
> nslookup
Default Server: dns01.adatum.com
Address: 10.1.2.3

> set type=SRV
```

You then need to issue the following query to retrieve all domain controllers for the specified domain:

```
> _ldap._tcp.<DomainDNSName>
```

You can issue a similar query to retrieve global catalogs, but since they are forest-wide, the query is based on the forest name:

```
> _gc._tcp.<ForestDNSName>
```

An alternate query to find Global Catalogs via *nslookup* would be to query for _gc._msdcs.*<ForestDNSName>*.

You can even find the domain controllers or global catalogs that are in a particular site or that *cover* a particular site by querying the following:

```
> _ldap._tcp.<SiteName>._sites.<DomainDNSName>
> _gc._tcp.<SiteName>._sites.<ForestDNSName>
```

See Recipe 11.20 for more information on site coverage.

Discussion

One of the benefits of Active Directory over its predecessor Windows NT is that it relies on DNS for name resolution, which is the standard for name resolution on the Internet and on most TCP/IP-based networks. Active Directory uses DNS to locate servers that serve a particular function, such as a domain controller for a domain, global catalog server, PDC Emulator, or KDC. It also uses the site topology information stored in Active Directory to populate site-specific records for domain controllers.

The DC locator process relies on this information in DNS to direct clients to the most optimal server when logging in. Reliance on DNS makes it easy to troubleshoot problems related to clients finding domain controllers. If you know the site a client is in, you can make a few DNS queries to determine which domain controller they should be using to authenticate.

The resource records that a domain controller registers in DNS can be restricted, if you have a lag site configured, for example, so querying DNS may return only a subset of the actual domain controllers that are available. See Recipes 12.14 and 12.15 for more information.

See Also

Recipe 12.14, Recipe 12.15, and Recipe 3.35 for finding the PDC Emulator via DNS, MS KB 267855 (Problems with Many Domain Controllers with Active Directory Integrated DNS Zones), and RFC 2782, "A DNS RR for Specifying the Location of Services (DNS SRV)"

3.29 Changing the Preference for a Domain Controller

Problem

You want a particular domain controller to be used less frequently for client requests or not at all. This may be necessary if a particular domain controller is overloaded, perhaps due to numerous application requests.

Solution

You can modify the `Priority` or `Weight` fields in SRV resource records by modifying the registry on the domain controller. Open *regedit* or *regedt32* on the domain controller and browse to the following key: `HKLM\SYSTEM\CurrentControlSet\Services\Netlogon\Parameters`. To configure the priority, add a `REG_DWORD` with the name `LdapSrvPriority`. To configure the weight, add a `REG_DWORD` with the name `LdapSrvWeight`.

After you make the change, the *%SystemRoot%\System32\Config\netlogon.dns* file should be updated and the DDNS updates sent to the DNS server within an hour. You can also restart the NetLogon service to expedite the process.

Discussion

Each domain controller registers several SRV records that clients use as part of the DC locator process to find the closest domain controller. Two fields of the SRV record let clients determine which server to use when multiple possibilities are returned. The `Priority` field is used to dictate if a specific server or set of servers should always be contacted over others unless otherwise unavailable. A server with a higher priority (i.e., lower `Priority` field value) will always be contacted before a server with a lower priority. For example, if DC1 has an SRV priority of 5 and DC2 has an SRV priority of 10, DC1 will always be used unless it is unavailable.

The `Weight` field, on the other hand, determines the percentage of time clients should use a particular server. You can easily calculate the percentage by dividing the weight by the sum of all weights for servers with the same priority. If servers DC1, DC2, and DC3 have weights of 1, 2, and 3, respectively, then DC1 will be contacted one out of six times or (1 / (3 + 2 + 1)), DC2 will be contacted two out of every six times or 1/3 (2 / (3 + 2 + 1)), and DC3 will be contacted three out of every six times or 1/2 (3 / (3 + 2 + 1)). Here is an example of how the SRV records look with these weights:

```
C:\> nslookup -type=SRV _ldap._tcp.dc._msdcs.adatum.com
Server: dns01.adatum.com
Address: 171.70.168.183

_ldap._tcp.dc._msdcs.adatum.com SRV service location:
        priority      = 0
        weight        = 1
        port          = 389
        svr hostname  = dc1.adatum.com
_ldap._tcp.dc._msdcs.adatum.com SRV service location:

priority      = 0

weight        = 2
        port          = 389
        svr hostname  = dc2.adatum.com
_ldap._tcp.dc._msdcs.datum.com SRV service location:
        priority      = 0
```

```
weight       = 3
port         = 389
svr hostname = dc3.datum.com
```

In certain situations, having this capability can come in handy. For example, the server acting as the PDC FSMO role owner typically receives more traffic from clients simply because of the nature of tasks that the PDC FSMO has to handle. If you find a certain server, like the PDC FSMO, has considerably higher load than the rest of the servers, you could change the priority or weight of the SRV records so that the server is used less often during the DC locator process. You can increase the `Priority` to eliminate its use unless all other domain controllers fail, or modify the `Weight` to reduce how often it will be used.

You can modify this information manually within the DNS Management Console, or for multiple DCs using Group Policy Objects in the `Computer Configuration \Administrative Templates\System\Net Logon\DC` Locator DNS Records GPO node.

See Also

MS KB 232025 (Description of the DNS SRV Resource Record Type)

3.30 Disabling the Global Catalog Requirement During a Domain Login

Problem

You want to disable the requirement for a global catalog server to be reachable when a user logs into a Windows 2000, Windows Server 2003, or Windows Server 2008 domain.

Solution

Using a graphical user interface

1. Open the Registry Editor (regedit).
2. In the left pane, expand HKEY_LOCAL_MACHINE→ System→Current-ControlSet→Control.
3. Right-click on LSA and select New→Key.
4. Enter `IgnoreGCFailures` for the key name and hit Enter.
5. Restart the server.

Using a command-line interface

```
> reg add HKLM\SYSTEM\CurrentControlSet\Control\LSA\IgnoreGCFailures /ve
> shutdown /r
```

Using VBScript

```
' This code enables the IgnoreGCFailres registry setting and reboots
strLSA = "HKLM\SYSTEM\CurrentControlSet\Control\LSA\IgnoreGCFailures\"
Set objWSHShell = WScript.CreateObject("WScript.Shell")
objWSHShell.RegWrite strLSA, ""
WScript.Echo "Successfully created key"
WScript.Echo "Rebooting server . . . "
objWSHShell.Run "rundll32 shell32.dll,SHExitWindowsEx 2"
```

Discussion

Beginning with Windows 2000 native mode, a global catalog server must be contacted for every login attempt; otherwise, the login will fail (unless there is no network connectivity, which would result in a user being logged on with cached credentials). This is necessary to process all universal security groups a user may be a member of. When a client attempts to authenticate with a domain controller, that domain controller contacts a global catalog server behind the scenes to enumerate the user's universal groups. (See Recipe 7.13 for more details.) If you have domain controllers in remote sites and they are not enabled as global catalog servers, you may run into a situation where users cannot log in if the network connection to the network with the closest global catalog server fails.

The only option you have available with Windows 2000 is to have the domain controllers ignore GC lookup failures (Recipe 7.13 provides a different solution for Windows Server 2003 and Windows Server 2008).

You can do this by adding an `IgnoreGCFailures` registry key under `HKLM\SYSTEM \CurrentControlSet\Control\LSA` on the domain controller(s) you want this to apply to. If you use universal groups in any capacity, having the domain controllers ignore GC failures can create a significant security hole because a user's token will not get updated with the appropriate universal group memberships.

See Also

Recipe 7.13 for enabling universal group caching, MS KB 216970 (Global Catalog Server Requirement for User and Computer Logon), and MS KB 241789 (How to Disable the Requirement that a Global Catalog Server Be Available to Validate User Logons)

3.31 Disabling the Global Catalog Requirement for Windows Server 2003 or Windows Server 2008

Problem

You want to disable the requirement for a global catalog server to be reachable when a user logs into a Windows 2003 or Windows Server 2008 domain.

This recipe requires a minimum of Windows Server 2003 forest functional level.

Solution

See Recipe 7.13 for information on enabling universal group caching, which can reduce the need to contact a global catalog server during logon for universal group expansion.

3.32 Finding the FSMO Role Holders

Problem

You want to find the domain controllers that are acting as one of the FSMO roles.

Solution

Using a graphical user interface

For the Schema Master:

1. Open the Active Directory Schema snap-in.
2. Right-click on Active Directory Schema in the left pane and select Operations Master.

For the Domain Naming Master:

1. Open the Active Directory Domains and Trusts snap-in (*domain.msc*).
2. Right-click on Active Directory Domains and Trusts in the left pane and select Operations Master.

For the PDC Emulator, RID Master, and Infrastructure Master:

1. Open the Active Directory Users and Computers snap-in (*dsa.msc*).
2. Make sure you've targeted the correct domain.
3. Right-click on Active Directory Users and Computers in the left pane and select Operations Master.
4. There are individual tabs for the PDC, RID, and Infrastructure roles.

Using a command-line interface

In the following command, you can leave out the /Domain <*DomainDNSName*> option to query the domain you are currently logged into:

```
> netdom query fsmo /Domain:<DomainDNSName>
```

To query the owner of an individual FSMO role, you can use the `dsquery server` command shown here, where `<Role>` can be schema, name, infr, pdc, or rid:

```
> dsquery server -hasfsmo <Role>
```

You can also obtain `fsmo` information using AdFind, as follows:

```
> adfind -sc fsmo
```

Using VBScript

```
' This code prints the FSMO role
' owners for the specified domain.
' ------ SCRIPT CONFIGURATION ------
strDomain = "<DomainDNSName>" ' e.g. emea.rallencorp.com
' ------ END CONFIGURATION --------

set objRootDSE = GetObject("LDAP://" & strDomain & "/RootDSE")
strDomainDN = objRootDSE.Get("defaultNamingContext")
strSchemaDN = objRootDSE.Get("schemaNamingContext")
strConfigDN = objRootDSE.Get("configurationNamingContext")

' PDC Emulator
set objPDCFsmo = GetObject("LDAP://" & strDomainDN)
Wscript.Echo "PDC Emulator: " & objPDCFsmo.fsmoroleowner

' RID Master
set objRIDFsmo = GetObject("LDAP://cn=RID Manager$,cn=system," & strDomainDN)
Wscript.Echo "RID Master: " & objRIDFsmo.fsmoroleowner

' Schema Master
set objSchemaFsmo = GetObject("LDAP://" & strSchemaDN)
Wscript.Echo "Schema Master: " & objSchemaFsmo.fsmoroleowner

' Infrastructure Master
set objInfraFsmo = GetObject("LDAP://cn=Infrastructure," & strDomainDN)
Wscript.Echo "Infrastructure Master: " & objInfraFsmo.fsmoroleowner

' Domain Naming Master
set objDNFsmo = GetObject("LDAP://cn=Partitions," & strConfigDN)
Wscript.Echo "Domain Naming Master: " & objDNFsmo.fsmoroleowner
```

Using PowerShell

```
$dom = [System.DirectoryServices.ActiveDirectory.Domain]::getCurrentDomain()
$for = [System.DirectoryServices.ActiveDirectory.Forest]::getCurrentForest()
$for.NamingRoleOwner
$for.SchemaRoleOwner
$dom.PdcRoleOwner
$dom.RidRoleOwner
$dom.InfrastructureRoleOwner
```

Discussion

Several Active Directory operations are sensitive, such as updating the schema, and therefore need to be restricted to a single domain controller to prevent corruption of the AD database. This is because Active Directory cannot guarantee the proper evaluation of these functions in a situation where they may be invoked from more than one DC. The FSMO mechanism is used to limit these functions to a single DC.

There are five designated FSMO roles that correspond to these sensitive functions. A FSMO role can apply either to an entire forest or to a specific domain. Each role is stored in the fSMORoleOwner attribute on various objects in Active Directory depending on the role. Table 3-5 contains a list of FSMO roles.

Table 3-5. FSMO roles

Role	Description	fSMORoleOwner location	Domain- or forest-wide?
Schema	Processes schema updates	CN=Schema,CN=Configuration,*<ForestDN>*	Forest
Domain Naming	Processes the addition, removal, and re-naming of domains	CN=Partitions CN=Configuration,*<ForestDN>*	Forest
Infrastructure	Maintains references to objects in other domains	CN=Infrastructure,*<DomainDN>*	Domain
RID	Handles RID pool allocation for the domain controllers in a domain	CN=RidManager$,CN=System, *<DomainDN>*	Domain
PDC Emulator	Acts as the Windows NT master browser and also as the PDC for downlevel clients and Windows NT Backup Domain Controllers (BDCs) in Windows 2000 and Windows Server 2003	*<DomainDN>*	Domain

Using VBScript

If you want to get the DNS name for each FSMO, you'll need to get the parent object of the nTDSDSA object and use the dNSHostName attribute, similar to Recipe 3.14. The code for getting the Schema Master could be changed to the following to retrieve the DNS name of the DC:

```
set objSchemaFsmo = GetObject("LDAP://cn=Schema,cn=Configuration," & strForestDN)
set objSchemaFsmoNTDS = GetObject("LDAP://" & objSchemaFsmo.fsmoroleowner)
set objSchemaFsmoServer = GetObject(objSchemaFsmoNTDS.Parent)
Wscript.Echo "Schema Master: " & objSchemaFsmoServer.Get("dNSHostName")
```

Using PowerShell

For a quick method of retrieving the FSMO role holders in a forest or domain, simply retrieve the properties of the forest or domain object, as follows:

```
$dom = [System.DirectoryServices.ActiveDirectory.Domain]::getCurrentDomain()
$dom
$for = [System.DirectoryServices.ActiveDirectory.Forest]::getCurrentForest()
$for
```

See Also

Recipe 3.14, MS KB 197132 (Windows 2000 Active Directory FSMO Roles), MS KB 223346 (FSMO Placement and Optimization on Windows 2000 Domain Controllers), MS KB 234790 (How to Find Servers That Hold Flexible Single Master Operations Roles), and MS KB 324801 (How to View and Transfer FSMO Roles in Windows Server 2003)

3.33 Transferring a FSMO Role

Problem

You want to transfer a FSMO role to a different domain controller. This may be necessary if you need to take a current FSMO role holder down for maintenance.

Solution

Using a graphical user interface

1. Use the same directions as described in Recipe 3.32 for viewing a specific FSMO, except target (i.e., right-click and select Connect to Domain Controller) the domain controller you want to transfer the FSMO *to* before selecting Operations Master.

2. Click the Change button.

3. Click OK twice.

4. You should then see a message stating whether the transfer was successful.

Using a command-line interface

The following would transfer the PDC Emulator role to *<NewRoleOwner>* (see the section called "Discussion" to see about transferring the other roles):

```
> ntdsutil roles conn "co t s <NewRoleOwner>" q "transfer PDC" q q
```

Using VBScript

```
' This code transfers the PDC Emulator role to the specified owner.
' See the discussion to see about
' transferring the other roles.
' ------ SCRIPT CONFIGURATION ------
strNewOwner = "<NewRoleOwner>" ' e.g. dc2.rallencorp.com
' ------ END CONFIGURATION ---------

Set objRootDSE = GetObject("LDAP://" & strNewOwner & "/RootDSE")
```

```
Set domainNC = GetObject("LDAP://" & objRootDSE.get("defaultNamingContext"))
domainSID = domainNC.objectSid
objRootDSE.Put "becomePDC", domainSID
objRootDSE.SetInfo
```

Using PowerShell

The following code will transfer the PDC Emulator role to another DC:

```
$dom = [ADSI]""
$domainSID = $dom.objectSID
$dcDSE = [ADSI]"LDAP://<DC>/rootDSE"
$role = "becomePdc"
$dcDSE.put($role,$domainSID)
$dcDSE.Setinfo()
```

The following will transfer the RID Master role to another DC; this syntax can be used for all FSMO role holders except for the PDC Emulator:

```
$dcDSE = [ADSI]"LDAP://<DC>/rootDSE"
$role = "becomeRID"
$dcDSE.put($role,1)
$dcDSE.Setinfo()
```

Discussion

The first domain controller in a new forest is assigned the two forest-wide FSMO roles (schema and domain naming). The first domain controller in a new domain gets the other three domain-wide roles. It is very likely you'll need to move the roles around to different domain controllers at some point. Also, when you need to decommission a domain controller that is currently a FSMO role owner (either permanently or for a significant period of time), you'll want to transfer the role beforehand.

If you plan to install a hotfix or do some other type of maintenance that only necessitates a quick reboot, you may not want to go to the trouble of transferring the FSMO role. This is because some FSMO roles are more time-critical than others, and some come into use on a far more frequent basis. For example, the PDC Emulator role is used extensively (and therefore should be transferred to a domain controller of equal or better capacity as a best practice), but the Schema Master is needed only when you are extending the schema by installing a new software package, such as Microsoft Exchange. If a FSMO role owner becomes unavailable before you can transfer it, you'll need to seize the role (see Recipe 3.34).

Using a command-line interface

Any role can be transferred using *ntdsutil* by replacing "transfer PDC" in the solution with one of the following:

- "transfer domain naming master"
- "transfer infrastructure master"

- "transfer RID master"
- "transfer schema master"

Using VBScript

FSMO roles can be transferred programmatically by setting the become<FSMORole> operational attribute on the RootDSE of the domain controller to transfer the role to. The following are the available attributes that can be set that correspond to each FSMO role:

- becomeDomainMaster
- becomeInfrastructureMaster
- becomePDC
- becomeRidMaster
- becomeSchemaMaster

Using PowerShell

The PowerShell example in this recipe uses the same operational attributes as the VBScript sample to transfer the PDC Emulator role. To transfer the other FSMO roles, substitute the operational attributes listed above.

See Also

Recipe 3.32 for finding FSMO role holders, Recipe 3.34 for seizing a FSMO role, MS KB 223787 (Flexible Single Master Operation Transfer and Seizure Process), MS KB 255504 (Using Ntdsutil.exe to Seize or Transfer FSMO Roles to a Domain Controller), and MS KB 324801 (How to View and Transfer FSMO Roles in Windows Server 2003)

3.34 Seizing a FSMO Role

Problem

You need to seize a FSMO role because the current role holder is down and will not be restored.

Solution

Using a command-line interface

The following would seize the PDC Emulator role to <NewRoleOwner>:

```
> ntdsutil roles conn "co t s <NewRoleOwner>" q "seize PDC" q q
```

Any of the other roles can be transferred as well using *ntdsutil* by replacing "seize PDC" in the previous solution with one of the following:

- "seize domain naming master"
- "seize infrastructure master"
- "seize RID master"
- "seize schema master"

Using VBScript

Seizing a FSMO role is typically not something you would want to do programmatically, but you could. All you need to do is set the `fSMORoleOwner` attribute for the object that represents the FSMO role (as described in Recipe 3.32) with the distinguished name of `nTDSDSA` object of the new role owner. However, this can be an extremely dangerous operation in the case of the RID Master FSMO, since it maintains extensive information that needs to be gracefully moved from one DC to another to avoid corruption of the AD database. In the case of the RID master, you should use `ntdsutil` to transfer or seize the role whenever possible.

Discussion

Seizing a FSMO role should not be done lightly. The general recommendation is to seize a FSMO role only when you cannot possibly bring the previous role holder back online. One reason that seizing a role is problematic is that you could possibly lose data. For example, let's say that you extended the schema and immediately after it was extended the Schema FSMO went down. If you could not bring that server back online, those extensions may not have replicated before the server went down. You would need to determine if any of the schema extensions replicated and, if not, re-extend the schema. Other issues can result from losing the RID FSMO, where duplicate RID pools may be allocated. See Recipe 3.32 for more information.

See Also

Recipe 3.32 for finding FSMO role holders, Recipe 3.33 for transferring a FSMO role, MS KB 223787 (Flexible Single Master Operation Transfer and Seizure Process), and MS KB 255504 (Using Ntdsutil.exe to Seize or Transfer FSMO Roles to a Domain Controller)

3.35 Finding the PDC Emulator FSMO Role Owner via DNS

Problem

You want to find the PDC Emulator for a domain using DNS.

Solution

Using a command-line interface

```
> nslookup -type=SRV _ldap._tcp.pdc._msdcs.<DomainDNSName>
```

Discussion

The PDC Emulator FSMO role is the only FSMO role that is stored in DNS. Like many of the other Active Directory-related DNS records, the PDC record is stored as an SRV record under `_ldap._tcp.pdc._msdcs.<DomainDNSName>` where `<DomainDNSName>` is the domain the PDC is in. This allows your Active Directory clients to use normal DNS name resolution to locate the PDC Emulator for their domain.

See Also

Recipe 3.28 for finding domain controllers via DNS

3.36 Finding the PDC Emulator FSMO Role Owner via WINS

Problem

You want to find the PDC Emulator for a domain using WINS.

Solution

Using a command-line interface

```
> netsh wins server \\<WINS server> show name netbiosname 1b
```

Discussion

In addition to registering a record with DNS, the PDC Emulator FSMO role will also register a record with a WINS server if it is configured to point to one. The PDC Emulator will register a record called "`<DomainName>` 1b"; this record corresponds to the Domain Master Browser record for the Browser service. Since the PDC Emulator will always be the domain master browser, this allows any downlevel clients to locate the PDC Emulator using NetBIOS name resolution.

See Also

Recipe 3.35 for finding the PDC Emulator via DNS

## CHAPTER 4

Searching and Manipulating Objects

4.0 Introduction

Active Directory is based on the Lightweight Directory Access Protocol (LDAP) and supports the LDAP version 3 specification defined in RFC 2251. And while many of the AD tools and interfaces, such as ADSI, abstract and streamline LDAP operations to make things easier, any good AD administrator or developer must have a thorough understanding of LDAP to fully utilize Active Directory. This chapter will cover some of the LDAP-related tasks you may need to perform when working with Active Directory, along with other tasks related to searching and manipulating objects within the directory.

The Anatomy of an Object

The Active Directory schema is composed of a hierarchy of classes that define the types of objects that can be created within Active Directory, as well as the different attributes that they can possess. These classes support *inheritance*, which enables developers to reuse existing class definitions for more than one type of object; for example, the `description` attribute is available with every type of AD object, but the attribute itself is only defined *once* within the schema. At the top of the inheritance tree is the top class, from which every class in the schema is derived. Table 4-1 contains a list of some of the attributes that are available from the top class, and subsequently are defined on every object that is created in Active Directory.

Table 4-1. Common attributes of objects

Attribute	Description
cn	RDN attribute for most object classes, also referred to as the *common name*.
whenCreated	Timestamp when the object was created. See Recipe 4.26 for more information.
description	Multivalued attribute that can be used as a generic field for storing a description of the object. Although this attribute is multivalued, objects such as users and groups can only have one value populated due to legacy support requirements.
displayName	Name of the object displayed in administrative interfaces.
distinguishedName	Distinguished name of the object.
whenChanged	Timestamp when the object was last changed by the local server. See Recipe 4.26 for more information.
name	RDN of the object. The value of this attribute will mirror the naming attribute (e.g., cn, ou, dc).
nTSecurityDescriptor	Security descriptor assigned to the object.
objectCategory	Used as a grouping mechanism for objects with a similar purpose (e.g., Person).
objectClass	List of classes from which the object's class was derived.
objectGUID	Globally unique identifier for the object.
uSNChanged	Update sequence number (USN) assigned by the local server after the last change to the object (can include creation).
uSNCreated	USN assigned by the local server when the object was created.

4.1 Viewing the RootDSE

Problem

You want to view attributes of the RootDSE, which can be useful for discovering basic information about a forest, domain, or domain controller without hardcoding the name of a particular naming context into a query.

Solution

Using a graphical user interface

1. Open LDP from the Windows Support Tools. (LDP is installed by default on a Windows Server 2008 domain controller.)
2. From the menu, select Connection→Connect.
3. For Server, enter a domain controller, domain name, or leave blank to do a serverless bind.
4. For Port, enter 389.
5. Click OK.
6. The contents of the RootDSE will be shown in the right pane.

Using a command-line interface

To display the RootDSE of a domain controller using AdFind, use the following syntax:

```
> adfind -rootdse
```

You'll see results similar to the following (truncated for readability):

```
>currentTime: 20051130204431.0Z
>subschemaSubentry: CN=Aggregate,CN=Schema,CN=Configuration,DC=contoso,DC=com
>dsServiceName: CN=NTDS Settings,CN=2K3-SP1-R2,CN=Servers,CN=Default-First-Site-
Name,CN=Sites,CN=Configuration,DC=contoso,DC=com
>namingContexts: DC=contoso,DC=com
>namingContexts: CN=Configuration,DC=contoso,DC=com
>namingContexts: CN=Schema,CN=Configuration,DC=contoso,DC=com
>namingContexts: DC=DomainDnsZones,DC=contoso,DC=com
>namingContexts: DC=ForestDnsZones,DC=contoso,DC=com
>defaultNamingContext: DC=contoso,DC=com
>schemaNamingContext: CN=Schema,CN=Configuration,DC=contoso,DC=com
>configurationNamingContext: CN=Configuration,DC=contoso,DC=com
>rootDomainNamingContext: DC=contoso,DC=com
>serverName: CN=2K3-SP1-R2,CN=Servers,CN=Default-First-Site-Name,CN=Sites,
CN=Configuration,DC=contoso,DC=com
>supportedCapabilities: 1.2.840.113556.1.4.800
>supportedCapabilities: 1.2.840.113556.1.4.1670
>supportedCapabilities: 1.2.840.113556.1.4.1791
>isSynchronized: TRUE
>isGlobalCatalogReady: TRUE
>domainFunctionality: 0
>forestFunctionality: 0
>domainControllerFunctionality: 2
```

Using VBScript

```
' This code prints the
' attributes of the RootDSE
set objRootDSE = GetObject("LDAP://RootDSE")
objRootDSE.GetInfo
for i = 0 to objRootDSE.PropertyCount - 1
    set strProp = objRootDSE.Item(i)
    WScript.Echo strProp.Name & " "
    for each strPropval in strProp.Values
        WScript.Echo " " & strPropval.CaseIgnoreString
    next
next
```

Using PowerShell

```
$root = [ADSI] "LDAP://RootDSE"
$colRootProps = $root | get-member
foreach ($prop in $colRootProps) { write-host $prop.Name -nonewline;
>> write-host ": " -nonewline;
>> write-host $root.($prop.Name)
>> }
>>
```

Discussion

The RootDSE was originally defined in RFC 2251 as part of the LDAPv3 specification. It is not part of the Active Directory namespace per se. It is a synthetic object that is maintained separately by each domain controller.

The RootDSE can be accessed anonymously using LDP; the command-line and VBScript solutions use the credentials of the currently logged-on user unless you specify an alternate username and password. In the CLI and VBScript solutions, serverless binds were used against the RootDSE. In that case, the DC Locator process is used to find a domain controller in the domain you authenticate against. This can also be accomplished with LDP by not entering a server name from the Connect dialog box.

The RootDSE is key to writing portable AD-enabled applications. It provides a mechanism to programmatically determine the distinguished names of the various naming contexts (among other things), which means that you do not need to hardcode that information in scripts and programs. Here is an example from LDP when run against a Windows Server 2003–based domain controller:

```
ld = ldap_open("dc01", 389);
Established connection to dc01.
Retrieving base DSA information ...
Result <0>: (null)
Matched DNs:
Getting 1 entries:
>> Dn:
1> currentTime: 07/26/2008 15:29:42 Pacific Standard Time Pacific Daylight Time;

1> subschemaSubentry:CN=Aggregate,CN=Schema,CN=Configuration,DC=adatum,DC=com;

1> dsServiceName: CN=NTDS Settings,CN=DC01,CN=Servers,CN=Default-First-Site-
Name,CN=Sites,CN=Configuration,DC=adatum,DC=com;

5> namingContexts: DC=adatum,DC=com; CN=Configuration,DC=adatum,DC=com;
CN=Schema,CN=Configuration,DC=adatum,DC=com;
DC=DomainDnsZones,DC=adatum,DC=com; DC=ForestDnsZones,DC=adatum,DC=com;

1> defaultNamingContext: DC=adatum,DC=com;

1> schemaNamingContext: CN=Schema,CN=Configuration,DC=adatum,DC=com;

1> configurationNamingContext: CN=Configuration,DC=adatum,DC=com;

1> rootDomainNamingContext: DC=adatum,DC=com;

21> supportedControl: 1.2.840.113556.1.4.319; 1.2.840.113556.1.4.801;
1.2.840.113556.
1.4.473; 1.2.840.113556.1.4.528; 1.2.840.113556.1.4.417; 1.2.840.113556.1.4.619;
1.2.
840.113556.1.4.841; 1.2.840.113556.1.4.529; 1.2.840.113556.1.4.805;
1.2.840.113556.1.
4.521; 1.2.840.113556.1.4.970; 1.2.840.113556.1.4.1338; 1.2.840.113556.1.4.474;
1.2.
```

```
840.113556.1.4.1339; 1.2.840.113556.1.4.1340; 1.2.840.113556.1.4.1413; 2.16.840.1.
113730.3.4.9; 2.16.840.1.113730.3.4.10; 1.2.840.113556.1.4.1504;
1.2.840.113556.1.4.
1852; 1.2.840.113556.1.4.802;

2> supportedLDAPVersion: 3; 2;

12> supportedLDAPPolicies: MaxPoolThreads; MaxDatagramRecv; MaxReceiveBuffer;
InitRecvTimeout; MaxConnections; MaxConnIdleTime; MaxPageSize; MaxQueryDuration;
MaxTempTableSize; MaxResultSetSize; MaxNotificationPerConn; MaxValRange;

1> highestCommittedUSN: 53242;

4> supportedSASLMechanisms: GSSAPI; GSS-SPNEGO; EXTERNAL; DIGEST-MD5;

1> dnsHostName: dc01.adatum.com;

1> ldapServiceName: adatum.com:dc01$@ADATUM.COM;

1> serverName: CN=DC01,CN=Servers,CN=Default-First-Site-
Name,CN=Sites,CN=Configuration,DC=adatum,DC=com;

3> supportedCapabilities: 1.2.840.113556.1.4.800; 1.2.840.113556.1.4.1670; 1.2.840.
113556.1.4.1791;

1> isSynchronized: TRUE;

1> isGlobalCatalogReady: TRUE;

1> domainFunctionality: 0 = ( DS_BEHAVIOR_WIN2000 );

1> forestFunctionality: 0 = ( DS_BEHAVIOR_WIN2000 );

1> domainControllerFunctionality: 2 = ( DS_BEHAVIOR_WIN2003 );
```

Using VBScript

All attributes of the RootDSE were retrieved and displayed. Typically, you will need
only a few of the attributes, in which case you'll want to use Get or GetEx as in the
following example:

```
strDefaultNC = objRootDSE.Get("defaultNamingContext")
```

Or if want to get an object based on the DN of one of the naming contexts, you can
call GetObject using an ADsPath:

```
set objUser = GetObject("LDAP://cn=administrator,cn=users," & _
                        objRootDSE.Get("defaultNamingContext") )
```

Using PowerShell

The PowerShell code in this example makes use of the foreach command, which allows
you to take a collection of objects (in this case, the properties of RootDSE), and perform
the same action on each one.

See Also

RFC 2251, MS KB 219005 (Windows 2000: LDAPv3 RootDSE), MSDN: IADsPropertyEntry, MSDN: IADsProperty Value, MSDN: IADs::Get, and MSDN: IADs::GetEx

4.2 Viewing the Attributes of an Object

Problem

You want to view one or more attributes of an object.

Solution

Using a graphical user interface

1. Open LDP from the Windows Support Tools or from the Windows Server 2008 command prompt.
2. From the menu, select Connection→Connect.
3. For Server, enter the name or IP address of a domain controller or domain that contains the object.
4. For Port, enter 389.
5. Click OK.
6. From the menu, select Connection→Bind.
7. Enter credentials of a user who can view the object (if necessary).
8. Click OK.
9. From the menu, select View→Tree.
10. For BaseDN, type the DN of the object you want to view.
11. For Scope, select Base.
12. Click OK.

Using a command-line interface

To obtain a list of attributes for a particular object using DSQuery, use the following syntax:

```
> dsquery * "<ObjectDN>" -scope base -attr *
```

For Windows 2000, use this command:

```
> enumprop "LDAP://<ObjectDN>"
```

To query for an object using AdFind, use the following syntax:

```
> adfind -b <Parent Container DN> -f cn=<Object CN> -tdcgt
```

For example, querying for the administrator user object produces the following output:

```
C:\>adfind -b dc=contoso,dc=com -f cn=administrator -tdc -tdcgt

AdFind V01.27.00cpp Joe Richards (joe@joeware.net) November 2005

Using server: 2k3-sp1-r2.contoso.com:389
Directory: Windows Server 2003

dn:CN=Administrator,CN=Users,DC=contoso,DC=com
>objectClass: top
>objectClass: person
>objectClass: organizationalPerson
>objectClass: user
>cn: Administrator
>description: Built-in account for administering the computer/domain
>distinguishedName: CN=Administrator,CN=Users,DC=contoso,DC=com
>instanceType: 4
>whenCreated: 05/26/2008-12:13:15 Eastern Daylight Time
>whenChanged:
05/26/2008-12:13:15 Eastern Daylight Time

>uSNCreated: 8194
>memberOf: CN=Group Policy Creator Owners,CN=Users,DC=contoso,DC=com
>memberOf: CN=Domain Admins,CN=Users,DC=contoso,DC=com
>memberOf: CN=Enterprise Admins,CN=Users,DC=contoso,DC=com
>memberOf: CN=Schema Admins,CN=Users,DC=contoso,DC=com
>memberOf: CN=Administrators,CN=Builtin,DC=contoso,DC=com
>uSNChanged: 13905
>name: Administrator
>objectGUID: {A5C30B01-535C-4BCF-83C1-ABA5D445B9F6}
>userAccountControl: 66048
>badPwdCount: 0
>codePage: 0
>countryCode: 0
>badPasswordTime: 0
>lastLogoff: 0
>lastLogon: 05/26/2008-23:09:03 Eastern Daylight Time
>pwdLastSet: 5/17/2008-18:09:27 Eastern Daylight Time
>primaryGroupID: 513
>objectSid: S-1-5-21-751427308-4037830757-4109730475-500
>adminCount: 1
>accountExpires: 00/00/0000-00:00:00
>logonCount: 7
>sAMAccountName: Administrator
>sAMAccountType: 805306368
>objectCategory: CN=Person,CN=Schema,CN=Configuration,DC=contoso,DC=com
>isCriticalSystemObject: TRUE

1 Objects returned
```

Using VBScript

```
' This code prints all default attributes for the specified object.
' ------ SCRIPT CONFIGURATION ------
strObjectDN = "<ObjectDN>" ' e.g. cn=jsmith,cn=users,dc=adatum,dc=com
' ------ END CONFIGURATION ---------

DisplayAttributes("LDAP://" & strObjectDN)

Function DisplayAttributes( strObjectADsPath )

    set objObject = GetObject(strObjectADsPath)
    objObject.GetInfo

    'Declare the hash (dictionary), constants and variables
    'Values taken from ADSTYPEENUM
    set dicADsType = CreateObject("Scripting.Dictionary")
    dicADsType.Add 0, "INVALID"
    dicADsType.Add 1, "DN_STRING"
    dicADsType.Add 2, "CASE_EXACT_STRING"
    dicADsType.Add 3, "CASE_IGNORE_STRING"
    dicADsType.Add 4, "PRINTABLE_STRING"
    dicADsType.Add 5, "NUMERIC_STRING"
    dicADsType.Add 6, "BOOLEAN"
    dicADsType.Add 7, "INTEGER"
    dicADsType.Add 8, "OCTET_STRING"
    dicADsType.Add 9, "UTC_TIME"
    dicADsType.Add 10, "LARGE_INTEGER"
    dicADsType.Add 11, "PROV_SPECIFIC"
    dicADsType.Add 12, "OBJECT_CLASS"
    dicADsType.Add 13, "CASEIGNORE_LIST"
    dicADsType.Add 14, "OCTET_LIST"
    dicADsType.Add 15, "PATH"
    dicADsType.Add 16, "POSTALADDRESS"
    dicADsType.Add 17, "TIMESTAMP"
    dicADsType.Add 18, "BACKLINK"
    dicADsType.Add 19, "TYPEDNAME"
    dicADsType.Add 20, "HOLD"
    dicADsType.Add 21, "NETADDRESS"
    dicADsType.Add 22, "REPLICAPOINTER"
    dicADsType.Add 23, "FAXNUMBER"
    dicADsType.Add 24, "EMAIL"
    dicADsType.Add 25, "NT_SECURITY_DESCRIPTOR"
    dicADsType.Add 26, "UNKNOWN"
    dicADsType.Add 27, "DN_WITH_BINARY"
    dicADsType.Add 28, "DN_WITH_STRING"

    for intIndex = 0 To (objObject.PropertyCount - 1)
        set objPropEntry = objObject.Item(intIndex)
        for Each objPropValue In objPropEntry.Values
            value = ""

            if (dicADsType(objPropValue.ADsType) = "DN_STRING") then
                value = objPropValue.DNString

            elseIf (dicADsType(objPropValue.ADsType) = "CASE_EXACT_STRING") then
```

```
                    value = objPropValue.CaseExactString

            elseIf (dicADsType(objPropValue.ADsType) = "CASE_IGNORE_STRING") then
                    value = objPropValue.CaseIgnoreString

            elseIf (dicADsType(objPropValue.ADsType) = "PRINTABLE_STRING") then
                    value = objPropValue.PrintableString

            elseIf (dicADsType(objPropValue.ADsType) = "NUMERIC_STRING") then
                    value = objPropValue.NumericString

            elseIf (dicADsType(objPropValue.ADsType) = "BOOLEAN") then
                    value = CStr(objPropValue.Boolean)

            elseIf (dicADsType(objPropValue.ADsType) = "INTEGER") then
                    value = objPropValue.Integer

            elseIf (dicADsType(objPropValue.ADsType) = "LARGE_INTEGER") then
                    set objLargeInt = objPropValue.LargeInteger
                    value = objLargeInt.HighPart * 2^32 + objLargeInt.LowPart

            elseIf (dicADsType(objPropValue.ADsType) = "UTC_TIME") then
                    value = objPropValue.UTCTime

            else
                    value = "<" & dicADsType.Item(objPropEntry.ADsType) & ">"


            end if
            WScript.Echo objPropEntry.Name & " : " & value
        next
    next
End Function
```

Using PowerShell

```
$obj = [ADSI]("LDAP://" + "<Object DN>")
$colObjProps = $obj | get-member
foreach ($prop in $colObjProps) {
  write-host $prop.Name -nonewline
  write-host ": " -nonewline
  write-host $obj.($prop.Name)
}
```

Discussion

Objects in Active Directory are made up of a collection of attributes. Attributes can be single- or multivalued. Each attribute also has an associated syntax that is defined in the schema. See Recipe 10.7 for a complete list of syntaxes.

Using a graphical user interface

You can customize the list of attributes returned from a search with LDP by modifying the Attributes: field under Options→Search. To include all attributes, enter an asterisk

(*). To modify the default subset of attributes that are returned, enter a semicolon-separated list of attributes. You can also use the numeric attribute ID instead of the attribute name, such as using `1.1` in place of `distinguishedName`.

Using a command-line interface

The `-attr` option for the `dsquery` command accepts a whitespace-separated list of attributes to display. Using an asterisk (*) will return all default attributes.

For the `enumprop` command, you can use the `/ATTR` option and a comma-separated list of attributes to return. In the following example, only the `name` and `whenCreated` attributes are returned:

```
> enumprop /ATTR:name,whenCreated "LDAP://<ObjectDN>"
```

When using AdFind, you have several shortcut switches to reduce the amount of typing you need to do. If you are searching for an object in the default container, you can use the `-default` switch rather than something like `-b dc=contoso,dc=com`. Likewise, if you are querying the Configuration NC, you can use the `-config` switch, `-root` for the root partition, or `-schema` for the Schema partition. If you want to query a subcontainer of one of these partitions, you can add the `-rb` switch, which stands for *Relative Base*.

Using VBScript

The `DisplayAttributes` function prints the attributes that contain values for the object passed in. After using `GetObject` to bind to the object, the `IADs::GetInfo` method was used to populate the local property cache with all of the object's attributes from AD. To print each value of a property, you have to know its type or syntax. The `ADsType` method returns an integer from the `ADSTYPEENUM` enumeration that corresponds with a particular syntax (e.g., `Boolean`). Based on the syntax, you call a specific method (e.g., Boolean) that can properly print the value. If you didn't incorporate this logic and tried to print all values, using the `CaseIgnoreString` method for example, an error would get generated when the script encountered an octet string because octet strings (i.e., binary data) do not have a `CaseIgnoreString` representation.

The values from the `ADSTYPEENUM` enumeration are stored in key/value pairs in a dictionary object (i.e., `Scripting.Dictionary`). In the dictionary object, the key for the dictionary is the `ADSTYPEENUM` integer and the value is a textual version of the syntax. The dictionary object was used to print the textual syntax of each attribute. You iterated over all the properties in the property cache using `IADsPropertyList` and `IADsPropertyEntry` objects, which are instantiated with the `IADsPropertyList::Item` method.

> The `DisplayAttributes` function is used throughout the book in examples where the attributes for a given type of object are displayed.

Using PowerShell

The PowerShell example in this recipe can also make use of the free Quest Active Directory cmdlets, specifically the Get-QADObject cmdlet.

See Also

Chapter 1 for more information about the Quest Active Directory cmdlets, Recipe 10.7, MSDN: IADsPropertyEntry, MSDN: IADsPropertyList, MSDN: ADSTYPEENUM, MSDN: IADs::GetInfo, and Chapter 20 of *Active Directory*, Fourth Edition, Brian Desmond et al. (O'Reilly).

4.3 Counting Objects in Active Directory

Problem

You want to retrieve the number of directory objects that meet the result of an LDAP query.

Solution

Using a graphical user interface

1. Open LDP from the Windows Support Tools.
2. From the menu, select Connection→Connect.
3. For Server, enter the name or IP address of a domain controller or domain that contains the object.
4. For Port, enter 389.
5. Click OK.
6. From the menu, select Connection→Bind.
7. Enter credentials of a user who can view the object (if necessary).
8. Click OK.
9. From the menu, select Browse→Search.
10. Enter the base DN, scope, and the LDAP filter of the objects that you're looking for.
11. Click on Options and remove the checkmark next to Display Results. This will display the number of objects returned by the query without displaying the details of the items that are returned.
12. Click OK and then click Run to perform the query.

Using a command-line interface

To retrieve a count of objects that match a particular query, use the following syntax:

```
> adfind -b <Search Base> -s <Scope> -f <Search Filter> -c
```

For example, retrieving the number of user objects in the *adatum.com* domain would use the following syntax:

```
> adfind -default -f "(&(objectclass=user)(objectcategory=person))" -c
>
> AdFind V01.27.00cpp Joe Richards (joe@joeware.net) November 2005
>
> Using server: 2k3-sp1-r2.adatum.com:389
> Directory: Windows Server 2003
> Base DN: DC=adatum,DC=com
>
> 5 Objects returned
```

Using VBScript

```
' This code lists the number of objects
' returned based on the specified criteria.
' ------ SCRIPT CONFIGURATION ------
strBase   = "<LDAP://<BaseDN>>;" ' BaseDN should be the search base
strFilter = "<Filter>;"          ' Valid LDAP search filter
strAttrs  = "<AttrList>;"        ' Comma-separated list
strScope  = "<Scope>"            ' Should be one of Subtree, Onelevel, or Base
' ------ END CONFIGURATION ---------

set objConn = CreateObject("ADODB.Connection")
objConn.Provider = "ADsDSOObject"
objConn.Open "Active Directory Provider"
set objRS = objConn.Execute(strBase & strFilter & strAttrs & strScope)
Wscript.Echo(objRS.RecordCount & " objects returned.")
```

Using PowerShell

The following example will query Active Directory for a list of user objects, and return the count:

```
$col = Get-QADObject -ldapfilter '(&(objectcategory=person)(objectclass=user))'
$col.Count
```

Discussion

Using VBScript

The VBScript solution uses the `RecordCount` property of an ADO Recordset, which contains the number of records that were returned by a particular query. The script listed here does not enable paging, so it will not work if more than 1,000 records will be returned by a query unless you specify the `"Page size"` property of the connection object, similar to the following:

```
objConn.Properties("Page size") = <PageSize>
```

Using PowerShell

The PowerShell code here can be shortened to a single line through the use of parentheses, as follows:

```
(Get-QADObject -ldapfilter '(&(objectcategory=person)(objectclass=user))').Count
```

4.4 Using LDAP Controls

Problem

You want to use an LDAP control as part of an LDAP operation.

Solution

Using a graphical user interface

1. Open LDP from the Windows Support Tools.
2. From the menu, select Options→Controls.
3. For the Windows Server 2003 version of LDP, select the control you want to use under Load Predefined. The control should automatically be added to the list of Active Controls.

   For the Windows 2000 version of LDP, you'll need to type the object identifier (OID) of the control under Object Identifier.
4. Enter the value for the control under Value.
5. Select whether the control is server- or client-side under Control Type.
6. Check the box beside Critical if the control is critical.
7. Click the Check-in button.
8. Click OK.
9. At this point, you will need to invoke the LDAP operation (e.g., Search) that will use the control. In the dialog box for any operation, be sure that the "Extended" option is checked before initiating the operation.

Using a command-line interface

The AdFind and AdMod utilities will enable a number of LDAP controls, either by default or through the use of various command-line switches. For example, the -showdel switch will invoke the Show Deleted Objects LDAP control, and -stats will invoke the Show Stats control.

Using VBScript

None of the ADSI automation interfaces directly expose LDAP controls. That means they cannot be utilized from VBScript. On the other hand, many of the controls, such as paged searching or deleting a subtree, are wrapped within their own ADSI methods that can be used within VBScript.

Any LDAP-based API, such as the Perl Net::LDAP modules, can be used to set controls as part of LDAP operations.

Using PowerShell

You can leverage LDAP controls within the current version of PowerShell by setting various properties on a DirectorySearcher object, such as the Tombstone property to return deleted objects, the ReferralChasing property, etc. For example, the following code will search for deleted objects that have an objectClass of computer:

```
$strCategory = "computer"
$objDomain = New-Object System.DirectoryServices.DirectoryEntry
$objSearcher = New-Object System.DirectoryServices.DirectorySearcher
$objSearcher.SearchRoot = $objDomain
$objSearcher.Filter = ("(objectCategory=$strCategory)")
$objSearch.tombstone = $true
$colResults = $objSearcher.FindAll()
```

Discussion

LDAP controls were defined in the LDAPv3 specification as a way to extend LDAP and its operations without breaking the protocol. Many controls have been implemented, some of which are used when searching the directory (e.g., paged searching, Virtual List View [VLV], finding deleted objects, and attribute scoped query), and some are needed to do certain modifications to the directory (e.g., cross-domain object moves, tree delete, and permissive modify). Controls can be marked as critical, which means they must be processed with the request or an error is returned. If an unsupported control is not flagged as critical, the server can continue to process the request and ignore the control.

The complete list of controls supported by Active Directory is included in Table 4-2.

Table 4-2. LDAP controls supported by Active Directory

Name	OID	Description
Permit No-Opt Modify	1.2.840.113556.1.4.1413	Allows duplicate adds of the same value for an attribute or deletion of an attribute that has no values to succeed (normally, it would fail in that situation).
Return Deleted Objects	1.2.840.113556.1.4.417	Used to inform the server to return any deleted objects that matched the search criteria.
Cross Domain Move	1.2.840.113556.1.4.521	Used to move objects between domains.
Set change notifications	1.2.840.113556.1.4.528	Used by clients to register for notification of when changes occur in the directory.

Name	OID	Description
Delayed Write	1.2.840.113556.1.4.619	Used to inform the server to return after directory modifications have been written to memory, but before they have been written to disk. This can speed up processing of a lot of modifications.
Security Descriptor Flags	1.2.840.113556.1.4.801	Used to pass flags to the server to control certain security descriptor options.
Subtree Delete	1.2.840.113556.1.4.805	Used to delete portions of the directory tree, including any child objects.
Verify Name Existence	1.2.840.113556.1.4.1338	Used to target a specific GC server that is used to verify DN-valued attributes that are processed during addition or modification operations.
No referrals generated	1.2.840.113556.1.4.1339	Informs the server not to generate any referrals in a search response.
Domain or phantom scope	1.2.840.113556.1.4.1340	Used to pass flags to the server to control search options.
Search Stats	1.2.840.113556.1.4.970	Used to return statistics about an LDAP query. See Recipe 15.10 for an example.
Attribute Scoped Query	1.2.840.113556.1.4.1504	Used to force a query to be based on a specific DN-valued attribute. This control is new to Windows Server 2003. See Recipe 4.8 for an example.
Extended DN	1.2.840.113556.1.4.529	Used to return an object's GUID and SID (for security principals) as part of its distinguished name.
Quota SID	1.2.840.113566.1.4.1852	Used to pass the SID of a security principal in order to query constructed attributes such as ms-DS-Quota-Effective and ms-DS-Quota-Used.
Paged Results	1.2.840.113556.1.4.319	Instructs the server to return search results in "pages."
DIRSYNC	1.2.840.113556.1.4.841	Used to find objects that have changed over a period of time.
Server-side Sort Request	1.2.840.113556.1.4.473	Used to inform the server to sort the results of a search.
Server-side Sort Response	1.2.840.113556.1.4.474	Returned by the server in response to a sort request.
VLV Request	2.16.840.1.113730.3.4.9	Used to request a virtual list view of results from a search. This control is new to Windows Server 2003.
VLV Response	2.16.840.1.113730.3.4.10	Response from a server returning a virtual list view of results from a search. This control is new to Windows Server 2003.

See Also

Recipe 4.8, Recipe 15.10, RFC 2251 (Lightweight Directory Access Protocol [v3]) for a description of LDAP controls, MSDN: Extended Controls, and MSDN: Using Controls

4.5 Using a Fast or Concurrent Bind

Problem

You want to perform an LDAP bind using a concurrent bind, also known as a fast bind. Concurrent binds are typically used in situations where you need to authenticate a lot of users, and those users either do not need to directly access the directory or else the directory access is done with another account.

Solution

 This capability was added in Windows Server 2003.

Using a graphical user interface

1. Open LDP from the Windows Support Tools.
2. From the menu, select Connection→Connect.
3. For Server, enter the name of a DC.
4. For Port, enter 389.
5. Click OK.
6. From the menu, select Options→Connection Options.
7. Under Option Name: select LDAP_OPT_F*_CONCURRENT_BIND.
8. Click the Set button.
9. From the menu, select Connection→Bind.
10. Enter credentials of a user.
11. Click OK.

Discussion

Unlike simple binding, concurrent binding does not generate a security token or determine a user's group memberships during the authentication process. It only determines if the authenticating user has a valid enabled account and password, which makes it much faster than a typical bind. This is usually used pro grammatically for AD-enabled applications to improve the speed of AD authentication; it's not something that you'll typically do on the fly. Concurrent binding is implemented as a session option that is set after you establish a connection to a domain controller, but before any bind attempts are made. After the option has been set, any bind attempt made with the connection will be a concurrent bind.

There are a couple of caveats when using concurrent binds. First, you cannot enable signing or encryption, which means that all data for concurrent binds will be sent over the network in clear text. Secondly, because the user's security token is not generated, access to the directory is done anonymously and access restrictions are based on the ANONYMOUS LOGON principal.

It is worth mentioning that there is another type of bind—a fast bind—which has been available since Windows 2000, but it is completely different from the procedure just described. This fast bind is implemented within ADSI, and simply means that when you fast bind to an object, the objectClass attribute for the object is not retrieved; therefore, the object-specific IADs class interfaces are not available. For example, if you bound to a user object using an ADSI fast bind, then only the basic IADs interfaces would be available, not the IADsUser interfaces.

This is the complete list of interfaces that are available for objects retrieved with fast binds:

- IADs
- IADsContainer
- IDirectoryObject
- IDirectorySearch
- IADsPropertyList
- IADsObjectOptions
- ISupportErrorInfo
- IADsDeleteOps

You must use the IADsOpenDSObject::OpenDSObject interface to enable fast binds. If you call IADsContainer::GetObject on a child object of a parent you used a fast bind with, the same fast bind behavior applies. Unlike concurrent binds, ADSI fast binds do not impose any restrictions on the authenticating user. This means that the object-specific IADs interfaces will not be available. Also, no check is done to verify the object exists when you call OpenDSObject.

ADSI fast binds are useful when you need to make a lot of updates to objects that you know exist (perhaps from an ADO query that returned a list of DNs) and you do not need any IADs-specific interfaces. Instead of two trips over the network per object binding, there would only be one.

See Also

MSDN: Using Concurrent Binding and MSDN: ADS_AUTHENTICATION_ENUM

4.6 Connecting to an Object GUID

Problem

You want to bind to a container using its Globally Unique Identifier (GUID).

Solution

Using a graphical user interface

1. Open LDP from the Windows Support Tools.
2. From the menu, select Connection→Connect.
3. For Server, enter the name of a domain controller (or leave blank to do a serverless bind).
4. For Port, enter 389.
5. Click OK.
6. From the menu, select Connection→Bind.
7. Enter credentials of a user.
8. Click OK.
9. From the menu, select Browse→Search.
10. For BaseDN, enter the GUID of the object that you're searching for in the following format:

    `<GUID=758A39F4A44A0C48A16016457C1AE9E9>`
11. For Scope, select the appropriate scope.
12. For Filter, enter an LDAP filter.
13. Click Run.

Using a command-line interface

```
> adfind -b "<GUID=ObjectGUID>"
```

Using VBScript

```
' This code illustrates how to bind to an object GUID.
' ------ SCRIPT CONFIGURATION ------
strDomain = "<DomainDNSName>" ' e.g. apac.adatum.com
strGUID = "<GUID>" ' e.g. "aa312825768811d1aded00c04fd8d5cd"
                        ' for the default Computers container
' ------ END CONFIGURATION --------

set objRootDSE = GetObject("LDAP://" & strDomain & "/RootDSE")
set objContainer = GetObject("LDAP://<GUID=" & _
                             strGUID & "," & _
```

```
                       objRootDSE.Get("defaultNamingContext") & ">" )
        WScript.Echo objContainer.Get("distinguishedName")
```

Using PowerShell

```
$obj = [System.DirectoryServices.DirectoryEntry] "LDAP://<GUID=<ObjectGUID>>"
```

Discussion

Each object in Active Directory has a GUID associated with it, stored in the `objectGUID` attribute. The GUID is for most purposes a unique identifier that retains its value even if an object is updated, renamed, or moved. This makes the GUID the preferable means of binding to an object, rather than hardcoding a reference to an object name that might change or by using a potentially complex LDAP query.

See Also

For a more in-depth discussion of the `objectGUID` attribute, see "GUIDs, or Having Unique in the Name Doesn't Make It So" (*http://blog.joeware.net/2005/06/19/42/*), MSDN: IADs.GUID, MSDN: Using objectGUID to Bind to an Object, and Recipe 4.7

4.7 Connecting to a Well-Known GUID

Problem

You want to connect to LDAP using one of the well-known GUIDs in Active Directory.

Solution

Using a graphical user interface

1. Open LDP.
2. From the menu, select Connection→Connect.
3. For Server, enter the name of a domain controller (or leave blank to do a serverless bind).
4. For Port, enter 389.
5. Click OK.
6. From the menu, select Connection→Bind.
7. Enter credentials of a domain user.
8. Click OK.
9. From the menu, select View→Tree.
10. For the DN, enter:

```
<WKGUID=<WKGUID>,<DomainDN>>
```

where *<WKGUID>* is the well-known GUID that you want to connect to, and *<DomainDN>* is the distinguished name of a domain.

11. Click OK. In the lefthand menu, you can now browse the container corresponding to the well-known GUID that you specified.

Using a command-line interface

To enumerate the well-known GUIDs in the Domain NC, use the following syntax:

```
> adfind -default -s base wellknownObjects
```

To display the WKGUIDs in the Configuration NC, replace **–default** with **–config** in the previous syntax.

To connect to a well-known GUID in the Domain NC using AdFind, use the following syntax:

```
> adfind -b "<WKGUID=<WKGUID>,<DomainDN>>" -s base -dn
```

Because of additional security settings attached to the Deleted Objects container, if you specify this GUID you must also use the **–showdel** switch in adfind.

Using VBScript

```
' This code illustrates how to bind to the default computer's container.
' ------ SCRIPT CONFIGURATION ------
strDomain = "<DomainDNSName>" ' e.g. apac.adatum.com
strWKGUID = "<WKGUID>" ' e.g. "aa312825768811d1aded00c04fd8d5cd"
                       ' for the default Computer's container
' ------ END CONFIGURATION --------

set objRootDSE = GetObject("LDAP://" & strDomain & "/RootDSE")
set objCompContainer = GetObject("LDAP://<WKGUID=" & _
                          strWKGUID & "," & _
                          objRootDSE.Get("defaultNamingContext") & ">" )
WScript.Echo objCompContainer.Get("distinguishedName")
```

Using PowerShell

```
$obj = [ADSI] "LDAP://<WKGUID=<Well-Known GUID>,<Domain DN>>"
```

Discussion

The domain NC in Active Directory contains a number of well-known GUIDs that correspond to containers that exist in every AD implementation. These GUIDs are stored as wellKnownObjects attributes within the *<DomainDN>* object, and allow administrators and developers to consistently connect to critical containers even if they are moved or renamed. The *<DomainDN>* container possesses the following objects that correspond to well-known GUIDs:

- CN=NTDS Quotas,*<DomainDN>*
- CN=Microsoft,CN=Program Data,*<DomainDN>*
- CN=Program Data,*<DomainDN>*
- CN=ForeignSecurityPrincipals,*<DomainDN>*
- CN=Deleted Objects,*<DomainDN>*
- CN=Infrastructure,*<DomainDN>*
- CN=LostAndFound,*<DomainDN>*
- CN=System,*<DomainDN>*
- OU=Domain Controllers,*<DomainDN>*
- CN=Computers,*<DomainDN>*
- CN=Users,*<DomainDN>*

The Configuration NC adds these additional WKGUIDs:

- CN=NTDS Quotas,CN=Confguration,*<ForestRootDN>*
- CN=LostAndFoundConfig,CN=Configuration,*<ForestRootDN>*
- CN=Deleted Objects,CN=Configuration,*<ForestRootDN>*

See Also

MSDN: Binding to Well-Known Objects Using WKGUID

4.8 Searching for Objects in a Domain

Problem

You want to find objects in a domain that match certain criteria.

Solution

Using a graphical user interface

1. Open LDP from the Windows Support Tools.
2. From the menu, select Connection→Connect.
3. For Server, enter the name of a domain controller (or leave blank to do a serverless bind).
4. For Port, enter 389.
5. Click OK.
6. From the menu, select Connection→Bind.
7. Enter credentials of a user.

8. Click OK.

9. From the menu, select Browse→Search.

10. For BaseDN, type the base distinguished name where the search will start. (You can leave this blank if you wish to connect to the domain NC as the base DN.)

11. For Scope, select the appropriate scope.

12. For Filter, enter an LDAP filter.

13. Click Run.

Using a command-line interface

To run a query using the built-in DSQuery tool, use the following syntax:

```
> dsquery * <BaseDN> -scope <Scope> -filter "<Filter>" -attr "<AttrList>"
```

To retrieve the SAM account name for all user objects within the *adatum.com* domain, for example, use the following syntax:

```
> dsquery * dc=adatum,dc=com -filter
"(&(objectclass=user)(objectcategory=person))" -attr sAMAccountName
```

To run a query using adfind, use the following syntax:

```
> adfind -b <BaseDN> -s <Scope> -f <Filter> <Attributes>
```

Querying for SAM account names of user objects with adfind takes the following syntax:

```
> adfind -b dc=adatum,dc=com -f "(&(objectclass=user)(objectcategory=person))"
sAMAccountName
```

 Both DSQuery and AdFind assume a default search scope of subtrees; you only need to specify the search scope if you want to use a different one.

Using VBScript

```
' This code searches
' for objects based on the specified criteria.
' ------ SCRIPT CONFIGURATION ------
strBase   = "<LDAP://<BaseDN>>;" ' BaseDN should be the search base
strFilter = "<Filter>;"              ' Valid LDAP search filter
strAttrs  = "<AttrList>;"            ' Comma-separated list
strScope  = "<Scope>"                ' Should be one of Subtree, Onelevel, or Base
' ------ END CONFIGURATION --------

set objConn = CreateObject("ADODB.Connection")
objConn.Provider = "ADsDSOObject"
objConn.Open "Active Directory Provider"
set objRS = objConn.Execute(strBase & strFilter & strAttrs & strScope)
objRS.MoveFirst
While Not objRS.EOF
```

```
        Wscript.Echo objRS.Fields(0).Value
        objRS.MoveNext
    Wend
    WScript.Echo("Search complete!")
```

Using PowerShell

The following example will search for user objects within an Active Directory domain using the Quest `get-QADObject` cmdlet:

```
get-QADObject -ldapfilter '(&(objectcategory=person)(objectclass=user))'
```

Another option is to use the `DirectorySearcher` class from the .NET Framework, as follows:

```
$strCategory = "computer"
$objDomain = New-Object System.DirectoryServices.DirectoryEntry
$objSearcher = New-Object System.DirectoryServices.DirectorySearcher
$objSearcher.SearchRoot = $objDomain
$objSearcher.Filter = ("(objectCategory=$strCategory)")
$colResults = $objSearcher.FindAll()
```

Discussion

Most tools that can be used to search Active Directory require a basic understanding of how to perform LDAP searches using a base DN, search scope, and search filter, as described in RFC 2251 and 2254. The base DN is where the search begins in the directory tree. The search scope defines how far down in the tree to search from the base DN. The search filter is a prefix notation string that contains equality comparisons of attribute and value pairs.

The scope can be `base`, `onelevel` (or `one`), or `subtree` (or `sub`). A `base` scope will only match the base DN, `onelevel` will only match objects that are contained directly under the base DN, and `subtree` will match everything from the base DN and any objects beneath it.

 There are no LDAP query scopes that will walk backward "up" the tree.

The search filter syntax is a powerful way to represent simple and complex queries. For example, a filter that matches all of the `user` objects would be `(&(objectclass=user)(objectcategory=Person))`. For more information on filters, see RFC 2254.

Using a graphical user interface

To customize the list of attributes returned for each matching object, look at the GUI discussion in Recipe 4.2.

Using a command-line interface

<AttrList> should be a space-separated list of attributes to return. To return all attributes that have been populated with a value, leave this field blank or use an asterisk (*).

Using VBScript

The VBScript solution uses ADO to perform the search. When using ADO, you must first create a connection object with the following three lines:

```
set objConn = CreateObject("ADODB.Connection")
objConn.Provider = "ADsDSOObject"
objConn.Open "Active Directory Provider"
```

At this point you can pass parameters to the Execute method, which will return a ResultSet object. You can iterate over the ResultSet by using the MoveFirst and MoveNext methods.

See Recipe 4.9 for more information on specifying advanced options in ADO like the page size.

Using PowerShell

A DirectorySearcher can be further customized by modifying additional properties related to the directory search, such as $objSearcher.SearchScope = [System.Directory Services.SearchScope]::OneLevel to specify a One Level LDAP search.

See Also

Recipe 4.2 for viewing attributes of objects, Recipe 4.9 for setting advanced ADO options, RFC 2251 (Lightweight Directory Access Protocol [v3]), RFC 2254 (Lightweight Directory Access Protocol [v3]), MSDN: Searching with ActiveX Data Objects (ADO), and for a good white paper on performing queries with LDAP, see *http://www.microsoft.com/windows2000/techinfo/howitworks/activedirectory/ldap.asp*

4.9 Searching the Global Catalog

Problem

You want to perform a forest-wide search using the global catalog.

Solution

Using a graphical user interface

1. Open LDP from the Windows Support Tools.
2. From the menu, select Connection→Connect.

3. For Server, enter the name of a global catalog server.

4. For Port, enter 3268.

5. Click OK.

6. From the menu, select Connection→Bind.

7. Enter the credentials of a user.

8. Click OK.

9. From the menu, select Browse→Search.

10. For BaseDN, type the base distinguished name of where to start the search.

11. For Scope, select the appropriate scope.

12. For Filter, enter an LDAP filter.

13. Click Run.

Using a command-line interface

To query the global catalog using DSQuery, use the following syntax:

```
> dsquery * <BaseDN> -gc -scope <Scope> -filter "<Filter>" -attr "<AttrList>"
```

To run a query using AdFind, use the following syntax:

```
> adfind -gc -b <BaseDN> -s <Scope> -f <Filter> <Attributes>
```

Using VBScript

```
' This code searches the global catalog
' ------ SCRIPT CONFIGURATION ------
strBase   = "<GC://<BaseDN>>;"
strFilter = "<Filter>;"
strAttrs  = "<AttrList>;"
strScope  = "<Scope>"
' ------ END CONFIGURATION ---------

set objConn = CreateObject("ADODB.Connection")
objConn.Provider = "ADsDSOObject"
objConn.Open "Active Directory Provider"
set objRS = objConn.Execute(strBase & strFilter & strAttrs & strScope)
objRS.MoveFirst
while Not objRS.EOF
    Wscript.Echo objRS.Fields(0).Value
    objRS.MoveNext
wend
```

Using PowerShell

To query the global catalog using the Quest AD cmdlets, use the following syntax to create the global catalog connection, and then use get-QADObject as described in previous recipes:

```
get-QADService -UseGlobalCatalog
```

To query the global catalog using the `DirectorySearcher` class, use the following syntax:

```
$strCategory = "computer"
$objGC = [System.DirectoryServices.DirectoryEntry] "GC://<DomainDN>"
$objGCSearcher = New-Object System.DirectoryServices.DirectorySearcher
$objGCSearcher.SearchRoot = $objGC
$objSearcher.Filter = ("(objectCategory=$strCategory)")
$colResults = $objSearcher.FindAll()
```

Discussion

The global catalog facilitates forest-wide searches. When you perform a normal LDAP search over port 389, you are searching against a particular partition within Active Directory, whether that is the Domain naming context, Configuration naming context, Schema naming context, or an application partition. If you have multiple domains in your forest, this type of search will not search against all domains but only the domain that you specify.

The global catalog, by contrast, contains a subset of the attributes for all objects in the forest (excluding objects in application partitions). Think of it as a subset of all the naming contexts combined. Every object in the directory will be contained in the global catalog (except for objects contained within application partitions), but only some of the attributes of those objects will be available. For that reason, if you perform a global catalog search and do not get values for attributes you were expecting to, make sure those attributes are included in the global catalog, also known as the partial attribute set (PAS). See Recipe 10.15 for more information on adding information to the PAS. As an alternative, you can query a DC within the domain containing the object to return a list of all attributes configured for that object.

Using a graphical user interface

The only difference between this solution and Recipe 4.8 is that the port has changed to 3268, which is the standard GC port.

Using a command-line interface

The only difference between this solution and Recipe 4.8, both for DSQuery and AdFind, is the addition of the -gc flag.

Using VBScript

The only difference between this solution and Recipe 4.8 is that the `strBase` variable changed to use the `GC:` progID:

```
strBase = "<GC://<BaseDN>>;"
```

See Also

Recipe 4.8 for searching for objects, Recipe 10.15, and MSDN: Searching with ActiveX Data Objects (ADO)

4.10 Searching for a Large Number of Objects

Problem

Your search is returning exactly 1,000 objects, which is only a subset of the objects you expected, and you want it to return all matching objects.

Solution

You might notice that searches with large numbers of matches stop displaying after 1,000. By default, domain controllers return a maximum of 1,000 entries from a search unless paging is enabled. This is done to prevent queries from consuming excessive resources on domain controllers by retrieving the results all at once instead of in pages or batches. The following examples are variations of Recipe 4.8, which will show how to enable paging and return all matching entries.

Using a graphical user interface

1. Open LDP from the Windows Support Tools.
2. From the menu, select Connection→Connect.
3. For Server, enter the name of a domain controller (or leave blank to do a serverless bind).
4. For Port, enter 389.
5. Click OK.
6. From the menu, select Connection→Bind.
7. Enter the credentials of a user.
8. Click OK.
9. From the menu, select Browse→Search.
10. For BaseDN, type the base distinguished name of where the search will start. (You can leave this blank if you wish to connect to the domain NC as the base DN.)
11. For Scope, select the appropriate scope.
12. For Filter, enter an LDAP filter.
13. Click Options to customize the options for this query.
14. For Timeout(s), enter a value such as 10.
15. For Page size, enter the number of objects to be returned with each page (e.g., 1,000).

---

16. Under Search Call Type, select Paged.

17. Click OK and then Run to perform the query. A page of results (i.e., 1,000 entries) will be displayed each time you click Run until all results have been returned.

Using a command-line interface

```
> dsquery * <BaseDN> -limit 0 -scope <Scope> -filter "<Filter>" -attr "<AttrList>"
```

Using VBScript

```
' This code enables paged searching
' ------ SCRIPT CONFIGURATION ------
strBase   = "<LDAP://<BaseDN>>;"
strFilter = "<Filter>;"
strAttrs  = "<AttrList>;"
strScope  = "<Scope>"
' ------ END CONFIGURATION ---------
set objConn = CreateObject("ADODB.Connection")
objConn.Provider = "ADsDSOObject"
objConn.Open "Active Directory Provider"
set objComm = CreateObject("ADODB.Command")
objComm.ActiveConnection = objConn
objComm.Properties("Page Size") = 1000
objComm.CommandText = strBase & strFilter & strAttrs & strScope
set objRS = objComm.Execute
objRS.MoveFirst
while Not objRS.EOF
    Wscript.Echo objRS.Fields(0).Value
    objRS.MoveNext
wend
```

Using PowerShell

```
$strCategory = "computer"
$objDomain = New-Object System.DirectoryServices.DirectoryEntry
$objSearcher = New-Object System.DirectoryServices.DirectorySearcher
$objSearcher.SearchRoot = $objDomain
$objSearcher.PageSize = 1000
$objSearcher.Filter = ("(objectCategory=$strCategory)")
$colResults = $objSearcher.FindAll()
```

Discussion

Paged searching support is implemented via an LDAP control. LDAP controls were defined in RFC 2251 and the Paged control in RFC 2696. Controls are extensions to LDAP that were not built into the protocol, so not all directory vendors support the same ones.

> In Active Directory, you can change the default maximum page size of 1,000 by modifying the LDAP query policy. See Recipe 4.27 for more information.

If you need searches to return hundreds of thousands of entries, Active Directory will return a maximum of only 262,144 entries even when paged searching is enabled. This value is defined in the LDAP query policy and can be modified like the maximum page size (see Recipe 4.27).

Using a graphical user interface

A word of caution when using LDAP to display a large number of entries—by default, only 2,048 lines will be displayed in the right pane. To change that value, go to Options→General and change the Line Value under Buffer Size to a larger number.

Using a command-line interface

The only difference between this solution and Recipe 4.8 is the addition of the `-limit` 0 flag. With `-limit` set to 0, paging will be enabled according to the default LDAP query policy; matching objects will be returned within those parameters. If `-limit` is not specified, a maximum of 100 entries will be returned.

 AdFind enables paged searches by default; it will return any number of objects from a query without any modification.

Using VBScript

To enable paged searching in ADO, you must instantiate an ADO `Command` object. A `Command` object allows for various properties of a query to be set, such as size limit, time limit, and page size. See MSDN for the complete list.

Using PowerShell

To enable paged searches in PowerShell, you will need to modify the `PageSize` property of the `DirectorySearcher` object.

The `get-QADObject` cmdlet also includes a `-PageSize` switch that will indicate the maximum results that should be returned, with a default value of 50. Similar to the `-limit` switch in `dsquery`, invoking this switch will cause paging to be enabled according to the default LDAP query policy.

See Also

Recipe 4.8 for searching for objects, Recipe 4.27 for viewing the default LDAP policy, RFC 2251 (Lightweight Directory Access Protocol [v3]), RFC 2696 (LDAP Control Extension for Simple Paged Results Manipulation), and MSDN: Searching with ActiveX Data Objects (ADO)

4.11 Searching with an Attribute-Scoped Query

This recipe requires the Windows Server 2003 forest functional level or better.

Problem

You want to perform a search using an individual value within a multivalued attribute as part of the search criteria. An attribute-scoped query can do this in a single query, instead of the previous method, which required multiple queries.

Solution

Using a graphical user interface

1. Follow the steps in Recipe 4.4 to enable an LDAP control.
2. Select the Attribute Scoped Query control (you can select controls by name with the Windows Server 2003 and Windows Server 2008 version of LDP). For the Windows 2000 version of LDP, add a control with an OID of 1.2.840.113556.1.4.1504.
3. For Value, enter the multivalued attribute name (e.g., member).
4. Click the "Check in" button.
5. Click OK.
6. From the menu, select Browse→Search.
7. For BaseDN, type the DN of the object that contains the multivalued attributes.
8. For Scope, select Base.
9. For Filter, enter an LDAP filter to match against the objects that are part of the multivalued DN attribute.
10. Click Run.

Attribute-scoped queries can only be performed using a Base scope.

Using a command-line interface

AdFind allows attribute-scoped queries by using the -asq switch; for example:

```
adfind -b cn=somegroup,cn=users,dc=domain,dc=group -asq member -f objectclass=user
samaccountname
```

Using VBScript

You cannot use attribute-scoped queries with ADSI, ADO, and VBScript. In an ADO search, you can use the `ADSI Flags` property as part of a `Connection` object to set the search preference, but there is no way to set the attribute that should be matched, which must be included as part of the LDAP control.

Using PowerShell

The Quest AD cmdlets will allow you to perform an attribute-scoped query as follows:

```
Get-QADObject -SearchRoot <ObjectDN> -AttributeScopeQuery '<Attribute>'
```

You can also use the native ADSI methods in PowerShell:

```
$group  = New-Object System.DirectoryServices.DirectoryEntry(
    "LDAP://CN=Domain Admins,CN=Users,<DomainDN>")
$source = New-Object System.DirectoryServices.DirectorySearcher

$source.SearchRoot  = $group
$source.SearchScope = [System.DirectoryServices.SearchScope]::Base
$source.Filter      = "(objectClass=*)"

$source.PropertiesToLoad.Add("member")
$source.PropertiesToLoad.Add("sAMAccountName")

$source.AttributeScopeQuery = "member"

$results = $source.FindAll()
```

Discussion

When dealing with **group** objects, you may have encountered the problem where you wanted to search against the members of a group to find a subset or to retrieve certain attributes about each member. This normally involved performing a query to retrieve all of the members, and additional queries to retrieve whatever attributes you needed for each member. This was less than ideal, so an alternative was developed for Windows Server 2003.

With an attribute-scoped query, you can perform a single query against the **group** object and return whatever properties you need from the member's object, or return only a subset of the members based on certain criteria. Let's look at the LDAP search parameters for an attribute-scoped query:

Attribute-scoped query control value
  The value to set for this control should be the DN attribute that you want to iterate over (e.g., member).

Base DN
  This must be the DN of the object that contains the DN attribute (e.g., cn=Domain Admins,cn=users,dc=adatum,dc=com).

Scope

    This must be set to **Base** to query only the **group** object itself.

Filter

    The filter will match against objects defined in the Control Value. For example, a filter of (`objectClass=user`) would match **user** objects only. You can also use any other attributes that are available with those objects. The following filter would match all **user** objects that have a **department** attribute equal to "Sales":

```
(&(objectclass=user)(department=Sales))
```

Attributes

    This should contain the list of attributes to return for the objects matched in the DN attribute.

When performing an attribute-scoped query against a member attribute, it's important to remember that primary group membership is handled as a special case; as such you may experience unpredictable results in this situation.

See Also

Recipe 4.4, MSDN: Performing an Attribute Scoped Query, and MSDN: Searching with ActiveX Data Objects (ADO)

4.12 Searching with a Bitwise Filter

Problem

You want to search against an attribute that contains a *bit flag*, which requires you to use a bitwise filter to perform the search.

Solution

Using a graphical user interface

1. Open LDP from the Windows Support Tools.
2. From the menu, select Connection→Connect.
3. For Server, enter the name of a domain controller (or leave blank to do a serverless bind).
4. For Port, enter 389.
5. Click OK.
6. From the menu, select Connection→Bind.
7. Enter credentials of a user.
8. Click OK.

9. From the menu, select Browse→Search.

10. For BaseDN, type the base distinguished name of where the search will start. (You can leave this blank if you wish to connect to the domain NC as the base DN.)

11. For Scope, select the appropriate scope.

12. For the Filter, enter the bitwise expression, such as the following, which will find all universal groups:

```
(&(objectCategory=group)(groupType:1.2.840.113556.1.4.804:=8))
```

13. Click Run.

Using a command-line interface

The following query finds universal groups in the *adatum.com* domain by using a bitwise AND filter:

```
> dsquery * dc=adatum,dc=com -scope subtree -attr "name" -filter
"(&(objectclass=group)(objectCategory=group)
(groupType:1.2.840.113556.1.4.804:=8) )"
```

The following query finds disabled user accounts in the *adatum.com* domain by using a bitwise AND filter:

```
> dsquery * dc=adatum,dc=com -attr name -scope subtree -filter
"(&(objectclass=user)(objectcategory=person)(useraccountcontrol:1.2.840.113556.1.4.
803:=2))"
```

You can also perform queries that use bitwise filters using AdFind. The following will find all disabled user accounts in the *adatum.com* domain:

```
> adfind -default -bit -f useraccountcontrol:AND:=2
```

Similarly, the following will return all universal groups in the *adatum.com* domain using a bitwise filter:

```
> adfind -default -bit -f groupType:AND:=8
```

Using VBScript

```
' The following query finds all disabled user accounts in the
' adatum.com domain
strBase   = "<LDAP://dc=adatum,dc=com>;"
strFilter = "(&(objectclass=user)(objectcategory=person)" & _
            "(useraccountcontrol:1.2.840.113556.1.4.803:=2));"
strAttrs  = "name;"
strScope  = "subtree"

set objConn = CreateObject("ADODB.Connection")
objConn.Provider = "ADsDSOObject"
objConn.Open "Active Directory Provider"
set objRS = objConn.Execute(strBase & strFilter & strAttrs & strScope)
objRS.MoveFirst
while Not objRS.EOF
    Wscript.Echo objRS.Fields(0).Value
```

```
        objRS.MoveNext
    wend
```

Using PowerShell

```
$objDomain = New-Object System.DirectoryServices.DirectoryEntry
$objSearcher = New-Object System.DirectoryServices.DirectorySearcher
$objSearcher.SearchRoot = $objDomain
$objSearcher.Filter =
("(&(objectclass=user)(objectcategory=person)(useraccountcontrol:1.2.840.113556.1.4
.803:=2))")
$colResults = $objSearcher.FindAll()
```

Discussion

Many attributes in Active Directory are composed of bit flags. A bit flag is often used to encode properties about an object into a single attribute. For example, the groupType attribute on group objects is a bit flag that is used to determine the group scope and type.

The userAccountControl attribute on user and computer objects is used to describe a whole series of properties, including account status (i.e., enabled or disabled), account lockout, password not required, smartcard authentication required, etc.

The searchFlags and systemFlags attributes on attributeSchema objects define, among other things, whether an attribute is constructed, indexed, and included as part of Ambiguous Name Resolution (ANR).

To search against these types of attributes, you need to use bitwise search filters. There are two types of bitwise search filters you can use, one that represents a logical OR and one that represents a logical AND. This is implemented within a search filter as a *matching rule*. A matching rule is simply a way to inform the LDAP server (in this case, a domain controller) to treat part of the filter differently. Here is an example of what a matching rule looks like:

```
(userAccountControl:1.2.840.113556.1.4.803:=514)
```

The format is (*attributename:MatchingRuleOID:=value*), though AdFind allows you to use an easier syntax for bitwise queries. As mentioned, there are two bitwise matching rules, which are defined by OIDs. The logical AND matching rule OID is 1.2.840.113556.1.4.803 and the logical OR matching rule OID is 1.2.840.113556.1. 4.804. These OIDs instruct the server to perform special processing on the filter. A logical OR filter will return success if any bit specified by *value* is stored in *attributename*. Alternatively, the logical AND filter will return success if all bits specified by *value* match the value of *attributename*. Perhaps an example will help clarify this.

To create a normal user account, you have to set userAccountControl to 514. The number 514 was calculated by adding the normal user account flag of 512 together with the disabled account flag of 2 (512 + 2 = 514). If you use the following logical OR matching rule against the 514 value, as shown here:

```
(useraccountcontrol:1.2.840.113556.1.4.804:=514)
```

then all normal user accounts (flag 512) OR disabled accounts (flag 2) would be returned. This would include enabled user accounts (from flag 512), disabled computer accounts (from flag 2), and disabled user accounts (from flag 2). In the case of userAccountControl, flag 2 can apply to both user and computer accounts, which is why both would be included in the returned entries.

One of the benefits of bitwise matching rules is that they allow you to combine a bunch of comparisons into a single filter. In fact, it may help to think that the OR filter could also be written using two expressions:

```
(|(useraccountcontrol:1.2.840.113556.1.4.804:=2)
(useraccountcontrol:1.2.840.113556.
1.4.804:=512))
```

Just as before, this will match userAccountControl attributes that contain either the 2 or 512 flags; we're performing two OR operations against the same value, first ORing the value against 2, then against 512.

For the logical AND operator, similar principles apply. Instead of any of the bits in the flag being a possible match, *all* of the bits in the flag must match for it to return a success. If the userAccountControl example was changed to use logical AND, it would look like this:

```
(useraccountcontrol:1.2.840.113556.1.4.803:=514)
```

In this case, only normal user accounts that are also disabled would be returned. The same filter could be rewritten using the & operator instead of | as in the following:

```
(&(useraccountcontrol:1.2.840.113556.1.4.803:=2)
(useraccountcontrol:1.2.840.113556.1.4.803:=512))
```

An important subtlety to note is that when you are comparing only a single bit flag value, the logical OR and logical AND matching rule would return the same result. So if you wanted to find any normal user accounts you could search on the single bit flag of 512 using either of the following:

```
(useraccountcontrol:1.2.840.113556.1.4.803:=512)
```

```
(useraccountcontrol:1.2.840.113556.1.4.804:=512)
```

Using PowerShell

Searching on a bitwise operator in PowerShell is done using a DirectorySearcher object with the appropriate LDAP filter, as you can see. In future chapters we will look at individual AD cmdlets that "mask" the bitwise search into a more human-readable operation, such as the Enable-QADUser and Disable-QADUser Quest cmdlets.

See Also

MSDN: Enumerating Groups by Scope or Type in a Domain, MSDN: Determining Which Properties Are Non-Replicated, Constructed, Global Catalog, and Indexed, and MS KB 305144 (How to Use the UserAccountControl Flags to Manipulate User Account Properties)

4.13 Creating an Object

Problem

You want to create an object.

Solution

In each solution below, an example of adding a user object is shown. Modify the examples as needed to include whatever class and attributes you need to create.

Using a graphical user interface

1. Open ADSI Edit from the Windows Support Tools in Windows 2000 and Windows Server 2003. (ADSI Edit is a native MMC snap-in in Windows Server 2008.)
2. If an entry for the naming context you want to browse is not already displayed, do the following:
   a. Right-click on ADSI Edit in the right pane and click "Connect to...".
   b. Fill in the information for the naming context, container, or OU you want to add an object to. Click on the Advanced button if you need to enter alternate credentials.
3. In the left pane, browse to the container or OU you want to add the object to. Once you've found the parent container, right-click on it and select New→Object.
4. Under Select a Class, select user.
5. For the cn, enter jsmith and click Next.
6. For sAMAccountName, enter jsmith and click Next.
7. Click the More Attributes button to enter additional attributes.
8. Click Finish.

You can also create an object using LDP as follows:

1. Open LDP from the Windows Support Tools.
2. From the menu, select Connection→Connect.
3. For Server, enter the name of a domain controller (or leave blank to do a serverless bind).

4. For Port, enter 389.

5. Click OK.

6. From the menu, select Connection→Bind.

7. Enter credentials of a user.

8. Click OK.

9. Click Browse→Add Child. For DN, enter the Distinguished Name of the object that you want to create.

10. Under Attribute and Values, enter the name of any attribute that you want to populate along with its associated value, and then click Enter. Repeat this until you've added all of the required attributes for the type of object you are creating, as well as any optional attributes that you want to populate.

11. Click Run to create the object.

Using a command-line interface

Create an LDIF file called *create_object.ldf* with the following contents:

```
dn: cn=jsmith,cn=users,dc=adatum,dc=com
changetype: add
objectClass: user
samaccountname: jsmith
```

Then run the following command:

```
> ldifde -v -i -f create_object.ldf
```

It is also worth noting that you can add a limited number of object types with the dsadd command. Run dsadd /? from a command line for more details.

You can also create objects using AdMod; to create a new user object in the *adatum.com* domain use the following syntax:

```
> admod -b "cn=Joe Smith,cn=users,dc=adatum,dc=com"

objectclass::user samaccountname::jsmith -add
```

Using VBScript

```
set objUsersCont = GetObject("LDAP://cn=users,dc=adatum,dc=com")
set objUser = objUsersCont.Create("user", "CN=jsmith")
objUser.Put "sAMAccountName", "jsmith" ' mandatory in Windows 2000
objUser.SetInfo
```

Using PowerShell

To create an object using the Quest AD cmdlets, use the following syntax:

```
new-QADObject -ParentContainer "ou=Workstations,dc=adatum,dc=com" -type 'computer'
-name 'comp1' -ObjectAttributes @{samAccountName='comp1';description='New Vista
Workstation'}
```

To create an object using `System.DirectoryServices`, use the following syntax:

```
$parentOU = [System.DirectoryServices.DirectoryEntry]
"LDAP://ou=Workstations,dc=adatum,dc=com"
$newWS = $parentOU.Create("computer","test1")
$newWS.put("samaccountName,"test1")
$newWS.put("description","New Vista Workstation")
$newWS.SetInfo()
```

Discussion

To create an object in Active Directory, you have to specify the `objectClass`, RDN value, and any other mandatory attributes that are not automatically set by Active Directory. Some of the automatically generated attributes include `objectGUID`, `instanceType`, and `objectCategory`.

In the `jsmith` example, the object class was `user`, the RDN value was `jsmith`, and the only other attribute set was `sAMAccountName`: this attribute is only mandatory in Windows 2000; it is optional in Windows Server 2003, and cannot, by default, be set in ADAM. Admittedly, this user object is unusable in its current state because it will be disabled by default and no password was set, but it should give you an idea of how to create an object. In the case of a user object, you'll need to configure a password that meets any existing password complexity requirements before enabling the user.

Using a graphical user interface

Other tools, such as AD Users and Computers, could be used to do the same thing, but ADSI Edit is useful as a generic object editor.

One attribute that you will not be able to set via ADSI Edit is the password (`unicodePwd` attribute). It is stored in binary form and needs to be edited using a secure connection. If you want to set the password for a user through a GUI, you can do it with the AD Users and Computers snap-in.

Using a command-line interface

For more on *ldifde*, see Recipe 4.28.

With DSAdd, you can set numerous attributes when creating an object. The downside is that you can create only the following object types: computer, contact, group, OU, quota, and user.

Using VBScript

The first step in creating an object is to call `GetObject` on the parent container. Then call the `Create` method on that object and specify the `objectClass` and RDN for the new object. The `sAMAccountName` attribute is then set by using the `Put` method. Finally, `SetInfo` commits the change. If `SetInfo` is not called, the creation will not get committed to the domain controller.

See Also

Recipe 4.28, Recipe 4.29 for importing objects with LDIF, MSDN: IADsContainer::GetObject, MSDN: IADsContainer::Create, MSDN: IADs::Put, and MSDN: IADs::SetInfo

4.14 Modifying an Object

Problem

You want to modify one or more attributes of an object.

Solution

The following examples set the last name (sn) attribute for the jsmith user object.

Using a graphical user interface

1. Open ADSI Edit.
2. If an entry for the naming context you want to browse is not already displayed, do the following:
   a. Right-click on ADSI Edit in the right pane and click "Connect to...".
   b. Fill in the information for the naming context, container, or OU you want to add an object to. Click on the Advanced button if you need to enter alternate credentials.
3. In the left pane, browse to the container or OU that contains the object you want to modify. Once you've found the object, right-click on it and select Properties.
4. Right-click the sn attribute and select Edit.
5. Enter Smith and click OK.
6. Click Apply, followed by OK.

You can also modify an object using LDP as follows:

1. Open LDP from the Windows Support Tools.
2. From the menu, select Connection→Connect.
3. For Server, enter the name of a domain controller (or leave blank to do a serverless bind).
4. For Port, enter 389.
5. Click OK.
6. From the menu, select Connection→Bind.
7. Enter credentials of a user.
8. Click OK.

9. Click Browse→Modify. For DN, enter the Distinguished Name of the object that you want to modify.

10. Under Attribute and Values, enter the name of any attribute that you want to modify along with its associated value, and then click Enter. Repeat this until you've added all of the attributes that you want to modify.

11. Click Run to modify the object.

Using a command-line interface

Create an LDIF file called *modify_object.ldf* with the following contents:

```
dn: cn=jsmith,cn=users,dc=adatum,dc=com
changetype: modify
replace: givenName
givenName: Jim
-
```

Then run the following command:

```
> ldifde -v -i -f modify_object.ldf
```

To modify an object using AdMod, you'll use the following general syntax:

```
> admod -b <ObjectDN> <attribute>:<operation>:<value>
```

For example, you can add a description to a user object using the following syntax:

```
> admod -b cn="Joe Smith,cn=Users,dc=adatum,dc=com"
        description::Consultant
```

You can modify a limited number of object types with the `dsmod` command. Run `dsmod /?` from a command line for more details.

Using VBScript

```
strObjectDN = "cn=jsmith,cn=users,dc=adatum,dc=com"
set objUser = GetObject("LDAP://" & strObjectDN)
objUser.Put "sn", "Smith"
objUser.SetInfo
```

Using PowerShell

To modify an object using the Quest AD cmdlets, use the following syntax:

```
set-QADObject -Identity <ObjectDN> @{attribute1=<Value>;attribute2=<Value>}
```

To modify an object using ADSI, use the following:

```
$objWS = [System.DirectoryServices.DirectoryEntry] "LDAP://<ObjectDN>"
$objWS.put("description","New Workstation Description")
$objWS.SetInfo()
```

Discussion

Using a graphical user interface

If the parent container of the object you want to modify has a lot of objects in it, you may want to add a new connection entry for the DN of the target object. This will be easier than trying to hunt through a container full of objects. You can do this by right-clicking ADSI Edit and selecting "Connect to...". Under Connection Point, select Distinguished Name and enter the DN of the object.

Using a command-line interface

For more on *ldifde*, see Recipe 4.28.

As of the publication of this book, the only types of objects you can modify with DSMod are the following: computer, contact, group, OU, server, quota, and user.

As you saw in the recipe, the basic format of the AdMod command when used to modify an attribute is as follows:

```
> admod -b <ObjectDN> <attribute>:<operation>:<value>
```

The value used for `<operation>` can be any one of the following:

`<blank>`
: Updates the attribute with the new value. (In practical terms, this leads to a syntax of `<attribute>::<value>`, with nothing included between the two colons.)

`+`
: Adds a value to an attribute.

`-`
: Clears an attribute.

`++`
: Adds multiple values to an attribute.

`--`
: Removes multiple values from an attribute.

 To change a user's password using AdMod, encrypt the connection by using the `-kerbenc` switch, and then modify the `unicodepwd` attribute.

Using VBScript

If you need to do anything more than simple assignment or replacement of a value for an attribute, you'll need to use the `PutEx` method instead of `Put`. `PutEx` allows for greater control of assigning multiple values, deleting specific values, and appending values.

PutEx requires three parameters: update flag, attribute name, and an array of values to set or unset. The update flags are defined by the ADS_PROPERTY_OPERATION_ENUM collection and listed in Table 4-3. Finally, SetInfo commits the change. If SetInfo is not called, the creation will not get committed to the domain controller.

Table 4-3. ADS_PROPERTY_OPERATION_ENUM

Name	Value	Description
ADS_PROPERTY_CLEAR	1	Remove all value(s) of the attribute.
ADS_PROPERTY_UPDATE	2	Replace the current values of the attribute with the ones passed in. This will clear any previously set values.
ADS_PROPERTY_APPEND	3	Add the values passed into the set of existing values of the attribute.
ADS_PROPERTY_DELETE	4	Delete the values passed in.

In the sample below, each update flag is used while setting the otherTelephoneNumber attribute:

```
strObjectDN = "cn=jsmith,cn=users,dc=adatum,dc=com"

const ADS_PROPERTY_CLEAR  = 1
const ADS_PROPERTY_UPDATE = 2
const ADS_PROPERTY_APPEND = 3
const ADS_PROPERTY_DELETE = 4

set objUser = GetObject("LDAP://" & strObjectDN)

' Add/Append two values
objUser.PutEx ADS_PROPERTY_APPEND, "otherTelephoneNumber", _
          Array("555-1212", "555-1213")
objUser.SetInfo
' Now otherTelephoneNumber = 555-1212, 555-1213

' Delete one of the values
objUser.PutEx ADS_PROPERTY_DELETE, "otherTelephoneNumber", Array("555-1213")
objUser.SetInfo
' Now otherTelephoneNumber = 555-1212

' Change values
objUser.PutEx ADS_PROPERTY_UPDATE, "otherTelephoneNumber", Array("555-1214")
objUser.SetInfo
' Now otherTelephoneNumber = 555-1214

' Clear all values
objUser.PutEx ADS_PROPERTY_CLEAR, "otherTelephoneNumber", vbNullString
objUser.SetInfo
' Now otherTelephoneNumber = <empty>
```

Using PowerShell

As of this writing, there is a bug in PowerShell relating to the use of the `PutEx` method to clear an attribute value. If you use the following code to clear an object's description, for example, you will still be able to retrieve the last value set for this value even after issuing the `SetInfo()` command:

```
$obj = [System.DirectoryServices.DirectoryEntry] "LDAP://<ObjectDN>"
$obj.PutEx(1, "description", 0)
$obj.SetInfo()
```

Despite this bug in PowerShell, if you view the object within AD Users and Computers or another interface, you will see that the attribute value has actually been cleared.

When working with the Quest cmdlets, if you are attempting to modify a multivalued attribute, the `-ObjectAttributes` switch requires you to format the values to be added to attribute as an array, using the `@(…)` syntax. As written, this syntax will overwrite any existing information within the multivalued attribute. In order to append values using the Quest tools, you will need to create and use a `Dictionary` object as follows:

```
[Collections.DictionaryEntry] $de = New-Object Collections.DictionaryEntry
-argumentList Append, @('<Value1>',<Value2>')
set-QADObject -Identity <Object DN> -ObjectAttributes @{siteLink=$de}
```

To delete values from a multivalued attribute, change `-argumentList Append` to `-argumentList Delete`.

See Also

MSDN: IADs::Put, MSDN: IADs::PutEx, MSDN: IADs::SetInfo, and MSDN: ADS_PROPERTY_OPERATION_ENUM

4.15 Modifying a Bit Flag Attribute

Problem

You want to safely modify an attribute that contains a bit flag, without blindly overwriting its existing contents.

Solution

Using VBScript

```
' This code safely modifies a bit flag attribute
' ------ SCRIPT CONFIGURATION ------
strObject = "<ObjectDN>" ' e.g. cn=jsmith,cn=users,dc=adatum,dc=com
strAttr = "<AttrName>" ' e.g. adatum-UserProperties
boolEnableBit = <TRUEorFALSE> ' e.g. FALSE
intBit = <BitValue> ' e.g. 16
' ------ END CONFIGURATION --------
```

```
set objObject = GetObject("LDAP://" & strObject)
intBitsOrig = objObject.Get(strAttr)
intBitsCalc = CalcBit(intBitsOrig, intBit, boolEnableBit)

if intBitsOrig <> intBitsCalc then
   objObject.Put strAttr, intBitsCalc
   objObject.SetInfo
   WScript.Echo "Changed " & strAttr & " from " & intBitsOrig & " to " & intBitsCalc
else
   WScript.Echo "Did not need to change " & strAttr & " (" & intBitsOrig & ")"
end if

Function CalcBit(intValue, intBit, boolEnable)

   CalcBit = intValue

   if boolEnable = TRUE then
      CalcBit = intValue Or intBit
   else
      if intValue And intBit then
         CalcBit = intValue Xor intBit
      end if
   end if

End Function
```

Using PowerShell

To set the userAccountControl bit value using a logical OR operation, use the following
syntax:

```
$objUser = [ADSI] "LDAP://cn=testuser,cn=users,dc=adatum,dc=com"
$newUAC = ($objUser.userAccountControl.ToString()) -bor 2
$objUser.Put("userAccountControl", $newValue)
$objUser.SetInfo()
```

Discussion

Recipe 4.12 described how to search against attributes that contain a bit flag, which is
used to encode various settings about an object in a single attribute. As a quick recap,
you need to use a logical OR operation to match any bits being searched against, and
a logical AND to match a specific set of bits. If you want to set an attribute that is a bit
flag, you need to take special precautions to ensure you don't overwrite an existing bit.
Let's consider an example. Adatum wants to secretly store some politically incorrect
information about their users, such as whether the user is really old or has big feet.
They don't want to create attributes such as adatum-UserHasBigFeet, so they decide to
encode the properties in a single bit flag attribute. They decide to call the attribute
adatum-UserProperties with the possible bit values shown in Table 4-4.

Table 4-4. Sample bit flag attribute values

Value	Description
1	User is overweight
2	User is very tall
4	User has big feet
8	User is very old

After they extend the schema to include the new attribute, Adatum needs to initially populate the attribute for all their users. To do so they can simply logically OR the values together that apply to each user. So if settings 4 and 8 apply to the `jsmith` user, his `adatum-UserProperties` would be set to 12 (4 OR 8). No big deal so far. The issue comes in when they need to modify the attribute in the future.

> You will, however, find that searching for information based on a bit flag attribute is not terribly efficient. This is because bit flags cannot be indexed; you need to calculate the value for every object populated with the bit flag attribute in question.

They later find out that `jsmith` was a former basketball player and is 6'8". They need to set the 2 bit (for being tall) in his `adatum-UserProperties` attribute. To set the 2 bit they need to first determine if it has already been set. If it has already been set, then there is nothing to do. If the 2 bit hasn't been set, they need to logical OR 2 with the existing value of `jsmith`'s `adatum-UserProperties` attribute. If they simply set the attribute to 2, it would overwrite the 4 and 8 bits that had been set previously. In the VBScript solution, they could use the `CalcBit` function to determine the new value:

```
intBitsCalc = CalcBit(intBitsOrig, 2, TRUE)
```

The result would be 14 (12 OR 2).

The same logic applies if they want to remove a bit, except the XOR logical operator is used.

> Active Directory contains numerous bit flag attributes, most notably `options` (which is used on several different object classes) and `userAccountControl` (which is used on `user` objects). We do not recommend blindly setting those attributes unless you know what you are doing. It is preferable to use a script from this recipe so that it calculates the new value based on the existing value.

You should note that it's certainly possible to modify bitwise attributes using a GUI tool like ADSI Edit or a command-line tool like DsMod. However, it will require a certain amount of manual effort as you'll first need to make note of the existing attribute value and then calculate the new value using a calculator or some other method. The

VBScript solution presented here simply automates that process by performing the lookup and calculations for you.

Using PowerShell

The PowerShell solution makes use of the built-in -bor operator in PowerShell, which performs a Boolean OR. You can also use -bxor to perform a Boolean XOR to clear the value set for a particular bit.

See Also

Recipe 4.12 for searching with a bitwise filter

4.16 Dynamically Linking an Auxiliary Class

 This recipe requires Windows Server 2003 or better forest functional level.

Problem

You want to dynamically link an auxiliary class to an existing object instance.

Solution

In each solution below, an example of adding the custom adatum-SalesUser auxiliary class to the jsmith user object will be described.

Using a graphical user interface

1. Open ADSI Edit.
2. If an entry for the naming context you want to browse is not already displayed, do the following:
   a. Right-click on ADSI Edit in the right pane and click "Connect to...".
   b. Fill in the information for the naming context, container, or OU you want to add an object to. Click on the Advanced button if you need to enter alternate credentials.
3. In the left pane, browse to the container or OU that contains the object you want to modify. Once you've found the object, right-click on it and select Properties.
4. Right-click the sn attribute and select Edit.
5. Click the More Attributes button to enter additional attributes.
6. Edit the values for the objectClass attribute.

7. For "Value to add," enter `adatum-SalesUser`.

8. Click Add.

9. Click OK twice.

Using a command-line interface

Create an LDIF file called *dynamically_link_class.ldf* with the following contents:

```
dn: cn=jsmith,cn=users,dc=adatum,dc=com
changetype: modify
add: objectClass
objectClass: adatum-SalesUser
-
```

Then run the following command:

```
> ldifde -v -i -f dynamically_link_class.ldf
```

Alternatively, you can use AdMod as follows:

```
> admod -b <ObjectDN> objectClass:+:<Dynamic Object Class>
```

Using VBScript

```
const ADS_PROPERTY_APPEND = 3
set objUser = GetObject("LDAP://cn=jsmith,cn=users,dc=adatum,dc=com")
objUser.PutEx ADS_PROPERTY_APPEND,"objectClass",Array("adatum-SalesUser")
objUser.SetInfo
```

Using PowerShell

```
set-variable -name ADS_PROPERTY_APPEND -value 3 -option constant
$objUser = [ADSI] "LDAP://cn=testuser,cn=users,dc=adatum=,dc=com"
$objUser.PutEx(ADS_PROPERTY_APPEND, "objectClass", @("adatum-SalesUser"))
$objUser.SetInfo()
```

Discussion

Dynamically linking an auxiliary class to an object is an easy way to use new attributes without modifying the existing object class definition in the schema. In Windows 2000, auxiliary classes could only be statically linked in the schema. Beginning with Windows Server 2003, you can dynamically link them by appending the auxiliary class name to the `objectClass` attribute of an object.

A situation in which it makes more sense to dynamically link auxiliary classes rather than link them statically is when several organizations or divisions within a company maintain their own user objects and want to add new attributes to the user class. Under Windows 2000, each organization would need to create their new attributes and auxiliary class in the schema, and then modify the user class to include the new auxiliary class. If you have 10 organizations that want to do the same thing, user objects in the forest could end up with a lot of attributes that would go unused. In Windows Server 2003, each division can instead create the new attributes and auxiliary class, and then dynamically link the auxiliary class with the specific objects that they want to have the new attributes. This eliminates the step of modifying the user class in the schema to contain the new auxiliary classes.

It is also worth mentioning that extensive use of dynamically linked auxiliary classes can lead to problems. If several groups are using different auxiliary classes, it might become hard to determine what attributes you can expect on your user objects. Essentially, you could end up with many variations of a user class that each group has implemented through the use of dynamic auxiliary classes. For this reason, use of dynamic auxiliary classes should be closely monitored. In addition, some tools that access Active Directory may not work properly with auxiliary classes.

See Also

Recipe 4.14 for modifying an object

4.17 Creating a Dynamic Object

 This recipe requires the Windows Server 2003 or better forest functional level.

Problem

You want to create an object that is automatically deleted after a period of time unless it is refreshed.

Solution

Using a graphical user interface

1. Open LDP. Click Connection→Connect and click OK.
2. Click Connection→Bind. Enter the appropriate user credentials, or just click OK.
3. Click View→Tree. Enter the DN of the parent container of the object you want to create, then click OK.
4. Click Browse→Add Child. The Add window appears.
5. In the DN text box, enter the DN of the new object.
6. In the Attribute text box, enter objectClass. In the Values: text box, enter the object class of the object you are creating, such as 'user'. Click Enter. In the Values: text box, enter dynamicObject and click Enter.
7. In the Attribute text box, enter entryTTL. In the Values: text box, enter the TTL of the object you are creating, such as '3600'. Click Enter.

8. Enter any other attributes and values that you wish to populate in the Attribute and Values: text boxes.

9. Click Run.

Using a command-line interface

Create an LDIF file called *create_dynamic_object.ldf* with the following contents:

```
dn: cn=jsmith,cn=users,dc=adatum,dc=com
changetype: add
objectClass: user
objectClass: dynamicObject
entryTTL: 1800
sAMAccountName: jsmith
```

Then run the following command:

```
> ldifde -v -i -f create_dynamic_object.ldf
```

Using VBScript

```
' This code creates a
' dynamic user object with a TTL of 30 minutes (1800 secs)
set objUsersCont = GetObject("LDAP://cn=users,dc=adatum,dc=com")
set objUser = objUsersCont.Create("user", "CN=jsmith")
objUser.Put "objectClass", "dynamicObject"
objUser.Put "entryTTL", 1800
objUser.Put "sAMAccountName", "jsmith" ' mandatory attribute
objUser.SetInfo
```

Using PowerShell

```
set-variable -name ADS_PROPERTY_APPEND -value 3 -option constant
$parentOU = [System.DirectoryServices.DirectoryEntry]
"LDAP://ou=adatumUsers,dc=adatum,dc=com"
$objUser = $parentOU.Create("user","TestUser1")
$objUser.put("samaccountName","testuser1")
$objUser.put("description","New Vista Workstation")
$objUser.Put("objectClass", "dynamicObject")
$objUser.Put("entryTTL", "1800)
$objUser.Put("sAMAccountName', "jsmith")
$objUser.SetInfo()
```

Discussion

The ability to create dynamic objects was introduced in Windows Server 2003. This gives you the ability to create objects that have a limited lifespan before they are automatically removed from the directory. To create a dynamic object, you simply need to specify the objectClass to have a value of dynamicObject in addition to its structural objectClass (e.g., user) value when instantiating the object. The entryTTL attribute can also be set to the number of seconds before the object is automatically deleted. If entryTTL is not set, the object will use the dynamicObjectDefaultTTL attribute specified in the domain. The `entryTTL` cannot be lower than the `dynamicObjectMinTTL` for the domain. See Recipe 4.19 for more information on how to view and modify these default values.

Dynamic objects have a few special properties worth noting:

- A static object cannot be turned into a dynamic object. The object must be marked as dynamic when it is created.
- Dynamic objects cannot be created in the Configuration NC and Schema NC.
- Dynamic objects do not leave behind tombstone objects.
- Dynamic objects that are containers cannot have static child objects.
- A dynamic container will not expire prior to any child objects contained within it. If the dynamic container has a lower TTL value than any of the children, once the container's TTL expires, it will be reset to the highest TTL value of the children plus one second.

See Also

Recipe 4.18 for refreshing a dynamic object and Recipe 4.19 for modifying the default dynamic object properties

4.18 Refreshing a Dynamic Object

 This recipe requires the Windows Server 2003 or Windows Server 2008 forest functional level.

Problem

You want to refresh a dynamic object to keep it from expiring and getting deleted from Active Directory.

Solution

In each solution below, an example of adding a **user** object is used. Modify the examples as needed to refresh whatever object is needed.

Using a graphical user interface

1. Open LDP.
2. From the menu, select Connection→Connect.
3. For Server, enter the name of a domain controller (or leave it blank to do a serverless bind).

4. For Port, enter 389.

5. Click OK.

6. From the menu, select Connection→Bind.

7. Enter credentials of a user who can modify the object.

8. Click OK.

9. Select Browse→Modify.

10. For DN, enter the DN of the dynamic object you want to refresh.

11. For Attribute, enter entryTTL.

12. For Values, enter the new time to live (TTL) for the object in seconds.

13. Under Operation, select Replace.

14. Click Enter.

15. Click Run.

Using a command-line interface

Create an LDIF file called *refresh_dynamic_object.ldf* with the following contents:

```
dn: cn=jsmith,cn=users,dc=adatum,dc=com
changetype: modify
replace: entryTTL
entryTTL: 1800
-
```

Then run the following command:

```
> ldifde -v -i -f refresh_dynamic_object.ldf
```

You can also use AdMod with the following syntax:

```
> admod -b <ObjectDN> entryTTL::<TTL in Seconds>
```

Using VBScript

```
set objUser = GetObject("LDAP://cn=jsmith,cn=users,dc=adatum,dc=com")
objUser.Put "entryTTL", "1800"
objUser.SetInfo
```

Using PowerShell

To refresh a dynamic object using the Quest AD cmdlets, use the following syntax:

```
set-QADObject -Identity <ObjectDN> @{entryTTL=1800}
```

To modify an object using ADSI, use the following:

```
$objDyn = [System.DirectoryServices.DirectoryEntry] "LDAP://<ObjectDN>"
$objDyn.put("entryTTL","1800")
$objDyn.SetInfo()
```

Discussion

Dynamic objects expire after their TTL becomes 0. You can determine when a dynamic object will expire by looking at the current value of an object's entryTTL attribute or by querying msDS-Entry-Time-To-Die, which contains the seconds remaining until expiration. If you've created a dynamic object and need to refresh it so that it will not get deleted, you must reset the entryTTL attribute to a new value. There is no limit to the number of times you can refresh a dynamic object. As long as the entryTTL value does not reach 0, the object will remain in Active Directory.

See Also

Recipe 4.14 for modifying an object and Recipe 4.17 for creating a dynamic object

4.19 Modifying the Default TTL Settings for Dynamic Objects

Problem

You want to modify the minimum and default TTLs for dynamic objects.

Solution

In each solution below, we'll show how to set the DynamicObjectDefaultTTL setting to 172800. Modifying the DynamicObjectMinTTL can be done in the same manner.

Using a graphical user interface

1. Open ADSI Edit.
2. If an entry for the Configuration naming context is not already displayed, do the following:
   a. Right-click on ADSI Edit in the right pane and click "Connect to...".
   b. Fill in the information for the naming context for your forest. Click on the Advanced button if you need to enter alternate credentials.
3. In the left pane, browse to the following path under the Configuration naming context: Services→Windows NT→Directory Service.
4. Right-click cn=Directory Service and select Properties.
5. Edit the msDS-Other-Settings attribute.
6. Click on DynamicObjectDefaultTTL= <xxxxx> and click Remove.
7. The attribute/value pair should have been populated in the "Value to add" field.
8. Edit the number part of the value to be 172800.
9. Click Add.
10. Click OK twice.

Using a command-line interface

The following `ntdsutil` command connects to *<DomainControllerName>*, displays the current values for the dynamic object TTL settings, sets the `DynamicObjectDefaultTTL` to 172800, commits the change, and displays the results:

```
> ntdsutil "config settings" connections "connect to server <DomainControllerName>"
q "show values" "set DynamicObjectDefaultTTL to 172800" "commit changes"
"show values" q q
```

Using VBScript

```
' This code modifies the
' default TTL setting for dynamic objects in a forest
' ------ SCRIPT CONFIGURATION ------
strNewValue = 172800

' Could be DynamicObjectMinTTL instead if you wanted to set that instead
strTTLSetting = "DynamicObjectDefaultTTL"
' ------ END CONFIGURATION --------

const ADS_PROPERTY_APPEND = 3
const ADS_PROPERTY_DELETE = 4

set objRootDSE = GetObject("LDAP://RootDSE")
set objDS = GetObject("LDAP://CN=Directory Service,CN=Windows NT," & _
                      "CN=Services,CN=Configuration," & _
                      objRootDSE.Get("rootDomainNamingContext"))
for each strVal in objDS.Get("msDS-Other-Settings")
    Set objRegEx = New RegExp
    objRegEx.Pattern = strTTLSetting & "="
    objRegEx.IgnoreCase = True
    Set colMatches = objRegEx.Execute(strVal)
    For Each objMatch in colMatches
        Wscript.Echo "Deleting " & strVal
        objDS.PutEx ADS_PROPERTY_DELETE, "msDS-Other-Settings", Array(strVal)
        objDS.SetInfo
    Next
Next

Wscript.Echo "Setting " & strTTLSetting & "=" & strNewValue
objDS.PutEx ADS_PROPERTY_APPEND, _
            "msDS-Other-Settings", _
            Array(strTTLSetting & "=" & strNewValue)
objDS.SetInfo
```

Discussion

Two configuration settings apply to dynamic objects:

`dynamicObjectDefaultTTL`
> Defines the default TTL that is set for a dynamic object at creation time unless another one is set via `entryTTL`.

dynamicObjectMinTTL

    Defines the smallest TTL that can be configured for a dynamic object.

Unfortunately, these two settings are not stored as discrete attributes. Instead, they are stored as attribute value assertions (AVAs) in the msDS-Other-Settings attribute on the cn=DirectoryServices,cn=WindowsNT,cn=Configuration,<ForestRootDN> object. AVAs are used occasionally in Active Directory on multivalued attributes, in which the values take the form of *Setting1=Value1,Setting2=Value2*, etc.

For this reason, you cannot simply manipulate AVA attributes as you would another attribute. You have to be sure to add or replace values with the same format, as they existed previously.

Using a command-line interface

You can use *ntdsutil* in interactive mode or in single-command mode. In this solution, we've included all the necessary commands on a single line. You can, of course, step through each command by simply running *ntdsutil* in interactive mode and entering each command one by one.

Using VBScript

Because you are dealing with AVAs, the VBScript solution is not very straightforward. Getting a pointer to the Directory Service object is easy, but then you must step through each value of the mSDS-Other-Settings attribute until you find the one you are looking for. It is not straightforward because you do not know the exact value of the setting you are looking for; all you know is that it begins with DynamicObjectDefaultTTL=. That is why it is necessary to resort to regular expressions. With a regular expression, you can compare each value against DefaultObjectDefaultTTL= and if you find a match, delete that value only. After you've iterated through all of the values and hopefully deleted the one you are looking for, you append the new setting using PutEx. Simple as that!

See Also

Recipe 4.14 for modifying an object and MSDN: Regular Expression (RegExp) Object

4.20 Moving an Object to a Different OU or Container

Problem

You want to move an object to a different container or OU.

Solution

Using a graphical user interface

1. Open ADSI Edit.
2. If an entry for the naming context you want to browse is not already displayed, do the following:

    a. Right-click on ADSI Edit in the right pane and click "Connect to...".

    b. Fill in the information for the naming context, container, or OU containing the object. Click on the Advanced button if you need to enter alternate credentials.

3. In the left pane, browse to the container or OU that contains the object you want to modify. Once you've found the object, right-click on it and select Move.
4. Browse to the new parent of the object, select it, and click OK.

 You can also move most objects within the Active Directory Users and Computers MMC snap-in (*dsa.msc*) by navigating to the object in question, right-clicking on it, and selecting Move. In Windows Server 2003 and later, you can also drag-and-drop the object to its new location.

Using a command-line interface

To move an object to a new parent container within the same domain, you can use either dsmove or admod, as follows:

```
> dsmove "<ObjectDN>" -newparent "<NewParentDN>"
```

Or:

```
> admod -b <ObjectDN> -move <NewParentDN>
```

Using VBScript

```
' This code moves an object from one location to another in the same domain.
' ------ SCRIPT CONFIGURATION ------
strNewParentDN = "LDAP://<NewParentDN>"
strObjectDN    = "LDAP://cn=jsmith,<OldParentDN>"
strObjectRDN   = "cn=jsmith"
' ------ END CONFIGURATION --------

set objCont = GetObject(strNewParentDN)
objCont.MoveHere strObjectDN, strObjectRDN
```

Using PowerShell

To move an Active Directory object using the Quest AD cmdlets, use the following syntax:

```
move-QADObject -identity <ObjectDN> -newparent <NewParentDN>
```

To use the .NET methods, use the following syntax:

```
$obj = [ADSI] "LDAP://<Object DN>"
$newParent = [ADSI] "LDAP://<New Parent DN>"
$obj.psbase.MoveTo($newParent)
```

Discussion

Using a graphical user interface

If the parent container of the object you want to move has a lot of objects in it, you may want to add a new connection entry for the DN of the object you want to move. This may save you time searching through the list of objects in the container. You can do this by right clicking ADSI Edit and selecting "Connect to…". Under Connection Point, select Distinguished Name and enter the DN of the object you want to move.

Using a command-line interface

The DSMove utility can work against any type of object (it has no limitations, as with DSAdd and DSMod). The first parameter is the DN of the object to be moved. The second parameter is the new parent container of the object. The -s parameter can additionally be used to specify a specific server to work against.

Using VBScript

The MoveHere method can be tricky, so an explanation of how to use it to move objects is in order. First, you need to call GetObject on the new parent container. Then call MoveHere on the parent container object with the ADsPath of the object to move as the first parameter and the RDN of the object to move as the second.

The reason for the apparent duplication of cn=jsmith in the MoveHere method is that the same method can also be used for renaming objects within the same container (see Recipe 4.23).

 Regardless of the method you use to move objects, you need to ensure that the user who is performing the move has the appropriate permissions to create objects in the destination container and delete objects from the source container.

Using PowerShell

When using the .NET methods within PowerShell, a number of these methods are actually presented within a PowerShell *wrapper* to allow you to call many different methods in a similar fashion. You can think of this wrapper as being similar to a view in a database table, where you are being presented with a specific way of looking at the information, but there may be (and likely is) a great deal more lurking under the surface.

In cases where you need to get "under the surface" in PowerShell, you will use the psbase keyword, which will allow you access to all available .NET methods. Using psbase exposes a number of additional methods and properties, including `MoveTo()`.

See Also

Recipe 4.23, MS KB 313066 (How to Move Users, Groups, and Organizational Units Within a Domain in Windows 2000), and MSDN: IADsContainer::MoveHere

4.21 Moving an Object to a Different Domain

Problem

You want to move an object to a different domain.

Solution

Using a graphical user interface

To migrate user, computer, group, or OU objects between domains in the same forest, use the following steps:

1. Open the Active Directory Migration Tool (ADMT) MMC snap-in.
2. Right-click on the Active Directory Migration Tool folder, and select one of the following:
   - User Account Migration Wizard
   - Group Account Migration Wizard
   - Computer Migration Wizard

Using a command-line interface

To migrate objects from the command line using the ADMT utility, use the following syntax:

```
> ADMT [ USER | GROUP | COMPUTER | SECURITY | SERVICE |
        REPORT | KEY | PASSWORD | CONFIG | TASK ] <Options>
```

For example, to migrate a computer object, you would use the following syntax:

```
> ADMT COMPUTER /N <ComputerName> /SD:<Source Domain> /TD:<Target Domain>
/TO:<Target OU>
```

To move an object using the movetree Resource Kit utility, use the following syntax:

```
> movetree /start /s SourceDC /d TargetDC /sdn SourceDN /ddn TargetDN
```

In the following example, the cn=jsmith object in the *amer.adatum.com* domain will be moved to the *emea.adatum.com* domain:

```
> movetree /start /s dc-amer1 /d dc-emea1\
  /ddn cn=jsmith,cn=users,dc=amer,dc=adatum,dc=com\
  /sdn cn=jsmith,cn=users,dc=emea,dc=adatum,dc=com\
```

 Movetree should only be used to migrate object types such as contact objects that cannot currently be migrated by ADMT. In all other cases, Microsoft recommends using ADMT to move objects between domains.

Using VBScript

```
set objObject = GetObject("LDAP://TargetDC/TargetParentDN")
objObject.MoveHere "LDAP://SourceDC/SourceDN", vbNullString
```

In the following example, the cn=jsmith object in the *amer.adatum.com* domain will be moved to the *emea.adatum.com* domain:

```
set objObject = GetObject( _
   "LDAP://dc-amer1/cn=users,dc=amer,dc=adatum,dc=com")
objObject.MoveHere _
   "LDAP://dc-emea1/cn=jsmith,cn=users,dc=emea,dc=adatum,dc=com", _
   vbNullString
```

Discussion

You can move objects between domains assuming you follow a few guidelines:

- The user performing the move operation must have permission to modify objects in the parent container of both domains.
- You need to explicitly specify the target DC (serverless binds usually do not work). This is necessary because the "Cross Domain Move" LDAP control is being used behind the scenes. For more information on controls, see Recipe 4.4.
- The move operation must be performed against the RID master for both domains.
- Both domains must be in Windows 2000 native mode or higher.
- When you move a **user** object to a different domain, its **objectSID** is replaced with a new SID (based on the new domain), and the old SID is optionally added to the **sIDHistory** attribute.

See Also

Recipe 4.4 for more information on LDAP controls, MS KB 238394 (How to Use the MoveTree Utility to Move Objects Between Domains in a Single Forest), MSDN: IADs-Container::MoveHere, and MS KB 326480 (How to Use Active Directory Migration Tool version 2 to migrate from Windows 2000 to Windows Server 2003)

4.22 Referencing an External Domain

Problem

You need to create a reference to an external Active Directory domain.

Solution

Using a graphical user interface

1. Open ADSI Edit from the Windows Support Tools.
2. If an entry for the naming context you want to browse is not already displayed, do the following:
   a. Right-click on ADSI Edit in the right pane and click "Connect to…".
   b. Fill in the information for the naming context, container, or OU you want to add an object to. Click on the Advanced button if you need to enter alternate credentials.
3. Right-click on the top-level node and open a connection to the Configuration NC.
4. Right-click on the Partitions container and select New→Object. Click Next.
5. Right-click on `crossRef` and click Next.
6. For the `cn` attribute, enter the FQDN of the external domain, *othercorp.com* for example. Click Next.
7. For the `nCName` attribute, enter the DN of the external domain, such as `dc=othercorp,dc=com`. Click Next.
8. For the `dnsRoot` attribute, enter the DNS name of a server that can respond to LDAP queries about the domain in question, such as *dc1.othercorp.com*.
9. Click Next and then Finish to create the `crossRef` object.

Using a command-line interface

Create an LDIF file called *create_crossref.ldf* with the following contents:

```
dn: cn=othercorp.com,cn=partitions,cn=configuration,dc=adatum,dc=com
changetype: add
objectClass: crossRef
cn: othercorp.com
nCName: dc=othercorp,dc=com
dnsRoot: dc1.othercorp.com
```

Then run the following command:

```
> ldifde -v -i -f create_crossref.ldf
```

You can also create a **crossRef** using AdMod as follows:

```
> admod -config -rb cn=othercorp.com,cn=partitions
objectClass::crossRef cn::othercorp.com nCName::dc=othercorp,dc=com
dnsRoot::dc1.othercorp.com -add
```

Using VBScript

```
set objPartitions =
GetObject("LDAP://cn=partitions,cn=configuration,dc=adatum,dc=com")
set objCrossRef = objPartitions.Create("crossRef", "CN=othercorp.com")
objCrossRef.Put "cn", "othercorp.com" ' mandatory attribute
objCrossRef.Put "nCName", "dc=othercorp,dc=com" ' mandatory attribute
objCrossRef.Put "dnsRoot", "dc1.othercorp.com" ' mandatory attribute
objCrossRef.SetInfo
```

Using PowerShell

To create a **crossref** object using the Quest AD cmdlets, use the following syntax:

```
new-QADObject -ParentContainer "cn=partitions,cn=configuration,<Forest Root DN>"
-type 'crossref' -name 'othercorp.com' -ObjectAttributes
@{cn='othercorp.com';nCName='dc=othercorp,dc=com';'dnsRoot'='dc1.othercorp.com'}
```

To create an object using **System.DirectoryServices**, use the following syntax:

```
$parentOU = [System.DirectoryServices.DirectoryEntry]
"LDAP://cn=Partitions,cn=Configuration,<Forest Root DN>"
$newCrossRef = $parentOU.Create("crossRef","othercorp.com")
$newCrossRef.put("cn","cn=othercorp.com")
$newCrossRef.put("nCName","dc=othercorp,dc=com")
$newCrossRef.put("dnsRoot","dc1.othercorp.com")
$newCrossRef.SetInfo()
```

Discussion

Similar to the way in which DNS servers use iterative queries to resolve hostnames that can only be resolved by remote servers, LDAP uses *referrals* to resolve queries for objects contained in naming contexts that are not hosted by the local DC. When a DC receives any query, it will search the Partitions container for a **crossRef** object containing the DN that's being used as the Base DN of the query. If the DC locates a **crossRef** that matches the search base of the query, and that **crossRef** indicates a naming context that's hosted by the domain controller itself, then the DC will perform the search locally. If the **crossRef** refers to an NC that's hosted on a remote server, the DC generates a *referral* to the server that is pointed to by the **crossRef** object. If the DC can't locate a relevant **crossRef** object, it will use DNS to attempt to generate an additional location to refer the client to.

In most cases, Active Directory will generate LDAP referrals automatically. However, you should manually create a **crossRef** object to generate LDAP referrals for an external domain, such as referrals to *othercorp.com* that are generated by the *adatum.com* domain.

See Also

MS KB 241737 (How to Create a Cross-Reference to an External Domain in Active Directory), MS KB 817872 (How to Create crossRef Objects for a DNS Namespace Subordinate of an Existing Active Directory Forest), MSDN: Referrals [Active Directory], and MSDN: When Referrals Are Generated [Active Directory]

4.23 Renaming an Object

Problem

You want to rename an object and keep it in its current container or OU.

Solution

Using a graphical user interface

1. Open ADSI Edit.
2. If an entry for the naming context you want to browse is not already displayed, do the following:
   a. Right-click on ADSI Edit in the right pane and click "Connect to...".
   b. Fill in the information for the naming context, container, or OU that contains the object you want to rename. Click on the Advanced button if you need to enter alternate credentials.
3. In the left pane, browse to the container or OU that contains the object you want to modify. Once you've found the object, right-click on it and select Rename.
4. Enter the new name and click OK.

You can also rename a `leaf` object by using LDP as follows:

1. Open LDP from the Windows Support Tools.
2. From the menu, select Connection→Connect.
3. For Server, enter the name of a domain controller (or leave blank for a serverless bind).
4. For Port, enter 389.
5. Click OK.
6. From the menu, select Connection→Bind.
7. Enter credentials of a user.
8. Click OK.
9. Click Browse→Modify RDN. For Old DN, enter the Distinguished Name of the object that you want to rename. For New DN, enter the object's new name.

10. Click Run to rename the object.

Using a command-line interface

To rename an object using the built-in DSMove utility, use the following syntax:

```
> dsmove "<ObjectDN>" -newname "<NewName>"
```

To use AdMod, use the following:

```
> admod -b "<ObjectDN>" -rename "<NewName>"
```

Using VBScript

```
' This code renames an object and leaves it in the same location.
' ------ SCRIPT CONFIGURATION ------
strCurrentParentDN = "<CurrentParentDN>"
strObjectOldName = "cn=<OldName>"
strObjectNewName = "cn=<NewName>"
' ------ END CONFIGURATION --------

set objCont = GetObject("LDAP://" & strCurrentParentDN)
objCont.MoveHere "LDAP://" & strObjectOldName & "," & _
                  strCurrentParentDN, strObjectNewName
```

Using PowerShell

To rename an object using the Quest AD cmdlets, use the following syntax:

```
Rename-QADObject -identity '<Object DN>' -NewName '<New Value of 'name'
attribute>'
```

To rename an object using the .NET methods, use the following:

```
$obj = [ADSI] "LDAP://<Object DN>"
$newName = "<New Value of 'name' Attribute>"
$obj.psbase.Rename($newName)
```

Discussion

Before you rename an object, you should ensure that no applications reference it by name. You can make objects rename-safe by requiring all applications that must store a reference to an object to use the GUID of the object, rather than the name.

The GUID (stored in the `objectGUID` attribute) is effectively unique and does not change when an object is renamed.

> Keep in mind that you may wish to perform other cleanup tasks when renaming an object. In the case of a user who is changing her name, you may wish to update her Display Name and `sn` attributes to match the new CN.

Using a graphical user interface

If the parent container of the object you want to rename has a lot of objects in it, you may want to add a new connection entry for the DN of the object you want to rename. This may save you time searching through the list of objects in the container. You can do this by right-clicking ADSI Edit and selecting "Connect to..." under Connection Point; select Distinguished Name and enter the DN of the object you want to rename.

You can also rename most objects within the Active Directory Users and Computers MMC snap-in (*dsa.msc*) by navigating to the object in question, right-clicking on it, and selecting Rename.

Using a command-line interface

The two parameters that are needed to rename an object are the original DN of the object and the new RDN (-newname). The -s option can also be used to specify a server name to work against.

Using VBScript

The MoveHere method can be tricky to use, so an explanation of how to use it to rename objects is in order. First, you need to call GetObject on the parent container of the object you want to rename. Then call MoveHere on the parent container object and specify the ADsPath of the object to rename as the first parameter. The new RDN, including the prefix (e.g., cn=) of the object, should be the second parameter.

See Also

MSDN: IADsContainer::MoveHere

4.24 Deleting an Object

Problem

You want to delete an individual object.

Solution

Using a graphical user interface

1. Open ADSI Edit.
2. If an entry for the naming context you want to browse is not already displayed, do the following:
   a. Right-click on ADSI Edit in the right pane and click "Connect to...".
   b. Fill in the information for the naming context, container, or OU that contains the object you want to delete. Click on the Advanced button if you need to enter alternate credentials.
3. In the left pane, browse to the object you want to delete.
4. Right-click on the object and select Delete.
5. Click Yes to confirm.

You can also delete an object using LDP, as follows:

1. Open LDP from the Windows Support Tools.
2. From the menu, select Connection→Connect.
3. For Server, enter the name of a domain controller (or leave blank for a serverless bind).
4. For Port, enter 389.
5. Click OK.
6. From the menu, select Connection→Bind.
7. Enter credentials of a user.
8. Click OK.
9. Click Browse→Delete. For DN, enter the Distinguished Name of the object that you want to delete.
10. Click Run to delete the object.

Using a command-line interface

You can delete an object using the built-in *dsrm* utility, as well as AdMod. For *dsrm*, use the following syntax:

```
> dsrm "<ObjectDN>"
```

For AdMod, enter the following:

```
> admod -b "<ObjectDN>" -del
```

Using VBScript

```
strObjectDN = "<ObjectDN>"
set objUser = GetObject("LDAP://" & strObjectDN)
objUser.DeleteObject(0)
```

Using PowerShell

To delete an object using the Quest AD cmdlets, use the following syntax:

```
remove-QADObject -identity <Object DN>
```

To delete an object using the .NET methods, use the following:

```
$obj = [ADSI] "LDAP://<Object DN>"
$obj.DeleteObject(0)
```

Discussion

This recipe covers deleting individual objects. If you want to delete a container or OU and all the objects in it, take a look at Recipe 4.25.

Using a graphical user interface

If the parent container of the object you want to delete has a lot of objects in it, you may want to add a new connection entry for the DN of the object you want to delete. This can save you time searching through the list of objects in the container and could help avoid accidental deletions. You can do this by right-clicking ADSI Edit and selecting "Connect to...". Under Connection Point, select Distinguished Name and enter the DN of the object you want to delete.

You can also delete most objects within the Active Directory Users and Computers MMC snap-in (*dsa.msc*) by navigating to the object in question, right-clicking on it, and selecting Delete.

Using a command-line interface

The *dsrm* utility can be used to delete any type of object (there are no limitations based on object type, as with dsadd and dsmod). The only required parameter is the DN of the object to delete. You can also specify -noprompt to keep it from asking for confirmation before deleting. The -s parameter can be used as well to specify a specific server to target. AdMod will not prompt you in this manner.

Using VBScript

Using the DeleteObject method is straightforward. Passing 0 as a parameter is required, but does not have any significance at present.

An alternate and perhaps safer way to delete objects is to use the IADsCon tainer::Delete method. To use this method, you must first bind to the parent container of the object. You can then call `Delete` by passing the object class and RDN of the object you want to delete. Here is an example for deleting a `user` object:

```
set objCont = GetObject("LDAP://ou=Sales,dc=adatum,dc=com")
objCont.Delete "user", "cn=rallen"
```

`Delete` is safer than `DeleteObject` because you have to be more explicit about what you are deleting. With `DeleteObject` you only need to specify a distinguished name and it will be deleted. If you happen to mistype the DN or the user input to a web page that uses this method is mistyped, the result could be disastrous.

See Also

Recipe 4.25 for deleting a container, MS KB 258310 (Viewing Deleted Objects in Active Directory), MSDN: IADsContainer::Delete, and MSDN: IADsDeleteOps:: DeleteObject

4.25 Deleting a Container That Has Child Objects

Problem

You want to delete a container or organizational unit and all child objects contained within.

Solution

Using a graphical user interface

Open ADSI Edit and follow the same steps as in Recipe 4.24. The only difference is that you'll be prompted to confirm twice instead of once before the deletion occurs.

Using a command-line interface

You can delete a container and its child objects using the built-in *dsrm* utility, as well as AdMod. For *dsrm*, use the following syntax:

```
> dsrm "<ObjectDN>" -subtree
```

For AdMod, enter the following:

```
> admod -b "<ObjectDN>" -del -treedelete
```

Using VBScript

The same code from Recipe 4.24 will also delete containers and objects contained within them.

Using PowerShell

To delete an object using the Quest AD cmdlets, use the following syntax:

```
remove-QADObject -identity <Object DN> -DeleteTree
```

To delete an object using the .NET methods, use the following:

```
$obj = [System.DirectoryServices.DirectoryEntry] "LDAP://<Object DN>"
$obj.psbase.DeleteTree()
```

Discussion

As you can see from the solutions, there is not much difference between deleting a leaf node versus deleting a container that has child objects. However, there is a distinction in what is happening in the background.

Deleting an object that has no children can be done with a simple LDAP delete operation. On the other hand, to delete a container and its children, the tree-delete LDAP control has to be used. If you were to do the deletion from an LDAP-based tool like LDP (the Active Directory Administration Tool), you would first need to enable the Subtree Delete control, which has an OID of 1.2.840.113556.1.4.805. LDP provides another option to do a Recursive Delete from the client side. That will essentially iterate through all the objects in the container, deleting them one by one. The Subtree Delete is much more efficient, especially when dealing with large containers.

As with the other operations we've discussed in this chapter (create, rename, move, etc.), the user performing the delete operation needs to have the necessary permissions to delete the object or objects in question. Active Directory permissions are discussed more extensively in Chapter 14.

Using PowerShell

As you can see, deleting a container object through PowerShell is similar to deleting a leaf object, and should be used with care as a result. The Quest AD cmdlet requires the use of the –DeleteTree switch in order to delete a container object rather than a leaf object.

See Also

Recipe 4.24 for information about deleting objects, Chapter 14, and MSDN: IADsDeleteOps::DeleteObject

4.26 Viewing the Created and Last Modified Timestamp of an Object

Problem

You want to determine when an object was either created or last updated.

Solution

Using a graphical user interface

1. Follow the steps in Recipe 4.2.
2. Ensure that createTimestamp and modifyTimestamp are included in the list of attributes to be returned by looking at Attributes under Options→Search.

Using a command-line interface

You can view the created and modified timestamps using the built-in DSQuery utility, as well as AdFind. For DSQuery, use the following syntax:

```
> dsquery * "<ObjectDN>" -attr name createTimestamp modifyTimestamp
```

For AdFind, use the following:

```
> adfind -default -rb cn=Users -f "cn=Joe Smith"
createTimestamp modifyTimestamp
```

Using VBScript

```
' This code prints the created and last modified timestamp
' for the specified object.
' ------ SCRIPT CONFIGURATION ------
strObjectDN = "<ObjectDN>"
' ------ END CONFIGURATION --------

set objEntry = GetObject("LDAP://" & strObjectDN)
Wscript.Echo "Object Name: " & objEntry.Get("name")
Wscript.Echo " Created: " & objEntry.Get("createTimestamp")
Wscript.Echo " Changed: " & objEntry.Get("modifyTimestamp")
```

Using PowerShell

The following code uses first the Quest AD cmdlets, followed by the .NET methods:

```
$obj1 = get-QADObject 'cn=administrator,cn=users,dc=adatum,dc=com'
$obj1.DirectoryEntry.whenChanged
$obj2 = [System.DirectoryServices.DirectoryEntry] "LDAP://<ObjectDN>"
$obj2.whenCreated
```

Discussion

When an object is created or modified in Active Directory, the `createTimestamp` and `modifyTimestamp` attributes get set with the current time. The `createTimestamp` attribute is replicated between domain controllers, so assuming the latest modification of the object in question has replicated to all domain controllers, they will all contain the timestamp when the object was created. `whenChanged` and `modifyTimestamp` are not replicated, which means that their values will be local to an individual domain controller. Additionally, `modifyTimestamp` is a constructed attribute.

See Also

Recipe 4.2 for viewing the attributes of an object and Chapter 12 for a more detailed description of the Active Directory replication process

4.27 Modifying the Default LDAP Query Policy

Problem

You want to view or modify the default LDAP query policy of a forest. The query policy contains settings that restrict search behavior, such as the maximum number of entries that can be returned from a search.

Solution

Using a graphical user interface

1. Open ADSI Edit.
2. In the Configuration partition, browse to Services→Windows NT→Directory Service→Query Policies.
3. In the left pane, click on the Query Policies container, then right-click on the Default Query Policy object in the right pane, and select Properties.
4. Double-click on the `lDAPAdminLimits` attribute.
5. Click on the attribute you want to modify and click Remove.
6. Modify the value in the "Value to add" box and click Add.
7. Click OK twice.

Using a command-line interface

To view the current settings, use the following command:

```
> ntdsutil "ldap pol" conn "con to server <DomainControllerName>" q "show values"
```

To change the `MaxPageSize` value to 2000, you can do the following:

```
> ntdsutil "ldap pol" conn "con to server <DomainControllerName>" q
ldap policy: set MaxPageSize to 2000
ldap policy: Commit Changes
```

Using VBScript

```
' This code modifies a setting of the default
' query policy for a forest
' ------ SCRIPT CONFIGURATION ------
pol_attr  = "MaxPageSize" ' Set to the name of the setting you want to modify
new_value = 1000          ' Set to the value of the setting you want modify
' ------ END CONFIGURATION ---------
Const ADS_PROPERTY_APPEND = 3
Const ADS_PROPERTY_DELETE = 4

set rootDSE = GetObject("LDAP://RootDSE")
set ldapPol = GetObject("LDAP://cn=Default Query Policy,cn=Query-Policies," & _
                "cn=Directory Service,cn=Windows NT,cn=Services," & _
                rootDSE.Get("configurationNamingContext") )
set regex = new regexp
regex.IgnoreCase = true
regex.Pattern = pol_attr & "="
for Each prop In ldapPol.GetEx("ldapAdminLimits")
   if regex.Test(prop) then
      if prop = pol_attr & "=" & new_value then
         WScript.Echo pol_attr & " already equal to " & new_value
      else
         ldapPol.PutEx ADS_PROPERTY_APPEND, "lDAPAdminLimits", _
                   Array( pol_attr & "=" & new_value )
         ldapPol.SetInfo
         ldapPol.PutEx ADS_PROPERTY_DELETE, "lDAPAdminLimits", Array(prop)
         ldapPol.SetInfo
         WScript.Echo "Set " & pol_attr & " to " & new_value
      end if
      Exit For
   end if
next
```

Discussion

The LDAP query policy contains several settings that control how domain controllers handle searches. By default, one query policy is defined for all domain controllers in a forest, but you can create additional ones and apply them to a specific domain controller or even at the site level (so that all domain controllers in the site use that policy).

Query policies are stored in the Configuration NC as `queryPolicy` objects. The default query policy is located at: `cn=Default Query Policy,cn=Query-Policies,cn=Directory Service,cn=Windows NT,cn=Services, <ConfigurationPartitionDN>`. The attribute `lDAPAdminLimits` of a `queryPolicy` object is multivalued and contains each setting for the policy in name/value pairs. Table 4-5 contains the available settings.

Table 4-5. LDAP query policy settings

Name	Default value	Description
MaxPoolThreads	4 per proc	Maximum number of threads that are created by the DC for query execution.
MaxDatagramRecv	4096	Maximum number of datagrams that can be simultaneously processed by the DC.
MaxReceiveBuffer	10485760	Maximum size in bytes for an LDAP request that the server will attempt to process. If the server receives a request that is larger then this value, it will close the connection.
InitRecvTimeout	120 secs	Initial receive timeout.
MaxConnections	5000	Maximum number of open connections.
MaxConnIdleTime	900 secs	Maximum amount of time a connection can be idle.
MaxActiveQueries	20	Maximum number of queries that can be active at one time.
MaxPageSize	1000	Maximum number of records that will be returned by LDAP responses.
MaxQueryDuration	120 secs	Maximum length of time the domain controller can execute a query.
MaxTempTableSiz	10000	Maximum size of temporary storage that is allocated to execute queries.
MaxResultSetSize	262144	Controls the total amount of data that the domain controller stores for this kind of search. When this limit is reached, the domain controller discards the oldest of these intermediate results to make room to store new intermediate results.
MaxNotificationPerConn	5	Maximum number of notifications that a client can request for a given connection.

Since the settings are stored as name/value pairs inside a single attribute, also referred to as AVAs, the VBScript solution has to iterate over each value and use a regular expression to determine when the target setting has been found. It does this by matching <*SettingName*>= at the beginning of the string. See Recipe 4.19 for more on AVAs.

You should not change the default query policy in production unless you've done plenty of testing. Changing some of the settings may result in unexpected application or domain controller behavior, such as a significant failure of your Active Directory domain controllers.

Instead of modifying the default LDAP query policy, you can create a new one from scratch. In the Query Policies container (where the default query policy object is located), create a new queryPolicy object and set the lDAPAdminLimits attribute as just described based on the settings you want configured. Then modify the attribute queryPolicyObject on the nTDSDSA object of a domain controller you want to apply the new policy to. This can be done via the Active Directory Sites and Services snap-in by browsing to the nTDSDSA object of a domain controller (cn=NTDS Settings), right-clicking on it, and selecting Properties. You can then select the new policy from a drop-down menu beside Query Policy. Click OK to apply the new policy.

See Also

Recipe 4.19 and MS KB 315071 (How to View and Set LDAP Policy in Active Directory by Using Ntdsutil.exe)

4.28 Exporting Objects to an LDIF File

Problem

You want to export objects to an LDAP Data Interchange Format (LDIF) file.

Solution

Using a graphical user interface

None of the standard Microsoft tools support exporting LDIF from a GUI.

Using a command-line interface

```
> ldifde -f output.ldf -l <AttrList> -p <Scope> -r "<Filter>" -d "<BaseDN>"
```

Using VBScript

There are no COM or VBScript-based interfaces to LDIF. With Perl you can use the `Net::LDAP::LDIF` module, which supports reading and writing LDIF files.

Discussion

The LDIF specification defined in RFC 2849 describes a well-defined file-based format for representing directory entries. The format is intended to be both human and machine parseable, which adds to its usefulness. LDIF is the de facto standard for importing and exporting a large number of objects in a directory and is supported by virtually every directory vendor, including Microsoft.

Using a command-line interface

The `-f` switch specifies the name of the file to use to save the entries to, `-s` is the DC to query, `-l` is the comma-separated list of attributes to include, `-p` is the search scope, `-r` is the search filter, and `-d` is the base DN. If you encounter any problems using `ldifde`, the `-v` switch enables verbose mode and can help identify problems.

See Also

Recipe 4.29 for importing objects using LDIF, RFC 2849 (The LDAP Data Interchange Format [LDIF]—Technical Specification), and MS KB 237677 (Using LDIFDE to Import and Export Directory Objects to Active Directory)

4.29 Importing Objects Using an LDIF File

Problem

You want to import objects into Active Directory using an LDIF file. The file could contain object additions, modifications, and deletions.

Solution

Using a command-line interface

To import objects using the *ldifde* utility, you must first create an LDIF file with the objects to add, modify, or delete. Here is an example LDIF file that adds a user, modifies the user twice, and then deletes the user:

```
dn: cn=jsmith,cn=users,dc=adatum,dc=com
changetype: add
objectClass: user
samaccountname: jsmith
sn: JSmith

dn: cn=jsmith,cn=users,dc=adatum,dc=com
changetype: modify
add: givenName
givenName: Jim
-
replace: sn
sn: Smith
-

dn: cn=jsmith,cn=users,dc=adatum,dc=com
changetype: delete
```

Once you've created the LDIF file, you just need to run the `ldifde` command to import the new objects:

```
> ldifde -i -f input.ldf
```

Discussion

For more information on the LDIF format, check RFC 2849.

Using a command-line interface

To import with *ldifde*, simply specify the `-i` switch to turn on import mode and `-f` `<filename>` for the file. It can also be beneficial to use the `-v` switch to turn on verbose mode to get more information in case of errors. The Windows Server 2003 version of *ldifde* also includes the `-j` switch that will create a logfile for troubleshooting purposes.

See Also

Recipe 4.28 for information on LDIF, RFC 2849 (The LDAP Data Interchange Format [LDIF]—Technical Specification), and MS KB 237677 (Using LDIFDE to Import and Export Directory Objects to Active Directory)

4.30 Exporting Objects to a CSV File

Problem

You want to export objects to a comma-separated variable (CSV) file. The CSV file can then be opened and manipulated from a spreadsheet application or with a text editor.

Solution

Using a command-line interface

You can export objects to a CSV file using the built-in *csvde* utility, as well as AdFind. For *csvde*, use the following syntax:

```
> csvde -f output.csv -l <AttrList> -p <Scope> -r "<Filter>" -d "<BaseDN>"
```

You can also export information to a CSV file using adfind:

```
> adfind -b <SearchBase> -f <Filter> -csv <Attr1> <Attr2> <Attr3>
```

Using PowerShell

You can export objects to a CSV file in PowerShell using the Quest AD cmdlets or the native ADSI methods, as follows:

```
 get-QADObject -identity <ObjectDN> -IncludeProperty <Property1> <Property2> ... |
Select <Property1> <Property2> ... | export-csv adobjects.csv

$obj = [ADSI]"LDAP://<Object DN>"
$record = ""
foreach ($property in ($obj | get-member)) { $record += $property.name + "|" }
$record | out-file -force adobjects.csv
$record = ""
foreach ($property in ($obj | get-member)) { $record += $obj.($property.name) + "|" }
$record | out-file -append adobjects.csv
```

Discussion

Once you have a CSV file containing entries, you can use a spreadsheet application such as Excel to view, sort, and manipulate the data.

Using a command-line interface

The parameters used by *cvsde* are nearly identical to those used by *ldifde*. The -f switch specifies the name of the file to use to save the entries to, -s is the DC to query, -1 is the comma-separated list of attributes to include, -p is the search scope (base, onelevel, or subtree), -r is the search filter, and -d is the base DN. If you encounter any issues, the -v switch enables verbose mode and can help identify problems.

AdFind offers a number of additional switches to customize the behavior of CSV file output, including:

-csv xxx
> CSV output. xxx is an optional string that specifies value to use for empty attributes.

-csvdelim x
> Delimiter to use for separating attributes in CSV output. The default is (,).

-csvmvdelim x
> Delimiter to use for separating multiple values in output. The default is (;).

-csvq x
> Character to use for quoting attributes. The default is (").

See Also

Recipe 4.31 for importing objects using a CSV file

4.31 Importing Objects Using a CSV File

Problem

You want to import objects into Active Directory using a CSV file.

Solution

Using a command-line interface

To import objects using the *csvde* utility, you must first create a CSV file containing the objects to add. The first line of the file should contain a comma-separated list of attributes you want to set, with DN being the first attribute. Here is an example:

```
DN,objectClass,cn,sn,userAccountControl,sAMAccountName,userPrincipalName
```

The rest of the lines should contain entries to add. If you want to leave one of the attributes unset, then leave the value blank (followed by a comma). Here is a sample CSV file that would add two user objects:

```
DN,objectClass,sn,userAccountControl,sAMAccountName,userPrincipalName
"cn=jim,cn=users,dc=adatum,dc=com",user,Smith,512,jim,jim@adatum.com
"cn=john,cn=users,dc=adatum,dc=com",user,,512,john,john@adatum.com
```

Once you've created the CSV file, you just need to run *cvsde* to import the new objects:

```
> csvde -i -f input.csv
```

Discussion

The major difference between *csvde* and *ldifde* is that you can only use *csvde* to import objects; unlike *ldifde*, you can't use it to modify existing objects. Note that each line of the CSV import file, except the header, should contain entries to add objects. You cannot modify attributes of an object or delete objects using *csvde*; however, you can accomplish this using *admod*. If you have a spreadsheet containing objects you want to import, first save it as a CSV file and use *csvde* to import it.

Using a command-line interface

To import with *csvde*, simply specify the -i switch to turn on import mode and -f <filename> for the file. It can also be beneficial to use the -v switch to turn on verbose mode to get more information in case of errors.

See Also

Recipe 4.30 for exporting objects in CSV format and MS KB 327620 (How to Use Csvde to Import Contacts and User Objects into Active Directory)

## CHAPTER 5

Organizational Units

5.0 Introduction

An LDAP directory such as Active Directory stores data in a hierarchy of *containers* and *leaf nodes* called the directory information tree (DIT). Leaf nodes are end points in the tree, while containers can store other containers and leaf nodes. In Active Directory, the two most common types of containers are organizational units (OUs) and container objects. The *container objects* are generic containers that do not have any special properties about them other than the fact that they can contain objects. *Organizational units*, on the other hand, have some special properties, such as the ability to link a Group Policy Object (GPO) to an OU. In most cases when designing a hierarchy of objects in Active Directory, especially users and computers, you should use OUs instead of containers. There is nothing you can do with a container that you can't do with an OU, but the reverse is certainly not the case.

The Anatomy of an Organizational Unit

Organizational units can be created as a child of a domain object or another OU; by default, OUs cannot be added as a child of a container object. (See Recipe 5.13 for more on how to work around this.) OUs themselves are represented in Active Directory by organizationalUnit objects. Table 5-1 contains a list of some interesting attributes that are available on organizationalUnit objects.

Table 5-1. Attributes of organizationalUnit objects

Attribute	Description
description	Textual description of the OU.
gPLink	List of GPOs that have been linked to the OU.
gpOptions	Contains 1 if GPO inheritance is blocked and 0 otherwise.
msDS-Approx-Immed-Subordinates	Approximate number of direct child objects in the OU. See Recipe 5.11 for more information.
managedBy	DN of user or group that is in charge of managing the OU.
ou	Relative distinguished name of the OU.
modifyTimestamp	Timestamp of when the OU was last modified.
createTimestamp	Timestamp of when the OU was created.

5.1 Creating an OU

Problem

You want to create an OU.

Solution

Using a graphical user interface

1. Open the ADUC snap-in.
2. If you need to change domains, right-click on the Active Directory Users and Computers label in the left pane, select Connect to Domain, enter the domain name, and click OK.
3. In the left pane, browse to the parent container of the new OU, right-click on it, and select New→Organizational Unit.
4. Enter the name of the OU and click OK.
5. To enter a description for the new OU, right-click on the OU in the left pane and select Properties.
6. Click OK after you are done.

Using a command-line interface

You can create a new OU using the built-in DSAdd utility, as well as AdMod. To create an OU using DSAdd, use the following syntax:

```
> dsadd ou "<OrgUnitDN>" -desc "<Description>"
```

To create an OU with AdMod, use the following syntax:

```
> admod -b <OrgUnitDN> objectclass::organizationalUnit
  description::"<Description>" -add
```

For example, creating the Finance OU with the description of "Finance OU" in the *adatum.com* domain would look like this:

```
> admod -b ou=Finance,dc=adatum,dc=com
  objectclass::organizationalUnit
  description::"Finance OU" -add

> AdMod V01.10.00cpp Joe Richards (joe@joeware.net) February 2007

>
> DN Count: 1
> Using server: 2k3-sp1-r2.adatum.com
> Adding specified objects...
>    DN: ou=Finance,dc=adatum,dc=com...
>
> The command completed successfully
```

Using VBScript

```
' This code creates an OU
' ------ SCRIPT CONFIGURATION ------
strOrgUnit       = "<OUName>" '      e.g. Tools
strOrgUnitParent = "<ParentDN>" '      e.g. ou=Engineering,dc=adatum,dc=com
strOrgUnitDescr  = "<Description>" ' e.g. Tools Users
' ------ END CONFIGURATION ---------

set objDomain = GetObject("LDAP://" & strOrgUnitParent)
set objOU = objDomain.Create("organizationalUnit", "OU=" & strOrgUnit)
objOU.Put "description", strOrgUnitDescr
objOU.SetInfo
WScript.Echo "Successfully created " & objOU.Name
```

Using PowerShell

To create an organizational unit using the Quest AD cmdlets, use the following syntax:

```
new-QADObject -parentcontainer '<Parent Container DN>' -type 'organizationalunit'
-name 'Marketing' -ObjectAttributes @{description='Marketing OU'}
```

To create an OU using `System.DirectoryServices`, use the following:

```
$objParentDN = [System.DirectoryServices.DirectoryEntry] "LDAP://<Parent Container DN>"
$objNewOU = $objParentDN.Create("organizationalunit", "ou=Sales")
$objNewOU.put("description", "Sales OU")
$bjNewOU.setInfo()
```

Discussion

OUs are used to structure data within Active Directory. Typically, there are four reasons you might need to create an OU:

Segregate objects

It is common practice to group related data into an OU. For example, user objects and computer objects are typically stored in separate containers (in fact, this is the default configuration with Active Directory). One reason for this is to make searching the directory easier.

Delegate administration

Perhaps the most common reason for creating an OU is to delegate administration. With OUs you can give a person or group of people rights to perform certain administrative functions on objects within the OU.

Apply a GPO

An OU is the smallest container object that a GPO can be applied to. If you have different types of users within your organization that need to apply different GPOs, the easiest way to set that up is to store the users in different OUs and apply GPOs accordingly.

Control visibility of objects

You can use OUs as a way to restrict what users can see in the directory.

In each solution in this recipe, the description attribute of the new OU was set. This is not a mandatory attribute, but it is good practice to set it so that others browsing the directory have a general understanding of the purpose of the OU. Also, consider setting the managedBy attribute to reference a user or group that is the owner of the OU.

See Also

MS KB 308194 (How to Create Organizational Units in a Windows 2000 Domain)

5.2 Enumerating the OUs in a Domain

Problem

You want to enumerate all containers and OUs in a domain, which effectively displays the structure of the domain.

Solution

Using a graphical user interface

1. Open the Active Directory Users and Computers snap-in.

2. If you need to change domains, right-click on "Active Directory Users and Computers" in the left pane, select Connect to Domain, enter the domain name, and click OK.

3. In the left pane, you can browse the directory structure.

Using a command-line interface

The following command will enumerate all OUs in the domain of the user running the command using the built-in DSQuery utility:

```
> dsquery ou domainroot
```

You can also retrieve this information with AdFind, using the following syntax:

```
> adfind -default -f "objectcategory=organizationalUnit" -dn
```

This adfind syntax can be shortened as follows:

```
> adfind -default -sc oudmp
```

Output from the adfind command will resemble the following:

```
> adfind -default -f "objectcategory=organizationalUnit" -dn
>
> AdFind V01.27.00cpp Joe Richards (joe@joeware.net) November 2005
>
> Using server: dc1.adatum.com:389
> Directory: Windows Server 2003
> Base DN: DC=adatum,DC=com
>
> dn:OU=Domain Controllers,DC=adatum,DC=com
> dn:OU=Finance,DC=adatum,DC=com
> dn:OU=FinanceTemps,OU=Finance,DC=adatum,DC=com
>
> 3 Objects returned
```

Using VBScript

```
' This code recursively displays all container and organizationalUnit
' objects under a specified base. Using "" for the second parameter means
' that there will be no indention for the first level of objects displayed.
Call DisplayOUs(LDAP://<DomainDN>", "")


'
DisplayOUs takes the ADsPath of the object to display
' child objects for and the number of spaces (indention) to
' use when printing the first parameter
Function DisplayOUs( strADsPath, strSpace)
   set objObject = GetObject(strADsPath)
   Wscript.Echo strSpace & strADsPath
   objObject.Filter = Array("container","organizationalUnit")
   for each objChildObject in objObject
      Call DisplayOUs(objChildObject.ADsPath, strSpace & " ")
   next
End Function
```

Using PowerShell

To enumerate all OUs using the Quest AD cmdlets, use the following syntax:

```
get-QADObject -SearchRoot <Base Search DN> -LdapFilter
'(objectcategory=organizationalunit)'
```

To enumerate OUs using `System.DirectoryServices`, use the following:

```
$strCategory = "organizationalunit"
$objDomain = New-Object System.DirectoryServices.DirectoryEntry
$objSearcher = New-Object System.DirectoryServices.DirectorySearcher
$objSearcher.SearchRoot = $objDomain
$objSearcher.Filter = ("(objectCategory=$strCategory)")
$colResults = $objSearcher.FindAll()
```

Discussion

Using a graphical user interface

If you want to expand all containers and OUs within an OU, you have to manually expand each one within ADUC; there is no "expand all" option.

Using a command-line interface

To enumerate both OUs and containers, you have to a use a more generic `dsquery` command. The following command will display all containers and OUs in the domain of the user running the command:

```
> dsquery * domainroot -filter
"(|(objectcategory=container)(objectcategory=organizationalunit))"
-limit 0
```

Using VBScript

When iterating over the contents of an OU using a `for each` loop, paging will be enabled so that all child objects will be returned (instead of only 1,000 per the administrative limit). To display all child container objects regardless of depth, use a recursive function called `DisplayOUs`.

 It should be noted that, in larger directories, the command-line and PowerShell solutions will provide better performance than the VBScript solution in this recipe.

5.3 Finding an OU

Problem

You want to find a specific OU within an Active Directory domain.

Solution

Using a graphical user interface

1. Open the ADUC snap-in.
2. If you need to change domains, right-click on the Active Directory Users and Computers label in the left pane, select Connect to Domain, enter the domain name, and click OK.
3. Right-click on the domain node and select Find.
4. In the Find drop-down box, select Organizational Unit. In the Named: text box, enter the name of the OU.
5. Click Find Now.

Using a command-line interface

```
> adfind -default -f "ou=<OU Name>"
```

Using VBScript

```
Set objCommand = CreateObject("ADODB.Command")
Set objConnection = CreateObject("ADODB.Connection")
objConnection.Provider = "ADsDSOObject"
objConnection.Open "Active Directory Provider"
objCommand.ActiveConnection = objConnection

strBase = "<LDAP://<DomainDN>>"
strOUName = "Finance"
strFilter = "(&(objectCategory=organizationalUnit)" _
   "&(name=" & strOUName & "))"
strAttributes = "distinguishedName"
strQuery = strBase & ";" & strFilter & ";" & strAttributes & ";subtree"

objCommand.CommandText = strQuery
objCommand.Properties("Page Size") = 100
objCommand.Properties("Timeout") = 30
objCommand.Properties("Cache Results") = False
Set objRecordSet = objCommand.Execute

While Not objRecordSet.EOF
   strName = objRecordSet.Fields("distinguishedName").Value
   Wscript.Echo "Distinguished Name: " & strName
   objRecordSet.MoveNext
Wend

objConnection.Close
```

Using PowerShell

To find a specific OU using the Quest AD cmdlets, use the following syntax:

```
get-QADObject -SearchRoot <Base Search DN> -LdapFilter '(ou=<OU Name>)'
```

To find a specific OU using `System.DirectoryServices`, use the following:

```
$objDomain = New-Object System.DirectoryServices.DirectoryEntry
$objSearcher = New-Object System.DirectoryServices.DirectorySearcher
$objSearcher.SearchRoot = $objDomain
$objSearcher.Filter = "(ou=<OU Name>)"
$objSearcher.FindAll()
```

Discussion

In a heavily nested environment, you may need to locate an OU based on its name when you don't necessarily know its location. By using the ADUC GUI or a command-line tool with a search scope of subtree, you can easily recurse through the entire domain structure to find an OU based on its name, description, or any other attribute. In VBScript, you can use an ADO query to find objects that possess the specific attributes that you're looking for.

 When designing your Active Directory structure, you should try to keep OU nesting from becoming too deep, since processing many levels of Group Policy Objects can greatly increase the logon times for your clients. In the interests of keeping things simple, it's often a good idea to keep your OU structure shallow whenever possible.

See Also

Recipes 5.2, 5.4, and MSDN: VBScript ADO Programming

5.4 Enumerating the Objects in an OU

Problem

You want to enumerate all the objects in an OU.

Solution

The following solutions will enumerate all the objects directly under an OU. Look at the "Discussion" section for more on how to display all objects under an OU regardless of the number of objects involved.

Using a graphical user interface

1. Open the ADUC snap-in.
2. If you need to change domains, right-click on "Active Directory Users and Computers" in the left pane, select Connect to Domain, enter the domain name, and click OK.
3. In the left pane, browse to the OU you want to view.

4. The contents of the OU will be displayed in the right pane.

Using a command-line interface

To list the contents of an OU using the built-in DSQuery utility, use the following syntax:

```
> dsquery * "<OU DN>" -limit 0 -scope onelevel
```

You can also use AdFind, as follows:

```
> adfind -b "<OU DN>" -s one -dn
```

Using VBScript

```
set objOU = GetObject("LDAP://<OU DN>")
for each objChildObject in objOU
    Wscript.Echo objChildObject.ADSPath
next
```

Using PowerShell

To enumerate the contents of an OU using the Quest AD cmdlets, use the following syntax:

```
get-QADObject -searchRoot <OU DN>
```

To perform the same task using System.DirectoryServices, use the following:

```
([ADSI]"LDAP://<OU DN>").psbase.Children
```

Discussion

Using a graphical user interface

By default, ADUC will display only 2,000 objects. To view more than 2,000 objects, select View→Filter Options. Then modify the maximum number of items displayed per folder.

Using a command-line interface

Using -limit 0, all objects under the OU will be displayed. If -limit is not specified, 100 will be shown by default. You can also specify your own number if you want to only display a limited number of objects.

The -scope onelevel or -s one (for AdFind) option causes only direct child objects of the OU to be displayed. Displaying all objects regardless of depth is referred to as the subtree scope, which is the default search scope for AdFind and DSQuery. If you want to return all objects regardless of depth, including the OU being searched, simply omit the -scope switch entirely.

To save on typing, you can use the `-default` switch with AdFind, which automatically uses the Domain DN as its search base. You can use this in combination with the `-rb` (Relative Base) switch, which will only require you to type in the relative DN of the OU that you want to search. So to list the objects in the cn=Finance,dc=adatum,dc=com OU, you can use the following abbreviated AdFind syntax:

```
> adfind -default -rb ou=Finance -s one -dn
```

Another option would be to use the `-incldn` switch, which will return objects that contain a particular search string anywhere within the Distinguished Name. So specifying `-incldn "ou=Finance"` would return the cn=Finance,dc=adatum,dc=com OU, as well as the cn=FinanceTemps,cn=Finance,dc=adatum,dc=com OU.

Using VBScript

When a `for each` loop iterates over the contents of an OU, paging will be enabled so that all child objects will be returned regardless of how many there are. If you want to display all child objects and objects contained in any child OUs, you need to implement a recursive function such as the following:

```
' Using "" for the second parameter means that there will be no
' indention for the first level of objects displayed.
DisplayNestedOUs "LDAP://<OrgUnitDN>", ""
' DisplayObjects takes the ADsPath of the object to display child
' objects for and the second is the number of spaces (indention)
' to use when printing the first parameter
Function
DisplayNestedOUs( strADsPath, strSpace)
   set objObject = GetObject(strADsPath)
   Wscript.Echo strSpace & strADsPath
   for each objChildObject in objObject
      DisplayObjects objChildObject.ADsPath, strSpace & " "
   next
End Function
```

This code is nearly identical to that shown in Recipe 5.2. The only difference is that the `Filter` method to restrict the type of objects displayed was not used.

Using PowerShell

The Quest cmdlet uses a default search scope of subtree, which will return the OU being searched and all child objects recursively. To restrict the search to only the immediate children of the OU, add the `-searchscope 'onelevel'` switch to the Quest cmdlet.

The `System.DirectoryServices` syntax again makes use of the `psbase` keyword to access the `Children` property.

See Also

Recipe 5.2

5.5 Deleting the Objects in an OU

Problem

You want to delete all child objects in an OU, but not the OU itself.

Solution

Using a graphical user interface

1. Open the ADUC snap-in.
2. If you need to change domains, right-click on "Active Directory Users and Computers" in the left pane, select Connect to Domain, enter the domain name, and click OK.
3. In the left pane, browse to and select the OU that contains the objects you want to delete.
4. Highlight all the objects in the right pane and press the Delete key on your keyboard.
5. Press F5 to refresh the contents of the OU. If objects still exist, repeat the previous step.

Using a command-line interface

To delete all objects within an OU, but not the OU itself, you need to use the -subtree and -exclude options with the dsrm command:

```
> dsrm "<OrgUnitDN>" -subtree -exclude
```

You can also perform this task by piping the results of an adfind query into admod, as follows:

```
>adfind -default -rb ou=<OU Name> -s one -dsq | admod -unsafe -del
```

Using VBScript

```
' This code deletes the objects in an OU, but not the OU itself
set objOU = GetObject("LDAP://<OrgUnitDN>")
for each objChildObject in objOU
    Wscript.Echo "
Deleting " & objChildObject.ADSPath
    objChildObject.DeleteObject(0)
next
```

Using PowerShell

To delete the child objects within an OU using the Quest cmdlets, use the following:

```
get-QADObject -searchRoot <OU DN> | remove-QADObject -force
```

To use the `System.DirectoryServices` methods, use this syntax:

```
$objOU = [ADSI] "LDAP://<OU DN>"
$objOU.psbase.Children() |% $_.psbase.DeleteObject(0)
```

Discussion

If you want to delete the objects in an OU and re-create the OU, you can either delete the OU itself, which will delete all child objects, or you could just delete the child objects. The benefit to the latter approach is that you do not need to reconfigure the ACL on the OU or relink any Group Policy Objects after you've re-created the OU.

See Also

Recipe 5.4 for enumerating objects in an OU, Recipe 5.6 for deleting an OU, and MSDN: IADsDeleteOps::DeleteObject

5.6 Deleting an OU

Problem

You want to delete an OU and all objects in it.

Solution

Using a graphical user interface

1. Open the ADUC snap-in.
2. If you need to change domains, right-click on "Active Directory Users and Computers" in the left pane, select Connect to Domain, enter the domain name, and click OK.
3. In the left pane, browse to the OU you want to delete, right-click on it, and select Delete.
4. Click Yes.
5. If the OU contains child objects, you will be asked for confirmation again before deleting it. Click Yes to continue.

Using a command-line interface

To delete an OU and all objects contained within, use the `-subtree` option with the `dsrm` command. If you don't use `-subtree` and the object you are trying to delete has child objects, the deletion will fail:

```
> dsrm "<OrgUnitDN>" -subtree
```

You can also delete an OU and all of its contents using the following `admod` command:

```
> admod -b "<OrgUnitDN>" -del -treedelete
Using VBScript' This code deletes an OU and all child objects of the OU
set objOU = GetObject("LDAP://<OrgUnitDN>")
objOU.DeleteObject(0)
```

Using PowerShell

To delete an OU and its contents using the Quest AD cmdlets, use the following syntax:

```
remove-QADObject -identity '<OU DN>' -DeleteTree
```

To use `System.DirectoryServices`, use the following:

```
$objOU = [System.DirectoryServices.DirectoryEntry] "LDAP://<OU DN>"
$objOU.psbase.DeleteTree()
```

Discussion

Deleting OUs that do not contain objects is just like deleting any other type of object. Deleting an OU that contains objects, however, requires a special type of delete operation. The Tree Delete LDAP control (OID: 1.2.840.113556.1.4.805) must be used by the application or script to inform AD to delete everything contained in the OU. All three solutions in this case use the control behind the scenes, but if you were going to perform the operation via an LDAP utility such as LDP, you would need to enable the control first.

See Also

Recipe 4.4 for using LDAP controls and MSDN: IADsDeleteOps::DeleteObject

5.7 Moving the Objects in an OU to a Different OU

Problem

You want to move some or all of the objects in an OU to a different OU. You may need to do this as part of a domain restructuring effort.

Solution

Using a graphical user interface

1. Open the ADUC snap-in.
2. If you need to change domains, right-click on the Active Directory Users and Computers node in the lefthand pane, select Connect to Domain, enter the domain name, and click OK.
3. In the left pane, browse to and select the OU that contains the objects you want to move.

4. Highlight the objects in the right pane you want to move, right-click on them, and select Move.

5. Browse to and select the parent container you want to move the objects to, and then click OK.

6. Press F5 to refresh the contents of the OU. If objects still exist, repeat the previous three steps.

Using a command-line interface

To move each object from one OU to another, you can use **dsquery** as part of a **for do** loop as follows:

```
> for /f "usebackq delims=""" %i in (`dsquery * "<Old OU DN>" -scope
Onelevel') do dsmove -newparent "<New OU DN>" %i
```

An alternative is to pipe the results of an **adfind** query into **admod** using the following syntax:

```
> adfind -b "<Old OU DN>" -s one -dsq |
        admod -move "<New OU DN>"
```

Using VBScript

```
' This code moves objects from the "old" OU to the "new" OU
' ------ SCRIPT CONFIGURATION -----
strOldOU = "<Old OU DN>" ' e.g. ou=EngTools,dc=adatum,dc=com
strNewOU = "<New OU DN>" ' e.g. ou=Tools,dc=adatum,dc=com
' ------ END CONFIGURATION --------

set objOldOU = GetObject("LDAP://" & strOldOU)
set objNewOU = GetObject("LDAP://" & strNewOU)
for each objChildObject in objOldOU
    Wscript.Echo "
Moving " & objChildObject.Name
    objNewOU.MoveHere objChildObject.ADsPath, objChildObject.Name
next
```

Using PowerShell

To move all users from one OU to another using the Quest AD cmdlets, use the following syntax:

```
get-QADObject -searchroot '<Old OU DN>' | move-QADObject -newparent '<New OU DN>'
```

To move objects using **System.DirectoryServices**, use the following:

```
$objOldOU = [ADSI] "LDAP://<Old OU DN>"
$objNewOU = [ADSI] "LDAP://<New OU DN>"
$objOldOU.psbase.Children |% $_.psbase.MoveTo($objNewOU)
```

Neither of these syntaxes can move objects recursively; if an OU contains a child OU that itself contains child objects, either of these methods will generate an error.

Discussion

When you move objects from one OU to another, you need to be aware of two significant Active Directory design factors that can affect the behavior of the objects that you're moving: delegation and Group Policy Object inheritance.

The first factor to be aware of is *delegation*. As an administrator, you can delegate permissions at the OU level so that specific users and groups can (or cannot) access or modify information concerning the objects contained within that OU. When you move an object from one OU to another, that object inherits the delegation settings from its new parent OU. This means that a user or group who had rights to an object before it was moved may no longer have rights to it afterward, and a user or group who did not have rights to the object before may have been delegated rights to the destination OU. You need to be aware of this setting to be sure that you do not allow or prevent object access unintentionally. Active Directory security and delegation is discussed further in Chapter 14.

The second factor to keep in mind is that of GPO inheritance. You can link a GPO at the site, domain, or OU level; any child objects that you move to a new OU will cease to receive the GPO settings that were applied to the old OU and will receive those settings associated with the new OU instead.

The one exception to this would be if you were moving an object from a parent OU to its child OU, for example moving from `ou=Finance,dc=adatum,dc=com` to `ou=Finance Temps,ou=Finance,dc=adatum,dc=com`. In this example, the rules of GPO inheritance would cause the moved objects to receive any GPO settings linked to the Finance OU, followed by any GPO settings linked to the Finance Temps OU. Again, you need to be certain that moving an object from one OU to another does not create any unintended effects.

You can use the Group Policy Management Console's Resultant Set of Policy (Modeling) wizard to simulate the effect that the move will have on objects within the originating OU before you actually perform the move.

Using a graphical user interface

If you want to move more than 2,000 objects at one time, you will need to modify the default number of objects displayed as described in the section called "Discussion" of Recipe 5.4.

Using a command-line interface

Since dsmove can move only one object at a time, you need to use a for do loop to iterate over each child object returned. Also note that if you want to move more than 100 objects, you'll need to specify the -limit xx option with dsquery, where xx is the maximum number of objects to move (use 0 for all).

Similarly, AdMod will only move 10 objects at a time by default. To move more objects than this, you need to either specify the -safety xx option, where xx is the maximum number of objects to modify, or else use -unsafe to move an unlimited number of objects.

Using VBScript

For more information on the MoveHere method, see Recipe 5.8.

See Also

Recipe 4.20 for moving objects, Recipe 5.4 for enumerating objects in an OU, and MSDN: IADsContainer::MoveHere

5.8 Moving an OU

Problem

You want to move an OU and all its child objects to a different location in the directory tree.

Solution

Using a graphical user interface

1. Open the ADUC snap-in.
2. If you need to change domains, right-click on "Active Directory Users and Computers" in the left pane, select Connect to Domain, enter the domain name, and click OK.
3. In the left pane, browse to the OU you want to move.
4. Right-click on the OU and select Move.
5. Select the new parent container for the OU and click OK.

Using a command-line interface

You can move an OU from one location to another by using either DSMove or AdMod. The DSMove syntax is as follows:

```
> dsmove "<OrgUnitDN>" -newparent "<NewParentDN>"
```

If you wish to move an OU with AdMod, use the following syntax:

```
> admod -b "<OrgUnitDN>" -move "<NewParentDN>"
```

Using VBScript

```
set objOU = GetObject("LDAP://<NewParentDN>")
objOU.MoveHere "LDAP://<OrgUnitDN>", "<OrgUnitRDN>"
```

Using PowerShell

To move an OU from one location to another, use either of the following syntaxes:

```
move-QADObject -identity '<OU DN>' -newparent '<Destination DN>'

$objOU = [ADSI] "LDAP://<OU DN>"
$newParent = [ADSI] "LDAP://<Destination DN>'
$objOU.psbase.MoveTo($newParent)
```

Discussion

One of the benefits of Active Directory is the ability to structure and restructure data easily. Moving an OU, even one that contains a complex hierarchy of other OUs and objects, can be done without impacting the child objects.

If any applications have a dependency on the location of specific objects, you need to ensure they are either updated with the new location or preferably reference the objects by GUID, not by distinguished name.

You should also be mindful of the impact of inherited ACLs and the effect of any new GPOs that are linked to the new parent OU. Keep in mind that any GPOs that were already linked to the OU will stay intact and the link will follow the OU to its new location in the directory structure.

See Also

MS KB 313066 (How to Move Users, Groups, and Organizational Units Within a Domain in Windows 2000) and MSDN: IADsContainer::MoveHere

5.9 Renaming an OU

Problem

You want to rename an organizational unit in your domain.

Solution

Using a graphical user interface

1. Open the ADUC snap-in.
2. If you need to change domains, right-click on "Active Directory Users and Computers" in the left pane, select Connect to Domain, enter the domain name, and click OK.
3. In the left pane, browse to the OU you want to move.
4. Right-click on the OU and select Rename.
5. Type in the new name for the OU and press Enter.

Using a command-line interface

To rename an object using the built-in DSMove utility, use the following syntax:

```
> dsmove "<ObjectDN>" -newname "<NewName>"
```

To use admod, use the following:

```
> admod -b "<ObjectDN>" -rename "<NewName>"
```

Using VBScript

```
' This code renames an object and leaves it in the same location.
' ------ SCRIPT CONFIGURATION -----
strCurrentParentDN = "<CurrentParentDN>"
strObjectOldName   = "ou=<OldName>"
strObjectNewName   = "ou=<NewName>"
' ------ END CONFIGURATION --------

set objCont = GetObject("LDAP://" & strCurrentParentDN)
objCont.MoveHere "LDAP://" & strObjectOldName & "," & _
                 strCurrentParentDN, strObjectNewName
```

Using PowerShell

You can rename an OU using either the Quest AD cmdlets or using a method in the System.DirectoryServices namespace, as follows:

```
Rename-QADObject -identity '<OU DN>' -newname '<New OU Name>'

$objOU = [ADSI] "LDAP://<OU DN>"
$objOU.psbase.Rename("<New OU Name>")
```

Discussion

Before you rename an OU, ensure that none of your production applications reference it by name. You can make objects rename-safe by requiring all applications that must store a reference to an object to use the GUID of the object, rather than the name. The

GUID (stored in the `objectGUID` attribute) is effectively unique within a forest and does not change when an object is renamed.

Using a command-line interface

The two parameters needed to rename an object are the original DN of the object and the new RDN (`-newname`). The `-s` option can also be used to specify a server name to work against.

Using VBScript

The `MoveHere` method can be tricky to use, so an explanation of how to use it to rename objects is in order. First, you need to call `GetObject` on the parent container of the object you want to rename. Then call `MoveHere` on the parent container object and specify the ADsPath of the object to rename as the first parameter. The new RDN, including prefix (e.g., `ou=`) of the object, should be the second parameter.

See Also

Recipe 4.23 and MSDN: IADsContainer::MoveHere

5.10 Modifying an OU

Problem

You want to modify one or more attributes of an OU.

Solution

The following examples set the description (`description`) attribute for the `Finance` Organizational Unit.

Using a graphical user interface

1. Open ADSI Edit.
2. If an entry for the naming context you want to browse is not already displayed, do the following:
   a. Right-click on ADSI Edit in the right pane and click "Connect to...".
   b. Fill in the information for the naming context, container, or OU you want to add an object to. Click on the Advanced button if you need to enter alternate credentials.
3. In the left pane, browse to the container or OU that contains the object you want to modify. Once you've found the object, right-click on it and select Properties.
4. Right-click the description attribute and select Edit.

5. Enter Finance Department and click OK.

6. Click Apply, followed by OK.

Using a command-line interface

To modify an object using AdMod, you'll use the following general syntax:

```
> admod -b <ObjectDN> <attribute>:<operation>:<value>
```

For example, you can add a description to an OU object using the following syntax:

```
> admod -b cn="ou=Finance,dc=adatum,dc=com"
    description::"Finance Department"
```

You can modify a limited number of object types with DSMod. Run `dsmod /?` from a command line for more details.

Using VBScript

```
strObjectDN = "ou=Finance,dc=adatum,dc=com"
set objUser = GetObject("LDAP://" & strObjectDN)
objUser.Put "description", "Finance Department"
objUser.SetInfo
```

Using PowerShell

```
set-QADObject -identity '<OU DN>' -ObjectAttributes
@{'<Attribute1>'='<Value>';'<Attribute2>'='<Value>'...}

$objOU = [System.DirectoryServices.DirectoryEntry] "LDAP://<OU DN>"
$objOU.put("<Attribute1>","<Value>")
$objOU.put("<Attribute2>","<Value>")
$objOU.SetInfo()
```

Discussion

Modifying the attributes of an OU is a relatively straightforward process that's similar to modifying other types of objects within Active Directory. You can modify most attributes of an OU using the Active Directory Computers and Users MMC snap-in, but some attributes will be available for editing only by using ADSI Edit or a command-line or scripting utility.

Using VBScript

To simply view some common properties of an OU, use the following code:

```
strOUDN = ou="<OU DN>" ' i.e. "ou=Finance,dc=adatum,dc=com"
Set objContainer = GetObject("LDAP://" & strOUDN)

For Each strValue in objContainer.description
  WScript.Echo "Description: " & strValue
Next
```

```
Wscript.Echo "Street Address: " & strStreetAddress
Wscript.Echo "Province/State: " & objContainer.st
Wscript.Echo "Postal/ZIP Code: " & objContainer.postalCode
Wscript.Echo "
Country: " & objContainer.c
```

To clear a property of an OU, you need to use the PutEx method in combination with the ADS_PROPERTY_CLEAR value, as follows:

```
Const ADS_PROPERTY_CLEAR = 1
strOUDN = ou="<OU DN>" ' i.e. "ou=Finance,dc=adatum,dc=com"

Set objContainer = GetObject("LDAP://" & strOUDN)

objContainer.PutEx ADS_PROPERTY_CLEAR, "description", 0
objContainer.PutEx ADS_PROPERTY_CLEAR, "street", 0
objContainer.PutEx ADS_PROPERTY_CLEAR, "st", 0
objContainer.PutEx ADS_PROPERTY_CLEAR, "postalCode", 0
objContainer.PutEx ADS_PROPERTY_CLEAR, "c", 0
objContainer.SetInfo
```

See Also

MSDN: IADs::Put, MSDN: IADs::PutEx, MSDN: IADs::SetInfo, and MSDN: ADS_PROPERTY_OPERATION_ENUM

5.11 Determining Approximately How Many Child Objects an OU Has

Problem

You want to quickly determine a rough approximation of how many child objects, if any, an OU contains.

Solution

Using a graphical user interface

1. Open LDP.
2. From the Menu, select Browse→Search.
3. For Base DN, enter <OrgUnitDN>.
4. For Filter, enter (objectclass=*).
5. For Scope, select Base.
6. Click the Options button and enter msDS-Approx-Immed-Subordinates for attributes.
7. Click OK and then Run.

8. The results will be displayed in the righthand pane.

 Another option would be to run a search using the `onelevel` scope and count the number of objects returned by the query. In LDP you can suppress the display of results so that it only displays the number of objects returned rather than displaying the specifics of each item.

Using a command-line interface

You can retrieve the number of child objects that are contained in an OU using either DSQuery or AdFind. To perform this task using DSQuery, use the following syntax:

```
> dsquery * "<OrgUnitDN>" -scope base -attr
msDS-Approx-Immed-Subordinates
```

The syntax for AdFind is as follows:

```
> adfind -b "<OrgUnitDN>" -s base msDS-Approx-Immed-Subordinates
```

Using VBScript

```
' This code displays the approximate number of child objects for an OU
set objOU = GetObject("LDAP://<OU DN>")
objOU.GetInfoEx Array("msDS-Approx-Immed-Subordinates"), 0
WScript.Echo "Number of child objects: " & _
            objOU.Get("msDS-Approx-Immed-Subordinates")
```

Discussion

The `msDS-Approx-Immed-Subordinates` attribute was introduced in Windows Server 2003. It contains the approximate number of direct child objects in a container or organizational unit. Note that this is an approximation and can be off by 10 percent or more, sometimes significantly more, of the actual total for large containers. (For instance, we ran this query for a container with 2,008 objects in it that reported a value of 1306 for the `msDS-Appox-Immed-Subordinates` attribute.) The main reason for adding this attribute was to give applications an idea of the rough order of magnitude of how many objects a container has so that it can display them accordingly.

`msDS-Approx-Immed-Subordinates` is a constructed attribute, i.e., the value is not actually stored in Active Directory like other attributes. Rather, Active Directory computes the value when an application asks for it. In the VBScript solution, the `GetInfoEx` method needs to be called because some constructed attributes, such as this one, are not retrieved when `GetInfo` or `Get` is called.

You can accomplish similar functionality with Windows 2000 Active Directory, but you need to perform a `onelevel` search against the OU and then count the number of objects returned. This method is by no means as quick as using `msDS-Approx-Immed-Subordinates` in Windows Server 2003, but it produces the most accurate results.

See Also

MSDN: GetInfoEx

5.12 Delegating Control of an OU

Problem

You want to delegate administrative access of an OU to allow a group of users to manage objects in the OU.

Solution

Using a graphical user interface

1. Open the ADUC snap-in.
2. If you need to change domains, right-click on "Active Directory Users and Computers" in the left pane, select Connect to Domain, enter the domain name, and click OK.
3. In the left pane, browse to and select the target OU, and then select Delegate Control.
4. Select the users and/or groups to delegate control to by using the Add button, and then click Next.
5. Select the type of privilege to grant to the users or groups you selected in step 4, and then click Next.
6. Click Finish.

Using a command-line interface

ACLs can be set via a command-line with the *dsacls* utility from the Windows 2000 and Windows Server 2003 Support Tools, or built directly into the Windows Server 2008 operating system. See Recipe 14.13 for more information.

Discussion

Although you can delegate control of an OU to a particular user, it is almost universally a better practice to use a group instead. Even if there is only one user to delegate control to, you should create a group, add that user as a member, and use that group in the ACL. That way in the future when you have to replace that user with someone else, you can simply make sure the new person is in the correct group instead of modifying ACLs again. The Delegation of Control wizard is discussed further in Recipe 14.6.

See Also

Recipe 14.13 for changing the ACL on an object and Recipe 14.6

5.13 Assigning or Removing a Manager for an OU

Problem

You want to assign or remove a manager for an OU.

Solution

Using a graphical user interface

1. Open the ADUC snap-in.
2. If you need to change domains, right-click on Active Directory Users and Computers in the left pane, select Connect to Domain, enter the domain name, and click OK.
3. In the left pane, right-click on the domain and select Find.
4. Right-click on the OU and select Properties.
5. Select the Managed By tab.
6. Click the Change button.
7. Locate the group or user to delegate control to and click OK.
8. To remove a manager from an OU, return to the Managed By tab and click Clear.

Using a command-line interface

To add a manager for an OU, use the following syntax:

```
> admod -b <ObjectDN> managedBy::<ManagerDN>
```

To clear the managedBy attribute, use the following:

```
> admod -b <ObjectDN> managedBy:-
```

Using VBScript

```
strObjectDN = "ou=Finance,dc=adatum,dc=com"
strUserDN = "cn=Joe Smith,ou=Finance,dc=adatum,dc=com"
set objUser = GetObject("LDAP://" & strObjectDN)
objUser.Put "managedBy", strUserDN
objUser.SetInfo
```

Using PowerShell

```
Set-QADObject -identity <OU DN> -objectAttributes @{'managedBy'='<User DN>'}

$objOU = [ADSI] "LDAP://<OU DN>"
$objOU.put("managedBy", "<User DN>"
$objOU.SetInfo()
```

Discussion

In the case of an OU, specifying a user, group, computer, or another OU in the Managed By tab does not confer any particular rights onto the manager; this is used as a strictly informational field. When you configure a manager for an OU, the manager's DN is placed in the OU's managedBy attribute, and the OU's DN is placed in the manager's managedObjects attribute. managedObjects is the backlink attribute of managedBy, showing all objects where that manager is specified.

See Also

MSDN: Managed-by attribute [AD Schema] and MSDN: Managed-Objects [AD Schema]

5.14 Linking a GPO to an OU

Problem

You want to apply the settings in a GPO to the users and/or computers within an OU, also known as linking the GPO to the OU.

Solution

Using a graphical user interface

1. Open the GPMC snap-in.
2. Expand Forest in the left pane.
3. Expand Domain and navigate down to the OU in the domain you want to link the GPO to.
4. Right-click on the OU and select either "Create and Link a GPO Here" (if the GPO does not already exist) or "Link an Existing GPO" (if you have already created the GPO).
5. To unlink a GPO, right-click on an existing link and remove the checkmark next to Link Enabled.

Using VBScript

```
' This code links a GPO to an OU in the specified domain
' ------ SCRIPT CONFIGURATION -----
strDomainDN = "<DomainDN>" '  e.g. dc=adatum,dc=com
strGPO      = "<GPOName>" '   e.g. WorkstationsGPO
strOUDN     = "<OrgUnitDN>" ' e.g. ou=Workstations,dc=adatum,dc=com

' ------ END CONFIGURATION --------

strBaseDN = "<LDAP://cn=policies,cn=system,dc=" & strDomainDN & ">;"
strFilter = "(&(objectcategory=grouppolicycontainer)" & _
              "(objectclass=grouppolicycontainer)" & _
              "(displayname=" & strGPO & "));"
strAttrs = "ADsPath;"
strScope = "OneLevel"

set objConn = CreateObject("ADODB.Connection")
objConn.Provider = "ADsDSOObject"
objConn.Open "Active Directory Provider"
set objRS = objConn.Execute(strBaseDN & strFilter & strAttrs & strScope)
if objRS.EOF <> TRUE then
   objRS.MoveFirst
end if

if objRS.RecordCount = 1 then
   strGPOADsPath = objRS.Fields(0).Value
   WScript.Echo "GPO Found: " & strGPOADsPath
elseif objRS.RecordCount = 0 then
   WScript.Echo "Did not founding matching GPO for: " & strGPO
   Wscript.Quit
elseif objRS.RecordCount > 1 then
   WScript.Echo "More than 1 GPO found matching: " & strGPO
   Wscript.Quit
end if

set objOU = GetObject("LDAP://" & strOUDN)

on error resume next
strGPLink = objOU.Get("gpLink")
if Err.Number then
   if Err.Number <> -2147463155 then
      WScript.Echo "Fatal error while retrieving gpLink attribute: " & _
                   Err.Description
      Wscript.Quit
   end if
end if
on error goto 0

objOU.Put "gpLink", strGPLink & "[" & strGPOADsPath & ";0]"
objOU.SetInfo
WScript.Echo "GPO successfully linked"

' The following code segment will remove any GPOs that
' are linked to an OU
```

```
Const ADS_PROPERTY_CLEAR = 1

Set objContainer = GetObject _
  ("LDAP://<OU DN>") ' i.e. "ou=Finance,dc=adatum,dc=com"
objContainer.PutEx ADS_PROPERTY_CLEAR, "gPLink", 0
objContainer.PutEx ADS_PROPERTY_CLEAR, "gPOptions", 0
objContainer.SetInfo
```

Using PowerShell

To link the "Marketing" Group Policy Object to the Marketing OU in *adatum.com*, use
the following free GPO cmdlet from SDM Software:

```
add-sdmgplink -name "Marketing" -scope "ou=marketing,dc=adatum,dc=com"
```

Discussion

The GPOs that are linked to an OU are stored in the gpLink attribute of the OU. The
format of the gpLink attribute is kind of strange, so you have to be careful when programmatically or manually setting that attribute. Since multiple GPOs can be linked to
an OU, the gpLink attribute has to store multiple values; unfortunately, it does not store
them as you might expect in a multivalued attribute. Instead, the links are stored as
part of the single-valued gpLink attribute. The ADsPath of each linked GPO is con-
catenated into a string, with each enclosed in square brackets. The ADsPath for each
GPO is followed by ;0 to signify the link is enabled or ;1 to signify the link is disabled.
Here is an example gpLink with two GPOs linked:

```
[LDAP://cn={6491389E-C302-418C-8D9D-
BB24E65E7507},cn=policies,cn=system,DC=adatum,DC=com;0]
[LDAP://cn={6AC1786C-016F-
11D2-945F-00C04fB984F9},cn=policies,cn=system,DC=adatum,DC=com;0]
```

A much better VBScript solution for linking GPOs is described in Recipe 9.14, which
uses the GPMC APIs.

Using PowerShell

The PowerShell sample in this recipe makes use of the SDM Software GPMC cmdlets,
a free collection of Group Policy-related PowerShell cmdlets maintained by Group Policy MVP Darren Mar-Elia. We will discuss this collection of Group Policy cmdlets
extensively in Chapter 9.

See Also

Recipe 9.14 for more information on GPMC and MS KB 248392 (Scripting the Addition
of Group Policy Links)

5.15 Protecting an OU Against Accidental Deletion

Problem

You want to prevent an Organizational Unit object from being accidentally deleted by an administrator who selects the incorrect option in Active Directory Users and Computers.

Solution

Using a graphical user interface (Windows Server 2008 only)

1. Open Active Directory Users and Computers. Click on View and confirm that Advanced Features is selected.
2. Drill down to the current domain. To connect to a different domain, right-click on the top-level node and click Change domain; select the appropriate domain and then drill down to it.
3. Right-click on the OU that you want to modify and click Properties.
4. Click on the Object tab.
5. Place a checkmark next to "Protect object from accidental deletion."
6. Click OK.

Using a command-line interface (all versions)

```
dsacls <OU DN> /d EVERYONE:SDDT
```

Using PowerShell (all versions)

```
Add-QADPermission -identity <OU DN> -Account 'EVERYONE' -Rights 'Delete,DeleteTree'
-ApplyTo 'ThisObjectOnly'
```

Discussion

One of the challenges in delegating permissions within Active Directory is the potential for accidental deletions, particularly when administrators delete an entire Organizational Unit when they had only intended to delete a single object within that OU. Windows Server 2008 exposes a new option in the Active Directory Users and Computers and the Active Directory Sites and Services MMC that will prevent an object from being deleted by means of a "fat-finger" deletion. By default, all new OUs that are created in Windows Server 2008 via the Active Directory Users and Computers MMC will have this protection enabled; however, any pre-existing OUs or OUs created through other methods will not unless you enable it manually using one of the methods shown above. Additionally, built-in Active Directory containers such as the BUILTIN, Computers, and Users containers, as well as the Domain Controllers OU and other built-in containers, do *not* have this protection enabled by default. If you attempt to delete an OU that is protected using this option, even when signed on as a Domain Admin or other similarly elevated account, you will receive an "Access Denied" message until you manually remove the checkbox or manually remove the DENY ACE associated with it.

If you wish to enable this protection for all OUs that were present in your environment prior to a Windows Server 2008 upgrade, you can automate the use of dsacls with a for do loop, as follows:

```
for /f "tokens=*" %i in ('dsquery ou -limit 0') do dsacls %i /d everyone:SDDT
```

You can also automate the process through PowerShell by piping the results of a Get-QADObject query into the Add-QADPermission cmdlet, as follows:

```
get-QADObject -type 'organizationalunit' | add-QADPermission -Account 'EVERYONE' -
Rights 'Delete,DeleteTree' -ApplyTo 'ThisObjectOnly'
```

One advantage to using the command-line or PowerShell methods is that this protection can be applied to container and leaf objects in *all* versions of Windows Server, even though the GUI checkbox is only available in Windows Server 2008.

## CHAPTER 6

Users

6.0 Introduction

User accounts are some of the most frequently used objects in Active Directory; they create the means of authenticating and authorizing someone to access resources on your network. Because Windows 2000 and newer Windows server systems manage users primarily through Active Directory, many key issues that system administrators deal with are covered in this chapter. In particular, Active Directory manages information regarding user passwords; group membership; enabling, disabling, or expiring user accounts; and keeping track of when users have logged on to your network.

The Anatomy of a User

The default location for user objects in a domain is the `cn=Users` container directly off the domain root. You can, of course, create `user` objects in other containers and organizational units in a domain, or move them to these containers after they've been created. Table 6-1 contains a list of some of the interesting attributes that are available on `user` objects. This is by no means a complete list. There are many other informational attributes that we haven't included.

Table 6-1. Attributes of user objects

Attribute	Description
accountExpires	Large integer representing when the user's account is going to expire. See Recipe 6.31 for more information.
cn	Relative distinguished name of user objects. This is commonly the username or the display name of the user.
displayName	Typically the full name of a user. This attribute is used in administrative tools to display a user's descriptive name.
givenName	First name of the user.

Attribute	Description
homeDirectory	Local or UNC path of user's home directory. See Recipe 6.31 for more information.
homeDrive	Defines the drive letter to map the user's home directory to. See Recipe 6.31 for more information.
lastLogon	The last time that a user logged onto a particular DC. This information is not replicated among domain controllers.
lastLogonTimestamp	Approximate last logon timestamp, which is replicated among domain controllers. This attribute was introduced in Windows Server 2003. See Recipe 6.37 for more information.
managedObjects	Multivalued, linked attribute (with managedBy) that contains a list of DNs of objects the user manages.
lockoutTime	Large integer representation of the timestamp for when a user was locked out. See Recipe 6.13 for more information.
memberOf	Backlink listing of DNs of the groups the user is a member of. See Recipe 6.21 for more information.
objectSID	Octet string representing the SID of the user.
primaryGroupID	ID of the primary group for the user. See Recipe 6.23 for more information.
profilePath	UNC path to profile directory. See Recipe 6.31 for more information.
pwdLastSet	Large integer denoting the last time the user's password was set. See Recipe 6.27 for more information.
sAMAccountName	NetBIOS style name of the user. This is limited to 20 characters to support legacy applications.
sIDHistory	Multivalued attribute that contains a list of SIDs that are associated with the user.
scriptPath	Path and filename of logon script. See Recipe 6.33 for more information.
sn	Last name of user.
tokenGroups	List of SIDs for the groups in the domain the user is a member of (both directly and via nesting).

Attribute	Description
unicodePwd	Octet string that contains a hash of a user's password. This attribute cannot be directly queried.
userAccountControl	Account flags that define such things as account status and password change status.
userPrincipalName	Internet-style account name for a user, which the user can use to log on to a computer. In most cases this should map to the user's email address, but this does not always need to be the case.
userWorkstations	List of computers a user can log on to, stored as a Unicode string.
msDS-PSOApplied	New to Windows Server 2008. A backlink that lists the Password Settings Objects that are applied to a user object.
msDS-ResultantPSO	New to Windows Server 2008. A constructed attribute that indicates which PSO is in effect for a user object.
msDS-UserPasswordExpiryTimeComputed	New to Windows Server 2008. A constructed attribute that indicates when a user's password is going to expire.
msDS-FailedInteractiveLogonCount	New to Windows Server 2008. Indicates the number of failed interactive logons for a user account since the Interactive Logon Count feature was enabled.
msDS-FailedInteractiveLogonCountAtLastSuccessfulLogon	New to Windows Server 2008. Indicates the number of failed interactive logons for a user account since the last time the user successfully logged on interactively.
msDS-LastFailedInteractiveLogonTime	New to Windows Server 2008. Indicates the last time and date that the user performed an unsuccessful interactive logon.
msDS-LastSuccessfulInteractiveLogonTime	New to Windows Server 2008. Indicates the last time and date that the user performed a successful interactive logon.
msDS-AuthenticatedAtDC	New to Windows Server 2008. A multivalued attribute listing the RODCs through which a user has successfully authenticated to a full DC.
msDS-RevealedDSAs	New to Windows Server 2008. Backlink indicating which RODCs have cached a user's password secrets.

6.1 Modifying the Default Display Name Used When Creating Users in ADUC

Problem

You want to modify how the default display name gets generated when you create a new user through the ADUC snap-in.

Solution

Using a graphical user interface

1. Open ADSI Edit.
2. In the Configuration Naming Context, browse to DisplaySpecifiers→*<Locale>* where *<Locale>* is the locale for your language (e.g., the U.S. English locale is 409).
3. Double-click on cn=user-Display.
4. Edit the createDialog attribute with the value you want the new default to be (e.g., %*<sn>*, %*<givenName>*).
5. Click OK.

Using a command-line interface

```
> admod -config -rb cn=user-Display,cn=409,cn=DisplaySpecifiers,
 createDialog::"%<sn>, %<givenName>"
```

Using VBScript

```
' This code modifies the default ADUC display name.
' ------ SCRIPT CONFIGURATION ------
strNewDefault = "%<sn>, %<givenName>"
strForestName = "<ForestDNSName>" ' e.g. adatum.com
' ------ END CONFIGURATION ---------

Set objRootDSE = GetObject("LDAP://" & strForestName & "/RootDSE")
Set objDispSpec = GetObject("LDAP://cn=User-Display,cn=409," & _
                            "cn=DisplaySpecifiers," & _
                            objRootDSE.Get("ConfigurationNamingContext"))
objDispSpec.Put "createDialog", strNewDefault
objDispSpec.SetInfo
WScript.Echo "New default for user's display name has been set to: " & _
             strNewDefault
```

Using PowerShell

To modify display specifiers using the Quest AD cmdlets, use the following syntax:

```
$strNewDefault = "%<sn>, %<givenName>"
$objDN =
    "cn=User-Display,cn=409,cn=DisplaySpecifiers,cn=Configuration,<Forest Root DN>"
get-QADObject -identity $objDN | set-QADObject
    -ObjectAttributes @{createDialog=$strNewDefault}
```

To modify display specifiers using `System.DirectoryServices`, use the following:

```
$root = [ADSI]"LDAP://RootDSE"
$strNewDefault = "%<sn>, %<givenName>"
$objDN = "cn=User-Display,cn=409,cn=DisplaySpecifiers,cn=Configuration,"
$obj = [ADSI]("LDAP://" + $objDN + $root.rootDomainNamingContext)
$obj.Put("createDialog", $strNewDefault)
$obj.SetInfo()
```

Discussion

When you create a new user object in the Active Directory Users and Computers snap-in, it will automatically fill in the Full Name field as you type in the First Name, Initials, and Last Name fields. As a convenience, you may want to alter that behavior so that it automatically fills in a different value. To do that, you need to modify the `User-Display` display specifier, which has the following distinguished name:

cn=user-Display,cn=<Locale>,cn=DisplaySpecifiers,cn=Configuration,<ForestRootDN>

<Locale> should be replaced with your language-specific locale and <ForestRootDN> should contain the distinguished name for your forest root domain. You need to modify the `createDialog` attribute, which by default has no value. Replacement variables are presented by %<attribute>, where attribute is an attribute name. For example, if you wanted the default to be "LastName, FirstName", you would use the following value:

%<sn>, %<givenName>

See Also

MS KB 250455 (XADM: How to Change Display Names of Active Directory Users)

6.2 Creating a User

Problem

You want to create a user object.

Solution

Using a graphical user interface

1. Open the ADUC snap-in.
2. If you need to change domains, right-click on "Active Directory Users and Computers" in the left pane, select Connect to Domain, enter the domain name, and click OK.
3. In the left pane, browse to and select the container where the new user should be located and select New→User.
4. Enter the values for the first name, last name, full name, and user logon name fields as appropriate and click Next.
5. Enter and confirm password, set any of the password flags, and click Next.
6. Click Finish.

Using a command-line interface

You can create a user with the built-in DSAdd utility or by using AdMod. Using DSAdd requires the following syntax:

```
> dsadd user "<UserDN>" -upn <UserUPN> -fn "<UserFirstName>"
-ln "<UserLastName>" -display "<UserDisplayName>" -pwd <UserPasswd>
```

To create a user account with AdMod, use the following syntax:

```
> admod -b "<UserDN>" -add objectClass::user
    sAMAccountName::<SAMAccount> unicodepwd::<password> userAccountControl::512
-kerbenc
```

Using VBScript

```
' Taken from ADS_USER_FLAG_ENUM
Const ADS_UF_NORMAL_ACCOUNT = 512

set objParent = GetObject("LDAP://<ParentDN>")
set objUser = objParent.Create("user", "cn=<UserName>") ' e.g. joes
objUser.Put "sAMAccountName", "<UserName>"    ' e.g. joes
objUser.Put "userPrincipalName", "<UserUPN>" ' e.g. joes@adatum.com
objUser.Put "givenName", "<UserFirstName>"    ' e.g. Joe
objUser.Put "sn", "<UserLastName>"            ' e.g. Smith
objUser.Put "displayName", "<UserFirstName> <UserLastName>" ' e.g. Joe Smith
objUser.SetInfo
objUser.SetPassword("<Password>")

objUser.Put "userAccountControl", ADFS_UF_NORMAL_ACCOUNT
objUser.SetInfo
```

Using PowerShell

To create a new Active Directory user with the Quest AD cmdlets, use the following syntax:

```
new-QADUser -name '<User CN>' -parentContainer '<Parent DN>' -UserPassword
'<Password>' -FirstName '<User First Name>' -LastName '<User Last Name>'
-UserPrincipalName '<User UPN>'
```

To create a new Active Directory user with `System.DirectoryServices`, use the following:

```
Set-Variable -name ADS_UF_NORMAL_ACCOUNT -value 512 -option Constant
$objParent = [ADSI] "LDAP://<ParentDN>"
$objUser = $objParent.Create("user", "cn=<User CN>")
$objUser.put("samaccountname", "<UserName>")
$objUser.Put("userPrincipalName", "<UserUPN>")
$objUser.Put("givenName", "<UserFirstName>")
$objUser.Put("sn", "<UserLastName>")
$objUser.Put("displayName", "<UserFirstName> <UserLastName>")
$objUser.SetInfo()
$objUser.SetPassword("<Password>")
$objUser.SetInfo()
$objUser.Put("userAccountControl", $ADS_UF_NORMAL_ACCOUNT)
$objUser.SetInfo()
```

Discussion

The only mandatory attribute that must be set when creating a user is sAMAccountName, which is the legacy account name—and even this attribute is only mandatory in Windows 2000. To make the account immediately available for a user to use, you'll need to make sure the account is enabled, which is accomplished by setting userAccountControl to 512 after you've set a password that follows any password complexity rules in place for the user (order is important in this case). If you only set the sAMAccountName when creating a user object, the account will be disabled by default.

With Windows Server 2003 and newer, you can also create user accounts using the inetOrgPerson class, which is described in Recipe 6.4. inetOrgPerson objects can be used for user authentication and restricting access to resources in much the same way as user objects.

Using a graphical user interface

To set additional attributes, double-click on the user account after it has been created. There are several tabs to choose from that contain attributes that are grouped together based on function (e.g., Profile).

Using a command-line interface

Several additional attributes can be set with the dsadd user command. Run dsadd user /? for the complete list. When creating a user with AdMod, you must specify the `objectClass` and `sAMAccount` attributes as a minimum. You can add additional attributes with the `admod` command by using the *`<attributename>::<value>`* syntax.

Using VBScript

Take a look at Recipe 6.31 for more information on the `userAccountControl` attribute and the various flags that can be set for it.

Using PowerShell

As you can see, the native PowerShell syntax to create a user is very similar to the VBScript syntax to perform the same task. When using the Quest AD cmdlets, the available switches to create a user account are very similar to those available through `dsadd user`, and include the following:

- `-city`
- `-company`
- `-department`
- `-firstname`
- `-lastname`
- `-homephone`
- `-fax`
- `-title`

See Also

Recipe 6.3 for creating users in bulk, Recipe 6.4 for creating an `inetOrgPerson` user, Recipe 6.31, and MSDN: ADS_USER_FLAG_ENUM

6.3 Creating a Large Number of Users

Problem

You want to create a large number of user objects, either for testing purposes or to initially populate Active Directory with your employee, customer, or student user accounts.

Solution

Using a command-line interface

The following example uses a `for do` loop in combination with `dsadd` to create 1,000 users under the `bulk` OU in the *adatum.com* domain with usernames such as *User1,*

User2, User3, etc. The password is set, but no other attributes are configured. You can modify the *dsadd* syntax to populate additional attributes, as well:

```
> for /F %i in (1,1,1000) do dsadd user cn=User%i,ou=bulk,dc=adatum,dc=com
-pwd User%i
```

You can also use the *ldifde* utility to perform a bulk import of unique usernames. Create an *.LDF* file using the following syntax (separate multiple entries with a blank line in between):

```
dn: CN=Joe Richards, OU=Engineering, DC=adatum, DC=com
changetype: add
cn: Joe Richards
objectClass: user
samAccountName: jrichards
```

Once you've created the LDIF file containing your user records, import the file using the following command:

```
> ldifde -i -f <filename.ldf> -s <servername>
```

You may notice that the LDIF file does not specify the user's password; this attribute must be modified after the user object has been created.

You can also use admod to automate this task as follows. The code below will create 4,000 users named "TestUser_1", "TestUser_2", "TestUser_3":

```
> admod -sc adau:4000;MyPassword1!;cn=testuser,ou=testou,dc=adatum,dc=com
```

Using VBScript

```
' This code creates a large number of users with incremented user names
' e.g. User1, User2, User3, ....
' ------ SCRIPT CONFIGURATION ------

intNumUsers = 1000                 ' Number of users to create
strParentDN = "<ParentDN>" ' e.g. ou=bulk,dc=emea,dc=adatum,dc=com
' ------ END CONFIGURATION --------

' Taken from ADS_USER_FLAG_ENUM
Const ADS_UF_NORMAL_ACCOUNT = 512

set objParent = GetObject("LDAP://" & strParentDN)
for i = 1 to intNumUsers
   strUser = "User" & i
   Set objUser = objParent.Create("user", "cn=" & strUser)
   objUser.Put "sAMAccountName", strUser
   objUser.SetPassword(strUser)
   objUser.SetInfo
   objUser.Put "userAccountControl", ADS_UF_NORMAL_ACCOUNT
   objUser.SetInfo
   WScript.Echo "Created " & strUser
next
WScript.Echo ""
WScript.Echo "Created " & intNumUsers & " users"
```

Using PowerShell

```
$parentDN = "<ParentDN>"
$strPass = "MyPassword1"
For ($i = 1; $i -le 1000; $i++) {
  $strUserName = "User" + $i
  New-QADUser -name $strUserName -parentContainer $parentDN -UserPassword $strPass
}
```

Discussion

Using ADSI, PowerShell, and the command-line utilities, you can create hundreds and even thousands of users far more easily and quickly than you would be able to do through a graphical user interface. You can also modify the examples to pull real data from a data source, such as an employee database.

Using a command-line interface

The AdMod syntax makes use of the -adau shortcut, which will add *X* number of users with *Y* as their starting password, so that "-adau:4000;MyPassword1" will create 4,000 users with a starting password of "MyPassword1". If the starting password is not specified, a unique random complex password will be generated for each user.

See Also

Recipe 6.2 for creating a user and MS KB 263911 (How to Set a User's Password using LDIFDE)

6.4 Creating an inetOrgPerson User

Problem

You want to create an inetOrgPerson object, which is the standard LDAP object class to represent users.

Solution

Using a graphical user interface

1. Open the ADUC snap-in.
2. If you need to change domains, right-click on "Active Directory Users and Computers" in the left pane, select Connect to Domain, enter the domain name, and click OK.
3. In the left pane, browse to the parent container of the new user, right-click on it, and select New→InetOrgPerson.

4. Enter first name, last name, and user logon name fields as appropriate and click Next.

5. Enter and confirm the password, set any of the password flags, and click Next.

6. Click Finish.

Using a command-line interface

DSAdd does not support creating `inetOrgPerson` objects, so use *ldifde* or *AdMod* instead. First, you need to create an LDIF file called *create_inetorgperson.ldf* with the following contents:

```
dn: <UserDN>
changetype: add
objectclass:
inetorgperson
sAMAccountName: <UserName>

dn: <UserDN>
changetype: modify
add: userAccountControl
userAccountControl: 512
```

Be sure to replace *<UserDN>* with the distinguished name of the user you want to add and *<UserName>* with the user's username. Then run the following command:

```
> ldifde -i -f create_inetorgperson.ldf
```

You can also use the admod utility to create an `inetOrgPerson` object, as follows:

```
> admod -b "cn=inetOrgPerson,cn=Users,dc=adatum,dc=com"
    objectclass::inetOrgPerson sAMAccountName::inetOrgPerson -add
```

Using VBScript

```
' This code creates an inetOrgPerson object

set objParent = GetObject("LDAP://<ParentDN>")
set objUser = objParent.Create("inetorgperson", "cn=<UserName>")

' Taken from ADS_USER_FLAG_ENUM
Const ADS_UF_NORMAL_ACCOUNT = 512

objUser.Put "sAMAccountName", "<UserName>"
objUser.Put "userPrincipalName", "<UserUPN>"
objUser.Put "givenName", "<UserFirstName>"
objUser.Put "sn", "<UserLastName>"
objUser.Put "displayName", "<UserFirstName> <UserLastName>"
objUser.SetInfo
objUser.SetPassword("<Password>")
objUser.SetInfo
objUser.Put "userAccountControl", ADS_UF_NORMAL_ACCOUNT
objUser.SetInfo
```

Using PowerShell

To create an `inetOrgPerson` object using the Quest AD cmdlets, use the following syntax:

```
new-QADObject -ParentContainer "ou=Users,dc=adatum,dc=com" -type 'inetOrgPerson' -
name '<UserName>' -ObjectAttributes
@{samAccountName='<UserName>';userPrincipalName='<UserUPN>'}
```

To create an object using `System.DirectoryServices`, use the following syntax:

```
$parentOU = [System.DirectoryServices.DirectoryEntry]
"LDAP://ou=Users,dc=adatum,dc=com"
$newInet = $parentOU.Create("inetOrgPerson","cn=test1")
$newInet.put("samaccountName","test1")
$newInet.SetInfo()
$newInet.Invoke("setpassword", "MyPassword1")
$newInet.SetInfo()
$newInet.Put("userAccountControl", 512)
$newInet.SetInfo()
```

Discussion

The `inetOrgPerson` object class was defined in RFC 2798. It is the closest thing in the LDAP world to a standard representation of a user, and most LDAP vendors support the `inetOrgPerson` class. Unfortunately, Microsoft did not support `inetOrgPerson` with the initial release of Active Directory. Even though they provided an add-on later to extend the schema to support it, the damage had been done. Most Active Directory implementations were already using the **user** object class and were unlikely to convert, which required vendors to build in support for the **user** class.

Starting with Windows Server 2003 Active Directory, `inetOrgPerson` is supported natively. You can create `inetOrgPerson` objects for your users, who can use them to authenticate just like accounts of the **user** object class. If you haven't deployed Active Directory yet and you plan on integrating a lot of third-party LDAP-based applications that rely on `inetOrgPerson`, you may want to consider using it instead of the **user** class. You won't be losing any information or functionality because the `inetOrgPerson` class inherits directly from the **user** class. For this reason, the `inetOrgPerson` class has even more attributes than the Microsoft **user** class.

The one potential downside is that some of the Microsoft tools, such as the DS utilities, do not support modifying `inetOrgPerson` objects. (You can, however, use AdMod to perform these modifications.)

See Also

Recipe 6.2 for creating a user, MS KB 314649, and RFC 2798 (Definition of the InetOrgPerson LDAP Object Class)

6.5 Converting a user Object to an inetOrgPerson Object (or Vice Versa)

Problem

You want to convert one or more user objects to inetOrgPerson objects to improve interoperability in a heterogeneous environment.

Using a graphical user interface

 This requires at least Windows Server 2003 forest functional level.

1. Open ADSI Edit.
2. If an entry for the naming context you want to browse is not already displayed, do the following:
   a. Right-click on ADSI Edit in the right pane and click "Connect to…".
   b. Fill in the information for the domain naming context, container, or OU that contains the object you want to modify. Click on the Advanced button if you need to enter alternate credentials.
3. In the left pane, browse to the naming context, container, or OU containing the user object that you want to view. Once you've found the object, right-click on it and select Properties.
4. Scroll to objectClass and select Edit.
5. Under Value to add, enter inetOrgPerson and click Add.
6. Click OK twice to save your changes.

Using a command-line interface

To convert a user object to an inetOrgPerson object, use the following syntax:

```
> admod -b "<UserDN>" objectClass:+:inetOrgPerson
```

 To revert the object back to a regular user, replace + with - in the previous syntax.

Using VBScript

```
' This code will convert a user object to inetOrgPerson.
' ------ SCRIPT CONFIGURATION ------
strUserDN = "<UserDN>" ' e.g. cn=jsmith,cn=Users,dc=adatum,dc=com
strClass = "inetOrgPerson"
' ------ END CONFIGURATION --------

set objUser = GetObject("LDAP://" & strUserDN)
objUsr.PutEx ADS_PROPERTY_APPEND,"objectClass",Array(strClass)
objUsr.SetInfo
```

Using PowerShell

```
set-variable -name $ADS_PROPERTY_APPEND -value 3 -option constant
$strClass = "inetOrgPerson"
$objUser = "LDAP://<UserDN>"
$objUser.PutEx($ADS_PROPERTY_APPEND, "objectClass", @($strClass))
$objUser.SetInfo()
```

Discussion

In a heterogeneous environment, you may wish to convert one or more Active Directory user objects to inetOrgPerson objects. Since the inetOrgPerson class inherits from the user class, making this modification is a simple matter of adding the "inetOrgPerson" value to an object's objectClass attribute. It's important to note that this is the only instance in which you can modify structural classes in this manner; you can't simply modify a user object with whatever class you wish, even if that class inherits from the user class.

You can easily modify the command-line, VBScript, and PowerShell recipes to convert all user accounts in your domain (or just in a particular OU) to inetOrgPerson objects. For example, the following combination of adfind and admod will search for all user accounts in the "Marketing" OU and convert each one to an inetOrgPerson object: (the -unsafe switch is necessary if you need to modify more than 10 objects at a time; you can also use the -safety X switch and specify the actual number of objects that you expect to modify for X):

```
adfind -default -rb "OU=Marketing" -f
"(&(objectcategory=person)(objectclass=User))" | admod
objectcategory:+:inetOrgPerson -unsafe
```

See Also

MS KB 307998 (Changing the Naming Attribute of the inetOrgPerson Class)

6.6 Modifying an Attribute for Several Users at Once

Problem

You want to modify an attribute for several users at once.

Solution

Using a graphical user interface

 This capability first became available in the Windows Server 2003 version of the ADUC snap-in.

1. Open the ADUC snap-in.
2. If you need to change domains, right-click on "Active Directory Users and Computers" in the left pane, select Connect to Domain, enter the domain name, and click OK.
3. In the left pane, browse to the parent container of the objects you want to modify.
4. In the right pane, highlight each object you want to modify, right-click, and select Properties.
5. Check the box beside the attribute(s) you want to modify and edit the fields for the attributes.
6. Click OK.

Using a command-line interface

The following command sets the home directory of all users under a parent container (*<ParentDN>*) to be on a particular file server (*<FileServer>*). The folder name is automatically replaced with the **sAMAccountName** for the user by using the **$username$** syntax:

```
> dsquery user "<ParentDN>" -limit 0 -scope onelevel | dsmod user -hmdir
"\\<FileServerName>\$username$"
```

Using VBScript

```
' This code sets the home drive of all users under a container
' to be on a file server where the share name is the same as the user's
' sAMAccountName.
set objParent = GetObject("LDAP://<ParentDN>")
objParent.Filter = Array("user")
for each objUser in objParent
    strSAM = objUser.Get("sAMAccountName")
    Wscript.Echo "
Modifying " & strSAM
```

```
         objUser.HomeDirectory = "\\<FileServerName>\" & _
                                  strSAM
      objUser.SetInfo
   next
```

Using PowerShell

```
$strfileServer = "\\Server1\"
$objOU = [ADSI] "LDAP://<OU DN>"
$objOU.psbase.Children |% {
    $uac = [int](($_.userAccountControl).ToString())
    if (($_.objectClass -eq "user") -and (($uac -band 2) -eq 0))
    {
        $_.put("homeDirectory", $strFileServer + $_.sAMAccountName)
        $_.SetInfo()
    }
}
```

Discussion

It is often necessary to update several users at once due to an organizational, geographic, or file server change. In each solution, we showed how to modify all users within a parent container, but you may need to use different criteria for locating the users.

Within ADUC, it may appear that you are limited to modifying multiple users that belong to the same container. However, with the Windows Server 2003 version of ADUC you can create a Saved Query that returns users based on any criteria you specify. You can then highlight those users and modify them as described in the GUI solution.

With the CLI solution, you can modify the dsquery user command to search on whatever criteria you want. The same applies in the VBScript solution, but you'll need to use an ADO query instead of the Filter method if you want to do anything more complex.

See Also

Recipe 4.8 for more information on searching with ADO

6.7 Deleting a User

Problem

You want to delete a user object.

Solution

Using a graphical user interface

1. Open Active Directory Users and Computers.

---

2. In the left pane, browse to the parent container or OU of the user that you want to delete. Alternatively, right-click on the domain and click Find..., then enter the name of the user and click Find Now.

3. Right-click on the user object and select Delete.

4. Click Yes to confirm.

You can also delete a user through LDP, as follows:

1. Open LDP from the Windows Support Tools.

2. From the menu, select Connection→Connect.

3. For Server, enter the name of a domain controller (or leave blank for a serverless bind).

4. For Port, enter 389.

5. Click OK.

6. From the menu, select Connection→Bind.

7. Enter credentials of a user.

8. Click OK.

9. Click Browse → Delete. For DN, enter the Distinguished Name of the user that you want to delete.

10. Click Run to delete the user.

Using a command-line interface

You can delete a user using the built-in *dsrm* utility, as well as AdMod. For *dsrm*, use the following syntax:

```
> dsrm "<UserDN>"
```

For AdMod, enter the following:

```
> admod -b "<UserDN>" -del
```

Using VBScript

```
strUserDN = "<UserDN>"
set objUser = GetObject("LDAP://" & strUserDN)
objUser.DeleteObject(0)
```

Using PowerShell

To delete an object using the Quest AD cmdlets, use the following syntax:

```
remove-QADObject -identity <User DN>
```

To delete an object using the .NET methods, use the following:

```
$usr = [ADSI] "LDAP://<User DN>"
$usr.DeleteObject(0)
```

Discussion

This recipe covers deleting individual users. If you want to delete a container or OU and all the objects in it, take a look at Recipe 4.25.

Using VBScript

Using the `DeleteObject` method is straightforward. Passing 0 as a parameter is required, but does not have any significance at present.

An alternate and perhaps safer way to delete objects is to use the `IADsContainer::Delete` method. To use this method, you must first bind to the parent container of the object. You can then call `Delete` by passing the object class and RDN of the object you want to delete. Here is an example for deleting a **user** object:

```
set objCont = GetObject("LDAP://ou=Sales,dc=adatum,dc=com")
objCont.Delete "user", "cn=rallen"
```

`Delete` is safer than `DeleteObject` because you have to be more explicit about what you are deleting. With `DeleteObject` you only need to specify a distinguished name and `DeleteObject` will delete it. If you happen to mistype the DN or if the user input to a web page that uses this method is mistyped, the result could be disastrous.

See Also

Recipe 4.25 for deleting a container, MS KB 258310 (Viewing Deleted Objects in Active Directory), MSDN: IADsContainer::Delete, and MSDN: IADsDeleteOps:: DeletesObject

6.8 Setting a User's Profile Attributes

Problem

You want to set one or more of the user profile attributes.

Solution

Using a graphical user interface

1. Open the ADUC snap-in.
2. In the left pane, right-click on the domain and select Find.
3. Select the appropriate domain beside In.
4. Beside Name, type the name of the user and click Find Now.
5. In the Search Results window, double-click on the user.
6. Click the Profile tab.

7. Modify the various profile settings as necessary.

8. Click OK.

Using a command-line interface

You can update a user's profile attributes using either DSMod or AdMod. DSMod uses the following syntax:

```
> dsmod user "<UserDN>" -loscr <ScriptPath> -profile <ProfilePath>
-hmdir <HomeDir> -hmdrv <DriveLetter>
```

AdMod uses the following syntax:

```
> admod -b "<UserDN>" <attribute>::<NewValue>
```

Using VBScript

```
' This code sets the various profile related attributes for a user.
strUserDN = "<UserDN>" ' e.g. cn=jsmith,cn=Users,dc=adatum,dc=com
set objUser = GetObject("LDAP://" & strUserDN)
objUser.Put "
homeDirectory", "\\fileserver\" & objUser.Get("sAMAccountName")
objUser.Put "
homeDrive", "z:"
objUser.Put "profilePath", "\\fileserver\" & _
             objUser.Get("sAMAccountName") & "\profile"
objUser.Put "scriptPath", "login.vbs"
objUser.SetInfo
Wscript.Echo "Profile info for " & objUser.Get("sAMAccountName") & " updated"
```

Using PowerShell

To modify user profile attributes using the Quest AD cmdlets, use the following syntax:

```
get-QADUser -identity "<User DN>" | set-QADUser -HomeDirectory '\\server1\jsmith'
-HomeDrive 'Z:' -ProfilePath '\\server1\profiles\jsmith' -scriptpath
'\\dc1\netlogon\script.vbs'
```

To modify these attributes using System.DirectoryServices, use the following syntax:

```
([ADSI]"LDAP://<User DN>") |% {
    $_.put("homeDirectory", "\\server1\" + $_.sAMAccountName)
    $_.put("homeDrive", "Z:")
    $_.put("profilePath", "\\server1\profiles\" + $_.sAMAccountName)
    $_.put("scriptPath", "\\dc1\netlogon\script.vbs")
    $_.SetInfo()
}
```

Discussion

The four attributes that make up a user's profile settings include:

homeDirectory
    UNC path to home directory

homeDrive
> Drive letter (e.g., Z:) to map home directory

profilePath
> UNC path to profile directory

scriptPath
> Path to logon script

When you set the homeDirectory attribute, the folder being referenced needs to already exist. For an example on creating shares for users, see MS KB 234746.

See Also

MS KB 234746 (How to Create User Shares for All Users in a Domain with ADSI), MS KB 271657 (Scripted Home Directory Paths Require That Folders Exist), and MS KB 320043 (How to Assign a Home Directory to a User)

6.9 Moving a User

Problem

You want to move a user object to a different container or OU.

Solution

Using a graphical user interface

1. Open the ADUC snap-in.
2. If you need to change domains, right-click on "Active Directory Users and Computers" in the left pane, select Connect to Domain, enter the domain name, and click OK.
3. In the left pane, right-click on the domain and select Find.
4. Type the name of the user and click Find Now.
5. In the Search Results window, right-click on the user and select Move.
6. Browse to and select the new parent container or OU.
7. Click OK.

 In Windows Server 2003 and newer, you can also drag and drop objects from one container or OU into another.

Using a command-line interface

You can move an object using either the built-in DSMove utility or AdMod. DSMove takes the following syntax:

```
> dsmove "<UserDN>" -newparent "<NewParentDN>"
```

To move an object using AdMod, do the following:

```
> admod -b "<Current User DN>" -move "<New Parent DN>"
```

Using VBScript

```
' This code moves a user from one container to another.
' ------ SCRIPT CONFIGURATION ------
strUserDN = "<UserDN>"       ' e.g. cn=rallen,cn=users,dc=adatum,dc=com
strOUDN = "<NewParentDN>" ' e.g. ou=Sales,dc=adatum,dc=com
' ------ END CONFIGURATION ---------
Set objUser = GetObject("LDAP://" & strUserDN)
Set objOU = GetObject("LDAP://" & strOUDN)
objOU.MoveHere objUser.ADsPath, objUser.Name
```

Using PowerShell

To move a user with the Quest AD cmdlets, use the following syntax:

```
move-QADObject -Identity <UserDN> -NewParentContainer <New OU DN>
```

To move a user with the `System.DirectoryServices` methods, use the following:

```
$objUser = [ADSI] "LDAP://<UserDN>"
$objNewOU = [ADSI] "LDAP://<New Parent OU DN>"
$objUser.psbase.MoveTo($objNewOU)
```

Discussion

Moving a `user` object between OUs in the same domain has no direct impact on the actual user in terms of any security or distribution groups that the user is a member of. The things to be cautious of when moving the user to a new OU are different security settings, different GPOs, and the possibility of breaking applications that have the user's DN hardcoded into them.

See Also

Recipe 4.20 for moving objects between OUs

6.10 Redirecting Users to an Alternative OU

This solution requires at least Windows Server 2003 domain functional level.

Problem

You want to redirect all new users from the default OU (i.e., `cn=Users`) into the destination OU that you specify.

Using a graphical user interface

1. Open LDP.
2. From the menu, select Connection→Connect.
3. For Server, enter the name of a domain controller (or leave blank to do a serverless bind).
4. For Port, enter 389.
5. Click OK.
6. From the menu, select Connection→Bind.
7. Enter credentials of a domain user.
8. Click OK.
9. From the menu, select Browse→Modify.
10. For DN, enter the distinguished name of the `domainDNS` object of the domain you want to modify.
11. For Attribute, enter `wellKnownObjects`.
12. For Values, enter the following:

    ```
    B:32:A9D1CA15768811D1ADED00C04FD8D5CD:CN=Users,<DomainDN>
    ```

    where `<DomainDN>` is the same as the DN you enter for the DN field.

13. Select Delete for the Operation and click the Enter button.
14. Go back to the Values field and enter the following:

    ```
    B:32:A9D1CA15768811D1ADED00C04FD8D5CD:<NewUsersParent>,<DomainDN>
    ```

    where `<NewUsersParent>` is the new parent container for new computer objects (e.g., `"ou=Adatum Users"`).

15. Select Add for the Operation and click the Enter button.
16. Click the Run button.
17. The result of the operations will be displayed in the right pane of the main LDP window.

Using the command-line interface

To redirect the default OU that new users will be created into, use the following syntax:

```
> redirusr "<DestinationDN>"
```

Discussion

Most modern methods for creating user accounts, including the ADUC MMC snap-in, AdFind, and DSAdd, allow you to specify which OU a new user should be created in. However, some utilities such as `net user` or the WinNT ADSI provider still rely on a legacy API that will create a user only in its default location until it is manually moved to another OU by an administrator. The default location in Windows Server 2003 is the `cn=Users` container; this can create issues applying Group Policy to new user objects since the `Users` container cannot have a GPO linked to it. To ensure that all newly created users receive the necessary Group Policy settings as soon as they are created, use the *redirusr.exe* utility to redirect all new users that are not otherwise placed into a designated OU into the destination OU that you specify. You only need to run this utility once per domain, and the destination OU needs to exist before you run the utility.

See Also

MS KB 324949 (Redirecting the Users and Computers Containers in Windows Server 2003)

6.11 Renaming a User

Problem

You want to rename a user.

Solution

Using a graphical user interface

1. Open the ADUC snap-in.
2. In the left pane, right-click on the domain and select Find.
3. Type the name of the user and click Find Now.
4. In the Search Results window, right-click on the user and select Rename.
5. You can modify the Full Name, Last Name, First Name, Display Name, User Principal Name (logon name), and SAM Account Name (pre-Windows 2000).
6. Click OK after you are done.

Using a command-line interface

The following command will rename the RDN of the user:

```
> dsmove "<UserDN>" -newname "<NewUserName>"
```

You can modify the UPN (-upn), First Name (-fn), Last Name (-ln), and Display Name (-display) using the dsmod user command. For example, the following command would change the user's UPN and last name:

```
> dsmod user "<UserDN>" -upn "<NewUserUPN>" -ln "<NewUserLastName>"
```

You can also rename a user by using AdMod with the following syntax:

```
> admod -b "<UserDN>" -rename "<NewUserName>"
```

Using VBScript

```
' This code renames the RDN of a user and the sAMAccountName attribute.
' ------ SCRIPT CONFIGURATION ------
strParentDN = "<ParentDN>" ' e.g. cn=Users,dc=adatum,dc=com
strUserOldName = "<OldUserName>" ' e.g. jsmith
strUserNewName = "<NewUserName>" ' e.g. jim
' ------ END CONFIGURATION --------

set objCont = GetObject("LDAP://" & strParentDN)
objCont.MoveHere "LDAP://cn=" & strUserOldName & "," & strParentDN, _
                 "cn=" & strUserNewName
set objUser = GetObject("LDAP://cn=" & strUserNewName & "," & strParentDN)
objUser.Put "sAMAccountName", strUserNewName
objUser.SetInfo
WScript.Echo "Rename successful"
```

Using PowerShell

To rename a user object using the Quest cmdlets, use the following:

```
Get-QADUser -Identity <UserDN>
  | Rename-QADObject -NewName '<NewCN>'
```

To rename a user object through System.DirectoryServices, use the following syntax:

```
$objUser = [ADSI] "LDAP://<UserDN>"
$strNewName = "<New User CN>"
$objUser.psbase.Rename($strNewName)
```

Discussion

Renaming a user object can have a couple different meanings in Active Directory. In the generic object sense, renaming an object consists of changing the RDN for the object to something else, as when cn=jsmith becomes cn=joe. Typically, though, you need to rename more than that with users. For example, let's say you had a username naming convention of FirstInitialLastName so Joe Smith's username would be jsmith. Let's pretend that Joe decides one day that Smith is way too common and he wants to be unique by changing his last name to Einstein. Now his username should be jeinstein. The following attributes would need to change to complete a rename of his object:

- His RDN should change from cn=jsmith to cn=jeinstein.
- His sAMAccountName should change to jeinstein.
- His userPrincipalName (UPN) should change to jeinstein@adatum.com.
- His mail (email address) attribute should change to jeinstein@adatum.com.
- His sn (last name) attribute should change to Einstein.

While this example may be contrived, it shows that renaming Joe Smith to Joe Einstein can take up to five attribute changes in Active Directory, or more if you include updates to proxy addresses and other attributes that are typically tied to the user's name. It is also important to note that if you change any of the first three in the bulleted list (RDN, UPN, or SAM Account Name), you should have the user log off and log back on after the changes have replicated. Since most applications and services rely on user GUID or SID, which doesn't change during a user rename, the person should not be affected, but you want to have him log off and back on anyway, just in case.

See Also

Recipe 4.23 for renaming objects

6.12 Copying a User

Problem

You want to copy an existing user account, which may be serving as a template, to create a new account.

Solution

Using a graphical user interface

1. Open the ADUC snap-in.
2. In the left pane, browse to the parent container of the template user object.
3. In the right pane, right-click on the user and select Copy.
4. Enter the name information for the new user and click Next.
5. Enter a password, check any options you want enabled, and click Next.
6. Click Finish.

Using VBScript

```
' This code copies the attributes in the Attrs array from an
' existing object to a new one.
' ------ SCRIPT CONFIGURATION ------
arrAttrs = Array("department","co","title","l", "c", "st")
strParentDN = "<ParentContainer>" ' e.g. cn=Users,dc=adatum,dc=com
```

```
strTemplateUser = "<TemplateUserName>" ' e.g. template-user-sales
strNewUser = "<NewUserName>" ' e.g. jdoe
strPassword = "<Password>"
' ------ END CONFIGURATION ---------

Const ADS_UF_NORMAL_ACCOUNT = 512 ' from ADS_USER_FLAG_ENUM

Set objTemplate = GetObject("LDAP://cn=" & strTemplateUser & _
                           "," & strParentDN)
Set objParent = GetObject("LDAP://" & strParentDN)
Set objUser = objParent.Create("user", "cn=" & strNewUser)

objUser.Put "sAMAccountName", strNewUser

for each strAttr in arrAttrs
    objUser.Put strAttr, objTemplate.Get(strAttr)
next

objUser.SetInfo
objUser.SetPassword(strPassword)
objUser.SetInfo

objUser.Put "userAccountControl", ADS_UF_NORMAL_ACCOUNT
objUser.AccountDisabled = FALSE
objUser.SetInfo

WScript.Echo "Successfully created user"
```

Using PowerShell

```
$objTemplateUser = [ADSI] "LDAP://<TemplateUserDN>"
$strNewUsername = "<NewUsername>"
$strNewUserCN = "cn=<New User CN>"
$objParentDN = [ADSI] "LDAP://<Parent DN for New User>"
$arrAttrs = "department","co","title","l", "c", "st"
$objNewUser = $objParentDN.Create("user", $strNewUserCN)
$objNewUser.put("samaccountname",$strNewUserName)
$objNewUser.SetInfo()
$objNewUser.psbase.Invoke("setPassword", "MyPassword1")
$objNewUser.SetInfo()
$objNewUser.put("userAccountControl", 512)
$objNewUser.SetInfo()
foreach ($attr in $arrAttrs) {
>> $newAttr = $objTemplateUser.$attr
>> $objNewUser.put("" + $attr, "" + $newAttr)
}
$objNewUser.SetInfo()
```

Discussion

Copying a user consists of copying the attributes that are common among a certain user base, which can include department, address, and perhaps even organizational information. ADUC actually uses attributes that are marked in the schema as "Copied when duplicating a user" to determine which attributes to copy. The VBScript solution just used a hardcoded set of attributes. If you are interested in finding the attributes that are configured in the schema to get copied, see Recipe 10.12.

Using a graphical user interface

To copy a user in ADUC, you have to browse to the user object. If you locate the user by using Find instead, the Copy option is not available when right-clicking a user in the search results window.

See Also

Recipe 10.12 for finding the attributes that should be copied when duplicating a user

6.13 Finding Locked-Out Users

Problem

You want to find users whose accounts are locked out.

Solution

Using a command-line interface

The following command finds all locked-out users in the domain of the specified domain controller:

```
> unlock <DomainControllerName> * -view
```

Using PowerShell

The following Quest AD cmdlet would find all locked-out users in a specified domain:

```
Get-QADuser -locked
```

Discussion

Despite the deceptively simple command just shown, finding the accounts that are currently locked out is a surprisingly complicated task. You would imagine that you could run a query using DSQuery or AdFind (similar to the one to find disabled users in Recipe 6.20), but unfortunately, it is not that easy.

The lockoutTime attribute is populated with a timestamp when a user is locked. One way to find locked-out users would be to find all users that have something populated in lockoutTime (i.e., lockoutTime=*). That query would definitely find all the currently locked users, but it would also find all the users that subsequently became unlocked and have yet to log in since being unlocked; the lockoutTime attribute doesn't get reset until the next time the user logs on successfully. This is where the complexity comes into play.

To determine the users that are currently locked out, you have to query the attribute `lockoutDuration` stored on the domain object (e.g., `dc=adatum,dc=com`). This attribute defines the number of minutes that an account will stay locked before becoming automatically unlocked. You need to take this value and subtract it from the current time to derive a timestamp that would be the outer marker for which users could still be locked. You can then compare this timestamp with the `lockoutTime` attribute of the `user` object. The search filter to find all locked users once you've determined the locked timestamp would look something like this:

```
(&(objectcategory=Person)(objectclass=user)(lockoutTime>DerivedTimestamp))
```

For any users that have a `lockoutTime` that is less than the derived timestamp, their account has already been automatically unlocked per the `lockoutDuration` setting.

None of the current standard GUI or CLI tools incorporates this kind of logic, but fortunately joe Richards wrote the *unlock.exe* utility, which does. And as its name implies, you can also unlock locked accounts with it. Thanks, joe!

See Also

MS KB 813500 (Support WebCast: Microsoft Windows 2000 Server and Windows Server 2003: Password and Account Lockout Features)

6.14 Unlocking a User

Problem

You want to unlock a locked-out user.

Solution

Using a graphical user interface

1. Open the ADUC snap-in.
2. In the left pane, right-click on the domain and select Find.
3. Select the appropriate domain beside In.
4. Type the name of the user beside Name and click Find Now.
5. In the Search Results window, right-click on the user and select Unlock.
6. Click OK.

Using a command-line interface

To unlock all locked user accounts in your domain, use *unlock.exe* with the following syntax:

```
> unlock . *
```

To unlock a specific user object, replace * with the user's sAMAccountName or distinguished name, as follows:

```
> unlock . joe.smith
```

Using VBScript

```
' This code unlocks a locked user.
' ------ SCRIPT CONFIGURATION ------
strUsername = "<UserName>"             ' e.g. jsmith
strDomain = "<NetBiosDomainName>" ' e.g. ADATUM
' ------ END CONFIGURATION --------

set objUser = GetObject("WinNT://" & strDomain & "/" & strUsername)
if objUser.IsAccountLocked = TRUE then
   objUser.IsAccountLocked = FALSE
   objUser.SetInfo
   WScript.Echo "Account unlocked"
else
   WScript.Echo "Account not locked"
end if
```

Using PowerShell

```
Unlock-QADUser -Identity <UserDN>
```

Discussion

If you've enabled account lockouts for an Active Directory domain (see Recipe 6.13), users will inevitably get locked out. A user can get locked out for a number of reasons, but generally it is because a user mistypes her password a number of times, changes her password and does not log off and log on again, or has services or scheduled tasks running under the security context of her individual user account rather than a security account.

You can use ADSI's IADsUser::IsAccountLocked method to determine if a user is locked out. You can set IsAccountLocked to FALSE to unlock a user. You can also query the msDS-User-Account-Control-Computed attribute of an object.

See Also

Recipe 6.13 for finding locked out users, Recipe 6.15 for viewing the account lockout policy, MS KB 250873 (Programmatically Changing the Lockout Flag in Windows 2000), and MSDN: Account Lockout

6.15 Troubleshooting Account Lockout Problems

Problem

A user is having account lockout problems and you need to determine from where and how the account is getting locked out.

Solution

Using a graphical user interface

LockoutStatus is a new program available for WindowsActive Directory that can help identify which domain controller's users are getting locked out. It works by querying the lockout status of a user against all domain controllers in the user's domain.

To determine the lockout status of a user:

1. Launch LockoutStatus and select File→Select Target from the menu.
2. Enter the target username and the domain of the user.
3. Click OK.

At this point, each domain controller in the domain will be queried and the results will be displayed.

Discussion

The *lockoutstatus.exe* tool is just one of many that are available in the "Account Lockout and Management" toolset provided by Microsoft. These new lockout tools are intended to help administrators with account lockout problems that were very difficult to troubleshoot given the tools available under Windows 2000. Along with the tool mentioned in the section called "Solution", here are a few others that are included in the set:

ALockout.dll
> A script that uses this DLL, called *EnableKerbLog.vbs* (included with the toolset), can be used to enable logging of application authentication. This can help identify applications that are using bad credentials and causing account lockouts.

ALoInfo.exe
> Displays services and shares that are using a particular account name. It can also print all the users and their password age.

NLParse.exe
> A filter tool for the *netlogon.log* files. You can use it to extract just the lines that relate to account lockout information.

EventCombMT
> A utility to parse Event Logs from multiple servers, either to collect all entries together or to search for individual events across multiple computers. This is

extremely useful when troubleshooting user account lockouts, for example, by determining which computer is causing the account lockout.

All of the new Account Lockout tools can be downloaded from *http://microsoft.com/ downloads/details.aspx?familyid=7AF2E69C-91F3-4E63-8629-B999ADDE0B9E&dis playlang=en*.

See Also

MS KB 813500 (Support WebCast: Microsoft Windows 2000 Server and Windows Server 2003: Password and Account Lockout Features)

6.16 Viewing the Domain-Wide Account Lockout and Password Policies

Problem

You want to view the domain-wide account lockout and password policies for a domain.

Solution

Using a graphical user interface

1. Open the Domain Security Policy snap-in.
2. In the left menu, expand Default Domain Policy→Computer Configuration→Windows Settings→Security Settings→Account Policies.
3. Click on Password Policy or Account Lockout Policy and double-click the property you want to set or view in the right frame.

Using a command-line interface

To view the account lockout and password properties of your domain, use the following AdFind query:

```
> adfind -default -s base Lockoutduration lockoutthreshold lockoutobservationwindow
maxpwdage minpwdage minpwdlength pwdhistorylength pwdproperties
```

Using VBScript

```
' This code displays the current settings for the password
' and account lockout policies.
' ------ SCRIPT CONFIGURATION ------
strDomain = "<DomainDN>" ' e.g. adatum.com
' ------ END CONFIGURATION --------

set objRootDSE = GetObject("LDAP://" & strDomain & "/RootDSE")
```

```
set objDomain = GetObject("LDAP://" & _
objRootDSE.Get("defaultNamingContext") )

' Hash containing the domain password and lockout policy attributes
' as keys and the units (e.g. minutes) as the values
set objDomAttrHash = CreateObject("Scripting.Dictionary")
objDomAttrHash.Add "lockoutDuration", "minutes"
objDomAttrHash.Add "lockoutThreshold", "attempts"
objDomAttrHash.Add "lockoutObservationWindow", "minutes"
objDomAttrHash.Add "maxPwdAge", "minutes"
objDomAttrHash.Add "minPwdAge", "minutes"
objDomAttrHash.Add "minPwdLength", "characters"
objDomAttrHash.Add "pwdHistoryLength", "remembered"
objDomAttrHash.Add "pwdProperties", " "

' Iterate over each attribute and print it .
for each strAttr in objDomAttrHash.Keys
   if IsObject( objDomain.Get(strAttr) ) then
      set objLargeInt = objDomain.Get(strAttr)
      if objLargeInt.LowPart = 0 then
         value = 0
      else
         value = Abs(objLargeInt.HighPart * 2^32 + objLargeInt.LowPart)
         value = int ( value / 10000000 )
         value = int ( value / 60 )
      end if
   else
      value = objDomain.Get(strAttr)
   end if
   WScript.Echo strAttr & " = " & value & " " & objDomAttrHash(strAttr)
next

'Constants from DOMAIN_PASSWORD_INFORMATION
Set objDomPassHash = CreateObject("Scripting.Dictionary")
objDomPassHash.Add "DOMAIN_PASSWORD_COMPLEX", &h1
objDomPassHash.Add "DOMAIN_PASSWORD_NO_ANON_CHANGE", &h2
objDomPassHash.Add "DOMAIN_PASSWORD_NO_CLEAR_CHANGE", &h4
objDomPassHash.Add "DOMAIN_LOCKOUT_ADMINS", &h8
objDomPassHash.Add "DOMAIN_PASSWORD_STORE_CLEARTEXT", &h16
objDomPassHash.Add "DOMAIN_REFUSE_PASSWORD_CHANGE", &h32

' The PwdProperties attribute requires special processing because
' it is a flag that holds multiple settings.
for each strFlag In objDomPassHash.Keys
   if objDomPassHash(strFlag) and objDomain.Get("PwdProperties") then
     WScript.Echo " " & strFlag & " is enabled"
   else
     WScript.Echo " " & strFlag & " is disabled"
   end If
next
```

Using PowerShell

To quickly retrieve details of the domain-wide password policy for the *adatum.com*
domain using the Quest AD cmdlets, use the following syntax:

```
Get-QADObject adatum.com | format-list Name, *password*, *lockout*
```

By piping the `get-QADObject` command into `Format-List`, you will receive output similar to the following:

```
Name                    :  adatum.com
MinimumPasswordAge      :  1 day
MaximumPasswordAge      :  42 days
PasswordHistoryLength   :  24 passwords remembered
MinimumPasswordLength   :  7 characters
LockoutDuration         :  30 minutes
LockoutThreshold        :  3 invalid login attempts
ResetLockoutCounterAfter :  30 minutes
```

Discussion

Several parameters controlling account lockout and password complexity can be set on a domain-linked Group Policy Object such as the Default Domain Policy. The properties that can be set for the password and account lockout policies include:

Account lockout duration
> Number of minutes an account will be locked before being automatically unlocked. A value of 0 indicates accounts will be locked out indefinitely, i.e., until an administrator manually unlocks them.

Account lockout threshold
> Number of failed logon attempts after which an account will be locked.

Reset account lockout counter after
> Number of minutes after a failed logon attempt that the failed logon counter for an account will be reset to 0.

The properties that can be set for the "Password Policy" include:

Enforce password history
> Number of passwords to remember before a user can reuse a previous password.

Maximum password age
> Maximum number of days a password can be used before a user must change it.

Minimum password age
> Minimum number of days a password must be used before it can be changed.

Minimum password length
> Minimum number of characters a password must be.

Password must meet complexity requirements
> If enabled, passwords must meet all of the following criteria:

- Not contain all or part of the user's account name
- Be at least six characters in length
- Contain characters from three of the following four categories:
  — English uppercase characters (A–Z)
  — English lowercase characters (a–z)
  — Base 10 digits (0–9)
  — Nonalphanumeric characters (e.g., !, $, #, %)

Store passwords using reversible encryption

If enabled, passwords are stored in such a way that they can be retrieved and decrypted. This is essentially the same as storing passwords in plain text, and should be avoided unless it is absolutely necessary.

In Windows 2000 and Windows Server 2003, administrators can only configure one password and account lockout policy per domain; if a group of users require a different policy in 2000 and 2003, a separate domain (and all of the hardware requirements and administrative overhead associated with managing that separate domain) is needed. Windows Server 2008 allows for the creation of Fine-Grained Password Policies (FGPPs), which allow you to configure multiple password policies within a single domain.

Using a graphical user interface

On a domain controller or machine that has *adminpak.msi* or the Remote Server Administration Tools (RSAT) installed, the Domain Security Policy snap-in is present from the Start menu under Administrative Tools. On a member server, you need to open the GPO snap-in and locate the Domain Security policy. See Recipe 9.0 for more information on GPOs.

Using a command-line interface

There is no standard CLI that can be used to modify a GPO, but you can use AdFind to view each of the attributes on the domain object that make up the account lockout and password policy settings.

Using VBScript

The VBScript solution requires quite a bit of code to perform the simple task of printing out the account lockout and password policy settings. First, create a `Dictionary` object with each of the six attributes as the keys and the unit's designation for each key (e.g., minutes) as the value. Then iterate over each key, printing it along with the value retrieved from the domain object.

Some additional code is necessary to distinguish between the values returned from some of the attributes. In the case of the time-based attributes, such as `lockoutDuration`, an

`IADsLargeInteger` object was returned from the `Get` method instead of a pure integer or string value. `IADsLargeInteger` objects represent 64-bit, also known as Integer8, numbers. 32-bit systems, which make up the majority of systems today, have to break 64-bit numbers into two parts (a high and low part) to store them. Unfortunately, VBScript cannot natively handle a 64-bit number and stores it as a double precision. To convert a 64-bit number into something VBScript can handle, you have to first multiply the high part by 4,294,967,296 (2^{32}) and then add the low part to the result:

```
value = Abs(objLargeInt.HighPart * 2^32 + objLargeInt.LowPart)
```

Then you divide by 10,000,000 or 10^7, which represents the number of 100-nanosecond intervals per second:

```
value = int ( value / 10000000 )
```

You then use the `int` function to discard any remainder and finally divide the result by 60 (number of seconds):

```
value = int ( value / 60 )
```

The last part of the code iterates over another `Dictionary` object that contains constants representing various flags that can be set as part of the `pwdProperties` attribute.

 Note that the result is only an approximation in minutes and can be off by several minutes, hours, or even days, depending on the original value.

See Also

Recipe 9.0 , MS KB 221930 (Domain Security Policy in Windows 2000), MS KB 255550 (Configuring Account Policies in Active Directory), MSDN: IADsLargeInteger, and MSDN: DOMAIN_PASSWORD_INFORMATION

6.17 Applying a Fine-Grained Password Policy to a User Object

Problem

You want to apply a Fine-Grained Password Policy to a **User** object in a Windows Server 2008 domain.

Solution

Using a graphical user interface

1. Open ADSI Edit. Right-click on the top-level node and click "Connect To...". In the Connection Settings screen, click OK.

2. In the righthand pane, double-click on "Default naming context," then double-click on the domain node (i.e., `dc=adatum,dc=com`).

3. Browse to `CN=System`, then `CN=Password Settings Container`.

4. Right-click on the PSO that you wish to modify and click Properties.

5. In the Select an Attribute to View drop-down box, select `msDS-PSOAppliesTo`.

6. In the Edit Attribute text box, enter the DN of the user object that this password policy should apply to, such as `cn=msteele,ou=Corp,dc=adatum,dc=com`.

7. Click Add, then click OK.

8. Click OK.

Using a command-line interface

The following will add the `'cn=joer'` user to the list of groups that a PSO will apply to:

```
psomgr -applyto CN=joer,CN=Users,DC=ADATUM,DC=COM -pso TestPSO -forreal
```

Using PowerShell

To add a group to the list of groups that a PSO will apply to, use the following syntax:

```
Add-QADPasswordSettingsObjectAppliesTo -Identity <PSO DN> -AppliesTo <User DN>
```

Discussion

Once a `PasswordSettingsObject` has been created, you can modify the password and account lockout settings controlled by the object, as well as the users and groups that the PSO should apply to. Since the `PasswordSettingsObject` is an Active Directory object class, these modifications can be made using any interface that can modify objects. When working from the command line, the *psomgr* tool from *http://www.joeware.net/ freetools* allows you to modify one or multiple PSOs at a time, and can also create "starter" PSOs using the `-quickstart` command-line switch. The full syntax for *psomgr.exe* can be obtained by typing `psomgr.exe /?` at a command prompt, or by visiting the *joeware* website.

See Also

Chapter 9

6.18 Viewing the Fine-Grained Password Policy That Is in Effect for a User Account

Problem

You want to determine which FGPP is in effect for a particular user.

Solution

Using a graphical user interface

1. Open Active Directory Users and Computers. Click on View, and confirm that there is a checkmark next to Advanced Features.

2. Browse to the user or group in question; right-click on the object and click Properties.

3. Click on the Attribute Editor tab. Click Filter, and confirm that there is a checkmark next to Show read-only attributes: Constructed and Backlinks.

4. Scroll to the `msDS-PSOApplied`.

5. Click OK.

Using a command prompt

```
psomgr.exe -effective <User DN>
```

Using PowerShell

```
get-QADUser -Identity <UserDN> -IncludedProperties msDS-ResultantPSO | format-list
dn,msDS-ResultantPSO
```

Discussion

Within a Windows Server 2008 domain, each user object contains a constructed back-link attribute called `msDS-ResultantPSO` that indicates which `PasswordSettingsObject` is in effect for that user. The precedence rules for `PasswordSettingsObjects` are as follows:

1. If a PSO has been applied directly to the user object, this PSO will take precedence. If multiple PSOs have been applied to a single user, the following tiebreakers will be used:

   • A PSO with a lower-numbered Precedence attribute (e.g., 5) will be applied over a higher-numbered one (e.g., 50).

   • If multiple PSOs have been configured with the same Precedence attribute, the PSO with the lowest GUID will take final precedence

2. If no PSOs have been applied directly to the user, any PSO that has been applied to a group that the user is a member of, whether directly or indirectly, will be applied. The same tiebreakers will be used here as in #1, above.

3. If no PSOs have been applied to the user or any groups that the user is a member of, the default domain PSO will be applied.

See Also

Recipes 6.18 and 9.29

6.19 Enabling and Disabling a User

Problem

You want to enable or disable a user account.

Solution

Using a graphical user interface

1. Open the ADUC snap-in.
2. In the left pane, right-click on the domain and select Find.
3. Select the appropriate domain beside In.
4. Type the name of the user beside Name and click Find Now.
5. In the Search Results window, right-click on the user and select Enable Account to enable or Disable Account to disable.
6. Click OK.

Using a command-line interface

To enable a user, use the following command:

```
> dsmod user <UserDN> -disabled no
```

To disable a user, use the following command:

```
> dsmod user <UserDN> -disabled yes
```

Using VBScript

```
' This code will enable or disable a user.
' ------ SCRIPT CONFIGURATION ------
' Set to FALSE to disable account or TRUE to enable account
strDisableAccount = FALSE
strUserDN = "<UserDN>" ' e.g. cn=jsmith,cn=Users,dc=adatum,dc=com
' ------ END CONFIGURATION --------

set objUser = GetObject("LDAP://" & strUserDN)
if objUser.AccountDisabled = TRUE then
   WScript.Echo "Account for " & objUser.Get("cn") & " currently disabled"
   if strDisableAccount = FALSE then
      objUser.AccountDisabled = strDisableAccount
      objUser.SetInfo
      WScript.Echo "Account enabled"
   end if
else
   WScript.Echo "Account currently enabled"
   if strDisableAccount = TRUE then
      objUser.AccountDisabled = strDisableAccount
      objUser.SetInfo
```

```
        WScript.Echo "Account disabled"
    end if
end if
```

Using PowerShell

To use the Quest AD cmdlets to enable or disable a user account, use the following syntax:

```
enable-QADUser -Identity <User DN>
disable-QADUser -Identity <User DN>
```

To use the System.DirectoryServices methods to disable a user, use the following:

```
$objUser = [ADSI] "LDAP://<UserDN>"
$objUser.psbase.InvokeSet('AccountDisabled', $true)
$objUser.psbase.CommitChanges()

---------alternate method
$objUser = [ADSI] "LDAP://<UserDN>"
$objUser.userAccountControl = ([int]$objUser.userAccountControl.ToString()) -bOR 2
$objUser.SetInfo()
```

To enable a user, use $false instead of $true (or in the alternate method, change the bOR to bXOR).

Discussion

Account status is used to control whether a user is allowed to log on or not. When an account is disabled, the user is not allowed to log on to his workstation with the account or to access AD controlled resources. Much like the lockout status, the account status is stored as a flag in the userAccountControl attribute (see Recipe 6.31).

There is an IADsUser::AccountDisabled property that allows you to determine and change the status. Set the method FALSE to enable the account or TRUE to disable.

See Also

Recipe 6.20 for finding disabled users and Recipe 6.31 for more on the attribute userAccountControl

6.20 Finding Disabled Users

Problem

You want to find disabled users in a domain.

Solution

Using a graphical user interface

1. Open the ADUC snap-in.
2. In the left pane, connect to the domain you want to query.
3. Right-click on the domain and select Find.
4. Beside Find, select Common Queries.
5. Check the box beside "disabled accounts."
6. Click the Find Now button.

Using a command-line interface

You can enumerate all disabled user objects in your domain by using the built-in DSQuery utility, as follows:

```
> dsquery user <DomainDN> -disabled
```

You can also use a bitwise query in AdFind to produce the same output, using the following syntax:

```
> adfind -bit -b <DomainDN> -f
"&(objectcategory=person)(objectclass=user)(useraccountcontrol:AND:=2)"
```

 You can replace *<DomainDN>* with the DN of a specific Organizational Unit if you wish to restrict the results of your AdFind query.

Using VBScript

```
' This code finds all disabled
' user accounts in a domain.
' ------ SCRIPT CONFIGURATION ------
strDomainDN = "<DomainDN>" ' e.g. dc=adatum,dc=com
' ------ END CONFIGURATION --------

strBase = "<LDAP://" & strDomainDN & ">;"
strFilter = "(&(objectclass=user)(objectcategory=person)" & _
            "(useraccountcontrol:1.2.840.113556.1.4.803:=2));"
strAttrs = "name;"
strScope = "subtree"

set objConn = CreateObject("ADODB.Connection")
objConn.Provider = "ADsDSOObject"
objConn.Open "Active Directory Provider"
set objRS = objConn.Execute(strBase & strFilter & strAttrs & strScope)
objRS.MoveFirst
while Not objRS.EOF
    Wscript.Echo objRS.Fields(0).Value
```

```
        objRS.MoveNext
    wend
```

Using PowerShell

To locate all disabled users in a domain using the Quest AD cmdlets, use the following syntax:

```
get-qaduser -disabled
```

To locate all disabled users using the `System.DirectoryServices` method, use the following:

```
$strFilter = "(&(objectcategory=person)(objectclass=user))"
$objDomain = New-Object System.DirectoryServices.DirectoryEntry
$objSearcher = New-Object System.DirectoryServices.DirectorySearcher
$objSearcher.SearchRoot = $objDomain
$objSearcher.Filter = ($strFilter) useraccountcontrol:1.2.840.113556.1.4.803:=2))")
$objSearcher.FindAll()
```

Discussion

Users in Active Directory can either be enabled or disabled. A disabled user cannot log in to the domain. Unlike account lockout, which is an automatic process that is based on the number of times a user incorrectly enters a password, an account has to be manually enabled or disabled.

All disabled user accounts have the bit that represents 2 (`0010 base 2`) set in their `userAccountControl` attribute. This doesn't mean that the attribute will be equal to 2, it just means that the bit that equals 2 will be enabled—other bits may also be set. See Recipes 4.12 and 4.15 for a more detailed explanation of bit flags.

See Also

Recipe 4.12, Recipe 4.15, and Recipe 6.19 for enabling and disabling users

6.21 Viewing a User's Group Membership

Problem

You want to view the group membership of a user.

Solution

Using a graphical user interface

1. Open the ADUC snap-in.
2. In the left pane, right-click on the domain and select Find.
3. Select the appropriate domain beside In.

4. Type the name of the user beside Name and click Find Now.

5. In the Search Results window, double-click on the user.

6. Click the Member Of tab.

7. To view all indirect group membership (from nested groups), you'll need to double-click on each group.

Using a command-line interface

The following command displays the groups *<UserDN>* is a member of. Use the -expand switch to list nested group membership as well:

```
> dsget user <UserDN> -memberof [-expand]
```

You can also use the GetUserInfo tool (another tool available from *http://www.joeware .net*) with the following syntax:

```
> getuserinfo \\<Domain>\<Username>
```

A third option would be to use the *whoami* tool, as follows:

```
> whoami /groups
```

To round out the command-line options for viewing group memberships, you can use the MemberOf *joeware* utility with the following syntax:

```
> memberof -u <Domain>\<User>
```

 To query group membership from a specific domain controller using MemberOf, use the -s switch followed by the name of the DC.

Using VBScript

```
' This code displays the
' group membership of a user.
' It avoids infinite loops due to circular group nesting by
' keeping track of the groups that have already been seen.
' ------ SCRIPT CONFIGURATION ------
strUserDN = "<UserDN>" ' e.g. cn=jsmith,cn=Users,dc=adatum,dc=com
' ------ END CONFIGURATION --------

set objUser = GetObject("LDAP://" & strUserDN)
Wscript.Echo "Group membership for " & objUser.Get("cn") & ":"
strSpaces = ""
set dicSeenGroup = CreateObject("Scripting.Dictionary")
DisplayGroups("LDAP://" &
strUserDN, strSpaces, dicSeenGroup)

Function DisplayGroups ( strObjectADsPath, strSpaces, dicSeenGroup)

    set objObject = GetObject(strObjectADsPath)
    WScript.Echo strSpaces & objObject.Name
```

```
    on error resume next ' Doing this to avoid an error when
                          ' memberOf is empty
    if IsArray( objObject.Get("memberOf") ) then
        colGroups = objObject.Get("memberOf")
    else
        colGroups = Array( objObject.Get("memberOf") )
    end if

    for each strGroupDN In colGroups
        if Not dicSeenGroup.Exists(strGroupDN) then
            dicSeenGroup.Add strGroupDN, 1
            DisplayGroups "LDAP://" & strGroupDN, strSpaces & " ", dicSeenGroup
        end if
    next
End Function
```

Using PowerShell

```
get-QADGroupMember -Identity <Group DN> -Indirect
```

Discussion

The memberOf attribute on user objects is multivalued and contains the list of distinguished names for groups of which the user is a member. memberOf is actually linked
with the member attribute on group objects, which holds the distinguished names of its
members. For this reason, you cannot directly modify the memberOf attribute; you must
instead modify the member attribute on the group.

The primary group of a user, which the user is technically a member of, will not be
shown in either the CLI or VBScript solutions except in the case of the MemberOf
utility. This is due to the fact that the primary group is not stored in the memberOf
attribute like the rest of the groups. See Recipes 6.23 and 7.12 for more on finding the
primary group of a user.

Using PowerShell

The -Indirect switch will "chase" nested group memberships; if you omit this switch,
the get-QADGroupMember cmdlet will display only the direct members of a group. If you
want to list only the indirect members of a group, you can use the Compare-Object cmdlet
as follows:

```
Compare-Object (Get-QADGroupMember -Identity <Group DN>)(Get-QADGroupMember
-Identity <Group DN> -Indirect)
```

See Also

Recipe 6.23, Recipe 7.4 for more on viewing the nested members of a group, Rec-
ipe 7.12, Recipe 10.17 for more information on linked attributes, and MS KB 906208
(When You Try to Log Onto a Windows Server 2003-Based Domain by Using a Domain
User Account, the Logon Request Fails)

6.22 Removing All Group Memberships from a User

Problem

You want to remove all group membership information from a user object.

Solution

Using a graphical user interface

1. Open the ADUC snap-in.
2. In the left pane, right-click on the domain and select Find.
3. Select the appropriate domain beside In.
4. Type the name of the user beside Name and click Find Now.
5. In the Search Results window, double-click on the user.
6. Click the Member Of tab.
7. Highlight all groups listed in the Member Of tab and select Remove. Click Yes to confirm.
8. Click OK.

Using a command-line interface

You can accomplish this task at the command line using a combination of AdFind and AdMod:

```
> adfind -b <DomainDN> -f  member=<UserDN> -dsq  | admod member:-:<UserDN> -unsafe
```

Using VBScript

```
Const ADS_PROPERTY_DELETE = 4
Const E_ADS_PROPERTY_NOT_FOUND = &h8000500D

Set objUser = GetObject("LDAP://<UserDN>")
arrMemberOf = objUser.GetEx("memberOf")

If Err.Number = E_ADS_PROPERTY_NOT_FOUND Then
    WScript.Echo "No group memberships found."
    WScript.Quit
End If

For Each Group in arrMemberOf
    Set objGroup = GetObject("LDAP://" & Group)
    objGroup.PutEx ADS_PROPERTY_DELETE, _
        "member", Array("<UserDN>")
    objGroup.SetInfo
Next
```

Using PowerShell

To remove group memberships using the Quest AD cmdlets, use the following syntax:

```
$objUser = get-QADUser -identity <User DN>
foreach ($strGroup in $objUser.memberOf) {
    $objGroup = get-QADGroup -identity $group
    remove-QADGroupMember $objGroup -member $objUser
}
```

To remove group memberships using ADSI, use the following:

```
$objUser = [ADSI] "LDAP://<User DN>"
foreach ($strGroup in $objUser.memberOf) {
    $objGroup = [ADSI]( "LDAP://" + $strGroup)
    $objGroup.PutEx(4, "member", @($objUser.distinguishedName))
    $objGroup.SetInfo()
}
```

Discussion

Using VBScript

The memberOf attribute on the **user** object is constructed; therefore, the code necessary to clear a user's group memberships actually involves modifying each **group** object in turn, rather than modifying the **user** object itself.

See Also

MSDN: Adding Members to Groups in a Domain [Active Directory] and MSDN: Group Objects [Active Directory]

6.23 Changing a User's Primary Group

Problem

You want to change the primary group of a user.

Solution

Using a graphical user interface

1. Open the ADUC snap-in.
2. In the left pane, right-click on the domain and select Find.
3. Select the appropriate domain beside In.
4. Type the name of the user beside Name and click Find Now.
5. In the Search Results window, double-click on the user.
6. Click the Member Of tab.

7. Click on the name of the group you want to set as the primary group.

8. Click the Set Primary Group button.

9. Click OK.

Using VBScript

```
' This code first checks to see if the user's primary group is already
' set to the specified group. If not it will a) add the user to the group
' if not already a member and b) set the primary group id to the group.
' ------ SCRIPT CONFIGURATION ------
strUserDN = "<UserDN>"    ' e.g. cn=rallen,ou=Sales,dc=adatum,dc=com
strGroupDN = "<GroupDN>" ' e.g. cn=SalesGroup,ou=Sales,dc=adatum,dc=com
' ------ END CONFIGURATION ---------

Const ADS_PROPERTY_APPEND = 3

set objUser = GetObject("LDAP://" & strUserDN )
WScript.Echo

set objGroup = GetObject("LDAP://" & strGroupDN )
objGroup.GetInfoEx Array("primaryGroupToken"), 0

if objGroup.Get("primaryGroupToken") = objUser.Get("primaryGroupID") then
    WScript.Echo "Primary group for user already set to " & strGroupDN
    WScript.Quit
end if

intAddMember = 1
for each strMemberDN in objUser.GetEx("memberOf")
    if LCase(strMemberDN) = LCase(strGroupDN) then
        intAddMember = 0
        Exit for
    end if
next

if intAddMember > 0 then
    objGroup.PutEx ADS_PROPERTY_APPEND, "member", Array(strUserDN)
    objGroup.SetInfo
    WScript.Echo "Added " & strUserDN & " as member of " & strGroupDN
end if

objUser.Put "primaryGroupID", objGroup.Get("primaryGroupToken")
objUser.SetInfo
WScript.Echo "Changed primary group id of " & strUserDN & _
             " to " & objGroup.Get("primaryGroupToken")
```

Using PowerShell

This PowerShell script performs similar functionality to the VBScript—it first checks to see if the user is a member of the group in question, adds the user if she is not, and then sets the primaryGroupID attribute to be that of the group's primarygroupToken:

```
$objGroup = Get-QADGroup -Identity <GroupDN>
$objUser = Get-QADUser -Identity <UserDN>
$bool = $false
$strGroupID = $objGroup.primaryGroupToken
$colMembers = get-qadgroupmember -identity <GroupDN> -indirect
foreach ($user in $colMembers) {
>> if ($user.distinguishedName -eq $objUser.distinguishedName) { $bool = $true }
if ($bool -eq $true) {
>> add-QADMember -identity $objGroup -member $objUser
}
set-QADUser -Identity $objUser -ObjectAttributes @{primaryGroupID=$strGroupID}
```

Discussion

The primary group is a holdover from Windows NT that was used to support Macintosh and POSIX clients. That said, you might have some legacy applications that depend on the primary group and therefore you may have to change some users' primary groups.

Changing the primary group is not difficult, but it is not straightforward, either. The primary group is stored on **user** objects in the **primaryGroupID** attribute, which contains the RID of the primary group. You can obtain this value by querying the **primary GroupToken** attribute on the target **group** object. Before you can set the **primaryGroupID** on the **user** object, you have to first make sure the user is a member of the group. If you try to set the **primaryGroupID** for a group in which the user is not a member, you will get an error.

The default **primaryGroupID** is set to 513 (Domain Users) for all users.

See Also

Recipe 7.12 for determining the group name given a group ID, MS KB 297951 (How to Use the PrimaryGroupID Attribute to Find the Primary Group for a User), MS KB 321360 (How to Use Native ADSI Components to Find the Primary Group), and MS KB 243330 (Well-Known Security Identifiers in Windows Operating Systems)

6.24 Copying a User's Group Membership to Another User

Problem

You want to copy one user's group membership to another user.

Solution

Using a graphical user interface

1. Open the ADUC snap-in.
2. In the left pane, right-click on the domain and select Find.

3. Select the appropriate domain beside In.

4. Beside Name, type the name of the user you want to transfer groups from and click Find Now.

5. In the Search Results window, double-click on the user.

6. Click the Member Of tab.

7. For each group you want to add another user in, do the following:

    a. Double-click on the group.

    b. Click the Members tab.

    c. Click the Add button.

    d. Find the user you want to add in the object picker and click OK.

    e. Click OK.

Using a command-line interface

The following command line will add *<NewUserDN>* to all of the groups that *<CurrentUserDN>* is a member of:

```
> for /F "usebackq delims=""" %i in ('dsget user
"<CurrentUserDN>" -memberof') do dsmod group %i -addmbr "<NewUserDN>"
```

If you want to get fancy and remove *<CurrentUserDN>* from each of the groups in the same operation, simply add an -rmmbr option on the end:

```
> for /F "usebackq delims=""" %i in ('dsget user
"<CurrentUserDN>" -memberof') do dsmod group %i -addmbr "<NewUserDN>"
-rmmbr "<CurrentUserDN>"
```

You can also accomplish this using a combination of AdFind and AdMod, as follows:

```
> adfind -b <DomainDN> -f member=<Source User DN> -dsq | admod member:+:<Dest. User
DN> -unsafe
```

Using VBScript

```
' This code adds the "new" user to the groups the "current"
' user is a member of
' ------ SCRIPT CONFIGURATION -----
strCurrentUserDN = "<CurrentUserDN>"
' e.g. cn=jsmith,ou=Sales,dc=adatum,dc=com
strNewUserDN = "<NewUserDN>"

' ------ SCRIPT CONFIGURATION ------

Const ADS_PROPERTY_APPEND = 3
set
objCurrentUser = GetObject("LDAP://" &
strCurrentUserDN )
set objNewUser = GetObject("LDAP://" & strNewUserDN )

on error resume next
```

```
    WScript.Echo "Transfering groups from " & strCurrentUserDN & " to " & strNewUserDN
    for each strGroupDN in objCurrentUser.GetEx("memberOf")
        set objGroup = GetObject("LDAP://" & strGroupDN)
        objGroup.PutEx ADS_PROPERTY_APPEND, "member", Array( strNewUserDN )
        objGroup.SetInfo
        if Err then
            WScript.Echo "Error adding user to group: " & strGroupDN
        else
            WScript.Echo "Added user to group: " & strGroupDN
        end if
    next
```

Using PowerShell

To copy group memberships using the Quest AD cmdlets, use the following syntax:

```
$objCurrentUser = get-QADUser -Identity <CurrentUserDN>
$objNewUser = get-QADUser -Identity <NewUserDN>
$colGroups = $objCurrentUser.memberOf
foreach ($group in $colGroups) {
>> add-QADGroupMember -Identity $group -member $objNewUser
>> }
```

To copy group memberships using System.DirectoryServices, use the following:

```
$objCurrentUser = [ADSI] "LDAP://<CurentUserDN>"
$objNewUser = [ADSI] "LDAP://<NewUserDN>"
foreach ($strGroup in $objCurrentUser.memberOf) {
    $objGroup = [ADSI]("LDAP://" + $strGroup)
    $objGroup.PutEx(3, "member", @($objNewUser.distinguishedName))
    $objGroup.SetInfo()
}
```

Discussion

Employees come and go; people take on new responsibilities and move on to new jobs. It is common to have movement within an organization. When this happens, typically someone is replacing the person that is moving on. The administrator needs to get the new person up to speed as quickly as possible, including setting up accounts and granting access to any necessary resources. A big part of this process includes adding the new user to the correct groups. You can help facilitate this by using one of the processes outlined in the "Solution" section to help the user gain access to the exact same groups that the former employee was a member of.

One important issue to point out is that the memberOf attribute, which was used in the "Solution" section to determine a user's group membership, contains only the groups that are visible to the DC that's being queried; this can vary depending on whether the DC in question is a Global Catalog and whether the user belongs to any universal groups. Any groups the user is a member of outside of the user's domain will not be transferred. To transfer universal group membership outside of a domain, you will need to perform a query against the global catalog for all group objects that have a member attribute that contains the DN of the user. You can also search the Global Catalog for the memberOf attribute for a given user to determine a user's universal group memberships.

See Also

Recipe 7.5 for adding and removing members of a group

6.25 Setting a User's Password

Problem

You want to set the password for a user.

Solution

Using a graphical user interface

1. Open the ADUC snap-in.
2. In the left pane, right-click on the domain and select Find.
3. Select the appropriate domain beside In.
4. Type the name of the user beside Name and click Find Now.
5. In the Search Results window, right-click on the user and select Reset Password.
6. Enter and confirm the new password.
7. Click OK.

Using a command-line interface

This command changes the password for the user specified by *<UserDN>*. Using * after the -pwd option prompts you for the new password. You can replace * with the password you want to set, but it is not a good security practice since other users that are logged into the machine may be able to see it:

```
> dsmod user <UserDN> -pwd *
```

You can modify the unicodepwd attribute directly by encrypting the admod connection using the -kerbenc switch:

```
> admod -b "<UserDN>" unicodepwd::<Password> -kerbenc
```

You can also use admod with the #setpwd# switch:

```
> admod -b "<UserDN>" #setpwd#::<NewPassword>
```

Using VBScript

```
' This code sets the password for a user.
' ------ SCRIPT CONFIGURATION ------
strUserDN = "<UserDN>" ' e.g. cn=jsmith,cn=Users,dc=adatum,dc=com
```

```
strNewPasswd = "<NewPasword>"
' ------ END CONFIGURATION --------

set objUser = GetObject("LDAP://" & strUserDN)
objUser.SetPassword(strNewPasswd)
Wscript.Echo "Password set for " & objUser.Get("cn")
```

Using PowerShell

To set a user's password with the Quest AD cmdlets, use the following syntax:

```
set-QADUser -Identity <UserDN> -UserPassword '<PasswordString>'
```

To set a password using `System.DirectoryServices`, use the following:

```
$objUser = [ADSI] "LDAP://<UserDN>"
$objUser.SetPassword("<PasswordString>")
$objUser.SetInfo()
```

Discussion

A one-way hash of a user's password is stored in the `unicodePwd` attribute. There are several supported methods to modify this attribute directly, or you can use one of the supported APIs to do so.

With the VBScript solution, you can use the `IADsUser::SetPassword` method or `IADsUser::ChangePassword`. The latter requires the existing password to be known before setting it. This is the method you'd want to use if you've created a web page that accepts the previous password before allowing a user to change it.

See Also

MS KB 225511 (New Password Change and Conflict Resolution Functionality in Windows), MS KB 264480 (Description of Password-Change Protocols in Windows 2000), MSDN: IADsUser::SetPassword, and MSDN: IADsUser::Change-Password

6.26 Preventing a User from Changing a Password

Problem

You want to disable a user's ability to change a password.

Solution

Using a graphical user interface

1. Open the ADUC snap-in.
2. In the left pane, right-click on the domain and select Find.
3. Select the appropriate domain beside In.

4. Beside Name, type the name of the user you want to modify and click Find Now.

5. In the Search Results window, double-click on the user.

6. Click the Account tab.

7. Under Account options, check the box beside "User cannot change password."

8. Click OK.

Using a command-line interface

```
> dsmod user <UserDN> -canchpwd no
```

Using VBScript

```
' This code disables a user's ability to change a password
' ------ SCRIPT CONFIGURATION ------
strUserDN = "<UserDN>" ' e.g. cn=rallen,ou=Sales,dc=adatum,dc=com
' ------ END CONFIGURATION ---------

Const ACETYPE_ACCESS_DENIED_OBJECT = 6
Const ACEFLAG_OBJECT_TYPE_PRESENT = 1
Const RIGHT_DS_CONTROL_ACCESS = 256
Const CHANGE_PASSWORD_GUID = "{ab721a53-1e2f-11d0-9819-00aa0040529b}"

set objUser = GetObject("LDAP://" & strUserDN)
set objSD = objUser.Get("ntSecurityDescriptor")
set objDACL = objSD.DiscretionaryAcl

' Add a deny ACE for Everyone
set objACE = CreateObject("AccessControlEntry")
objACE.Trustee = "Everyone"
objACE.AceFlags = 0
objACE.AceType = ACETYPE_ACCESS_DENIED_OBJECT
objACE.Flags = ACEFLAG_OBJECT_TYPE_PRESENT
objACE.ObjectType = CHANGE_PASSWORD_GUID
objACE.AccessMask = RIGHT_DS_CONTROL_ACCESS
objDACL.AddAce objACE

' Add a deny ACE for Self
' (This is only necessary to prevent a user from
' changing their own password.)
set objACE = CreateObject("AccessControlEntry")
objACE.Trustee = "Self"
objACE.AceFlags = 0
objACE.AceType = ACETYPE_ACCESS_DENIED_OBJECT
objACE.Flags = ACEFLAG_OBJECT_TYPE_PRESENT
objACE.ObjectType = CHANGE_PASSWORD_GUID
objACE.AccessMask = RIGHT_DS_CONTROL_ACCESS
objDACL.AddAce objACE

objSD.DiscretionaryAcl = objDACL
objUser.Put "nTSecurityDescriptor", objSD
objUser.SetInfo
WScript.Echo "Enabled no password changing for " & strUserDN
```

Discussion

Even though in the GUI solution you check and uncheck the "User cannot change password" setting, actually making the change in Active Directory is a little more complicated, as is evident in the VBScript solution. Not allowing a user to change his password consists of setting two deny Change Password ACEs on the target `user object`. One deny ACE is for the `Everyone` account and the other is for `Self`.

The VBScript solution should work as is, but it is not very robust in terms of checking to see if the ACEs already exist and making sure they are in the proper order. If you need to make the code more robust, we suggest checking out MS KB 269159 for more information on setting ACEs properly.

See Also

MS KB 269159 (How to Use Visual Basic and ADsSecurity.dll to Properly Order ACEs in an ACL)

6.27 Requiring a User to Change a Password at Next Logon

Problem

You want to require a user to change her password the next time she logs on to the domain.

Solution

Using a graphical user interface

1. Open the ADUC snap-in.
2. In the left pane, right-click on the domain and select Find.
3. Select the appropriate domain beside In.
4. Beside Name, type the name of the user you want to modify and click Find Now.
5. In the Search Results window, double-click on the user.
6. Click the Account tab.
7. Under Account options, check the box beside "User must change password at next logon."
8. Click OK.

Using a command-line interface

You can configure the "User must change password" using either DSMod or AdMod. To modify this setting using DSMod, use the following syntax:

```
> dsmod user "<UserDN>" -mustchpwd yes
```

For AdMod, do the following:

```
> admod -b "<UserDN>" pwdLastSet::0
```

Using VBScript

```
' This code sets the flag that requires a
' user to change their password
' ------ SCRIPT CONFIGURATION ------
strUserDN = "<UserDN>" ' e.g. cn=rallen,ou=Sales,dc=adatum,dc=com
' ------ END CONFIGURATION --------
set objUser = GetObject("LDAP://" & strUserDN)
objUser.Put "pwdLastSet", 0
objUser.SetInfo
WScript.Echo "User must change password at next logon: " & strUserDN
```

Using PowerShell

To flag a user's password to change on next logon using the Quest AD cmdlets, use the following syntax:

```
set-QADUser -Identity <UserDN> -UserMustChangePassword
```

To use the `System.DirectoryServices` methods, use the following:

```
$objUser = [ADSI] "LDAP://<UserDN>"
$objUser.Put("pwdLastSet", 0)
$objUser.SetInfo()
```

Discussion

When a user changes a password, a timestamp is written to the `pwdLastSet` attribute of the `user` object. When the user logs in to the domain, this timestamp is compared to the effective maximum password age that is defined for the user to determine if the password has expired. To force a user to change his password at next logon, set the `pwdLastSet` attribute of the target user to zero, and verify that the user's account doesn't have the "password never expires" option enabled.

To disable this option so that a user does not have to change his password, set `pwdLastSet` to `-1`. These two values (`0` and `-1`) are the only ones that can be set on the `pwdLastSet` attribute.

6.28 Preventing a User's Password from Expiring

Problem

You want to prevent a user's password from expiring.

Solution

Using a graphical user interface

1. Open the ADUC snap-in.
2. In the left pane, right-click on the domain and select Find.
3. Select the appropriate domain beside In.
4. Beside Name, type the name of the user you want to modify and click Find Now.
5. In the Search Results window, double-click on the user.
6. Click the Account tab.
7. Under Account options, check the box beside "Password never expires."
8. Click OK.

Using a command-line interface

```
> dsmod user "<UserDN>" -pwdneverexpires yes
```

Using VBScript

```
' This code sets a user's password to never expire
' See Recipe 4.12 for the code for the CalcBit function
' ------ SCRIPT CONFIGURATION ------
strUserDN = "<UserDN>" ' e.g. cn=rallen,ou=Sales,dc=adatum,dc=com
' ------ END CONFIGURATION --------

intBit = 65536
strAttr = "userAccountControl"

set objUser = GetObject("LDAP://" & strUserDN)
intBitsOrig = objUser.Get(strAttr)
intBitsCalc = CalcBit(intBitsOrig, intBit, TRUE)
if intBitsOrig <> intBitsCalc then
    objUser.Put strAttr, intBitsCalc
    objUser.SetInfo
    WScript.Echo "Changed " & strAttr & " from " & _
                 intBitsOrig & " to " & intBitsCalc
else
    WScript.Echo "Did not need to change " & strAttr & " (" & _
                 intBitsOrig & ")"
end if
```

Using PowerShell

To prevent a user's password from expiring using the Quest AD cmdlets, use the following syntax:

```
set-QADUser -Identity <UserDN> -PasswordNeverExpires
```

To use the `System.DirectoryServices` methods, use the following:

```
$objUser = [ADSI] "LDAP://<UserDN>"
$currentUAC = [int]($objUser.userAccountControl.ToString())

$newUAC = $currentUAC -bor 65536
$objUser.put("userAccountControl", $newValue)
$objUser.SetInfo()
```

Discussion

Setting a user's password to never expire overrides any password aging policy you've defined in the domain. To disable password expiration, you need to set the bit equivalent of 65,536 (i.e., 10000000000000000) in the userAccountControl attribute of the target user.

Using PowerShell

The PowerShell solution makes use of the built-in -bor operator in PowerShell, which performs a bitwise OR. You can also use -bxor to perform a Boolean XOR to clear the value set for a particular bit. userAccountControl is presented by PowerShell as a constructed property. The only common interface on constructed properties is ToString(), which exists both explicitly and implicitly on all PSObjects. When explicit, it is used for serialization of the object. When implicit, it is presented as the name of the base type of the object.

See Also

Recipe 4.15 for more on modifying a bit flag attribute and Recipe 6.31 for more on setting the userAccountControl attribute

6.29 Finding Users Whose Passwords Are About to Expire

Problem

You want to find the users whose passwords are about to expire.

Solution

Using a command-line interface

```
> dsquery user -stalepwd <NumDaysSinceLastPwdChange>
```

You can also use the FindExpAcc *joeware* tool with the following syntax:

```
> findexpacc -pwd
```

Discussion

When a Windows-based client logs on to Active Directory, a check is done against the domain password policy and the user's `pwdLastSet` attribute to determine if the user's password has expired. If it has, the user is prompted to change it. In a pure Windows-based environment, this notification process may be adequate, but if you have a lot of non-Windows-based computers that are joined to an Active Directory domain (e.g., Kerberos-enabled Unix clients), or you have a lot of application and service accounts, you'll need to develop your own user password expiration notification process. Even in a pure Windows environment, cached logins present a problem because when a user logs into the domain with cached credentials (i.e., when the client is not able to reach a domain controller), this password expiration notification check is not done.

The process of finding users whose passwords are about to expire is a little complicated. Fortunately, the new `dsquery user` command helps by providing an option for searching for users that haven't changed their password for a number of days (`-stalepwd`). The downside to the `dsquery user` command is that it will not only find users whose password is about to expire, but also users that must change their password at next logon (i.e., `pwdLastSet = 0`). The Perl solution does not suffer from this limitation.

Using a command-line interface

You can use the FindExpAcc tool to query Active Directory for expired user or computer accounts, as well as active accounts with expired passwords. It also includes switches that are familiar from AdFind and AdMod, such as `-b` to specify the Base DN, `-f` to specify an LDAP filter, etc.

The `findexpacc` utility can also be used to query for user accounts that are about to expire, in addition to accounts with expiring passwords.

See Also

Recipe 6.16 for more on the password policy for a domain, Recipe 6.20, Recipe 6.25 for how to set a user's password, and Recipe 6.28 for how to set a user's password to never expire

6.30 Viewing the RODCs That Have Cached a User's Password

Problem

You wish to view the RODCs that have cached a user account's password secrets in a Windows Server 2008 domain.

Solution

Using a graphical user interface

1. Open the ADUC snap-in.
2. Click View→Advanced Features. In the left pane, right-click on the domain and select Find.
3. Select the appropriate domain beside In.
4. Beside Name, type the name of the user and click Find Now.
5. In the Search Results window, double-click on the user.
6. Select the Attribute Editor tab. Click Filter and ensure that there is a checkmark next to Backlinks.
7. Scroll to the msDS-RevealedDSAs attribute to view a list of RODCs that have cached this user's password secrets.
8. Click OK after you're done.

Using a command-line interface

```
> adfind -b <UserDN> msDS-RevealedDSAs
```

Using VBScript

```
' ------ SCRIPT CONFIGURATION ------
strUserDN = "<UserDN>" ' e.g. cn=rallen,ou=Sales,dc=adatum,dc=com
' ------ END CONFIGURATION --------

set objUser = GetObject("LDAP://" & strUserDN)
strRODCs = objUser.Get("msDS-RevealedDSAs")
WScript.Echo strRODCs
```

Using PowerShell

```
> $objUser = [ADSI] "LDAP://<UserDN>"
> $objUser.psbase.InvokeGet("msDS-RevealedDSAs")
```

Discussion

As discussed in Chapter 3, Windows Server 2008 introduces the Read-Only Domain Controller (RODC) to improve the security of branch office and other remote environments. One of the security measures introduced by the RODC is the Password Replication Policy (PRP), which specifies a list of users and groups that can and cannot have their password secrets cached on one or more DCs. Each RODC maintains a forward-link attribute called msDS-RevealedUsers, which lists the user accounts for whom each RODC has cached password secrets. Each user account, in turn, maintains a backlink called msDS-RevealedDSAs. This backlink can be queried to determine which

RODCs have stored password information for a particular user account; however, like all backlinks, this attribute cannot be modified directly.

See Also

Recipes 3.2 and 3.4.

6.31 Setting a User's Account Options (userAccountControl)

Problem

You want to view or update the userAccountControl attribute for a user. This attribute controls various account options, such as if the user must change her password at next logon and if the account is disabled.

Solution

Using a graphical user interface

1. Open the ADUC snap-in.
2. In the left pane, right-click on the domain and select Find.
3. Select the appropriate domain beside In.
4. Beside Name, type the name of the user and click Find Now.
5. In the Search Results window, double-click on the user.
6. Select the Account tab.
7. Many of the userAccountControl flags can be set under Account options.
8. Click OK after you're done.

Using a command-line interface

The dsmod user command has several options for setting various userAccountControl flags, as shown in Table 6-2. Each switch accepts yes or no as a parameter to either enable or disable the setting.

Table 6-2. dsmod user options for setting userAccountControl

dsmod user switch	Description
-mustchpwd	Sets whether the user must change password at next logon
-canchpwd	Sets whether the user can change his password
-disabled	Sets account status to enabled or disabled
-reversiblepwd	Sets whether the user's password is stored using reversible encryption
-pwdneverexpires	Sets whether the user's password never expires

Using VBScript

```
' This code enables or disables a bit value in the userAccountControl attr.
' See Recipe 4.12 for the code for the CalcBit function.
' ------ SCRIPT CONFIGURATION ------
strUserDN = "<UserDN>" ' e.g. cn=rallen,ou=Sales,dc=adatum,dc=com
intBit = <BitValue> ' e.g. 65536
boolEnable = <TrueOrFalse> ' e.g. TRUE
' ------ END CONFIGURATION --------

strAttr = "
userAccountControl"
set objUser = GetObject("LDAP://" & strUserDN)
intBitsOrig = objUser.Get(strAttr)
intBitsCalc = CalcBit(intBitsOrig, intBit, boolEnable)
if intBitsOrig <> intBitsCalc then
    objUser.Put strAttr, intBitsCalc
    objUser.SetInfo
    WScript.Echo "Changed " & strAttr & " from " & _
                 intBitsOrig & " to " & intBitsCalc
else
    WScript.Echo "Did not need to change " & strAttr & " (" & _
                 intBitsOrig & ")"
end if
```

Using PowerShell

To modify user properties associated with the userAccountControl attribute, you have several switches available through the set-QADUser Quest cmdlet, including the following:

```
set-QADUser -Identity <UserDN> -PasswordNeverExpires
set-QADUser -Identity <UserDN> -UserMustChangePassword
enable-QADUser -Identity <UserDN>
disable-QADUser - Identity <UserDN>
```

To use the System.DirectoryServices methods to set a bitwise attribute, use the following (to clear a bit value, use -bxor instead of -bor):

```
$intBit = <BitValue>
$objUser = [ADSI] "LDAP://<UserDN>"
$currentUAC = [int]($objUser.userAccountControl.ToString())

$newUAC = $currentUAC -bor $intBit
$objUser.put("userAccountControl", $newValue)
```

$objUser.SetInfo()Discussion

The userAccountControl attribute on user (and computer) objects could be considered the kitchen sink of miscellaneous and sometimes completely unrelated user account properties. If you have to work with creating and managing user objects very much, you'll need to become intimately familiar with this attribute.

The userAccountControl attribute is a bit flag, which means you have to take a couple extra steps to search against it or modify it. See Recipe 4.12 for more on searching with a bitwise filter and Recipe 4.15 for modifying a bit flag attribute.

The dsmod user command can be used to modify a subset of userAccountControl properties, as shown in Table 6-2, and Table 6-3 contains the complete list of userAccount Control properties as defined in the ADS_USER_FLAG_ENUM enumeration.

Table 6-3. ADS_USER_FLAG_ENUM values

Name	Value	Description
ADS_UF_SCRIPT	1	Logon script is executed.
ADS_UF_ACCOUNTDISABLE	2	Account is disabled.
ADS_UF_HOMEDIR_REQUIRED	8	View-only attribute. Indicates that Home Directory is required.
ADS_UF_LOCKOUT	16	Account is locked out.
ADS_UF_PASSWD_NOTREQD	32	A password is not required.
ADS_UF_PASSWD_CANT_CHANGE	64	Read-only flag that indicates if the user cannot change her password.
ADS_UF_ENCRYPTED_TEXT_PASSWORD_ALLOWED	128	Store password using reversible encryption.
ADS_UF_NORMAL_ACCOUNT	512	Enabled user account.
ADS_UF_INTERDOMAIN_TRUST_ ACCOUNT	2048	A permit to trust account for a system domain that trusts other domains.
ADS_UF_WORKSTATION_TRUST_ACCOUNT	4096	Enabled computer account.
ADS_UF_SERVER_TRUST_ACCOUNT	8192	Computer account for backup domain controller.
ADS_UF_DONT_EXPIRE_PASSWD	65536	Password will not expire.
ADS_UF_MNS_LOGON_ACCOUNT	131072	MNS logon account.
ADS_UF_SMARTCARD_REQUIRED	262144	Smart card is required for logon.
ADS_UF_TRUSTED_FOR_DELEGATION	524288	Allow Kerberos delegation.
ADS_UF_NOT_DELEGATED	1048576	Do not allow Kerberos delegation even if ADS_UF_TRUSTED_FOR_DELEGATION is enabled.
ADS_UF_USE_DES_KEY_ONLY	2097152	Requires DES encryption for keys.
ADS_UF_DONT_REQUIRE_PREAUTH	4194304	Account does not require Kerberos pre-authentication for logon.
ADS_UF_PASSWORD_EXPIRED	8388608	Read-only flag indicating account's password has expired. Only used with the WinNT provider.
ADS_UF_TRUSTED_TO_AUTHENTICATE_FOR_DELEGATION	16777216	Account is enabled for delegation.

See Also

Recipe 4.12, Recipe 4.15 for setting a bit flag attribute, and MSDN: ADS_USER_FLAG_ENUM

6.32 Setting a User's Account to Expire

Problem

You want a user's account to expire at some point in the future.

Solution

Using a graphical user interface

1. Open the ADUC snap-in.
2. In the left pane, right-click on the domain and select Find.
3. Select the appropriate domain beside In.
4. Beside Name, type the name of the user you want to modify and click Find Now.
5. In the Search Results window, double-click on the user.
6. Click the Account tab.
7. Under "Account expires," select the radio button beside "End of."
8. Select the date the account should expire.
9. Click OK.

Using a command-line interface

Valid values for the -acctexpires flag include a positive number of days in the future when the account should expire, for instance at the end of the day, or to never expire the account:

```
> dsmod user "<UserDN>" -acctexpires <NumDays>
```

Using VBScript

```
' This code sets the
' account expiration date for a user.
' ------ SCRIPT CONFIGURATION ------
strExpireDate = "<Date>" ' e.g. "07/10/2004"
strUserDN = "<UserDN>" ' e.g. cn=rallen,ou=Sales,dc=adatum,dc=com
' ------ END CONFIGURATION --------

set objUser = GetObject("LDAP://" & strUserDN)
objUser.AccountExpirationDate = strExpireDate
objUser.SetInfo
WScript.Echo "Set user " & strUserDN & " to expire on " & strExpireDate
```

```
' These two lines would disable
account expiration for the user
' objUser.Put "
accountExpires", 0
' objUser.SetInfo
```

Using PowerShell

```
set-QADUser -Identity <UserDN> -AccountExpires "08/08/2008"
```

Discussion

User accounts can be configured to expire on a certain date. Account expiration is stored in the `accountExpires` attribute on a `user` object. This attribute contains a large integer representation of the date in which the account expires, expressed in 100-nanosecond intervals since January 1, 1601. If you set this attribute to 0, it disables account expiration for the user (i.e., the account will never expire). Note that this is different than the `dsmod user` command where a value of `0` with `-acctexpires` will cause the account to expire at the end of the day.

See Also

MS KB 278359 (Account Expiration for a Migrated User Appears to be One Day Ahead of or Behind the Date in the Source Domain) and MSDN: Account Expiration

6.33 Determining a User's Last Logon Time

 This recipe requires at least Windows Server 2003 forest functional level.

Problem

You want to determine the last time a user logged into a domain.

Solution

Using a graphical user interface

If you install the *AcctInfo.dll* extension to ADUC in Windows Server 2003, you can view the last logon timestamp:

1. Open the ADUC snap-in.
2. In the left pane, right-click on the domain and select Find.

3. Select the appropriate domain beside In.

4. Beside Name, type the name of the user you want to locate and click Find Now.

5. In the Search Results window, double-click on the user.

6. Click the Additional Account Info tab.

7. View the value for `Last-Logon-Timestamp`.

 AcctInfo.dll can be downloaded from the Microsoft download site as a part of the Account Lockout and Management Tools:

http://microsoft.com/downloads/details.aspx?FamilyId=7AF2E69C -91F3-4E63-8629-B999ADDE0B9E&displaylang=en

In Windows Server 2008, you do not need to install additional DLLs to view this information in ADUC. To view the last logon timestamp in ADUC in Windows Server 2008, do the following:

1. Open the ADUC snap-in

2. Click View and confirm that Advanced Features has a checkmark next to it.

3. Right-click on the domain and select Find.

4. Select the appropriate domain beside In.

5. Beside Name, type the name of the user you want to locate and click Find Now.

6. In the Search Results window, double-click on the user.

7. Click the Attribute Editor tab.

8. View the value for the `lastLogonTimestamp` attribute.

Using a command-line interface

```
> adfind -b <UserDN> lastLogonTimestamp -tdc
```

 The `-tdc` and `-tdcs` switches will display attributes such as `lastLogonTimestamp` in a human-readable format.

Using VBScript

```
' This code prints the
' last logon timestamp for a user.
' ------ SCRIPT CONFIGURATION ------
strUserDN = "<UserDN>" ' e.g. cn=rallen,ou=Sales,dc=adatum,dc=com
' ------ END CONFIGURATION --------

set objUser = GetObject("LDAP://" & strUserDN)
set objLogon = objUser.Get("
lastLogonTimestamp")
```

```
intLogonTime = objLogon.HighPart * (2^32) + objLogon.LowPart
intLogonTime = intLogonTime / (60 * 10000000)
intLogonTime = intLogonTime / 1440
WScript.Echo "Approx
last logon timestamp: " & intLogonTime + #1/1/1601#
```

 Note that due to how the math is handled in this script, the result is only an approximation in minutes and can be off by several minutes, hours, or even days depending on the original value.

Discussion

Trying to determine when a user last logged on has always been a challenge in the Microsoft NOS environment. In Windows NT, you could retrieve a user's last logon timestamp from a PDC or BDC, but this timestamp was the last time the user logged on to the individual PDC or BDC itself. That means to determine the actual last logon, you'd have to query every domain controller in the domain. In large environments, this wasn't practical. With Windows 2000 Active Directory, things did not improve. A lastLogon attribute is used to store the last logon timestamp, but unfortunately, this attribute isn't replicated. So again, to get an accurate picture, you'd have to query every domain controller in the domain for the user's last logon attribute and keep track of the most recent one.

Starting with Windows Server 2003 forest functional level, we finally have a viable solution. A new attribute called lastLogonTimestamp was added to the schema for user objects. This attribute is similar to the lastLogon attribute that was available previously, with two distinct differences. First, and most importantly, this attribute is replicated. That means when a user logs in, the lastLogonTimestamp attribute will get populated and then replicate to all domain controllers in the domain.

The second difference is that since lastLogonTimestamp is replicated, special safeguards needed to be put in place so that users who logged in repeatedly over a short period of time did not cause unnecessary replication traffic. So, the lastLogonTimestamp is updated only if the last update occurred between 9 and 14 days ago by default. (This window is configurable by modifying the msDS-LogonTimeSyncInterval on the domain NC.) This means that the lastLogonTimestamp attribute could be more than a week off in terms of accuracy with a user's actual last logon. Ultimately, this shouldn't be a problem for most situations because lastLogonTimestamp is intended to address the common problem where administrators want to run a query and determine which users have not logged in over the past month or more.

See Also

Recipe 6.34 for finding users who have not logged on recently

6.34 Finding Users Who Have Not Logged On Recently

 This recipe requires at least Windows Server 2003 domain functional level.

Problem

You want to determine which users have not logged on recently.

Solution

Using a graphical user interface

1. Open the ADUC snap-in.
2. In the left pane, right-click on the domain and select Find.
3. Beside Find, select Common Queries.
4. Select the number of days beside "Days since last logon."
5. Click the Find Now button.

Using a command-line interface

You can locate users who have not logged on for a certain amount of time using either the built-in DSQuery tool or the OldCmp utility from *http://www.joeware.net*:

```
> dsquery user -inactive <NumWeeks>
```

OldCmp can create a report of all user objects based on several criteria. To create a report of all users in the *adatum.com* domain who haven't logged on in more than 90 days, for example, use the following syntax:

```
> oldcmp -report -users -b dc=adatum,dc=com -llts -age 90-sh
```

Discussion

As discussed in Recipe 6.33, in Windows Server 2003 a new attribute on user objects called lastLogonTimestamp contains the approximate last time the user logged on. Using this to find the users that have not logged on in a number of weeks is much easier than the option with Windows 2000, where we would need to query every domain controller in the domain. However, the lastLogonTimestamp attribute has a certain amount of latency associated with it to cut down on replication traffic; the date contained in this attribute can be anywhere from 9 to 14 days off in a default Windows Server 2003 domain. This latency can be made longer or shorter by modifying the attribute msDS-LogonTimeSyncInterval of the Domain NC.

See Also

Recipe 6.29 for more on computing large integer timestamps and Recipe 6.33 for more on finding a user's last logon timestamp

6.35 Viewing and Modifying a User's Permitted Logon Hours

Problem

You want to see the hours that a user is permitted to log onto the network.

Solution

Using a graphical user interface

1. Open the ADUC snap-in.
2. If you need to change domains, right-click on "Active Directory Users and Computers" in the left pane, select Connect to Domain, enter the domain name, and click OK.
3. Right-click on the user and select Properties. From the Account tab, click on Logon Hours.
4. Select the hours that you want to allow or disallow, and click Logon Permitted or Logon Denied. Click OK.
5. Click Apply, followed by OK.

Using VBScript

```
Days = Array _
("Sunday", "Monday", "Tuesday", "Wednesday", "Thursday", "Friday", "Saturday")
Set objUser = GetObject("LDAP://<UserDN>")
arrHours = objUser.Get("logonHours")

For i = 1 To LenB(arrHours)
    arrHoursBytes(i-1) = AscB(MidB(arrHours, i, 1))
    WScript.Echo "MidB returns: " & MidB(arrHours, i, 1)
    WScript.Echo "arrHoursBytes: " & arrHoursBytes(i-1)
    wscript.echo vbcrlf
Next

intCounter = 0
intLoopCounter = 0
WScript.echo "Day Byte 1 Byte 2 Byte 3"
For Each HourByte In arrHoursBytes
    arrHourBits = DisplayLogonHourBits(HourByte)

    If intCounter = 0 Then
        WScript.STDOUT.Write Days(intLoopCounter) & Space(2)
        intLoopCounter = intLoopCounter + 1
```

```
            End If

        For Each HourBit In arrHourBits
            WScript.STDOUT.Write HourBit
            intCounter = 1 + intCounter

            If intCounter = 8 or intCounter = 16 Then
                Wscript.STDOUT.Write Space(1)
            End If

            If intCounter = 24 Then
                WScript.echo vbCr
                intCounter = 0
            End If
        Next
    Next

    Function DisplayLogonHourBits(x)
        Dim arrBits(7)
        For i = 7 to 0 Step -1
            If x And 2^i Then
                arrBits(i) = 1
            Else
                arrBits(i) = 0
            End If
        Next
        DisplayLogonHourBits = arrBits
    End Function
```

Using PowerShell

```
    # similar algorithm to vbscript, but easier to understand
    # output is identical

    ## user DN
    $userDN = "LDAP://<UserDN>"

    ## powers of two in a single byte
    ## can use [System.Math]::Pow(), but this is faster
    $pow2 = @(1, 2, 4, 8, 16, 32, 64, 128)

    ## bit-state - a bit is either off (0) or on (1)
    $onoff = @("0", "1")

    function dump($byte)
    {
        $result = ""
        for ($i = 0; $i -lt 8; $i++)
        {
            $result += $onoff[($byte -band $pow2[$i]) -ne 0]
        }
        return $result
    }

    # days of the week, zero based
```

```
$days = @("Sunday", "Monday", "Tuesday", "Wednesday", "Thursday",
"Friday", "Saturday")
$day = 0

# main
$obj = [ADSI]$userDN
$arr = $obj.logonHours.Value

for ($i = 0; $i -lt $arr.Length; $i += 3)
{
    $days[$day]
    (dump $arr[$i]) + " " + (dump $arr[$i+1]) + " " + (dump $arr[$i+2])
    $day += 1
}
```

Discussion

Using VBScript and PowerShell

The logonHours attribute of a user object is represented as an octet string, rather than a simple string like most of the other attributes we've discussed. As a result, manipulating it directly is a bit trickier than simply inserting a new string in place of an old one. An octet string is simply another name for an array of bytes containing arbitrary binary data. For the logonHours attribute, each hour of a day is represented as a single bit within a byte. Each byte contains eight (8) bits, so it takes three bytes to represent all of the hours in a day. It goes from low-order to high-order (that is, the low-order bit in the lowest byte for a given day is midnight to one a.m.). The information is stored in the logonHours attribute in UTC and translated by the user interface into local time. Finally, since there are 7 days in a week, and each day takes 3 bytes of information, the attribute will have 21 elements.

In the VBScript example shown in this recipe, we use a VBScript function that manipulates the various bits of the attribute to produce the correct values. In the PowerShell example, we pre-generate an array containing the powers-of-2 contained with a byte and process each day as a subarray of the entire attribute. Using the bitwise and function in PowerShell allows us to map binary values directly into array subscripts, which reduces the complexity of the routine.

See Also

MS KB 816666 (How to Limit User Logon Time in a Domain in Windows Server 2003) and MSDN: Logon-Hours attribute [AD Schema]

6.36 Viewing a User's Managed Objects

Problem

You want to view the objects that are owned by a user.

Solution

Using a graphical user interface

1. Open ADSI Edit.
2. If an entry for the naming context you want to browse is not already displayed, do the following:
    a. Right-click on ADSI Edit in the right pane and click "Connect to...".
    b. Fill in the information for the naming context, container, or OU you want to add an object to. Click on the Advanced button if you need to enter alternate credentials.
3. In the left pane, browse to the naming context, container, or OU of the object you want to view. Once you've found the object, right-click on it and select Properties.
4. View the managedObjects attribute.

Using a command-line interface

```
> adfind -b "<UserDN>" managedObjects
```

Using VBScript

```
' This code displays the
' managed objects for a user
' ------ SCRIPT CONFIGURATION ------
strUserDN = "<UserDN>" ' e.g. cn=jsmith,cn=Users,dc=adatum,dc=com
' ------ END CONFIGURATION ---------

On Error Resume Next
set objUser = GetObject("LDAP://" & strUserDN)
Wscript.Echo objUser.Get("cn") & "'s
Managed Objects:"
colObjects = objUser.GetEx("managedObjects")
if Err.Number = -2147463155 then
    Wscript.Echo " none"
else
    for each strObjectDN in colObjects
        Wscript.Echo " " & strObjectDN
    next
end if
```

Using PowerShell

To retrieve a user's managedObjects property using the System.DirectoryServices methods, use the following syntax:

```
$obj = [ADSI] "LDAP://<UserDN>"
$obj.managedObjects
```

To use the Quest AD cmdlets, use the following:

```
$obj = get-QADUser -identity "<UserDN>"
$obj.DirectoryEntry.managedObjects
```

Discussion

The `managedObjects` attribute is linked to the `managedBy` attribute that can be set on certain objects in Active Directory like computers, OUs, and groups. Setting the `managedBy` attribute provides a quick way to define who owns an object. If you do use it, you can use the `managedObjects` attribute on user, contact, or group objects to get the list of objects for which the user has been configured in the `managedBy` attribute.

6.37 Creating a UPN Suffix for a Forest

Problem

You want users to have a different UPN suffix from the default provided by your forest.

Solution

Using a graphical user interface

1. Open the Active Directory Domains and Trusts snap-in.
2. In the left pane, right-click Active Directory Domains and Trusts and select Properties.
3. Under Alternative UPN suffixes, type the name of the suffix you want to add.
4. Click Add and OK.

Using a command-line interface

```
> admod -config -rb cn=Partitions
    uPNSuffixes:+:treyresearch.com
```

 The *attributeName:+:attributeValue* syntax will add an additional value to an existing list of values in a multivalued attribute. Using *attributeName::attributeValue* would overwrite the existing values with the value you specify.

Using VBScript

```
' This code adds a new UPN suffix.
' ------ SCRIPT CONFIGURATION ------
Const ADS_PROPERTY_APPEND = 3
strNewSuffix = "<NewSuffix>" ' e.g. othercorp.com
strDomain = "<DomainDNSName>" ' e.g. adatum.com
' ------ END CONFIGURATION --------
set objRootDSE = GetObject("LDAP://" & strDomain & "/RootDSE")
```

```
set objPartitions = GetObject("LDAP://cn=Partitions," & _
                              objRootDSE.Get("ConfigurationNamingContext"))
objPartitions.PutEx ADS_PROPERTY_APPEND, "uPNSuffixes", Array(strNewSuffix)
objPartitions.SetInfo
```

Using PowerShell

```
set-variable -name $ADS_PROPERTY_APPEND -value 3 -option constant
$strDN = "LDAP://cn=Partitions,cn=Configuration,<ForestDN>"
$strNewSuffix = "<NewSuffix>"
$objPart = [ADSI] $strDN
$objPart.PutEx($ADS_PROPERTY_APPEND, "uPNSuffixes", @($strNewSuffix))
$objPart.SetInfo()
```

Discussion

The UPN allows users to log on with a friendly name that may even correspond to their email address. UPN logons also do not require the domain to be known so that it can be abstracted away from the user. You may need to create an additional UPN suffix (e.g., @*adatum.com*) if you want UPNs to map to email addresses, but your AD forest is rooted at a different domain name (e.g., *ad.adatum.com*) than the domain name used in email addresses (e.g., *treyresearch.com*).

Using VBScript

UPN suffixes are stored in the multivalued uPNSuffixes attribute on the Partitions container in the Configuration naming context. The default forest UPN suffix is assumed and not stored in that attribute.

See Also

MS KB 243280 (Users Can Log On Using User Name or User Principal Name), MS KB 243629 (How to Add UPN Suffixes to a Forest), and MS KB 269441 (How to Use ADSI to List the UPN Suffixes that Are Defined in Active Directory)

6.38 Restoring a Deleted User

Problem

You want to restore a user object that has been inadvertently deleted, as well as restore its members.

Solution

Using a graphical user interface

1. Reboot the domain controller in Directory Services Restore Mode.

2. Perform a System State restore.

3. Before rebooting the server, perform the steps listed in the following section.

Using a command line interface

1. To restore the user and group accounts, use the following sequence of commands. Replace *<GroupDN>* with the name of the user object that needs to be restored (the `activate instance ntds` line is only necessary in Windows Server 2008):

```
> ntdsutil
> activate instance ntds
> authoritative restore
> restore object <UserDN>
> quit
> exit
```

2. Reboot the domain controller into normal mode and wait for replication to complete.

Discussion

In most cases, it is sufficient when restoring a deleted object within Active Directory to simply perform an *authoritative* restore of the individual object. Performing this authoritative restore will allow the restored user object to be replicated to other DCs within the domain along with all attributes that were present at the time that the System State backup was taken.

See Also

MS KB 216993 (Useful Shelf Life of a System-State Backup of Active Directory), MS KB 840001 (How to Restore Deleted User Accounts and Their Group Memberships in Active Directory), and Chapter 16 for more on recovering and restoring Active Directory

6.39 Protecting a User Against Accidental Deletion

Problem

You want to prevent a user object from being accidentally deleted by an administrator who selects the incorrect option in Active Directory Users and Computers.

Solution

Using a graphical user interface (Windows Server 2008 only)

1. Open Active Directory Users and Computers. Click on View and confirm that Advanced Features is selected.

2. Drill down to the current domain. To connect to a different domain, right-click on the top-level node and click Change domain; select the appropriate domain and then drill down to it.

3. Right-click on the object that you want to modify and click Properties.

4. Click on the Object tab.

5. Place a checkmark next to "Protect object from accidental deletion."

6. Click OK.

Using a command-line interface (all versions)

```
dsacls <User DN> /d EVERYONE:SDDT
```

Using PowerShell (all versions)

```
Add-QADPermission -identity <User DN> -Account 'EVERYONE' -Rights
'Delete,DeleteTree' -ApplyTo 'ThisObjectOnly'
```

Discussion

By default, all new OUs that are created in Windows Server 2008 will have this protection enabled; however, no other object types are configured with this default protection. If you attempt to delete a group that is protected using this option, even when signed on as a Domain Admin or other similarly elevated account, you will receive an "Access Denied" message until you manually remove the checkbox or manually remove the DENY ACE associated with it.

By using the command-line or PowerShell methods, this protection can be applied to group objects in *all* versions of Windows Server, even though the GUI checkbox is only available in Windows Server 2008.

## CHAPTER 7

Groups

7.0 Introduction

A group is a simple concept that has been used in many different types of standalone
and networked systems over the years. In generic terms, a group is just a collection of
objects. Groups are often used to apply security in an efficient manner, where you create
a collection of users and assign certain permissions or rights to that group, rather than
to each individual user within the group. When applying security settings, it's much
easier to use a group rather than individual users, because you only need to apply the
security setting once instead of once per user. In addition, groups are also frequently
used to send email messages to an entire group of users at once rather than requiring
the sender to address each person individually.

In Active Directory, groups are flexible objects that can contain virtually any other type
of object as a member, although they'll generally only contain users, `inetOrgPerson`s,
computers, and other groups. Active Directory groups can be used for many different
purposes, including controlling access to resources, defining a filter for the application
of group policies, and as an email distribution list.

The ways in which a group can be used in an Active Directory forest are defined by the
group's *scope* and *type*. The *type* of a group can be either *security* or *distribution*. Security
groups can be used to restrict access to Windows resources, whereas distribution
groups can be used only as a simple grouping mechanism for sending email messages
or for some other non-Windows security-related function. Both security and distribution groups can be used as email lists, but only security groups can be used to assign
access to resources.

The *scope* of a group determines where members of the group can be located within
the forest and where in the forest you can use the group in an ACL. The supported
group scopes include *universal, global*, and *domain local*. Universal groups and domain
local groups can have members that are part of any domain in the same forest (or a
separate forest if a cross-forest trust exists), whereas global groups can only have members that are part of the same domain that the group is contained in. When assigning
permissions to group objects, universal and global groups can be assigned permissions

to resources anywhere in the forest, whereas domain local groups can only be assigned permissions to resources in the same domain. (In this way, domain local and global groups are functional opposites of one another.)

The Anatomy of a Group

Groups are represented in Active Directory by **group** objects. Table 7-1 contains a list of some of the noteworthy attributes that are available on **group** objects.

Table 7-1. Attributes of group objects

Attribute	Description
cn	Relative distinguished name of group objects.
whenCreated	Timestamp of when the OU was created.
description	Textual description of the group.
groupType	Flag containing the group scope and type. See Recipe 7.8 for more information.
info	Additional notes about a group.
primaryGroupToken	Local RID for the group. This matches the primaryGroupID attribute that is set on user objects.
managedBy	DN of a user or group that is the owner of the group.
managedObjects	List of DNs of objects for which this group is listed in the managedBy attribute.
Member	List of DNs of members of the group.
memberOf	List of DNs of the groups this group is a member of.
whenChanged	Timestamp of when the OU was last modified.
sAMAccountName	Downlevel account name for the group. Typically this is the same as the cn attribute.
wWWHomePage	URL of the home page for the group.
sAMAccountType	Describes the type of account that was created for an object, such as a domain object, a group object, a normal user account, etc.

7.1 Creating a Group

Problem

You want to create a group.

Solution

Using a graphical user interface

1. Open the ADUC snap-in.
2. If you need to change domains, right-click on Active Directory Users and Computers in the left pane, select Connect to Domain, enter the domain name, and click OK.

3. In the left pane, browse to the parent container of the new group, right-click on it, and select New→Group.

4. Enter the name of the group and select the group scope (global, domain local, or universal) and group type (security or distribution).

5. Click OK.

Using a command-line interface

In the following example, *<GroupDN>* should be replaced with the DN of the group to create, *<GroupScope>* should be l, g, or u for domain local, global, and universal groups, respectively, and -secgrp should be set to yes if the group is a security group or no otherwise. Another recommended option is to set -desc for specifying a group description:

```
> dsadd group "<GroupDN>" -scope <GroupScope> -secgrp yes|no -desc "<GroupDesc>"
```

You can also create a group object with admod, using the following syntax:

```
> admod -b "<GroupDN>" objectClass::group groupType::
"<GroupType>" sAMAccountName::"<Pre-Windows2000Name>" -add
```

For example, to create a global security group called "Finance Users" in the Finance OU of the *adatum.com* domain, you can use either of the following commands:

```
> dsadd group "cn=Finance Users,ou=Finance,dc=adatum,dc=com"-scope global-
secgrp yes
```

```
> admod-b "cn=Finance Users,ou=Finance,dc=adatum,dc=com" groupType::-2147483646
sAMAccountName::"Finance Users" -add
```

In the case of AdMod, you must specify the numeric value for the group type, which can be any one of those listed in Table 7-2.

Table 7-2. Numeric values for group types

Group type	Numeric value
Universal Distribution Group	8
Universal Security Group	−2147483640
Domain Local Distribution Group	4
Domain Local Security Group	−2147483644
Global Distribution Group	2
Global Security Group	−2147483646

These values are defined in the ADS_GROUP_TYPE_ENUM enumeration; see Recipe 7.8 for more information.

If you omit the sAMAccountName attribute when creating the group, it will be automatically populated with a random string.

Using VBScript

```
' The following code creates a global security group.
' ------ SCRIPT CONFIGURATION ------
strGroupParentDN = "<GroupParentDN>" ' e.g. ou=Groups,dc=adatum,dc=com
strGroupName     = "<GroupName>"     ' e.g. ExecAdminsSales
strGroupDescr    = "<GroupDesc>"     ' e.g. Executive Admins for Sales group
' ------ END CONFIGURATION ---------

' Constants taken from ADS_GROUP_TYPE_ENUM
Const ADS_GROUP_TYPE_GLOBAL_GROUP      = 2
Const ADS_GROUP_TYPE_DOMAIN_LOCAL_GROUP = 4
Const ADS_GROUP_TYPE_SECURITY_ENABLED  = -2147483648
Const ADS_GROUP_TYPE_UNIVERSAL_GROUP   = 8

set objOU = GetObject("LDAP://" & strGroupParentDN)
set objGroup = objOU.Create("group","cn=" & strGroupName)
objGroup.Put "groupType", ADS_GROUP_TYPE_GLOBAL_GROUP _
                     Or ADS_GROUP_TYPE_SECURITY_ENABLED
objGroup.Put "sAMAccountName", strGroupName
objGroup.Put "description", strGroupDescr
objGroup.SetInfo
```

Using PowerShell

To create a group using the Quest cmdlets, use the following syntax:

```
new-QADGroup -ParentContainer '<Parent OU DN>' -name '<GroupName>' -samaccountname
'<GroupName> -grouptype 'Distribution' -groupscope 'Universal'
```

To create a group in PowerShell using ADSI, use the following syntax:

```
set-variable ADS_GROUP_TYPE_GLOBAL_GROUP      2            -option constant
set-variable ADS_GROUP_TYPE_DOMAIN_LOCALGROUP 4            -option constant
set-variable ADS_GROUP_TYPE_UNIVERSAL_GROUP   8            -option constant
set-variable ADS_GROUP_TYPE_SECURITY_ENABLED -2147483648 -option constant

$groupType = $ADS_GROUP_TYPE_GLOBAL_GROUP -bor $ADS_GROUP_TYPE_SECURITY_ENABLED

$objParent = [ADSI] "LDAP://<Parent DN>"
$objGroup = $objParent.Create("group", "cn=<Group Name>")
$objGroup.Put("groupType", $groupType.ToString())
$objGroup.Put("samaccountname", "<Group Name>")
$objGroup.SetInfo()
```

Discussion

In each solution, a group was created with no members. For more information on how to add and remove members, see Recipe 7.5.

The `groupType` attribute contains a flag indicating both group scope and type. The available flag values are defined in the `ADS_GROUP_TYPE_ENUM` enumeration. Recipe 7.8 contains more information on setting the group scopes and types.

See Also

Recipe 7.5 for adding and removing group members, Recipe 7.8 for setting group scope and type, MS KB 231273 (Group Type and Scope Usage in Windows), MS KB 232241 (Group Management with ADSI in Windows 2000), MS KB 816302 (How to Manage Groups in Active Directory in Windows Server 2003), and MSDN: ADS_GROUP_TYPE_ENUM

7.2 Viewing the Permissions of a Group

Problem

You want to list the AD object permissions that have been assigned to a **group** object.

Solution

Using a graphical user interface

1. Open the Active Directory Users and Computers (ADUC) snap-in. Click on View and confirm that there is a checkmark next to Advanced Features.
2. If you need to change domains, right-click on Active Directory Users and Computers in the left pane, select Connect to Domain, enter the domain name, and click OK.
3. In the left pane, right-click on the domain and select Find.
4. Enter the name of the group and click Find Now.
5. Double-click on the group in the bottom results pane.
6. Click on the Security tab. The users and groups that have been assigned permissions to the object are listed in the bottom pane; select each entry to view the permissions that have been assigned to it.
7. Click on Advanced to view the owner of the group, as well as any auditing that has been configured.

Using a command-line interface

```
> dsacls "<GroupDN>"
```

You can also obtain this information using AdFind, as follows:

```
adfind -gcb -f name=<Group Name> ntsecuritydescriptor -sddl++ -resolvesids
```

Using VBScript

```
Const SE_DACL_PROTECTED = &H1000

Set objGroup = GetObject("LDAP://<GroupDN>")

Set objNtSecurityDescriptor = objGroup.Get("nTSecurityDescriptor")

Control = objNtSecurityDescriptor.Control

WScript.Echo "Group Permissions"
If (intNtSecurityDescriptorControl And SE_DACL_PROTECTED) Then
    Wscript.Echo "Permission inheritance is disabled."
Else
    WScript.Echo "Permission inheritance is enabled."
End If
WScript.Echo

Set objDACL = objNtSecurityDescriptor.DiscretionaryAcl
DisplayAceInformation objDACL, "DACL"

Sub DisplayAceInformation(SecurityStructure, strType)
    Const ADS_ACETYPE_ACCESS_ALLOWED = &H0
    Const ADS_ACETYPE_ACCESS_DENIED = &H1
    Const ADS_ACETYPE_ACCESS_ALLOWED_OBJECT = &H5
    Const ADS_ACETYPE_ACCESS_DENIED_OBJECT = &H6
    intAceCount = 0
    For Each objAce In SecurityStructure
        strTrustee = Mid(objAce.Trustee,1,12)
        If StrComp(strTrustee, "NT AUTHORITY", 1) <> 0 Then
            intAceCount = intAceCount + 1
            WScript.Echo strType & " permission entry: " & intAceCount
            WScript.Echo "Name: " & objAce.Trustee

            intAceType = objAce.AceType
            If (intAceType = ADS_ACETYPE_ACCESS_ALLOWED Or _
                intAceType = ADS_ACETYPE_ACCESS_ALLOWED_OBJECT) Then
                WScript.Echo "Allow ACE"
            ElseIf (intAceType = ADS_ACETYPE_ACCESS_DENIED Or _
                intAceType = ADS_ACETYPE_ACCESS_DENIED_OBJECT) Then
                WScript.Echo "Deny ACE"
            Else
                WScript.Echo "Unknown ACE."
            End If
            ReadBitsInAccessMask(objAce.AccessMask)
            WScript.Echo VbCr
        End If
    Next
End Sub

Sub ReadBitsInAccessMask(AccessMask)
    Const ADS_RIGHT_DELETE = &H10000
    Const ADS_RIGHT_READ_CONTROL = &H20000
    Const ADS_RIGHT_WRITE_DAC = &H40000
    Const ADS_RIGHT_WRITE_OWNER = &H80000
    Const ADS_RIGHT_DS_CREATE_CHILD = &H1
```

```
        Const ADS_RIGHT_DS_DELETE_CHILD = &H2
        Const ADS_RIGHT_ACTRL_DS_LIST = &H4
        Const ADS_RIGHT_DS_SELF = &H8
        Const ADS_RIGHT_DS_READ_PROP = &H10
        Const ADS_RIGHT_DS_WRITE_PROP = &H20
        Const ADS_RIGHT_DS_DELETE_TREE = &H40
        Const ADS_RIGHT_DS_LIST_OBJECT = &H80
        Const ADS_RIGHT_DS_CONTROL_ACCESS = &H100

        WScript.Echo VbCrLf & "Standard Access Rights"
        If (AccessMask And ADS_RIGHT_DELETE) Then _
            WScript.Echo vbTab & "-Delete an object."
        If (AccessMask And ADS_RIGHT_READ_CONTROL) Then _
            WScript.Echo vbTab & "-Read permissions."
        If (AccessMask And ADS_RIGHT_WRITE_DAC) Then _
            WScript.Echo vbTab & "-Write permissions."
        If (AccessMask And ADS_RIGHT_WRITE_OWNER) Then _
            WScript.Echo vbTab & "-Modify owner."

        WScript.Echo VbCrLf & "Directory Service Specific Access Rights"
        If (AccessMask And ADS_RIGHT_DS_CREATE_CHILD) Then _
            WScript.Echo vbTab & "-Create child objects."
        If (AccessMask And ADS_RIGHT_DS_DELETE_CHILD) Then _
            WScript.Echo vbTab & "-Delete child objects."
        If (AccessMask And ADS_RIGHT_ACTRL_DS_LIST) Then _
            WScript.Echo vbTab & "-Enumerate an object."
        If (AccessMask And ADS_RIGHT_DS_READ_PROP) Then _
            WScript.Echo vbTab & "-Read the properties of an object."
        If (AccessMask And ADS_RIGHT_DS_WRITE_PROP) Then _
            WScript.Echo vbTab & "-Write the properties of an object."
        If (AccessMask And ADS_RIGHT_DS_DELETE_TREE) Then _
            WScript.Echo vbTab & "-Delete a tree of objects"
        If (AccessMask And ADS_RIGHT_DS_LIST_OBJECT) Then _
            WScript.Echo vbTab & "-List a tree of objects."

        WScript.Echo VbCrLf & "Control Access Rights"
        If (AccessMask And ADS_RIGHT_DS_CONTROL_ACCESS) + _
            (AccessMask And ADS_RIGHT_DS_SELF) = 0 Then
            WScript.Echo "-None"
        Else
            If (AccessMask And ADS_RIGHT_DS_CONTROL_ACCESS) Then _
                WScript.Echo vbTab & "-Extended access rights."
            If (AccessMask And ADS_RIGHT_DS_SELF) Then
                WScript.Echo vbTab & "-Active Directory must validate a property "
                WScript.Echo vbTab & " write operation beyond the schema " & _
                    "definition "
                WScript.Echo vbTab & " for the attribute."
            End If
        End If
    End Sub
```

Using PowerShell

To retrieve DACL and SACL information using the Quest PowerShell cmdlets, use the following syntax:

```
Get-QADPermission -identity <Group DN> -Inherited -SchemaDefault
```

If you have Exchange 2007 or above management tools installed on your workstation, you can also retrieve DACL and SACL information using the following Exchange cmdlet:

```
Get-ADPermission -Identity <Group Name>
```

Discussion

In an Active Directory environment, you can set permissions on an object within the directory in much the same way that you can set NTFS permissions on files and folders. Each AD object has a Security Descriptor (SD) associated with it that is made up of a Discretionary Access Control List (DACL) that dictates which users and groups can access an object, and a System Access Control List (SACL) that controls which users' or groups' activities should be audited. The DACL and SACL are each made up of one or more Access Control Entries (ACEs), one for each user or group and its associated permission.

Using PowerShell

By default, the Get-QADPermission cmdlet will only display those DACL and SACL entries that have been explicitly defined on the group object. The -Inherited switch will show entries that have been inherited from a container higher in the domain structure, and the -SchemaDefault switch will show those DACL and SACL entries that were applied by default.

See Also

MSDN: Creating a DACL [Security], MSDN: Order of ACEs in a DACL [Security], MSDN: SACL Access Right [Security], and MSDN: Retrieving an Object's SACL [Security]

7.3 Viewing the Direct Members of a Group

Problem

You want to view the direct members of a group.

Solution

Using a graphical user interface

1. Open the ADUC snap-in.
2. If you need to change domains, right-click on Active Directory Users and Computers in the left pane, select Connect to Domain, enter the domain name, and click OK.
3. In the left pane, right-click on the domain and select Find.
4. Enter the name of the group and click Find Now.
5. Double-click on the group in the bottom results pane.
6. Click the Members tab.

Using a command-line interface

You can enumerate the direct members of a group using the built-in DSGet utility, or AdFind. Using DSGet requires the following syntax:

```
> dsget group "<GroupDN>" -members
```

To list group members with AdFind, enter the following:

```
> adfind -b "<GroupDN>" member
```

Using VBScript

```
' This code prints the direct members of the specified group.
' ------ SCRIPT CONFIGURATION -----
strGroupDN = "<GroupDN>" ' e.g. cn=SalesGroup,ou=Groups,dc=adatum,dc=com
' ------ END CONFIGURATION --------

set objGroup = GetObject("LDAP://" & strGroupDN)
Wscript.Echo "Members of " & objGroup.Name & ":"
for each objMember in objGroup.Members
    Wscript.Echo objMember.Name
next
```

Using PowerShell

To enumerate direct group membership, use either the Quest AD cmdlet `Get-QADGroup Member` or ADSI syntax, as shown here:

```
Get-QADGroupMember -identity <Group DN>
[ADSI] "LDAP://<Group DN>".Member
```

Discussion

The member attribute of a group object contains the distinguished names of the direct members of the group. By direct members, we mean the members that have been directly added to the group. This is in contrast to indirect group members, which are members of the group due to nested group membership. See Recipe 7.4 for how to find the nested membership of a group.

The memberOf attribute is a *backlink* to member. This means that, for each group membership listed in a group's member attribute, the DN of the group itself appears in that user/computer/group's memberOf attribute. Think of it this way: if the *FinanceUsers* group has Jane as a member, then Jane is a member of the *FinanceUsers* group. In this way, Active Directory uses forward links and backlinks to maintain consistency between groups and their membership.

See Also

Recipe 7.4 for viewing nested group membership

7.4 Viewing the Nested Members of a Group

Problem

You want to view the nested membership of a group.

Solution

Using a graphical user interface

1. Open the ADUC snap-in.
2. If you need to change domains, right-click on Active Directory Users and Computers in the left pane, select Connect to Domain, enter the domain name, and click OK.
3. In the left pane, right-click on the domain and select Find.
4. Enter the name of the group and click Find Now.
5. Double-click on the group in the bottom results pane.
6. Click the Members tab.
7. You must now double-click on each group member to view its membership.

Using a command-line interface

```
> dsget group "<GroupDN>" -members -expand
```

You can also obtain this information using the *joeware* MemberOf utility:

```
> memberof -group <GroupDN>
```

Using VBScript

```
' This code prints the nested membership of a group.
' ------ SCRIPT CONFIGURATION ------
```

```
strGroupDN = "<GroupDN>" ' e.g. cn=SalesGroup,ou=Groups,dc=adatum,dc=com
' ------ END CONFIGURATION ---------

strSpaces = " "
set dicSeenGroupMember = CreateObject("Scripting.Dictionary")
Wscript.Echo "Members of " & strGroupDN & ":"
DisplayMembers("LDAP://" & strGroupDN, strSpaces, dicSeenGroupMember)

Function
DisplayMembers ( strGroupADsPath, strSpaces,dicSeenGroupMember)

    set objGroup = GetObject(strGroupADsPath)
    for each objMember In objGroup.Members
        Wscript.Echo strSpaces & objMember.Name
        if objMember.Class = "group" then
            if dicSeenGroupMember.Exists(objMember.ADsPath) then
                Wscript.Echo strSpaces & " ^ already seen group member " & _
                                    "(stopping to avoid loop)"
            else
                dicSeenGroupMember.Add objMember.ADsPath, 1
                DisplayMembers objMember.ADsPath, strSpaces & " ", _
                            dicSeenGroupMember
            end if
        end if
    next

End Function
```

Using PowerShell

The simplest method of listing nested group membership in PowerShell is using the Quest AD cmdlets, as follows:

```
Get-QADGroupMember -identity <Group DN> -indirect
```

Discussion

As described in Recipe 7.3, group membership is stored in the multivalued `member` attribute on `group` objects. But that attribute will not show the complete picture because group nesting is allowed in Active Directory after you've transitioned from mixed mode. To view the complete group membership, you have to recurse through each group's members. (The exception to this is the `memberof` command-line utility, which correctly displays primary group memberships.)

In the VBScript example, we used a dictionary object (referred to as a hash or associative array in other languages) to ensure that we did not get in an infinite loop. The dictionary object stores each group member; before the `DisplayMembers` function is called, a check is performed to determine if the group has already been evaluated. If so, a message is displayed indicating the group will not be processed again. If this type of checking was not employed and you had a situation where group A was a member of group B, group B was a member of group C, and group C was a member of group A, the loop would repeat without terminating.

See Also

Recipe 7.3 for viewing group membership and MSDN: IADsMember

7.5 Adding and Removing Members of a Group

Problem

You want to add or remove members of a group.

Solution

Using a graphical user interface

1. Open the ADUC snap-in.
2. If you need to change domains, right-click on Active Directory Users and Computers in the left pane, select Connect to Domain, enter the domain name, and click OK.
3. In the left pane, right-click on the domain and select Find.
4. Enter the name of the group and click Find Now.
5. Double-click on the group in the bottom results pane.
6. Click the Members tab.
7. To remove a member, click on the member name, click the Remove button, click Yes, and click OK.
8. To add a member, click on the Add button, enter the name of the member, and click OK twice.

Using a command-line interface

The -addmbr option in dsmod adds a member to a group:

```
> dsmod group "<GroupDN>" -addmbr "<MemberDN>"
```

To add a group member with admod, use the following syntax:

```
> admod -b "<GroupDN>" member:+:"<MemberDN>"
```

The -rmmbr option in dsmod removes a member from a group:

```
> dsmod group "<GroupDN>" -rmmbr "<MemberDN>"
```

To remove a group member with admod, use the following syntax:

```
> admod -b "<GroupDN>" member:-:"<MemberDN>"
```

The -chmbr option in dsmod replaces the complete membership list:

```
> dsmod group "<GroupDN>" -chmbr "<Member1DN Member2DN ... >"
```

To replace the membership of a group with **admod**, use the following command:

```
> admod -b "<GroupDN>" member:+-:"<Member1DN>;<Member2DN>;<Member3DN>"
```

Using VBScript

```
' This code adds a member to a group.
' ------ SCRIPT CONFIGURATION ------
strGroupDN = "<GroupDN>" ' e.g. cn=SalesGroup,ou=
Groups,dc=adatum,dc=com
strMemberDN = "<MemberDN>" ' e.g. cn=jsmith,cn=users,dc=adatum,dc=com
' ------ END CONFIGURATION ---------

set objGroup = GetObject("LDAP://" & strGroupDN)
' Add a member

objGroup.Add("LDAP://" & strMemberDN)
' This code removes a member from a group.
' ------ SCRIPT CONFIGURATION ------
strGroupDN = "<GroupDN>" ' e.g. cn=SalesGroup,ou=Groups,dc=adatum,dc=com
strMemberDN = "<MemberDN>" ' e.g. cn=jsmith,cn=users,dc=adatum,dc=com
' ------ END CONFIGURATION ---------

set objGroup = GetObject("LDAP://" & strGroupDN)
' Remove a member
objGroup.Remove("LDAP://" & strMemberDN)
```

Using PowerShell

To add and remove users from groups using the Quest AD cmdlets, use the following syntax:

```
Add-QADGroupMember -Identity <GroupDN> -Member <UserDN>
Remove-QADGroupMember -Identity <GroupDN> -Member <UserDN>
```

To add a group member using ADSI, use the following syntax:

```
$objGroup = [ADSI] "LDAP://<Group DN>"
$objGroup.Add("LDAP://<User DN>")
```

To remove a group member using ADSI, use the following syntax:

```
$objGroup = [ADSI] "LDAP://<Group DN>"
$objGroup.Remove("LDAP://<User DN>")
```

Discussion

Since there are no restrictions on what distinguished names you can put in the **member** attribute, you can essentially have any type of object as a member of a group. Although OUs are typically used to structure objects that share certain criteria, **group** objects can be used to create loose collections of objects.

The benefit of using **group** objects as a collection mechanism is that the same object can be a member of multiple groups, whereas an object can only be a part of a single OU. Another key difference is that you can assign permissions on resources to groups because they are considered security principals in Active Directory, whereas OUs are not. This is different from some other directories, such as Novell NetWare, where OUs act more like security principals.

See Also

Recipe 7.3 for viewing group membership, MSDN: IADsGroup::Add, and MSDN: IADsGroup::Remove

7.6 Moving a Group Within a Domain

Problem

You want to move a group to a different OU or container within the same domain.

Solution

Using a graphical user interface

1. Open ADSI Edit.
2. If an entry for the naming context you want to browse is not already displayed, do the following:
   a. Right-click on ADSI Edit in the right pane and click "Connect to...".
   b. Fill in the information for the naming context, container, or OU containing the object. Click on the Advanced button if you need to enter alternate credentials.
3. In the left pane, browse to the container or OU that contains the group you want to move. Once you've found the object, right-click on it and select Move.
4. Browse to the new parent of the object, select it, and click OK.

Using a command-line interface

To move an object to a new parent container within the same domain, you can use either DSMove or AdMod, as follows:

```
> dsmove "<GroupDN>" -newparent "<NewParentDN>"
```

or:

```
> admod -b "<GroupDN>" -move "<NewParentDN>"
```

Using VBScript

```
' This code moves an object from one location to another in the same domain.
' ------ SCRIPT CONFIGURATION -----
strNewParentDN = "LDAP://<NewParentDN>"
```

```
strGroupRDN  = "<GroupRDN>" ' i.e. "cn=Finance"
strGroupDN   = "LDAP://cn=<GroupRDN>,<OldParentDN>"
' ------ END CONFIGURATION --------

set objCont = GetObject(strNewParentDN)
objCont.MoveHere strGroupDN,strGroupRDN
```

Using PowerShell

To move a group with the Quest AD cmdlets, use the following syntax:

```
move-QADObject -Identity <GroupDN> -NewParentContainer <New OU DN>
```

To move a group with the System.DirectoryServices methods, use the following:

```
$objGroup = [ADSI] "LDAP://<GroupDN>"
$objNewOU = [ADSI] "LDAP://<New Parent OU DN>"
$objGroup.psbase.MoveTo($objNewOU)
```

Discussion

Using a command-line interface

The DSMove utility can work against any type of object, including groups. The first parameter is the DN of the group that you want to move. The second parameter is the new parent container of the group. The -s parameter can additionally be used to specify a specific server to work against.

Using VBScript

The MoveHere method can be tricky, so an explanation of how to use it to move objects is in order. First, you need to call GetObject on the new parent container. Then call MoveHere on the parent container object with the ADsPath of the object to move as the first parameter and the RDN of the group being moved as the second.

The reason for the apparent duplication of cn=<GroupName> in the MoveHere method is that the same method can also be used for renaming objects (including groups) within the same container (see Recipe 4.20).

See Also

Recipe 4.20 for moving an object to a different OU, Recipe 4.21 for moving an object to a different domain, Recipe 7.8 for changing group scope and type, MS KB 313066 (How to Move Users, Groups, and Organizational Units Within a Domain in Windows 2000), and MSDN: IADsContainer::MoveHere

7.7 Moving a Group to Another Domain

Problem

You want to move a group to a different domain.

Solution

Using a graphical user interface

To migrate user, computer, group, or OU objects between domains in the same forest, use the following steps:

1. Open the ADMT MMC snap-in.
2. Right-click on the Active Directory Migration Tool folder, and select the Group Account Migration Wizard.
3. On the Test or Migrate Changes screen, click Migrate Now?
4. On the Domain Selection screen, enter the DNS or NetBIOS name of the source and target domains and click Next.
5. On the Group Selection screen, select the **group** objects that you wish to migrate and click Next. (You cannot migrate built-in or well-known groups such as Domain Users or Domain Admins using this process.)
6. On the Organizational Unit Selection screen, enter the name of the target OU or select Browse to open up an object picker in the target domain. Click Next to continue.
7. On the Group Options screen, select one or more of the following and click Next:

    Update user rights
    > Copies any user rights that are assigned in the source domain to the target domain.

    Copy group members
    > Specifies whether the user objects that belong to the group should be migrated along with the group. If you don't select this option, the group will be created in the target domain with no members.

    Update previously migrated objects
    > Supports migrations that take place over time by comparing the source and target groups and migrating any changes that have taken place.

    Fix membership of group
    > Adds any migrated user accounts to groups in the target domain if the user accounts were members of the source groups in the source domain.

    Migrate group SIDs to target domain
    > Adds the security identifiers (SIDs) of the migrated group accounts in the source domain to the SID history of the new group in the target domain.

8. On the Naming Conflicts screen, select whether you want to migrate **group** objects that conflict with objects in the target domain and click Next.

9. Follow the remainder of the wizard to complete the migration.

Using a command-line interface

To migrate a group from the command line using the ADMT utility, use the following syntax:

```
> ADMT GROUP /N "<GroupName1>" "<GroupName2>" /IF:YES /SD:"<SourceDomainDN>"
/TD:"<TargetDomainDN>" /TO:"<TargetOUDN>"
```

Using VBScript

```
set objObject = GetObject("LDAP://TargetDC/TargetParentDN")
objObject.MoveHere "LDAP://SourceDC/SourceDN", vbNullString
```

In the following example, the **"cn=Finance Users"** group in the *amer.adatum.com* domain will be moved to the *emea.adatum.com* domain:

```
set objObject = GetObject( _
    "LDAP://dc-amer1/cn=Finance Users,dc=amer,dc=adatum,dc=com")
objObject.MoveHere _
    "LDAP://dc-emea1/cn=Finance Users,cn=users,dc=emea,dc=adatum,dc=com", _
    vbNullString
```

Discussion

The only type of group that can be moved between domains using the built-in operating system tools is universal groups; additionally, the RID Master for both the source and the target domains needs to be available in order to complete the move. If you want to move a global or domain local group to a different domain, first convert it to a universal group, move the group, then convert it back to a global or domain local group.

When you convert a group between types, you may encounter problems because different groups have different membership restrictions. See Recipe 7.0 for more information on group type membership restrictions.

Another way to accomplish interdomain group moves is by using ADMT, which might be quite useful if you need to move a large number of groups. With ADMT, you can move and restructure groups without needing to go to all the trouble of converting the group to a universal group and then modifying the group membership. For more on the latest version of ADMT, see *http://www.microsoft.com/windowsserver2003/technol ogies/directory/activedirectory/default.mspx*.

7.8 Changing the Scope or Type of a Group

Problem

You want to change the scope or type of a group.

Solution

Using a graphical user interface

1. Open the ADUC snap-in.
2. If you need to change domains, right-click on Active Directory Users and Computers in the left pane, select Connect to Domain, enter the domain name, and click OK.
3. In the left pane, right-click on the domain and select Find.
4. Enter the name of the group you want to modify and click Find Now.
5. Double-click on the group in the results pane.
6. In the group properties dialog box, select the new scope or type, and click OK.

Using a command-line interface

The following example changes the group scope for *<GroupDN>* to *<NewScope>*, which should be l for domain local group, g for global group, or u for universal group:

```
> dsmod group "<GroupDN>" -scope <NewScope>
```

The following example changes the group type for *<GroupDN>*. For the -secgrp switch, specify yes to change to a security group or no to make the group a distribution group:

```
> dsmod group "<GroupDN>" -secgrp yes|no
```

To change the scope and/or type of a group using AdMod, use the following syntax:

```
> admod -b <GroupDN> groupType::<GroupType>
```

Just as when you created a group using AdMod, you must specify the numeric value for the group type; refer back to Recipe 7.1 for more information.

Using VBScript

```
' This code sets the scope and type of the specified group
' to a universal security group.
' ------ SCRIPT CONFIGURATION ------
strGroupDN = "<GroupDN>" ' e.g. cn=SalesGroup,ou=
Groups,dc=adatum,dc=com
' ------ END CONFIGURATION ---------

' Constants taken from ADS_GROUP_TYPE_ENUM
ADS_GROUP_TYPE_GLOBAL_GROUP       = 2
ADS_GROUP_TYPE_DOMAIN_LOCAL_GROUP = 4
```

```
ADS_GROUP_TYPE_UNIVERSAL_GROUP       = 8
ADS_GROUP_TYPE_SECURITY_ENABLED      = -2147483648

set objGroup = GetObject("LDAP://" & strGroupDN )
objGroup.Put "
groupType", ADS_GROUP_TYPE_UNIVERSAL_GROUP _
                   Or ADS_GROUP_TYPE_SECURITY_ENABLED
objGroup.SetInfo
```

Using PowerShell

To modify a group's type or scope using the Quest AD cmdlets, use the following syntax. Use `'Security'` or `'Distribution'` as the group type, and `'Global'`, `'Universal'`, or `'DomainLocal'` as the group scope:

```
set-QADGroup -GroupType '<GroupType>' -GroupScope '<GroupScope>'
```

To modify group information using ADSI, use the following syntax. The **groupType** attribute is used to establish both the type and the scope of a **group** object by using a bit-wise OR:

```
set-variable ADS_GROUP_TYPE_GLOBAL_GROUP       2            -option constant
set-variable ADS_GROUP_TYPE_DOMAIN_LOCALGROUP  4            -option constant
set-variable ADS_GROUP_TYPE_UNIVERSAL_GROUP    8            -option constant
set-variable ADS_GROUP_TYPE_SECURITY_ENABLED -2147483648 -option constant

$groupType = $ADS_GROUP_TYPE_GLOBAL_GROUP -bor $ADS_GROUP_TYPE_SECURITY_ENABLED

$objGroup = [ADSI] "LDAP://<Group DN>"
$objGroup.Put("groupType", $groupType.ToString())
$objGroup.SetInfo()
```

Discussion

Group scope and type are stored as a flag in the **groupType** attribute on **group** objects. To directly update **groupType**, you must logically OR the values associated with each type and scope, as shown in the API solution, or use the raw numeric values listed in Recipe 7.1 when using AdMod. Note that there is no specific value for the distribution list type. If you want to create a distribution list, just do not include the **ADS_GROUP_TYPE_SECURITY_ENABLED** flag when setting **groupType**. To convert a group from one scope to another, the domain must be at least Windows 2000 native domain functional level. There are also additional group types that are available through Authorization Manager, which are discussed in Recipe 7.10.

> For a good description of the usage scenarios for each group type, see Chapter 11 of *Active Directory*, Fourth Edition, by Brian Desmond et al. (O'Reilly).

See Also

Recipes 7.1 and 7.10, MS KB 231273 (Group Type and Scope Usage in Windows), MSDN: ADS_GROUP_TYPE_ENUM, and MSDN: What Type of Group to Use

7.9 Modifying Group Attributes

Problem

You want to modify one or more attributes of an object.

Solution

Using a graphical user interface

1. Open ADSI Edit.

2. If an entry for the naming context you want to browse is not already displayed, do the following:

    a. Right-click on ADSI Edit in the right pane and click "Connect to…".

    b. Fill in the information for the naming context, container, or OU containing the group that you want to modify. Click on the Advanced button if you need to enter alternate credentials.

3. In the left pane, browse to the container or OU that contains the group you want to modify. Once you've found the group, right-click on it and select Properties.

4. Right-click the attribute that you want to modify and select Edit.

5. Enter the new value that you want to use and click OK.

6. Click Apply, followed by OK.

Using a command-line interface

Create an LDIF file called *modify_object.ldf* with the following contents:

```
dn: cn=Finance Users,cn=users,dc=adatum,dc=com
changetype: modify
add: description
description: Members of the Finance Department
-
```

Then run the following command:

```
> ldifde -v -i -f modify_object.ldf
```

To modify a group using AdMod, you'll use the following general syntax:

```
> admod-b <GroupDN> <attribute>:<operation>:<value>
```

For example, you can add a description to a **group** object using the following syntax:

```
> C:\>admod -b cn="Finance Users,cn=Users,dc=adatum,dc=com"
    description::"Members of the Finance Department"
```

You can also modify **group** objects with the **dsmod group** command using the following syntax:

```
> dsmod group <GroupDN> <options>
```

The available options for **dsmod** include the following:

-samid *<NewSAMName>*
> Updates the **sAMAccountName** attribute of the **group** object

-desc *<NewDescription>*
> Updates the **description** attribute of the **group** object

-secgrp {yes | no}
> Configures the **group** object as a security group (**yes**) or a distribution group (**no**)

-scope {l | g | u}
> Configures the group scope as domain local (**l**), global (**g**), or universal (**u**)

{-addmbr | -rmmbr | -chmbr} *<MemberDN1> <MemberDN2>*
> Adds the specified objects to the group (**addmbr**), removes the specified objects (**rmmbr**), or replaces the membership list wholesale with only the specified objects (**chmbr**)

Using VBScript

```
strGroupDN = "cn=Finance Users,cn=users,dc=adatum,dc=com"
set objGroup = GetObject("LDAP://" & strGroupDN)
objGroup.Put "description", "Members of the Finance Department"
objGroup.SetInfo
```

Using PowerShell

You can modify a group's properties using either the **set-QADGroup** Quest cmdlet, or else by using the native ADSI methods:

```
set-QADGroup -Identity <Group DN> -GroupType
'<GroupType>' -GroupScope '<GroupScope>' -description '<Description>'

$objGroup = [ADSI] "LDAP://<Group DN>"
$objGroup.Put("<attribute>", "<value>")
$objGroup.SetInfo()
```

Discussion

Using a graphical user interface

If the parent container of the object you want to modify has a lot of objects in it, you may want to add a new connection entry for the DN of the target object. This will be easier than trying to hunt through a container full of objects. You can do this by right-clicking ADSI Edit and selecting "Connect to…" under Connection Point, then selecting Distinguished Name and entering the DN of the object.

Using a command-line interface

For more on *ldifde*, see Recipe 4.28.

Using VBScript

If you need to do anything more than simple assignment or replacement of a value for an attribute, you'll need to use the `PutEx` method instead of `Put`. `PutEx` allows greater control when assigning multiple values, deleting specific values, and appending values.

`PutEx` requires three parameters: update flag, attribute name, and an array of values to set or unset. The update flags are defined by the `ADS_PROPERTY_OPERATION_ENUM` collection and listed in Recipe 4.14. Finally, `SetInfo` commits the change. If `SetInfo` is not called, the creation will not get committed to the domain controller.

Using PowerShell

The `set-QADGroup` cmdlet has the following switches that allow you to modify specific attributes of a group object:

- `-managedBy`
- `-Notes`
- `-Email`
- `-GroupType`
- `-GroupScope`
- `-SamAccountName`
- `-Description`
- `-DisplayName`

If you need to modify one or more attributes that are not covered by these switches, you can use the `-ObjectAttributes` switch to modify one or more attributes defined in an array, as follows: `-ObjectAttributes @{"<Attribute 1>"="<Value1>";"<Attribute 2>"="<Values 2>";"<Attribute 3>"="<Value 3>"}`, and so forth.

See Also

Recipes 4.14 and 4.28, MSDN: IADs::Put, MSDN: IADs::PutEx, MSDN: IADs::SetInfo, and MSDN: ADS_PROPERTY_OPERATION_ENUM

7.10 Creating a Dynamic Group

Problem

You want to create a dynamic group using the optional Authorization Manager (Az-Man) component.

Solution

Using a graphical user interface

1. Install the Authorization Manager component through Add/Remove Programs, if it is not already present.
2. Open the Authorization Manager MMC snap-in.
3. Right-click on the Authorization Manager node and select Open Authorization Store.
4. Under "Select authorization store type," select one of the following:

   Active Directory (in Windows Server 2008, this will read 'Active Directory or Active Directory Application Mode (ADAM)')
   > Enter the name of the application partition, for example, `cn=ERP,cn=Program Data,dc=adatum,dc=com`, or click Browse to select it from the Active Directory tree.

   XML file
   > Enter the path to the XML file, or click Browse to select it from the filesystem.

   Microsoft SQL (Windows Server 2008 only)
   > This will be a URL in the format `MSSQL://<Connection String>/<Database Name>/<Policy Store Name>`

5. Drill down to Console Root→Authorization Manager→Authorization Share→Application Name→Groups.
6. Right-click on Groups and select New→Group.

> This will create a group that is scoped to the entire authorization store. You can drill down to an individual application to create a group that is only applicable within the app itself.

7. From the New Application Group screen, enter the name of the group and a description. Under Group Type, select LDAP query. Click OK to create the group.
8. Right-click on the group you just created and select Properties. From the LDAP tab, enter the LDAP attributes that will make up the group. For example, you can configure the group to include only Managers by entering (`title=Manager`).

9. Click OK to finish creating the group.

Using a command-line interface

The following syntax will create an application group that's based on an LDAP query:

```
> admod -b <GroupDN> groupType::32 sAMAccountType::1073741825 msDS-AzLDAPQuery::
"(&(objectcategory=person)(objectclass=user))" -add
```

Using VBScript

```
' The following code will create an application group
' that is scoped to an individual application rather than
' the entire authorization store

AzManStore = CreateObject("AzRoles.AzAuthorizationStore")

Set Application1 = AzManStore.OpenApplication("ERP")
Set AppGroup = _
    Application1.CreateApplicationGroup("HR Managers",VT_EMPTY)
AppGroup.Type = AZ_GROUPTYPE_LDAP_QUERY
AppGroup.Description = "Users with hiring authority"
AppGroup.LdapQuery = _
    "(memberOf= CN=HR Managers,OU=Distribution Lists,DC=enterprise,DC=com)"

'----- Persist the changes to the application group and then the app ------
AppGroup.Submit
Application1.Submit
```

Discussion

Authorization Manager was introduced in Windows Server 2003 as a feature that allows application developers to create role-based authorization groups based on a company's organizational structure. Groups created through Authorization Manager are similar to the ones that you would create using Active Directory Users and Computers or a corresponding command-line utility or script, except that AzMan groups are created and maintained for use by a single application or a specific set of applications created by a developer. An application developer or administrator can create AzMan groups without having administrative rights to the domain as a whole, and group membership can be configured so that it is dynamically determined; that is, you can configure a group of users based on a dynamic set of criteria rather than needing to discretely specify each individual group member one at a time. Once a developer or administrator has created a group using Authorization Manager, these groups can be assigned specific roles within an application that allow them to perform certain tasks. These groups are not Windows Security-enabled groups and although they have an SID, cannot currently be used to secure Windows resources.

A number of new features have been made available for Authorization Manager in Windows Server 2008, including the following:

- Authorization Manager data can be stored in an SQL database, as well as in AD DS, AD LDS (ADAM in Windows Server 2003), or in an XML file.
- Business rule groups, that is, groups whose membership is determined at runtime by a script, are now available.
- Custom object pickers, which allow application administrators to use the Authorization Manager snap-in for applications that use AD LDS/ADAM or SQL user accounts, can now be used.

In addition to these new features, AzMan in Windows Server 2008 has made a number of improvements to existing features, such as the following:

- The Authorization Manager application programming interface (API) has been improved to optimize common functions and to use simpler, faster versions of commonly used methods.
- Lightweight Directory Access Protocol (LDAP) queries are not limited to only user objects.
- Additional events are recorded in the event log if auditing is active.

In Windows Server 2008, business rules and authorizations are disabled by default. In earlier versions of Windows, these rules were enabled by default.

See Also

MSDN: Qualifying Access with Business Logic in Scripts, MSDN: Using Dynamic Business Rules in Windows Server 2003 Authorization Manager, MSDN: Authorization Manager Model [Security], MS KB 324470 (How to Install and Administer the Authorization Manager in Windows Server 2003), and MSDN: Dynamic Groups in Windows Server 2003 Authorization Manager

7.11 Delegating Control for Managing Membership of a Group

Problem

You want to delegate the ability to manage the membership of a group.

Solution

Using a graphical user interface

This requires Windows Server 2003 or later version of ADUC.

1. Open the ADUC snap-in.

2. If you need to change domains, right-click on Active Directory Users and Computers in the left pane, select Connect to Domain, enter the domain name, and click OK.

3. In the left pane, right-click on the domain and select Find.

4. Enter the name of the group and click Find Now.

5. Double-click on the group in the results pane.

6. Select the Managed By tab.

7. Click the Change button.

8. Locate the group or user to delegate control to and click OK.

9. Check the box beside "Manager can update membership list."

10. Click OK.

Using a command-line interface

```
> dsacls <GroupDN> /G <GroupName>@DomainName:WP;member;
```

In the following example, the *SalesAdmin* group will be given rights to modify membership of the *PreSales* group:

```
> dsacls cn=presales,ou=sales,dc=adatum,dc=com /G salesadmins@adatum.com:
WP;member;
```

Using VBScript

```
' This code grants write access to the member attribute of a group.
' ------ SCRIPT CONFIGURATION -----
strGroupDN = "<GroupDN>" ' e.g. cn=SalesGroup,ou=Sales,dc=adatum,dc=com"
strUserOrGroup = "<UserOrGroup>" ' e.g. joe@adatum.com or ADATUM\joe
' ------ END CONFIGURATION --------

set objGroup = GetObject("LDAP://" & strGroupDN)
'###########################
' Constants
'###########################
' ADS_ACETYPE_ENUM
Const ADS_ACETYPE_ACCESS_ALLOWED_OBJECT = &h5
Const ADS_FLAG_OBJECT_TYPE_PRESENT = &h1
Const ADS_RIGHT_DS_WRITE_PROP = &h20

' From schemaIDGUID of member attribute
Const MEMBER_ATTRIBUTE = "{bf9679c0-0de6-11d0-a285-00aa003049e2}"

'###########################
' Create ACL
'###########################
set objSD = objGroup.Get("nTSecurityDescriptor")
set objDACL = objSD.DiscretionaryAcl
```

```
' Set WP for member attribute
set objACE = CreateObject("AccessControlEntry")
objACE.Trustee    = strUserOrGroup
objACE.AccessMask = ADS_RIGHT_DS_WRITE_PROP
objACE.AceFlags   = 0
objACE.Flags      = ADS_FLAG_OBJECT_TYPE_PRESENT
objACE.AceType    = ADS_ACETYPE_ACCESS_ALLOWED_OBJECT
objACE.ObjectType = MEMBER_ATTRIBUTE

objDACL.AddAce objACE

'############################
' Set ACL
'############################

objSD.DiscretionaryAcl = objDACL
objGroup.Put "nTSecurityDescriptor", objSD
objGroup.SetInfo
WScript.Echo "Delegated control of member attribute for " & _
             strGroupDN & " to " & strUserOrGroup
```

Using PowerShell

```
add-QADPermission -Identity <Group DN> -Account <User/Group DN> -Rights
'WriteProperty' -Property 'member' -ApplyTo 'ThisObjectOnly'
```

You can also use a PowerShell console on a computer where the Exchange Server 2007 or above management tools have been installed:

```
Add-ADPermission -Identity <Group Name> -User <User or Group Name> -AccessRights
WriteProperty -Properties "members"
```

Discussion

To grant a user or group the ability to manage group membership, you have to grant the write property (WP) permission on the member attribute of the target group. You can add this ACE directly using dsacls, or more indirectly with ADUC. Beginning in Windows Server 2003, ADUC has a new feature that allows you to simply check a box to grant the ability to modify group membership to the object represented by the managedBy attribute.

If you want to configure additional permissions, such as the ability to modify the description attribute for the group, you will need to go to the Security tab in ADUC, or specify the appropriate attribute with the /G switch with dsacls. For example, this will grant write property on the description attribute:

```
/G <GroupName>@<DomainDNSName>:WP;description;
```

See Also

Recipe 14.6 for delegating control in Active Directory

7.12 Resolving a Primary Group ID

Problem

You want to find the name of a user's primary group.

Solution

Using a graphical user interface

1. Open the ADUC snap-in.
2. If you need to change domains, right-click on Active Directory Users and Computers in the left pane, select Connect to Domain, enter the domain name, and click OK.
3. In the left pane, right-click on the domain and select Find.
4. Type the name of the user and click Find Now.
5. In the Search Results window, double-click on the user.
6. Click the Member Of tab.
7. The Primary Group name is shown on the bottom half of the dialog box.

Using VBScript

```
' This code prints the group name of a user's primary group
'-----------SCRIPT CONFIGURATION----------------------------
strUserDN = "<UserDN>" ' i.e. "cn=jsmith,dc=adatum,dc=com"
strDomain = "<DomainNetBIOSName>" ' i.e. ADATUM
'-----------------------------------------------------------

' Grab the primary group's RID from the user object
set objUser = GetObject("LDAP://" & strUserDN)
strGroupRID = objUser.Get("primaryGroupID")

' Grab the user's SID to obtain the domain SID
strUserName = objUser.sAMAccountName
Set WMIUser = GetObject("winmgmts:{impersonationlevel=impersonate}!" _
    & "/root/cimv2:
Win32_UserAccount.Domain='" & strDomain & "'" _
    & ",Name='" & strUserName & "'")
strUserSID = WMIUser.SID
strDomainSID = mid(strUserSID,1,(InStrREV(strUserSID,"-")))

' Now construct the Primary Group SID
strGroupSID = strDomainSID & strGroupRID

' Bind to the primary group using its SID and echo its name
set objGroup = GetObject("LDAP://<SID=" & strGroupSID &">")
strGroupDN = objGroup.distinguishedName
WScript.Echo(strGroupDN)
```

Using PowerShell

```
# This code prints the group name of a user's primary group

$strUserDN = "<UserDN>" # i.e. "cn=jsmith,cn=users,dc=adatum,dc=com"

# bind to the user object
$objUser = [ADSI]("LDAP://" + $strUserDN)

# get the user's primary group ID
$grpID = $objUser.primaryGroupID

# get the user's SID into a byte array
$sid = $objUser.objectSID.Value

# create a .NET SID object
$objSID = new-object System.Security.Principal.SecurityIdentifier($sid, 0)

# build the SID of the primary group
$grp = $objSID.AccountDomainSid.Value + "-" + $objUser.primaryGroupID.ToString()

# bind to the group object
$objGroup = [ADSI]("LDAP://<SID=" + $grp + ">")

# output the group name
$objGroup.distinguishedName
```

Discussion

When trying to determine a user's group membership, you have to look at the user's memberOf attribute, which contains a list of DNs for each group the user is a member of, as well as the user's primary group. By default, all users are assigned *Domain Users* as their primary group. Therefore, by default all users in a domain are implicitly members of the *Domain Users* group. Unfortunately, a user's primary group will not show up in the memberOf attribute.

> Services for Macintosh and POSIX-based applications are the main users of primary groups. If you don't use either of those, you usually don't need to worry about changing a user's primary group.

The primary group is stored in the **primaryGroupID** attribute on **user** objects. Unfortunately, the information that's stored in that attribute is the relative identifier (RID) of the group, not the DN or even **sAMAccountName** as you might expect. **group** objects have a **primaryGroupToken** attribute, which contains the same value, but is a constructed attribute. Because Active Directory dynamically constructs it, you cannot utilize it in search filters. So even if you have the **primaryGroupID** of a user (e.g., 513), you cannot do a simple query to find out which group it is associated with. You can find the name of a user's primary group relatively easily using the Active Directory Users and Computers snap-in, as described in the GUI solution.

Using VBScript

The VBScript solution uses a combination of WMI and ADSI to retrieve the distinguished name of the user's primary group by constructing and deconstructing various SIDs. Every user, computer, and group object in Active Directory possesses a SID that is composed of two parts: the SID for the Active Directory domain, followed by the RID for the object. The domain SID will be identical for all objects that exist in the same AD domain; only the RID will differ. Because of this, you can retrieve the user object's SID using the `Win32_UserAccount` WMI namespace, and then remove the final `-xxxx` to obtain the domain SID. Once you have the domain SID, it's fairly simple to append the primary group RID to the end of it, thus creating a usable SID for the primary group itself.

Using PowerShell

The PowerShell solution uses a combination of ADSI and the .NET Framework to retrieve the distinguished name of the user's primary group. When you map the `object SID` attribute to the .NET class `System.Security.Principal.SecurityIdentifier`, one of the attributes exposed is the SID of the domain for that `objectSID`. As described earlier, you can simply suffix the RID of a user's primary group to that string and do a lookup of the group object using ADSI.

See Also

MS KB 297951 (How to Use the PrimaryGroupID Attribute to Find the Primary Group for a User) and MS KB 321360 (How to Use Native ADSI Components to Find the Primary Group)

7.13 Enabling Universal Group Membership Caching

This recipe requires at least Windows Server 2003 forest functional level.

Problem

You want to enable universal group membership caching so that a global catalog server is not needed during most user logins.

Solution

Using a graphical user interface

1. Open the Active Directory Sites and Services snap-in.
2. In the left pane, browse to the site you want to enable group caching for and click on it.
3. In the right pane, double-click on the `NTDS Site Settings` object.
4. Under Universal Group Membership Caching, check the box beside Enable Universal Group Caching.
5. If you want to force the cache refresh from a particular site, select a site or else leave the default set to `<Default>`.
6. Click OK.

Using a command-line interface

You can use a combination of the `dsquery site` and `dsget site` commands to find if a site has group caching enabled:

```
> dsquery site -name <SiteName> | dsget site -dn -cachegroups -prefGCSite
```

You can use *ldifde* to enable group caching. Create a file called *enable_univ_cache.ldf* with the following contents, but change `<SiteName>` to the name of the site you want to enable, and `<ForestRootDN>` to the distinguished name of the forest root domain:

```
dn: cn=NTDS Site Settings,cn=<SiteName>,cn=sites,cn=configuration,<ForestRootDN>
changetype: modify
replace: options
options: 32
-
```

Then use the following command to import the change:

```
> ldifde -i -f enable_univ_cache.ldf
```

You can also perform this change by using a combination of AdFind and AdMod with the following syntax:

```
> adfind -config -rb "cn=NTDS Settings,cn=<SiteName>,cn=Sites"
options -adcsv | admod options::{{.:SET:32}}
```

Using VBScript

```
' This code enables universal group
' caching for the specified site.
' ------ SCRIPT CONFIGURATION -----
strSiteName = "<SiteName>" ' e.g. Default-First-Site-Name
' ------ END CONFIGURATION --------

set objRootDSE = GetObject("LDAP://RootDSE")
set objSite = GetObject("LDAP://cn=NTDS Site Settings,cn=" & strSiteName & _
```

```
                     ",cn=sites," & objRootDSE.Get("configurationNamingContext") )
     objSite.Put "options", 32
     objSite.SetInfo
     WScript.Echo "Successfully enabled universal group caching for " & _
                 strSiteName
```

Using PowerShell

```
     set-QADObject -Identity "cn=NTDS Site Settings,cn=<Site Name>,cn=Sites,<Config DN>"
     -ObjectAttributes @{options="32"}

     $objSite = [ADSI] "LDAP://cn=NTDS Site Settings,cn=<Site Name>,cn=Sites,<Config DN>"
     $options = [int]$objSite.options.ToString()
     $objSite.put("options", $options -bor 32)
     $objSite.SetInfo()
```

Discussion

When a client logs on to a Windows 2000 Active Directory domain controller, the domain controller that authenticates the user needs to contact a global catalog server in order to fully authenticate the client. This is necessary because global catalogs are the only servers that store universal group information, which is needed to completely determine a user's group memberships upon logon. (If the DC that authenticates the user is itself a GC, then it does not need to contact any other servers to complete the authentication process.)

Universal groups can be created and used anywhere in a forest. Objects located any-where in a forest can be added as members of a universal group. Since a universal group could be created in a domain other than where the user object resides, it is necessary to store universal group membership in the global catalog. That way, during logon, domain controllers can query a global catalog to determine all universal groups a user is a member of. Microsoft's primary reason for making this a requirement during logon is that a user could be part of a universal group that has been explicitly denied access to certain resources. If universal groups aren't evaluated, a user could gain access to resources that are supposed to be restricted.

To remove this limitation, Windows Server 2003 Active Directory introduced *universal group caching*. Universal group caching can be enabled on a per site basis and allows domain controllers to cache universal group information locally, thus removing the need to query the global catalog during client logon.

You can enable universal group caching manually by enabling the 10000 bit (32 in decimal) on the `options` attribute of the `NTDS Site Settings` object. With the exception of the AdFind/AdMod syntax, the CLI and VBScript solutions listed here blindly wrote 32 to that attribute, which is not ideal. See Recipe 4.15 for more information on properly setting a bit flag attribute. (The second PowerShell solution shows you how to do it properly using the ADSI interface in PowerShell.) The Sites and Services snap-in hides this logic and just requires you to check a box. Another setting can also be configured that relates to universal group caching. By default, domain controllers will use the site topology to determine the optimal site to use to query a global catalog server for universal group information. You can override this feature and explicitly set which site domain controllers should use by selecting the site in the Sites and Services snap-in or by setting the attribute `msDS-Preferred-GC-Site` on the `NTDS Site Settings` object to the DN of the target site.

See Also

Recipe 4.15

7.14 Restoring a Deleted Group

Problem

You want to restore a `group` object that has been inadvertently deleted, as well as restore its members.

Solution

Using a graphical user interface

1. Reboot the domain controller in Directory Services Restore Mode.
2. Perform a System State restore.
3. Before rebooting the server, perform the steps listed in the following section.

Using a command line interface

1. To restore the user and group accounts, use the following sequence of commands. Replace *<ContainerDN>* with the name of the container or OU containing the user and `group` objects that need to be restored. (The activate instance `ntds` line is only necessary in Windows Server 2008):

   ```
   > ntdsutil
   > activate instance ntds
   > authoritative restore

   > restore subtree <ContainerDN>
   > quit
   > exit
   ```

2. Reboot the domain controller into normal mode and wait for replication to complete.
3. Reboot the domain controller into Directory Services Restore Mode again. Perform the commands in Step 1 a second time. (It is only necessary to mark the restore as authoritative a second time; you do not need to perform the actual System State restore again.)

4. Restart the domain controller after running these commands.

Discussion

In most cases, it is sufficient when restoring a deleted object within Active Directory to simply perform an *authoritative* restore of the object or container. However, things get a bit more complicated when you're restoring `group` objects as well as the users who were members of those groups. Because you cannot easily control the order in which objects are restored to the AD database, you may run into a situation where a `group` object gets restored *before* the users who were members of that group. In this case, when Active Directory attempts to populate the restored group's member attribute, it can only populate it with user objects that already exist within the directory. Put another way, if some or all of the users or other groups that are referenced in the restored group's `member` attribute have not yet been restored, they will not be included in the restored group's member `attribute`. This will leave the restored group in an inconsistent state, since it will not possess all of the members that it had before it was deleted.

To correct this issue, it's necessary to perform the authoritative restore process *twice* when restoring groups and their members. The first authoritative restore will re-create all users that should be members of the `group` objects. The second pass will go back and correctly repopulate the `member` attribute of any restored groups, now that all of the needed user objects exist within Active Directory.

See Also

MS KB 216993 (Useful Shelf Life of a System-State Backup of Active Directory), MS KB 840001 (How to Restore Deleted User Accounts and Their Group Memberships in Active Directory), and Chapter 16 for more on recovering and restoring Active Directory

7.15 Protecting a Group Against Accidental Deletion

Problem

You want to prevent a `group` object from being accidentally deleted by an administrator who selects the incorrect option in Active Directory Users and Computers.

Solution

Using a graphical user interface (Windows Server 2008 only)

1. Open Active Directory Users and Computers. Click on View and confirm that Advanced Features is selected.

2. Drill down to the current domain. To connect to a different domain, right-click on the top-level node and click Change domain; select the appropriate domain and then drill down to it.

3. Right-click on the group that you want to modify and click Properties.

4. Click on the Object tab.

5. Place a checkmark next to "Protect object from accidental deletion."

6. Click OK.

Using a command-line interface (all versions)

```
dsacls <Group DN> /d EVERYONE:SDDT
```

Using PowerShell (all versions)

```
Add-QADPermission -identity <Group DN> -Account 'EVERYONE' -Rights
'Delete,DeleteTree' -ApplyTo 'ThisObjectOnly'
```

If you have Exchange 2007 installed in your environment, you can also use the following Exchange cmdlet to modify this information:

```
Add-ADPermission -Identity <Group Name> -User <User or Group Name>
   -AccessRights Delete,DeleteTree -Deny $true
```

Discussion

By default, all new OUs that are created in Windows Server 2008 will have this protection enabled; however, no other object types are configured with this default protection. If you attempt to delete a group that is protected using this option, even when signed on as a Domain Admin or other similarly elevated account, you will receive an "Access Denied" message until you manually remove the checkbox or manually remove the DENY ACE associated with it.

By using the command-line or PowerShell methods, this protection can be applied to group objects in *all* versions of Windows Server, even though the GUI checkbox is only available in Windows Server 2008.

7.16 Applying a Fine-Grained Password Policy to a Group Object

Problem

You want to apply a Fine-Grained Password Policy to a Group object in a Windows Server 2008 domain.

Solution

Using a graphical user interface

1. Open ADSI Edit. Right-click on the top-level node and click "Connect to…". In the Connection Settings screen, click OK.
2. In the righthand pane, double-click on Default naming context, then double-click on the domain node (i.e., `dc=adatum,dc=com`).
3. Browse to `CN=System`, then `CN=Password Settings` Container.
4. Right-click on the PSO that you wish to modify and click Properties.
5. In the Select an Attribute to View drop-down box, select `msDS-PSOAppliesTo`.
6. In the Edit Attribute text box, enter the DN of the `group` object that this password policy should apply to, such as `cn=Marketing,ou=Corp,dc=adatum,dc=com`.
7. Click Add, then click OK.
8. Click OK.

Using a command-line interface

The following will add the `Marketing` group to the list of groups that a PSO will apply to:

```
C:> psomgr -applyto CN=Marketing,CN=Users,DC=ADATUM,DC=COM -pso TestPSO -forreal
```

Using PowerShell

To add a group to the list of groups that a PSO will apply to, use the following syntax:

```
Add-QADPasswordSettingsObjectAppliesTo -Identity <PSO DN> -AppliesTo <Group DN>
```

Discussion

Once a `PasswordSettingsObject` has been created, you can modify the password and account lockout settings controlled by the object, as well as the users and groups that the PSO should apply to. Since the `PasswordSettingsObject` is an Active Directory object class, these modifications can be made using any interface that can modify objects. When working from the command line, the *psomgr* tool from *http://www.joeware.net/freetools* allows you to modify one or multiple PSOs at a time, and can also create "starter" PSOs using the `-quickstart` command-line switch. The full syntax for *psomgr.exe* can be obtained by typing `psomgr.exe /?` at a command prompt, or by visiting the *joeware* website.

See Also

Chapter 9 of *Active Directory*

## CHAPTER 8

Computer Objects

8.0 Introduction

As far as Active Directory is concerned, computers are very similar to users. In fact, computer objects inherit directly from the user object class, which is used to represent user accounts. That means that computer objects possess all of the attributes of user objects and then some. Computers need to be represented in Active Directory for many of the same reasons users do, including the need to access resources securely, utilize GPOs, and have permissions assigned to them.

To participate in a domain, computers need a *secure channel* to a domain controller. A secure channel is an authenticated connection that can transmit encrypted data. To set up the secure channel, a computer must present a password to a domain controller. Similar to the way in which it authenticates a user account, Active Directory will use Kerberos authentication to verify the identity of a computer account. Without the computer object and, by association, the password stored with it that is changed behind the scenes on a regular basis by the operating system, there would be no way for the domain controller to verify a computer is what it claims to be.

8.1 The Anatomy of a computer Object

The default location for computer objects in a domain is the cn=Computers container located directly off the domain root. You can, however, create computer objects anywhere in a domain. Beginning with Windows Server 2003, you can modify the default location for computer objects as described in Recipe 8.14. Table 8-1 contains a list of some of the interesting attributes that are available on computer objects.

Table 8-1. *Attributes of computer objects*

Attribute	Description
cn	Relative distinguished name of computer objects.
dnsHostName	Fully qualified DNS name of the computer.
lastLogonTimestamp	The approximate timestamp of the last time the computer logged in to the domain. This attribute was introduced in Windows Server 2003.
managedBy	The distinguished name (DN) of the user or group that manages the computer.
memberOf	List of DNs of the groups the computer is a member of.
msDS-AuthenticatedToAccountList	New to Windows Server 2008. A backlink attribute that identifies users who have successfully authenticated to a full DC via a particular RODC.
msDS-RevealedUsers	New to Windows Server 2008. Identifies the list of users and computers whose secrets have been replicated to an RODC.
operatingSystem	Textual description of the operating system running on the computer. See Recipe 8.15 for more information.
operatingSystemHotFix	Currently not being used, but will hopefully be populated at some point.
operatingSystemServicePack	Service pack version installed on the computer. See Recipe 8.15 for more information.
operatingSystemVersion	Numeric version of the operating system installed on the computer. See Recipe 8.15 for more information.
pwdLastSet	Large integer that can be translated into the last time the computer's password was set. See Recipe 8.11 for more information.
sAMAccountName	NetBIOS-style name of the computer. This is typically the name of the computer with $ at the end.
userAccountControl	Account flag that defines various account properties. In the case of a computer object, this specifies whether the computer is a member computer or a domain controller.

8.2 Creating a Computer

Problem

You want to create a computer account.

Solution

Using a graphical user interface

1. Open the ADUC snap-in.
2. If you need to change domains, right-click on Active Directory Users and Computers in the left pane, select "Connect to Domain," enter the domain name, and click OK.

3. In the left pane, browse to the parent container for the computer, right-click on it, and select New→Computer.

4. Enter the name of the computer. If necessary, place a checkmark next to "Assign this computer as a pre-Windows 2000 computer" or "Assign this computer as a backup domain controller." Click Next to continue.

5. If you will be using this computer account as part of an RIS deployment, place a checkmark next to "This is a managed computer" and enter the GUID that it should use, and then click Next. Otherwise, just click Next to continue.

6. Click Finish.

Using a command-line interface

You can create a computer object using either the built-in DSAdd utility or AdMod. To create an account using DSAdd, use the following syntax:

```
> dsadd computer "<ComputerDN>" -desc "<Description>"
```

To create a computer account using AdMod, enter the following:

```
> admod -b "<ComputerDN>" objectclass::computer
  sAMAccountName::<ComputerName>$ userAccountControl::4096
  description::"<Description>" -add
```

Using VBScript

```
' This code creates a computer object.
' ------ SCRIPT CONFIGURATION -------
strBase = "<ParentComputerDN>" ' e.g. cn=Computers,dc=adatum,dc=com
strComp = "<ComputerName>"      ' e.g. joe-xp
strDescr = "<Description>"      ' e.g. Joe's Windows XP workstation
' ------ END CONFIGURATION ---------

' ADS_USER_FLAG_ENUM
Const ADS_UF_WORKSTATION_TRUST_ACCOUNT = &h1000 ' 4096

set objCont = GetObject("LDAP://" & strBase)
set objComp = objCont.Create("computer", "cn=" & strComp)
objComp.Put "sAMAccountName", strComp & "$"
objComp.Put "description", strDesc
objComp.Put "userAccountControl", ADS_UF_WORKSTATION_TRUST_ACCOUNT
objComp.SetInfo
Wscript.Echo "Computer account for " & strComp & " created"
```

Using PowerShell

To create a computer account using the Quest cmdlets, use the `new-QADObject` cmdlet as follows:

```
new-QADObject -ParentContainer <OU DN> -type 'computer' -name '<ComputerName>'
-ObjectAttributes @{samAccountName='<ComputerName>$';userAccountControl='4096'}
```

To use ADSI, use the following syntax:

```
set-variable ADS_UF_WORKSTATION_TRUST_ACCOUNT 0x1000 -option constant

$objParent = [ADSI] "LDAP://<Parent OU DN>"
$objComp = $objParent.Create("computer", "cn=<ComputerName>")
$objComp.Put("samAccountName", "<ComputerName>$")
$objComp.Put("userAccountControl", ADS_UF_WORKSTATION_TRUST_ACCOUNT)
$objComp.SetInfo()
```

Discussion

Creating a `computer` object in Active Directory is not much different from creating a `user` object. We set the `description` attribute in the CLI and API solutions, but it is not a mandatory attribute. The only mandatory attribute is `sAMAccountName`, which should be set to the name of the computer with $ appended. Also note that these solutions simply create a `computer` object. This does not mean any user can join a computer to the domain with that computer account. For more information on creating a computer object and allowing a specific user or group to join the computer to the domain, see Recipe 8.3.

See Also

Recipe 8.3 for creating a computer for a user, MS KB 222525 (Automating the Creation of Computer Accounts), MS KB 283771 (How to Prestage Windows 2000 Computers in Active Directory), MS KB 315273 (Automating the Creation of Computer Accounts), MS KB 320187 (How to Manage Computer Accounts in Active Directory in Windows 2000), and MSDN: ADS_USER_FLAG_ENUM

8.3 Creating a Computer for a Specific User or Group

Problem

You want to create a computer account for a specific user or group to join to the domain. This requires setting permissions on the computer account so that the user or group can modify certain attributes.

Solution

Using a graphical user interface

1. Open the ADUC snap-in.
2. If you need to change domains, right-click on Active Directory Users and Computers in the left pane, select "Connect to Domain," enter the domain name, and click OK.

3. In the left pane, browse to the parent container for the computer, right-click on it, and select New→Computer.

4. Enter the name of the computer.

5. Under "The following user or group can join this computer to a domain," click the Change button.

6. Use the Object Picker to select a user or group to join the computer to the domain.

7. Click OK.

Using a command-line interface

In the following solution, replace *<ComputerDN>* with the distinguished name of the computer object and *<UserOrGroup>* with the user principal name or NT-style name of a user or group you want to manage the computer:

```
> dsadd computer <ComputerDN>
> dsacls <ComputerDN> /G <UserOrGroup>:CALCGRSDDTRC;;
> dsacls <ComputerDN> /G <UserOrGroup>:WP;description;
> dsacls <ComputerDN> /G <UserOrGroup>:WP;sAMAccountName;
> dsacls <ComputerDN> /G <UserOrGroup>:WP;displayName;
> dsacls <ComputerDN> /G <UserOrGroup>:WP;userAccountControl;
> dsacls <ComputerDN> /G <UserOrGroup>:WS;"Validated write to service principal\
name";
> dsacls <ComputerDN> /G <UserOrGroup>:WS;"Validated write to DNS host name";
```

 You can replace the first line of this code with the AdMod code from Recipe 8.2 if you choose.

Using VBScript

```
' This code creates a computer object and grants a
user/group rights over it.
' ------ SCRIPT CONFIGURATION -------
strComputer = "<ComputerName>"  ' e.g. joe-xp
strUser     = "<UserOrGroup>"   ' e.g. joe@adatum.com or ADATUM\joe
strDescr    = "<ComputerDescr>" ' e.g. Joe's workstation
strDomain   = "<ComputerDomain>" ' e.g. adatum.com
' ------ END CONFIGURATION ---------

'#############################
' Constants
'#############################

' ADS_USER_FLAG_ENUM
Const ADS_UF_PASSWD_NOTREQD            = &h0020
Const ADS_UF_WORKSTATION_TRUST_ACCOUNT = &h1000

' ADS_ACETYPE_ENUM
Const ADS_ACETYPE_ACCESS_ALLOWED       = &h0
```

```
Const ADS_ACETYPE_ACCESS_ALLOWED_OBJECT = &h5

' ADS_FLAGTYPE_ENUM
Const ADS_FLAG_OBJECT_TYPE_PRESENT = &h1

' ADS_RIGHTS_ENUM
Const ADS_RIGHT_DS_SELF           = &h8
Const ADS_RIGHT_DS_WRITE_PROP     = &h20
Const ADS_RIGHT_DS_CONTROL_ACCESS = &h100
Const ADS_RIGHT_ACTRL_DS_LIST     = &h4
Const ADS_RIGHT_GENERIC_READ      = &h80000000
Const ADS_RIGHT_DELETE            = &h10000
Const ADS_RIGHT_DS_DELETE_TREE    = &h40
Const ADS_RIGHT_READ_CONTROL      = &h20000

' schemaIDGUID values
Const DISPLAY_NAME      = "{bf967953-0de6-11d0-a285-00aa003049e2}"
Const SAM_ACCOUNT_NAME  = "{3e0abfd0-126a-11d0-a060-00aa006c33ed}"
Const DESCRIPTION       = "{bf967950-0de6-11d0-a285-00aa003049e2}"

' controlAccessRight rightsGUID values
Const USER_LOGON_INFORMATION      = "{5f202010-79a5-11d0-9020-00c04fc2d4cf}"
Const USER_ACCOUNT_RESTRICTIONS   = "{4C164200-20C0-11D0-A768-00AA006E0529}"
Const VALIDATED_DNS_HOST_NAME     = "{72E39547-7B18-11D1-ADEF-00C04FD8D5CD}"
Const VALIDATED_SPN               = "{F3A64788-5306-11D1-A9C5-0000F80367C1}"

'###########################
' Create Computer
'###########################

set objRootDSE = GetObject("LDAP://" & strDomain & "/RootDSE")
set objContainer = GetObject("LDAP://cn=Computers," & _
                             objRootDSE.Get("defaultNamingContext"))
set objComputer = objContainer.Create("Computer", "cn=" & strComputer)

objComputer.Put "sAMAccountName", strComputer & "$"
objComputer.Put "userAccountControl", _
                ADS_UF_PASSWD_NOTREQD Or ADS_UF_WORKSTATION_TRUST_ACCOUNT
objComputer.Put "description", strDescr
objComputer.SetInfo

'###########################
' Create ACL
'###########################

set objSD = objComputer.Get("nTSecurityDescriptor")
set objDACL = objSD.DiscretionaryAcl

' Special: Control Rights, List Children
'          Generic Read, Delete,
'          Delete Subtree, Read Permission
set objACE1 = CreateObject("AccessControlEntry")
objACE1.Trustee    = strUser
objACE1.AccessMask = ADS_RIGHT_DS_CONTROL_ACCESS Or _
                     ADS_RIGHT_ACTRL_DS_LIST Or _
```

```
                      ADS_RIGHT_GENERIC_READ Or _
                      ADS_RIGHT_DELETE Or _
                      ADS_RIGHT_DS_DELETE_TREE Or ADS_RIGHT_READ_CONTROL
objACE1.AceFlags    = 0
objACE1.AceType     = ADS_ACETYPE_ACCESS_ALLOWED

' Write Property: description
set objACE2 = CreateObject("AccessControlEntry")
objACE2.Trustee     = strUser
objACE2.AccessMask  = ADS_RIGHT_DS_WRITE_PROP
objACE2.AceFlags    = 0
objACE2.Flags       = ADS_FLAG_OBJECT_TYPE_PRESENT
objACE2.AceType     = ADS_ACETYPE_ACCESS_ALLOWED_OBJECT
objACE2.ObjectType  = DESCRIPTION

' Write Property: sAMAccountName
set objACE3 = CreateObject("AccessControlEntry")
objACE3.Trustee     = strUser
objACE3.AccessMask  = ADS_RIGHT_DS_WRITE_PROP
objACE3.AceFlags    = 0
objACE3.Flags       = ADS_FLAG_OBJECT_TYPE_PRESENT
objACE3.AceType     = ADS_ACETYPE_ACCESS_ALLOWED_OBJECT
objACE3.ObjectType  = SAM_ACCOUNT_NAME

' Write Property: displayName
set objACE4 = CreateObject("AccessControlEntry")
objACE4.Trustee     = strUser
objACE4.AccessMask  = ADS_RIGHT_DS_WRITE_PROP
objACE4.AceFlags    = 0
objACE4.Flags       = ADS_FLAG_OBJECT_TYPE_PRESENT
objACE4.AceType     = ADS_ACETYPE_ACCESS_ALLOWED_OBJECT
objACE4.ObjectType  = DISPLAY_NAME

' Write Property: Logon Information

set objACE5 = CreateObject("AccessControlEntry")
objACE5.Trustee     = strUser
objACE5.AccessMask  = ADS_RIGHT_DS_WRITE_PROP
objACE5.AceFlags    = 0
objACE5.AceType     = ADS_ACETYPE_ACCESS_ALLOWED_OBJECT
objACE5.Flags       = ADS_FLAG_OBJECT_TYPE_PRESENT
objACE5.ObjectType  = USER_LOGON_INFORMATION

' Write Property: Account Restrictions
set objACE6 = CreateObject("AccessControlEntry")
objACE6.Trustee     = strUser
objACE6.AccessMask  = ADS_RIGHT_DS_WRITE_PROP
objACE6.AceFlags    = 0
objACE6.AceType     = ADS_ACETYPE_ACCESS_ALLOWED_OBJECT
objACE6.Flags       = ADS_FLAG_OBJECT_TYPE_PRESENT
objACE6.ObjectType  = USER_ACCOUNT_RESTRICTIONS

' Write Self: Validated SPN
set objACE7 = CreateObject("AccessControlEntry")
objACE7.Trustee     = strUser
```

```
objACE7.AccessMask = ADS_RIGHT_DS_SELF
objACE7.AceFlags   = 0
objACE7.AceType    = ADS_ACETYPE_ACCESS_ALLOWED_OBJECT
objACE7.Flags      = ADS_FLAG_OBJECT_TYPE_PRESENT
objACE7.ObjectType = VALIDATED_SPN

' Write Self: Validated DNS Host Name
set objACE8 = CreateObject("AccessControlEntry")
objACE8.Trustee    = strUser
objACE8.AccessMask = ADS_RIGHT_DS_SELF
objACE8.AceFlags   = 0
objACE8.AceType    = ADS_ACETYPE_ACCESS_ALLOWED_OBJECT
objACE8.Flags      = ADS_FLAG_OBJECT_TYPE_PRESENT
objACE8.ObjectType = VALIDATED_DNS_HOST_NAME

objDACL.AddAce objACE1
objDACL.AddAce objACE2
objDACL.AddAce objACE3
objDACL.AddAce objACE4
objDACL.AddAce objACE5
objDACL.AddAce objACE6
objDACL.AddAce objACE7
objDACL.AddAce objACE8

'############################
' Set ACL
'############################
objSD.DiscretionaryAcl = objDACL
objComputer.Put "nTSecurityDescriptor", objSD
objComputer.SetInfo
WScript.Echo "Successfully created " & strComputer & _
             " and gave rights to " & strUser
```

Discussion

By default, members of the *Authenticated Users* group can join up to 10 computers to an Active Directory domain. If you've modified this default behavior or need to allow a user to add computers to the domain on a regular basis, you need to grant certain permissions so that the user has rights to modify the **computer** object. When you create a computer via the ADUC snap-in, you have the option to select a user or group to manage the **computer** object and join a computer to the domain using that object. When you use that method, eight ACEs are added to the ACL of the **computer** object. They are:

- List Contents, Read All Properties, Delete, Delete Subtree, Read Permissions, All Extended Rights (i.e., Allowed to Authenticate, Change Password, Send As, Receive As, Reset Password)
- Write Property for **description**
- Write Property for **sAMAccountName**
- Write Property for **displayName**
- Write Property for Logon Information

- Write Property for Account Restrictions
- Validate write to DNS hostname
- Validate write for service principal name

Using a graphical user interface

If you want to modify the default permissions that are applied when you select a user or group through the GUI, double-click on the `computer` object after you've created it and go to the Security tab. For the Security tab to be visible, you have to select View→Advanced Features.

Using a command-line interface

With the *dsacls* utility, you can specify either a UPN (*user@domain*) or downlevel-style (*DOMAIN\user*) account name when applying permissions. Also, *dsacls* requires that the `displayName` of the attribute, property set, or extended right you are setting the permission on be used instead of the `lDAPDisplayName`, as you might expect. That is why we had to use "Validated write to service principal name," which is the `displayName` for the `Validated-SPN controlAccessRight` object, with the ACE for the SPN-validated write. *dsacls* is also case-sensitive, so be sure to specify the correct case for the words in the `displayName`.

Using VBScript

After creating the `computer` object, similar to Recipe 8.2, create an ACE object for each of the eight ACEs previously listed using the `IADsAccessControlEntry` interface.

To apply the ACEs, retrieve the current security descriptor for the computer object, which is stored in the `nTSecurityDescriptor` attribute, and then add the eight ACEs. Finally, call `SetInfo` to commit the change to Active Directory. For more information on setting ACEs and ACLs programmatically, see the `IADsAccessControlEntry` documentation in MSDN.

See Also

Recipe 8.2 for creating a computer account, MS KB 238793 (Enhanced Security Joining or Resetting Machine Account in Windows 2000 Domain), MS KB 283771 (How to Prestage Windows 2000 Computers in Active Directory), MS KB 320187 (How to Manage Computer Accounts in Active Directory in Windows 2000), MSDN: IADsAccessControlEntry, MSDN: ADS_ACETYPE_ENUM, and MSDN: ADS_RIGHTS_ENUM, MSDN: ADS_FLAGTYPE_ENUM

8.4 Deleting a Computer

Problem

You want to delete a computer account.

Solution

Using a graphical user interface

1. Open the ADUC snap-in.
2. If you need to change domains, right-click on Active Directory Users and Computers in the left pane, select "Connect to Domain," enter the domain name, and click OK.
3. In the left pane, browse to the parent container for the computer, right-click on it, and select Find....
4. In the Find: drop-down box, select Computers. Enter the name of the computer account and click Find Now.
5. Right-click on the computer and click Delete. Click Yes to confirm.

Using a command-line interface

You can delete a computer using the built-in *dsrm* utility, as well as AdMod. For *dsrm*, use the following syntax:

```
> dsrm "<Computer DN>"
```

For AdMod, enter the following:

```
> admod -b "<Computer DN>" -del
```

Using VBScript

```
strCompDN = "<Computer DN>"
set objComp = GetObject("LDAP://" & strCompDN)
objComp.DeleteObject(0)
```

Using PowerShell

To delete an object using the Quest AD cmdlets, use the following syntax:

```
remove-QADObject -identity <Computer DN>
```

To delete an object using the .NET methods, use the following:

```
$obj = [ADSI] "LDAP://<Computer DN>"
$obj.DeleteObject(0)
```

8.5 Joining a Computer to a Domain

Problem

You want to join a computer to a domain after the **computer** object has already been created in Active Directory.

Solution

Using a graphical user interface

1. Log on to the computer you want to join to the domain and open the Control Panel.
2. Open the System applet.
3. Click the Computer Name tab.
4. Click the Change button.
5. Under "Member of," select Domain.
6. Enter the domain you want to join and click OK.
7. You may be prompted to enter credentials that grant permission to join the computer.
8. Reboot the computer.

   Note that the tabs in the System applet vary between Windows 2000, Windows XP, and Windows Server 2003.

Using a command-line interface

```
> netdom join <ComputerName> /Domain <DomainName> /UserD <DomainUserUPN>
/PasswordD * /UserO <ComputerAdminUser> /PasswordO * /Reboot
```

Using VBScript

```
' This code joins a computer to a domain ' ------ SCRIPT CONFIGURATION ------
strComputer     = "<ComputerName>"        ' e.g. joe-xp
strDomain       = "<DomainName>"          ' e.g. adatum.com
strDomainUser   = "<DomainUserUPN>"       ' e.g. administrator@adatum.com
strDomainPasswd = "<DomainUserPasswd>"
strLocalUser    = "<ComputerAdminUser>"   ' e.g. administrator
strLocalPasswd  = "<ComputerUserPasswd>"
' ------ END CONFIGURATION ---------

'#########################
' Constants
'#########################
Const JOIN_DOMAIN          = 1
Const ACCT_CREATE          = 2
Const ACCT_DELETE          = 4
Const WIN9X_UPGRADE        = 16
Const DOMAIN_JOIN_IF_JOINED = 32
```

```
Const JOIN_UNSECURE           = 64
Const MACHINE_PASSWORD_PASSED = 128
Const DEFERRED_SPN_SET        = 256
Const INSTALL_INVOCATION      = 262144


'###########################
' Connect to Computer
'###########################
set objWMILocator = CreateObject("WbemScripting.SWbemLocator")
objWMILocator.Security_.AuthenticationLevel = 6
set objWMIComputer = objWMILocator.ConnectServer(strComputer, _
                                        "root\cimv2", _
                                        strLocalUser, _
                                        strLocalPasswd)
set objWMIComputerSystem = objWMIComputer.Get( _
                            "Win32_ComputerSystem.Name='" & _
                            strComputer & "'")


'###########################
' Join Computer
'###########################
rc = objWMIComputerSystem.JoinDomainOrWorkGroup(strDomain, _
                                        strDomainPasswd, _
                                        strDomainUser, _
                                        vbNullString, _
                                        JOIN_DOMAIN)
if rc <> 0 then
    WScript.Echo "Join failed with error: " & rc
else
    WScript.Echo "Successfully joined " & strComputer & " to " & strDomain
end if
```

Discussion

When trying to add a computer to Active Directory, you can either pre-create the computer object as described in Recipes 8.2 and 8.3 before joining it to the domain, or you can perform both operations at the same time.

Using a graphical user interface

If you have the correct permissions in Active Directory, you can actually create a computer object at the same time as you join it to a domain via the instructions described in the GUI solution. Since the System applet doesn't allow you to specify an OU for the computer object, if it needs to create a computer object, it will do so in the default Computers container. See Recipe 8.17 for more information on the default computers container and how to change it.

Using a command-line interface

The netdom command will attempt to create a computer object for the computer during a join if one does not already exist. An optional /OU switch can be added to specify the

---

OU in which to create the **computer** object. To do so, you'll need to have the necessary permissions to create and manage **computer** objects in the OU.

There are some restrictions on running the **netdom join** command remotely. If a Windows XP machine has the **ForceGuest** security policy setting enabled, you cannot join it remotely. Running the **netdom** command directly on the machine works regardless of the **ForceGuest** setting. Additionally, the remote computer will need to have the Windows Firewall configured so that it is accessible over the network from the administrative workstation.

You can unjoin a computer from a domain at the command line by using *unjoin.exe*, another free download from the *joeware* website. *unjoin.exe* will not remove the computer account from the Active Directory domain; it will merely change the domain membership locally on the machine itself.

Using VBScript

In order for the **Win32_ComputerSystem::JoinDomainOrWorkGroup** method to work remotely, you have to use an **AuthenticationLevel** equal to 6 so that the traffic between the two machines (namely the passwords) is encrypted. You can also create **computer** objects using **JoinDomainOrWorkGroup** by using the **ACCT_CREATE** flag in combination with **JOIN_DOMAIN**.

 This function is not available for Windows 2000 and earlier machines.

Just like with the *netdom* utility, you cannot run this script against a remote computer if that computer has the **ForceGuest** setting enabled, and the Windows Firewall must be configured appropriately to allow remote access from the administrative workstation.

See Also

MS KB 238793 (Enhanced Security Joining or Resetting Machine Account in Windows 2000 Domain), MS KB 251335 (Domain Users Cannot Join Workstation or Server to a Domain), MS KB 290403 (How to Set Security in Windows XP Professional That Is Installed in a Workgroup), and MSDN: Win32_ComputerSystem::JoinDomainOr-Work-group, MSDN: NetJoinDomain; more information on the **ForceGuest** setting can be found at *http://www.microsoft.com/resources/documentation/Windows/XP/all/reskit/en-us/prde_ffs_ypuh.asp*

8.6 Moving a Computer Within the Same Domain

Problem

You want to move a `computer` object to a different container or OU within the same domain.

Solution

Using a graphical user interface

1. Open the ADUC snap-in.
2. If you need to change domains, right-click on Active Directory Users and Computers in the left pane, select "Connect to Domain," enter the domain name, and click OK.
3. In the left pane, right-click on the domain and select Find.
4. Beside Find, select Computers.
5. Type the name of the computer and click Find Now.
6. In the Search Results window, right-click on the computer and select Move.
7. Browse to and select the new parent container or OU.
8. Click OK.

 Starting with the Windows Server 2003 version of Active Directory Users and Computers, you can also use the new drag-and-drop functionality to move computers and other objects.

Using a command-line interface

You can move a computer object to a new container using the built-in DSMove utility or AdMod. To use DSMove, enter the following syntax:

```
> dsmove "<ComputerDN>" -newparent "<NewParentDN>"
```

To move a computer object using AdMod, use the following:

```
> admod -b "<ComputerDN>" -move "<NewParentDN>"
```

Using VBScript

```
' This code moves a computer
' to the specified container/OU.
' ------ SCRIPT CONFIGURATION -------
strCompDN = "<ComputerDN>" ' e.g. cn=joe-xp,cn=Users,dc=adatum,dc=com
strOUDN = "<NewParentDN>"  ' e.g. ou=workstations,dc=adatum,dc=com
' ------ END CONFIGURATION --------
```

```
set objComp = GetObject("LDAP://" & strCompDN)
set objOU = GetObject("LDAP://" & strOUDN)
objOU.MoveHere objComp.ADsPath, objComp.Name
```

Using PowerShell

To move an Active Directory computer account using the Quest AD cmdlets, use the following syntax:

```
move-QADObject -identity <ComputerDN> -newparent <NewParentDN>
```

To use the .NET methods, use the following syntax:

```
$obj = [ADSI] "LDAP://<Computer DN>"
$newParent = [ADSI] "LDAP://<New Parent DN>"
$obj.psbase.MoveTo($newParent)
```

Discussion

You can move computer objects around a domain without much impact on the computer itself. You just need to be cautious of the security settings on the new parent OU, which may impact a user's ability to manage the computer object in Active Directory. Also, if GPOs are used differently on the new parent, it could impact booting and logon times, and how the computer's operating system behaves after a user has logged on.

See Also

Recipe 4.20 for moving an object to a different OU and Recipe 8.7 for moving a computer to a different domain

8.7 Moving a Computer to a New Domain

Problem

You want to move a computer object to a different domain.

Solution

Using a graphical user interface

To migrate a computer object between domains in the same forest, use the following steps:

1. Open the ADMT MMC snap-in.
2. Right-click on the Active Directory Migration Tool folder and select the Computer Account Migration Wizard.
3. On the Domain Selection page, enter the DNS or NetBIOS name of the source and target domains. Click Next.

4. On the Translate Objects screen, specify which objects should have new ACLs applied in the new domain. Select any, none, or all of the following, and then click Next to continue:

   - Files and folders
   - Local groups
   - Printers
   - Registry
   - Shares
   - User profiles
   - User rights

5. On the Security Migration Options screen, select the following options to determine how local user accounts will be migrated into the new domain. Select one of the following and click Next to continue:

   Replace
   > Replaces any references to objects from the source domain with references to objects in the target domain.

   Add
   > Adds references to objects in the target domain while leaving the source domain objects intact.

   Remove
   > Removes all references to source domain objects.

6. On the Naming Conflicts page, configure how the wizard should handle naming conflicts during the migration process. Select one of the following and click Next to continue:

   - Ignore conflicting accounts and don't migrate.
   - Replace conflicting accounts.
   - Rename conflicting accounts by adding a designated prefix or suffix.

7. On the Options screen, select the amount of time the wizard should wait before rebooting the target computer into the new domain.

8. Click Next to review your choices and begin the migration process.

Using a command-line interface

The following command migrates a `computer` object from the *adatum.com* domain to the *emea.adatum.com* domain. It will place the migrated object in the Finance OU and will wait two minutes before rebooting the target computer:

```
ADMT COMPUTER /N "FIN101-A" "FIN101-A" /SD:"emea.adatum.com"
/TD:"emea.adatum.com" /TO:"Finance" /RDL:2
```

Using VBScript

```
set objObject = GetObject("LDAP://<TargetDC>/<TargetParentDN>")
objObject.MoveHere "LDAP://<SourceDC>/<SourceDN>", vbNullString
```

Discussion

You can move objects between domains assuming you follow a few guidelines:

- The user requesting the move must have permission to modify objects in the parent container of both domains.

- You need to explicitly specify the target DC (serverless binds usually do not work). This is necessary because the Cross Domain Move LDAP control is being used behind the scenes. (For more information on controls, see Recipe 4.4.)

- The move operation must be performed against the RID master for both domains. This is done to ensure that two objects that are being moved simultaneously don't somehow get assigned the same RID.

- Both domains must be in Windows 2000 native mode or better.

See Also

Recipe 4.4 for more on LDAP controls, MSDN: IADsContainer::MoveHere, and MS KB 326480 (How to Use Active Directory Migration Tool Version 2 to Migrate from Windows 2000 to Windows Server 2003)

8.8 Renaming a Computer

Problem

You want to rename a computer.

Solution

Using a graphical user interface

1. Log on to the computer either directly or with a remote console application such as Terminal Services.
2. Open the Control Panel and double-click on the System applet.
3. Select the Computer Name tab and click the Change button.
4. Under Computer Name, type the new name of the computer and click OK until you are out of the System applet.
5. Reboot the machine.

Using a command-line interface

You can rename a computer object by using the built-in *netdom* utility with the following syntax:

```
> netdom renamecomputer <ComputerName> /NewName <NewComputerName>
/UserD<DomainUserUPN> /PasswordD * /UserO <ComputerAdminUser> /PasswordO * /Reboot
```

Using VBScript

```
' This code renames a computer in AD and on the host itself.
' ------ SCRIPT CONFIGURATION -------
strComputer       = "<ComputerName>"        ' e.g. joe-xp
strNewComputer    = "<NewComputerName>"      ' e.g. joe-pc
strDomainUser     = "<DomainUserUPN>"        ' e.g. administrator@adatum.com
strDomainPasswd = "<DomainUserPasswd>"
strLocalUser      = "<ComputerAdminUser>" 'e.g. joe-xp\administrator
strLocalPasswd  = "<ComputerAdminPasswd>"
' ------ END CONFIGURATION ---------

'############################
' Connect to Computer
'############################
set objWMILocator = CreateObject("WbemScripting.SWbemLocator")
objWMILocator.Security_.AuthenticationLevel = 6
set objWMIComputer = objWMILocator.ConnectServer(strComputer, _
                                                 "root\cimv2", _
                                                 strLocalUser, _
                                                  strLocalPasswd)

set objWMIComputerSystem = objWMIComputer.Get( _
                              "Win32_ComputerSystem.Name='" & _
                              strComputer & "'")
'############################
' Rename Computer
'############################
rc = objWMIComputerSystem.Rename(strNewComputer, _
                                 strDomainPasswd, _
                                 strDomainUser)
if rc <> 0 then
    WScript.Echo "Rename failed with error: " & rc
else
    WScript.Echo "Successfully renamed " & strComputer & " to " & _
                 strNewComputer
end if

WScript.Echo "Rebooting ... "
set objWSHShell = WScript.CreateObject("WScript.Shell")
objWSHShell.Run "rundll32 shell32.dll,SHExitWindowsEx 2"
```

Using PowerShell

```
$objComp = get-WMIObject Win32_ComputerSystem -Comp <ComputerName>
$objComp.Rename("<NewComputerName>")
$os = get-wmiobject win32_operatingsystem -comp <ComputerName>
$os.Reboot()
```

Discussion

Renaming a computer consists of two operations: renaming the **computer** object in Active Directory and renaming the hostname on the machine itself. To do it in one step, an option that each of the three solutions offers, you must have permission in Active Directory to rename the account and administrator permissions on the target machine. For the rename operation to be complete, you must reboot the computer.

> In some cases, renaming a computer can adversely affect services running on the computer. For example, you cannot rename a machine that is a domain controller, Exchange Server, or a Windows Certificate Authority without taking additional (and often significant) steps and precautions.

Using a graphical user interface

After you rename the computer, you will be prompted to reboot the machine. You can cancel if necessary, but you'll need to reboot at some point to complete the rename operation.

Using a command-line interface

The `renamecomputer` option in *netdom* was introduced with Windows Server 2003. It can run remotely and includes a `/Reboot` switch that allows you to automatically reboot the computer after the rename is complete.

Using VBScript

The `Win32_ComputerSystem::Rename` method must be run on the local machine unless the computer is a member of a domain. Unlike the GUI and CLI solutions, you cannot specify alternate credentials for the connection to the computer other than domain credentials. For this reason, the user and password you use with the `Rename` method must have administrative privileges on the target machine (i.e., part of the Administrators group) and on the **computer** object in Active Directory.

> The `Rename` method was introduced in Windows XP and Windows Server 2003, and is not available on Windows 2000 and earlier machines.

See Also

Recipe 4.23 for renaming objects, MS KB 228544 (Changing Computer Name in Windows 2000 Requires Restart), MS KB 238793 (Enhanced Security Joining or Resetting Machine Account in Windows 2000 Domain), MS KB 260575 (How to Use Netdom.exe to Reset Machine Account Passwords of a Windows 2000 Domain

Controller), MS KB 325354 (How to Use the Netdom.exe Utility to Rename a Computer in Windows Server 2003), and MSDN: Win32_ComputerSystem::Rename

8.9 Adding or Removing a Computer Account from a Group

Problem

You want to add or remove a computer account from an Active Directory security group.

Solution

Using a graphical user interface

1. Open the ADUC snap-in.
2. If you need to change domains, right-click on "Active Directory Users and Computers" in the left pane, select "Connect to Domain," enter the domain name, and click OK.
3. In the left pane, browse to the parent container of the objects you want to modify.
4. In the right pane, highlight each object you want to modify, right-click, and select Properties.
5. On the "Member of" tab, click Add.
6. Click the group to which you want to add the computer, and then click Add. To add the computer to more than one group, press Ctrl while selecting the groups you want to add the computer to, and then click Add.
7. To remove a group, select the **group** object and click Remove.
8. Click OK to finish.

Using a command-line interface

To add a **computer** object to a group, use the following syntax:

```
> admod -b "<GroupDN>" member:+:"<ComputerDN>"
```

 To remove an object, replace `:+:` with `:-:` in the previous syntax.

Using VBScript

```
' This code adds and removes a computer object from a group.
' ------ SCRIPT CONFIGURATION ------
strGroupDN = "<GroupDN>" ' e.g. cn=SalesGroup,ou=Groups,dc=adatum,dc=com
```

```
strComputerDN = "<ComputerDN>" ' e.g. cn=Fin101,cn=Computers,dc=adatum,dc=com
' ------ END CONFIGURATION ---------

set objGroup = GetObject("LDAP://" & strGroupDN)
' Add a member
objGroup.Add("LDAP://" & strComputerDN)

' Remove a member
objGroup.Remove("LDAP://" & strComputerDN)
```

Using PowerShell

To add a computer account to a group using the Quest AD cmdlets, use the following syntax:

```
$objComp = get-QADComputer -identity "<ComputerDN>"
add-QADGroupMember -identity "<GroupDN>" -member $objComputer
```

To add a computer to a group using ADSI, use the following:

```
$objGroup = [ADSI]("LDAP://" + "<Group DN>")
$objGroup.Add("LDAP://" + "<Computer DN>")
#
# to remove a computer from the group instead
#
$objGroup.Remove("LDAP://" + "<Computer DN>")
```

Discussion

In Active Directory, both **user** and **computer** objects are security principals that can be assigned rights and permissions within a domain. As such, **computer** objects can be added to or removed from **group** objects to make for simpler resource administration. You can make this change through ADUC or ADSI Edit, or by manually editing the **member** attribute of the appropriate group object.

See Also

MSDN: NT-Group-Members attribute [AD Schema] and MSDN: Member Attribute [AD Schema]

8.10 Testing the Secure Channel for a Computer

Problem

You want to test the secure channel of a computer.

Solution

Using a command-line interface

```
> nltest /server:<ComputerName> /sc_query:<DomainName>
```

Discussion

Every member computer in an Active Directory domain establishes a secure channel with a domain controller. The computer's password is stored locally in the form of an LSA secret and in Active Directory. This password is used by the NetLogon service to establish the secure channel with a domain controller. If for some reason the LSA secret and computer password become out of sync, the computer will no longer be able to authenticate in the domain. The `nltest /sc_query` command can query a computer to verify its secure channel is working. Here is sample output from the command when things are working:

```
Flags: 30 HAS_IP HAS_TIMESERV
Trusted DC Name \\dc1.adatum.com
Trusted DC Connection Status Status = 0 0x0 NERR_Success
The command completed successfully
```

If a secure channel is failing, you'll need to reset the computer as described in Recipe 8.11. Here is sample output when things are not working:

```
Flags: 0
Trusted DC Name
Trusted DC Connection Status Status = 1311 0x51f ERROR_NO_LOGON_SERVERS
The command completed successfully
```

See Also

Recipe 8.11 for resetting a computer and MS KB 216393 (Resetting Computer Accounts in Windows 2000 and Windows XP)

8.11 Resetting a Computer Account

Problem

You want to reset a computer because its secure channel is failing.

Solution

Using a graphical user interface

1. Open the ADUC snap-in.
2. If you need to change domains, right-click on Active Directory Users and Computers in the left pane, select "Connect to Domain," enter the domain name, and click OK.
3. In the left pane, right-click on the domain and select Find.
4. Beside Find, select Computers.
5. Type the name of the computer and click Find Now.

6. In the Search Results, right-click on the computer and select Reset Account.

7. Click Yes to verify.

8. Click OK.

9. Rejoin the computer to the domain.

Using a command-line interface

You can use the DSMod utility to reset a computer's password. You will need to rejoin the computer to the domain after doing this:

```
> dsmod computer "<ComputerDN>" -reset
```

Another option is to use the `netdom` command, which can reset the secure channel between the computer and the domain controller without affecting the computer's password, so that you do not need to rejoin it to the domain:

```
> netdom reset <ComputerName> /Domain <DomainName> /UserO <UserUPN> /PasswordO *
```

You can also use the `nltest` command to reset a secure channel using the following syntax:

```
> nltest /sc_reset:<DomainName>\<DCName>
```

Using VBScript

```
' This resets an existing computer object's password to initial default.
' You'll need to rejoin the computer after doing this.
set objComputer = GetObject("LDAP://<ComputerDN>")
objComputer.SetPassword "<ComputerName>"
```

Discussion

When you've identified that a computer's secure channel has failed, you'll need to reset the computer object, which consists of setting the computer object password to the name of the computer. This is the default initial password for new computers. Every 30 days, Windows 2000 and newer systems automatically change their passwords in the domain. After you've set the password, you'll need to rejoin the computer to the domain since it will no longer be able to communicate with a domain controller due to unsynchronized passwords. However, the `netdom reset` command will try to reset the password on both the computer and in Active Directory, which will not necessitate rejoining it to the domain if successful.

From a practical standpoint, you should first attempt to reset the secure channel between the computer and the domain using the `netdom` or `nltest` syntaxes, since doing so will not require you to unjoin and rejoin the computer to the domain; in particular, this will save you from performing the associated reboots involved with rejoining the domain. If resetting the secure channel does not correct the issue you're facing, you can then resort to resetting the computer's password.

See Also

Recipe 8.5 for joining a computer to a domain, Recipe 8.10 for testing a secure channel, MS KB 216393 (Resetting Computer Accounts in Windows 2000 and Windows XP), and MS KB 325850 (How to Use Netdom.exe to Reset Machine Account Passwords of a Windows Server 2003 Domain Controller)

8.12 Finding Inactive or Unused Computers

Problem

You want to find inactive computer accounts in a domain.

Solution

These solutions might only apply to Windows-based machines. Other types of machines—e.g., Unix, Mac, Network Attached Storage (NAS)—that have accounts in Active Directory might not update their login timestamps or passwords, which are used to determine inactivity.

Using a command-line interface

The following query will locate all inactive computers in the current forest:

```
> dsquery computer forestroot -inactive <NumWeeks>
```

You can also use **domainroot** in combination with the **-d** option to query a specific domain:

```
> dsquery computer domainroot -d <DomainName> -inactive <NumWeeks>
```

or you can target your query at a specific container:

```
> dsquery computer ou=MyComputers,dc=adatum,dc=com -inactive <NumWeeks>
```

These commands can only be run against a Windows Server 2003 domain functional level or higher domain.

You can also use the OldCmp *joeware* utility to create a report of all computer accounts whose passwords are older than a certain number of days (90 by default) by using the following syntax:

```
> oldcmp -report
```

To specify an alternate password age with `oldcmp`, use the `-age x` switch. You can also use the `-llts` switch to use the `lastLogonTimeStamp` attribute to perform the age calculations. (Without this switch, `oldcmp` will use `pwdLastSet` by default, which will work against any version of Active Directory in any domain mode.)

Discussion

Using a command-line interface

The `dsquery computer` command is very handy for finding inactive computers that have not logged in to the domain for a number of weeks or months. You can pipe the results of the query to the *dsrm* command-line utility if you want to remove the inactive `computer` objects from Active Directory in a single command. Here is an example that would delete all computers in the current domain that have been inactive for 12 weeks or longer:

```
> for /F "usebackq" %i in (`dsquery computer domainroot -inactive 12`) do dsrm %i
```

You can also use OldCmp to disable inactive accounts, and then either delete them or move them to an alternate OU. OldCmp has a number of safeties built into the utility to prevent you from deleting a large number of computer accounts without meaning to. For example, OldCmp will not delete an account unless it has first been disabled, it will not modify more than 10 objects at a time unless you manually specify a higher limit, and it simply will not do anything at all to a domain controller computer account under any circumstances. Unless you have a requirement for quickly removing unused `computer` objects, we'd recommend allowing them to remain inactive for at least three months before removing them. If you don't really care when the objects get removed, use a year (i.e., 52 weeks) to be on the safe side.

See Also

Recipe 6.28 for finding users whose passwords are about to expire

8.13 Changing the Maximum Number of Computers a User Can Join to the Domain

Problem

You want to grant users the ability to join more or fewer than 10 computers to a domain. This limit is called the *machine account quota*.

Solution

Using a graphical user interface

1. Open the ADSI Edit MMC snap-in and connect to the Domain Naming Context.
2. Right-click on the domainDNS object for the domain you want to change and select Properties.
3. Edit the ms-DS-MachineAccountQuota attribute and enter the new quota value.
4. Click OK twice.

Using a command-line interface

In the following LDIF code, replace *<DomainDN>* with the distinguished name of the domain you want to change, and replace *<Quota>* with the new machine account quota:

```
dn: <DomainDN>
changetype: modify
replace: ms-DS-MachineAccountQuota
ms-DS-MachineAccountQuota: <Quota>
-
```

If the LDIF file was named *change_computer_quota.ldf*, you would then run the following command:

```
> ldifde -v -i -f change_computer_quota.ldf
```

You can also make this change using AdMod, as follows:

```
> admod -b <DomainDN> ms-DS-MachineAccountQuota::<Quota>
```

Using VBScript

```
' This code sets the
' machine account quota for a domain.
' ------ SCRIPT CONFIGURATION ------
intQuota = <Quota>
strDomain = "<DomainDNSName>" ' e.g. emea.adatum.com
' ------ END CONFIGURATION --------

set objRootDSE = GetObject("LDAP://" & strDomain & "/RootDSE")
set objDomain = GetObject("LDAP://" & objRootDSE.Get("defaultNamingContext"))
objDomain.Put "
ms-DS-MachineAccountQuota", intQuota
objDomain.SetInfo
WScript.Echo "Updated user quota to " & intQuota
```

Using PowerShell

You can modify the MachineAccountQuota attribute using either the Quest cmdlets or ADSI, as follows:

```
set-QADObject '<DomainDN>' -ObjectAttributes
@('ms-DS-MachineAccountQuota'='<NewQuota>')
```

```
$objDom = [System.DirectoryServices.ActiveDirectory.Domain]::getCurrentDomain()
$objDom.Put("ms-DS-MachineAccountQuota","<NewQuota>")
$objDom.SetInfo()
```

Discussion

In a default Active Directory installation, members of the Authenticated Users group can add and join up to 10 computer accounts in the default Computers container. The number of computer accounts that can be created is defined in the attribute ms-DS-MachineAccountQuota on the domainDNS object for a domain. The default setting is artificially set to 10, but you can easily change that to whatever number you want, including 0, via the methods described in the "Solution" section. If you set it to 0, users have to be granted explicit permissions in Active Directory to join computers; refer to Recipe 8.5 for instructions on granting these permissions.

Another method for granting users the right to add computer objects, although not recommended, is via Group Policy. If you grant the "Add workstation to domain" right via Computer Configuration→Windows Settings→Security Settings→Local Policies→User Rights Assignment on a GPO that's been linked to the Domain Controllers OU, then users will be able to create computer accounts even if they do not have create child permissions on the default Computers container. This is a holdover from Windows NT to maintain backward compatibility and should not be used unless absolutely necessary. In fact, a good security best practice would be to remove this user right from any user or group objects that do not require it.

See Also

Recipe 8.5 for permissions needed to join computers to a domain, MS KB 251335 (Domain Users Cannot Join Workstation or Server to a Domain), and MS KB 314462 ("You Have Exceeded the Maximum Number of Computer Accounts" Error Message When You Try to Join a Windows XP Computer to a Windows 2000 Domain)

8.14 Modifying the Attributes of a computer Object

Problem

You want to modify one or more attributes of a computer object.

Solution

Using a graphical user interface

1. Open ADSI Edit.
2. If an entry for the naming context you want to browse is not already displayed, do the following:

a. Right-click on ADSI Edit in the right pane and click "Connect to...".

b. Fill in the information for the naming context, container, or OU you want to add an object to. Click on the Advanced button if you need to enter alternate credentials.

c. In the left pane, browse to the container or OU that contains the computer object you want to modify. Once you've found the object, right-click on it and select Properties.

4. Right-click the attribute you want to modify and select Edit.

5. Enter the new value and click OK.

6. Click Apply, followed by OK.

Using a command-line interface

Create an LDIF file called *modify_object.ldf* with the following contents:

```
dn: <ComputerDN>
changetype: modify
add: <AttributeName>
<AttributeName>: <AttributeValue>
-
```

Then run the following command:

```
> ldifde -v -i -f modify_object.ldf
```

To modify an object using AdMod, you'll use the following general syntax:

```
> admod -b <ComputerDN> <attribute>:<operation>:<value>
```

For example, you can add a location to a **computer** object using the following syntax:

```
> admod -b cn="Fin101,cn=Computers,dc=adatum,dc=com" location::"Berlin, Germany"
```

Using VBScript

```
' The following code will modify the location attribute
' of a computer object.

Set objComputer = GetObject ("LDAP://<ComputerDN>")

objComputer.Put "Location" , "<NewLocationValue>"
objComputer.SetInfo
```

Using PowerShell

```
set-QADObject -identity <ComputerDN> -ObjectAttributes
@{'<attribute1>'='<Value>';'<attribute2>'='<Value>'...}

$objComp = [ADSI] "LDAP://<ComputerDN>"
$objComp.Put("<attribute>","<Value>")
$objComp.SetInfo()
```

Discussion

Like all objects within Active Directory, `computer` objects have various attributes that can be queried, modified, and deleted during the day-to-day management of your domain. Because `computer` objects inherit from the user class, they include similar informational attributes to the `user` objects, as well as attributes that are specific to `computer` objects, including:

- Location
- Description
- operatingSystemVersion
- operatingSystemServicePack
- sAMAccountName
- pwdLastSet
- primaryGroupID

See Also

Recipe 8.12 for finding inactive or unused computers, Recipe 8.15 for finding computers with a particular OS, and MSDN: Computer System Hardware Classes [WMI]

8.15 Finding Computers with a Particular OS

Problem

You want to find computers that have a certain OS version, release, or service pack in a domain.

Solution

Using a graphical user interface

1. Open LDP.
2. From the menu, select Connection→Connect.
3. For Server, enter the name of a domain controller (or leave blank to do a serverless bind).
4. For Port, enter 389.
5. Click OK.
6. From the menu, select Connection→Bind.
7. Enter credentials of a user to perform the search.
8. Click OK.

9. From the Menu, select Browse→Search.

10. For Base DN, enter the base of where you want your search to begin.

11. For Filter, enter a filter that contains the OS attribute you want to search on. For example, a query for all computers that are running Windows XP would look like the following:

```
(&(objectclass=computer)(objectcategory=computer)(operatingSystem=Windows XP
Professional))
```

12. Select the appropriate Scope based on how deep you want to search.

13. Click the Options button if you want to customize the list of attributes returned for each matching object.

14. Click Run, and the results will be displayed in the right pane.

You can also perform this search using the Active Directory Users and Computers MMC snap-in (*dsa.msc*), as follows:

1. Open the ADUC MMC snap-in.

2. Right-click on the domain, OU, or container that you wish to search, and click Find.

3. In the Find drop-down box, select Computers.

4. Click on the Advanced tab. Click on Field and select Operating System.

5. Select the Condition that you want to search on from one of the following:
   - Starts with
   - Ends with
   - Is (exactly)
   - Is not
   - Present
   - Not present

6. In the Value field, enter the value that you want to search for, such as "Windows Server 2003."

7. Click Find Now.

Using a command-line interface

You can query for computer objects of a particular operating system using either DSQuery or AdFind. To perform the query with DSQuery, use the following syntax:

```
> dsquery * <DomainDN> -scope subtree -attr "*" -filter "(&(objectclass=
computer)(objectcategory=computer)(operatingSystem=Windows Server 2003))"
```

To use AdFind, enter the following:

```
> adfind -b <DomainDN> -f  "(&(objectcategory=computer)
  (operatingSystem=Windows Server 2003))"
```

Using VBScript

```
' This code searches for computer objects that have Service Pack 1 installed.
' ------ SCRIPT CONFIGURATION ------
strBase = "<LDAP://" & "<DomainDN>" & ">;"
' ------ END CONFIGURATION --------

strFilter = "(&(objectclass=computer)(objectcategory=computer)" & _
            "(operatingSystemServicePack=Service Pack 1));"
strAttrs  = "cn,operatingSystem,operatingSystemVersion," & _
            " operatingSystemServicePack;"
strScope  = "subtree"

set objConn = CreateObject("ADODB.Connection")
objConn.Provider = "ADsDSOObject"
objConn.Open "Active Directory Provider"
Set objRS = objConn.Execute(strBase & strFilter & strAttrs & strScope)
objRS.MoveFirst
while Not objRS.EOF
    Wscript.Echo objRS.Fields(0).Value
    Wscript.Echo objRS.Fields(1).Value
    Wscript.Echo objRS.Fields(2).Value
    Wscript.Echo objRS.Fields(3).Value
    Wscript.Echo objRS.Fields(4).Value
    WScript.Echo
    objRS.MoveNext
wend
```

Using PowerShell

To search for computers based on operating system or service pack revision using the Quest tools, use the **get-QADComputer** cmdlet, as follows:

```
get-QADComputer -OSVersion '<Operating System>' -OSServicePack '<ServicePackLevel>'
```

To search for computers using ADSI, use the following code:

```
$strQuery = "(&(objectcategory=computer)(operatingSystemServicePack=Service Pack 1))"
$objDomain = New-Object System.DirectoryServices.DirectoryEntry
$objSearcher = New-Object System.DirectoryServices.DirectorySearcher
$objSearcher.SearchRoot = $objDomain
$objSearcher.Filter = $strQuery
$colResults = $objSearcher.FindAll()
```

Discussion

When a computer joins an Active Directory domain, the operating system attributes are updated for the **computer** object. There are four of these attributes, which can be used in queries to find computers that match certain OS-specific criteria, like service pack level.

These attributes include the following:

`operatingSystem`

Descriptive name of the installed Operating System—e.g., Windows Server 2003, Windows 2000 Server, and Windows XP Professional. The values of this attribute in Windows Vista and Windows Server 2008 now include special characters such as the copyright symbol, which makes this attribute a poor choice for searching.

`operatingSystemVersion`

Numerical representation of the operating system—e.g., 5.0 (2195) and 5.2 (3757).

`operatingSystemServicePack`

Current service pack level if one is installed—e.g., Service Pack 2 and Service Pack 3.

This recipe typically applies only to Windows-based machines. Other types of machines (e.g., Unix) that have accounts in Active Directory might not automatically update their OS attributes, though some newer Unix or Linux-based NAS devices have been configured to do so. Additionally, the `operatingSystem` attribute does not distinguish between Windows NT 4 server and Windows NT 4 workstation.

8.16 Binding to the Default Container for Computers

This recipe requires the Windows Server 2003 or Windows Server 2008 domain functional level.

Problem

You want to bind to the default container that new computer objects are created in.

Solution

Using a graphical user interface

1. Open LDP.
2. From the menu, select Connection→Connect.
3. For Server, enter the name of a domain controller (or leave blank to do a serverless bind).
4. For Port, enter 389.
5. Click OK.
6. From the menu, select Connection→Bind.
7. Enter credentials of a domain user.
8. Click OK.

9. From the menu, select View→Tree.

10. For the DN, enter:

   ```
   <WKGUID=aa312825768811d1aded00c04fd8d5cd,<DomainDN>>
   ```

   where *<DomainDN>* is the distinguished name of a domain.

11. Click OK.

12. In the lefthand menu, you can now browse the default computers container for the domain.

Using a command-line interface

By default, all computer objects created in an Active Directory domain are placed into the built-in Computers container. This default container has a significant limitation, in that you are unable to link Group Policy Objects (GPOs) to the built-in container. If you have one or more GPOs that you wish to apply to all computer objects in your domain, you should modify the default location for computer accounts in AD. You can use the *redircmp* utility to change this default location, as we will discuss in Recipe 8.17.

Using VBScript

```
' This code illustrates how to bind to the default computers container.
' ------ SCRIPT CONFIGURATION ------
strDomain = "<DomainDNSName>" ' e.g. apac.adatum.com
' ------ END CONFIGURATION --------

' Computer GUID as defined in ntdsapi.h
Const ADS_GUID_COMPUTRS_CONTAINER = "aa312825768811d1aded00c04fd8d5cd"

set objRootDSE = GetObject("LDAP://" & strDomain & "/RootDSE")
set objCompContainer = GetObject("LDAP://<WKGUID=" & _
                       ADS_GUID_COMPUTRS_CONTAINER & "," & _
                       objRootDSE.Get("defaultNamingContext") & ">" )
WScript.Echo objCompContainer.Get("distinguishedName")
```

Using PowerShell

```
$obj = [ADSI] "LDAP://<WKGUID= aa312825768811d1aded00c04fd8d5cd>,<Domain DN>>"
#
# or .....
#
$strDomain = "<DomainDNSName>" ' e.g. apac.adatum.com

Set-Variable ADS_GUID_COMPUTERS_CONTAINER aa312825768811d1aded00c04fd8d5cd

$rootDSE = [ADSI]("LDAP://" + $strDomain + "/RootDSE")
$container = [ADSI]("LDAP://<WKGUID=" + $ADS_GUID_COMPUTERS_CONTAINER + "," +
                   $rootDSE.defaultNamingContext + ">")
$container.distinguishedName
```

Discussion

In much the same way that the TCP/IP protocol defines a list of well-known ports that are commonly used by industry applications (TCP 20 and 21 for FTP, TCP port 80 for HTTP, etc.), Active Directory defines Well-Known GUIDs that map to container objects that are present in every AD installation. The Domain NC defines the following WKGUIDs:

- `Users`
- `Computers`
- `System`
- `Domain Controllers`
- `Infrastructure`
- `Deleted Objects`
- `Lost and Found`

The Configuration NC also defines its own `Deleted Objects` WKGUID.

For example, the default computers container has the following WKGUID:

```
aa312825768811d1aded00c04fd8d5cd
```

You can use the GUID to bind to the default computers container in the domain using the following ADsPath:

```
LDAP://<WKGUID=aa312825768811d1aded00c04fd8d5cd,dc=apac,dc=adatum,dc=com>
```

The list of well-known objects for a domain is contained in the `wellKnownObjects` attribute of the `domainDNS` object for the domain. The `wellKnownObjects` attribute is multivalued with DNWithBinary syntax. The following is an example of what that attribute looks like for the *adatum.com* domain:

```
B:32:AA312825768811D1ADED00C04FD8D5CD:CN=Computers,DC=adatum,DC=com;
B:32:F4BE92A4C777485E878E9421D53087DB:CN=Microsoft,CN=Program
Data,DC=adatum,DC=com;
B:32:09460C08AE1E4A4EA0F64AEE7DAA1E5A:CN=Program Data,DC=adatum,DC=com;
B:32:22B70C67D56E4EFB91E9300FCA3DC1AA:
CN=ForeignSecurityPrincipals,DC=adatum,DC=com;
B:32:18E2EA80684F11D2B9AA00C04F79F805:CN=Deleted Objects,DC=adatum,DC=com;
B:32:2FBAC1870ADE11D297C400C04FD8D5CD:CN=Infrastructure,DC=adatum,DC=com;
B:32:AB8153B7768811D1ADED00C04FD8D5CD:CN=LostAndFound,DC=adatum,DC=com;
B:32:AB1D30F3768811D1ADED00C04FD8D5CD:CN=System,DC=adatum,DC=com;
B:32:A361B2FFFFD211D1AA4B00C04FD7D83A:OU=Domain Controllers,DC=adatum,DC=com;
B:32:A9D1CA15768811D1ADED00C04FD8D5CD:CN=Users,DC=adatum,DC=com;
```

Each value has the format of:

```
B:NumberofBytes:GUID:DistinguishedName
```

As you can see, the GUID for the first value is the same as the one we used in the ADsPath above to bind to the default computers container.

See Also

Recipe 8.17 for changing the default computers container and MSDN: Binding to Well-Known Objects Using WKGUID

8.17 Changing the Default Container for Computers

Problem

You want to change the container that computers are created in by default.

Solution

Using a graphical user interface

1. Open LDP.
2. From the menu, select Connection→Connect.
3. For Server, enter the name of a domain controller (or leave blank to do a serverless bind).
4. For Port, enter 389.
5. Click OK.
6. From the menu, select Connection→Bind.
7. Enter credentials of a domain user.
8. Click OK.
9. From the menu, select Browse→Modify.
10. For DN, enter the distinguished name of the `domainDNS` object of the domain you want to modify.
11. For Attribute, enter `wellKnownObjects`.
12. For Values, enter the following:

        B:32:AA312825768811D1ADED00C04FD8D5CD:CN=Computers,<DomainDN>

    where `<DomainDN>` is the same as the DN you enter for the DN field.
13. Select Delete for the Operation and click the Enter button.
14. Go back to the Values field and enter the following:

        B:32:AA312825768811D1ADED00C04FD8D5CD:<NewComputersParent>,<DomainDN>

    where `<NewComputersParent>` is the new parent container for new computer objects (e.g., `ou=Adatum Computers`).
15. Select Add for the Operation and click the Enter button.
16. Click the Run button.

The result of the operations will be displayed in the right pane of the main LDP window.

Using a command-line interface

```
> redircmp "<NewParentDN>"
```

Using VBScript

```
' This code changes the
' default computers container.
' ------ SCRIPT CONFIGURATION ------
strNewComputersParent = "<NewComputersParent>" ' e.g. OU=Adatum Computers
strDomain              = "<DomainDNSName>"      ' e.g. adatum.com
' ------ END CONFIGURATION ---------

Const COMPUTER_WKGUID = "B:32:AA312825768811D1ADED00C04FD8D5CD:"
' ADS_PROPERTY_OPERATION_ENUM
Const ADS_PROPERTY_APPEND = 3
Const ADS_PROPERTY_DELETE = 4

set objRootDSE = GetObject("LDAP://" & strDomain & "/RootDSE")
set objDomain = GetObject("LDAP://" & objRootDSE.Get("
defaultNamingContext"))
set objCompWK = GetObject("LDAP://" & _
                          "<WKGUID=AA312825768811D1ADED00C04FD8D5CD," & _
                          objRootDSE.Get("defaultNamingContext") & ">")

objDomain.PutEx ADS_PROPERTY_DELETE, "wellKnownObjects", _
                Array( COMPUTER_WKGUID & objCompWK.Get("distinguishedName"))
objDomain.PutEx ADS_PROPERTY_APPEND, "wellKnownObjects", _
                Array( COMPUTER_WKGUID & strNewComputersParent & "," & _
                       objRootDSE.Get("defaultNamingContext") )
objDomain.SetInfo
WScript.Echo "New default Computers container set to " & _
             strNewComputersParent
```

Discussion

Most Active Directory administrators do not use the Computers container within the Domain Naming context as their primary computer repository. One reason is that since it is a container and not an OU, you cannot apply Group Policy Objects to it. If you have another location where you store computer objects, you might want to consider changing the default container used to bind to the computers container by changing the well-known objects attribute, as shown in this recipe. This can be beneficial if you want to ensure computers cannot sneak into Active Directory without having the appropriate group policies applied to them. While you can also apply GPOs at the site or the domain level, forcing new computers into a particular Organizational Unit ensures that those computers receive the Group Policy settings that you want them to receive through GPOs linked at the OU level. However, this does not protect you from an administrator (whether intentionally or accidentally) explicitly creating a computer

---

object in the incorrect OU; this only protects you from applications or utilities that do not allow or do not require you to specify an OU when creating the computer.

 See Recipe 8.16 for more information on how well-known objects are specified in Active Directory.

See Also

MS KB 324949 (Redirecting the Users and Computers Containers in Windows Server 2003 Domains)

8.18 Listing All the Computer Accounts in a Domain

Problem

You want to obtain a list of all computer accounts in an Active Directory domain.

Solution

Using a graphical user interface

1. Open the Active Directory Users and Computers MMC snap-in.
2. Right-click on the domain node and select Find.
3. In the Find drop-down box, select Computers and click Find Now.
4. All computer objects in the domain will be displayed in the Search Results window.

Using a command-line interface

```
> adfind -default -f objectCategory=computer
```

Using VBScript

```
' The following script will enumerate all computer accounts
' within an Active Directory domain.

Const ADS_SCOPE_SUBTREE = 2
strDomain = "<DomainDN>"

Set objConnection = CreateObject("ADODB.Connection")
Set objCommand = CreateObject("ADODB.Command")
objConnection.Provider = "ADsDSOObject"
objConnection.Open "Active Directory Provider"

Set objCOmmand.ActiveConnection = objConnection
objCommand.CommandText = _
```

```
            "Select Name, Location from 'LDAP://" & strDomain & "' " _
                & "Where objectCategory='computer'"
        objCommand.Properties("Page Size") = 1000
        objCommand.Properties("Searchscope") = ADS_SCOPE_SUBTREE
        Set objRecordSet = objCommand.Execute
        objRecordSet.MoveFirst

        Do Until objRecordSet.EOF
            Wscript.Echo "Computer Name: " & objRecordSet.Fields("Name").Value
            Wscript.Echo "Location: " & objRecordSet.Fields("Location").Value
            objRecordSet.MoveNext
        Loop
```

Using PowerShell

You can obtain a listing of computer accounts using either the Quest AD cmdlets or the native ADSI methods, as shown here:

```
get-QADObject -ldapfilter 'objectclass=computer'

$strCategory = "computer"
$objDomain = New-Object System.DirectoryServices.DirectoryEntry
$objSearcher = New-Object System.DirectoryServices.DirectorySearcher
$objSearcher.SearchRoot = $objDomain
$objSearcher.Filter = "(objectCategory=$strCategory)"
$objSearcher.FindAll()
```

Discussion

Using VBScript and PowerShell

To obtain a list of domain controllers, rather than just computer objects, you should query the Configuration NC rather than the domain NC, and replace "where object Category=computer" with "where objectCategory=ntDSDSA".

See Also

MSDN: Object Class and Object Category [Active Directory] and MSDN: Object-Class Attribute [AD-Schema]

8.19 Identifying a Computer Role

Problem

You want to identify the role that a particular computer serves in an Active Directory domain.

Solution

Using a graphical user interface

1. Open the Active Directory Users and Computers MMC snap-in.
2. Right-click on the domain node and select Find.
3. In the Find drop-down box, select Computers and click Find Now.
4. The role of each computer will be displayed in the Machine Role column in the Search Results window.

Using a command-line interface

```
> wmic computersystem get domainrole
```

For a domain controller that holds the PDC Emulator FSMO role, this will return the following output:

```
DomainRole
5
```

 For a DC that doesn't hold the PDCe FSMO, this command will return a value of 4.

Using VBScript

```
' The following code will return the domain role of the
' local computer.
strComputer = "."
Set objWMIService = GetObject("winmgmts:" _
    & "{impersonationLevel=impersonate}!\\" _
    & strComputer & "\root\cimv2")
Set colComputers = objWMIService.ExecQuery _
    ("Select DomainRole from Win32_ComputerSystem")
For Each objComputer in colComputers
    Select Case objComputer.DomainRole
        Case 0
            strComputerRole = "Standalone Workstation"
        Case 1
            strComputerRole = "Member Workstation"
        Case 2
            strComputerRole = "Standalone Server"
        Case 3
            strComputerRole = "Member Server"
        Case 4
            strComputerRole = "Backup Domain Controller"
        Case 5
            strComputerRole = "Primary Domain Controller"
    End Select
```

```
        Wscript.Echo strComputerRole
    Next
```

Discussion

Using a command-line interface

WMIC is the command-line component of the Windows Management Instrumentation that uses aliases to enable you to easily access WMI namespaces from the command line. To run `wmic` against a remote computer, specify the `/node:"<ComputerFQDN>"` switch.

Using VBScript

Rather than relying on an `if...else` construct to produce output, this script uses `Select Case`. In situations where there are numerous possible outcomes for a conditional statement, `Select Case` can produce far more elegant code than using numerous `if...else` statements.

8.20 Protecting a Computer Against Accidental Deletion

Problem

You want to prevent a `computer` object from being accidentally deleted by an administrator who selects the incorrect option in Active Directory Users and Computers.

Solution

Using a graphical user interface (Windows Server 2008 only)

1. Open Active Directory Users and Computers. Click on View and confirm that Advanced Features is selected.
2. Drill down to the current domain. To connect to a different domain, right-click on the top-level node and click "Change domain"; select the appropriate domain and then drill down to it.
3. Right-click on the computer that you want to modify and click Properties.
4. Click on the Object tab.
5. Place a checkmark next to "Protect object from accidental deletion."
6. Click OK.

Using a command-line interface (all versions)

```
dsacls <Computer DN> /d EVERYONE:SDDT
```

Using PowerShell (all versions)

```
Add-QADPermission -identity <Computer DN> -Account 'EVERYONE' -Rights
'Delete,DeleteTree' -ApplyTo 'ThisObjectOnly'
```

If you have Exchange 2007 installed in your environment, you can also obtain this information using the Exchange 2007 Management Tools, as follows:

```
Add-ADPermission -Identity <Computer Name> -User EVERYONE
    -AccessRights Delete,DeleteTree -Deny $true
```

Discussion

By default, all new OUs that are created in Windows Server 2008 will have this protection enabled; however, no other object types are configured with this default protection. If you attempt to delete a computer object that is protected using this option, even when signed on as a Domain Admin or other similarly elevated account, you will receive an "Access Denied" message until you manually remove the checkbox or manually remove the Deny ACE associated with it.

Using the command-line or PowerShell methods can apply this protection to **group** objects in *all* versions of Windows Server, even though the GUI checkbox is only available in Windows Server 2008.

8.21 Viewing the RODCs That Have Cached a Computer's Password

Problem

You wish to view the RODCs that have cached a computer account's password secrets in a Windows Server 2008 domain.

Solution

Using a graphical user interface

1. Open the ADUC snap-in.
2. Click View→Advanced Features. In the left pane, right-click on the domain and select Find.
3. In the Find drop-down box, select Computers. Select the appropriate domain beside In.
4. Beside Name, type the name of the computer account and click Find Now.
5. In the Search Results window, double-click on the user.
6. Select the Attribute Editor tab. Click Filter and ensure that there is a checkmark next to Backlinks.

---

7. Scroll to the msDS-RevealedDSAs attribute to view a list of RODCs that have cached this user's password secrets.

8. Click OK.

Using a command-line interface

```
> adfind -b <ComputerDN> msDS-RevealedDSAs
```

Using VBScript

```
' ------ SCRIPT CONFIGURATION ------
stCompDN = "<ComputerDN>" ' e.g. cn=rallen,ou=Sales,dc=adatum,dc=com
' ------ END CONFIGURATION --------

set objComp = GetObject("LDAP://" & strCompDN)
strRODCs = objComp.Get("msDS-RevealedDSAs")
WScript.Echo strRODCs
```

Using PowerShell

```
> $objComp = [ADSI] "LDAP://<CompDN>"
> $objComp.psbase.InvokeGet("msDS-RevealedDSAs")
```

Discussion

As discussed in Chapter 3, Windows Server 2008 introduces the Read-Only Domain Controller (RODC) to improve the security of branch office and other remote environments. One of the security measures introduced by the RODC is the Password Replication Policy (PRP), which specifies a list of users, computers, and groups that can and cannot have their password secrets cached on one or more DCs. Each RODC maintains a forward-link attribute called msDS-RevealedUsers, which lists the user and computer accounts for whom each RODC has cached password secrets. Each computer account, in turn, maintains a backlink called msDS-RevealedDSAs. This backlink can be queried to determine which RODCs have stored password information for a particular user account; however, like all backlinks, this attribute cannot be modified directly.

See Also

Recipes 3.2 and 3.4

## CHAPTER 9

Group Policy Objects

9.0 Introduction

Active Directory Group Policy Objects (GPOs) can customize virtually any aspect of a computer or user's desktop. They can also be used to install applications, secure a computer, run logon/logoff or startup/shutdown scripts, and much more. You can assign a GPO to a local computer, site, domain, or Organizational Unit. This is called scope of management (SOM), because only the users or computers that fall under the scope of the computer, OU, site, or domain will process the GPO. Assigning a GPO to a SOM is referred to as *linking* the GPO. You can further restrict the application of GPOs by using security groups to filter which users or groups they will apply to.

With Windows Server 2003 and newer servers and Windows XP and newer workstations, you can also use a WMI filter to restrict the application of a GPO. A WMI filter is simply a WMI query that can search against any information on a client's computer. If the WMI filter returns a true value (i.e., the client computer matches the conditions that are specified in the filter), the GPO will be processed; otherwise, it will not. So not only do you have all of the SOM options for applying GPOs, you can now use any WMI information available on the client's computer to determine whether GPOs should be applied. For more on the capabilities of GPOs, we recommend Chapter 7 of *Active Directory*, Fourth Edition, by Brian Desmond et al. (O'Reilly).

Group Policies are defined by a set of files that are replicated to each domain controller in a domain and a `groupPolicyContainer` (GPC) object that is stored in the `cn=Policies,cn=System,<DomainDN>` container. GPC objects contain information related to software deployment, wireless deployments, IPSec assignments, and metadata about the version of the GPO. GPC objects are used for linking to OUs, sites, and domains. The guts of GPOs are stored on the filesystem of each domain controller in group policy template (GPT) files and can be found in the *%SystemRoot%\SYSVOL\sysvol\<DomainDNSName>\Policies* directory.

So why are there two storage points for GPOs? The need for the Active Directory object is obvious: to be able to link GPOs to other types of objects, the GPOs need to be represented in Active Directory. Group Policy Templates are stored in the filesystem to reduce the amount of data that needs to be replicated within Active Directory.

For Windows 2000, Windows Server 2003, and Windows XP clients, each Group Policy object store individual copies of Administrative templates (*.adm* files) in the SYSVOL folder. In an environment containing numerous GPOs, this can significantly add to the amount of data that must be replicated to the SYSVOL share on all domain controllers in a domain. Beginning with Windows Vista, GPO settings are deployed using a new XML-based *.ADMX* format, and administrators have the option to configure a single Central Store to provide a storage instance for all GPOs in a domain.

Furthermore, Windows Server 2008 introduces Group Policy Preferences (GPP), a new group of GPO settings that can be used to manage configuration items that could not previously be managed (or that could not be managed particularly well) via GPO, including managing the creation of file shortcuts, ODBC connections, drive mappings, printer connections, and more. Group Policy Preferences can be deployed on a Windows Server 2003 Active Directory, so long as you have a Windows Server 2008 computer or a Windows Vista workstation from which to run the updated GPMC that includes support for Group Policy Preferences. In addition, you will need to install the Client-Side Extensions for Group Policy Preferences, which can be downloaded and deployed via Windows Software Update Services (WSUS) or similar centralized patch-management software.

Managing GPOs

While the new capabilities of GPOs were significant in Windows 2000 Active Directory, the one obvious thing that was lacking was good tools for managing them. The dual storage nature of GPOs creates a lot of problems. First, Microsoft did not provide a scriptable interface for accessing and manipulating GPO settings. Second, there were no tools for copying or migrating GPOs from a test environment to production. In Windows 2000, the primary tool for managing GPOs was the Group Policy Editor (GPE), now known as the Group Policy Object Editor (GPOE). The main function of GPOE is to modify GPO settings; it does not provide any other management capabilities.

Microsoft realized these were major issues for group policy adoption, so they developed the Group Policy Management Console (GPMC) with the release of Windows Server 2003. The GPMC is a MMC snap-in that provides the kitchen sink of GPO management capabilities: you can create, delete, import, copy, back up, restore, and model GPO processing from a single interface. Perhaps what is even better is the scriptable API that comes with the GPMC. Pretty much every function you can accomplish with the GPMC tool, you can do via a script.

The only major feature that is still lacking is the ability to directly modify the settings of a GPO via command line or script. Previously, this could be done with only the GPOE, but there are third-party options that can provide this type of functionality. The GPMC still provides numerous options for migrating GPOs, which addresses the majority of the problems people face today.

Prior to Windows Server 2008, GPMC is an out-of-band download that can be obtained from the following site: *http://www.microsoft.com/windowsserver2003/gpmc/default.mspx*. In Windows Server 2008, GPMC is built into the Active Directory Domain Services administrative tools, and it can be installed on Windows Vista computers as part of the Remote Server Administration Tools (RSAT). It requires at least version 1.1 of the .NET Framework on Windows Server 2003 or Windows XP SP1 or SP2. (Windows XP SP 1 requires hotfix Q326469 as well.) The GPMC cannot be run on Windows 2000. You can, however, manage Windows 2000-based Active Directory GPOs with the GPMC as long as you run it from one of the previously mentioned platforms.

Another tool that you can download from the Microsoft website is GPInventory. This is an incredibly useful tool that will allow you to perform a software inventory for users and computers in a domain or OU, and to track information about the rollout of GPOs in AD, such as computers that have not applied new GPO information. Additionally, the Group Policy Best Practice Analyzer (GP BPA) is a free download that can help you identify Group Policy configuration errors within your environment.

The majority of solutions presented in this chapter use GPMC. It is for this reason that we highly recommend becoming familiar with it. Most of the command-line solutions we provide will use one of the scripts provided in the GPMC install. A whole host of pre-canned scripts have already been written, in a mix of VBScript and JavaScript, which serve as great command-line tools and good examples to start scripting GPOs. These scripts are available by default in the *%ProgramFiles%\GPMC\scripts* directory on a Windows Server 2003 or R2 server that has had the GPMC installed on it, or you can download them from the Microsoft Downloads site for use on Windows Server 2008 or Windows Vista computers. You can execute them in one of two ways, either by using *cscript*:

```
> cscript listallgpos.wsf
```

or, if you make *cscript* your default WSH interpreter, by executing the file directly. To make *cscript* your default interpreter, run this command:

```
> cscript //H:cscript
```

The complete documentation for the GPM API is available in the *gpmc.chm* file in the *%ProgramFiles%\GPMC\scripts* directory or from MSDN (*http://msdn.microsoft.com*).

At the time of this writing, there is no native PowerShell provider available for Group Policy. However, there are a number of free third-party Group Policy cmdlets available from SDM software at *http://www.sdmsoftware.com/freeware.php*. The majority of the PowerShell solutions in this chapter are written using the SDM Group Policy cmdlets.

9.1 Finding the GPOs in a Domain

Problem

You want to find all of the GPOs that have been created in a domain.

Solution

Using a graphical user interface

1. Open the GPMC snap-in.
2. In the left pane, expand the Forest container.
3. Expand the Domains container.
4. Browse to the domain of the target GPO.
5. Expand the Group Policy Objects container. All of the GPOs in the domain will be listed under that container.

Using a command-line interface

You can generate a list of all GPOs in a domain using the *listastallgpos.wsf* script, as well as DSQuery and AdFind:

```
> listallgpos.wsf [/domain:<DomainDNSName>] [/v]

> dsquery * domainroot -filter (objectcategory=grouppolicycontainer)
-attr displayname

> adfind -default -f (objectcategory=grouppolicycontainer) displayname
```

You can also use the *gpotool* utility from the Windows Server 2003 Resource Kit to display the GPOs:

```
> gpotool [/domain:<DomainDNSName>] [/verbose]
```

Using VBScript

```
' This code displays
' all of the GPOs for a domain.
' ------ SCRIPT CONFIGURATION ------
strDomain = "<DomainDNSName>" ' e.g. adatum.com
' ------ END CONFIGURATION --------

set objGPM = CreateObject("GPMgmt.GPM")
set objGPMConstants = objGPM.GetConstants()

' Initialize the Domain object
```

```
set objGPMDomain = objGPM.GetDomain(strDomain, "", objGPMConstants.UseAnyDC)

' Create an empty search criteriaset objGPMSearchCriteria =
objGPM.CreateSearchCriteria
set objGPOList =
objGPMDomain.SearchGPOs(objGPMSearchCriteria)

' Print the GPOs
WScript.Echo "Found " & objGPOList.Count & " GPOs in " & strDomain & ":"
for each objGPO in objGPOList
    WScript.Echo "    " & objGPO.DisplayName
next
```

Using PowerShell

```
get-SDMgpo *
```

Discussion

See the "Introduction" to this chapter for more on how GPOs are stored in Active Directory.

Using VBScript

You can find the GPOs in a domain by using the `GPMDomain.SearchGPOs` method. The only parameter you need to pass to `SearchGPOs` is a `GPMSearchCriteria` object, which can be used to define criteria for your search. In this case, we created a object `GPMSearchCriteria` without additional criteria so that all GPOs are returned. The `SearchGPOs` method returns a `GPMGPOCollection` object, which is a collection of `GPMGPO` objects.

Using PowerShell

You can obtain the details from a single GPO by replacing * with the `-Name` parameter, followed by the friendly name of the GPO, such as `get-SDMgpo -Name "Default Domain Policy"`.

See Also

MS KB 216359 (How to Identify Group Policy Objects in the Active Directory and SYSVOL) and MSDN: GPMDomain.SearchGPOs

9.2 Creating a GPO

Problem

You want to create a Group Policy Object within Active Directory.

Solution

Using a graphical user interface

1. Open the GPMC snap-in.
2. In the left pane, expand the Forest container, expand the Domains container, and browse to the domain of the target GPO.
3. Right-click on the Group Policy Objects container and select New.
4. Enter the name of the GPO and click OK.

Using a command-line interface

```
> creategpo.wsf <GPOName> [/domain:<DomainDNSName>]
```

Using VBScript

```
' This code creates an empty GPO.
' ------ SCRIPT CONFIGURATION -----
strGPO = "<GPOName>"              ' e.g. "Sales GPO"
strDomain = "<DomainDNSName>" ' e.g. "adatum.com"
' ------ END CONFIGURATION --------

set objGPM = CreateObject("GPMgmt.GPM")
set objGPMConstants = objGPM.GetConstants()

' Initialize the Domain object
set objGPMDomain = objGPM.
GetDomain(strDomain, "", objGPMConstants.UseAnyDC)

' Create the GPO and print the results
set objGPO = objGPMDomain.CreateGPO()
WScript.Echo "Successfully created GPO"
objGPO.DisplayName = strGPO
WScript.Echo "Set GPO name to " & strGPO
```

Using PowerShell

To create a GPO called "Marketing GPO" in the *adatum.com* domain, use the following syntax:

```
new-SDMgpo -name "Marketing GPO" -domain "adatum.com"
```

If the GPO is successfully created, the cmdlet will output the display name of the GPO, along with the GUID and the Distinguished Name of the GPC that resides in the cn=Policies,cn=System,<DomainDN> container.

Discussion

When you create a GPO through the GPMC, it is initially empty with no settings or links configured. See Recipe 9.6 for more on modifying GPO settings, and Recipe 9.14 for creating a link.

Using VBScript

To create a GPO, first instantiate a `GPMDomain` object for the domain to add the GPO to. This is accomplished with the `GPM.GetDomain` method. Then it is just a matter of calling the `GPMDomain.CreateGPO` method (with no parameters) to create an empty GPO. A `GPM.GPO` object is returned from this method, which you then use to set the display name of the GPO.

See Also

MS KB 216359 (How to Identify Group Policy Objects in the Active Directory and SYSVOL) and MSDN: GPMDomain.CreateGPO

9.3 Copying a GPO

Problem

You want to copy the properties and settings of a GPO into another GPO.

Solution

Using a graphical user interface

1. Open the GPMC snap-in.
2. In the left pane, expand the Forest container, expand the Domains container, browse to the domain of the source GPO, and expand the Group Policy Objects container.
3. Right-click on the source GPO and select Copy.
4. Right-click on the Group Policy Objects container and select Paste.
5. Select whether you want to use the default permissions or to preserve the existing permissions from the GPO being copied, and click OK.
6. A status window will pop up that will indicate whether the copy was successful. Click OK to close.
7. Rename the new GPO by right-clicking it in the left pane and selecting Rename.

Using a command-line interface

```
> copygpo.wsf <SourceGPOName> <TargetGPOName>
```

Using VBScript

```vbscript
' This code copies a source GPO to a new GPO.
' ------ SCRIPT CONFIGURATION ------
strSourceGPO = "<SourceGPOName>" ' e.g. SalesGPO
strNewGPO    = "<NewGPOName>"    ' e.g. Marketing GPO
strDomain    = "<DomainDNSName>" ' e.g. adatum.com
' ------ END CONFIGURATION ---------

set objGPM = CreateObject("GPMgmt.GPM")
set objGPMConstants = objGPM.GetConstants()
' Initialize the Domain object
set objGPMDomain = objGPM.GetDomain(strDomain, "", objGPMConstants.UseAnyDC)

' Find the source GPO
set objGPMSearchCriteria = objGPM.CreateSearchCriteria
objGPMSearchCriteria.Add objGPMConstants.SearchPropertyGPODisplayName, _
                         objGPMConstants.SearchOpEquals, cstr(strSourceGPO)
set objGPOList = objGPMDomain.
SearchGPOs(objGPMSearchCriteria)
if objGPOList.Count = 0 then
   WScript.Echo "Did not find GPO: " & strGPO
   WScript.Echo "Exiting."
   WScript.Quit
elseif objGPOList.Count > 1 then
   WScript.Echo "Found more than one matching GPO. Count: " & _
                objGPOList.Count
   WScript.Echo "Exiting."
   WScript.Quit
else
   WScript.Echo "Found GPO: " & objGPOList.Item(1).DisplayName
End if

' Copy from source GPO to target GPO
set objGPMResult = objGPOList.Item(1).CopyTo(0, objGPMDomain, strNewGPO)

' This will throw an exception if there were any errors
' during the actual operation.
on error resume next
objGPMResult.OverallStatus()
if objGPMResult.Status.Count > 0 then
   WScript.Echo "Status message(s): " & objGPMResult.Status.Count
   for i = 1 to objGPMResult.Status.Count
      WScript.Echo objGPMResult.Status.Item(i).Message
   next
   WScript.Echo vbCrLf
end if

' Display the results
if Err.Number <> 0 then
   WScript.Echo "Error copying GPO."
   WScript.Echo "Error: " & Err.Description
else
   WScript.Echo "Copy successful to " & strNewGPO & "."
end if
```

Discussion

Prior to the GPMC tool, two of the big problems with managing GPOs in large environments were migrating them from one forest to another and copying them from one domain to another within the same forest. It is common to have a test forest where GPOs are initially created, configured, and tested before moving them into production. The problem before GPMC was that once you had the GPO the way you wanted it in the test forest, there was no easy or well-publicized way to move it to the production forest.

With the GPMC, you can simply copy GPOs between domains and even forests. Copying GPOs between forests requires a trust to be in place between the two target domains (or a cross-forest trust in place between the two forests). If this is not possible, you can import GPOs, which is similar to a copy operation except that a trust is not needed. A GPO import uses a backup of the source GPO in order to create the new GPO. See Recipe 9.7 for more information on importing a GPO.

Some properties of GPOs, such as security group filters, UNC paths, and Restricted Groups may vary slightly from domain to domain; for example, a logon script that runs from \\SERVERA\share in the source domain may need to run on \\SERVERB\share in the target domain. In that case, you can use a GPMC migration table to help facilitate the transfer of those types of references to the target domain. For more information on migration tables, see the GPMC help file and Recipe 9.8.

Using VBScript

To copy a GPO, you have to first find the source GPO. Use a `GPMSearchCriteria` object to find the GPO that is equal to the display name of the GPO specified in the configuration section. Use an `if else` conditional statement to ensure that only one GPO is returned. If `0` is returned or more than `1` is returned, you have to abort the script.

Now that you have a `GPMGPO` object, you're ready to copy the GPO using the `GPMGPO.CopyTo` method. The first parameter to `CopyTo` is a flag that indicates how permissions in the source GPO should be handled when copying them to the new GPO. Specify `0` to use the default setting (see the GPMC help file for the other values). The second parameter is the `GPMDomain` object of the domain the GPO should be copied to. The last parameter is the display name of the new GPO.

Using PowerShell

Unfortunately, the current release of the SDM PowerShell cmdlets does not provide the ability to copy a Group Policy Object. The SDM cmdlets do, however, allow you to copy Starter GPOs, as we will discuss later in this chapter.

See Also

Recipe 9.7 for importing a GPO, Recipe 9.8, and MSDN: GPMGPO.CopyTo

9.4 Deleting a GPO

Problem

You want to delete a GPO.

Solution

Using a graphical user interface

1. Open the GPMC snap-in.
2. In the left pane, expand the Forest container, expand the Domains container, browse to the domain of the target GPO, and expand the Group Policy Objects container.
3. Right-click on the target GPO and select Delete.
4. Click OK to confirm.

Using a command-line interface

```
> deletegpo.wsf <GPOName> [/domain:<DomainDNSName>]
```

 To retain the links to the deleted GPO (in case you will be re-creating it with the same name), use the /keeplinks switch. Otherwise, all links will be deleted along with the GPO.

Using VBScript

```
' This code deletes the specified GPO.
' ------ SCRIPT CONFIGURATION ------
strGPO = "<GPOName>"           ' e.g. "My New GPO"
strDomain = "<DomainDNSName>"  ' e.g. "adatum.com"
' ------ END CONFIGURATION --------

set objGPM = CreateObject("GPMgmt.GPM")
set objGPMConstants = objGPM.GetConstants()

' Initialize the Domain object
set objGPMDomain = objGPM.GetDomain(strDomain, "", objGPMConstants.UseAnyDC)

' Find the GPO
set objGPMSearchCriteria = objGPM.CreateSearchCriteria
objGPMSearchCriteria.Add objGPMConstants.SearchPropertyGPODisplayName, _
                    objGPMConstants.SearchOpEquals, cstr(strGPO)
set objGPOList =
objGPMDomain.SearchGPOs(objGPMSearchCriteria)
if objGPOList.Count = 0 then
   WScript.Echo "Did not find GPO: " & strGPO
   WScript.Echo "Exiting."
```

```
       WScript.Quit
    elseif objGPOList.Count > 1 then
        WScript.Echo "Found more than one matching GPO. Count: " & _
                    objGPOList.Count
        WScript.Echo "Exiting."
        WScript.Quit
    else
        WScript.Echo "Found GPO: " & objGPOList.Item(1).DisplayName
    end if
    ' Delete the GPO
    objGPOList.Item(1).Delete
    WScript.Echo "Successfully deleted GPO: " & strGPO
```

Using PowerShell

```
remove-SDMgpo -Name "<GPO Friendly Name>"
```

Discussion

When you delete a GPO through the GPMC, it attempts to find all links to the GPO in the domain and will delete them if the user has permissions to delete the links. If the user does not have the necessary permissions to remove the links, the GPO will still get deleted, but the links will remain intact. Any links external to the domain the GPO is in are not automatically deleted. For this reason, it is a good practice to view the links to the GPO before you delete it. Links to deleted GPOs show up as "Not Found" in GPMC.

Using VBScript

Use a `GPMSearchCriteria` object to find the GPO that is equal to the display name of the GPO specified in the configuration section. Use an `if else` conditional statement to ensure that only one GPO is returned. If 0 or more than 1 is returned, abort the script. If only 1 is returned, use the `GPMGPO.Delete` method to delete the GPO.

Using PowerShell

To delete a GPO in a remote domain, use the `-DomainName` switch, followed by the FQDN of the domain.

See Also

Recipe 9.13 for viewing the links for a GPO and MSDN: GPMGPO.Delete

9.5 Viewing the Settings of a GPO

Problem

You want to view the settings that have been defined on a GPO.

Solution

Using a graphical user interface

1. Open the GPMC snap-in.
2. In the left pane, expand the Forest container, expand the Domains container, browse to the domain of the target GPO, and expand the Group Policy Objects container.
3. Click on the target GPO.
4. In the right pane, click on the Settings tab.
5. Click the Show All link to display all configured settings.

Using a command-line interface

```
> getreportsforgpo.wsf "<GPOName>" <ReportLocation> [/domain:<DomainDNSName>]
```

Using VBScript

```vbscript
' This code generates a HTML report of all the properties
' and settings for a GPO.
' ------ SCRIPT CONFIGURATION ------
strGPO        = "<GPOName>"           ' e.g. Sales GPO
strDomain     = "<DomainDNSName>"     ' e.g. adatum.com
strReportFile = "<FileNameAndPath>"   ' e.g. c:\gpo_report.html
' ------ END CONFIGURATION --------

set objGPM = CreateObject("GPMgmt.GPM")
set objGPMConstants = objGPM.GetConstants()

' Initialize the Domain object
set objGPMDomain = objGPM.GetDomain(strDomain, "", objGPMConstants.UseAnyDC)

set objGPMSearchCriteria = objGPM.CreateSearchCriteria
objGPMSearchCriteria.Add objGPMConstants.SearchPropertyGPODisplayName, _
                         objGPMConstants.SearchOpEquals, cstr(strGPO)
set objGPOList = objGPMDomain.SearchGPOs(objGPMSearchCriteria)

if objGPOList.Count = 0 then
   WScript.Echo "Did not find GPO: " & strGPO
   WScript.Echo "Exiting."
   WScript.Quit
elseif objGPOList.Count > 1 then
   WScript.Echo "Found more than one matching GPO. Count: " & _
                objGPOList.Count
   WScript.Echo "Exiting."
   WScript.Quit
else
   WScript.Echo "Found GPO: " & objGPOList.Item(1).DisplayName
end if

set objGPMResult = objGPOList.Item(1).GenerateReportToFile( _
```

```
                 objGPMConstants.ReportHTML, _
                             strReportFile)

' This will throw an exception if there were any errors
' during the actual operation.
on error resume next
objGPMResult.OverallStatus()

if objGPMResult.Status.Count > 0 then
   WScript.Echo "Status message(s): " & objGPMResult.Status.Count
   for i = 1 to objGPMResult.Status.Count
      WScript.Echo objGPMResult.Status.Item(i).Message
   next
   WScript.Echo vbCrLf
end if
' Display the result
if Err.Number <> 0 then
   WScript.Echo "Error generating report."
   WScript.Echo "Error: " & Err.Description
else
   WScript.Echo "Reported saved to " & strReportFile
end if
```

Using PowerShell

```
out-SDMgpsettingsreport -Name <GPO Friendly Name> -FileName <File Name> -ReportHTML
```

Discussion

The GPMC can generate an XML or HTML report that contains all of the settings in a GPO. See Recipe 9.6 for more on how to modify GPO settings.

Using VBScript

Use a `GPMSearchCriteria` object to find the GPO that is equal to the display name of the GPO specified in the configuration section. Use an `if else` conditional statement to ensure that only one GPO is returned. If zero or more than one are returned, abort the script. If only one is returned, you can use the `GPMGPO.GenerateReportToFile` method to generate a report of all the settings in the GPO. The first parameter for `GenerateReportToFile` is a constant that determines the type of report to generate (i.e., HTML or XML). The second parameter is the path of the file to store the report.

Using PowerShell

The `out-SDMgpsettingsreport` cmdlet can produce output in either XML or HTML format, by using the `-ReportXML` or `-ReportHTML` switches, respectively.

See Also

MSDN: GPMGPO.GenerateReportToFile

9.6 Modifying the Settings of a GPO

Problem

You want to modify the settings associated with a GPO.

Solution

Using a graphical user interface

1. Open the GPMC snap-in.
2. In the left pane, expand the Forest container, expand the Domains container, browse to the domain of the target GPO, and expand the GPO container.
3. Right-click on the target GPO and select Edit. This will bring up the GPOE.
4. Browse through the Computer Configuration or User Configuration settings and modify them as necessary.

Using PowerShell

You can find a pre-made PowerShell function to copy the settings from one GPO to another in the May 2007 issue of *Technet Magazine*, available online at *http://technet .microsoft.com/en-us/magazine/cc162355.aspx*.

Using a command-line interface, VBScript, or PowerShell

You cannot modify the settings of a GPO with any of the command-line tools or APIs, but you can copy and import settings as described in Recipes 9.3 and 9.7.

Discussion

The one function that the GPMC tool and APIs cannot accomplish is modifying GPO settings. This still must be done from within the GPOE. You can, however, launch GPOE from within GPMC as described in the GUI solution. Not having a scriptable way to modify GPO settings has been a big roadblock with managing GPOs, especially across multiple forests. Copying or importing GPOs can help with migrating settings across forests.

See Also

Recipe 9.3 for copying a GPO, Recipe 9.5 for viewing the settings of a GPO, and Recipe 9.7 for importing settings into a GPO

9.7 Importing Settings into a GPO

Problem

You want to import settings from one GPO to another.

Solution

Using a graphical user interface

1. Open the GPMC snap-in.
2. In the left pane, expand the Forest container, expand the Domains container, browse to the domain of the target GPO, and expand the Group Policy Objects container.
3. Right-click on the target GPO and select Import Settings.
4. Click Next.
5. Click the Backup button if you want to take backup of the GPO you are importing into.
6. Click Next.
7. Select the backup folder location and click Next.
8. Select the backup instance you want to import from and click Next.
9. It then will scan to see if there are any security principals or UNC paths in the GPO being imported from. If there are, it will give you an option to modify those settings.
10. Click Next.
11. Click Finish.

Using a command-line interface

```
> importgpo.wsf "<GPOBackupLocation>" "<OrigGPOName>" "<NewGPOName>"
```

Using VBScript

```
' This code imports the settings from a GPO that has been backed up into
' an existing GPO.
' ------ SCRIPT CONFIGURATION ------
strGPOImportTo    = "<GPOName>"           ' e.g. "Sales GPO"
strDomain         = "<DomainDNSName>"     ' e.g. "adatum.com"
strBackupLocation = "<BackupLocation>"    ' e.g. "c:\GPMC Backups"

' GUID representing the specific backup
' e.g.{3E53B39B-C29B-44FF-857B-8A84528804FF}
strBackupID       = "<BackupGUID>"
' ------ END CONFIGURATION --------

set objGPM = CreateObject("GPMgmt.GPM")
set objGPMConstants = objGPM.GetConstants()
```

```
' Initialize the Domain object
set objGPMDomain = objGPM.GetDomain(strDomain, "", objGPMConstants.UseAnyDC)

' Locate GPO backup
set objGPMBackupDir = objGPM.GetBackupDir(strBackupLocation)
set objGPMBackup = objGPMBackupDir.GetBackup(strBackupID)
WScript.Echo "Backup found:"
WScript.Echo " ID: " & objGPMBackup.ID
WScript.Echo " Timestamp: " & objGPMBackup.TimeStamp
WScript.Echo " GPO ID: " & objGPMBackup.GPOID
WScript.Echo " GPO Name: " & objGPMBackup.GPODisplayName
WScript.Echo " Comment: " & objGPMBackup.Comment
WScript.Echo

' Find GPO to import into
set objGPMSearchCriteria = objGPM.CreateSearchCriteria
objGPMSearchCriteria.Add objGPMConstants.SearchPropertyGPODisplayName, _
                         objGPMConstants.SearchOpEquals, cstr(strGPOImportTo)
set objGPOList =
objGPMDomain.SearchGPOs(objGPMSearchCriteria)
if objGPOList.Count = 0 then
   WScript.Echo "Did not find GPO: " & strGPO
   WScript.Echo "Exiting."
   WScript.Quit
elseif objGPOList.Count > 1 then
   WScript.Echo "Found more than one matching GPO. Count: " & _
                objGPOList.Count
   WScript.Echo "Exiting."
   WScript.Quit
else
   WScript.Echo "Found GPO: " & objGPOList.Item(1).DisplayName
end if

' Perform the import
set objGPMResult = objGPOList.Item(1).Import(0,objGPMBackup)

' This will throw an exception if there were any errors
' during the actual operation.
on error resume next
objGPMResult.OverallStatus()

if objGPMResult.Status.Count > 0 then
   WScript.Echo "Status message(s): " & objGPMResult.Status.Count
   for i = 1 to objGPMResult.Status.Count
      WScript.Echo objGPMResult.Status.Item(i).Message
   next
   WScript.Echo vbCrLf
end if

' Print results
if Err.Number <> 0 then
   WScript.Echo "Error importing GPO " & objGPMBackup.GPODisplayName
   WScript.Echo "Error: " & Err.Description
else
```

```
    WScript.Echo "Import successful."
    WScript.Echo "GPO '" & objGPMBackup.GPODisplayName & _
                 "' has been imported into GPO '" &
                 objGPOList.Item(1).DisplayName & "'"
end if
```

Using PowerShell

```
Import-SDMGPO -ID <GUID of GPO Backup> -Name <Friendly Name of Target GPO>
```

Discussion

The GPMC import function uses a backup of the source GPO to create the new "imported" GPO. This means you must first back up the source GPO using GPMC. You can then import the settings from that GPO into a new GPO, which may be in the same domain or a completely different forest. Importing a GPO is a great way to help facilitate transferring GPO settings from a test environment to production.

Some properties of GPOs, such as security group filters or UNC paths, may vary slightly from domain to domain; a logon script that runs from \\SERVERA\share in the source domain may need to run on \\SERVERB\share in the target domain, for example. In this case, you can use a GPMC migration table to help facilitate the transfer of those kinds of references to the target domain. For more information on migration tables, see the GPMC help file and Recipe 9.8.

Using VBScript

To import the settings of a backup, you have to first instantiate a GPMBackup object of the source backup by specifying the backup ID (a GUID) with the GPMBackupDir.Get Backup method. If you need to programmatically search for the backup ID, you can use the GPMBackup.SearchBackups method to find the most recent backup or a backup with a particular display name.

Next, instantiate a GPMGPO object of the GPO you're importing into. To do this, use a GPMSearchCriteria object to find the GPO that is equal to the display name of the GPO specified in the configuration section. Use an if else conditional statement to ensure that only one GPO is returned. If zero or more than one are returned, abort the script. If only one is returned, use the GPMGPO.Import method to import the settings. The first parameter to the Import method is a flag that determines how security principals and UNC path mapping is done; 0 is the default to not copy security settings. You can also use a migration table to do mappings if necessary. The second parameter is the GPMBackup object instantiated earlier. The rest of the script performs some error handling and prints the results.

Using PowerShell

The `Import-SDMGPO` cmdlet takes the following two mandatory arguments: `-ID <GUID>`, where `<GUID>` corresponds to the GUID of the backup that you are using as the source of the import. It's important to note that this is not the GUID of the GPO, but the GUID of the GPO backup. The second mandatory argument is `-Name <String>`, where `<String>` corresponds to the friendly name of the GPO that you are importing settings into. Be aware that the target GPO will be overwritten by the contents of the GPO backup during the import operation.

See Also

Recipe 9.3 for copying a GPO, Recipe 9.8, Recipe 9.23 for backing up a GPO, and MSDN: GPMGPO.Import

9.8 Creating a Migration Table

Problem

You want to create a migration table to assist in copying or migrating a GPO from one domain or forest to another.

Solution

Using a graphical user interface

1. Open the Group Policy Management Console. Navigate to the forest and domain containing the GPOs you wish to migrate or copy.
2. Right-click on the Group Policy Objects node and select Open Migration Table Editor.
3. You will begin with a blank migration table. To populate the source fields from existing data, click on Tools→Populate from GPO or Tools→Populate from Backup. Select the GPO or the backup that you wish to import. Optionally, place a checkmark next to "During scan, include security principals from the DACL on the GPO." Click OK.
4. Modify the Destination Name column of any entries to match their format in the destination forest or domain.
5. To add a new entry, enter the name of the item in the Source Name column. In the Source Type column, select one of the following:
   - User
   - Computer
   - Domain Local Group
   - Domain Global Group

- Universal Group
- UNC Path
- Free Text or SID

6. To delete an entry, right-click on the entry and select Delete.

7. To configure an entry to use the same information as configured in the source GPO, right-click on the entry and select Set Destination→Same As Source.

8. To configure an entry to use the relative name of the destination, right-click on the entry and select Set Destination→Map by Relative Name. For example, if you have an entry for the *salesuser@adatum.com* user in a GPO that you wish to copy to the *mycompany.com* forest, selecting Map by Relative Name will populate the entry in the destination GPO as *salesuser@mycompany.com*.

9. To ensure that you have properly formatted all entries in the table, click Tools→Validate Table, then click File→Save or File→Save As to save the migration table.

Using a command-line interface

```
> createmigrationtable.wsf <DestinationFileName> /GPO:<DestinationGPO> /MapByName
```

Discussion

One of the convenient new features of the GPMC is the ability to copy a GPO's settings from one GPO to another, or to migrate GPOs between domains or forests. In some cases, certain entries in the GPO may need to be modified to suit the needs of the destination domain or forest. For example, a UNC for user home directories will likely need to be modified to correspond to a server or DFS share in the destination, as well as individual user or group names. To address this need, you can create and populate a migration table to automatically transform the necessary entries on one or more GPOs.

Using a command-line interface

To create a migration table from the command line, use the *createmigrationtable.wsf* script that is included in the *~\Scripts* folder of the GPMC. The script will require two arguments: the destination filename and the GPO that it should be populated from.

As an alternative to the /GPO: switch, you can use /BackupLocation: to populate the migration table from a GPO backup. By default, a migration table that you create using this script will use Same As Source mapping, or you can specify the /MapByName parameter to use relative name mapping.

See Also

Recipe 9.3 for more on copying a GPO and Recipe 9.7 for information on importing settings into a GPO

9.9 Creating Custom Group Policy Settings

Problem

You want to deploy settings via Group Policy that are not covered by the default set of GPO templates that come with Active Directory.

Solution

Windows 2000, XP, and 2003 Group Policy Objects come preloaded with a number of default *templates* (also called *ADM files*) that define a number of settings that can be controlled via GPO. To control and deploy settings for additional or third-party applications, you'll need to create your own custom ADM files to manage the settings you require. You'll create this file in Notepad or another simple text editor, and save it as *<FileName>.adm*. For example, the following ADM file will allow you to disable dynamic DNS registration for Windows 2000 clients:

```
Class Machine

Category !!AdministrativeServices

Category !!DNSClient

Policy !!DisableDynamicUpdate
Keyname "System\CurrentControlSet\Services\Tcpip\Parameters"
Explain !!DisableDynamicUpdate_Help
Valuename "DisableDynamicUpdate"
End Policy

End Category ;;DNS Client

End Category ;;AdministrativeServices

[strings]
AdministrativeServices="System"
DNSClient="DNS Client"
DisableDynamicUpdate="Disable Dynamic Update"
DisableDynamicUpdate_Help="Stops the client from dynamically registering all
adapters
with DNS.\n\nWhen this setting is enabled it changes the DisableDynamicUpdate value
to 1 in
HKEY_LOCAL_MACHINE\SYSTEM\CurrentControlSet\Services\Tcpip\Parameters\n\nWhen
this setting is disabled, the value is set back to its default of zero. Note that
when the policy is disabled, the registry value may be deleted from the
registry.\n\
nSee Q246804 for more details."

;End of Strings
```

To import custom ADM settings into the GPE, follow these steps:

1. Open the GPMC snap-in.

2. In the left pane, expand the Forest container, expand the Domains container, browse to the domain of the target GPO, and expand the Group Policy Objects container.

3. Drill down to User Configuration or Computer Configuration, as appropriate. Right-click on Administrative Templates and select Add/Remove Template.

4. Click Add and browse to the location of the ADM file you created, and then click Open.

5. Click Close, and then browse to the new node you've just added to the Administrative Templates folder.

6. If you don't see the new settings you've created, right-click on the right pane, select View → Filtering, and remove the checkmark next to "Only show policy settings that can be fully managed." Then click OK to return to the GPO Editor. (This happens because the GPO Editor displays only *policy* settings by default, while the settings contained in a custom ADM file are considered *preferences*.)

ADMX files in Windows Server 2008 have a significantly different format, as they are based on the Extensible Markup Language (XML) format. For example, the following demonstrates how to add a new search provider to Internet Explorer using a customized ADMX file:

```xml
<?xml version="1.0" encoding="utf-8"?> <policyDefinitions
  xmlns:xsd="http://www.w3.org/2001/XMLSchema"
  xmlns:xsi="http://www.w3.org/2001/XMLSchema-instance" revision="1.0"
  schemaVersion="1.0"
 xmlns="http://www.microsoft.com/GroupPolicy/PolicyDefinitions">
  <policyNamespaces>
    <target prefix="search" namespace="Microsoft.Policies.search" />
    <using prefix="inetres" namespace="Microsoft.Policies.InternetExplorer" />
  </policyNamespaces>
  <resources minRequiredRevision="1.0" />
  <policies>
    <policy name="PopulateSearchProviderList_1" class="User"
      displayName="$(string.PopulateSearchProviderList)"
      explainText="$(string.IE_Explain_PopulateSearchProviderList)"
      key="Software\Policies\Microsoft\Internet Explorer\SearchScopes">
      <parentCategory ref="inetres:InternetExplorer" />
      <supportedOn ref="inetres:SUPPORTED_IE7Vista"/>
      <enabledList>
        <item key="Software\Policies\Microsoft\Internet Explorer\SearchScopes"
          valueName="Version">
          <value>
            <decimal value="VERSION" />
          </value>
        </item>
        <item key="Software\Policies\Microsoft\Internet
          Explorer\SearchScopes\SUBKEY1" valueName="DisplayName">
          <value>
            <string>NAME1</string>
```

```
            </value>
          </item>
          <item key=" Software\Policies\Microsoft\Internet
            Explorer\SearchScopes\SUBKEY1" valueName="URL">
            <value>
               <string>URL1</string>
            </value>
          </item>
       </enabledList>
     </policy>
     <policy name="PopulateSearchProviderList_2" class="Machine"
       displayName="$(string.PopulateSearchProviderList)"
       explainText="$(string.IE_Explain_PopulateSearchProviderList)"
       key="Software\Policies\Microsoft\Internet Explorer\SearchScopes">
       <parentCategory ref="inetres:InternetExplorer" />
       <enabledList> Insert same as user policy above </enabledList>
     </policy>
   </policies>
 </policyDefinitions>
```

In addition to the ADMX file, you will need to create an ADML file using a format
similar to the following:

```
<?xml version="1.0" encoding="utf-8"?>
  <policyDefinitionResources xmlns:xsd=http://www.w3.org/2001/XMLSchema
    xmlns:xsi="http://www.w3.org/2001/XMLSchema-instance" revision="1.0"
schemaVersion="1.0"
    xmlns="http://www.microsoft.com/GroupPolicy/PolicyDefinitions">
    <displayName>enter display name here</displayName>
    <description>enter description here</description>
    <resources>
      <stringTable>
        <string id="PopulateSearchProviderList">Populate List of search
providers</string>
        <string id="IE_Explain_PopulateSearchProviderList">
This policy setting will allow you to populate a list of search providers
that will be displayed in Internet Explorer's search box. If you enable
this policy setting and if the "Restrict search providers to a specific list of search
providers" Group Policy setting is enabled, this list will be the only list that
appears in the Internet Explorer drop-down list. If the "Add a specific list of
search providers to the user's search provider list" Group Policy setting is enabled,
this list will be added to the user's list of search providers. If you disable
this policy setting or do not configure it, users will have complete
freedom
        to create their own search provider list.</string>
      </stringTable>
    </resources>
  </policyDefinitionResources>
```

Discussion

When you create a custom ADM file for a Group Policy Object, the new template is
automatically uploaded to the *%SystemRoot%\SYSVOL\sysvol\domain name\Policies\
{GPO GUID}\Adm* folder on the DC that is performing the updates to the GPO,

typically the PDC Emulator. Because the *SYSVOL* folder is included in the Active Directory replication process, the new ADM file will be automatically replicated to all other instances of the GPO.

When you create a custom ADMX file, save it to the *%windir%\policydefinitions* folder, while the ADML file will be saved in the *%windir%\policydefinitions\<Definition Language>* folder.

See Also

MS KB 323639 (How to Create Custom Administrative Templates in Windows 2000), MS KB 259576 (Group Policy Application Rules for Domain Controllers), MS KB 316977 (Group Policy Template Behavior in Windows Server 2003), MS KB 816662 (Recommendations for Managing Group Policy Administrative Template [.adm] Files)

9.10 Assigning Logon/Logoff and Startup/Shutdown Scripts in a GPO

Problem

You want to assign either user logon/logoff scripts or computer startup/shutdown scripts in a GPO.

Solution

Using a graphical user interface

1. Open the GPMC snap-in.
2. In the left pane, expand the Forest container, expand the Domains container, browse to the domain of the target GPO, and expand the Group Policy Objects container.
3. Right-click on the target GPO and select Edit. This will bring up the GPOE.
4. In the Windows 2000 and Windows Server 2003 GPMC, if you want to assign a computer startup or shutdown script, browse to Computer Configuration→Windows Settings→Scripts. If you want to assign a user logon or logoff script, browse to User Configuration→Windows Settings→Scripts.
5. In the Windows Server 2008 GPMC, browse to Computer Configuration→Policies→Windows Settings→Scripts. If you want to assign a user logon or logoff script, browse to User Configuration→Policies→Windows Settings→Scripts.
6. In the right pane, double-click on the type of script you want to add.
7. Click the Add button.
8. Select the script by typing its name or browsing to its location.

9. Optionally, type any script parameters in the Script Parameters field.

10. Click OK twice.

Discussion

When you assign a script in a GPO, you can either reference a script that is stored locally on the domain controller somewhere under the *SYSVOL* share, or in a UNC path to a remote file server. The default storage location is in the *SYSVOL* share in the *<DomainName>\scripts* folder—e.g., *\\adatum.com\sysvol\adatum.com\scripts*. The logon script can also be set as an attribute of the user object (`scriptPath`). This is provided as legacy support for users migrated from NT 4.0 domains and requires the script to be stored in the *Netlogon* share. You should choose one method of specifying the logon script or the other—but not both, as this will cause the logon script to run twice.

9.11 Installing Applications with a GPO

Problem

You want to install an application on a group of computers using a GPO.

Solution

Using a graphical user interface

1. Open the GPMC snap-in.

2. In the left pane, expand the Forest container, expand the Domains container, browse to the domain of the target GPO, and expand the Group Policy Objects container.

3. Right-click on the target GPO and select Edit. This will bring up the GPOE.

4. Expand Software Settings under Computer Configuration or User Configuration, depending on which you want to target the installation for. In the Windows Server 2008 version of GPMC, browse to Computer Configuration→Policies or User Configuration→Policies.

5. Right-click on Software Installation and select New→Package.

6. Browse to the network share that has the MSI package for the application and click OK. Be sure to specify a UNC path such as *\\servername\share\installer.msi*. If you enter a local file path on the DC such as *c:\packages\pro.msi*, the client will not be able to access the installer.

7. Select whether you want to assign the application or publish it, and click OK. You can also click Advanced to further define how you want to deploy the software installation package.

Discussion

Installing applications with a GPO is a powerful feature, but you must be careful about the impact it can have on your network throughput and clients. If the MSI package you are installing is several megabytes in size, it will take a while for it to download to the client computer. This can result in sluggish performance on the client, especially over a heavily utilized connection. (Software installation does not occur over slow links, by default.) You'll also want to make sure you've thoroughly tested the application before deployment. After you've configured the GPO to install an application, it will be only a short period of time before it has been installed on all targeted clients. If there is a bug in the application or the installer program is faulty, the impact could be severe to your user base and support staff alike.

Your two options for deploying an application are to assign it or publish it. If you assign an application using the "deploy at logon" option, it will get automatically installed on the targeted clients when users log on to those machines. If you publish an application or assign it without choosing this option, it will be installed the first time a user double-clicks on a shortcut to the application or attempts to open a file that requires the application. A published application can also be installed manually from the Add/Remove Programs applet in the Control Panel on the target computers. You can assign an application to both `user` and `computer` objects, but you can publish applications only to `user`s.

 If you need to exert more granular control over your software installations than is enabled by Group Policy, you should investigate leveraging the additional capabilities of dedicated deployment software such as Microsoft's Systems Management Server (SMS) or System Center Configuration Manager (SCCM).

9.12 Disabling the User or Computer Settings in a GPO

Problem

You want to disable either the user or computer settings of a GPO.

Solution

Using a graphical user interface

1. Open the GPMC snap-in.
2. In the left pane, expand the Forest container, expand the Domains container, browse to the domain of the target GPO, and expand the Group Policy Objects container.
3. Right-click on the target GPO and select GPO Status.

4. You can either select User Configuration Settings Disabled to disable the user settings or Computer Configuration Settings Disabled to disable the computer settings.

Using VBScript

```
' This code can enable or disable the user or computer settings of a GPO.
' ------ SCRIPT CONFIGURATION ------
strGPO    = "<GPOName>"          ' e.g. "Sales GPO"
strDomain = "<DomainDNSName>"    ' e.g. "adatum.com"
boolUserEnable = False
boolCompEnable = True
' ------ END CONFIGURATION --------

set objGPM = CreateObject("GPMgmt.GPM")
set objGPMConstants = objGPM.GetConstants()

' Initialize the Domain object
set objGPMDomain = objGPM.GetDomain(strDomain, "", objGPMConstants.UseAnyDC)

' Find the specified GPO
set objGPMSearchCriteria = objGPM.CreateSearchCriteria
objGPMSearchCriteria.Add objGPMConstants.SearchPropertyGPODisplayName, _
                         objGPMConstants.SearchOpEquals, cstr(strGPO)
set objGPOList =
objGPMDomain.SearchGPOs(objGPMSearchCriteria)
if objGPOList.Count = 0 then
    WScript.Echo "Did not find GPO: " & strGPO
    WScript.Echo "Exiting."
    WScript.Quit
elseif objGPOList.Count > 1 then
    WScript.Echo "Found more than one matching GPO. Count: " & _
                  objGPOList.Count
    WScript.Echo "Exiting."
    WScript.Quit
else
    WScript.Echo "Found GPO: " & objGPOList.Item(1).DisplayName
end if

' You can comment out either of these if you don't want to set one:

objGPOList.Item(1).
SetUserEnabled boolUserEnable
WScript.Echo "User settings: " & boolUserEnable

objGPOList.Item(1).
SetComputerEnabled boolCompEnable
WScript.Echo "Computer settings: " & boolCompEnable
```

Using PowerShell

```
$gpm = New-Object -ComObject GPMgmt.GPM
$gpmConstants = $gpm.GetConstants()
$objDomain = $gpm.GetDomain("<Domain FQDN>", "", $gpmConstants.UseAnyDC)
$objGpo = $objDomain.GetGPO("{<GPO GUID>}")
$objGpo.SetComputerEnabled($true)
$objGpo.SetUserEnabled($false)
```

Discussion

GPOs consist of two parts, a user and a computer section. The user section contains settings that are specific to a user that logs in to a computer, while the computer section defines settings that apply to the computer regardless of which user logs in. You can enable or disable either the user configuration or computer configuration sections of a GPO, or both. By disabling both, you effectively disable the GPO. This can be useful if you want to stop a GPO from applying settings to clients, but you do not want to delete it, remove the links, or clear the settings.

Disabling the user configuration or the computer configuration is useful in environments that have separate OUs for computers and users. Typically, you would disable the computer configuration for GPOs linked to the users' OU, and vice versa. Disabling half of the GPO in this way makes GPO processing more efficient and can improve performance both during logon and when Group Policy Objects perform a background refresh (every 5 minutes by default on domain controllers, every 90 minutes by default on clients and member servers).

Using VBScript

First, we have to find the target GPO. To do this, we use a `GPMSearchCriteria` object to find the GPO that is equal to the display name of the GPO specified in the configuration section. We use an `if else` conditional statement to ensure that only one GPO is returned. If zero or more than one are returned, we abort the script. If only one is returned, we call the `SetUserEnabled` and `SetComputerEnable` methods to either enable or disable the settings per the configuration.

See Also

MSDN: GPMGPO.SetUserEnabled and MSDN: GPMGPO.SetComputerEnabled

9.13 Listing the Links for a GPO

Problem

You want to list all of the links for a particular GPO.

Solution

Using a graphical user interface

1. Open the GPMC snap-in.
2. In the left pane, expand the Forest container, expand the Domains container, browse to the domain of the target GPO, and expand the Group Policy Objects container.
3. Click on the GPO you want to view the links for.
4. In the right pane, the defined links for the GPO will be listed under Links.

Using a command-line interface

```
> dumpgpoinfo.wsf "<GPOName>"
```

Using VBScript

```
' This code lists all the sites, OUs, and domains a GPO is linked to.
' ------ SCRIPT CONFIGURATION ------
strGPO    = "<GPOName>"      ' e.g. "SalesGPO"
strForest = "<ForestName>"   ' e.g. "adatum.com"
strDomain = "<DomainDNSName>" ' e.g. "adatum.com"
' ------ END CONFIGURATION ---------

set objGPM = CreateObject("GPMgmt.GPM")
set objGPMConstants = objGPM.GetConstants()

' Initialize the Domain object
set objGPMDomain = objGPM.GetDomain(strDomain, "", objGPMConstants.UseAnyDC)
' Initialize the Sites Container object
set objGPMSitesContainer = objGPM.GetSitesContainer(strForest, _
                           strDomain, "", objGPMConstants.UseAnyDC)
' Find the specified GPO
set objGPMSearchCriteria = objGPM.CreateSearchCriteria
objGPMSearchCriteria.Add objGPMConstants.SearchPropertyGPODisplayName, _
                         objGPMConstants.SearchOpEquals, cstr(strGPO)
set objGPOList =
objGPMDomain.SearchGPOs(objGPMSearchCriteria)
if objGPOList.Count = 0 then
   WScript.Echo "Did not find GPO: " & strGPO
   WScript.Echo "Exiting."
   WScript.Quit
elseif objGPOList.Count > 1 then
   WScript.Echo "Found more than one matching GPO. Count: " & _
                objGPOList.Count
   WScript.Echo "Exiting."
   WScript.Quit
else
   WScript.Echo "Found GPO: " & objGPOList.Item(1).DisplayName
end if

' Search for all SOM links for this GPO
```

```
set objGPMSearchCriteria = objGPM.CreateSearchCriteria
objGPMSearchCriteria.Add objGPMConstants.SearchPropertySOMLinks, _
                        objGPMConstants.SearchOpContains, objGPOList.Item(1)
set objSOMList =
objGPMDomain.SearchSOMs(objGPMSearchCriteria)
set objSiteLinkList =
objGPMSitesContainer.SearchSites(objGPMSearchCriteria)

if objSOMList.Count = 0 and objSiteLinkList.Count = 0 Then
    WScript.Echo "No Site, Domain, or OU links found for this GPO"
else
    WScript.Echo "Links:"
    for each objSOM in objSOMList
        select case objSOM.Type
            case objGPMConstants.SOMDomain
                strSOMType = "Domain"
            case objGPMConstants.SOMOU
                strSOMType = "OU"
        end select
        ' Print GPO Domain and OU links
        WScript.Echo " " & objSOM.Name & " (" & strSOMType & ")"
    next

    ' Print GPO Site Links
    for each objSiteLink in objSiteLinkList
        WScript.Echo " " & objSiteLink.Name & " (Site)"
    next
end if
```

Using PowerShell

```
Get-SDMGPLink -Name <GPO Friendly Name>
```

Discussion

See Recipe 9.0 for more information on GPO linking and SOMs.

Using VBScript

First, we have to find the target GPO. To do this, we use a `GPMSearchCriteria` object to find the GPO that is equal to the display name of the GPO specified in the configuration section. We use an `if else` conditional statement to ensure that only one GPO is returned. If none or more than one are returned, we abort the script. If only one is returned, we search for all SOMs (domain, OUs, and sites) that have the GPO linked using the `GPMSitesContainer.SearchSites` and `GPMDomain.SearchSOMs` methods.

Using PowerShell

The `-Name <GPO Friendly Name>` switch allows you to search for all links to a particular GPO within a particular domain. If you instead wish to retrieve a list of all GPOs that are linked at a particular level of the AD infrastructure, such as an OU, you would instead use the `-Scope <DistinguishedName>` switch, indicating the domain, site, or OU that you wish to query.

See Also

Recipe 9.0, Recipe 9.14 for creating a GPO link to an OU, MSDN: GPMDomain.SearchSOMs, and MSDN: GPMSitesContainer.SearchSites

9.14 Creating a GPO Link to an OU

Problem

You want to apply the GPO settings to the users and/or computers in an OU. This is called *linking* a GPO to an OU.

Solution

Using a graphical user interface

1. Open the GPMC snap-in.
2. In the left pane, expand the Forest container, expand the Domains container, and browse to the target domain.
3. Right-click on the OU you want to link and select Link an Existing GPO.
4. Select from the list of available GPOs and click OK.

Using VBScript

```
' This code links a GPO to an OU
' ------ SCRIPT CONFIGURATION ------
strGPO     = "<GPOName>"          ' e.g. "Sales GPO"
strDomain  = "<DomainDNSName>"    ' e.g. "adatum.com"
strOU      = "<OrgUnitDN>"        ' e.g. "ou=Sales,dc=adatum,dc=com"
intLinkPos = -1 ' set this to the position the GPO evaluated at
                ' a value of -1 signifies appending it to the end of the list
' ------ END CONFIGURATION ---------

set objGPM = CreateObject("GPMgmt.GPM")
set objGPMConstants = objGPM.GetConstants()

' Initialize the Domain object
set objGPMDomain = objGPM.GetDomain(strDomain, "", objGPMConstants.UseAnyDC)

' Find the specified GPO
set objGPMSearchCriteria = objGPM.CreateSearchCriteria
objGPMSearchCriteria.Add objGPMConstants.SearchPropertyGPODisplayName, _
objGPMConstants.SearchOpEquals, cstr(strGPO)
set objGPOList = objGPMDomain.SearchGPOs(objGPMSearchCriteria)
if objGPOList.Count = 0 then
```

```
      WScript.Echo "Did not find GPO: " & strGPO
      WScript.Echo "Exiting."
      WScript.Quit
   elseif objGPOList.Count > 1 then
      WScript.Echo "Found more than one matching GPO. Count: " & _
                   objGPOList.Count
      WScript.Echo "Exiting."
      WScript.Quit
   else
      WScript.Echo "Found GPO: " & objGPOList.Item(1).DisplayName
   end if

   ' Find the specified OU
   set objSOM = objGPMDomain.
   GetSOM(strOU)
   if IsNull(objSOM) then
      WScript.Echo "Did not find OU: " & strOU
      WScript.Echo "Exiting."
      WScript.Quit
   else
      WScript.Echo "Found OU: " & objSOM.Name
   end if

   on error resume next

   set objGPMLink = objSOM.
   CreateGPOLink( intLinkPos, objGPOList.Item(1) )

   if Err.Number <> 0 then
      WScript.Echo "There was an error creating the GPO link."
      WScript.Echo "Error: " & Err.Description
   else
      WScript.Echo "Sucessfully linked GPO to OU"
   end if
```

Using PowerShell

```
add-SDMgplink -Name "<GPO Display Name>" -Scope "<Container DN>"
```

Discussion

Linking a GPO is the process whereby you assign a scope of management (SOM), which can be an OU, site, or domain. The solutions show how to link a GPO to an OU, but they could be easily modified to link to a site or domain.

See Recipe 5.14 for details on how to link an OU by modifying the gpLink attribute, instead of using the GPMC interface.

Using VBScript

To link a GPO, we first have to find the target GPO. We use a GPMSearchCriteria object to find the GPO that is equal to the display name of the GPO specified in the configuration section. We use an if else conditional statement to ensure that only one GPO is returned. If zero or more than one are returned, we abort the script. If only one GPO is returned, we instantiate a `GPMSOM` object by passing the name of the OU to be linked to the `GPMDomain.GetSOM` method. Once we instantiate this object, we can call `GPMSOM.CreateGPOLink` to create a GPO link to the OU.

 If the OU in question already has GPOs linked to it, the VBScript solution will, by default, insert the new link at the end of the list of linked GPOs.

Using PowerShell

To modify the link order of the GP link using the SDM cmdlets, use the `-Location` switch. A value of `-1` places the link at the bottom of the list; a value of `1` places it at the top of the processing order, etc.

See Also

MS KB 248392 (Scripting the Addition of Group Policy Links) and MSDN: GPM-SOM.CreateGPOLink

9.15 Blocking Inheritance of GPOs on an OU

Problem

You want to block inheritance of GPOs on an OU.

Solution

Using a graphical user interface

1. Open the GPMC snap-in.
2. In the left pane, expand the Forest container, expand the Domains container, and browse to the target domain.
3. Right-click on the OU you want to block inheritance for and select Block Inheritance.

Using VBScript

```
' This code blocks inheritance of GPOs on the specified OU
' ------ SCRIPT CONFIGURATION ------
strDomain = "<DomainDNSName>" ' e.g. "adatum.com"
strOU     = "<OrgUnitDN>"      ' e.g. "ou=Sales,dc=adatum,dc=com"
boolBlock = TRUE               ' e.g. set to FALSE
to not block inheritance
' ------ END CONFIGURATION --------
```

```
set objGPM = CreateObject("GPMgmt.GPM")
set objGPMConstants = objGPM.GetConstants()

' Initialize the Domain object
set objGPMDomain = objGPM.GetDomain(strDomain, "", objGPMConstants.UseAnyDC)

' Find the specified OU
set objSOM = objGPMDomain.GetSOM(strOU)
if IsNull(objSOM) then
   WScript.Echo "Did not find OU: " & strOU
   WScript.Echo "Exiting."
   WScript.Quit
else
   WScript.Echo "Found OU: " & objSOM.Name
end if

' on error resume next

objSOM.GPOInheritanceBlocked = boolBlock

if Err.Number <> 0 then
   WScript.Echo "There was an error blocking inheritance."
   WScript.Echo "Error: " & Err.Description
else
   WScript.Echo "Successfully set inheritance blocking on OU to " & boolBlock
end if
```

Using PowerShell

```
$gpm = New-Object -ComObject GPMgmt.GPM
$gpmConstants = $gpm.GetConstants()
$objDomain = $gpm.GetDomain("<Domain FQDN>", "", $gpmConstants.UseAnyDC)
$objOU = $objDomain.GetSOM("<OU DN>")
$objOU.GPOInheritanceBlocked = $true
```

Discussion

By default, GPOs are inherited down through the directory tree. If you link a GPO to a top-level OU, that GPO will apply to any objects within the child OUs. Sometimes that may not be what you want, and you can disable inheritance as described in the solutions.

Try to avoid blocking inheritance when possible because it can make determining what settings should be applied to a user or computer difficult. If someone sees that a GPO is applied at a top-level OU, he may think it applies to any object under it. Using the Resultant Set of Policies (RSoP) snap-in can help identify what settings are applied to a user or computer (see Recipe 9.25).

Using VBScript

To block inheritance, we first have to get a `GPMSOM` object for the OU by calling the `GPMDomain.GetSOM` method. The only parameter to this method is the DN of the OU (or you can leave the reference to the domain itself blank). Next, we call the `GPMSOM.GPO InheritanceBlocked` method, which should be set to either `TRUE` or `FALSE`, depending on if you want inheritance blocked or not.

See Also

Recipe 9.25, MSDN: GPMSOM, GPOInheritanceBlocked, and MSDN: GPMDomain.GetSOM

9.16 Enforcing the Settings of a GPO Link

Problem

You want to ensure that a GPO's settings are enforced regardless of any Block Inheritance settings that have been enforced further down the scope of management.

Solution

Using a graphical user interface

1. Open the GPMC snap-in.
2. In the left pane, expand the Forest container, expand the Domains container, browse to the domain of the target GPO, and expand the container containing the link you want to enforce.
3. Right-click on the link you want to configure and place a checkmark next to Enforced. To remove the Enforced setting, right-click on the link and remove the checkmark.

Using VBScript

```
' This code enforces a link to a GPO.
' ------ SCRIPT CONFIGURATION ------
strGPO      = "<GPOName>"    ' e.g. SalesGPO
strForest   = "<ForestName>" ' e.g. adatum.com
strDomain   = "<DomainName>" ' e.g. adatum.com
strLinkName = "<LinkName>"   ' e.g. "Finance" for an OU link,
                             ' "adatum.com" for a domain,
                             ' "Default-First-Site-Link" for a site

boolEnforced = TRUE                ' FALSE to disable the enforced setting
' ------ END CONFIGURATION ---------

set objGPM = CreateObject("GPMgmt.GPM")
set objGPMConstants = objGPM.GetConstants()
```

```
' Initialize the Domain object
set objGPMDomain = objGPM.GetDomain(strDomain, "", objGPMConstants.UseAnyDC)
' Initialize the Sites Container object
set objGPMSitesContainer = objGPM.GetSitesContainer(strForest, _
                            strDomain, "", objGPMConstants.UseAnyDC)
' Find the specified GPO
set objGPMSearchCriteria = objGPM.CreateSearchCriteria
objGPMSearchCriteria.Add objGPMConstants.SearchPropertyGPODisplayName, _
                          objGPMConstants.SearchOpEquals, cstr(strGPO)
set objGPOList =
objGPMDomain.SearchGPOs(objGPMSearchCriteria)
if objGPOList.Count = 0 then
   WScript.Echo "Did not find GPO: " & strGPO
   WScript.Echo "Exiting."
   WScript.Quit
elseif objGPOList.Count > 1 then
   WScript.Echo "Found more than one matching GPO. Count: " & _
                objGPOList.Count
   WScript.Echo "Exiting."
   WScript.Quit
else
   WScript.Echo "Found GPO: " & objGPOList.Item(1).DisplayName
   strGUID = objGPOList.Item(1).ID
end if
' Search for all SOM links for this GPO
set objGPMSearchCriteria = objGPM.CreateSearchCriteria
objGPMSearchCriteria.Add objGPMConstants.SearchPropertySOMLinks, _
                          objGPMConstants.SearchOpContains,
objGPOList.Item(1)
set objSOMList = objGPMDomain.SearchSOMs(objGPMSearchCriteria)
set objSiteLinkList = objGPMSitesContainer.SearchSites(objGPMSearchCriteria)

if objSOMList.Count = 0 and objSiteLinkList.Count = 0 Then
   WScript.Echo "No Site, Domain, or OU links found for this GPO"
else
    for each objSOM in objSOMList
        if strcomp(objSOM.Name, strLinkName, vbTextCompare) = 0 then
            set colGPOLinks = objSOM.getGPOLinks()
            for each objGPOLink in colGPOLinks
                if strcomp(objGPOLink.GPOID,strGUID,vbTextCompare) = 0 then
                    objGPOLink.Enforced = boolEnforced
                    WScript.Echo("Enforced GPO " & strGPO & _
                                 " link to " & strLinkName)
                end if
            next
        end if
    next

    ' Print GPO Site Links
    for each objSiteLink in objSiteLinkList
        if strcomp(objSiteLink.Name, strLinkName, vbTextCompare) = 0 then
            set colGPOLinks = objSiteLink.getGPOLinks()
            for each objGPOLink in colGPOLinks
                if strcomp(objGPOLink.GPOID,strGUID,vbTextCompare) = 0 then
                    objGPOLink.Enforced = boolEnforced
```

```
            WScript.Echo("Enforced GPO " & strGPO & _
                         " link to " & strLinkName)
                end if
            next
        end if
    next
end if
```

Discussion

As a counterpoint to the ability to block inheritance of a GPO for a particular site, domain, or OU, an administrator can configure a particular GPO link as Enforced, meaning that the settings contained in that GPO will be configured for that SOM regardless of the presence of any Block Inheritance configuration. This is useful in a decentralized environment, for example, where a central IT department has configured a certain Group Policy baseline that it wishes to enforce regardless of what individual departments may have configured on their own. Just like security filtering and Block Inheritance, though, we recommend that you use this function sparingly, as it can create complex troubleshooting issues when trying to determine where and how Group Policy application is failing.

 Remember that the Enforced setting is configured against a particular *link* to a GPO, not against the GPO itself. This means that one GPO can be linked to several locations, but not all of those links need to be enforced.

Using VBScript

It is unfortunately not possible to zero in on an individual Group Policy link through VBScript, since the `IGPMSearchCriteria` interface does not allow you to search for a particular link by any sort of display name or GUID. As such, the script in this recipe will set the Enforced flag for every link associated with a particular GPO, which may or may not be what you intended to achieve.

See Also

Recipe 9.15, MSDN:IGPMSearchCriteria, and MSDN:GPMC Object Model

9.17 Applying a Security Filter to a GPO

Problem

You want to configure a GPO so that it applies only to members of a particular security group.

Solution

Using a graphical user interface

1. Open the GPMC snap-in.
2. In the left pane, expand the Forest container, expand the Domains container, browse to the target domain, and expand the Group Policy Objects container.
3. Click on the GPO you want to modify.
4. In the right pane under Security Filtering, click the Add button.
5. Use the Object Picker to select a group and click OK.
6. Highlight Authenticated Users and click the Remove button.
7. Click OK to confirm.

Using a command-line interface

```
> setgpopermissions.wsf "<GPOName>" "<GroupName>" /permission:Apply
> setgpopermissions.wsf "<GPOName>" "Authenticated Users" /permission:None
```

Using VBScript

```
' This code adds a security group filter permission to a GPO
' and removes the Authenticated Users filter permission.
' ------ SCRIPT CONFIGURATION ------
strGPO         = "<GPOName>"        ' e.g. "Sales GPO"
strDomain      = "<DomainDNSName>"  ' e.g. "adatum.com"
strGroupAdd    = "<GroupName>"      ' e.g. "SalesUsers"
strGroupRemove = "Authenticated Users"
' ------ END CONFIGURATION ---------

set objGPM = CreateObject("GPMgmt.GPM")
set objGPMConstants = objGPM.GetConstants()

' Initialize the Domain object
set objGPMDomain = objGPM.GetDomain(strDomain, "", objGPMConstants.UseAnyDC)

' Find the specified GPO
set objGPMSearchCriteria = objGPM.CreateSearchCriteria
objGPMSearchCriteria.Add objGPMConstants.SearchPropertyGPODisplayName, _
                    objGPMConstants.SearchOpEquals, cstr(strGPO)
set objGPOList =
objGPMDomain.SearchGPOs(objGPMSearchCriteria)
if objGPOList.Count = 0 then
   WScript.Echo "Did not find GPO: " & strGPO
   WScript.Echo "Exiting."
   WScript.Quit
elseif objGPOList.Count > 1 then
   WScript.Echo "Found more than one matching GPO. Count: " & _
                objGPOList.Count
   WScript.Echo "Exiting."
   WScript.Quit
```

```
else
    WScript.Echo "Found GPO: " & objGPOList.Item(1).DisplayName
end if

' Get permission objects to Apply GPO
set objGPMPerm1 = objGPM.CreatePermission(strGroupAdd, _
                       objGPMConstants.PermGPOApply, False)
set objGPMPerm2 = objGPM.CreatePermission(strGroupRemove, _
                       objGPMConstants.PermGPOApply, False)

' Get the existing set of permissions on the GPO
set objSecurityInfo = objGPOList.Item(1).GetSecurityInfo()

' Add the new permission
objSecurityInfo.Add objGPMPerm1
' Remove Authenticate users
objSecurityInfo.Remove objGPMPerm2

on error resume next

' Apply the permission to the GPO
objGPOList.Item(1).SetSecurityInfo objSecurityInfo
if Err.Number <> 0 then
    WScript.Echo "There was an error setting the
security filter."
    WScript.Echo "Error: " & Err.Description
else
    WScript.Echo "Added Apply permission for group " & strGroupAdd
    WScript.Echo "Removed Apply permission for group " & strGroupRemove
end if
```

Using PowerShell

```
add-SDMgposecurity -Name "<GPO Display Name>" -Trustee "<Domain>\<Username>" -
PermApply
```

Discussion

You can use security filtering to restrict the users, groups, or computers that a GPO applies to by granting or denying the Apply Group Policy permission on the ACL of the GPO. By default, *Authenticated Users* are granted the Apply Group Policy right on all new GPOs, so you will also need to remove this right if you want to restrict the GPO to be applied only to members of one specific group.

As a rule, you should avoid using Deny permissions as part of any custom security filter, because this can lead to confusion with accounts that are members of groups with conflicting filter settings. For example, if a user is a member of a group that has Deny set in the filter and is also a member of a group that is allowed to apply the policy, the Deny setting will always win. This can be difficult to troubleshoot, particularly if nested group memberships are involved.

Be very careful when changing permissions on GPOs. If you create a very restricted GPO and apply a security filter to it, be sure to also put tight controls on who can modify the GPO and how. If for some reason that security filter were removed (resulting in no security filters), the restrictive GPO could be applied to every user or computer in the domain.

Using VBScript

First, we have to find the target GPO. We use a `GPMSearchCriteria` object to find the GPO that is equal to the display name of the GPO specified in the configuration section. We use an `if else` conditional statement to ensure that only one GPO is returned. If none or more than one were returned, we abort the script. If only one GPO is returned, we create two `GPM.CreatePermission` objects for the group we want to add as a security filter and for the *Authenticated Users* group. Next, we use the object `GPMGPO.GetSecurityInfo` to retrieve the current ACL on the GPO. Finally, we add the permission to the ACL for the group we want as the new security filter, and we remove the permission for *Authenticated Users*.

Using PowerShell

The SDM cmdlets allow you to apply one of the following preconfigured permissions:

- `-PermApply`
- `-PermEdit`
- `-PermEditSecurityAndDelete`
- `-PermRead`

In addition to the `add-SDMgposecurity` cmdlet, you can also retrieve and remove security entries using the `get-SDMgposecurity` and `remove-SDMgposecurity` cmdlets, respectively.

See Also

MSDN: GPM.CreatePermission and MSDN: GPMGPO.GetSecurityInfo

9.18 Delegating Administration of GPOs

Problem

You want to delegate permissions on GPOs and related tasks within Active Directory.

Solution

Using a graphical user interface

To delegate the ability to create GPOs, do the following:

1. Open the Group Policy Management Console.
2. Navigate to the Group Policy Objects node and click on the Delegation tab.
3. To add permissions for a new user or group to create GPOs, click Add. Use the object picker to select the object you want and click OK.

To delegate permissions on a particular GPO, follow these steps:

1. Open the Group Policy Management Console.
2. Navigate to the GPO that you want to delegate permissions for and click on the Delegation tab.
3. To add permissions for a new user or group, click Add. Use the object picker to select the object you want and click OK.
4. In the Permissions drop-down box, select "Read, Edit Settings" or "Edit Settings, Delete, and Modify Security," then click OK.

To delegate Group Policy-related tasks on a particular site, domain, or OU, do the following:

1. Open the Group Policy Management Console.
2. Navigate to the site, domain, or OU that you want to delegate permissions for and click on the Delegation tab.
3. In the Permission drop-down, select Link GPOs, Perform Group Policy Modeling Analyses, or Read Group Policy Results Data.
4. To add permissions for a new user or group, click Add. Use the object picker to select the object you want and click OK.
5. In the Permissions drop-down box, select "This container only" or "This container and all child containers," then click OK.

Discussion

In addition to using Active Directory users and groups to control how GPOs are applied within a site, domain, or OU, you can also use ACLs to delegate permissions over GPOs to allow you to decentralize the administration of them in your organization.

You can delegate the ability to do the following:

- Create GPOs
- Manage the settings of an individual GPO
- Link GPOs to a site, domain, or OU

- Create WMI filters
- Manage an individual WMI filter

While the ability to delegate administration in this manner is quite simple to implement, it's critical that you fully understand the security implications that it carries. For example, the ability to link GPOs to an entire site or domain should be granted only to highly trusted administrators since it can have far-reaching implications for the performance and behavior of your network.

See Also

MS KB 250842 (Troubleshooting Group Policy Application Problems) and Recipe 9.17 for more on using security filtering to control GPO behavior

9.19 Importing a Security Template

Problem

You want to import a security template into a GPO.

Solution

Using a graphical user interface

1. Open the GPMC snap-in.
2. In the left pane, expand the Forest container, expand the Domains container, browse to the domain of the GPO you want to target, and expand the Group Policy Objects container.
3. Right-click on the target GPO and select Edit.
4. Navigate to Computer Configuration→Windows Settings.
5. Right-click on Security Settings and select Import Policy.
6. Browse to the template you want to import and click Open.

Discussion

Rather than manually configuring the plethora of security settings available in Windows 2000 and Windows Server 2003, you can use a template.

Some common security templates include the following:

compatws.inf
   Used for workstations that need backward compatibility with legacy applications or networks.

hisec*.inf

   Used for a high-security configuration. *hisecdc.inf* corresponds to a domain controller. *hisecws.inf* is for a secure workstation or member server.

secure*.inf

   Used for situations in which you want a secure configuration, but the settings in the *hisec*.inf* templates are a bit over-the-top. Sufficient for most environments.

It's important to test the settings created by these templates before deploying them in a production network, since it may be necessary to modify one or more to meet the needs of your unique environment.

 To configure security settings for a local computer or for computers not configured in an Active Directory domain, you can use the `secedit` command-line utility with the `/configure` switch.

See Also

Windows Server 2003 Security Guide (*http://www.microsoft.com/technet/security/prod tech/windowsserver2003/w2003hg/sgch00.mspx*), Windows Server 2008 Security Guide (*http://technet.microsoft.com/en-us/library/cc264463.aspx*), MS KB 216735 (Methods Used to Apply Security Settings Throughout an Enterprise), MS KB 816297 (How to Define Security Templates by Using the Security Templates Snap-in in Windows Server 2003), and MS KB 816585 (How to Apply Predefined Security Templates in Windows Server 2003)

9.20 Creating a WMI Filter

 WMI filters can be configured only on Windows Server 2003 and newer domain controllers, and they will not apply to Windows 2000 computers.

Problem

You want to create a WMI filter.

Solution

Using a graphical user interface

   1. Open the GPMC snap-in.

2. In the left pane, expand the Forest container, expand the Domains container, browse to the target domain, and click the WMI Filters container.

3. Right-click on the WMI Filters container and select New.

4. Enter a name and description for the filter.

5. Click the Add button.

6. Select the appropriate namespace, enter a WQL query, and click OK.

7. Repeat steps 5 and 6 for as many queries as you need to add.

8. Click the Save button.

Using VBScript

At the time of publication of this book, there were no GPM methods available for creating WMI filters.

Discussion

WMI filters are new in Windows Server 2003 and provide another way to filter how GPOs are applied to clients. WMI filters live in Active Directory as objects under the `WMIPolicy` container within the `System` container for a domain. A WMI filter consists of a WMI Query Language (WQL) query that when linked to a GPO will be run against all clients that the GPO applies to. If the WQL returns a `true` value (that is, it returns nonempty results from the WQL query), the GPO will continue to process. If the WQL query returns `false` (nothing is returned from the query), the GPO will not be processed.

The great thing about WMI filters is that the vast amount of information that is available in WMI on a client becomes available to filter GPOs. You can query against CPU, memory, disk space, hotfixes installed, service packs installed, applications installed, running processes, and the list goes on and on.

For example, if you want to create a GPO that applies only to computers that are running Windows XP Professional, it would have been really difficult to accomplish under Windows 2000 Active Directory. You would have either needed to create a security group that contained all of those computers as members (and apply a security filter) or to move all of those workstations to a particular OU. With a WMI filter, this becomes trivial to create. (Bear in mind, however, that there is client performance overhead associated with WMI queries, as each computer will need to process the WMI query to determine whether a particular GPO should or should not be applied.) Here is a sample WQL query that would return `true` when run on a Windows XP Professional workstation (however, since Windows 2000 workstations and servers cannot process WMI filters, any GPO filtered with this WMI filter would be processed on both XP and 2000 computers):

```
select * from Win32_OperatingSystem
where Caption = "Microsoft Windows XP Professional"
```

The introduction of Group Policy Preferences creates significant new options in terms of how GPOs can be targeted and filtered. Prior to the introduction of Group Policy Preferences, you were limited to filtering using only WMI filters to control whether the entire GPO is applied. With WMI filters, you cannot specify individual settings within a GPO. Group Policy Preferences, on the other hand, support item-level targeting, where individual settings can be targeted based on criteria such as IP address, if that machine is a laptop or desktop, security group membership, and so on.

See Also

Recipe 9.21 for applying a WMI filter to a GPO and MSDN: Querying with WQL

9.21 Applying a WMI Filter to a GPO

 WMI filters can be configured only on a Windows Server 2003 domain controller, and they will apply only to Windows Server 2003 and Windows XP-based clients.

Problem

You want to apply a WMI filter to a GPO.

Solution

Using a graphical user interface

1. Open the GPMC snap-in.
2. In the left pane, expand the Forest container, expand the Domains container, browse to the domain of the GPO you want to target, and expand the Group Policy Objects container.
3. Click on the target GPO.
4. At the bottom of the right pane, you can select from the list of WMI filters.
5. After you've selected the WMI filter, click Yes to confirm.

Using VBScript

```
' This code links an existing WMI filter with a GPO.
' ------ SCRIPT CONFIGURATION ------
strGPO        = "<GPOName>"       ' e.g. "Sales GPO"
strDomain     = "<DomainDNSName>" ' e.g. "adatum.com"

' e.g. {D715559A-7965-45A6-864D-AEBDD9934415}
strWMIFilterID = "<WMIFilterID>"
' ------ END CONFIGURATION --------
```

```
set objGPM = CreateObject("GPMgmt.GPM")
set objGPMConstants = objGPM.GetConstants()

' Initialize the Domain object
set objGPMDomain = objGPM.GetDomain(strDomain, "", objGPMConstants.UseAnyDC)
' Find the GPO
set objGPMSearchCriteria = objGPM.CreateSearchCriteria
objGPMSearchCriteria.Add objGPMConstants.SearchPropertyGPODisplayName, _
                         objGPMConstants.SearchOpEquals, _
                         cstr(strGPO)
set objGPOList = 
objGPMDomain.SearchGPOs(objGPMSearchCriteria)
if objGPOList.Count = 0 then
   WScript.Echo "Did not find GPO: " & strGPO
   WScript.Echo "Exiting."
   WScript.Quit
elseif objGPOList.Count > 1 then
   WScript.Echo "Found more than one matching GPO. Count: " & _
                objGPOList.Count
   WScript.Echo "Exiting."
   WScript.Quit
else
   WScript.Echo "Found GPO: " & objGPOList.Item(1).DisplayName
end if

on error resume next

' Retrieve the WMI filter
strWMIFilter = "MSFT_SomFilter.Domain=""" & _
               strDomain & """,ID=""" & _
               strWMIFilterID & """"
set objWMIFilter = objGPMDomain.GetWMIFilter(strWMIFilter)
if Err.Number <> 0 then
   WScript.Echo "Did not find WMI Filter: " & strWMIFilterID
   WScript.Echo "Exiting."
   WScript.Quit
else
   WScript.Echo "Found WMI Filter: " & objWMIFilter.Name
end if

' Link the filter and print the result
objGPOList.Item(1).SetWMIFilter(objWMIFilter)
if Err.Number <> 0 then
   WScript.Echo "Failed
to set WMI filter."
   WScript.Echo "Error: " & err.description
else
   WScript.Echo "Set WMI filter successfully."
end if
```

Using PowerShell

```
add-SDMWMIFilterLink -Name <GPO Friendly Name> -FilterName <WMI Filter Friendly
Name>
```

Discussion

You can link only one WMI filter to a GPO at any time. This is not an overly restrictive limitation, though, because you can still link more than one GPO to a site, domain, or OU. If you need multiple WMI filters to apply to a GPO, copy the GPO and apply a different WMI filter to it. See Recipe 9.20 for more information on WMI filters.

 Keep in mind that requiring your clients to process multiple WMI filters will have an impact on their performance at logon time and during the GPO background refresh process.

Using VBScript

We use a `GPMSearchCriteria` object to find the GPO that is equal to the display name of the GPO specified in the configuration section. We use an `if else` conditional statement to ensure that only one GPO is returned. If no GPOs are returned or if more than one is returned, we abort the script. If only one GPO is returned, we call `GPMDomain.GetWMIFilter` to instantiate a `GPMWMIFilter` object based on the WMI filter GUID specified in the configuration section. (If you need to programmatically search for the WMI filter ID, you can use the `GPMDomain.SearchWMIFilters` method.) After we retrieve the `GPMWMIFilter` object, we call the `GPMGPO.SetWMIFilter` method to set the filter for the GPO.

Using PowerShell

The SDM GPO cmdlets include a corresponding `Remove-SDMGPOFilterLink` cmdlet to remove a WMI filter from a particular GPO.

See Also

MSDN: GPMDomain.GetWMIFilter and MSDN: GPMGPO.SetWMIFilter

9.22 Configuring Loopback Processing for a GPO

Problem

You want to configure a GPO to use loopback processing that will enforce consistent computer settings regardless of which user logs on to a computer.

Solution

Using a graphical user interface

1. Open the GPMC snap-in.

2. Navigate to the GPO that you want to configure. Right-click on the GPO and select Edit Settings.

3. Navigate to Computer Configuration→System→Group Policy. Double-click on "User Group Policy loopback processing mode." Select the radio button next to Enabled.

4. In the Mode drop-down box, select either Merge or Replace. (See the section called "Discussion" of this recipe for more information on these two options.)

5. Click OK.

Discussion

GPOs are applied to user/computer combinations on an Active Directory network based on the site, domain, and OU that the **user** and **computer** objects belong to. If the user and computer are located in two separate locations, the user will receive the GPOs that apply to the user's container combined with those that apply to the computer's container. However, there may be cases where you want a user to receive GPOs based solely on the location of the **computer** objects. In this case, you will enable loopback processing in one of two modes:

Merge Mode
> In this mode, any GPOs that are associated with the user will be applied first. The GPOs associated with the **computer** object will be applied after the GPOs associated with the **user** object, thereby giving them a higher precedence than the user GPOs. In this case, the user will still receive any GPO settings associated with her **user** object, but settings configured for the computer will override in the case of any conflicts.

Replace Mode
> In this mode, only the list of GPOs that apply to the **computer** object will be applied.

See Also

MS KB 231287 (Loopback Processing of Group Policy)

9.23 Backing Up a GPO

Problem

You want to back up a GPO.

Solution

Using a graphical user interface

1. Open the GPMC snap-in.
2. In the left pane, expand the Forest container, expand the Domains container, browse to the domain of the GPO you want to back up, and expand the Group Policy Objects container.
3. Right-click on the GPO you want to back up and select Back Up.
4. For Location, enter the folder path to store the backup files.
5. For Description, enter a descriptive name for the backup.
6. Click the Back Up button.
7. You will see a progress bar and status message that indicates if the backup was successful.
8. Click OK to exit.

Using a command-line interface

```
> backupgpo.wsf "<GPOName>" "<BackupFolder>" /comment:"<BackupComment>"
```

Using VBScript

```
' This code backs up a GPO to the specified backup location.
' ------ SCRIPT CONFIGURATION ------
strGPO      = "<GPOName>"          ' e.g. "Default Domain Policy"
strDomain   = "<DomainDNSName>";"' e.g. "adatum.com"
strLocation = "<BackupFolder>"    ' e.g. "c:\GPMC Backups"
strComment  = "<BackupComment>"   ' e.g. "Default Domain Policy Weekly"
' ------ END CONFIGURATION ---------

set objGPM = CreateObject("GPMgmt.GPM")
set objGPMConstants = objGPM.GetConstants()

' Initialize the Domain object
set objGPMDomain = objGPM.GetDomain(strDomain, "", objGPMConstants.UseAnyDC)

' Find the GPO you want to back up
set objGPMSearchCriteria = objGPM.CreateSearchCriteria
objGPMSearchCriteria.Add objGPMConstants.SearchPropertyGPODisplayName, _
                    objGPMConstants.SearchOpEquals, cstr(strGPO)
set objGPOList =
objGPMDomain.SearchGPOs(objGPMSearchCriteria)
if objGPOList.Count = 0 then
   WScript.Echo "Did not find GPO: " & strGPO
   WScript.Echo "Exiting."
   WScript.Quit
elseif objGPOList.Count > 1 then
   WScript.Echo "Found more than one matching GPO. Count: " & _
              objGPOList.Count
```

```
    WScript.Echo "Exiting."
    WScript.Quit
else
    WScript.Echo "Found GPO: " & objGPOList.Item(1).DisplayName
End if

' Kick off the backup
On Error Resume Next
set objGPMResult = objGPOList.Item(1).Backup(strLocation, strComment)
' Call the OverallStatus method on the GPMResult.
' This will throw an exception if there were any
' errors during the actual operation.
objGPMResult.OverallStatus()
if objGPMResult.Status.Count > 0 then
    WScript.Echo "Status messages:" & objGPMResult.Status.Count
    for i = 1 to objGPMResult.Status.Count
    WScript.Echo objGPMResult.Status.Item(i).Message
    next
    WScript.Echo vbCrLf
end if

' Print the results
if Err.Number <> 0 then
    WScript.Echo "The backup failed."
    WScript.Echo "Attempted to backup GPO '" & strGPO & "' to location " &
strLocation
    WScript.Echo "Error: " & err.description
else
    set objGPMBackup = objGPMResult.Result
    WScript.Echo "Backup completed successfully."
    WScript.Echo "GPO ID: " & objGPMBackup.GPOID
    WScript.Echo "Timestamp: " & objGPMBackup.TimeStamp
    WScript.Echo "Backup ID: " & objGPMBackup.ID
end if
```

Using PowerShell

```
export-SDMgpo -Name "<GPO Display Name>" -Location "<Path to Backup Folder>"
-Description "<Backup Description>"
```

Discussion

The GPMC provides a way to back up individual (or all) GPOs. A GPO backup consists of a set of folders and files that catalog the GPO settings, filters, and links, and is created in the backup location you specify. You can back up a GPO to a local drive or over the network to a file server. Restoring a GPO is just as easy and is described in Recipe 9.24.

Prior to GPMC, the only way to back up GPOs was by backing up the System State on a domain controller. The System State includes Active Directory and the SYSVOL share (both components are needed to completely back up a GPO). To restore a GPO using this method, you'd have to boot into DS Restore mode and perform an authoritative restore of the GPO(s) you were interested in. Needless to say, the GPMC method is significantly easier.

A good practice is to back up your GPO backups. Since all the backup information is captured in a series of files, you can back up that information to media, which provides two levels of restore capability. You could restore the last backup taken, which could be stored on a domain controller or file server, or you could go to tape and restore a previous version.

In the folder you specify to store the GPO backups is a list of folders that have GUIDs for names. This does not make it very easy to distinguish which backups are for which GPOs. A quick way to find that out is to use the *querybackuplocation.wsf* script. This will list each of the folder GUID names and the corresponding GPO it is for:

```
> querybackuplocation.wsf "c:\gpmc backups"
```

Using VBScript

We use a `GPMSearchCriteria` object to find the GPO that is equal to the display name of the GPO specified in the configuration section. We use an `if else` conditional statement to ensure that only one GPO is returned. If none or more than one is returned, we abort the script. If only one is returned, we call the `GPMGPO.Backup` method to back up the GPO. The first parameter is the directory to store the GPO backup files, and the second parameter is a comment that can be stored with the backup. This comment may come in handy later for doing searches against the backups on a server, so you may want to think about what to put for it.

Using PowerShell

The `-Location` switch allows you to back up GPOs to either a local file location such as *C:\GPOBackups*, or else a remote UNC path, such as *\\SERVER1\GPOBackups*.

See Also

Recipe 9.24 for restoring a GPO and MSDN: GPMGPO.Backup

9.24 Restoring a GPO

Problem

You want to restore a GPO.

Solution

Using a graphical user interface

1. Open the GPMC snap-in.

2. In the left pane, expand the Forest container, expand the Domains container, browse to the domain of the GPO you want to back up, and expand the Group Policy Objects container.

3. Right-click on the GPO you want to restore, and select "Restore from Backup."

4. Click Next.

5. Select the backup folder location and click Next.

6. Select the backup you want to restore and click Next.

7. Click Finish.

8. You will see the restore status window. After it completes, click OK to close the window.

Using a command-line interface

```
> restoregpo.wsf "<BackupFolder>" "<GPOName>"
```

Using VBScript

```
' This code restores a GPO from a backup.
' ------ SCRIPT CONFIGURATION ------
strGPO      = "<GPOName>"        ' e.g. "Sales Users GPO"
strDomain   = "<DomainDNSName>"  ' e.g. "adatum.com"
strLocation = "<BackupFolder>"   ' e.g. "c:\GPMC Backups"
strBackupID = "<BackupGUID>"     ' e.g. "{85CA37AC-0DB3-442B-98E8-537291D26ED3}"
' ------ END CONFIGURATION --------
set objGPM = CreateObject("GPMgmt.GPM")
set objGPMConstants = objGPM.GetConstants()

' Initialize the Domain object
set objGPMDomain = objGPM.GetDomain(strDomain, "", objGPMConstants.UseAnyDC)

' Make sure backup location and ID are valid
set objGPMBackupDir = objGPM.GetBackupDir(strLocation)
set objGPMBackup = objGPMBackupDir.GetBackup(strBackupID)
WScript.Echo "Backup found:"
WScript.Echo "  ID: " & objGPMBackup.ID
WScript.Echo "  Timestamp: " & objGPMBackup.TimeStamp
WScript.Echo "  GPO ID: " & objGPMBackup.GPOID
WScript.Echo "  GPO Name: " & objGPMBackup.GPODisplayName
WScript.Echo "  Comment: " & objGPMBackup.Comment
WScript.Echo

' Perform restore
set objGPMResult = objGPMDomain.RestoreGPO(objGPMBackup, _
                                    objGPMConstants.DoNotValidateDC)
' This will throw an exception if there were any errors
' during the actual operation.
on error resume next
objGPMResult.OverallStatus()
if objGPMResult.Status.Count > 0 then
   WScript.Echo "Status message(s): " & objGPMResult.Status.Count
```

```
        for i = 1 to objGPMResult.Status.Count
            WScript.Echo objGPMResult.Status.Item(i).Message
        next
        WScript.Echo vbCrLf
    end if

    ' Print result
    if Err.Number <> 0 then
        WScript.Echo "Error restoring GPO " & objGPMBackup.GPODisplayName
        WScript.Echo "Error: " & Err.Description
    else
        WScript.Echo "Restore successful."
        WScript.Echo "GPO '" & objGPMBackup.GPODisplayName & _
                     "' has been restored."
    end if
```

Using PowerShell

```
import-SDMgpo -Name "<GPO Display Name>" -Backup Location "<Backup Location>"
```

Discussion

To restore a GPO using GPMC, you first need a valid backup of the GPO. The procedure for backing up a GPO is described in Recipe 9.23. You can then restore the GPO, even if the GPO has been deleted. To restore a deleted GPO, use the following steps:

1. Right-click on the Group Policy Objects container in the target domain and select Manage Backups.
2. Highlight the GPO you want to restore and click the Restore button.
3. Click Yes to confirm.
4. Click OK after the restore completes.

If you don't have a valid backup of the GPO, but you do have another GPO that is identical or similar to the one you want to restore (perhaps in another forest), you can copy that GPO to replace the one you want to restore.

Keep in mind that restoring a GPO does not restore the links that were associated with that GPO, since the gpLink attribute is configured on the container that the GPO was linked to and not the container itself. See Recipe 9.3 for more on copying GPOs.

Using VBScript

To restore a GPO, you have to first get a handle to the backup you are going to restore from. Instantiate an object to the backup location with GPM.GetBackupDir and then call GPMBackupDir.GetBackup with the GUID of the backup to be restored. To programmatically search for the backup ID, use the GPMBackup.SearchBackups method to find the most recent backup or a backup with a particular display name.

After obtaining a GPMBackup object, call the GPMDomain.RestoreGPO method. The first parameter is the GPMBackup object that represents the backup to restore. The second parameter is a validation flag—use the constant that causes the restore to not be validated against a domain controller.

See Also

Recipe 9.3 for copying a GPO, Recipe 9.23 for backing up a GPO, and MSDN: GPMDomain.RestoreGPO

9.25 Simulating the RSoP

Problem

You want to simulate the Resultant Set of Policies (RSoP) based on OU, site, and security group membership. This is also referred to as Group Policy Modeling.

Solution

 This must be run against a Windows Server 2003 or newer domain controller.

Using a graphical user interface

1. Open the GPMC snap-in.
2. In the left pane, right-click Group Policy Modeling and select Group Policy Modeling Wizard.
3. Select a domain controller to process the query and click Next.
4. Under User Information and/or Computer Information, either select the container you want to simulate to contain the user or computer, or select a specific user or computer account, and click Next.
5. Select a site if necessary, and specify whether you wish to simulate a slow link or loopback processing, and then click Next.
6. If you selected a target user container or user account in step 4, you will be presented with an option to simulate different group membership. Click Next when you are done.
7. If you selected a target computer container or computer account in step 4, you will be presented with an option to simulate different group membership. Click Next when you are done.
8. If you selected a target user container or user account in step 4, you will be presented with an option to simulate any additional WMI filters. Click Next when you are done.

9. If you selected a target computer container or computer account in step 4, you will be presented with an option to simulate any additional WMI filters. Click Next when you are done.

10. Click Next to start the simulation.

11. Click Finish.

12. In the right pane of the GPMC window, the results of the simulation will be displayed.

Discussion

With GPMC, you can simulate the RSoP based on user-defined OU, site, group, and domain membership. This is very powerful because it allows you to create one or more GPOs, simulate them being applied to a user and computer, and determine whether any changes are necessary before deployment.

See Also

Recipe 9.26 for viewing the RSoP

9.26 Viewing the RSoP

Problem

You want to view the actual RSoP for a user and computer. This is a great tool for determining if policies are being applied correctly on a client.

Solution

Using a graphical user interface

 The RSoP snap-in is available only on Windows Server 2003 and newer.

Open the RSoP snap-in by running *rsop.msc* from the command line. This will cause the RSoP snap-in to evaluate the group policies for the target computer and pop open an MMC console so that you can browse the applied settings.

You can target a different computer by right-clicking the top of the tree in the left pane and selecting Change Query. You will then be prompted for the name of the computer to query.

You can also gather this information by using the Group Policy Results Wizard in the GPMC.

Using a command-line interface

```
> gpresult
```

With the Windows Server 2003 and newer versions of *gpresult*, you can specify a /S option and the name of a computer to target, which allows you to run the command remotely. With Windows 2000, there is a /S option, but it enables super-verbose mode. There is no way to target another computer with the Windows 2000 version. For a complete list of options with either version, run gpresult /? from a command line.

Discussion

If you implement more than a few GPOs, it can get confusing as to what settings will apply to users. To address this problem, you can query the resultant set of policies on a client to determine what settings have been applied.

The registry on the target computer is another source of information. You can view the list of policies that were applied to the computer by viewing the subkeys under this key:

```
HKEY_CURRENT_USER\Software\Microsoft\Windows\CurrentVersion\Group Policy\History
```

The settings that were applied are not stored in the registry, but you can obtain the GPO name, distinguished name, SYSVOL location, version, and where the GPO is linked.

See Also

Recipe 9.25 for simulating the RSoP

9.27 Refreshing GPO Settings on a Computer

Problem

You've made some changes to a GPO and want to apply them to a computer by refreshing the group policies for the computer.

Solution

Using a command-line interface

On Windows XP or newer computer, use this command:

```
> gpupdate [/target:{Computer | User}]
```

On Windows 2000, use this command:

```
> secedit /refreshpolicy [machine_policy | user_policy]
```

Using PowerShell

```
update-SDMgp -Target "<Machine FQDN>"
```

Discussion

By default, Group Policy settings will refresh automatically every 5 minutes on a domain controller and every 90 minutes on clients and member servers. To force GPO settings to refresh sooner than that, you will need to run the *gpupdate* utility on the client computer. The new *gpupdate* command is a much-needed improvement over the older *secedit* utility that was used to refresh Group Policy in Windows 2000. With *gpupdate*, you can force all settings to be applied with the /force option (the default is only changed settings). You can apply the computer or user settings of GPOs using the /target option, and you can force a logoff or reboot after the settings have been applied using the /logoff and /boot options.

Using PowerShell

The update-SDMgp cmdlet includes a number of optional switches that map to the *gpupdate.exe* command-line option, including -Computer, -User, -Force, -Logoff, -Boot, -Sync. In addition, you can use the -Username and -Password switches to provide alternate credentials to connect to the remote computer.

See Also

MS KB 298444 (A Description of the Group Policy Update Utility)

9.28 Restoring a Default GPO

Problem

You've made changes to the Default Domain Security Policy, Default Domain Controller Security Policy, or both, and now want to reset them to their original configuration.

Solution

Using a command-line interface

The following command would replace both the Default Domain Security Policy and Default Domain Controller Security Policy on a Windows Server 2003 domain controller. You can specify Domain or DC instead of Both, to only restore one or the other:

```
> dcgpofix /target:Both
```

Note that this must be run from a domain controller in the target domain where you want to reset the GPO.

To re-create the default GPOs in a Windows 2000 domain, download the Windows 2000 Default Group Policy Restore Tool (*recreatedefpol.exe*) from *http://www.microsoft .com/downloads/details.aspx?FamilyID=b5b685ae-b7dd-4bb5-ab2a-976d6873129d& DisplayLang=en.*

Discussion

If you've made changes to the default GPOs in Windows Server 2003 or newer Active Directory and would like to revert back to the original settings, the *dcgpofix* utility is your solution. *dcgpofix* works with a particular version of the schema. If the version it expects to be current is different from what is in Active Directory, it will not restore the GPOs. You can work around this by using the /ignoreschema switch, which will restore the GPO according to the version *dcgpofix* thinks is current. The only time you might experience this issue is if you install a service pack on a domain controller (*dc1*) that extends the schema but the changes have not yet replicated to a second domain controller (*dc2*). If you try to run *dcgpofix* from *dc2*, you will receive the error since a new version of the schema and the *dcgpofix* utility was installed on *dc1*.

In Windows 2000, the *recreatedefpols.exe* utility will instruct you to log out after running the utility, and then log back on to complete the process using the administrative account that should be added as an EFS Recovery Agent.

9.29 Creating a Fine-Grained Password Policy

Problem

You want to create a Fine-Grained Password Policy in a Windows Server 2008 domain.

Solution

Using a graphical user interface

1. Open ADSI Edit. Right-click on the top-level node and click "Connect to...". In the Connection Settings screen, click OK.

2. In the right pane, double-click on Default naming context, then double-click on the domain node (i.e., dc=adatum,dc=com).

3. Browse to CN=System, then CN=Password Settings Container. Right-click on CN=Password Settings Container and click New→Object....

4. The Create Object screen appears. Click Next. In the Value text box, enter a name for the Fine-Grained Password Policy, such as "20CharacterNoExpiry". Click Next.

5. The Password Settings Precedence screen appears. In the Value text box, enter the value for the precedence of the password policy, such as "1". Click Next.

6. The Password reversible encryption status for user accounts screen appears. In the Value text box, enter FALSE. Click Next.

7. The Password history length for user accounts screen appears. In the Value text box, enter the number of passwords that should be retained in password history, such as 24. Click Next.

8. The Password complexity status for user accounts screen appears. In the Value text box, enter TRUE if you want complex passwords enabled, FALSE if you do not. Click Next.

9. The "Minimum password length for user accounts" screen appears. In the Value text box, enter the minimum length of a password defined by this policy, such as 20. Click Next.

10. The "Minimum password age for user accounts" screen appears. In the Value text box, enter the minimum age for a password defined by this policy (in days) before it can be changed by the user, in the format D:HH:MM:SS. For a value of 2 days, for example, enter 2:00:00:00. Click Next.

11. The "Maximum password age for user accounts" screen appears. In the Value text box, enter 0 to configure nonexpiring passwords. (To define the maximum age for a password defined by this policy, enter a value in the format days:hours:minutes:seconds after which the password will expire, such as 42:00:00:00.)

12. The "Lockout threshold for lockout of user accounts" screen appears. In the Value text box, enter the number of bad password attempts that will cause an account to be locked out, such as 50. Click Next.

13. The "Observation Window for lockout of user accounts" screen appears. In the Value text box, enter the value in minutes during which the number of bad password attempts will lock out the account. For a value of 30 minutes, enter 0:0:30:00. Click Next.

14. The "Lockout duration for locked out user accounts" screen appears. In the Value text box, enter the value in minutes for how long an account will remain locked out. For a value of 30 minutes, enter 0:00:30:00. For a "hard lockout," in which the account must be manually unlocked by an administrator, enter a value of 0. Click Next.

15. Click More Attributes. In the Select an Attribute to View drop-down box, select msDS-PSOAppliesTo.

16. In the Edit Attribute text box, enter the DN of the user or group object that this password policy should apply to, such as cn=Marketing,ou=Corp,dc=adatum,dc=com.

17. Click Add, then click OK.

18. Click Finish.

Using a command-line interface

Fine-Grained Password Policy objects can be created at the command line using the *psomgr.exe* tool from *http://www.joeware.net*. The following example will create a policy with the following parameters:

- name: 20CharNoExpiry
- displayname: 20CharactersNoExpiration
- precedence: 1
- maxpwdage: 0 (no expiration)
- minlength: 20
- lockout count: 50
- lockout duration: 30 minutes
- lockout observation window: 60 minutes
- minpwdage: 2 days
- complexity: TRUE
- reversible encryption enabled: FALSE

```
C:> psomgr -add
20CharNoExpiry:20CharactersNoExpiration:1:0:20:50:30:60:2:TRUE:FALSE -forreal
```

Using PowerShell

Fine-Grained Password Policy objects can be created in PowerShell using the Quest AD cmdlets tools, as follows:

```
New-QADPasswordSettingsObject -Name '45DayExpiry' -Precedence 10
-MaximumPasswordAge (new-timespan -days 45 -hour 0 -minute 0)
-PasswordComplexityEnabled 'true'
```

Discussion

In Windows 2000 and Windows Server 2003, only one password and account lockout policy is allowed per domain; this has been updated in Windows Server 2008 once you reach the Windows Server 2008 domain functional level. These Fine-Grained Password Policies are controlled by creating one or more msDS-PasswordSettingsObjects, or PSOs for short, in the CN=Password Settings Container,CN=System,CN=<Domain DN> container. Each PSO can apply to one or more user or group objects, and each is assigned a precedence that will allow Active Directory to determine which PSO to enforce if more than one can apply to a particular user.

Using a command-line interface

The *psomgr.exe* utility from *http://www.joeware.net/freetools* provides an extremely rich environment from which you can create and manage PSOs at the command line. Some of the available command-line switches allow you to `-view`, `-add`, `-rename`, and `-mod` (modify) `PasswordSettingsObjects`, as well as to control which users and groups a particular PSO should apply to.

See Also

Recipes 6.18 and 9.30 and Chapter 9 of *Active Directory*

9.30 Editing a Fine-Grained Password Policy

Problem

You want to modify a Fine-Grained Password Policy in a Windows Server 2008 domain.

Solution

Using a graphical user interface

1. Open ADSI Edit. Right-click on the top-level node and click "Connect to...". In the Connection Settings screen, click OK.
2. In the right pane, double-click on Default naming context, then double-click on the domain node (i.e., `dc=adatum,dc=com`).
3. Browse to CN=System, then CN=Password Settings Container.
4. Right-click on the PSO that you wish to modify and click Properties.
5. Click Finish.

Using a command-line interface

The following command renames a `PasswordSettingsObject`:

```
psomgr -rename newname -pso oldname -forreal
```

The following modifies a PSO's maximum password age to 60 days:

```
psomgr -mod -pso TestPSO -pwdlen 60 -forreal
```

The following adds the `Marketing` group to the list of groups that a PSO will apply to:

```
psomgr -applyto CN=Marketing,CN=Users,DC=ADATUM,DC=COM -pso TestPSO -forreal
```

The following removes the `Marketing` group from the list of groups that a PSO will apply to:

```
psomgr -unapplyto CN=Marketing,CN=Users,DC=ADATUM,DC=COM -pso TestPSO -forreal
```

You can also use the *Domain**sAMAccountName* syntax instead of a distinguished name.

Using PowerShell

The following renames a PSO using the AD cmdlets:

```
rename-QADObject -Identity <PSO DN> -NewName <New PSO CN>
```

To rename a PSO using the .NET methods, use the following:

```
$objPSO = [System.DirectoryServices.DirectoryEntry] "LDAP://<PSO DN>"
$newName = "<New Value of 'name' Attribute>"
$objPSO.psbase.Rename($newName)
```

To add a group to the list of groups that a PSO will apply to, use the following syntax:

```
Add-QADPasswordSettingsObjectAppliesTo -Identity <PSO DN> -AppliesTo <Group DN>
```

To remove a group from the list of groups that a PSO will apply to, use the following syntax:

```
Remove-QADPasswordSettingsObjectAppliesTo -Identity <PSO DN> -AppliesTo <Group DN>
```

Discussion

Once a `PasswordSettingsObject` has been created, you can modify the password and account lockout settings controlled by the object, as well as the users and groups that the PSO should apply to. Since the `PasswordSettingsObject` is an Active Directory object class, these modifications can be made using any interface that can modify objects.

When working from the command-line, the *psomgr* tool from *http://www.joeware.net/ freetools* allows you to modify one or multiple PSOs at a time, and can also create "starter" PSOs using the `psomgr -quickstart -forreal` syntax. The `-quickstart` switch creates a PSO that replicates the domain-linked password policy, as well as the following two PSOs:

cn=pwd_policy_admin
> Creates a PSO with a minimum password length of 15, with passwords that expire every 35 days and that are subject to 30-minute lockout after 25 bad password attempts

cn=pwd_policy_serviceid
> Creates a PSO with a minimum length of 15, with passwords that expire every 364 days and that are not subject to account lockout

The full syntax for *psomgr.exe* can be obtained by typing `psomgr.exe /?` at a command prompt, or by visiting the *joeware* website.

See Also

Recipes 6.18 and 9.29 and Chapter 9 of *Active Directory*

9.31 Viewing the Effective PSO for a User

Problem

You want to determine which PSO is in effect for a particular user.

Solution

Using a graphical user interface

1. Open Active Directory Users and Computers. Click on View and confirm that there is a checkmark next to Advanced Features.
2. Browse to the user or group in question; right-click on the object and click Properties.
3. Click on the Attribute Editor tab. Click Filter, and confirm that there is a checkmark next to Show read-only attributes: Constructed and Backlinks.
4. Scroll to the `msDS-PSOApplied`.
5. Click OK.

Using a command-line interface

```
psomgr.exe -effective <User DN>
```

Using PowerShell

```
get-QADUser -Identity <UserDN> -IncludedProperties msDS-ResultantPSO | format-list
dn,msDS-ResultantPSO
```

Discussion

Within a Windows Server 2008 domain, each user object contains a constructed back-link attribute called `msDS-ResultantPSO` that indicates which `PasswordSettingsObject` is in effect for that user. The precedence rules for `PasswordSettingsObjects` are as follows:

1. If a PSO has been applied directly to the user object, it will take precedence. If multiple PSOs have been applied to a single user, the following tiebreakers will be used:
   - A PSO with a lower-numbered `Precedence` attribute (e.g., 5) will be applied over a higher-numbered one (e.g., 50).
   - If multiple PSOs have been configured with the same `Precedence` attribute, the PSO with the lowest GUID will take final precedence.

2. If no PSOs have been applied directly to the user, any PSO that has been applied to a group that the user is a member of, whether directly or indirectly, will be applied. The same tiebreakers will be used here as in #1, above.

3. If no PSOs have been applied to the user or any groups that the user is a member of, the default domain PSO will be applied.

See Also

Recipes 6.18 and 9.29 and Chapter 9 of *Active Directory*

## CHAPTER 10

Schema

10.0 Introduction

The Active Directory schema contains the blueprint for how objects are structured and secured, what data they can contain, and even how they can be viewed. Having a good understanding of the schema is paramount for any Active Directory administrator, designer, or architect. Understanding key concepts, such as class inheritance, class types, attribute syntax, and attribute indexing options is critical to being able to adequately design an Active Directory infrastructure and should be considered mandatory for any developer who is writing applications or automation scripts that utilize Active Directory.

If you are one of the lucky few who is designated as a schema administrator (i.e., a member of the *Schema Admins* group), then the importance of the schema is already well known to you. This chapter serves as a guide to accomplishing many of the day-to-day tasks of schema administrators. For a more in-depth discussion of the schema, we suggest reading *Active Directory*, Fourth Edition, by Brian Desmond et al. (O'Reilly).

The Anatomy of Schema Objects

An interesting feature of Active Directory not common among other LDAP implementations is that the schema is stored within Active Directory itself as a set of objects. This means that you can use similar interfaces and programs to manage the schema as you would any other type of object without any need to shut down or restart Active Directory.

All schema objects are stored in the `Schema` container (for example, `cn=schema,cn=configuration, <ForestRootDN>`). The schema is comprised of two classes of objects, `classSchema` and `attributeSchema`. Unsurprisingly, the `classSchema` objects define classes and `attributeSchema` objects define attributes. The `Schema` container contains a third type of object called `subSchema`, also known as the abstract schema, which is defined in the LDAP version 3 specification (RFC 2251). There is only a single `subSchema` object in the `Schema` container, named `cn=Aggregate`, and it contains a summary of the entire schema.

Tables 10-1 and 10-2 contain useful attributes of `classSchema` objects and `attributeSchema` objects, respectively.

Table 10-1. Attributes of classSchema objects

Attribute	Description
adminDescription	Description of the class.
auxiliaryClass	Multivalued attribute containing any auxiliary classes defined for the class.
cn	Relative distinguished name of the class.
defaultHidingValue	Boolean that determines whether objects of this class are hidden by default in administrative GUIs.
defaultSecurityDescriptor	Default security descriptor applied to objects of this class.
governsID	OID for the class.
isDefunct	Boolean that indicates whether the class is defunct (i.e., deactivated).
lDAPDisplayName	Name used when referencing the class in searches or when instantiating or modifying objects of this class.
mayContain	Multivalued attribute that contains a list of attributes that can be optionally set on the class.
mustContain	Multivalued attribute that contains a list of attributes that must be set on the class.
objectClassCategory	Integer representing the class's type. Can be one of 1 (structural), 2 (abstract), 3 (auxiliary), or 0 (88).
possibleInferiors	Multivalued list of other object classes this object can contain.
possSuperiors	Multivalued list of object classes this object can be subordinate to.
rDNAttID	Naming attribute (i.e., RDN) of instances of the class.
schemaIDGUID	GUID of the class.
showInAdvancedViewOnly	Boolean that indicates whether instances of this class should be shown only in Advanced mode in the administrative GUIs.
subClassOf	Parent class.
systemAuxiliaryClass	Multivalued attribute containing any auxiliary classes defined for the class. This can be modified only internally by Active Directory.
systemFlags	Integer representing additional properties of the class.
systemMayContain	Multivalued attribute that contains a list of attributes that can be optionally set on the class. This can be modified only internally by Active Directory.
systemMustContain	Multivalued attribute that contains a list of attributes that must be set on the class. This can be modified only internally by Active Directory.
systemPossSuperiors	Multivalued list of object classes this object can be subordinate to. This can be modified only internally by Active Directory.

Table 10-2. *Attributes of attributeSchema objects*

Attribute	Description
adminDescription	Description of the attribute.
attributeID	OID for the attribute.
attributeSecurityGUID	GUID of the property set (if any) that an attribute is a member of.
attributeSyntax	OID representing the syntax of the attribute. This is used in conjunction with oMSyntax to define a unique syntax.
cn	Relative distinguished name of the attribute.
isDefunct	Boolean that indicates if the attribute is defunct (i.e., deactivated).
isMemberOfPartialAttributeSet	Boolean that indicates if the attribute is a member of the partial attribute set (i.e., the global catalog).
isSingleValued	Boolean that indicates whether the attribute is single-valued or multivalued.
linkID	If this is populated, it will contain an integer that represents a link (either forward or backward) to another attribute.
lDAPDisplayName	Name used when referencing the attribute in searches or when populating it on objects. Note that this value may not be the same as cn.
oMSyntax	An integer representing the OSI Abstract Data Manipulation (OM) type of the attribute. This is used in conjunction with attributeSyntax to determine a unique syntax for the attribute.
schemaIDGUID	GUID of the attribute.
searchFlags	Integer representing special properties related to searching with the attribute. This includes how the attribute is indexed and if it is used in ANR searches.
systemFlags	Integer representing additional properties of the attribute.

10.1 Registering the Active Directory Schema MMC Snap-in

Problem

You want to use the Active Directory Schema MMC snap-in for the first time on an administrative computer.

Solution

Before you can use the Active Directory Schema MMC snap-in, you have to register the DLL associated with it. This can be done with the *regsvr32* utility using the following command:

```
> regsvr32 schmmgmt.dll
```

If the command is successful, you'll see the following message:

```
DllRegisterServer in schmmgmt.dll succeeded.
```

Discussion

Most of the Active Directory MMC snap-ins do not require that you manually register the associated DLL. Microsoft requires this with the Active Directory Schema snap-in, however, due to the sensitive nature of modifying the schema. This doesn't actually do much to prevent users from using it, but at least it isn't available by default. And regardless, only members of the *Schema Admins* group have permission to modify the schema anyway, so making this snap-in available should not pose any risk.

The *schmmgmt.dll* file is installed as part of the *adminpak.msi* Administrative Tools installer in Windows 2000, XP, and Windows Server 2003, or else it is installed by default on domain controllers when they are first promoted. It is also installed with the Remote Server Administration Tool (RSAT) for Windows Vista workstations. If you want to use the Schema snap-in on a domain member server or workstation machine and you have not installed the *adminpak.msi* package or RSAT, you'll need to specify the full path to *schmmgmt.dll* when using *regsvr32*.

See Also

MS KB 320337 (How to Manage the Active Directory Schema in Windows 2000) and MS KB 326310 (How to Manage the Active Directory Schema in Windows Server 2003 Enterprise Edition)

10.2 Enabling Schema Updates

 This is necessary only when the Schema FSMO role owner is running Windows 2000.

Problem

You want to enable schema modifications on a Windows 2000 Schema FSMO. This is a necessary first step before you can extend the schema.

Solution

Using a graphical user interface

1. Open the Active Directory Schema snap-in.
2. Click on Active Directory Schema in the left pane.
3. Right-click on Active Directory Schema and select Operations Master.
4. Check the box beside "Allow schema modifications."
5. Click OK.

Using a command-line interface

To enable modifications to the schema, use the following command:

```
> reg add HKEY_LOCAL_MACHINE\System\CurrentControlSet\Services\NTDS\Parameters /t
REG_DWORD /v "Schema Update Allowed" /d 1
```

To disable modifications to the schema, use the following command:

```
> reg delete HKEY_LOCAL_MACHINE\System\CurrentControlSet\Services\NTDS\Parameters
/v "Schema Update Allowed" /f
```

Using VBScript

```
' This code enables or disables schema mods on Schema FSMO.
' ------ SCRIPT CONFIGURATION ------
' TRUE to enable schema mods and FALSE to disable
boolSetReg = TRUE

' Name of the Schema FSMO or "." to run locally
strDC = "<SchemaFSMOName>"
' ------ END CONFIGURATION --------

const HKEY_LOCAL_MACHINE = &H80000002
set objReg = GetObject("winmgmts:\\" & strDC & "\root\default:StdRegProv")
strKeyPath  = "System\CurrentControlSet\Services\NTDS\Parameters"
strValueName = "Schema Update Allowed"

if boolSetReg = TRUE then
    strValue = 1
    intRC = objReg.SetDWORDValue(HKEY_LOCAL_MACHINE,strKeyPath, _
                          strValueName,strValue)
    if intRC > 0 then
       WScript.Echo "Error occurred: " & intRC
    else
       WScript.Echo strValueName & " value set to " & strValue
    end if
else
    intRC = objReg.DeleteValue(HKEY_LOCAL_MACHINE,strKeyPath,strValueName)
    if intRC > 0 then
       WScript.Echo "Error occurred: " & intRC
    else
       WScript.Echo strValueName & " value deleted"
    end if
end if
```

Discussion

When the Schema FSMO role owner is running Windows 2000, you must explicitly enable schema modifications on the server before extending the schema. To enable this, you need to create a key value called Schema Update Allowed with a value of 1 under the following key:

```
HKEY_LOCAL_MACHINE\System\CurrentControlSet\Services\NTDS\Parameters
```

To disable schema modifications, set the value to 0 or delete it from the registry.

This is no longer necessary when the Schema FSMO owner is Windows Server 2003 or newer. Microsoft removed the need to perform this registry modification as a requirement for extending the schema.

See Also

MS KB 285172 (Schema Updates Require Write Access to Schema in Active Directory)

10.3 Generating an OID to Use for a New Class or Attribute

Problem

You want to generate an OID to use with a new class or attribute that you intend to add to the schema.

Solution

To implement schema extensions for production use, you should use an OID from your company or organization's OID branch. To determine if your company already has an assigned OID, see these sites:

- *http://www.iana.org/assignments/enterprise-numbers*
- *http://www.alvestrand.no/objectid/*

If your organization does not have an assigned OID, go to your country's national registry to request one. The list of registries can be found at the following site: *http://www.iso.ch/iso/en/aboutiso/isomembers/index.html*.

Once you have a base OID, you can create branches from that OID however you want. For example, if you had a base OID of 1.2.3.4, you could start new class OIDs under 1.2.3.4.1 and new attributes under 1.2.3.4.2. In that case, the first class OID you would create would be 1.2.3.4.1.1 and the first attribute OID would be 1.2.3.4.2.1.

Discussion

An OID is nothing more than a string of numbers separated by periods (.). OIDs were initially defined by the ITU-T in X.208 and have been used to uniquely identify a variety of things, including SNMP MIB objects and LDAP schema classes and attributes. OIDs are hierarchical, and the national registries are responsible for managing and assigning OID branches.

See Also

Recipe 10.2 for more on enabling schema updates

10.4 Extending the Schema

Problem

You want to extend the schema to support new classes and attributes in Active Directory.

Solution

Extending the schema is a straightforward process that consists of adding new classes or attributes, or modifying existing ones in the schema. While extending the schema is not hard, due to the sensitive nature of the schema you should implement a schema extension process that thoroughly tests any extensions before you put them in your production forest. Here is a suggested summary of what your schema extension process should be:

1. Meet with clients and determine if there is a business justification for integrating their application with Active Directory. Determine if there are any existing attributes that would fulfill the desired requirements.

2. Examine the extensions and determine what impact, if any, they will have on your Active Directory environment (e.g., adding an attribute to the global catalog).

3. Try out the extensions in a test environment. Observe any peculiarities.

4. Document the extensions.

5. Extend the schema in your production Active Directory.

For more information on defining a schema extension process, see Chapter 12 of *Active Directory*.

Discussion

One thing to be cautious of when developing a schema extension process is not to make it an overly bureaucratic process that can require several weeks to complete. At the same time, you want to ensure that any schema changes that you make are well thought out, tested, and documented thoroughly to avoid encountering issues later. While some organizations may want to strictly limit schema extensions, there is nothing inherently bad about properly extending the schema; it is one of the core features and advantages over Active Directory's predecessor, Windows NT 4.0.

See Also

Recipe 10.7 for adding a new attribute, Recipe 10.9 for adding a new class, and MS KB 283791 (How to Modify Schema Information Using the Ldifde Utility)

10.5 Preparing the Schema for an Active Directory Upgrade

Problem

You want to prepare the Active Directory schema for an application installation, such as an Active Directory upgrade.

Solution

From a graphical user interface

To prepare your Active Directory forest for a Windows upgrade, do the following:

1. Log on to the Schema Master FSMO of your AD forest.
2. Click Start→Run or open a command prompt.
3. Run the command `adprep /forestprep`. Read the warning message that appears and press C, followed by Enter.

To determine whether `adprep /forestprep` has completed for a Windows Server 2003 upgrade, check for the existence of the following object, where *<ForestRootDN>* is the distinguished name of the forest root domain:

    cn=Windows2003Update,cn=ForestUpdates,cn=Configuration,<ForestRootDN>

To determine whether `adprep/forestprep` has completed for a Windows Server 2008 upgrade, check for the existence of the following object, where *<ForestRootDN>* is the distinguished name of the forest root domain:

    cn=ActiveDirectoryUpdate,cn=ForestUpdates,cn=Configuration,<ForestRootDN>

To extend an Active Directory domain to prepare for a Windows Server 2003 or Windows Server 2008 upgrade, follow these steps:

1. Log on to the Infrastructure Master FSMO for the domain.
2. Click Start→Run or open a command prompt.
3. Run the command `adprep /domainprep`. Read the warning message that appears and press C, followed by Enter.

Discussion

Just like some third-party applications, major upgrades to the Windows operating system itself will usually require that the Active Directory schema be extended with new classes and attributes. To automate this process, Active Directory includes the *adprep* utility to perform these modifications. *adprep* needs to be run once for the entire forest using the `/forestprep` switch and once for each domain that will be upgraded using the `/domainprep` switch. In the case of a Windows Server 2003 upgrade, you can view the schema extensions that will be performed by this utility by looking at the *.ldf* files in the \i386 directory on the Windows Server 2003 CD. These files contain LDIF entries for adding and modifying new and existing classes and attributes. Since the /forestprep process extends and modifies the schema, you must perform this task using credentials that belong to both the *Schema Admins* and *Enterprise Admins* groups.

After /forestprep has completed, /domainprep will create new containers and objects within each Domain NC, as well as modify ACLs on some objects and the behavior of the *Everyone* security principal. Before you can run /domainprep, you need to ensure that the updates from /forestprep have replicated to all domain controllers in the forest using the method described in this recipe. /domainprep needs to be run on the *Infrastructure Master* of the domain, using *Domain Admin* credentials.

To prepare to add the first Windows Server 2003 R2 domain controller to an existing domain, you will need to run the version of *adprep* contained on Disc 2 of the R2 media. The R2 preparation also includes a third *adprep* switch that will update permissions on existing Group Policy Objects (GPOs) to allow for updated functionality in the Group Policy Management Console (GPMC):

```
> adprep /domainprep /gpprep
```

The Windows Server 2008 preparation, in addition to /forestprep, /domainprep, and /domainprep /gpprep, also includes /rodcprep to allow for the installation of Read-Only Domain Controllers (RODCs), which we discussed in Chapter 3.

See Also

Recipe 3.10 for more on verifying the promotion of a domain controller, MS KB 325379 (How to Upgrade Windows 2000 Domain Controllers to Windows Server 2003), MS KB 331161 (Hotfixes to Install on Windows 2000 Domain Controllers Before Running adprep/forestprep), and MS KB 314649 (Windows Server 2003 adprep/forestprep Command Causes Mangled Attributes in Windows 2000 Forests that Contain Exchange 2000 Servers)

10.6 Documenting Schema Extensions

Problem

You want to document your schema extensions.

Solution

There are several different ways you can document schema extensions. If you require LDIF files of the schema extensions before you extend the schema, you can use the files themselves as a simple self-documenting system. You can put comments in LDIF files by putting # at the beginning of a line, or else use the new schema analyzer functionality available with Active Directory Application Mode (ADAM, referred to as the Active

Directory Lightweight Directory Service, or AD LDS, in Windows Server 2008). We recommend a combination of these options, and recommend that any company that needs to extend the schema of their customer's Active Directory should include LDIF files, regardless of whether you use that method to actually extend the schema.

The AD Schema Analyzer is a useful new tool that can document your existing schema, as well as create a file to help you modify the schema. To use the Schema Analyzer, do the following:

1. In Windows Server 2003, click Start→All Programs→ADAM→ADAM Tools Command Prompt. In Windows Server 2008, open a command prompt and cd to the *Windows\ADAM* directory. Run the program *adschemaanalyzer* from the command prompt.

2. Click File→Load target schema. To load the current Active Directory schema, enter your username, password, and domain name, and then click OK.

3. Click File→Load base schema. Enter your username, password, and domain name, and then click OK.

4. Place a checkmark next to each class, attribute, and property set that you wish to export.

5. Click File→Create LDIF file. Enter a path and name of the file to export, and click Save.

Discussion

There are no hard and fast rules for documenting schema extensions. Documenting schema extensions in some fashion, even a rudimentary one, should be a requirement of any schema extension process you adopt. If you have the resources and time, you can even develop a much more elaborate documentation system using the Web or even an object-modeling system.

See Also

RFC 2849 (The LDAP Data Interchange Format (LDIF)—Technical Specification)

10.7 Adding a New Attribute

Problem

You want to add a new attribute to the schema.

Solution

 For Windows 2000 Active Directory, you need to enable schema modifications before proceeding. See Recipe 10.2 for more information.

Using a graphical user interface

1. Open the Active Directory Schema snap-in.
2. In the left pane, right-click on the Attributes folder and select Create Attribute.
3. Click the Continue button to confirm that you want to extend the schema.
4. Enter the information for the new attribute.
5. Click OK.

Using a command-line interface

You can create new attributes by using *ldifde* and an LDIF file that contains the properties to be set on the attribute. The following text shows a sample LDIF file called *create_attr.ldf* that creates an attribute called adatum-LanguagesSpoken:

```
dn: cn=adatum-LanguagesSpoken,cn=schema,cn=configuration,<ForestRootDN>
changetype: add
objectclass: attributeSchema
lDAPDisplayName: adatumLanguagesSpoken
attributeId: 1.3.6.1.4.1.999.1.1.28.3
oMSyntax: 20
attributeSyntax: 2.5.5.4
isSingleValued: FALSE
searchFlags: 1
description: "Languages a user speaks"
```

Then run the following command:

```
> ldifde -v -i -f create_attr.ldf
```

You can also use AdMod to add a schema attribute as follows:

```
> admod -schema -rb cn=adatumLanguagesSpoken
  objectClass::attributeSchema
    lDAPDisplayName::adatumLanguagesSpoken
    attributeId::1.3.6.1.4.1.999.1.1.28.3
    oMSyntax::20
    attributeSyntax::2.5.5.4
    isSingleValued::FALSE
    searchFlags::1
    description::"Languages a user speaks"
    -add
```

Using VBScript

```
' This code illustrates how to create an attribute
' called adatum-LanguagesSpoken.

set objRootDSE = GetObject("LDAP://RootDSE")
set objSchemaCont = GetObject("LDAP://" & _
                              objRootDSE.Get("schemaNamingContext") )
set objAttr = objSchemaCont.Create("attributeSchema", _
                                   "cn=adatum-LanguagesSpoken")
objAttr.Put "lDAPDisplayName", "adatum-LanguagesSpoken"
objAttr.Put "attributeId", "1.3.6.1.4.1.999.1.1.28.3"
objAttr.Put "oMSyntax", 20
objAttr.Put "attributeSyntax", "2.5.5.4"
objAttr.Put "isSingleValued", FALSE
objAttr.Put "description", "Languages a user speaks"
objAttr.Put "searchFlags", 1 ' index the attribute
objAttr.SetInfo
WScript.Echo "Attribute created"
```

Using PowerShell

To create a schema attribute using the Quest tools, use the `new-QADObject` cmdlet as follows:

```
new-QADObject -ParentContainer 'cn=schema,cn=configuration,<ForestRootDN>' -type
'attributeSchema' -name 'adatum-LanguagesSpoken' -ObjectAttributes
@{lDAPDisplayName='adatum-LanguagesSpoken';
attributeId='1.3.6.1.4.1.999.1.1.28.3';oMSyntax='20';attributeSyntax='2.5.5.4';
isSingleValued='FALSE';description='Language a user speaks';searchFlags='1'}
```

To create a schema attribute using native PowerShell functionality, use the following syntax:

```
$root = [ADSI]"LDAP://RootDSE"
$schema = $root.schemaNamingContext
$parentCont = [ADSI]("LDAP://" + $schema)
$newAttr = $parentCont.Create("attributeSchema","adatum-LanguagesSpoken")
$newAttr.put("lDAPDisplayName","adatum-LanguagesSpoken")
$newAttr.put("attributeId","1.3.6.1.4.1.999.1.1.28.3")
$newAttr.put("oMSyntax", 20)
$newAttr.put("attributeSyntax", "2.5.5.4")
$newAttr.put("isSingleValued", $false)
$newAttr.put("description", "Languages a user speaks")
$newAttr.put("searchFlags", 1)
$newAttr.SetInfo()
```

Discussion

To create an attribute, you need to add an `attributeSchema` object to the `Schema` container. Typically, when you extend the schema, you perform several additions or modifications at once. The order of your extensions is very important. You can't create a class, assign an attribute, and then create the attribute; you obviously need to create the attribute before it can be assigned to the class. Even if you create the attribute before you assign it to a class, you must reload the schema before doing the class assignment. Reloading the schema is described in more detail in Recipe 10.25.

Most of the attributes that can be set on `attributeSchema` objects are pretty straightforward, but a couple of them require a little explanation. The `attributeSyntax` and `oMSyntax` attributes together define the syntax, or the type of data that can be contained in the attribute. Table 10-3 shows the possible combinations of these two attributes and the resulting syntax.

Table 10-3. attributeSyntax and oMSyntax combinations

Name	attributeSyntax	oMSyntax	Description
AccessPointDN	2.5.5.14	127	Type of distinguished name taken from X.500.
Boolean	2.5.5.8	1	TRUE or FALSE value.
CaseExactString	2.5.5.3	27	Case-sensitive string.
CaseIgnoreString	2.5.5.4	20	Case-insensitive string.
DirectoryString	2.5.5.12	64	Case-insensitive Unicode string.
DN	2.5.5.1	127	String representing a distinguished name.
DNWithBinary	2.5.5.7	127	Octet string that has the following format: `B:CharCount:BinaryValue:ObjectDN` where *CharCount* is the number of hexadecimal digits in BinaryValue, *BinaryValue* is the hexadecimal representation of the binary value, and *ObjectDN* is a distinguished name.
DNWithString	2.5.5.14	127	Octet string that contains a string value and a DN. A value with this syntax has the following format: `S:CharCount:StringValue:ObjectDN` where *CharCount* is the number of characters in the *StringValue* string and *ObjectDN* is a distinguished name of an object in Active Directory.
Enumeration	2.5.5.9	10	Defined in X.500 and treated as an integer.
GeneralizedTime	2.5.5.11	24	Time-string format defined by ASN.1 standards. See ISO 8601 and X.680.
IA5String	2.5.5.5	22	Case-sensitive string containing characters from the IA5 character set.
Integer	2.5.5.9	2	32-bit integer.
Integer8	2.5.5.16	65	64-bit integer, also known as a large integer.
NTSecurityDescriptor	2.5.5.15	66	Octet string that contains a security descriptor.
NumericString	2.5.5.6	18	String that contains digits.
OctetString	2.5.5.10	4	Array of bytes used to store binary data.
OID	2.5.5.2	6	String that contains digits (0–9) and decimal points (.).
ORName	2.5.5.7	127	Taken from X.400; used for X.400 to RFC 822 map ping.
PresentationAddress	2.5.5.13	127	String that contains OSI presentation addresses.

Name	attributeSyntax	oMSyntax	Description
PrintableString	2.5.5.5	19	Case-sensitive string that contains characters from the printable character set.
ReplicaLink	2.5.5.10	127	Used by Active Directory internally.
Sid	2.5.5.17	4	Octet string that contains a security identifier (SID).
UTCTime	2.5.5.11	23	Time-string format defined by ASN.1 standards.

The `searchFlags` attribute is a bit flag that defines special properties related to searching with the attribute. Table 10-4 contains the values that can be set for this attribute. The values are cumulative, so to index an attribute and include it in ANR searches, you would set a value of 5 (1 + 4).

Table 10-4. searchFlags bit values

Value	Description
1	Index over attribute. See Recipe 10.11 for more information.
2	Index over container and attribute.
4	Include as part of Ambiguous Name Resolution (ANR). Should be used in addition to 1. See Recipe 10.14 for more information.
8	Preserve attribute in tombstone objects. This will ensure that the value of a particular attribute will be retained when the object is tombstoned, so that it will be repopulated automatically if you need to reanimate the object.
16	Copy attribute when duplicating an object. See Recipe 10.12 for more information.
32	Create a tuple index for this attribute. This improves the response time for searches that put a wildcard in front of the search string for the attribute (e.g., `givenname=*on`).
64	Create an index on which to assist with VLV performance.
128	Set the confidential bit on this attribute, which requires normal users to be assigned additional permissions to be able to read its contents. (This is new with Windows Server 2003 Service Pack 1.)
256	Disable security auditing for the attribute. Applicable to Windows Server 2008 or higher.
512	The attribute should be added to the Read-Only Filtered Attribute Set (RO-FAS), preventing the attribute from being replicated to any RODCs in the environment.

See Also

Recipe 4.15 for setting a bit flag, Recipe 10.9 for adding a new class, and Recipe 10.25 for reloading the schema

10.8 Viewing an Attribute

Problem

You want to view the properties of an attribute.

Solution

Using a graphical user interface

1. Open the Active Directory Schema snap-in.
2. In the left pane, click on the Attributes folder.
3. In the right pane, double-click the attribute you want to view.
4. Click on each tab to view the available properties.

Using a command-line interface

In the following command, replace *<AttrCommonName>* with the common name (not LDAP display dame) of the attribute you want to view:

```
> dsquery * cn=schema,cn=configuration,<ForestRootDN> -scope onelevel -attr *
-filter "(&(objectcategory=attributeSchema)(cn=<AttrCommonName>))"
```

You can also use AdFind to view the properties of an attribute as follows:

```
> adfind -schema -f (ldapdisplayname=<AttributeName>)
```

You can also use a shortcut syntax for this command, as follows:

```
> adfind -sc s:<AttributeName>
```

Using VBScript

```
' This code displays the
' attributes for the specified attributeSchema object
' Refer to Recipe 4.2 for the DisplayAttributes()
' function code.
' ------ SCRIPT CONFIGURATION ------
' Set to the common name (not LDAP display dame) of the attribute
strAttrName = "<AttrCommonName>" ' e.g. surname
' ------ END CONFIGURATION --------

set objRootDSE = GetObject("LDAP://RootDSE")
set objAttr = GetObject("LDAP://cn=" & strAttrName & "," & _
                        objRootDSE.Get("schemaNamingContext"))
objAttr.GetInfo
WScript.Echo "Properties for " & strAttrName & ":"
DisplayAttributes(objAttr.ADsPath)
```

Using PowerShell

You can view the properties of a schema attribute using the Quest AD cmdlets or native ADSI commands, as follows:

```
$attr = get-QADObject -LdapFilter
"(&(objectcategory=attributeSchema)(cn=<AttrCommonName>))"
$attr.psbase.getProperties() | format-table PropertyName, Value

$strAttrName  "<AttrCommonName>"  ## e.g., surname
```

```
$root = [ADSI]"LDAP://RootDSE"
$obj = [ADSI]("LDAP://cn=" + $strAttrName + "," + $root.schemaNamingContext)
$obj.psbase.Properties | ft PropertyName, Value
```

Discussion

In the CLI and VBScript solutions, we mention that you need to specify the common name (or cn) of the attribute you want to view. The common name is a source of confusion for many people. For example, the surname attribute has the following distinguished name in the *adatum.com* forest:

```
cn=surname,cn=schema,cn=configuration,dc=adatum,dc=com
```

The problem is that most applications refer to attributes by their LDAP display name as defined in the lDAPDisplayName attribute for the attributeSchema object, which is typically different from the cn attribute. As an example, the surname attribute uses surname for its common name (cn), but sn for its LDAP display name (lDAPDisplayName).

In the CLI solution, to use the LDAP display name instead of cn when using DSQuery, simply change (cn=*<AttrCommonName>*) to (lDAPDisplayName= *<AttrLDAPName>*). In the VBScript solution, it is not that simple. When using cn, we can call GetObject since we know the DN of the attributeSchema object. If you want to use the lDAPDisplayName attribute instead, you'll need to do an ADO query and use search criteria similar to those in the CLI solution.

AdFind includes the shortcut adfind -sc s:<name>, which will check both the LDAP Display Name and the cn automatically. Additionally, this shortcut will decode various properties when it produces its output.

One attribute of note that is defined on attributeSchema objects is the systemFlags bit flag, which is used to define a few miscellaneous properties about an attribute. Table 10-5 contains the bits associated with systemFlags. The values are cumulative, so a value of 17 (1 + 16) would indicate that the attribute is part of the base Active Directory installation and is not replicated.

Table 10-5. systemFlags bit values

Value	Description
1	Not replicated among domain controllers.
4	Dynamically constructed by Active Directory.
16	Part of the base Active Directory installation. This value cannot be set.

See Also

Recipe 4.2 for viewing the attributes of an object and Recipe 4.12 for searching with a bitwise filter

10.9 Adding a New Class

Problem

You want to add a new class to the schema.

Solution

 For Windows 2000 Active Directory, you need to enable schema modifications before proceeding. See Recipe 10.2 for more information.

Using a graphical user interface

1. Open the Active Directory Schema snap-in.
2. In the left pane, right-click on the Classes folder and select "Create Class...".
3. Click the Continue button to confirm that you want to extend the schema.
4. Enter the information for the new class and click Next.
5. Enter any mandatory and optional attributes and click Finish.

Using a command-line interface

You can create new classes by using *ldifde* and an LDIF file that contains the properties to be set on the class. The following text shows a sample LDIF file called *create_class.ldf* that creates a class called `adatum-SalesUser`:

```
dn: cn=adatum-SalesUser,cn=schema,cn=configuration,<ForestRootDN>
changetype: add
objectclass: classSchema
lDAPDisplayName: adatum-SalesUser
governsId: 1.3.6.1.4.1.999.1.1.28.4
objectClassCategory: 3
subClassOf: top
description: Auxiliary class for Sales user attributes
adminDescription: Auxiliary class for Sales user
attributes
mayContain: adatum-Building
mayContain: adatum-Theatre
```

Then run the following command:

```
> ldifde -v -i -f create_class.ldf
```

You can also add a new class using AdMod, as follows:

```
> admod -schema -rb cn=adatum-SalesUser
    objectclass::classSchema lDAPDisplayName::adatum-SalesUser
    governsId::1.3.6.1.4.1.999.1.1.28.4 objectClassCategory::3
    subClassOf::top
```

```
description::"Auxiliary class for Sales user"
adminDescription::"Auxiliary class for Sales user"
mayContain::adatum-Building;adatum-Theatre
-add
```

Using VBScript

```
' This code creates a class in the schema called adatum-SalesUser.
' It is assumed that the script is being run by a member of Schema Admins

set objRootDSE = GetObject("LDAP://RootDSE")
set objSchemaCont = GetObject("LDAP://" & _
                              objRootDSE.Get("schemaNamingContext") )
set objClass = objSchemaCont.Create("classSchema", _
                                    "cn=adatum-SalesUser")
objClass.Put "lDAPDisplayName", "adatum-SalesUser"
objClass.Put "governsId", "1.3.6.1.4.1.999.1.1.28.4"
objClass.Put "objectClassCategory", 3
objClass.Put "subClassOf", "top"
objClass.Put "adminDescription", "Auxilliary class for Sales user attributes"
objClass.Put "mayContain", Array("adatum-Building","adatum-Theatre")
objClass.SetInfo
WScript.Echo "Class created"
```

Using PowerShell

To create a schema class using the Quest tools, use the **new-QADObject** cmdlet as follows:

```
new-QADObject -ParentContainer 'cn=schema,cn=configuration,<ForestRootDN>' -type
'classSchema' -name 'adatum-SalesUser' -ObjectAttributes @{lDAPDisplayName='adatum-
SalesUser';
governsId='1.3.6.1.4.1.999.1.1.28.4';objectClassCategory='3';subClassOf='top';admin
Description='Auxilliary class for Sales user
attributes';mayContain=@('description';'adatum-Theatre')}
```

To create a schema class using ADSI commands, use the following syntax:

```
$ADS_PROPERTY_APPEND=2
$parentCont = [ADSI] "LDAP://cn=schema,cn=configuration,<ForestRootDN>"
$newClass = $parentCont.Create("classSchema","adatum-SalesUser")
$newClass.put("lDAPDisplayName","adatum-SalesUser")
$newClass.put("governsId","1.3.6.1.4.1.999.1.1.28.4")
$newClass.put("objectClassCategory","3")
$newClass.put("subClassOf","top")
$newClass.put("adminDescription","Auxilliary class for Sales user attributes")
$newClass.putEx($ADS_PROPERTY_APPEND, "mayContain", @("adatum-Building","adatum-
Theatre"))
$newClass.SetInfo()
```

Discussion

To create a new class, you need to create a **classSchema** object in the **Schema** container. The important attributes to set include:

`governsId`
> Defines the OID for the class

`objectClassCategory`
> Defines the class type

`subClassOf`
> Defines the parent class

`mayContain` *and* `mustContain`
> Defines any optional and mandatory attributes for instantiated objects of the class

The `lDAPDisplayName` also needs to be set and should be equal to the common name (`cn`) as a general rule. Even though many of the default classes do not use the same name for the common name and LDAP display name, using the same name is highly recommended to avoid confusion when referencing the class. Another best practice is to set the `schemaIDGUID` of the class.

See Also

Recipe 10.0 for attributes of `classSchema` objects, Recipe 10.3 for generating an OID, Recipe 10.18 for more on object class type, Recipe 10.20 for setting the default security for a class, and Recipe 10.25 for reloading the schema cache

10.10 Viewing a Class

Problem

You want to view the attributes of a class.

Solution

Using a graphical user interface

1. Open the Active Directory Schema snap-in.
2. In the left pane, click on the Classes folder.
3. In the right pane, double-click the class you want to view.
4. Click on each tab to view the available properties.

Using a command-line interface

In the following command, replace *<ClassCommonName>* with the common name (not LDAP display name) of the class you want to view:

```
> dsquery * cn=<ClassCommonName>,cn=schema,cn=configuration,<ForestRootDN> -scope
base -attr *
```

You can also use AdFind to view the properties of a class as follows:

```
> adfind -schema -rb cn=<ClassCommonName>
```

You can also use a shortcut syntax for this command, as follows:

```
> adfind -sc s:<ClassCommonName or ClassLDAPDisplayName>
```

Using VBScript

```
' This code prints out the attributes for the specified class.
' Recipe 4.2 for the code for the DisplayAttributes()
' function.
' ------ SCRIPT CONFIGURATION ------
' Set to the common name (not LDAP display dame)
' of the class you want to view.
strClassName = "<ClassCommonName>" ' e.g. user
' ------ END CONFIGURATION --------

set objRootDSE = GetObject("LDAP://RootDSE")
set objClass = GetObject("LDAP://cn=" & strClassName & "," & _
                         objRootDSE.Get("schemaNamingContext"))
objClass.GetInfo
WScript.Echo "Properties for " & strClassName
DisplayAttributes(objClass.ADsPath)
```

Using PowerShell

```
$objClass = get-QADObject -Identity "cn=<Class
Name>,cn=schema,cn=Configuration,<ForestRootDN>"
$objClass.psbase.getProperties() | format-table PropertyName, Value

$root = [ADSI]"LDAP://RootDSE"
$obj = [ADSI]("LDAP://cn=" + $strClassName + "," + $root.schemaNamingContext)
$obj.psbase.Properties | ft PropertyName, Value
```

Discussion

See Table 10-1, at the beginning of this chapter, for a list of the important classSchema attributes and their descriptions.

See Also

Recipe 4.2 for viewing the attributes of an object

10.11 Indexing an Attribute

Problem

You want to index an attribute so that searches using that attribute are faster.

Solution

 For Windows 2000 Active Directory you need to enable schema modifications before proceeding. See Recipe 10.2 for more information.

Using a graphical user interface

1. Open the Active Directory Schema snap-in.
2. In the left pane, click on the Attributes folder.
3. In the right pane, double-click the attribute you want to index.
4. Check the box beside "Index this attribute in the Active Directory."
5. Click OK.

Using a command-line interface

You can index an attribute by using the *ldifde* utility and an LDIF file that contains the following:

```
dn: cn=<AttrCommonName>,cn=schema,cn=configuration,<ForestRootDN>
changetype: modify
replace: searchFlags
searchFlags: 1
-
```

If the LDIF file were named *index_attribute.ldf*, you would run the following command:

```
> ldifde -v -i -f index_attribute.ldf
```

You can also enable the appropriate `searchFlags` value using `admod`, as follows:

```
> admod -schema -rb cn=<AttrCommonName> searchFlags::1
```

Using VBScript

```
' This code indexes an attribute.
' ------ SCRIPT CONFIGURATION ------
' Set to the common name (not LDAP display name) of the attribute
strAttrName = "<AttrCommonName>" ' e.g. adatum-LanguagesSpoken
' ------ END CONFIGURATION --------

set objRootDSE = GetObject("LDAP://RootDSE")
set objAttr = GetObject("LDAP://cn=" & strAttrName & "," &
                        objRootDSE.Get("schemaNamingContext"))
objAttr.Put "searchFlags", 1
objAttr.SetInfo
WScript.Echo "
Indexed attribute: " & strAttrName
```

The CLI and VBScript solutions assume that searchFlags wasn't previously set; if a value is present, they just blindly overwrite it. See Recipe 4.15 for a better solution that will enable the bit value you want without overwriting any previous settings.

Using PowerShell

To set the searchFlags bit value using a bitwise OR operation, use the following syntax:

```
$strAttrName = "<AttrCommonName>"  # e.g. adatum-LanguagesSpoken

$root = [ADSI]"LDAP://RootDSE"
$objAttr = [ADSI]("LDAP://cn=" + $strAttrName + "," + $root.schemaNamingContext)
$objAttr.put("searchFlags", $objAttr.searchFlags.Value -bor 1)
$objAttr.setInfo()
```

Discussion

To index an attribute, you need to set bit 0 (0001) in the searchFlags attribute for the attributeSchema object.

searchFlags is a bit flag attribute that is used to set various properties related to searching with the attribute. Table 10-5, earlier in this chapter, contains the various bit flags that can be set with searchFlags. When setting searchFlags, you may often need to set a couple bits together. For example, all Ambiguous Name Resolution (ANR) attributes must also be indexed, which means searchFlags should be set to 5 (1 + 4).

You can find the attributes that are indexed in the schema by using the following search criteria:

Base
> cn=Schema,cn=Configuration,*<ForestRootDN>*

Filter
> (&(objectcategory=attributeSchema)(searchFlags:1.2.840.113556.1.4.803:=1))

Scope
> onelevel

Alternatively, to find attributes that aren't indexed, change the previous search filter to the following:

> (&(objectcategory=attributeSchema)(!(searchFlags:1.2.840.113556.1.4.803:=1)))

Beginning in Windows Server 2008, the objectclass attribute is now indexed by default. This allows you to perform simpler searches by querying directly against objectclass, rather than using the more complex query of "(&(objectcategory=ABC)(objectClass=XYZ))".

You can also find indexed attributes using AdFind, as follows:

```
adfind -sc indexed
```

See Also

Recipe 4.15 for modifying a bit flag attribute, Recipe 10.7 for adding a new attribute, and MS KB 243311 (Setting an Attribute's searchFlags Property to Be Indexed for ANR)

10.12 Modifying the Attributes That Are Copied When Duplicating a User

Problem

You want to add an attribute to the list of attributes that are copied when duplicating a user with the ADUC snap-in.

Solution

 For Windows 2000 Active Directory you need to enable schema modifications before proceeding. See Recipe 10.2 for more information.

Using a graphical user interface

1. Open the Active Directory Schema snap-in.
2. In the left pane, click on the Attributes folder.
3. In the right pane, double-click the attribute you want to edit.
4. Check the box beside "Attribute is copied when duplicating a user."
5. Click OK.

Using a command-line interface

You can cause an attribute to get copied when duplicating a user by using the *ldifde* utility and an LDIF file that contains the following:

```
dn: cn=adatum-LanguagesSpoken,cn=schema,cn=configuration,<ForestRootDN>
changetype: modify
replace: searchFlags
searchFlags: 16
-
```

If the LDIF file were named *add_dup_user_attr.ldf*, you would run the following command:

```
> ldifde -v -i -f add_dup_user_attr.ldf
```

You can also modify the **searchFlags** attribute using AdMod, as follows:

```
> admod -b <AttributeDN> searchFlags::16
```

Using VBScript

```
' This code adds an attribute to the list of
' attributes that get
' copied when duplicating a user.
' ------ SCRIPT CONFIGURATION ------
' Set to the common name (not LDAP display dame) of the attribute
strAttrName = "<AttrCommonName>" ' e.g. adatum-LanguagesSpoken
' ------ END CONFIGURATION --------

set objRootDSE = GetObject("LDAP://RootDSE")
set objAttr = GetObject("LDAP://cn=" & strAttrName & "," & objRootDSE.
Get("schemaNamingContext"))
objAttr.Put "searchFlags", 16
objAttr.SetInfo
WScript.Echo "New copied attribute: " & strAttrName
```

 The CLI and VBScript solutions assume that **searchFlags** wasn't previously set; if a value is present, they just blindly overwrite it. See Recipe 4.15 for a better solution that will enable the bit you want without overwriting any previous settings.

Using PowerShell

To set the **searchFlags** bit value using a bit-wise OR operation, use the following syntax:

```
$strAttrName = "<AttrCommonName>"  # e.g. adatum-LanguagesSpoken

$root = [ADSI]"LDAP://RootDSE"
$objAttr = [ADSI]("LDAP://cn=" + $strAttrName + "," + $root.schemaNamingContext)
$objAttr.put("searchFlags", $objAttr.searchFlags.Value -bor 16)
$objAttr.setInfo()
```

Discussion

The Active Directory Users and Computers snap-in queries the schema for the list of attributes that should be copied whenever you right-click on a user and select Copy. This flag is purely informational and does not impose any restrictions or result in any impact on the DIT, unlike indexing an attribute.

To find out which attributes are copied when duplicating a user, use the following search criteria:

Base
    cn=Schema,cn=Configuration,<ForestRootDN>

Filter

```
(&(objectcategory=attributeSchema)
 (searchFlags:1.2.840.113556.1.4.803:=16))
```

Scope

```
onelevel
```

Alternatively, to find attributes that aren't copied, change the previous search filter to the following:

```
(&(objectcategory=attributeSchema)(!(searchFlags:1.2.840.113556.1.4.803:=16)))
```

You can also find a list of these attributes using AdFind, as follows:

```
adfind -sc copy
```

See Also

Recipe 4.15 for modifying a bit flag attribute and Recipe 10.7 for adding a new attribute

10.13 Adding Custom Information to ADUC

Problem

You want schema information that you've created to be visible in the ADUC MMC snap-in.

Solution

This recipe is only required for Windows 2000 and Windows Server 2003. In the Windows Server 2008 version of ADUC, you can access all available attributes for an object using the Attribute Editor tab.

Using VBScript

```
Set oFileSystem = WScript.CreateObject("Scripting.FileSystemObject")
sSystemFolder = oFileSystem.GetSpecialFolder(1)
set oRootDSE = Getobject("LDAP://RootDSE")

' The display specifier for US English is 409; modify this
' for another locale if necessary.
set oCont = GetObject("LDAP://" & "CN=409, CN=DisplaySpecifiers," &
oRootDSE.get("configurationNamingContext"))
Set oDisp = oCont.GetObject("displaySpecifier","cn=user-Display")

'Add Attribute Display Names
oDisp.PutEx 3,"attributeDisplayNames" , Array("BudgetCode,BudgetCode")
oDisp.SetInfo

'Add this field to the Right-Click Context Menu
iCount = 0
If Not IsEmpty(oDisp.shellContextMenu) Then
```

```
    aMenu = oDisp.GetEx("shellContextMenu")
    iCount = iCount + 1
End If
sNewMenu = CStr(iCount) & ",&Budget code…,budgetshell.vbs"
oDisp.PutEx 3,"shellContextMenu" , Array(sNewMenu)
oDisp.SetInfo
Set sOutFile = oFileSystem.CreateTextFile(sSystemFolder & "\budgetshell.vbs",True)
sOutFile.WriteLine "Set Args = Wscript.Arguments"
sOutFile.WriteLine "Set oUser = GetObject(Args(0))"
sOutFile.WriteLine "MsgBox " & Chr(34) & "Budget Code" & Chr(34) & " & vbCRLF & " &
Chr(34) & "Budget Code: " & Chr(34) & " & oUser.BudgetCode & vbCRLF & " & Chr(34)
sOutFile.WriteLine "Set oUser = Nothing"
sOutFile.WriteLine "WScript.Quit"
sOutFile.Close
'Allow for updates
iCount = 0
If Not IsEmpty(oDisp.adminContextMenu) Then
    aMenu = oDisp.GetEx("adminContextMenu")
    iCount = iCount + 1
End If
sNewMenu = CStr(iCount) & ",&Budget Code…,budgetadmin.vbs"
oDisp.PutEx 3,"adminContextMenu" , Array(sNewMenu)
oDisp.SetInfo
MsgBox " Adding Admin Context Menu Program"
Set sOutFile = oFileSystem.CreateTextFile(sSystemFolder & "\budgetadmin.vbs",True)
sOutFile.WriteLine "Set Args = Wscript.Arguments"
sOutFile.WriteLine "Set oUser = GetObject(Args(0))"
sOutFile.WriteLine "temp = InputBox(" & Chr(34) & "Current Budget Code: " & Chr(34)
& " & oUser.BudgetCode & vbCRLF & " & Chr(34) & "New Budget Code" & Chr(34) & ")"
sOutFile.WriteLine "if temp <> " & Chr(34) & Chr(34) & " then oUser.Put " & Chr(34)
& "BudgetCode" & Chr(34) & ",temp"sOutFile.WriteLine "oUser.SetInfo"
sOutFile.WriteLine "Set oUser = Nothing"
sOutFile.WriteLine "WScript.Quit"
sOutFile.Close
Set oDisp = Nothing
Set oCont = Nothing
Set oRoot = Nothing
Set oFileSystem = Nothing
WScript.Quit
```

 It's important that you run the script listed in this recipe only one time; otherwise you may wind up with duplicate entries in the ADUC context menu.

Discussion

Modifying the default MMC snap-ins is a nontrivial task, but it can be accomplished using VBScript to add information to the display specifiers in the Configuration NC. Let's say that you've extended the user class in your forest with an auxiliary class that stores the user's budget code for his expense reports, and you want to be able to view and edit this information using ADUC. You can create a VBScript that will display and modify this information from the right-click context menu, as shown in this recipe.

Another option would be to create a VBScript file that simply displays the necessary message boxes to display and/or update the user attribute in question, after which you could use ADSI Edit or AdMod to configure your display specifiers to call that script whenever appropriate.

If you saved such a script to the *dc1**share**updatebudget.vbs* path, for example, you could then add the following information to the `adminContextMenu` attribute of `cn=user-Display,cn=409,cn=DisplaySpecifiers,cn=Configuration,<ForestRootDN>`:

```
4, &Update Budget Information,\\dc1\share\updatebudget.vbs
```

In the Windows Server 2008 version of ADUC, you can view all available attributes for an object from the Attribute Editor tab. If you do not see this tab when accessing the properties of an object, be sure that the Advanced Features option on the View menu has been selected.

See Also

MSDN: Display Specifiers and MS KB 299646 (How to Add Custom Attributes to the DSFind Pick List)

10.14 Modifying the Attributes Included with ANR

Problem

You want to modify the attributes that are included as part of ANR.

Solution

 For Windows 2000 Active Directory, you need to enable schema modifications before proceeding. See Recipe 10.2 for more information.

Using a graphical user interface

1. To proceed, you must have first indexed the attribute.
2. Open the Active Directory Schema snap-in.
3. In the left pane, click on the Attributes folder.
4. In the right pane, double-click the attribute you want to edit.
5. Check the box beside ANR.
6. Click OK.

Using a command-line interface

You can include an attribute as part of ANR by using the *ldifde* utility and an LDIF file that contains the following:

```
dn: cn=adatum-LanguagesSpoken,cn=schema,cn=configuration,<ForestRootDN>
changetype: modify
replace: searchFlags
searchFlags: 5
-
```

If the LDIF file were named *add_anr_attr.ldf*, you'd run the following command:

```
> ldifde -v -i -f add_anr_attr.ldf
```

You can also modify the **searchFlags** attribute using AdMod, as follows:

```
> admod -b <AttributeDN> searchFlags::5
```

Using VBScript

```
' This code will make an attribute part of the ANR set.
' ------ SCRIPT CONFIGURATION ------
' Set to the common name (not LDAP display dame) of the attribute
strAttrName = "<AttrCommonName>" ' e.g. adatum-LanguagesSpoken
' ------ END CONFIGURATION --------

set objRootDSE = GetObject("LDAP://RootDSE")
set objAttr = GetObject("LDAP://cn=" & strAttrName & "," & _
                        objRootDSE.Get("
schemaNamingContext"))
objAttr.Put "searchFlags", 5
objAttr.SetInfo
WScript.Echo "New ANR attribute: " & strAttrName
```

 The CLI and VBScript solutions assume that **searchFlags** wasn't previously set; if a value is present, they just blindly overwrite it. Check out Recipe 4.15 for a better solution that will enable the bit you want without overwriting any previous settings.

Using PowerShell

To set the ANR bit value using a bitwise OR operation, use the following syntax:

```
$strAttrName = "<AttrCommonName>"  # e.g. adatum-LanguagesSpoken

$root = [ADSI]"LDAP://RootDSE"
$objAttr = [ADSI]("LDAP://cn=" + $strAttrName + "," + $root.schemaNamingContext)
$objAttr.put("searchFlags", $objAttr.searchFlags.Value -bor 5)
$objAttr.setInfo()
```

Discussion

ANR is an efficient search algorithm that allows for a complex search filter to be written using a single comparison. For example, a search for (anr=Jim Smith) would translate into the following query:

- An OR filter with every attribute in the ANR set against Jim Smith*
- A filter for givenName = Jim* and sn = Smith*
- A filter for givenName = Smith* and sn = Jim*

These filters are ORed together and then processed by Active Directory. Since all ANR attributes are also indexed, the query return should come back quickly.

Here is a list of the default attributes that are included as part of ANR searches. The LDAP display name of the attribute is shown first, with the common name in parentheses:

- displayName (Display-Name)
- givenName (Given-Name)
- legacyExchangeDN (Legacy-Exchange-DN)
- msDS-AdditionalSamAccountName (ms-DS-Additional-Sam-Account-Name)
- physicalDeliveryOfficeName (Physical-Delivery-Office-Name)
- name (RDN)
- sAMAccountName (SAM-Account-Name)
- sn (Surname)

 msDS-AdditionalSamAccountName was added as an ANR attribute in Windows Server 2003.

One requirement of any new ANR attribute is that the attribute must also be indexed. ANR searches are intended to be very fast, so if a nonindexed attribute were added to the set, it could dramatically impact the performance of the searches. Therefore, Active Directory requires that each added attribute be indexed.

You can use `adfind` with the `-stats+only` switch to verify what the ANR expansion actually looks like. You can find out which attributes are included in the ANR set by using the following search criteria:

Base
```
cn=Schema,cn=Configuration,<ForestRootDN>
```
Filter
```
(&(objectcategory=attributeSchema)(searchFlags:1.2.840.113556.1.4.803:=4))
```
Scope
```
onelevel
```

You can also find attributes that are included in ANR using AdFind, as follows:
```
adfind -sc anr
```

Alternatively, to find attributes that aren't included in ANR, change the previous search filter to the following:
```
(&(objectcategory=attributeSchema)(!(searchFlags:1.2.840.113556.1.4.803:=4)))
```

See Also

Recipe 4.15 for modifying a bit flag attribute, Recipe 10.7 for adding a new attribute, MS KB 243299 (Ambiguous Name Resolution for LDAP in Windows 2000), and MS KB 243311 (Setting an Attribute's searchFlags Property to Be Indexed for ANR)

10.15 Modifying the Set of Attributes Stored on a Global Catalog

Problem

You want to add or remove an attribute in the global catalog.

Solution

 For Windows 2000 Active Directory, you need to enable schema modifications before proceeding. See Recipe 10.2 for more information.

Using a graphical user interface

1. Open the Active Directory Schema snap-in.
2. In the left pane, click on the Attributes folder.
3. In the right pane, double-click the attribute you want to edit.

4. Check the box beside "Replicate this attribute to the Global Catalog" to add to the global catalog, or uncheck to remove the global catalog.

5. Click OK.

Using a command-line interface

You can add an attribute to the global catalog by using the *ldifde* utility and an LDIF file that contains the following:

```
dn: cn=<AttrCommonName>,cn=schema,cn=configuration,<ForestRootDN>
changetype: modify
replace:
isMemberOfPartialAttributeSet
isMemberOfPartialAttributeSet: TRUE
-
```

If the LDIF file were named *add_gc_attr.ldf*, you would run the following command:

```
> ldifde -v -i -f add_gc_attr.ldf
```

You can also modify this property using AdMod, as follows:

```
> admod -schema -rb cn=<AttrCommonName> isMemberOfPartialAttributeSet::TRUE
```

Using VBScript

```
' This code adds an attribute to the global catalog.
' ------ SCRIPT CONFIGURATION ------
' Set to the common name (not LDAP display name) of the attribute.
strAttrName = "<AttrCommonName>" ' e.g. User
' Set to TRUE to add to GC, set to FALSE to remove from GC
boolAddtoGC = TRUE
' ------ END CONFIGURATION --------

set objRootDSE = GetObject("LDAP://RootDSE")
set objAttr = GetObject("LDAP://cn=" & strAttrName & "," & _
                        objRootDSE.Get("schemaNamingContext"))
objAttr.Put "isMemberOfPartialAttributeSet", boolAddtoGC
objAttr.SetInfo
WScript.Echo "Added attribute to GC: " & strAttrName
```

Using PowerShell

To add an attribute to the Partial Attribute Set using the Quest cmdlets, use the following:

```
$boolAddToGC = $true
$attr = get-QADobject -Identity 'cn=<Attribute
Name>,cn=schema,cn=configuration,<ForestRootDN> -IncludedProperties
'isMemberOfPartialAttributeSet'
$attr.isMemberOfPartialAttributeSet = $boolAddToGC
```

To use the native PowerShell commands, use the following syntax:

```
$strAttrName = "<AttrCommonName>"  # e.g. adatum-LanguagesSpoken
$boolAddToGC = $true    ## $true to "Add", $false to "Remove"
$root = [ADSI] "LDAP://RootDSE"
$objAttr = [ADSI]("LDAP://cn=" + $strAttrName + "," + $root.schemaNamingContext)
$objAttr.Put("isMemberOfPartialAttributeSet", $boolAddToGC)
$objAttr.setInfo()
```

Discussion

Each domain controller in a forest replicates a copy of the Domain naming context for its own domain, as well as copies of the forest-wide Configuration and Schema partitions. However, domain controllers do not replicate Domain naming contexts for other domains in the forest. When enabled as a global catalog server, a domain controller will make partial, read-only replicas of all the objects in other domains in the forest.

Searching against the global catalog is useful when you need to perform a single search across several naming contexts at once. The global catalog stores only a subset of each object's attributes, which is why it is considered a partial replica. Attributes stored in the global catalog are considered part of the PAS. Any attributes that you add to the PAS should be ones you'd want to use as part of global catalog searches that are not present already.

You can add to the attributes that are stored in the global catalog by setting the `isMemberOfPartialAttributeSet` attribute of an `attributeSchema` object to `TRUE`. Likewise, to remove an attribute from the PAS, set `isMemberOfPartialAttributeSet` to `FALSE` for the target attribute.

 With Windows 2000, anytime you added an attribute to the PAS a full sync of all of the global catalog contents was done for every global catalog server. This could have a major impact on replication in some multidomain environments, as the amount of data that needed to replicate across your forest could be significant. Fortunately, this limitation was removed in Windows Server 2003 so that a full sync is no longer performed. Removing an attribute from the partial attribute list does not force a global catalog sync, even under Windows 2000.

You can find which attributes are included in the global catalog by using a query with the following criteria:

Base
    cn=Schema,cn=Configuration,<ForestRootDN>

Filter
    (&(objectcategory=attributeSchema)(isMemberOfPartialAttributeSet=TRUE))

Scope
    onelevel

You can also find attributes that are included in the PAS using AdFind, as follows:

```
adfind -sc pas
```

Alternatively, to find attributes that aren't in the global catalog, you only need to change part of the previous filter to the following:

```
(isMemberOfPartialAttributeSet=FALSE)
```

See Also

MS KB 229662 (How to Control What Data Is Stored in the Global Catalog), MS KB 230663 (How to Enumerate Attributes Replicated to the Global Catalog), MS KB 232517 (Global Catalog Attributes and Replication Properties), MS KB 248717 (How to Modify Attributes That Replicate to the Global Catalog), MS KB 257203 (Common Default Attributes Set for Active Directory and Global Catalog), and MS KB 313992 (How to Add an Attribute to the Global Catalog in Windows 2000)

10.16 Finding Nonreplicated and Constructed Attributes

Problem

You want to find the attributes that are not replicated or that are constructed by Active Directory.

Solution

Using a graphical user interface

1. Open LDP.
2. From the menu, select Connection→Connect.
3. For Server, enter the name of a domain controller (or leave blank to do a serverless bind).
4. For Port, enter 389.
5. Click OK.
6. From the menu, select Connection→Bind.
7. Enter credentials of a domain user.
8. Click OK.
9. From the menu, select Browse→Search.
10. For BaseDN, type the Schema Container DN (for example, cn=schema,cn=configuration,dc=adatum,dc=com).
11. For Scope, select One Level.
12. To find nonreplicated attributes, use the following for Filter:

```
        (&(objectcategory=attributeSchema)(systemFlags:1.2.840.113556.1.4.803:=1))
```

13. To find constructed attributes, use the following for Filter:

```
        (&(objectcategory=attributeSchema)(systemFlags:1.2.840.113556.1.4.803:=4))
```

14. Click Run.

Using a command-line interface

To find the nonreplicated attributes using DSQuery, use the following command:

```
> dsquery * cn=schema,cn=configuration,<ForestRootDN> -attr "cn" -filter
"(&(objectcategory=attributeSchema)(systemFlags:1.2.840.113556.1.4.803:=1))"
```

To find the nonreplicated attributes using AdFind, use the following:

```
> adfind -sc norepl
```

To find the constructed attributes using DSQuery, use the following command:

```
> dsquery * cn=schema,cn=configuration,<ForestRootDN> -attr "cn" -filter
"(&(objectcategory=attributeSchema)(systemFlags:1.2.840.113556.1.4.803:=4))"
```

To find the constructed attributes using AdFind, use the following:

```
> adfind -sc constructed
```

Using VBScript

```
' This script will print out the nonreplicated
' and constructed attributes.
set objRootDSE = GetObject("LDAP://RootDSE")
strBase = "<LDAP://" & objRootDSE.Get("SchemaNamingContext") & ">;"
strFilter = "(&(objectcategory=attributeSchema)" _
            & "(
systemFlags:1.2.840.113556.1.4.803:=1));"
strAttrs = "cn;"
strScope = "onelevel"

set objConn = CreateObject("ADODB.Connection")
objConn.Provider = "ADsDSOObject"
objConn.Open "Active Directory Provider"
set objRS = objConn.Execute(strBase & strFilter & strAttrs & strScope)
objRS.MoveFirst
WScript.Echo "Nonreplicated attributes: "
while Not objRS.EOF
    Wscript.Echo " " & objRS.Fields(0).Value
    objRS.MoveNext
wend

strFilter = "(&(objectcategory=attributeSchema) " _
            & "(systemFlags:1.2.840.113556.1.4.803:=4));"
set objRS = objConn.Execute(strBase & strFilter & strAttrs & strScope)
objRS.MoveFirst
WScript.Echo ""
WScript.Echo "
Constructed attributes: "
```

```
        while Not objRS.EOF
            Wscript.Echo " " & objRS.Fields(0).Value
            objRS.MoveNext
        wend
```

Using PowerShell

You can obtain information about nonreplicated and constructed attributes using the Quest AD cmdlets or ADSI, as follows:

```
"Non-Replicated Attributes:"
get-QADObject -SearchRoot "cn=schema,cn=configuration,<ForestRootDN>" -LdapFilter
"(&(objectcategory=attributeSchema)(systemFlags:1.2.840.113556.1.4.803:=1))"

"Constructed Attributes:"
get-QADObject -SearchRoot "cn=schema,cn=configuration,<ForestRootDN>" -LdapFilter
"(&(objectcategory=attributeSchema)(systemFlags:1.2.840.113556.1.4.803:=4))"

function search([string]$searchDN, [string]$localfilter)
{
    $searcher = New-Object System.DirectoryServices.DirectorySearcher
    $searcher.SearchRoot = [ADSI]("LDAP://" + $searchDN)
    $searcher.PageSize = 1000
    $searcher.Filter = $localfilter

    return $searcher.FindAll()
}

$root = [ADSI]"LDAP://RootDSE"
$filter = "(&(objectCategory=attributeSchema)(systemFlags:1.2.840.113556.1.4.803:="

"Non-Replicated Attributes"
search $root.schemaNamingContext ($filter + "1))")

"Constructed Attributes"
search $root.schemaNamingContext ($filter + "4))")
```

Discussion

The systemFlags attribute of attributeSchema objects defines a few special attribute properties, including whether an attribute is not replicated between domain controllers and whether it is dynamically constructed by Active Directory.

Most attributes are replicated after they are updated on an object, but some never replicate between domain controllers. These attributes are considered nonreplicated. An example of a nonreplicated attribute you may be familiar with is the lastLogon attribute, which stores the last logon time for user and computer objects. Whenever a user or computer logs in to Active Directory, the authenticating domain controller updates the user or computer's lastLogon attribute, but the update does not get replicated out to other domain controllers.

Constructed attributes are automatically maintained by Active Directory and cannot be set manually. A good example of a constructed attribute is the new msDS-Approx-Immed-Subordinates that first became available in Windows Server 2003. That attribute contains the approximate number of child objects within a container. Obviously this attribute wouldn't be of much value if you had to maintain it, so Active Directory does it automatically.

One of the downsides to constructed attributes is that you cannot search against them. For example, we cannot perform a search to find all containers that have more than 10 objects in them (i.e., msDS-Approx-Immed-Subordinates>10). This would return an operations error. Constructed attributes can be returned only as part of the attribute set for a query and cannot be used as part of the query itself.

To find the nonreplicated or constructed attributes, you have to use a bitwise LDAP filter against attributeSchema objects. A bit value of 1 indicates the attribute is nonreplicated and a value of 4 indicates the attribute is constructed.

See Also

Recipe 4.12 for searching with a bitwise filter

10.17 Finding the Linked Attributes

Problem

You want to find attributes that are linked.

Solution

Using a graphical user interface

1. Open LDP.
2. From the menu, select Connection→Connect.
3. For Server, enter the name of a domain controller (or leave blank to do a serverless bind).
4. For Port, enter 389.
5. Click OK.
6. From the menu, select Connection→Bind.
7. Enter credentials of a domain user.
8. Click OK.
9. From the menu, select Browse→Search.
10. For BaseDN, type the Schema container DN (e.g., cn=schema, cn=configuration,dc=adatum,dc=com).
11. For Scope, select One Level.

12. To find linked attributes, use the following for Filter:

```
(&(objectcategory=attributeSchema)(linkid=*))
```

13. Click Run.

Using a command-line interface

You can return a list of linked attributes using either the built-in DSQuery tool or AdMod. To use DSQuery, use the following syntax:

```
> dsquery * cn=schema,cn=configuration,<ForestRootDN> -scope onelevel -filter
"(&(objectcategory=attributeSchema)(linkid=*))" -attr cn linkID
```

To return a list of linked attributes with AdFind, use the following:

```
> adfind -sc linked
```

Using VBScript

```
' This code prints out all of the attributes that are linked
' and their corresponding linkID values.
set objRootDSE = GetObject("LDAP://RootDSE")
strBase   = "<LDAP://" & objRootDSE.Get("SchemaNamingContext") & ">;"
strFilter = "(&(objectcategory=attributeSchema)(linkid=*));"
strAttrs  = "cn,linkid;"
strScope  = "onelevel"

set objConn = CreateObject("ADODB.Connection")
objConn.Provider = "ADsDSOObject"
objConn.Open "Active Directory Provider"
set objRS = objConn.Execute(strBase & strFilter & strAttrs & strScope)
objRS.MoveFirst
while Not objRS.EOF
    Wscript.Echo objRS.Fields(1).Value & " : " & objRS.Fields(0).Value
    objRS.MoveNext
wend
```

Using PowerShell

You can obtain linked attribute information using the Quest AD cmdlets or ADSI, as follows:

```
get-QADObject -SearchRoot "cn=schema,cn=configuration,<ForestRootDN>" -LdapFilter
"(&(objectcategory=attributeSchema)(linkId=*))"

function search([string]$searchDN, [string]$localfilter)
{
    $searcher = New-Object System.DirectoryServices.DirectorySearcher
    $searcher.SearchRoot = [ADSI]("LDAP://" + $searchDN)
    $searcher.PageSize = 1000
    $searcher.SearchScope = [System.DirectoryServices.SearchScope]::OneLevel
    $searcher.Filter = $localfilter

    return $searcher.FindAll()
}
```

```
$root = [ADSI]"LDAP://RootDSE"
$filter = "(&(objectcategory=attributeSchema)(linkId=*))"

$results = search $root.schemaNamingContext $filter
foreach ($r in $results) {
    $r.Properties.cn.Item(0).ToString() + " : " + $r.Properties.linkid.Item(0)
}
```

Discussion

The values of some attributes in Active Directory are linked. For example, if you set the manager attribute on one user object to be the DN of a second user object, the reports attribute on the second user object will automatically contain the first user object's DN. In this example, the manager attribute, or the attribute that gets set, is considered the *forward link*, and the reports attribute, or the attribute that automatically gets calculated, is called the *back link*. Another common example is group membership. The member attribute of the group object represents the forward link, while the memberOf attribute of the corresponding object (e.g., *user*) represents the backlink.

You can identify which attributes are linked in the schema by searching for attribute Schema objects that have a linkID attribute that contains some value. The linkID value for a forward-link attribute will be an even, positive number. The corresponding back-link attribute will be the forward linkID plus 1. For example, the manager attribute linkID is 42, and the backlink reports attribute has a linkID of 43.

10.18 Finding the Structural, Auxiliary, Abstract, and 88 Classes

Problem

You want to list the structural, auxiliary, abstract, and 88 classes.

Solution

Using a graphical user interface

1. Open the Active Directory Schema snap-in.
2. In the left pane, click on the Classes folder.
3. In the right pane, the list of all the classes will be displayed. The Type column contains the type of class. Even though you can click on the column header, it currently does not sort the classes by type.

Using a command-line interface

You can return the list of Active Directory classes using either DSQuery or AdFind. DSQuery takes the following syntax:

```
> dsquery * cn=schema,cn=configuration,<ForestRootDN> -limit 0 -scope onelevel
-filter "(objectcategory=classSchema)" -attr lDAPDisplayName objectclasscategory
```

AdFind requires the following syntax:

```
> adfind -schema -f "(objectcategory=classSchema)" lDAPDisplayName
objectClassCategory
```

Using VBScript

```
' This code prints out classes of a particular type
' ------ SCRIPT CONFIGURATION ------
' Set the following to TRUE or FALSE depending if you want to
' view or not view classes of the type defined by the variable
boolShowStructural = TRUE
boolShowStructural = TRUE
boolShowAuxiliary  = TRUE
boolShowAbstract   = TRUE
boolShow88         = TRUE
' ------ END CONFIGURATION ---------

set objRootDSE = GetObject("LDAP://RootDSE")
set objSchemaCont = GetObject("LDAP://cn=schema," & _
                              objRootDSE.Get("configurationNamingContext"))
objSchemaCont.Filter = Array("classSchema")
WScript.Echo "Loading classes, this will take a few seconds."
for each objClass in objSchemaCont
   WScript.StdOut.Write(".")
   if objClass.Get("
objectClassCategory") = 0 then
       str88 = str88 & vbTab & objClass.Get("lDAPDisplayName") & vbCrlf
   elseif objClass.Get("objectClassCategory") = 1 then
       strStruct = strStruct & vbTab & _
                   objClass.Get("lDAPDisplayName") & vbCrlf
   elseif objClass.Get("objectClassCategory") = 2 then
       strAbst = strAbst & vbTab & objClass.Get("lDAPDisplayName") & vbCrlf
   elseif objClass.Get("objectClassCategory") = 3 then
       strAux = strAux & vbTab & objClass.Get("lDAPDisplayName") & vbCrlf
   else
       WScript.Echo "Unknown class type: " & _
                   objClass.Get("lDAPDisplayName") & vbCrlf
   end if
next
WScript.Echo vbCrlf

if boolShowStructural = TRUE then
   WScript.Echo " Structural Classes: "
   WScript.Echo strStruct
   WScript.Echo
end if

if boolShowAbstract = TRUE then
   WScript.Echo " Abstract Classes: "
   WScript.Echo strAbst
   WScript.Echo
end if
```

```
if boolShowAuxiliary = TRUE then
    WScript.Echo "Auxiliary Classes: "
    WScript.Echo strAux
    WScript.Echo
end if

if boolShow88 = TRUE then
    WScript.Echo "88 Classes: "
    WScript.Echo str88
    WScript.Echo
end if
```

Using PowerShell

You can obtain information about different class types using the Quest cmdlets or by using ADSI, as follows:

```
$str88 = 0
$strStruct = 1
$strAbstr = 2
$strAux = 3
Write-Host "88 classes:"
get-QADObject -SearchRoot "cn=schema,cn=configuration,<ForestRootDN>" -LdapFilter
"(&(objectcategory=classSchema)(objectClassCategory=$str88))"
Write-Host "Structural classes:"
get-QADObject -SearchRoot "cn=schema,cn=configuration,<ForestRootDN>" -LdapFilter
"(&(objectcategory=classSchema)(objectClassCategory=$strStruct))"
Write-Host "Abstract classes:"
get-QADObject -SearchRoot "cn=schema,cn=configuration,<ForestRootDN>" -LdapFilter
"(&(objectcategory=classSchema)(objectClassCategory=$strAbstr))"
Write-Host "Auxilliary classes:"
get-QADObject -SearchRoot "cn=schema,cn=configuration,<ForestRootDN>" -LdapFilter
"(&(objectcategory=classSchema)(objectClassCategory=$strAux))"

function search([string]$searchDN, [string]$localfilter)
{
    $searcher = New-Object System.DirectoryServices.DirectorySearcher
    $searcher.SearchRoot = [ADSI]("LDAP://" + $searchDN)
    $searcher.PageSize = 1000
    $searcher.Filter = $localfilter

    return $searcher.FindAll()
}
function display ($results)
{
    foreach ($r in $results) {
        "`t" + $r.Properties.ldapdisplayname.Item(0)
    }
}

$root = [ADSI]"LDAP://RootDSE"
$filter = "(&(objectcategory=classSchema)(objectClassCategory="

"88 Classes:"
```

```
display (search $root.schemaNamingContext ($filter + "0))"))

"Structural Classes:"
display (search $root.schemaNamingContext ($filter + "1))"))

"Abstract Classes:"
display (search $root.schemaNamingContext ($filter + "2))"))

"Auxilliary Classes:"
display (search $root.schemaNamingContext ($filter + "3))"))
```

Discussion

There are four supported class types in the Active Directory schema. The class type is defined by the `objectClassCategory` attribute on `classSchema` objects. Each class type is used for a different purpose relating to organizing and inheriting classes. Table 10-6 describes each type.

Table 10-6. Object class category values

Name	Value	Description
88	0	Legacy class type defined by the original X.500 standards. It should not be used for new classes.
Structural	1	Used for instantiating objects. Can be comprised of abstract, auxiliary, and other structural classes.
Abstract	2	Used to define a high-level grouping of attributes that can be used as part of other abstract or structural class definitions. Objects cannot be instantiated using an abstract class.
Auxiliary	3	Used as a collection of attributes that can be applied to other abstract, auxiliary, or structural classes.

10.19 Finding the Mandatory and Optional Attributes of a Class

Problem

You want to view the mandatory and optional attributes of a class.

Solution

Using a graphical user interface

1. Open the Active Directory Schema snap-in.
2. In the left pane, click on the Classes folder.
3. In the right pane, double-click the class you want to view.
4. Click on the Attributes tab.

Using a command-line interface

You can enumerate the mandatory and optional attributes of a class using either DSQuery or AdFind. DSQuery takes the following syntax:

```
> dsquery * cn=<ClassCommonName>,cn=schema,cn=configuration,<ForestRootDN> -l
-attr mayContain mustContain systemMayContain systemMustContain
```

To list these attributes using AdFind, use the following syntax:

```
> adfind -schema -rb cn=<ClassCommonName> mayContain mustContain systemMayContain
systemMustContain
```

Using VBScript

```
' This code displays the mandatory and optional attributes for a class.
' ------ SCRIPT CONFIGURATION -----
' Set to common name of class to view
strClassName = "<ClassCommonName>" ' e.g. Surname
' ------ END CONFIGURATION --------

set objRootDSE = GetObject("LDAP://RootDSE")
set objClass = GetObject("LDAP://cn=" & strClassName & "," & _
                         objRootDSE.Get("schemaNamingContext"))

WScript.Echo "Class: " & strClassName & vbCrlf

' Need to enable this so that if an attribute is not set, the code won't fail
on error resume next

WScript.Echo "mayContain:"
for each strVal in objClass.Get("mayContain")
    WScript.Echo vbTab & strVal
next

WScript.Echo vbCrlf & "systemMayContain:"
for each strVal in objClass.Get("systemMayContain")
    WScript.Echo vbTab & strVal
next

WScript.Echo vbCrlf & "mustContain:"
for each strVal in objClass.Get("mustContain")
    WScript.Echo vbTab & strVal
next

WScript.Echo vbCrlf & "systemMustContain:"
for each strVal in objClass.Get("systemMustContain")
    WScript.Echo vbTab & strVal
next
```

Using PowerShell

```
$obj = get-QADObject -Identity "cn=<Class Name>,cn=schema,cn=configuration,Forest
Root DN>" -IncludedProperties maycontain, mustcontain, systemmaycontain,
systemmustcontain
$obj.mayContain
$obj.mustContain
$obj.systemMayContain
$obj.systemMustContain

$strClassName = "<ClassCommonName>"  # e.g. User
```

```
#
$root = [ADSI] "LDAP://RootDSE"

$obj = [ADSI]( "LDAP://cn=" + $strClassName + "," + $root.schemaNamingContext)
"mayContain: "
foreach ($val in $obj.mayContain) { "`t" + $val; }
"`nmustContain: "
foreach ($val in $obj.mustContain) { "`t" + $val; }
"`nsystemMayContain: "
foreach ($val in $obj.systemMayContain) { "`t" + $val; }
"`nsystemMustContain: "
foreach ($val in $obj.systemMustContain) { "`t" + $val; }
```

Discussion

The mayContain and systemMayContain attributes define the optional attributes for a class, while the mustContain and systemMustContain attributes contain the mandatory attributes. The systemMayContain and systemMustContain attributes are set by Active Directory itself and cannot be modified. You can only populate the mustContain attribute when a class is first created; you cannot add attributes to it after the fact. This is so that you are not inadvertently able to modify a class such that existing instances of that class become invalid.

It is also worth noting that each of the solutions displays only the attributes defined directly on the class. It will not show any inherited attributes that are defined by inherited classes.

10.20 Modifying the Default Security of a Class

Problem

You want to modify the default security that is applied to objects instantiated from a particular structural class.

Solution

For Windows 2000 Active Directory, you need to enable schema modifications before proceeding. See Recipe 10.2 for more information.

Using a graphical user interface

1. Open the Active Directory Schema snap-in.
2. In the left pane, click on the Classes folder.
3. In the right pane, double-click the class you want to modify the security for.

4. Click the Default Security tab.

5. Modify the security as necessary.

6. Click OK.

Using a command-line interface

```
> admod -schema -rb cn=<ClassShortName>
defaultSecurityDescriptor::"O:AOG:DAD:(A;;RPWPCCDCLCSWRCWDWOGA;;;S-1-0-0)"
```

Using VBScript

```
' This code modifies the defaultSecurityDescriptor of a class
' ------ SCRIPT CONFIGURATION -----
' Set to the common name (not LDAP display dame) of the class
strClassName = "<ClassCommonName>" ' e.g. User
' ------ END CONFIGURATION --------

set objRootDSE = GetObject("LDAP://RootDSE")
set objClass = GetObject("LDAP://cn=" & strAttrName & "," & _
                          objRootDSE.Get("schemaNamingContext"))
objClass.Put "defaultSecurityDescriptor", _
  "O:AOG:DAD:(A;;RPWPCCDCLCSWRCWDWOGA;;;S-1-0-0)"
objClass.SetInfo
WScript.Echo "Default Security Descriptor modified"
```

Using PowerShell

```
get-QADObject -Identity "cn=<Class Name>,cn=schema,cn=configuration,<Forest Root
  DN>" -IncludeAllProperties | set-QADObject -ObjectAttributes
@{defaultSecurityDescriptor=" O:AOG:DAD:(A;;RPWPCCDCLCSWRCWDWOGA;;;S-1-0-0)"}

$strClassName = "<ClassCommonName>"  # e.g. User

# what is the new default security for the object?
$strSDDL = O:AOG:DAD:(A;;RPWPCCDCLCSWRCWDWOGA;;;S-1-0-0)"

$root = [ADSI]"LDAP://RootDSE"

$obj = [ADSI]("LDAP://cn=" + $strClassName + "," + $root.schemaNamingContext)
$obj.Put("defaultSecurityDescriptor", $strSDDL)
$obj.SetInfo()
```

Discussion

Whenever a new object is created in Active Directory, if a security descriptor is not specified in the object creation, a default security descriptor (SD) is applied to it. Then any inherited security from its parent container is applied. The default security descriptor is stored in the defaultSecurityDescriptor attribute of the classSchema object. If you modify the default SD, every new object will get that SD, but it does not affect any existing objects.

Using a command-line interface

The `defaultSecurityDescriptor` attribute is stored in Active Directory using the Security Descriptor Definition Language (SDDL) format, and will return data formatted similar to the following:

```
"O:AOG:DAD:(A;;RPWPCCDCLCSWRCWDWOGA;;;S-1-0-0)"
```

For more information on formulating SDDL strings, see the Platform Software Development Kit (SDK) or MSDN.

 When creating your own Active Directory classes, we recommend against setting a default security descriptor, as this feature can create issues when working with delegated permissions.

When modifying the `defaultSecurityDescriptor` attribute using the CLI, VBscript, or PowerShell, it's important to remember that this is a single-valued attribute. This means that if you put any value into this attribute, it will overwrite all existing Security Descriptors that have been defined on the object. If you wish to append a new entry onto the default security descriptor, you will need to retrieve the existing value in the attribute, append the new entry that you wish to add, and then write the full string back to the attribute.

See Also

MS KB 265399 (How to Change Default Permissions for Objects That Are Created in the Active Directory) and MSDN: Security Descriptor String Format

10.21 Managing the Confidentiality Bit

Problem

You want to manage the confidentiality of a schema attribute.

Solution

Using a command-line interface

```
admod -schema -rb cn=<AttrName> searchFlags::128
```

Using VBScript

```
' This code safely modifies the
' confidentiality bit of an attribute.
' ------ SCRIPT CONFIGURATION ------
strAttribute = "<schemaAttributeDN>"
  ' e.g. "cn=SalesUser-Description,cn=Schema,
```

```
      ' cn=Configuration,dc=adatum,dc=com"
strAttr = "searchFlags"           ' e.g. adatum-UserProperties
boolEnableBit = <TRUEorFALSE>     ' e.g. TRUE
intBit = 128
' ------ END CONFIGURATION --------

set objAttribute = GetObject("LDAP://" & strAttribute)
intBitsOrig = objAttribute.Get(strAttr)
intBitsCalc = CalcBit(intBitsOrig, intBit, boolEnableBit)

if intBitsOrig <> intBitsCalc then
    objObject.Put strAttr, intBitsCalc
    objObject.SetInfo
    WScript.Echo "Changed " & strAttr & " from " & intBitsOrig & " to " & intBitsCalc
else
    WScript.Echo "Did not need to change " & strAttr & " (" & intBitsOrig & ")"
end if

Function CalcBit(intValue, intBit, boolEnable)

    CalcBit = intValue

    if boolEnable = TRUE then
        CalcBit = intValue Or intBit
    else
        if intValue And intBit then
            CalcBit = intValue Xor intBit
        end if
    end if

End Function
```

Using PowerShell

To set the searchFlags bit value using a logical OR operation, use the following syntax:

```
$objAttr = [ADSI] "LDAP://cn=<AttrName>,cn=schema,cn=Configuration,<ForestRootDN>"
$currentSearchFlags = $objAttr.searchFlags.Value
$newSearchFlags = $currentSearchFlags -bor 128
$objAttr.put("searchFlags", $newSearchFlags)
$objAttr.setInfo()
```

Discussion

The confidentiality bit was introduced in Windows Server 2003 Service Pack 1; it is a feature that allows you to restrict access to attributes that should not be accessible to all users. For example, you may have created an attribute to store users' Social Security Number information. Even though this attribute may be populated for every user object in the directory, you will likely wish to restrict access to that specific attribute to only a subset of your personnel. The confidentiality bit is set in the searchFlags attribute by setting bit 7 (128) to a value of 1. Once you've done this, the Read permission on that attribute will not be sufficient to access the information stored in it; you'll need to grant the Control_Access permission to allow a user or group to view the contents of the attribute using LDP. (Unfortunately, the current version of *dsacls* does not allow you to set the `Control_Access` permission via the command line.)

While the confidentiality bit is a great improvement in Active Directory security, it does have two significant limitations. The first is that there is no supported mechanism to set the confidentiality bit on any attributes that are a part of the base schema; you can, however, obtain a list of these attributes by searching for attributes that have bit 4 (16 in decimal) set to 1.

Second, there are certain default permissions included with Active Directory that will still allow certain security principals to access the information stored in confidential attributes; these groups include the *Administrators*, *Account Operators*, and any user or group who has the Full Control permission on an object containing a confidential attribute.

See Also

Recipe 4.15 for more on modifying a bitwise attribute and "How the Active Directory Schema Works" at *http://www.microsoft.com/technet/prodtechnol/windowsserver2003/library/TechRef/e3525d00-a746-4466-bb87-140acb44a603.mspx*

10.22 Adding an Attribute to the Read-Only Filtered Attribute Set (RO-FAS)

Problem

You want to add an attribute to the RO-FAS to prevent it from being replicated to any Read-Only Domain Controllers (RODCs) in your environment.

Solution

Using a command-line interface

```
admod -schema -rb cn=<AttrName> searchFlags::512
```

Using VBScript

```
' This code safely adds an attribute to the Read-Only Filtered Attribute Set.
' ------ SCRIPT CONFIGURATION ------
strAttribute = "<schemaAttributeDN>"
  ' e.g. "cn=adatum-EmplID,cn=Schema,
  ' cn=Configuration,dc=adatum,dc=com"
strAttr = "searchFlags"
boolEnableBit = <TRUEorFALSE> ' e.g. TRUE
intBit = 512
' ------ END CONFIGURATION --------

set objAttribute = GetObject("LDAP://" & strAttribute)
```

```
    intBitsOrig = objAttribute.Get(strAttr)
    intBitsCalc = CalcBit(intBitsOrig, intBit, boolEnableBit)

    if intBitsOrig <> intBitsCalc then
        objObject.Put strAttr, intBitsCalc
        objObject.SetInfo
        WScript.Echo "Changed " & strAttr & " from " & intBitsOrig & " to " & intBitsCalc
    else
        WScript.Echo "Did not need to change " & strAttr & " (" & intBitsOrig & ")"
    end if

    Function CalcBit(intValue, intBit, boolEnable)

        CalcBit = intValue

        if boolEnable = TRUE then
            CalcBit = intValue Or intBit
        else
            if intValue And intBit then
                CalcBit = intValue Xor intBit
            end if
        end if

    End Function
```

Using PowerShell

To set the searchFlags bit value using a logical OR operation, use the following syntax:

```
$objAttr = [ADSI] "LDAP://cn=<AttrName>,cn=schema,cn=Configuration,<ForestRootDN>"
$currentSearchFlags = $objAttr.searchFlags.Value
$newSearchFlags = $currentSearchFlags -bor 512
$objAttr.put("searchFlags", $newSearchFlags)
$objAttr.setInfo()
```

Discussion

As discussed in Chapter 3, Read-Only Domain Controllers contain a read-only copy of all partitions that are held by a writable domain controller, with the exception of attributes that are configured as part of the RO-FAS, as well as user credentials, except for those that are specifically configured so that they are allowed to be cached to one or more RODCs.

Attributes that are configured as part of the RO-FAS are not replicated to any RODCs within an Active Directory forest. Because this data is not replicated to RODCs, the data will not be resident on an RODC if it is compromised or stolen. Administrators can add any attribute to the RO-FAS that is not a system-critical attribute; that is, any attribute that does not have a schemaFlagsEx attribute of TRUE.

As a best practice, Microsoft recommends that the forest functional level be set to Windows Server 2008 before configuring the RO-FAS, and that any attributes destined for the RO-FAS be configured as such before any RODCs are deployed in the environment. Both of these recommendations will ensure that data contained in the RO-FAS will never be replicated to an RODC. Additionally, any attribute that is configured as part of the RO-FAS should also be configured with the confidentiality bit for further security.

For additional information on Read-Only Domain Controllers and the RO-FAS, we suggest reading Chapter 7 of *Active Directory*.

See Also

Recipe 10.21 for more on managing confidential data in Active Directory

10.23 Deactivating Classes and Attributes

Problem

You want to deactivate a class or attribute in the schema because you no longer need it.

Solution

Using a graphical user interface

1. Open the Active Directory Schema snap-in.
2. In the left pane, click on the Classes folder or the Attributes folder.
3. In the right pane, double-click the class or attribute you want to deactivate.
4. Uncheck the box beside "Class is active" or "Attribute is active."
5. Click OK.

Using a command-line interface

You can deactivate a class using the *ldifde* utility and an LDIF file that contains the following lines:

```
dn: cn=<SchemaObjectCommonName>,cn=schema,cn=configuration,<ForestRootDN>
changetype: modify
replace: isDefunct
isDefunct: TRUE
-
```

If the LDIF file were named *deactivate_class.ldf*, you would run the following command:

```
> ldifde -v -i -f deactivate_class.ldf
```

You can also deactivate a class using AdMod, as follows:

```
> admod -schema -rb cn=<SchemaObjectCommonName>
isDefunct::TRUE
```

Using VBScript

```
' This code deactivates a
' class or attribute.
' ------ SCRIPT CONFIGURATION ------
strName = "<SchemaObjectCommonName>" ' e.g. adatum-LanguagesSpoken
' ------ END CONFIGURATION --------
set objRootDSE = GetObject("LDAP://RootDSE")
set objSchemaObject = GetObject("LDAP://cn=" & strName & "," & _
                                objRootDSE.Get("schemaNamingContext"))
objSchemaObject.Put "isDefunct", TRUE
objSchemaObject.SetInfo
WScript.Echo "Schema object deactivated: " & strName
```

Using PowerShell

To deactivate a schema attribute or class using the Quest cmdlets, use the following syntax:

```
get-QADObject -Identity "cn=<ObjectName>,cn=schema,cn=configuration,<ForestRootDN>
-IncludedProperties 'isDefunct' | set-QADObject -ObjectAttributes
@{isDefunct="TRUE"}
```

To deactivate a schema object using native PowerShell methods, use the following:

```
$obj = [ADSI] "LDAP://cn=<ObjectName>,cn=schema,cn=configuration,<ForestRootDN>"
$obj.put("isDefunct", $true)
$obj.SetInfo()
```

Discussion

There is no supported way to delete classes or attributes defined in the schema. You can, however, deactivate them, also known as making them *defunct*. Before you deactivate a class, make sure that no instantiated objects of that class exist. If you want to deactivate an attribute, you should make sure no object classes define the attribute as mandatory. After you've verified the class or attribute is no longer being used, you can deactivate by setting the isDefunct attribute to TRUE. You can always reactivate it at a later time by simply setting isDefunct to FALSE. With Windows Server 2003 and Windows Server 2008 Active Directory, you can even redefine the class or attribute while it is defunct. This gives you much more flexibility over reusing classes or attributes you may have added before, but no longer want.

See Also

Recipe 10.24 for redefining classes and attributes

10.24 Redefining Classes and Attributes

 This recipe requires the Windows Server 2003 or Windows Server 2008 forest functional level.

Problem

You want to redefine a class or attribute that was previously created.

Solution

To redefine a class or attribute, you must first deactivate it by setting the `isDefunct` attribute to `TRUE` (see Recipe 10.23 for more details). If you are deactivating a class, make sure that no objects are instantiated that use the class. If you are deactivating an attribute, make sure that it isn't populated on any objects and remove it from any classes that have it defined as part of `mayContain` and `mustContain`. After the class or attribute has been deactivated, you can modify (i.e., redefine) the LDAP display name (`lDAPDisplayName`), the OID (`governsID` or `attributeID`), the syntax (`attributeSyntax` and `oMSyntax`), and the `schemaIDGUID`. The one attribute that you cannot modify is the common name.

Discussion

Redefining schema objects became available in Windows Server 2003. Although you still cannot delete schema objects, you can work around many of the reasons that would cause you to want to delete a schema object by redefining it instead. Redefining schema objects comes in handy if you accidentally mistype an OID (`governsID/attributeID`) or `lDAPDisplayName`, or no longer need an attribute you previously created. You can reuse it by renaming the attribute and giving it a different syntax.

See Also

Recipe 10.23 for deactivating classes and attributes

10.25 Reloading the Schema Cache

Problem

You want to reload the schema cache so that schema extensions will take effect immediately.

Solution

Using a graphical user interface

1. Open the Active Directory Schema snap-in.
2. In the left pane, click on Active Directory Schema.
3. Right-click on the label and select "Reload the Schema."

Using a command-line interface

You can reload the schema by using the *ldifde* utility and an LDIF file that contains the following:

```
dn:
changetype: modify
add: schemaUpdateNow
schemaUpdateNow: 1
-
```

If the LDIF file were named *reload.ldf*, you would run the following command:

```
> ldifde -v -i -f reload.ldf
```

You can also reload the schema cache using AdMod, as follows:

```
> admod -sc refreshschema
```

Using VBScript

```
set objRootDSE = GetObject("LDAP://dc1/RootDSE")
objRootDSE.Put "schemaUpdateNow", 1
objRootDSE.SetInfo
WScript.Echo "Schema reloaded"
```

Using PowerShell

```
$objRootDSE = [ADSI] "LDAP://<DCName>/RootDSE" # Specify the Schema Master FSMO
$objRootDSE.put("schemaUpdateNOW", 1)
$objRootDSE.SetInfo()
```

Discussion

Each domain controller maintains a complete copy of the schema in memory to make access to the schema very fast. This is called the *schema cache*. When you extend the schema on the Schema FSMO role owner, the change is written to the schema cache, and not committed to disk yet. The schema automatically commits any changes to the schema every five minutes if a change has taken place, but you can also do it manually/ programmatically by writing to the schemaUpdateNow operational attribute of the RootDSE on the Schema FSMO role owner. Once that is done, any changes to the schema cache are written to disk. ·

It is necessary to force a schema cache update if your schema extensions reference newly created attributes or classes. For example, let's say that you want to create one new auxiliary class that contains one new attribute. To do that, you would first need to create the attribute and then create the auxiliary class. As part of the auxiliary class's definition, you would need to reference the new attribute, but unless you reload the schema cache, an error would be returned stating that the attribute does not exist. For this reason, you need to add an additional step. First, create the attribute, then reload the schema cache, and finally create the auxiliary class. Here is what an LDIF representation would look like:

```
dn: cn=adatum-TestAttr,cn=schema,cn=configuration,dc=adatum,dc=com
changetype: add
objectclass: attributeSchema
lDAPDisplayName: adatum-TestAttr
attributeId: 1.3.6.1.4.1.999.1.1.28.312
oMSyntax: 20
attributeSyntax: 2.5.5.4
isSingleValued: FALSE
searchFlags: 1

dn:
changetype: modify
add: schemaUpdateNow
schemaUpdateNow: 1
-

dn: cn=adatum-TestClass,cn=schema,cn=configuration,dc=adatum,dc=com
changetype: add
objectclass: classSchema
lDAPDisplayName: adatum-TestClass
governsId: 1.3.6.1.4.1.999.1.1.28.311
subClassOf: top
objectClassCategory: 3
mayContain: adatum-TestAttr
```

See Also

Recipe 10.7 for adding a new attribute to the schema and Recipe 10.9 for adding a new class to the schema

10.26 Managing the Schema Master FSMO

Problem

You want to view, transfer, or seize the Schema Master FSMO for your Active Directory Forest.

Solution

Using a graphical user interface

To view the current Schema Master FSMO role holder, do the following:

1. Open the Active Directory Schema snap-in.
2. Right-click on Active Directory Schema in the left pane and select Operations Master.

To transfer the Schema Master to another server, follow these steps:

1. Open the Active Directory Schema snap-in. Right-click on Active Directory Schema and select "Connect to Domain Controller." Select the DC that you wish to transfer the FSMO role to.
2. Right-click on Active Directory Schema in the left pane and select Operations Master.
3. Click the Change button.
4. Click OK twice.
5. You should then see a message stating whether the transfer was successful.

Using a command-line interface

To query the owner of the Schema Master FSMO role, you can use the `dsquery server` or `adfind` commands shown here:

```
> dsquery server -hasfsmo schema
> adfind -sc fsmo:schema
```

To transfer the Schema Master to another server, follow these steps:

```
> ntdsutil roles conn "co t s <NewRoleOwner>" q "transfer Schema Master" q q
```

To forcibly seize the Schema Master to another DC, do the following:

```
> ntdsutil roles conn "co t s <NewRoleOwner>" q "seize Schema Master" q q
```

Using VBScript

```
' This code prints the Schema Master role owner for the specified forest.

strSchemaDN = objRootDSE.Get("schemaNamingContext")

' Schema Master
set objSchemaFsmo = GetObject("LDAP://" & strSchemaDN)
Wscript.Echo "Schema Master: " & objSchemaFsmo.fsmoroleowner

' This code transfers the Schema Master role to the local server
Set dse = GetObject("LDAP://localhost/RootDSE")
set myDomain = GetObject("LDAP://" & dse.get("defaultNamingContext"))
dse.Put "becomeSchemaMaster",1
```

```
dse.SetInfo

' This code seizes the Schema Master role to another server
set myDomain = GetObject("LDAP://" & dse.get("defaultNamingContext"))
dse.Put "becomeSchemaMaster",1
dse.SetInfo
```

Using PowerShell

```
$dcDSE = [ADSI]"LDAP://<DC>/rootDSE"
$role = "becomeSchemaMaster" $dcDSE.put($role,1)
$dcDSE.Setinfo()
```

Discussion

Several Active Directory operations, such as updating the schema, are sensitive and therefore need to be restricted to a single domain controller to prevent corruption of the AD database. This is because Active Directory cannot guarantee the proper evaluation of these functions in a situation where they may be invoked from more than one DC. The FSMO mechanism is used to limit these functions to a single DC.

The first domain controller in a new forest is assigned the two forest-wide FSMO roles, the schema master and domain naming master. The first domain controller in a new domain gets the other three domain-wide roles. If you need to decommission the domain controller that is currently the Schema Master role owner (either permanently or for a significant period of time), you'll want to transfer the role beforehand.

If the Schema Master becomes unavailable before you can transfer it, you'll need to seize the role (see Recipe 3.34).

 If you seize the Schema Master FSMO to another server, you should reformat and reinstall the original role holder and perform a metadata cleanup in Active Directory before returning it to your production environment.

See Also

Recipe 3.32, Recipe 3.33, and Recipe 3.34 for more on viewing, transferring, and seizing FSMO roles; and MS KB 324801 (How to View and Transfer FSMO roles in Windows Server 2003)

## CHAPTER 11

Site Topology

11.0 Introduction

Active Directory needs information about the underlying network to determine how domain controllers should replicate and what domain controller(s) are optimal for a given client to authenticate with. This network information is often referred to as the site or replication *topology*, and consists of numerous object types that represent various aspects of the network.

At a high level, a site is a logical collection of high-speed LAN segments. One or more subnets can be associated with a site, and this mapping is used to determine which site a client belongs to, based on its IP address. Sites are connected via site links, which are analogous to WAN connections. Finally, each domain controller in a site has one or more `connection` objects, which define a replication connection to another domain controller.

These site topology objects are contained under the `Sites` container within the Configuration naming context. Figure 11-1 shows an example of the site topology hierarchy using the Active Directory Sites and Services snap-in.

Directly under the `Sites` container are the individual site containers, plus containers that store the site link objects (`cn=Inter-site Transports`) and subnets (`cn=Subnets`). There are three objects included within a site:

- An `NTDS Site Settings` (`nTDSSiteSettings`) object that contains attributes that can customize replication behavior for the whole site

- A `License Site Settings` (`licensingSiteSettings`) object that can be used to direct hosts within the site to the appropriate licensing server

- A `Servers` container

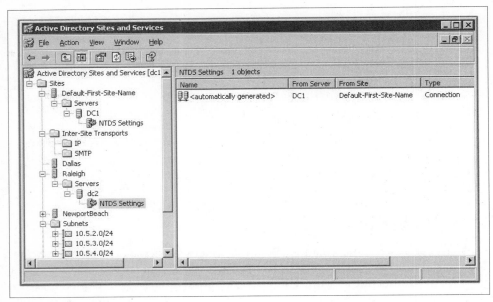

Figure 11-1. Site topology hierarchy

The `Servers` container contains a `server` object for each of the domain controllers that are members of the site, along with any other servers that need to be represented in the site topology (e.g., DFS servers). Figure 11-1 shows the site topology hierarchy.

A `server` object can contain an `NTDS Settings` (`nTDSDSA`) object, which distinguishes domain-controller `server` objects from other `server` objects. The `NTDS Settings` object stores several attributes that are used to customize replication behavior for a specific domain controller. The `NTDS Settings` object can contain one or more `nTDSConnection` objects, which define the replication connections between domain controllers.

The Anatomy of Site Topology Objects

Tables 11-1 through 11-7 contain some of the important attributes of the various site topology objects.

Table 11-1. Attributes of site objects

Attribute	Description
cn	RDN of the object. This is the name of the site (e.g., Raleigh).
gpLink	Contains a prioritized list of GPOs that are linked to the site.
siteObjectBL	Multivalued attribute that contains a list of distinguished names for each subnet that is associated with the site.

Table 11-2. *Attributes of nTDSSiteSettings objects*

Attribute	Description
cn	RDN of the object, which is always equal to NTDS Site Settings.
interSiteTopologyGenerator	Distinguished name of the NTDS Settings object of the current ISTG.
msDS-Preferred-GC-Site	If universal group caching is enabled, this contains the distinguished name of the site that domain controllers should refresh their cache from. This attribute was first introduced in Windows Server 2003. See Recipe 7.13 for more information.
options	Bit flag that determines if universal group caching is enabled, whether site link transitivity is disabled, and if replication schedules should be ignored. For more information see Recipe 11.6.
schedule	Octet string that represents the default replication schedule for the site.

Table 11-3. *Attributes of subnet objects*

Attribute	Description
cn	RDN of the object. Contains the network number and bit mask for the subnet (e.g., 10.1.3.0/24).
siteObject	Distinguished name of the site object the subnet is associated with.

Table 11-4. *Attributes of siteLink objects*

Attribute	Description
cn	RDN of the object. Contains the name of the link.
cost	Number that represents the site link cost. See Recipe 11.15 for more information.
replInterval	Interval in minutes that replication occurs over the site link.
schedule	Octet string that represents the replication schedule for the site link.
siteList	Multivalued list of distinguished names of each site that is associated with the site link. See Recipe 11.13 for more information.

Table 11-5. *Attributes of server objects*

Attribute	Description
bridgeheadTransportList	Multivalued attribute that contains the list of transports (e.g., IP or SMTP) for which the server is a preferred bridgehead server.
cn	RDN of the object. This is set to the hostname of the associated server.
dNSHostName	Fully qualified domain name of the server. This attribute is automatically maintained for domain controllers.
serverReference	Distinguished name of the corresponding computer object contained within one of the domain-naming contexts.

Table 11-6. Attributes of nTDSDSA (NTDS Settings) objects

Attribute	Description
cn	RDN of the object, which is always equal to NTDS Settings.
invocationID	GUID that represents the DIT (*ntds.dit*) on the domain controller.
hasMasterNCs	Multivalued attribute containing the list of writable naming contexts (does not include application partitions) stored on the domain controller.
hasPartialReplicaNCs	Multivalued attribute containing the list of read-only naming contexts stored on the domain controller. This will be populated only if the domain controller is a global catalog server.
msDS-Behavior-Version	Number that represents the functional level (i.e., operating system) of the domain controller. This attribute was first introduced in Windows Server 2003.
msDS-HasDomainNCs	Contains the distinguished name of the writable domain naming context stored on the domain controller. This attribute was first introduced in Windows Server 2003.
msDs-HasInstantiatedNCs	A combination of all available read-only and writable naming contexts stored on the domain controller. This attribute was first introduced in Windows Server 2003.
msDS-hasPartialReplicaNCs	Multivalued attribute that contains distinguished names of each read-only naming context stored on the domain controller. This will be populated only if the domain controller is a global catalog server. This attribute was first introduced in Windows Server 2003.
msDS-hasMasterNCs	Multivalued attribute that contains distinguished names of each writable naming context and application partition stored on the domain controller. This attribute was first introduced in Windows Server 2003.
options	Bit flag that determines if domain controller is a global catalog server.
queryPolicyObject	If set, the distinguished name of the LDAP query policy object to be used by the domain controller.

Table 11-7. Attributes of nTDSConnection objects

Attribute	Description
cn	RDN of the object. For KCC-generated connections, this is a GUID.
enabledConnection	Boolean that indicates if the connection is available to be used.
fromServer	Distinguished name of the NTDS Settings object of the domain controller this connection replicates with.
ms-DS-ReplicatesNCReason	Multivalued attribute that stores reason codes for why the connection exists. There will be one entry per naming context the connection is used for.
options	Bit flag where a value of 1 indicates the connection was created by the KCC and a value of 0 means the connection was manually created. See Recipe 11.29 for more information.
schedule	Octet string that represents the replication schedule for the site link.
transportType	Distinguished name of the transport type (e.g., IP or SMTP) that is used for the connection.

11.1 Creating a Site

Problem

You want to create a site.

Solution

Using a graphical user interface

1. Open the Active Directory Sites and Services snap-in.
2. Right-click on the Sites container and select New Site.
3. Beside Name, enter the name of the new site.
4. Under Link Name, select a site link for the site.
5. Click OK twice.

Using a command-line interface

Create an LDIF file called *create_site.ldf* with the following contents:

```
dn: cn=<SiteName>,cn=sites,cn=configuration,<ForestRootDN>
changetype: add
objectclass: site

dn: cn=Licensing Site Settings,cn=<SiteName>,cn=sites,cn=configuration,<ForestRootDN>
changetype: add
objectclass: licensingSiteSettings

dn: cn=NTDS Site Settings,cn=<SiteName>,cn=sites,cn=configuration,<ForestRootDN>
changetype: add
objectclass: nTDSSiteSettings

dn: cn=Servers,cn=<SiteName>,cn=sites,cn=configuration,<ForestRootDN>
changetype: add
objectclass: serversContainer
```

Then run the following command:

```
> ldifde -v -i -f create_site.ldf
```

You can also create a site by issuing the following four AdMod commands:

```
> admod -config -rb "cn=<SiteName>,cn=sites" -add
> admod -config -rb "cn=Licensing Site Settings,cn=<SiteName>,
cn=sites" objectclass::licensingSiteSettings -add
> admod -config -rb "cn=NTDS Site Settings,cn=<SiteName>,
cn=sites" objectclass::nTDSSiteSettings -add
> admod -config -rb cn=Servers,cn=<SiteName>,cn=sites"
objectclass::serversContainer -add
```

Using VBScript

```
' This code creates the objects that make up a site.
' ------ SCRIPT CONFIGURATION ------
strSiteName = "<SiteName>" ' e.g. Dallas
' ------ END CONFIGURATION --------

set objRootDSE = GetObject("LDAP://RootDSE")

set objSitesCont = GetObject("LDAP://cn=sites," & _
                          objRootDSE.Get("configurationNamingContext") )
' Create the site
set objSite = objSitesCont.Create("site","cn=" & strSiteName)
objSite.SetInfo

' Create the Licensing Site Settings object
set objLicensing = objSite.Create("licensingSiteSettings", _
                               "cn=Licensing Site Settings")

objLicensing.SetInfo

' Create the NTDS Site Settings object
set objNTDS = objSite.Create("nTDSSiteSettings","cn=NTDS Site Settings")
objNTDS.SetInfo

' Create the Servers container
set objServersCont = objSite.Create("
serversContainer","cn=Servers")
objServersCont.SetInfo

WScript.Echo "Successfully created site " & strSiteName
```

Using PowerShell

To create a new site using the Quest cmdlets, use the following four commands:

```
new-QADObject -name "<SiteName>" -type "site" -ParentContainer
"cn=sites,cn=configuration,<ForestRootDN>"
new-QADObject -name "Licensing Site Settings" -type "licensingSiteSettings"
-ParentContainer "cn=<SiteName>,cn=sites,cn=configuration,<ForestRootDN>"
new-QADObject -name "NTDS Site Settings" -type "nTDSSiteSettings" -ParentContainer
"cn=<SiteName>,cn=sites,cn=configuration,<ForestRootDN>"
new-QADObject -name "Servers" -type "serversContainer" -ParentContainer
"cn=<SiteName>,cn=sites,cn=configuration,<ForestRootDN>"
```

To use the native PowerShell commands, use the following syntax:

```
$objCont = [ADSI] "LDAP://cn=Sites,cn=Configuration,<ForestRootDN>"
$objSite = $objCont.Create("sites", "cn=<SiteName>"
$objSite.SetInfo()
$objLic = $objSite.Create("licensingSiteSettings", "cn=Licensing Site Settings")
$objLic.SetInfo()
$objNTDS = $objSite.Create("ntdsSiteSettings", "cn=NTDS Site Settings")
$objNTDS.SetInfo()
$objServers = $objSite.Create("serversContainer", "cn=Servers")
$objServers.SetInfo()
```

Discussion

To create a site in Active Directory, you have to create a number of objects. The first is a `site` object, which is the root of all the other objects. The `site` object contains the following:

`licensingSiteSettings`
> This object isn't mandatory but is created automatically when creating a site with AD Sites and Services. It is intended to point clients to a license server for the site.

`nTDSSiteSettings`
> This object stores replication-related properties about a site, such as the replication schedule, current ISTG role holder, and whether universal group caching is enabled.

`serversContainer`
> This container is the parent of the `server` objects that are part of the site. All the domain controllers that are members of the site will be represented in this container.

After these objects are created, you've essentially created an empty site. If you didn't do anything else, the site would not be of much value. To make it usable, you need to assign `subnet` objects to it (see Recipe 11.11), and add the site to a `siteLink` object to link the site to other sites (see Recipe 11.14). At that point, you can promote or move domain controllers into the site, and it should be fully functional.

See Also

Recipes 11.11 and 11.14, and MS KB 318480 (How to Create and Configure an Active Directory Site in Windows 2000)

11.2 Listing Sites in a Forest

Problem

You want to obtain the list of sites in a forest.

Solution

Using a graphical user interface

1. Open the Active Directory Sites and Services snap-in.
2. Click on the Sites container.
3. The list of sites will be displayed in the right pane.
4. Double-click on a site to view its properties.

Using a command-line interface

Run one of the following commands to list the sites in a forest:

```
> dsquery site
```

or:

```
> adfind -sites -f (objectcategory=site)
```

Run one of the following commands to view the properties for a particular site:

```
> dsget site "<SiteName>"
```

or:

```
> adfind -sites -rb "cn=<SiteName>"
```

Using VBScript

```
' This code lists all of the site objects.

set objRootDSE = GetObject("LDAP://RootDSE")
set objSitesCont = GetObject("LDAP://cn=sites," & _
                       objRootDSE.Get("configurationNamingContext") )
objSitesCont.Filter = Array("site")
for each objSite in objSitesCont
   Wscript.Echo " " & objSite.Get("cn")
next
```

Using PowerShell

You can obtain a list of sites in a forest using either native PowerShell syntax or the Quest cmdlets, as follows:

```
$strCategory = "site"
$objForest = [System.DirectoryServices.ActiveDirectory.Forest]::getCurrentForest()
$objSearcher = New-Object System.DirectoryServices.DirectorySearcher
$objSearcher.SearchRoot = $objForest
$objSearcher.Filter = ("(objectCategory=$strCategory)")
$colResults = $objSearcher.FindAll()

get-QADObject -searchroot "cn=sites,cn=configuration,<ForestRootDN>" -ldapfilter
"objectcategory=site"
```

Discussion

Site objects are stored in the Sites container (for example, cn=sites,cn=configuration,dc=adatum,dc=com) in the Configuration Naming Context (CNC). For more information on creating sites, see Recipe 11.1.

11.3 Renaming a Site

Problem

You want to rename a site.

Solution

Using a graphical user interface

1. Open the Active Directory Sites and Services snap-in.
2. Click on the Sites container.
3. In the right pane, right-click the site you want to rename and select Rename.
4. Enter the new name of the site and press Enter.

Using a command-line interface

The following command will change the RDN of a site:

```
> dsmove "<SiteDN>" -newname "<NewSiteName>"
```

You can also rename a site using AdMod, using the following syntax:

```
> admod -b "<SiteDN>" -rename "<NewSiteName>"
```

Using VBScript

```
' This code renames a site object.
' ------ SCRIPT CONFIGURATION ------
strSiteOldName = "<OldSiteName>" ' e.g. Raleigh
strSiteNewName = "<NewSiteName>" ' e.g. Raleigh-Durham
' ------ END CONFIGURATION ---------

Set objRootDSE = GetObject("LDAP://RootDSE")
strConfigurationNC = objRootDSE.Get("configurationNamingContext")

strSitesContainer = "LDAP://cn=Sites," & strConfigurationNC
strOldSiteDN = "LDAP://cn=" & strSiteOldName & ",cn=Sites," & strConfigurationNC

Set objSitesContainer = GetObject(strSitesContainer)
objSitesContainer.MoveHere strOldSiteDN, strSiteNewName
```

Using PowerShell

To rename a site using the Quest AD cmdlets, use the following syntax:

```
Rename-QADObject -identity '<Site DN>' -NewName '<New site name>'
```

To rename a site using native PowerShell methods, use the following:

```
$obj = [ADSI] "LDAP://<Site DN>"
$newName = "<New site name>"
$obj.psbase.Rename($newName)
```

Discussion

Renaming a site in Active Directory involves changing the cn of the site object. The largest concern with renaming a site, as with any other AD object, is to ensure that no applications reference the site by name. A best practice to avoid this pitfall is to reference AD objects by their GUIDs, which will not change even when the object is renamed.

See Also

MSDN: Object Names and Identities and MSDN: Using objectGUID to Bind to an Object

11.4 Deleting a Site

Problem

You want to delete a site.

Solution

Using a graphical user interface

1. Open the Active Directory Sites and Services snap-in.
2. Click on the Sites container.
3. In the right pane, right-click the site you want to delete and select Delete.
4. Click Yes twice.

Using a command-line interface

```
> dsrm <SiteDN> -subtree -noprompt
```

Alternatively, you can remove a site and its associated objects by issuing the following AdMod command:

```
> admod -b "cn=<SiteName>,cn=sites,cn=configuration,<ForestRootDN>" -del -treedelete
```

Using VBScript

```
' This code deletes a site and all child containers.
' ------ SCRIPT CONFIGURATION ------
strSiteName = "<SiteName>" ' e.g. Dallas
' ------ END CONFIGURATION --------
```

```
set objRootDSE = GetObject("LDAP://RootDSE")
set objSite = GetObject("LDAP://cn=" & strSiteName & ",cn=sites," & _
                        objRootDSE.Get("configurationNamingContext") )
objSite.DeleteObject(0)
WScript.Echo "Successfully deleted site " & strSiteName
```

Using PowerShell

To delete a site using the Quest AD cmdlets, use the following syntax:

```
remove-QADObject -identity <Site DN>
```

To delete a site using ADSI, use the following:

```
$objSite = [ADSI] "LDAP://<Site DN>"
$objSite.psbase.DeleteTree()
```

Discussion

When deleting a site, be very careful to ensure that no active **server** objects exist within it. If you delete a site that contains domain controllers, it will disrupt replication for all domain controllers in that site. A more robust VBScript solution would be to first perform an ADO query for all **server** objects using the distinguished name of the site as the base DN. If no servers were returned, then you could safely delete the site. If **server** objects were found, you should move them before deleting the site.

It is also worth noting that deleting a site does not delete any of the subnets or site links that are associated with the site. This would be another good thing to add to the VBScript solution. That is, before you delete the site, delete any subnets and site links that are associated with the site or, more likely, associate them with a different site.

See Also

Recipe 11.1 for more on creating a site and Recipe 11.7 for creating a subnet

11.5 Delegating Control of a Site

Problem

You want to delegate permission of an AD site to allow it to be administered by another user or group.

Solution

Using a graphical user interface

The following example will delegate administration of the managedBy attribute of a site:

1. Open the Active Directory Sites and Services snap-in.
2. Click on the Sites container.

3. In the right pane, right-click the site you want to delegate and select Delegate Control.

4. Click Next to bypass the initial Welcome screen of the Delegation of Control wizard.

5. Click Add to select the users or groups that you want to delegate control to. Click Next to continue.

6. Select "Create a custom task to delegate" and click Next.

7. Click "Only the following objects in the folder." Place a checkmark next to site objects and click Next.

8. Place a checkmark next to "Write managedBy." Click Next to continue.

9. Click Finish.

Using a command-line interface

The following code will allow a group called *SiteAdmins* to manage the managedBy attribute of sites within *adatum.com*:

```
> dsacls cn=Sites,cn=Configuration,dc=adatum,dc=com /I:S /G
adatum.com\SiteAdmins:WP;;managedBy
```

Using VBScript

```
' This VBScript code grants write access to the managedBy attribute of a site.

' ------ SCRIPT CONFIGURATION -------
strSiteDN = "<SiteDN>"  ' e.g. cn=SalesGroup,ou=Sales,dc=adatum,dc=com"
strUserOrGroup = "<UserOrGroup>"  ' e.g. joe@adatum.com or ADATUM\joe
' ------ END CONFIGURATION ---------

set objSite = GetObject("LDAP://" & strSiteDN)

'###########################
' Constants
'###########################
' ADS_ACETYPE_ENUM
Const ADS_ACETYPE_ACCESS_ALLOWED_OBJECT = &h5
Const ADS_FLAG_OBJECT_TYPE_PRESENT = &h1
Const ADS_RIGHT_DS_WRITE_PROP = &h20

' From schemaIDGUID of managedBy attribute
Const MANAGEDBY_ATTRIBUTE = "{0296c120-40da-11d1-a9c0-0000f80367c1}"

'###########################
' Create ACL
'###########################
set objSD = objSite.Get("nTSecurityDescriptor")
set objDACL = objSD.DiscretionaryAcl

' Set WP for member attribute
set objACE = CreateObject("AccessControlEntry")
```

```
objACE.Trustee      = strUserOrGroup
objACE.AccessMask   = ADS_RIGHT_DS_WRITE_PROP
objACE.AceFlags     = 0
objACE.Flags        = ADS_FLAG_OBJECT_TYPE_PRESENT
objACE.AceType      = ADS_ACETYPE_ACCESS_ALLOWED_OBJECT
objACE.ObjectType   = MANAGEDBY_ATTRIBUTE

objDACL.AddAce objACE

'############################
' Set ACL
'############################
objSD.DiscretionaryAcl = objDACL
objSite.Put "nTSecurityDescriptor", objSD
objSite.SetInfo
WScript.Echo "Delegated control of description attribute for " & strSiteDN & " to " _
& strUser
```

Using PowerShell

The following Quest PowerShell cmdlet will delegate the authority to modify the description attribute of a site object:

```
add-QADPermission -Identity <Site DN> -Account <User/Group DN> -Rights
'WriteProperty' -Property 'managedBy' -ApplyTo 'ThisObjectOnly'
```

Discussion

Using a graphical user interface

Delegating control over a site can be done via the Delegation of Control wizard, or by using *dsacls* at the command line or a VBScript. The Delegation of Control wizard allows you to delegate one preconfigured task—managing Group Policy links—or create a custom task to delegate. When delegating a custom task, you must first determine whether you are delegating permission over the entire site and all objects contained therein or whether you are only going to delegate control over specific child objects. (For example, you can delegate control over all computer objects within a site.) Once you've made this determination, you'll then specify the specific permissions that you're delegating; you can delegate anything from Full Control of the entire object down to granting read permissions on a single attribute.

See Also

MS KB 310997 (Active Directory Services and Windows 2000 or Windows Server 2003 domains) and MS KB 315676 (How to Delegate Administrative Authority in Windows 2000)

11.6 Configuring Universal Group Caching for a Site

 This recipe requires the Windows Server 2003 forest functional level or higher.

Problem

You want to configure a site so that it does not require access to a global catalog server during most user logins.

Solution

Using a graphical user interface

1. Open the Active Directory Sites and Services snap-in.
2. In the left pane, browse to the site you want to enable group caching for and click on it.
3. In the right pane, double-click on the NTDS Site Settings object.
4. Under Universal Group Membership Caching, check the box beside Enable Universal Group Caching.
5. If you want to force the cache refresh from a particular site, select a site; otherwise, leave the default set to *<Default>*.
6. Click OK.

Using a command-line interface

You can use *ldifde* to enable universal group caching. Create a file called *enable_univ_cache.ldf* with the following contents, but change *<SiteName>* to the name of the site you want to enable, and *<ForestRootDN>* to the distinguished name of the forest root domain:

```
dn: cn=NTDS Site Settings,cn=<SiteName>,cn=sites,cn=configuration,<ForestRootDN>
changetype: modify
replace: options
options: 32
-
```

Then use the following command to import the change:

```
> ldifde -i -f enable_univ_cache.ldf
```

You can also perform this change using a combination of AdFind and AdMod, using the following syntax:

```
> adfind -config -rb "cn=NTDS Settings,cn=<SiteName>,cn=Sites"
options -adcsv | admod options::{{.:SET:32}}
```

 To explicitly set the site that domain controllers in this site should use to refresh universal group membership, configure the msDS-Preferred-GC-Site attribute on the NTDS Site Settings object with the DN of the desired site.

Using VBScript

```
' This code safely enables universal group caching for the specified site.
' ------ SCRIPT CONFIGURATION ------
strNTDS = "cn=NTDS Site Settings,<SiteDN>"      ' e.g. cn=NTDS Site
                                                ' Settings,cn=Raleigh,
                                                ' cn=Sites,cn=Configuration,
                                                ' dc=adatum,dc=com
strAttr = "options"
boolEnableCaching = TRUE   ' Set to false to disable UG caching
intBit = 32
' ------ END CONFIGURATION --------

set objNTDS = GetObject("LDAP://" & strNTDSDN)
intBitsOrig = objNTDS.Get(strAttr)
intBitsCalc = CalcBit(intBitsOrig, intBit, boolEnableBit)

if intBitsOrig <> intBitsCalc then
    objNTDS.Put strAttr, intBitsCalc
    objNTDS.SetInfo
    WScript.Echo "Changed " & strAttr & " to " & boolEnableCaching
else
    WScript.Echo "Did not need to change " & strAttr & " value."
end if

Function CalcBit(intValue, intBit, boolEnable)

    CalcBit = intValue

    if boolEnableCaching = TRUE then
       CalcBit = intValue Or intBit
    else
       if intValue And intBit then

           CalcBit = intValue Xor intBit
       end if
    end if

End Function
```

To set the options bit value attribute using a logical OR operation, use the following syntax:

```
$objNTDS = [ADSI] "LDAP://cn=NTDS Site Settings,<Site DN>"
$currentOptions = [int]($objNTDS.options.ToString())
$newOptions = $currentOptions -bor 32
$objNTDS.put("options", $newOptions)
$objNTDS.setInfo()
```

Discussion

In Windows 2000 Active Directory, an authenticating domain controller is required to contact a global catalog server (if it is not one itself) in order to process any client authentication requests. This is necessary because of the need to verify universal group memberships for any clients attempting to access the domain. *Universal group caching* was introduced in Windows Server 2003 to reduce the impact of this requirement. Universal group caching can be enabled on a site-by-site basis and allows domain controllers to cache universal group information locally. This largely removes the need to query the global catalog during client logon, though a global catalog will still need to be contacted the first time a new user logs on because no membership information will be cached in that case. The local DC will also need to contact a GC at regular intervals to update its cached information.

You can enable universal group caching manually by enabling bit 5 (32 in decimal) on the options attribute of the NTDS Site Settings object. With the exception of the Ad-Find/AdMod solution, the CLI solutions blindly write a value of 32 to that attribute, which is not ideal since it will overwrite any existing values that may already be in place. The VBScript solution provides a safer and more elegant solution for setting a bit flag attribute such as options.

See Also

Recipe 4.12 for more on viewing bitwise attributes, Recipe 4.15 for information on configuring bitwise values, and MS KB 269181 (How to Query Active Directory by Using a Bitwise Filter)

11.7 Creating a Subnet

Problem

You want to create a subnet.

Solution

Using a graphical user interface

1. Open the Active Directory Sites and Services snap-in.
2. Right-click on the Subnets container and select New Subnet.
3. Enter the Address and Mask and then select the site the subnet is part of.
4. Click OK.

Using a command-line interface

Create an LDIF file called *create_subnet.ldf* with the following contents:

```
dn: cn=<Subnet>,cn=subnets,cn=sites,cn=configuration,<ForestRootDN>
changetype: add
objectclass: subnet
siteObject: cn=<SiteName>,cn=sites,cn=configuration,<ForestRootDN>
```

Then run the following command:

```
> ldifde -v -i -f create_subnet.ldf
```

You can also create a subnet using AdMod, as follows:

```
> admod -b "cn=<Subnet>,cn=subnets,cn=sites,cn=configuration,<ForestRootDN>"
objectClass::subnet siteObject::"cn=<SiteName>,
cn=sites,cn=configuration,<ForestRootDN>" -add
```

Using VBScript

```
' This code creates a subnet object and associates it with a site.
' ------ SCRIPT CONFIGURATION ------
strSubnet = "<Subnet>"    ' e.g. 10.5.3.0/24
strSite   = "<SiteName>" ' e.g. Dallas
' ------ END CONFIGURATION --------

set objRootDSE = GetObject("LDAP://RootDSE")
set objSubnetsCont = GetObject("LDAP://cn=subnets,cn=sites," & _
                          objRootDSE.Get("configurationNamingContext") )
set objSubnet = objSubnetsCont.Create("subnet", "cn=" & strSubnet)
objSubnet.Put "siteObject", "cn=" & strSite & ",cn=sites," & _
                          objRootDSE.Get("configurationNamingContext")
objSubnet.SetInfo
WScript.Echo "Successfully created subnet " & strSubnet
```

Using PowerShell

You can create a subnet object and associate it with an existing site using the Quest cmdlets or else by using the native PowerShell commands, as follows:

```
new-QADObject -parentcontainer 'cn=subnets,cn=sites,cn=configuration,<ForestRootDN>
-type 'subnet' -name '10.10.10.0/24' -ObjectAttributes @{siteObject='<SiteDN>'

$parentDN = [ADSI] "LDAP://cn=subnets,cn=sites,cn=configuration,<ForestRootDN>"
$newSubnet = $parentDN.Create("subnet","cn=10.10.10.0/24")
$newSubnet.put("siteObject","<SiteDN>")
$newSubnet.SetInfo()
```

Discussion

Subnet objects reside in the Subnets container in the Configuration NC (e.g., cn=subnets,cn=sites,cn=configuration,dc=adatum,dc=com). The RDN of the subnet should be the subnet address and bit-mask combination (e.g., 10.5.3.0/24). The other important attribute to set is siteObject, which should contain the DN of the site that the subnet is associated with.

See Also

MS KB 323349 (How to Configure Subnets in Windows Server 2003 Active Directory)

11.8 Listing the Subnets

Problem

You want to list the subnet objects in Active Directory.

Solution

Using a graphical user interface

1. Open the Active Directory Sites and Services snap-in.
2. Click on the Subnets container.
3. The list of subnets will be displayed in the right pane.
4. To view the properties of a specific subnet, double-click on the one you want to view.

Using a command-line interface

The following command will list all subnets:

```
> dsquery subnet
```

The following command will display the properties for a particular subnet. Replace *<Subnet>* with the subnet address and mask (e.g., 10.5.3.0/24):

```
> dsget subnet "<Subnet>"
```

You can also list all configured subnets with AdFind, as follows:

```
> adfind -subnets -f (objectCategory=subnet)
```

To display the properties of a particular subnet with AdFind, use this syntax:

```
> adfind -subnets -rb "cn=<Subnet>"
```

Using VBScript

```
' This code lists all the subnets stored in Active Directory.
set objRootDSE = GetObject("LDAP://RootDSE")
set objSubnetsCont = GetObject("LDAP://cn=subnets,cn=sites," & _
                               objRootDSE.Get("configurationNamingContext") )
objSubnetsCont.Filter = Array("subnet")
for each objSubnet in objSubnetsCont
   Wscript.Echo " " & objSubnet.Get("cn")
next
```

Using PowerShell

```
get-QADObject -searchRoot cn=subnets,cn=sites,cn=configuration,<ForestRootDN>
-lDAPFilter "objectcategory=subnet"

$strCategory = "subnet"
$objForest = [System.DirectoryServices.ActiveDirectory.Forest]::getCurrentForest()
$objSearcher = New-Object System.DirectoryServices.DirectorySearcher
$objSearcher.SearchRoot = $objForest
$objSearcher.Filter = ("(objectCategory=$strCategory)")
$colResults = $objSearcher.FindAll()
```

Discussion

To display the site that subnets are associated with, include the `siteObject` attribute as one of the attributes to return from the query. For example, the second-to-last line of the VBScript solution could be modified to return the site by using this code:

```
Wscript.Echo " " & objSubnet.Get("cn") & " : " & objSubnet.Get("siteObject")
```

See Also

MS KB 323349 (How to Configure Subnets in Windows Server 2003 Active Directory)

11.9 Finding Missing Subnets

Problem

You want to find the subnets that are missing from your site topology. Missing subnets can result in clients not authenticating against the most optimal domain controller, which can degrade performance.

Solution

Having all of your subnets in Active Directory is important because a client that attempts to log on from a subnet that is not associated with any site may authenticate with any domain controller in the domain. This can result in the logon process taking longer to complete. Unfortunately, Microsoft has not provided an easy way to rectify this problem.

Under Windows 2000, the only source of missing subnet information is the System event 5778. Here is an example:

```
Event Type:        Information
Event Source:      NETLOGON
Event Category:      None
Event ID:        5778
Date:              1/27/2007
Time:              12:07:04 AM
User:              N/A
Computer:        DC2
Description:
'JSMITH-W2K' tried to determine its site by looking up its IP address
('10.21.85.34')
in the Configuration\Sites\Subnets container in the DS. No subnet matched the IP
address. Consider adding a subnet object for this IP address.
```

The only way to dynamically determine missing subnets is to query each domain controller for 5778 events and map the IP addresses specified within the events to a subnet you add to the site topology.

As of Windows Server 2008, things are not that much better. One of the issues with the 5778 events under Windows 2000 is that they can easily fill up your System event log if you have many missing subnets. Starting in Windows 2003, Microsoft decided to instead display a summary event 5807 that states that some number of connection attempts have been made by clients that did not map to a subnet in the site topology. Here is an example:

```
Event Type:        Warning
Event Source:      NETLOGON
Event Category:    None

Event ID:          5807
Date:              1/10/2007
Time:              10:59:53 AM
User:              N/A
Computer:          DC1
Description:
During the past 4.18 hours there have been 21 connections to this Domain Controller
from client machines whose IP addresses don't map to any of the existing sites in
the enterprise. Those clients, therefore, have undefined sites and may connect to any
Domain Controller including those that are in far distant locations from the
clients.
A client's site is determined by the mapping of its subnet to one of the existing
sites. To move the above clients to one of the sites, please consider creating
```

subnet object(s) covering the above IP addresses with mapping to one of the existing sites.

The names and IP addresses of the clients in question have been logged on this computer in the following log file '%SystemRoot%\debug\netlogon.log' and, potentially, in the log file '%SystemRoot%\debug\netlogon.bak' created if the former log becomes full. The log(s) may contain additional unrelated debugging information.

To filter out the needed information, please search for lines which contain text 'NO_CLIENT_SITE:'. The first word after this string is the client name and the second word is the client IP address. The maximum size of the log(s) is controlled by the following registry DWORD value 'HKEY_LOCAL_MACHINE\SYSTEM\CurrentControlSet\Services\ Netlogon\Parameters\LogFileMaxSize'; the default is 20000000 bytes. The current maximum size is 20000000 bytes. To set a different maximum size, create the above registry value and set the desired maximum size in bytes.

For more information, see Help and Support Center at http://go.microsoft.com/fwlink/events.asp.

Instead of scraping the event logs on every domain controller, you can look at the *%SystemRoot%\debug\netlogon.log* file on each domain controller and parse out all of the NO_CLIENT_SITE entries. This is still far from an easy process, but at least the event logs are no longer cluttered with 5778 events.

Here is an example of some of the NO_CLIENT_SITE entries from the *netlogon.log* file:

```
01/16 15:50:07 ADATUM: NO_CLIENT_SITE: ADATUM-TEST4 164.2.45.157
01/16 15:50:29 ADATUM: NO_CLIENT_SITE: SJC-BACKUP 44.25.26.142
01/16 16:19:58 ADATUM: NO_CLIENT_SITE: ADATUM-TEST4 164.2.45.157
01/16 16:20:07 ADATUM: NO_CLIENT_SITE: ADATUM-TEST4 164.2.45.157
01/16 16:50:07 ADATUM: NO_CLIENT_SITE: ADATUM-TEST4 164.2.45.157
01/16 16:57:00 ADATUM: NO_CLIENT_SITE: JSMITH-W2K1 10.61.80.19
01/16 17:20:08 ADATUM: NO_CLIENT_SITE: ADATUM-TEST4 164.2.45.157
01/16 17:50:08 ADATUM: NO_CLIENT_SITE: ADATUM-TEST4 164.2.45.157
```

If you wanted to get creative and automate a solution to do this, you could write a script that goes out to each domain controller, opens the *netlogon.log* file, and retrieves NO_CLIENT_SITE entries. You could then examine all of the IP addresses and create subnets in Active Directory that would contain them. You could associate all of those subnets with a default site or even use the Default-First-Site-Name site. Then once a week (or whenever), you could look at the sites that were created or that were associated with the default site and determine what site they should actually be associated with.

Another potential solution would be to create a subnet object that is a *supernet* of all of the physical subnets on your network, and then associate this logical subnet with a site that would not otherwise be authenticating users. Any users that authenticate against this site will do so only because their specific subnet is not defined elsewhere in Active Directory.

See Also

MS KB 909423 (TechNet Support WebCast: Configuring Subnets for Active Directory Sites in Windows Server 2003)

11.10 Deleting a Subnet

Problem

You want to delete a subnet object.

Solution

Using a graphical user interface

1. Open the Active Directory Sites and Services snap-in.
2. Click on the Subnets container.
3. The list of subnets will be displayed in the right pane.
4. Right-click on the subnet you wish to remove and select Delete.
5. Click Yes to confirm.

Using a command-line interface

You can delete a subnet object using the built-in *dsrm* utility or AdMod. The *dsrm* utility takes the following syntax:

```
> dsrm cn=<SubnetName>,cn=subnets,cn=sites,cn=configuration,<ForestRootDN>
```

To remove a subnet using AdMod, use this syntax:

```
> admod -b cn=<SubnetName>,cn=subnets,cn=sites,cn=configuration,<ForestRootDN> -del
```

Using VBScript

```
strSubnetName = "cn=<SubnetName>" ' e.g. "cn=10.0.0.0/8"
strParentDN = cn=subnets,cn=sites,cn=configuration," _
            & strForestDN
strForestDN = "<ForestRootDN>" ' e.g. "dc=adatum,dc=com"

set objContainer = GetObject("LDAP://" & strParentDN)
objContainer.Delete "subnet", strSubnetName
```

Using PowerShell

To delete a site using the Quest AD cmdlets, use the following syntax:

```
remove-QADObject -identity <Subnet DN>
```

To delete a site using ADSI, use the following:

```
$objSubnet = [ADSI] "LDAP://<Subnet DN>"
$objSubnet.psbase.DeleteTree()
```

Discussion

Using VBScript

This script example uses the `IADsContainer::Delete` method to delete the subnet object. To use this method, you must first bind to the parent container of the object. You then call `Delete` by passing the object class along with the RDN of the object that you want to delete.

The `Delete` method is a safer alternative to the `DeleteObject` method because you need to be more explicit about what you are deleting. With `DeleteObject`, you only have to specify the distinguished name of an object and it will summarily delete it. For example, the following code will delete a subnet object using `DeleteObject`:

```
strSubnetDN = "<SubnetDN>"
set objSubnet = GetObject("LDAP://" & strObjectDN)
objSubnet.DeleteObject(0)
```

As you can see, if a user accidentally or maliciously mistypes an inappropriate DN, the result could be disastrous. Using the `DeleteObject` method puts more constraints on the delete operation.

See Also

Recipe 4.25 for deleting a container object, MS KB 258310 (Viewing Deleted Objects in Active Directory), MSDN: IADsDeleteOps::DeleteObject, and MSDN: IADsContainer::Delete

11.11 Changing a Subnet's Site Assignment

Problem

You want to change the site object that a particular subnet is associated with.

Solution

Using a graphical user interface

1. Open the Active Directory Sites and Services MMC snap-in (*dssite.msc*).
2. Browse to Sites→Subnets, then right-click on the subnet that you wish to modify and select Properties.
3. In the Site drop-down box, select the name of the site that this subnet should be associated with and click OK.

Using a command-line interface

```
> admod cn=<SubnetName>,cn=Subnets,cn=Sites,cn=Configuration,<ForestRootDN>
siteObject::<NewSiteDN>
```

 For *<SubnetName>*, use the format "192.168.1.0/24", for example.

Using VBScript

```
' This code updates the
' site assignment of a subnet object.
' ------ SCRIPT CONFIGURATION ------
strNewSiteName = "<SiteName>" ' e.g. "Raleigh"
strSubnetName = "<SubnetName>" ' e.g. "192.168.1.0/24"
' ------ END CONFIGURATION --------

set objRootDSE = GetObject("LDAP://RootDSE")
set objSiteSettings = GetObject("LDAP://cn=" & _strSubnetName & _
                                "cn=subnets,cn=sites," & _
                                objRootDSE.Get("ConfigurationNamingContext"))

objSiteSettings.Put "siteObject", _
                    "cn=" & strNewSiteName & ",cn=sites," & _
                    objRootDSE.Get("ConfigurationNamingContext")
objSiteSettings.SetInfo
WScript.Echo("Site membership updated successfully!")
```

Using PowerShell

```
set-QADObject -Identity <SubnetDN> -ObjectAttributes @{siteObject='<NewSiteDN>'}

$objSubnet = [ADSI] "LDAP://<SubnetDN>"
$objSubnet.put("siteObject","<SiteDN>")
$objSubnet.SetInfo()
```

Discussion

Since the site topology that you create in Active Directory is meant to map to your physical network topology, an Active Directory subnet object can be associated with only a single AD site at any one time. If you modify your site configuration or need to delete a site object for any reason, you should configure any subnets associated with that site that are still active on your network so that they are associated with another Active Directory site. This will ensure that any clients that reside on those subnets will be able to locate resources such as domain controllers appropriately, without sending authentication requests across site links unnecessarily.

See Also

Recipe 11.9 to find missing subnets on your network and Recipe 11.10 for more on deleting subnet objects

11.12 Creating a Site Link

Problem

You want to create a site link to connect two or more sites together.

Solution

Using a graphical user interface

1. Open the Active Directory Sites and Services snap-in.
2. Expand the Sites container.
3. Expand the Inter-Site Transports container.
4. Right-click on IP (or SMTP) and select New Site Link.
5. For Name, enter the name for the site link.
6. Under "Sites not in this site link," select at least two sites and click the Add button.
7. Click OK.

Using a command-line interface

The following LDIF would create a site link connecting the SJC and Dallas sites:

```
dn: cn=Dallas-SJC,cn=IP,cn=inter-site
transports,cn=sites,cn=configuration,<ForestRootDN>
changetype: add
objectclass: siteLink
siteList: cn=SJC,cn=sites,cn=configuration,<ForestRootDN>
siteList: cn=Dallas,cn=sites,cn=configuration,<ForestRootDN>
```

If the LDIF file were named *create_site_link.ldf*, you'd then run the following command:

```
> ldifde -v -i -f create_site_link.ldf
```

You can also create a site link using AdMod, as follows:

```
> admod -b "cn=<SiteLinkName>,cn=IP,cn=inter-site
   transports,cn=sites,cn=configuration,<ForestRootDN>"
   objectclass::sitelink
   "sitelist:++:cn=<FirstSite>,cn=sites,cn=configuration,
   <ForestRootDN>;
   cn=<SecondSite>,cn=sites,cn=configuration,<ForestRootDN>"
   cost::50 replInterval::180
   -add
```

Using VBScript

```
' This code creates a site link.
' ------ SCRIPT CONFIGURATION ------
intCost = 100            ' site link cost
intReplInterval = 180    ' replication interval in minutes
strSite1 = "<Site1>"     ' e.g. SJC
strSite2 = "<Site2>"     ' e.g. Dallas
strLinkName = strSite1 & " - " & strSite2
' ------ END CONFIGURATION ---------

' Taken from ADS_PROPERTY_OPERATION_ENUM
const ADS_PROPERTY_UPDATE = 2

set objRootDSE = GetObject("LDAP://RootDSE")
set objLinkCont = GetObject( _
                "LDAP://cn=IP,cn=Inter-site Transports,cn=sites," & _
                objRootDSE.Get("configurationNamingContext") )
set objLink = objLinkCont.Create("siteLink", "cn=" & strLinkName)
strSite1DN = "cn=" & strSite1 & ",cn=sites," & _
                objRootDSE.Get("configurationNamingContext")
strSite2DN = "cn=" & strSite2 & ",cn=sites," & _
                objRootDSE.Get("configurationNamingContext")
objLink.PutEx ADS_PROPERTY_UPDATE, "siteList", Array(strSite1DN,strSite2DN)
objLink.Put "cost", intCost
objLink.Put "replInterval", intReplInterval
objLink.SetInfo

WScript.Echo "Successfully created link: " & strLinkName
```

Using PowerShell

You can create a site link object using either the Quest AD cmdlets or native PowerShell commands, as follows:

```
new-QADObject -ParentContainer "cn=IP,cn=Inter-site
Transports,cn=sites,cn=configuration,<Forest Root DN>" -type "siteLink" -name
"Site1-Site2" -ObjectAttributes @{cost=<Site Link Cost>;replInterval=<Replication
interval>";siteList=@('<Site1 DN>','<Site2 DN>')}
```

Discussion

Without site links, domain controllers would not be able to determine the optimal partners to replicate with. The cost that is associated with a site defines how expensive the link is. A lower cost is less expensive (or faster) than a higher cost. Link costs are inversely proportional to bandwidth, so a faster link should be configured with a lower cost than a low-speed one. Site link costs are manually configured items, which means that the administrator can control how inter-site replication should take place on the network.

Using PowerShell

Because `siteList` is a multivalued attribute, the `-ObjectAttributes` switch requires you to format the values to be added to `siteList` as an array, using the @(…) syntax. As written, this syntax will overwrite any existing information within the mutlivalued attribute. In order to append values using the Quest tools, you will need to create and use a `Dictionary` object as follows:

```
[Collections.DictionaryEntry] $de = New-Object Collections.DictionaryEntry -
argumentList Append, @('<Value1>','<Value2>')
set-QADObject -Identity <Object DN> -ObjectAttributes @{siteLink=$de}
```

To delete values from a multivalued attribute, change `-argumentList Append` to `-argumentList Delete`.

See Also

Chapter 12 for more information on replication and MS KB 316812 (How to Create and Configure a Site Link in Active Directory in Windows 2000)

11.13 Finding the Site Links for a Site

Problem

You want to list the site links that are associated with a site.

Solution

Using a graphical user interface

1. Open LDP and from the menu, select Connection→Connect.
2. For Server, enter the name of a domain controller (or leave blank to do a serverless bind).
3. For Port, enter 389.
4. Click OK.
5. From the menu, select Connection→Bind.
6. Enter the credentials of the domain user.
7. Click OK.
8. From the menu, select Browse→Search.
9. For BaseDN, type the Inter-Site Transports container DN (e.g., `cn=Inter-siteTransports,cn=sites,cn=configuration,dc=adatum,dc=com`).
10. For Scope, select Subtree.

11. For Filter, enter the following:

```
(&(objectcategory=siteLink)(siteList=cn=<SiteName>,
cn=sites,cn=configuration,<ForestRootDN>))
```

12. Click Run.

Using a command-line interface

You can list the site links associated with a particular site using DSQuery or AdFind. DSQuery requires the following syntax:

```
> dsquery * "cn=inter-site transports,cn=sites,cn=configuration,<ForestRootDN>"
-filter "(&(objectcategory=siteLink)(siteList=cn=<SiteName>,
cn=sites,cn=configuration,<ForestRootDN>))" -scope subtree -attr name
```

To obtain this information using AdFind, use the following:

```
> adfind -config -f "(&(objectcategory=siteLink)(siteList=cn=<SiteName>,
cn=sites,cn=configuration,<ForestRootDN>))" name
```

Using VBScript

```
' This code displays the site links associated with the specified site.
' ------ SCRIPT CONFIGURATION ------
strSiteName = "<SiteName>" ' e.g. Raleigh
' ------ END CONFIGURATION --------

set objRootDSE = GetObject("LDAP://RootDSE")
strSiteDN = "cn=" & strSiteName & ",cn=sites," & _
            objRootDSE.Get("ConfigurationNamingContext")

strBase    = "<LDAP://cn=Inter-site Transports,cn=sites," _
                & objRootDSE.Get("ConfigurationNamingContext") & ">;"
strFilter  = "(&(objectcategory=siteLink)" & _
                "(siteList=" & strSiteDN & "));"
strAttrs   = "name;"
strScope   = "subtree"

set objConn = CreateObject("ADODB.Connection")
objConn.Provider = "ADsDSOObject"
objConn.Open "Active Directory Provider"
set objRS = objConn.Execute(strBase & strFilter & strAttrs & strScope)

WScript.Echo "Total site links for " & strSiteName & ": " & objRS.RecordCount
if objRS.RecordCount > 0 then

    objRS.MoveFirst
    while Not objRS.EOF
        Wscript.Echo vbTab & objRS.Fields(0).Value
        objRS.MoveNext
    wend
end if
```

Using PowerShell

```
get-QADObject -searchRoot "cn=sites,cn=configuration,dc=adatum,dc=com" -lDAPFilter
"(&(objectcategory=siteLink)(siteList="<Site DN>"))"

$strCategory = "siteLink"
$objForest = [System.DirectoryServices.ActiveDirectory.Forest]::getCurrentForest()
$objSearcher = New-Object System.DirectoryServices.DirectorySearcher
$objSearcher.SearchRoot = $objForest
$objSearcher.Filter = ("(&(objectcategory=siteLink)(siteList="<Site DN>"))")
$colResults = $objSearcher.FindAll()
```

Discussion

A site can be included as a part of zero or more site links. A site with no site links would be considered orphaned from the site topology, since there is no way to determine how and where it connects into the topology. Branch office sites may have only a single site link back to a hub, while a hub site may have numerous links that connect it to the rest of the world.

Finding the site links associated with a site consists of performing a query for all siteLink objects that have the DN of the site included in the siteList attribute for a link. The siteList attribute is a multivalued attribute that contains all the sites that are connected via the site link.

11.14 Modifying the Sites That Are Part of a Site Link

Problem

You want to modify the sites associated with a site link.

Solution

Using a graphical user interface

1. Open the Active Directory Sites and Services snap-in.
2. In the left pane, expand Sites→Inter-Site Transports.
3. Click either the IP or SMTP folder, depending where the site link is stored.
4. In the right pane, double-click on the link you want to modify.
5. Under the General tab, you can add and remove sites that are associated with the site link.
6. Click OK.

Using a command-line interface

Create an LDIF file called *modify_site_link.ldf* with the following contents. Replace *<LinkName>* with the name of the link and *<SiteName>* with the site to add to the link:

```
dn: cn=<LinkName>,cn=IP,cn=inter-site
transports,cn=sites,cn=configuration,<ForestRootDN>
changetype: modify
add: siteList

siteList: cn=<SiteName>,cn=sites,cn=configuration,<ForestRootDN>
-
```

Then run the following command:

```
> ldifde -v -i -f modify_site_link.ldf
```

You can also add sites to a site link using AdMod, as follows:

```
> admod -b "cn=<LinkName>,cn=IP,cn=inter-site
transports,cn=sites,cn=configuration,<ForestRootDN>" siteList:+:"cn=<SiteName>
,cn=sites,cn=configuration,<ForestRootDN>"
```

Using VBScript

```
' This code adds a site to an existing site link.
' ------ SCRIPT CONFIGURATION ------
strSite = "<SiteName>" ' e.g. Burlington
strLink = "<LinkName>" ' e.g. DEFAULTIPSITELINK
' ------ END CONFIGURATION --------

' Taken from ADS_PROPERTY_OPERATION_ENUM
const ADS_PROPERTY_APPEND = 3

set objRootDSE = GetObject("LDAP://RootDSE")
set objLink = GetObject("LDAP://cn=" & strLink & _
                    ",cn=IP,cn=Inter-site Transports,cn=sites," & _
                    objRootDSE.Get("configurationNamingContext") )
strSiteDN = "cn=" & strSite & ",cn=sites," & _
            objRootDSE.Get("configurationNamingContext")
objLink.PutEx ADS_PROPERTY_APPEND, "siteList", Array(strSiteDN)
objLink.SetInfo

WScript.Echo "Successfully modified link: " & strLink
```

Using PowerShell

To append one or more values to the list of sites within a site link using the Quest tools, use the following syntax:

```
[Collections.DictionaryEntry] $de = New-Object Collections.DictionaryEntry
-argumentList Append, @('<Site1 DN>','<Site2 DN>')
set-QADObject -Identity <SiteLink DN> -ObjectAttributes @{siteLink=$de}
```

To perform this task using the PutEx ADSI method, use the following:

```
$objSiteLink = [ADSI] "LDAP://<SiteLink DN>"
$strSite1DN = "<Site1 DN>"
$strSite2DN = "<Site2 DN>"
$ADS_PROPERTY_APPEND = 3
$objSiteLink.PutEx($ADS_PROPERTY_APPEND, "siteList" @($strSite1DN, $strSite2DN))
$objSiteLink.SetInfo()
```

Discussion

To associate a site with a site link, add the DN of the site to the siteList attribute of the siteLink object that represents the link. To remove a site from a link, remove the DN associated with the site from the siteList attribute. For example, to remove a site from a site link using AdMod, replace siteList:+: with siteList:-:.

Using PowerShell

To remove one or more sites from a site link using the Quest cmdlets, replace -argumentList Append with -argumentList Delete. To remove one or more site links using ADSI, use a PutEx value of "4" for ADS_PROPERTY_DELETE rather than a value of "3" for ADS_PROPERTY_APPEND. To remove all sites from a site link, use the following syntax to clear the multivalued attribute:

```
$ADS_PROPERTY_CLEAR = 1
$objSiteLink.PutEx($ADS_PROPERTY_CLEAR,"siteList",0)
```

See Also

Recipe 11.13 for finding the links associated with a site

11.15 Modifying the Cost for a Site Link

Problem

You want to modify the cost for a site link.

Solution

Using a graphical user interface

1. Open the Active Directory Sites and Services snap-in.
2. In the left pane, expand Sites→Inter-Site Transports.
3. Click either the IP or SMTP folder, depending on where the site link is stored.
4. In the right pane, double-click on the link you want to modify.
5. Under the General tab, you can change the cost for the site link.
6. Click OK.

Using a command-line interface

Create an LDIF file called *modify_site_link_cost.ldf* with the following contents. Replace *<LinkName>* with the name of the link you want to modify and *<LinkCost>* with the cost:

```
dn: cn=<LinkName>,cn=IP,cn=inter-site
transports,cn=sites,cn=configuration,<ForestRootDN>
changetype: modify
replace: cost
cost: <LinkCost>
-
```

Then run the following command:

```
> ldifde -v -i -f modify_site_link_cost.ldf
```

You can also modify the cost of a site link using AdMod, as follows:

```
> admod -b "cn=<LinkName>,cn=IP,cn=inter-site
transports,cn=sites,cn=configuration,<ForestRootDN>" cost::<LinkCost>
```

Using VBScript

```
' This code modifies the cost attribute of a site link.
' ------ SCRIPT CONFIGURATION ------
strLink = "<SiteLink>" ' e.g. DEFAULTIPSITELINK
intCost = <LinkCost>    ' e.g. 200
' ------ END CONFIGURATION ---------

set objRootDSE = GetObject("LDAP://RootDSE")
set objLink = GetObject("LDAP://cn=" & strLink & _
                    ",cn=IP,cn=Inter-site Transports,cn=sites," & _
                    objRootDSE.Get("configurationNamingContext") )
objLink.Put "cost", intCost
objLink.SetInfo

WScript.Echo "Successfully modified link: " & strLink
```

Using PowerShell

You can modify the cost of a site link using the Quest cmdlets or ADSI, as follows:

```
set-QADObject -Identity <SiteLinkDN> -ObjectAttributes @{cost=<New Cost>}

$objSiteLink = [ADSI] "LDAP://<SiteLinkDN>"
$objSiteLink.put("cost", "<New Cost>")
$objSiteLink.SetInfo()
```

Discussion

The cost attribute is one of the most important attributes of siteLink objects. cost is used by the KCC to determine what connection objects should be created to allow domain controllers to replicate data.

cost is inversely proportional to bandwidth; the lower the cost, the greater the bandwidth. The number you use for the cost is also arbitrary; the default is 100. You could use 100–1,000 as the range for your site link costs, or you could use 1–10. The actual number isn't important, so long as you configure the values to be relative based on the other site links you've configured. The costs that you assign to your site links should be configured according to the physical topology of your network, where you assign the lowest costs to the highest-speed links, and higher costs to lower-speed links such as a backup ISDN link between two sites.

11.16 Enabling Change Notification for a Site Link

Problem

You want to enable change notification between sites so that replication will occur as changes occur rather than according to a set schedule.

Solution

Using a graphical user interface

1. Open ADSI Edit. Create or open a connection to the Configuration Container, then browse to CN=Configuration,*<ForestRootDN>*→CN=Sites→CN=Inter-Site Transports→CN=IP.

2. Right-click on the site link object that you want to modify and select Properties.

3. Scroll to the options attribute. If the attribute has not been set, click Edit and enter a value of 1. Click OK.

4. If there is an existing value in place, perform a bitwise OR with 1 and the existing value, click Edit, and enter the new value. Click OK.

Using a command-line interface

```
>  adfind -b cn=<SiteLinkName>,cn=IP,cn=Inter-site
Transports,cn=Sites,cn=Configuration,cn=<ForestRootDN>"
options -adcsv | admod options::{{.:SET:1}}
```

Using VBScript

```
' This code safely modifies a bit flag attribute.
' ------ SCRIPT CONFIGURATION -------
strSiteLink = "<SiteLinkDN>"    ' e.g. cn=jsmith,cn=users,dc=adatum,dc=com
strAttr = "options"
boolEnableBit = <TRUEorFALSE>   ' e.g. TRUE to enable
intBit = 1
' ------ END CONFIGURATION ---------

set objSiteLink = GetObject("LDAP://" & strSiteLink)
intBitsOrig = objSiteLink.Get(strAttr)
intBitsCalc = CalcBit(intBitsOrig, intBit, boolEnableBit)
```

```
   if intBitsOrig <> intBitsCalc then
       objSiteLink.Put strAttr, intBitsCalc
       objSiteLink.SetInfo
       WScript.Echo "Changed " & strAttr & " from " & intBitsOrig & " to " &
intBitsCalc
   else
       WScript.Echo "Did not need to change " & strAttr & " (" & intBitsOrig & ")"
   end if

   Function CalcBit(intValue, intBit, boolEnable)
       CalcBit = intValue

       if boolEnable = TRUE then
           CalcBit = intValue Or intBit
       else
           if intValue And intBit then
               CalcBit = intValue Xor intBit
           end if
       end if

   End Function
```

Using PowerShell

```
$objSiteLink = [ADSI] "<Site Link DN>"
$currentOptions = [int]($objSiteLink.options.ToString())
$newOptions = $currentOptions -bor 1
$objSiteLink.put("options", $newOptions)
$objSiteLink.setInfo()
```

Discussion

By default, intra-site replication occurs on the basis of change notifications where replication occurs almost immediately after a change occurs, while domain controllers in
different sites will, by default, only replicate with each other on a set schedule. To
configure a particular site link to use the change-notification mechanism for replication,
you can set bit 1 of its options attribute. Keep in mind that this will create more frequent
replication traffic on the site link in question, but it will ensure that changes made in
one site can be replicated to the other site much more quickly than by using the default
inter-site replication schedules.

See Also

Recipe 4.15 for more on modifying bitwise attributes and Recipe 11.17 for more on
modifying replication schedules

11.17 Modifying Replication Schedules

Problem

You want to change the times of day or week that a particular site link (IP or SMTP) is available for replication.

Solution

1. Open the Active Directory Sites and Services snap-in.
2. In the left pane, expand Sites→Inter-Site Transports.
3. Click either the IP or SMTP folder, depending on where the site link is stored.
4. In the right pane, double-click on the link you want to modify.
5. On the General tab, click Change Schedule.
6. Click OK.
7. Select the times and days of the week that you wish to allow or disallow, and select the Replication Available or Replication Not Available radio button, as appropriate.
8. Click OK twice to save your changes.

Using a command-line interface

To configure a site link to be available 24 hours a day, 7 days a week, use the following syntax:

```
> admod -b cn=<SiteLinkName>,cn=<TransportName>,cn=Inter-site
Transports,cn=sites,cn=configuration,<ForestRootDN> schedule::0
```

Using VBScript

```
' The following script will display the availability schedule
' for a particular site link.

Days = Array _
    ("Sunday", "Monday", "Tuesday", "Wednesday", "Thursday", "Friday", "Saturday")

Set objSiteLink = GetObject _
    ("LDAP://<SiteLinkDN>")
arrHours = objSiteLink.Get("schedule")

For i = 1 To LenB(arrHours)
    arrHoursBytes(i-1) = AscB(MidB(arrHours, i, 1))
    WScript.Echo "MidB returns: " & MidB(arrHours, i, 1)
    WScript.Echo "arrHoursBytes: " & arrHoursBytes(i-1)
    wscript.echo vbcrlf
Next

intCounter = 0
```

```
intLoopCounter = 0
WScript.echo "Day Byte 1 Byte 2 Byte 3"
For Each HourByte In arrHoursBytes
    arrHourBits = DisplayLogonHourBits(HourByte)

    If intCounter = 0 Then
        WScript.STDOUT.Write Days(intLoopCounter) & Space(2)
        intLoopCounter = intLoopCounter + 1
    End If

    For Each HourBit In arrHourBits
        WScript.STDOUT.Write HourBit
        intCounter = 1 + intCounter

        If intCounter = 8 or intCounter = 16 Then
            Wscript.STDOUT.Write Space(1)
        End If

        If intCounter = 24 Then
            WScript.echo vbCr
            intCounter = 0
        End If
    Next
Next

Function DisplayLogonHourBits(x)
    Dim arrBits(7)
    For i = 7 to 0 Step -1
        If x And 2^i Then
            arrBits(i) = 1
        Else
            arrBits(i) = 0
        End If
    Next
    DisplayLogonHourBits = arrBits
End Function
```

Discussion

When you configure an inter-site replication link, you can specify a particular schedule
during which the link will be available for replication. By default, inter-site links can
pass replication traffic 24 hours a day, 7 days a week, but you can restrict this so that
it is only available for specific hours of the day and/or days of the week. This might be
useful for a heavily utilized link that you do not want to have overloaded with replication traffic. For example, a bank headquarters may wish to prevent replication traffic
from being initiated during a two-hour time period at the end of every day while its
branch offices are transmitting daily report information.

Using VBScript

The `schedule` attribute of a `siteLink` object is a binary object, rather than a simple string like most of the other attributes we've discussed. Because of this, manipulating it directly is a bit trickier than simply inserting a new string in place of an old one. In the VBScript example shown in this recipe, we use a VBScript function that manipulates the various bits of the attribute to display the correct values.

See Also

Recipe 12.4 to force replication from one DC to another, MS KB 232263 (Replication Schedule for Intra-site Replication Partners), and MSDN: schedule Attribute [AD Schema]

11.18 Disabling Site Link Transitivity or Site Link Schedules

Problem

You want to disable site link transitivity to control replication manually.

Solution

Using a graphical user interface

1. Open the Active Directory Sites and Services snap-in.
2. In the left pane, expand Sites→Inter-Site Transports.
3. Right-click either the IP or SMTP folder, depending on which protocol you want to disable transitivity or ignore schedules for.
4. Select Properties.
5. To disable site link transitivity, uncheck "Bridge all site links."
6. To ignore site link schedules, check "Ignore schedules."
7. Click OK.

Using a command-line interface

You can modify the `options` attribute of a site link object using an LDIF file and *ldifde*, but since the attribute is a bit flag, you are better off using the GUI, VBScript, or PowerShell solutions that look at the current value of `options` and modify it accordingly. *ldifde* doesn't handle this type of logic.

Using VBScript

```
' This code can disable site link transitivity and site
' schedules for all links of the IP transport.
' The code for the CalcBit function can be found in Recipe 4.15
```

```
' ------ SCRIPT CONFIGURATION ------
boolDisableTrans = <TrueOrFalse>    ' e.g. TRUE
boolIgnoreSchedules = <TrueOrFalse> ' e.g. FALSE
' ------ END CONFIGURATION ---------

set objRootDSE = GetObject("LDAP://RootDSE")
set objLink = GetObject( _
              "LDAP://cn=IP,cn=Inter-site Transports,cn=sites," & _
              objRootDSE.Get("configurationNamingContext") )

intBitsOrg = objLink.Get("options")
intBits = CalcBit(intBitsOrg, 2, boolDisableTrans)
intBits = CalcBit(intBitsOrg, 1, boolIgnoreSchedules)

if objLink.Get("options") <> intBits then
   objLink.Put "options", intBits
   objLink.SetInfo
   WScript.Echo "Successfully modified link transitivity for " & strLink
else
   WScript.Echo "Did not need to modify link transitivity for " & strLink
end if
```

Using PowerShell

```
$objIP = [ADSI] "LDAP://cn=IP,cn=Inter-site
Transports,cn=sites,cn=configuration,<ForestRootDN>"
$currentOptions = [int]($objIP.options.ToString())
$newOptions = $currentOptions -bor 2
$newOptions = $currentOptions -bor 1
$objIP.put("options", $newOptions)
$objIP.setInfo()
```

Discussion

Active Directory site links, by default, are transitive, which means that if site A is linked
to site B, and site B is linked to site C, then site A is also linked (through site B) to site
C. The KCC uses transitivity when making decisions about creating connection objects.
You can, however, disable this behavior if you so choose. Typically, this is not something you'll want to do without a very good reason. Disabling transitivity may be necessary, for example, in some Windows 2000 deployments that have a lot of sites and
find that the KCC is having a hard time keeping up. Starting with Windows Server
2003, the KCC has been greatly improved and site link transitivity should not cause
these problems.

The other reason you might want to disable transitivity is if you need to make replication
more deterministic—that is, you want to exert more manual control over the process.
Disabling transitivity makes it much easier to determine where the KCC will attempt
to establish connection objects, because the KCC on a domain controller will not be
able to replicate with domain controllers that are not in sites that are directly linked.

We mention site link schedules here primarily because the same attribute (i.e.,
options) that determines site link transitivity also determines if link schedules are

enforced. If you enable the `ignore schedules` option for a particular transport (i.e., IP or SMTP), the KCC ignores any preconfigured link schedules. If you later disable this setting, link schedules will go back into effect.

See Also

Recipe 4.15 for more on setting a bit flag attribute

11.19 Creating a Site Link Bridge

Problem

You want to create a site link bridge because you've disabled site link transitivity.

Solution

Using a graphical user interface

1. Open the Active Directory Sites and Services snap-in.
2. In the left pane, expand Sites→Inter-Site Transports.
3. Right-click either the IP or SMTP folder, depending on which protocol you want to create a site link bridge for.
4. Select New Site Link Bridge.
5. Highlight two or more site links in the left box.
6. Click the Add button.
7. Click OK.

Using a command-line interface

Create an LDIF file called *create_site_link_bridge.ldf* with the following contents, where *<Link1>* and *<Link2>* refer to the site links to be bridged:

```
dn: cn=<BridgeName>,cn=IP,cn=inter-site
transports,cn=sites,cn=configuration,<ForestRootDN>
changetype: add
objectclass: siteLinkBridge
siteLinkList: cn=<Link1>,cn=IP,cn=Inter-site
Transports,cn=sites,cn=configuration,<ForestRootDN>
siteLinkList: cn=<Link2>,cn=IP,cn=Inter-site
Transports,cn=sites,cn=configuration,<ForestRootDN>
```

Then run the following command:

```
> ldifde -v -i -f create_site_link_bridge.ldf
```

You can also create a site link bridge using AdMod, as follows:

```
> admod -b "cn=<BridgeName>,cn=IP,cn=inter-site
     transports,cn=sites,cn=configuration,<ForestRootDN>"
     objectclass::sitelinkBridge
     "sitelist:++:cn=<FirstSiteLink>,cn=IP,cn=inter-site
     transports,cn=sites,cn=configuration,<ForestRootDN>;
     cn=<SecondSiteLink>,cn=IP,cn=inter-site
     transports,cn=sites,cn=configuration,<ForestRootDN>"
     -add
```

Using VBScript

```
' This code creates a site link bridge between two site links.
' ------ SCRIPT CONFIGURATION -------
strLink1 = "<Link1>"       ' e.g. AMS-LON
strLink2 = "<Link2>"       ' e.g. SJC-RTP
strBridge = "<BridgeName>"' e.g. AMER-EUR
' ------ END CONFIGURATION --------

set objRootDSE = GetObject("LDAP://RootDSE")
set objLinkCont = GetObject( _
                "LDAP://cn=IP,cn=Inter-site Transports,cn=sites," & _
                objRootDSE.Get("configurationNamingContext") )
set objBridge = objLinkCont.Create("siteLinkBridge", "cn=" & strBridge)
strLink1DN = "cn=" & strLink1 & _
             ",cn=IP,cn=Inter-site Transports,cn=sites," & _
             objRootDSE.Get("configurationNamingContext")
strLink2DN = "cn=" & strLink2 & _
             ",cn=IP,cn=Inter-site Transports,cn=sites," & _
             objRootDSE.Get("configurationNamingContext")
objBridge.Put "siteLinkList", Array(strLink1DN,strLink2DN)
objBridge.SetInfo

WScript.Echo "Successfully created bridge: " & strBridge
```

Using PowerShell

To create a site link bridge using the Quest cmdlets, use the following syntax:

```
$strSiteLink1 = <SiteLink1 DN>
$strSiteLink2 = <SiteLink2 DN>
new-QADObject -parentContainer "cn=IP,cn=Inter-site
Transports,cn=sites,cn=configuration,<ForestRootDN>" -type "siteLinkBridge" -name
"New SiteLinkBridge" -ObjectAttributes
@{siteLinkList=@($strSiteLink1,$strSiteLink2)}
```

To create a site link bridge using ADSI, use the following:

```
$ADS_PROPERTY_APPEND = 3
$strSiteLink1 = <SiteLink1 DN>
$strSiteLink2 = <SiteLink2 DN>
$objLinkCont = [ADSI] "LDAP://cn=IP,cn=Inter-site
Transports,cn=sites,cn=configuration,<ForestRootDN>"
$objBridge = $objLinkCont.Create("siteLinkBridge","cn=NewSiteLinkBridge")
$objBridge.putEx($ADS_PROPERTY_APPEND,"siteLinkList",@($strSiteLink1,$strSiteLink2)}
```

Discussion

If you've disabled site link transitivity or have networks that lack direct routes between sites, you will need to create *site link bridges*. Creating a site link bridge to link several links is analogous to creating a site link to link several sites. Let's take an example where site link transitivity is disabled and we have four sites, among which site A has a link to site B and site C has a link to site D. If we want domain controllers in sites A and B to replicate with sites C and D, we need to create a site link bridge to bridge the A–B link with the C–D link.

See Also

Recipe 11.18 for disabling site link transitivity

11.20 Finding the Bridgehead Servers for a Site

Problem

You want to find the bridgehead servers for a site.

Solution

Using a graphical user interface

1. The *replmon.exe* utility is no longer available in Windows Server 2008; for 2008 servers, the command-line interface option is the appropriate option. Open the Replication Monitor from the Support Tools (*replmon.exe*).

2. From the menu, select View→Options.

3. In the left pane, right-click on Monitored Servers and select Add Monitored Server.

4. Use the Add Monitored Server Wizard to add a server in the site you want to find the bridgehead server(s) for.

5. In the left pane, right-click on the server and select Show BridgeHead Servers→In This Server's Site.

Using a command-line interface

```
> repadmin /bridgeheads [<ServerName>] [/verbose]
```

The `/bridgeheads` option is valid only with the Windows Server 2003 version of *repadmin*. There is no such option in the Windows 2000 version.

Using VBScript

```
' This code finds the bridgehead servers for the specified site.
' ------ SCRIPT CONFIGURATION ------
strServer = "<ServerName>" ' server to target query against, e.g. dc01
```

```
strSite = "<SiteName>" ' name of site to query
                       ' e.g. Default-First-Site-Name
' ------ END CONFIGURATION --------

set objIadsTools = CreateObject("IADsTools.DCFunctions")
intRes = objIadsTools.GetBridgeHeadsInSite(Cstr(strServer),Cstr(strSite),0)

if intRes = -1 then
    Wscript.Echo "Bridge heads: " & objIadsTools.LastErrorText
    WScript.Quit
end if

for count = 1 to intRes
    WScript.Echo vbTab & objIadsTools.BridgeHeadName(count)
next
```

Discussion

Bridgehead servers are responsible for replicating data between sites. Instead of all domain controllers replicating the same naming contexts outside of the site, the bridgehead servers act as a funnel for replication into and out of a site. Any domain controller in a site can become a bridgehead server, and bridgeheads are designated by the KCC for each writable partition in the site. You can control which servers are designated as bridgehead servers by defining preferred bridgehead servers (see Recipe 11.21 for more on how to do this).

See Also

MS KB 271997 (Description of Bridgehead Servers in Windows 2000)

11.21 Setting a Preferred Bridgehead Server for a Site

Problem

You want to set a preferred bridgehead server for a site.

Solution

Using a graphical user interface

1. Open the Active Directory Sites and Services snap-in.
2. In the left pane, expand Sites, expand the site where the server you want to set as a bridgehead is contained, and expand the Servers container.
3. Right-click on the server you want to set as the bridgehead and select Properties.
4. Highlight IP, SMTP, or both, depending on the protocol(s) for which you want the server to be a bridgehead.
5. Click the Add button.

6. Click OK.

Using a command-line interface

Create an LDIF file called *set_bridgehead_server.ldf* with the following contents:

```
dn: cn=<DCName>,cn=servers,cn=<SiteName>,cn=sites,cn=configuration,<ForestRootDN>
changetype: modify
add: bridgeheadTransportList
bridgeheadTransportList: cn=IP,cn=Inter-site
Transports,cn=sites,cn=configuration,<ForestRootDN>
-
```

Then run the following command:

```
> ldifde -v -i -f set_bridgehead_server.ldf
```

You can also set the preferred bridgehead server with AdMod, using the following syntax:

```
Admod -b cn=<DCName>,cn=servers,cn=<SiteName>,
cn=sites,cn=configuration,<ForestRootDN> bridgeheadTransportList:+:"cn=IP,
cn=Inter-site transports,cn=sites,cn=configuration,<ForestRootDN>"
```

Using VBScript

```
' This code sets a preferred bridgehead server for a particular transport.
' ------ SCRIPT CONFIGURATION ------
strServer     = "<DomainControllerName>"  ' e.g. dc1
strServerSite = "<SiteName>"              ' e.g. Default-First-Site-Name
strTransport  = "<TransportName>"         ' e.g. either IP or SMTP
' ------ END CONFIGURATION --------

set objRootDSE = GetObject("LDAP://RootDSE")

set objServer = GetObject("LDAP://cn=" & strServer & ",cn=Servers,cn=" & _
                          strServerSite & ",cn=sites," & _
                          objRootDSE.Get("configurationNamingContext") )
objServer.Put "bridgeHeadTransportList", _
              "cn=" & strTransport & ",cn=Inter-site Transports,cn=sites," _
              & objRootDSE.Get("configurationNamingContext")
objServer.SetInfo

WScript.Echo "Successfully set bridgehead server: " & strServer
```

Using PowerShell

You can set a preferred bridgehead server using either of the syntaxes listed here:

```
set-QADObject -Identity "cn=<DC Name>,cn=servers,cn=<Site
Name>,cn=sites,cn=configuration,<ForestRootDN>" -ObjectAttributes
@{bridgeHeadTransportList="cn=IP,cn=Inter-site
Transports,cn=sites,cn=configuration,<ForestRootDN>"}

$objDC = [ADSI] "LDAP://n=<DC Name>,cn=servers,cn=<Site
Name>,cn=sites,cn=configuration,<ForestRootDN>"
```

```
$objDC.put("bridgeHeadTransportList","cn=IP,cn=Inter-site
Transports,cn=sites,cn=configuration,<ForestRootDN>"
$objDC.SetInfo()
```

Discussion

Setting a preferred bridgehead server can give you more control over which domain controllers participate in inter-site replication, but it is also limiting. The KCC typically selects bridgehead servers dynamically, but if you set preferred bridgehead servers, the KCC will not select new ones if the preferred servers become unavailable. Therefore, you should ensure that if you do select preferred bridgehead servers, you select at least two for a given partition in a site.

 As a general rule, you shouldn't set preferred bridgehead servers if at all possible.

See Also

MS KB 271997 (Description of Bridgehead Servers in Windows 2000)

11.22 Listing the Servers

Problem

You want to list the server objects in the site topology.

Solution

Using a graphical user interface

1. Open LDP.
2. From the menu, select Connection→Connect.
3. For Server, enter the name of a domain controller (or leave blank to do a serverless bind).
4. For Port, enter 389.
5. Click OK.
6. From the menu, select Connection→Bind.
7. Enter the credentials of a domain user.
8. Click OK.
9. From the menu, select Browse→Search.

10. For BaseDN, type the Sites container's DN (for example, `cn=sites,cn=configuration,dc=adatum,dc=com`).

11. For Scope, select Subtree.

12. For Filter, enter (`objectcategory=server`).

13. Click Run.

You can also view the servers in your site topology by using the Active Directory Sites and Services MMC snap-in (*dssite.msc*) and manually browsing the site topology.

Using a command-line interface

```
> dsquery server [-site <SiteName>]
```

To list all servers in the site topology using AdFind, use the following syntax:

```
> adfind -sites -f (objectcategory=server)
```

To restrict the results to a specific site, do the following:

```
> adfind -config -rb cn=<SiteName>,cn=sites -f (objectcategory=server)
```

Using VBScript

```
' This code lists the server objects in the site topology.

set objRootDSE = GetObject("LDAP://RootDSE")
strBase     = "<LDAP://cn=sites," & _
                  objRootDSE.Get("ConfigurationNamingContext") & ">;"
strFilter = "(objectcategory=server);"
strAttrs = "distinguishedName;"
strScope = "subtree"

set objConn = CreateObject("ADODB.Connection")
objConn.Provider = "ADsDSOObject"
objConn.Open "Active Directory Provider"
set objRS = objConn.Execute(strBase & strFilter & strAttrs & strScope)
objRS.MoveFirst
while Not objRS.EOF
    Wscript.Echo objRS.Fields(0).Value
        objRS.MoveNext
wend
```

Using PowerShell

```
get-QADObject -SearchRoot "cn=sites,cn=configuration,<ForestRootDN>" -lDAPFilter
"objectcategory=server"

$strCategory = "server"
$objRoot = [ADSI] "LDAP://cn=sites,cn=configuration,<ForestRootDN>"
$objSearcher = New-Object System.DirectoryServices.DirectorySearcher
$objSearcher.SearchRoot = $objForest
$objSearcher.Filter = ("(objectCategory=$strCategory)")
$colResults = $objSearcher.FindAll()
```

Discussion

Each Active Directory domain controller is represented in the site topology by a **server** object that is associated with a specific site. Replication decisions are made based on links from this site to other sites that contain domain controllers.

Other types of services can also add **server** objects to the site topology. The way you can distinguish which ones are domain controllers is the presence of an NTDS Settings (nTDSDSA) object that is a child of the **server** object. Only domain controllers will have that object.

11.23 Moving a Domain Controller to a Different Site

Problem

You want to move a domain controller to a different site. This may be necessary if you promoted the domain controller without first adding its subnet to Active Directory. In that case, the domain controller may not be added to the appropriate site.

Solution

Using a graphical user interface

1. Open the Active Directory Sites and Services snap-in.
2. In the left pane, expand Sites, expand the site where the server you want to move is contained, and expand the Servers container.
3. Right-click on the server you want to move and select Move.
4. Select the site to move the server to.
5. Click OK.

 Starting with Windows Server 2003, you can also drag-and-drop the server object from one site to another, if desired.

Using a command-line interface

You can move a domain controller to a new site using either the built-in DSMove utility or AdMod. DSMove takes the following syntax:

```
> dsmove "cn=<ServerName>,cn=servers,cn=<CurrentSite>,
cn=sites,cn=configuration,<ForestRootDN>" -newparent "cn=servers,cn=<NewSite>,
cn=sites,cn=configuration,<ForestRootDN>"
```

To move a DC using AdMod, use the following:

```
> admod -b "cn=<ServerName>,cn=servers,cn=<CurrentSite>,
cn=sites,cn=configuration,<ForestRootDN> -move "cn=servers,cn=<NewSite>,
cn=sites,cn=configuration,<ForestRootDN>
```

Using VBScript

```
' This code moves a server to a different site.
' ------ SCRIPT CONFIGURATION ------
' Should contain the common name of the server object
strDC = "<DomainControllerName>" ' e.g. dc02
' Name of servers current site
strCurrentSite = "<CurrentSite>" ' e.g. Default-First-Site-Name
' Name of site you want to move server to

strNewSite = "<NewSite>"           ' e.g. Raleigh
' ------ END CONFIGURATION --------

strConfigDN = GetObject("LDAP://RootDSE").Get("configurationNamingContext")
strServerDN = "LDAP://cn=" & strDC & ",cn=servers,cn=" &
                          strCurrentSite & ",cn=sites," & strConfigDN
strNewParentDN = "LDAP://cn=servers,cn=" & strNewSite & ",cn=sites," & strConfigDN

Set objCont = GetObject(strNewParentDN)
objCont.MoveHere strServerDN, "cn=" & strDC
```

Using PowerShell

To move a domain controller to a new site using the Quest AD cmdlets, use the following syntax:

```
move-QADObject -identity "cn=<DC
Name>,cn=servers,cn=<CurrentSiteName>,cn=sites,cn=configuration,<ForestRootDN>"
-newparent "cn=servers,cn=<NewSiteName>,cn=sites,cn=configuration,<ForestRootDN>"
```

To use ADSI, use the following syntax:

```
$obj = [System.DirectoryServices.DirectoryEntry] "LDAP://cn=<DC
Name>,cn=servers,cn=<CurrentSiteName>,cn=sites,cn=configuration,<ForestRootDN>"
$newParent = [ADSI]
"LDAP://cn=servers,cn=<NewSiteName>,cn=sites,cn=configuration,<ForestRootDN>"
$obj.psbase.MoveTo($newParent)
```

Discussion

After you move a server to a new site, you might want to monitor replication to and from that server to make sure that any new connections that are needed get created and start replicating. See Recipe 12.2 for more on viewing the replication status of a server.

See Also

MS KB 214677 (Automatic Detection of Site Membership for Domain Controllers)

11.24 Configuring a Domain Controller to Cover Multiple Sites

Problem

You want to configure a domain controller to cover multiple sites, which will cause clients in all of those sites to use that domain controller for authentication and directory lookups.

Solution

Using a graphical user interface

1. Run *regedit.exe* from the command line or click Start→Run.
2. In the left pane, expand *HKEY_LOCAL_MACHINE\SYSTEM\CurrentControlSet\Services\Netlogon\Parameters*.
3. If the SiteCoverage value does not exist, right-click on Parameters in the left pane and select New→Multi-String Value. For the name, enter SiteCoverage.
4. In the right pane, double-click on the value and enter each site the server should cover on a separate line.
5. Click OK.

Using a command-line interface

```
> reg add HKLM\System\CurrentControlSet\Services\Netlogon\Parameters /v
"SiteCoverage" /t REG_MULTI_SZ /d <Site1>\0<Site2>
```

Using VBScript

```
' This code configures a domain controller to cover multiple sites.
' ------ SCRIPT CONFIGURATION ------
strDC = "<DomainControllerName>" ' e.g. dc01
arrSites = Array("<Site1>","<Site2>") ' Array of sites to cover
' ------ END CONFIGURATION ---------

strNTDSReg = "SYSTEM\CurrentControlSet\Services\Netlogon\Parameters"
const HKLM = &H80000002
set objReg = GetObject("winmgmts:\\" & strDC & "\root\default:StdRegProv")
objReg.SetMultiStringValue HKLM, strNTDSReg, _
                    "SiteCoverage", _
                    arrSites
WScript.Echo "Site coverage set for " & strDC
```

Using PowerShell

```
$strRegPath = "HKLM:\System\CurrentControlSet\Services\Netlogon\Parameters"
$arrSites = "<Site1 DN>", "<Site2 DN>"
new-ItemProperty -path $strRegPath -name "SiteCoverage" -type MultiString
set-ItemProperty -path $strRegPath -name "SiteCoverage -value $arrSites
```

Discussion

In an Active Directory environment, it is perfectly valid to have a site that does not contain its own domain controller. In fact, if you model the site topology after your real network, some sites will lack their own domain controllers unless you've deployed a branch office architecture or have very few sites. If you create sites without any domain controllers, the site links between the sites will determine which domain controllers will *cover* or advertise their services to the site. When a domain controller covers for a remote site, it needs to publish site-specific DNS resource records that clients in the remote site can use to find the domain controller. Active Directory will select DCs to cover DC-less sites automatically, but you can hardcode the list of sites a specific domain controller should cover by modifying the Registry as described in the section called "Solution".

Using PowerShell

Because the Windows Server 2008 release of PowerShell contains a provider for the Windows Registry, it is extremely intuitive to navigate and manage the Registry. For example, you can use the cd command to change directories within the Registry just as you might when navigating the filesystem from a command prompt. In this example you also see how simple it is to create an array of strings in PowerShell; you simply specify the values in the array separated by commas.

See Also

MS KB 200498 (Configure a Domain Controller for Membership in Multiple Sites)

11.25 Viewing the Site Coverage for a Domain Controller

Problem

You want to view the sites that a domain controller covers.

Solution

Using a command-line interface

In the following command, replace *<DomainControllerName>* with the name of the domain controller you want to view site coverage for:

```
> nltest /server:<DomainControllerName> /DsGetSiteCov
```

Using VBScript

Although you cannot use it directly from a scripting language like VBScript, Microsoft provides a DsGetDcSiteCoverage method that can be used by languages such as Visual

Basic and C++ to retrieve site coverage information. In fact, the `nltest` command shown in the CLI solution is a wrapper around this method.

Discussion

Recipe 11.24 describes how to configure a domain controller to cover multiple sites. Recipe 11.26 describes how you can prevent a domain controller from covering for any sites other than its own.

See Also

MSDN: DsGetDcSiteCoverage

11.26 Disabling Automatic Site Coverage for a Domain Controller

Problem

You want to prevent a domain controller from covering sites outside of the one in which it resides.

Solution

Using a graphical user interface

1. Run *regedit.exe* from the command line or Start→Run.
2. Expand *HKEY_LOCAL_MACHINE\SYSTEM\CurrentControlSet\Services \Netlogon\Parameters*.
3. Right-click on Parameters and select New→DWORD Value.
4. For the name, enter `AutoSiteCoverage`.
5. Double-click on the new value, enter 0 under Value data, and click OK.

Using a command-line interface

```
> reg add HKLM\System\CurrentControlSet\Services\Netlogon\Parameters /v
AutoSiteCoverage /t REG_DWORD /d 0
```

Using VBScript

```
' This code disables auto site coverage.
strNetlogonReg = "SYSTEM\CurrentControlSet\Services\Netlogon\Parameters"
const HKLM = &H80000002
Set objReg = GetObject("winmgmts:root\default:StdRegProv")

objReg.SetDWORDValue HKLM, strNetlogonReg, "AutoSiteCoverage", 0
WScript.Echo "Site coverage disabled"
```

Using PowerShell

```
$strRegPath = "HKLM:\System\CurrentControlSet\Services\Netlogon\Parameters"
set-ItemProperty -path $strRegPath -name "AutoSiteCoverage" -value 0
```

Discussion

If you want to reduce the load on a domain controller, one way is to prevent it from covering for other sites. Automatic site coverage happens when a site does not contain any member domain controllers.

See Also

Recipe 11.25 for viewing the site coverage for a domain controller

11.27 Finding the Site for a Client

Problem

You want to find which site a client computer is located in.

Solution

Using a command-line interface

In the following command, replace *<HostName>* with the name of the host you want to find the site for:

```
> nltest /server:<HostName> /DsGetSite
```

 You'll use the /server: *<HostName>* parameter even if you are specifying a client computer.

Using VBScript

Although you cannot use it directly from a scripting language like VBScript, Microsoft provides a DsGetSiteName method that can be used by languages such as Visual Basic and C++ to retrieve site coverage information. In fact, the nltest command shown in the CLI solution is a wrapper around this method.

The IADsTool interface provides a wrapper around this method:

```
set objIadsTools = CreateObject("IADsTools.DCFunctions")
strSite = objIadsTools.DsGetSiteName("<HostName>")
Wscript.Echo "Site: " & strSite
```

Discussion

Each domain controller has a **server** object that is contained within a site. Clients are different—they are associated with a site based on their IP address, and the corresponding subnet that it matches is in the **Subnets** container. The client site information is important because it determines the domain controller the client authenticates with. If the client's IP address does not match the subnet range of any of the subnets stored in Active Directory, it will randomly pick a site to use, which means it could authenticate against any domain controller in the domain. See Recipe 11.28 for a way to hardcode the site association for a client.

See Also

Recipe 11.28 for forcing a host into a particular site, MS KB 247811 (How Domain Controllers Are Located in Windows), and MSDN: DsGetSiteName

11.28 Forcing a Host into a Particular Site

Problem

You want to force a host to be in a particular site.

Solution

Using a graphical user interface

1. Run *regedit.exe* from the command line or Start→Run.
2. Expand *HKEY_LOCAL_MACHINE\SYSTEM\CurrentControlSet\Services \Netlogon\Parameters*.
3. Right-click on Parameters and select New→String Value.
4. Enter `SiteName` for the name.
5. Double-click on the new value, enter the name of the site under Value data, and click OK.

Using a command-line interface

```
> reg add HKLM\System\CurrentControlSet\Services\Netlogon\Parameters /v SiteName /t
REG_SZ /d <SiteName>
```

Using VBScript

```
' This code forces the host the script is run on to use a particular host.
' ------ SCRIPT CONFIGURATION ------
strSite = "<SiteName>" ' e.g. Raleigh
' ------ END CONFIGURATION ---------
```

```
strNetlogonReg = "SYSTEM\CurrentControlSet\Services\Netlogon\Parameters"
const HKLM = &H80000002
set objReg = GetObject("winmgmts:root\default:StdRegProv")
objReg.SetStringValue HKLM, strNetlogonReg, "SiteName", strSite
WScript.Echo "Set SiteName to " & strSite
```

Using PowerShell

```
$strRegPath = "HKLM:\System\CurrentControlSet\Services\Netlogon\Parameters"
set-ItemProperty -path $strRegPath -name "SiteName" -value "<SiteName>"
```

Discussion

You can bypass the part of the DC Locator process that determines a client's site by hardcoding it in the Registry. This is generally not recommended and should primarily be used as a troubleshooting tool. If a client is experiencing authentication delays due to a misconfigured site or subnet object, you can hardcode its site so that it temporarily points to a more optimal location (and domain controller) to see if this alleviates the problem. However, in a situation like this, your ultimate goal should be to properly configure your sites and subnets so that the DC Locator process can function without this kind of manual intervention.

See Also

Recipe 11.27 for finding the site for a client and MS KB 247811 (How Domain Controllers Are Located in Windows)

11.29 Creating a Connection Object

Problem

You want to create a connection object to manually set up replication between two servers.

Solution

Using a graphical user interface

1. Open the Active Directory Sites and Services snap-in.
2. In the left pane, expand Sites, expand the site that contains the connection object you want to check, expand the Servers container, and expand the server for which you want to create the connection object.
3. Right-click on the NTDS Settings object and select Create New Active Directory Connection.
4. Select the replication partner and click OK.
5. Enter the name for the connection and click OK.

Using a command-line interface

```
> repadmin /add <PartitionDN> <DC1DNSName> <DC2DNSName>
```

Discussion

Hopefully you will not need to create connection objects manually, since creating and maintaining connection objects is the job of the KCC. It can be a lot of work to keep your connection objects up-to-date by yourself, especially if you have a large topology. The KCC uses complex algorithms to determine the best partners for a domain controller to replicate with. The Windows 2000 KCC had problems generating very large topologies, but the Windows Server 2003 version is significantly better.

It is sometimes necessary to create connections manually if you find a replication problem and need to get replication going again between one or more sites. By creating a connection and forcing replication to occur over that connection, you can get servers back in sync quickly.

See Also

Recipe 11.30 for listing the connection objects for a server

11.30 Listing the connection Objects for a Server

Problem

You want to view the connection objects associated with a domain controller.

Solution

Using a graphical user interface

1. Open the Active Directory Sites and Services snap-in.
2. In the left pane, expand Sites, expand the site that contains the connection object you want to check, expand the Servers container, expand the server that contains the connection object, and click on the NTDS Settings object.
3. In the right pane, under the name column, it will display which connection objects were automatically generated by the KCC and which ones were manually generated.

Using a command-line interface

```
> repadmin /showconn [<DomainControllerName>]
```

Using VBScript

```
' This code lists the connection objects for a server.
' ------ SCRIPT CONFIGURATION ------
strServer = "<ServerName>" ' e.g. dc01
strSite = "<SiteName>"     ' e.g. MySite1
' ------ END CONFIGURATION ---------

set objRootDSE = GetObject("LDAP://RootDSE")
set objNTDSCont = GetObject("LDAP://cn=NTDS Settings,cn=" & strServer & _
                       ",cn=servers,cn=" & strSite & ",cn=sites," & _
                       objRootDSE.Get("configurationNamingContext") )

objNTDSCont.Filter = Array("ntdsConnection")
WScript.Echo " Connection objects for " & strSite & "\" & strServer
for each objConn in objNTDSCont
   if objConn.Get("options") = 0 then
      Wscript.Echo " " & objConn.Get("cn") & " (MANUAL)"
   else
      Wscript.Echo " " & objConn.Get("cn") & " (AUTO)"
   end if
next
```

 Another option for programmatically getting the connection objects for a server is to use the GetDSAConnections method from the IADsTool interface.

Using PowerShell

```
get-QADObject -SearchRoot "cn=NTDS Settings,cn=<DC Name>,cn=servers,cn=<Site
Name>,cn=configuration,<ForestRootDN>" -lDAPFilter "objectclass=ntdsConnection"

$strCategory = "ntdsConnection"
$objSearchRoot = [ADSI] "LDAP://cn=NTDS Settings,cn=<DC Name>,cn=servers,
cn=<SiteName>,cn=configuration,<ForestRootDN>"
$objSearcher = New-Object System.DirectoryServices.DirectorySearcher
$objSearcher.SearchRoot = $objForest
$objSearcher.Filter = ("(objectCategory=$strCategory)")
$colResults = $objSearcher.FindAll()
```

Discussion

connection objects are used to replicate inbound changes to a domain controller. By viewing the connection objects for a server, you can see what domain controllers it receives updates from. connection objects are created automatically by the KCC, but can be created manually if necessary.

See Also

Recipe 11.29 for creating a connection object

11.31 Load-Balancing connection Objects

Problem

You want to evenly distribute `connection` objects between bridgehead servers in a site.

Solution

Using a command-line interface

To see what changes the Active Directory Load Balancing (ADLB) utility would make, run the following command without the `/commit` option. To actually make the changes in Active Directory, use the `/commit` option:

```
> adlb /server:<DomainControllerName> -site:<SiteName> [/commit] [/verbose]
```

 This utility is available in the Windows Server 2003 Resource Kit.

Discussion

Bridgeheads can become overloaded or end up with too many `connection` objects in relation to other bridgeheads in the domain. The ADLB tool allows you to balance the load of `connection` objects among bridgehead servers within a site. The Windows Server 2003 algorithms are much better than Windows 2000 at load-balancing `connection` objects across servers, but that process happens only when new `connection` objects are added. You can use the *adlb* tool to load-balance existing `connection` objects more efficiently at any time.

We recommend first viewing the changes *adlb* would make before using the `/commit` option. Though the tool has matured to the point that it will typically make good decisions for your topology, it is still always good to do a sanity check to ensure *adlb* doesn't mess up your replication topology.

11.32 Finding the ISTG for a Site

Problem

You want to find the Inter-Site Topology Generator (ISTG) for a site.

Solution

Using a graphical user interface

1. Open the Active Directory Sites and Services snap-in.
2. Click on the site you are interested in.
3. In the right pane, double-click on the NTDS Site Settings object.
4. The ISTG will be displayed under ISTG if one is present.

Using a command-line interface

In Windows Server 2003, you can query for this information using *repadmin* or DSQuery:

```
> repadmin /istg <DomainControllerName>

> dsquery * "cn=NTDS Site Settings,cn=<SiteName>,cn=sites,<ForestRootDN>" -attr
intersitetopologygenerator
```

 You can leave off the *<DomainControllerName>* switch to query the local DC for this information.

These commands are available only with Windows Server 2003. You can also use AdFind for both Windows 2000 and Windows Server 2003, as follows:

```
> adfind -config -rb "cn=ntds site settings,cn=<SiteName>,cn=sites"
intersitetopologygenerator
```

Using VBScript

```
' This code finds the ISTG for the specified site.
' ------ SCRIPT CONFIGURATION ------
strSiteName = <SiteName> ' e.g. Raleigh
' ------ END CONFIGURATION ---------

set objRootDSE = GetObject("LDAP://RootDSE")
set objSiteSettings = GetObject("LDAP://cn=NTDS Site Settings,cn=" & _
                                strSiteName & ",cn=sites," & _
                                objRootDSE.Get("ConfigurationNamingContext"))
on error resume next
strISTGDN = objSiteSettings.Get("interSiteTopologyGenerator")
if (strISTGDN <> "") then
   set objNTDSSettings = GetObject("LDAP://" & strISTGDN)
   set objServer = GetObject( objNTDSSettings.Parent )
   WScript.Echo "ISTG for site " & strSiteName & " is " & _
                objServer.Get("dnsHostName")
else
```

```
        WScript.Echo "No ISTG found for site " & strSiteName
    end if
```

Discussion

One domain controller in every site is picked as the ISTG for that site. While each domain controller is responsible for creating its own intra-site connection objects, the ISTG for a site is responsible for creating the inter-site connection objects for the bridgehead servers in the site.

The current ISTG for a site is stored in the interSiteTopologyGenerator attribute of the site's NTDS Site Settings object. The distinguished name of ISTG's NTDS Settings object is stored in the interSiteTopologyGenerator attribute.

Disabling inter-site topology generation is synonymous with disabling the KCC for a site. See Recipe 11.36 for more information on disabling the KCC.

See Also

Recipe 11.33 for moving the ISTG, Recipe 11.36, MS KB 224815 (The Role of the Inter-Site Topology Generator in Active Directory Replication), and MS KB 224599 (Determining the Inter-Site Topology Generator (ISTG) of a Site in the Active Directory)

11.33 Transferring the ISTG to Another Server

Problem

You want to move the ISTG for a site to another domain controller. This happens automatically if you take the current ISTG offline, but you may want to transfer the role to a server that is more optimal in your environment.

Solution

Using a graphical user interface

1. Open ADSI Edit.
2. Connect to the Configuration NC if it is not already displayed in the left pane.
3. In the left pane, browse to Configuration NC→Sites.
4. Click on the site you want to transfer the ISTG for.
5. In the right pane, double-click CN=NTDS Site Settings.
6. Modify the interSiteTopologyGenerator attribute to include the NTDS Settings object of the domain controller you want to transfer the ISTG role to.
7. Click OK.

Using a command-line interface

```
> admod -b "cn=NTDS Site Settings,cn=<SiteName>,
cn=sites,cn=configuration,<ForestRootDN>" interSiteTopologyGenerator::"cn=NTDS Site
Settings,cn=<NewISTGName>,cn=servers,cn=<SiteName>,
cn=sites,cn=configuration,<ForestRootDN>
```

Using VBScript

```
' This code forces a new ISTG in a site.
' ------ SCRIPT CONFIGURATION ------
' Name of site to transfer ISTG in
strSiteName = "<SiteName>" ' e.g. Raleigh
' Site the new ISTG server is in
strNewISTGSite = "<ISTGSiteName>" ' e.g. Raleigh
' Common name of server object for new ISTG
strNewISTGName = "<DomainControllerName>" ' e.g. dc01
' ------ END CONFIGURATION ---------

set objRootDSE = GetObject("LDAP://RootDSE")
set objSiteSettings = GetObject("LDAP://cn=NTDS Site Settings,cn=" & _
                                strSiteName & ",cn=sites," & _
                                objRootDSE.Get("ConfigurationNamingContext"))
strCurrentISTG = objSiteSettings.Get("interSiteTopologyGenerator")

objSiteSettings.Put "interSiteTopologyGenerator", _
                cn=NTDS Settings,cn=" & strNewISTGName & _
                ",cn=servers,cn=" & strNewISTGSite & ",cn=sites," & _
                objRootDSE.Get("ConfigurationNamingContext")
objSiteSettings.SetInfo
WScript.Echo "ISTG for " & strSiteName & " changed from:"
WScript.Echo " " & strCurrentISTG
WScript.Echo "To"
WScript.Echo " " & objSiteSettings.Get("interSiteTopologyGenerator")
```

Using PowerShell

You can modify the Inter-Site Topology Generator for an AD site using the Quest cmdlets or ADSI methods, as follows:

```
$strNewISTG = "cn=NTDS Settings,cn=<DC
Name>,cn=servers,cn=<SiteName>,cn=configuration,<ForestRootDN>"
set-QADObject -Identity "cn=NTDS
Settings,cn=<SiteName>,cn=Configuration,<ForestRootDN>" -ObjectAttributes
@{interSiteTopologyGenerator=$strNewISTG}

$strNewISTG = "cn=NTDS Settings,cn=<DC
Name>,cn=servers,cn=<SiteName>,cn=configuration,<ForestRootDN>"
$objSiteSettings = [ADSI] "LDAP://cn=NTDS
Settings,cn=<SiteName>,cn=Configuration,<ForestRootDN>"
$objSiteSettings.put("interSiteTopologyGenerator", $strNewISTG)
$objSiteSettings.SetInfo()
```

Discussion

The current ISTG for a site is stored in the `interSiteTopologyGenerator` attribute of the site's `NTDS Site Settings` object. The distinguished name of the ISTG's `NTDS Settings` object is stored in that attribute as well.

Domain controllers communicate their presence as the ISTG by writing to the `interSiteTopologyGenerator` attribute at a set interval. If you want another domain controller to assume the role of the ISTG, you need to write the distinguished name of that domain controller's `NTDS Settings` object to the `interSiteTopologyGenerator` attribute of the `NTDS Site Settings` object for the site.

Two registry settings govern the ISTG registration process, both of which are stored under the *HKEY_LOCAL_MACHINE\System\CurrentControlSet\Services\NTDS \Parameters* key. The interval (in minutes) in which the current ISTG should write to the `interSiteTopologyGenerator` attribute to inform the other DCs in the site that it is still the ISTG is stored in the `KCC site generator renewal interval (minutes)` value. The default is 30 minutes. The other value is named `KCC site generator failover (minutes)` and contains the time in minutes that each domain controller in the site should wait for the `interSiteTopologyGenerator` attribute to be written to before attempting to register itself as the ISTG. The default is 60 minutes.

See Also

MS KB 224815 (The Role of the Inter-Site Topology Generator in Active Directory Replication)

11.34 Triggering the KCC

Problem

You want to trigger the KCC.

Solution

Using a graphical user interface

1. Open the Active Directory Sites and Services snap-in.
2. In the left pane, browse to the `NTDS Settings` object for the server you want to trigger the KCC for.
3. Right-click on `NTDS Settings`, select All Tasks, and check Replication Topology.
4. Click OK.

Using a command-line interface

```
> repadmin /kcc <DomainControllerName>
```

Using VBScript

```
' This code triggers the KCC on a DC.
' ------ SCRIPT CONFIGURATION ------
strDC = "<DomainControllerName>" ' e.g. dc01
' ------ END CONFIGURATION ---------

set objIadsTools = CreateObject("IADsTools.DCFunctions")
intRes = objIadsTools.TriggerKCC(Cstr(strDC),0)

if intRes = -1 then
    Wscript.Echo objIadsTools.LastErrorText
else
    Wscript.Echo "KCC successfully triggered"
end if
```

Discussion

The KCC runs every 15 minutes by default on all domain controllers to generate the intra-site topology connections. The KCC that runs on the server that is selected as the ISTG generates inter-site topology connections to other sites from the bridgehead servers in its site. In some situations—such as when you create new site, siteLink, or subnet objects—you may want to run the KCC immediately so that any new connections between domain controllers are created right away.

See Also

Recipe 11.35 for determining if the KCC is completing successfully, the *iadstools.doc* file that is installed with the Support Tools for more information on IADsTools, and MS KB 224815 (The Role of the Inter-Site Topology Generator in Active Directory Replication)

11.35 Determining Whether the KCC Is Completing Successfully

Problem

You want to determine whether the KCC is completing successfully.

Solution

Using a graphical user interface

1. Open the Event Viewer of the target domain controller.
2. Click on the Directory Service log.

3. In the right pane, click on the Source heading to sort by that column.

4. Scroll down to view any events with `Source: NTDS KCC`.

Using a command-line interface

The following command will display any KCC errors found in the Directory Service log:

```
> dcdiag /v /test:kccevent /s:<DomainControllerName>
```

Using PowerShell

The following syntax will query the Directory Service log for all events that have a source of "NTDS KCC":

```
get-Eventlog "Directory Service" | where-object {$_.Source -eq "NTDS KCC" } |
format-list
```

Discussion

The only way to debug issues with the KCC is by looking for NTDS KCC events in the Directory Service event log. If you suspect a problem or perhaps are seeing errors, you can increase the amount of logging in the event log by enabling diagnostics logging for the KCC. When KCC diagnostics logging is enabled, each KCC exception logs a significant amount of information to the event log that may help you pinpoint the problem. See Recipe 15.2 for more information on enabling diagnostics logging.

11.36 Disabling the KCC for a Site

Problem

You want to disable the KCC for a site and generate your own replication connections between domain controllers.

Solution

Using a graphical user interface

1. Open ADSI Edit.

2. Connect to the Configuration Naming Context if it is not already displayed.

3. In the left pane, browse to the *cn=Sites* folder.

4. Click on the site you want to disable the KCC for.

5. In the right pane, double-click `CN=NTDS Site Settings`.

6. Modify the options attribute. To disable only intra-site topology generation, enable bit 0 (decimal 1). To disable inter-site topology generation, enable bit 4 (decimal 16). To disable both, enable both bit 4 and bit 1 (decimal 17).

---

7. Click OK.

Using a command-line interface

You can disable the KCC for *\<SiteName\>* by using the *ldifde* utility and an LDIF file that contains the following:

```
dn: cn=NTDS Site Settings,<SiteName>,cn=sites,cn=configuration,<ForestRootDN>
changetype: modify
replace: options
options: <OptionsValue>
-
```

If the LDIF file were named *disable_kcc.ldf*, you would run the following command:

```
> ldifde -v -i -f disable_kcc.ldf
```

You can also perform this change using a combination of AdFind and AdMod, as follows:

```
> adfind -b "cn=NTDS Settings,cn=<SiteName>,cn=Sites,cn=configuration,<ForestRootDN>"
options -adcsv | admod options::{{.:SET:<OptionsValue>}}
```

The LDIFDE solution simply overwrites the value of the options attribute without checking to see if any current value may be in place. See Recipe 4.15, or use the AdFind/AdMod solution for a safer method to modify bitwise values.

Using VBScript

```
' This code disables the KCC for a site.
' ------ SCRIPT CONFIGURATION ------
strSiteName = "<SiteName>" ' e.g. Default-First-Site-Name
boolDisableIntra = TRUE     ' set to TRUE/FALSE to disable/enable intra-site
boolDisableInter = TRUE     ' set to TRUE/FALSE to disable/enable inter-site
' ------ END CONFIGURATION ---------

strAttr = "options"
set objRootDSE = GetObject("LDAP://RootDSE")
set objObject = GetObject("LDAP://cn=NTDS Site Settings,cn=" _
                    & strSiteName & ",cn=sites," & _
                    objRootDSE.Get("configurationNamingContext") )

intBitsOrig = objObject.Get(strAttr)
intBitsCalc = CalcBit(intBitsOrig, 1, boolDisableIntra)
WScript.Echo "Checking the KCC Intra-site generation flag:"
if intBitsOrig <> intBitsCalc then
    objObject.Put strAttr, intBitsCalc
    objObject.SetInfo
    WScript.Echo "  Changed " & strAttr & " from " _
                & intBitsOrig & " to " & intBitsCalc

else
   WScript.Echo " Did not need to change " & strAttr & _
```

```
                " (" & intBitsOrig & ")"
    end if

    intBitsOrig = objObject.Get(strAttr)
    intBitsCalc = CalcBit(intBitsOrig, 16, boolDisableInter)
    WScript.Echo "Checking the KCC Inter-site generation flag:"
    if intBitsOrig <> intBitsCalc then
        objObject.Put strAttr, intBitsCalc
        objObject.SetInfo
        WScript.Echo " Changed " & strAttr & " from " & intBitsOrig & _
                    " to " & intBitsCalc
    else
        WScript.Echo " Did not need to change " & strAttr & " (" & _
                    intBitsOrig & ")"
    end if
```

Using PowerShell

```
$objNTDS = [ADSI] "LDAP://cn=<Site DN>"

$currentOptions = [int]($objNTDS.options.ToString())

$newOptions = $currentOptions -bor <Options Value> # 1, 16, or 17
$objNTDS.put("options", $newOptions)
$objNTDS.setInfo()
```

Discussion

In some cases, you may want to disable the KCC from generating the intra-site topology connections, inter-site topology connections, or both. The connection objects that the KCC dynamically creates determine how domain controllers replicate with each other. Disabling the KCC was sometimes necessary with Windows 2000 due to scalability issues with the KCC and very large topologies. In Windows Server 2003, the KCC has been greatly improved, and, hopefully, you will not need to disable the KCC. We recommend against disabling the KCC unless you have really good reasons, because you will have to pay close attention to any domain controller or site topology changes and manually adjust the connection objects accordingly.

Disabling the KCC can be done only at the site level. You have to modify the NTDS Site Settings object of the site for which you want to disable the KCC. The options attribute (a bit flag) on this object determines whether the KCC runs. If the 00001 bit is enabled, intra-site topology generation is disabled; if the 10000 bit is enabled (16 in decimal), inter-site topology generation is disabled. See Recipe 4.15 for more on the proper way to set bit flags.

See Also

Recipe 4.15 for more on setting bit flags, Recipe 11.29 for creating a connection object manually, MS KB 242780 (How to Disable the Knowledge Consistency Checker from

Automatically Creating Replication Topology), and MS KB 245610 (How to Disable the Knowledge Consistency Checker Inter-Site Topology Generation for All Sites)

11.37 Changing the Interval at Which the KCC Runs

Problem

You want to change the interval at which the KCC runs.

Solution

Using a graphical user interface

1. Run *regedit.exe* from the command line or Start→Run.
2. Expand *HKEY_LOCAL_MACHINE\SYSTEM\CurrentControlSet\Services\NTDS \Parameters*.
3. Right-click on Parameters and select New→DWORD Value.
4. Enter the following for the name: `Repl topology update period (secs)`.
5. Double-click on the new value, and under "Value data" enter the KCC interval in number of seconds (900 is the default).
6. Click OK.

Using a command-line interface

```
> reg add HKLM\System\CurrentControlSet\Services\NTDS\Parameters /v "Repl topology
update period (secs)" /t REG_DWORD /d <NumSecs>
```

Using VBScript

```
' This code changes the interval in which the KCC runs.
' ------ SCRIPT CONFIGURATION -------
intNumSecs = <NumSecs> ' Number of seconds between intervals
                       ' 900 is default
' ------ END CONFIGURATION ---------

strNetlogonReg = "SYSTEM\CurrentControlSet\Services\NTDS\Parameters"
const HKLM = &H80000002
Set objReg = GetObject("winmgmts:root\default:StdRegProv")
objReg.SetDWORDValue HKLM, strNetlogonReg, _
                    "Repl topology update period (secs)", _
                    intNumSecs
WScript.Echo "KCC interval set to " & intNumSecs
```

Using PowerShell

```
$strRegPath = "HKLM:\System\CurrentControlSet\Services\NTDS\Parameters"
set-ItemProperty -path $strRegPath -name "Repl topology update period (secs)" -
value "<# of secs>
```

Discussion

By default, the KCC checks its connections every 15 minutes and makes changes as necessary. You can modify this interval by simply modifying the registry. This was necessary with many Windows 2000 implementations that had large topologies. In that case, the KCC might have taken longer than 15 minutes to run, or else it would have monopolized the CPU. Changing the KCC to run every hour instead of 15 minutes helps ensure that it has enough time to complete. With Windows Server 2003, Microsoft made significant improvements to the scalability of the KCC, and we recommend running the KCC at the default interval.

There is another related registry setting you should also be aware of. By default, the KCC waits five minutes after Active Directory starts up before it runs. You can change this delay by creating a `REG_DWORD` value called `Repl topology update delay (secs)` under the *HKLM\System\CurrentControlSet\Services\NTDS\Parameters* key. The data for the value should be the number of seconds to wait after startup before the KCC starts. The default is 300, which is 5 minutes.

See Also

MS KB 271988 (Replication Topology Updates)

Replication

12.0 Introduction

Replication is one of the most important and perhaps complex components of Active Directory. The infrastructure behind Active Directory replication, including the site topology, `connection` objects, and the KCC, was covered in Chapter 11. This chapter focuses strictly on some of the tasks and processes associated with replicating data and checking replication health. For an in-depth overview of how replication works in Active Directory, we suggest reading *Active Directory*, Fourth Edition, Brian Desmond et al. (O'Reilly).

12.1 Determining Whether Two Domain Controllers Are in Sync

Problem

You want to determine whether two domain controllers are in sync and have no objects to replicate to each other.

Solution

Using a command-line interface

By running the following command you can compare the up-to-dateness vector on the two DCs:

```
> repadmin /showchanges <DestinationDC's FQDN> <SourceDCGUID> <NamingContext>
```

For example, the following illustrates the syntax needed to compare the up-to-dateness vectors using *dc2.adatumadatum.com* as the destination DC and the GUID of *dc1.adatum.com* as the source, checking replication on the Domain NC:

```
> repadmin /showchanges dc1.adatum.com 5f09d979-1795-4ca1-9fc3-04efd
2bb721 dc=adatum,dc=com
Building starting position from destination server dc1.adatum.com

Source Neighbor:
dc=adatum,dc=com
==== INBOUND NEIGHBORS =======================================

dc=adatum,dc=com
    Default-First-Site-Name\DC2 via RPC
        DC object GUID: 5f09d979-1795-4ca1-9fc3-04efd22bb721
        Address: 5f09d979-1795-4ca1-9fc3-04efd22bb721._msdcs.adatum.com
        DC invocationID: accbf436-4577-4191-9a42-16f49e01db5d
        SYNC_ON_STARTUP DO_SCHEDULED_SYNCS WRITEABLE
        USNs: 12384/OU, 12384/PU
        Last attempt @ 2006-02-26 10:04:08 was successful.

Destination's up-to-date vector:
accbf436-4577-4191-9a42-16f49e01db5d @ USN 12393
e197616c-7465-43f2-a502-bac90df20b09 @ USN 14059

==== SOURCE DC: 5f09d979-1795-4ca1-9fc3-04efd22bb721._msdcs.adatum.com ====

No Changes
```

The Windows 2000 version of *repadmin* requires you to use a different syntax, running a command against both DCs to allow you to manually compare the information that's automatically displayed by the **/showchanges** switch in Windows Server 2003. Here is the equivalent syntax:

```
> repadmin /showvector <NamingContextDN> <DC1Name>
> repadmin /showvector <NamingContextDN> <DC2Name>
```

Using VBScript

```
' This code prints the
' up-to-dateness vector for the DCs defined in
' the array arrDCList for the naming context defined by strNCDN.
' ------ SCRIPT CONFIGURATION -----
' Set to the DN of the naming context you want to check the DCs against
strNCDN = "<NamingContextDN>" ' e.g. dc=amer,dc=adatum,dc=com
' Enter 2 or more DCs to compare
arrDCList = Array("<DC1Name>","<DC2Name>")
' ------ END CONFIGURATION --------

set objIadsTools = CreateObject("IADsTools.DCFunctions")

for each strDC in arrDCList
   WScript.Echo "
Replication partner USNs for " & strDC & ":"
   intUSN = objIadsTools.GetHighestCommittedUSN(Cstr(strDC),0)
   if intUSN = -1 then
       Wscript.Echo "Error retrieving USN: " & objIadsTools.LastErrorText
       WScript.Quit
   end if
```

```
WScript.Echo vbTab & strDC & " = " & intUSN

intRes = objIadsTools.GetReplicationUSNState(Cstr(strDC), _
                                      Cstr(strNCDN),0,0)
   if intRes = -1 then
      Wscript.Echo "Error retrieving USNs: " & objIadsTools.LastErrorText
      WScript.Quit
   end if
   for count = 1 to intRes
      WScript.Echo vbTab & objIadsTools.ReplPartnerName(count) & _
            " = " & objIadsTools.ReplPartnerUSN(count)
   next
   WScript.Echo
next
```

Using PowerShell

```
Write-Host $domain =
[System.DirectoryServices.ActiveDirectory.Domain]::GetCurrentDomain()
$NC = "DC={0}" -f ($domain.Name -replace "\.",",DC=")
foreach($dc in $domain.DomainControllers)
{
   Write-Host "$($DC.Name)"
   Write-Host "================"
   $UDTV = $dc.GetReplicationCursors($NC)
   $GUID =
@{n='DSA';e={if($_.SourceServer){$_.SourceServer}else{$_.SourceInvocationId}}}
   $UDTV | Select-Object $GUID,UpToDatenessUsn,LastSuccessfulSyncTime | Sort-Object
DSA -desc
}
```

Discussion

To determine if two or more DCs are in sync from a replication standpoint, you need
to compare their up-to-dateness vectors. Each domain controller stores what it thinks
is the highest update sequence number (USN) for every DC that replicates a naming
context. This is called the *up-to-dateness vector*. If you want to compare DC1 and DC2,
you'd first want to get the up-to-dateness vector for DC1 and compare DC1's highest
USN against what DC2 thinks DC1's highest USN is. If they are different, then you can
deduce that DC2 has not yet replicated all the changes from DC1. Next, compare the
reverse to see if DC1 is in sync with DC2.

See Also

IadsTools.doc in the Support Tools for more information on the IADsTools' interface

12.2 Viewing the Replication Status of Several Domain Controllers

Problem

You want to take a quick snapshot of replication activity for one or more domain controllers.

Solution

Using a command-line interface

The following command will show the replication status of all the domain controllers in the forest, as shown in the output that follows:

```
> repadmin /replsum

Replication Summary Start Time: 2006-02-26 11:01:34

Beginning data collection for replication summary, this may take awhile:
  .....

Source DC          largest delta  fails/total %% error
DC1                     15m:22s     0 /   3   0
DC2                        :12s     0 /   3   0

Destination DC largest delta     fails/total %% error
DC1                        :05s     0 /   3   0
DC2                     15m:22s     0 /   3   0
```

You can also use * as a wildcard character to view the status of a subset of domain controllers. The following command will display the replication status of only the servers that begin with the name **dc-rtp**:

```
> repadmin /replsum dc-rtp*
```

 This command is available starting with the Windows Server 2003 version of *repadmin*.

Discussion

The new **/replsum** option in *repadmin* is a great way to quickly determine if there are any replication issues. This command should be your starting point if you suspect any replication problems. If you are running **/replsum** against a lot of domain controllers, you can use the **/sort** option to sort the returned table output by any of the table columns. You can also use the /errorsonly option to display only the replication partners who are encountering errors.

12.3 Viewing Unreplicated Changes Between Two Domain Controllers

Problem

You want to find the unreplicated changes between two domain controllers.

Solution

Using a graphical user interface

1. Open the Replication Monitor from the Support Tools (*replmon.exe*).
2. From the menu, select View→Options.
3. On the General tab, check the boxes beside Show Transitive Replication Partners and Extended Data.
4. Click OK.
5. In the left pane, right-click on Monitored Servers and select Add Monitored Server.
6. Use the Add Monitored Server Wizard to add one of the domain controllers you want to compare (we'll call it *dc1*).
7. In the left pane, under the server you just added, expand the naming context that you want to check for unreplicated changes.
8. Right-click on the other domain controller you want to compare (we'll call it *dc2*) and select "Check Current USN and Un-replicated Objects."
9. Enter credentials if necessary and click OK.
10. If some changes have not yet replicated from *dc2* to *dc1*, a box will pop up that lists the unreplicated objects.
11. To find out what changes have yet to replicate from *dc1* to *dc2*, repeat the same steps, except add *dc2* as a monitored server and check for unreplicated changes against *dc1*.

Using a command-line interface

Run the following command to find the differences between two domain controllers. Use the /statistics option to view a summary of the changes:

```
> repadmin /showchanges <DC1Name> <DC2GUID> <NamingContextDN>
> repadmin /showchanges <DC2Name> <DC1GUID> <NamingContextDN>
```

The Windows 2000 version of *repadmin* has a different syntax to accomplish the same thing. Here is the equivalent syntax:

```
> repadmin /getchanges <NamingContextDN> <DC1Name> <DC2GUID>
> repadmin /getchanges <NamingContextDN> <DC2Name> <DC1GUID>
```

Using VBScript

```
' This code uses the IADsTools interface to print the unreplicated
' changes for the naming context defined by strNCDN for the DCs
' defined by strDC1Name and strDC2Name.
' ------ SCRIPT CONFIGURATION ------
strNCDN    = "<NamingContextDN>" ' e.g. dc=adatum,dc=com
strDC1Name = "<DC1Name>"         ' e.g. dc1.adatum.com
strDC2Name = "<DC2Name>"         ' e.g. dc2.adatum.com
' ------ END CONFIGURATION ---------

set objIadsTools = CreateObject("IADsTools.DCFunctions")


' ---------------------------------
' Have to get the GUIDs of both servers in order to identify
' the correct partner in the GetReplicationUSNState call
' ---------------------------------
strDC1GUID = objIadsTools.GetGuidForServer(Cstr(strDC1Name), _
                                   Cstr(strDC1Name),0)
strDC2GUID = objIadsTools.GetGuidForServer(Cstr(strDC2Name), _
                                   Cstr(strDC2Name),0)
' ---------------------------------
' Need to get what each DC thinks is the highest USN for the other
' The USN is needed in the call to GetMetaDataDifferences to return
' the unreplicated changes
' ---------------------------------
intRes = objIadsTools.GetReplicationUSNState(Cstr(strDC1Name), _
                                   Cstr(strNCDN),0,0)
if intRes = -1 then
   Wscript.Echo objIadsTools.LastErrorText
   WScript.Quit
end if
for count = 1 to intRes
   if strDC2GUID = objIadsTools.ReplPartnerGuid(count) then
      intDC2USN = objIadsTools.ReplPartnerUSN(count)
   end if
next
if intDC2USN = "" then
   WScript.Echo strDC2Name & " is not a replication partner with " & _
             strDC1Name
end if
intRes = objIadsTools.GetReplicationUSNState(Cstr(strDC2Name), _
                                   Cstr(strNCDN),0,0)
if intRes = -1 then
   Wscript.Echo objIadsTools.LastErrorText
   WScript.Quit
end if
for count = 1 to intRes
   if strDC1GUID = objIadsTools.ReplPartnerGuid(count) then
```

```
            intDC1USN = objIadsTools.ReplPartnerUSN(count)
        end if
    next
    if intDC2USN = "" then
        WScript.Echo strDC1Name & " is not a replication partner with " & _
                    strDC2Name
    end if


    ' ---------------------------------
    ' Now that we have retrieved the highest USN for both partners,
    ' the GetMetaDataDifferences method will return what needs to be
    ' replicated
    ' ---------------------------------
    intRes = objIadsTools.GetMetaDataDifferences(Cstr(strDC1Name), _
                                                 Cstr(intDC1USN), _
                                                 Cstr(strNCDN),0)
    if intRes = -1 then
        Wscript.Echo objIadsTools.LastErrorText
        WScript.Quit
    end if
    WScript.Echo "Data on " & strDC1Name & " but not " & strDC2Name & ":"
    for count = 1 to intRes
        WScript.Echo count & ". " & _
                    objIadsTools.MetaDataDifferencesObjectDN(count)
        WScript.Echo vbTab & " Attribute: " & _
                    objIadsTools.MetaDataDifferencesAttribute(count)
        WScript.Echo vbTab & " Write time: " & _
                    objIadsTools.MetaDataDifferencesLastWriteTime(count)
        WScript.Echo vbTab & " Orig Server: " & _
                    objIadsTools.MetaDataDifferencesOrigServer(count)
        WScript.Echo vbTab & " Orig USN: " & _
                    objIadsTools.MetaDataDifferencesOrigUSN(count)
    next
    WScript.Echo

    intRes = objIadsTools.GetMetaDataDifferences(Cstr(strDC2Name), _
                                                 Cstr(intDC2USN), _
                                                 Cstr(strNCDN), 0)
    if intRes = -1 then
        Wscript.Echo objIadsTools.LastErrorText
        WScript.Quit
    end if
    WScript.Echo "Data on " & strDC2Name & " but not " & strDC1Name & ":"
    for count = 1 to intRes
        WScript.Echo count & ". " & _
                    objIadsTools.MetaDataDifferencesObjectDN(count)
        WScript.Echo vbTab & " Attribute: " & _
                    objIadsTools.MetaDataDifferencesAttribute(count)
        WScript.Echo vbTab & " Write time: " & _
                    objIadsTools.MetaDataDifferencesLastWriteTime(count)
        WScript.Echo vbTab & " Orig Server: " & _
                    objIadsTools.MetaDataDifferencesOrigServer(count)
        WScript.Echo vbTab & " Orig USN: " & _
                    objIadsTools.MetaDataDifferencesOrigUSN(count)
    next
```

Discussion

All three solutions show how to display the current unreplicated changes between two domain controllers. This can be useful in troubleshooting replication on your network, particularly if you are finding inconsistent information between one or more domain controllers. The `repadmin /showchanges` command has several additional options you can use to display the changes, including saving the output to a file for later comparison. Also, with the `/statistics` option, you can view a summary of the changes.

See Also

IadsTools.doc in the Support Tools for more information on the IADsTools interface

12.4 Forcing Replication from One Domain Controller to Another

Problem

You want to force replication between two partners.

Solution

Using a graphical user interface

1. Open the Active Directory Sites and Services snap-in.
2. Browse to the NTDS Setting object for the domain controller you want to replicate to.
3. In the right pane, right-click on the `connection` object corresponding to the domain controller you want to replicate from and select Replicate Now.

Using a command-line interface

The following command will perform a replication sync from *<DC2Name>* to *<DC1Name>* of the naming context specified by *<NamingContextDN>*:

```
> repadmin /replicate <DC1Name> <DC2Name> <NamingContextDN>
```

The Windows 2000 version of *repadmin* has a different syntax to accomplish the same thing. Here is the equivalent syntax:

```
> repadmin /sync <NamingContextDN> <DC1Name> <DC2GUID>
```

Using VBScript

```
' This code initiates a replication event between two DCs
' for a naming context
' ------ SCRIPT CONFIGURATION -----
strDC1Name = "<DC1Name>" ' e.g. dc1
strDC2Name = "<DC2Name>" ' e.g. dc2
strNamingContextDN = "<NamingContextDN>" ' e.g. dc=adatum,dc=com
' ------ END CONFIGURATION --------

set objIadsTools = CreateObject("IADsTools.DCFunctions")
intRes = objIadsTools.ReplicaSync(Cstr(strDC1Name),_
                        Cstr(strNamingContextDN),_
                        Cstr(strDC2Name), 0, 0)

if intRes = -1 then
    Wscript.Echo "Error: " & objIadsTools.LastErrorText
else
    WScript.Echo "Replication intitiated from " & strDC2Name & _
            " to " & strDC1Name
end if
```

Using PowerShell

```
$strDCname = <DomainDNSName>
$context = New-Object
System.DirectoryServices.ActiveDirectory.DirectoryContext('DirectoryServer',
$strDCname)
$dc =
[System.DirectoryServices.ActiveDirectory.DomainController]::getDomainController
($context)
$strPartDN = "<Partition DN>"
$dc.TriggerSyncReplicaFromNeighbors($strPartDN)
```

Discussion

Each solution shows how to replicate all unreplicated changes from a source domain controller to a destination domain controller. This sync is a one-way operation. If you want to ensure that both domain controllers are in sync, you'll need to follow the same procedure in the opposite direction, replicating both from DC1 to DC2 and from DC2 to DC1. It's important to remember that all replication takes place as a *pull* operation. For example, DC2 notifies DC1 that it has changes available, after which DC1 pulls the changes it needs from DC2. For replication to occur in the opposite direction, DC1 will notify DC2 that it has changes available, and DC2 will pull those changes from DC1.

> With *repadmin*, you can replicate a single object instead of any unreplicated object in a naming context by using the /replsingleobj option. This option is available starting with the Windows Server 2003 version of *repadmin*.

Using PowerShell

The PowerShell method in this solution will prompt the DC to trigger replication for all of its configured replication partners, not just an individual remote domain controller.

See Also

Recipe 12.3 for viewing unreplicated changes between two domain controllers, MS KB 232072 (Initiating Replication Between Active Directory Direct Replication Partners), and *IadsTools.doc* in the Support Tools for more information on the IADsTools interface

12.5 Enabling and Disabling Replication

Problem

You want to enable or disable inbound or outbound replication on a domain controller.

Solution

Using a command-line interface

To disable outbound replication on a domain controller, use the following syntax:

```
> repadmin /options +DISABLE_OUTBOUND_REPL
```

To re-enable outbound replication, enter the following:

```
> repamin /options -DISABLE_OUTBOUND_REPL
```

To disable inbound replication, use the following syntax:

```
> repadmin /options +DISABLE_INBOUND_REPL
```

To re-enable inbound replication, use the following:

```
> repadmin /options -DISABLE_INBOUND_REPL
```

Discussion

When you are making major changes to Active Directory, particularly in cases where you are extending the schema, it is recommended that you disable outbound replication on the DC that you're modifying. This will allow you to test any changes that you've made on a single DC without propagating those changes to the remainder of your directory. If you make a mistake or find that the changes you've made are otherwise unacceptable, you can restore a single DC rather than being faced with the prospect of performing a disaster recovery operation on your entire domain.

It's important to note that disabling outbound replication on a domain controller will not have any effect on inbound replication; the DC in question will still receive updates from its other replication partners unless you disable inbound replication on them as well.

In a worst-case scenario, you can disable replication for an entire forest by issuing the following command:

```
> repadmin /options * +DISABLE_INBOUND_REPL
```

See Also

MS KB 321153 (How to Disable or Enable Active Directory Replication in Windows 2000)

12.6 Changing the Intra-Site Replication Interval

Problem

You want to change the number of seconds that a domain controller in a site waits before replicating within the site.

Solution

Using a graphical user interface

1. Run *regedit.exe* from the command line or Start→Run.
2. Expand *HKEY_LOCAL_MACHINE\SYSTEM\CurrentControlSet\Services\NTDS \Parameters*.
3. If a value entry for Replicator notify pause after modify (secs) does not exist, right-click on Parameters and select New→DWORD Value. For the name, enter Replicator notify pause after modify (secs).
4. Double-click on the value and enter the number of seconds to wait before notifying intra-site replication partners.
5. Click OK.

Using a command-line interface

```
> reg add HKLM\System\CurrentControlSet\Services\NTDS\Parameters /v "Replicator
notify pause after modify (secs)" /t REG_DWORD /d <NumSeconds>
```

Using VBScript

```
' This code sets the intra-site delay interval.
' ------ SCRIPT CONFIGURATION -----
strDC = "<DomainControllerName>" ' DC you want to configure
intNumSeconds = <NumSeconds> ' Time in seconds to delay
```

```
'  ------ END CONFIGURATION --------

const HKLM = &H80000002
strNTDSReg = "SYSTEM\CurrentControlSet\Services\NTDS\Parameters"
set objReg = GetObject("winmgmts:\\" & strDC & _
                       "\root\default:StdRegProv")
objReg.SetDWORDValue HKLM, strNTDSReg, _
                    "Replicator notify pause after modify (secs)", _
                    intNumSeconds
WScript.Echo "Intra-site replication delay set to " & intNumSeconds
```

Using PowerShell

```
$strRegPath = "HKLM:\System\CurrentControlSet\Services\Netlogon\Parameters"
$strKeyName = "Replicator notify pause after modify (secs)"
$intSeconds = <NumSeconds>
Set-ItemProperty -path $strRegPath -name $strKeyName -value $intSeconds
```

Discussion

After a change has been made to a domain controller's local copy of Active Directory, it waits for a period of time before sending change-notification requests to its intra-site replication partners. The default delay on Windows 2000 domain controllers is 5 minutes; for Windows Server 2003, the default delay has been changed to 15 seconds. You can customize this notification delay by changing the registry value `Replicator notify pause after modify (secs)` on the domain controllers, as described in the "Solution" section.

 If you are upgrading a Windows 2000 domain controller to Windows Server 2003, Microsoft recommends removing the 5-minute value after upgrading to Windows Server 2003 in order to utilize the new default of 15 seconds.

See Also

MS KB 214678 (How to Modify the Default Intra-Site Domain Controller Replication Interval)

12.7 Changing the Intra-Site Notification Delay

Problem

You want to change how long a domain controller waits before notifying domain controllers within a site that updates are available.

Solution

Using a graphical user interface

1. Open ADSI Edit.
2. If an entry for the Configuration naming context you want to browse is not already displayed, do the following:
   a. Right-click on ADSI Edit in the right pane and click "Connect to...".
   b. Fill in the information for the Configuration NC. Click on the Advanced button if you need to enter alternate credentials.
3. In the left pane, browse to CN=Configuration, <ForestRootDN>→CN=Partitions. Right-click on the domain partition designated by the short name of the domain (CN=ADATUM for *adatum.com*) and select Properties.
4. Double-click on the following attributes and modify their values as appropriate:
   - msDS-Replication-Notify-First-DSA-Delay
   - msDS-Replication-Notify-Subsequent-DSA-Delay

Using a command-line interface

Create a file called *modify_replication_interval.ldf* with the following contents:

```
dn: <DomainPartitionCrossRefDN>
changetype: modify
replace: msDS-Replication-Notify-First-DSA-Delay
msDS-Replication-Notify-First-DSA-Delay: <FirstDelayInSeconds>
-
replace: msDS-Replication-Notify-Subsequent-DSA-Delay
msDS-Replication-Notify-Subsequent-DSA-Delay: <NextDelayInSeconds>
```

Then import the changes into Active Directory using the following syntax:

```
ldifde -i -v modify_replication_interval.ldf
```

You can also make the changes using AdMod, as follows:

```
admod -b cn=<DomainPartition>,cn=Partitions,cn=Configuration,<ForestRootDN> msDS-
Replication-Notification-First-DSA-Delay::<FirstDelayInSeconds> msDS-
Replication-Notify-Subsequent-DSA-Delay::<NextDelayInSeconds>
```

Using VBScript

```
' This code sets the
' replication delay for an application partition.
' ------ SCRIPT CONFIGURATION -----
strDomainPartDN = "<DomainPartitionDN>" ' e.g. cn=adatum,dc=adatum,dc=com
intFirstDelay = <FirstDelayInSeconds>
intNextDelay = <NextDelayInSeconds>
' ------ END CONFIGURATION --------

set objRootDSE = GetObject("LDAP://RootDSE")
```

```
strBase = "<LDAP://cn=Partitions," & _
          objRootDSE.Get("ConfigurationNamingContext") & ">;"
strFilter = "(&(objectcategory=crossRef)(nCName=" & strDomainPartDN & "));"
strAttrs = "cn,distinguishedName;"
strScope = "onelevel"
set objConn = CreateObject("ADODB.Connection")
objConn.Provider = "ADsDSOObject"
objConn.Open "Active Directory Provider"
set objRS = objConn.Execute(strBase & strFilter & strAttrs & strScope)

if objRS.RecordCount <> 1 then
   WScript.Echo "Did not find a match for " & strDomainPartDN
else
   objRS.MoveLast
   set objAppPart = GetObject("LDAP://" & _
                    objRS.Fields("distinguishedName").Value )
   objAppPart.Put "msDS-Replication-Notify-First-DSA-Delay", intFirstDelay
   objAppPart.Put "msDS-Replication-Notify-Subsequent-DSA-Delay", intNextDelay
   objAppPart.SetInfo
   Wscript.Echo "Modified " & objRS.Fields("distinguishedName").Value
end if
```

Using PowerShell

To modify the intra-site replication parameters, you can use the Quest AD cmdlets or ADSI methods, as follows:

```
set-QADObject -Identity
cn==<DomainPartition>,cn=Partitions,cn=Configuration,<ForestRootDN> -
ObjectAttributes @{ Replication-Notification-First-DSA-
Delay="<FirstDelayInSeconds>";msDS-
Replication-Notify-Subsequent-DSA-Delay::"<NextDelayInSeconds>"}

$objPart = cn=<DomainPartition>,cn=Partitions,cn=Configuration,<ForestRootDN>
$objPart.Put("Replication-Notification-First-DSA-Delay", "<FirstDelayInSeconds>")
$objPart.Put("msDS-Replication-Notify-Subsequent-DSA-Delay",
"<NextDelayInSeconds>")
$objPart.SetInfo()
```

Discussion

Because Active Directory assumes that DCs within a site are connected by high-speed links, intra-site replication occurs as changes are made rather than adhering to a specific schedule. In Windows 2000, anytime you made a change on a domain controller, that DC would wait five minutes before beginning to notify its replication partners that it had changes available, as we discussed in the previous recipe. The 2000 DC would then notify all of its configured partners one at a time in 30-second intervals. To change these values in Windows 2000, you need to modify the following Reg_DWORD values in the Windows 2000 Registry:

```
HKEY_LOCAL_MACHINE\SYSTEM\CurrentControlSet
\Services\NTDS\Parameters\Replicator notify pause after modify (secs)

HKEY_LOCAL_MACHINE\SYSTEM\CurrentControlSet
\Services\NTDS\Parameters\Replicator notify pause between DSAs(secs)
```

In Windows Server 2003, the intra-site replication intervals have been reduced so that the initial delay is 15 seconds, after which a 2003 DC will notify its replication partners in 3-second intervals. This greatly reduces the *convergence time* within a site—that is, the amount of time it takes for domain controllers within a site to synchronize with one another.

 There are some updates that are deemed of sufficient importance that the initial 15-second delay does not apply. This is known as *urgent replication*, and applies to critical directory updates such as locking out an account, changing the account lockout or password policy of a domain, and changing the password of a domain-controller computer account.

See Also

MS KB 214678 (How to Modify the Default Intra-Site Domain Controller Replication Interval), and MS KB 305476 (Initial Synchronization Requirements for Windows 2000 Server and Windows Server 2003 Operations Master Role Holders)

12.8 Changing the Inter-Site Replication Interval

Problem

You want to set the replication schedule for a site link.

Solution

Using a graphical user interface

1. Open the Active Directory Sites and Services snap-in.
2. Expand the Inter-Site Transport container.
3. Click on the IP container.
4. In the right pane, double-click on the site link you want to modify the replication interval for.
5. Enter the new interval beside "Replicate every."
6. Click OK.

Using a command-line interface

To change the replication interval, create an LDIF file named *set_link_rep_interval.ldf* with the following contents:

```
dn: cn=<LinkName>,cn=ip,cn=Inter-Site Transports,cn=sites,
cn=configuration,<ForestRootDN>
changetype: modify
replace: replInterval
replInterval: <NewInterval>
-
```

Then run the following command:

```
> ldifde -v -i -f set_link_rep_interval.ldf
```

You can also make this change using AdMod, as follows:

```
> admod -b cn=<LinkName>,cn=ip,cn=Inter-Site
Transports,cn=sites,cn=configuration,<ForestRootDN>
replInterval::<NewInterval>
```

Using VBScript

```
' This code sets the
' replication interval for a site link.
' ------ SCRIPT CONFIGURATION -----
strLinkName     = "<LinkName>" ' cn of the link you want to configure
intNewInterval = <NewInterval> ' replication interval in minutes
' ------ END CONFIGURATION --------

set objRootDSE = GetObject("LDAP://RootDSE")
set objLink = GetObject("LDAP://cn=" & strLinkName & _
                        ",cn=IP,cn=Inter-site Transports,cn=sites," & _
                        objRootDSE.Get("configurationNamingContext") )
objLink.Put "replInterval", intNewInterval
objLink.SetInfo
WScript.Echo "Set interval for link " & objLink.Get("cn") & _
             " to " & intNewInterval
```

Using PowerShell

```
set-QADObject -Identity "cn=<LinkName>,cn=ip,cn=Inter-Site
Transports,cn=sites,cn=configuration,<ForestRootDN>" -objectAttributes
@{replInterval="<newInterval>"}

$objSiteLink = [ADSI] "cn=<LinkName>,cn=ip,cn=Inter-Site
Transports,cn=sites,cn=configuration,<ForestRootDN>"
$objSiteLink.Put("replInterval", "<newInterval>")
$objSiteLink.SetInfo()
```

Discussion

To configure the inter-site replication interval between two sites, you need to set the `replInterval` attribute on the site-link object that connects the two sites. The value of the attribute should be the replication interval in minutes. The default value is 180 minutes (3 hours), and the minimum is 15 minutes.

These solutions assume the use of IP transport, but SMTP transport can be used as well. However, keep in mind that you cannot use an SMTP link to replicate the Domain naming context, only the Schema and Configuration NCs as well as Global Catalog information.

See Also

MS KB 224815 (The Role of the Inter-Site Topology Generator in Active Directory Replication), and "Administering Inter-Site Replication" in the Windows Server 2003 Operations Guide

12.9 Disabling Inter-Site Compression of Replication Traffic

Problem

You want to disable inter-site compression of replication traffic.

Solution

You need to modify the options attribute of the site-link object that connects the sites you want to disable compression for. Site-link objects are stored in the following location:

```
cn=IP,cn=Inter-site Transports,cn=Sites,cn=Configuration,<ForestRootDN>
```

The options attribute is a bit flag. In order to disable compression, you must set bit 2, or 0100 in binary. If the attribute is currently unset, you can simply set it to 4.

Using a command-line interface

```
> adfind -b cn=IP,cn=Inter-site Transports,cn=Sites,cn=Configuration,<ForestRootDN>
options -adcsv | admod options::{{.:SET:4}}
```

Using VBScript

```
' This code safely modifies a bit flag attribute
' ------ SCRIPT CONFIGURATION ------
strSiteLink = "cn=<LinkName>,cn=IP" &
  ",cn=Inter-site Transports,cn=Sites,cn=Configuration,<ForestRootDN>"
strAttr = "options"
boolEnableBit = <TRUEorFALSE> ' e.g. FALSE
intBit = 4
' ------ END CONFIGURATION --------

set objSiteLink = GetObject("LDAP://" & strSiteLink)
intBitsOrig = objObject.Get(strAttr)
intBitsCalc = CalcBit(intBitsOrig, intBit, boolEnableBit)
```

```
if intBitsOrig <> intBitsCalc then
   objSiteLink.Put strAttr, intBitsCalc
   objSiteLink.SetInfo
   WScript.Echo "Changed " & strAttr & " from " & intBitsOrig & " to " &
intBitsCalc
else
   WScript.Echo "Did not need to change " & strAttr & " (" & intBitsOrig & ")"
end if

Function CalcBit(intValue, intBit, boolEnable)

   CalcBit = intValue

   if boolEnable = TRUE then
      CalcBit = intValue Or intBit
   else
      if intValue And intBit then
         CalcBit = intValue Xor intBit
      end if
   end if

End Function
```

Using PowerShell

To set the options bit value using a bitwise OR operation, use the following syntax:

```
$objSiteLink = [ADSI]("LDAP:// cn=<LinkName>,cn=IP," +
   "cn=Inter-site Transports,cn=Sites,cn=Configuration,<ForestRootDN>")
$currentOptions = $objSiteLink.options.Value
$newOptions = $currentOptions -bor 4
$objSiteLink.Put("options", $newOptions)
$objSiteLink.SetInfo()
```

Discussion

By default, data replicated inter-site is compressed. By contrast, intra-site replication traffic is not compressed. It is useful to compress inter-site traffic if the traffic is going over a WAN on the assumption that the less traffic the better. The trade-off to reducing WAN traffic is increased CPU utilization on the bridgehead servers replicating the data. If CPU utilization is an issue on your bridgehead servers and you aren't as concerned about the amount of traffic being replicated, you should consider disabling inter-site compression.

See Also

Recipe 4.15 for setting bit flag attributes

12.10 Checking for Potential Replication Problems

Problem

You want to determine whether replication is succeeding.

Solution

The following two commands will help identify problems with replication on a source domain controller:

```
> dcdiag /test:replications
> repadmin /showrepl /errorsonly
```

Discussion

For a more detailed report, you can use the Replication Monitor (*replmon.exe*). The `Generate Status Report` option will produce a lengthy report of site topology and replication information, and will provide details on any errors encountered. The Directory Service event log can also be an invaluable source of information on replication and KCC problems.

See Also

Recipe 12.2 for viewing the replication status of several domain controllers

12.11 Enabling Enhanced Logging of Replication Events

Problem

You want to enable enhanced logging of replication events.

Solution

Enable diagnostics logging for five Replication Events. See Recipe 15.2 for more information.

See Also

MS KB 220940 (How to Enable Diagnostic Event Logging for Active Directory Services)

12.12 Enabling Strict or Loose Replication Consistency

Problem

You want to enable strict or loose replication consistency.

Solution

Using a graphical user interface

1. Run *regedit.exe* from the command line or Start→Run.

2. Expand *HKEY_LOCAL_MACHINE\SYSTEM\CurrentControlSet\Services\NTDS\Parameters*.

3. If the `Strict Replication Consistency` value does not exist, right-click on Parameters and select New→DWORD Value. For the name, enter `Strict Replication Consistency`.

4. In the right pane, double-click on the value and enter 1 to enable strict consistency or 0 to enable loose consistency.

5. Click OK.

Using a command-line interface

To enable strict consistency, run the following command:

```
> reg add HKLM\System\CurrentControlSet\Services\NTDS\Parameters /v "Strict
Replication Consistency" /t REG_DWORD /d 1
```

To enable loose consistency, run the following command:

```
> reg add HKLM\System\CurrentControlSet\Services\NTDS\Parameters /v "Strict
Replication Consistency" /t REG_DWORD /d 0
```

You can also enable and disable strict replication using `repadmin`. You can either specify an individual domain controller in the `<DC Name>` field, or use a * to enable or disable strict replication on every DC in the forest, as follows:

```
repadmin /regkey <DCName> +strict
repadmin /regkey <DCName> -strict
```

Using VBScript

```
' This code enables strict or loose consistency on the specified DC.
' ------ SCRIPT CONFIGURATION -----
intEnableStrict = 1 ' 1 = strict consistency, 0 = loose consistency
strDC = "<DomainControllerName>"
' ------ END CONFIGURATION --------

const HKLM = &H80000002
strNTDSReg = "SYSTEM\CurrentControlSet\Services\NTDS\Parameters"
set objReg = GetObject("winmgmts:\\" & strDC & _
                       "\root\default:StdRegProv")
objReg.SetDWORDValue HKLM, strNTDSReg, "
Strict Replication Consistency", _
                     intEnableStrict
WScript.Echo "Strict Replication Consistency value set to " & _
             intEnableStrict
```

Using PowerShell

```
$strRegPath = "HKLM:\System\CurrentControlSet\Services\NTDS\Parameters"
Set-ItemProperty -path $strRegPath -name "Strict Replication Consistency" -value
"1"
```

Discussion

Up until Windows 2000 Service Pack 3, domain controllers followed a *loose replication consistency* model whereby lingering objects could get reinjected into Active Directory and replicate among all the domain controllers. A *lingering object* is one that was previously deleted, but got reintroduced because a domain controller did not successfully replicate for the duration of the time defined by the tombStoneLifetime attribute, or because the object was restored using a backup older than the tombStoneLifetime. See Recipe 16.0 for more on the tombStoneLifetime attribute. Windows 2000 SP2 and earlier domain controllers would replicate the lingering object throughout the naming context. Loose consistency thus has the potential to cause some security risks since an object you thought was deleted is now back in the forest again.

Some post-SP2 hotfixes and SP3 introduced *strict replication consistency*. Under strict replication, a domain controller will stop replicating with a destination domain controller when it determines that the source is attempting to replicate a lingering object. Event ID 1084 will get logged in the Directory Service event log, indicating that the domain controller couldn't replicate the lingering object. Although strict replication can halt replication, it is the preferable method, and a good way to check that lingering objects do not infiltrate your forest. For this reason, you must monitor your domain controllers to ensure they are replicating on a regular basis and that they do not have any 1084 events.

See Also

Recipe 16.0 for more on the tombStoneLifetime attribute, MS KB 317097 (Lingering Objects Prevent Active Directory Replication from Occurring), and MS KB 314282 (Lingering Objects May Remain After You Bring an Out-of-Date Global Catalog Server Back Online)

12.13 Finding Conflict Objects

Problem

You want to find conflict objects that are a result of replication collisions.

Solution

Using a graphical user interface

1. Open LDP from the Windows Support Tools.
2. From the menu, select Connection→Connect.
3. For Server, enter the name of a domain controller (or leave blank to do a serverless bind).
4. For Port, enter 389 or 3268 for the global catalog.
5. Click OK.
6. From the menu, select Connection→Bind.
7. Enter credentials (if necessary) of a user who can view the object.
8. Click OK.
9. From the menu, select Browse→Search.
10. For BaseDN, type the base DN from where you want to start the search.
11. For Scope, select the appropriate scope.
12. For Filter, enter (name=*\0ACNF:*).
13. Click Run.

Using a command-line interface

The following command finds all conflict objects within the whole forest:

```
> dsquery * forestroot -gc -attr distinguishedName -scope subtree -filter
"(name=*\0ACNF:*)"
```

You can also perform this query with AdFind as follows:

```
> adfind -b -gc -f "(name=*\0ACNF:*)" -dn
```

Using VBScript

```
' This code finds any
' conflict objects in a forest.
' If the search times out, you may need to change strBase to
' a specific OU or container
' ------ SCRIPT CONFIGURATION ------
strBase = "<GC://" & "<ForestRootDN>" & ">;"
' ------ END CONFIGURATION --------

strFilter = "(name=*\0ACNF:*);"
strAttrs = "distinguishedName;"
strScope = "Subtree"

set objConn = CreateObject("ADODB.Connection")
objConn.Provider = "ADsDSOObject"
objConn.Open
```

```
Set objRS = objConn.Execute(strBase & strFilter & strAttrs & strScope)

WScript.Echo objRS.RecordCount & "
conflict objects found"
while not objRS.EOF
  Wscript.Echo objRS.Fields.Item("distinguishedName").Value
  objRS.MoveNext
wend
```

Using PowerShell

The following example will search for conflict objects within an Active Directory domain using the Quest `get-QADObject` cmdlet:

```
get-QADObject -ldapfilter 'name=*\0ACNF:*'
```

Another option is to use the `DirectorySearcher` class from the .NET Framework, as follows:

```
$strFilter = "name=*\0ACNF:*"
$objDomain = New-Object System.DirectoryServices.DirectoryEntry
$objSearcher = New-Object System.DirectoryServices.DirectorySearcher
$objSearcher.SearchRoot = $objDomain
$objSearcher.Filter = ($strFilter)
$colResults = $objSearcher.FindAll()
```

Discussion

Any distributed multimaster system has to deal with replication collisions, and Active Directory is no different. A collision can occur if an object is created on one domain controller and before that object has time to replicate out, an object with at least the same name is created on a different domain controller. So which object wins? With Active Directory, the following steps are used to determine which object is retained as is and which one is considered a conflict object:

1. AD will compare the version number of the objects. In Active Directory, version numbers are incremented every time you make a change to an object; the higher the version number, the more changes have been made to the object.

2. If the version numbers are the same, AD then compares the timestamps of when each object was created. The object that was created more recently will be retained and the older one will be renamed.

3. If the statistically improbable happens and two objects or attributes possess identical timestamps and version numbers, AD will take one final step to resolve the conflict by maintaining the object that originated from the DC with the higher GUID, and renaming the object that originated from the DC with the lower GUID.

When the losing object is renamed, the format of the renamed object is:

```
<ObjectName>\0CNF:<ObjectGUID>
```

where `<ObjectName>` is the original name of the object, followed by a null termination character, followed by `CNF:`, followed by the object's GUID.

It is good to periodically scan your Active Directory tree to ensure you do not have a lot of conflict objects hanging around and to remove any that exist. It is a bit problematic to find conflict objects in a single query because the filter to find them is not optimized. In all three solutions, you have to perform a leading- and trailing-match pattern search (with *), and this can easily time out if you have a lot of objects. You may want to restrict your initial search to a few containers so that the search is quicker.

See MS KB 297083 for more information on how to handle conflict objects after you've identified them.

See Also

MS KB 218614 (Replication Collisions in Windows 2000), and MS KB 297083 (How to Rename an Object After a Replication Collision Has Occurred)

12.14 Finding Orphaned Objects

Problem

You want to find orphaned objects within Active Directory

Solution

Using a graphical user interface

1. Open the ADUC snap-in.
2. If you need to change domains, right-click on "Active Directory Users and Computers" in the left pane, select "Connect to Domain," enter the domain name, and click OK.
3. If the LostAndFound container is not visible in the lefthand pane, click on View and place a checkmark next to Advanced Features.

   You will see a list of any orphaned objects in the righthand pane.

Using a command-line interface

You can query for orphaned objects using either the built-in DSQuery utility or AdFind. DSQuery takes the following syntax:

```
> dsquery * cn=LostAndFound,<DomainDN> -scope onelevel -attr *
```

To use AdFind, enter the following:

```
> adfind -default -rb cn=LostAndFound -s onelevel
```

Using VBScript

```
' Using "" for the second parameter means that there will be no
' indentation for the first level of objects displayed.
DisplayLostAndFound "LDAP://cn=LostAndFound,<DomainDN>", ""

' DisplayLostAndFound takes the ADsPath of the
LostAndFound container
' and recursively displays all objects contained within it
Function DisplayLostAndFound( strADsPath, strSpace)
    set objObject = GetObject(strADsPath)
    Wscript.Echo strSpace & strADsPath
    for each objChildObject in objObject
        DisplayLostAndFound objChildObject.ADsPath, strSpace & " "
    next
End Function
```

Using PowerShell

```
get-QADObject -searchroot 'cn=LostAndFound,<DomainDN>' -searchScope 'OneLevel'
```

Another option is to use the `DirectorySearcher` class from the .NET Framework, as follows:

```
$objRoot = [ADSI] "LDAP://cn=LostAndFound,<DomainDN>"
$objSearcher = New-Object System.DirectoryServices.DirectorySearcher
$objSearcher.SearchRoot = $objRoot
$objSearcher.SearchScope = [System.DirectoryServices.SearchScope]::OneLevel
$colResults = $objSearcher.FindAll()
```

Discussion

Because of the distributed nature of Active Directory, there exists the possibility that an administrator working on one DC can attempt to create or move a user into a container object such as an OU at the same time that another administrator *deletes* that OU from another DC. When this occurs, the leaf object becomes orphaned and is moved into the `LostAndFound` container within the Domain NC. You can view the `lastKnownParent` attribute of an object in this container to determine the OU or container that was deleted, and then delete the object or move it to a different container as appropriate.

From a procedural standpoint, objects being moved to the `LostAndFound` container should be a rare event. If it is happening frequently or if there are a large number of objects in the container, you should review the change-control procedures that are in place on your network to ensure that object moves and deletions are more tightly coordinated.

See Also

MS KB 271946 (Replication Does Not Work When There Is a Name Conflict on a Global Catalog) and MSDN: Lost-And-Found Class [AD Schema]

12.15 Listing the Replication Partners for a DC

Problem

You want to find the replication partners for a particular DC.

Solution

Using a graphical user interface

1. Open Active Directory Sites and Services.

2. Browse to Sites→<*SiteName*>→Servers→<*DCName*>→NTDS Settings.

3. The replication partners that have been configured for the DC in question will appear in the righthand pane. Double-click on any connection object to view its properties.

Using a command-line interface

You can query for replication connections using either the built-in DSQuery utility or AdFind. DSQuery takes the following syntax:

```
> dsquery * "cn=NTDS Settings,cn=<DCName>,cn=Servers,cn=<SiteName>,
cn=Sites,cn=Configuration,<ForestRootDN> -filter (objectcategory=NTDSConnection)
-attr *
```

To use AdFind, enter the following:

```
> adfind -config -rb "cn=NTDS
Settings,cn=<DCName>,cn=Servers,cn=<SiteName>,cn=Sites"
-f (objectcategory=NTDSConnection)
```

Using VBScript

```
' This code searches for ntdsConnection Objects within the Sites container.
' ------ SCRIPT CONFIGURATION ------
strSite = "<SiteName>" ' e.g. "cn=Raleigh"
strForestDN = "<ForestRootDN>" ' e.g. "dc=adatum,dc=com"
strBaseDN = "<LDAP://" & strSite & _
            ",cn=Sites,cn=Configuration," & strForestDN & ">;"
            ' BaseDN should be the search base
strFilter = "(objectclass=NTDSConnection);"
strAttrs = "fromServer;"
strScope = "Subtree"
' ------ END CONFIGURATION ---------

set objConn = CreateObject("ADODB.Connection")
objConn.Provider = "ADsDSOObject"
objConn.Open "Active Directory Provider"
set objRS = objConn.Execute(strBaseDN & strFilter & strAttrs & strScope)
objRS.MoveFirst
While Not objRS.EOF
```

```
        Wscript.Echo objRS.Fields(0).Value
        objRS.MoveNext
    Wend
    WScript.Echo("Search complete!")
```

Using PowerShell

```
$strdcName = "win2003-dc.essential.local"

$cType = [DirectoryServices.ActiveDirectory.DirectoryContextType]::DirectoryServer
$context = new-object DirectoryServices.ActiveDirectory.DirectoryContext($cType,
$strDCname)
$dc =
[DirectoryServices.ActiveDirectory.DomainController]::GetDomainController($context)
$dc.GetAllReplicationNeighbors()
```

Discussion

By default, Active Directory's replication topology is created by the KCC, which runs on every DC to dynamically create and maintain connection objects. (The KCC will run every 15 minutes by default to determine if there have been any changes to the site topology that require modifications to the connection objects KCC has created.) Each connection object corresponds to an inbound replication connection—that is, a remote DC that will contact the local DC whenever it has changes available. Any connection object that is listed as <automatically generated> in Active Directory Sites and Services was created by the KCC. You can create additional connection objects manually, but these objects will not be kept up-to-date by the KCC in the event that a remote DC is relocated or taken offline.

See Also

MS KB 251250 (NTFRS Event ID 13557 Is Recorded When Duplicate NTDS Connection Objects Exist) and MS KB 232538 (Unsuccessful Replication Without Partner Listed)

12.16 Viewing Object Metadata

Problem

You want to view metadata for an object. The object's replPropertyMetaData attribute stores metadata information about the most recent updates to every attribute that has been set on the object.

Solution

Using a graphical user interface

1. Open LDP.
2. From the menu, select Connection→Connect.
3. For Server, enter the name of a domain controller or domain that contains the object.
4. For Port, enter 389.
5. Click OK.
6. From the menu, select Connection→Bind.
7. Enter credentials (if necessary) of a user that can view the object.
8. Click OK.
9. From the menu, select Browse→Replication→View Metadata.
10. For Object DN, type the distinguished name of the object you want to view.
11. Click OK.

Using a command-line interface

In the following command, replace *<ObjectDN>* with the distinguished name of the object for which you want to view metadata:

```
> repadmin /showobjmeta <DomainControllerName> <ObjectDN>
```

This command was called /showmeta in the Windows 2000 version of *repadmin*. Also, the parameters were switched in that version; *<ObjectDN>* came before *<DomainControllerName>*.

You can also obtain object metadata for a single object using AdFind, as follows:

```
> adfind -sc objmeta:<ObjectDN>
```

To obtain the object metadata for all objects within a container, use the following syntax:

```
> adfind -sc objsmeta:<ContainerDN>
```

Using VBScript

```
' This code displays the metadata for the specified object.
' ------ SCRIPT CONFIGURATION -----
strObjectDN = "<ObjectDN>"          ' e.g. dc=adatum,dc=com
strDC = "<DomainControllerName>" ' e.g. dc1
' ------ END CONFIGURATION --------

set objIadsTools = CreateObject("IADsTools.DCFunctions")
intRes = objIadsTools.
GetMetaData(Cstr(strDC),Cstr(strObjectDN),0)
```

```
  if intRes = -1 then
    Wscript.Echo objIadsTools.LastErrorText
    WScript.Quit
  end if

  for count = 1 to intRes
    WScript.Echo count & ". " & objIadsTools.MetaDataName(count)
    WScript.Echo vbTab & " Version: " & _
                         objIadsTools.MetaDataVersionNumber(count)
    WScript.Echo vbTab & " Last Write: " & _
                         objIadsTools.MetaDataLastWriteTime(count)
    WScript.Echo vbTab & " Local USN: " & _
                         objIadsTools.MetaDataLocalUSN(count)
    WScript.Echo vbTab & " Source USN: " & _
                         objIadsTools.MetaDataSourceUSN(count)
    WScript.Echo vbTab & " Server: " & _
                         objIadsTools.MetaDataServerName(count)
  next
```

Using PowerShell

```
$strdcName = "<DC FQDN>"

$cType = [DirectoryServices.ActiveDirectory.DirectoryContextType]::DirectoryServer
$context = new-object DirectoryServices.ActiveDirectory.DirectoryContext($cType,
$strDCname)
$dc =
[DirectoryServices.ActiveDirectory.DomainController]::GetDomainController($context)
$configContainer = "CN=Configuration,{0}" -f ([ADSI]"").distinguishedName.Value
$dc.GetReplicationMetadata($configContainer).cn
```

Discussion

Object metadata can be an invaluable source of information when you need to troubleshoot replication problems or find out the last time an attribute was set for a particular object. In fact, a quick way to determine if two domain controllers have the same
copy of an object is to look at the metadata for the object on both servers. If they both
have the same metadata, then they have the same version of the object.

Unfortunately, the replPropertyMetaData attribute is stored as an octet string, so in
Windows 2000, you could not simply read the attribute to view all of the metadata
information. In the VBScript solution, the IADsTools GetMetaData method is a wrapper
around the DsReplicaGetInfo method call. This method understands the format of the
replPropertyMetaData attribute and can return it in a readable format. The following
data is stored for each attribute that has been set on the object:

Attribute ID
    Attribute that was updated.

Attribute version
    Number of originating writes to the property.

Local USN

USN of the property on the local DC. This will be the same as the originating DC if the originating DC and local DC are the same.

Originating USN

USN stored with the property when the update was made on the originating DC.

Originating DC

DC that the originating write was made on.

Time/Date

Time and date that the property was changed in UTC.

Starting with Windows Server 2003 and ADAM, you also have access to the msDS-ReplAttributeMetaData and msDS-ReplValueMetaData attributes, which provide much object metadata in XML-formatted output, as shown through this AdFind query:

```
> adfind -default -rb cn=administrator,cn=users msds-replattributemetadata

Using server: dc2.adatum.com:389
Directory: Windows Server 2003
Base DN: cn=administrator,cn=users,DC=adatum,DC=com

dn:CN=Administrator,CN=Users,DC=adatum,DC=com
>msDS-ReplAttributeMetaData: <DS_REPL_ATTR_META_DATA>
    <pszAttributeName>isCriticalSystemObject</pszAttributeName>
    <dwVersion>1</dwVersion>
    <ftimeLastOriginatingChange>2006-02-26T14:24:08Z</ftimeLastOriginatingChange>
    <uuidLastOriginatingDsaInvocationID>e197616c-7465-43f2-a502-
bac90df20b09</uuidLastOriginatingDsaInvocationID>
    <usnOriginatingChange>8194</usnOriginatingChange>
    <usnLocalChange>7298</usnLocalChange>
    <pszLastOriginatingDsaDN>CN=NTDS Settings,CN=DC1,CN=Servers,CN=Default-First-
Site-Name,CN=Sites,CN=Configuration,DC=adatum,DC=com</pszLastOriginatingDsaDN>
</DS_REPL_ATTR_META_DATA>
>msDS-ReplAttributeMetaData: <DS_REPL_ATTR_META_DATA>
    <pszAttributeName>objectCategory</pszAttributeName>
    <dwVersion>1</dwVersion>
    <ftimeLastOriginatingChange>2006-02-26T14:24:08Z</ftimeLastOriginatingChange>
    <uuidLastOriginatingDsaInvocationID>e197616c-7465-43f2-a502-
bac90df20b09</uuidLastOriginatingDsaInvocationID>
    <usnOriginatingChange>8194</usnOriginatingChange>
    <usnLocalChange>7298</usnLocalChange>
    <pszLastOriginatingDsaDN>CN=NTDS Settings,CN=DC1,CN=Servers,CN=Default-First-
Site-Name,CN=Sites,CN=Configuration,DC=adatum,DC=com</pszLastOriginatingDsaDN>
</DS_REPL_ATTR_META_DATA>
```

See Also

IadsTools.doc in the Support Tools for more information on the IADsTools interface

## CHAPTER 13

DNS and DHCP

13.0 Introduction

Active Directory is tightly coupled with the Domain Name System (DNS) name resolution service. Windows clients (running Windows 2000 or later) and domain controllers alike use DNS to locate domain controllers that are housed in a particular site or that serve a particular function (like a Global Catalog server). Each domain controller registers numerous resource records (RRs) in DNS to advertise its services as a domain controller, global catalog server, PDC Emulator, etc.

One of the innovative uses of Active Directory is as a store for DNS data. Instead of using the primary and secondary zone transfer method, or even the more recent NO-TIFY method (RFC 1996) to replicate zone data between non-AD-integrated DNS servers, AD-integrated zones store the zone data in Active Directory and use the same replication process used to replicate other data between domain controllers. The one catch with AD-integrated zones is that the DNS server must also be a domain controller, and overloading DNS server responsibilities on your domain controllers may not be something you want to do if you plan on supporting a large volume of DNS requests. You can integrate forward and reverse lookup zones into Active Directory, as well as *stub zones*, a feature introduced in Windows Server 2003 that is used to maintain information about remote DNS zones and to reduce zone transfer traffic across WAN links. Additionally, Windows Server 2008 introduces the GlobalNamesZone (GNZ), a manually maintained zone that is used to provide short name resolution on a DNS network: GNZ allows clients to resolve *server1* via DNS instead of a fully qualified domain name such as *server1.adatum.com*. For a detailed description of resource records, zone types, and much more on DNS, see Chapter 6 in *Active Directory*, Fourth Edition, by Brian Desmond et al. (O'Reilly).

The Anatomy of a DNS Object

The only time DNS data is stored in Active Directory is if you have a zone that is AD-integrated. When using standard primary and secondary zones that are not AD-integrated, the DNS data is stored locally in the filesystem of each DNS server in *zone files*. If you have an AD-integrated zone under Windows 2000, a container is created in the following location: `cn=<ZoneName>,cn=MicrosoftDNS,cn=System,<DomainDN>`, where *<ZoneName>* is the name of the zone.

Starting with Windows Server 2003, you can use application partitions to store DNS data in an alternate location. By default, there are three options:

- Store DNS data on all domain controllers in a domain (this is the only option available for Windows 2000).
- Store DNS data on all domain controllers that are DNS servers in the domain.
- Store DNS data on all domain controllers that are DNS servers in the forest.

The default location for the second option is `dc=DomainDNSZones,<DomainDN>`; for the third option, it is `dc=ForestDNSZones,<ForestDN>`. These two locations are actually application partitions that are replicated only to the domain controllers that are DNS servers in the domain or forest, respectively.

Inside the `MicrosoftDNS` container is a `dnsZone` object for each AD-integrated zone. Inside the `dnsZone` container are `dnsNode` objects that store all resource records associated with a particular node. In the following textual representation of an A record, the *dc1.adatum.com* name is considered a node (generally the left side of the resource record):

```
dc1.adatum.com. 600 IN A 6.10.57.21
```

There could be multiple resource records associated with the *dc1.adatum.com* name, so Microsoft decided to implement each distinct name as a `dnsNode` object. The `dnsNode` object has a `dnsRecord` attribute, which is multivalued and contains all of the resource records associated with that node. Unfortunately, the contents of that attribute are stored in a binary format and are not directly readable.

Tables 13-1 and 13-2 contain some of the interesting attributes that are available on `dnsZone` and `dnsNode` objects.

Table 13-1. Attributes of dnsZone objects

Attribute	Description
dc	Relative distinguished name of the zone. For example, the dc=domaindns zones,dc=adatum,dc=com dnsZone object has a dc attribute value of *adatum.com*.
dnsProperty	Binary-formatted string that stores configuration information about the zone.
msDS-Approx-Immed-Subordinates	Approximate number of nodes contained within the zone. This became available in Windows Server 2003.

Table 13-2. Attributes of dnsNode objects

Attribute	Description
dc	Relative distinguished name of the node.
dnsRecord	Binary-formatted multivalued attribute that stores the resource records associated with the node.
dnsTombstoned	Boolean that indicates whether the node is marked for deletion. FALSE means it is not and TRUE means that it is.

13.1 Creating a Forward Lookup Zone

Problem

You want to create a forward lookup zone. A forward lookup zone maps FQDNs to IP addresses or other names.

Solution

Using a graphical user interface

1. Open the DNS Management snap-in.
2. If an entry for the DNS server you want to connect to does not exist, right-click on DNS in the left pane and select "Connect to DNS Server." Select "This computer" or "The following computer," then enter the server you want to connect to (if applicable), and click OK.
3. Expand the server in the left pane and click on Forward Lookup Zones.
4. Right-click on Forward Lookup Zones and select New Zone.
5. Click Next.
6. Select the zone type and click Next.
7. If you selected to store the zone data in Active Directory, next you will be asked which servers you want to replicate the DNS data to. Click Next after you make your selection.

 Step 7 applies only to DNS servers that are Windows Server 2003 or newer domain controllers. If you still have Windows 2000 DNS servers in your environment, choose the option to replicate the zone to all domain controllers in your domain.

8. Enter the zone name and click Next.
9. Fill out the information for the remaining screens. They will vary depending on whether you are creating a primary, secondary, or stub zone.

Using a command-line interface

The following command creates an AD-integrated zone:

```
> dnscmd <DNSServerName> /zoneadd <ZoneName> /DsPrimary
```

Using VBScript

```
' This code creates an AD-integrated forward zone.
' ------ SCRIPT CONFIGURATION ------
strServer = "<DNSServerName>" ' e.g. dc1.adatum.com
strNewZone = "<ZoneName>"      ' e.g. othercorp.com
' ------ END CONFIGURATION --------
set objDNS = GetObject("winMgmts:\\" & strServer & "\root\MicrosoftDNS")
set objDNSZone = objDNS.Get("MicrosoftDNS_Zone")
strNull = objDNSZone.CreateZone(strNewZone, 0 , True)
WScript.Echo "Created zone " & strNewZone
```

Using PowerShell

The following PowerShell code will create an Active Directory-integrated forward lookup zone:

```
$zoneName = "<DNS Zone FQDN>"
$wmi = [WMIClass]"\\<DNSServerName>\root\MicrosoftDNS:MicrosoftDNS_Zone"
$wmi.CreateZone($zoneName, 0, $true)
```

Discussion

Using a command-line interface

When you create an AD-integrated zone with the /DsPrimary switch, you can additionally include a /dp switch and specify an application partition to add the zone to. Here is an example:

```
> dnscmd /zoneadd <ZoneName> /DsPrimary /dp domaindnszones.adatum.com
```

Using VBScript

The DNS WMI Provider is Microsoft's first comprehensive DNS API. You can create and modify zones, query and manage resource records, and manipulate DNS server configuration. In the VBScript solution, the CreateZone method of the MicrosoftDNS_Zone class was used to create the forward zone. The DNS WMI Provider is available only for Windows Server 2003 DNS; it cannot be used on Windows 2000 DNS servers. The CreateZone method will create an Active Directory-integrated zone with a replication scope of the domain NC of the domain in question, rather than DomainDNSZones or ForestDNSZones.

Using PowerShell

Since there is no native provider for DNS in PowerShell, it is very similar to VBScript, as the PowerShell commands leverage the same WMI provider to perform tasks.

See Also

Recipe 13.2 for creating a reverse lookup zone, MS KB 323445 (How to Create a New Zone on a DNS Server in Windows Server 2003), MSDN: DNS WMI Provider, and MSDN: CreateZone Method of the MicrosoftDNS_Zone Class

13.2 Creating a Reverse Lookup Zone

Problem

You want to create a reverse lookup zone. A reverse lookup zone maps IP addresses to names.

Solution

Using a graphical user interface

1. Open the DNS Management snap-in.
2. If an entry for the DNS server you want to connect to does not exist, right-click on DNS in the left pane and select "Connect to DNS Server." Select "This computer" or "The following computer," then enter the server you want to connect to (if applicable) and click OK.
3. Expand the server in the left pane and click on Reverse Lookup Zones.
4. Right-click on Reverse Lookup Zones and select New Zone.
5. Click Next.
6. Select the zone type (Primary, Secondary, or Stub zone). To AD-integrate the zone, place a checkmark next to "Store the zone in Active Directory (available only if DNS server is a domain controller)" and click Next.
7. If you selected to store the zone data in Active Directory, next you will be asked which servers you want to replicate the DNS data to: all DNS servers in the forest, all DNS servers in the domain, all domain controllers in the domain, or all DCs that are hosting a particular application partition. Click Next after you make your selection.

 Step 7 applies only to DNS servers that are installed on Windows Server 2003 or higher domain controllers. If you still have Windows 2000 DNS servers in your environment, choose the option to replicate the zone to all domain controllers in your domain.

8. Type the Network ID for the reverse zone or enter a reverse zone name to use.

9. Fill out the information for the remaining screens. They will vary depending on if you are creating a primary, secondary, or stub zone.

Using a command-line interface

The following command creates an AD-integrated reverse zone:

```
> dnscmd <DNSServerName> /zoneadd <ZoneName> /DsPrimary
```

Using VBScript

```
' This code creates an
' AD-integrated reverse zone.
' ------ SCRIPT CONFIGURATION ------
strServer = "<DNSServerName>" ' e.g. dc1.adatum.com
strNewZone = "<ZoneName>" ' e.g. 8.10.192.in-addr.arpa.
' ------ END CONFIGURATION --------

set objDNS = GetObject("winMgmts:\\" & strServer & "\root\MicrosoftDNS")
set objDNSZone = objDNS.Get("MicrosoftDNS_Zone")
strNull = objDNSZone.CreateZone(strNewZone, 0 , True)
WScript.Echo "Created zone " & strNewZone
```

Using PowerShell

The following PowerShell code will create an Active Directory-integrated reverse look-up zone:

```
$zoneName = "<Reverse Lookup Zone FQDN>" # e.g., "8.10.192.in-addr.arpa"
$wmi = [WMIClass]"\\<DNSServerName>\root\MicrosoftDNS:MicrosoftDNS_Zone"
$wmi.CreateZone($zoneName, 0, $true)
```

Discussion

Creating a reverse zone is very similar to creating a forward zone. See Recipe 13.1 for more information.

See Also

MS KB 323445 (How to Create a New Zone on a DNS Server in Windows Server 2003) and MSDN: CreateZone Method of the MicrosoftDNS_Zone Class

13.3 Viewing a Server's Zones

Problem

You want to view the zones on a server.

Solution

Using a graphical user interface

1. Open the DNS Management snap-in.
2. Right-click on DNS in the left pane and select "Connect to DNS Server."
3. Enter the server you want to connect to and click Enter.
4. In the left pane, expand the server and click Forward Lookup Zones and Reverse Lookup Zones to view the hosted zones.

Using a command-line interface

```
> dnscmd <DNSServerName> /enumzones
```

Using VBScript

```
' This code lists the zones that are hosted by the specified server.
' ------ SCRIPT CONFIGURATION ------
strServer = "<DNSServerName>" ' e.g. dc1.adatum.com
' ------ END CONFIGURATION --------

set objDNS = GetObject("winMgmts:\\" & strServer & "\root\MicrosoftDNS")
set objDNSServer = objDNS.Get("MicrosoftDNS_Server.Name="".""")
set objZones = objDNS.ExecQuery("Select * from MicrosoftDNS_Zone " & _
                                "Where DnsServerName = '" & _
                                objDNSServer.Name & "'")
WScript.Echo "Zones on " & objDNSServer.Name
for each objZone in objZones
   WScript.Echo " " & objZOne.Name
next
```

Using PowerShell

```
$computername = "<Server FQDN>"
$server = Get-WmiObject -Class MicrosoftDNS_Zone -computer $computername -Namespace
root\MicrosoftDNS
$server | format-list ContainerName
```

Discussion

Using a graphical user interface

When you click on either the Forward Lookup Zones or Reverse Lookup Zones in the lefthand pane of the DMS MMC, the right pane contains a Type column that displays the zone type for each zone.

Using a command-line interface

When using the /enumzones switch without any more parameters, it displays all zones on the server. You can specify additional filters that limit the types of zones returned.

With the Windows 2000 version of *dnscmd*, you can specify up to two filters (for example, using the `/enumzones /primary /forward` switch combination will display all primary forward zones on the server):

```
Filter1:
    /Primary
    /Secondary
    /Cache
    /Auto-Created
Filter2:
    /Forward
    /Reverse
```

Starting with the Windows Server 2003 version of *dnscmd*, the filter behavior has changed. Instead of having two levels of criteria, you can specify one or more of the following:

`/Primary`
> Lists both standard and Active Directory–integrated primary zones

`/Secondary`
> Lists all standard secondary zones

`/Forwarder`
> Lists all zones that forward unresolvable queries to another DNS server

`/Stub`
> Lists all stub zones hosted on a server

`/Cache`
> Lists zones that are loaded into cache on the server

`/Auto-Created`
> Lists zones that were created automatically during the DNS server installation

`/Forward`
> Lists all forward lookup zones

`/Reverse`
> Lists all reverse lookup zones

`/Ds`
> Lists all Active Directory–integrated zones

`/File`
> Lists zones that are stored in text files

`/DomainDirectoryPartition`
> Lists zones that are stored in the `DomainDNSZones` partition

`/ForestDirectoryPartition`
> Lists zones that are stored in the `ForestDNSZones` partition

`/CustomDirectoryPartition`
> Lists zones that are stored in a user-created directory partition

`/LegacyDirectoryPartition`
> Lists zones that are stored in the domain NC

`/DirectoryPartition <PartitionName>`
> Lists zones that are stored in a particular application partition

Using VBScript

A WQL query was used to find all `MicrosoftDNS_Zone` objects. You can add additional criteria to the WQL `Select` statement to return a subset of zones supported on the server.

Using PowerShell

You can display all properties of the DNS zones that reside on a server by omitting the `' | format-list ContainerName'` syntax.

See Also

MSDN: MicrosoftDNS_Zone

13.4 Converting a Zone to an AD-Integrated Zone

Problem

You want to convert a standard primary zone to an AD-integrated zone. This causes the contents of the zone to be stored and replicated in Active Directory instead of in a text file on the local server.

Solution

Using a graphical user interface

1. Open the DNS Management snap-in.
2. Right-click on DNS in the left pane and select "Connect to DNS Server."
3. Enter the server you want to connect to and click Enter.
4. If you want to convert a forward zone, expand the Forward Lookup Zone folder. If you want to convert a reverse zone, expand the Reverse Lookup Zone folder.
5. Right-click on the zone you want to convert and select Properties.
6. Beside Type, click the Change button.
7. Check the box beside "Store the zone in Active Directory."
8. Click OK twice.

Using a command-line interface

```
> dnscmd <ServerName> /zoneresettype <ZoneName> /DsPrimary
```

Using VBScript

```
' This code converts a zone to AD-integrated.
' ------ SCRIPT CONFIGURATION ------
strZone = "<ZoneName>"     ' e.g. adatum.com
strServer = "<ServerName>" ' e.g. dc1.adatum.com
' ------ END CONFIGURATION --------

set objDNS = GetObject("winMgmts:\\" & strServer & "\root\MicrosoftDNS")
set objDNSServer = objDNS.Get("MicrosoftDNS_Server.Name=""."""")
set objDNSZone = objDNS.Get("MicrosoftDNS_Zone.ContainerName=""" & _
                   strZone & """,DnsServerName=""" & _
                   objDNSServer.Name & """,Name=""" & strZone & """")
strNull = objDNSZone.ChangeZoneType(0, True)
objDNSZone.Put_
WScript.Echo "Converted " & strZone & " to
AD-Integrated"
```

Discussion

See Recipe 13.0, Recipe 13.5, and Chapter 6 of *Active Directory* for more on AD-integrated zones.

See Also

MS KB 198437 (How to Convert DNS Primary Server to Active Directory Integrated), MS KB 227844 (Primary and Active Directory Integrated Zones Differences), and MSDN: ChangeZoneType Method of the MicrosoftDNS_Zone Class

13.5 Moving AD-Integrated Zones into an Application Partition

 This recipe requires at least Windows Server 2003 domain functional level.

Problem

You want to move AD-integrated zones into an application partition.

Solution

Using a graphical user interface

1. Open the DNS Management snap-in.

---

2. If an entry for the DNS server you want to connect to does not exist, right-click on DNS in the left pane and select Connect to DNS Server. Select "This computer" or "The following computer," then enter the server you want to connect to (if applicable), and click OK.

3. Expand the server in the left pane and expand either Forward Lookup Zones or Reverse Lookup Zones, depending on the type of zone.

4. Right-click on the name of the zone and select Properties.

5. Click on the Change button beside Replication.

6. Select the application partition you want to move the zone into.

7. Click OK twice.

Using a command-line interface

The following command will move a zone to the default application partition that replicates across all domain controllers in the domain that are configured as DNS servers:

```
> dnscmd <DNSServerName> /zonechangedirectorypartition <ZoneName> /domain
```

Using VBScript

At the time of publication of this book, the DNS WMI Provider did not support programmatically moving a zone into an application partition.

Discussion

With Windows 2000 Active Directory, if you had AD-integrated zones, those zones were replicated to every domain controller in the domain where they were stored. In many cases, not every domain controller also served as a DNS server, which resulted in increased and unnecessary traffic to replicate zone changes to DCs that did not require the data.

Windows Server 2003 and higher provides an elegant solution to this issue by using application partitions. Application partitions are user-defined partitions that can be configured to replicate with any domain controller in a forest. This provides a lot more flexibility for how you store and replicate your AD-integrated zones. You could, in fact, have a few domain controllers from each domain act as DNS servers for all of your AD domains.

See Also

Chapter 17 for more information on application partitions

13.6 Configuring Zone Transfers

Problem

You want to enable zone transfers to specific secondary nameservers.

Solution

Using a graphical user interface

1. Open the DNS snap-in.
2. In the left pane, expand the server node and expand either Forward Lookup Zone or Reverse Lookup Zone depending on the type of zone you want to manage.
3. Right-click on the zone and select Properties.
4. Select the Zone Transfers tab.
5. Select either the option to restrict zone transfers to those servers listed on the Name Servers tab or the option to restrict zone transfers to specific IP addresses. See the "Discussion" section for more on these two options.

Using a command-line interface

The following command enables zone transfers for the *test.local* zone and specifies they can only occur with servers that have NS records in the zone (i.e., servers listed within the Name Servers tab of the DNS snap-in):

```
> dnscmd <ServerName> /ZoneResetSecondaries test.local /SecureNs
```

The next command enables zone transfers for the same zone, but specifies they can only occur with hosts whose IP addresses are 172.16.11.33 and 172.16.11.34:

```
> dnscmd <ServerName> /ZoneResetSecondaries test.local /SecureList 172.16.11.33
172.16.11.34
```

Using VBScript

```
' This code configures the allowed secondaries for zone transfer and notify

' XFR constants
const ZONE_SECSECURE_NO_SECURITY = 0
const ZONE_SECSECURE_NS_ONLY = 1
const ZONE_SECSECURE_LIST_ONLY = 2
const ZONE_SECSECURE_NO_XFR = 3

' NOTIFY constants
const ZONE_NOTIFY_OFF = 0
const ZONE_NOTIFY_ALL_SECONDARIES = 1
const ZONE_NOTIFY_LIST_ONLY = 2

' ------ SCRIPT CONFIGURATION -------
```

```
strZone = "<ZoneName>" ' e.g. adatum.com
strServer = "<ServerName>" ' e.g. dc1.adatum.com

' use one of the above XFR constants
intSecureSecondaries = ZONE_SECSECURE_LIST_ONLY
arrSecondaries = Array("1.1.1.2","1.1.1.3")

' use one of the above NOTIFY constants
intNotify = ZONE_NOTIFY_LIST_ONLY
arrNotify = Array("<IP1>","<IP2>")
' ------ END CONFIGURATION ---------

set objDNS = GetObject("winMgmts:\\" & strServer & "\root\MicrosoftDNS")
set objDNSServer = objDNS.Get("MicrosoftDNS_Server.Name=""."""")
set objDNSZone = objDNS.Get("MicrosoftDNS_Zone.ContainerName=""" & _
                 strZone & """,DnsServerName=""" & _
                 objDNSServer.Name & """,Name=""" & strZone & """")
strNull = objDNSZone.ResetSecondaries(arrSecondaries,intSecureSecondaries, _
                 arrNotify,intNotify)
objDNSZone.Put_
WScript.Echo "Updated secondaries for zone transfer and notify"
```

Using PowerShell

```
$zone = Get-WmiObject -Class MicrosoftDNS_Zone -computer $computername -Namespace
root\MicrosoftDNS -Filter 'ContainerName="<Zone Name>"'
$zone.SecondaryServers="<IPAddress1>","<IPAddress2>"
$zone.SecureSecondaries = $true
$zone.Notify = $true
$zone.Put()
```

Discussion

Depending on your environment, your DNS implementation may require that you create secondary zones to allow for load balancing for busy DNS servers or remote sites connected by slow links. In this situation, you want to allow zone transfers to occur between your AD-integrated DNS servers and your secondary servers, but you want to restrict which hosts can initiate zone transfers with your AD-integrated name servers. Allowing anyone to initiate a zone transfer with your domain controllers could provide an attacker with information for mapping out your network; it is therefore critical that you limit which hosts can pull zone transfers from your servers.

If you are using only Active Directory-integrated zones, the Name Servers tab will be automatically populated with a list of all name servers that are authoritative for the selected zone, and this is the recommended choice when you have a large network with many name servers deployed. If any of your name servers are using standard zone files, however, you will need to populate this tab manually for any secondary name servers you deploy.

Specifying a list of IP addresses for hosts that can initiate zone transfers may be more secure since it is more specific, but this approach has the trade-off of creating the additional management overhead of keeping track of the IP addresses of all name servers on your network, so you should follow this approach only if your network is small and you have relatively few name servers deployed. Another disadvantage of this approach is that if you forget to add some IP addresses of name servers to your list, zone information stored on those servers could become stale, causing name resolution to fail for some of your clients. This could result in some of your users experiencing difficulties in accessing network resources.

Note that on Windows 2000 name servers, the default setting is to allow zone transfers with any host that requests them. This setting is inherently insecure as it allows attackers to use *nslookup* to display all resource records on your servers, so be sure to use the steps outlined in this recipe to change the setting on your servers to one of the two settings described here. Beginning with Windows Server 2003, DNS is more secure by default because in the case of file-based zones, it is configured to allow zone transfers only with servers listed on the Name Servers tab of a zone. In the case of Active Directory integrated zones, DNS is configured to disallow zone transfers entirely—they generally aren't needed in an Active Directory environment because the data replicates through Active Directory replication.

See Also

MS KB 164017 (Explanation of a DNS Zone Transfer)

13.7 Configuring Forwarding

Problem

You want to configure forwarding to allow for name resolution outside of your corporate network.

Solution

Using a graphical user interface

1. Open the DNS Management snap-in.
2. Connect to the DNS Server you want to modify. In the left pane, right-click on DNS and select "Connect to DNS Server." Select "The following computer" and enter the target server name. Click OK.
3. Right-click on the server and select Properties.
4. Click the Forwarders tab.
5. To configure a global forwarder, make sure "All other DNS domains" is selected under DNS domain, type an IP under "Selected domain's forwarder IP address list," click Add, and then click Apply.

6. To configure a conditional forwarder for a specific domain, click the New button.

7. Enter the domain name and click OK.

8. Add IPs as described for global forwarders in step 5.

9. From the Forwarders tab, you can also set the number of seconds that the server waits before forward queries time out. You can also disable the use of recursion for certain domains. Both of these can be set on a per-domain basis.

Using a command-line interface

The following command sets the default forwarders. Replace *<IPsOfForwarders>* with a space-separated list of IP addresses for the name servers to forward requests to:

```
> dnscmd <ServerName> /resetforwarders <IPsOfForwaders>
```

For example:

```
> dnscmd dns01 /resetforwarders 10.22.3.4 10.22.3.5
```

The following command creates a domain-based forwarder:

```
> dnscmd <ServerName> /zoneadd <DomainName> /forwarder <IPsOfForwarders>
```

The following command configures the default forwarder timeout:

```
> dnscmd <ServerName> /config /forwardingtimeout <NumSeconds>
```

The following command configures the forwarder timeout for a specific domain:

```
> dnscmd <ServerName> /config <DomainName> /forwardertimeout <NumSeconds>
```

Using VBScript

```
' This code enumerates the default forwarders.
' ------ SCRIPT CONFIGURATION ------
strServer = "<ServerName> " ' e.g. dns1.adatum.com
' ------ END CONFIGURATION --------

set objDNS = GetObject("winMgmts:\\" & strServer & "\root\MicrosoftDNS")
set objDNSServer = objDNS.Get("MicrosoftDNS_Server.Name="".""")
for each strForwarder in objDNSServer.Forwarders
    Wscript.Echo strForwarder
Next

' This code sets the default forwarders.
' ------ SCRIPT CONFIGURATION ------
strServer = "<ServerName>" ' e.g. dns1.adatum.com
arrForwarders = Array("<IP1>","<IP2>")
' ------ END CONFIGURATION --------

set objDNS = GetObject("winMgmts:\\" & strServer & "\root\MicrosoftDNS")
set objDNSServer = objDNS.Get("MicrosoftDNS_Server.Name="".""")
objDNSServer.Forwarders = arrForwarders
objDNSServer.Put_
Wscript.Echo "Successfully set default forwarders"
' This code sets the
```

```
' forwarders for a specific domain.
' ------ SCRIPT CONFIGURATION ------
strServer = "<ServerName>" ' e.g. dns01
strNewZone = "<ZoneName>"  ' e.g. othercorp.com
arrMasterIPs = Array("<IP1>","<IP2>") ' replace &lt;IPx&gt; with IPs of master server
' ------ END CONFIGURATION --------
on error resume next
set objDNS = GetObject("winMgmts:\\" & strServer & "\root\MicrosoftDNS")
set objDNSZone = objDNS.Get("MicrosoftDNS_Zone")
strNull = objDNSZone.CreateZone(strNewZone,3,false,"",arrMasterIPs)
if Err then
    WScript.Echo "Error occurred creating zone: " & Err.Description
else
    WScript.Echo "Domain forwarder created."
end if
```

Using PowerShell

```
$server = Get-WmiObject -Class MicrosoftDNS_Server -computer "<DNS Server FQDN>"
-namespace root\MicrosoftDNS
$server.Forwarders = "<IP Address 1>", "<IP Address 2>"
$server.Put()
```

Discussion

Name servers have long supported the notion of *forwarders*. Rather than sending all unresolved queries to the root Internet name servers, you can use forwarders to send queries to a specific server or set of servers, perhaps hosted by your ISP or by a partner corporation. This allows you to better control the name resolution process on your network.

Beginning in Windows Server 2003, Microsoft has extended this capability to support *conditional forwarding*. With conditional forwarding, you can forward unresolved queries for specific domains to different nameservers. The most common use of conditional forwarding is when you have two or more noncontiguous namespaces. Consider, for example, a merger between the *adatum.com* and *othercorp.com* corporations. Normally, for the nameservers of *adatum.com* to resolve queries for *othercorp.com*, the queries would have to first be forwarded to the root Internet nameservers. With conditional forwarding, you can configure the *adatum.com* DNS servers so that all requests for *othercorp.com* should be sent directly to the *othercorp.com* nameservers and all other unresolved queries should be sent to the Internet, and vice versa. The trade-off for this feature is the additional CPU processing that's necessary to examine each query and forward it to the appropriate server, rather than just funneling all unresolved queries to a single external server.

See Also

MS KB 304491 (Conditional Forwarding in Windows Server 2003) and MS KB 811118 (Support WebCast: Microsoft Windows Server 2003 DNS: Stub Zones and Conditional Forwarding)

13.8 Delegating Control of an Active Directory Integrated Zone

Problem

You want to delegate control of managing the resource records in a zone.

Solution

Using a graphical user interface

1. Open the DNS Management snap-in.
2. If an entry for the DNS server you want to connect to does not exist, right-click on DNS in the left pane and select "Connect to DNS Server." Select "This computer" or "The following computer," then enter the server you want to connect to (if applicable) and click OK.
3. Expand the server in the left pane and expand either Forward Lookup Zones or Reverse Lookup Zones, depending on the type of zone.
4. Right-click on the name of the zone and select Properties.
5. Click on the Security tab.
6. Click the Add button.
7. Use the Object Picker to locate the user or group to which you want to delegate control.
8. Under Permissions, check the Full Control box.
9. Click OK.

Using a command-line interface

The following command grants full control over managing the resource records in an AD-Integrated zone:

```
> dsacls dc=<ZoneName>,cn=MicrosoftDNS,<DomainOrAppPartitionDN> /G
<UserOrGroup>:GA;;
```

Using VBScript

```
' This code grants full control for the specified user or group over
' an AD-Integrated zone.
' ------ SCRIPT CONFIGURATION -------
strZoneDN = "dc=<ZoneName>,cn=MicrosoftDNS,<DomainOrAppPartitionDN>"
strUserOrGroup = "<UserOrGroup>" ' e.g. joe@adatum.com or ADATUM\joe
' ------ END CONFIGURATION ---------

set objZone = GetObject("LDAP://" & strZoneDN)
'###########################
' Constants
'###########################
```

```
' ADS_ACETYPE_ENUM
Const ADS_ACETYPE_ACCESS_ALLOWED_OBJECT = &h5

' ADS_FLAGTYPE_ENUM
Const ADS_FLAG_OBJECT_TYPE_PRESENT = &h1

' ADS_RIGHTS_ENUM
Const ADS_RIGHT_GENERIC_ALL = &h10000000

'##########################
' Create ACL
'##########################

set objSD = objZone.Get("nTSecurityDescriptor")
set objDACL = objSD.DiscretionaryAcl

' Full Control
set objACE1 = CreateObject("AccessControlEntry")
objACE1.Trustee    = strUserOrGroup
objACE1.AccessMask = ADS_RIGHT_GENERIC_ALL
objACE1.AceFlags   = 0
objACE1.Flags      = ADS_FLAG_OBJECT_TYPE_PRESENT
objACE1.AceType    = ADS_ACETYPE_ACCESS_ALLOWED_OBJECT

objDACL.AddAce objACE1

'##########################
' Set ACL
'##########################
objSD.DiscretionaryAcl = objDACL
objZone.Put "nTSecurityDescriptor", objSD
objZone.SetInfo
WScript.Echo "Delegated
control of " & strZoneDN & " to " & strUserOrGroup
```

Using PowerShell

The following Quest cmdlet delegates Full Control of an AD-integrated DNS zone to a particular user or group:

```
add-QADPermission -Identity <Group DN> -Account <User/Group DN> -Rights
'GenericAll'-ApplyTo 'All'
```

Discussion

By default, members of the *DNSAdmins* group have control over DNS server and zone configuration. You can delegate control of individual AD-integrated zones by modifying permissions on the zone object in AD. The solutions show examples for how to grant Full Control to an additional user or group over a particular zone.

See Also

MS KB 256643 (Unable to Prevent DNS Zone Administrator from Creating New Zones)

13.9 Creating and Deleting Resource Records

Problem

You want to create and delete resource records in a zone.

Solution

Using a graphical user interface

1. Open the DNS Management snap-in.
2. If an entry for the DNS server you want to connect to does not exist, right-click on DNS in the left pane and select "Connect to DNS Server." Select "This computer" or "The following computer," then enter the server you want to connect to (if applicable) and click OK.
3. If you want to add or delete a record in a forward zone, expand the Forward Lookup Zone folder. If you want to add or delete a record for a reverse zone, expand the Reverse Lookup Zone folder.

To create a resource record, do the following:

1. In the left pane, right-click the zone and select the option that corresponds to the record type you want to create—e.g., New Host (A).
2. Fill in all required fields.
3. Click OK.

To delete a resource record, do the following:

1. In the left pane, click on the zone the record is in.
2. In the right pane, right-click on the record you want to delete and select Delete.
3. Click Yes to confirm.

Using a command-line interface

To add a resource record, use the following command:

```
> dnscmd <DNSServerName> /recordadd <ZoneName> <NodeName> <RecordType> <RRData>
```

The following command adds an A record in the *adatum.com* zone:

```
> dnscmd dc1 /recordadd adatum.com wins01 A 19.25.52.2.25
```

To delete a resource record, use the following command:

```
> dnscmd <DNSServerName> /recorddelete <ZoneName> <NodeName> <RecordType> <RRData>
```

The following command deletes an A record in the *adatum.com* zone:

```
> dnscmd dc1 /recorddelete adatum.com wins01 A 19.25.52.2.25
```

Using VBScript

```
' This code shows how to add an A record and PTR record using
' the DNS WMI Provider.
' ------ SCRIPT CONFIGURATION ------
strForwardRRAdd = "test-xp.adatum.com. IN A 192.32.64.13"
strReverseRRAdd = "13.64.32.192.in-addr.arpa IN PTR test-xp.adatum.com"
strForwardDomain = "adatum.com"
strReverseDomain = "192.in-addr.arpa."
' ------ END CONFIGURATION --------

set objDNS = GetObject("winMgmts:root\MicrosoftDNS")
set objRR = objDNS.Get("MicrosoftDNS_ResourceRecord")
set objDNSServer = objDNS.Get("MicrosoftDNS_Server.Name="".""")

' Create the A record
strNull = objRR.CreateInstanceFromTextRepresentation( _
                    objDNSServer.Name, _
                    strForwardDomain, _
                    strForwardRRAdd, _
                    objOutParam)
set objRR2 = objDNS.Get(objOutParam)
WScript.Echo "Created Record: " & objRR2.TextRepresentation

' Create the PTR record
strNull = objRR.CreateInstanceFromTextRepresentation( _
                    objDNSServer.Name, _
                    strReverseDomain, _
                    strReverseRRAdd, _
                    objOutParam)
set objRR2 = objDNS.Get(objOutParam)
WScript.Echo "Created Record: " & objRR2.TextRepresentation

' This code shows how to delete an A and PTR record for the record
' we created in the previous example.

strHostName = "test-xp.adatum.com."

set objDNS = GetObject("winMgmts:root\MicrosoftDNS")
set objDNSServer = objDNS.Get("MicrosoftDNS_Server.Name="".""")

set objRRs = objDNS.ExecQuery(" select * " & _
                        " from MicrosoftDNS_ResourceRecord " & _
                        " where OwnerName = """ & strHostName & """" & _
                        " Or RecordData = """ & strHostName & """")
if objRRs.Count < 1 then
    WScript.Echo "No matches found for " & strHostName
else
    for each objRR in objRRs
        objRR.Delete_
        WScript.Echo "Deleted " & objRR.TextRepresentation
    next
end if
```

Using PowerShell

The following syntax will create an A record within a DNS zone:

```
$server = "<DNS Server FQDN>"
$zone = "<DNS Zone>"
$name = "<A Record FQDN>"
$class = 1 # 1 corresponds to the 'IN' record class
$ttl = 3600
$address = "<IP Address>"
$newRecord = [WmiClass]\\<ServerName>\root\MicrosoftDNS:MicrosoftDNS_AType
$newRecord.CreateInstanceFromPropertydata($server, $zone, $name, $class, $ttl,
$address
```

The following will delete an A record that corresponds to a particular IP address:

```
$record = Get-WmiObject -ComputerName <Server Name> -Namespace 'root\MicrosoftDNS'
-Class MicrosoftDNS_AType  -Filter "IPAddress = '<IP Address>'"
$record.psbase.Delete()
```

Discussion

Using a graphical user interface

The DNS Management snap-in is good for creating a small number of records, but if you need to add or delete more than a couple of dozen, then we'd recommend writing a batch file around *dnscmd* or using the DNS WMI Provider to automate the process.

Using a command-line interface

Adding A, CNAME, and PTR resource records is pretty straightforward as far as the data you must enter, but other record types, such as SRV, require quite a bit more data. The help pages for /recordadd and /recorddelete display the required information for each record type. For example, to add an SRV record using *dnscmd*, you need to specify the priority, weight, port, and hostname of the record as in the following example:

```
> dnscmd /recordadd dc1.adatum.com SRV 50 100 88 _kerberos
```

Using VBScript

The first example creates A and PTR records using the CreateInstance FromTextRepresentation method, which is a MicrosoftDNS_ResourceRecord method that allows you to create resource records by passing in the textual version of the record. This is the textual representation of the A record used in the example:

```
test-xp.adatum.com IN A 192.32.64.13
```

The first parameter to this method is the DNS server name, the second is the name of the domain to add the record to, the third is the resource record, and the last is an out parameter that returns a reference to the new resource record.

The second example finds all resource records that match a certain hostname and deletes them. This is done by first using a WQL query to find all resource records where the OwnerName equals the target hostname (this will match any A records) and where RecordData equals the target hostname (this will match any PTR records). The Delete_ method is called on each matching record, removing them from the DNS server.

See Also

MSDN: MicrosoftDNS_ResourceRecord

13.10 Querying Resource Records

Problem

You want to query resource records.

Solution

Using a graphical user interface

The DNS Management snap-in does not provide an interface for searching resource records.

Using a command-line interface

In the following command, replace *<RecordType>* with the type of resource record you want to find (e.g., A, CNAME, SRV) and *<RecordName>* with the name or IP address of the record to match:

```
> nslookup -type=<RecordType> <RecordName>
```

Using VBScript

```
' This code prints the
' resource records that match
' the specified name.
' ------ SCRIPT CONFIGURATION ------
strQuery = "<RecordName>"
' ------ END CONFIGURATION --------

set objDNS = GetObject("winMgmts:root\MicrosoftDNS")
set objDNSServer = objDNS.Get("MicrosoftDNS_Server.Name=""."""")
set objRRs = objDNS.ExecQuery(" select * " & _
                    " from MicrosoftDNS_ResourceRecord" & _
                    " where OwnerName = """ & strQuery & """" & _
                    " Or DomainName = """ & strQuery & """" & _
                    " Or RecordData = """ & strQuery & """")

if objRRs.Count < 1 then
    WScript.Echo "No matches found for " & strHostName & " of " _
                & strRecordType & " type"
```

```
else
    for each objRR in objRRs
        WScript.Echo objRR.TextRepresentation
    next
end if
```

Using PowerShell

```
Get-WmiObject -ComputerName <ServerName> -Namespace 'root\MicrosoftDNS' -Class
MicrosoftDNS_AType  -Filter "ContainerName ='<ZoneName>'" | Where-Object
{$_.ownername -eq "<Record FQDN>" | Select OwnerName, IPAddress
```

Discussion

Using a command-line interface

You can leave off the -type switch, and the command will find any A, PTR, and CNAME records that match <RecordName>.

You can also run *nslookup* from interactive mode, which can be entered by typing nslookup at a command prompt with no additional parameters, or switch back and forth between query types by using the q=ANY command to reset *nslookup*.

Using VBScript

In the VBScript solution, a WQL query was used to find all matching resource records. This is a good example of how powerful the DNS WMI Provider can be. The query attempts to find any object of the MicrosoftDNS_ResourceRecord class that has an OwnerName, DomainName, or RecordData field equal to the <RecordName>. This is not the most efficient query if the server supports multiple large zones, so you may want to restrict it to search for specific types of records by adding criteria to match RecordType = <Type>.

See Also

MSDN: MicrosoftDNS_ResourceRecord, RFC 1035 (Domain Names—Implementation and Specification), and RFC 1700 (DNS Parameters)

13.11 Modifying the DNS Server Configuration

Problem

You want to modify the DNS Server settings.

Solution

Using a graphical user interface

1. Open the DNS Management snap-in.
2. If an entry for the DNS server you want to connect to does not exist, right-click on DNS in the left pane and select "Connect to DNS Server." Select "This computer" or "The following computer," then enter the server you want to connect to (if applicable), and click OK.
3. Right-click on the server and select Properties.
4. There will be several tabs you can choose from to edit the server settings.
5. Click OK to commit the changes after you complete your modifications.

Using a command-line interface

With the following command, replace <Setting> with the name of the setting to modify and <Value> with the value to set:

```
> dnscmd <DNSServerName> /config /<Setting> <Value>
```

The following command enables the EnableDnsSec setting on *dns01*:

```
> dnscmd dns01 /config /EnableDnsSec 1
```

The following command disables the NoTcp setting on the local host:

```
> dnscmd /config /NoTcp 0
```

The following command sets the DsPollingInterval setting to 60 on *dns02*:

```
> dnscmd dns02 /config /DsPollingInterval 60
```

For the complete list of settings, run dnscmd /config from the command line.

Using VBScript

```
set objDNS = GetObject("winMgmts:root\MicrosoftDNS")
set objDNSServer = objDNS.Get("MicrosoftDNS_Server.Name=""."""")
objDNSServer.<Setting> = <Value> ' e.g. objDNSServer.AllowUpdate = TRUE
objDNSServer.Put_
```

Using PowerShell

```
$server = Get-WmiObject -Class MicrosoftDNS_Server -computer "<Server FQDN>"
-namespace root\MicrosoftDNS
$server.<Setting> = <Value> # e.g. $server.EnableDNSSec = $false
$server.Put()
```

Discussion

The Microsoft DNS server supports a variety of settings to configure everything from scavenging and forwarders to logging. With the DNS Management snap-in, the settings are spread over several tabs in the Properties property page. You can get a list of these settings by simply running `dnscmd /config` from a command line. For the CLI and VBScript solutions, the setting names are nearly identical. In the VBScript solution, be sure to call the `Put_` method after you are done configuring settings in order for the changes to take effect.

See Also

MSDN: MicrosoftDNS_Server

13.12 Scavenging Old Resource Records

Problem

You want to scavenge old resource records. DNS scavenging is the process whereby resource records are automatically removed if they are not updated after a period of time. Typically, this applies only to resource records that were added via DDNS, but you can also scavenge manually created static records as well. DNS scavenging is a recommended practice so that your DNS zones are automatically kept clean of stale resource records.

Solution

The following solutions will show how to enable automatic scavenging on all AD-integrated zones.

Using a graphical user interface

1. Open the DNS Management snap-in.
2. If an entry for the DNS server you want to connect to does not exist, right-click on DNS in the left pane and select "Connect to DNS Server." Select "This computer" or "The following computer," then enter the server you want to connect to (if applicable), and click OK.
3. Click on the server, right-click on it, and select "Set Aging/Scavenging for all zones."
4. Check the box beside "Scavenge stale resource records."
5. Configure the No-Refresh and Refresh intervals as necessary, and click OK.
6. Check the box beside "Apply these settings to the existing Active Directory-integrated zones" and click OK.
7. Right-click on the server again and select Properties.
8. Select the Advanced tab.
9. Check the box beside "Enable automatic scavenging of stale resource records."

10. Configure the scavenging period as necessary.

11. Click OK.

Using a command-line interface

```
> dnscmd <DNSServerName> /config /ScavengingInterval < ScavengingMinutes>
> dnscmd <DNSServerName> /config /DefaultAgingState 1
> dnscmd <DNSServerName> /config /DefaultNoRefreshInterval <NoRefreshMinutes>
> dnscmd <DNSServerName> /config /DefaultRefreshInterval <RefreshMinutes>
> dnscmd <DNSServerName> /config ..AllZones /aging 1
```

Using VBScript

```
' This code enables scavenging for all AD-integrated zones.
' ------ SCRIPT CONFIGURATION ------
strServer = "<DNSServerName>"
intScavengingInterval = <ScavengingMinutes>
intNoRefreshInterval  = <NoRefreshMinutes>
intRefreshInterval    = <RefreshMinutes>
' ------ END CONFIGURATION --------

set objDNS = GetObject("winMgmts:\\" & strServer & "\root\MicrosoftDNS")
set objDNSServer = objDNS.Get("MicrosoftDNS_Server.Name=""."""")

objDNSServer.ScavengingInterval       = intScavengingInterval
objDNSServer.DefaultNoRefreshInterval = intNoRefreshInterval
objDNSServer.DefaultRefreshInterval   = intRefreshInterval
objDNSServer.DefaultAgingState        = TRUE
objDNSServer.Put_
WScript.Echo "Configured server scavenging settings"

set objZones = objDNS.ExecQuery("Select * from MicrosoftDNS_Zone " & _
                    "Where DnsServerName = '" & _
                            objDNSServer.Name & "'" & _
                    " And DsIntegrated = TRUE")
WScript.Echo "Configuring AD-integrated zones: "
for each objZone in objZones
   WScript.Echo " " & objZone.Name & " HERE: " & objZone.Aging
   objZone.Aging = 1
   objZone.Put_
next
```

Using PowerShell

```
$server = Get-WmiObject -Class MicrosoftDNS_Server -computer "<Server FQDN>"
-namespace root\MicrosoftDNS
$server.ScavengingInterval = <Scavenging Interval>
$server.DefaultNoRefreshInterval = <No Refresh Interval>
$server.DefaultRefreshInterval = <Refresh Interval>
$server.DefaultAgingState = $true
$server.Put()
```

Discussion

There are four settings that you need to be aware of before enabling scavenging. You must use caution when enabling scavenging, because an incorrect configuration could lead to resource records getting deleted by mistake.

The first setting you have to configure is the *scavenging interval*. This is the interval in which the DNS server will kick off the scavenging process. It is disabled by default so that scavenging does not take place unless you enable this setting. The default value is 168 hours, which is equivalent to 7 days.

The second setting is the *default aging configuration setting* for new zones. If you want all new zones to be configured for scavenging, set this to 1.

The next two settings control how records get scavenged. The *no-refresh interval* determines how long before a dynamically updated record can be updated again. This setting is necessary to reduce how often a DNS server has to update its timestamp of the resource record. The default value is 168 hours (7 days). This means that after a resource record has been dynamically updated, the server will not accept another dynamic update for the same record for another 7 days. However, if the IP address or some other data for the record changes, the server will still accept the new information.

The *refresh interval* setting is the amount of time after the no-refresh interval during which a client can update its record before it is considered old or stale. The default value for this setting is also 168 hours (7 days). If you use the default values, the combination of the no-refresh interval and refresh interval would mean that a dynamically updated record would not be considered stale for up to 14 days after its most recent update. Combine this with the default scavenging interval, and it could be up to 21 days before a record is deleted if the record became stale immediately after the last scavenge process completed: 7 days (no refresh) + 7 days (refresh) + up to 7 days (scavenge process).

The solutions in this recipe show you how to configure these settings for all zones that are hosted on a server; however, you can configure these settings for individual zones as well. In the GUI solution, you would do this by accessing the Properties sheet of an individual zone rather than the server node; in *dnscmd*, simply specify the zone name after /aging, /scavenginginterval, /defaultagingstate, /defaultnorefreshinterval, or /defaultrefreshinterval.

13.13 Clearing the DNS Cache

Problem

You want to clear the DNS cache. The DNS cache contains resource records that are cached by the server or workstation for a period of time in memory so that repeated requests for the same record can be returned immediately. There are two types of DNS cache. One pertains to the cache on the Windows DNS *client* resolver (this can refer to both server and workstation operating systems when they are requesting DNS information from a server), and the other refers to the cache used by the Microsoft DNS *server* software.

Solution

To flush the client resolver cache, use the following command:

```
> ipconfig /flushdns
```

To flush the DNS server cache, use any of the following solutions.

Using a graphical user interface

1. Open the DNS Management snap-in.
2. Right-click on DNS in the left pane and select "Connect to DNS Server."
3. Enter the server you want to connect to and click Enter.
4. Right-click on the server and select Clear Cache.

Using a command-line interface

The following command will clear the cache on `<DNSServerName>`. You can leave out the `<DNSServerName>` parameter to simply run the command against the local server:

```
> dnscmd <DNSServerName> /clearcache
```

Using VBScript

```
' This code clears the DNS server cache on the specified server.
' ------ SCRIPT CONFIGURATION ------
strServer = "<DNSServerName>" ' e.g. dc1.adatum.com
' ------ END CONFIGURATION --------

set objDNS = GetObject("winmgmts:\\" & strServer & "\root\MicrosoftDNS")
set objDNSServer = objDNS.Get("MicrosoftDNS_Server.Name=""."""")
set objDNSCache = objDNS.Get("MicrosoftDNS_Cache.ContainerName=""""..Cache""""" & _
                            ",DnsServerName=""""" & objDNSServer.Name & _
                            """"",Name=""""..Cache""""")

objDNSCache.ClearCache
WScript.Echo "Cleared server cache"
```

Using PowerShell

```
$cache = Get-WmiObject -Class MicrosoftDNS_Cache -computer "<Server FQDN>"
-namespace root\MicrosoftDNS
$cache.ClearCache()
```

Discussion

The client resolver cache is populated whenever a DNS lookup is performed on a workstation or server (e.g., with *nslookup*). It's important to remember that this cache will store both positive DNS responses as well as negative ones. For example, if lost network connectivity causes DNS queries for an external resource like a mail server to fail, those queries will continue to fail until the cache refreshes: the queries have been *negatively cached*.

The second type of cache is in place on Microsoft DNS servers and on some third-party DNS servers. It is a cache of all DNS requests that the server has made while processing queries from various clients. You can view this cache by browsing the Cached Lookups folder for a server in the DNS Management snap-in. This folder is not shown by default, so you'll need to select Advanced from the View menu.

With both the client and server cache, records are removed from the cache after the record's TTL value expires. The TTL is used to age records so that clients and servers will request an updated copy of the record at a later point in order to receive any changes that may have occurred.

13.14 Verifying That a Domain Controller Can Register Its Resource Records

Problem

You want to verify DNS is configured correctly so that a domain controller can register its resource records, which are needed for clients to be able to locate various AD services.

Solution

Using a command-line interface

 This test is available only with the Windows Server 2003 and newer versions of *dcdiag*.

With the following *dcdiag* command, replace *dc1* with the DNS name of the domain that the domain controller is in. This command has to be run from the domain controller you want to test, not from an administrative workstation:

```
> dcdiag /test:RegisterInDNS /DnsDomain:dc1

Starting test: RegisterInDNS
```

```
    DNS configuration is sufficient to allow this domain controller to
    dynamically register the domain controller Locator records in DNS.

    The DNS configuration is sufficient to allow this computer to dynamically
    register the A record corresponding to its DNS name.

    ...................... dc1 passed test RegisterInDNS
```

Discussion

With the default setup, domain controllers attempt to dynamically register the resource records necessary for them to be located by Active Directory clients and other domain controllers. Domain controllers must have their resource records populated in DNS in order to function, but it can be very tedious and error-prone to register all of the records manually. This is why allowing the domain controllers to use dynamic DNS (DDNS) to automatically register and update their records can be much easier from a support standpoint.

The Windows Server 2003 and newer versions of *dcdiag* provide a `RegisterInDNS` switch that allows you to test whether or not the DC can register its records. In the solution above, we showed the output if the domain controller passes the test.

Here is the output if an error occurs:

```
    Starting test: RegisterInDNS
        This domain controller cannot register domain controller Locator DNS
        records. This is because either the DNS server with IP address
        6.10.45.14 does not support dynamic updates or the zone adatum.com is
        configured to prevent dynamic updates.

        In order for this domain controller to be located by other domain members
        and domain controllers, the domain controller Locator DNS records must be
        added to DNS. You have the following options:

        1. Configure the adatum.com zone and the DNS server with IP address
        6.10.45.14 to allow dynamic updates. If the DNS server does not
        support dynamic updates, you might need to upgrade it.

        2. Migrate the adatum.com zone to a DNS server that supports dynamic
        updates (for example, a Windows 2000 DNS server).

        3. Delegate the zones _msdcs.adatum.com, _sites.adatum.com,
        _tcp.adatum.com, and _udp.adatum.com to a DNS server that supports
        dynamic updates (for example, a Windows 2000 DNS server); or

        4. Manually add to the DNS records specified in the
        systemroot\system32\config\netlogon.dns file.

        DcDiag cannot reach a conclusive result because it cannot interpret the
        following message that was returned: 9501.

        ...................... dc1 failed test RegisterInDNS
```

As you can see, the output of *dcdiag* offers several options for resolving the problem. The information provided will also vary depending on the error encountered.

See Also

Recipe 13.16 for registering a domain controller's resource records

13.15 Enabling DNS Server Debug Logging

Problem

You want to enable DNS debug logging to troubleshoot issues related to DNS queries or updates.

Solution

Using a graphical user interface

1. From the Administrative Tools, open the DNS Management snap-in.
2. Connect to the DNS Server you want to modify. In the left pane, right-click on DNS and select "Connect to DNS Server." Select "The following computer" and enter the target server name. Click OK.
3. Right-click on the server and select Properties.
4. Click on the Debug Logging tab (or the Logging tab in Windows 2000).
5. Select what you want to log and the location of the logfile (in Windows 2000, the logfile location is hardcoded to *%systemroot%\system32\dns\dns.log*).
6. Click OK.

Using a command-line interface

Use the following four commands to enable debug logging. For the log level, you have to add together the event codes you want logged and specify the result in hex. The available event codes can be found in Table 13-3:

```
> dnscmd <ServerName> /Config /LogLevel <EventFlagSumInHex>
```

Use the following command to specify the location of the logfile:

```
> dnscmd <ServerName> /Config /LogFilePath <DirectoryAndFilePath>
```

Use the following command to log only entries that pertain to certain IP addresses:

```
> dnscmd <ServerName> /Config /LogIPFilterList <IPAddress1>[,<IPAddress2>...]
```

Use the following command to specify the maximum logfile size:

```
> dnscmd <ServerName> /Config /LogFileMaxSize <NumberOfBytesInHex>
```

Use the following command to disable debug logging:

```
> dnscmd <ServerName> /Config /LogLevel 0
```

Using VBScript

```
' This code enables
' DNS debug logging.
' ------ SCRIPT CONFIGURATION -------
strServer = "<ServerName>" ' e.g. dc1
' The log level must be in decimal, not hex like dnscmd
intLogLevel = <EventFlagSumInDecimal> ' e.g. 65535
arrFilterList = Array("<IPAddress1>") ' e.g. 192.168.1.12
strFilePath = <DirectoryAndFilePath> ' e.g. c:\dnslog.txt
intFileSize = <NumberOfBytesInDecimal> ' e.g. 50000000
' ------ END CONFIGURATION ---------

set objDNS = GetObject("winMgmts:\\" & strServer & "\root\MicrosoftDNS")
set objDNSServer = objDNS.Get("MicrosoftDNS_Server.Name="".""")
objDNSServer.LogLevel = intLogLevel
objDNSServer.LogIPFilterList = arrFilterList

objDNSServer. LogFilePath = strFilePath
objDNSServer.LogFileMaxSize = intFileSize
objDNSServer.Put_
WScript.Echo "Enabled DNS  Debug Logging on " & strServer

' To disable debug logging, set the intLogLevel variable to 0
```

Using PowerShell

```
$arrFilterList = "<IPAddress1>", "<IPAddress2>"
$server = Get-WmiObject -Class MicrosoftDNS_Server -computer "<Server FQDN>"
-namespace root\MicrosoftDNS
$server.LogLevel = <Log Level> # i.e., 65535
$server.LogIPFilterList = $arrFilterList
$server.LogFilePath = "<File Path>"
$server.LogFileMaxSize = "<Max File Size>"
$server.Put()
```

Discussion

With the DNS Server debug log, you can record all DNS operations received and initiated by the server, including queries, updates, zone transfers, etc. If you need to troubleshoot a particular host, you can use the LogIPFilterList setting in *dnscmd* or the WMI DNS Provider to restrict the log to operations performed only for or by that host.

The most important debug log setting is the log level. With the DNS snap-in, you can select from a list of available options. With Windows Server 2003, the DNS snap-in provides an intuitive interface for selecting the required options. On Windows 2000, you are presented with a list of checkboxes and you have to figure out which ones need to be used in conjunction with one another. You have a similar issue with CLI and VBScript solutions, where you need to determine what log level you want to set.

Table 13-3 contains all of the event codes with their hexadecimal and decimal values.

Table 13-3. DNS debug logging event codes

Hexadecimal value	Decimal value	Descriptions
0x0	0	No logging. This is the default.
0x1	1	Query transactions.
0x10	16	Notifications transactions.
0x20	32	Update transactions.
0xFE	254	Nonquery transactions.
0x100	256	Question packets.
0x200	512	Answer packets.
0x1000	4096	Send packets.
0x2000	8192	Receive packets.
0x4000	16384	UDP packets.
0x8000	32768	TCP packets.
0xFFFF	65535	All packets.
0x10000	65536	AD write transactions.
0x20000	131072	AD update transactions.
0x1000000	16777216	Full packets.
0x80000000	2147483648	Write-through transactions.

DNS debug logging can come in handy if you want to look at the dynamic update requests a particular DNS Server is processing. For example, if a client or DHCP server is attempting to dynamically register records, you can enable the Update Transactions log category on the DNS Server you think should be processing the updates. If you don't see any update transactions, this can indicate that another server is processing the dynamic update requests.

 Transactions are not immediately written to the debug logfile as they occur. They are buffered and written to the file after a certain number of requests are processed.

See Also

MSDN: MicrosoftDNS_Server

13.16 Registering a Domain Controller's Resource Records

Problem

You want to manually force registration of a domain controller's resource records. This may be necessary if you've made some configuration changes on your DNS servers to allow your domain controllers to start dynamically registering resource records.

Solution

Using a command-line interface

```
> nltest /dsregdns /server:<DomainControllerName>
```

Discussion

Beginning with the Windows Server 2003 version of *nltest*, a /dsregdns switch allows you to force registration of the domain-controller-specific resource records. You can also force reregistration of its resource records by restarting the NetLogon service on the domain controller. The NetLogon service automatically attempts to reregister a domain controller's resource records every hour, so if you can wait that long, you do not need to use *nltest*.

See Also

Recipe 13.14 for verifying if a domain controller is registering its resource records

13.17 Deregistering a Domain Controller's Resource Records

Problem

You want to manually deregister a domain controller's resource records.

Solution

Using a command-line interface

With the following *nltest* command, replace *<DomainControllerName>* with the FQDN of the domain controller you want to deregister and *<DomainDNSName>* with the FQDN of the domain of which the domain controller is a member:

```
> nltest /dsderegdns: <DomainControllerName> /dom:<DomainDNSName>
```

Discussion

When a domain controller is demoted from a domain, it dynamically deregisters its resource records. This is a nice feature of the demotion process because it means you do not have to manually remove all of the resource records or wait for scavenging to remove them. If, however, you have a domain controller that crashes and you do not plan on bringing it back online, you'll need to remove the records manually or wait for the scavenging process to take place.

You can use the DNS Mgmt MMC snap-in and even the *dnscmd.exe* utility to manually remove them one by one, or you can use *nltest*, as shown in the solution.

The /dsderegdns switch also has /DomGUID and /DsaGUID options if you want to delete the records that are based on the domain GUID and DSA GUID, respectively. You need to know the actual GUIDs of the domain and domain controller to use those switches, so if you don't have them handy, it would be easier to delete them using the DNS Management MMC snap-in.

13.18 Preventing a Domain Controller from Dynamically Registering All Resource Records

Problem

You want to prevent a domain controller from dynamically registering its resource records using DDNS. If you manually register a domain controller's resource records, you'll want to prevent those domain controllers from attempting to dynamically register them. If you do not disable them from sending dynamic update requests, you may see annoying error messages on your DNS servers that certain DDNS updates are failing.

Solution

Using a command-line interface

```
> reg add HKLM\System\CurrentControlSet\Services\Netlogon\Parameters /v
UseDynamicDNS /t REG_DWORD /d 0
The operation completed successfully.

> net stop netlogon
The Net Logon service is stopping.
The Net Logon service was stopped successfully.

> del %SystemRoot%\system32\config\netlogon.dnb

> net start netlogon
The Net Logon service is starting.......
The Net Logon service was started successfully.
```

Using VBScript

```
' This code prevents a DC from registering resource records dynamically.
' It must be run directly on the server.

' Create Registry Value
const HKLM = &H80000002
set oReg=GetObject("winmgmts:root\default:StdRegProv")
strKeyPath = "System\CurrentControlSet\Services\Netlogon\Parameters"
if oReg.SetDWORDValue(HKLM,strKeyPath,"UseDynamicDNS",0) <> 0 then
    WScript.Echo "Error creating registry value"
else
    WScript.Echo "Created registry value successfully"
end if

' Stop Netlogon service
strService = "Netlogon"
set objService = GetObject("WinMgmts:root/cimv2:Win32_Service.Name='" & _
                           strService & "'")
if objService.StopService <> 0 then
    WScript.Echo "Error stopping " & strService & " service"
else
    WScript.Echo "Stopped " & strService & " service successfully"
end if

' Delete netlogon.dnb file
set WshShell = CreateObject("WScript.Shell")
set objFSO = CreateObject("Scripting.FileSystemObject")
set objFile = objFSO.GetFile( _
                 WshShell.ExpandEnvironmentStrings("%SystemRoot%") _
                 & "\system32\config\netlogon.dnb" )

objFile.Delete
WScript.Echo "Deleted netlogon.dnb successfully"

' Start Netlogon service
if objService.StartService <> 0 then
    WScript.Echo "Error starting " & strService & " service"
else
    WScript.Echo "Started " & strService & " service successfully"
end if

WScript.Echo
WScript.Echo "Done"
```

Using PowerShell

```
$strRegPath = "HKLM:\System\CurrentControlSet\Services\Netlogon\Parameters"
new-ItemProperty -path $strRegPath -name "UseDynamicDNS" -type DWORD
set-ItemProperty -path $strRegPath -name "UseDynamicDNS" -value "0"

Stop-Service netlogon
$strPath = join-path (get-content env:SystemRoot) system32\config\netlogon.dnb
Remove-Item $strPath
Start-Service netlogon
```

Discussion

By default, domain controllers attempt to dynamically register their Active Directory-related resource records every hour via the NetLogon service. You can prevent a domain controller from doing this by setting the UseDynamicDNS value to 0 under *HKEY_LOCAL_MACHINE\System\CurrentControlSet\Services\Netlogon\Parameters*. After you set that value, you should stop the NetLogon service, remove the *%System-Root%\system32\config\netlogon.dnb* file, and then restart NetLogon. It is necessary to remove the *netlogon.dnb* file because it maintains a cache of the resource records that are dynamically updated. This file will get re-created when the NetLogon service restarts.

See Also

Recipe 13.19 for preventing certain resource records from being dynamically registered, MS KB 198767 (How to Prevent Domain Controllers from Dynamically Registering DNS Names), and MS KB 246804 (How to Enable/Disable Windows 2000 Dynamic DNS Registrations)

13.19 Preventing a Domain Controller from Dynamically Registering Certain Resource Records

Problem

You want to prevent a domain controller from dynamically registering certain resource records. It is sometimes advantageous to prevent certain resource records from being dynamically registered. For example, if you want to reduce the load on the PDC Emulator for a domain, you can prevent some of its SRV records from being published, which would reduce the amount of client traffic the server receives.

Solution

Using a graphical user interface

> This is only available on Windows Server 2003 and higher domain controllers.

1. Open the Group Policy Management Console.
2. Create a GPO linked to the Domain Controllers OU, or else edit an existing GPO.
3. Navigate to Computer Configuration→Administrative Templates→System→Net Logon→DC Locator DNS Records (in Windows Server 2003 and R2) or Computer

Configuration→Policies→Administrative Templates→System→Net Logon→DC Locator DNS Records (in Windows Server 2008).

4. Enable the "DC Locator DNS records not registered by the DCs" setting, and list one or more of the following SRV record types that should not be registered:

- Dc
- DcByGuid
- Gc
- GcIpAddress
- GenericGc
- Kdc
- Ldap
- LdapIpAddress
- Rfc1510Kdc
- Rfc1510Kpwd
- Rfc1510UdpKdc
- Rfc1510UdpKpwd

Using a command-line interface

This command will disable the Ldaps' Gc, and GcIpAddress resource records from being dynamically registered:

```
> reg add HKLM\System\CurrentControlSet\Services\Netlogon\Parameters /v
DnsAvoidRegisterRecords /t REG_MULTI_SZ /d Ldap\0Gc\0GcIpAddress
The operation completed successfully.

> net stop netlogon
The Net Logon service is stopping.
The Net Logon service was stopped successfully.

> del %SystemRoot%\system32\config\netlogon.dnb

> net start netlogon
The Net Logon service is starting.......
The Net Logon service was started successfully.
```

Using VBScript

```
' This code prevents a DC from registering the resource records
' associated with the Ldap, Gc, and GcIpAddress mnemonics and must be run
' directly on the server.

' Create Registry Value
const HKLM = &H80000002
set objReg = GetObject("winmgmts:root\default:StdRegProv")
strKeyPath = "System\CurrentControlSet\Services\Netlogon\Parameters"
' prevent Ldap, Gc, and GCIpAddress records from being registered
```

```
    arrValues = Array("Ldap","Gc","GcIpAddress")
    if objReg.SetMultiStringValue(HKLM,strKeyPath,"DnsAvoidRegisterRecords", _
                                  arrValues) <> 0 then
       WScript.Echo "Error creating registry value"
    else
       WScript.Echo "Created registry value successfully"
    end if


    ' Stop Netlogon service
    strService = "Netlogon"
    set objService = GetObject("WinMgmts:root/cimv2:Win32_Service.Name='" & _
                               strService & "'")
    if objService.StopService <> 0 then
       WScript.Echo "Error stopping " & strService & " service"
    else
       WScript.Echo "Stopped " & strService & " service successfully"
    end if


    ' Delete netlogon.dnb file
    On Error Resume Next
    set WshShell = CreateObject("WScript.Shell")
    set objFSO = CreateObject("Scripting.FileSystemObject")
    set objFile = objFSO.GetFile( _
                       WshShell.ExpandEnvironmentStrings("%systemroot%") _
                       & "\system32\config\netlogon.dnb")
    objFile.Delete
    if (Err.Number <> 0) then
       WScript.Echo "Error deleting netlogon.dnb: " & Err.Description
    else
       WScript.Echo "Deleted netlogon.dnb successfully"
    end if


    ' Start Netlogon service
    if objService.StartService <> 0 then
       WScript.Echo "Error starting " & strService & " service"
    else
       WScript.Echo "Started " & strService & " service successfully"
    end if

    WScript.Echo
    WScript.Echo "Done"
```

Using PowerShell

```
$strRegPath = "HKLM:\System\CurrentControlSet\Services\Netlogon\Parameters"
$arrValues = "Ldap", "Gc", "GcIpAddress"
new-ItemProperty -path $strRegPath -name "DnsAvoidRegisterRecords" -type
MultiString
set-ItemProperty -path $strRegPath -name "DnsAvoidRegisterRecords" -value
$arrValues

Stop-Service netlogon
$strPath = join-path (get-content env:SystemRoot) system32\config\netlogon.dnb
Remove-Item $strPath
Start-Service netlogon
```

Discussion

The procedure to disable registration of certain resource records is very similar to that described in Recipe 13.18 for preventing all resource records from being dynamically registered, however, in this case you need to create a value called DnsAvoidRegisterRecords under the *HKEY_LOCAL_MACHINE\System\CurrentControlSet\Services\Netlogon\Parameters* key. The type for DnsAvoidRegisterRecords should be REG_MULTI_SZ, and the data should be a whitespace-separated list of mnemonics. Mnemonics are used to represent various resource records that domain controllers register. The complete list of mnemonics is included in Table 13-4.

 You can also control these values using Group Policy, in *Computer Configuration\Administrative Templates\System\Netlogon*.

Table 13-4. Registry mnemonics for resource records

Registry mnemonic	Resource record type	Resource record name
LdapIpAddress	A	*<DnsDomainName>*
Ldap	SRV	_ldap._tcp.*<DnsDomainName>*
LdapAtSite	SRV	_ldap._tcp.*<SiteName>*._sites.*<DnsDomainName>*
Pdc	SRV	_ldap._tcp.pdc._msdcs.*<DnsDomainName>*
Gc	SRV	_ldap._tcp.gc._msdcs.*<DnsForestName>*
GcAtSite	SRV	_ldap._tcp.*<SiteName>*._sites.gc._msdcs.*<DnsForestName>*
DcByGuid	SRV	_ldap._tcp.*<DomainGuid>*.domains._msdcs.*<DnsForestName>*
GcIpAddress	A	_gc._msdcs.*<DnsForestName>*
DsaCname	CNAME	*<DsaGuid>*._msdcs.*<DnsForestName>*
Kdc	SRV	_kerberos._tcp.dc._msdcs.*<DnsDomainName>*
KdcAtSite	SRV	_kerberos._tcp.dc._msdcs.*<SiteName>*._sites. *<DnsDomainName>*
Dc	SRV	_ldap._tcp.dc._msdcs.*<DnsDomainName>*
DcAtSite	SRV	_ldap._tcp.*<SiteName>*._sites.dc._msdcs.*<DnsDomainName>*
Rfc1510Kdc	SRV	_kerberos._tcp.*<DnsDomainName>*
Rfc1510KdcAtSite	SRV	_kerberos._tcp.*<SiteName>*._sites.*<DnsDomainName>*
GenericGc	SRV	_gc._tcp.*<DnsForestName>*
GenericGcAtSite	SRV	_gc._tcp.*<SiteName>*._sites.*<DnsForestName>*
Rfc1510UdpKdc	SRV	_kerberos._udp.*<DnsDomainName>*
Rfc1510Kpwd	SRV	_kpasswd._tcp.*<DnsDomainName>*
Rfc1510UdpKpwd	SRV	_kpasswd._udp.*<DnsDomainName>*

If you configure DCs not to register these domain-wide SRV records, such as in a branch office environment, your branch office clients will still fail over to DCs in your hub site if their local DC becomes unavailable. Clients will continue to use the hub site DCs until they are rebooted, even if the local DC comes back online. MS KB 939252 provides a hotfix that will improve client failover behavior in this scenario.

See Also

Recipe 13.18 for preventing all resource records from being dynamically registered, MS KB 246804 (How to Enable/Disable Windows 2000 Dynamic DNS Registrations), MS KB 267855 (Problems with Many Domain Controllers with Active Directory Integrated DNS Zones), and the Windows Server 2003 Branch Office Planning and Deployment Guide (*http://go.microsoft.com/fwlink/?LinkId=28523*)

13.20 Allowing Computers to Use a Different Domain Suffix Than Their AD Domain

Problem

You want to allow computers to use a different domain suffix than their AD domain.

Solution

The following solutions work only for Windows Server 2003 domains. Read the section called "Discussion" for a workaround for Windows 2000.

Using a graphical user interface

1. Open ADSI Edit.
2. Connect to the domain you want to edit.
3. Right-click on the domainDNS object and select Properties.
4. Edit the msDS-AllowedDNSSuffixes attribute and the DNS suffix you want to add.
5. Click OK.

Using a command-line interface

Create an LDIF file called *add_dns_suffix.ldf* with the following contents:

```
dn: <DomainDN>
changetype: modify
add: msDS-AllowedDNSSuffixes
msDS-AllowedDNSSuffixes: <DNSSuffix>
-
```

Then run the following command:

```
> ldifde -v -i -f add_dns_suffix.ldf.ldf
```

You can also make this change using AdMod, as follows:

```
> admod -b <DomainDN> msDS-AllowedDNSSuffixes:+:<DNSSuffix>
```

Using VBScript

```
' This code adds a domain suffix that can be used by clients in the domain.
' ------ SCRIPT CONFIGURATION ------
strDNSSuffix = "<DNSSuffix>"   ' e.g. othercorp.com
strDomain = "<DomainDNSName>" ' e.g. amer.adatum.com
' ------ END CONFIGURATION --------

set objRootDSE = GetObject("LDAP://" & strDomain & "/RootDSE")
set objDomain = GetObject("LDAP://" & objRootDSE.Get("defaultNamingContext") )
objDomain.Put "msDS-AllowedDNSSuffixes", strDNSSuffix
objDomain.SetInfo

WScript.Echo "Added " & strDNSSuffix & " to suffix list."
```

Using PowerShell

You can modify the list of allowed DNS suffixes for a domain using the Quest cmdlets or ADSI, as follows:

```
set-QADObject -Identity "<Domain DN>" -ObjectAttributes @{msDS-
AllowedDNSSuffixes="<DomainDNSName>"}

$objDom = [ADSI] "LDAP://<Domain DN>"
$strSuffix = "<DomainDNSName>"
$objDom.PutEx(3, "msDS-AllowedDNSSuffixes", @($strSuffix))
$objDom.SetInfo()
```

Discussion

Windows 2000, Windows XP, and Windows Server 2003 member computers dynamically maintain the dNSHostName and servicePrincipalName attributes of their corresponding computer object in Active Directory with their current hostname. By default, those attributes can only contain hostnames that have a DNS suffix equal to the Active Directory domain the computer is a member of.

If the computer's DNS suffix is not equal to the Active Directory domain, as may be the case during a domain migration or a corporate merger or consolidation, 5788 and 5789 events will be generated in the System event log on the domain controllers the clients attempt to update. These events report that the dnsHostName and servicePrincipalName attributes could not be updated due to an incorrect domain suffix. For Windows Server 2003 and Windows Server 2008 domains, you can avoid this by adding the computer's DNS suffix to the msDS-AllowedDNSSuffixes attribute on the domain object (e.g., dc=adatum,dc=com).

With Windows 2000, the only workaround for this issue is to grant the `Self` principal the ability to write the `dNSHostName` and `servicePrincipalName` attribute for `computer` objects. Here are the steps:

1. Open ADSI Edit.
2. Right-click on the domain object and select Properties.
3. Click the Security tab.
4. Click the Add button.
5. Enter Self in the object picker and click OK.
6. Click the Advanced button.
7. Under the Name column, double-click on SELF.
8. Click the Properties tab.
9. Beside "Apply onto," select Computer objects.
10. Under Permissions, check the Allow box for `Write dNSHostName` and `Write service PrincipalName`.
11. Click OK until you close all the windows.

 It is worth noting that if you implement this method, it is possible for someone to cause a computer to write any name into those attributes and, therefore, advertise itself as another computer.

See Also

MS KB 258503 (DNS Registration Errors 5788 and 5789 When DNS Domain and Active Directory Domain Name Differ)

13.21 Authorizing a DHCP Server

Problem

You want to permit (i.e., authorize) a DHCP server to process DHCP requests from clients. This is necessary only if the DHCP server is a member of an Active Directory domain.

Solution

Using a graphical user interface

 Windows 2000 DHCP servers cannot be authorized with the Windows Server 2003 version of the DHCP snap-in unless the DHCP server has Service Pack 2 or higher installed.

1. Open the DHCP snap-in.
2. In the left pane, right-click on DHCP and select Add Server.
3. Type in the name of the DHCP server you want to target and click OK.
4. Click on the server entry in the left pane.
5. Right-click on the server and select Authorize.

 If the DHCP server is not a member of an Active Directory domain, you will not see the Authorize option.

Using a command-line interface

The following command authorizes a DHCP server in Active Directory:

```
> netsh dhcp add server <DHCPServerName> <DHCPServerIP>
```

This example shows how to authorize the DHCP server named *dhcp01.adatum.com* with IP 192.168.191.15:

```
> netsh dhcp add server dhcp01.adatum.com 192.168.191.15
```

Discussion

Windows-based DHCP servers that belong to an Active Directory domain must be authorized before they can give leases to clients. This feature helps reduce the danger of a rogue Windows DHCP server that an end user sets up, perhaps even unintentionally.

However, this still doesn't prevent someone from plugging in a non-Windows DHCP server (e.g., a Linksys router with the DHCP server enabled) and causing clients to receive bad leases. A rogue DHCP server can provide incorrect lease information or deny lease requests altogether, ultimately causing a denial of service for clients on your network.

If the DHCP server service is enabled on a domain controller, it is automatically authorized. A DHCP server that is a member server of an Active Directory domain performs a query in Active Directory to determine whether it is authorized. If it is, it will respond to DHCP requests; if not, it will not respond to requests.

A standalone Windows DHCP server that is not a member of an Active Directory domain sends out a DHCPINFORM message when it first initializes. If an authorized DHCP server responds to the message, the standalone server will not respond to any further DHCP requests. If it does not receive a response from a DHCP server, it will respond to client requests and distribute leases.

DHCP servers are represented in Active Directory as objects of the dhcpClass class, in the cn=NetServices,cn=Services,cn=Configuratation,<ForestRootDN> container. The relative distinguished name of these objects is the IP address of the DHCP server. There is also an object in the same container named cn=dhcpRoot, which is created after the first DHCP server is authorized. It has an attribute named dhcpServers that contains all authorized servers. By default, only members of the *Enterprise Admins* group can authorize DHCP servers. However, you can delegate the rights to authorize a DHCP server. Do the following to delegate the necessary permissions to a group called *DHCP Admins*:

1. Open ADSI Edit from the Support Tools while logged on as a member of the *Enterprise Admins* group.
2. In the left pane, expand the Configuration Container→CN=Configuration→CN=Services→CN=NetServices.
3. Right-click on CN=NetServices and select Properties.
4. Select the Security tab.
5. Click the Advanced button.
6. Click the Add button.
7. Use the object picker to select the *DHCP Admins* group.
8. Check the boxes under "Allow for Create dHCPClass objects" and "Delete dHCPClass objects."
9. Click OK until all dialog boxes are closed.
10. Back in ADSI Edit, right-click on CN=dhcpRoot (if you've previously authorized DHCP Servers) and select Properties.
11. Select the Security tab.
12. Click the Advanced button.
13. Click the Add button.
14. Use the object picker to select the *DHCP Admins* group.
15. Check the boxes under Allow for "Write All Properties."
16. Click OK until all dialog boxes are closed.

Using a graphical user interface

You can quickly determine whether a DHCP server has been authorized by looking at its server node in the left pane of the DHCP snap-in. If the icon has a little red flag, it isn't authorized; if the flag is green, it is authorized.

Using a command-line interface

To see the list of authorized servers using the command line, run the following command:

```
> netsh dhcp show server
```

See Also

MS KB 279908 (Unexpected Results in the DHCP Service Snap-In After Using NETSH to Authorize DHCP), MS KB 300429 (How to Install and Configure a DHCP Server in an Active Directory Domain in Windows 2000), MS KB 303351 (How to Use Netsh.exe to Authorize, Unauthorize, and List DHCP Servers in Active Directory), and MS KB 306925 (After a New DHCP Server Is Authorized, the Original DHCP Server Becomes Unauthorized and Cannot Be Authorized Again in Windows 2000 Server)

13.22 Locating Unauthorized DHCP Servers

Problem

You want to locate any unauthorized or rogue DHCP servers on your network.

Solution

Using a command-line interface

Here's how to search for rogue DHCP servers from a workstation with an IP address of 10.0.0.101 while disregarding a known, valid DHCP server residing on 10.0.0.200:

```
> dhcploc 10.0.0.101 10.0.0.200
```

Discussion

The DHCP authorization process in Active Directory will prevent any newer Windows DHCP servers from offering up IP addresses without first being authorized by a member of the *Enterprise Admins* group. However, this mechanism does not extend to Windows NT 4.0 DHCP servers or non-Windows devices, such as a Linksys router that also functions as a DHCP server. The *dhcploc* utility in the Windows Support Tools in Windows 2000 and Windows Server 2003 will display an output of all DHCP traffic that it receives, with a *** displayed next to traffic that it receives from unauthorized servers, as follows:

```
14:24:28 (IP)0.0.0.0      NACK   (S)10.0.0.40    ***

14:24:28 (IP)10.0.0.103   OFFER  (S)10.0.0.60    ***

14:24:28 (IP)10.0.0.201   ACK    (S)10.0.0.30

14:24:23 (IP)10.0.0.203   ACK    (S)10.0.0.30

14:24:25 (IP)10.0.0.4     OFFER  (S)10.0.0.30

14:24:35 (IP)10.0.0.2     OFFER  (S)10.0.0.40

14:24:36 (IP)10.0.0.3     OFFER  (S)10.0.0.26    ***
```

The *dhcploc* utility is no longer available in Windows Server 2008.

See Also

Recipe 13.21 for more on authorizing DHCP servers in Active Directory

13.23 Restricting DHCP Administrators

Problem

You want to restrict who can administer your DHCP servers in your domain.

Solution

Using a graphical user interface

1. Open the Active Directory Users and Computers MMC snap-in.
2. In the console tree, click Active Directory Users and Computers→Domain-Name→Users.
3. In the details pane, click DHCP Administrators.
4. Click Action→Properties→Members.
5. Remove all users and groups you do not want to have administering your DHCP server by clicking their names and then clicking Remove.
6. To add new DHCP administrators, click Add, provide the user or group name, and then click OK.
7. Click OK.

Using a command-line interface

Add a member to a group with DSMod by passing the -addmbr option:

```
> dsmod group "<GroupDN>" -addmbr "<MemberDN>"
```

To add a group member with AdMod, use the following syntax:

```
> admod -b "<GroupDN>" member:+:"<MemberDN>"
```

Remove a member from a group with DSMod by passing the -rmmbr option:

```
> dsmod group "<GroupDN>" -rmmbr "<MemberDN>"
```

To remove a group member with AdMod, use the following syntax:

```
> admod -b "<GroupDN>" member:-:"<MemberDN>"
```

Replace the complete membership list with DSMod by passing the `-chmbr` option:

```
> dsmod group "<GroupDN>" -chmbr "<Member1DN Member2DN ...>"
```

To replace the membership of a group with AdMod, use the following command:

```
> admod -b "<GroupDN>" member:+-:"<Member1DN>;<Member2DN>;<Member3DN>"
```

Using VBScript

```
' This code adds a member to the DHCP Administrators group.
' ------ SCRIPT CONFIGURATION ------
strGroupDN = "<GroupDN>" ' e.g. "cn=
DHCP Administrators,cn=Users,<DomainDN>
strMemberDN = "<MemberDN>" ' e.g. cn=jsmith,cn=users,dc=adatum,dc=com
' ------ END CONFIGURATION --------

set objGroup = GetObject("LDAP://" & strGroupDN)
' Add a member
objGroup.Add("LDAP://" & strMemberDN)

' This code removes a member from the
' DHCP Administrators group.

set objGroup = GetObject("LDAP://" & strGroupDN)
objGroup.Remove("LDAP://" & strMemberDN)
```

Using PowerShell

You can modify the membership of the *DHCP Administrators* group using the Quest AD cmdlets or using ADSI methods, as follows:

```
Add-QADGroupMember -Identity "cn=DHCP Administrators,cn=Users,<Domain DN>" -Member
"<User DN>"
RemoveQADGroupMember -Identity "cn=DHCP Administrators,cn=Users,<Domain DN>"
-Member "<User DN>"
```

To add a group member using ADSI, use the following syntax:

```
$objGroup = [ADSI] "LDAP://cn=DHCP Administrators,cn=Users,<Domain DN>"
$objGroup.Add("LDAP://<User DN>")
```

To remove a group member using ADSI, use the following syntax:

```
$objGroup = [ADSI] "LDAP://cn=DHCP Administrators,cn=Users,<Domain DN>"
$objGroup.Remove("LDAP://<User DN>")
```

Discussion

Windows Server 2003 is better than its predecessors about supporting role separation. Most roles can be assigned independently of one another rather than just by making a user a Domain Admin or an Enterprise Admin. This is great for security administrators who want to ensure that users have only enough rights to perform their assigned tasks. For example, a user *Fred* might need to modify an enterprise-wide object. You could just add *Fred* to the *Enterprise Admin* groups to solve the problem. However, *Fred* now has access to virtually any object in the entire forest and could cause irreparable harm to your network, not to mention compromise all security in place. Instead, you can grant *Fred* access to just that object.

This can be done in separate ways. One method is the "Delegation of Control" wizard. Another way is that Windows has several built-in groups that are created and populated when specific services are installed. One such group is *DHCP Administrators*, which is created when the first DHCP server is brought up in a domain. You can control administrative access to the DHCP function of these servers through this group membership.

Nondomain joined computers also have a *DHCP Administrators* group. This is a local group on each computer and must be managed separately on each sever.

See Also

"To Add a User or Group as a DHCP Administrator" in the Windows Server 2003 documentation, and "Delegate Ability to Authorize DHCP server to a Nonenterprise Administrator" in the Windows Server 2003 documentation

## CHAPTER 14

Security and Authentication

14.0 Introduction

The default Windows 2000 installation of Active Directory was not as secure as it could have been out of the box. It allowed anonymous queries to be executed, which could take up valuable processing resources, and it did not place any requirements on encrypting or signing traffic between clients and domain controllers. As a result, usernames, passwords, and search results could be sent over the network in clear text. Fortunately, beginning with Windows Server 2003, things have been tightened up significantly. LDAP traffic is signed by default, and anonymous queries are disabled by default. Additionally, Transport Layer Security (TLS), the more flexible cousin of Secure Sockets Layer (SSL), is supported, allowing for end-to-end encryption of traffic between domain controllers and clients.

Active Directory's ACL model provides ultimate flexibility for securing objects throughout a forest; you can restrict access down to the attribute level if you need to. With this flexibility comes increased complexity. An object's ACL is initially generated from the default ACL for the object's class, inherited permissions, and permissions directly applied on the object.

An ACL is a collection of ACEs, which defines the permission and properties that a security principal can use on the object to which the ACL is applied. Defining these entries and populating the ACL is the foundation of Active Directory security and delegation.

In this chapter, we will explore some of the common tasks of managing permissions in Active Directory. If you are looking for a detailed guide to Active Directory permissions, we suggest reading *Active Directory*, Fourth Edition, by Brian Desmond et al. (O'Reilly).

In order for ACLs to be of use, a user must first authenticate to Active Directory. *Kerberos* is the primary network authentication system used by Active Directory. Kerberos is a standards-based system originally developed at MIT that has been widely implemented at universities. We will also be covering some Kerberos-related tasks in this chapter that you will be likely to encounter in an Active Directory environment. For a complete review of Kerberos, we recommend *Kerberos: The Definitive Guide* by Jason Garman (O'Reilly).

14.1 Enabling SSL/TLS

Problem

You want to enable SSL/TLS access to your domain controllers so clients can encrypt LDAP traffic to the servers.

Solution

Using a graphical user interface in Windows 2000 Server and Windows Server 2003

1. Open the Control Panel on a domain controller.
2. Open the "Add or Remove Programs" applet.
3. Click on Add/Remove Windows Components.
4. Check the box beside Certificate Services and click Yes to verify.
5. Click Next.
6. Select the type of authority you want the domain controller to be (select "Enterprise root CA" if you are unsure) and click Next.
7. Type the common name for the CA, select a validity period, and click Next.
8. Enter the location for certificate database and logs, and click Next.
9. After the installation completes, click Finish.
10. Now open the Domain Controller Security Policy GPO.
11. Navigate to Computer Configuration→Windows Settings→Security Settings→Public Key Policies.
12. Right-click on Automatic Certificate Request Settings and select New→Automatic Certificate Request.
13. Click Next.
14. Under Certificate Templates, click on Domain Controller and click Next.
15. Click Finish.
16. Right-click on Automatic Certificate Request Settings and select New→Automatic Certificate Request.
17. Click Next.
18. Under Certificate Templates, click on Computer and click Next.
19. Click Finish.

Using a graphical user interface in Windows Server 2008

1. Open Server Manager.
2. Click Add Roles, and then click Next.
3. Check the box beside Active Directory Certificate Services and click Next.
4. The Select Role Services screen appears. Ensure that there is a checkmark next to Certification Authority and then click Next.
5. Select the setup type that you want (select "Enterprise" if you are unsure) and click Next.
6. Select the CA type that you want the domain controller to be (select "Root CA" if you are unsure) and click Next.
7. The Set Up Private Key screen appears. Click Next.
8. The Configure Cryptography for CA screen appears. Click Next.
9. Type the common name for the CA, and click Next.
10. Select a validity period, and click Next.
11. Enter the location for certificate database and logs, and click Next.
12. Click Install, and then click Close when the installation completes.
13. Now open the Default Domain Controller GPO, or another GPO that is linked to the Domain Controllers OU, within the GPMC.
14. Navigate to Computer Configuration→Policies→Windows Settings→Security Settings→Public Key Policies.
15. Right-click on Automatic Certificate Request Settings and select New→Automatic Certificate Request.
16. Click Next.
17. Under Certificate Templates, click on Domain Controller and click Next.
18. Click Finish.
19. Right-click on Automatic Certificate Request Settings and select New→Automatic Certificate Request.
20. Click Next.
21. Under Certificate Templates, click on Computer and click Next.
22. Click Finish.

Discussion

After Active Directory domain controllers obtain certificates, they open up ports 636 and 3289. Port 636 is for LDAP over SSL/TLS and port 3269 is used for global catalog queries performed over SSL/TLS. See Recipe 14.2 for more information on how to query a domain controller using SSL/TLS.

Installing and configuring a Public Key Infrastructure (PKI) to support the certificate templates and certificate requests described here is outside the scope of this book; for more information, please refer to *Windows Server 2003 Security Cookbook* by Mike Danseglio and Robbie Allen (O'Reilly).

See Also

MS KB 247078 (How to Enable Secure Socket Layer [SSL] Communication Over LDAP For Windows 2000 Domain Controllers), MS KB 281271 (Windows 2000 Certification Authority Configuration to Publish Certificates in Active Directory of Trusted Domain), and MS KB 321051 (How to Enable LDAP over SSL with a Third-Party Certification Authority)

14.2 Encrypting LDAP Traffic with SSL, TLS, or Signing

Problem

You want to encrypt LDAP traffic using SSL, TLS, or signing.

Solution

Using a graphical user interface

Most of the GUI-based tools, beginning with Windows 2000 Server Service Pack 3 running on both workstation and server computers, will automatically sign and encrypt traffic between the server and client. This includes the following tools:

- Active Directory Domains and Trusts
- Active Directory Sites and Services
- Active Directory Schema
- Active Directory Users and Computers
- ADSI Edit
- Group Policy Management Console
- Object Picker

With ADSI Edit, you can also specify the port number to use when browsing a partition. View the settings for a connection by right-clicking on the partition and selecting Settings. Click the Advanced button and enter 636 for LDAP over SSL or 3269 for the global catalog over SSL.

Starting with Windows Server 2003, LDAP supports encryption using the StartTLS and StopTLS operations, which are available from the Options→TLS menu. With the Windows 2000 version, you can use SSL by going to Connection→Connect and entering 636 or 3269 for the port.

Using a command-line interface

The DS command-line tools support LDAP signing and encryption when run from Windows Server 2003, Windows Server 2008, Windows XP, or Windows Vista against Windows 2000 SP3 or newer domain controllers. This includes DSAdd, DSMod, DSrm, DSMove, DSGet, and DSQuery. The *joeware* utilities also support connecting using SSL security.

Using VBScript

```
' Constants taken from ADS_AUTHENTICATION_ENUM

ADS_SECURE_AUTHENTICATION = 1
ADS_USE_SSL = 2

'This code shows how to enable SSL and secure authentication using ADSI.
set objLDAP = GetObject("LDAP:")
set objOU = objLDAP.OpenDSObject("LDAP://ou=Sales,dc=adatum,dc=com", _
                                 "administrator@adatum.com", _
                                 "MyAdminPassword", _
                                 ADS_SECURE_AUTHENTICATION + ADS_USE_SSL)
WScript.Echo objOU.Get("ou")
' This code shows how to enable SSL and secure authentication using ADO.
set objConn = CreateObject("ADODB.Connection")
objConn.Provider = "ADsDSOObject"
objConn.Properties("User ID") = "administrator@adatum.com"
objConn.Properties("Password") = "MyAdminPassword"
objConn.Properties("Encrypt Password") = True
objConn.Properties("ADSI Flag") = ADS_SECURE_AUTHENTICATION + ADS_USE_SSL
objConn.Open "Active Directory Provider"
set objRS = objConn.Execute("<LDAP://cn=users,dc=adatum,dc=com>;" & _
                            "(cn=*);" & "cn;" & "onelevel")
objRS.MoveFirst
while Not objRS.EOF
    Wscript.Echo objRS.Fields(0).Value
    objRS.MoveNext
wend
```

Discussion

An out-of-the-box installation of Windows 2000 Active Directory did not provide any default data encryption over the network between clients and domain controllers when using most of the standard tools. If you run Network Monitor (*netmon.exe*) while using tools that perform simple LDAP binds, you'll see LDAP requests, usernames, and passwords going over the network in plain text. Obviously this is not the most secure configuration; beginning with Windows Server 2003, most of the AD tools sign and encrypt traffic from the clients to the domain controllers by default.

To use the more secure Windows tools against Windows 2000 domain controllers, you need to install at least Service Pack 3 on the Windows 2000 domain controllers. The new versions of the tools cannot be run directly on Windows 2000, so you must use a Windows XP/Vista or Windows Server 2003/2008 machine to host them.

See Also

Recipe 14.1 for enabling SSL/TLS, Recipe 14.3 for disabling LDAP encryption, MS KB 325465 (Windows 2000 Domain Controllers Require SP3 or Later When Using Windows Server 2003 Administration Tools), MS KB 304718 (Administering Windows Server-Based Computers Using Windows XP Professional-Based Clients), and MSDN: ADS_AUTHENTICATION_ENUM

14.3 Disabling LDAP Signing or Encryption

Problem

You want to disable LDAP signing and/or encryption.

Solution

Using the Registry

If you need to temporarily disable LDAP encryption or signing for troubleshooting purposes, browse to the *HKLM\Software\Microsoft\Windows\CurrentVersion\AdminDebug\ADsOpenObjectFlags* key on the client that is running the administrative tool. Create a DWORD entry called `ADsOpenObjectFlags` and set it to one of the following values:

1

    To disable LDAP signing

2

    To disable LDAP encryption

3

    To disable both LDAP signing and LDAP encryption

Using PowerShell

```
$strRegPath =
"HKLM:\Software\Microsoft\Windows\CurrentVersion\AdminDebug\ADsOpenObjectFlags"
new-ItemProperty -path $strRegPath -name "ADsOpenObjectFlags" -type DWORD
set-ItemProperty -path $strRegPath -name " ADsOpenObjectFlags" -value
"<Signing/Encryption Setting>"
```

Discussion

If you want to take advantage of some of the new features of the Active Directory administration tools, but have not installed SP3 on your Windows 2000 domain controllers yet, you can disable signing on the Windows XP/Vista or Windows Server 2003/2008 machine. It is worth stating the obvious that this is insecure and defeats one of the major benefits of the new tools, but you may have no other choice.

See Also

Recipe 14.2 to enable LDAP signing and encryption

14.4 Enabling Anonymous LDAP Access

Problem

You want to enable anonymous LDAP access for clients. In Windows 2000 Active Directory, anonymous queries were enabled by default, although they were restricted. With Windows Server 2003 Active Directory, anonymous queries are disabled by default except for querying the RootDSE.

Solution

Using a graphical user interface

1. Open ADSI Edit.
2. In the Configuration partition, browse to `cn=Services`→`cn=Windows NT`→`cn=Directory Service`.
3. In the left pane, right-click on the Directory Service object and select Properties.
4. Double-click on the `dSHeuristics` attribute.
5. If the attribute is empty, set it with the value `0000002`.
6. If the attribute has an existing value, make sure the seventh digit is set to `2`.
7. Click OK twice.

Using VBScript

```
' This code enables or disables anonymous query mode for a forest.
' ------ SCRIPT CONFIGURATION -----
boolEnableAnonQuery = 2 ' e.g. 2 to enable, 0 to disable
' ------ END CONFIGURATION --------

set objRootDSE = GetObject("LDAP://RootDSE")
set objDS = GetObject( _
           "LDAP://cn=Directory Service,cn=Windows NT,cn=Services," _
           & objRootDSE.Get("configurationNamingContext") )
```

```
strDSH = objDS.Get("dSHeuristics")

for i = len(strDSH) to 6
    strDSH = strDSH & "0"
next

strNewDSH = Left(strDSH,6) & boolEnableAnonQuery
strNewDSH = strNewDSH & Right(strDSH, len(strDSH) - 7 )

WScript.Echo "Old value: " & strDSH
WScript.Echo "New value: " & strNewDSH
if strDSH <> strNewDSH then
    objDS.Put "
dSHeuristics", strNewDSH
    objDS.SetInfo
    WScript.Echo "Successfully set anon query mode to " & boolEnableAnonQuery
else
    WScript.Echo "Anon query mode already set to " & boolEnableAnonQuery
end if
```

Using PowerShell

```
$root = [ADSI]"LDAP://RootDSE"
$obj  = [ADSI]("LDAP://cn=Directory Service,cn=Windows NT,cn=Services," +
        $root.configurationNamingContext)

$dsHeuristics = $obj.dsHeuristics.value
if ($dsHeuristics -eq $null)
{
    "dsHeuristics was null (not previously set)"
    $dsHeuristics = "0000000"      # seven zeroes
}

$len = $dsHeuristics.Length
if ($len -lt 7)
{
    $dsHeuristics = $dsHeuristics + ("0000000").SubString(0, (7 - $len))
    $len = 7
}

# we've ensured that $dsHeuristics is AT LEAST seven chars long now
# it may be 13 chars or more. we really don't care about that!

$char = $dsHeuristics.SubString(6, 1)
if ($char -eq "2")
{
    "Anonymous query mode already set to 2"
}
else
{
    $upd = $dsHeuristics.SubString(0, 6) + "2"
    if ($dsHeuristics.Length -gt 7)
    {
        $dsHeuristics.SubString(7, $len)
    }
```

```
    $obj.dsHeuristics = $upd
    $obj.SetInfo()

    "Anonymous query mode set to 2"
    "New value of dsHeuristics equal to $upd"
}
```

Discussion

To enable anonymous access, you have to modify the dSHeuristics attribute of the cn=Directory Service,cn=Windows NT,cn=Services,ConfigurationDN object. The dSHeuristics attribute is an interesting attribute used to control certain behavior in Active Directory. For example, you can enable List Object Access mode (see Recipe 14.19) by setting the dSHeuristics flag.

The dSHeuristics attribute consists of a series of digits that, when set, enable certain functionality. To enable anonymous access, the seventh digit must be set to 2. By default, dSHeuristics does not have a value. If you set it to enable anonymous access, the value would be 0000002.

After enabling anonymous access, the assumption is you'll want to grant access for anonymous users to retrieve certain data from Active Directory. To do that, grant the ANONYMOUS LOGON user access to the parts of the directory you want anonymous users to search. You must grant the access from the root of the directory down to the object of interest. See MS KB 320528 for an example of how to enable the anonymous user to query the email addresses of user objects.

See Also

Recipe 14.19, MS KB 320528 (How to Configure Active Directory to Allow Anonymous Queries), MS KB 326690 (Anonymous LDAP Operations to Active Directory Are Disabled on Windows Server 2003 Domain Controllers), and DS-Heuristics Attribute in MSDN (*http://msdn.microsoft.com/en-us/library/ms675656(VS.85).aspx*)

14.5 Restricting Anonymous Access to Active Directory

Problem

You want to enable or disable anonymous access to the information stored in the Active Directory database.

Solution

Using a graphical user interface

1. Open the Active Directory Users and Computers (ADUC) snap-in.

2. If you need to change domains, right-click on Active Directory Users and Computers in the left pane, select "Connect to Domain," enter the domain name, and click OK.

3. Navigate to the Builtin container. Double-click on the Pre-Windows 2000 Compatible Access group.

4. Click the Members tab.

5. Select the *Everyone* group and click the Remove button. Click Yes and then OK to confirm.

6. Select the Anonymous Logon user and click the Remove button. Click Yes and then OK to confirm.

7. If the *Authenticated Users* group is not present in the group membership list, click Add to include it and then click OK.

Using a command-line interface

You have three command-line choices to modify the Pre-Windows 2000 Access security group: `net localgroup`, DSMod, or AdMod. `net localgroup` takes the following syntax:

```
> net localgroup "Pre-Windows 2000 Compatible Access" Everyone /delete
> net localgroup "Pre-Windows 2000 Compatible Access" "Anonymous Logon" /delete
> net localgroup "Pre-Windows 2000 Compatible Access" "Authenticated Users" /add
```

To update the group membership using DSMod so that it only includes Authenticated Users, enter the following:

```
> dsmod group "cn=Pre-Windows 2000 Compatible Access,cn=Builtin,
  <DomainDN>" -chmbr "cn=S-1-5-11,cn=ForeignSecurityPrincipals,<DomainDN>"
```

To use AdMod, use the following syntax:

```
> admod -b "cn=Pre-Windows 2000 Compatible Access,cn=Builtin,
  <DomainDN>" member::"cn=S-1-5-11,cn=ForeignSecurityPrincipals,<DomainDN>"
```

Using VBScript

```
' This code clears the membership of the Pre-Windows 2000 Compatible Access group
' and then adds "Authenticated Users" back as the only member.
' ------ SCRIPT CONFIGURATION ------
strAnonAccessDN = "cn=Pre-Windows 2000 Compatible Access," & _
   cn=Builtin,<DomainDN>"
strAuthUsersDN = "cn=S-1-5-11,cn=ForeignSecurityPrincipals,<DomainDN>"
Const ADS_PROPERTY_CLEAR = 1 ' Used to clear the existing membership
' ------ END CONFIGURATION --------

set objAnonAccessDN = GetObject("LDAP://" & strAnonAccessDN)

' Remove any existing groups with anonymous access
objAnonAccessDN.PutEx ADS_PROPERTY_CLEAR, "member", 0
objAnonAccessDN.SetInfo
```

```
' Now add auth users only
objGroup.Add("LDAP://" & strAuthUsersDN)
```

Discussion

Anonymous access to Active Directory is controlled by membership in the *Pre-Windows 2000 Compatible Access* security group, located in the `cn=Builtin` container. This group exists because some legacy applications and operating systems, most notably Windows NT 4.0 RAS servers, required anonymous access to the information stored in AD in order to function properly. The default membership of this group depends on whether you selected "Permissions compatible with pre-Windows 2000 operating systems" or "Permissions compatible with only Windows 2000 and Windows 2003" when you ran *dcpromo*. If you selected the former, the *Everyone* group and the *Anonymous Logon* SID were added to Pre-Windows 2000 Compatible Access; if the latter, only *Authenticated Users* was added.

In the DSMod, AdMod, and VBScript solutions, the *Authenticated Users* group was specified using a SID. This group is represented by an object residing in the `ForeignSecurityPrincipals` container. This is because *Well-Known SIDs* such as *Everyone* (`S-1-1-0`) and *Authenticated Users* (`S-1-5-11`) are not actual groups within Active Directory itself and are therefore stored in the FSP container.

See Also

MS KB 303973 (How to Add Users to the Pre-Windows 2000 Compatible Access Group) and MS KB 243330 (Well-Known Security Identifiers in Windows Operating Systems)

14.6 Using the Delegation of Control Wizard

Problem

You want to delegate control over objects in Active Directory to a user or group.

Solution

Using a graphical user interface

1. Open the Active Directory Users and Computers (ADUC) or Active Directory Sites and Services snap-in, depending on the type of object you want to delegate.
2. In the left pane, browse to the object you want to delegate control on.
3. Right-click on the object and select Delegate Control. Only certain objects support the "Delegation of Control Wizard," so this option will not show up for every type of object.
4. Click Next.

5. Click the Add button and use the Object Picker to select the users or groups you want to delegate control to.

6. Click Next.

7. If the task you want to delegate is an option under "Delegate the following common tasks," place a checkmark next to it and click Next. If the task is not present, select "Create a custom task to delegate" and click Next. If you selected the latter option, you will need to perform four additional steps:

   a. Select the object type you want to delegate.

   b. Click Next.

   c. Select the permissions you want to delegate.

   d. Click Next.

5. Click Finish.

Using a command-line interface

To grant permissions from the command line, use the following syntax:

```
> dsacls <ObjectDN> /g <Permissions>
```

For example, the following syntax will delegate the permission to read and write information to the description property:

```
> dsacls <ObjectDN> /g RPWP;description;
```

Using PowerShell

The following syntax will delegate read permission to the description property of a single object, without delegating permissions to any child objects:

```
Add-QADPermission -Identity <ObjectDN> -Account <Delegated User/Group DN> -Rights
'ReadProperty' -Property 'description' -ApplyTo 'ThisObjectOnly'
```

Discussion

The Delegation of Control Wizard is Microsoft's attempt to ease the pain of trying to set permissions for common tasks. Because Active Directory permissions are so granular, they can also be cumbersome to configure. The Delegation of Control Wizard helps in this regard, but it is still limited in functionality. The default tasks that can be delegated are fairly minimal, although you can add more tasks as described in Recipe 14.7. Another limitation is that you can only add new permissions; you cannot undo or remove permissions that you previously set with the wizard. To do that, you have to use the ACL Editor directly as described in Recipe 14.9 or use *dsrevoke*.

See Also

Recipe 14.7 for customizing the Delegation of Control wizard and Recipe 14.8 for more on using *dsrevoke*

14.7 Customizing the Delegation of Control Wizard

Problem

You want to add or remove new delegation options in the Delegation of Control Wizard.

Solution

Open the Delegation of Control Wizard INF file (*%SystemRoot%\Inf\Delegwiz.inf*) in Windows Server 2000 and Windows Server 2003, and *%SystemRoot%\System32\Delegwiz.inf* in Windows Server 2008) on the computer you want to modify the wizard for.

Under the [DelegationTemplates] section, you'll see a line like the following:

```
Templates = template1, template2, template3, template4, template5, template6,
template7, template8, template9,template10, template11, template12, template13
```

You need to append a new template name. In this case, we'll follow the same naming convention and create a template named template14. The line now looks like this:

```
Templates = template1, template2, template3, template4, template5, template6,
template7, template8, template9,template10, template11, template12, template13,
template14
```

Scroll to the end of the file and append a new template section. You can use the other template sections as examples. Here is the generic format:

```
[<TemplateName>]
AppliesToClasses = <CommaSeparatedOfObjectClassesInvokedFrom>

Description = "<DescriptionShownInWizard>"

ObjectTypes = <CommaSeparatedListOfObjectClassesThatAreSet>

[<TemplateName>.SCOPE]<Permission entries for Scope>

[<TemplateName>.<ObjectClass1>]<Permission entries for ObjectClass1>

[<TemplateName>.<ObjectClass2>]<Permission entries for ObjectClass2>

...
```

<TemplateName> is the same as what we used in the [DelegationTemplates] section—i.e., template14.

In the AppliesToClasses line, replace <CommaSeparatedObjectClassesInvokedFrom> with a comma-separated list of LDAP display names of the classes that can be delegated. This delegation action will show up on the classes listed here only when you select Delegate Control from a snap-in. To make our new template entry apply to domain objects, OUs, and containers, we would use this line:

```
AppliesToClasses = domainDNS,organizationalUnit,container
```

In the `Description` line, replace `<DescriptionShownInWizard>` with the text you want shown in the wizard that describes the permissions being delegated. Here is a sample description for delegating full control over `inetOrgPerson` objects:

```
Description = "Create, delete, and manage user and inetOrgPerson accounts"
```

In the `ObjectTypes` line, replace `<CommaSeparatedListOfObjectClassesThatAreSet>` with a comma-separated list of object classes to be delegated. In this example, permissions will be modified for `user` and `inetOrgPerson` objects:

```
ObjectTypes = user,inetOrgPerson
```

Next, define the actual permissions to set when this action is selected. You can define two different types of permissions. You can use a `[<TemplateName>.SCOPE]` section to define permissions that are set on the object that is used to start the wizard. This will be one of the object classes defined in the `AppliesToClass` line. This is commonly used in the context of containers and organizational units to specify create, modify, or delete child objects of a particular type. For example, to grant the ability to create (CC) or delete (DC) `user` and `inetOrgPerson` objects, you would use the following:

```
[template14.SCOPE]
user=CC,DC
inetOrgPerson=CC,DC
```

As you can see, each permission (e.g., create child) is abbreviated to a two-letter code (e.g., CC). Table 14-1 lists the valid codes.

Table 14-1. Permissions and abbreviated codes

Abbreviated code	Permission
RP	Read Property
WP	Write Property
CC	Create Child
DC	Delete Child
GA	Full Control

It is perfectly valid to leave out a `SCOPE` section if it is not needed. The rest of the lines are used to specify permissions that should be set on the object classes defined by the `ObjectTypes` line.

To grant full control over all existing `user` and `inetOrgPerson` objects, we'll use these entries:

```
[template14.user]
@=GA

[template14.inetOrgPerson]
@=GA
```

This is very similar to the previous example, except that here SCOPE is replaced with the names of the object classes the permissions apply to. The @ symbol is used to indicate that the permission applies to all attributes on the object. You can get more granular by replacing @ with the name of the attribute the permission applies to. For example, this would grant read and write permissions on the department attribute for inetOrgPerson objects:

```
[template14.inetOrgPerson]
department=RP,WP
```

You can also enable control access rights using the CONTROLRIGHT designator instead of @ or an attribute name; you just need to specify the LDAP display name of the control access right you want to enable. The following section enables the Reset Password right on inetOrgPerson objects and enables read and write access to the pwdLastSet attribute:

```
[template14.inetOrgPerson]
CONTROLRIGHT="Reset Password"
pwdLastSet=RP,WP
```

Discussion

You can completely customize the tasks that can be delegated with the Delegation of Control Wizard, but you still have the problem of getting the *Delegwiz.inf* file on all the clients that need to use the new settings. You can manually copy it to the computers that need it, or you can use Group Policy to automate the distribution of it.

See Also

Recipe 14.6 for more on using the Delegation of Control wizard

14.8 Revoking Delegated Permissions

Problem

You want to remove permissions that you've delegated to a domain or an OU.

Solution

Using a graphical user interface

1. Open the Active Directory Users and Computers MMC snap-in (*dsa.msc*). Right-click on the object that you wish to modify and select Properties.
2. From the Security tab, highlight the permissions entry that you wish to revoke and click Remove, then OK.

Using a command-line interface

The following command will remove any permissions that have been delegated directly to the ADATUM\jsmith user over the Finance Organizational Unit:

```
> dsrevoke /remove "/root:ou=Finance,dc=adatum,dc=com" ADATUM\jsmith
```

Using PowerShell

The following will retrieve all ACLs assigned to a particular user for an Active Directory object, and then will remove those ACEs using the remove-QADPermission cmdlet:

```
Get-QADPermission -Identity <ObjectDN> -Account (<User DN>) | remove-QADPermission
-Identity <ObjectDN>
```

Discussion

While the Delegation of Control wizard makes it trivial to grant permissions to objects within Active Directory, one thing that it lacks is an Undo button. To help address this, Microsoft has made the *dsrevoke* command-line utility a free download from its site (*http://www.microsoft.com/downloads/details.aspx?FamilyID=77744807-c403-4bda -b0e4-c2093b8d6383&DisplayLang=en*). The *dsrevoke* utility will remove any permissions that have been delegated to a security principal on a domain or an OU, with the following limitations:

- You can use *dsrevoke* only on a domain or an OU; if you've delegated permissions over individual objects, you'll need to remove these manually.
- *dsrevoke* removes only object permissions; if you've assigned any user rights through Group Policy, they'll need to be removed separately.
- You can't use *dsrevoke* to remove any permissions that have been delegated to the Schema or Configuration NCs.

See Also

Best Practices for Delegating Active Directory Administration, located at *http://www .microsoft.com/downloads/details.aspx?FamilyID=631747a3-79e1-48fa-9730 -dae7c0a1d6d3&DisplayLang=en*

14.9 Viewing the ACL for an Object

Problem

You want to view the ACL for an object.

Solution

Using a graphical user interface

1. Open the ACL Editor. You can do this by viewing the properties of an object (right-click on the object and select Properties) with a tool such as ADUC or ADSI Edit. Select the Security tab. To see the Security tab with ADUC, you must select View→Advanced Features from the menu.
2. Click the Advanced button to view a list of the individual ACEs.

Using a command-line interface

```
> dsacls <ObjectDN>
```

Using VBScript

Unfortunately, the code to view the ACEs in an ACL is quite messy and long. This will be included as part of the code on the website for the book (*http://www.oreilly.com/catalog/9780596521103*).

Using PowerShell

```
get-QADObject -Identity <ObjectDN> -SecurityMask DACL | Get-QADPermission
-Inherited -SchemaDefault
```

Discussion

Viewing an object's ACL is a common task and should already be familiar to most administrators. The ACL Editor is useful for checking the permissions that have been set on objects, especially after running the Delegation of Control Wizard. In addition to viewing permissions, the options available in the GUI include viewing auditing settings and the owner of the object. Knowing the owner of an object is important because ownership confers certain inherent rights.

Because the ACL Editor is the same for NTFS permissions and properties as it is for Active Directory objects, you should feel comfortable with the look and feel of the interface; it is exactly the same as file and folder permissions. We also highly recommend getting familiar with the Advanced View of the ACL Editor, as this is truly the view in which you can determine what is going on with permissions. The Basic view presents a list of security principals that have permissions configured, but it will not always show every configured ACE entry. The Advanced view will show the complete picture, including the scope of permissions for ACEs down to the object and even the attribute level.

See Also

Recipe 14.13 for changing an ACL and Recipe 15.15 for auditing of object access

14.10 Customizing the ACL Editor

Problem

You want to set permissions on attributes that do not show up in the default Active Directory Users and Computers ACL Editor.

Solution

The ACL Editor in ADUC shows only a subset of the object's attributes on which permissions can be set. These can be seen in the ACL Editor by clicking the Advanced button, adding or editing a permission entry, and selecting the Properties tab.

An attribute can have a read permission, write permission, or both, either of which can be set to Allow or Deny. If the attribute you want to secure is not in the list, you will need to modify the *dssec.dat* file on the computer that you're running the ACL Editor from.

There are sections for each object class represented in square brackets—e.g., [user]. Underneath that heading is a list of attributes that you can configure to display or not display in the ACL Editor.

These are the first few lines for the [user] section:

```
[user]
aCSPolicyName=7
adminCount=7
allowedAttributes=7
```

The value to the right of the attribute determines whether it is shown in the ACL Editor. The valid values include the following:

0

Both Read Property and Write Property are displayed for the attribute.

1

Write property is displayed for the attribute.

2

Read property is displayed for the attribute.

7

No entries are displayed for the attribute.

If the attribute is not defined, then the default value (specified by @, if present) is used.

Discussion

Much like the Delegation of Control Wizard, you can customize the attributes that are shown in the ACL Editor, but you still need to distribute the *dssec.dat* file to all computers that need to see the change.

A good example of when this recipe is needed is for delegating the ability to unlock accounts. This is common in larger organizations when you want to assign this task to the help desk without giving them additional rights on user objects. In this case, you need to set the `lockoutTime` to 0 in the [user] section of the *dssec.dat* file.

See Also

MS KB 296490 (How to Modify the Filtered Properties of an Object) and MS KB 294952 (How to Delegate the Unlock Account Right)

14.11 Viewing the Effective Permissions on an Object

Problem

You want to view the effective permissions that a user or group has for a particular object.

Solution

Using a graphical user interface

1. Open the ACL Editor. You can do this by viewing the properties of an object (right-click on the object and select Properties) with a tool such as ADUC or ADSI Edit. Select the Security tab. To see the Security tab with ADUC, you must select View→Advanced Features from the menu.
2. Click the Advanced button.
3. Select the Effective Permissions tab.
4. Click the Select button to bring up the Object Editor.
5. Find the user or group for which you want to see the effective permissions.
6. The results will be shown under Effective Permissions.

> The Effective Permissions tab is available beginning with the Windows Server 2003 version of the ACL Editor. For Windows 2000, you'll need to use the *acldiag* command-line solution. *acldiag* is not available in Windows Server 2008.

Using a command-line interface

```
> acldiag <ObjectDN> /geteffective:<UserOrGroup>
```

Discussion

Viewing the permissions on an object does not tell the whole story as to what the actual translated permissions are for a user or group on that object. The *effective permissions* of an object take into account all group membership and any inherited permissions that might have been applied further up the tree. While this is a useful tool to analyze permissions, it is still unfortunately only a best guess; there are still some situations in which certain permissions will not be reflected.

See Also

MS KB 323309 (Effective Permissions Are Displayed Incorrectly)

14.12 Configuring Permission Inheritance

Problem

You want to configure permission inheritance on an Active Directory container to determine whether a child object should automatically receive any permissions that you've granted to its parent object.

Solution

1. Open the ACL Editor. You can do this by viewing the properties of an object (right-click on the object and select Properties) with a tool such as Active Directory Users and Computers (ADUC) or ADSI Edit. Select the Security tab. If the Security tab is not visible within ADUC, you must select View→Advanced Features from the menu.
2. Click the Advanced button to view a list of the individual ACEs.
3. To turn off inheritance, remove the checkmark next to "Allow inheritable permissions from the parent to propagate to this object and all child objects. Include these with entries defined explicitly here."
4. You will be given the option to "Copy the existing permissions onto the object as explicitly assigned permissions," to "Remove all inherited permissions (all explicitly assigned permissions will remain in place)," or to "Cancel the operation."
5. To re-enable permission inheritance from objects further up the directory structure, reinsert the checkmark listed in Step 3.

Using a VBScript

To disable permission inheritance (i.e., to configure an object such that only explicitly assigned permissions apply), use the following syntax:

```
> dsacls <ObjectDN> /P:Y
```

To enable permission inheritance, do the following:

```
> dsacls <ObjectDN> /P:N
```

Using VBScript

```
' This code enables or disables the "Allow inheritable permissions..."
' setting on an AD object.
' ------ SCRIPT CONFIGURATION ------
Const SE_DACL_PROTECTED = &H1000 ' set to 0 to enable inheritance
strObject = "<ObjectDN>" ' e.g. ou=Finance,dc=adatum,dc=com
' ------ END CONFIGURATION ---------

Set objObject = GetObject("LDAP://" & strObject)
Set objntSD = objObject.Get("nTSecurityDescriptor")
intNTSDControl = objNtSD.Control

' Disable the bit for "allow inheritable permissions".
intNTSDControl = intNTSDControl And SE_DACL_PROTECTED
objntSD.Control = intNTSDControl
objObject.Put "nTSecurityDescriptor", objntSD
objObject.SetInfo

Wscript.Echo "Inheritable permissionss disabled!"
```

Using PowerShell

The following syntax will prevent an object from receiving inherited permissions that have been applied at a higher level in the tree so that the object is only affected by permissions that have been explicitly configured on the object itself:

```
Set-QADObjectSecurity -Identity <ObjectDN> -LockInheritance -Remove
```

The following syntax will configure an AD object so that it will receive inherited permissions that have been applied at a higher level in the directory tree:

```
Set-QADObjectSecurity -Identity <ObjectDN> -UnlockInheritance
```

Discussion

Similar to NTFS permissions on the filesystem, Active Directory permissions on container objects can be set to inherit or trickle down to objects further down the directory structure. This process can greatly simplify assigning permissions, as you can assign a common set of permissions high up in the directory structure and have those permissions filter down to all of the OUs and objects below. In some cases, though, you might want to turn off permissions inheritance to configure a different set of permissions entirely for a child object or container.

One thing to keep in mind when enabling or disabling inheritance is that there are a number of AD security principals protected by the AdminSDHolder process that will receive a specific set of permissions regardless of the inheritance settings you configure. These groups include *Enterprise Admins, Schema Admins, Domain Admins*, and *Administrators* in Windows 2000, with the addition of *Account Operators, Server Operators, Print Operators, Backup Operators*, and *Cert Publishers* in Windows Server 2003 or with certain hotfixes in Windows 2000. In addition, some Active Directory-aware applications depend on inheritance being in place in order to function efficiently.

See Also

"AdminSDHolder, or where did my permissions go?" at *http://msmvps.com/blogs/ulfb simonweidner/archive/2005/05/29/49659.aspx* and MS KB 232199 (Description and Update of the Active Directory AdminSDHolder Object)

14.13 Changing the ACL of an Object

Problem

You want to change the ACL on an object to grant or restrict access to it for a user or group.

Solution

Using a graphical user interface

1. Open the ACL Editor. You can do this by viewing the properties of an object (right-click on the object and select Properties) with a tool such as ADUC or ADSI Edit. Select the Security tab. To see the Security tab with ADUC, you must select Views→Advanced Features from the menu.
2. Click the Advanced button to view a list of the individual ACEs.
3. Click Add to specify a new user or group, then place checkmarks next to the permissions that you want to assign and click OK.
4. To remove an ACE, highlight the entry and click Remove. If the Permissions entry is inherited from further up the directory tree, the option to remove the permission will not be available unless you remove the checkmark next to "Allow inheritable permissions from the parent to propagate to this object and all child objects...". With this checkmark in place, you will only have the option to remove any permissions that have `<not inherited>` listed in the "Inherited From" column.

Using a command-line interface

To grant permissions from the command line, use the following syntax:

```
> dsacls <ObjectDN> /g <Permissions>
```

To deny permissions, replace /g with /d.

Using VBScript

See Recipe 7.11, Recipe 8.3, Recipe 13.8, and Recipe 17.9 for several examples of modifying an ACL with VBScript.

Using PowerShell

To add an entry to the ACL of an object, use the `Add-QADPermission` Quest AD cmdlet. To remove an existing ACL entry, use the `Remove-QADPermission` cmdlet.

Discussion

Changing the ACL of an object is a common task for administrators in any but the most basic AD implementations because, as shown in Recipes 14.6 and 14.7, the Delegation of Control Wizard is limited and cumbersome to extend and deploy. The GUI and command-line methods are useful for one-off changes to permissions, but for making global changes to a number of objects, you should consider using a script to automate the process.

See Also

Recipes 7.11, 8.3, 13.8, 14.6, 14.7, 17.9, and MS KB 281146 (How to Use Dsacls.exe in Windows 2000)

14.14 Changing the Default ACL for an Object Class in the Schema

Problem

You want to change the default ACL for an object class in the schema.

Solution

Using a graphical user interface

1. Open the Active Directory Schema snap-in.
2. In the left pane, browse to the class you want to modify.
3. Right-click on it and select Properties.
4. Select the Default Security tab.
5. Use the ACL Editor to change the ACL.
6. Click OK.

 The Default Security tab is available only in the Windows Server 2003 and newer versions of the Active Directory Schema snap-in. See MS KB 265399 for the manual approach that is needed with Windows 2000.

Discussion

Each instantiated object in Active Directory has an associated structural class that defines a default security descriptor (the `defaultSecurityDescriptor` attribute). When an object is created and a security descriptor isn't specified, the default security descriptor is applied to it. This, along with inheritable permissions from the parent container, determines how an object's security descriptor is initially defined. If you find that you are modifying the default security descriptor on a particular type of object every time it is created, you may want to modify its default security descriptor. (Another option would be to use a script that would modify the individual object's ACL at the same time that the object was created.)

See Also

Recipe 10.1 for more on registering the Active Directory Schema snap-in, Recipe 14.15 for comparing the ACL of an object to the default defined in the schema, Recipe 14.16 for resetting the ACL of an object to the default defined in the schema, and MS KB 265399 (How to Change Default Permissions for Objects That Are Created in the Active Directory)

14.15 Comparing the ACL of an Object to the Default Defined in the Schema

Problem

You want to determine if an object has the permissions defined in the schema for its object class as part of its ACL.

Solution

Using a command-line interface

```
> acldiag <ObjectDN> /schema
```

Discussion

For more on the default security descriptor (SD), see Recipe 14.14. *acldiag* will determine if the object possesses the security descriptor that's defined in the schema—if you've modified the security descriptor, *acldiag* will compare the object's SD against the currently defined SD, not the Active Directory default.

The *acldiag* tool is available in the Windows Server 2003 Resource Kit; it is not supported in Windows Server 2008.

See Also

Recipe 14.16 for resetting an object's ACL to the default defined in the schema

14.16 Resetting an Object's ACL to the Default Defined in the Schema

Problem

You want to reset an object's ACL to the one defined in the schema for the object's object class.

Solution

Using a graphical user interface

 This is available only in the Windows Server 2003 and newer versions of the ACL Editor.

1. Open the ACL Editor. You can do this by viewing the properties of an object (right-click on the object and select Properties) with a tool such as ADUC or ADSI Edit. Select the Security tab. To see the Security tab with ADUC, you must select View→Advanced Features from the menu.
2. Click the Advanced button.
3. Click the Default button.
4. Click OK twice.

Using a command-line interface

```
> dsacls <ObjectDN> /s
```

Discussion

For more on the default security descriptor, see Recipe 14.14.

14.17 Preventing the LM Hash of a Password from Being Stored

Problem

You want to prevent the LM hash for new passwords from being stored in Active Directory. The LM hash is primarily used for backward compatibility with Windows 95 and 98 clients; it is susceptible to brute force attacks.

Solution

For Windows 2000, you need to create the following Registry key on all domain controllers: `HKLM\SYSTEM\CurrentControlSet\Control\Lsa\NoLMHash`. Note that this is a key and not a value entry. Also, this is supported only on Windows 2000 SP2 and later domain controllers.

For Windows Server 2003, the `NoLMHash` key has turned into a DWORD value entry under the `HKLM\SYSTEM\CurrentControlSet\Control\Lsa` key. This value should be set to `1`. You can accomplish this by modifying the Default Domain Controller Security Policy as described next.

Using a graphical user interface

1. Open the Default Domain Controller Group Policy Object in the GPMC.
2. In the left pane, expand Computer Configuration→Policies→Windows Settings→Security Settings→Local Policies→Security Options.
3. In the right pane, double-click on "Network security: Do not store LAN Manager hash value on next password change."
4. Check the box beside "Define this policy setting."
5. Click the Enabled radio button.

Discussion

If you do not have Windows 98 or older clients in your domain, you should disable the storage of the LM password hash for users. The LM hash uses an old algorithm (pre-Windows NT 4.0) and is considered to be relatively weak compared to the NT hash that is also stored.

 The LM hash is generated only for passwords that are shorter than 15 characters. So if you have a password longer than this, the LM hash is not stored for you.

In addition to making this change on the server side, you should configure your network clients as described in Recipe 14.18. Finally, to clear any existing LM hashes that have already been stored in AD, you will need to force a password change for the users in question.

See Also

MS KB 299656 (How to Prevent Windows from Storing a LAN Manager Hash of Your Password in Active Directory and Local SAM Databases)

14.18 Enabling Strong Domain Authentication

Problem

You want to ensure that users can only authenticate to Active Directory using strong authentication protocols.

Solution

Using a graphical user interface

1. Open the Group Policy Management Console snap-in.
2. In the left pane, expand the Forest container, expand the Domains container, browse to the domain you want to administer, and expand the Group Policy Objects container.
3. Right-click on the GPO that controls the configuration of your domain controllers and select Edit. (By default, this is the Default Domain Controller Policy, but it may be a different GPO in your environment.) This will bring up the Group Policy Object Editor.
4. Browse to Computer Configuration→Policies→Windows Settings→Security Settings→Local Policies→Security Options.
5. Double-click on "Network security: LAN Manager Authentication Level." Place a checkmark next to "Define this policy setting."
6. Select "Send NTLMv2 responses only/refuse LM & NTLM." Click OK.
7. Wait for Group Policy to refresh, or type `gpupdate /force` from the command prompt of a Windows Server 2003 or higher domain controller. On a Windows 2000 DC, use the `secedit` command with the `/refreshpolicy` switch.

Discussion

Microsoft operating systems have supported different flavors of LM and NT LAN Manager (NTLM) authentication since the earliest days of Windows. LM authentication is an extremely old and weak authentication protocol that should no longer be used in production environments unless absolutely necessary. By default, Windows 2000 Active Directory supported client authentication attempts using LM, NTLM, or

NTLMv2; Windows Server 2003 and above supports only NTLM and NTLMv2 out of the box.

The strongest NTLM authentication scheme you can select is to refuse LM and NTLM authentication from any client, and to only respond to clients using NTLMv2. Depending on your client configuration, though, enabling this option may require changes on the client side as well. You can apply the same setting to a GPO linked to your Active Directory domain to ensure that all of your clients will use NTLMv2 instead of older, weaker protocols.

Windows Server 2008 Active Directory has a default value of "Send NTLMv2 response only" for this GPO setting.

See Also

MS KB 239869 (How to Enable NTLM 2 Authentication) and MS KB 299656 (How to Prevent Windows from Storing a LAN Manager Hash of Your Password in Active Directory and Local SAM databases)

14.19 Enabling List Object Access Mode

Problem

You want to prevent any authenticated user from being able to browse the contents of Active Directory by default. Enabling List Object Access mode means that users will need explicit permissions to see directory listings of containers.

Solution

Using a graphical user interface

1. Open ADSI Edit.
2. In the Configuration partition, browse to `cn=Services`→`cn=Windows NT`→`cn=Directory Service`.
3. In the left pane, right-click on the Directory Service object and select Properties.
4. Double-click on the `dSHeuristics` attribute.
5. If the attribute is empty, set it with the value `001`. If the attribute has an existing value, make sure the third digit (from the left) is set to `1`.
6. Click OK twice.

Using VBScript

```
On Error Resume Next ' necessary if dsHeuristics is not
                     ' already set

' This code enables or disables list object mode for a forest.
' ------ SCRIPT CONFIGURATION -----
boolEnableListObject = 1 ' e.g. 1 to enable, 0 to disable
' ------ END CONFIGURATION --------

set objRootDSE = GetObject("LDAP://RootDSE")
set objDS = GetObject( _
              "LDAP://cn=Directory Service,cn=Windows NT,cn=Services," _
              & objRootDSE.Get("configurationNamingContext") )
strDSH = objDS.Get("dSHeuristics")
if len(strDSH) = 1 then
   strDSH = strDSH & "0"
end if
strNewDSH = Left(strDSH,2) & boolEnableListObject
if len(strDSH) > 3 then
   strNewDSH = strNewDSH & Right(strDSH, len(strDSH) - 3)
end if

WScript.Echo "Old value: " & strDSH
WScript.Echo "New value: " & strNewDSH

if strDSH <> strNewDSH then
   objDS.Put "
dSHeuristics", strNewDSH
   objDS.SetInfo
   WScript.Echo "Successfully set list object mode to " & _
              boolEnableListObject
else
   WScript.Echo "List object mode already set to " & boolEnableListObject
end if
```

Discussion

List Object Access mode is useful if you want your users to view only a subset of objects when doing a directory listing of a particular container, or you do not want them to be able to list the objects in a container at all. By default, the *Authenticated Users* group is granted the List Contents access control right over objects in a domain. If you remove or deny this right on a container by modifying the ACL, users will not be able to get a listing of the objects in that container using tools such as ADUC or ADSI Edit.

To limit the objects that users can see when they pull up an object listing, you first need to enable List Object Access mode as described in the solution. You should then remove the List Contents access control right on the target container. Lastly, you'll need to grant the List Object right to the objects that the users or groups should be able to list.

Enabling List Object Access mode can significantly increase the administration overhead for configuring ACLs in Active Directory. It can also impact performance on a domain controller since it will take considerably more time to verify ACLs before returning information to a client.

Using VBScript

While we discussed error handling in Chapter 1, this script actually requires the `On Error Resume Next` command in order to function. Without this line in place, the script will throw an error if the `dsHeuristics` attribute is not set.

See Also

MSDN: Controlling Object Visibility and Microsoft's High-Volume Hosting Site at *http://www.microsoft.com/serviceproviders/deployment/hvh_ad_deploy.asp*

14.20 Modifying the ACL on Administrator Accounts

Problem

You want to modify the ACL for user accounts that are members of one of the administrative groups.

Solution

Using one of the methods described in Recipe 14.13, modify the ACL on the `cn=AdminSDHolder,cn=Systems,<DomainDN>` object in the domain that the administrator accounts reside in. The ACL on this object gets applied every hour to all user accounts that are members of the administrative groups.

Discussion

If you've ever tried to directly modify the ACL on a user account that was a member of one of the administrative groups in Active Directory, or you modified the ACL on the OU containing an administrative account, and then wondered why the account's ACL was overwritten later, you've come to the right place. The Admin SD Holder feature of Active Directory is one that many administrators stumble upon after much grinding of teeth. However, after you realize the purpose for it, you'll understand it is a necessary feature.

Once an hour, a process on the PDC Emulator that we'll refer to as the Admin SD Holder process compares the ACL on the `AdminSDHolder` object to the ACL on the accounts that are in administrative groups in the domain as well as the groups themselves. If it detects a difference, it will overwrite the account or Group ACL and disable inheritance.

If you later remove a user from an administrative group, you will need to reapply any inherited permissions and enable inheritance if necessary. The Admin SD Holder process will not take care of this for you.

The Admin SD Holder process is intended to subvert any malicious activity by a user that has been delegated rights over an OU or container that contains an account that is in one of the administrative groups. An OU administrator could, for example, modify permissions inheritance on an OU to attempt to lock out the *Domain Admins* group; this permission change would be reverted the next time the `AdminSDHolder` thread runs.

These are the groups included as part of the Admin SD Holder processing:

- *Administrators*
- *Account Operators*
- *Cert Publishers*
- *Backup Operators*
- *Domain Admins*
- *Enterprise Admins*
- *Print Operators*
- *Schema Admins*
- *Server Operators*

The *administrator* and *krbtgt* user accounts are also specifically checked during the Admin SD Holder process.

See Also

MS KB 232199 (Description and Update of the Active Directory AdminSDHolder Object), MS KB 306398 (AdminSDHolder Object Affects Delegation of Control for Past Administrator Accounts), and MS KB 817433 (Delegated Permissions Are Not Available and Inheritance Is Automatically Disabled)

14.21 Viewing and Purging Your Kerberos Tickets

Problem

You want to view and possibly purge your Kerberos tickets.

Solution

Both the *kerbtray* and *klist* utilities can be found in the Windows Server 2003 Resource Kit.

The *kerbtray* utility is not supported under Windows Server 2008. *Klist* is supported under Windows Server 2008 and is built into the Active Directory Domain Services role.

Using a graphical user interface

1. Run *kerbtray.exe* from the command line or Start→Run.
2. A new icon (green) should show up in the system tray. Double-click on that icon. This will allow you to view your current tickets.
3. To purge your tickets, right-click on the *kerbtray* icon in the system tray and select Purge Tickets.
4. Close the *kerbtray* window and reopen it by right-clicking on the *kerbtray* icon and selecting List Tickets.

Using a command-line interface

Run the following command to list your current tickets:

```
> klist tickets
```

Run the following command to purge your tickets:

```
> klist purge
```

Discussion

Active Directory uses Kerberos as its preferred network authentication system. When you authenticate to a Kerberos Key Distribution Center (KDC), which in Active Directory terms is a domain controller, you are issued one or more tickets. These tickets identify you as a certain principal in Active Directory and can be used to authenticate you to other Kerberized services. This type of ticket is known as a *ticket-granting ticket*, or TGT. Once you've obtained a TGT, the client can use the TGT to gain access to a Kerberized service by querying the Ticket Granting Service on the KDC; if the KDC verifies that the user is authorized to access the service in question, it will issue a *service ticket* that allows the client to use the particular service.

Kerberos is a fairly complicated system and we can't do it justice in a single paragraph. If you want more information on tickets and how the Kerberos authentication system works, see Jason Garman's *Kerberos: The Definitive Guide* (O'Reilly).

See Also

RFC 1510 (The Kerberos Network Authentication Service V5) and MS KB 232179 (Kerberos Administration in Windows 2000)

14.22 Forcing Kerberos to Use TCP

Problem

Clients are experiencing authentication problems, and you've determined it is due to UDP fragmentation of Kerberos traffic. You want to force Kerberos traffic to use the TCP protocol instead.

Solution

Using a graphical user interface

1. Run *regedit.exe* from the command line or from Start→Run.
2. In the left pane, expand HKEY_LOCAL_MACHINE→System→Current-ControlSet→Control→Lsa→Kerberos→Parameters.
3. Right-click on Parameters and select New→DWORD value. Enter `MaxPacketSize` for the value name.
4. In the right pane, double-click on MaxPacketSize and enter `1`.
5. Click OK.

Using a command-line interface

```
> reg add "HKLM\SYSTEM\CurrentControlSet\Control\Lsa\Kerberos\Parameters" /v
"MaxPacketSize" /t REG_DWORD /d 1
```

Using VBScript

```
' This code forces Kerberos to use TCP.
' ------ SCRIPT CONFIGURATION -----
strComputer = "<ComputerName>" ' e.g. rallen-w2k3
' ------ END CONFIGURATION -------

const HKLM = &H80000002
strRegKey = "SYSTEM\CurrentControlSet\Control\Lsa\Kerberos\Parameters"
set objReg = GetObject("winmgmts:\\" & strComputer & _
                       "\root\default:StdRegProv")
objReg.SetDwordValue HKLM, strRegKey, "MaxPacketSize", 1
WScript.Echo "Kerberos forced to use TCP for " & strComputer
```

Using PowerShell

```
$strRegPath = "HKLM:\System\CurrentControlSet\Lsa\Kerberos\Parameters"
New-ItemProperty -path $strRegPath -name "MaxPacketSize" -type DWORD
Set-ItemProperty -path $strRegPath -name "MaxPacketSize" -value "1"
```

Discussion

If you have users that are experiencing extremely slow logon times (especially over VPN) or they are seeing the infamous "There are currently no logon servers available to service the logon request" message, then they may be experiencing UDP fragmentation of Kerberos traffic. This occurs because UDP is a *connectionless protocol*, so UDP packets that arrive out of order will be dropped by the destination router. One way to help identify if there is a problem with Kerberos is to have the users run the following command:

```
> netdiag /test:kerberos
```

Another source of information (such as in Windows Server 2008 where `netdiag` is not available) is the System event log on the clients. Various Kerberos-related events are logged there if problems with authentication occur.

For more information about Kerberos and UDP, see MS KB 244474 (How to Force Kerberos to Use TCP Instead of UDP).

See Also

MS KB 244474 (How to Force Kerberos to Use TCP Instead of UDP in Windows Server 2003, in Windows XP, and in Windows 2000)

14.23 Modifying Kerberos Settings

Problem

You want to modify the default Kerberos settings that define things, such as maximum ticket lifetime.

Solution

Using a graphical user interface

1. Open the Default Domain Group Policy Object, or another domain-linked GPO, in the Group Policy Management Console.
2. Navigate to Computer Configuration→Policies→Account Policies→Kerberos Policy.
3. In the right pane, double-click on the setting you want to modify.
4. Enter the new value and click OK.

Discussion

There are several Kerberos-related settings you can customize, most of which revolve around either increasing or decreasing the maximum lifetime for Kerberos user and service tickets. In most environments, the default settings are sufficient, but the ones you can modify are listed in Table 14-2.

 Change the default Kerberos policy settings with caution, as doing so can cause operational problems and compromise security if done incorrectly.

Table 14-2. Kerberos policy settings

Setting	Default value
Enforce user logon restrictions	Enabled
Maximum lifetime for service ticket	600 minutes
Maximum lifetime for user ticket	10 hours
Maximum lifetime for user ticket renewal	7 days
Maximum tolerance for computer clock synchronization	5 minutes

See Also

MS KB 231849 (Description of Kerberos Policies in Windows 2000) and MS KB 232179 (Kerberos Administration in Windows 2000)

14.24 Viewing Access Tokens

Problem

You want to view the access tokens that are created for a user account that has authenticated to Active Directory.

Using a command-line interface

```
> tokensz /compute_tokensize /
package:negotiate /target_server:host/<DCName>
/user:<Username> /domain:<DomainName> /password:<Password> /dumpgroups
```

Discussion

When an Active Directory security principal receives a TGT from the Kerberos Key Distribution Center, the TGT contains a Privilege Attribute Certificate (PAC). This PAC contains several pieces of authentication data, such as the groups that a user belongs to (including all nested group memberships). In the majority of AD environments, this PAC is created without issue, but some larger environments can run into instances of token bloat. This occurs when a user belongs to a large number of groups (estimates start around 70 to 120), and the size of the PAC becomes too large for the TGT to handle. This issue can manifest itself through authentication issues or through Group

Policy Objects not applying properly. You can use the *tokensz.exe* utility, downloadable from *http://go.microsoft.com/fwlink/?LinkId=25830*, to compute the token size for a user relative to the maximum allowable size, as well as to list the groups that a user belongs to.

You can resolve this issue by streamlining the number of groups that the user or users belong to, which has the added benefit of simplifying the process of assigning permissions and applying Group Policy Objects. If this isn't possible, you can apply the hotfix referenced in MS KB 327825 or modify the `HKLM\System\CurrentControlSet\Control\Lsa\Kerberos\Parameters\MaxTokenSize` DWORD value on your domain computers. This issue is more relevant on Windows 2000 domain controllers, since Windows Server 2003 has made a number of improvements to alleviate the need to modify this value.

If you determine that you need to modify the `MaxTokenSize` value, use the following formula as an approximate guideline:

```
1200 + 40d + 80s
```

In this equation, 1200 denotes a suggested amount of overhead that's used by the PAC; you can use the *tokensz* utility to determine the size for the domain in question. `d` refers to the number of domain local security groups that a representative user is a member of, plus any universal security groups in other domains that the user belongs to, plus any groups represented in the user's `sIDHistory` attribute. `s` refers to the number of global security groups a representative user belongs to, plus any universal security groups within the user's own domain.

See Also

MS KB 327825 (New Resolution for Problems That Occur When Users Belong to Many Groups), MS KB 263693 (Group Policy May Not Be Applied to Users Belonging to Many Groups), MS KB 280830 (Kerberos Authentication May Not Work If User Is a Member of Many Groups), and Troubleshooting Kerberos Errors at *http://www.microsoft.com/technet/prodtechnol/windowsserver2003/technologies/security/tkerberr.mspx*

## CHAPTER 15

Logging, Monitoring, and Quotas

15.0 Introduction

This chapter deals with tracking the activity and usage of various Active Directory components. When you need to troubleshoot a problem, often the first place you look is the logfiles. With Active Directory, there are several different logfiles, and each has different ways to increase or decrease the verbosity of the information that is logged. Viewing log messages can be a useful troubleshooting step, but you should also look at *performance metrics* to determine if system hardware or a particular service is being overutilized. In this chapter, we'll review a couple of ways you can view performance metrics, as well as monitor Active Directory performance. For more extensive monitoring, we suggest looking at NetPro's Active Directory monitoring tools (*http://www .netpro.com/*), Microsoft System Center Operations Manager (*http://microsoft.com/ scom/*), or similar products from other vendors such as NetIQ or Quest. In addition to the typical items that you would monitor on a Windows Server (e.g., disk space usage, physical and virtual memory errors, processor utilization), you should also monitor AD-specific performance metrics. This extends to monitoring replication activity, Event Log information, and the status of services like the File Replication Service (FRS).

We'll also cover a somewhat-related topic called *quotas*, which allow you to monitor and limit the number of objects that a security principal (user, group, or computer) can create within a partition. This feature, introduced in Windows Server 2003, attempts to close a hole that existed in Windows 2000 where users who had access to create objects in Active Directory could create as many of those objects as they wanted. These users could even cause a denial-of-service attack by creating objects until the disk drive on the domain controllers filled to capacity. This kind of attack is not likely to happen in most environments, but you should still consider the possibility and protect against it.

The Anatomy of a Quota Object Container

Quota objects became available in Windows Server 2003. They are stored in the `NTDSQuotas` container of the naming contexts and application partitions except for the schema naming context (quotas cannot be associated with the schema NC). By default, this container is hidden from view within tools such as Active Directory Users and Computers, but can be seen by selecting View → Advanced Features from the menu. The `quota` object container has an `objectClass` of `msDS-QuotaContainer` and contains several attributes that define default quota behavior. Table 15-1 lists some of the important attributes of `msDS-QuotaContainer` objects.

Table 15-1. Attributes of msDS-QuotaContainer objects

Attribute	Description
cn	RDN of quota container objects. By default, this is equal to `NTDSQuotas`.
msDS-DefaultQuota	The default quota applied to all security principals that do not have another quota specification applied. See Recipe 15.20 for more details.
msDS-QuotaEffective	A constructed attribute that contains the effective quota of the security principal that is viewing the attribute. See Recipe 15.21 for more details.
msDS-QuotaUsed	A constructed attribute that contains the quota usage of the security principal that is viewing the attribute. See Recipe 15.21 for more details.
msDS-TombstoneQuotaFactor	Percentage that tombstone objects count against a quota. The default is 100, which means a tombstone object has equal weighting to a normal object. See Recipe 15.19 for more details.
msDS-TopQuotaUsage	Multivalued attribute that contains information about the security principals with the top quota usage. See Recipe 15.21 for more details.

The Anatomy of a Quota Object

Quota objects have an `objectClass` of `msDS-QuotaControl`, which defines three attributes that relate to quotas. Table 15-2 contains these attributes and provides a description for each.

Table 15-2. Attributes of msDS-QuotaControl objects

Attribute	Description
cn	RDN of the quota object.
msDS-QuotaAmount	Number of objects that can be created by the security principals that the quota applies to. See Recipe 15.17 for more information.
msDS-QuotaTrustee	SID of the security principal that the quota applies to. This can be a user, group, or computer SID. See Recipe 15.17 for more information.

15.1 Enabling Extended dcpromo Logging

Problem

You want to enable extended *dcpromo* logging. This can be useful if you are experiencing problems during the Domain Controller promotion or demotion process and the *dcpromo* logfiles are not providing enough information to indicate the problem.

Solution

These solutions are slightly different on Windows 2000. See the section called "Discussion" for more information. To enable the maximum amount of logging, use 16711683 (FF0003 in hexadecimal) as the flag value. For a complete description of the possible bit values, see MS KB 221254.

Using a graphical user interface

1. Run *regedit.exe* from the command line or Start→Run.
2. In the left pane, expand *HKEY_LOCAL_MACHINE\Software\Microsoft\Windows \CurrentVersion\AdminDebug\dcpromoui*.
3. If the `LogFlags` value does not exist, right-click on *dcpromoui* in the left pane and select New→DWORD Value. For the name, enter `LogFlags`.
4. In the right pane, double-click on the `LogFlags` value and enter the flag value you want to set.
5. Click OK.

Using a command-line interface

In the following command, `<FlagValue>` needs to be the decimal version (not hexadecimal) of the flag value:

```
> reg add HKLM\Software\Microsoft\Windows\CurrentVersion\AdminDebug\dcpromoui /v
"LogFlags" /t REG_DWORD /d <FlagValue>
```

Using VBScript

```
' This code sets the dcpromoui logging flag (for Windows Server 2003 only).
' ------ SCRIPT CONFIGURATION ------
strDC = "<DomainControllerName>" ' e.g. dc01
intFlag = <FlagValue>            ' Flag value in decimal, e.g. 16711683
' ------ END CONFIGURATION --------

const HKLM = &H80000002
strDcpromoReg =
"Software\Microsoft\Windows\CurrentVersion\AdminDebug\dcpromoui\LogFlags"
set objReg = GetObject("winmgmts:\\" & strDC & "\root\default:StdRegProv")
objReg.SetDwordValue HKLM, strDcpromoReg, "LogFlags", intFlag
WScript.Echo "Dcpromoui flag set to " & intFlag
```

Using PowerShell

```
$strRegPath =
"HKLM:\Software\Microsoft\Windows\CurrentVersion\AdminDebug\dcpromoui\LogFlags"
New-ItemProperty -path $strRegPath -name "LogFiles" -type DWORD
Set-ItemProperty -path $strRegPath -name "LogFiles" -value "<FlagValue>"
```

Discussion

As described in Recipe 3.9, the *dcpromo* wizard creates a couple of logfiles in
%SystemRoot%\debug when it is executed, which can be useful in troubleshooting
promotion or demotion problems. Typically, the default amount of logging that is done
in the *dcpromoui.log* file is sufficient to identify most problems, but you can increase it
as described in the "Solution" section.

The location of the log flags registry value changed from Windows 2000 to Windows
Server 2003. In Windows 2000, the value is located here:

```
HKLM\Software\Microsoft\Windows\CurrentVersion\AdminDebug\dcpromoui
```

In Windows Server 2003 and newer, the value is located here (this is the value that was
used in the "Solution" section):

```
HKLM\Software\Microsoft\Windows\CurrentVersion\AdminDebug\dcpromoui\LogFlags
```

See Also

Recipe 3.9 for more on troubleshooting *dcpromo* problems and MS KB 221254 (Registry
Settings for Event Detail in the Dcpromoui.log File)

15.2 Enabling Diagnostics Logging

Problem

You want to enable diagnostics event logging because the current level of logging is not
providing enough information to help pinpoint the problem you are troubleshooting.

Solution

Using a graphical user interface

1. Run *regedit.exe* from the command line or Start→Run.
2. In the left pane, expand the following Registry key: *HKEY_LOCAL_MACHINE
   \System\CurrentControlSet\Services\NTDS\ Diagnostics*.
3. In the right pane, double-click on the diagnostics logging entry you want to increase, and enter a number (0–5) based on how much you want logged.
4. Click OK.

Using a command-line interface

```
> reg add HKLM\SYSTEM\CurrentControlSet\Services\NTDS\Diagnostics /v
"<LoggingSetting>" /t REG_DWORD /d <0-5>
```

Using VBScript

```
' This code sets the specified
' diagnostics logging level.
' ------ SCRIPT CONFIGURATION ------
strDC = "<DomainControllerName>"    ' e.g. dc01
strLogSetting = "<LoggingSetting>" ' e.g. 1 Knowledge Consistency Checker
intFlag = <FlagValue>              ' Flag value in decimal, e.g. 5
' ------ END CONFIGURATION ---------

const HKLM = &H80000002
strRegKey = "SYSTEM\CurrentControlSet\Services\NTDS\
Diagnostics"
set objReg = GetObject("winmgmts:\\" & strDC & "\root\default:StdRegProv")
objReg.SetDwordValue HKLM, strRegKey, "LogFlags", intFlag
WScript.Echo "
Diagnostics logging for " & strLogSetting _
                & " set to " & intFlag
```

Using PowerShell

```
$strRegPath = "HKLM:\SYSTEM\CurrentControlSet\Services\NTDS\Diagnostics"
Set-ItemProperty -path $strRegPath -name "<LoggingSetting>" -value "<FlagValue>"
```

Discussion

A useful way to troubleshoot specific problems you are encountering with Active Directory is to increase the diagnostics logging level. Diagnostics logging can be enabled for individual components of AD. For example, if you determine the KCC is not completing every 15 minutes, you can enable diagnostics logging for the "1 Knowledge Consistency Checker" setting.

These settings are stored under *HKLM\SYSTEM\CurrentControlSet\Services\NTDS \Diagnostics*. By default, all settings are set to 0, which disables diagnostic logging, but you can increase it by setting it to a number from 1 through 5. As a general rule, a value of 1 is used for minimum logging, 3 for medium logging, and 5 for maximum logging. It is a good practice to ease your way up to 5 because some diagnostics logging settings can generate a bunch of events in the event log, which may make it difficult to read, along with increasing resource utilization on the domain controller.

Here is the complete list of diagnostics logging settings for Windows Server 2003 and Windows Server 2008. Note that settings 20–24 are not available on Windows 2000-based domain controllers:

```
1 Knowledge Consistency Checker
2 Security Events
3 ExDS Interface Events
4 MAPI Interface Events
```

```
 5 Replication Events
 6 Garbage Collection
 7 Internal Configuration
 8 Directory Access
 9 Internal Processing
10 Performance Counters
11 Initialization/Termination
12 Service Control
13 Name Resolution
14 Backup
15 Field Engineering
16 LDAP Interface Events
17 Setup
18 Global Catalog
19 Inter-site Messaging
20 Group Caching
21 Linked-Value Replication
22 DS RPC Client
23 DS RPC Server
24 DS Schema
```

See Also

MS KB 220940 (How to Enable Diagnostic Event Logging for Active Directory Services)

15.3 Enabling NetLogon Logging

Problem

You want to enable NetLogon logging to help with troubleshooting client account logon, lockout, or domain-controller location issues.

Solution

Using a command-line interface

To enable NetLogon logging, use the following command:

```
> nltest /dbflag:0x2080ffff
```

To disable NetLogon logging, use the following command:

```
> nltest /dbflag:0x0
```

Discussion

The *netlogon.log* file located in *%SystemRoot%\Debug* can be invaluable for trouble-shooting client logon and related issues. When enabled at the highest setting (0x2080ffff), it logs useful information such as the site the client is in, the domain controller the client authenticated against, additional information related to the DC

Locator process, account password expiration information, account lockout information, and even Kerberos failures.

The NetLogon logging level is stored in the following registry value:

```
HKLM\System\CurrentControlSet\Services\Netlogon Parameters\DBFlag
```

 If you set that registry value manually instead of using *nltest*, you'll need to restart the NetLogon service for it to take effect.

One of the issues with the *netlogon.log* file is that it can quickly grow to several megabytes, which makes it difficult to peruse. A new tool available for Windows XP, Windows Server 2003 and Windows Server 2008 called *nlparse* can filter the contents of the *netlogon.log* file so that you'll see only certain types of log entries. The *nlparse* tool is part of the Account Lockout and Management Tools that Microsoft made available from the following web page (assuming the tools haven't moved):

> *http://www.microsoft.com/downloads/details.aspx?FamilyID=7af2e69c-91f3-4e63-8629-b999adde0b9e&DisplayLang=en*

See Also

MS KB 109626 (Enabling Debug Logging for the Netlogon Service), MS KB 247811 (How Domain Controllers Are Located in Windows), and MS KB 273499 (Description of Security Event 681)

15.4 Enabling GPO Client Logging

Problem

You want to troubleshoot GPO processing issues on a client or server by enabling additional logging in the Application event log.

Solution

Using a graphical user interface

1. Run *regedit.exe* from the command line or Start→Run.
2. In the left pane, expand the appropriate key from the table in the section called "Discussion".
3. Create and populate the appropriate key value.
4. Click OK.

Using a command-line interface

```
> reg add "<Key Value>" /v "<Value Name>" /t REG_DWORD /d <Value>
```

Using VBScript

```
' This code enables
' GPO logging on a target computer.
' ------ SCRIPT CONFIGURATION ------
strComputer = "<ComputerName>" ' e.g. rallen-w2k3
strRegKey = "<Key Name>"
strValueName = "<Value Name>"
strValue = "<Value>"
' ------ END CONFIGURATION ---------

const HKLM = &H80000002
strRegKey = "SOFTWARE\Microsoft\Windows NT\CurrentVersion\Diagnostics"
set objReg = GetObject("winmgmts:\\" & strComputer _
                       & "\root\default:StdRegProv")
objReg.SetDwordValue HKLM, strRegKey, strValueName, strValue
WScript.Echo "Enabled
GPO logging for " & strComputer
```

Discussion

If you experience problems with client GPO processing, such as a GPO not getting applied even though you think it should, there are a number of different Registry keys that can help you troubleshoot the problem. One way to get detailed information about what GPOs are applied on a client is by enabling additional GPO event logging. Table 15-3 lists a number of Registry settings that can be configured to enable Group Policy logging, as well as the files that are created when these settings are enabled.

Table 15-3. Registry settings to enable Group Policy logging

Logging for the CSE	Located	Enable verbose logging by adding this key or value ...	... to this registry key
Group Policy core (UserEnv) and registry CSE	%windir%\debug\usermode\UserEnv.log	UserEnvDebugLevel = REG_DWORD 30002	HKEY_LOCAL_MACHINE\Software\Microsoft\Windows NT\CurrentVersion\Winlogon
Security CSE	%windir%\security\logs\winlogon.log	ExtensionDebugLevel = REG_DWORD 0x2	HKEY_LOCAL_MACHINE\Software\Microsoft\Windows NT\CurrentVersion\Winlogon\GpExtensions\{827d319e-6eac-11d2-a4ea-00c04f79f83a}\
Folder Redirection CSE	windir%\debug\usermode\fdeploy.log	FdeployDebugLevel = Reg_DWORD 0x0f	HKEY_LOCAL_MACHINE\Software\Microsoft\Windows NT\CurrentVersion\Diagnostics
Software Installation CSE	%windir%\debug\usermode\appmgmt.log	Appmgmtdebuglevel=dword:0000009b	HKEY_LOCAL_MACHINE\Software\Microsoft\Windows NT\CurrentVersion\Diagnostics
Windows Installer (deployment-related actions)	%windir%\temp\MSI*.log	Logging = voicewarmup Debug = DWORD: 00000003	HKEY_LOCAL_MACHINE\Software\Policies\Microsoft\Windows\Installer
Windows Installer (user-initiated actions)	%temp%\MSI*.log	Logging = voicewarmup Debug = DWORD: 00000003	HKEY_LOCAL_MACHINE\Software\Policies\Microsoft\Windows\Installer

Windows Vista and Windows Server 2008 have eliminated the *Userenv.log* file in favor of a Group Policy-specific view within the Windows Event Viewer.

See Also

MS KB 186454 (How to Enable User Environment Event Logging in Windows 2000)

15.5 Enabling Kerberos Logging

Problem

You want to enable Kerberos logging on a domain controller to troubleshoot authentication problems.

Solution

Using a graphical user interface

1. Run *regedit.exe* from the command line or Start→Run.
2. In the left pane, expand *HKEY_LOCAL_MACHINE\System\CurrentControlSet \Control\Lsa\Kerberos\Parameters*.
3. If the LogLevel value doesn't already exist, right-click on Parameters and select New→DWORD value. Enter LogLevel for the value name and click OK.
4. In the right pane, double-click on LogLevel and enter 1.
5. Click OK.

Using a command-line interface

```
> reg add HKLM\SYSTEM\CurrentControlSet\Control\Lsa\Kerberos\Parameters /v
"LogLevel" /t REG_DWORD /d 1
```

Using VBScript

```
' This code enables Kerberos logging for the specified domain controller.
' ------ SCRIPT CONFIGURATION ------
strDC = "<DomainControllerName>" ' e.g. dc01
' ------ END CONFIGURATION --------

const HKLM = &H80000002
strRegKey = "SYSTEM\CurrentControlSet\Control\Lsa\Kerberos\Parameters"
set objReg = GetObject("winmgmts:\\" & strDC & "\root\default:StdRegProv")
objReg.SetDwordValue HKLM, strRegKey, "LogLevel", 1
WScript.Echo "Enable Kerberos logging for " & strDC
```

Using PowerShell

```
$strRegPath = "HKLM:\SYSTEM\CurrentControlSet\Control\Lsa\Kerberos\Parameters"
New-ItemProperty -path $strRegPath -name "LogLevel" -type DWORD
Set-ItemProperty -path $strRegPath -name "LogLevel" -value "1"
```

Discussion

If you are experiencing authentication problems or would like to determine whether you are experiencing any Kerberos-related issues, enabling Kerberos logging will cause Kerberos errors to be logged in the System event log. The Kerberos events can point out if the problem is related to clock skew, an expired ticket, an expired password, etc. For a good overview of some of the Kerberos error messages, see MS KB 230476.

Here is a sample event:

```
Event Type:        Error
Event Source:      Kerberos
Event Category:    None
Event ID:          3
Date:              5/26/2003
Time:              5:53:43 PM
User:              N/A
Computer:          DC01
Description:
A Kerberos Error Message was received:
         on logon session
 Client Time:
 Server Time: 0:53:43.0000 5/27/2003 Z
 Error Code: 0xd KDC_ERR_BADOPTION
 Extended Error: 0xc00000bb KLIN(0)
 Client Realm:
 Client Name:
 Server Realm: ADATUM.COM
 Server Name: host/dc01.adatum.com
 Target Name: host/dc01.adatum.com@ADATUM.COM
 Error Text:
 File: 9
 Line: ab8
 Error Data is in record data.
```

See Also

MS KB 230476 (Description of Common Kerberos-Related Errors in Windows 2000) and MS KB 262177 (How to Enable Kerberos Event Logging)

15.6 Viewing DNS Server Performance Statistics

Problem

You want to view DNS Server performance statistics.

Solution

Using a graphical user interface

1. Open the Performance Monitor.
2. Click on System Monitor in the left pane.
3. In the right pane, click the + button. This will bring up the page to add counters.
4. Under "Select counters from computer," enter the DNS server you want to target.
5. Select the DNS performance object.
6. Select the counters you want to add and click the Add button.
7. Click Close.

Using a command-line interface

```
> dnscmd <DNSServerName> /statistics
```

Using VBScript

```
' This code displays all statistics for the specified DNS server.
' ------ SCRIPT CONFIGURATION ------
strServer = "<DNSServerName>" ' e.g. dc1.adatum.com
' ------ END CONFIGURATION ---------

set objDNS = GetObject("winmgmts:\\" & strServer & "\root\MicrosoftDNS")
set objDNSServer = objDNS.Get("MicrosoftDNS_Server.Name="".""")
set objStats = objDNS.ExecQuery("Select * from MicrosoftDNS_Statistic ")
for each objStat in objStats
    WScript.Echo " " & objStat.Name & " : " & objStat.Value
next
```

Using PowerShell

```
get-eventlog | where-object { $_.logDisplayName = "DNS Server"}
```

Discussion

The Microsoft DNS Server keeps track of dozens of performance metrics. These metrics include the number of queries, updates, transfers, directory reads, and directory writes processed by the server. If you can pump these metrics into an enterprise management system, you can track DNS usage and growth over time.

These statistics can also be useful to troubleshoot load-related issues. If you suspect a DNS Server is being overwhelmed with DNS update requests, you can look at the Dynamic Update Received/sec counter and see if it is processing an unusually high number of updates.

Using a command-line interface

You can obtain a subset of the statistics by providing a *statid* after the /statistics option. Each statistics category has an associated number (i.e., statid). For a complete list of categories and their statids, run the following command:

```
> dnscmd /statistics /?
```

Here is an example of viewing the Query (statid = 2) and Query2 (statid = 4) statistics:

```
> dnscmd /statistics 6
DNS Server . statistics:

Queries and Responses:
----------------------
Total:
    Queries Received =   14902
    Responses Sent   =   12900
UDP:
    Queries Recvd    =   14718
    Responses Sent   =   12716
    Queries Sent     =   23762
    Responses Recvd  =       0
TCP:
    Client Connects  =     184
    Queries Recvd    =     184
    Responses Sent   =     184
    Queries Sent     =       0
    Responses Recvd  =       0

Queries:
--------
Total        =   14902
    Notify   =       0
    Update   =    2207
    TKeyNego =     184
    Standard =   12511
    A        =    1286
    NS       =      29
    SOA      =    2263
    MX       =       0
    PTR      =       1
    SRV      =    8909
    ALL      =       0
    IXFR     =       0
    AXFR     =       0
    OTHER    =      23

Command completed successfully.
```

Using VBScript

You can obtain a subset of statistics by adding a **where** clause to the WQL query. The following query matches only counters that start with "Records":

```
select * from MicrosoftDNS_Statistic where Name like 'Records%'
```

See Also

MSDN: MicrosoftDNS_Statistic

15.7 Monitoring the File Replication Service

Problem

You want to monitor the performance of the File Replication Service (FRS).

Solution

Using a graphical user interface

1. Double-click on *frsdiag.exe* in the Windows Resource Kit.
2. Under Target Server(s), select Local Machine, or click Browse to select a remote machine to diagnose.
3. Click GO.

Using a command-line interface

The following will display the polling interval for *dc1.adatum.com*:

```
> ntfrsutl poll dc1.adatum.com
```

The **sets** parameter will display all active replication sets on *dc1.adatum.com*, as follows:

```
> ntfrsutl sets dc1.adatum.com
```

Discussion

Windows 2000, Windows Server 2003, and Windows Server 2008 use FRS by default to replicate the contents of the *SYSVOL* shared folder, as well as any Distributed File System (DFS) folders you've configured on pre-Windows Server 2003 R2 servers. R2 and Windows Server 2008 provide the new DFS-R file replication mechanism, which is a significant improvement over FRS in terms of scalability and manageability. While DFS-R cannot be used for replicating *SYSVOL* in Windows Server 2003 R2, it is the preferred replication mechanism for *SYSVOL* in Windows Server 2008.

Anytime FRS detects a change that's been made to a file or folder within one of these shared folders, it will replicate the updated object to other servers within the replica set. Because FRS allows for multimaster file replication (similar to the database replication performed by AD itself), any server in the replica set is able to make changes to *SYSVOL* or DFS folders, and the File Replication Service will distribute those changes accordingly.

You can monitor the File Replication Service using either *frsdiag* from the Windows Server 2003 Resource Kit, or the Ultrasound utility, which is a free download from the Microsoft website. Ultrasound requires access to a database to store its information: either a SQL server instance or the free MSDE database that can also be downloaded from the Microsoft site.

See Also

MS KB 221111 (Description of FRS Entries in the Registry), MS KB 319553 (How to Restrict FRS Replication Traffic to a Specific Static Port), and MS KB 272279 (How to Troubleshoot the File Replication Service and the Distributed File System)

15.8 Monitoring the Windows Time Service

Problem

You want to verify the correct functioning of the Windows Time Service.

Solution

Using a command-line interface

The following syntax verifies that the Windows Time Service is functioning on *dc1.adatum.com* and *dc2.adatum.com*:

```
> w32tm /monitor /computers:dc1.adatum.com,dc2.adatum.com
```

Discussion

Because Active Directory relies on Kerberos for authentication, it's critical that all of your domain controllers, member servers, and clients maintain a consistent time across the network; if any computer's clock is off by more than five minutes by default, it will not be able to authenticate to Active Directory. You can use the *w32tm* utility to verify time synchronization on one or more computers using the /monitor switch, as well as using the /resync switch to prompt a computer to immediately resynchronize its clock with its authoritative time source.

See Also

Recipe 3.20 to configure a DC to use an external time source, MS KB 257187 (RPC Error Messages Returned for Active Directory Replication When Time Is Out of

Synchronization), and MS KB 816042 (How to Configure an Authoritative Time Server in Windows Server 2003)

15.9 Enabling Inefficient and Expensive LDAP Query Logging

Problem

You want to log inefficient and expensive LDAP queries to the Directory Services event log.

Solution

To log a summary report about the total number of searches, total expensive searches, and total inefficient searches to the Directory Services event log, set the 15 Field Engineering diagnostics logging setting to 4. This summary is generated every 12 hours during the garbage collection cycle.

To log an event to the Directory Services event log every time an expensive or inefficient search occurs, set the 15 Field Engineering diagnostics logging setting to 5.

See Recipe 15.2 for more on enabling diagnostics logging.

Discussion

A search is considered *expensive* if it has to visit a large number of objects in Active Directory. The default threshold for an expensive query is 10,000. That means any search that visits 10,000 or more objects would be considered expensive. A search is considered *inefficient* if it returns less than 10 percent of the total objects it visits. If a query visited 10,000 objects and only returned 999 of them (less than 10 percent), it would be considered inefficient. The default bottom limit for an inefficient query is 1,000. If the query returned 1,000 instead, it would not be considered inefficient. To summarize, with 1,000 as the default bottom threshold, no search that visits less than 1,000 entries (even if it visited 999 and returned 0) would be considered inefficient.

Here is a sample summary report event that is logged when 15 Field Engineering is set to 4:

```
Event Type:       Information
Event Source:     NTDS General
Event Category:   Field Engineering
Event ID:         1643
Date:             5/24/2003
Time:             7:24:24 PM
User:             NT AUTHORITY\ANONYMOUS LOGON
Computer:         DC1
Description:
Internal event:   Active Directory performed the following number of search
operations
within this time interval.
```

```
Time interval (hours): 9
Number of search operations: 24679

During this time interval, the following number of search operations were
characterized as either expensive or inefficient.

Expensive search operations: 7
Inefficient search operations: 22
```

If you set 15 Field Engineering to 5, the summary event is logged during the garbage
collection cycle, and event 1644 is generated every time an expensive or inefficient
search occurs. Setting this value can provide useful information if you are running
applications that regularly generate expensive or inefficient queries. Notice that this
event provides details on all aspects of the search, including the client IP, authenticating
user, search base DN, search filter, attributes, controls, number of entries visited, and
number of entries returned. This was taken from a Windows Server 2003 domain controller. Windows 2000 does not provide quite as much detail:

```
Event Type:         Information
Event Source:       NTDS General
Event Category:     Field Engineering
Event ID:           1644
Date:               5/24/2003
Time:               7:50:40 PM
User:               ADATUM\rallen
Computer:           DC1
Description:
Internal event:     A client issued a search operation with the following options.

Client: 192.168.4.14
Starting node: DC=adatum,DC=com
Filter: (description=*)
Search scope: subtree
Attribute selection: cn
Server controls:

Visited entries: 10340
Returned entries: 1000
```

With the default settings, the query shown in the above event is considered both expensive and inefficient. It is expensive because it visited more than 10,000 entries. It is
inefficient because it returned less than 10 percent of those entries.

You can customize what a domain controller considers *expensive* and *inefficient* by
creating a couple of registry values under the *HKLM\SYSTEM\CurrentControlSet\Serv-
ices\NTDS\Parameters* key. You can create a value named Expensive Search Results
Threshold of type DWORD and specify the number of entries a search would need to
visit to be considered expensive. Similarly, you can create a value named Inefficient
Search Results Threshold of type DWORD and specify the minimum number of entries
visited where a match returning less than 10 percent would be considered inefficient.

If you want to see all the LDAP queries that are being sent to a domain controller, a quick way to do that would be to set the 15 Field Engineering setting to 5 and Expensive Search Results Threshold to 0. This would cause the domain controller to consider every search as expensive and log all the LDAP searches. While this can be very useful, you should use it with care as it could quickly fill your event log. Be sure to allow sufficient disk space for your Event Logs to avoid any issues with low disk space on your domain controllers.

See Also

Recipe 15.2 for enabling diagnostics logging

15.10 Using the STATS Control to View LDAP Query Statistics

Problem

You want to use the STATS LDAP control to test the efficiency of a query.

Solution

Using a graphical user interface

1. Open LDP from the Windows Support Tools. (In Windows Server 2008, LDP is built into the AD DS binaries.)
2. From the menu, select Connection→Connect.
3. For Server, enter the name of a domain controller (or leave blank to do a serverless bind).
4. For Port, enter 389.
5. Click OK.
6. From the menu, select Connection→Bind.
7. Enter the credentials of a user to perform the search.
8. Click OK.
9. From the menu, select Options→Control.
10. For the Windows Server 2003 or Windows Server 2008 versions of LDP, you can select Search Stats from the Load Predefined selection. For Windows 2000, add a control with the OID 1.2.840.113556.1.4.970.
11. Click OK.
12. From the menu, select Browse→Search.
13. Enter your search criteria and then click the Options button.

14. Under Search Call Type, be sure that Extended is selected.

15. Click OK and then click Run.

Using a command-line interface

The AdFind command-line utility has four switches that will display efficiency statistics for any query:

`-stats`

Enables the STATS control to return statistics about the query, along with the actual results of the query.

`-statsonly`

Returns *only* the statistics about the query, and suppresses the actual query results.

`-stats+`

Similar to `-stats`, but also displays additional advanced analysis about the query.

`-stats+only`

Just like `-stats+`, but will suppress the actual results of the query and only display the query statistics.

Discussion

The STATS control is a useful way to obtain statistics about the performance of an LDAP query. With the STATS control, you can find out information such as the amount of time it took the server to process the query, how many entries were visited versus returned, what the search filter expanded to, and if any indexes were used. Here is an example of what the STATS control returns for a search for all **group** objects in the cn=Users container:

```
Statistics
=====================================================
Elapsed time: 0 (ms)
Returned 18 of 23 visited - (78.26%)

Used Filter:
  (objectCategory=CN=Group,CN=Schema,CN=Configuration,CN=adatum,CN=com

Used Indices:
  Ancestors_index:23:N

Pages referenced: 332
Pages read from disk: 0
Pages pre-read from Disk: 0

Analysis
-------------------------------------------------

Indices used:

Index name: Ancestors_index
```

```
Record count: 23 (estimate)
Index type: Normal attribute index
Ancestor index used, possibly inefficient, verify filter
```

A couple things are worth noting here. First, the search visited 23 entries and ended up returning 18. In terms of the definitions defined in Recipe 15.9, this query is both *inexpensive* and *efficient*. You can also see that the filter used, (objectcategory=group), was expanded to:

```
(objectCategory=CN=Group,CN=Schema,CN=Configuration,DC=adatum,DC=com)
```

The syntax of the objectCategory attribute is a distinguished name, but Active Directory provides a shortcut so that you need to use only the LDAP display name of the class instead. Internally, Active Directory converts the display name to the distinguished name, as shown here. Finally, we can see that our search used an index, INTER SECT_INDEX:17:I.

Let's look at another example, except this time we'll perform an ANR search for Jim Smith:

```
***Searching ...
ldap_search_ext_s(ld, "ou=Sales,DC=adatum,DC=com", 2, "(anr=Jim Smith)",
attrList, 0, svrCtrls, ClntCtrls, 20, 1000 ,&msg)
Result <0>:
Matched DNs:
Stats:
        Call Time:          20 (ms)
        Entries Returned:       1
        Entries Visited:        2
        Used Filter:        ( | (displayName=Jim Smith*) (givenName=Jim Smith*)
(legacyExchangeDN=Jim Smith)  (msDS-AdditionalSamAccountName=Jim Smith*)
(physicalDeliveryOfficeName=Jim Smith*)  (proxyAddresses=Jim Smith*) (name=Jim
Smith*)  (sAMAccountName=Jim Smith*)
(sn=Jim Smith*)  ( & (givenName=Jim*)  (sn=Smith*) )  ( & (givenName=Smith*)
(sn=Jim*) ) )
        Used Indexes:
idx_givenName:10:N;idx_givenName:10:N;idx_sn:9:N;idx_
sAMAccountName:8:N;idx_name:7:N;idx_proxyAddresses:6:N;idx_
physicalDeliveryOfficeName:5:N;idx_msDS-AdditionalSamAccountName:4:N;idx_
legacyExchangeDN:3:N;idx_givenName:2:N;idx_displayName:1:N;
```

You can see from the second line that we used a very simple filter (anr=Jim Smith). If you look down a little farther at Used Filter:, you can see a better example of search-filter expansion. Like the objectCategory example earlier, ANR is a shorthand way to do something complex. A simple one-term search filter expands into a multiterm filter that searches across numerous attributes. (For more on the behavior of ANR, see Recipe 10.14.) The point of showing this is to illustrate that the STATS control is very powerful and can be an invaluable tool when trying to troubleshoot or optimize LDAP queries.

See Also

Recipe 4.4 for using LDAP controls, Recipe 4.8 for searching for objects, Recipe 10.14 for more on ANR, and Recipe 15.9 for more on expensive and inefficient searches

15.11 Monitoring the Performance of AD

Problem

You want to use the Performance Monitor to examine the performance of Active Directory.

Solution

Using a graphical user interface

1. Open the Performance Monitor (Reliability and Performance Monitor in Windows Server 2008).
2. Click on System Monitor in the left pane (Performance Monitor in Windows Server 2008).
3. Press Ctrl-I. This will bring up the page to add counters.
4. Under "Select counters from computer," enter the name of the domain controller you want to target.
5. Select the NTDS performance object.
6. Select the counters you want to monitor.
7. After you're done with your selections, click Close.

Discussion

There are several Performance Monitor counters that can be very valuable for monitoring and troubleshooting Active Directory. The NTDS performance object has counters for address book lookups; inbound and outbound replication; LDAP reads, writes, and searches; Kerberos authentication; and the Security Account Manager (SAM).

Here is a list of some of the most useful NTDS counters. We've also included their Performance Monitor explanation, which you can view by clicking on the Explain button in the Add Counters dialog box:

DRA Inbound Bytes Total/sec
> Shows the total number of bytes replicated in. It is the sum of the number of uncompressed bytes (never compressed) and the number of compressed bytes (after compression).

DRA Inbound Objects/sec
> Shows the number of objects received from neighbors through inbound replication. A *neighbor* is a domain controller from which the local domain controller replicates locally.

DRA Inbound Values Total/sec
> Shows the total number of object property values received from inbound replication partners. Each inbound object has one or more properties, and each property has zero or more values. A zero value indicates property removal.

DRA Outbound Bytes Total/sec
> Shows the total number of bytes replicated out. It is the sum of the number of uncompressed bytes (never compressed) and the number of compressed bytes (after compression).

DRA Outbound Objects/sec
> Shows the number of objects replicated out.

DRA Outbound Values Total/sec
> Shows the number of object property values sent to outbound replication partners.

DRA Pending Replication Synchronizations
> Shows the number of directory synchronizations that are queued for this server but not yet processed.

DS Client Binds/sec
> Shows the number of *ntdsapi.dll* binds per second serviced by this DC.

DS Directory Reads/sec
> Shows the number of directory reads per second.

DS Directory Searches/sec
> Shows the number of directory searches per second.

DS Directory Writes/sec
> Shows the number of directory writes per second.

KDC AS Requests
> Shows the number of Authentication Server (AS) requests serviced by the Kerberos Key Distribution Center (KDC) per second. AS requests are used by the client to obtain a ticket-granting ticket.

KDC TGS Requests
> Shows the number of Ticket Granting Server (TGS) requests serviced by the KDC per second. TGS requests are used by the client to obtain a ticket to a resource.

Kerberos Authentications
> Shows the number of times per second that clients use a ticket for this DC to authenticate to this DC.

LDAP Bind Time
> Shows the time, in milliseconds, taken for the last successful LDAP bind.

LDAP Client Sessions
> Shows the number of currently connected LDAP client sessions.

LDAP Searches
> Shows the percentage of directory searches coming from LDAP.

LDAP Searches/sec
> Shows the rate at which LDAP clients perform search operations.

LDAP Successful Binds
> Shows the percentage of LDAP bind attempts that are successful.

LDAP Successful Binds/sec
> Shows the number of LDAP binds per second.

LDAP Writes
> Shows the percentage of directory writes coming from LDAP.

LDAP Writes/sec
> Shows the rate at which LDAP clients perform write operations.

15.12 Using Perfmon Trace Logs to Monitor AD

Problem

You want to enable Trace Logs to view system-level calls related to Active Directory.

Solution

Using Windows 2000 and Windows Server 2003

1. Open the Performance Monitor.

2. In the left pane, expand Performance Logs and Alerts.

3. Right-click on Trace Logs and select New Log Settings.

4. Enter a name for the log and click OK.

5. Click the Add button.

6. Highlight one or more of the Active Directory providers and click OK.

7. Use the tabs to configure additional settings about the log.

8. When you are done, click OK.

9. Unless you've scheduled it to run at a different time, the Trace Log you created should show up in the right pane next to a green icon, which indicates that it is running.

10. To stop the Trace Log, right-click on it in the right pane and select Stop.

11. Now open up a command prompt (*cmd.exe*).

12. Use `cd` to change into the directory where the Trace Log files are stored (*c:\perflogs* by default).

13. Run the following command:

```
> tracerpt <LogFileName>
```

Using Windows Server 2008

1. Open Reliability and Performance Monitor.

2. In the left pane, expand Data Collector Sets.

3. Right-click Event Trace Sessions and click New → Data Collector Sets.

4. In the Name: field, enter AD Trace Log. Click Next.

5. Click Add. In the Event Trace Providers screen, click Active Directory Domain Services: Core. Click OK.

6. Click Next twice. Click the "Start this data collector set now" radio button and click Finish.

7. Right-click on AD Trace Log and click Properties. On the File tab, take note of the location of the *.etl* file. Click OK.

8. Open a command prompt and run the following command:

```
tracerpt <LogFileName>
```

Discussion

Trace Logs capture detailed system- and application-level events. Applications support Trace Log capability by developing a Trace Log Provider. Active Directory supports several providers that log low-level system calls related to Kerberos, LDAP, and DNS, to name a few. This can be an extremely valuable tool for debugging or just exploring the inner workings of Active Directory. Trace Logs can be resource-intensive, so you should enable them with care.

The *tracerpt* command is available by default with Windows Server 2003 and Windows Server 2008. On Windows 2000, you'll need to use the Resource Kit utility called *tracedmp.exe* with the same syntax.

The *tracerpt/tracedmp* commands generate a *summary.txt* file that summarizes all of the events by total. A second file called *dumpfile.csv* is created that can be imported into Excel or viewed with a text viewer to show the details of each event.

Here is an example of what the *summary.txt* file looks like on a domain controller that had all of the Active Directory-related Trace Log Providers enabled:

```
Files Processed:
        AD_000001.etl
Total Buffers Processed 5
Total Events Processed 193
Total Events Lost   0
Start Time           Friday, May 23, 2003
End Time             Friday, May 23, 2003
Elapsed Time         24 sec
+----------------------------------------------------------------------+
|Event Count Event Name          Event Type  Guid
|
+----------------------------------------------------------------------
-+
|  1         EventTrace          Header   {68fdd900-4a3e-11d1-84f4-
0000f80464e3}|
| 69         SamNameById         Start    {25059476-899f-11d2-819e-
0000f875a064}|
| 69         SamNameById         End      {25059476-899f-11d2-819e-
0000f875a064}|
|  2         KerbInitSecurityContext  End  {52e82f1a-7cd4-47ed-b5e5-
fde7bf64cea6}|
|  2         KerbInitSecurityContext  Start {52e82f1a-7cd4-47ed-b5e5-
fde7bf64cea6}|
|  1         KerbAcceptSecurityContext Start {94acefe3-9e56-49e3-9895-
7240a231c371}|
|  1         KerbAcceptSecurityContext End  {94acefe3-9e56-49e3-9895-
7240a231c371}|
|  1         SamGetAliasMem      Start    {1cf5fd19-1ac1-4324-84f7-
970a634a91ee}|
|  1         SamGetAliasMem      End      {1cf5fd19-1ac1-4324-84f7-
970a634a91ee}|
| 14         LdapRequest         End      {b9d4702a-6a98-11d2-b710-
00c04fb998a2}|
| 14         LdapRequest         Start    {b9d4702a-6a98-11d2-b710-
00c04fb998a2}|
|  1         DsLdapBind          Start    {05acd009-daeb-11d1-be80-
00c04fadfff5}|
|  1         DsLdapBind          End      {05acd009-daeb-11d1-be80-
00c04fadfff5}|
|  8         DsDirSearch         End      {05acd000-daeb-11d1-be80-
00c04fadfff5}|
|  8         DsDirSearch         Start    {05acd000-daeb-11d1-be80-
00c04fadfff5}|
+----------------------------------------------------------------------
-+
```

Here you can see that over a 24-second period, there was 1 LDAP bind request (DsLdapBind), 8 directory searches (DsDirSearch), and 14 total LDAP requests (LdapRequest).

The *dumpfile.csv* contains entries for every event that was generated during the time period. Here is an example of an entry for one of the DsDirSearch requests (note that the lines will wrap due to their length so we've added a blank line in between for separation):

```
DsDirSearch, Start, 0x000003F4, 126982224636242128, 61350, 440530, "DS", 3, 3,
1141178432, 2694848000, "192.168.5.26", "deep", "OU=Sales,DC=adatum,DC=com", "0,
0

DsDirSearch, End, 0x000003F4, 126982224636342271, 61350, 440540, "DS", 3, 5,
1157955648, 2694848000, "0", "
(&(objectCategory=CN=Person,CN=Schema,CN=Configuration,DC=adatum,DC=com)
(objectClass=user)) 0, 0
```

Based on just those two lines (disregarding most of the numeric values), we can deduce that a user on the host with IP address 192.168.5.26 performed an LDAP query for user objects in the Sales OU. Pretty neat, huh?

See Also

MS KB 302552 (How to Create and Configure Performance Monitor Trace Logs in Windows 2000)

15.13 Creating an Administrative Alert

Problem

You want to define a threshold for a performance counter that should cause an alert to be generated.

Solution

Using Windows 2000 or Windows Server 2003

1. Open the Performance Monitor.
2. In the left pane, expand "Performance Logs and Alerts."
3. Right-click on Alerts and select New Alert Settings.
4. Enter a name for the alert and click OK.
5. On the General tab, enter a description for the alert in the Comment field.
6. Click the Add button.
7. Highlight one or more of the Active Directory providers and click OK.
8. For each counter, for "Alert when the value is...," specify Under or Over. For Limit, specify the threshold value that should trigger the alert.
9. For "Sample data every," specify how often the performance counter should be updated.
10. On the Schedule tab, specify the time that the scan should begin and end.
11. On the Action tab, specify the action that the OS should take when the alert is generated. You can choose from one or more of the following:

- Log an entry in the application event log.
- Send a network message.
- Start a performance data log.
- Run an external program.

12. Click OK.

Using Windows Server 2008

1. Open the Reliability and Performance Monitor.
2. Expand Data Collector Sets. Right-click User-Defined and click New→Data Collector Set.
3. In the Name text box, enter "AD Performance Alert." Select the Create manually radio button and click Next.
4. Click the Performance Counter Alert radio button and click Next.
5. Click Add. Select the counter that you wish to be alerted about. Click Add and click OK.
6. In the "Alert when:" drop-down box, click Above or Below. In the Limit text box, enter the threshold value that you wish to monitor. Click Next.
7. Click the "Start this data collector now" radio button. Click Finish.

Discussion

There are any number of options for monitoring the ongoing performance of the Windows operating system, whether the machine in question is a domain controller, member server, or workstation. For larger environments, you can look into add-on tools like the SCOM or third-party utilities from NetPro, NetIQ, and others. For a built-in solution, however, the Performance MMC snap-in can monitor performance metrics and send various administrative alerts.

See Also

Recipe 15.14 for configuring an alert to email an operator or administrator, MS KB 243625 (How to Configure Administrative Alerts in Windows 2000), and MS KB 248345 (How to Create a Log Using System Monitor in Windows)

15.14 Emailing an Administrator on a Performance Alert

Problem

You want to create an alert that will notify an administrator via email if a performance alert is generated.

Solution

Using VBScript

```
' This code will send a simple email message
' from a computer that is running its own SMTP server

'------------Script Configuration--------------------
strSubject = "Low hard disk space on server dc1."
strFromLine = "admin@adatum.com"
strToLine = "oncall@adatum.com"
strText = "Available disk space on the C:\ drive of dc1." & _
    "adatum.com has gone below 100MB."
'----------------------------------------------------

Set objMessage = CreateObject("CDO.Message")
objMessage.Subject = strSubject
objMessage.From = strFromLine
objMessage.To = strToLine
objMessage.TextBody = strText
objMessage.Send
```

Using PowerShell

```
#send-mail.ps1
param ([string]$SMTPserver    = "<SMTP Server IP Address>",
    [string]$SMTPport         = "<SMTP Port>",
    [string]$From             = "from@example.com",
    [string]$To               = "to@example.com",
    [string]$Subject          = "simple subject",
    [string]$Body             = "simple body"
)

$var = (new-object net.mail.smtpclient($SMTPserver, $SMTPport))
$var.Send($From, $To, $Subject, $Body)
```

Discussion

A common request among Windows system administrators is to have the ability to email an on-call administrator when a critical performance alert is generated—for example, when a domain controller is experiencing a critical hardware failure. It is a relatively simple matter to send email through VBScript using Collaborative Data Objects (CDOs), which are built into Windows XP and Windows Server 2003. You can either hardcode the appropriate alert messages into the VBScript code and maintain multiple scripts for the various alerts that you create, or you can generate command-line arguments within the Performance Alert and use those alerts to customize the output of a single, more generic script. Using the Performance MMC or the Reliability and Performance Monitor, you can submit one or more of the following as command-line arguments to a script that's been fired in response to an alert:

- Date/time

- The value that was measured by the alert
- The name of the alert
- The name of the counter being measured
- The value of the limit that was exceeded
- A manually defined text string

You can also use a number of third-party tools to implement this solution, such as the open source Blat (*http://www.blat.net*) SourceForge project, which allows you to send SMTP or NNTP messages from a command line.

Using VBScript

The script example in this recipe assumes that the computer that's running the script is itself running the SMTP service. To send a message using a remote SMTP server, you'll need to specify the following additional information before sending the message:

```
objMessage.Configuration.Fields.Item _
("http://schemas.microsoft.com/cdo/configuration/sendusing") = 2

'Name or IP of the remote SMTP Server
objMessage.Configuration.Fields.Item _
("http://schemas.microsoft.com/cdo/configuration/smtpserver") = "smtp.myserver.com"

'Port being used by the SMTP server (port 25 by default)
objMessage.Configuration.Fields.Item _
("http://schemas.microsoft.com/cdo/configuration/smtpserverport") = 25

objMessage.Configuration.Fields.Update
```

See Also

MS KB 280391 (How to Send Digitally Signed Messages by Using CDOSYS/CDOEX) and MS KB 248698 (How to Send Mail from an Active Server Page by Using CDOEX with Exchange 2000 Server or Exchange Server 2003)

15.15 Enabling Auditing of Directory Access

Problem

You want to enable auditing of directory access and modifications. Audit events are logged to the Security event log.

Solution

Using a graphical user interface

1. Open the Domain Controller Security Policy snap-in.

2. In the left pane, expand Local Policies and click on Audit Policy.

3. In the right pane, double-click "Audit directory service access."

4. Make sure the box is checked beside "Define these policy settings."

5. Check the box beside Success and/or Failure.

6. Click OK.

Using a command-line interface

```
> auditpol \\<DomainControllerName> /enable /directory:all
```

Discussion

You can log events to the Security event log for every successful and/or failed attempt to access or modify the directory, which is referred to as *auditing*. Auditing is enabled via the Security Settings section of a GPO that's linked to the Domain Controllers OU, using the "Audit directory service access" setting. Once this is enabled, you need to use the ACL Editor to define auditing in the SACL of the objects and containers you want to monitor.

By default, the domain object has an inherited audit entry for the *Everyone* security principal for all object access and modifications. That means once you enable auditing in the Domain Controller Security Policy and this configuration change replicates out, domain controllers will log events for any directory access or modification to any part of the directory. As you can imagine, auditing every access to Active Directory can generate a lot of events, so you'll either want to disable auditing of the *Everyone* group and apply more specific auditing instead, or else keep a close eye on your domain controllers to ensure that they are not adversely affected while auditing is enabled.

Here is a sample event that was logged after the *Administrator* account created a contact object called foobar in the Sales OU:

```
Event Type:        Success Audit
Event Source:      Security
Event Category:    Directory Service Access
Event ID:          566
Date:              5/26/2007
Time:              7:24:10 PM
User:              ADATUM\administrator
Computer:          DC1
Description:
Object Operation:
        Object Server:      DS
        Operation Type:     Object Access
        Object Type:        organizationalUnit
        Object Name:        OU=Sales,DC=adatum,DC=com
        Handle ID:          -
        Primary User Name:  DC1$
        Primary Domain:     ADATUM
        Primary Logon ID:   (0x0,0x3E7)
        Client User Name:   administrator
```

```
Client Domain:       ADATUM
Client Logon ID:     (0x0,0x3B4BE)
Accesses:            Create Child

 Properties:
Create Child
contact

Additional Info:     CN=foobar,OU=Sales,DC=adatum,DC=com
Additional Info2:    CN=foobar,OU=Sales,DC=adatum,DC=com
Access Mask:         0x1
```

 It can also be useful to enable Audit Account Management in the GPO that's linked to the Domain Controllers OU. This provides additional information about account-management operations—for example, finding what account deleted a certain object.

Windows Server 2008 also enables additional auditing functionality of Directory Services events, including capturing "before" and "after" values on changes and deletions to Active Directory objects. You can enable this functionality with the *auditpol.exe* tool discussed earlier, using syntax similar to the following:

```
auditpol /set /subcategory:"directory service changes"
```

Once you have enabled auditing of Directory Service Changes and configured auditing on the relevant objects or containers, the Directory Services Event Viewer will record detailed entries whenever an AD object is created, modified, moved, or deleted, as follows:

- Event 5136 will be logged when an object is modified. In the case of a modify event, you will see two discrete 5136 entries: one containing the deletion of the old value (for example, the old description attribute), and a second containing the addition of the new value (for example, the new description attribute).
- Event 5137 will be logged when an object is created.
- Event 5138 will be logged when an object is undeleted.
- Event 5139 will be logged when an object is moved, indicating both the old DN and the new DN
- Event 5141 will be logged when an object is deleted.

See Also

MS KB 232714 (How to Enable Auditing of Directory Service Access), MS KB 314955 (How to Audit Active Directory Objects in Windows 2000), MS KB 314977 (How to Enable Active Directory Access Auditing in Windows 2000), and MS KB 814595 (How to Audit Active Directory Objects in Windows Server 2003)

15.16 Enabling Auditing of Registry Keys

Problem

You want to enable auditing of any changes to one or more Registry keys.

Using a graphical user interface

To enable auditing of a Registry key on an individual domain controller, do the following:

1. Create a Group Policy Object (or enable an existing GPO) that enables the following settings under Computer Configuration→Window Settings→Security Settings→Local Policies→Audit Policy:
   - Audit object access: Success
   - Audit object access: Failure
2. Link the GPO to the container containing the DC you wish to audit.
3. On the DC you want to audit, open *regedit.exe* from the command line or from Start→Run.
4. Navigate to the Registry key that you want to enable auditing on.
5. Right-click on the key and select Permissions. Click Advanced and select the Auditing tab.
6. Click Add to select a user or group to audit, then click OK. For Apply Onto, select "This key only," "This key and subkeys," or "Subkeys only."
7. Under Access, select the actions that should be audited, and click OK.

If you need to enable auditing of the same Registry keys on multiple computers, a much more efficient solution would be to use a GPO as follows:

1. Create a Group Policy Object (or modify an existing GPO) that enables the following settings under Computer Configuration → Window Settings → Security Settings → Local Policies → Audit Policy:
   - Audit object access: Success
   - Audit object access: Failure
2. Navigate to Computer Configuration→Windows Settings→Security Settings→Registry.
3. Right-click on Registry and select "Add key." On the "Select Registry key" screen, navigate to the key that you want to audit and click OK.
4. Right-click on the key and select Permissions. Click Advanced and select the Auditing tab.
5. Click Add to select a user or group to audit, then click OK. For Apply Onto, select "This key only," "This key and subkeys," or "Subkeys only."

---

6. Under Access, select the actions that should be audited, and click OK.

7. Link the GPO to the container containing the DC you wish to audit.

Discussion

Before you can enable auditing on specific Registry keys, you must create an audit policy that enables auditing of object access events, both Success and Failure events. You can enable auditing by modifying an existing Group Policy Object or by creating a brand-new GPO that you've created expressly for this purpose. Maintaining a number of single-purpose GPOs can make for easier Group Policy troubleshooting, but can lead to performance implications if clients need to process too many GPOs at logon and during the background refresh of Group Policy. As is usually the case, the definition of "too many" will vary from one environment to the next; it's important to monitor the performance of your clients to determine which approach is appropriate for your network. Once you've enabled auditing of a specific key or keys, information about the activity that you've chosen to audit will appear in the Security event log of the computer where the event took place.

See Also

Recipe 9.6 for more on modifying the settings of a Group Policy Object, MS KB 810088 (CPU Usage May Be High After You Turn On Auditing for HKEY_LOCAL_ MACHINE\System), and MS KB 841001 (Event IDs 560 and 562 appear many times in the security event log)

15.17 Creating a Quota

 This recipe requires a Windows Server 2003 or newer domain controller.

Problem

You want to limit the number of objects a security principal can create in a partition by creating a quota.

Solution

Using a command-line interface

```
> dsadd
quota -part <PartitionDN> -qlimit <QuotaLimit> -acct <PrincipalName>
[-rdn <QuotaName>]
```

The following command creates a quota specification that allows the *ADATUM\rallen* user to create only five objects in the dc=adatum,dc=com partition:

```
> dsadd quota -part dc=adatum,dc=com -qlimit 5 -acct ADATUM\rallen
```

Discussion

Quotas were introduced in Windows Server 2003; they allow an administrator to limit the number of objects that a user (or group of users) can create. This is similar in nature to the quota for creating computer objects found in Windows 2000 (see Recipe 8.14 for more details), except that the quotas in Windows Server 2003 apply to the creation of all object types.

There are three things that need to be set when creating a quota specification, including:

Partition
> Currently, quotas can apply only to an entire partition. You cannot create a quota that pertains only to a subtree in a partition. You can create quotas for any partition, including application partitions, except for the schema naming context. The reasoning behind this restriction is that the schema is a highly protected area of the directory, and you shouldn't need to restrict how many objects get created there.

Target security principal
> A quota can be defined for any type of security principal. The msDS-QuotaTrustee attribute on the quota object stores the target principal in the form of an SID.

Limit
> This determines how many objects the target security principal can create.

The quota limit is a combination of the new objects that a user creates plus any tombstone objects that are created by that user. If a user creates an object and then deletes another object, that would still count as two objects toward any quotas that apply to the user. This is because when an object is deleted, it isn't removed; it is simply marked as tombstoned. Once the tombstone object is removed from Active Directory, which happens after 60 days by default (or 180 in an AD forest created on a 2003 Service Pack 1 server), the user's quota will be decremented accordingly. By default, a tombstone object counts as one object, but that is configurable. See Recipe 15.19 for more on changing the tombstone quota factor.

Since quotas can be assigned to both users and groups, it is conceivable that multiple quotas may apply to a user. In this case, the quota with the highest limit will be in force for the user. You can also create a default quota for a partition that applies to all security principals. See Recipe 15.20 for more information on configuring the default quota.

 Quotas do not apply to members of the *Enterprise Admins* and *Domain Admins* groups. Even if you've configured a default quota for all users, members of those administrative groups will not have any restrictions.

See Also

Recipe 8.14 for more on the computer object quota, Recipe 15.0 for more on the attributes of quota objects, Recipe 15.18 for finding the quotas assigned to a security principal, Recipe 15.19 for changing the tombstone quota factor, and Recipe 15.20 for setting a default quota

15.18 Finding the Quotas Assigned to a Security Principal

 This recipe requires a Windows Server 2003 or newer domain controller.

Problem

You want to find the quotas that have been configured for a security principal (i.e., user, group, or computer).

Solution

Using a command-line interface

```
> dsquery quota <PartitionDN> -acct <PrincipalName>
```

The following command searches for quotas that have been assigned to the *ADATUM \rallen* user in the dc=adatum,dc=com partition:

```
> dsquery quota dc=adatum,dc=com -acct ADATUM\rallen
```

Discussion

The DSQuery solution will find only quotas that have been directly assigned to a security principal; it will not list quotas that have been assigned to any group objects that the principal may be a member of. The msDS-QuotaTrustee attribute on quota objects defines a SID that the quota applies to. The dsquery quota command will look up the SID for the specified account and match that against quota objects that reference that SID. Unfortunately, this doesn't quite show the whole picture. A user could have a quota assigned directly, which the DSQuery command would show, but the user could also be part of one or more groups that have quotas assigned. These won't show up using DSQuery.

A more robust solution would entail retrieving the tokenGroups attribute of the user, which contains a list of SIDs for all expanded group memberships, and then querying each of those groups to determine whether any of them have quotas assigned. This is actually the type of algorithm that is used to determine a user's effective quota, as shown in Recipe 15.21.

See Also

Recipe 15.17 for creating a quota and Recipe 15.21

15.19 Changing How Tombstone Objects Count Against Quota Usage

 This recipe requires a Windows Server 2003 or newer domain controller.

Problem

You want to change the relative weight of tombstone objects in quota calculations.

Solution

Using a graphical user interface

1. Open ADSI Edit.
2. Connect to the partition on which you want to modify this setting (this setting must be changed for each partition that you want to configure).
3. In the left pane, expand the root of the partition.
4. Right-click on cn=NTDS Quotas and select Properties.
5. Set the msDS-TombstoneQuotaFactor attribute to a value between 0 and 100.
6. Click OK.

Using a command-line interface

Create an LDIF file called *change_ tombstone_quota.ldf* with the following contents:

```
dn: cn=NTDS Quotas,<PartitionDN>
changetype: modify
replace:
msDs-TombstoneQuotaFactor
msDs-
TombstoneQuotaFactor: <0-100>
-
```

Then run the following command:

```
> ldifde -v -i -f
change_tombstone_quota.ldf
```

You can also make the change using DSMod or AdMod. DSMod takes the following syntax:

```
> dsmod partition <PartitionDN> -qtmbstawt <0-100>
```

You can make the change with AdMod, as follows:

```
> admod -b <PartitionDN> msDs-TombstoneQuotaFactor::<0-100>
```

Using VBScript

```
' This code modifies the
' tombstone quota factor for the specified partition.
' ------ SCRIPT CONFIGURATION ------
strPartitionDN = "<PartitionDN>" ' e.g. dc=adatum,dc=com
intTombstoneFactor = <0-100>      ' e.g. 50
' ------ END CONFIGURATION ---------

set objPart = GetObject("LDAP://cn=NTDS Quotas," & strPartitionDN )
objPart.Put "msDs-TombstoneQuotaFactor", intTombstoneLifetime
objPart.SetInfo
WScript.Echo "Set the tombstone quota factor for " & _
             strPartitionDN & " to " & intTombstoneFactor
```

Using PowerShell

You can modify the tombstone quota factor using the Quest AD cmdlets or else using native PowerShell commands, as follows:

```
Set-QADObject -Identity <PartitionDN> -ObjectAttributes @{msDs-
TombstoneQuotaFactor='<QuotaValue>'}

$obj = [ADSI] "LDAP://<PartitionDN>"
$obj.Put("msDS-TombstoneQuotaFactor", "<QuotaValue>")
$obj.SetInfo()
```

Discussion

The tombstone quota factor is a percentage that determines how much each tombstone object counts against a security principal's quota usage. By default, tombstone objects count as one object. This means if a user's quota is set to 10 and the user deletes 10 objects, that user will not be able to create or delete any other objects until those tombstone objects have been purged from Active Directory.

The msDs-TombstoneQuotaFactor attribute on the NTDS Quota container for each partition defines the tombstone quota factor. As mentioned previously, the default is that tombstone objects count 100 percent of a normal object; thus, the attribute msDs-TombstoneQuotaFactor contains 100 by default. If you modify this attribute to contain a value of 50 and a user has a quota limit of 10, then that user could delete a maximum of 20 objects (i.e., create 20 tombstone objects) because 20 × 50 percent =

10. As another example, you may not care about how many objects your users delete; in this case, you'd want to set the tombstone quota factor to 0 so that tombstoned objects would not count against a user's NTDS Quota at all.

See Also

MSDN: ms-DS-Tombstone-Quota-Factor attribute [AD Schema] and MSDN: ms-DS-Quota-Container class [AD Schema]

15.20 Setting the Default Quota for All Security Principals in a Partition

 This recipe requires a Windows Server 2003 or newer domain controller.

Problem

You want to set a default quota for all security principals.

Solution

Using a graphical user interface

1. Open ADSI Edit.
2. Connect to the partition you want to modify (this setting must be changed for each partition that you want to configure).
3. In the left pane, expand the root of the partition.
4. Right-click on cn=NTDS Quotas and select Properties.
5. Set the msDS-DefaultQuota attribute to the number of objects that security principals should be allowed to create if they are not assigned another quota.
6. Click OK.

Using a command-line interface

Create an LDIF file called *set_default_quota.ldf* with the following contents:

```
dn: cn=NTDS Quotas,<NTDS Quotas DN>
changetype: modify
replace: msDs-
DefaultQuota
msDs-
```

```
DefaultQuota: <NumberOfObjects>
-
```

Then run the following command:

```
> ldifde -v -i -f set_default_quota.ldf
```

You can also make the change using DSMod or AdMod. DSMod takes the following syntax:

```
> dsmod partition <NTDS Quotas DN> -qdefault <DefaultQuota>
```

You can make the change with AdMod, as follows:

```
> admod -b <NTDS Quotas DN>
msDs-DefaultQuota::<DefaultQuota>
```

Using VBScript

```
' This code sets the
' default quota for the specified partition.
' ------ SCRIPT CONFIGURATION ------
strPartitionDN = "<PartitionDN>"          ' e.g. dc=adatum,dc=com
intDefaultQuota = <NumberOfObjects>       ' e.g. 10
' ------ END CONFIGURATION ---------

set objPart = GetObject("LDAP://cn=NTDS Quotas," & strPartitionDN )
objPart.Put "msDs-DefaultQuota", intDefaultQuota
objPart.SetInfo
WScript.Echo "Set the default quota for " & _
             strPartitionDN & " to " & intDefaultQuota
```

Using PowerShell

You can modify the tombstone quota factor using the Quest AD cmdlets or else using native PowerShell commands, as follows:

```
set-QADObject -Identity "cn=NTDS Quotas,<PartitionDN>"
-ObjectAttributes @{msDs-DefaultQuota='QuotaValue'}

$obj = [ADSI] "LDAP://cn=NTDS Quotas,<PartitionDN>"
$obj.Put("msDS-DefaultQuota", "<QuotaValue>")
$obj.SetInfo()
```

Discussion

The easiest way to apply a default quota to all of your users is to modify the msDS-DefaultQuota attribute on the NTDS Quotas container for the target partition. This attribute contains the default quota limit that is used if no other quotas have been assigned to a security principal. A value of -1 means that no quota exists; security principals can create and/or tombstone as many objects as they wish.

You should be careful when setting the default quota because it applies to every non-administrator security principal. If you set the default to 0, for example, computers would not be able to dynamically update their DNS records in an AD-integrated zone because that creates an object. This may not be applicable in your environment, but the point is that you need to consider the impact of the default quota and test it thoroughly before implementing it.

15.21 Finding the Quota Usage for a Security Principal

 This recipe requires a Windows Server 2003 or newer domain controller.

Problem

You want to find the quota usage for a certain security principal.

Solution

The quota usage of a security principal can be determined a few different ways. First, you can use DSGet. Here is an example:

```
> dsget user "<UserDN>" -part <PartitionDN> -qlimit -qused
```

This displays the effective quota limit and how much of the quota has been used for a particular user. You can use similar parameters with `dsget computer` and `dsget group` to find the quota usage for those types of objects.

Users can find their own quota usage by querying the `msDs-QuotaUsed` and `msDs-QuotaEffective` attributes on the `cn=NTDS Quotas` container for a partition. These two attributes are constructed, which means they are dynamically calculated based on the user that is accessing them (see Recipe 10.16 for more on constructed attributes). The `msDs-QuotaUsed` attribute returns how much of the quota has been used by the user, and the `msDs-QuotaEffective` attribute contains the quota limit.

Alternatively, view the `msDs-TopQuotaUsage` attribute on a partition's `cn=NTDS Quotas` container, which contains the users with the top quota usage. This attribute is multi-valued, with each value being XML-like text that contains the SID and how much of the quota the principal has used. See the "Discussion" section for an example.

Discussion

If you implement quotas, you'll certainly need to tell users what their quotas are (or provide instructions on how they can find out for themselves). Currently, there are a few ways to determine quota usage, as outlined in the "Solution" section.

Perhaps the most interesting is obtaining the top-quota usage. Each value of the `msDs-TopQuotaUsage` attribute contains an entry that details the top quota users in the database, listed in decreasing order of quota usage. Each value of the `msDs-TopQuotaUsage`

---

attribute contains blocks of data formatted in an XML-like language. Each block has the SID of the security principal (`<ownerSID>`), quota used (`<quotaUsed>`), number of tombstone objects created (`<tombstonedCount>`), and the number of objects that are still active (`<liveCount>`) (i.e., not tombstoned). Here is an example of what the attribute can contain:

```
>> Dn: CN=NTDS Quotas,DC=adatum,DC=com
      3> msDS-TopQuotaUsage:
<MS_DS_TOP_QUOTA_USAGE>
        <partitionDN> DC=adatum,DC=com </partitionDN>
        <ownerSID> S-1-5-21-1422208173-2062366415-1864960452-512 </ownerSID>
        <quotaUsed> 152 </quotaUsed>
        <tombstonedCount> 2 </tombstonedCount>
        <liveCount> 150 </liveCount>
</MS_DS_TOP_QUOTA_USAGE>
;
<MS_DS_TOP_QUOTA_USAGE>
        <partitionDN> DC=adatum,DC=com </partitionDN>
        <ownerSID> S-1-5-18 </ownerSID>
        <quotaUsed> 43 </quotaUsed>
        <tombstonedCount> 32 </tombstonedCount>
        <liveCount> 11 </liveCount>
</MS_DS_TOP_QUOTA_USAGE>
;
<MS_DS_TOP_QUOTA_USAGE>
        <partitionDN> DC=adatum,DC=com </partitionDN>
        <ownerSID> S-1-5-32-544 </ownerSID>
        <quotaUsed> 14 </quotaUsed>
        <tombstonedCount> 0 </tombstonedCount>
        <liveCount> 14 </liveCount>
</MS_DS_TOP_QUOTA_USAGE>
```

Additionally, AdFind has switches that can decode this output in a much friendlier format as follows:

```
adfind -b "cn=ntds quotas, <PartitionDN>" msDs-TopQuotaUsage;binary -resolvesids
```

This command will return results similar to the following:

```
cn=NTDS Quotas,dc=adatum,dc=com
> msDs-TopQuotaUsage;binary: NC: dc=adatum,dc=com Owner: ADATUM\Domain Admins
Used:175 Tombstone: 0 LiveCount: 175
cn=NTDS Quotas,dc=adatum,dc=com
> msDs-TopQuotaUsage;binary: NC: dc=adatum,dc=com Owner: NT AUTHORITY\SYSTEM Used:
62 Tombstone: 29 LiveCount: 33
> msDs-TopQuotaUsage;binary: NC dc=adatum,dc=com Owner: BUILTIN\Administrators
Used: 14 Tombstone: 0 LiveCount: 14
```

See Also

Recipe 15.18 for more on finding the quotas that are assigned to a security principal

## CHAPTER 16

Backup, Recovery, DIT Maintenance, and Deleted Objects

16.0 Introduction

The AD Directory Information Tree (DIT) is implemented as a transactional database using the Extensible Storage Engine (ESE). The primary database file is named *ntds.dit* and is stored in the *%SystemRoot%\NTDS* folder by default, but can be relocated during the initial promotion process or manually via *ntdsutil* (see Recipe 16.12 for more details).

Each database write transaction is initially stored in a logfile called *edb.log*, which is stored in the same directory as *ntds.dit* by default, though you can modify this either during or after the initial **dcpromo** process. That logfile can grow to 10 MB in size, after which additional logfiles are created (e.g., *edb00001.log)*, each of which can also grow to up to 10 MB in size. After the transactions in the logfiles are committed to the database, the logfiles are purged, beginning with the log containing the oldest transactions. (This process is referred to as *circular logging*.) These logfiles are useful when a domain controller is shut down unexpectedly because when the DC comes back online, Active Directory can replay the logfiles and apply any transactions that might not have been written to disk before the DC shut down. The *edb.chk* file stores information about the last transaction that was actually committed to the database; AD uses this information to determine which transactions in the logfiles still need to be committed. Finally, two 10 MB files called *res1.log* and *res2.log* are used as placeholders in case the disk runs out of space; if this happens, these files are deleted to free up enough space to allow Active Directory to commit any final changes before the DC is shut down.

In order to recover portions of Active Directory, or the entire directory itself, you need to have a solid backup strategy in place. You can back up Active Directory while it is online, which means you do not need to worry about scheduling regular downtime simply to perform backups. Restoring Active Directory is also a relatively simple process. To do any type of restore in Windows 2000 and Windows Server 2003, you have to boot into offline mode, more commonly referred to as Directory Services (DS) Restore Mode, in which the Active Directory database is not active. You can then restore a single object, an entire subtree, or the entire database if necessary. For a detailed discussion on backing up and restoring Active Directory, see *Active Directory*, Fourth Edition, by Brian Desmond et al. (O'Reilly).

You also need to be familiar with how deleted objects are treated in Active Directory, which can affect your backup procedures. When an object is requested to be deleted, it is actually marked as a tombstone and moved to the Deleted Object container. This *tombstone object* has most of the original object's attribute values removed to save space in the *NTDS.DIT* file. These objects are stored in the `cn=Deleted Objects` container in the naming context that the original object was located in. The deleted object is named using the following format: `<OrigName>\0ADEL:<ObjectGUID>`, where `<OrigName>` is the original RDN of the object, `<ObjectGUID>` is the GUID of the object, and `\0A` is a null-terminated character. For example, if you deleted the `jsmith` user object, its tombstone object would have a distinguished name similar to the following:

```
CN=jsmith\0ADEL:fce1ca8e-a5ec-4a29-96e1-c8013e533d2c,CN=Deleted
Objects,DC=adatum,DC=com
```

In Windows Server 2008, the Active Directory Domain Service is now restartable, meaning that you can stop the AD DS service to perform some (but not all) maintenance operations without needing to reboot the domain controller into DSRM. Some of the operations you can perform on a 2008 DC while the AD DS service is stopped include:

- Performing an offline defragmentation
- Moving the AD database files
- Performing a nonauthoritative restore. However, performing an authoritative restore still requires a full reboot into DSRM.

You can stop the Active Directory Domain Services service using familiar interfaces such as the Services MMC snap-in, Server Manager, the `net stop` command-line utility, or the `Stop-Service` PowerShell cmdlet. Be aware that when you stop the Active Directory Domain Services service, one or more of the following dependent services will be stopped as well; you will need to take this into consideration when restarting the AD DS service so that all associated services are also restarted:

- File Replication
- Kerberos Key Distribution Center
- Intersite Messaging
- DNS Server (on DCs that are running the DNS Server service)

- DFS Replication

After a period of time known as the *tombstone lifetime* (60 days is the default for Windows Server 2003 and Windows Server 2003 R2 forests), the tombstone object is finally removed from Active Directory. At that point, no remnants of the former object exist in Active Directory.

> The default tombstone lifetime changed with Windows Server 2003 Service Pack 1, Windows Server 2003 Service Pack 2, and Windows Server 2008 and beyond. A 2003 RTM or 2003 R2 forest that has been upgraded to a subsequent service pack or operating system will retain the original 60-day tombstone lifetime; however, a forest created from scratch with SP1, SP2, or Windows Server 2008 will have a default tombstone lifetime of 180 days.

Tombstone objects are important to understand with regard to your backup strategy because you should not keep backups longer than the tombstone lifetime. If you attempt to restore a backup that is older than the tombstone lifetime, it may introduce objects that were deleted, but for which a tombstone object no longer exists. Under normal conditions, if you do a nonauthoritative restore from backup, objects that were valid when the backup was taken but that were subsequently deleted will be deleted during the first replication cycle after the DC is rebooted normally. If the tombstone object has already expired (e.g., the backup is older than 60 days), Active Directory has no way to determine if the object was previously deleted and will happily readd it outright. Re-injected deleted objects are referred to as *lingering* or *zombie objects*.

The tombstone lifetime value is stored in the `tombstoneLifetime` attribute on the following object: `cn=Directory Service,cn=Windows NT,cn=Services,cn=Configuration,` `<ForestRootDN>`.

The Anatomy of a Deleted Object

Deleted objects are generally stored in the `Deleted Objects` container of a naming context. You cannot browse that container by default. You need to enable an LDAP control, as explained in Recipe 16.22, to view deleted objects. Table 16-1 contains some of the attributes that are stored with deleted objects.

> The attributes that are preserved in tombstone objects are determined by `attributeSchema` objects that have bit 3 enabled (8 in decimal) in the `searchFlags` attribute.

Table 16-1. *Useful attributes of deleted objects*

Attribute	Description
isDeleted	The value for this attribute is TRUE for deleted objects.
lastKnownParent	Distinguished name of container the object was contained in. This was introduced in Windows Server 2003.
Name	RDN of the object's current location.
userAccountControl	This attribute is retained when the original object is deleted. This applies only to `user` and `computer` objects.
objectSID	This attribute is retained when the original object is deleted. This applies only to `user` and `computer` objects.
sAMAccountName	This attribute is retained when the original object is deleted. This applies only to `user` and `computer` objects.
sidHistory	Beginning with Windows Server 2003 Service Pack 1, the `sidHistory` attribute is now included in this list of attributes that are retained with tombstoned objects.

To aid in Active Directory backup and recovery, Windows Server 2008 introduces a new *snapshot* feature that allows you to take point-in-time snapshots of the Active Directory database, and then mount those snapshots to view the contents and compare them to the current contents of the AD database. Using scripts or third-party tools, you can even copy information from an Active Directory snapshot directly into the live AD database without needing to reboot the domain controller to perform a traditional restore operation.

16.1 Backing Up Active Directory in Windows 2000 and Windows Server 2003

Problem

You want to back up Active Directory to tape or disk in Windows 2000 or Windows Server 2003.

Solution

Back up the System State, which includes, among other things, the Active Directory-related files on the domain controller. Here are the directions for backing up the System State using the NTBackup utility that comes installed on Windows 2000 and Windows Server 2003 computers.

Using a graphical user interface

1. Go to Start→All Programs (or Programs for Windows 2000)→Accessories→System Tools→Backup.
2. Click the Advanced Mode link.

3. Click the Backup tab.

4. Check the box beside System State.

5. Check the box beside any other files, directories, or drives you would also like to back up.

6. For "Backup destination," select either File or Tape, depending on where you want to back up the data to.

7. For "Backup media or file name," type either the name of a file or select the tape to save the backup to.

8. Click the Start Backup button twice.

Using a command-line interface

The NTBackup utility supports several command-line parameters that you can use to initiate backups without ever bringing up the GUI.

For the complete list of supported commands on Windows 2000, see MS KB 300439 (How to Use Command Line Parameters With the "NTbackup" Command).

For the complete list of supported commands on Windows Server 2003, see MS KB 814583 (How to Use Command-Line Parameters with the NTbackup Command in Windows Server 2003).

Discussion

Fortunately, domain controllers can be backed up while online. Having the ability to perform online backups makes the process very easy. And since Active Directory is included as part of the System State on domain controllers, you are required to back up only the System State, although you can back up other folders and drives as necessary. (As a best practice, it is also a good idea to back up the system drive as well.) On a domain controller, the System State includes the following:

- Boot files
- Registry
- COM+ class registration database
- Active Directory files
- System Volume (SYSVOL)
- Certificates database (if running Certificate Server)

See Also

Recipe 16.25 for modifying the tombstone lifetime, MS KB 216993 (Backup of the Active Directory Has 60-Day Useful Life), MS KB 240363 (How to Use the Backup Program to Back Up and Restore the System State in Windows 2000), MS KB 300439 (How to Use Command-Line Parameters with the "Ntbackup" Command), MS KB

326216 (How to Use the Backup Feature to Back Up and Restore Data in Windows Server 2003), and MS KB 814583 (How to Use Command Line Parameters with the Ntbackup Command in Windows Server 2003)

16.2 Backing Up Active Directory in Windows Server 2008

Problem

You want to back up the Active Directory database in Windows Server 2008.

Solution

 This recipe applies to Windows Server 2008 domain controllers only.

Using a command-line interface

```
> wbadmin start systemstatebackup –backuptarget:<BackupTarget>
```

Discussion

New to Windows Server 2008, the wbadmin command is used to create a System State Backup of the Active Directory Database. The steps in this recipe assume that you have installed the Windows Server Backup feature in Windows Server 2008. To install the Windows Server Backup command-line tools, you will also need to install Windows PowerShell.

See Also

Recipe 16.3 for information on creating Active Directory snapshots and Recipe 16.4 for more on mounting and using snapshots

16.3 Creating an Active Directory Snapshot

Problem

You want to create a snapshot of the Active Directory database.

Solution

 This recipe applies to Windows Server 2008 domain controllers only.

Using a command-line interface

```
> ntdsutil
> ntdsutil: activate instance ntds
> ntdsutil: snapshot
> snapshot: create
```

Discussion

New to Windows Server 2008, the Active Directory Domain Services snapshot feature leverages the Volume Shadow Copy Service (VSS) to allow administrators to create "shadow copies" of the Active Directory database from previous points in time. Once a snapshot has been created, you can use the *ntdsutil* and *dsamain* command-line utilities to mount the snapshot as a read-only copy of the Active Directory database. Once the snapshot is mounted, you can view it using customary tools such as ADSI Edit and LDP, as well as using third-party tools to copy information from a snapshot into the live Active Directory Database.

See Also

Recipe 16.4 for more on mounting and using snapshots

16.4 Mounting an Active Directory Snapshot

Problem

You want to mount a snapshot of the Active Directory database that you created previously using either *ntdsutil* or a System State backup.

Solution

 This recipe applies to Windows Server 2008 domain controllers only.

Using a command-line interface

If you want to view a snapshot in *ntdsutil*, you must first mount the snapshot within *ntdsutil* as follows:

```
> ntdsutil
> ntdsutil: activate instance ntds
> ntdsutil: snapshot
> snapshot: list all
```

The `list all` command generates a list of snapshots that have been created on the domain controller in question, each with a corresponding number. You will then issue the `mount<Number>` command to mount the snapshot that you want. Once the snapshot is mounted, *ntdsutil* will list the physical path that the database has been mounted to, such as *C:\$SNAP_200808011002_VOLUMEC$*.

Once you have mounted the snapshot you want, you'll use the *dsamain* command to expose the snapshot as an LDAP server. When using *dsamain*, you will need to provide an alternate LDAP port since 389 is in use by the live AD database. You can also specify an alternate LDAPS port, Global Catalog port, and secure Global Catalog port. Use the *dsamain* tool as follows:

```
> dsamain /dbpath <Path to database file> /ldapport <Port #>
```

The mounted snapshot will be exposed as an LDAP server as long as the command window remains open. Use Ctrl-C to "switch off" the snapshot functionality.

Discussion

The *dsamain* utility can be used to expose an Active Directory snapshot that has been created using *ntdsutil*, or it can use the contents of a System State backup that has been restored to an alternate location on the local hard drive. (Network or UNC paths are not supported.) Once a snapshot or restored backup is exposed using *dsamain*, it can be accessed in a read-only manner using Active Directory tools such as LDP or ADSI Edit, as well as scripts and PowerShell.

See Also

Recipe 16.3 for more on creating snapshots and Recipe 16.5 for more on accessing and manipulating information contained in a snapshot

16.5 Accessing Active Directory Snapshot Data

Problem

You want to access data contained within a snapshot of the Active Directory database that you created previously using either *ntdsutil* or a System State backup.

Solution

 This recipe applies to Windows Server 2008 domain controllers only.

Using VBScript

```
' The following code will extract a user's description field
' from an AD snapshot, and then inserts it into the "live"
' copy of Active Directory
'--------------- SCRIPT CONFIGURATION ----------------
strComputerName = "<ComputerName>" ' Use "localhost" for the local DC
strPort = "<PortNumber>"            ' the snapshot port number to connect to
strObjDN = "<ObjectDN>"             ' the DN of the object to connect to
'-----------------------------------------------------

Set objSnapshot = GetObject("LDAP://" & strComputerName & _
                            ":" & strPort & "/" & strObjDN)
Set objLive = GetObject("LDAP://" & strObjDN)

strSnapshotDesc = objSnapshot.description
objLive.put("description", strSnapshotDesc)
ObjLive.SetInfo()
```

Using PowerShell

```
$objSnapshot = [ADSI] "LDAP://<DC Name>:<PortNumber>/<ObjectDN>"
$objLive = [ADSI] "LDAP://<ObjectDN>"
$strDesc = $objSnapshot.Description
$objLive.Put("description", $strDesc)
$objLive.SetInfo()
```

Discussion

An Active Directory snapshot provides a read-only view of the Active Directory database as it existed at a particular point in time, whether the snapshot was created using *ntdsutil* or whether you are using *dsamain* to mount the *ntds.dit* contained in a System State backup. While the current release of Windows Server 2008 does not provide a simple "cut-and-paste" GUI interface to insert values from a snapshot into the live Active Directory database, you can do so using scripting, PowerShell, or a third-party tool. You can also view the contents of a snapshot using tools such as LDP or ADSI Edit by simply indicating the alternate LDAP port number that you specified when you mounted the snapshot.

See Also

Recipe 16.4 for more on mounting and using snapshots

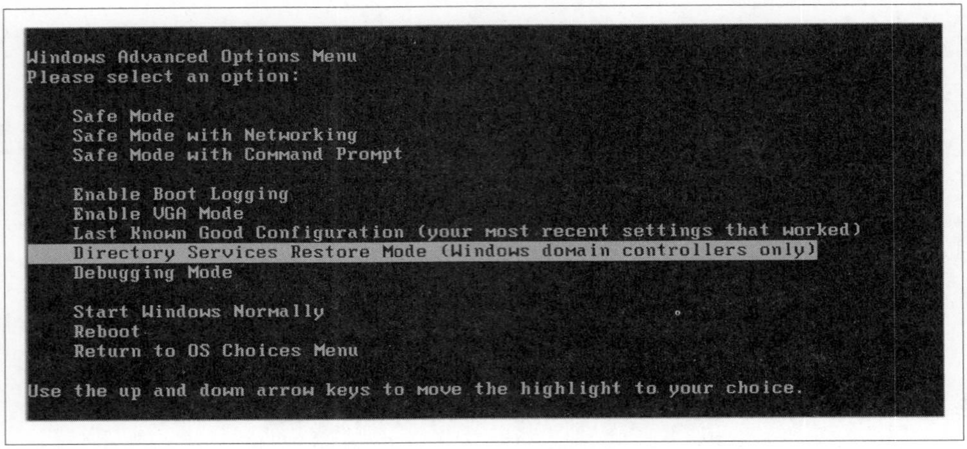

Figure 16-1. Boot options

16.6 Restarting a Domain Controller in Directory Services Restore Mode

Problem

You want to restart a domain controller in DS Restore Mode.

Solution

To enter DS Restore Mode, you must reboot the server at the console. Press F8 after the power-on self test (POST), which will bring up a menu, as shown in Figure 16-1. From the menu, select Directory Services Restore Mode.

In Windows Server 2008, you can also enable DSRM prior to rebooting a server by entering the following command:

```
> bcdedit /set safeboot dsrepair
```

Once you have completed the maintenance on the DC and wish to return to a normal startup mode, enter the following prior to rebooting:

```
> bcdedit /deletevalue safeboot
```

Discussion

The Active Directory database is live and locked by the system whenever a domain controller is booted into normal mode. In Windows 2000 and Windows Server 2003, if you want to perform integrity checks, restore part of the database, or otherwise manipulate the Active Directory database in some way, you have to reboot into DS Restore Mode. In this mode, Active Directory does not start up and the database files (e.g., *ntds.dit*) are not locked. In Windows Server 2008, you have a new Restartable AD DS service that allows you to perform certain maintenance tasks, such as performing an offline defrag, without needing to reboot the domain controller into DSRM. Even in 2008, though, certain critical operations such as an authoritative restore will still need to be performed in Directory Services Restore Mode.

It is not always practical to be logged into the console of the server when you need to reboot it into DS Restore Mode. You can work around this by modifying the *boot.ini* file for a Windows 2000 or Windows Server 2003 server to automatically boot into DS Restore Mode after reboot. You can then use Terminal Services to log on to the machine remotely while it is in that mode. See MS KB 256588 for more information on how to enable this capability. Be careful if you try to access DS Restore Mode via Terminal Services. Unless you have configured everything properly, you may end up with the domain controller booted into DS Restore Mode and not be able to access it via Terminal Services.

See Also

MS KB 256588 (Using Terminal Services for Remote Administration of Windows 2000 DCs in Directory Service Restore Mode)

16.7 Resetting the Directory Service Restore Mode Administrator Password

Problem

You want to reset the DS Restore Mode administrator password. This password is set individually (i.e., not replicated) on each domain controller and is initially configured when you promote the domain controller into a domain.

Solution

Using a graphical user interface

For this to work you must be booted into DS Restore Mode (see Recipe 16.6 for more information):

1. Go to Start→Run.
2. Type compmgmt.msc and press Enter.
3. In the left pane, expand System Tools→Local Users and Computers.
4. Click on the Users folder.
5. In the right pane, right-click on the Administrator user and select Set Password.
6. Enter the new password and confirm, then click OK.

Using a command-line interface

With the Windows Server 2003 and Windows Server 2008 version of *ntdsutil*, you can change the DS Restore Mode administrator password of a domain controller while it is live (i.e., not in DS Restore Mode). Another benefit of this new option is that you can run it against a remote domain controller. Here is the command sequence as used in Windows Server 2003 (in Windows Server 2008, you will need to enter the `activate instance ntds` command prior to the `auth restore` command):

```
> ntdsutil
> set dsrm password
> reset password on server DC1
```

Microsoft added a new utility called *setpwd* in Windows 2000 Service Pack 2 and later to reset the DSRM password in Windows 2000. It works similarly to the Windows Server 2003 and 2008 versions of *ntdsutil* by allowing you to reset the DS Restore Mode password while a domain controller is live. It can also be used remotely.

Discussion

You may be thinking that having a separate DS Restore Mode administrator password can be quite a pain. Yet another thing you have to maintain and update on a regular basis, right? But if you think about it, you'll see that it is quite necessary.

Generally, you boot a domain controller into DS Restore Mode when you need to perform some type of maintenance on the Active Directory database. To do this, the database needs to be offline. But if the database is offline, then there is no way to authenticate against it. Because of this, the system has to use another user repository, so it reverts back to the legacy SAM database. The DS Restore Mode administrator account and password are stored in the SAM database, just as with standalone Windows servers.

The one disadvantage to the solutions presented in this recipe is that you have to reset the DSRM password on one machine at a time. To help automate this process, Directory Services MVP Dean Wells has created a batch script that will change the password on every DC in a forest. The script requires the Windows 2000 *setpwd* utility to be present in the system path on each DC that it's being run on, and can be found here: *http://www.mail-archive.com/activedir@mail.activedir.org/msg29990.html*.

See Also

Recipe 16.6 for booting into Directory Services Restore Mode, MS KB 239803 (How to Change the Recovery Console Administrator Password on a Domain Controller), and MS KB 322672 (How to Reset the Directory Services Restore Mode Administrator Account Password in Windows Server 2003)

16.8 Performing a Nonauthoritative Restore

Problem

You want to perform a nonauthoritative restore of a domain controller. This can be useful if you want to quickly restore a domain controller that failed due to a hardware problem.

Solution

Using a graphical user interface (for Windows 2000 and Windows Server 2003)

1. You must first reboot into Directory Services Restore Mode (see Recipe 16.6 for more information).
2. Open the NT Backup utility; go to Start→All Programs (or "Programs for Windows 2000")→Accessories→System Tools→Backup.
3. Click the Advanced Mode link.
4. Under the Welcome tab, click the Restore Wizard button and click Next.
5. Check the box beside System State and any other drives you want to restore and click Next.
6. Click the Advanced button.
7. Select "Original location" for "Restore files to."
8. For the "How to Restore" option, select "Replace existing files" and click Next.
9. For the Advanced Restore Options, be sure that the following are checked: "Restore Security Settings," "Restore junction points," and "Preserve existing mount volume points." Then click Next.
10. Click Finish.
11. Restart the computer.

Using a command-line interface (for Windows Server 2008)

To perform a system state recovery in Windows Server 2008, you will need to know the date and timestamp of the system state backup that you want to recover from. You can perform a nonauthoritative restore by rebooting the DC into DSRM, or else by stopping the Active Directory Domain Services service; you can stop this service from the Services MMC snap-in, from Server Manager, or by using the net stop command-line utility:

```
> wbadmin start systemstaterecovery -version:<BackupDate>-<BackupTime>
```

Discussion

If you encounter a failed domain controller that you cannot bring back up (e.g., multiple hard disks fail), you have two options for restoring it. One option is to remove the domain controller completely from Active Directory (as outlined in Recipe 3.11) and then repromote it back in. This is known as the *restore from replication* method, because you are essentially bringing up a brand-new domain controller and letting replication restore all the data on the server. On Windows Server 2003 domain controllers, you can also use the Install From Media option described in Recipes 3.5 and 3.6 to expedite this process.

The other option is described in the section called "Solution". You can restore the domain controller from a good backup. This method involves getting into DS Restore Mode (in Windows 2000 and Windows Server 2003), restoring the System State and any necessary system drive(s), and then rebooting. As long as the domain controller comes up clean, it should start participating in Active Directory replication once again and replicate any changes that have occurred since the backup was taken. This method is generally the fastest for restoring a domain controller, particularly if the server is the only DC located in a remote site. This option becomes even quicker in Windows Server 2008, as you can perform a nonauthoritative restore without rebooting into DSRM because of the new "restartable Active Directory" functionality.

For a detailed discussion of the advantages and disadvantages of each option, see *Active Directory*.

See Also

Recipe 16.6 for getting into Directory Services Restore Mode, MS KB 240363 (How to Use the Backup Program to Back Up and Restore the System State in Windows 2000), and MS KB 811944 (Computer Does Not Start After You Use Windows Backup to Restore the System State)

16.9 Performing an Authoritative Restore of an Object or Subtree

Problem

You want to perform an authoritative restore of one or more objects, but not the entire Active Directory database.

Solution

Follow the same steps as Recipe 16.8, except that once the restore has completed, do not restart the computer.

In Windows Server 2008, activate the appropriate database instance by typing `activate instance ntds` and then pressing Enter again before entering the `auth restore` command. To restore a single object, run the following:

```
> ntdsutil
> auth restore
> restore object cn=jsmith,ou=Sales,dc=adatum,dc=com
> q
```

To restore an entire subtree, run the following:

```
> ntdsutil
> auth restore
> restore subtree ou=Sales,dc=adatum,dc=com
> q
```

Restart the computer.

There are some issues related to restoring user, group, computer, and trust objects that you should be aware of. See MS KB 216243 and MS KB 280079 for more information.

Discussion

If an administrator or user accidentally deletes an important object or entire subtree from Active Directory, you can restore it. Fortunately, the process isn't very painful. The key is having a good backup that contains the objects you want to restore. If you don't have a backup with the objects in it, you are, for the most part, out of luck. (See Recipe 16.23 for another option to restore deleted objects in Windows Server 2003.)

To restore one or more objects, you need to follow the same steps as when performing a nonauthoritative restore. The only difference is that after you do the restore, you need to use *ntdsutil* to mark the objects in question as authoritative on the restored domain controller. After you reboot the domain controller, it will then receive information from its replication partners and process updates for any objects that have been changed since the backup that was restored on the machine, except for the objects or subtree that were marked as authoritative. For those objects, Active Directory modifies the restored objects in such a way that they will become authoritative and replicate out to the other domain controllers.

> Performing an authoritative restore of **user** or **group** objects will require additional considerations, as detailed in MS KB 280079. (Authoritative restore of groups can result in inconsistent membership information across domain controllers.)

You can also use *ntdsutil* without first doing a restore in situations where an object has accidentally been deleted, but the change has not yet replicated to all domain controllers. The trick here is that you need to find a domain controller that has not had the deletion replicated yet, and either stop it from replicating or make the object authoritative before it sends its replication updates. Take a look at Recipe 12.5 for more information on controlling inbound and outbound replication on a domain controller.

 Even with the new "restartable Active Directory" functionality in Windows Server 2008, an authoritative restore is a sufficiently sensitive operation that you must still reboot a 2008 domain controller into Directory Services Restore mode before performing the restore.

See Also

Recipe 16.6 for booting into Directory Services Restore Mode, Recipe 16.23 for restoring a deleted object, MS KB 216243 (Authoritative Restore of Active Directory and Impact on Trusts and Computer Accounts), and MS KB 280079 (Authoritative Restore of Groups Can Result in Inconsistent Membership Information Across Domain Controllers)

16.10 Performing a Complete Authoritative Restore

Problem

You want to perform a complete authoritative restore of the Active Directory database because a significant failure has occurred.

Solution

Follow the same steps as in Recipe 16.8, except that after the restore has completed, do not restart the computer.

Run the following command to restore the entire database (in Windows Server 2008, you will need to enter the `activate instance ntds` command prior to the `auth restore` command):

```
> ntdsutil
> auth restore
> restore database
> q
```

Restart the computer.

Discussion

In a production environment, you should never have to perform an authoritative restore of the entire Active Directory database unless you have encountered a drastic situation such as a forest recovery scenario. It is a drastic measure, and you will almost inevitably lose data as a result. Before you even attempt such a restore, you may want to contact Microsoft Support to make sure that all options have been exhausted. However, you should still test the authoritative restore process in a lab environment and make sure that you have the steps properly documented in case you ever do need to use it.

 Even with the new "restartable Active Directory" functionality in Windows Server 2008, an authoritative restore is a sufficiently sensitive operation that you must still reboot a 2008 domain controller into Directory Services Restore mode before performing the restore.

See Also

Recipe 16.6 for getting into Directory Services Restore Mode, MB KB 216243 (Authoritative Restore of Active Directory and Impact on Trusts and Computer Accounts), MS KB 241594 (How to Perform an Authoritative Restore to a Domain Controller in Windows 2000), and MS KB 280079 (Authoritative Restore of Groups Can Result in Inconsistent Membership Information Across Domain Controllers)

16.11 Checking the DIT File's Integrity

Problem

You want to check the integrity and semantics of the DIT file to verify that there is no corruption or bad entries.

Solution

Using a command-line interface

On a Windows 2000 or Windows Server 2003 domain controller, reboot into Directory Services Restore Mode. On a Windows Server 2008 DC, this recipe can be performed while the Active Directory Domain Services service is in the Stopped state; it is not necessary to reboot the DC into DSRM.

 In Windows Server 2008, activate the appropriate database instance by typing `activate instance ntds` and then pressing Enter before running the files and the semantic database analysis commands.

Once the DC is prepared as needed, run the following commands:

```
> ntdsutil
> files
> integrity
> q
> q
> ntdsutil
```

```
> semantic database analysis
> verbose on
> go
```

Discussion

The Active Directory DIT file (*ntds.dit*) is implemented as a transactional database. Microsoft uses the ESE database (also called Jet Blue) for Active Directory, which has been used for years in other products such as Microsoft Exchange.

Since the Active Directory DIT is ultimately a database, it can suffer from many of the same issues as traditional databases. The `ntdsutil integrity` command checks for any low-level database corruption and ensures that the database headers are correct and the tables are in a consistent state. It reads every byte of the database and can take quite a while to complete, depending on how large your DIT file is. The time it takes is also greatly dependent on your hardware, but some early estimates from Microsoft for Windows 2000 put the rate at 2 GB an hour.

Whereas the `ntdsutil integrity` command verifies the overall structure and health of the database files, the `ntdsutil semantics` command looks at the contents of the database. It will verify, among other things, reference counts, replication metadata, and security descriptors. If any errors are reported back, you can run `go fixup` to attempt to correct them. You should have a recent backup handy before doing this and perform this step only as a troubleshooting option, preferably under the direction of a Microsoft PSS engineer, since in the worst case the corruption cannot be fixed or the state of your AD database may even become worse after the `go fixup` command completes.

See Also

Recipe 16.6 for booting into Directory Services Restore Mode and MS KB 315136 (How to Complete a Semantic Database Analysis for the Active Directory Database by Using Ntdsutil.exe)

16.12 Moving the DIT Files

Problem

You want to move the Active Directory DIT files to a new drive to improve performance or capacity.

Solution

Using a command-line interface

On a Windows 2000 or Windows Server 2003 domain controller, reboot into Directory Services Restore Mode. On a Windows Server 2008 DC, this recipe can be performed while the Active Directory Domain Services service is in the Stopped state; it is not necessary to reboot the DC into DSRM.

Once the DC is prepared as needed, run the following commands, in which *<DriveAndFolder>* is the new location where you want to move the files (e.g., *d:\NTDS*):

```
> ntdsutil
> files
> move db to <DriveAndFolder>
> q
> q
> ntdsutil
> files
> move logs to <DriveAndFolder>
> q
> q
```

> In Windows Server 2008, activate the appropriate database instance by typing `activate instance ntds` and then pressing Enter before running the `file` commands.

Discussion

You can move the Active Directory database file (*ntds.dit*) independently of the logfiles. The first command in the solution moves the database, and the second moves the logs. You may also want to consider running an integrity check against the database after you've moved it to ensure that nothing went wrong during the move. See Recipe 16.11 for more details.

See Also

Recipe 16.6 for booting into Directory Services Restore Mode, Recipe 16.11 for checking DIT file integrity, MS KB 257420 (How to Move the Ntds.dit File or logfiles), MS KB 315131 (How to Use Ntdsutil to Manage Active Directory Files from the Command Line in Windows 2000), and MS KB 816120 (How to Use Ntdsutil to Manage Active Directory Files from the Command Line in Windows Server 2003)

16.13 Repairing or Recovering the DIT

Problem

You need to repair or perform a soft recovery of the Active Directory DIT because a power failure or some other failure caused the domain controller to enter an unstable state.

Solution

Using a command-line interface

On a Windows 2000 or Windows Server 2003 domain controller, reboot into Directory Services Restore Mode. On a Windows Server 2008 DC, this recipe can be performed while the Active Directory Domain Services service is in the Stopped state; it is not necessary to reboot the DC into DSRM.

Once the DC is prepared as appropriate, open a command prompt, type `ntdsutil` and press Enter.

Run the following command to perform a soft recovery of the transaction logfiles:

 In Windows Server 2008, activate the appropriate database instance by typing `activate instance ntds` and then pressing Enter again before entering the `files` command.

```
> ntdsutil
> files
> recover
> q
> q
```

If you continue to experience errors, you may need to run a repair, which does a low-level repair of the database but can result in loss of data:

```
> ntdsutil
> files
> repair
> q
> q
```

 The `repair` option from the *ntdsutil* files menu is not available in Windows Server 2008.

If either the recover or repair operations are successful, you should then check the integrity of the AD database (see Recipe 16.11).

Discussion

You should (hopefully) never need to recover or repair your Active Directory database. A recovery may be needed after a domain controller unexpectedly shuts down, perhaps due to a power loss, and certain changes were never committed to the database. When it boots back up, a soft recovery is automatically done in an attempt to reapply any changes that were contained in the transaction logfiles. Since Active Directory does this automatically, it is unlikely that running the `ntdsutil recover` command will be of much help. `ntdsutil repair`, on the other hand, can fix low-level problems, but it can also result in a loss of data, which cannot be predicted. *Use at your own peril!*

We recommend that you use extreme caution when performing a repair and you may wish to engage Microsoft Support first in case something goes wrong. If you try the repair and it makes things worse, you should consider rebuilding the domain controller from scratch. See Recipe 3.11 for forcibly removing a failed domain controller from your domain.

See Also

Recipe 16.6 for booting into Directory Services Restore Mode, Recipe 16.11 for checking the integrity of the DIT, MS KB 315131 (How to Use Ntdsutil to Manage Active Directory Files from the Command Line in Windows 2000), and MS KB 816120 (How to Use Ntdsutil to Manage Active Directory Files from the Command Line in Windows Server 2003)

16.14 Performing an Online Defrag Manually

 This recipe must be run against a Windows Server 2003 or newer domain controller.

Problem

You want to initiate an online defragmentation to optimize the disk space that's being used by the *ntds.dit* file.

Solution

Using a graphical user interface

1. Open LDP from the Windows Support Tools. (LDP is installed natively with Active Directory Domain Services in Windows Server 2008.)
2. From the menu, select Connection→Connect.
3. For Server, enter the name of the target domain controller.
4. For Port, enter 389.
5. Click OK.
6. From the menu, select Connection→Bind.
7. Enter the credentials of a user from one of the administrator groups.
8. Click OK.

9. From the menu, select Browse→Modify.

10. Leave the Dn blank.

11. For Attribute, enter "DoOnlineDefrag".

12. For Values, enter "oy, sor180".

13. For Operation, select Add.

14. Click Enter.

15. Click Run.

Using a command-line interface

Create an LDIF file called *online_defrag.ldf* with the following contents:

```
dn:
changetype: modify
replace:
DoOnlineDefrag
DoOnlineDefrag: 180
-
```

Then run the following command:

```
> ldifde -v -i -f online_defrag.ldf
```

You can also perform an online defrag using AdMod:

```
> admod -b "" doOnlineDefrag::180
```

Using VBScript

```
' This code kicks off an online defrag to run for up to 180 seconds.
' ------ SCRIPT CONFIGURATION ------
strDC = "<DomainControllerName>" ' e.g. dc01
' ------ END CONFIGURATION --------

set objRootDSE = GetObject("LDAP://" & strDC & "/RootDSE")
objRootDSE.Put "DoOnlineDefrag", 180
objRootDSE.SetInfo
WScript.Echo "Successfully initiated an online defrag"
```

Using PowerShell

```
$rootDSE = [ADSI] "LDAP://<DomainControllerName>/RootDSE"
$rootDSE.put("DoOnlineDefrag", "180")
$rootDSE.SetInfo()
```

Discussion

Starting in Windows Server 2003 we were given the ability to initiate an online defragmentation. By default, the online defrag process runs every 12 hours on each domain controller after the garbage collection process completes. This process defrags the

Active Directory database (*ntds.dit*) by combining whitespace generated from deleted objects, but does not reduce the size of the database file.

To start an online defrag, simply write the `DoOnlineDefrag` attribute to the RootDSE with a value equal to the maximum time the defrag process should run (in seconds). You must be a member of one of the administrator groups in the domain controller's domain in order to write to this attribute.

See Also

Recipe 16.18 for performing an offline defrag and MS KB 198793 (The Active Directory Database Garbage Collection Process)

16.15 Performing a Database Recovery

Problem

You want to perform a recovery of the Active Directory database when other methods have failed.

Solution

Using a command-line interface

On a Windows 2000 or Windows Server 2003 domain controller, reboot into Directory Services Restore Mode. On a Windows Server 2008 DC, this recipe can be performed while the Active Directory Domain Services service is in the Stopped state; it is not necessary to reboot the DC into DSRM.

Once the DC is prepared as needed, to perform an integrity check of the Active Directory database, enter the following:

```
> esentutl /g "<PathToNTDS.DIT>"/!10240 /8 /o
```

To perform a recovery of the AD database, enter the following:

```
> esentutl /r "<PathToNTDS.DIT>" /!10240 /8 /o
```

To perform a repair of the database, use the following syntax:

```
> esentutl /p "<PathToNTDS.DIT>" /!10240 /8 /o
```

Discussion

When attempting to recover the *ntds.dit* database, you may occasionally encounter a situation where *ntdsutil* is unable to repair whatever damage has occurred. You may run into error messages similar to the following:

```
Operation failed because the database was inconsistent.
```

```
Initialize jet database failed; cannot access file.

Error while performing soft recovery.
```

Because the AD database is based on the ESE, you also have access to the *esentutl* database utility, which can perform a number of operations against the *ntds.dit* file, including defragmentation, database recovery or repair, and integrity checks. (For a complete description of each operation, type `esentutl /?` at the command line.)

If the *ntdsutil* recovery options listed elsewhere in this chapter fail, you can attempt to repair AD using this ESE utility. Many of the operations that you can perform with *esentutl* have the potential to exacerbate data loss, so be certain that you have a viable backup in place before attempting any of them. In fact, in some cases it may actually be simpler and quicker to simply restore from a known good backup to get your domain or forest back online again.

See Also

MS KB 305500 (Cannot Repair the Active Directory Database by Using the Ntdsutil Tool) and MS KB 280364 (How to Recover from Event ID 1168 and Event ID 1003 Error Messages)

16.16 Creating a Reserve File

Problem

You want to create another reserve file on the disk containing the *ntds.dit* file to guard against AD failures caused by disk space shortages.

Solution

Using a command-line interface

The following command will create an empty reserve file, 250 MB in size, in the same directory as the *ntds.dit* file:

```
> fsutil file createnew <PathToNTDS.DIT>\reservefile 256000000
```

For example, the following will create the reserve file in *c:\windows\ntds*:

```
> fsutil file createnew c:\windows\ntds\reservefile 256000000
```

Discussion

By default, Active Directory creates two files called *res1.log* and *res2.log* in the same directory as the *ntds.dit* database. Each of these files is 10 MB in size and is used to hold in reserve the last 20 MB of space on the drive hosting the AD database files. If a domain controller runs out of space on that drive, Active Directory will use the space being held by *res1.log* and *res2.log* to commit any uncommitted transactions before shutting down so that no information is lost. If you wish to set aside more space than this, you can create a reserve file to set aside additional space; this reserve file can then be manually deleted to free up disk space. This can provide an additional safeguard against a user or administrator inadvertently filling up the drive that's hosting the *ntds.dit* file, or to guard against a virus or a malicious user performing a denial-of-service attack by intentionally filling up the drive.

 To prevent accidental or malicious bloating of the *ntds.dit* file itself, you can also establish quotas to restrict the number of objects that can be created by a user.

See Also

Recipe 15.17 for more on creating Active Directory quotas and Recipe 15.19 for configuring how tombstoned objects affect quotas

16.17 Determining How Much Whitespace Is in the DIT

Problem

You want to find the amount of whitespace in your DIT. A lot of whitespace in the DIT may mean that you could regain enough space on the disk to warrant performing an offline defrag.

Solution

Using a graphical user interface

1. Run *regedit.exe* from the command line or Start→Run.
2. Expand *HKEY_LOCAL_MACHINE\SYSTEM\CurrentControlSet\Services\NTDS \Diagnostics*.
3. In the right pane, double-click on 6 Garbage Collection.
4. For Value data, enter 1.
5. Click OK.

Using a command-line interface

```
> reg add HKLM\System\CurrentControlSet\Services\NTDS\Diagnostics /v "6 Garbage
Collection" /t REG_DWORD /d 1
```

Using VBScript

```
' This code enables logging of DIT
' whitespace information in the event log.
' ------ SCRIPT CONFIGURATION ------
strDCName = "<DomainControllerName>" ' e.g. dc1
' ------ END CONFIGURATION --------

const HKLM = &H80000002
strNTDSReg = "SYSTEM\CurrentControlSet\Services\NTDS\Diagnostics"
set objReg = GetObject("winmgmts:\\" & strDCName & "\root\default:StdRegProv")
objReg.SetDWORDValue HKLM, strNTDSReg, "6 Garbage Collection", 1
WScript.Echo "Garbage Collection logging set to 1"
```

Using PowerShell

```
$strRegPath = "HKLM:\System\CurrentControlSet\Services\NTDS\Parameters"
Set-ItemProperty -path $strRegPath -name "6 Garbage Collection" -value "1"
```

Discussion

By setting the 6 Garbage Collection diagnostics logging option, event 1646 will get generated after the garbage collection process runs. Here is a sample 1646 event:

```
Event Type:          Information
Event Source:        NTDS Database
Event Category:      Garbage Collection
Event ID:            1646
Date:                5/25/2003
Time:                9:52:46 AM
User:                NT AUTHORITY\ANONYMOUS LOGON
Computer:            DC1
Description:
Internal event:      The Active Directory database has the following amount of free
hard disk space remaining.

Free hard disk space (megabytes): 100
Total allocated hard disk space (megabytes): 1024
```

This shows that domain controller Dc1 has a 1 GB DIT file with 100 MB that is free (i.e., whitespace).

See Also

Recipe 16.18 for performing an offline defrag

16.18 Performing an Offline Defrag to Reclaim Space

Problem

You want to perform an offline defrag of the Active Directory DIT to reclaim whitespace in the DIT file.

Solution

Using a command-line interface

On a Windows 2000 or Windows Server 2003 domain controller, reboot into Directory Services Restore Mode. On a Windows Server 2008 DC, this recipe can be performed while the Active Directory Domain Services service is in the Stopped state; it is not necessary to reboot the DC into DSRM.

1. Once the DC is prepared as necessary, check the integrity of the DIT as outlined in Recipe 16.11.

2. Now, you are ready to perform the defrag operation. Run the following command to create a compacted copy of the DIT file. You should check to make sure the drive on which you create the copy has plenty of space. A rule of thumb is that it should have at least 115 percent of the size of the current DIT available:

   ```
   > ntdsutil files "compact to <TempDriveAndFolder>" q q
   ```

3. Next, you need to delete the transaction logfiles in the current NTDS directory:

   ```
   > del <CurrentDriveAndFolder>\*.log
   ```

4. You may want to keep a copy of the original DIT file for a short period of time to ensure that nothing catastrophic happens to the compacted DIT. This does not replace the need for a System State backup and a backup of the domain controller's system drive; it is simply a temporary measure to provide a fallback if the move process itself goes wrong. If you are going to copy or move the original version, be sure you have enough space in its new location:

   ```
   > move <CurrentDriveAndFolder>\ntds.dit <TempDriveAndFolder>\ntds_orig.dit
   > move <TempDriveAndFolder>\ntds.dit <CurrentDriveAndFolder>\ntds.dit
   ```

5. Repeat the steps in Recipe 16.11 to ensure the new DIT is not corrupted. If it is clean, reboot into normal mode and monitor the event log. If no errors are reported in the event log, make sure the domain controller is backed up as soon as possible.

Discussion

Performing an offline defragmentation of your domain controllers can reclaim disk space if you've deleted a large number of objects from Active Directory. You should perform an offline defrag when (and if) this occurs only if you actively require the disk space back—e.g., when following a spin-off in which you've migrated a large number of objects into a separate domain. The database will reuse whitespace and grow organically as required. Typically, the database grows year over year as more objects are added, so an offline defrag should seldom be required. An offline defrag always carries a small element of risk, so it should not be done unnecessarily.

You might want to consider doing an offline defrag after the upgrade from Windows 2000, as a feature called *single instance storage for security descriptors* initially released with Windows Server 2003 can greatly reduce the amount of space your DIT requires.

With this new feature, unique security descriptors are stored once regardless of how many times they are used, whereas in Windows 2000 the same security descriptor would be stored individually on each object that used it.

The key thing to plan ahead of time is your disk space requirements. If you plan on creating the compacted copy of the DIT on the same drive as the current DIT, you need to make sure that drive has 115 percent of the size of the DIT available. If you plan on storing the original DIT on the same drive, you'll need to make sure you have at least that much space available.

See Also

Recipe 16.6 for booting into Directory Services Restore Mode, Recipe 16.11 for checking the integrity of the DIT, MS KB 198793 (The Active Directory Database Garbage Collection Process), MS KB 229602 (Defragmentation of the Active Directory Database), and MS KB 232122 (Performing Offline Defragmentation of the Active Directory Database)

16.19 Changing the Garbage Collection Interval

Problem

You want to change the default garbage collection interval.

Solution

Using a graphical user interface

1. Open ADSI Edit.
2. In the left pane, expand cn=Configuration → cn=Services → cn=Windows NT.
3. Right-click on cn=Directory Service and select Properties.
4. Edit the garbageColPeriod attribute and set it to the interval in hours that the garbage collection process should run (the default is 12 hours).
5. Click OK.

Using a command-line interface

Create an LDIF file called *change_garbage_period.ldf* with the following contents:

```
dn: cn=Directory Service,cn=Windows NT,cn=Services,cn=Configuration,<ForestRootDN>
changetype: modify
replace: garbageCollPeriod
garbageCollPeriod: <IntervalInHours>
-
```

Then run the following command:

```
> ldifde -v -i -f change_garbage_period.ldf
```

You can also modify the garbage collection period using AdMod:

```
> adfind -config -rb "cn=Directory Servce,cn=Windows NT,cn=Services" -s base -dsq |
admod garbageCollPeriod::<IntervalInHours>
```

Using VBScript

```
' This code changes the default garbage-collection interval.
' ------ SCRIPT CONFIGURATION ------
intGarbageColl = <IntervalInHours>
' ------ END CONFIGURATION --------

set objRootDSE = GetObject("LDAP://RootDSE")
set objDSCont = GetObject("LDAP://cn=Directory Service,cn=Windows NT," & _
                "cn=Services," & objRootDSE.Get("configurationNamingContext") )
objDSCont.Put "garbageCollPeriod", intGarbageColl
objDSCont.SetInfo
WScript.Echo "Successfully set the garbage collection interval to " & _
             intGarbageColl
```

Using PowerShell

```
set-QADObject -Identity "cn=Directory Service,cn=Windows
NT,cn=Services,cn=Configuration,<ForestRootDN> -ObjectAttributes
@{garbageCollPeriod=<IntervalInHours>}

$ds = [ADSI] "LDAP:// cn=Directory Service,cn=Windows
NT,cn=Services,cn=Configuration,<ForestRootDN>"
$ds.Put("garbageCollPeriod", "<IntervalInHours>"
$ds.SetInfo()
```

Discussion

When an object is deleted from the Configuration naming context, a Domain naming context, or an application partition, the object is *tombstoned* by renaming the object, moving it to the Deleted Object container, and clearing the value of most of its attributes to save space in the *ntds.dit* file. This tombstone object remains in Active Directory for the duration of the tombstone lifetime (60 days for Windows Server 2003, 180 days for forest installations with 2003 Service Pack 1) before it gets completely removed. See Recipe 16.25 for more information on the tombstone lifetime.

A garbage collection process runs on each domain controller that automatically removes expired tombstone objects. This process runs every 12 hours by default, but you can change it to run more or less frequently by setting the garbageCollPeriod attribute on the following object to the frequency in hours:

```
cn=DirectoryService,cn=WindowsNT,cn=Services,cn=Configuration,<RootDomainDN>
```

See Also

Recipe 16.20 for logging the number of tombstones that get garbage collected, Recipe 16.25 for modifying the tombstone lifetime, and MS KB 198793 (The Active Directory Database Garbage Collection Process)

16.20 Logging the Number of Expired Tombstone Objects

Problem

You want to log the number of expired tombstone objects that are removed from Active Directory during each garbage collection cycle.

Solution

Using a graphical user interface

1. Run *regedit.exe* from the command line or Start→Run.
2. Expand *HKEY_LOCAL_MACHINE\SYSTEM\CurrentControlSet\Services\NTDS \Diagnostics*.
3. In the right pane, double-click on 6 Garbage Collection.
4. For Value data, enter 3.
5. Click OK.

Using a command-line interface

```
> reg add HKLM\System\CurrentControlSet\Services\NTDS\Diagnostics /v "6 Garbage
Collection" /t REG_DWORD /d 3
```

Using VBScript

```
' This code enables garbage-collection logging.
' ------ SCRIPT CONFIGURATION ------
strDCName = "<DomainControllerName>"
intValue = 3
' ------ END CONFIGURATION --------

const HKLM = &H80000002
strNTDSReg = "SYSTEM\CurrentControlSet\Services\NTDS\Diagnostics"
set objReg = GetObject("winmgmts:\\" & strDCName & "\root\default:StdRegProv")
objReg.SetDWORDValue HKLM, strNTDSReg, "6 Garbage Collection," intValue
WScript.Echo "Garbage Collection logging enabled"
```

Using PowerShell

```
$strRegPath = "HKLM:\System\CurrentControlSet\Services\NTDS\Parameters"
Set-ItemProperty -path $strRegPath -name "6 Garbage Collection" -value "3"
```

Discussion

Here is a sample event that is logged when the 6 Garbage Collection diagnostics logging level is set to 3 or higher:

```
Event Type:        Information
Event Source:      NTDS General
Event Category:    Garbage Collection
Event ID:          1006
Date:              6/24/2008
Time:              11:29:31 AM
User:              NT AUTHORITY\ANONYMOUS LOGON
Computer:          DC1
Description:
Internal event: Finished removing deleted objects that have expired (garbage
collection). Number of expired deleted objects that have been removed: 229.
```

See Also

Recipe 15.2 for more on diagnostics logging and Recipe 16.19 for more on the garbage collection process

16.21 Determining the Size of the Active Directory Database

Problem

You want to determine the size of the Active Directory database.

Solution

Using a command-line interface in Windows Server 2003

If you are in DS Restore Mode, you can use *ntdsutil* to report the size of the Active Directory database:

```
> ntdsutil files info
```

If you are not in DS Restore Mode and run this command, you will receive the following error message:

```
*** Error: Operation only allowed when booted in DS restore mode
"set SAFEBOOT_OPTION=DSREPAIR" to override - NOT RECOMMENDED!
```

As you can see, it is possible to override this failure by setting the SAFEBOOT_OPTION environment variable to DSREPAIR, but we do not recommend this unless you know what you are doing. By setting this environment variable, the *ntdsutil* command will not stop you from performing other commands that should not be done while the database is online. This can obviously be quite dangerous.

Using a command-line interface in Windows Server 2008

In Windows Server 2008, you can obtain the file size information without booting into Directory Services Restore Mode by temporarily stopping the Active Directory Domain Services service, as follows:

```
net stop "active directory domain services"
```

You will receive a message indicating that the following four dependent services will also be stopped:

- Key Distribution Center
- Intersite Messaging
- DNS Server
- DFS Replication

Once the AD DS service has been stopped, you can display file information using the following syntax:

```
ntdsutil
ntdsutil: activate instance "ntds"
ntdsutil: files
file maintenance: info
file maintenance: quit
ntdsutil: quit
```

When you are finished, don't forget to restart the AD DS service, as well as any dependent services that halted when you stopped Active Directory Domain Services.

Discussion

The size of the Active Directory database on a domain controller is the size of the *ntds.dit* file. This file can vary slightly in size between domain controllers, even within the same domain, due to unreplicated changes, differences with nonreplicated data, and whitespace from purged objects.

You should monitor the size of this file on one or more domain controllers in each of your domains to ensure that you have adequate disk space. Also, by knowing the average size of your DIT, you can quickly recognize if it spikes dramatically, perhaps due to a new application that is writing data to the directory.

If you find that you are running out of disk space, you have a couple of options. You could move the Active Directory files to a new drive with more capacity. Alternatively, you can perform an offline defragmentation if the DIT file contains a lot of whitespace.

In Windows Server 2008, obtaining information about the size of the AD database is one of the tasks that you can perform while the AD DS service is stopped, without needing to reboot the server into Directory Services Restore Mode.

See Also

Recipe 16.12 for moving the DIT files, Recipe 16.17 for determining how much white-space is in the DIT, and Recipe 16.18 for performing an offline defragmentation of the Active Directory database

16.22 Searching for Deleted Objects

Problem

You want to search for deleted objects.

Solution

Using a graphical user interface

1. Open LDP from the Windows Support Tools.
2. From the menu, select Connection→Connect.
3. For Server, enter the name of a domain controller you want to target (or leave blank to do a serverless bind).
4. For Port, enter 389.
5. Click OK.
6. From the menu, select Connection→Connect.
7. Enter credentials of a user who is an administrator for the domain.
8. Click OK.
9. From the menu, select Options→Controls.
10. For Windows Server 2003, select the Return Deleted Objects control under Load Predefined. For Windows 2000, type `1.2.840.113556.1.4.417` for the Object Identifier and click the Check In button.
11. Click OK.
12. From the menu, select Browse→Search.
13. For BaseDN, enter "cn=Deleted Objects,<*DomainDN*>".
14. For Scope, select One Level.
15. For Filter, enter "(isDeleted=TRUE)".
16. Click the Options button.
17. Under Search Call Type, select Extended.
18. Click OK.
19. Click Run.

Using a command-line interface

To view all of the deleted objects in the current domain, use the following syntax:

```
> adfind -default -rb "cn=Deleted Objects" -showdel
```

You can also use the *adrestore.exe* utility from the Microsoft website by simply typing `adrestore` from the command line.

Using VBScript

It is currently not possible to search for deleted objects with ADSI or ADO.

Using PowerShell

You can search for tombstoned objects using the SDM AD Tombstone Reanimation cmdlets, which are freeware cmdlets available from *http://www.sdmsoftware.com*, using the following syntax:

```
Get-SDMADTombstone
```

Discussion

When an object is deleted in Active Directory, it is not really deleted, at least not immediately. The object is renamed, most of its attributes are cleared, and it is moved to the `Deleted Objects` container within the naming context that it was deleted from. See Recipe 16.0 for more on tombstone objects.

 Not all objects are moved to the `Deleted Objects` container. If you are unable to find a given deleted object, open the search scope to the whole naming context the object previously existed in.

Both the `Deleted Objects` container and tombstone objects themselves are hidden by default in tools such as ADUC and ADSI Edit. To query tombstone objects, you need to enable the Return Deleted Objects LDAP control, which has an OID of `1.2.840.113556.1.4.417`. When that control is enabled, you can perform searches for tombstone objects by specifying a search filter that contains (`isDeleted=TRUE`) in it. Only members of the administrator groups can perform searches for tombstone objects.

See Also

MSDN: Retrieving Deleted Objects

16.23 Undeleting a Single Object

Problem

You want to undelete or *reanimate* an object that has been deleted from your Windows Server 2003 Active Directory domain.

 This recipe requires Windows Server 2003 or newer Active Directory.

Solution

Using a graphical user interface

1. Open LDP from the Windows Support Tools.
2. From the menu, select Connection→Connect.
3. For Server, enter the name of a domain controller or domain that contains the object.
4. For Port, enter 389.
5. Click OK.
6. From the menu, select Connection→Bind.
7. Enter the credentials of a user who can view deleted objects.
8. Click OK.
9. Click on Options→Controls. In the Load Pre-defined drop-down box, select "Return deleted objects." Click OK.
10. From the menu, select View→Tree.
11. For BaseDN, type "<CN=Deleted Objects,<*DomainDN*>".
12. Click OK.
13. Click the + sign next to the `Deleted Objects` container in the righthand pane to browse the deleted objects in your domain.
14. Double-click on the object that you want to undelete.
15. Right-click on the object and select Modify.
16. In the Edit Entry Attribute box, enter "isDeleted." Leave the Value box blank. Select Delete from the Operation radio buttons, and then click Enter.
17. Enter "distinguishedName" in the Edit Entry Attribute box, and enter the DN that the restored object should have. Select Replace from the Operation radio buttons, and then click Enter.

18. Once you've entered both changes, click Run.

Using a command-line interface

```
adfind -default -f "name=<ObjectRDN>*" -showdel -dsq | admod -undel
```

Discussion

When an Active Directory object is deleted, it is placed in the `cn=Deleted Objects` container within the domain naming context. To save space in the *ntds.dit* file, most of the object's attribute values are cleared; only a small subset are actually retained, including:

- SID
- ObjectGUID
- LastKnownParent
- sAMAccountName
- SIDHistory (Windows Server 2003 SP1 and later)

Once you've manually reanimated an object, you'll need to manually restore any additional attributes that were not saved when the object was tombstoned; e.g., for a user object, you'll want to reconfigure their home directory, logon script information, and the like. You'll also need to re-enter the user into any necessary security and distribution groups so that she can receive the necessary access to resources that she possessed before her account was deleted.

Another option when restoring a single object is to perform a System State restore on a domain controller, and then use *ntdsutil* to mark the individual object *authoritative*. This has the downside of causing downtime on a domain controller, since you'll need to reboot it into Directory Services Restore mode to perform the restore. However, it saves you the manual effort of re-establishing most user account attributes since these will be automatically repopulated as part of the restore process.

Using a command-line interface

In addition to the *joeware* tools, Microsoft offers the *adrestore* command-line utility that will enumerate the deleted objects in a domain and give you the option to undelete them.

See Also

MS KB 840001 (How to Restore Deleted User Accounts and Their Group Membership in Active Directory), MSDN: Considerations for Active Directory Services Backup, and the other recipes in this chapter for more on AD backups, restores, snapshots, and disaster recovery

16.24 Undeleting a Container Object

Problem

You want to undelete a container object such as an OU that contained other objects when it was deleted.

This recipe requires Windows Server 2003 or newer Active Directory.

Solution

Using a graphical user interface

Use the steps in Recipe 16.23 to first undelete the container object. Then undelete each individual child object that was contained within the container, specifying the container's DN in the restored object's DN. Alternately, perform a System State restore and use *ntdsutil* to mark the restored OU as authoritative, as described in Recipe 16.9.

Performing an authoritative restore of **user** or **group** objects will require additional considerations, as detailed in MS KB 280079 (Authoritative Restore of Groups Can Result in Inconsistent Membership Information Across Domain Controllers).

Using a command-line interface

```
> adfind -default -rb "cn=Deleted Objects" -f "(name=<ContainerRDN>*)"
-showdel -dsq | admod -undel
> adfind -default -rb "cn=Deleted Objects" -f
("lastKnownParent=<ParentContainerDN>") -showdel -dsq | admod -undel
```

Discussion

When you delete an Active Directory container object, it also deletes any child objects that are housed within that container. Restoring an entire OU, for example, therefore requires you to restore both the container itself as well as all of the child objects contained within it. This is relatively simple to perform from the command line since you can restrict your query to those objects that have the appropriate value listed in the lastKnownParent attribute. However, just as when you reanimate an individual object, each of these child objects will need to have its individual attributes re-established. Therefore, when restoring a container object, your most efficient method will be to perform a System State restore and to use *ntdsutil* to mark the restored OU as authoritative.

See Also

MSDN: Restoring Deleted Object [Active Directory]

16.25 Modifying the Tombstone Lifetime for a Domain

Problem

You want to change the default tombstone lifetime for a domain.

Solution

Using a graphical user interface

1. Open ADSI Edit.
2. In the left pane, expand cn=Configuration→cn=Services→cn=Windows NT.
3. Right-click on "cn=Directory Service" and select Properties.
4. Set the tombstoneLifetime attribute to the number of days that tombstone objects should remain in Active Directory before getting removed completely (the default is 60 days in Windows Server 2003, and 180 days for AD environments installed from scratch on a Service Pack 1 server).
5. Click OK.

Using a command-line interface

Create an LDIF file called *change_tombstone_lifetime.ldf* with the following contents:

```
dn: cn=Directory Service,cn=Windows NT,cn=Services,cn=Configuration,<ForestRootDN>
changetype: modify
replace: tombstoneLifetime
tombstoneLifetime: <NumberOfDays>
-
```

Then run the following command:

```
> ldifde -v -i -f change_tombstone_lifetime.ldf
```

You can also make this change using AdMod, as follows:

```
> admod -b "cn=Directory Service,cn=Windows
NT,cn=Services,cn=Configuration,<ForestRootDN> tombstoneLifetime::<NumberOfDays>
```

Using VBScript

```
' This code modifies the default
' tombstone lifetime.
' ------ SCRIPT CONFIGURATION ------
intTombstoneLifetime = <NumberOfDays>
' ------ END CONFIGURATION --------
```

```
set objRootDSE = GetObject("LDAP://RootDSE")
set objDSCont = GetObject("LDAP://cn=Directory Service,cn=Windows NT," & _
                "cn=Services," & objRootDSE.Get("configurationNamingContext") )
objDSCont.Put "tombstoneLifetime", intTombstoneLifetime
objDSCont.SetInfo
WScript.Echo "Successfully set the
tombstone lifetime to " & _
                intTombstoneLifetime
```

Using PowerShell

```
Set-QADObject -Identity LDAP://cn=Directory
Service,cn=WindowsNT,cn=Services,cn=Configuration,<ForestRootDN>" -ObjectAttributes
@{tombstoneLifetime=<NumberOfDays>}

$ds = [ADSI] "LDAP://cn=Directory
Service,cn=WindowsNT,cn=Services,cn=Configuration,<ForestRootDN>"
$ds.put("tombstoneLifetime", <NumberOfDays>)
$ds.SetInfo()
```

Discussion

In Windows Server 2003 RTM and Windows Server 2003 R2, the default tombstone lifetime for Active Directory is 60 days. This was increased to 180 days in Service Pack 1 due to numerous customers needing to extend this value from its original default, but you will see this value populated automatically only in a forest that was created from scratch on a server that already has Windows Server 2003 Service Pack 1 or Service Pack 2 installed, as well as Windows Server 2008 RTM and beyond. If you upgrade an existing 2003 or R2 domain controller to an updated service pack level or to Windows Server 2008, the tombstone lifetime will stay at 60 days unless you manually increase it using one of the solutions in this recipe.

It is not recommended that you lower the tombstone lifetime unless you have a very good reason for doing so, since lowering this value below the 60-day default also lowers the length of time a backup of Active Directory is good for. See Recipes 16.0 and 16.22 for more information on tombstone (deleted) objects and the tombstone lifetime.

See Also

Recipe 16.19 for more on the garbage collection process, MS KB 198793 (The Active Directory Database Garbage Collection Process), MS KB 216993 (Backup of the Active Directory Has 60-Day Useful Life), and MS KB 314282 (Lingering Objects May Remain After You Bring an Out-of-Date Global Catalog Server Back Online)

## CHAPTER 17

Application Partitions

17.0 Introduction

Active Directory domain controllers, when first installed, host three predefined partitions. The *Configuration naming context* is replicated to all domain controllers in the forest, and contains information that is needed forest-wide, such as the site topology and LDAP query policies. The *Schema naming context* is also replicated forest-wide and contains all of the schema objects that define how data is stored and structured in Active Directory. The third partition is the *Domain naming context*, which is replicated to all of the domain controllers that host a particular domain.

Windows Server 2003 introduced a new type of partition, called an *application partition*, which is very similar to the other naming contexts except that you can configure which domain controllers in the forest will replicate the data that's contained within it. Examples include the *DomainDnsZones* partition, which is replicated across all AD-Integrated DNS servers in the same domain, and *ForestDnsZones*, which is replicated across all AD-integrated DNS servers in the forest. This capability gives administrators much more flexibility over how they can store and replicate the data that is contained in Active Directory. If you need to replicate a certain set of data to only two different sites, for example, you can create an application partition that will only replicate the data to the domain controllers in those two sites rather than replicating the data to additional DCs that have no need of it.

See Chapter 13 for more on DNS-related management tasks, as well as *Active Directory*, Fourth Edition, by Brian Desmond et al. (O'Reilly) for more details on application partitions.

> Application partitions are new to Windows Server 2003, so this entire chapter applies only to Windows Server 2003 and Windows Server 2008 domain controllers. Windows 2000 domain controllers cannot host application partitions.

The Anatomy of an Application Partition

Application partitions are stored in Active Directory in a similar fashion as a Domain NC. In fact, application partitions and Domain NCs consist of the same two types of objects: a domainDNS object and a crossRef object that resides under the Partitions container in the Configuration naming context (CNC). Application partitions have a similar naming convention as domains and can be named virtually anything you want. You can create an application partition that uses the current namespace within the forest. For example, in the *adatum.com* (dc=adatum,dc=com) forest, you could create an *apps.adatum.com* (dc=apps,dc=adatum,dc=com) application partition. Alternatively, a name that is part of a new tree can also be used, for example, *apps.local* (dc=apps,dc=local). Application partitions can also be subordinate to other application partitions.

Tables 17-1 and 17-2 contain some of the interesting attributes of domainDNS and crossRef objects as they apply to application partitions.

Table 17-1. Attributes of domainDNS objects

Attribute	Description
dc	Relative distinguished name of the application partition.
instanceType	This attribute must be set to 5 when creating an application partition. See Recipe 17.1 for more information.
msDs-masteredBy	List of nTDSDSA object DNs of the domain controllers that replicate the application partition. See Recipe 17.4 for more information.

Table 17-2. Attributes of crossRef objects

Attribute	Description
cn	Relative distinguished name of the crossRef object. This value is generally a GUID for application partitions.
dnsRoot	Fully qualified DNS name of the application partition.
msDS-NC-Replica-Locations	List of nTDSDSA object DNs of the domain controllers that replicate the application partition. See Recipe 17.4 for more information.
msDS-SDReferenceDomain	Domain used for security descriptor translation. See Recipe 17.8 for more information.
nCName	Distinguished name of the application partition's corresponding domainDNS object.
systemFlags	Bit flag that identifies if the crossRef represents an application. See Recipe 17.2 for more information.

17.1 Creating and Deleting an Application Partition

Problem

You want to create or delete an application partition. Application partitions are useful if you need to replicate data to a subset of locations where you have domain controllers. Instead of replicating the application data to all domain controllers in a domain, you can use an application partition to replicate the data to only the domain controllers of your choosing.

Solution

Using a command-line interface

Use the following command to create an application partition on a domain controller:

On a Windows Server 2008 domain controller, enter the command `activate instance ntds` prior to entering the `dom man` command.

```
> ntdsutil
> ntdsutil: dom man
> domain management: conn
> connections: conn to se <DomainControllerName>
> connections: q
> domain management: create nc <AppPartitionDN> NULL
> domain management: q
> ntdsutil: q
```

Use the following command to delete an application partition:

On a Windows Server 2008 domain controller, enter the command `activate instance ntds` prior to entering the `dom man` command.

```
> ntdsutil
> ntdsutil:dom man
> domain management: conn
> connections: conn to se <DomainControllerName>
> connections: q
> domain management: delete nc <AppPartitionFQDN>
> domain management: q
> ntdsutil: q
```

Discussion

To create an application partition, you'll use the *ntdsutil* utility to create a `domainDNS` object that serves as the root container for the partition. A `crossRef` object is automatically created in the `Partitions` container in the Configuration NC. Conversely, when removing an application partition, you only need to remove the `crossRef` object and the `domainDNS` is automatically deleted. When you delete an application partition, all objects within the partition also get deleted. Tombstone objects are not created for any of the objects within the application partition or for the application partition itself.

See Also

MS KB 322669 (How to Manage the Application Directory Partition and Replicas in Windows Server 2003), MSDN: Creating an Application Directory Partition, and MSDN: Deleting an Application Directory Partition

17.2 Finding the Application Partitions in a Forest

Problem

You want to find the application partitions that have been created in a forest.

Solution

Using a graphical user interface

1. Open LDP from the Windows Support Tools. (LDP is installed by default with the Active Directory Domain Services role in Windows Server 2008.)
2. From the menu, select Connection→Connect.
3. For Server, enter the name of a DC.
4. For Port, enter 389.
5. Click OK.
6. From the menu, select Connection→Bind.
7. Enter a user and password with the necessary credentials.
8. Click OK.
9. From the menu, select Browse→Search.
10. For BaseDN, type the DN of the Partitions container (for example, `cn=partitions,cn=configuration,dc=adatum,dc=com`).
11. For Filter, enter:

        (&(objectcategory=crossRef)(systemFlags:1.2.840.113556.1.4.803:=5))

12. For Scope, select One Level.

13. Click the Options button.

14. For Attributes, type **dnsRoot**.

15. Click OK.

16. Click Run.

Using a command-line interface

Use the following command to find all of the application partitions in a forest:

```
> dsquery * cn=partitions,cn=configuration,<ForestDN> -filter
"(&(objectcategory=crossRef)(systemFlags:1.2.840.113556.1.4.803:=5))"
-scope onelevel -attr dnsRoot
```

You can also find application partitions in a forest using AdFind:

```
> adfind -sc appparts+
```

Using VBScript

```
' This code displays the application partitions contained in the
' default forest

set objRootDSE = GetObject("LDAP://RootDSE")
strBase     = "<LDAP://cn=Partitions," & _
                objRootDSE.Get("ConfigurationNamingContext") & ">;"
strFilter = "(&(objectcategory=crossRef)" & _
            "(systemFlags:1.2.840.113556.1.4.803:=5));"

strAttrs = "cn,ncName;"
strScope = "onelevel"

set objConn = CreateObject("ADODB.Connection")
objConn.Provider = "ADsDSOObject"
objConn.Open "Active Directory Provider"
set objRS = objConn.Execute(strBase & strFilter & strAttrs & strScope)

objRS.MoveFirst
while not objRS.EOF
    Wscript.Echo objRS.Fields("nCName").Value
    objRS.MoveNext
wend
```

Using PowerShell

The following example will search for application partitions within an Active Directory domain using the Quest `get-QADObject` cmdlet:

```
Get-QADObject -ldapfilter
"(&(objectcategory=crossRef)(systemFlags:1.2.840.113556.1.4.803:=5))"
```

Another option is to use the `DirectorySearcher` class from the .NET Framework, as follows:

```
$strFilter = "(&(objectcategory=crossRef)(systemFlags:1.2.840.113556.1.4.803:=5))"
$objDomain = New-Object System.DirectoryServices.DirectoryEntry
$objSearcher = New-Object System.DirectoryServices.DirectorySearcher
$objSearcher.SearchRoot = $objDomain
$objSearcher.Filter = $strFilter
$objSearcher.SearchScope = [System.DirectoryServices.SearchScope]::OneLevel
$colResults = $objSearcher.FindAll()
```

Discussion

To get the list of application partitions in the "Solution," we queried all **crossRef** objects in the **Partitions** container that have the **systemFlags** attribute with the bits 0 and 2 set (5 in decimal). To do this, a logical AND bit-wise filter was used. See Recipe 4.12 for more on searching with a bitwise filter.

You can take a shortcut by not including the bitwise OID in the search filter, and changing it to **systemFlags=5**. This currently produces the same results in the test forest as with the bitwise filter, but there are no guarantees since it is a bit flag attribute. You may encounter circumstances in which an application partition would have another bit set in **systemFlags** that would yield a different value.

In each solution, the **dnsRoot** attribute was printed for each application partition, which contains the DNS name of the application partition. You can also retrieve the **nCName** attribute, which contains the distinguished name of the application partition.

See Also

Recipe 4.12

17.3 Adding or Removing a Replica Server for an Application Partition

Problem

You want to add or remove a replica server for an application partition. After you've created an application partition, you should make at least one other server a replica server in case the first server fails.

Solution

Using a command-line interface

Use the following command to add a replica server for an application partition:

```
> ntdsutil "dom man" conn "co to se <DomainControllerName>" q "add nc
replica<AppPartitionDN> <DomainControllerName>" q q
```

Use the following command to remove a replica server for an application partition:

```
> ntdsutil "dom man" conn "co to se <DomainControllerName>" q "remove nc
replica <AppPartitionDN> <DomainControllerName>" q q
```

You can also add a replica using AdMod:

```
> adfind -partitions -f "(dnsRoot=<PartitionDNSName>)" -dsq | admod
msDS-NC-Replica-Locations:+:"cn=ntds settings,
cn=<DCName>,cn=servers,cn=<SiteName>,cn=sites,cn=configuration,<ForestRootDN>"
```

Using VBScript

```
' This code adds or removes a replica server for the
' specified application partition
' ------ SCRIPT CONFIGURATION -----
strAppPart = "<AppPartitionFQDN>" ' DNS name of the application partition

' Hostname of server to add as replica for app partition.
' This needs to match the common name for the DC's server object.
strServer = "<DomainControllerName>" ' e.g. dc01

' Set to True to add server as new replica or False to remove
boolAdd = True
' ------ END CONFIGURATION --------

' Constants taken from ADS_PROPERTY_OPERATION_ENUM
const ADS_PROPERTY_APPEND = 3
const ADS_PROPERTY_DELETE = 4

set objRootDSE = GetObject("LDAP://RootDSE")

' --------------------------------------------------------
' First find the NTDS Settings object for the server
' --------------------------------------------------------
strBase     = "<LDAP://cn=Sites," & _
                objRootDSE.Get("ConfigurationNamingContext") & ">;"
strFilter   = "(&(objectcategory=server)(cn=" & strServer & "));"
strAttrs    = "cn,distinguishedName;"
strScope    = "subtree"
set objConn = CreateObject("ADODB.Connection")
objConn.Provider = "ADsDSOObject"
objConn.Open "Active Directory Provider"
set objRS = objConn.Execute(strBase & strFilter & strAttrs & strScope)
if objRS.RecordCount <> 1 then
   WScript.Echo "Did not find a match for server " & strServer
       WScript.Quit

else
   objRS.MoveLast
   strServerDN = "cn=NTDS Settings," & _
                  objRS.Fields("distinguishedName").Value
   ' Make sure the NTDS Settings object actually exists
   set objNTDSDSA = GetObject("LDAP://" & strServerDN)
   Wscript.Echo "Found server: "
   WScript.Echo strServerDN
   Wscript.Echo
end if
```

```
' ----------------------------------------------------------------
' Now need to find the crossRef object
' for the application partition
' ----------------------------------------------------------------
strBase   = "<LDAP://cn=Partitions," & _
            objRootDSE.Get("ConfigurationNamingContext") & ">;"
strFilter = "(&(objectcategory=crossRef)" & _
            "(dnsRoot=" & strAppPart & "));"
strAttrs  = "cn,distinguishedName;"
strScope  = "onelevel"
set objRS = objConn.Execute(strBase & strFilter & strAttrs & strScope)
if objRS.RecordCount <> 1 then
   WScript.Echo "Did not find a match for application partition " & _
                strAppPart
   WScript.Quit
else
   objRS.MoveLast
   set objAppPart = GetObject("LDAP://" & _
                    objRS.Fields("distinguishedName").Value )
   Wscript.Echo "Found app partition: "
   WScript.Echo objRS.Fields("distinguishedName").Value
   WScript.Echo
end if


' ----------------------------------------------
' Lastly, either add or remove the replica server
' ----------------------------------------------
if boolAdd = TRUE then
   objAppPart.PutEx ADS_PROPERTY_APPEND, "msDS-NC-Replica-Locations", _
                    Array(strServerDN)
   objAppPart.SetInfo
   WScript.Echo "Added server to replica set"
else
   objAppPart.PutEx ADS_PROPERTY_DELETE, "msDS-NC-Replica-Locations", _
                    Array(strServerDN)
   objAppPart.SetInfo
   WScript.Echo "Removed server from replica set"
end if
```

Using PowerShell

The following syntax will add a single entry to the list of replica locations, while leaving the rest of the list intact:

```
[Collections.DictionaryEntry] $de = new-object Collections.DictionaryEntry -
argumentList Append @('cn=NTDS
Settings,cn=<DCName>,cn=servers,cn=<SiteName>cn=sites,cn=configuration,<ForestRootD
N>')
get-QADObject -SearchRoot "cn=partitions,cn=configuration,<ForestRootDN>" -
SearchFilter "dnsRoot=<PartitionName>" | Set-QADObject -objectAttributes @{msDS-NC-
Replica-Locations=$de}
```

This syntax will remove a single entry from the replica location list without affecting any other entries:

```
[Collections.DictionaryEntry] $de = new-object Collections.DictionaryEntry -
argumentList Delete @('cn=NTDS
Settings,cn=<DCName>,cn=servers,cn=<SiteName>cn=sites,cn=configuration,<ForestRootD
N>')
get-QADObject -SearchRoot "cn=partitions,cn=configuration,<ForestRootDN>" -
SearchFilter "dnsRoot=<PartitionName>" | Set-QADObject -objectAttributes @{msDS-NC-
Replica-Locations=$de}
```

Discussion

When you initially create an application partition, there is only one domain controller
that hosts the application partition, namely the one you created the application partition on. You can add any other domain controllers in the forest as replica servers,
assuming the domain controllers are running Windows Server 2003 or newer operating
systems. The list of replica servers is stored in the msDS-NC-Replica-Locations attribute
on the crossRef object for the application partition in the Partitions container. That
attribute contains the distinguished name of each replica server's nTDSDSA object. To
add a replica server, simply add the DN of the new replica server. To remove a replica
server, remove the DN corresponding to the server you want to remove. Behind the
scene, the KCC gets triggered anytime there is a change to that attribute, at which point
it will either cause the application partition to get replicated to the target domain controller or it will remove the replica from the target DC. When a domain controller is
demoted, it should automatically remove itself as a replica server for any application
partitions that it replicated.

Using PowerShell

Because msDS-NC-Replica-Locations is a multivalued attribute, you need to create a
DictionaryEntry object in PowerShell in order to modify it. The Quest AD cmdlets
include the -argumentList Append and -argumentList Delete options for your use. If
you wanted to simply overwrite all existing entries in the multivalued attribute with
new ones that you specify, you would use syntax similar to the following:

```
-objectAttributes @{msDS-NC-Replica-Locations=@('<DN1>',<DN2>')}
```

It's more likely, however, that you will want to add or remove only one entry in the list
of replica locations, while leaving the rest of the list intact. To perform these steps,
follow the example syntax included in the recipe.

See Also

Recipe 17.4 for finding the replica servers for an application partition and MS KB
322669 (How to Manage the Application Directory Partition and Replicas in Windows
Server 2003)

17.4 Finding the Replica Servers for an Application Partition

Problem

You want to find the replica servers for an application partition.

Solution

Using a graphical user interface

1. Open ADSI Edit.
2. Connect to the configuration naming context of the forest the application partition is in, if it is not already present in the left pane.
3. Expand the configuration naming context and click on the Partitions container.
4. In the right pane, right-click on the crossRef object that represents the application partition and select Properties.
5. Under Attributes, select the msDS-NC-Replica-Locations attribute.

Using a command-line interface

```
> ntdsutil "dom man" conn "co to se <DomainControllerName>" q "list nc
replicas <AppPartitionDN>" q q
```

You can also list replica servers using AdFind:

```
> adfind -partitions -f "(dnsRoot=<PartitionDNSName>)" dnsRoot msDS-NC-
Replica-Locations
```

Using VBScript

```
' This code displays the DN of each domain controller's
' nTDSDSA object that is a replica server for the
' specified app partition
' ------ SCRIPT CONFIGURATION ------
' Fully qualified DNS name of app partition
strAppPart = "<AppPartitionFQDN>" ' e.g. apps.adatum.com
' ------ END CONFIGURATION ---------

set objRootDSE = GetObject("LDAP://RootDSE")
strBase    = "<LDAP://cn=Partitions," & _
             objRootDSE.Get("ConfigurationNamingContext") & ">;"
strFilter  = "(&(objectcategory=crossRef)(dnsRoot=" & strAppPart & "));"
strAttrs   = "
msDS-NC-Replica-Locations;"
strScope   = "onelevel"
set objConn = CreateObject("ADODB.Connection")
objConn.Provider = "ADsDSOObject"
objConn.Open "Active Directory Provider"
set objRS = objConn.Execute(strBase & strFilter & strAttrs & strScope)
if objRS.RecordCount <> 1 then
```

```
    WScript.Echo "Did not find a match for application partition " & _
              strAppPart
    WScript.Quit
else
    objRS.MoveLast
    if objRS.Fields("msDS-NC-Replica-Locations").Properties.Count > 0 then
        Wscript.Echo "There are no replica servers for app partition " & _
strAppPart
    else
        Wscript.Echo "Replica servers for app partition " & strAppPart & ":"
        for each strNTDS in objRS.Fields("msDS-NC-Replica-Locations").Value
            WScript.Echo " " & strNTDS
        next
    end if
end if
```

Using PowerShell

```
$objPart = get-QADObject -SearchRoot
"cn=partitions,cn=configuration,<ForestRootDN>" -SearchFilter
"dnsRoot=<PartitionName>"
$objPart.msDS-NC-Replica-Locations
```

Discussion

The list of replica servers for an application partition is stored in the multivalued msDS-NC-Replica-Locations attribute on the crossRef object for the application partition. This object is located in the Partitions container in the Configuration naming context.

See Also

Recipe 17.3 for adding and removing replica servers

17.5 Finding the Application Partitions Hosted by a Server

Problem

You want to find the application partitions that a particular server is hosting. Before you decommission a server, it is good to check to see if it hosts any application partitions and if so, to add another replica server to replace it.

Solution

Using a graphical user interface

1. Open LDP from the Windows Support tools. (On a Windows Server 2008 DC, LDP is installed by default.)
2. From the menu, select Connection→Connect.
3. For Server, enter the name of a DC.

4. For Port, enter 389.

5. Click OK.

6. From the menu, select Connection→Bind.

7. Enter a user and password with the necessary credentials.

8. Click OK.

9. From the menu, select Browse→Search.

10. For BaseDN, type the DN of the Partitions container (for example, `cn=partitions,cn=configuration,dc=adatum,dc=com`).

11. For Filter, enter:

```
(&(objectcategory=crossRef)(systemFlags:1.2.840.113556.1.4.803:=5)
(msDS-NC-Replica-Locations=cn=NTDS Settings,cn=<DomainControllerName>,
cn=servers,cn=<SiteName>,cn=sites,cn=configuration,<ForestDN>))
```

12. For Scope, select One Level.

13. Click the Options button.

14. For Attributes, type `dnsRoot`.

15. Click OK.

16. Click Run.

Using a command-line interface

Use the following command to find all of the application partitions hosted by a domain controller. To run this command, you need the distinguished name of the forest root domain (`<ForestDN>`), the common name of the DC's server object (`<DomainControllerName>`), and the common name of the `site` object the server is in (`<SiteName>`):

```
> dsquery * "cn=partitions,cn=configuration,<ForestDN>" -scope onelevel -attr
dnsRoot -filter "(&(objectcategory=crossRef)(systemFlags:1.2.840.113556.1.4.803:=5)
(msDS-NC-Replica-Locations=cn=NTDS Settings,cn=<DomainControllerName>,
cn=servers,cn=<SiteName>,cn=sites,cn=configuration,<ForestDN>))"
```

You can also display the application partitions hosted by a particular DC using AdFind:

```
> adfind -partitions -s onelevel -bit -f
"(&(objectcategory=crossRef)(systemFlags:AND:=5)(msDS-NC-Replica-Locations=cn=NTDS
Settings,cn=<DomainControllerName>,cn=servers,cn=<SiteName>,
cn=sites,cn=configuration,<ForestRootDN>))"
```

Using VBScript

```
' This code finds the application partitions
' hosted by the specified server.
' ------ SCRIPT CONFIGURATION ------
' Hostname of server to add as replica for app partition.
' This needs to match the common name for the DC's server object.
strServer = "<DomainControllerName>" ' e.g. dc01
```

```
' ------ END CONFIGURATION ---------

' ------------------------------------------------------------
' First need to find the NTDS Settings object for the server
' ------------------------------------------------------------
set objRootDSE = GetObject("LDAP://RootDSE")
strBase     = "<LDAP://cn=Sites," & _
                objRootDSE.Get("ConfigurationNamingContext") & ">;"
strFilter = "(&(objectcategory=server)(cn=" & strServer & "));"
strAttrs    = "cn,distinguishedName;"
strScope    = "subtree"
set objConn = CreateObject("ADODB.Connection")
objConn.Provider = "ADsDSOObject"
objConn.Open "Active Directory Provider"
set objRS = objConn.Execute(strBase & strFilter & strAttrs & strScope)
if objRS.RecordCount <> 1 then
   WScript.Echo "Did not find a match for server " & strServer
   WScript.Quit
else
   objRS.MoveLast
   strServerDN = "cn=NTDS Settings," & _
                objRS.Fields("distinguishedName").Value
   Wscript.Echo "Found server object: "
   WScript.Echo strServerDN
   Wscript.Echo
end if


' --------------------------------------------------------------------
' Find the crossRef objects that are hosted by the server
' --------------------------------------------------------------------
strBase = "<LDAP://cn=Partitions," & _
          objRootDSE.Get("ConfigurationNamingContext") & ">;"
strFilter =  "(&(objectcategory=crossRef)" & _
              "(msDS-NC-Replica-Locations=" & strServerDN & "));"

strAttrs    = "nCName;"
strScope    = "onelevel"
set objRS = objConn.Execute(strBase & strFilter & strAttrs & strScope)
if objRS.RecordCount = 0 then
   WScript.Echo "Server " & strServer & _
                        " does not host any
application partitions"
   WScript.Quit
else
   Wscript.Echo "App partitions
hosted by server " & strServer & ": "
   objRS.MoveFirst
   while not objRS.EOF
      WScript.Echo " " & objRS.Fields("nCName").Value
      objRS.MoveNext
   wend
end if
```

Using PowerShell

```
get-QADObject -SearchScope 'onelevel' -SearchRoot
cn=partitions,cn=configuration,<ForestRootDN> -SearchFilter
"(&(objectcategory=crossRef)(systemFlags:1.2.840.113556.1.4.803:=5)(msDS-NC-
Replica-Locations=cn=NTDS Settings,
cn=<DomainControllerName>,cn=servers,cn=<SiteName>,
cn=sites,cn=configuration,<ForestRootDN>))"
```

Discussion

As described in Recipes 17.3 and 17.4, the `msDS-NC-Replica-Locations` attribute on `crossRef` objects contains the list of replica servers for a given application partition. Each of the solutions illustrates how to perform a query using this attribute to locate all of the application partitions a particular domain controller is a replica server for. For the GUI and CLI solutions, you need to know the distinguished name of the `nTDSDSA` object for the target domain controller. The VBScript solution tries to dynamically determine the distinguished name given a server name.

See Also

Recipe 17.3 and Recipe 17.4 for finding the replica servers for an application partition

17.6 Verifying Application Partitions Are Instantiated on a Server Correctly

Problem

You want to verify that an application partition is instantiated on a replica server. After you add a domain controller as a replica server for an application partition, the data in the application partition needs to fully replicate to that domain controller before it can be used on that domain controller.

Solution

Using a command-line interface

Use the following command to determine if there are any problems with application partitions on a domain controller:

```
> dcdiag /test:checksdrefdom /test:verifyreplicas /test:crossrefvalidation
/s:<DomainControllerName>
```

 These tests are valid only with the Windows Server 2003 and newer versions of *dcdiag*.

You can also verify the state of a particular application partition by using *ntdsutil* as follows:

1. Type "ntdsutil".
2. If you are running these commands on a Windows Server 2008 domain controller, type "activate instance ntds".
3. Type "domain management" (or just "do ma") to go to the Domain Management menu.
4. Type "connections" (or just "co") to go to the Connections menu.
5. Type "connect to server *<ServerName>*."
6. Type "q" to return to the Domain Management menu.
7. Type "list nc replicas *<AppPartitionDN>*." (You can shorten "list nc replicas" to just "li nc rep".)

Discussion

The *dcdiag* CheckSDRefDom, VerifyReplicas, and CrossRefValidation tests can help determine if an application partition has been instantiated on a server and if there are any problems with it. Here is the *dcdiag* help information for those three tests:

CrossRefValidation
> This test looks for cross-references that are in some way invalid.

CheckSDRefDom
> This test checks that all application directory partitions have appropriate security descriptor reference domains.

VerifyReplicas
> This test verifies that all application directory partitions are fully instantiated on all replica servers.

Another way you can check to see if a certain application partition has been instantiated on a domain controller yet is to look at the msDS-HasInstantiatedNCs attribute for the server's nTDSDSA object. That attribute has DN with Binary syntax and contains a list of all the application partitions that have been successfully instantiated on the server. Unfortunately, tools such as ADSI Edit and DSQuery do not interpret DN with Binary attributes correctly, but it can be viewed with LDP. In addition, you can use AdFind as follows:

```
adfind -config -rb cn=dc1,cn=servers,cn=default-first-site-name,cn=site
s -f "msds-HasInstantiatedNCs=B:8:00000005:dc=apps,dc=local" -dn
```

This will return results similar to the following:

```
AdFind V01.27.00cpp Joe Richards (joe@joeware.net) November 2005

Using server: dc1.adatum.com:389
Directory: Windows Server 2003
Base DN: cn=dc1,cn=servers,cn=default-first-site-name,cn=sites,CN=Configuration,
```

```
DC=adatum,DC=com

dn:CN=NTDS Settings,CN=DC1,CN=Servers,CN=Default-First-Site-Name,CN=Sites,
CN=Configuration,DC=adatum,DC=com

1 Objects returned
```

See Also

MSDN: ms-DS-Has-Instantiated-NCs attribute [AD Schema]

17.7 Setting the Replication Notification Delay for an Application Partition

Problem

Two replication-related settings that you can customize for application partitions (or any naming context for which change notification is enabled) include the first and subsequent replication delay after a change to the partition has been detected. The first replication delay is the time that a domain controller waits before it notifies its first replication partner that there has been a change. The subsequent replication delay is the time that the domain controller waits after it has notified its first replication partner before it will notify its next partner. You may need to customize these settings so that replication happens as quickly as you need it to for data in the application partition.

Solution

Using a graphical user interface

1. Open ADSI Edit.
2. Connect to the configuration naming context of the forest that the application partition is in if a connection is not already present in the left pane.
3. Expand the configuration naming context and click on the Partitions container.
4. In the right pane, right-click on the crossRef object that represents the application partition and select Properties.
5. Set the msDS-Replication-Notify-First-DSA-Delay and msDS-Replication-Notify-Subsequent-DSA-Delay attributes to the number of seconds you want for each delay (see the section called "Discussion" for more details).
6. Click OK.

Using a command-line interface

The Windows Server 2003 and newer versions of *repadmin* support setting the notification delays:

```
> repadmin /notifyopt <AppPartitionDN> /first:<FirstDelayInSeconds>
/subs:<NextDelayInSeconds>
```

You can also change both of these parameters using AdMod, as follows:

```
> admod -b <AppPartitionCrossRefDN>
msDS-Replication-Notify-First-DSA-Delay::<FirstDelayInSeconds> msDS-Replication-
Notify-Subsequent-DSA-Delay::<NextDelayInSeconds>
```

Using VBScript

```
' This code sets the
' replication delay for an application partition
' ------ SCRIPT CONFIGURATION ------
strAppPartDN = "<AppPartitionDN>" ' e.g. dc=apps,dc=adatum,dc=com
intFirstDelay = <FirstDelayInSeconds>
intNextDelay = <NextDelayInSeconds>
' ------ END CONFIGURATION ---------

set objRootDSE = GetObject("LDAP://RootDSE")
strBase    = "<LDAP://cn=Partitions," & _
                objRootDSE.Get("ConfigurationNamingContext") & ">;"
strFilter  = "(&(objectcategory=crossRef)(nCName=" & strAppPartDN & "));"
strAttrs   = "cn,distinguishedName;"
strScope   = "onelevel"
set objConn = CreateObject("ADODB.Connection")
objConn.Provider = "ADsDSOObject"
objConn.Open "Active Directory Provider"
set objRS = objConn.Execute(strBase & strFilter & strAttrs & strScope)

if objRS.RecordCount <> 1 then
   WScript.Echo "Did not find a match for " & strAppPartDN
else
   objRS.MoveLast
   set objAppPart = GetObject("LDAP://" & _
                    objRS.Fields("distinguishedName").Value )
   objAppPart.Put "msDS-
Replication-Notify-First-DSA-Delay", intFirstDelay
   objAppPart.Put "msDS-Replication-Notify-Subsequent-DSA-Delay", intNextDelay
   objAppPart.SetInfo
   Wscript.Echo "Modified " & objRS.Fields("distinguishedName").Value
end if
```

Using PowerShell

To modify the initial and subsequent notification delays, you can use the Quest AD
cmdlets or ADSI methods, as follows:

```
Set-QADObject -Identity
cn=<AppPartition>,cn=Partitions,cn=Configuration,<ForestRootDN> -ObjectAttributes
@{ Replication-Notification-First-DSA-Delay="<FirstDelayInSeconds>";msDS-
Replication-Notify-Subsequent-DSA-Delay::"<NextDelayInSeconds>"}

$objPart = cn=<AppPartition>,cn=Partitions,cn=Configuration,<ForestRootDN>
$objPart.put("Replication-Notification-First-DSA-Delay", "<FirstDelayInSeconds>")
$objPart.put("msDS-Replication-Notify-Subsequent-DSA-Delay",
```

```
"<NextDelayInSeconds>")
$objPart.SetInfo()
```

Discussion

The settings that control the notification delay are stored in the `msDS-Replication-Notify-First-DSA-Delay` and `msDS-Replication-Notify-Subsequent-DSA-Delay` attributes on the application partition's `crossRef` object in the `Partitions` container. The time values are stored as seconds. The default for application partitions is 15 seconds for the first delay and 5 seconds for each subsequent delay.

See Also

MSDN: Application Directory Partition Replication [Active Directory], MSDN: Modifying Application Directory Partition Configuration [Active Directory], MSDN: ms-DS-Replication-Notify-First-DSA-Delay, and MSDN: ms-DS-Replication-Notify-Subsequent-DSA-Delay

17.8 Setting the Reference Domain for an Application Partition

Problem

Whenever you create an object in Active Directory, the default security descriptor that's defined in the schema for the object's class is applied to the object. This default security descriptor may reference specific groups, such as *Domain Admins*, but it is not specific to a domain. This makes a lot of sense for domain naming contexts, where the *Domain Admins* group in question would be the one that's defined in the domain in question. But for application partitions that don't contain a *Domain Admins* group, it is not so straightforward. Which domain's *Domain Admins* group do you use? To work around this issue, you can set a default security descriptor reference domain for an application partition by setting the `msDS-SDReferenceDomain` attribute of the partition's `crossRef` object.

Solution

Using a graphical user interface

1. Open ADSI Edit.
2. Connect to the Configuration naming context of the forest the application partition is in if it is not already present in the left pane.
3. Expand the Configuration naming context and click on the Partitions container.
4. In the right pane, right-click on the `crossRef` object that represents the application partition and select Properties.
5. Under Attributes, select the `msDS-SDReferenceDomain` attribute.

---

6. Enter the Distinguished Name for the appropriate domain and click OK.

Using a command-line interface

```
> ntdsutil "dom man" conn "co to se <DomainControllerName>" q "set nc ref domain
<AppPartitionDN> <DomainDN>" q q
```

You can also set the reference domain using AdMod:

```
> adfind -partitions -f "(dnsRoot=<PartitionDNSName>)" -dsq | admod
msDS-SDReferenceDomain::"<DomainDN>"
```

Using VBScript

```
' This code sets the SD
' reference domain for the specified app partition
' ------ SCRIPT CONFIGURATION -----
' DN of reference domain
strRefDomainDN = "<DomainDN>"          ' e.g. dc=emea,dc=adatum,dc=com
' Fully qualified DNS name of app partition
strAppPart = "<AppPartitionFQDN>"      ' e.g. app.adatum.com
' ------ END CONFIGURATION --------

set objRootDSE = GetObject("LDAP://RootDSE")
strBase = "<LDAP://cn=Partitions," & _
          objRootDSE.Get("ConfigurationNamingContext") & ">;"
strFilter  = "(&(objectcategory=crossRef)(dnsRoot=" & _
             strAppPart & "));"
strAttrs   = "nCName,
msDS-SDReferenceDomain,distinguishedName;"
strScope   = "onelevel"
set objConn = CreateObject("ADODB.Connection")
objConn.Provider = "ADsDSOObject"
objConn.Open "Active Directory Provider"
set objRS = objConn.Execute(strBase & strFilter & strAttrs & strScope)
if objRS.RecordCount <> 1 then
   WScript.Echo "Did not find a match for application partition " & _
               strAppPart
   WScript.Quit
else
   objRS.MoveLast
   WScript.Echo "Current Reference Domain: " & _
               objRS.Fields("msDS-SDReferenceDomain").Value
   set objCrossRef = GetObject("LDAP://" & _
                    objRS.Fields("distinguishedName").Value )
   objCrossRef.Put "msDS-SDReferenceDomain", strRefDomainDN
   objCrossRef.SetInfo
   WScript.Echo "New Reference Domain: " & _
               objCrossRef.Get("msDS-SDReferenceDomain")
end if
```

Using PowerShell

```
get-QADObject -SearchRoot "cn=partitions,cn=Configuration,<ForestRootDN>"
-SearchFilter "dnsRoot=<PartitionName>" | Set-QADObject -objectAttributes
@{msDS-SDReferenceDomain=<DomainDN>}
```

Discussion

If you don't set the `msDS-SDReferenceDomain` attribute for an application partition, then a specific hierarchy will be followed to determine the default security descriptor domain. These are the guidelines:

- If the application partition is created as part of a new tree, the forest root domain is used as the default domain.
- If the application partition is a child of a domain, the parent domain is used as the default domain.
- If the application partition is a child of another application partition, the parent application partition's default domain is used.

See Also

Recipe 10.20 for more on setting the default security descriptor for a class and Recipe 17.1 for creating an application partition

17.9 Delegating Control of Managing an Application Partition

Problem

You want to delegate control over the management of an application partition.

Solution

Using a graphical user interface

1. Open ADSI Edit.
2. Connect to the Configuration naming context of the forest the application partition is in if it is not already present in the left pane.
3. Expand the Configuration naming context and click on the Partitions container.
4. In the right pane, right-click on the `crossRef` object that represents the application partition and select Properties.
5. Click the Security tab.
6. Click the Advanced button.
7. Click the Add button.

---

8. Use the object picker to find the user or group you want to delegate control to and click OK.

9. Click the Properties tab.

10. Under Allow, check the boxes beside Write msDS-NC-Replica-Locations, Write msDS-SDReferenceDomain, Write msDS-Replication-Notify-First-DSA-Delay, and Write msDS-Replication-Notify-Subsequent-DSA-Delay.

11. Click OK.

Using a command-line interface

```
> dsacls <AppPartitionCrossRefDN> /G <UserOrGroup>:RPWP;msDS-NC-Replica-Locations
> dsacls <AppPartitionCrossRefDN> /G <UserOrGroup>:RPWP;msDS-SDReferenceDomain
> dsacls <AppPartitionCrossRefDN> /G <UserOrGroup>:RPWP;msDS-Replication-Notify-
First-DSA-Delay
> dsacls <AppPartitionCrossRefDN> /G <UserOrGroup>:RPWP;msDS-Replication-Notify-
Subsequent-DSA-Delay
```

 As is the case with most permissions, you should exercise care when delegating the ability to create or modify application partitions. Because application partitions reside within Active Directory, allowing them to be placed indiscriminately or setting the initial and subsequent replication delays too low can bring your network to a grinding halt.

Using VBScript

```
' This script delegates control over the four key attributes
' of an app partition to the specified user or group.
' ------ SCRIPT CONFIGURATION ------
' Fully qualified DNS name of app partition
strAppPart = "<AppPartitionFQDN>" ' e.g. apps.adatum.com
' User or group to delegate control to
strUser = "<UserOrGroup>" ' e.g. joe@adatum.com or ADATUM\joe
' ------ END CONFIGURATION ---------

'#############################
' Constants
'#############################

' ADS_ACETYPE_ENUM
Const ADS_ACETYPE_ACCESS_ALLOWED        = &h0
Const ADS_ACETYPE_ACCESS_ALLOWED_OBJECT = &h5

' ADS_FLAGTYPE_ENUM
Const ADS_FLAG_OBJECT_TYPE_PRESENT = &h1

' ADS_RIGHTS_ENUM
Const ADS_RIGHT_DS_WRITE_PROP = &h20
Const ADS_RIGHT_DS_READ_PROP  = &h10

' schemaIDGUID values
Const REPLICA_LOCATIONS            = "{97de9615-b537-46bc-ac0f-10720f3909f3}"
```

```
Const SDREFERENCEDOMAIN          = "{4c51e316-f628-43a5-b06b-ffb695fcb4f3}"
Const NOTIFY_FIRST_DSA_DELAY     = "{85abd4f4-0a89-4e49-bdec-6f35bb2562ba}"
Const NOTIFY_SUBSEQUENT_DSA_DELAY = "{d63db385-dd92-4b52-b1d8-0d3ecc0e86b6}"

'###########################
' Find App Partition
'###########################


set objRootDSE = GetObject("LDAP://RootDSE")
strBase = "<LDAP://cn=Partitions," & _
          objRootDSE.Get("ConfigurationNamingContext") & ">;"
strFilter  = "(&(objectcategory=crossRef)(dnsRoot=" & _
              strAppPart & "));"
strAttrs   = "cn,distinguishedName;"
strScope   = "onelevel"
set objConn = CreateObject("ADODB.Connection")
objConn.Provider = "ADsDSOObject"
objConn.Open "Active Directory Provider"

Set objRS = objConn.Execute(strBase & strFilter & strAttrs & strScope)
if objRS.RecordCount <> 1 then
   WScript.Echo "Did not find a match for " & strAppPart
else
   objRS.MoveLast
   set objAppPart = GetObject("LDAP://" & _
                    objRS.Fields("distinguishedName").Value )
end if

'###########################
' Create ACL
'###########################


set objSD = objAppPart.Get("ntSecurityDescriptor")
set objDACL = objSD.DiscretionaryAcl

' Read/Write Property: msDS-NC-Replica-Locations
set objACE1 = CreateObject("AccessControlEntry")
objACE1.Trustee    = strUser
objACE1.AccessMask = ADS_RIGHT_DS_WRITE_PROP Or ADS_RIGHT_DS_READ_PROP
objACE1.AceFlags   = 0
objACE1.Flags      = ADS_FLAG_OBJECT_TYPE_PRESENT
objACE1.AceType    = ADS_ACETYPE_ACCESS_ALLOWED_OBJECT
objACE1.ObjectType = REPLICA_LOCATIONS '

' Read/Write Property: msDS-SDReferenceDomain
set objACE2 = CreateObject("AccessControlEntry")
objACE2.Trustee    = strUser
objACE2.AccessMask = ADS_RIGHT_DS_WRITE_PROP Or ADS_RIGHT_DS_READ_PROP
objACE2.AceFlags   = 0
objACE2.Flags      = ADS_FLAG_OBJECT_TYPE_PRESENT
objACE2.AceType    = ADS_ACETYPE_ACCESS_ALLOWED_OBJECT
objACE2.ObjectType = SDREFERENCEDOMAIN

' Read/Write Property: msDS-Replication-Notify-First-DSA-Delay
```

```
set objACE3 = CreateObject("AccessControlEntry")
objACE3.Trustee    = strUser
objACE3.AccessMask = ADS_RIGHT_DS_WRITE_PROP Or ADS_RIGHT_DS_READ_PROP
objACE3.AceFlags   = 0
objACE3.Flags      = ADS_FLAG_OBJECT_TYPE_PRESENT
objACE3.AceType    = ADS_ACETYPE_ACCESS_ALLOWED_OBJECT
objACE3.ObjectType = NOTIFY_FIRST_DSA_DELAY

' Read/Write Property: msDS-Replication-Notify-Subsequent-DSA-Delay
set objACE4 = CreateObject("AccessControlEntry")
objACE4.Trustee    = strUser
objACE4.AccessMask = ADS_RIGHT_DS_WRITE_PROP Or ADS_RIGHT_DS_READ_PROP
objACE4.AceFlags   = 0
objACE4.Flags      = ADS_FLAG_OBJECT_TYPE_PRESENT
objACE4.AceType    = ADS_ACETYPE_ACCESS_ALLOWED_OBJECT
objACE4.ObjectType = NOTIFY_SUBSEQUENT_DSA_DELAY

objDACL.AddAce objACE1
objDACL.AddAce objACE2

objDACL.AddAce objACE3
objDACL.AddAce objACE4

'############################
' Set ACL
'############################
objSD.DiscretionaryAcl = objDACL
objAppPart.Put "ntSecurityDescriptor", objSD
objAppPart.SetInfo
WScript.Echo "Delegated control of " & strAppPart & " to " & strUser
```

Discussion

If you want to delegate control of management of application partitions, you must grant control over four key attributes. Here is a description of each attribute and what can be accomplished by having control over it:

msDS-NC-Replica-Locations
> A user can add replica servers for the application partition. See Recipe 17.3 for more information.

msDS-SDReferenceDomain
> A user can define the default security descriptor domain for the application partition. See Recipe 17.8 for more information.

msDS-Replication-Notify-First-DSA-Delay
> See Recipe 17.7 for more information.

msDS-Replication-Notify-Subsequent-DSA-Delay
> See Recipe 17.7 for more information.

If you want to delegate control over managing objects within the application partition, you need to follow the same procedures you would when delegating control over objects in a domain naming context. See Recipe 13.8 for more information on delegating control.

See Also

Recipe 13.8, Recipe 14.6 for delegating control, Recipe 17.3 for more on adding and removing replica servers, Recipe 17.7 for more on the replication delay attributes, and Recipe 17.8 for more on the default security descriptor domain

Active Directory Application Mode and Active Directory Lightweight Directory Service

18.0 Introduction

Active Directory Application Mode (ADAM) was released in November 2003 on the Microsoft website. ADAM is a lightweight LDAP platform that allows developers and administrators to work with AD objects such as users, groups, and organizational units, without worrying about the overhead of running a full-blown copy of the Active Directory directory service. ADAM can run on Windows XP or Windows 2003 computers, and you can run multiple instances of ADAM on a single machine. Because ADAM runs as a standalone service, you can start, stop, install, or remove ADAM instances without affecting or interfering with any underlying AD infrastructure. ADAM can leverage domain authentication, local machine users and groups, or it can authenticate users based on security principals that you've created within ADAM itself. (It's important to note that these are separate from Active Directory security principals, which cannot be created within an ADAM instance.) ADAM can also be used to replicate data between non-domain-joined computers such as ISA configuration between a farm of ISA 2004 servers configured as a workgroup.

With the release of Windows Server 2008, along with several other technologies, Microsoft renamed ADAM. The new name for ADAM is Active Directory Lightweight Directory Service (AD LDS). (Except where explicitly mentioned, the names ADAM and AD LDS will be used interchangeably.) The second version of version of ADAM, ADAM Service Pack 1, was packaged with Windows Server 2003 R2; it contained a number of improvements over the initial release of ADAM, including:

Creating user objects in the Configuration partition
By default, any ADAM user object you create is scoped to only the partition it was created in. By creating user objects in the Configuration partition, you can grant them permissions to resources in any partition within an ADAM instance. This also allows you to configure an ADAM user to administer ADAM, rather than requiring a Windows user to do so.

Password resets chained to Windows
Any password changes made within ADAM to a proxy object such as a userProxy can be forwarded through to the appropriate Windows authentication store.

VLV searching
This version of ADAM can leverage the VLV function of Windows Server 2003, which allows you to display a subset of the results of a query without needing to return every single entry.

With the release of Windows Server 2008, ADAM has been rebranded as Active Directory Lightweight Directory Services, or AD LDS. In addition to the feature set in ADAM and ADAM SP1, ADLDS includes the following new features:

Server Core support
AD LDS can be installed on computers that are running Server Core, the reduced-footprint installation option that was introduced with Windows Server 2008.

Auditing for AD LDS changes
The Directory Services Changes audit policy subcategory allows you to view old and new values when changes are made to AD LDS objects.

Database Mounting Tool (Dsamain.exe)
Similar to Active Directory Domain Services, you can use *dsamain* to mount snapshots of AD LDS partitions to view and compare information from previous points in time.

Support for Active Directory Sites and Services
You can now use the AD Sites & Services MMC to manage replication between ADLDS instances.

Unlike ADAM (V1.0 and SP1), currently there is no standalone installation package for AD LDS; it is only included in Window Server 2008. This means that you cannot install AD LDS on client operating systems such as Windows Vista or XP or even on previous Server operating systems such as Windows Server 2003. This is especially unfortunate as ADAM cannot be properly installed on Vista. For more detailed information on ADAM and AD LDS, refer to *Active Directory*, Fourth Edition, by Brian Desmond et al. (O'Reilly).

18.1 Installing ADAM/AD LDS

Problem

You want to install a new instance of ADAM.

Solution

Using a graphical user interface

To install AD LDS on a Windows Server 2008 server, do the following:

1. Click Start→Server Manager.
2. Browse to Roles. Click Add Roles. Click Next.
3. Place a checkmark next to Active Directory Lightweight Directory Services.
4. Click Next twice, and then click Install.

To install ADAM on a Windows Server 2003 R2 server, do the following:

1. Click Start→Control Panel→Add/Remove Programs.
2. Click Add/Remove Windows Components.
3. Select Active Directory Services, and click Details.
4. Place a checkmark next to Active Directory Application Mode (ADAM). Click OK and then Next to continue.
5. If prompted, provide the path to the Windows Server 2003 R2 Disc 2 media.
6. Click Finish when all files have copied.

To install ADAM on Windows XP or Windows Server 2003, do the following:

1. Double-click on the ADAM installer. Click Next to begin.
2. After reading the License Agreement, select the radio button next to "I agree" and click Next.
3. Click Finish when all files have copied.

Using a command-line interface

To perform a command-line install of AD LDS on Windows Server 2008, use the following syntax:

```
> servermanagercmd -install adlds
```

To perform a silent install of ADAM on 2003, R2, or XP, use the following syntax:

```
> <ADAM Installer File> /q
```

The /q switch is not supported by the ADAM installer that is included with R2; to perform an unattended install of an ADAM instance on R2, see Recipes 18.2 and 18.3.

Discussion

At its most basic level, an ADAM installation will simply copy the necessary program files and DLLs to the machine in question without creating an ADAM instance or performing any other configuration steps. This can be useful if you want to include AD LDS as part of a base image that you deploy to your application developers, while allowing them to create their own instances and configuration sets as they see fit. By using the /q switch on the ADAM installation file or using the **servermanagercmd** command in 2008, you can deploy it during Windows setup or through an automated batch file.

If the installation process encounters any errors, these will be logged in the *%windir%\Debug\adamsetup.log* file.

See Also

Recipes 18.2 and 18.3, MS KB 840991 (Active Directory Application Mode Does Not Function Correctly in Windows Server 2003 or Windows XP), MSDN: About Active Directory Application Mode [ADAM], and *Active Directory*

18.2 Creating a New ADAM/AD LDS Instance

Problem

You want to create a new ADAM/AD LDS instance.

Solution

Using a graphical user interface

1. Click on Start→All Programs→ADAM→Create an ADAM instance. Click Next to begin.

In Windows Server 2008, you will select Start→Administrative Tools→Active Directory Lightweight Directory Services Setup and then click Next.

2. Select the radio button next to "A unique instance" and click Next.

3. Enter the name of the instance and click Next.

4. Enter the LDAP and SSL port numbers that will be used to access this instance; these default to 50000 and 50001 on a domain controller or any computer that is already listening on the default LDAP port. Otherwise, the LDAP and SSL ports that ADAM/AD LDS chooses during the installation will be 389 and 636.

 If you've already installed an ADAM/AD LDS instance on ports 50000 and 50001, the ADAM installer will choose the next two ports available; the second ADAM instance would choose ports 50002 and 50003, then 50004 and 50005, and so on.

5. Click Next to continue.

6. Specify whether you want to create an Application Directory Partition for this instance. You can use any partition name isn't already being used, such as `cn=IntranetApplication,dc=adatum,dc=com`. Click Next to continue.

7. Specify the directory that will house the instance data as well as its data recovery files. These will both default to *c:\Program Files\Microsoft ADAM\<instance name>\data*. Click Next.

8. On the Service Account Selection screen, configure the account under whose security context this instance will run. By default, the `Network Service Account` is selected, or you can click the radio button next to "This account" and specify a different account.

9. On the ADAM (or AD LDS) administrator's screen, specify the user or group account that will have administrative rights to this ADAM instance. This defaults to the currently logged-on user, or you can click the radio button next to "This account" and specify a different user or group. Click Next.

10. Specify whether you want to import additional LDIF files into this instance. See Recipe 18.7 for more information.

11. Click Next twice and then Finish to create the new instance.

Using a command-line interface on all versions of ADAM and AD LDS

Create an answer file similar to the one listed here. Save it as *adam_install.txt*:

```
[ADAMInstall]

; Install a unique ADAM instance
InstallType=Unique

; Specify the name of the new instance
InstanceName=IntranetApplication

; Specify the ports to be used by LDAP.
LocalLDAPPortToListenOn=50000
```

```
LocalSSLPortToListenOn=50001

; Create a new application partition
NewApplicationPartitionToCreate="cn=IntranetApplication,dc=adatum,dc=com"

; The following line specifies the directory to use for ADAM data files.
DataFilesPath=C:\Program Files\Microsoft ADAM\IntranetApplication\data
; The following line specifies the directory to use for ADAM log files.
LogFilesPath=D:\ADAM Log Files\IntranetApplication\logs

; The following line specifies the .ldf files to import into the ADAM schema.
ImportLDIFFiles="ms-inetorgperson.ldf" "ms-user.ldf"
```

Then enter the following command at the Run line or from the Windows command prompt:

```
> adaminstall.exe /answer:<driveletter>:\<pathname>\<answerfile.txt>
```

Discussion

An ADAM/AD LDS *instance* refers to a single installation of ADAM/AD LDS on a particular server or workstation. A single Windows computer can host multiple instances of ADAM/AD LDS simultaneously; they are all independently managed and use different LDAP and LDAPS ports to communicate. Just as you can have multiple web servers operating on the same computer, with one using TCP port 80 and one using TCP port 8081, you can likewise have multiple ADAM instances running simultaneously on different ports.

When you create an ADAM/AD LDS instance, you also have the option to create an application directory partition to associate with the instance. An ADAM/AD LDS instance can have zero, one, or multiple application partitions associated with it that will be used to store application data such as security principals as well as user and group information.

See Also

Recipe 18.7, MSDN: Binding to an Instance [ADAM], and Chapter 20 of *Active Directory*

18.3 Creating a New Replica of an ADAM/AD LDS Configuration Set

Problem

You want to create a new replica of an existing ADAM or AD LDS configuration set.

Solution

Using a graphical user interface

1. Click on Start→All Programs→ADAM→Create an ADAM instance. Click Next to begin. (In Windows Server 2008 you will click Start→Administrative Tools→Active Directory Lightweight Directory Services Setup and then click Next.)

2. Select the radio button next to "A replica of an existing instance" and click Next.

3. Enter the name of the instance that you want to connect to and click Next.

4. Enter the LDAP and SSL port numbers that will be used to access this instance; these default to **50000** and **50001** on a domain controller or any computer that is already listening on the default LDAP port. Otherwise, the LDAP and SSL ports that ADAM chooses during the installation will be **389** and **636**.

 If you've already installed an ADAM instance on ports **50000** and **50001**, the ADAM installer will choose the next two ports available; the second ADAM instance would choose ports **50002** and **50003**, then **50004** and **50005**, and so on.

5. On the Join a Configuration Set screen, enter the name of a server hosting an existing replica of this instance, and the port number used to connect to it. Click Next to continue.

6. On the Administrative Credentials for the Configuration Set screen, specify a user or group account that has administrative rights to this ADAM instance. This defaults to the currently logged-on user, or you can click the radio button next to "This account" and specify a different user or group. Click Next.

7. On the Copy Application Partitions screen, select the application directory partitions that you would like to replicate to the local server. Use the Add, Remove, Select All, and Remove All buttons to select the appropriate partitions. Click Next to continue.

8. Specify the directory that will house the instance data as well as its data recovery files. These will both default to *c:\Program Files\Microsoft ADAM\<instance name>\data*. Click Next.

9. On the Service Account Selection screen, configure the account under whose security context this instance will run. By default, the `Network Service Account` is selected, or you can click the radio button next to "This account" and specify a different account.

10. On the ADAM (or AD LDS) Administrators screen, specify the user or group account that will have administrative rights to this instance. This defaults to the currently logged-on user, or you can click the radio button next to "This account" and specify a different user or group. Click Next.

11. Click Next and then Finish to create the new ADAM replica.

Using a command-line interface on all versions

Create an answer file similar to the one listed here. Save it as *new_replica_install.txt*:

```
[ADAMInstall]

[ADAMInstall]
; Install a replica of an existing ADAM instance.
InstallType=Replica
; Specify the name of the new replica.
InstanceName=IntranetApplication
; Specify the ports used for LDAP and SSL.
LocalLDAPPortToListenOn=50000
LocalSSLPortToListenOn=50001
; The following line specifies the directory to use for
; ADAM data files.
DataFilesPath=C:\Program Files\Microsoft ADAM\IntranetApplication\data
; The following line specifies the directory to use for ADAM log files.
LogFilesPath=D:\ADAM Log Files\IntranetApplication\logs
; Specify the name of the a computer hosting an existing replica
SourceServer=servername
SourceLDAPPort=389
```

Then enter the following command at the Run line or from the Windows command prompt:

```
> adaminstall.exe /answer:<driveletter>:\<pathname>\<answerfile.txt>
```

Discussion

Similar to Active Directory itself, ADAM and AD LDS use *multimaster replication* that allows multiple computers to host, read, and make updates to one or more *configuration sets*. An ADAM/AD LDS *replica* is a computer that is hosting one instance of a particular configuration set. Unlike Active Directory, you can host replica instances on computers that are running any Windows XP or Windows Server 2003 computer; you are not restricted to replicating data only to your domain controllers. Conversely, you are also no longer forced to replicate data to *all* of your domain controllers unnecessarily; this can be quite useful in the case of data that is locally interesting, but that perhaps doesn't need to be replicated throughout your entire AD environment.

See Also

Recipe 18.2 for creating a new ADAM instance, MSDN: Using Application Directory Partitions [ADAM], and Chapter 20 of *Active Directory*

18.4 Stopping and Starting an ADAM/AD LDS Instance

Problem

You want to start or stop an ADAM instance.

Solution

Using a graphical user interface

1. Open the Services MMC snap-in.
2. Select the name of the ADAM or AD LDS instance that you want to manage.
3. Right-click on the instance name and select Start, Stop, Pause, Resume, or Restart, as needed.

Using a command-line interface

To stop an ADAM or AD LDS instance, enter the following:

```
> net stop <instance_name>
```

To start an ADAM or AD LDS instance, enter the following:

```
> net start <instance_name>
```

Using VBScript

```
' The following code will stop or start an ADAM or AD LDS instance
'--------------- SCRIPT CONFIGURATION ---------------
strComputer = "."
strInstanceName = "<ADAM/AD LDS Instance>" ' ie "ADAM_IntranetApplication"
'---------------------------------------------------
Set objWMIService = GetObject("winmgmts:" _
    & "{impersonationLevel=impersonate}!\\" & strComputer & "\root\cimv2")
Set colServiceList = objWMIService.ExecQuery _
    ("Select * from Win32_Service where Name='" & strInstanceName & "'")

For Each objService in colServiceList
    errReturn = objService.StartService() ' change this method name to
                                          ' .StopService() to stop the
                                          ' ADAM instance.

Next
```

Using PowerShell

```
Start-Service "<ADAM/AD LDS Instance>"
Stop-Service "<ADAM/AD LDS Instance>"
```

Discussion

When you install an ADAM or AD LDS instance on a computer (regardless of whether it is a new or replica instance), the instance will advertise itself as a typical Windows service with the naming convention of ADAM_*<InstanceName>*, where *<InstanceName>* is the name you specified when you installed the instance. If you need to modify the display name of the service after you've installed the ADAM instance, you can use the built-in **sc** utility as follows:

```
> sc \\<servername> config <servicename> displayname = "<display name>"
```

See Also

Recipe 18.6 for listing the ADAM instances installed on a computer, MSDN: Service-ControllerStatusEnumeration, MSDN: Service Control Utilities [SDK Tools], and Chapter 20 of *Active Directory*

18.5 Changing the Ports Used by an ADAM/AD LDS Instance

Problem

You want to change the LDAP or SSL ports that are being used by a particular ADAM instance.

Solution

```
> dsdbutil
    > activate instance <instancename>
    > LDAP port <port>
    > SSL port <port>
> quit
```

Discussion

If you need to change the LDAP and/or SSL port that an instance is using to communicate, you must first stop the instance using one of the methods specified in Recipe 18.4. Once the instance has stopped, use *dsdbutil* as shown in the section called "Solution".

See Also

Recipe 18.4 for more on starting and stopping ADAM/AD LDS instances and *Active Directory*

18.6 Listing the ADAM Instances Installed on a Computer

Problem

You want to list all of the ADAM instances installed on a computer.

Solution

Using a command-line interface

To list all ADAM instances installed on a computer, enter the following:

```
> dsdbutil
```

From the `dsbutil`: prompt, enter the following:

```
> list instances
```

Using VBScript

```
' The following code will list all instances whose name begins with
' "ADAM_" on the local computer
'---------------- SCRIPT CONFIGURATION ----------------
strComputer = "."
'------------------------------------------------------
Set objWMIService = GetObject("winmgmts:" _
    & "{impersonationLevel=impersonate}!\\" & strComputer & "\root\cimv2")

Set services = objWMIService.ExecQuery _
    ("Select * from Win32_Service where Name Like '% ADAM_%'")

If services.Count = 0 Then
   Wscript.Echo "No ADAM instances found."
Else
   For Each service in services
        Wscript.Echo service.Name & " -- " & service.State
   Next
End If
```

Using PowerShell

The following code will list all ADAM/AD LDS instances whose name begins with
"ADAM_" on the local computer:

```
Get-Service -include "ADAM_*"
```

Discussion

As we discussed in Recipe 18.4, a single computer can host multiple ADAM instances
running on different ports, each of which will advertise itself as a typical Windows
service. In Windows Server 2003, R2, and XP, these services will have a naming convention of `ADAM_<InstanceName>`, where *<InstanceName>* is the name that you specified
when you installed the instance. (The name of the service will remain the same even if
you change the display name or description of the service at a later time, which can
make the *services.msc* snap-in a less-than-desirable option for stopping and starting
ADAM instances if you make a habit of renaming them.) By querying for service names
that include the string "ADAM" using something like '%ADAM_%' in the WQL query,
you can return the ADAM instances that are installed on a local or remote computer.
The method discussed in this recipe will not help you, however, if someone has modified the Registry key containing the name of the ADAM instance. Locating ADAM
services can be a difficult task if someone in your organization is trying to hide his
ADAM instances. One possible solution if you are having difficulty with this type of
information gathering would be to perform a port scan on one or more target

computers; once you've obtained a list of listening ports, you can connect to each one in turn and look for an LDAP response.

In Windows Server 2008, the `"ADAM_"` prefix has been dropped from the service name, which makes the `dsbutil` option the most appropriate option for listing AD LDS instances on a Windows Server 2008 instance.

See Also

Recipe 18.4, MSDN: Querying with WQL [WMI], MSDN: WQL Operators [WMI], and Chapter 20 of *Active Directory*

18.7 Extending the ADAM/AD LDS Schema

Problem

You want to extend the ADAM/AD LDS Schema with new classes or attributes.

Solution

Using a command-line interface

To extend the ADAM/AD LDS Schema from the command line, you'll need to create an LDIF file containing the necessary schema extensions, and then import it using the LDIFDE command, or use a tool like AdMod to perform the changes. ADAM comes with a number of such LDIF files pre-installed that you can import during the ADAM installation process. If you did not import these files during installation, you can do so after the fact using the following syntax:

```
> ldifde -i -f <driveletter>:\<pathname>\contact.ldf -s <servername>:<portnumber>
-k -j . -c "CN=Schema,CN=Configuration" #schemaNamingContext
```

Discussion

The schema that you receive when you install ADAM/AD LDS contains a subset of the classes and attributes that exist in the Active Directory Schema. You have the same ability to extend the schema in ADAM as you do in AD, which means that you can expand and modify the schema to be the same as the AD Schema, or to match any changes made by your third-party or home-grown applications. Because of this, ADAM is a great place to test potential schema modifications that you want to make in Active Directory. Because the schema extension process works the same in both AD and ADAM, and because you can easily install, uninstall, and reinstall ADAM instances, you can use ADAM to quickly test new extensions, tweaking the definitions until you get exactly what you want.

Every instance of ADAM will have at least two partitions: the Configuration partition and the Schema partition; you can create additional application partitions during or after installation, as described in *Active Directory*. Similar to the Active Directory Schema NC, the ADAM Schema partition contains definitions of classes and attributes that can be used to create objects within a particular ADAM instance. An ADAM Schema is unique to an individual ADAM instance; changes to the schema in one instance will not affect the schema in other, separate instances. ADAM comes with a number of pre-configured LDIF files that you can import to create common object types such as user, contact, and inetOrgPerson objects. You can import these LDIF files during the initial creation of an ADAM instance as well as after the instance has been created.

Using a command-line interface

When updating the ADAM Schema, be sure to use the version of *ldifde* that came with ADAM/AD LDS rather than any earlier versions of the utility.

See Also

Recipe 18.2, MSDN: Adding User Classes [ADAM], MSDN: Adding Contact Classes [ADAM], MSDN: Extending the Active Directory Application Mode Schema [ADAM], and Chapter 20 of *Active Directory*

18.8 Managing ADAM/AD LDS Application Partitions

Problem

You want to add or remove an application partition to house ADAM data.

Solution

Using a graphical user interface

To add an application partition, do the following:

1. Open *ldp.exe* from the *%windir%\ADAM* folder. (LDP is installed by default on a Windows Server 2008 server running the AD LDS role.) Click Connection→Connect to bind to the desired instance, and Connection→Bind to provide credentials to bind to the instance.

2. Click on Browse→Add child.

3. For DN, enter a distinguished name for the application partition.

4. Under "Edit entry," enter "ObjectClass" in the Attribute box and "container" in the Values box and then click Enter.

5. Under "Edit entry," enter "instanceType" for the Attribute and "5" in the Values box, and then click Enter.

6. Click Run.

To remove an application partition, do the following:

1. Open ADAM ADSI Edit in Windows Server 2003, R2, or XP; in Windows Server 2008, simply open ADSI Edit. If necessary, create and bind to a connection of your ADAM/AD LDS instance.

2. Browse to the Partitions container (`CN=Partitions`). Right-click on the application directory partition that you want to delete, and then click Delete.

3. Click Yes to confirm.

Using a command-line interface

Use the following sequence of commands to create an ADAM application partition:

```
> dsmgmt
    > create nc <ApplicationPartitionDN> container <ComputerName>:<PortNumber>
    > quit
> quit
```

Use the following command to delete an application partition:

```
> dsmgmt
    > delete nc <ApplicationPartitionDN>
    > quit
> quit
```

Using VBScript

```
' This code creates an application partition off of the
' root of the default forest.
' ------ SCRIPT CONFIGURATION ------
strAppPart = "<AppPartitionName>" ' DN of the app partition to delete
strServer = "<DomainControllerName>" ' DNS name of DC to host app partition
strDescr = "<Description>" ' Descriptive text about the app partition
' ------ END CONFIGURATION --------

set objRootDSE = GetObject("LDAP://" & strServer & "/RootDSE")
set objLDAP = GetObject("LDAP://" & strServer & "/" & _
                        objRootDSE.Get("rootDomainNamingContext") )
set objAppPart = objLDAP.Create("domainDNS", "dc=" & strAppPart)
objAppPart.Put "instancetype", 5
objAppPart.Put "description", strDescr
objAppPart.SetInfo
WScript.Echo "Created application partition: " & strAppPart

' This code deletes the specified application partition
' ------ SCRIPT CONFIGURATION ------
strAppPart = "<AppPartitionDN>" ' DN of the app partition to delete
' ------ END CONFIGURATION ---------

set objRootDSE = GetObject("LDAP://RootDSE")
strBase = "<LDAP://cn=Partitions," & _
            objRootDSE.Get("ConfigurationNamingContext") & ">;"
strFilter = "(&(objectcategory=crossRef)(nCName=" & _
            strAppPart & "));"
```

```
strAttrs = "cn,distinguishedName;"
strScope = "onelevel"

set objConn = CreateObject("ADODB.Connection")
objConn.Provider = "ADsDSOObject"
objConn.Open "Active Directory Provider"
set objRS = objConn.Execute(strBase & strFilter & strAttrs & strScope)

if objRS.RecordCount <> 1 then
    WScript.Echo "Did not find a match for " & strAppPart
else
    objRS.MoveLast
    set objAppPart = GetObject("LDAP://" & _
                         objRS.Fields("distinguishedName").Value )

    objAppPart.DeleteObject(0)
    Wscript.Echo "Deleted " & objRS.Fields("distinguishedName").Value
end if
```

Discussion

An ADAM or AD LDS installation creates up to three partitions by default: Configuration, Schema, and an application. The Configuration and Schema partitions get created automatically during the creation of a new ADAM instance; you can create application partitions during the initial installation or after the instance has been created. If you're installing a replica of an existing configuration set, the existing Schema and Configuration partitions are automatically replicated to the new instance. The Configuration partition stores information about ADAM replication and partitions, while the Schema partition contains definitions for the types of objects that you can create within the instance. (These partitions correspond quite closely to the Configuration and Schema naming contexts within Active Directory.)

When you create a new application directory partition, you need to specify a *distinguished name* for the partition; this name needs to be unique within your environment.

See Also

MSDN: Using Application Directory Partitions [ADAM], MSDN: Creating an Application Directory Partition [ADAM], MSDN: Deleting an Application Directory Partition [ADAM], and Chapter 20 of *Active Directory*

18.9 Managing ADAM/AD LDS Organizational Units

Problem

You want to create or delete OUs within an ADAM or AD LDS instance.

Solution

Using a graphical user interface

1. Open ADAM ADSI Edit. If necessary, create and bind to a connection of your instance.
2. Right-click on the instance and select New→Object.
3. Under "Select a class," click on `organizationalUnit` and click Next.
4. For the value of the `ou` attribute, type `AdamUsers` and click Next.
5. Click Finish.
6. To delete an OU, right-click on the object in question and select Delete.

Using a command-line interface

To create an ADAM OU from the command line, use the following syntax:

```
> admod -h <ComputerName>:<PortNumber> -b <OU DN>
objectClass::organizationalUnit -add
```

To delete an OU, replace the –add switch with –del in the previous statement.

 A useful option in AdFind and AdMod for working with ADAM is the ability to create environment variables to specify long or often-used switches. In this example, it would be quite useful to define an environment variable of `adam-h` that has a value of `<ComputerName>:<PortNumber>` and then that portion of the command can be shorted to `-e adam`. See the AdFind usage screens for more information. If you work with multiple ADAM instances, you can specify multiple environment variables such as `adam1-h`, `adam2-h`, and `adam3-h` and then specify `-e adam1`, `-e adam2`, or `-e adam3` to access the different instances. You can even specify `adamx-u` and `adamx-up` environment variables to specify alternate credentials to connect to the various ADAM instances.

Using VBScript

```
' The following code will add a new OU to an
' ADAM or AD LDS instance
'---------------- SCRIPT CONFIGURATION ----------------
strComputerName = "<ComputerName>" ' Use "localhost" for the local computer
strPort = "<PortNumber>"           ' the LDAP port number to connect to
strAppPart = "<Application Partition DN>"
'------------------------------------------------------

Set objDomain = GetObject("LDAP://" & strComputerName & _
                          ":" & strPort & "/" & strAppPart)
Set objOU = objDomain.Create("organizationalUnit", "ou=Finance")
objOU.SetInfo
```

```
' The following code will delete the OU you just created
objOU.Delete "organizationalUnit", "ou=Finance"
```

Using PowerShell

To create an Organizational Unit using the Quest AD cmdlets, use the following syntax:

```
new-QADObject -Service "<Computer Name>:<Port Number>" -parentcontainer '<Parent
Container DN>' -type 'organizationalunit' -name 'Marketing' -ObjectAttributes
@{description='Marketing OU'}
```

To create an OU using `System.DirectoryServices`, use the following:

```
$objParentDN = [ADSI] "LDAP://<ComputerName>:<PortNumber>/<Parent Container DN>"
$objNewOU = $objParentDN.Create("organizationalunit", "ou=Sales")
$objNewOU.put("description", "Sales OU")
$bjNewOU.setInfo()
```

Discussion

Creating OUs in ADAM and AD LDS is identical to creating them within Active Directory. Just like in AD, ADAM/AD LDS OUs are containers that can contain other objects such as users, groups, contacts, or other OUs. You can also delegate permissions to an OU, allowing a user or group to have rights to the OU itself and to objects within that OU.

Using a command-line interface

A useful feature of AdFind and AdMod is that, if you are working on ADAM or AD on the local machine, you can use a period (.) for the hostname and it will expand that into *localhost* for you.

See Also

Recipe 18.20 for more on managing ADAM and AD LDS permissions, Chapter 5 for more on managing Active Directory OUs, and Chapter 20 of *Active Directory*

18.10 Managing ADAM Users

Problem

You want to create or delete user objects within an ADAM instance.

Solution

Using a graphical user interface

1. Open ADAM ADSI Edit, or ADSI Edit in Windows Server 2008. If necessary, create a connection and bind to the necessary ADAM or AD LDS instance.

---

2. Right-click on the container that should house the user and select New→Object.

3. Under "Select a class," click on "user" and click Next.

4. For the value of the cn attribute, type Joe Smith and click Next.

5. Click Finish.

Using a command-line interface

```
> admod -h <ComputerName>:<PortNumber> -b <User DN>
objectClass::user -add
```

Using VBScript

```
' The following code will add a new OU to an ADAM instance
'--------------- SCRIPT CONFIGURATION ---------------
strComputerName = "<ComputerName>" ' Use "localhost" for the local computer
strPort = "<PortNumber>"              ' the LDAP port number to connect to
strAppPart = "<Application Partition DN>" ' ie "o=adatum,c=us"
strUserDN = "<UserDN>"               ' ie "Joe Smith"
strUPN = "<UserPrincipalName>"       ' ie "joe@adatum.com"
'----------------------------------------------------

Set objOU = GetObject("LDAP://" & strComputerName & _ ":" & strPort & _
                      "/" & strAppPart))
Set objUser = objOU.Create("user", strUserDN)
objUser.Put "displayName", strUserDN
objUser.Put "userPrincipalName", strUPN
objUser.SetInfo
```

Using PowerShell

To create a new ADAM/AD LDS user with the Quest AD cmdlets, use the following syntax:

```
new-QADUser -service "<Computer Name>:<Port Number>" -name '<User CN>' -
parentContainer '<Application Partition DN/<Parent DN>' -UserPrincipalName '<User
UPN>' -UserPassword "<Password>"
```

To create a new Active Directory user with System.DirectoryServices, use the following:

```
$objParent = [ADSI]
"LDAP://<ComputerName>:<PortNumber>/<ApplicationPartitionDN>/<ParentDN>")
$objUser = $objParent.Create("user", "cn=<User CN>")
$objUser.Put("userPrincipalName", "<UserUPN>")
$objUser.Put("displayName", "<UserFirstName> <UserLastName>")
$objUser.SetInfo()
$objUser.Put("userPassword", "<Password>")
$objUser.SetInfo()
```

Discussion

Creating users in ADAM or AD LDS is quite similar to creating users in Active Directory. The most significant difference is that ADAM/AD LDS users do not have the sAMAccountName attribute. You could conceivably define such an attribute within ADAM and associate it with the user class, but it will not have the same properties that it does in Active Directory, particularly the AD constraint in which sAMAccountName uniqueness is enforced across a domain. ADAM also would not be able to use a manually created attribute like that for user logons the way that sAMAccountName is used in AD.

 If you create an ADAM user on a Windows Server 2003 or R2 computer without creating a password for it, the object will be disabled until you enable it using LDP or an ADSI script.

See Also

Recipe 18.11 to configure the password for an ADAM/AD LDS user, MSDN: Managing Users [ADAM], MSDN: Set or Modify the Password of an ADAM User [ADAM], and Chapter 20 of *Active Directory*

18.11 Changing the Password for an ADAM or AD LDS User

Problem

You want to change the password for an ADAM or AD LDS user.

Solution

Using a graphical user interface

1. Open LDP from the Windows Support Tools. (In Windows Server 2008, LDP is installed by default on a server that is running the AD DS or AD LDS server roles.)
2. Click Connection→Connect, and then enter the server name and port number used by your ADAM or AD LDS instance.
3. Click Options→Connection Options.
4. In the Option Name drop-down, select LDAP_OPT_SIGN, type "1" in Value, and then click Set.
5. Select LDAP_OPT_ENCRYPT, type "1" in Value, click Set and then Close.
6. Click Connection→Bind, and then enter a username and password to bind to the ADAM or AD LDS instance.
7. Click on View→Tree. Leave the BaseDN value blank and click OK.

8. Navigate to the DN of the container within the application partition containing the ADAM or AD LDS user in question.

9. Right-click the CN=*<UserName>* user object, and then click Modify.

10. Enter "userpassword" as the attribute to be modified, and then enter the new password under Values.

11. Click Enter, and then click Run.

Using VBScript

```
' The following code will set the password for an ADAM user
'---------------- SCRIPT CONFIGURATION -----------------
Const ADS_SECURE_AUTHENTICATION = 1
Const ADS_USE_SSL              = 2

Const ADS_USE_SIGNING         =  64
Const ADS_USE_SEALING         = 128

Const ADS_OPTION_PASSWORD_PORTNUMBER = 6
Const ADS_OPTION_PASSWORD_METHOD    = 7

Const ADS_PASSWORD_ENCODE_REQUIRE_SSL = 0
Const ADS_PASSWORD_ENCODE_CLEAR      = 1

strComputerName = "<ComputerName>" ' Use "localhost" for the local computer
strPort = "<PortNumber>"           ' the LDAP port number to connect to
intPort = CInt(strPort)
strUserDN = "<UserDN>"

lngAuth = ADS_USE_SIGNING Or ADS_USE_SEALING Or _
          ADS_SECURE_AUTHENTICATION
'------------------------------------------------------

' Bind to the user whose password you want to change
Set objUser = GetObject _
    ("LDAP://" & strComputerName & ":" & strPort & "/" & strUserDN, _
      vbNullString, vbNullString, lngAuth)

' Set the password for the user.
objUser.SetOption ADS_OPTION_PASSWORD_PORTNUMBER, intPort
objUser.SetOption ADS_OPTION_PASSWORD_METHOD, _
                  ADS_PASSWORD_ENCODE_CLEAR

' In a production script, this should be read in as a script argument
' rather than being embedded in clear-text
' within the script itself
objUser.SetPassword "
ADAMComplexPassword1234"

If Err.Number <>0 Then
    WScript.Echo "Error:      Set password failed with error " _
                              & Hex(Err.Number)
Else
    WScript.Echo "Success:    Password set for user"
```

```
    WScript.Echo "              " & objUser.ADsPath
End If
```

Using PowerShell

```
Set-QADUser -Service "<ComputerName>:<PortNumber>" -Identity "<User DN>"
-userPassword <NewPassword>
```

Discussion

To create user objects within an ADAM instance, you first need to import the optional
LDIF files that are provided with the ADAM installer into the ADAM schema, including
ms-User.ldf, ms-InetOrgPerson.ldf, and *ms-UserProxy.ldf*. The *ms-user.ldf* file allows
you to create `Person`, `organizational-Person`, and `User` objects. Any ADAM user objects
that you create on Windows Server 2003, R2, or Windows Server 2008 computers will
adhere to whatever local or domain password and account lockout policies are in place
on the server that's hosting the instance. You can use the procedures listed here to
change the password for an ADAM/AD LDS user, or to set a password for an ADAM/
AD LDS user that was created without specifying an initial password.

Using a command-line interface

You can also use *ldifde* to set or change an ADAM or AD LDS user's password, but it
requires a 128-bit SSL connection with a certificate installed on the computer that's
running the instance.

You can also perform this using the `-kerbenc` switch in `admod`, as follows:

```
> admod -h . -b cn=jsmith,o=test userpassword::mypasswordQ1 -kerbenc
```

See Also

MS KB 263991 (How to Set a User's Password with LDIFDE), MSDN: Setting User
Passwords [ADAM], and Chapter 20 of *Active Directory*

18.12 Enabling and Disabling an ADAM User

Problem

You want to enable or disable an ADAM user object.

Solution

Using a graphical user interface

1. Open ADAM ADSI Edit, or ADSI Edit in Windows Server 2008. If necessary, create
   and bind to a connection of your ADAM or AD LDS instance.
2. Navigate to the user in question, right-click, and select Properties.

3. Scroll to the `msDS-UserAccountDisabled` attribute and click Edit.

4. Click True, and then click OK.

5. To re-enable the ADAM user account, modify the `msDS-UserAccountDisabled` attribute to have a value of `False`.

Using a command-line interface

To disable an ADAM user from the command line, enter the following syntax:

```
> admod -h <ComputerName>:<PortNumber> -b <User DN>
msDS-UserAccountDisabled::TRUE
```

To enable or re-enable a user account, change `TRUE` to `FALSE` in the previous command.

 When configuring this attribute, `TRUE` and `FALSE` are case-sensitive and must be specified using all uppercase letters.

Using VBScript

```
' The following code will enable
' or disable an ADAM user
'---------------- SCRIPT CONFIGURATION ----------------
strComputerName = "<ComputerName>" ' Use "localhost" for the local computer
strPort = "<PortNumber>"           ' the LDAP port number to connect to
strUserDN = "<UserDN>"
'------------------------------------------------------

Set objUser = GetObject _
    ("LDAP://" & strComputerName & ":" & strPort & "/" & strUserDN)

objUser.Put " msDS-UserAccountDisabled", "FALSE" ' set this to TRUE to disable
objUser.SetInfo
```

Using PowerShell

```
Enable-QADUser -Identity <User DN> -Service "<ComputerName>:<PortNumber>"
Disable-QADUser -Identity <User DN> -Service "<ComputerName>:<PortNumber>"

$objUser = GetObject("LDAP://<ComputerName>:<PortNumber>/<UserDN>")
$objUser.Put("msDS-UserAccountDisabled", "FALSE")
$objUser.SetInfo()
```

Discussion

ADAM or AD LDS users can be enabled or disabled by modifying the `msDS-UserAccountDisabled` property. A new user will be enabled by default when you first create it, unless the password you've assigned for it doesn't meet the requirements of the password policy, which is in effect on the machine. This restriction doesn't apply to ADAM instances that are being housed on Windows XP Professional computers.

Since ADAM support on XP is primarily intended for standalone development tasks rather than hosting enterprise-caliber applications it doesn't enforce password policies.

See Also

Recipe 18.11 for more on setting the password of an ADAM user, MSDN: ms-DS-User-Account-Disabled Attribute [AD Schema], and Chapter 20 of *Active Directory*

18.13 Creating ADAM or AD LDS Groups

Problem

You want to create or delete a **group** object within ADAM.

Solution

Using a graphical user interface

1. Open ADAM ADSI Edit or ADSI Edit on Windows Server 2008. If necessary, create and bind to a connection of your ADAM instance.
2. Right-click on the instance and select New→Object.
3. Under "Select a class," click on group and click Next.
4. For the value of the **cn** attribute, type "AdamGroup" and click Next.
5. Leave the value of the **groupType** attribute blank to create a security-enabled global group and click Next.
6. Click Finish.
7. To delete a **group** object, right-click on the object in question and select Delete.

Using a command-line interface

To create an ADAM or AD LDS group from the command line, enter the following syntax:

```
> admod -h <ComputerName>:<PortNumber> -b <Group DN>
objectClass::group -add
```

 To delete a **group** object, change **-add** to **-del** in the previous command.

Using VBScript

```
' The following code will create a group object
'--------------- SCRIPT CONFIGURATION ---------------
strComputerName = "<ComputerName>" ' Use "localhost" for the local computer
strPort = "<PortNumber>"           ' the LDAP port number to connect to
strOUDN = "<OUDN>"                 ' ie "ou=AdamUsers,o=adatum,c=us"
strGroupName = "<GroupName>"       ' ie "cn=FinanceGroup"
'----------------------------------------------------

Set objOU = GetObject("LDAP://" & strComputerName _
                      & ":" & strPort & "/" & strOUDN)
Set objGroup = objOU.Create("group", strGroupName)
objGroup.SetInfo

' The following code snippet will delete the group you just created
objOU.delete "group", strGroupName
```

Using PowerShell

To create a **group** object using the Quest AD cmdlets, use the following syntax:

```
new-QADObject -Service "<Computer Name>:<Port Number>" -parentcontainer '<Parent
Container DN>' -type 'group' -name 'MarketingGroup'
```

To create an OU using **System.DirectoryServices**, use the following:

```
$objParentDN = [ADSI] "LDAP://<ComputerName>:<PortNumber>/<Parent Container DN>"
$objNewGroup = $objParentDN.Create("group", "cn=SalesGroup")
$objNewGroup.setInfo()
```

Discussion

Group objects in ADAM and AD LDS are greatly simplified compared to their Active Directory counterparts, since the notion of security and distribution groups as two separate entities does not exist. In addition, all ADAM/AD LDS groups have the same scope: a group that has been created within an application partition can only be used within that partition, whereas a security principal that's been created in the Configuration NC can be used in all naming contexts in that instance. This means that a group or user that was created in **Instance1** cannot be used to assign permissions on objects in **Instance2** or be added to a group in **Instance2**. Windows security principals can be assigned permissions in any application partition. And just like ADAM/AD LDS user objects, ADAM/AD LDS **group** objects do not contain the **sAMAccountName** attribute.

 When you first install an ADAM or AD LDS instance, you have four default groups that are installed in the **CN=Roles** container: *Administrators, Instances, Readers*, and *Users*.

See Also

MSDN: Enumerating Users and Groups [ADAM], MSDN: Creating Groups [ADAM], MSDN: Deleting Groups [MSDN], and Chapter 20 of *Active Directory*

18.14 Managing ADAM or AD LDS Group Memberships

Problem

You want to manage the groups that an AD, ADAM, or AD LDS user is a member of.

Solution

Using a graphical user interface

1. Open ADAM ADSI Edit or ADSI Edit in Windows Server 2008. Connect and bind to the instance you want to manage.
2. Navigate to the group in question, right-click, and select Properties.
3. Scroll to the member attribute and click Edit.
4. To add a Windows user to the group, click Add Windows Account and enter the name of the Windows account. To add an ADAM or AD LDS user, click Add ADAM Account and enter the DN of the user you wish to add. Repeat this to add additional users.
5. To remove members, click on the CN of the object you wish to remove, and then click Remove. Repeat this to remove additional users from the group.

Using a command-line interface

To add a Windows user to a group from the command line, enter the following syntax:

```
> admod -h <ComputerName>:<PortNumber> -b <Group DN>
member:+:"<SID=<UserSID>>"
```

To add multiple users at one time, change + to ++ in the previous command and separate the User DNs with a semicolon.

To remove a single user, change + to - in the previous command.

To remove multiple users, change + to -- in the previous command and separate the User DNs with a semicolon.

Using VBScript

```
' The following code will modify an
' ADAM or AD LDS group membership
'--------------- SCRIPT CONFIGURATION ----------------
Const ADS_PROPERTY_DELETE = 4
strComputerName = "<ComputerName>" ' Use "localhost" for the local computer
```

```
strPort = "<PortNumber>"              ' the LDAP port number to connect to
strGroupDN = "<GroupDN>"        ' ie "cn=FinanceGroup,ou=..."
strUserDN = "<UserDN>"          ' ie "cn=Joe Smith,
                                         ' ou=AdamUsers,o=adatum,c=us"
'-------------------------------------------------------------------

Set objGroup = GetObject _
        ("LDAP://" & strComputerName & ":" & strPort & "/" & strGroupDN)
Set objUser = GetObject _
        ("LDAP://" & strComputerName & ":" & strPort & "/" & strUserDN)

' the following code will add a user object to a group
objGroup.Add objUser.AdsPath

' the following code will remove a user object from a group
objGroup.PutEx ADS_PROPERTY_DELETE, "member", _ Array(strUserDN)
objGroup.SetInfo

' the following code will enumerate all members of a group
For Each objUser in objGroup.Members
    Wscript.Echo objUser.Name
```

NextUsing PowerShell

To add and remove users from ADAM or AD LDS groups using the Quest AD cmdlets, use the following syntax:

```
Add-QADGroupMember -Identity <GroupDN> -Service <ComputerName>:<PortNumber> -Member
<UserDN>
Remove-QADGroupMember -Identity <GroupDN> -Service <ComputerName>:<PortNumber>
-Member <UserDN>
```

To add a group member using ADSI, use the following syntax:

```
$objGroup = [ADSI] "LDAP://<ComputerName>:<PortNumber>/<Group DN>"
$objUser = [ADSI] "LDAP://<ComputerName>:<PortNumber>/<User DN>"
$objGroup.PutEx(3, "member", @($objUser))
$objGroup.SetInfo()
```

To remove a group member using ADSI, use the following syntax:

```
$objGroup = [ADSI] "LDAP://<ComputerName>:<PortNumber>/<Group DN>"
$objUser = [ADSI] "LDAP://<ComputerName>:<PortNumber>/<User DN>"
$objGroup.PutEx(4, "member", @($objUser))
$objGroup.SetInfo()
```

Discussion

ADAM/AD LDS group objects can contain both ADAM/AD LDS users and Windows security principals, which allows you to assign permissions to data stored in ADAM/AD LDS instances using a consistent method. In the case of groups that were created within a specific application partition, they can only be assigned permissions within that partition; groups that were created within the Configuration partition can be assigned permissions to objects in any partition within the instance.

Using a command-line interface

To insert a Windows principal into an ADAM/AD LDS group, you need to either know the `ForeignSecurityPrincipal` or the `userProxy` object that the Windows user is tied to within the instance; otherwise, you need to add the user by its SID as done here.

See Also

MSDN: Adding a User to a Group [ADAM], MSDN: Removing Members from Groups [ADAM], and Chapter 20 of *Active Directory*

18.15 Viewing and Modifying ADAM Object Attributes

Problem

You want to view the attributes of an object within an ADAM instance.

Solution

Using a graphical user interface

1. Open ADAM ADSI Edit. If necessary, create and bind to a connection of your ADAM instance.
2. Navigate to the object in question, right-click, and select Properties. To view only the mandatory attributes for an object, remove the checkmark next to "Show optional attributes." To view only the optional attributes for an object, place a checkmark next to "Show optional attributes" and remove the checkmark next to "Show mandatory attributes."
3. Scroll through the object's properties. To modify a particular property, select the property and select Edit.
4. To insert a value into a single-valued attribute, enter the value and click OK. To remove a value from a single-valued attribute, click Clear.
5. To insert one or more values into a multivalued attribute, enter each value and click Add. To remove one or more values from a multivalued attribute, select the value and click Remove.

Using a command-line interface

To view the attributes of an object, enter the following:

```
> adfind -h <ComputerName>:<PortNumber> -b <Object DN> -s base
```

To restrict the AdFind output to only a few attributes, specify the name of each attribute you want to view after the ObjectDN; to view multiple attributes, separate each one with spaces in between. You can also use the -excl switch to display all but one or two attributes.

To insert a value into a single-valued attribute, enter the following syntax:

```
> admod -h <ComputerName>:<PortNumber> -b <Object DN> <AttributeName>::<Value>
```

To insert multiple values into a multivalued attribute, change + to ++ in the previous command and separate the values with a semicolon.

To clear an attribute's value (whether a single- or a multivalued attribute), enter the following:

```
> admod -h <ComputerName>:<PortNumber> -b <Object DN> <AttributeName> :-
```

To remove a single value from a multivalued attribute, change - to -- in the previous command.

Using VBScript

```
' The following code will list all attributes of an object
'--------------- SCRIPT CONFIGURATION ---------------
strComputerName = "<ComputerName>" ' Use "localhost" for the local computer
strPort = "<PortNumber>"                ' the LDAP port number to connect to
strObjectDN = "<ObjectDN>"              ' ie "ou= AdamUsers,o=adatum,c=us"
strObjectType = "<ObjectType>"          ' ie "organizationalunit", "group", "user"
strAttributeName = "<AttributeName>"  ' ie "description
strAttributeValue = "<AttributeValue>" ' ie "Description of this object"
'----------------------------------------------------

Set objObject = GetObject _
        ("LDAP://" & strComputerName & ":" & strPort & "/" & strObjectDN)
Set objObjectProperties = GetObject("LDAP://" & strComputerName & _
                                ":" & strPort & "/schema/" & _
                                strObjectType

For Each strAttribute in objObjectProperties.MandatoryProperties
    strValues = objObject.GetEx(strAttribute)
    For Each strItem in strValues
        Wscript.Echo strAttribute & " -- " & strItem
    Next
Next

For Each strAttribute in objObjectProperties.OptionalProperties
    strValues = objObject.GetEx(strAttribute)
    If Err = 0 Then
        For Each strItem in strValues
            Wscript.Echo strAttribute & " -- " & strItem
        Next
    Else
        Wscript.Echo strAttribute & " -- No value set"
        Err.Clear
```

```
        End If
    Next

    ' the following code will update an attribute value
    objObject.Put strAttributeName, strAttributeValue
    objObject.SetInfo
```

Using PowerShell

You can view and modify an ADAM/AD LDS object's properties using either the get-QADObject and set-QADObject Quest cmdlets, or else by using the native ADSI methods:

```
Get-QADObject -Service <ComputerName>:<PortNumber> -Identity <ObjectDN>
-IncludeAllProperties
Set-QADObject -Service <ComputerName>:<PortNumber> -Identity <ObjectDN>
-ObjectAttributes @{<attribute1>=<value1>;<attribute2>=<value2>}
$objADAMObj = [ADSI] "LDAP://<ComputerName>:<PortNumber/<Object DN>"
$objADAMObj.Put("<attribute>", "<value>")
$objADAMObj.SetInfo()
```

Discussion

Just like in Active Directory, each ADAM or AD LDS instance possesses a schema that defines what types of objects you can create and what sorts of attributes those objects possess. One of the major advantages of working with ADAM is that you can make changes to the schema of an ADAM instance without affecting the AD schema, thus allowing for more flexible application development that doesn't run the risk of making permanent or far-reaching changes to an entire Active Directory forest. Similar to AD, object classes can have both *mandatory* and *optional* attributes that you can view.

See Also

MSDN: Active Directory Application Mode Schema [ADAM], MSDN: Extending the Active Directory Application Mode Schema [ADAM], and Chapter 20 of *Active Directory*

18.16 Importing Data into an ADAM or AD LDS Instance

Problem

You want to perform a bulk import of object data into an ADAM or AD LDS instance.

Solution

Using a command-line interface

To import objects using the *ldifde* utility, you must first create an LDIF file with the objects to add, modify, or delete. Here is an example LDIF file that adds three users to an ADAM or AD LDS application partition:

```
dn: cn=Joe Smith,cn=users,ou=AdamUsers,o=adatum,c=us
changetype: add
objectClass: user
cn: Joe Smith
name: Joe Smith

dn: cn=Richard Mahler,cn=users,ou=AdamUsers,o=adatum,c=us
changetype: add
objectClass: user
cn: Richard Mahler
name: Richard Mahler

dn: cn=Doug Martin,cn=users,ou= AdamUsers,o=adatum,c=us
changetype: add
objectClass: user
cn: Doug Martin
name: Doug Martin
```

Once you've created the LDIF file, you just need to run *ldifde* to import the new objects:

```
> ldifde -i -f c:\import.ldf -s <servername>:<portnumber> -k -j
```

 Be sure to use the most current version of *ldifde* available.

Discussion

For more information on the LDIF format, check RFC 2849.

Using a command-line interface

To import with *ldifde*, simply specify the -i switch to turn on import mode and -f <filename> for the file. It can also be beneficial to use the -v switch to turn on verbose mode to get more information in case of errors.

See Also

Recipe 4.29 for information on importing data using LDIF files, RFC 2849 (The LDAP Data Interchange Format [LDIF]—Technical Specification), MS KB 237677 (Using LDIFDE to Import and Export Directory Objects to Active Directory), and Chapter 20 of *Active Directory*

18.17 Configuring Intra-site Replication

Problem

You want to create a replication schedule for an ADAM or AD LDS application partition that is hosted on multiple computers within a single site.

Using a graphical user interface

1. In Windows Server 2003 R2, open ADAM ADSI Edit. In Windows Server 2008, open Active Directory Sites and Services. If necessary, create and bind to a connection of your ADAM instance.

    In order to use the AD Sites & Services MMC snap-in to manage AD LDS replication in Windows Server 2008, you must use the *MS-ADLDS-DisplaySpecifiers.LDF* file to extend the schema of the configuration set that you are managing.

2. Navigate to the Sites container and the name of the site you need to modify.
3. Right-click on `CN=NTDS Site Settings`, and then click Schedule.
4. Select the block of time that should be available for replication; for every available block of time, you can configure the replication frequency to None, Once per Hour, Twice per Hour, or Four Times per Hour. Click OK when you're finished.

Discussion

Like Active Directory, ADAM and AD LDS use multimaster replication to copy information between replicas of each member of a configuration set. By default, all ADAM/AD LDS instances that you create will be placed within a single site, `Default-First-Site-Name`. Similar to AD, ADAM/AD LDS's intra-site replication takes place through *update notifications*, where replication partners are notified as changes occur.

See Also

MSDN: Active Directory Application Mode Schema [ADAM], MSDN: Using Application Directory Partitions [ADAM], and Chapter 20 of *Active Directory*

18.18 Forcing ADAM/AD LDS Replication

Problem

You want to force immediate replication of an ADAM or AD LDS application partition.

Solution

Using a command-line interface

```
> repadmin /syncall <servername>:<port> <AppPartitionDN>
```

Discussion

The *repadmin* command-line tool that comes with both AD and ADAM is primarily used to display and manage the replication topology of multiple directory servers. But *repadmin* can do much more, such as allowing you to view object metadata, update Service Principal Names (SPNs), and display information on trust relationships. You can see all of the basic options that are available by typing `repadmin /?` at a command prompt. Once you've familiarized yourself with these switches, you can then start learning about the more advanced features available by typing `repadmin/experthelp`. *repadmin* is one of those indispensable tools for an AD or ADAM administrator; it's well worth the time to learn its ins and outs to help you monitor and troubleshoot your network.

See Also

MS KB 229896 (Using Repadmin.exe to Troubleshoot Active Directory Replication), MS KB 905739 (TechNet Support WebCast: Troubleshooting Active Directory replication using the Repadmin tool), and Chapter 20 of *Active Directory*

18.19 Managing AD LDS Replication Authentication

Problem

You want to manage the security of AD LDS replication.

Solution

Using a graphical user interface

1. Open ADSI Edit. Connect and bind to the Configuration container of the AD LDS instance that you wish to manage.

2. Double-click on `Configuration [<ComputerName>:<PortNumber>]`.

3. Right-click on `CN=Configuration,<ApplicationDN>` and click Properties.

4. Scroll to `msDS-ReplAuthenticationMode`. Double-click on the attribute and enter one of the following values:

   2

   Mutual authentication with Kerberos

1

    Negotiated authentication

0

    Negotiated pass-through authentication

Using a command-line interface

```
> admod -h <ComputerName>:<PortNumber> -b <ConfigDN>
msDS-ReplAuthenticationMode::<AuthenticationMode>
```

Using VBScript

```
' The following code will modify the replication authentication mode of a
' configuration set
'---------------- SCRIPT CONFIGURATION ----------------
strComputerName = "<ComputerName>" ' Use "localhost" for the local computer
strPort = "<PortNumber>"           ' the LDAP port number to connect to
strConfigPart = "<Configuration Partition DN>" ' ie "cn=configuration,cn=adatum,c=us"
'------------------------------------------------------

Set objConfig = GetObject("LDAP://" & strComputerName & _ ":" & strPort & _
                    "/" & strConfigPart))
objConfig.put("msDS-ReplAuthenticationMode", <AuthenticationMode>"
objConfig.SetInfo
```

Using PowerShell

```
set-QADObject -Service <ComputerName>:<PortNumber> -Identity <ConfigDN>
-ObjectAttributes @{"msDS-ReplAuthenticationMode"="<AuthenticationMode>"}

$objConfig = [ADSI] "LDAP://<ComputerName>:<PortNumber>/<ConfigDN>"
$objConfig.Put("msDS-ReplAuthenticationMode", "<AuthenticationMode>")
$objConfig.SetInfo()
```

Discussion

To ensure replication security, AD LDS will authenticate replication partners within a configuration set before replication begins. The method used for replication authentication will depend on the value of the msDS-ReplAuthenticationMode attribute on the configuration directory partition. After replication partners have successfully authenticated, all replication traffic between the two partners is encrypted. AD LDS uses Security Support Provider Interface (SSPI) to establish the appropriate authentication security level between replication partners, and replication authentication always occurs over a secure channel.

Table 18-1 lists the security levels for replication authentication in Windows Server 2008. The default replication security level for a new, unique AD LDS instance is 1, unless a local workstation user account is specified as the AD LDS service account, in which case the replication security level is set to 0.

Table 18-1. Description of the msDS-ReplAuthenticationMode values

Value	Description
0—Negotiated pass-through	All AD LDS instances in the configuration set use an identical account name and password as the AD LDS service account. Using this replication authentication value, a configuration set can include computers that are joined to one or more workgroups and/or computers that are joined to one or more untrusted domains or forests. This is the default value if a local user account is specified as the AD LDS service account for the configuration set.
1—Negotiated	Kerberos authentication (using SPNs) is attempted first. If Kerberos fails, NTLM authentication is attempted. If NTLM fails, the AD LDS instances will not replicate. This is the default value for a configuration set, unless it is configured with a local account as the AD LDS service account.
2—Mutual authentication with Kerberos	Kerberos authentication, using service principal names (SPNs), is required. If Kerberos authentication fails, the AD LDS instances will not replicate. If this value is selected, the configuration set must be fully contained within an AD DS domain or within computers belonging to trusted domains or forests.

See Also

MSDN: Active Directory Application Mode Schema [ADAM], MSDN: Using Application Directory Partitions [ADAM], and Chapter 20 of *Active Directory*

18.20 Managing ADAM/AD LDS Permissions

Problem

You want to manage permissions within an ADAM instance.

Solution

Using a graphical user interface

1. Open the version of LDP that was installed with ADAM, either ADAM SP1, the ADAM that is installed with Windows Server 2003 R2, or the version of LDP that is installed along with the AD LDS server role in Windows Server 2008.

2. Connect and bind to the object or container that you wish to modify.

3. Right-click on the object or container and select Advanced/Security Descriptor. To display and edit auditing information in addition to the Discretionary Access Lists (DACLs) associated with the object, place a checkmark next to SACL.

4. Click OK.

5. To delete an Access Control Entry (ACE), highlight the entry and click Delete.

6. To add an entry, click Add.

7. In the Trustee text box, enter the name of the **user** or **group** object that you wish to apply permissions to. In the ACE mask section, select whether you are creating *Allow ACE* or *Deny ACE*.

8. In the Access mask section, place checkmarks next to the permissions that you are allowing or denying.

9. Click OK when you are finished.

Using a command-line interface

To view the effective permissions on an ADAM object, use the following syntax:

```
> dsacls \\<servername>:<port>\<ObjectDN>
```

To grant permissions on an ADAM object, use the following:

```
> dsacls "\\<servername>:<port>\<ObjectDN>" /G <User or Group Receiving
Permissions>:<Permission Statement>
```

To deny permissions on an ADAM object, use the following:

```
> dsacls "\\<servername>:<port>\<ObjectDN>" /D <User or Group Receiving
Permissions>:<Permission Statement>
```

Discussion

One of the great new features introduced with ADAM SP1 was the version of the LDP utility included with it, which provides you the ability to modify both DACL and SACL entries at an extremely granular level; this feature has been carried over into the version of LDP installed with Windows Server 2008. You also have the familiar *dsacls* utility that will allow you to delegate permissions from the command line. When delegating permissions, you must first determine whether you are delegating permission over an entire container and all objects contained therein, or whether you are only going to delegate control over specific child objects. (For example, you can delegate control over all ADAM/AD LDS user objects within an OU.) Once you've made this determination, you'll then specify the specific permissions that you're delegating; you can delegate anything from full control of the entire object down to granting read permissions on a single attribute.

Using a command-line interface

dsacls requires a specific syntax for the permission statement used to grant or deny permissions, formatted in this manner:

```
[PermissionBits];[{Object|Property}];[InheritedObjectType]
```

[PermissionBits] here refers to any of the values listed in Table 18-2; you can specify one or more together with no spaces between them.

Table 18-2. Description of the PermissionBits values

Value	Description
GR	Generic read
GE	Generic execute
GW	Generic write
GA	Generic all (FULL CONTROL)
SD	Delete
DT	Delete an object and all its child objects (DELETE TREE)
RC	Read security information
WD	Change security information
WO	Change owner information
LC	List child objects
CC	Create child objects
DC	Delete child objects
WS	Write to self
RP	Read property
WP	Write property
CA	Control access
LO	List object access

The [Object | Property] option allows you to delegate permissions for an entire object, or for only specific properties of that object. For example, you can delegate the Write Property permission for all properties of an object, or only one or two specific properties.

See Also

MS KB 310997 (Active Directory Services and Windows 2000 or Windows Server 2003 domains), MS KB 315676 (How to Delegate Administrative Authority in Windows 2000), MS KB 281146 (How to Use Dsacls.exe in Windows Server 2003 and Windows 2000), and Chapter 20 of *Active Directory*

18.21 Enabling Auditing of AD LDS Access

Problem

You want to enable auditing of directory access and modifications. Audit events are logged to the Security event log.

Solution

Using a graphical user interface

1. Open the Group Policy Object (GPO) that is linked to the computer(s) hosting the AD LDS instance that you wish to audit.
2. In the left pane, expand Local Policies and click on Audit Policy.
3. In the right pane, double-click "Audit directory service access."
4. Make sure the box is checked beside "Define these policy settings."
5. Check the box beside Success and/or Failure.
6. Click OK.

Using a command-line interface

```
> auditpol \\<DomainControlerName> /enable /directory:all
```

Discussion

Windows Server 2008 also enables additional auditing functionality of Directory Services events, including capturing **"before"** and **"after"** values on changes and deletions to Active Directory objects. You can enable this functionality using the *auditpol.exe* tool discussed earlier, using syntax similar to the following:

```
Auditpol /set /subcategory:"directory service changes"
```

Here is a sample event that was logged after the *Administrator* account created a user object called foobar in the Sales OU:

```
Event Type:          Success Audit
Event Source:        Security
Event Category:      Directory Service Access
Event ID:            566
Date:                5/26/2003
Time:                7:24:10 PM
User:                ADATUM\administrator
Computer:            DC1
Description:
Object Operation:
        Object Server:        DS
        Operation Type:       Object Access
        Object Type:          organizationalUnit
        Object Name:          OU=Sales,DC=adatum,DC=com
        Handle ID:            -
        Primary User Name:    DC1$
        Primary Domain:       ADATUM
        Primary Logon ID:     (0x0,0x3E7)
        Client User Name:     administrator
        Client Domain:        ADATUM
        Client Logon ID:      (0x0,0x3B4BE)
        Accesses:             Create Child
```

```
Properties:
Create Child
user

Additional Info:      CN=foobar,OU=Sales,DC=adatum,DC=com
Additional Info2:     CN=foobar,OU=Sales,DC=adatum,DC=com
Access Mask:          0x1
```

 In an Active Directory environment it can also be useful to enable Audit Account Management in the GPO that's linked to the Domain Controllers OU. This provides additional information about account-management operations—for example, finding what account deleted a certain object.

See Also

MS KB 232714 (How to Enable Auditing of Directory Service Access), MS KB 314955 (How to Audit Active Directory Objects in Windows 2000), MS KB 314977 (How to Enable Active Directory Access Auditing in Windows 2000), and MS KB 814595 (How to Audit Active Directory Objects in Windows Server 2003)

## CHAPTER 19

Active Directory Federation Services

19.0 Introduction

Active Directory Federation Services (AD FS) was introduced in Windows Server 2003 R2, and updated for Windows Server 2008. It is used to allow single sign-on (SSO) capabilities to web applications hosted by multiple organizations without the need to configure an Active Directory trust relationship between them. This task is performed by using AD FS servers to separate the process of *authentication* (proving who a user *is*) from that of *authorization* (specifying what a user can *do*). AD FS allows this separation by configuring *account partners* to authenticate users and groups, and then providing *claims* to *resource partners* that control the actual access to resources.

This relationship between account partners and resource partners is called a *federated trust*. This verbiage can sometimes lead to confusion, since it seems to imply that AD FS requires an Active Directory trust relationship to exist between account and resource partners. In this case, the word *trust* merely refers to a business agreement between two organizations that have agreed to this type of distributed authentication and authorization arrangement. A federated trust refers to a scenario in which the AD FS Federation Service has been properly configured by both the organization that performs user authentication and the organization that controls access to web resources.

While an Active Directory trust relationship is not a requirement to configure AD FS, you can, however, combine AD FS with an Active Directory forest trust to create a *Federated Web SSO with Forest Trust* configuration. This is typically used within a single organization that has one forest configured in a perimeter network or DMZ, and a second forest configured on an internal network. In this case, AD FS allows users on the internal network to be able to access resources on the perimeter network without needing to maintain two separate accounts. The other common AD FS configuration, *Federated Web SSO*, will be more commonly used by two separate organizations (most notably in a B2B relationship) for whom an Active Directory forest trust would create too much access for users on both sides of the equation or where Selective Authentication would require too much ongoing maintenance.

Using a Graphical User Interface

You'll notice throughout this chapter that most of the management options available to you are only those within a graphical user interface: either the AD FS MMC snap-in or the Internet Services Manager snap-in. In its current release, AD FS lacks the ability to perform many enterprise-level tasks, such as managing remote servers or performing command-line administration.

19.1 Installing AD FS Prerequisites for Windows Server 2003 R2

Problem

You want to install the necessary prerequisites to configure AD FS on a Windows Server 2003 R2 server.

Solution

Using a graphical user interface

To install IIS on a Windows Server 2003 R2 server, follow these steps:

1. Click Start→Control Panel→Add or Remove Programs.
2. Select Add/Remove Windows Components.
3. Click on the Application Server checkbox and select Details.
4. Place a checkmark next to ASP.NET and Internet Information Service (IIS), then click OK.
5. Click Next to begin installing the necessary components, then click Finish.

To enable SSL for the Default Web Site, do the following:

1. Open the Internet Service Manager snap-in.
2. Navigate to the server that you want to manage, and click on Web Sites.
3. Right-click the Default Web site and select Properties.
4. On the Directory Security tab, select Server Certificate in the Secure Communications section. Click Next to begin the wizard.
5. Select "Create a new certificate" and click Next.
6. Select "Prepare the request now, but send it later" and then click Next.
7. Enter a name for the certificate, and the bit length of the certificate. Select Server Gated Cryptography if your users will be accessing your site from countries that have any sort of encryption restrictions.
8. Enter your organization name and organizational unit, and then click Next.
9. Enter the FQDN of the server name and click Next.

10. Enter your location information, and then click Next.

11. Enter the path and filename that you want to save the certificate information to, and then click Next to continue.

12. Click Next to create the certificate request.

Once you have submitted the certificate request to a Certification Authority and have received a .CER file in return, use these steps to install the certificate:

1. Right-click on the Default Web Site and select Properties.

2. On the Directory Security tab, click Server Certificate. Click Next to continue.

3. Select "Process the pending request," install the certificate, and click Next.

4. Browse to the location of the certificate that you received from the Certification Authority. Click Next twice, followed by Finish, to install the certificate.

Using a command-line interface

To perform an unattended install of IIS, you must create an answer file containing a [Components] section and an optional [InternetServer] section, similar to the following:

```
[Components]
iis_common = on
aspnet = on
complusnetwork = on

[InternetServer]
PathWWWServer = "d:\docs\webfiles"
```

Save the unattended file as *unattended.txt*, then run the following command:

```
> sysocmgr /i:sysoc.inf /u:<PathToUnattendedFile>
```

Discussion

Because AD FS is primarily used to enable web-based SSO solutions, AD FS requires the following components installed as a prerequisite:

- IIS
- ASP.NET
- COM+

These components can be installed during the initial operating system install or after the fact using Add/Remove Programs or the *sysocmgr* utility.

To improve the security of an AD FS installation, you will also need to install an SSL certificate on the Default Web Site before the AD FS install can continue. This can be a certificate purchased from a third-party CA such as VeriSign, or one issued by an internal Certificate Authority. For a test environment, you can also use the

SelfSSL.exe utility from the IIS 6 Resource Kit to install a self-signed certificate; however, this option should never be used for a production application.

See Also

MS KB 309506 (How to Perform an Unattended Installation of IIS 6.0) and MS KB 299875 (How to Implement SSL in IIS)

19.2 Installing AD FS Prerequisites for Windows Server 2008

Problem

You want to install the necessary prerequisites to configure AD FS on a Windows Server 2008 server.

Solution

Using a graphical user interface

To install IIS on a Windows Server 2008 server, follow these steps:

1. Click Start→Server Manager.
2. In the lefthand pane, click Roles.
3. In the righthand pane, click "Add roles" and then click Next.
4. Place a checkmark next to Web Server (IIS). If prompted, click Add Required Features. Click Next twice.
5. Place a checkmark next to ASP.NET and Windows Authentication. If prompted, click Add Required Role Services.
6. Click Next, and then click Install.
7. When the installation completes, click Close.

To enable SSL for the Default Web Site, do the following:

1. Open the Internet Information Service (IIS) Manager snap-in.
2. Drill down to *<server name>*. In the righthand pane, double-click on Server Certificates.
3. Click on Create Certificate Request. Enter the identifying information for the certificate request. Click Next.
4. Select the desired Cryptographic Service Provider and Bit length, and then click Next.
5. Specify a name for the Certificate request and then click Next.

Once you have submitted the certificate request to a Certification Authority and have received a .CER file in return, use these steps to install the certificate:

1. Navigate to *<server name>* if you have not done so already. Click "Complete certificate request."

2. Browse to the appropriate CER file, and enter the FQDN of the server in the Friendly name field. Click OK.

3. Browse to Sites→Default Web Site. Right-click on Default Web Site and click Edit Bindings....

4. Click Add. In the Type: drop-down box, select *https*. In the IP Address: drop-down box, select the IP address of the server. Confirm that the Port text box reads 443. In the "SSL certificate:" drop-down box, select the SSL certificate that you installed in steps 1 and 2.

5. Click OK, then click Close.

6. In the middle pane, double-click on SSL Settings. On the SSL Settings page, place a checkmark next to Require SSL. In the "client certificates:" radio buttons, select Accept. Click Apply.

Using a command-line interface

The following command will install the Web Server (IIS) role and all necessary subcomponents.

```
> servermanagercmd web-server web-asp-net
```

To generate a certificate request via the command line, you must first create a *request.inf* file similar to the following:

```
;----------------- request.inf -----------------

[Version]

Signature="$Windows NT$

[NewRequest]

Subject = "CN=<DC fqdn>" ; replace with the FQDN of the DC
KeySpec = 1
KeyLength = 1024
; Can be 1024, 2048, 4096, 8192, or 16384.
; Larger key sizes are more secure, but have
; a greater impact on performance.
Exportable = TRUE
MachineKeySet = TRUE
SMIME = False
PrivateKeyArchive = FALSE
UserProtected = FALSE
UseExistingKeySet = FALSE
ProviderName = "Microsoft RSA SChannel Cryptographic Provider"
ProviderType = 12
RequestType = PKCS10
KeyUsage = 0xa0
```

```
[EnhancedKeyUsageExtension]

OID=1.3.6.1.5.5.7.3.1 ; this is for Server Authentication

;------------------------------------------------
```

Once you have created the appropriate *request.inf* file, issue the following *certreq.exe* command:

```
> certreq -new request.inf request.req
```

Once you have submitted the certificate request to a Certification Authority and have received a .CER file in return, use the following command to install the certificate:

```
> certreq -accept newcert.cer
```

Discussion

Because IIS underwent significant modifications between Windows Server 2003 and Windows Server 2008, the steps needed to install IIS as a precursor to installing AD FS have been similarly modified. The Web Server (IIS) role in Windows Server 2008 can be installed using the Server Manager MMC console, or from the command-line interface using the *servermanagercmd.exe* utility.

Just like on 2003 servers, you need to install an SSL certificate on the IIS server before installing and configuring AD FS. You can configure a certificate from a commercial CA or one internal to your environment, or else you can install a self-signed certificate if you are operating in a test environment. Again, self-signed certificates should not be used in any production or public-facing server environment.

See Also

MS KB 321051 (How to Enable LDAP Over SSL with a Third-Party Certification Authority)

19.3 Installing the Federation Service in Windows Server 2003 R2

Problem

You want to install the AD FS Federation Service on a Windows Server 2003 R2 computer.

> Installing the Federation Service assumes that the server in question is joined to an Active Directory domain.

Solution

Using a graphical user interface

1. Click Start→Control Panel→Add or Remove Programs.
2. Select Add/Remove Windows Components.
3. Click on the Active Directory Services checkbox, and select Details.
4. Click on Active Directory Federation Services (ADFS) and select Details.
5. Place a checkmark next to Federation Service, then click OK.
6. If you have not enabled ASP.NET 2.0, you will receive a warning message asking if you want to enable it. Click Yes to continue.
7. Click OK twice and then Next to begin the installation.
8. In the token-signing certificate section, select either "Create a self-signed token-signing certificate" or "Select token-signing certificate" to browse for an existing one.
9. In the Trust policy section, select either "Create a new trust policy" or "Use an existing trust policy" to browse for an existing one.
10. Click Next and then Finish to complete the installation.

Using a command-line interface

To perform an unattended install of the AD FS Federation Services, you must create an answer file containing a [Components] section, an [ADFS] section, and an [ADFSFederationServer] section, similar to the following:

```
[Components]
ADFSFederationServer = On

[ADFS]
UseASPNet = 1

[ADFSFederationServer]
SignCertificateThumbprintFS = ""
TrustPolicyPath = "d:\ADFS\TrustPolicies\defaulttrust.xml"
```

Save the unattended file as *unattended.txt*, then run the following command:

```
> sysocmgr /i:sysoc.inf /u:<PathToUnattendedFile>
```

Discussion

In an AD FS environment, *federation servers* are servers that have the Federation Service component installed on them. These servers are responsible for routing authentication requests between the different organizations involved in a federated trust, or from external (i.e., Internet) clients accessing a Web SSO application.

A federation server will perform slightly different tasks depending on whether your organization is an *account partner* (an organization that hosts user accounts that need access to resources) or the *resource partner* (the organization hosting the actual resources being accessed). When configured by an account partner, federation servers are used to validate users against an Active Directory or ADAM account store, and to issue the initial security tokens that those accounts can use to access applications hosted by the resource partner. Federation servers in the resource partner organization will then validate the security tokens that were issued by the federation servers for the account partner. Resource partner federation servers can also issue cookies to a user's web browser to enable single sign-on capabilities if they need to access multiple applications that are hosted by the resource partner.

See Also

Recipe 19.1 and Windows Server Tech Center: AD FS Server Roles

19.4 Installing the Federation Service on Windows Server 2008

Problem

You want to install the AD FS Federation Service on a Windows Server 2008 computer.

 Installing the Federation Service assumes that the server in question is joined to an Active Directory domain.

Solution

Using a graphical user interface

1. Click Start→Server Manager.
2. In the lefthand pane, click Roles.
3. In the righthand pane, click "Add roles" and then click Next.
4. Place a checkmark next to Active Directory Federation Services. If prompted, click Add Required Features. Click Next twice.
5. Place a checkmark next to Federation Service.
6. Click Next. Select an existing token-signing certificate, or select the option to create a self-signed token-signing certificate if you are working in a test environment.
7. Click Next through the remaining wizard screens, then click Install.
8. When the installation completes, click Close.

Using a command-line interface

```
> servermanagercmd -i ADFS-Federation
```

Discussion

The functionality of the AD FS Federation Service in Windows Server 2008 is fundamentally identical to the same service running on a 2003 R2 server. To add the AD FS server role in 2008, you will once again use the Server Manager console or the *servermanagercmd.exe* command-line utility.

See Also

Recipe 19.2 and Windows Server Tech Center: AD FS Server Roles

19.5 Configuring an Active Directory Account Store

Problem

You want to configure an AD FS account partner to use Active Directory for authentication.

Solution

Using a graphical user interface

1. Open the ADFS MMC snap-in. Navigate to Federation Service→Trust Policy→My Organization.
2. Right-click on Account Stores. Select New→Account Store... and click Next.
3. Select Active Directory for the type of account store and then click Next.
4. Click Finish to add the Active Directory account store.

Discussion

AD FS account partners rely on *account stores* to authenticate users and to retrieve whatever security claims are configured for a particular user. You can configure one or multiple account stores for any account partner that you've configured, and you can define relative priorities between multiple stores. When you configure an Active Directory account store, AD FS can examine attributes of Active Directory user objects in addition to simply authenticating the user. AD logon requests can be in the UPN format, like *jsmith@adatumadatum.com*, or in a domain\username format such as *ADATUM\jsmith*.

If you've configured multiple account stores, AD FS will attempt to process incoming authentication requests against each account store in order. You can modify this order by navigating to Federation Service→Trust Policy→My Organization. Right-click on

Account Stores and select Store Priority, then use the Up or Down buttons to modify the priority order of the account stores.

 You can only configure one Active Directory account store per account partner, but multiple ADAM or AD LDS account stores.

See Also

Recipe 19.6 for information on Configuring an ADAM or AD LDS Account Store and MSDN: System.Web.Security.SingleSignOn

19.6 Configuring an ADAM or AD LDS Account Store

Problem

You want to configure an AD FS account partner to use an instance of ADAM or AD LDS for authentication.

Solution

Using a graphical user interface

1. Open the ADFS MMC snap-in. Navigate to Federation Service→Trust Policy→My Organization.
2. Right-click on the Account Stores node, then select New→Account Store.... Click Next to bypass the initial Welcome screen.
3. Select Active Directory Application Mode (ADAM) for the Account Store Type for Windows Server 2003 R2; in Windows Server 2008, select Active Directory Light-weight Directory Services (AD LDS).Click Next.
4. Enter a display name and a Uniform Resource Identifier (URI) for the ADAM account store and click Next.
5. Specify the FQDN or IP address of the ADAM server, and the TCP/IP port that this instance is listening on.
6. For "LDAP search base distinguished name," enter the search base that should be used for any LDAP queries made against this ADAM instance; for example, dc=adatum,dc=us.
7. Enter the name of the ADAM username attribute, i.e., userPrincipalName.
8. Click Next to continue.
9. On the Identity Claims page, place a checkmark next to one or more of the following:

UPN
> Enter the LDAP attribute name that stores the UPN.

Email
> Enter the LDAP attribute name that stores the user's email address.

Common name
> Enter the LDAP attribute name that stores the user's CN.

10. Click Next and then Finish to enable the account store.

Discussion

ADAM/AD LDS account stores are configured quite similarly to Active Directory stores; but unlike an AD account store, you can configure multiple ADAM/AD LDS account stores on a given federation server. Configuring an ADAM/AD LDS account store requires the following configuration information:

- Server name/IP address of a server hosting the ADAM instance.
- Port number that the instance is using to communicate.
- LDAP search base, such as `dc=IntranetApp,dc=adatum,dc=com`.
- Username attribute, such as `userPrincipalName`. This is the attribute that ADFS will use to attempt to authenticate incoming requests.

You can also modify the default timeout period for searches; the default is five seconds. In addition, you can enable SSL/TLS to encrypt the connection between the federation server and the web server hosting the application.

See Also

Recipe 19.5 for information on configuring an Active Directory account store and Chapter 18 for more on configuring ADAM/AD LDS instances and application partitions

19.7 Creating Organizational Claims

Problem

You want to add a new type of claim that can be used by claims-aware or token-based web applications.

Solution

Using a graphical user interface

1. Open the ADFS MMC snap-in. Navigate to Federation Service→Trust Policy→My Organization.

2. Right-click on Organization Claims, then select New→Organizational Claim.

3. Enter a name for the claim, then select Group Claim or Custom Claim and click OK.

4. To map a Group Claim to an existing group, right-click on the claim that you just created and select Properties. On the Resource Group tab, place a checkmark next to "Map this claim to the following resource group." Manually enter the DN of the group or use the browse button to select it from the Active Directory tree. Click OK when you're done.

Discussion

AD FS *claims* are the foundation of authentication and authorization in federated applications. Administrators in account partners will configure organizational claims that will be presented by these users when accessing applications that are hosted by resource partners. There are three types of claims that are currently supported by the AD FS Federation Service: identity claims, group claims, and custom claims.

An *identity claim* refers to some type of identifier that's used to establish a user's identity within the account partner organization: this can be a UPN, an E-Mail address, or a Common Name. UPN and E-Mail claims are formatted in the familiar `user@adatum.com` format, while a Common Name claim is made up of an arbitrary string like `Adatum Employees` or `Joe Smith`. For this reason, you should avoid using Common Name claims as identity claims unless UPN or E-Mail claims are unfeasible in your environment.

 Although you can send multiple claim types from an account partner to a resource partner, you can only send one UPN and one E-Mail claim at a time. You can use custom claims if you need to configure additional claim types using E-Mail or UPN information.

A *group claim*, as the name would suggest, indicates that the user is a member of a particular group or role in the account partner organization. The resource partner can then make authorization decisions based on this group membership claim. (Again, the resource partner will do nothing to verify that the user is actually a member of the group they claim to be; it is up to the account partner to perform this authorization process before submitting the claim to the resource partner.)

You can create a *custom claim* to allow users in the account partner organization to use additional information to submit claims to the resource partner. Custom claims are simply attribute/value pairs that are submitted by users from the account partner when they attempt to access resource partner applications; this can include information such as an employee ID number or some other unique identifier.

See Also

Recipe 19.8 for more on configuring an account partner and Recipe 19.9 for more on configuring a resource partner

19.8 Creating an Account Partner

Problem

You want to configure an account partner to allow the organization's users to access applications that are managed by an AD FS resource partner.

Solution

Using a graphical user interface

1. Open the ADFS MMC snap-in. Navigate to Federation Service→Trust Policy→Partner Organizations.

2. Right-click on Account Partners, and select New→Account Partner.

3. To create an account partner manually, click No on the Import Policy File page and click Next.

4. On the Account Partner Details screen, enter the display name of the account partner, the Federation Service URI (such as *http://www.adatum.com/adfs*), and the Federation Service endpoint URL (such as *https://www.adatum.com/adfs/ls/clientlogon.aspx*). Click Next to continue.

5. On the Account Partner Verification Certificate screen, browse to or manually enter the path to the verification certificate and click Next.

6. For Federation Scenario, select one of the following:

   Federated Web SSO
   Choose this for a scenario with an external organization or one where you're not using a forest trust. To use this option, simply click Next to continue.

   Federated Web SSO with Forest Trust
   To configure this option, click Next, then select "All Active Directory domains and forests" to allow users from any domain in the organization to authenticate. To restrict the domains that can submit requests, click on "The following Active Directory domains and forests." Select the domain or forest that you want to accept logons from and click Add. Click Next to continue.

7. On the Account Partner Identity Claims screen, select one or more of the following:

UPN Claim

> This will take you to the Accepted UPN Suffixes page. From here you can select All UPN Suffixes, or else specify a suffix and click Add. Click Next to continue.

E-Mail Claim

> This will take you to the Accepted E-mail Suffixes page. From here you can select All E-mail Suffixes, or specify an accepted suffix and click Add. Click Next to continue.

Common Name Claim

> This option requires no additional configuration; simply click Next to continue.

8. Click Next and then Finish to create the Account Partner.

> The All UPN Suffixes and All E-Mail Suffixes options are only available when you are configuring a Federated Web SSO with Forest Trust.

Discussion

When configuring AD FS, you'll start by configuring one or more account partners to represent the organization that houses user accounts, either in AD or ADAM/AD LDS, which requires access to applications hosted by one or more resource partners. The AD FS Federation Server in the account partner's organization will create security tokens or claims that can be processed by the Federation Service in the resource partner and used to make authorization decisions.

> You can think of an account partner as being analogous to a trusted domain or forest in an Active Directory trust relationship; however, it is not necessary for an Active Directory trust relationship to be configured for AD FS to function in this manner.

You can configure an account partner in one of two AD FS scenarios: Federated Web SSO or Federated Web SSO with Forest Trust. In the Federated Web SSO scenario, there is no need for a forest trust to exist between the account partners and resource partners; this is typically used for two separate organizations that do not wish to create a forest trust between them. The Federated Web SSO with Forest Trust scenario is more typically used within a single organization to allow secure web access via the Internet.

> In the case of the Federated Web SSO with Forest Trust scenario, you can configure the account partner either to allow logon requests from any domain that is trusted by the account partner or to only accept logon requests from particular domains.

In addition to configuring the account partner, you also need to determine what types of claims will be sent by the account partner to the federation server hosted by the resource partner. You can send any combination of UPN, E-Mail, Common name, Group, or Custom claims. (Claims types are discussed further in Recipe 19.7.)

After you have configured account partner information, you'll need to configure the corresponding resource partner with information identifying the account partner. In Windows Server 2008, this process is simplified by the inclusion of XML-based configuration files; in 2003 R2, account partner information needs to be entered manually on the resource partner.

See Also

Recipe 19.7 for more on creating group or custom claims and Recipe 19.9 for information on configuring a resource partner

19.9 Configuring a Resource Partner

Problem

You want to configure a resource partner to allow access to a resource by users defined within an AD FS Federation Service account partner.

Solution

Using a graphical user interface

1. Open the ADFS MMC snap-in. Navigate to Federation Service→Trust Policy→Partner Organizations.
2. Right-click on Account Partners, and select New→Resource Partner.
3. To create a resource partner manually, click No on the Import Policy File page and click Next.
4. On the Resource Partner Details screen, enter the display name of the resource partner, the Federation Service URI (such as *http://www.adatum.com/adfs*), and the Federation Service endpoint URL (such as *https://www.adatum.com/adfs/ls/clientlogon.aspx*). Click Next to continue.
5. For Federation Scenario, select one of the following:

    Federated Web SSO
    Choose this for a scenario with an external organization or one where you're not using a forest trust. To use this option, simply click Next to continue.

    Federated Web SSO with Forest Trust
    Use this for federated trusts within the same organization.

6. Select one or more of the following on the Resource Partner Identity Claims screen:

UPN Claim

> This will bring up the Select UPN Suffixes screen. From here, either select "Pass all UPN Suffixes through unchanged" or "Replace all UPN suffixes with the following:," and specify the UPN suffix that you want to replace all incoming suffixes with. Click Next to continue.

E-Mail Claim

> This will bring up the Select E-Mail Suffixes screen. From here, either select "Pass all E-Mail Suffixes through unchanged" or "Replace all E-Mail Suffixes with the following:," and specify the email suffix that you want to replace all incoming suffixes with. Click Next to continue.

Common Name Claim

> This type of claim just denotes a string such as "Joe Smith" or "Adatum Employees."

7. Click Next and then Finish to create the Resource Partner.

Discussion

A resource partner is the necessary second piece of the AD FS puzzle, and is the organization that is hosting the web resources that need to be accessed by the account partner. It's important to note that resource partners do not actually authenticate users from the account partner's organization; rather, they simply process the claims that are forwarded to them after the account partner has performed any necessary authentication. This process cuts very much to the heart of AD FS—the resource partner trusts the account partner to perform whatever authentication is needed, after which the resource partner performs the authorization portion of the process using the claims that were produced by the account partner.

 Each web server in the resource partner organization that needs to be protected by the AD FS Federation Service needs to be configured with the AD FS Web Agent.

See Also

Recipe 19.7 for more on configuring a claim, Recipe 19.8 for more on creating an account partner, and Recipe 19.10 for more on configuring an application

19.10 Configuring an Application

Problem

You want to add a claims-based or token-based application to AD FS.

Solution

Using a graphical user interface

1. Open the ADFS MMC Snap-in. Browse to Federation Service→Trust Policy→My Organization.

2. Right-click on Applications and select New→Application. Click Next to continue.

3. On the Application Type screen, select either "Claims-aware application" or "Windows NT token-based application" and click Next.

4. On the "Application details" screen, enter the name of the application and the URL used to access the application. Click Next to continue.

5. On the Accepted Identity Claims page, place a checkmark next to one or more of the following:

   - UPN

   - E-Mail

   - Common Name (only available with a claims-aware application)

6. Click Next and then Finish to add the new application.

Discussion

You can use the AD FS Web Agent for two different types of web applications: *claims-aware applications* and *Windows NT token-based applications*. As the names imply, claims-aware applications can make authorization decisions based on claims submitted to them by the AD FS server in the account partner organization, while token-based applications can use only traditional Windows-based authorization mechanisms. Claims-aware applications can use a combination of identity claims, group claims, and custom claims to gain access to applications hosted by the resource partner. Windows NT token-based applications are not capable of handling AD FS claims, and instead use traditional Windows authorization. For a user to access a token-based application, the user needs to have an account in the resource web server's domain or any domain that is trusted by that domain; in many cases this will be a "shadow account" that maps back to the user's account in the account partner. In other words, token-based applications are far less flexible and far more limiting than claims-aware applications when used in AD FS implementations.

See Also

Recipe 19.7 for more on configuring a claim and Recipe 19.13 for more on configuring the AD FS Web Agent

19.11 Configuring a Forest Trust

Problem

You want to create a forest trust to enable AD FS to use the Web SSO with Forest Trust configuration.

Solution

Using a graphical user interface

1. Open the Active Directory Domains and Trusts snap-in.
2. In the left pane, right-click the forest root domain and select Properties.
3. Click on the Trusts tab.
4. Click the New Trust button.
5. After the New Trust Wizard opens, click Next.
6. Type the DNS name of the AD forest and click Next.
7. Select "Forest trust" and click Next.
8. Complete the wizard by stepping through the rest of the configuration screens.

Using a command-line interface

```
> netdom trust <Forest1DNSName> /Domain:<Forest2DNSName> /Twoway /Transitive /ADD
            [/UserD:<Forest2AdminUser> /PasswordD:*]
            [/UserO:<Forest1AdminUser> /PasswordO:*]
```

For example, to create a two-way forest trust from the AD forest *adatum.com* to the AD forest *othercorp.com*, use the following command:

```
> netdom trust adatum.com /Domain:othercorp.com /Twoway /Transitive /ADD
        /UserD:administrator@othercorp.com /PasswordD:*
        /UserO:administrator@adatum.com /PasswordO:*
```

Using PowerShell

The following code will create a two-way transitive trust between the local forest and a remote forest named *treyresearch.net*. This code will need to be mirrored on the opposite side of the trust in order for the trust to be fully functional:

```
$localFor = [System.DirectoryServices.ActiveDirectory.Forest]::getCurrentForest()
$strRemoteFor = 'treyresearch.net'
$strRemoteUser = 'administrator'
$strRemotePass = 'P@ssw0rd'
$remoteCon = New-Object
System.DirectoryServices.ActiveDirectory.DirectoryContext('Forest',$strRemoteFor,
$strRemoteUser,$strRemotePass)$trustDirection = 'Bidirectional'
$localFor.CreateTrustRelationship($remoteFor, $trustDirection)
```

Discussion

A new type of trust called a *forest trust* was introduced in Windows Server 2003. Under Windows 2000, if you wanted to create a fully trusted environment between two forests, you would have to set up individual external two-way trusts between every domain in both forests. If you have two Windows 2000 forests with three domains each and wanted to set up a fully trusted model, for example, you would need to set up nine individual one-way trusts.

With a forest trust, you can now define a single one-way or two-way transitive trust relationship that extends to all the domains in both forests. You may want to implement a forest trust if you merge or acquire a company and you want all of the new company's Active Directory resources to be accessible to users in your Active Directory environment and vice versa. To configure a forest trust, the forests on both sides of the trust need to be at the Windows Server 2003 forest functional level; by default, forest trusts also have SID filtering enabled, as do external trusts that are created on Windows Server 2003 DCs or Windows 2000 DCs that are running 2000 Service Pack 4 or later. For AD FS, you can implement a forest trust to leverage the Federated Web SSO with Forest Trust scenario, which will allow you additional options when configuring an AD FS account partner.

See Also

Recipe 19.8 and Recipe 2.16 for more on trust transitivity in a Windows Server 2003 environment

19.12 Configuring an Alternate UPN Suffix

Problem

You want to modify or add a new UPN suffix for the users in an Active Directory forest.

Solution

Using a graphical user interface

1. Open the Active Directory Domains and Trusts snap-in.
2. In the left pane, right-click Active Directory Domains and Trusts and select Properties.
3. Under Alternate UPN suffixes, type the name of the suffix you want to add.
4. Click Add and OK.

Using a command-line interface

```
> admod -config -rb cn=Partitions uPNSuffixes:+:treyresearch.com
```

The *attributeName* :+: *attributeValue* syntax will add an additional value to an existing list of values in a multivalued attribute. Using *attributeName::attributeValue* would add the value you specify and remove all other values.

Using VBScript

```
' This code adds a new UPN suffix.
' ------ SCRIPT CONFIGURATION -----
strNewSuffix = "<NewSuffix>" ' e.g. othercorp.com
strDomain = "<DomainDNSName>" ' e.g. adatum.com
' ------ END CONFIGURATION ---------
set objRootDSE = GetObject("LDAP://" & strDomain & "/RootDSE")
set objPartitions = GetObject("LDAP://cn=Partitions," & _
                               objRootDSE.Get("ConfigurationNamingContext"))
objPartitions.PutEx ADS_PROPERTY_APPEND, "
uPNSuffixes", Array(strNewSuffix)

objPartitions.SetInfo
```

Using PowerShell

```
set-variable -name $ADS_PROPERTY_APPEND -value 3 -option constant
$strDN = "LDAP://cn=Partitions,cn=Configuration,<ForestDN>"
$strNewSuffix = "<NewSuffix>"
$objPart = [ADSI] $strDN
$objPart.PutEx($ADS_PROPERTY_APPEND, "uPNSuffixes", @($strNewSuffix))
$objPart.SetInfo()
```

Discussion

The UPN allows users to log on with a friendly name that may or may not correspond to their email address. Also, UPN logons do not require the domain to be known, so that it can be abstracted away from the user. You may need to create an additional UPN suffix (e.g., *@adatum.com*) if you want UPNs to map to email addresses, but your AD forest is rooted at a different domain name (e.g., *ad.adatum.com*) than the domain name used in email addresses (e.g., *adatum.com*). In the case of AD FS identity claims, only one UPN claim can be used for a given application, so it may also be necessary to configure additional UPN suffixes to meet this requirement as well.

Keep in mind that shared UPN suffixes are not supported in cross-forest trust environments. In other words, the UPN suffixes must be different in either forest.

Using a command-line interface

Like many command-line recipes in this guide, this recipe references the admod utility that can be downloaded from *http://www.joeware.net*.

Using VBScript

UPN suffixes are stored in the multivalued `uPNSuffixes` attribute on the `Partitions` container in the Configuration naming context. The default forest UPN suffix is assumed and not stored in that attribute.

See Also

MS KB 243280 (Users Can Log On Using User Name or User Principal Name), MS KB 243629 (How to Add UPN Suffixes to a Forest), and MS KB 269441 (How to Use ADSI to List the UPN Suffixes that Are Defined in Active Directory)

19.13 Configuring the AD FS Web Agent

Problem

You want to install and configure the AD FS Web Agent to allow or deny access to an AD FS-aware web application.

Solution

Using a graphical user interface

To install the AD FS Web Agent in Windows Server 2003 R2, do the following:

1. Click Start→Control Panel→Add or Remove Programs.
2. Select Add/Remove Windows Components.
3. Click on the Active Directory Services checkbox, and select Details.
4. Click on Active Directory Federation Services (ADFS) and select Details.
5. Place a checkmark next to ADFS Web Agent, and then click OK.
6. Click OK twice and then Next to begin the installation.

To install the AD FS Web Agent in Windows Server 2008, do the following:

1. Click on Start→Server Manager. In the lefthand pane, click Roles.
2. Click Add Roles and then click Next twice to continue.
3. Place a checkmark next to "Claims-aware agent and/or Windows Token-based Agent." If prompted, click Add Required Role Services.

 In order to install the Windows Token-based Agent, the web server needs to be a member of an Active Directory domain. The Claims-aware agent does not have this requirement.

4. Click Next through the remainder of the wizard and then click Install.

5. When the installation completes, click Close.

To configure a website to use Windows NT token-based authentication, do the following:

1. Open the Internet Service Manager MMC snap-in.

2. Right-click on the Web Sites folder and select Properties. On the ADFS Web Agent tab, specify the Federation Service URL, for example, *http://www.adatum.com/ adfs/service.asmx*.

3. Next, right-click on the specific website you wish to configure and select Properties.

4. On the ADFS Web Agent tab, place a checkmark next to "Enable the ADFS Web Agent for Windows NT token-based applications." If needed, specify the cookie path, cookie domain, and the return URL being used by the application.

5. Click Apply and then OK to save your changes.

 To configure claims-based applications, you'll need to modify the *web.config* file for the claims-aware application. You can see an example of this in Microsoft Knowledge Base article 911687.

Using a command-line interface

To perform an unattended install of the AD FS Web Agent in Windows Server 2003 R2, you must create an answer file containing a [Components] section, similar to the following:

```
[Components]
ADFSClaims = On
ADFSTraditional = On
```

Save the unattended file as *unattended.txt*, and then run the following command:

```
> sysocmgr /i:sysoc.inf /u:<PathToUnattendedFile>
```

To install the AD FS Web Agent in Windows Server 2008, use the following servermanagercmd syntax:

```
> servermanagercmd.exe -i ADFS-Web-Agents
```

 To only install one agent type or the other, substitute ADFS-Web-Agents for either ADFS-Claims or ADFS-Windows-Token.

Discussion

For a web application that's hosted by a resource partner to process AD FS claims, it must have the AD FS Web Agent installed on it. The Web Agent is a standalone component of AD FS; you do not need to install the Federation Service itself on individual web servers. Rather, you configure the web agent to point to a Federation Service in the resource partner organization so that it can refer to it as needed.

See Also

Recipe 19.10 for more on configuring an AD FS application, Recipe 19.14 to enable auditing on a resource web server, and MS KB 911687 (You Cannot Use IIS Manager to Configure the Logging Settings for the AD FS Web Agent in Windows Server 2003)

19.14 Enabling Logging for the AD FS Web Agent

Problem

You want to enable logging for an application running on a web server in a resource partner's organization.

Solution

Using the registry

To enable auditing for a Windows NT token-based application, create or modify the following Registry keys:

```
HKLM\System\CurrentControlSet\Control\Lsa\WebSSO\Parameters\DebugLevel
DWORD - "FFFFFFFF"

HKLM\System\CurrentControlSet\Control\Lsa\ifssvc\Parameters\DebugPrintLevel
DWORD - "FFFFFFFF"

HKLM\Software\Microsoft\ADFS\WebServerAgent\DebugPrintLevel
DWORD - "FFFFFFFF"
```

 To modify the auditing level for a claims-based application, you need to modify the appropriate *web.config* file.

Using VBScript

```
' The following script creates the necessary DWORD values to
' configure logging for a token-based application

'-------------SCRIPT CONFIGURATION-------------------------
```

```
Const HKEY_LOCAL_MACHINE = &H80000002
strComputer = "."
'-----------------------------------------------------------

Set oRegistry=GetObject("winmgmts:{impersonationLevel=impersonate}!\\" & _
    strComputer & "\root\default:StdRegProv")

strKeyPath = "System\CurrentControlSet\Control\Lsa\WebSSO\Parameters"

strValueName = "DebugLevel"
dwValue = FFFFFFFF
oReg.SetDWORDValue HKEY_LOCAL_MACHINE,strKeyPath,strValueName,dwValue

strKeyPath = "System\CurrentControlSet\Control\Lsa\ifssvc\Parameters"
strValueName = "DebugPrintLevel"
oReg.SetDWORDValue HKEY_LOCAL_MACHINE,strKeyPath,strValueName,dwValue

strKeyPath = "Software\Microsoft\ADFS\WebServerAgent"
oReg.SetDWORDValue HKEY_LOCAL_MACHINE,strKeyPath,strValueName,dwValue
```

Using PowerShell

```
$strRegPath = "HKLM\System\CurrentControlSet\Control\Lsa\WebSSO\Parameters"
New-ItemProperty -path $strRegPath -name "DebugLevel" -type DWORD
Set-ItemProperty -path $strRegPath -name "DebugLevel" -value "FFFFFFFF"

$strRegPath = "HKLM\System\CurrentControlSet\Control\Lsa\ifssvc\Parameters"
New-ItemProperty -path $strRegPath -name "DebugPrintLevel" -type DWORD
Set-ItemProperty -path $strRegPath -name "DebugPrintLevel" -value "FFFFFFFF"

$strRegPath = "HKLM\Software\Microsoft\ADFS\WebServerAgent"
New-ItemProperty -path $strRegPath -name "DebugPrintLevel" -type DWORD
Set-ItemProperty -path $strRegPath -name "DebugPrintLevel" -value "FFFFFFFF"
```

Discussion

Unlike standard IIS logging, you cannot use the Internet Services Manager (ISM) MMC snap-in to configure logging for the AD FS Web Agent. Instead, you need to modify the Registry entries listed here in the case of a Windows NT token-based application. To configure logging for a claims-based application, you need to modify the contents of that application's *web.config* file.

See Also

MSDN: System.Web.Security.SingleSignOn and MSDN: StdRegProv.SetDWORDValue method [WMI]

## CHAPTER 20

Microsoft Exchange Server 2007 and Exchange Server 2003

20.0 Introduction

Microsoft Exchange Server is Microsoft's flagship messaging and collaboration server application. Exchange manages email messages through a proprietary MAPI protocol for rich use with Microsoft Outlook clients as well as the Internet standard protocols of POP3, IMAP4, and SMTP. It is a scalable enterprise solution from gateway to mailbox with expected functionality including backup and recovery, message hygiene, and mailbox management. Several features that have evolved over the years are still present in the latest version, including Outlook Web Access (OWA), Public Folders, cached Exchange mode, and Mobile device synchronization with ActiveSync. Other features have been added or improved significantly for 2007, such as message flow control with transport rules and new message hygiene options.

Exchange has a set of APIs that can be used to integrate custom applications or access specific Exchange data. Exchange can be an important component of a business collaboration system. We are not going to cover every single PowerShell cmdlet or all possible recipes for configuring Exchange Server, but we will introduce a good cross section of common tasks that Exchange implementers or administrators may need to perform their duties.

20.1 Exchange Server and Active Directory

Even with all the major changes in Exchange Server, one of the mainstays over the last three versions is the use of Windows Active Directory as the Directory Services provider. Exchange 2000 Server was one of the first AD-aware applications. Indeed, AD is partly based on the Exchange directory used in Exchange 5.5 and earlier. Installing Exchange requires first extending the AD schema with Exchange-specific attributes. A successful implementation of Microsoft Exchange Server is dependent therefore on a successful implementation of Active Directory. In addition, Exchange 2007 routing is now dependent on AD Site topology instead of its own routing engine as was present in 2000 and 2003.

This deep integration also means that AD topology design should also consider Exchange messaging requirements. If Exchange 2000 or 2003 is already installed, AD design is still a consideration for migration to Exchange 2007. The AD and Exchange relationship also makes an Exchange chapter a suitable addition to this book.

20.2 Exchange Server 2007 Architecture

Microsoft has made sweeping changes to Exchange Server with Exchange Server 2007. The whole underlying architecture for the latest version is radically different from Exchange 2000/2003 and as a result, so are the mechanisms for deploying and administering Exchange. Exchange no longer relies on Windows Server and Internet Information Services (IIS) for basic SMTP support. Exchange 2007 requires the 64-bit version of Windows Server 2003 or 2008. Exchange 2007 has embraced modularity by separating functionality into different server roles. It is no longer necessary to install the entire application and then lock it down specific to its intended use—mailbox server, bridgehead, etc.

There are five main Exchange 2007 roles to choose from at installation:

- Client Access Server
- Mailbox Server
- Hub Transport Server
- Unified Messaging Server
- Edge Transport Server

Only the selected roles are installed. Other installation options include Clustered Mailbox Roles and the Management Console. The Edge Transport role is a special independent role installed on a server that is not a domain member and typically resides in a perimeter network (DMZ). The other roles can share residence on a single server within an Active Directory domain structure or be placed on separate servers or even virtual machines as part of a deployment strategy.

20.3 Exchange Administration Tools

With the changes in Exchange from 2003 to 2007, a good rule of thumb is to use the Exchange 2003 tools to administer and configure objects on an Exchange 2003 server and use the Exchange 2007 tools to administer and configure objects on an Exchange 2007 server. The tools provided between the two versions are very different.

Exchange 2003 Tools

There are two main GUIs for administering Exchange Server 2003. Exchange configuration is done primarily through the Exchange System Manager (ESM). User and group administration is performed with Active Directory Users and Computers (ADUC), with additional Exchange tabs in object properties. These Exchange 2003 tools both use the Microsoft Management Console and are installed with the Exchange System Management Tools. The Exchange version of the ADUC is installed on machines that have the Exchange System Management tools installed. The ESM is used to configure global exchange settings, connectors, protocols, information store properties, mail policies, message queues, and more.

There really isn't a fully compatible command-line interface equivalent to the GUIs for Exchange 2003 administration. There are some command-line tools that can be used for a variety of user and group administrative tasks. These include AD tools such as *ldifde* and *csvde*, which we covered in Chapter 4.

WMI and Collaboration Data Objects for Exchange Management (CDOEXM) provide interfaces to Exchange Server information and data. VBScript can be used to access this content, especially to automate tasks. ADSI is used to return information from AD, and VBScript can call that interface as well.

PowerShell can be used to call WMI objects, though, which may be used to manage Exchange 2003 configuration. If you are still on Exchange 2003 and starting to use PowerShell, the `Get-WMIObject` cmdlet can be an alternative for accessing Exchange WMI providers:

```
Get-WmiObject -ComputerName <Exchange_Server> -Class <Exchange_WMI_Class>
```

Exchange 2007 Tools

Exchange Server 2007 administration is shared between the Exchange Management Shell (EMS) and the Exchange Management Console (EMC); however, the EMC is built upon the EMS. Every configuration performed in the console has an equivalent command-line entry using the shell. This is a big change from previous versions.

WMI and CDOEXM are not supported in Exchange 2007. VBScript calling WMI providers or CDOEXM to automate Exchange 2003 administration should be converted to equivalent PowerShell scripts for Exchange 2007.

Exchange Management Shell

As we have seen in the previous chapters, Windows PowerShell revolutionizes the command-line experience in Windows. Microsoft Exchange Server 2007 is the first Microsoft application to extend PowerShell for deployment and administration. With Exchange 2007 SP1, there are over 400 cmdlets to assist with Exchange management.

PowerShell uses an XML file as a console definition file to identify snap-ins to be loaded with PowerShell. For the EMS, this file is named `exshell.psc1` and is called with the parameter `-PSConsoleFile`. The Exchange Management Shell is an extension of PowerShell. The Windows start menu shortcut for the EMS actually uses the following command:

```
C:\WINDOWS\system32\windowspowershell\v1.0\powershell.exe -PSConsoleFile
"C:\Program Files\Microsoft\Exchange Server\bin\exshell.psc1" -noexit -command ".
'C:\Program Files\Microsoft\Exchange Server\bin\Exchange.ps1'"
```

The EMS snap-in referenced in the console definition file is called `Microsoft.Exchange.Management.PowerShell.Admin`. If you are already in a PowerShell window, another way to launch EMS is by adding the EMS snap-in as follows:

```
Add-PSSnapin Microsoft.Exchange.Management.PowerShell.Admin
```

The EMS looks much like a standard Command prompt window with some added bells and whistles. For the first time, Exchange Server has a full CLI for Exchange management.

Exchange Management Console

The EMC is built upon the EMS. It is a graphical representation of underlying shell commands in the EMS. When Exchange 2007 was first released, there were many components that required the EMS in order to configure. Exchange 2007 Service Pack 1 brought a lot of those into the console, including POP and IMAP administration, Public Folder configuration, and Message Tracking.

The EMC resides in the newer version of the Microsoft Management Console. The interface is separated into three panes: Navigation, Results, and Action. Both User/ Group and Server administration are performed using the EMC. The ADUC extensions for Exchange 2000 or 2003 are no longer present for Exchange 2007.

Exchange 2007 Scripts Folder

Not to be overlooked in terms of Exchange 2007 administration is the *scripts* folder. Installed with Exchange 2007, Microsoft includes several premade scripts that can be used to easily make specific changes or that can be amended to customize components:

```
C:\Program Files\Microsoft\Exchange Server\Scripts\
```

For example, in the scripts folder, there are PowerShell scripts to install anti-spam transport agents on a Hub Transport server and to export Message Classifications for distribution to Outlook 2007 clients. Administrators can also add their own custom Exchange scripts to this folder as it is added to the Windows Path environment variable when Exchange is installed. It is not necessary therefore to remember the entire path to the scripts folder when executing scripts from the command line.

Third-Party Tools

Sometimes innovative utilities are created by third parties that can accomplish a task with greater ease than the native tools. There are numerous products, both free and commercially available, that can assist Exchange management. joe Richards maintains several Active Directory and Exchange utilities through his website, *http://www.joeware .net*. A few tools that we use in this chapter, including ExchMbx, AdFind, and AdMod, are available as freeware at *http://joeware.net/freetools/tools/exchmbx/index.htm*.

Problem

You want to generate a reference list of all the Exchange 2007 cmdlets available in the Exchange Management Shell.

Exchange 2007 Solution

Using PowerShell

PowerShell has a cmdlet that can list all the available cmdlets in PowerShell or the EMS, called `Get-Command`. A subset of this cmdlet called `Get-ExCommand` returns only the cmdlets added to PowerShell with the installation of the EMS. To get a list of all the EMS cmdlets, execute the following cmdlet:

```
Get-ExCommand | fl Name,Definition >> c:\ExCommandList.txt
```

This will generate a formatted list of all of the EMS cmdlets and their definitions in a text file on the C:\ drive.

Discussion

The purpose of the `Get` cmdlets is really to serve as a search and query tool. When specific cmdlet properties are specified, `Get-Command` will return only the cmdlets representing the filter properties requested. `Get-ExCommand` is actually `Get-Command` with a built-in filter for cmdlets, called `Microsoft.Exchange.Management.PowerShell.Admin`, that are part of the PSSnapin, which we know as the Exchange Management Shell. For example, we can show all EMS cmdlets with the term "mailbox" as part of the object as follows:

```
Get-ExCommand *mailbox*
```

See Also

There is a nice PowerShell cmdlet directory with some third-party extensions as well, found at *http://powershellcommunity.org/Directories/Cmdlets.aspx*, and you can also download the Exchange Management Shell Quick Reference from Microsoft at *http:// go.microsoft.com/fwlink/?linkid=64647*

20.4 Preparing Active Directory for Exchange

Problem

You want to prepare your Active Directory forest and domains for the installation of your first Exchange Server.

Exchange 2003 Solution

Using a graphical user interface

The first phase of the installation is *ForestPrep* and it needs to be run once on the Schema FSMO domain controller:

1. Log on to the Schema FSMO forest root domain controller with an account that has both *Enterprise Admin* and *Schema Admin* rights.

2. Per your corporate standards, create either a global or a universal group for the initial Exchange administration delegation. Name the group in a descriptive way like *ExchangeRootAdmins*. See Chapter 7 for assistance on creating groups.

3. Insert the Exchange Server CD into the CD-ROM drive if needed.

4. On the Start menu, click Run, and type:

   ```
   <driveletter>:\setup\i386\setup.exe /forestprep
   ```

   where *<driveletter>* is the drive letter of your CD-ROM drive or installation file location.

    This path may vary for certain versions of Exchange Server such as MSDN or Select versions.

5. On the Welcome screen, click Next.

6. On the License Agreement screen, read through the agreement and if you agree, click "I agree" and click Next. Of course, agreement is mandatory for installation to continue.

7. If the Product Identification screen is presented, enter your Exchange Server product key and click Next.

    This screen may not appear for certain versions of Exchange Server, such as the MSDN or Select versions.

8. On the Component Selection screen, verify that the action specified is *ForestPrep*, and click Next.

---

9. On the Server Administrator Account screen, enter the group created in step 2 and click Next.

10. On the Completing the Microsoft Exchange Wizard screen, click Finish.

The second phase is *DomainPrep* and it needs to be run once for the forest root domain and once for every domain in the forest that will contain mail-enabled objects. Preferably, you will run this process on every domain in the forest. You will want to wait for the schema updates from the *ForestPrep* to replicate prior to starting *DomainPrep*:

1. Log on to a machine that is part of the domain with an account that is a member of the *Domain Admins* group.

2. Insert the Exchange Server CD into the CD-ROM drive.

3. On the Start menu, click Run, and then type:

        <driveletter>:\setup\i386\setup.exe /domainprep

   where *<driveletter>* is the drive letter of your CD-ROM drive or installation file location.

 This path may vary for certain versions of Exchange Server such as MSDN or Select versions.

4. On the Welcome screen, click Next.

5. On the License Agreement screen, read through the agreement and if you agree, click "I agree" and click Next.

6. If presented, on the Product Identification screen, enter your Exchange Server product key and click Next.

 This screen may not appear for certain versions of Exchange Server, such as the MSDN or Select versions.

7. On the Component Selection screen, verify that the action specified is *Domain-Prep* and click Next.

8. Depending on how your domain is configured for Pre-Windows 2000 Compatible Access, you may get a pop-up with a message saying "The domain "*<domain-name>*" has been identified as an insecure domain for mail-enabled groups with hidden DL membership...". If you get this pop-up, click OK.

9. On the Completing the Microsoft Exchange Wizard screen, click Finish.

Using a command-line interface

You cannot run *ForestPrep* from the command line. You can, however, run an unattended *DomainPrep*. You will need to create an unattended installation configuration file, which is described in Recipe 20.6. For further details on this process, see the Exchange Server 2003 Deployment Guide.

You can load the Exchange schema extensions to your forest before running *Forest-Prep*, allowing you to import the Exchange-specific schema modifications months in advance without needing to specify an organization name as you had to do in Exchange 2000.

Exchange 2007 Solution

Using a graphical user interface

As with Exchange 2003, the Active Directory forest schema needs to be extended. Exchange 2007 further extends AD with new attributes. This step is done automatically through the GUI setup process. Running setup from the GUI therefore requires Schema Admin rights.

There is no separate mechanism to apply schema extensions or prepare the domain independent of installing the Exchange 2007 binaries when using the GUI. This makes the GUI a reasonable option for smaller shops; however, larger businesses with division of administrative duties will certainly want to use the command-line option.

Using a command-line interface

Exchange 2007 uses *Setup.com* at the root of the CD to control aspects of preparation, installation, and even recovery. *Setup.com* can be run from the command line with the appropriate parameters applied. The command line allows for easier separation of administrative duties based on permission level. The Exchange administrator may not have schema admin rights on AD. For AD preparation, there are several parameters to be applied in order.

If you are adding an Exchange 2007 Server to an existing Exchange 2003 organization, then you must first run *Setup.com* with the /PrepareLegacyExchangePermissions switch, after ensuring at least one global catalog (GC) server is running Windows 2003 SP1 or higher and that there are no GCs running Windows 2000 Server:

/PrepareLegacyExchangePermissions
> With changes applied by the PrepareSchema switch, the Recipient Update Service (RUS) will no longer have permissions to certain user attributes. This switch configures those permissions in every domain where Exchange 2000 or 2003 is installed so the RUS won't fail.

/PrepareSchema
> This switch updates the Active Directory schema by importing a set of .*ldf* files for Exchange 2007. If the /PrepareLegacyExchangePermissions switch has not been run, the /PrepareSchema switch will run first if there are any Exchange 2000 or 2003 servers present. The Schema Master must be Windows Server 2003 SP1 or greater.

`/PrepareAD`

This switch creates the Exchange configuration container in AD, creates the Exchange-related universal security groups (USGs), and applies the appropriate permissions. The `/PrepareAD` switch will also run the `/PrepareSchema` and the `/PrepareLegacyExchangePermissions` steps if they have not been executed yet.

`/PrepareDomain`

Like *DomainPrep*, this switch configures the necessary permissions and configuration of the domain in preparation for installation of Exchange server.

`/PrepareAllDomains`

This switch prepares all the domains in the forest at once.

This series of setup steps are sequential. The schema needs to be extended before AD is configured and that must complete prior to the domains being prepared. Especially in a wide area topology, you should leave sufficient time in between steps to allow for AD replication between domain controllers.

Discussion

Microsoft Exchange will not run in an Active Directory forest unless the forest and the domains have been properly prepared. Microsoft did not make the assumptions that everyone or every AD forest would use Exchange and therefore did not include all of the Exchange attributes and classes in the base Active Directory schema. The ability to dynamically extend the schema for Active Directory makes it possible to require only those people running Exchange to install the Exchange infrastructure and only in the AD forests where they need Exchange.

In addition to schema changes, you have to make security changes to Active Directory and the domain policy, as well as create some basic Exchange infrastructure objects. All of this is completed in the AD and Domain preparation processes for Exchange. Do not confuse these with the Windows 2003 *ForestPrep* and *DomainPrep* processes (using the `adprep` command); the concept is the same but the specific changes are different.

You need to run the *ForestPrep* or the *PrepareSchema* and *PrepareAD* processes once per forest to make the schema changes, create the Exchange organization structure in the Configuration container, and set up Exchange-specific permissions. In Exchange 2003, the *ForestPrep* process is also responsible for the initial delegation of Exchange rights to a specific user or group for administrative control. We recommend that you create a security group in your root domain for this delegation. You could use a domain local group in a single domain forest in which you will never create another domain. In a multidomain forest, you must use a global group or a universal group. The group is used to assign rights to objects in the Configuration container. Whether you use a global or universal group is up to you—either will do the job. The *ForestPrep* process requires the person running the process to be part of both the *Enterprise Admins* and *Schema Admins* groups.

You need to run the *DomainPrep* or *PrepareDomain* processes in the root domain of the forest and for every domain that will contain mail-enabled objects. Normally, *DomainPrep* is run on every domain in an Active Directory forest. The process creates Exchange security principals, modifies the domain security policy, creates some Exchange-specific infrastructure objects, and assigns permissions to the domain's Active Directory partition. The *DomainPrep* or *PrepareDomain* processes require the person running the process to be a member of the *Domain Admins* group of the domain being prepared. Thankfully, Exchange 2007 adds a `/PrepareAllDomains` switch allowing this step to be run once and have it apply to all accessible domains. However, when running the `/PrepareAllDomains` step, the person running the process must be a member of the *Enterprise Admins* group of the forest being prepared.

Due to the depth of changes made to the overall structure of Active Directory, the *ForestPrep* or *PrepareAD* processes require Schema Admin and Enterprise Admin rights, and *DomainPrep* or *PrepareDomain* requires Domain Admin rights. This prevents anyone but the centralized administration group responsible for the overall Active Directory forest from initially installing Exchange into the forest.

For a more in-depth discussion of the Exchange Server 2003 and 2007 deployment requirements, considerations, and the specifics of what the preparation processes do, please see the Exchange Server Library at *http://technet.microsoft.com/en-us/library/ aa996058(EXCHG.80).aspx*. You should also review the Exchange Server 2003 Deployment Tools and the Exchange Best Practices Analyzer, available from the same site.

 Prior to updating the forest using a Windows 2008 Server, you must first install the Active Directory Services remote management tools. This is easily accomplished from the command line as follows:

```
ServerManagerCmd -I RSAT-ADDS
```

See Also

Chapters 7 and 11 for more on groups and the AD schema, MS KB 314649 (Windows Server 2003 adprep/forestprep Command Causes Mangled Attributes in Windows 2000 Forests that Contain Exchange 2000 Servers), MS KB 327757 (How to Extend the Active Directory Schema for Exchange Without Installing Exchange), and the Exchange Server 2003 Deployment Guide; in addition, MS KB 925821 (The Exchange 2007 Setup program unexpectedly exits when you run commands to prepare Active Directory for the installation of Exchange 2007) and the Exchange Server 2007 Setup Permissions Reference at *http://technet.microsoft.com/en-us/library/bb310770(EXCHG .80).aspx* and "How to Install Exchange 2007 SP1 Prerequisites on Windows Server 2008 or Windows Vista" located at *http://technet.microsoft.com/en-us/library/ bb691354(EXCHG.80).aspx*

20.5 Installing the First Exchange Server in an Organization

Problem

You want to install the first Exchange Server for a new Exchange organization.

Exchange 2003 Solution

Using a graphical user interface

1. Install and configure prerequisite services. See the "Discussion" section for more on these services.

2. Log on to a server that is a member of an Exchange-enabled domain with an account that is a member of the delegated group in Recipe 20.4. This account should also be a local administrator of the server.

3. Go to the Windows Update site and install any critical security patches, or use your organization's existing patch management solution, such as WSUS. Click on Start→All Programs→Windows Update.

4. Insert the Exchange Server CD into the CD-ROM drive or point to the file installation source.

5. On the Start menu, click Run, type *<driveletter>:\setup\i386\setup.exe*, and click OK. *<driveletter>* is the drive letter of your CD-ROM drive. The path to *setup.exe* may vary for certain versions of Exchange Server such as MSDN or Select versions.

6. On the Welcome screen, click Next.

7. On the License Agreement screen, read through the agreement and if you agree, click "I agree" and click Next.

8. If presented, on the Product Identification screen, enter your Exchange Server product key and click Next.

 This screen may not appear for certain versions of Exchange Server, such as the MSDN or Select versions.

9. On the Component Selection screen in the Action column, verify that the action selected is Typical. Verify the install path is correct for your installation and click Next. It is a common practice to load Exchange onto a drive other than the system drive.

10. On the Installation Type screen, verify that Create a new Exchange Organization is selected, and click Next.

11. On the Organization Name screen, enter the name you want for your Exchange organization, and click Next. You can leave the default name of "First Organization" or name it something specific to your installation (e.g., "ADATUMAIL").

12. On the License Agreement screen, select "I agree" and then click Next.

13. Review the Installation Summary screen and click Next.

14. On the Completing the Microsoft Exchange Wizard screen, click Finish.

15. Stop and disable the NNTP service unless you specifically wish to use newsfeeds within your Messaging environment.

16. Download and install the latest Exchange 2003 service pack. (As of the time of this writing, it is Service Pack 2.) See "Installing an Exchange Service Pack" for more on installing Exchange service packs.

17. Download and run the Exchange Best Practices Analyzer to determine its compliance with security and performance best practices.

Using a command-line interface

You cannot install the first Exchange 2003 server of the organization via the command line. However, you can install subsequent Exchange servers using an unattended installation.

Discussion

The first Exchange 2003 server you install is special. This is because in addition to installing the Exchange Server software on the server, the process is also creating Active Directory objects in the Configuration container for the Exchange organization. As such, the install is slightly different from any other Exchange Server installation you will do in the forest (see "Installing Additional Exchange Servers"). The difference is in Steps 10 and 11, which will not be present for any other Exchange Server Installations within the Exchange organization. In these steps you will choose whether you want to create a new Exchange organization or join an existing Exchange 5.5 organization. The additional, and considerable, amount of work involved in joining an existing Exchange 5.5 organization is outside the scope of this chapter. See the *Exchange Server Cookbook* by Paul Robichaux et al. (O'Reilly) for more information.

See Also

MS KB 822593 (Description of the /ChooseDC Switch in Exchange Server 2003), MS KB 822893 (Setup Options for Exchange Server 2003), and *Exchange Server Cookbook*

Exchange 2007 Solution

Using a graphical user interface

1. Install and configure prerequisite services. See the section called "Discussion" for more on these services.

2. Log on to a server that is a member of an Exchange-prepared domain with an account that is a member of the delegated group in Recipe 20.4.

3. Go to the Windows Update site and install any critical security patches, or use your organization's existing patch management solution, such as WSUS. Click on Start→All Programs→Windows Update.

4. Insert the Exchange Server CD into the CD-ROM drive or point to the file installation source.

5. On the Start menu, click Run, type "<driveletter>:\setup.exe", and click OK. *<driveletter>* is the drive letter of your CD-ROM drive.

 You could also type "<driveletter>:\setup.com". Without any parameters, it will in turn launch **setup.exe**. **setup.com** is used for the command line and **setup.exe** for the GUI setup wizard.

6. The main installation screen will show three sections on the right: Plan, Install, and Enhance. Under Install, there are five steps. The first three we should have completed as prerequisites. The uncompleted installation steps will be bold. When the prerequisites are completed, click on step 4: Install Microsoft Exchange Server 2007 SP1.

7. The Introduction is marketing information. Enjoy the read and click Next.

8. On the License Agreement screen, read through the agreement and if you agree, click "I accept the terms of the license agreement" and click Next. Obviously, this is mandatory to continue with the installation.

9. Microsoft then requests your assistance in error reporting so they can help make the product better. Select Yes or No and click Next.

10. There are two installation types: Typical and Custom. If you want a standard installation similar to the features from previous versions, select Typical. If you are installing Unified Messaging, Clustered Exchange, Stand-alone Management Tools, or an Edge Server, you must select Custom. Then click Next.

11. If you selected Custom, you will now need to choose which roles to install on this server. Click Next.

12. As the first Exchange Server in a new organization, enter the new Organization name. This value cannot be changed later. Then click Next.

13. The next screen asks if you need a Public Folder database. This is required for Outlook clients prior to Outlook 2007 and for Entourage. Click Next.

14. Setup works through a set of Readiness Checks, including online updates. It becomes annoying should one of the prerequisites fail at this point because we have to repeat these steps after resolving the cause of the failure. Click Install if there are no issues to correct.

15. Installation progress is shown in the GUI; when it is done, the Completion screen will be presented. Click on Finish to close the window.

Using a command-line interface

Unlike Exchange 2003, you can install Exchange 2007 from the command line. *Setup.com*, found in the root of the Exchange 2007 or Exchange 2007 SP1 CD, has several switches to break down installation into its components. We already covered the preparatory switches in an earlier recipe Preparing Active Directory for Exchange. The other command-line switches for *Setup.com* are as follows:

/Mode
> The Mode for *Setup.com* identifies whether you are performing an install, uninstall, or recovery. The default mode is Install.

/Roles
> These are the main roles that you can select for a custom installation in the GUI. The roles are Mailbox, Hub Transport, Client Access, Unified Messaging, and Edge Transport. Management Tools is also an option.

/OrganizationName
> For the first Exchange 2007 server in a new organization, this value is needed.

/TargetDir
> This is the destination directory for binary installation. By default, this is found in `%programfiles%\Microsoft\Exchange Server\`.

/SourceDir
> This parameter is used to direct *Setup.com* to use an alternate location for the source files for installation.

/UpdatesDir
> This parameter directs setup to check the specified directory for an *Updates.exe* file or any *.msp* files.

/DomainController
> Exchange 2007 installation requires communication with a domain controller running Windows Server 2003 SP1 or higher. This switch is used if there are domain controllers running earlier Windows versions and the installer needs to avoid those.

/AnswerFile
> Setup is directed to a text file with preset properties to apply during installation.

/EnableLegacyOutlook
> This switch could have been called "CreatePublicFolderDatabase" because that is what it does. It is also what is needed to support legacy versions of Outlook as

MAPI clients. Outlook 2000 and 2003 use public folders for Free/Busy information and the Offline Address Book.

/DoNotStartTransport

This switch prevents Exchange 2007 from automatically routing email when it first starts. The administrator may have additional software to install or configure before Exchange should be enabled.

/LegacyRoutingServer

Where Exchange 2000 or 2003 are still present, this is used to specify a routing group connector for communication between Exchange 2007 and those versions.

/EnableErrorReporting

As we saw in the GUI, Microsoft is interested in making the product better by automating error reports submitted to them. This is optional and the default is set to No.

/NoSelfSignedCertificate

For Unified Messaging and Client Access Servers, the administrator may already have certificates installed to secure communication between devices. In that case, there may not be a need to implement the self-signed certificates that install with Exchange 2007 by default.

/AddUmLanguagePack

Unified Messaging is available in several languages. Different companies have different language needs, and this switch allows for specific installation of only the language packs required.

/RemoveUmLanguagePack

As the name suggests, this switch is used to uninstall language packs that are no longer required.

/NewCms

This switch is used to create a new Clustered Mailbox Server (CMS).

/CmsName

This switch is used to define the unique name for the new CMS.

/CmsIpAddress

A CMS must also have a unique IP address for client connectivity, and this switch is used to configure it.

/CmsSharedStorage

This switch validates storage for Exchange 2007 clusters.

/CmsDataPath

This switch defines the shared storage data path to be used by the CMS.

/AdamLdapPort

This is used to specify a nondefault port for Edge Transport server to use for ADAM LDAP access.

`/AdamSslPort`

> Also for the Edge server, this switch directs the setup to apply a specific port for SSL access to ADAM.

For example, to install the Mailbox and Hub Transport roles on a new server in a nondefault destination folder with a Public Folder database, run:

```
setup.com /Mode:Install /Roles:Mailbox,HubTransport /TargetDir:"d:\exchange\"
/EnableLegacyOutlook
```

Using PowerShell

For small installations, PowerShell does not offer a great benefit for running the setup. *Setup.com* can be run from a classic command prompt or a PowerShell prompt. For larger organizations, especially with multiple simultaneous Exchange Server installations, PowerShell affords some opportunities to simplify the process, such as identifying Exchange Servers on the network based on specific hostname policies or confirming target directory availability.

Discussion

Like Exchange 2003, if this Exchange 2007 Server is the first Exchange Server in a new organization, then it has some specific responsibilities at installation. For example, the administrator must specify a name for the new Exchange Organization.

The local Exchange 2007 Server has a few main prerequisites, which are presented in the UI as follows:

- .NET Framework 2.0
- Microsoft Management Console 3.0
- Windows PowerShell 1.0

The forest also has prerequisites. The Schema Master must reside on a Windows 2003 Server with SP1or greater and a domain functional level must be at Windows 2000 Native or higher.

There is a Typical installation mirroring the complete set of available features found in Exchange 2003. A Custom installation provides us with the opportunity to select individual roles or a combination. The Management Tools are listed as a separate option, but they are automatically installed with any of the other roles. They are listed separately for installation on an administration workstation or server.

Exchange performs readiness checks based on the roles selected. Should a readiness check fail, the offending situation must be resolved and, if you're using the GUI, the setup must be restarted.

Exchange 2007 SP1 is not an add-on service pack. Exchange 2007 can be installed completely from the Service Pack 1 CD or download. This saves the administrator from having to install the RTM binaries and then apply the latest service pack. Installing directly to Exchange 2007 SP1 follows the same instructions as installing Exchange 2007 RTM.

Installing Exchange 2007 SP1 on Windows Server 2008 has a couple of specific prerequisites. For example, PowerShell is shipped with Windows 2008 but is not installed as a feature by default. Windows 2008 has a simple command to apply components. To implement prerequisites for a Typical Exchange installation on Windows 2008, run the following Windows 2008 commands:

```
ServerManagerCmd -i PowerShell
ServerManagerCmd -i Web-Server
ServerManagerCmd -i Web-ISAPI-Ext
ServerManagerCmd -i Web-Metabase
ServerManagerCmd -i Web-Lgcy-Mgmt-Console
ServerManagerCmd -i Web-Basic-Auth
ServerManagerCmd -i Web-Digest-Auth
ServerManagerCmd -i Web-Windows-Auth
ServerManagerCmd -i Web-Dyn-Compression
ServerManagerCmd -i Web-RPC-Over-HTTP-Proxy
```

Exchange 2007 SP1 is required for Exchange installation on Windows Server 2008.

See Also

The full set of installation requirements are available from the deployment section of the Exchange 2007 technical library, found at *http://technet.microsoft.com/en-us/library/aa996058(EXCHG.80).aspx*; also see "How to Install Exchange 2007 SP1 Prerequisites on Windows Server 2008 or Windows Vista" at *http://technet.microsoft.com/en-us/library/bb691354(EXCHG.80).aspx*

20.6 Creating Unattended Installation Files for Exchange Server

Problem

You want to create an unattended installation file for command-line installations and upgrades of Exchange Server.

Exchange 2003 Solution

Using a graphical user interface

1. Follow the procedures for a standard Exchange Server installation, Exchange Server Management Tools installation (Recipe 20.7), or Exchange Server service pack installation to the point where you enter the **setup** or **update** commands.

2. Append this option to the `run` command: `/createunattend <driveletter>:\<path>\ <filename>` `.ini`. Note that `<filename>` should be descriptive of the install or update. Examples include:

   - *e2k3-unattended-sp2-install.ini*
   - *e23k-tools-install.ini*

3. Follow all of the screen prompts of the normal installation or upgrade.

4. On the Completing the Microsoft Exchange Wizard screen, click Finish.

The unattended installation is in the location specified in the `/createunattend` option.

Exchange 2007 Solution

Using a command-line interface

Exchange 2007 can be installed in unattended mode simply using the command-line setup options. Some of the *Setup.com* switches can be listed within a text file that in turn is called by the `/AnswerFile` parameter. The *Setup.com* switches that can reside in an unattended installation answer file are `EnableLegacyOutlook`, `LegacyRoutingServer`, `ServerAdmin`, `ForeignForestFQDN`, `OrganizationName`, `DoNotStartTransport`, `UpdatesDir`, `EnableErrorReporting`, `NoSelfSignedCertificates`, `AdamLdapPort`, and `AdamSslPort`. These switches are listed in a text file without the backslash and saved as a text file such as *UnattendParams.txt*.

Setup.com references the answer file as follows:

```
Setup.com /Mode:Install /Roles:Mailbox /AnswerFile:C:\UnattendParams.txt
```

Discussion

Using unattended installation is a great way to install Exchange on many servers, deploy the Exchange tools to many admin workstations, update service packs for Exchange on many servers, or maintain consistency in installation configurations.

The basic process in Exchange 2003 is simply to add the `/createunattend` switch to the command line for either the *setup* or *update* command. You can also, if you so choose, create an encrypted unattended installation file by using the `/encryptedmode` option. To see a complete list of options, run the *setup* or *update* executable with the `/?` option. In Exchange 2007, the parameter is called `/AnswerFile` and is formed using parameters available with *Setup.com*. After you create an unattended installation answer file, you can use it to install additional Exchange servers.

See Also

Recipe 20.7 for more on installing the Exchange Management Tools, MS KB 822893 (Setup Options for Exchange Server 2003), and "How to Install Exchange 2007 in

Unattended Mode" located at *http://technet.microsoft.com/en-us/library/ aa997281(EXCHG.80).aspx*

20.7 Installing Exchange Management Tools

Problem

You want to install Exchange Management Tools onto a workstation or server that isn't running Exchange.

Exchange 2003 Solution

Using a graphical user interface

1. Install and configure prerequisite services. See the section called "Discussion" for the list of these services.
2. Go to the Windows Update site and install any critical security patches.
3. Load the Exchange Server CD into your CD-ROM drive or point to the installation source file location.
4. On the Start menu, click Run and then type "<driveletter>:\setup\i386\setup.exe" and click OK. *<driveletter>* is the drive letter of your CD-ROM drive or network share. This path may vary for certain versions of Exchange Server such as MSDN or Select versions.
5. On the Welcome screen, click Next.
6. On the License Agreement screen, read through the agreement and if you agree, select "I agree" and click Next.
7. If the Product Identification screen is presented, enter your Exchange Server product key and click Next.

 This screen may not appear for certain versions of Exchange Server such as the MSDN or Select versions.

8. On the Component Selection screen, select Custom in the top row of the Action column. Next to Microsoft Exchange System Management Tools, select Install. Verify that the install path is correct for your installation and click Next.
9. Review the Installation Summary screen and click Next.
10. On the Completing the Microsoft Exchange Wizard screen, click Finish.
11. Download and install the latest Exchange 2003 service pack. As of the time of this writing, it is Service Pack 2.

Using a command-line interface

Any Exchange Management Tools installations can be handled through the command line with the unattended installation process. You will need to generate and use the appropriate unattended install INI file. See Recipe 20.6 for more on creating an INI file.

Once you have an unattended file, use the following command to install:

```
> <driveletter>:\setup\i386\setup.exe /unattendfile <unattendfile>
```

Note that if there is an error during the install process it will be recorded in the Exchange Server setup log, which by default will be located in the root of the system drive, generally *C:*.

Discussion

Exchange Server 2003 has several software prerequisites for the Exchange Management Tools components, without which they will refuse to install. You must have the Windows Server 2003 Administration Tools Pack (*adminpak.msi*) installed on Windows XP SP1+, Windows 2000 SP3+, or Windows Server 2003 along with the following services:

- IIS
- WWW Service
- SMTP Service

See the *Windows Server Cookbook for Windows Server 2003 and Windows 2000* by Robbie Allen (O'Reilly) for more details on installation of these prerequisites.

Microsoft has a recommendation against installing Exchange tools on a machine that runs Outlook. We haven't had an issue with loading the Exchange tools on a workstation that had Outlook, but it is a point that we must mention. See MS KB 266418 for more details.

 You may or may not run into issues loading the Exchange Management Tools on a client computer that is running the Outlook email client. However, it is absolutely essential that you do not install Microsoft Outlook on the Exchange server itself.

Using a command-line interface

If you have only one or two machines you want to install the tools on, automating the Exchange Server Management Tools installation will probably not be of any value to you. However, if you have several machines you need to load the tools on, using the unattended installation feature can certainly lead to time savings, efficiency, and consistency.

Exchange 2007 Solution

Using a graphical user interface

Installing just the Exchange 2007 Management Tools requires a Custom installation:

1. Follow the standard installation steps outlined in Recipe 20.5 except for creating a new organization, up to the option for installation type.

2. Select Custom installation and click Next.

3. The different roles are available to select by checkbox. Select the Management Tools option at the bottom of the list. This will render the other roles unavailable for selection.

4. Setup works through a set of Readiness Checks, including online updates. It becomes annoying should one of the prerequisites fail at this point because we have to repeat these steps after resolving the cause of the failure. Click Install if there are no issues to correct.

5. Installation progress is shown in the GUI and when it is done, the Completion screen will be presented. Click on Finish to close the window.

Using a command-line interface

Setup.com provides a switch to select the roles to install. The role `ManagementTools` or `MT` is one of the options. After the prerequisites are applied, the Exchange 2007 Management Tools can be installed as follows:`setup.com /Mode:Install /Role:Management Tools`.

Discussion

Installing the Exchange Management Tools on a workstation or server that is not running Exchange Server is an alternative to using Remote Desktop administration of Exchange. The tools install the following components:

- Exchange Management Console
- Exchange Management Shell
- Exchange Best Practices Analyzer
- Exchange Help files
- Exchange Troubleshooting Assistant

Like the server installation, the management tools themselves have prerequisites for installation. They need the .NET Framework 2.0, Microsoft Management Console 3.0, and PowerShell 1.0. Exchange 2007 SP1 64-bit Management Tools are supported on Windows Vista 64-bit, Windows Server 2008 64-bit, Windows Server 2003 64-bit, and Windows XP x64 edition. The Management Tools only are supported in 32-bit, as well on the 32-bit versions of the operating systems listed for 64-bit with XP 32-bit and Windows 2003 Server at SP2 or higher.

See Also

Recipe 20.6 for more on unattended installation, MS KB 822593 (Description of the /ChooseDC Switch in Exchange Server 2003), MS KB 822893 (Setup Options for Exchange Server 2003), MS KB 266418 (Microsoft Does Not Recommend Installing Exchange Server and Outlook on the Same Computer), *Windows Server Cookbook for Windows Server 2003 and Windows 2000*, and "How to Install the Exchange 2007 Management Tools" located at *http://technet.microsoft.com/en-us/library/ bb232090(EXCHG.80).aspx*

20.8 Stopping and Starting Exchange Server

Problem

You want to stop or start Exchange Server.

Exchange 2003 Solution

Stopping and starting Exchange consists of stopping and starting the Exchange-related services through the Services MMC snap-in or the `net stop`/`net start` command-line utilities. See the section called "Discussion" for the list of Exchange services.

Using a graphical user interface

1. Open the Computer Management MMC snap-in (*compmgmt.msc*).
2. Navigate to Services.
3. Scroll to and select the service that you wish to manage.
4. Click Stop, Start, or Restart.

Using a command-line interface

The following command will stop a service:

```
> net stop <ServiceName>
```

The following command will start a service:

```
> net start <ServiceName>
```

The following will stop and start a service in a single command:

```
> net stop <ServiceName> && net start <ServiceName>
```

Net start and stop commands can easily be assembled in a batch file (*.bat*) as well. Calling the *.bat* file from the command line may be easier than waiting for individual `net start` or `net stop` commands.

Using VBScript

```
'-------------SCRIPT CONFIGURATION---------------------
strComputer = "<ComputerName>"
strServiceName = "<ServiceName>"

Set objWMIService = GetObject("winmgmts:" _
    & "{impersonationLevel=impersonate}!\\" & strComputer _
    & "\root\cimv2")

Set colServiceList = objWMIService.ExecQuery _
    ("Select * from Win32_Service where Name='" & strServiceName _
    _ & "'")

' The following code will start a service

For Each objService in colServiceList
    errReturn = objService.StartService()
Next

' The following code will stop a service

For Each objService in colServiceList
    errReturn = objService.StopService()
Next
```

Exchange 2007 Solution

Using PowerShell

Stopping and starting Exchange 2007 services is a little easier because almost every service has the term "exchange" in its name. The Microsoft Speech Engine required for Unified Messaging and the Edge Credential Service used by an Edge Transport Server are the only ones that are not captured by these scripts.

For a list of all of the services on the server with exchange in their display name:

```
Get-service *exchange* | ft Name, Status
```

PowerShell can call on WMI to perform the task as well, though not as cleanly as the `Get-Service` cmdlet:

```
Get-WMIObject -class "Win32_Service" -Namespace "root/CIMV2" | Where {$_.Name -like
"*exchange*"} | ft Name,Status
```

The Namespace `"root/CIMV2"` is the default namespace for the `Get-WMIObject` call.

PowerShell will return the services in alphabetical order. The results can be further piped to the Sort-Objects cmdlet to control how the list is presented.

To start services with exchange in the display name and Automatic start mode:

```
'------------SCRIPT CONFIGURATION---------------------
$strComputer = "."
Get-WMIObject -class "Win32_Service" -Namespace "root/CIMV2" -ComputerName
$strComputer | Where-Object {($_.DisplayName -like "*exchange*") -and ($_.StartMode
-eq "Auto")} | Start-service
```

The Get-Service cmdlet does not have a property for StartMode. WMI is needed to access that value. To stop services that are running and have exchange in the display name:

```
Get-service *exchange* | ? { $_.Status -eq "Running" } | stop-service
```

And again, the same function using the Get-WMIObject cmdlet:

```
'------------SCRIPT CONFIGURATION---------------------
$strComputer = "."

Get-WMIObject -class "Win32_Service" -Namespace "root/CIMV2" -ComputerName
$strComputer | Where-Object {($_.DisplayName -like '*exchange*') -and ($_.Started
-eq $True)} | Stop-service
```

Discussion

There are several services involved with Exchange Server, and stopping different services will accomplish different things. Typically, it is not necessary to stop services manually. The services are interdependent, so when you stop or start various services, you may see a message about having to stop dependent services. If you do stop dependent services, don't forget to restart them again when you restart the service that you began with.

Different servers could be running a combination of different services based on the complexity of the environment and the specific function of the server. Not all Exchange servers will run all Exchange services.

For the long list of Exchange Server services, some of which are very similar between Exchange 2003 and 2007, see Table 20-1.

Table 20-1. Exchange services

Exchange service	Version	Description
Microsoft Exchange POP3 (POP3Svc or MSExchangePOP3)	2003 2007	This service supplies POP3 protocol message server functionality. On Exchange 2007, this is only available on a CAS.
Microsoft Exchange IMAP4 (IMAP4Svc or MSExchangeIMAP4)	2003 2007	This service supplies IMAP4 protocol message server functionality. On Exchange 2007, this is only available on a CAS.
Microsoft Exchange Information Store (MSExchangeIS)	2003 2007	This service is used to access the Exchange mail and public folder stores. If this service is not running, users will not be able to use Exchange.
Microsoft Exchange System Attendant (MSExchangeSA)	2003 2007	This service provides monitoring, maintenance, and directory lookup services. One of the most important functions of the System Attendant in Exchange 2003 is the Recipient Update Service (RUS), which is responsible for mapping attributes in Active Directory to the Exchange subsystem and enforcing recipient policies.
MTA Stacks (MSExchangeMTA)	2003	This service is used to transfer X.400 messages sent to and from foreign systems, including Exchange 5.5 Servers. This service was extremely important in Exchange 5.5, which used X.400 as the default message transfer protocol. Before stopping or disabling this service, review MS KB 810489.
Management (MSExchangeMGMT)	2003	This service is responsible for various management functions available through WMI, such as message tracking.
Routing Engine (RESvc)	2003	This service is used for routing and topology information for routing SMTP-based messages.
Simple Mail Transfer Protocol (SMTPSVC)	2003	This service is responsible for supplying SMTP Protocol Server functionality.
Site Replication Service (MSExchangeSRS)	2003	This service is used in organizations that have Exchange 5.5 combined with Exchange 2000/2003.
Exchange Event (MSExchangeES)	2003	This service was used for launching event-based scripts in Exchange 5.5 when folder changes were detected. Exchange 2000 offered the ability to create Event Sinks directly, so this use of this service has decreased.
Network News Transfer Protocol (NntpSvc)	2003	This service is responsible for supplying NNTP Protocol Server functionality.
Active Directory Topology (MSExchangeADTopology)	2007	Queries Active Directory and returns configuration information and other data.
ADAM (ADAM_MSExchange)	2007	Manages Active Directory replicated content on an Edge Transport Server.
Anti-spam Update service (MSExchangeAntiSpamUpdate)	2007	Automatically downloads anti-spam filter updates from Microsoft.
Credential service (EdgeCredential-Sync)	2007	This service monitors any credential changes in ADAM and implements the changes on the Edge Transport Server.

Exchange service	Version	Description
EdgeSync (MSExchangeEdgeSync)	2007	Synchronizes data over LDAP between the Hub Transport and an Edge Transport Server.
File Distribution Service (MSExchangeFDS)	2007	The FDS copies the Offline Address Book files to web distribution points and distributes any custom prompts for Unified Messaging.
Mail submission service (MsExchangeMailSubmission)	2007	This service transfers messages from a mailbox server to a Hub Transport server.
Mailbox Assistants (MsExchange-MailboxAssistants)	2007	Manages the calendar, resource booking, Out-of-Office, and managed folder assistants.
Monitoring (MSExchangeMonitoring)	2007	This Exchange Monitoring service allows diagnostics using an RPC Server.
Replication (MSExchangeRepl)	2007	Performs log shipping services for LCR (Local Continuous Replication), SCR (Standby Continuous Replication), and CCR (Cluster Continuous Replication).
Search (MSFTESQL-Exchange)	2007	Maintains text index of mailbox databases and adds entries provided by the Search Indexer service.
Search Indexer (MSExchangeSearch)	2007	Collects new items and provides them to the Search service.
Service Host (MSExchangeService-Host)	2007	This service manages the IIS RPC Virtual Directory and Outlook Anywhere registry data.
Speech Engine (MSS)	2007	This service powers the Unified Messaging Speech processing services.
Transport (MSExchangeTransport)	2007	SMTP Services in Exchange 2007 are managed with this service.
Transport Log Search (MSExchange-TransportLogSearch)	2007	This service powers the Message Tracking functionality in Exchange.
Unified Messaging (MSExchangeUM)	2007	This service manages the Unified Messaging engine for Outlook Voice Access.

See Also

MS KB 810489 and MS KB 263094 (XADM: Internal Names of Exchange 2000 Server Services)

20.9 Mail-Enabling a User

Problem

You want to mail-enable an existing user.

Exchange 2003 Solution

Using a graphical user interface

1. Open the Users and Computers (ADUC) snap-in.

    This needs to be run on a workstation or server that has the Exchange Management Tools loaded (see Recipe 20.7).

2. If you need to change domains, right-click on Active Directory Users and Computers in the left pane, select Connect to Domain, enter the domain name, and click OK.

3. In the left pane, browse to the parent container of the user, right-click on the user, and select Exchange Tasks.

4. On the Welcome screen, click Next.

5. Select Establish E-mail Address and click Next.

6. Verify the mail alias is what you want.

7. Click Modify, select external email address type (generally SMTP Address), click OK, enter an external email address, and click OK.

    There is an Advanced tab on the Internet Address Properties screen. On this tab, you have the option to override the default handling of email sent to this recipient (e.g., you can force all email to be delivered as HTML or plain text, etc.).

8. On the Completion screen, click Finish.

Using a command-line interface

```
> exchmbx -b "<User DN>" -me <smtp email address>
```

Replace *<User DN>* with the user's distinguished name and *<smtp email address>* with the user's external email address.

To mail-enable the user *joe* with the email address *joe@zimbra.adatum.com*, execute the following command. The command should be contained on one line:

```
> exchmbx -b "cn=joe,cn=users,dc=adatum,dc=com" -me joe@zimbra.adatum.com
```

For an alternative Microsoft-native tool method, create an LDIF file called *mailenable_user.ldf* with the following contents:

```
dn: <User DN>
changetype: modify
replace: targetAddress
targetaddress: SMTP:<smtp email address>
```

```
-
replace: mailNickName
mailNickname: <mail nickname>
-
replace: mAPIRecipient
mAPIRecipient: FALSE
-
replace: legacyExchangeDN
legacyExchangeDN: <legacy exchange DN>
-
replace: internetEncoding
internetEncoding: 1310720
-
```

Replace *<User DN>* with the user's distinguished name, *<smtp email address>* with the user's external email address, and *<legacy exchange DN>* with the proper legacy exchange distinguished name value. Then run the following command to import the new settings into AD:

```
>ldifde -i -f mailenable_user.ldf
```

Using VBScript

```
' This code mail enables a user.
' ------ SCRIPT CONFIGURATION ------
strUserDN = "<UserDN>" ' e.g. cn=jsmith,cn=Users,dc=adatum,dc=com
strEmailAddr = "<EmailAddress>" 'e.g. jsmith@gmx.net
' ------ END CONFIGURATION ---------
Set objUser = GetObject("LDAP://" & strUserDN)
objUser.MailEnable strEmailAddr
objUser.Put "internetEncoding",1310720
objUser.SetInfo()
Wscript.Echo "Successfully mail-enabled user."
```

Discussion

A mail-enabled user is a user object that has at least one email address defined within Exchange, but does not have a mailbox. This does not give any access rights to the user within the Exchange system; it simply allows Exchange users to select the mail-enabled users from the GAL and easily send email to them. You would use a mail-enabled user when you have a user who needs to log in to the domain, but has an email address external to the forest's Exchange organization. The email address could be external to the company, or it could just be external to the Exchange organization of that forest. Examples would be users with mailboxes on external email systems or users with mailboxes on internal non-Exchange servers.

To mail-enable a user, you need to have permissions of Exchange View-Only Administrator or higher for the target administrative group.

When you create a mail-enabled user with ADUC or with VBScript, you call out to the CDOEXM interface, which is the Microsoft-supported method of managing Exchange attributes on users, groups, and contacts. The specific method in this case is

`MailEnable`. In the background, the specific changes made by the `MailEnable` method are on the **user** object in Active Directory and include changes to the following attributes:

- `targetAddress`
- `mailNickname`
- `mAPIRecipient`
- `legacyExchangeDN`

In addition to those attributes, the `internetEncoding` attribute should also be set for proper message handling. This is the attribute that is updated if you go into the Advanced tab of the Internet Address Properties screen. The default value for this attribute is **1310720**, which tells Exchange to use the default settings of the Internet Mail Service. You can specify other values to force email to be converted to various formats. Table 20-2 contains the list of alternate values for the `internetEncoding` attribute.

Table 20-2. internetEncoding attribute values

Value	Meaning
1310720	Use Internet Mail Service settings
917504	Allow plain text
1441792	Allow plain text or HTML
2228224	Allow plain text/uuencoding
131072	Allow plain text/uuencoding with BinHex

Once all of those attributes are in place, the RUS sets additional attributes on the user object to make it useable for Exchange.

Using a graphical user interface

Mail-enabling a user is a little more confusing if you are creating new users because you don't get prompted to mail-enable them. To create a mail-enabled user from scratch, create the user and, when prompted to create a mailbox, clear the "Create an Exchange Mailbox" checkbox. Once the user is created, follow the directions described in the solution.

Using a command-line interface

Command-line administration tools for Exchange 2000 and 2003 are rather rare. Luckily, the ExchMbx tool is available as a free download from *http://www.joeware.net*. This tool can turn a difficult process into something quite simple. If you need to modify the `internetEncoding` attribute, add the `-internetEncoding` option to the parameter list specifying the proper value from Table 20-2. For example:

```
>exchmbx -b <UserDN> -me <SmtpEmailAddress> -internetEncoding <Value>
```

If you prefer Microsoft-native solutions, the LDIF solution we described will work, but can be dangerous because there is the possibility of duplicating critical values within the Exchange organization. If you put duplicate mailNickname or legacyExchangeDN values into the system, you will have bad results in your Exchange organization that will almost certainly start producing nondelivery reports (NDRs) for the mail objects involved.

The mailNickname attribute can generally be set to be the same as the sAMAccountName, which has to be unique in the domain, though the mailNickname value must be unique across the entire forest. But what should you do you with legacyExchangeDN? If you aren't tied to a legacy 5.5 organization, you can follow the simple format the system currently uses. If you have a legacy 5.5 organization, you need to follow the structure for that organization. For assistance with this, contact Microsoft PSS or Microsoft Consulting Services.

The general format of legacyExchangeDN is:

```
/o=<Org>/ou=<AdministrativeGroup>/cn=<RecipientContainer>/cn=<MailNickName>
```

Assuming your mailNickName is unique (it had better be) and you know the values for the other variables, you can quickly construct a legacyExchangeDN like:

```
/o=CORPMAIL/ou=LASVEGAS/cn=Recipients/cn=OSCARJAMESON
```

You should always verify by searching Active Directory that the legacyExchangeDN you chose is not already used. The reason for this is that someone may have changed an existing user's mailNickname but, correctly, did not touch the legacyExchangeDN value. You could, of course, fix the legacyExchangeDN of that other user so that it properly fits the pattern, but you would impact the user's email functionality.

The attribute legacyExchangeDN is used in Exchange internally for addressing email. If you try to respond to an email sent to you by a user within the same Exchange organization who has had her legacyExchangeDN changed, you will get an NDR and the mail will not be delivered. So, if a user has a name change from Chris Smith to Chris Jones and her sAMAccountName and mailNickname both change from *csmith* to *cjones*, her legacyExchangeDN must remain the same so that anyone within the Exchange organization will be able to easily respond to emails she sent as *csmith*. The point is that you should always check that the legacyExchangeDN value you are setting is unique. The simple solution to follow if the value is already present is to append a -1, -2, or whatever dash value is required to get to a unique value.

You have the option of *not* specifying the `legacyExchangeDN` in the LDIF file. If the attribute is empty, Exchange will populate it for you. If there is already a value, Exchange will not change the attribute.

Unfortunately, if you are mail-enabling an object that was previously mail- or mailbox-enabled, it could have an existing value for `legacyExchangeDN`; this value may or may not be unique. One very specific case is that some tools will set the `legacyExchangeDN` value to `ADCDisabled` when an object is mail- or mailbox-disabled to alert the Active Directory Connector (ADC) to the object's status.

You can modify the `internetEncoding` attribute value in the LDIF file to any value in Table 20-2.

If you want to mail-enable multiple users at once, remove the `-b` option from the parameter list and pipe the distinguished names into ExchMbx from another tool or from a file. Run `exchmbx /?` for usage details.

Using VBScript

Creating a mail-enabled user from VBScript is quite simple; one call to the `MailEnable` method and the work is done. As we indicated in the CLI solution, you can modify the `internetEncoding` value to one of the other values in Table 20-2 depending on your needs.

See Also

Recipe 20.7, MS KB 275636 (Creating Exchange Mailbox-Enabled and Mail-Enabled Objects in Active Directory), and MS KB 281740 (XCON: Internet Mail Service Settings Are Not Overridden for Custom Recipients in Distribution List) for the values of `internetEncoding`

Exchange 2007 Solution

Using a graphical user interface

1. Open the EMC by clicking Start→All Programs→Microsoft Exchange Server 2007→Exchange Management Console.
2. Navigate to the Recipient Configuration container and select Mail Contact.
3. In the Action Pane, click on New Mail User.
4. In the new window, select the radio button for Existing User followed by the Choose button.
5. Navigate to and select the intended user and click OK.

6. Confirm the Domain\Username combination and click on Next.

7. Make any desired change to the Alias value.

8. Click on the Edit button to add a new external SMTP (or Custom) address and click Next.

9. Click New to confirm the summary and execute the change.

10. A completion screen shows what was run, including the underlying PowerShell cmdlet to perform the same task.

11. Click Finish to close the window.

This entry now represents a mail-enabled user. This user does not have a mailbox. The external SMTP address we entered can be seen in the E-mail Addresses tab in the user properties looking from the EMC. The mail-enabled user can be found in the Recipients Configuration container in the Mail Contacts folder, and this entry represents the primary SMTP address in the multivalued attribute called proxyAddresses.

Using PowerShell

This is one of those tasks that is simple on the surface but makes significant changes beneath. PowerShell and Exchange 2007 reduces mail-enabling an existing user to a simple one-line cmdlet:

```
Enable-MailUser -Identity <user_ID_parameter> -Alias <alias_Name>
-ExternalEmailAddress <SMTP:proxy_SMTP_Address>
```

An example of the cmdlet might look like this:

```
Enable-MailUser -Identity 'adadutm.com/Users/Kieran Lefkovics' -Alias 'Kieran'
-ExternalEmailAddress 'SMTP:kieran@gmx.com'
```

Discussion

In Exchange 2003, the Exchange Management Tools really only configured Exchange-related properties of AD objects like recipients and groups. Users and groups were configured using AD tools. With Exchange 2007, these controls are moved into the EMC and EMS. The Enable-MailUser cmdlet mail-enables an existing user; however, the Exchange 2007 management tools can also be used to configure new users.

20.10 Mail-Disabling a User

Problem

You want to mail-disable a user.

Exchange 2003 Solution

Using a graphical user interface

1. Open the Active Directory Users and Computers (ADUC) snap-in.

    This needs to be run on a workstation or server that has the Exchange Management Tools loaded (see Recipe 20.7).

2. If you need to change domains, right-click on Active Directory Users and Computers in the left pane, select Connect to Domain, enter the domain name, and click OK.

3. In the left pane, browse to the parent container of the user, right-click on the user, and select Exchange Tasks.

4. On the Welcome screen, click Next.

5. Select Remove Exchange Attributes and click Next.

6. Read the warning and click Next.

7. On the Completion screen, click Finish.

Using a command-line interface

```
> exchmbx -b "<User DN>" -clear
```

Replace *<User DN>* with the user's distinguished name.

For an alternative Microsoft-native tool method, create an LDIF file called *clearmailattribs.ldf* with the following contents:

```
dn: <UserDN>
changetype: modify
replace: altRecipient
altRecipient:
-
replace: authOrig
authOrig:
-
...<SEE DISCUSSION, NOT A COMPLETE LDIF FILE>
...
```

Replace *<UserDN>* with the user's distinguished name. Note that this is not a complete LDIF file, as there are many attributes that must be cleared; see the section called "Discussion" for further details. Once you've created the LDIF file, run the following command:

```
> ldifde -i -f clearmailattribs.ldf
```

Using VBScript

```
' This code mail disables a user.
' ------ SCRIPT CONFIGURATION ------
strUserDN = "<UserDN>"    ' e.g. cn=jsmith,cn=Users,dc=adatum,dc=com
' ------ END CONFIGURATION ---------
set objUser = GetObject("LDAP://" & strUserDN)
objUser.MailDisableobjUser.SetInfo()
Wscript.Echo "Successfully mail-disabled user."
```

Exchange 2007 Solution

Using a graphical user interface

1. Open the EMC by clicking Start→All Programs→Microsoft Exchange Server 2007→Exchange Management Console.
2. Navigate to the Recipient Configuration container and select Mail Contact. (You can use either the Recipient Configuration list or the Mail Contact list.)
3. Select the user to mail-disable.
4. Click Disable in the Action pane to remove the Exchange properties from the existing user.
5. Select Yes to confirm.

The mail-disabled user then disappears from the Recipient Configuration and Mail Contact container views; however, he still resides as a regular user in AD, stripped of his Exchange properties.

Using PowerShell

The logical cmdlet to mail-disable a user is as follows:

```
Disable-MailUser -Identity <user_ID_parameter>
```

An example of the cmdlet might look like this:

```
Disable-MailUser -Identity 'adadutm.com/Users/Kieran Lefkovics'
```

or:

```
Disable-MailUser kieran@gmx.com
```

The -Identity parameter can use the Distinguished Name, the User Principal Name, the Domain\Account name, or even the GUID. This cmdlet also only removes the Exchange properties for the user; it does not remove the user from AD. Because it is a significant change perhaps, there is a confirmation step after entering the above. The administrator will be prompted to complete the action, requiring a Yes, Yes to all, No, No to all, Suspend, or Help. This prompt can be suppressed or selected by assigning one of those values in the original cmdlet using the -Confirm parameter.

Discussion

This recipe removes the Active Directory Exchange attributes for a previously mail-enabled user. This is a simple process from ADUC and from VBScript, but behind the scenes, several attributes are being updated. For a complete list of the attributes that are modified, see MS KB 307350.

Mail-disabling a user requires Exchange View-Only Administrator or higher permissions, as well as Read and Write permissions to a number of object attributes. See the Microsoft Exchange Tech Center on the Microsoft website for a list of all necessary attributes.

Using a graphical user interface

This process is identical to the process for deleting a user's mailbox in both Exchange 2003 and 2007.

Using a command-line interface

The ExchMbx solution is simple and, unlike the VBScript solution, can be used on either mail-enabled or mailbox-enabled users.

 If you want to clear the Exchange mail attributes on several objects at once, remove the -b option from the parameter list and pipe the distinguished names into ExchMbx from another tool or from a file. Run exchmbx /? for usage details.

The LDIF file shown in the solution is not complete. There are about 90 attributes that need to be cleared, and therefore listed in the file. Check out MS KB 307350 for the current listing of attributes that should be cleared when removing Exchange attributes.

Using VBScript

The VBScript solution leverages the CDOEXM MailDisable method to mail-disable the user. Unfortunately, you cannot use this method to mailbox-disable a user. So, when you call this method, you should be sure that the user is mail-enabled versus mailbox-enabled. If you use this method on a mailbox-enabled user, you will get an error such as "E-mail addresses cannot be removed from this user because it has a mailbox." The quick way to ascertain whether a user has a mailbox or is simply mail-enabled is to check for the existence of the homeMDB attribute. If a user object has homeMDB populated, there is an associated mailbox for that account.

See Also

Recipes 20.7 and 20.9 for more on mail-enabling a user, MS KB 307350 (XGEN: Using the "Remove Exchange Attributes" Option), and "How to Disable Mail for a Mail-enabled User" at *http://technet.microsoft.com/en-us/library/aa996598(EXCHG.80).aspx*

20.11 Mailbox-Enabling a User

Problem

You want to create a mailbox for a user. This is also known as mailbox-enabling a user.

Exchange 2003 Solution

Using a graphical user interface

1. Open the Active Directory Users and Computers (ADUC) snap-in.

    This needs to be run on a workstation or server that has the Exchange Management Tools loaded (see Recipe 20.7).

2. If you need to change domains, right-click on Active Directory Users and Computers in the left pane, select Connect to Domain, enter the domain name, and click OK.

3. In the left pane, browse to the parent container of the user, right-click on the user, and select Exchange Tasks.

4. On the Welcome screen, click Next.

5. Select Create Mailbox and click Next.

6. Verify the mail alias is what you want, select the server you want the mailbox on, select which store you want the mailbox in, and click Next.

7. On the Completion screen, click Finish.

Using a command-line interface

```
> exchmbx -b "<UserDN>" -cr "<server>:<storage group>:<mail store>"
```

Or alternatively, run the following command:

```
> exchmbx -b <UserDN> -cr "<Home MDB URL>"
```

To mailbox-enable the user *joe* with a mailbox on Exchange Server SRV1, storage group SG1, and mailbox store DB1, execute the following command:

```
> exchmbx -b "cn=joe,cn=users,dc=adatum,dc=com" -cr "srv1:sg1:db1"
```

It is recommended that you keep your storage group and mailbox store names short, simple, and space-free. Spaces are troublesome to deal with at the command prompt and have caused many administrators unneeded grief. If you do not use spaces or other special characters, you can dispense with the quotes in all of the command-line examples.

Replace *\<UserDN\>* with the user's distinguished name, ***\<server\>*** with the Exchange server name, ***\<storage group\>*** with the storage group, ***\<mail store\>*** with the mail store, and *\<Home MDB URL\>* with the full homeMDB URL for the desired mailbox store.

Using VBScript

```
' This code creates a mailbox for a user.
' ------ SCRIPT CONFIGURATION ------
strUserDN = "<UserDN>"     ' e.g. cn=jsmith,cn=Users,dc=adatum,dc=com
strHomeMDB = "<Home MDB DN>"
' e.g. CN=Mailbox Store (SERVER),CN=First Storage Group,CN=InformationStore,
' CN=SERVER,CN=Servers,CN=First Administrative Group,CN=Administrative Groups,
'      CN=ADATUMMAIL,CN=Microsoft Exchange,CN=Services,
'      CN=Configuration,DC=adatum,DC=com"
' ------ END CONFIGURATION --------
set objUser = GetObject("LDAP://" & strUserDN)
objUser.CreateMailBox strHomeMDB
objUser.SetInfo()
Wscript.Echo "Successfully mailbox-enabled user."
```

Exchange 2007 Solution

Using a graphical user interface

1. Open the EMC by clicking Start→All Programs→Microsoft Exchange Server 2007→Exchange Management Console.

2. Navigate to the Recipient Configuration container.

3. In the Action pane, select New Mailbox.

4. The next window displays the different types of mailboxes to create. Leave User Mailbox selected and click Next.

5. Here, the process changes depending on whether we are creating a new user or adding Exchange attributes to an existing user. Select Existing user and click Add in green.

6. Identify the user(s) to Mailbox enable and select them. Click OK.

7. Click Next.

8. In this window, we can change the alias for this user; we need to browse to the preferred mailbox store for this new mailbox and select it.

9. Optionally, we can identify managed folder and Activesync policies to apply against this mailbox as well.

10. Click New to accept the confirmation summary.

11. Click Finish to close the window.

The EMC for this process allows you to select multiple users from AD to mailbox-enable using the Recipient selector in step 6.

Using PowerShell

In the EMS, we use the `Enable-Mailbox` cmdlet to apply the appropriate Exchange attributes to an existing user. A mailbox has to have an associated storage location, which is the message store where it is to reside:

```
Enable-Mailbox -Identity <User_ID_Parameter> -Alias <Name> -Database
<Storage_Group\Database>
```

An example of this cmdlet might read as follows:

```
Enable-Mailbox -Identity 'Adatum.com/Users/Alberto Contador' -Alias 'alberto'
-Database 'MAILO1MBX\First Storage Group\Mailbox Database'
```

To mailbox-enable a group of users, this command can be piped from a `Get-User` filter parameter as well:

```
Get-User -RecipientType User | Enable-Mailbox -Database 'MAILO1MBX\First Storage
Group\Mailbox Database'
```

This command retrieves all users with the Recipient Type of User and mail-enables them. After `Enable-Mailbox` is successfully applied to an object, the Recipient Type will show as `UserMailbox`.

If you have a set of users within an Organizational Unit that need to be mailbox-enabled, it is just a matter of applying a different filter parameter to the `Get-User` cmdlet:

```
Get-User -OrganizationalUnit "Sales" | Where-Object{$_.RecipientType -eq "User"} |
Enable-Mailbox -Database "MAILO1MBX\First Storage Group\Mailbox Database"
```

Discussion

A mailbox-enabled user is a user object that has a mailbox defined in the Exchange organization that the user object exists in. This is the most common object in an Exchange organization.

Mailbox-enabling a user requires Exchange View-Only Administrator or higher permissions, as well as Read and Write permissions to a number of object attributes. See the Microsoft Exchange Tech Center on the Microsoft website for a list of all necessary attributes.

When you create a mailbox for a user with the GUI or VBScript in Exchange 2003, you call out to the `CreateMailbox` CDOEXM interface. In the background, the specific changes made by the `CreateMailbox` method occur on the **user** object in Active Directory and include changes to the following attributes:

- mDBUseDefaults
- msExchUserAccountControl
- homeMTA
- msExchHomeServerName
- homeMDB
- mailNickname
- msExchMailboxGuid
- msExchMailboxSecurityDescriptor
- legacyExchangeDN

In Exchange 2003, once all the attributes are in place, the RUS sets additional attributes on the **user** object. The mailbox cannot be used nor receive email until the RUS has gone through this stamping process. It's also important to note that the mailbox will not be physically created until it is accessed for the first time or until it receives an item of mail.

Thankfully, the RUS goes away in Exchange 2007. Additional attributes are updated when a user is mailbox-enabled in Exchange 2007 as follows:

- mail
- msDS-ReplValueMetaData
- msExchPoliciesIncluded
- msExchRecipientDisplayType
- msExchRecipientTypeDetails
- msExchVersion
- proxyAddresses
- showInAddressBook

You can use ADSIEdit before and after the `Enable-Mailbox` cmdlet is run to see the different attributes of the object to which values have been added. Right-click on the user in ADSIEdit and select properties and then make sure the Attribute Editor tab is selected. Click on the box beside "Show only attributes that have values" to display the attributes in use for that user object. Doing this before and after engaging the `Enable-Mailbox` cmdlet will allow you to visualize the changes.

Using a command-line interface

Prior to the ExchMbx tool, there was no simple way to mailbox-enable a user from the command line in Exchange 2000 or 2003. The `LDIFDE` method is not feasible because the `msExchMailboxSecurityDescriptor` attribute is a binary value and difficult to manipulate with LDIF files and text editors. For flexibility, ExchMbx allows you to specify the entire homeMDB URL, or you can specify the server, storage group, and mailbox store. ExchMbx could possibly be used for Exchange 2007 to mailbox-enable a user as well; however, its author has not fully tested it against Exchange 2007. PowerShell really replaces the tools we had in Exchange 2003 for tasks like this.

 If you want to mailbox-enable multiple users at once, remove the **-b** option from the parameter list and pipe the distinguished names into ExchMbx from another tool or from a file. Run `exchmbx /?` for usage details.

Using VBScript

The trickiest part of creating a mailbox for an Exchange 2003 user with VBscript is to know what to use for the homeMDB attribute. If you use the wrong value you will get the error "The server is not operational," which isn't helpful feedback. This is where the GUI method is nice, because it looks up all of the possible values for you and lets you select from the list.

We present an alternative scripting method in Recipe 20.13, which lets you specify three well-known pieces of information to locate the proper homeMDB value.

Another alternative would be to search Active Directory for all valid homeMDB values, display them, and have the person running the script select from the list, just like ADUC does. This third method involves searching against the Configuration container of Active Directory with the following filter:

    (objectcategory=msExchPrivateMDB)

See Also

Recipes 20.7 and 20.13, MS KB 275636 (Creating Exchange Mailbox-Enabled and Mail-Enabled Objects in Active Directory), MS KB 253770 (XADM: Tasks Performed by the Recipient Update Service), and "Enable-Mailbox" at *http://technet.microsoft.com/en-us/library/aa998251(EXCHG.80).aspx*

20.12 Deleting a User's Mailbox

Problem

You want to delete a user's mailbox. This is also known as mailbox-disabling a user.

Exchange 2003 Solution

Using a graphical user interface

1. Open the Active Directory Users and Computers (ADUC) snap-in.

 This needs to be run on a workstation or server that has the Exchange Management Tools loaded (see Recipe 20.7).

2. If you need to change domains, right-click on Active Directory Users and Computers in the left pane, select Connect to Domain, enter the domain name, and click OK.
3. In the left pane, browse to the parent container of the user, right-click on the user, and select Exchange Tasks.
4. On the Welcome screen, click Next.
5. Select Remove Exchange Attributes and click Next.
6. Read the warning and click Next.
7. On the Completion screen, click Finish.

Using a command-line interface

See the command-line example for Recipe 20.10.

Using VBScript

```
' This code mail-disables a user.
' ------ SCRIPT CONFIGURATION ------
strUserDN = "<UserDN>" ' e.g. cn=jsmith,cn=Users,dc=adatum,dc=com
' ------ END CONFIGURATION --------
set objUser = GetObject("LDAP://" & strUserDN)
objUser.DeleteMailbox
objUser.SetInfo()
Wscript.Echo "Successfully deleted user's mailbox."
```

Exchange 2007 Solution

Using a graphical user interface

1. Open the EMC by clicking Start→All Programs→Microsoft Exchange Server 2007→Exchange Management Console.
2. Navigate to the Recipient Configuration container and select Mailbox. (You can use either the Recipient Configuration list or the Mailbox list.)
3. Select the user to mailbox-disable.

---

4. Click Disable in the Action pane to remove the Exchange properties from the existing user.

5. Select Yes to confirm.

This process disconnects the mailbox from the user object by removing the Exchange-specific attributes. In the EMC action pane, there is the option to `Disable` and also `Remove`. The latter will disconnect the mailbox and also delete the user from AD.

Using PowerShell

```
Disable-Mailbox -Identity <User_ID_Parameter>
```

A basic example might be:

```
Disable-Mailbox ray@adatum.com
```

It really is that easy. As with the other cmdlets, the `-Identity` parameter is assumed and does not need to be typed out in the command. The mailbox for *ray@adatum.com* will be disconnected from the user.

To delete mailboxes from a set of users, just pipe the output of a `Get-Mailbox` filter to the `Disable-Mailbox` cmdlet, similar to the examples in Recipe 20.11.

Discussion

Although the recipe title is "Deleting a User's Mailbox," these solutions don't really delete the mailbox. They actually just clear the Exchange attributes from the user object and that disassociates the mailbox from the user; the mailbox itself will still exist in the Exchange store. The length of time it will exist depends on the mailbox retention period, which is 30 days by default. While the mailbox exists in that state, it can be reconnected to the same or a different user object.

 Deleting a user requires Exchange View-Only Administrator or higher permissions, as well as Read and Write permissions to a number of object attributes. See the Microsoft Exchange Tech Center on the Microsoft website for a list of all necessary attributes.

Using VBScript

The VBScript solution leverages the CDOEXM `DeleteMailbox` method to delete the mailbox for the user. Unfortunately, you cannot use this method to mail-disable a user. So when you call this method, you should be sure that the user is mailbox-enabled versus mail-enabled. If you use this method on a mail-enabled user, you will get an error such as "This user does not have a mailbox." The quick way to ascertain whether a user has a mailbox or is simply mail-enabled is to check for the existence of the `homeMDB` attribute. If a user object has `homeMDB` populated, there is an associated mailbox for that account.

See Also

Recipes 20.7 and 20.10, MS KB 307350 (XGEN: Using the "Remove Exchange Attributes" Option), MS KB 274343 (How to Recover a Deleted Mailbox in Exchange), and "Disable-Mailbox," which you can find at *http://technet.microsoft.com/en-us/library/aa997210(EXCHG.80).aspx*

20.13 Moving a Mailbox

Problem

You want to move a mailbox to a new database, storage group, or server.

Exchange 2003 Solution

Using a graphical user interface

1. Open the Users and Computers (ADUC) snap-in.

    This needs to be run on a workstation or server that has the Exchange Management Tools loaded (see Recipe 20.7).

2. If you need to change domains, right-click on Active Directory Users and Computers in the left pane, select Connect to Domain, enter the domain name, and click OK.

3. In the left pane, browse to the parent container of the user, right-click on the user, and select Exchange Tasks.

4. On the Welcome screen, click Next.

5. Select Move Mailbox and click Next.

6. Select new values for Server and Mailbox Store and click Next.

7. Select how you want to handle corrupted messages and click Next.

8. Specify when to start processing the move task and click Next.

9. When the Completed screen is shown, click Finish. If there are errors, select the View Detailed Report checkbox to get a failure report.

Using a command-line interface

```
> exchmbx -b <UserDN> -move "<server>:<storage group>:<mail store>"
```

Or alternatively, run the following command:

```
> exchmbx -b <UserDN> -move "<Home MDB URL>"
```

Replace *<UserDN>* with the user's distinguished name, *<server>* with the Exchange server name, *<storage group>* with the storage group, *<mail store>* with the mail store, and *<Home MDB URL>* with the full homeMDB URL for the desired mailbox store.

To move an existing mailbox for the user *joe* to Exchange server **Srv1**, Storage group **SG1**, and mailbox store **DB1**, execute the following command.

```
> exchmbx -b "cn=joe,cn=users,dc=adatum,dc=com" -move "srv1:sg1:db1"
```

Using VBScript

```
' This code moves a mailbox.
' ------ SCRIPT CONFIGURATION ------
strUserDN = "<UserDN>" ' e.g. cn=jsmith,cn=Users,dc=adatum,dc=com
strServer = "<Exchange Server>"          ' e.g. Srv1
strSGName = "<Storage Group Name>"       ' e.g. SG1
strMailStoreName = "<MailBox Store Name>" ' e.g. DB1
' ------ END CONFIGURATION --------
' Find Storage Group URL and Generate Mailbox Store URL
strSearch = "cn=" & strSGName & ","
set objSrv = CreateObject("CDOEXM.ExchangeServer")
objSrv.DataSource.Open strServer
for each strSg in objSrv.StorageGroups
   if (instr(1,strSg,strSearch,1)>0) then
       strSGUrl = strSg
       exit for
   end if
next
strMBUrl = "LDAP://cn=" & strMailStoreName & "," & strSGUrl

' Attach to user and move mailbox
set objUser = GetObject("LDAP://" & strUserDN)
objUser.MoveMailbox(strMBUrl)
Wscript.Echo "Successfully moved mailbox."
```

Exchange 2007 Solution

Using a graphical user interface

1. Open the EMC by clicking Start→All Programs→Microsoft Exchange Server 2007→Exchange Management Console.

2. Navigate to the Recipient Configuration container and select Mailbox. (You can use either the Recipient Configuration list or the Mailbox list.)

3. Select the user or users to move.

4. Click Move Mailbox in the Action pane to remove the Exchange properties from the existing user.

5. The Move Mailbox wizard opens to the Introduction page. Select the destination mailbox store for the move. The Browse button allows you to see the different servers with available mailbox databases. Click Next.

6. Select the method for dealing with corrupt messages. You can either bypass the mailbox itself or just skip the message. There is also an option to skip the mailbox where the number of corrupt messages exceeds a configurable threshold.

7. If you want to select a specific Global Catalog Server or Domain Controller to access for the move, you can optionally do this here as well.

8. Finally, there is an option to exclude rule messages for Exchange 2000 and 2003 target databases. The wizard is not aware of what version the target is at this point. The checkbox is available in the GUI even if the destination mailbox store is on Exchange 2007. Click Next.

9. Select whether you want the move to happen immediately (default) or on a specified schedule. You can also choose here to cancel mailbox move instances that are not completed within a specific number of hours. Click Next.

10. After reviewing the mailbox move summary, click Move.

11. The mailbox move progress is shown on the screen. When completed, the wizard displays the underlying PowerShell commands that it used. You can view an *xml* logfile of the move by selecting the checkbox near the bottom of the window.

12. Click Finish to close the Move Mailbox wizard.

Using PowerShell

Of course, there is a simple PowerShell command to accomplish the same feat. The simple cmdlet to move a mailbox is as follows:

```
Move-Mailbox -Identity <User_name> -TargetDatabase <Server\Storage_Group\Database>
```

An example of such a move might be:

```
Move-Mailbox "Ceriana" -TargetDatabase "MAILMBX01\First Storage Group\Management"
```

Again, the `-Identity` parameter is assumed, so typing the actual parameter is optional. There are many times where you will have to move groups of mailboxes to new storage or a new database. There are several ways of accomplishing this. The easiest is probably to pipe the output from a `Get-Mailbox` cmdlet with the appropriate filters to the `Move-Mailbox` cmdlet. For example:

```
Get-Mailbox | where {$._<User_Property> -eq <Value>} | Move-Mailbox -TargetDatabase
<Server\Storage_Group_Database>
```

You can also assemble the mailboxes in an array that PowerShell can loop through using a `foreach` command. This works well if the array is loaded at the beginning of the script. If not, the mailboxes are then moved in serial—the next mailbox isn't moved until the previous one is completed. That is not the most efficient method. The array itself can be piped to the `Move-Mailbox` cmdlet to work through the items in a multi-threaded fashion:

```
$array = "UserA","UserB","UserC","UserD","UserE"
$array | Move-Mailbox -TargetDatabase <Server\Storage_Group\Database>
-Confirm:$false
```

The source must also be a CSV file with a list of usernames and the intended destination store for their mailbox. These are the two required values for the `Move-Mailbox` cmdlet. If all the mailboxes are to be moved to the same destination database, then the target database is best specified as part of the cmdlet and not pulled from the CSV for each mailbox. The `Import-CSV` cmdlet calls the *.csv* file by name and pipes the output to the `Move-Mailbox` command.

Assuming we have a *.csv* file with a column entitled `Username` beneath which our users with mailboxes to be moved are listed, we can import those values and move their mailboxes as follows:

```
Import-CSV <file_name>.csv | foreach {Move-Mailbox -Identity $_.Username
-TargetDatabase <Server\Storage Group\Database> -Confirm:$false}
```

The EMS allows us to move mailboxes across forest boundaries as well. This is done by passing authentication credentials within the script. To move an array of mailboxes from a Source forest to a target forest, we can use the EMS as follows:

```
$array = "UserA","UserB","UserC","UserD","UserE"
$sc = Read-Host "Enter Source Forest Credentials" -AsSecureString
$tc = Read-Host "Enter Target Forest Credentials" -AsSecureString
$array | get-mailbox $mbx -Credential $sc | move-mailbox -TargetDatabase
<Server\Storage Group\Database> -GlobalCatalog <target_GC> -SourceForestCredential
$sc -SourceForestGlobalCatalog <source_GC> -TargetForestCredential $tc -AllowMerge
-SourceMailboxCleanupOptions deletesourcemailbox
```

The Active Directory Migration Tool or another migration application needs to be used to create the same users in the target forest along with the users' SID history from the source forest. The `Import-CSV` cmdlet could also be incorporated into the cross-forest script as we did earlier as another source option for input of mailbox information into the `Move-Mailbox` cmdlet.

Discussion

Mailbox moves are commonly done in many Exchange organizations due to servers getting upgraded, server hardware issues, users migrating from Exchange 2000 to Exchange 2003 or Exchange 2003 to Exchange 2007, users changing locations, or if the administrators want to readjust the mailbox location for load balancing. Some properties are based on mailbox stores or storage groups and it may be necessary to move users to specific storage to accommodate specific feature settings.

Moving a mailbox in Exchange 2003 requires Read and Write permissions to the following attributes:

- msexchhomeservername
- homemdb
- homeMTA
- msExchOmaAdminWirelessEnable
- msExchOmaAdminExtendedSettings

- `targetAddress`

A mailbox move is an odd operation in terms of permissions. Logically, moving a mailbox is basically a combination of create and delete operations, which is something an Exchange administrator can do just fine. See MS KB 842033 for details of the permissions needed. You may also run into an error if the mailbox limits on the target store are lower than they were on the source store. For more details, go to *http://www.active dir.org/article.aspx?aid=58*.

Using a graphical user interface

The Move Mailbox Wizard is the only Exchange wizard that allows you to schedule when the changes will be made. This is obviously a handy feature for mailbox moves because it isn't something you tend to want to do in the middle of the day. This allows Exchange administrators who like to sleep at night to schedule the work to be done, and then go home with everyone else.

Interestingly, scheduling mailbox moves in Exchange 2007 requires that the Exchange Management Console remain open on the machine scheduled to perform the task, according to Microsoft KB 931748.

Using a command-line interface

Prior to the ExchMbx tool, there was no simple way to move a mailbox from the command line in Exchange 2003. The command structure to move a mailbox is very similar to the command structure to create a mailbox; see the command-line solution in Recipe 20.11.

If you want to move multiple mailboxes at once, remove the `-b` option from the parameter list and pipe the distinguished names into ExchMbx from another tool or from a file. Run `exchmbx /?` for usage details.

Of course, PowerShell changes this limitation. Moving mailboxes in Exchange 2007 is now done with a simple one-liner using the EMS.

Using VBScript

The trickiest part of moving a mailbox for a user is to know what the Home MDB URL is for the database you want to move the user to. The method used here allows you to specify three well-known components and arrive at the answer. In Recipe 20.11, we use another method to do this by entering the exact value for the mailbox store URL. A third alternative would be to search Active Directory for all valid `homeMDB` values, display them, and have the person running the script select from the list like ADUC does. To get the list of mailbox store URLs, search against the Configuration container in Active Directory (e.g., `cn=Configuration,dc=adatum,dc=com`) with the filter (`objectCategory=msExchPrivateMDB`).

Using PowerShell

There are several ways to perform this task using PowerShell, depending on the number of mailboxes to move. Looping through an array, importing a CSV file, or applying a cmdlet filter and piping the result to the `Move-Mailbox` command are all options. The EMS is required to move mailboxes across forest boundaries. This is certainly beneficial for migrations either resulting from corporate mergers or Exchange migrations.

The source and target authentication credentials are input by the administrator when the command is launched. The script will prompt the administrator and since it uses the `-AsSecureString` parameter, the input will only show as a series of asterisks, so type carefully. For the mailbox move, Exchange will prompt for user confirmation for the move. The `-Confirm` parameter can toggle the prompt on or off with `$true` to prompt and `$false` to accept the default of `Yes`.

Like the other solutions, PowerShell does not have a mechanism to migrate the dumpster. This is a consideration for companies that require access to the dumpster for compliance reasons. You may need to keep the last backup available prior to the mailbox move.

See Also

Recipes 20.7 and 20.11, MS KB 842033 ("Access Denied" Error Message When You Move Mailboxes by Using the Exchange Task Wizard in Exchange Server 2003), MS KB 316792 (Minimum Permissions Necessary to Perform Exchange-Related Tasks), MS KB 821829 (Moving Mailboxes in Exchange Server 2003), and MS KB 931748 (The Exchange Management Console Must Remain Open When You Schedule a Task to Move a Mailbox in Exchange 2007 or in Exchange 2003)

20.14 Viewing Mailbox Sizes and Message Counts

Problem

You want to view the sizes and message counts of all mailboxes on a server.

Exchange 2003 Solution

Using a graphical user interface

1. Open the Exchange System Manager (ESM) snap-in.
2. In the left pane, browse to the mailboxes container of the server, storage group, and database you want to view mailboxes in.

---

3. In the right pane, scroll down through the list of mailboxes, noting the Size and Total Items columns.

Using VBScript

```
' This code displays all mailboxes and their sizes
' ------ SCRIPT CONFIGURATION ------
strComputer = "<Exchange Server>" 'e.g. Svr2
' ------ END CONFIGURATION ---------

set objWMI = GetObject("winmgmts:\\" & strComputer & _
                       "\root\MicrosoftExchangeV2")
set objMbxs = objWMI.ExecQuery("Select * from Exchange_Mailbox",,48)
for each objMbx in objMbxs
  Wscript.Echo objMbx.MailBoxDisplayName & " " & objMbx.size & "KB " _
               & objMbx.TotalItems & " items"
Next
Wscript.Echo "Script completed successfully."
```

Exchange 2007 Solution

Using PowerShell

Again, this is another scenario where the EMS simplifies Exchange management. An important reporting cmdlet for mailbox reporting is `Get-MailboxStatistics`. It quantifies mailbox size, item count, last logon time, and more (see the section called "Discussion" for the list). To get summary statistics for a specific server, run the following:

```
Get-MailboxStatistics -Server <Server_name>
```

This lists the mailboxes and their size and message counts on the server specified. Data is easily sorted in ascending or descending order by any value in the `Get-MailboxStatistics` output. For example, to sort the list by mailbox size, and easily identify the largest mailboxes, we can use:

```
Get-MailboxStatistics -Server <Server_name> | Sort-Object TotalItemSize
-Descending | ft
```

Administrators often need to act on this information and need it in a timely manner. It is easy to write this information to file and attach it to a scheduled email using a PowerShell script.

This script assigns parts of the email message to variables, collects the data with `Get-MailboxStatistics` values, writes the report to a *.txt* file, and attaches it to an email to the administrator. It specifies only a Recipient Type of `UserMailbox`, which is a mailbox-enabled user. This also requires that the sending SMTP server can relay for the host sending the request:

```
$FromAddress = reports@adatum.com
$ToAddress = administrator@adatum.com
$MessageSubject = "Daily Mailbox Size Report"
$MessageBody = "The Daily Mailbox Size Report is attached."
```

```
$SendingServer = "MAILMBX01.adatum.com"

Get-Mailbox | where { $._RecipientType -eq "UserMailbox" } | Get-MailboxStatistics
| Sort-Object TotalItemSize -Descending | ft
DisplayName,@{label="TotalItemSize(KB)";expression={$_.TotalItemSize.Value.ToKB()}}
, ItemCount > c:\mbxreport.txt

$SMTPMessage = New-Object System.Net.Mail.MailMessage $FromAddress, $ToAddress,
$MessageSubject, $MessageBody
$Attachment = New-Object Net.Mail.Attachment("c:\mbxreport.txt")
$SMTPMessage.Attachments.Add($Attachment)

$SMTPClient = New-Object System.Net.Mail.SMTPClient $SendingServer
$SMTPClient.Send($SMTPMessage)
```

Save the script as a PowerShell file such as *MbxReportSend.ps1* and schedule it to run every morning so it is sitting in your inbox when you get to the office.

Discussion

Mailbox sizes and message counts are items on Exchange systems that administrators routinely want to know about for the purposes of reporting and metrics. Administrators want to know if their mail system is balanced and if users are spread across the mailbox stores evenly. Knowing the number of users and the size of their mailboxes in each mailbox store, the administrator can make better decisions about where new user mailboxes should be placed or if some leveling of mailboxes is required.

Using a graphical user interface

Click on the header of each of the columns displayed in the right pane of the ESM to sort by that value.

Using VBScript

This script can be modified to show several things for mailboxes. Some of the more notable items besides Size and Items are LastLogonTime, LastLoggedOnUserAccount, and DateDiscoveredAbsentInDS. Please reference the Exchange 2003 SDK for a complete list of items available in the Exchange_Mailbox WMI class.

The Exchange_Mailbox WMI class is deprecated in Exchange 2007, and replaced by the Get-MailboxStatistics cmdlet.

Using PowerShell

The Get-MailboxStatistics cmdlet is a powerful reporting resource. It can be used as a standalone command to review a snapshot of mailbox properties, or it can be used as a filter for other queries. The output can be saved on a regular basis to compare values over time and identify trends of how users leverage their mailboxes.

By running the cmdlet with the Format List option at the end, the full set of variables captured by `Get-MailboxStatistics` is displayed:

```
Get-MailboxStatistics -Identity william | fl

AssociatedItemCount     : 239
DeletedItemCount        : 20
DisconnectDate          :
DisplayName             : William Lefkovics
ItemCount               : 4222
LastLoggedOnUserAccount : ADATUM\william
LastLogoffTime          : 7/14/2008 3:47:40 AM
LastLogonTime           : 7/14/2008 3:47:40 AM
LegacyDN                : /O=ADATUM/OU=EXCHANGE ADMINISTRATIVE GROUP (FYDIBOHF2
                          3SPDLT)/CN=RECIPIENTS/CN=WILLIAM
MailboxGuid             : f3774890-ae27-4e00-8464-eeca8e34df81
ObjectClass             : Mailbox
StorageLimitStatus      : BelowLimit
TotalDeletedItemSize    : 1349B
TotalItemSize           : 3250300B
Database                : MAILMBX01\First Storage Group\Mailbox Database
ServerName              : MAILMBX01
StorageGroupName        : First Storage Group
DatabaseName            : Mailbox Database
Identity                : f3774890-ae27-4e00-8464-eeca8e34df81
IsValid                 : True
OriginatingServer       : mailmbx01.adatum.com
```

Any of these output values can be used to filter another cmdlet or be saved to file or database for reporting over time. The `LastLogonTime` is valuable in identifying stale mailboxes that have not been archived and deleted.

See Also

Exchange Server 2003 SDK: WMI Reference and Glen Scales' Mailbox Size GUI Script, version 5 at *http://gsexdev.blogspot.com/2008/05/version-5-of-mailbox-size-gui-script .html*

20.15 Configuring Mailbox Limits

Problem

You want to enable storage limits for user mailboxes on an Exchange server.

Exchange 2003 Solution

Using a graphical user interface

1. Open the Exchange System Manager (ESM) snap-in.

2. In the left pane, browse to the mailboxes container of the server, storage group, and database you want to configure a storage limit for.

3. Right-click the mailbox store. Select Properties, and then select the Limits tab.

4. Select one or more of the following checkboxes:

Issue warning at
> Warns users that they have exceeded the storage limit, but their mailbox will continue to function.

Prohibit send at
> Warns users that they have exceeded the storage limit and then prevents them from sending new messages until their mailboxes are brought back underneath the configured storage limit. Users can still receive messages.

Prohibit send and receive at
> Warns users that they have exceeded the storage limit and then prevents them from both sending and receiving messages until they have corrected the situation.

5. Specify the appropriate values for these settings in kilobytes (KB).

 The maximum value that you can configure for these items through the ESM is 2 GB (2,097,151 KB). To establish larger values than that, you need to use ADSIEdit or the command-line or script solutions listed next.

Using a command-line interface

To configure the size at which a warning will be issued, we call on the *joeware* utilities AdFind and AdMod. We use the following syntax:

```
> adfind -config -rb "cn=<StorageGroup>,cn=InformationStore,cn=<ServerName>,
cn=Servers,cn=<Administrative Group>,cn=Administrative Groups,cn=<ExchangeOrg>,
cn=Microsoft Exchange,cn=Services" -dsq | admod mDBStorageQuota::<LimitinKB>
```

To configure the size at which a user can receive mail but not send, use:

```
> adfind -config -rb "cn=<StorageGroup>,cn=InformationStore,cn=<ServerName>,
cn=Servers,cn=<Administrative Group>,cn=AdministrativeGroups,cn=<ExchangeOrg>,
cn=Microsoft Exchange,cn=Services" -dsq | admod mDBOverQuotaLimit::<LimitinKB>
```

To configure the limit at which a user can neither send nor receive messages, use:

```
> adfind -config -rb "cn=<StorageGroup>,cn=InformationStore,cn=<ServerName>,
cn=Servers,cn=<Administrative Group>,cn=Administrative Groups,cn=<ExchangeOrg>,
cn=Microsoft Exchange,cn=Services" -dsq | admod mDBOverHardQuotaLimit::<LimitinKB>
```

You can set multiple attributes in a single command by specifying more than one attribute in the AdMod portion of the command syntax, as follows:

```
> adfind -config -rb "cn=<StorageGroup>,cn=InformationStore,cn=<ServerName>,
cn=Servers,cn=<Administrative Group>,cn=Administrative Groups,cn=<ExchangeOrg>,
```

```
cn=Microsoft Exchange,cn=Services" -dsq | admod mDBStorageQuota::<LimitinKB>
mDBOverQuotaLimit::<LimitinKB> mDBOverHardQuotaLimit::<LimitinKB>
```

Using VBScript

```
' The following script will update the Warning, OverQuota, and
' HardOverQuota attributes of a mailbox store
'----------SCRIPT CONFIGURATION----------------------------
' strLDAPString = "cn=<StorageGroup>,cn=InformationStore," & _
"cn=<ServerName>,cn=Servers,cn=<AdministrativeGroup>," & _
"cn=Administrative Groups,cn=<ExchangeOrg>,cn=Microsoft Exchange," & _
"cn=Services,cn=Configuration,<ForestRootDN>"

strWarningLimit = "<WarningLimitinKB>"
strSoftQuotaLimit = "<ReceiveOnlyLimitinKB>"
strHardQuotaLimit = "<NoSendOrReceiveLimitinKB>"
'------------------END CONFIGURATION--------------------

Set objMaiboxStore = GetObject _
    ("LDAP://" & strLDAPString)

objMailboxStore.Put "mdBStorageQuota", strWarningLimit
objMailboxStore.Put "mdBOverQuotaLimit", strSoftQuotaLimit
objMailboxStore.Put "mdBOverHardQuotaLimit", strHardQuotaLimit

objMailboxStore.SetInfo
```

Exchange 2007 Solution

Using a graphical user interface

To configure Storage Quota settings on a database:

1. Open the EMC by clicking Start→All Programs→Microsoft Exchange Server
   2007→Exchange Management Console.
2. Navigate to the Server Configuration container and select Mailbox.
3. Select the Database that needs to have quota limits changed.
4. Right-click on the database and select Properties or click on properties in the Action
   pane.
5. Click on the Limits tab.
6. Set the values as required for the company for the levels of storage quota.

To configure Storage Quota settings on a mailbox:

1. Open the EMC by clicking Start→All Programs→Microsoft Exchange Server
   2007→Exchange Management Console.
2. Navigate to the Recipients Configuration container and select Mailbox. (You can
   use either the Recipient Configuration list or the Mailbox list.)
3. Select the Mailbox that needs to have quota limits changed.

4. Right-click on the Mailbox and select Properties or click on Properties in the Action pane.

5. Click on the Mailbox Settings tab.

6. Click on the Storage Quota option.

7. Deselect the box applying the database settings to the mailbox.

8. Set the storage quota values as required for the user.

Using PowerShell

Mailbox Storage Quota is configured at the user level or the database level and matches the descriptions just outlined in the section called "Exchange 2003 Solution". The default values of the quota settings on a mailbox database are as follows:

- `IssueWarningQuota`—1,991,680 KB
- `ProhibitSendQuota`—2,097,152 KB
- `ProhibitSendReceiveQuota`—2,411,520 KB

To set the different quota levels on a database, use the following command:

```
Set-MailboxDatabase <Storage_Group\Database> -IssueWarningQuota:<Value>
-ProhibitSendQuota:<Value> -ProhibitSendReceiveQuota:<Value>
```

An example of this cmdlet is as follows:

```
Set-MailboxDatabase "First Storage Group\Management" -IssueWarningQuota:1800MB
-ProhibitSendQuota:1900MB -ProhibitSendReceiveQuota:2000MB
```

To set the different quota levels on a mailbox use the following command:

```
Set-Mailbox <Mailbox_ID_Parameter> -UseDatabaseQuotaDefaults <$true|$False>
-IssueWarningQuota:<Value> -ProhibitSendQuota:<Value> -
ProhibitSendReceiveQuota:<Value>
```

Discussion

It's not uncommon for administrators to want to set reasonable size limits on individual users' mailboxes. You can configure this globally at the mailbox store level. Since you can have multiple stores on a single server, this allows you to create multiple stores with multiple storage limits for departments or groups that have greater storage needs. You can also override the mailbox store defaults for individual user accounts by modifying the Exchange General tab within Active Directory Users and Computers for an individual user account, or else by programmatically modifying the same three attributes and then setting the `mdBUseDefaults` attribute to `FALSE`. In Exchange 2007, this is an EMS parameter on the `Set-Mailbox` cmdlet called `-UseDatabaseQuotaDefaults`. You can also set mailbox limits in Exchange 2003 using a System Policy, and then apply the same policy to multiple stores.

The size limitation seen in Exchange Server 2003 does not exist in Exchange 2007. Indeed, you can set the units using PowerShell to KB, MB, GB, or even TB. Imagine a mailbox quota warning message issued at a mailbox quota size of 12 TB. The quota levels are relative to each other as well. The `IssueWarningQuota` should not be greater than the `ProhibitSendQuota`, which in turn should not be greater than the `ProhibitSendReceiveQuota` value.

See Also

MS KB 822938 (How to Use System Policies to Configure Mailbox Storage Limits in Exchange Server 2003), MS KB 823144 (How to Configure Storage Limits on Public Folders in Exchange 2003), MS KB 235895 (How to Monitor Mailbox Storage Limits in Event Viewer), and "How to Configure Storage Quotas on a Mailbox Database" at *http://technet.microsoft.com/en-us/library/bb201753(EXCHG.80).aspx*

20.16 Creating an Address List

Problem

You want to create an Address List.

Exchange 2003 Solution

Using a graphical user interface

1. Open the Exchange System Manager (ESM) snap-in.
2. In the left pane, browse to the Recipients→All Address Lists container.
3. Right-click on the All Address Lists container and select New→Address List.
4. Enter the Address List name.
5. Click on Filter Rules, configure the filter settings, and click OK.

 The filter should be a standard LDAP filter; for example, `(&(objectcategory=person)(objectclass=user)(homeMDB=*)(employeeType=FT))`.

6. Click Finish.

Using a command-line interface

First, create an LDIF file called *add_al.ldf* with the following contents:

```
dn: CN=<Address List Name>,<ParentDN>
changetype: add
cn: <Address List Name>
displayName: <Address List Name>
objectClass: addressBookContainer
```

```
purportedSearch: <LDAP Filter>
systemFlags: 1610612736
```

Replace *<Address List Name>* with the name of the Address List and *<ParentDN>* with the distinguished name of the Address Lists container in Active Directory, for example:

```
cn=All Address Lists,cn=Address Lists Container,cn=ADATUMMAIL,cn=Microsoft Exchange,
cn=Services,cn=Configuration,dc=adatum,dc=com
```

Then run the following command:

```
>ldifde -i -f add-al.ldf
```

Using VBScript

```
' This code creates an Address List.
' ------ SCRIPT CONFIGURATION ------
strParentDN  = "<DN to All Address Lists Container>"
' e.g CN=All Address Lists,CN=Address Lists Container,
' CN=ADATUMMAIL,CN=Microsoft Exchange,
' CN=Services,CN=Configuration,DC=adatum,DC=com

strObjClass = "addressBookContainer"
strALName = "<Address List Name>"    ' e.g. Sales Dept
strFilterAttrib = "purportedSearch"
strFilter = "<LDAP Filter>"    ' e.g. (&(department=sales)(homemdb=*))"

' ------ END CONFIGURATION ---------
' Set Dynamic values
set objOU = GetObject("LDAP://" & strParentDN)
set objNewObj = objOU.Create(strObjClass,"cn=" & strALName)
objNewObj.Put "displayName",strALName
objNewObj.Put strFilterAttrib,strFilter

' Set static values
objNewObj.Put "systemFlags",1610612736

' Save object
objNewObj.SetInfo
Wscript.Echo "Successfully created address list."
```

Exchange 2007 Solution

Using a graphical user interface

1. Open the EMC by clicking Start→All Programs→Microsoft Exchange Server 2007→Exchange Management Console.

2. Navigate to the Organization Configuration container and select Mailbox.

3. In the Action pane, click New Address List to launch the New Address List wizard.

4. Enter a name for the new list.

5. Select the container for the Address List.

6. Identify the recipient types to include in this Address List and click Next.

7. Choose the filter conditions for this list, such as geographical region or company department. Custom Attributes can be used here to filter Address List creation as well. Click Next.

8. The Schedule window allows the option of scheduling when the Address List is to be created and how long it should run. The default is Immediately. Click Next.

9. Review the Configuration summary and click Edit.

10. The cmdlets performed are displayed. Click Finish to close the window.

The Address List can also be applied at any time to incorporate changes using the `Apply` option found toward the bottom of the Action pane specific to the Address List selected.

Using PowerShell

As you probably predicted, there is a simple cmdlet for creating Address Lists in Exchange 2007, as follows:

```
New-AddressList -Name <AddressList_Name> -Container <AddressListIDParameter>
-IncludedRecipients
```

Here is an example of this cmdlet creating a new Address List container called Regions:

```
New-AddressList -Name 'Regions' -Container '\' -IncludedRecipients 'None'
```

In addition, there is an `Update-AddressList` to generate members independent of list creation or to apply any changes in list membership.

```
Update-AddressList -Identity <AddressListIDParameter>
```

And a custom Address List placed in the new Regions container based on a state, in this case Nevada, might read as follows:

```
new-AddressList -Name 'Nevada' -IncludedRecipients 'MailboxUsers, MailContacts,
MailGroups, MailUsers' -ConditionalStateOrProvince 'NV' -Container '\Regions'
```

After the list is created, it needs to be applied. This is done with a separate cmdlet as follows:

```
Update-AddressList -Identity '\Regions\Nevada'
```

Discussion

Address Lists are special groupings of email accounts that allow users to quickly find specific email users that are part of some logical grouping in the GAL. In essence, they are a subset of the GAL. In Exchange 2003, the RUS is responsible for creating and maintaining the Address List links to the mail-enabled objects. The RUS links an Address List to mail-enabled objects by adding the Address List's distinguished name to the object's `showInAddressBook` multivalue attribute. Once an Address List has been created, it can take hours or days for the RUS to fully populate the list by stamping all related objects' `showInAddressBook` attributes, depending on the size of your organization. Exchange 2007 no longer depends on an RUS and propagation is a little more responsive, though applying the Address List can now be scheduled even in the EMC. Exchange 2007 provides some precanned Address Lists and allows for more complete `Opath` filter creation with the `Recipient Filter` option.

Address Lists should employ friendly and descriptive names, as they are options for users to query in finding other users through Outlook. In addition, Address Lists should be added after consideration. Too many Address Lists can confuse users as to which one they should be using.

A curious point about Address Lists in Exchange 2003 is that even though an LDAP filter is used to specify who should and shouldn't be in the list, Exchange doesn't actually use the filter to do an LDAP lookup against Active Directory. Instead, the RUS does its own compare on objects one by one. This is why you can't specify a search base where the Address List should start; it encompasses the entire forest, including the configuration container. This means you need to be very careful with the filter so that it is limited to the objects you truly want displayed. A positive aspect of this implementation is that it doesn't matter if you select indexed attributes for the filter. Since the RUS isn't using LDAP to resolve the objects from the filter, performance is not affected by any indexes on the attributes.

 Be careful if you use the preview button in the Exchange System Manager to verify the list's validity. That method will use an LDAP query against Active Directory to display the values, and has no bearing on whether the list is built yet or even what will end up in it. It is possible in certain cases that the preview will not match with what you actually get in the Address List, for example if the RUS has not run or if the `HideFromAddressBook` property has been set for one or more members of the group.

Address Lists are represented in Active Directory by the `addressBookContainer` class. This is a simple class. In Exchange 2000 and 2003, the main value, the Address List filter, is stored in the `purportedSearch` attribute.

Using a graphical user interface

Using the GUI for this process is straightforward and is the most likely the way you'll want to create Address Lists unless you need to create a lot of them on the fly or you are importing them from a test lab. In Exchange 2007, the option to schedule the creation of the Address List is available.

Using a command-line interface

As mentioned previously, you need to be very careful with the filter you specify for the `purportedSearch` attribute. The slightest mistake can cause the filter to not produce any results or produce an incorrect or incomplete result set. A filter such as `(!attrib=value)` instead of `(!(attrib=value))`, while acceptable to Active Directory's

LDAP parser, will cause undefined results when interpreted by the RUS. The only way to verify that the list has been properly built is to manually compare what the query should generate with what has been generated.

To do this comparison, first generate a list of distinguished names that are members of the Address List. This is done by using LDAP to query for all mail-enabled objects that have the Address List distinguished name listed in the `showInAddressBook` attribute; for example:

```
(&(mailNickname=*)( showinaddressbook=cn=All Users,cn=All Address Lists,cn=Address
Lists Container,cn=ADATUM,cn=Microsoft Exchange,cn=Services,
cn=Configuration,dc=adatum,dc=com))
```

Next, generate a list of distinguished names that are matched by the query you used for the Address List. Finally, compare these lists.

Using VBScript

Using VBScript is very similar to using the command-line method. You simply set the same attributes on a newly created object. As in the command-line method, the single most important attribute is the `purportedSearch` attribute; see the command-line discussion in this recipe for more details.

Using PowerShell

There is a set of cmdlets to manage Address Lists in Exchange 2007. First the `New-AddressList` cmdlet is used to create the list. Subsequently, `Update-AddressList` is used to populate the Address List or specifically apply the filters and build the list, and even schedule when it should be updated. For larger enterprises with tens of thousands or hundreds of thousands of Active Directory recipients, Address List generation is not trivial.

See Also

MS KB 319213 (How to Use Address Lists to Organize Recipients in Exchange 2003), MS KB 253828 (How the Recipient Update Service Populates Address Lists), and "Filterable Properties for the -RecipientFilter Parameter in Exchange 2007 SP1" at *http://technet.microsoft.com/en-us/library/bb738157(EXCHG.80).aspx*

20.17 Creating a Storage Group

Problem

You want to create a new storage group to allow for more mailbox stores, faster backups, or a logical organization of mailboxes.

Exchange 2003 Solution

Using a graphical user interface

1. Open the Exchange System Manager (ESM) snap-in.
2. In the left pane, browse to the server that you want to create a new storage group for.
3. Right-click on the server and select New→Storage Group.
4. Enter a name, transaction log location, system path location for storage of temporary and recovered files, and click OK.

Using a command-line interface

First, create an LDIF file called *add_sg.ldf* with the following contents:

```
dn: CN=<Storage Group Name>,<ParentDN>
changetype: add
objectClass: msExchStorageGroup
cn: <Storage Group Name>
showInAdvancedViewOnly: TRUE
systemFlags: 1610612736
msExchESEParamEnableIndexChecking: TRUE
msExchESEParamEnableOnlineDefrag: TRUE
msExchESEParamSystemPath: <Path to store system files>
msExchESEParamPageFragment: 8
msExchESEParamPageTempDBMin: 0
msExchRecovery: TRUE
msExchESEParamZeroDatabaseDuringBackup: 0
msExchESEParamBaseName: E01
msExchESEParamCircularLog: 0
msExchESEParamEventSource: MsExchangeIS
msExchESEParamCheckpointDepthMax: 20971520
msExchESEParamCommitDefault: 0
msExchESEParamLogFilePath: <Path to log files>
msExchESEParamDbExtensionSize: 256
msExchESEParamLogFileSize: 5120
```

Replace `<Storage Group Name>` with the name of the storage group, `<ParentDN>` with the distinguished named for the storage groups container for the appropriate server, `<Path to store system files>` with the filesystem path where you want system files (temporary and recovered files), and `<Path to log files>` with the filesystem path where you want Exchange logfiles. Then run the following command:

```
>ldifde -i -f add-sg.ldf
```

Using VBScript

```
' This code creates a Storage Group.
' ------ SCRIPT CONFIGURATION ------
strServer = "<Exchange Server>"    ' e.g. ExchServer2
strName = "<Storage Group Name>"    ' e.g. SG1
strPath = "<File Path>" & strName   ' e.g. D:\Program Files\ExchSrvr
' ------ END CONFIGURATION ---------
```

```
' Create URL to Storage Group
Set objSrv = CreateObject("CDOEXM.ExchangeServer")
objSrv.DataSource.Open strServer

' This for loop is a bit of a hack to retrieve the first Storage Group
' in the collection. VBScript doesn't let you access specific elements
' of a collection the way Jscript can.
for each strSg in objSrv.StorageGroups
    strTemp = strSg
    exit for
next
strTemp = mid(strTemp,instr(2,strTemp,"cn",1))
strSGUrl = "LDAP://cn=" & strName & "," & strTemp

' Create/configure Storage Group and save it
set objSG = CreateObject("CDOEXM.StorageGroup")
objSG.MoveSystemFiles(strPath)
objSG.MoveLogFiles(strPath)
objSG.DataSource.SaveTo strSGUrl
Wscript.Echo "Successfully created storage group."
```

Exchange 2007 Solution

Using a graphical user interface

1. Open the EMC by clicking Start→All Programs→Microsoft Exchange Server 2007→Exchange Management Console.
2. Navigate to the Server Configuration container and select Mailbox.
3. Select the desired server in the top of the middle pane.
4. The Database Management tab in the bottom of the middle pane will show the current storage groups and databases.
5. Right-click in the lower pane and select New Storage Group from the context menu or select New Storage Group toward the bottom of the Action pane.
6. The New Storage Group wizard opens requesting first a descriptive friendly name.
7. The wizard then offers the default logfile and system file locations. Use the Browse button to change these to an alternate location if needed.
8. If Local Continuous Replication is desired for this storage group, select the option in the GUI.
9. Configure any changes to the default System files and Log files folders for the LCR copy.
10. Click New to create the new Storage Group and Click Finish to close the Wizard.

Using PowerShell

It should come as no surprise by now that the EMS has an unmistakable cmdlet for creating a new Storage Group, called New-StorageGroup:

```
New-StorageGroup -Server <Server_Name> -Name <Storage Group Name> -LogFolderPath
<Log File Path> -SystemFolderPath <System File Path>
```

An example of this command might be as follows:

```
New-StorageGroup -Server "mailmbx01" -Name "Canada" -LogFolderPath "c:\program
files\microsoft\exchange server\mailbox\Canada" -SystemLogFileFolder "c:\program
files\microsoft\exchange server\mailbox\Canada"
```

Optionally, the `-Recovery` parameter is used to define a Recovery Storage Group.

Discussion

Storage groups are used for physically breaking your databases up into smaller management groups. This is done for several reasons. Chief among them are so you will have more numerous but smaller databases, a logical organization of mailboxes, or faster Exchange backups and restores, since the Exchange Server can run one simultaneous backup for each storage group. For example, if you have four mailbox databases in a single storage group, you can only have one backup running for that storage group; if you spread those four mailbox databases across two storage groups, you can run two simultaneous backups. For more detailed information on Exchange backups and file structures, see the *Exchange Server Cookbook* by Paul Robichaux et al. (O'Reilly).

For Exchange 2003, depending on the version (Standard or Enterprise) of Exchange, you can have up to four storage groups per server and up to five mailbox stores per storage group. Exchange 2007 increases this to 50 databases, which can be distributed among up to 50 storage groups. ESM enforces these limits, but it is possible to directly modify Active Directory to exceed them. If you create more databases or storage groups than allowed by your version, the additional databases will not mount. In Exchange 2003, Microsoft recommends that you spread your mailboxes across as many stores and storage groups as possible; this is because of memory management improvements since Exchange 2000. Thanks to 64-bit in Exchange 2007, database and storage group options have increased.

Storage groups are represented in Active Directory by the `msExchStorageGroup` class. This class has several attributes that have fairly intuitive string values and names and can be matched up to the options in ESM. Unfortunately, the raw Active Directory objects and attributes and their valid values for Exchange are not well documented. You can experiment with their settings, but you should do so only in a lab environment.

Using a command-line interface

One negative aspect of creating storage groups by direct Active Directory object manipulation is that you will not get warnings concerning the maximum number of storage groups allowed.

Using VBScript

The process of calling the CDOEXM interfaces to create storage groups is rather straightforward once you have the URL for the location of the object in Active Directory. In this solution, to get the distinguished name of the storage group container for the server, the script loops through all storage groups on the server and sets `strTemp` to the URL value of the last storage group. This value is then parsed to get the parent container for the storage groups to build the new storage group URL.

Using PowerShell

The results of creating a new storage group are reflected immediately in the EMC. The new storage group is ready to receive Mailbox Stores.

See Also

MS KB 821748 (How to Add New Mailbox Stores in Exchange Server 2003), MS KB 890699 (How to Configure Storage Groups in Exchange Server 2003), and *Exchange Server Cookbook*

20.18 Creating a Mailbox Store

Problem

You want to create a mailbox store. The primary reason for creating additional mailbox stores is to decrease the size of the individual stores while supporting many users on one server.

Exchange 2003 Solution

Using a graphical user interface

1. Open the Exchange System Manager (ESM) snap-in.
2. In the left pane, browse to the server and storage group that you want to create a new mailbox store on.
3. Right-click on the storage group and select New→Mailbox Store.
4. Enter a name for the store, configure the settings on each tab, and click OK.
5. When prompted to mount the store, click Yes.

Using VBScript

```
' This code creates a Mailbox Store.
' ------ SCRIPT CONFIGURATION ------
strServer = "<Exchange Server>"        ' e.g. ExchServer2
strSGName = "<Storage Group Name>"      ' e.g. SG1
strMailStoreName = "<MailBox Store Name>" ' e.g. DB1
```

```
' ------ END CONFIGURATION ---------

' Find Storage Group URL
strSearch = "CN=" & strSGName & ","
set objSrv = CreateObject("CDOEXM.ExchangeServer")
objSrv.DataSource.Open strServer
for each strSg in objSrv.StorageGroups
    if (instr(1,strSg,strSearch,1)>0) then strSGUrl = strSg
next

' Generate Mailbox Store URL
strMBUrl = "LDAP://CN=" & strMailStoreName & "," & strSGUrl

' Create/configure Mailbox Store and save it
set objMb = CreateObject("CDOEXM.MailBoxStoreDB")
objMb.DataSource.SaveTo strMBUrl

' Mount DataBase
objMB.Mount
Wscript.Echo "Successfully created mailbox store."
```

Exchange 2007 Solution

Using a graphical user interface

1. Open the EMC by clicking Start→All Programs→Microsoft Exchange Server 2007→Exchange Management Console.

2. Navigate to the Server Configuration container and select Mailbox.

3. Select the desired server in the top of the middle pane.

4. The Database Management tab in the bottom of the middle pane will show the current storage groups and databases.

5. Select the desired Storage Group to host the new Mailbox database.

6. Right-click on the Storage Group and select New Mailbox Database from the context menu or highlight the New Storage Group and select New Mailbox Database toward the bottom of the Action pane.

7. This opens the New Mailbox Database wizard.

8. Assign the Mailbox database a relevant name and tab to the next field.

9. The default database file path is generated. Click Browse to make any changes to this path.

10. Click New to create the Mailbox Database.

11. Note the PowerShell commands needed to create the database. Click Finish to end the wizard.

At the bottom of the wizard, there is a lone checkbox. By default, new Mailbox databases are automatically mounted at startup. Deselect this box to prevent the new database from mounting automatically. If the box remains checked, the system will also run a `Mount-Database` command as a follow-up.

Using PowerShell

The cmdlet for creating a new mailbox database on Exchange 2007 looks much like this:

```
New-MailboxDatabase -StorageGroup <Storage Group Name> -Name <Name_ID_Parameter>
-EdbFilePath <EDB File Path>
```

An example of this cmdlet might be as follows:

```
New-MailboxDatabase -StorageGroup "MAILMBX01\Canada" -Name "Ontario" -EdbFilePath
"C:\program files\microsoft\exchange server\ontario.edb"
```

A final step for the PowerShell-generated database is to mount it if needed:

```
Mount-Database -Identity "Ontario"
```

Discussion

Mailbox stores, which are also called *mailbox databases* (especially in Exchange 2007), are where mailboxes are located. There are quite a few configuration settings for mailbox stores that are beyond the scope of this chapter, but going through the ESM GUI when manually creating a mailbox store should give you an idea of what can be configured.

In Exchange 2003, depending on the version (Standard or Enterprise) of Exchange, you can have up to four storage groups per server and up to five mailbox stores per storage group. ESM enforces these limits, but it is possible to directly modify Active Directory to exceed these limits. If you create more databases or storage groups than allowed, the additional databases will not mount. Exchange 2007 allows for up to 50 databases spread across up to 50 storage groups.

Mailbox stores are represented in Active Directory by the `msExchPrivateMDB` class. This class is not as simple as some of the other classes used by Exchange. In addition, several of the attributes hold binary data, so working with these Active Directory objects directly can be difficult via VBScript or command-line methods. One of the more notable attributes of the mailbox store objects is a backlink attribute called `homeMDBBL`. This is a multivalued attribute linking back to all of the `user` objects that have mailboxes in this mailbox store.

Using a command-line interface

Due to the binary attributes the mailbox store objects contain, they are not good candidates for the LDIFDE command-line tool.

Using VBScript

The process of calling the CDOEXM interface is rather straightforward once you have the URL for the location of the object in Active Directory. As with the GUI, there are many properties that can be configured through VBScript. To get a complete list of the various methods and properties available for the `MailBoxStoreDB` interface, see the Exchange Server 2003 SDK.

Using PowerShell

The Exchange 2007 tools make these tasks much more simple and intuitive.

See Also

MS KB 821748 (How to Add New Mailbox Stores in Exchange Server 2003)

20.19 Installing Anti-Spam Agents on the Hub Transport Servers

Problem

You want to install the Exchange 2007 anti-spam agents for SP1 on a hub transport server because you are not using an Edge Transport Server at this time.

Exchange 2007 Solution

Using the command-line interface

The anti-spam transport agents are installed as part of the Edge Transport role; however, not all Exchange 2007 deployments will use an Edge server. The anti-spam agents are not installed by default on a Hub Transport server, but can be added manually.

Within the scripts folder on any Exchange 2007 Server, there is a pre-canned PowerShell script to install the anti-spam transport agents. This is found in the *scripts* folder located by default at *c:\program files\Microsoft\exchange server\scripts*. You can navigate to this folder from within the EMS and run:

```
.\install-AntispamAgents.ps1
```

Alternatively, you can run `install-AntispamAgents` using the command line from any folder as the scripts folder is added to the Windows Path environment variable at installation. Open a command prompt, type `Path`, and hit Enter to show the different folders held in the `Path` variable.

Finally, the transport service needs to be restarted to apply the anti-spam agents:

```
Restart-Service MSExchangeTransport
```

If you are using another SMTP Server product to provide gateway services, you must designate that IP address as an internal SMTP Server. This is required for Connection Filtering to work correctly:

```
Set-TransportConfig -InternalSMTPServers <IP_Address>
```

Discussion

After the anti-spam agents are installed on a Hub Transport Server, the agents are available on all Hub Transports Servers. They are stored in Active Directory.

To confirm the installation, open up the EMC and navigate to the Hub Transport object under the Organization Configuration container. In the middle pane, a new tab should appear entitled "Anti-spam." That tab should show the set of installed and enabled transport agents as:

- Content Filtering
- IP Allow List
- IP Allow List Providers
- IP Block List
- IP Block List Providers
- Recipient Filtering
- Sender Filtering
- SenderID
- Sender Reputation

See Also

"How to Enable Anti-Spam Functionality on a Hub Transport Server" at *http://technet* *.microsoft.com/en-us/library/bb201691.aspx*

20.20 Enabling Message Tracking

Problem

You want to enable Message Tracking on an Exchange Server 2003 or Exchange 2007 computer.

Exchange 2003 Solution

Using a graphical user interface

1. Prepare a directory on the local hard drive (preferably on a separate physical disk from the Exchange stores) to accept the tracking log directory.
2. Open the Exchange System Manager (ESM) snap-in.
3. In the lefthand pane, browse to the server for which you wish to enable message tracking.

4. Right-click the Server object and select Properties.

5. On the General tab, place a checkmark next to "Enable message tracking" and "Remove log files." Enter the number of days you wish to retain the logfiles for and click Apply.

6. Click OK once you've read the warning message.

7. Ensure that the process has created a share called *%servername%.log* and that the share is accessible to those users whose responsibilities involve running message traces.

Using a command-line interface

```
> adfind -config -rb "<cn=ServerName>,cn=Servers,cn=<Administrative Group Name>,
cn=Administrative Groups,cn=<Exchange Organization>,cn=Microsoft
Exchange,cn=Services" -dsq | admod messageTrackingEnabled::TRUE
msExchTrkLogCleaningInterval::<Cleanup Interval in Days>
```

Once you have enabled these two settings in Active Directory, you should modify the following Registry key on the Exchange server in question to prevent the Message Tracking Logs from being stored in the same directory as the Information Store:

```
HKLM\System\CurrentControlSet\Services\MSExchangeSA\Parameters\<ServerName>]
LogDirectory - REG_SZ:<PathToLoggingDirectory>
```

Using VBScript

```
' This code enables
' Message Tracking for an Exchange Server.
' ------ SCRIPT CONFIGURATION ------
strConnectionDN = "<Server Name><ParentDN>"
strLogPath = "<LogFilePath>" ' e.g. D:\Program Files\ExchangSrvr\Logs
strCleanupInterval = "<CleanupInterval>" ' From 1 - 99
                                         ' Set to 0 to retain indefinitely

Const HKEY_LOCAL_MACHINE = &H80000002 ' For configuring the Registry
strComputer = "<ComputerName>" ' Use "." for the local computer
strKeyPath = "SYSTEM\CurrentControlSet\Services\" & _
             "MSExchangeSA\Parameters\<ServerName>"
strValueName = "LogDirectory"
strValue = "<PathToLoggingDirectory>"
' ------ END CONFIGURATION ---------

' First configure the relevant AD attributes

Set objServer = GetObject ("LDAP://" & strConnectionDN)

objServer.Put "messageTrackingEnabled", "TRUE"
objServer.Put "msExchTrkLogCleaningInterval", strCleanupInterval
objStorageGroup.SetInfo

' Now configure the relevant Registry key

Set oReg=GetObject("winmgmts:{impersonationLevel=impersonate}!\\" & _
```

```
strComputer & "\root\default:StdRegProv")
oReg.SetStringValue HKEY_LOCAL_MACHINE,strKeyPath,strValueName,strValue
```

Exchange 2007 Solution

Using a graphical user interface

Message Tracking in Exchange 2007 can be set on servers running the Hub or Edge Transports and also on a server with the Mailbox role installed. To enable Message Tracking on a Transport server:

1. Open the EMC by clicking Start→All Programs→Microsoft Exchange Server 2007→Exchange Management Console.

2. Navigate to the Hub Transport container under Server Configuration (select Edge Transport here for an Edge Server).

3. Select Properties in the Action pane.

4. In the Properties window, select the Log Settings tab.

5. Select or deselect the checkbox next to "Enable Message Tracking logging" to enable or disable this feature.

6. Click OK to close the Properties window.

Using PowerShell

A simple one-line cmdlet is used to toggle Message Tracking on or off for a transport server:

```
Set-TransportServer <Server_Name> -MessageTrackingLogEnabled <$True|$False>
```

The cmdlet is a little different for a mailbox server, as follows:

```
Set-MailboxServer <Server_Name> -MessageTrackingLogEnabled <$True|$False>
```

There are a few other parameters that are easily configured with these cmdlets. These include:

MessageTrackingLogPath
> This parameter is used to set a nondefault local path for the Message Tracking logs. The default location is *C:\Program Files\Microsoft\Exchange Server\TransportRoles \Logs\MessageTracking*.

MessageTrackingLogSubjectEnabled
> By default, message subjects are logged in Message Tracking; however, privacy or compliance policy may require subjects be omitted from logging content.

MessageTrackingLogMaxDirectorySize
> Controlling the directory size where Message Tracking logs are stored can prevent unexpected drive space usage.

MessageTrackingLogMaxFileSize

> The default file size for Message Tracking logs is 10 MB. To control the frequency of new logfiles and the number of files, it may be beneficial to increase or decrease the individual file size.

MessageTrackingLogMaxAge

> For policy, compliance, or storage reasons, it may benefit the enterprise to have logs expire.

A full example of this configuration might be:

```
Set-TransportServer MAILEXHT01 -MessageTrackingLogEnabled:$True
-MessageTrackingLogPath "e:\TrackLog\" -MessageTrackingLogMaxDirectorySize 1GB
```

Discussion

Message Tracking logs are an invaluable aid to troubleshooting message delivery in any Exchange Server environment. A message can be tracked from submission to the Information Store all the way through to its departure out of the Exchange environment. As long as the administrator doing the tracking has the rights to and can resolve the NetBIOS name of each server along the message path, the administrator will be able to see how a particular message traveled through the network and how long it took to go through each server.

 You can also configure Message Tracking using a System Policy in Exchange 2003, which allows you to apply the same setting to multiple servers.

Message Tracking is enabled by default on all Exchange 2007 servers running the Hub Transport, Mailbox, or Edge Transport roles. The ability to disable or re-enable Message Tracking in the GUI for transport servers was added with Exchange 2007 SP1. The EMS allows for full configuration of message tracking.

When changing the location of the Message Tracking logs, the existing logs are not automatically transferred to the new folder. In Exchange 2007, administrators can also control the size of the folder to prevent unexpected consumption of available drive space.

See Also

MS KB 246856 (How to Enable Message Tracking in Exchange 2000 Server and in Exchange Server 2003) and "How to Configure Message Tracking" at *http://technet .microsoft.com/en-us/library/aa997984(EXCHG.80).aspx*

20.21 Summary

Exchange Server 2003 administration is focused on the Exchange System Manager and the Active Directory Users and Computers interfaces. For many tasks, there are scripting or command-line solutions using a number of different APIs or even third-party applications to access configuration information and data. Exchange 2007 makes significant changes to architecture and design, resulting in a new set of management tools. Exchange 2007 is the first Microsoft application to extend PowerShell for administration. This chapter shows some uses of the EMC and EMS in Exchange 2007 Management while still covering some common Exchange 2003 tasks.

As an Exchange 2007 administrator, you are going to have to learn the Exchange Management Shell at least at the cmdlet level. It is not that difficult—my 20-month-old daughter already speaks in cmdlets: `Get-Milk` and `Eat-Cereal`. We have only scratched the surface for recipes and how-tos for configuring and administering Exchange Servers. With the Exchange Management Shell especially, this chapter could be its own book, and probably is.

## CHAPTER 21

Microsoft Identity Lifecycle Manager

21.0 Introduction

Microsoft Identity Lifecycle Manager (ILM) 2007 is a suite of application servers that includes the successor to the Microsoft Identity Integration Server (MIIS) 2003. The ILM 2007 product set also contains a separate but complementary server product called Certificate Lifecycle Manager (CLM), which is used to provide self-service for environments with a Public Key Infrastructure (PKI) that need to provide self-service and policy-based certificate management. While CLM is typically thought of as a solution for smart card enrollment and lifecycle management, it excels at providing policy management for any certificate type; however, the CLM components of the ILM 2007 suite are not covered in this chapter. In the light of the rename, the MIIS community has struggled to differentiate between what was the MIIS synchronization engine from the ILM suite itself, not wishing to drag CLM into what has typically been an MIIS conversation. In cases where differentiation is important, the two server products are usually referred to as the "synch engine" and CLM; however, for the purposes of simplification within this chapter, the term ILM is used to only refer to the synch engine from this point forward.

ILM is a robust .NET application platform built on Microsoft's highly successful database platform—SQL Server. ILM provides services for the synchronization and reconciliation of identity data, and in some cases passwords, between multiple disparate repositories, including:

* Enterprise directories
  — Active Director/Active Directory Application Mode
  — Novell eDirectory
  — Sun Directory Server
  — IBM Tivoli Directory Server

- Databases
  - Microsoft SQL
  - Oracle
  - IBM DB2
- Mainframe
  - IBM RACF and iSeries (OS/400)
  - CA ACF2 and Top Secret
- Email
  - Microsoft Exchange Server
  - Lotus Notes
- Flat text files
  - DSML
  - LDIF
  - Attribute Value Pair
  - CSV
  - Delimited
  - Fixed width

While ILM no longer provides a metadirectory service, ILM is nonetheless considered to be in a class of products known as *metadirectory synchronization* tools. This is in contrast to other products like virtual directories that have no central reconciliation or synchronization mechanism.

For an up-to-date list on supported ILM Management Agents, visit *http://www.micro soft.com/windowsserver/ilm2007/overview.mspx*.

While the depth of connector coverage for identity management products is often a popular topic, it is typically irrelevant for two reasons:

- ILM is a SQL Server application and with SQL Server comes connectivity via ODBC, Linked Servers, and Integration Services, all of which provide access to databases and systems that do not have native Management Agent support
- ILM has what is known as the Extensible MA for Connectivity (XMA or ECMA), which is a framework for writing your own MA to proprietary applications and platforms; the XMA allows you to write the connectivity components and hand them back to ILM using its standard interface

Given the options for aggregating data sources through SQL Server or creating an XMA to consume a custom interface or web service, ILM provides an extremely flexible platform on top of which to develop an identity management solution.

While the term MA is fairly common in the Microsoft community, the generic term *connector* is also commonly used across multiple identity management products.

Feature Pack Versus Feature Pack

In the past there were two versions of MIIS, the full Enterprise version and the *free* Identity Integration Feature Pack (IIFP). The original IIFP provided a scaled-down version of the full Enterprise server in the sense that it only supported a handful of MAs. While you may still be able to leverage IIFP in some cases, no further changes or fixes will be published for it or the MIIS 2003 Enterprise version after SP2. To make matters worse, an update to ILM debuted which was also dubbed a "Feature Pack." Make no mistake about it, the ILM 2007 Feature Pack 1 is not to be confused with the old IIFP product and is *only* available as a licensed product.

The principal feature, from an identity synchronization perspective, that ILM 2007 Feature Pack 1 added support for was Exchange 2007 mailbox provisioning support. Customers are recommended to update to FP1 if they deployed on ILM 2007 initially in order to maintain supportability for future hotfixes; there are no licensing costs to move from ILM 2007 to ILM 2007 FP1.

Requirements for ILM

ILM requires three components:

Windows Server 2003 Enterprise Edition x86
    The Standard Edition is not sufficient here, nor are x64 editions of the OS supported for the application server

SQL Server 2000 or 2005, Standard or Enterprise Edition
    Either version or edition is sufficient; however, x64 editions are only supported if the SQL Server and the ILM Server loaded onto separate servers

.NET Framework 2.0
    ILM 2007 relies on the 2.0 version of the framework and any new extensions will need to be compiled using this version; older rules extensions may work (in the case of an upgrade from MIIS 2003) with the 1.1 framework, but any change requiring a recompile will need the 2.0 framework support

While not strictly required, most deployments make use of Visual Studio to build and compile rules extensions, and given the requirements for the 2.0 framework, Visual Studio 2005 or 2008 become the only supported versions (see Figure 21-1).

Windows Server 2003 Enterprise x86
SQL Server 2000 SP3a + /2005 SP2 + Standard or Enterprise x86
Identity Lifecycle Manager 2007
.NET Framework 2.0

Single Server ILM with Local SQL

 Windows Server 2003 Enterprise x86
Identity Lifecycle Manager 2007
.NET Framework 2.0

 Windows Server 2003 Enterprise x86 or x64
SQL Server 2000 SP3a + /2005 SP2 + Standard or Enterprise x86 or x64
.NET Framework 2.0 (SQL Server 2005)

Single Server ILM with Remote SQL

 Windows Server 2003 Enterprise x86
Identity Lifecycle Manager 2007
.NET Framework 2.0

 Windows Server 2003 Enterprise x86 or x64
SQL Server 2000 SP3a + /2005 SP2 + Standard or Enterprise x86 or x64
.NET Framework 2.0 (SQL Server 2005)

Split Server ILM with Remote SQL Cluster

Figure 21-1. Deployment options

 In Visual Studio 2008 it is now possible to select the .NET Framework version under which to compile the product. While there is no official support statement at the time of this publication, Visual Studio 2008 projects compiled under the 3.0 and 3.5 frameworks work fine but make no use of the new extensions anyway. If you are concerned about supportability, it is recommended to select the 2.0 framework to compile under.

SQL and ILM collocation

MIIS and SQL traditionally performed optimally when placed on the same server, suffering as much as a 60% performance impact to transaction performance when separated. With the update to .NET Framework 2.0 and some optimizations in the sync engine processing, the performance lost is somewhat lessened, albeit still substantial enough to warrant the same recommendation: whenever possible, locate the SQL Server and ILM server on the same physical server. Based on personal experience, collocation still results in a 20% to 40% performance impact in ILM 2007.

While ILM does not technically require Active Directory, future versions of ILM (ILM "2") will require AD for much of its advanced functionality. In a world where more than 80% of enterprise customers have deployed Active Directory, this is rarely an issue, and customers that have either failed to deploy AD or who perhaps do not consider AD strategic will probably not consider ILM anyway.

If you've had some history with MIIS and consider yourself up-to-date concerning the transition to ILM, feel free to skip the primer. If you're still hazy on the whole thing, then prepare to be enthralled, mildly enlightened, or at least somewhat puzzled by the primer.

 While ILM itself does not officially support clustering of the application, both a cold and warm standby option are available. For more information on the Planning for High Availability, see *http://download.microsoft .com/download/2/8/a/28a574b9-b183-4925-814e-acf9db53bb20/higha vail.doc.*

ILM Primer

The really attractive thing about ILM is that it is a streamlined .NET engine for synchronizing and reconciling identity information. That, in effect, is all it does, and it does it really well. The thing that makes the product so versatile is that at pretty much any point in a data flow you can "go to code" via an extension, resolve the issue in your preferred .NET language, and return the manipulated data back to your data flow. All the product does is take information from one source, and transform it or flow it to another source. We're hoping the power of the tool will begin to make itself more apparent as you read on.

The synchronization engine is an application that relies completely on SQL Server, and all data, code, rule sets, attribute flows, as well as the consolidated data sets, are stored within SQL tables (see Figure 21-2).

Since ILM is a complex application and not something most AD administrators have experience with, we are going to discuss the basic features and terminology in more depth.

Importing data

There are several terms that you will hear attributed to a data source within ILM: data source, directory, or connected directory (CD). A "CD" can refer to a database, a flat file, or a full-fledged directory such as Active Directory.

There are two ways we can get data into the product for processing: full imports and delta imports. Since AD exposes delta changes natively via *DirSync*, you are spoiled into thinking you can do delta imports with any CD, but that is not the case. When data is brought in for processing, it's stored in a special location called the Connector Space (CS).

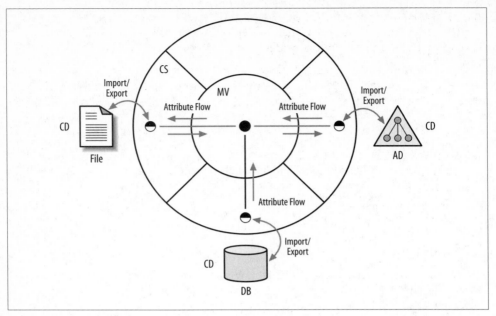

Figure 21-2. ILM architecture

Full imports (stage only)

Also called "staging"; reads the entire CD every time. They can be scoped or limited to specific containers or organizational units and the entire MA can be scoped to only process specific object types.

Delta imports (stage only)

If the CD is capable of differentiating changes like AD is, you can ask the CD for objects that have changed since your last full import. The caveat here is that you always have to start with at least one *error-free* full import in order to get a delta import.

 The way you get data into ILM is to "stage" the data into a special area called the Connector Space (CS) through a full import. Subsequent imports may be able to utilize delta imports if the CD supports it.

In Figure 21-3, the (A) actions depict the import process from CD to CS. While this could be a full or a delta import, the very first import should always be a full import.

The connector space

Technically speaking the connector space is just a table in SQL, but the important concepts to understand here are that the CS is where objects go once they've been staged

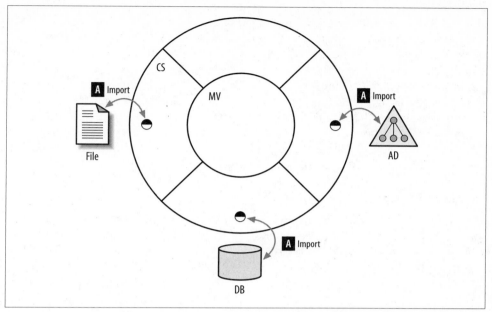

Figure 21-3. Importing data

(either through a full or delta import) and that the CS effectively becomes a localized copy of the CD you're connecting to. From that point on, all of the processing happens against the objects in the CS—not directly against the CD; this is an important distinction between a metadirectory product, like ILM, and a Virtual Directory. This is a good thing because you can grab a copy of the data and then build and validate your rules against it without risking data corruption, access rights, or network traffic. Getting objects staged into the CS takes minutes to set up and is limited only by your rights to read the directory and the time it takes to iterate through the directory and create the entries in SQL.

Now, this is very important: before you can read from an Active Directory connected directory, the account you will use to connect must have at least the "Replicating Directory Changes" right. For information on how to set that up, refer to the KB article at *http://support.microsoft.com/default.aspx?scid=kb;en-us;303972&Product=id serv2003*.

Beyond this detail, any authenticated user can read public attributes; however, sooner or later you may run into areas of the directory that require greater access rights.

Once objects have been staged into the connector space, they can synchronize with another section of the engine called the metaverse.

The Metaverse

The metaverse (MV) holds the consolidated representation of identities from each of the connector spaces. For instance, if you have an account in ADAM and an account in an AD domain, and both have been staged into their respective connector spaces, you can choose to represent those objects either independently through a process called *projection*, or as a single object through a process called a *join*. As a general practice, the MV holds a single object representing the consolidated identity information mined from objects in the individual data sources; think of it as a many (CS) to one (MV) relationship. Most importantly, the way data is synchronized from one CS to another CS is through the MV. Without an MV object, you cannot flow information between CSs. So what's this we were saying about projection and joins?

Projection and joins

One of the immutable laws of ILM is that *every MV object has to start out its lifecycle as a projection from one CS object*. Incidentally, the converse is also true: *once all of your CS objects are disconnected from an MV object, that MV object will cease to exist.* A projection rule simply states "create an MV object of a specific type for this specific CS object."

Once you've projected a set of CS objects into the MV, you can set up some rules for objects in other CSs to *join* the MV object. There are tons of ways you can specify this, but once you have two CSs joined via a common MV object, you can then synchronize data between the respective CS and MV objects, creating a "bridge" of sorts.

> After using a full or delta import to Stage data into the CS, we can then project those objects into the MV using a projection rule. Objects in separate CSs can be connected through an MV object through the join process, which allows for the synchronization of data between connected objects.

Now, projecting an object into the MV doesn't mean that any of its data goes with it. On the contrary, we have to create attribute flow rules to tell the engine exactly which CS attribute goes to which MV attribute. Before we can proceed on to how synchronization works, we need to talk briefly about connectors, what states they can be in, and how we can filter them.

In Figure 21-4, action (1) depicts the *projection* of a CS object into the metaverse, which results in the creation of the MV object, while action (2) depicts inbound attribute flow.

In Figure 21-5, action (3) and (5) depict *joins* occurring between CS objects in the File and AD CS respectively, while actions (4) and (6) depict inbound and outbound attribute flow.

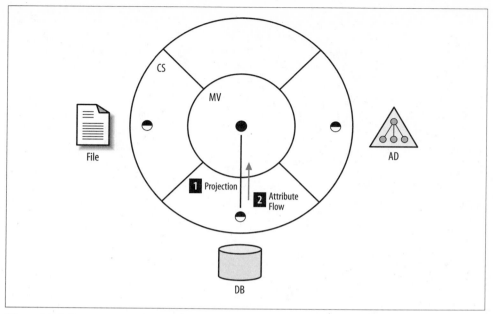

Figure 21-4. Projection

The many faces of the connector

Whenever you project a CS object into the MV, a *connector* is created. Of particular importance is the type of that connector—in this case it is considered a *normal connector*. You can also create connectors of type *explicit* and you can remove a connector by disconnecting it. When an object is first staged into the CS, it is a *normal disconnector*. If that object is joined or projected, it becomes a *normal connector*. Suffice it to say that normal connectors and disconnectors can become connectors again, whereby if it is explicit then it must be manually made a connector or disconnector. OK, stay with us now...

Now, if you disconnect an existing connector, you can place that *disconnector* as one of two types: a *normal disconnector* or an *explicit disconnector*. A connector is really just a special relationship between CS and MV objects that absolves the need to re-evaluate the relationship every time a sync is run, which makes the connector a static entity within the engine. This is an important concept to understand, as join rules for a particular CS object are only evaluated under two conditions: the CS object is not currently connected, and the CS object is not assigned as an explicit disconnector. Once a join is made the rule is never executed again for that CS object.

The bottom line here is *never create explicit anything and your life will be much easier*—explicit disconnectors are designed to provide a temporary state until information can be "bread crumbed" back into the originating system, and are not intended to be a

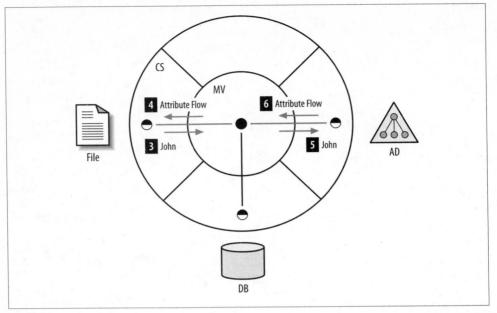

Figure 21-5. Joins

permanent solution (although for many people, they are a nonetheless a permanent problem).

State-based synchronization

There are two basic types of Identity Management (IdM) products on the market today, state-based and event-based. ILM is a state-based product, which simply means that *things happen when the state of an object or attribute changes state*. Where event-based systems are concerned, an event is generated based upon some predefined threshold or application trigger that tells the IdM system to do something. Without devolving into a religious discussion regarding which is better, the first truth you need to understand is that all systems on the market today have aspects of both systems. While one system may claim to be one or the other, all products include both state- and event-based aspects. The important thing to take note of is how you approach a problem with one system versus another. The only thing you need to understand is that as a synchronization engine, the product will process each object in turn (serially) and resolve the state of that object (and all of its attributes) completely each and every time that object is touched. This is probably the most difficult concept to understand with the product, and it generally confounds people trying to understand why full or delta synchronizations cause extensions in other management agents to fire (don't worry, we're not there yet).

The problem facing any IdM product vendor is that if you change the set of rules for synchronization of data, then how do you reapply those new rules to objects that have not been triggered by an event or state change? We'll come back to this, but suffice it to say that this product enforces the current set of rules against *all* objects when a *full synchronization* is run; so full synchronization reconciles every connector. Running a *delta synchronization* applies the current rule set to objects that have changed, or are currently disconnected, since the last full or delta import (i.e., the state changed).

Full synchronization

> Forces all rules and attribute flow to process every object in the CS. This ultimately will flow data from the CS to the MV and out to any other CS that is joined to the MV object in question.

Delta synchronization

> Forces all rules and attribute flows to process only the objects in the CS that have changed since the last synchronization. This will flow data from the CS to the MV only for changed objects.

It is important to recognize that the process of reconciliation is critical for issues of compliance. Products that do not ensure full reconciliation for all objects are not telling you the whole story.

 We use full or delta imports to stage data into the CS, but we also do full or delta syncs to copy data between the CS and the MV. The important thing to note is that while imports are always one-way (import, not export), synchronizations are always two-way (import and export). There is simply no way around this—if you have export attribute flow rules set up, they must be processed to complete the state evaluation of every object, even if you only intend this to happen in one place. If that CS object is tied to a CS object through an MV object (through a join), then a sync run on one CS will process changes all the way to the other CS object.

In Figure 21-6, normal synchronization convergence is depicted. Running a full or delta sync will cause synchronization to occur across all three connectors; however, *inbound attribute flow only occurs on the management agent that the synchronization was triggered from* (depicted as the DB-connected directory).

Now that we've talked about how to get data into the CS and sync it with a MV object, we need to talk more about management agents. We will touch on Attribute Flow in a moment.

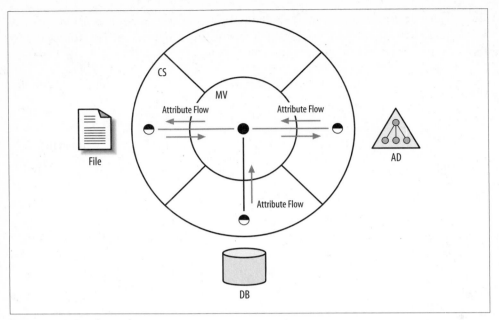

Figure 21-6. Synchronization

Management Agents

The management agent (MA) is a set of processes comprising the native APIs of the product we are connecting to combined with a nice little GUI to configure it. All the stuff we talked about, imports and syncs, joins and projections, and connector filters, are all part of the management agent itself. In actual fact, it is not an agent at all—at least not in the sense that you have to install anything on the CD. This is a fundamental difference between state-based and event-based products; event-based systems require some sort of agent or driver that must reside on the system or application in question, whereas state-based systems require nothing but a local instance of the APIs in question.

 To get the APIs needed for connectivity to Lotus Notes, the Lotus Notes client needs to be installed on the ILM server. The same can be said for Oracle connectivity requiring the Oracle client, SQL connectivity requiring the SQL client, and so on.

The MA is responsible for determining how you connect to the CD, which object types you want to see (like user, group, or computer), and which attributes you care to have copied to the CS. Only selected attributes can flow into the MV through attribute flow.

Sometimes the terms MA and CS are used interchangeably, but while they represent the entirety of the CS relative to the CD, they are much more. The MA is where you store the credentials for connecting to the CD, as well as all of the connectivity, scopes, filters, join and projection rules, attribute flows, deprovision rules, extension configuration, and password sync setup. Suffice it to say, you will have one MA for every CD you want to talk to, which will be represented by its own CS.

MAs also provide a way to store and represent sets of potentially schedulable operation profiles, called *run profiles*.

Run profiles

So, how do you tell ILM that you want to perform a full import or a delta sync? You do this by creating a series of run profiles that contain at least one of the following prebuilt operations:

- Full import (stage only)
- Delta import
- Full synchronization
- Delta synchronization
- Full import full synchronization (special)
- Delta import delta synchronization (special)
- Export

The export is solely for exporting pending changes in the CS out to the CD. This is critical for actually sending the changes back to the directory. You should feel reassured to know that the product cannot automatically affect the CD simply by manipulating objects in the MV or the CS. You *must* do an export to send changes out. Consequently, if the credentials you supplied to the MA do not have rights to modify the requested attributes or create a newly provisioned user, for example, the exports will fail. The credentials in the MA must have all of the appropriate rights to affect the pending changes.

You can also string combinations of operations together in one profile. For instance, you might want to start with a delta import and delta synchronization and follow that immediately with an export, followed by a delta import. That would get data in, process it, and send it directly back out with the changes, all in one run.

At this point, don't worry too much about the "special" run profiles; you'll touch on them more if you begin working with the full product. But suffice it to say, they pretty much do what you'd think, with one exception. The "Delta Import Delta Synchronization" profile will only synchronize changes that were imported as part of the current delta import. This is *not* the same as performing the same two operations in separate steps.

Now, before we talk about attribute flow we need to talk briefly about the Metaverse Designer.

The Metaverse Designer

Suppose that you have an attribute in your AD called `extensionAttribute3`, but it really represents your cost center. What you'd really like to do is just call it "Cost Center" in the MV, so that it actually makes sense when you decide to flow this to some other CS. With the Metaverse Designer you can create custom object types and attributes as needed and you don't have to have OID numbers like in AD. You can create `costCen` `ter` of type `String (indexable)`, make it multivalue or not, index it if you want to, and assign it to the `person` object class. You can then flow data into that from any CS as long as it is of type `String`.

The Metaverse Designer is what you use when you want to add custom attributes to objects in the metaverse.

Attribute flow rules

Simply stated, an *attribute flow rule* is a mapping between a CS attribute (such as `extensionAttribute3`) and an MV attribute (such as `costCenter`). An attribute flow can be either import or export, and either direction can be one of the following mapping types:

Direct
> Flowing data from a CS attribute to an MV attribute of the same type (e.g., `String/` `String`). The attribute names can be completely different, but you just want to flow the data over unaltered. For example, flow `EIN` into `employeeID`.

Advanced
> There are three types of advanced flows:

> *Extension*
>> Flows data from *one or more* CS attributes to a single MV attribute, whereby the data needs to be transformed or concatenated in some way. The attributes can even be of different types, as long you perform the type conversion within the code. The term *extension* implies that we have to write code to accomplish this mapping. For example, take a user's last name and add the first character of the first name to form the logon ID.

> *Constant*
>> Flows a constant or arbitrary `String` to a single MV object of type `string`. Since it's a constant, the data is not originating from any CS attribute. No code is required; however, if you want to "blank" out an attribute (flow a null), you have to do this with an *extension*—as of SP1, this was not an option available in the GUI. For example, everyone's company attribute is "My Company."

> *Distinguished Name*
>> Flows a component of a DN into an MV object of type `string`. You can pick apart a large DN by choosing which section of the string to flow across. No code is required, unless you want to transform the component itself and then you're back to the extension. For example, you know that the second

---

component of the DN is always the department name, so flow that information unaltered into the department attribute.

This is only available for import attribute flows into the metaverse; it cannot be used to export components of a DN to another CS. To do that, you need to flow the component into an MV attribute and then set up a direct export attribute flow to the CS.

With any rules extension, you have the opportunity to resolve the situation in any .NET language. The good news is that if you are a VB.NET or C# programmer, ILM will create the entire project template for you. You will find the greatest number of examples online in VB.NET, and that is the language we will use in this chapter.

MAs are used to connect natively to a CD; they define the objects in which you are interested, whether those objects should be filtered, how they are joined or projected, and what attribute flow rules exist between the CS and MV. You can create custom attributes to flow information into the MV through the Metaverse Designer, and run profiles are used to bundle together various methods to pull data into the CS and synchronize it with the MV.

ILM also supports password management via a web-based application and password synchronization from AD to other systems. Many additional scenarios are covered in the Microsoft Identity and Access Management Series (see the section called "See Also").

The scenario

Figure 21-7 outlines the example scenario of synchronizing AD from an HR database, which is used throughout this chapter. The numbered points will be referenced in later recipes.

We'll start with an employee database that runs on SQL Server, referred to from now on as the HR Database. You can download this database from *http://www.rallenhome .com/books/adcookbook2*.

Let's walk through how ILM will synchronize the HR Database with Active Directory, and define some of the specialized terms Microsoft uses to describe the process. The numbers in parentheses refer to the numbered points in the diagram.

First, we will *import* or *stage* (1) records from the HR Database into the HR Database MA connector space. The import process creates connector space objects (2).

Next, we will *synchronize* the data in the HR Database MA connector space. The first time we do this, and any time ILM discovers a new user record in the MA connector space, ILM will *project* (3) a new object (4) into the metaverse, and *join*, or link the HR

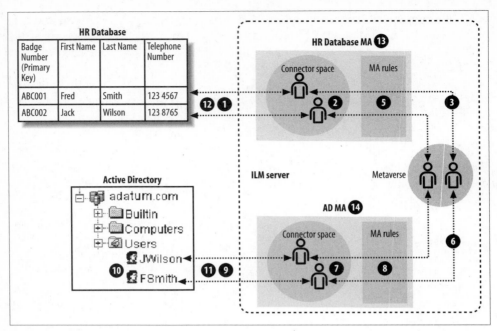

Figure 21-7. Example scenario

Database MA object to the metaverse object. ILM will then *flow* attribute data from the HR Database MA connector space object to the *joined* metaverse object through the MA's rules (5).

Synchronizing the HR Database MA will also *provision* (6) a new connector space object (7) in the Active Directory MA's connector space and join the new Active Directory connector space object to the metaverse object (4). ILM will then flow the appropriate attribute information from the metaverse object (4) into the AD connector space object (7) through the Active Directory MA's rules (8).

We will *export* (9) objects (7) from the AD connector space into Active Directory itself to create Active Directory user objects (10).

We will also import (11) the `telephoneNumber` attribute from AD user objects (10) into the related AD connector space objects (7) and synchronize the AD management agent. This will flow attribute data through the ADMA rules (8) and into the joined metaverse object (4); from there, attribute data will flow through the HR Database MA's rules (5) to the joined HR Database MA connector space object (2). At this stage, the updated HR Database MA connector space object (2) will be exported (12) to the HR Database, resulting in the [`telephoneNumber`] column being updated.

Deprovisioning will also be tested by deleting a row in the HR Database and then importing (1) objects from the HR Database in to the HR Database connector space. This will result in the related connector space object (2) being marked as deleted. Synchronizing the HR Database MA will cause the joined metaverse object (4) to be deleted. This will, in turn, cause the joined AD connector space object (7) to be deleted. Finally, the delete operation is exported to Active Directory, resulting in the deletion of an Active Directory user object (10).

See Also

Microsoft provides a great deal of useful documentation for MIIS on its website. This section lists some of the most useful documents:

The ILM help files
> ILM comes with a very useful and complete help file. You can find it in the ILM installation folder, typically at *C:\Program Files\Microsoft Identity Integration Server\UIShell\helpfiles*. There are two help files: *mms.chm* contains general help for configuring and running MIIS, and *mmsdev.chm* contains information about programming rules extensions and interpreting MIIS XML files. In addition, the ILM Developer Reference can be found at *http://msdn2.microsoft.com/en-us/library/ms698364.aspx*.

The ILM home page
> The ILM home page (*http://www.microsoft.com/ilm*) is the starting point for all the current information about ILM, including recent releases and other news.

Microsoft TechNet: Identity Lifecycle Manager TechCenter
> The most up-to-date information for both the MIIS and ILM product set can be found in the ILM TechCenter (*http://technet.microsoft.com/en-us/library/cc626295.aspx*) on TechNet.

Microsoft TechNet: Identity Lifecycle Manager TechCenter: Community
> For the latest links to both Microsoft and independently published blogs, check out the *Community* page on the ILM TechCenter. Here you can find the link to the TechNet-hosted forum for ILM, which is frequented by the ILM product team as well as many of the ILM MVPs (*http://technet.microsoft.com/en-us/ilm/cc511010.aspx*).

Microsoft Identity and Access Management Series Overview
> This document provides an overview of MIIS and describes how MIIS fits into Microsoft's overall identity architecture. You can download it from *http://www.microsoft.com/technet/security/topics/identitymanagement/idmanage/Overview.mspx*.

Identity Integration Feature Pack (IIFP) SP2 for Microsoft Windows Server Active Directory
> This provides identity integration/directory synchronization, account provisioning/deprovisioning, and password synchronization between Active Directory

directory services, ADAM, Microsoft Exchange Server 2000 or Exchange 2003 instances (the IIFP was *not* updated to support Exchange 2007): *http://www.micro soft.com/downloads/details.aspx?FamilyID=D9143610-C04D-41C4-B7EA -6F56819769D5&displaylang=en*.

MIIS 2003 Design and Planning collection
> The Design and Planning collection contains a series of work aids and methodologies that will aid you in your efforts to implement ILM. It's available at *http://www .microsoft.com/downloads/details.aspx?familyid=DADC5021-222B-4AF7-8C58 -2227C358756F&displaylang=en*.

ILM 2007 Design Concepts
> The Design Concepts series focuses on specific ILM concepts in detail and is recommended once you have a strong feel for the ILM architecture and terminology. It is located at *http://www.microsoft.com/downloads/details.aspx?FamilyID= 40a52201-a297-4c35-82e9-f0b4ca05daeb&displaylang=en*.

ILM 2007 Getting Started collection
> The Getting Started collection is a great extension to the scenario collection and focuses on specific common tasks, available at *http://www.microsoft.com/down loads/details.aspx?FamilyID=11fb01bc-94a9-4404-bb90-ceca1a206e32&Display Lang=en*.

Microsoft Identity Integration Server 2003 Scenarios
> The MIIS Scenarios documents describe how to use MIIS to solve common identity management problems, including account provisioning, global address list synchronization, and password management. Download the scenarios from *http:// www.microsoft.com/downloads/details.aspx?FamilyID=15032653-d78e-4d9d -9e48-6cf0ae0c369c&DisplayLang=en*.

TechNet Virtual Lab: Microsoft Identity Integration Server 2003
> There is a virtual lab you can use to try out some of the recipes in this chapter before investing the effort to build an MIIS server. The labs are available at *http://www .microsoft.com/technet/traincert/virtuallab/miis.mspx*.

 In recipes involving direct access to SQL, we are using SQL Server 2000 Enterprise Manager. The same operation using SQL Server 2005 Server Management Studio can be accomplished by expanding the *Root Node \Databases\HR\Tables*.

21.1 Creating the HR Database MA

Problem

You want to get employee records from the HR Database into ILM so that they can be used as the source for new accounts in AD.

Solution

You need to start by creating an MA for the HR Database (refer to (12) in Figure 21-7):

1. Open Identity Manager.
2. Click the Management Agents button on the toolbar.
3. In the Actions pane on the right, click Create.
4. In the Create Management Agent Designer, select SQL Server 7.0 or 2000 from the "Management Agent for" drop-down list.
5. Type HR Database into the Name text box.
6. Type a description in the Description field—this is where you can be creative.
7. Click Next.
8. In the Connect to Database pane on the right side:
   a. Type the SQL server name into the Server Name text box.
   b. Type the name of the database in the Database text box.
   c. Type the name of the table or view that contains the employee records in the Table/View text box.
   d. Leave the Delta View and Multivalue Table text boxes blank.
   e. Select the radio button for the type of authentication the SQL Server is set up to use.
   f. Fill in the User Name, Password, and Domain text boxes with the credentials of a user who has permissions to read and update the table we will create.
9. Click Next.
10. On the Configure Columns page:
    a. Click the Set Anchor button. This will display the Set Anchor dialog box.
    b. In the Set Anchor dialog box, select Badge Number and press the Add button.
    c. Click OK to save the anchor attribute definition.
11. On the Configure Connector Filter page, click Next.
12. On the Configure Join and Projection Rules page, click Next.
13. On the Configure Attribute Flow page, click Next.
14. On the Configure Deprovisioning page, click the "Make them disconnectors" radio button in the lefthand pane.
15. Click Next.
16. In the Configure Extensions page, click Finish.

Discussion

Following these steps will create an SQL Server management agent. Associated with the MA is a namespace known as the *connector space*. ILM will store the data from the relevant columns of the HR Database here and use them to provision, synchronize, and deprovision user accounts in Active Directory. Creating the HR Database MA is the first of several steps to get the data into ILM. You should now see a management agent in the management agent pane of the Identity Manager with the name and comments displayed.

See Also

Recipe 21.2 for more on creating the HR database MA

21.2 Creating an Active Directory MA

Problem

You want to provision user accounts into Active Directory from the records in the HR Database.

Solution

The first step to accomplish this is to create an Active Directory management agent (in Recipe 21.1, see (13) of Figure 21-7):

1. Open Identity Manager.
2. Click the Management Agents button on the toolbar.
3. In the Actions pane on the right side, click Create.
4. In the Management Agent Designer, select Active Directory from the "Management Agent for" drop-down list.
5. In the Name box, type a name. The forest name is usually a good choice.
6. If you feel creative, type a meaningful description into the Description text box.
7. Click Next.
8. In the Connect to Active Directory Forest pane on the right side:
   a. Type the fully qualified DNS name of the forest into the Forest Name text box.
   b. Fill in the username, password, and domain name of an appropriate user account. The account must have sufficient access permissions. See the section called "Discussion" for more details.
   c. Click Next.
9. In the Configure Directory Partitions pane on the right side:
   a. Select the domain(s) you wish to manage in the Select Directory Partitions field.

---

b. Click the Containers button in the lower-left portion of the dialog box.

c. In the Select Container dialog, select the containers you wish to manage.

d. Click OK.

e. Click Next.

10. In the Select Attributes pane on the right side, select the attributes you wish to manage from the Attributes field. You can check the Show All checkbox to display a full list of all attributes in the AD. Some AD attributes are mandatory; a typical minimal list would be: `cn`, `displayName`, `employeeID`, `givenName`, `sAMAccountName`, `sn`, `userAccountControl`, `userPrincipalName`, and `unicodePwd` (you need to select the Show All checkbox to see the `unicodePwd` attribute). Click Next to save the selected attributes.

6. In the Select Object Types pane on the right side, select "user" in the Object Types field and click Next.

 ILM requires that the `organizationUnit`, `domainDNS`, and `container` object types always be selected. ILM uses these objects to maintain the hierarchical structure of Active Directory in the MA's connector space.

7. In the Select Attributes pane on the right side, select the attributes you wish to manage from the Attributes field. You can check the Show All checkbox to display a full list of all attributes in the AD. Some AD attributes are mandatory; a typical minimal list would be: `cn`, `displayName`, `employeeID`, `givenName`, `sAMAccountName`, `sn`, `userAccountControl`, `userPrincipalName`, and `unicodePwd` (you need to select the Show All checkbox to see the `unicodePwd` attribute). Click Next to save the selected attributes.

8. On the Configure Connector Filter page, click Next.

9. On the Configure Join and Projection Rules page, click Next.

10. On the Configure Attribute Flow page, click Next.

11. On the Configure Deprovisioning page, click "Stage a delete on the object for the next export run", then click Next.

12. On the Configure Extensions page, click Finish.

Discussion

The account used to connect to AD must have the following rights to the containers that you intend to write to:

- Standard
- Read
- Write

- Advanced
- Delete
- Replicate directory changes
- Create all child objects
- Delete all child objects
- List contents
- Read all properties
- Write all properties
- Delete subtree
- Read permissions
- All validated writes

A popular question that surfaces in the discussion boards has to do with why ILM doesn't support the use of anonymous binds to LDAP directories. While there is quite a bit of development involved in connecting to a given directory's change log for the purposes of being able to process deltas, there was obviously a hard choice made during the original product planning to avoid direct support for binding anonymously. Most of the use cases involving ILM have to do with ongoing delta processing, so supporting an anonymous bind provides little or no value except for the small percentage of cases where a quick solution precipitates the need for an anonymous bind. If you find yourself in the latter situation, consider using LDIFDE or another tool to extract the directory to an LDIF file for processing or build an extensible MA (XMA).

See Also

Recipe 21.1 for more on creating the HR database MA, Recipes 21.5 and 21.8 for further configuration of this Active Directory MA

21.3 Setting Up a Metaverse Object Deletion Rule

Problem

You have decided on a single authoritative source for new employees: the HR Database. When a user record is deleted from it, you want ILM to delete the corresponding Active Directory account.

Solution

One of the configuration options required to have deletions propagated from the HR Database to Active Directory is the *metaverse object deletion rule*:

1. Open Identity Manager.

---

2. Click the Metaverse Designer button on the toolbar.

3. In the Actions pane on the far right side, click Configure Object Deletion Rule.

4. Select the "Delete metaverse object when connector from this management agent is disconnected" radio button and ensure the HR Database MA is selected in the drop-down list.

5. Click OK.

Discussion

The object deletion rule informs ILM of when to delete metaverse objects. Deleting a metaverse object does not necessarily cause anything to happen in the connected data source, but it *does* disconnect any connected objects in all of the connector spaces. This will cause the deprovisioning rule to fire for each disconnected object. The deprovisioning rule is configured for each management agent in the Configure Deprovisioning page for the management agent.

It is critical to plan accordingly for the lifecycle of every object. In many cases, deleting the MV object is not desirable if not all of the connectors are to be deleted. If you find yourself needing to maintain objects in other connected directories even after an authoritative source object has changed to an inactive status or been removed entirely (HR *very rarely* deletes records), consider leaving the connectors in place and allowing the default metaverse object deletion rule to prevail. This is incredibly helpful if you are doing any sort of reporting based off of aggregated identity data derived from the metaverse.

See Also

Recipe 21.1, Recipe 21.29 for deleting data in the connector space and metaverse, and Recipe 21.15 for the provisioning run profile

21.4 Setting Up Simple Import Attribute Flow—HR Database MA

Problem

You have already created the MAs needed, but you want to flow the column data from the HR Database to attributes in Active Directory.

Solution

You need to configure the ADMA's attribute flow rules page (in Recipe 21.1, refer to (5) in Figure 21-7):

1. Open Identity Manager.

2. Click the Management Agents button on the toolbar.

3. In the Management Agents pane, double-click the HR Database MA.

4. In the Management Agent Designer pane on the lefthand side, select Configure Attribute Flow.

5. Ensure "person" is selected in the data source object type drop-down list.

6. Ensure "person" is selected in the metaverse object type drop-down list.

7. In the Data Source attribute list, select the attribute whose data you wish to flow into the metaverse (see the section called "Discussion" for some suggestions).

8. In the Metaverse attribute list, select the attribute you want the data to flow into (see the "Discussion" section for some suggestions).

9. In the Mapping Type section of the dialog, select Direct.

10. In the Flow Direction section of the dialog, select Import.

11. Click New. The new attribute mapping will appear in the attribute mapping list, with an arrow indicating that it is an import attribute flow.

12. Click OK.

Discussion

ILM has been configured to flow an attribute from the HR Database MA's connector space into the metaverse. In general, we can map any attribute from the connected system to any attribute in the metaverse. However, if a Mapping Type of Direct is issued, the attributes in the MA and the metaverse must be of the same data type (e.g., string or integer). To map from one data type to another, configure the advanced attribute flow (see Recipe 21.6).

Here are some typical simple mappings:

- `FirstName→givenName`
- `LastName→sn`
- `Dept→department`
- `StaffNumber→employeeID`
- `TelNo→telephoneNumber`

You need to make your own decisions about what data in the HR Database maps onto what data in the metaverse attributes, but these are usually fairly obvious. If you want to construct a name—for example, you'd like the `sAMAccountName` to be derived from the first character of the first name prepended to the last name—you need an advanced flow.

As a rule of thumb (and personal preference), it is generally better to do advanced flows to assemble data on the inbound flow so that the correct information is contributed to the metaverse. This approach scales better since syncs process only the inbound attribute flow for the MA that the run profile was executed from, and having direct flows on all outbound attribute rules translates to less overhead for converging a single identity. So consider moving as many of your advanced rules to import flows, and use advanced rules only when necessary for export flows.

See Also

Recipe 21.1, Recipe 21.5 for a simple export attribute flow to AD, Recipe 21.6 for more advanced attribute flow, and Recipe 21.7 for writing a rules extension to take the advanced flow even further (all these flows are eventually exported to AD)

21.5 Setting Up a Simple Export Attribute Flow to AD

Problem

You want to flow attributes in the metaverse to attributes in AD. For example, the givenName field in the metaverse needs to map to the givenName field in AD.

Solution

You need to configure the attribute flow pages on the ADMA (in Recipe 21.1, refer to (8) in Figure 21-7):

1. Open Identity Manager.
2. Click the Management Agents button on the toolbar.
3. In the Management Agents pane, double-click the ADMA.
4. In the Management Agent Designer pane on the lefthand side, select Configure Attribute Flow.
5. Ensure "user" is selected in the data source object type drop-down list.
6. Ensure "person" is selected in the metaverse object type drop-down list.
7. In the data source attribute list, select the connector space attribute you want to flow data into. See the section called "Discussion" for some suggestions.
8. In the Metaverse attribute list, select the attribute you want to flow data from. See the section called "Discussion" for some suggestions.
9. In the Mapping Type section of the dialog, select Direct.
10. In the Flow Direction section of the dialog, select Export.
11. Click New. The new attribute mapping will appear in the attribute mapping list, with an arrow indicating that it is an export attribute flow.
12. Click OK.

Discussion

This will configure a simple export attribute flow from the metaverse to the ADMA. You need to determine what attributes in the metaverse should flow to AD attributes.

Here are some typical simple mappings:

- givenName→givenName
- sn→sn
- department→department
- employeeID→employeeID
- telephoneNumber→telephoneNumber
- cn→displayName
- cn→cn
- uid→sAMAccountName

In many ILM scenarios, data is manipulated on its way *in* to the metaverse, and then copied on its way out to other connected systems. In the above example, the cn comes from the displayName. This is because you will later create an advanced import flow that will write the first name followed by a space and the last name into the displayName in the metaverse. Something similar will be done for uid, only you will take the first character of the first name and append the last name; e.g., Fred Smith gets a sAMAccountName of *FSmith*.

See Also

Recipes 21.1, 21.4, Recipe 21.6, and 21.7 (these recipes are interesting because most of the data you are exporting to AD in this recipe was first imported from them)

21.6 Defining an Advanced Import Attribute Flow—HR Database MA

Problem

You want to create an Active Directory username using the first and last name from the HR Database. Simple attribute-to-attribute mapping is not sufficient. You need to take partial strings from different attributes and combine them to form a new name.

Solution

This will involve writing some VB or C# for an advanced attribute flow, which is covered in Recipe 21.7. To start with, you must define the *flow rule*—an entity that connects the UI elements to the coding we will do later (refer to (5) in Figure 21-7):

---

1. Open Identity Manager.

2. Click the Management Agents button on the toolbar.

3. In the Management Agents pane, double-click the HR Database MA.

4. In the Management Agent Designer pane on the lefthand side, select Configure Attribute Flow.

5. Ensure "person" is selected in the data source object type drop-down list.

6. Ensure "person" is selected in the metaverse object type drop-down list.

7. In the Mapping Type section of the dialog, select Advanced.

8. In the Flow Direction section of the dialog, select Import.

9. Select FirstName and LastName from the data source attributes text box (to select multiple entries, hold down the Ctrl key).

10. Select cn from the Metaverse attribute list.

11. Click New.

12. In the Advanced Attribute Flow Options dialog, delete the default name, type cn, and then click OK. The flow rule name you defined here will appear in the VB or C# you will write later. A convention among MIIS developers is to use the name of the destination attribute (in this case, cn).

13. Notice that in the Type column in the upper pane, the newly created attribute mapping is detailed as Rules-Extension. A rules extension is a unit of managed .NET code.

14. Select First Name and Last Name from the Data Source attribute mapping list (remember to use the Ctrl key to select multiple attributes).

15. Select uid from the Metaverse attribute mapping list.

16. Click New.

17. In the Advanced Import Attribute Flow Options dialog, type uid into the "Flow rule name" text box and click OK.

18. Notice in the Type column in the upper pane the newly created attribute mapping is detailed as Rules-Extension.

19. Select Configure Extensions in the lefthand pane.

20. Type HR DatabaseExtension into the Rules Extension Name text box.

21. Click OK.

Discussion

In this recipe, an advanced attribute flow rule was defined. The rule extension is implemented in managed .NET code in Recipe 21.7.

There are two additional types of advanced attribute flow. One is where a constant is defined that will always be written to the selected attribute. The second is used if you are flowing a distinguished name (the source attribute must be defined as a *Reference*

DN) and only wish to flow a specific component of the DN and not the entire DN itself into a string attribute in the metaverse. No rules extension code is required for either type of advanced attribute flow. However, if you need to manipulate the attributes being flowed using code, you must define an advanced attribute flow and provide a flow rule name. Even though you may not have created the DLL that will be used at this stage, you still have to put a name in the dialog to exit the MA designer.

See Also

Recipe 21.1, Recipe 21.4 for simple import attribute flow from the HR Database, Recipe 21.5, Recipe 21.7 for creating a rules extension to further extend advanced attribute flow, and Recipe 21.8 to export data to AD

21.7 Implementing an Advanced Attribute Flow Rules Extension—HR Database MA

Problem

You want to perform advanced attribute flow on the HR Database MA.

Solution

You've already defined an advanced attribute flow rule for the MA in the Identity Manager console. You now need to write the code and produce the DLL that implements that flow rule (refer to (5) in Figure 21-7):

1. Open Identity Manager.
2. Click the Management Agents button on the toolbar.
3. Select the HR Database MA in the Management Agents pane.
4. Click Create Extension Project in the Action pane on the far right side.
5. Ensure the dialog box is filled in similar to Figure 21-8 (you can specify your own name and location).

![Create Extension Project dialog box]

Create Extension Project	
Programming language:	Visual Basic
Project type:	Rules Extension
Project name:	RolesMAExtension
Project location:	C:\Documents and Settings\Administrator\My Docu Browse...
☑ Launch in VS.Net IDE	
	OK Cancel Help

Figure 21-8. Create Extension Project dialog

6. Click OK. This will launch Visual Studio.

 This recipe assumes that you have already installed Visual Studio 2005 or better on the machine running ILM. If you are doing your development on another machine, you have two choices. You can map a drive to the ILM server and modify the code through the mapped drive, or you can copy the entire project to your development machine and work on it there. In any case, you will have to be sure to copy the resulting DLL back to the ILM server anytime you make a code change.

7. In the Solution Explorer in the far righthand pane in Visual Studio, double-click the *HR DatabaseExtension.vb* node. This file contains the source code for your rules extension.

8. The main code window should show the automatically generated code (this auto-code generation is provided for VB and C#). The first few lines of code should look like this:

```
Imports Microsoft.MetadirectoryServices
Public Class MAExtensionObject
    Implements IMASynchronization
```

9. Scroll to the code section that looks like this:

```
Public Sub MapAttributesForImport(ByVal FlowRuleName As String, ByVal csentry As
    CSEntry, ByVal mventry As MVEntry) Implements
    IMASynchronization.MapAttributesForImport
        ' TODO: write your import
attribute flow code
        Select Case FlowRuleName
            Case "uid"
                ' TODO: remove the following statement and add your scripted
                 ' import attribute flow here
                Throw New EntryPointNotImplementedException()
```

```
                    Case "cn"
                        ' TODO: remove the following statement and add your scripted
                            ' import
attribute flow here
                        Throw New EntryPointNotImplementedException()

                    Case Else
                        ' TODO: remove the following statement and add your default
                            ' script here
                        Throw New EntryPointNotImplementedException()

                End Select
        End Sub
```

10. Edit this section to make the code look like this (the bold sections are new code that we typed in):

```
Select Case FlowRuleName
Case "uid"
If Not csentry("Last Name").IsPresent Then
    Throw New UnexpectedDataException("No Last Name!")
End If

If Not csentry("First Name").IsPresent Then
    Throw New UnexpectedDataException("No First Name!")
End If

mventry("uid").Value = csentry("First Name").StringValue.Substring(0, 1) + _
csentry("Last Name").Value

Case "cn"
If Not csentry("Last Name").IsPresent Then
    Throw New UnexpectedDataException("No Last Name!")
  End If
  If Not csentry("First Name").IsPresent Then
    Throw New UnexpectedDataException("No First Name!")
  End If
  mventry("cn").Value = csentry("First Name").Value + " " + _
    csentry("Last Name").Value

Case Else
    ' TODO: remove the following statement and add your default script here
    Throw New EntryPointNotImplementedException

End Select
```

11. Go to the Build menu and select Build Solution. Ensure you see a message in the output panel at the bottom of the screen like this:

```
--------------------- Done ---------------------

    Build: 1 succeeded, 0 failed, 0 skipped
```

12. Close Visual Studio.

13. Open Windows Explorer and browse to *C:\Program Files\Microsoft Identity Integration Server\Extensions* (this assumes you installed ILM on the *C:* drive in the default location; if you didn't, substitute the relevant parts of the path), and ensure the DLL is present. In this case, the DLL will be called *HR DatabaseExtension.dll*.

14. To be absolutely sure you have the correct rules extension selected in ILM, open Identity Manager.

15. Click the Management Agents button.

16. In the Management Agent pane, double-click the HR Database MA.

17. In the lefthand pane of the Management Agent Designer, click Configure Extensions.

18. Click the Select button.

19. Select *HR DatabaseExtension.dll* and click OK.

20. Click OK to close Management Agent properties.

21. Close Identity Manager.

Discussion

This code does some fairly simple string manipulation. This chapter doesn't venture into the world of advanced ILM coding, but there are many examples in the Developer Reference off the help menu in Identity Manager.

The ILM development environment is so flexible that human-driven digital identity business processes can be encapsulated in ILM rules. However, there is no workflow engine, which means you may have to call workflow processes on another engine, such as BizTalk.

The next release of Identity Lifecycle Manager (ILM "2") will support full Windows Workflow integration and activity assembly using a provided portal application based on Windows SharePoint Services 3.0. In addition, many of the current use cases for writing advanced attribute flow to do basic string manipulation will be supplanted with a declarative model, and much less coding will be required.

See Also

Recipe 21.1 and Recipe 21.8 for setting constants on certain attributes

21.8 Setting Up Advanced Export Attribute Flow in Active Directory

Problem

Simple attribute-to-attribute mapping is not flexible enough to create the attribute values you want. You want to set constant values on some attributes. In this case, there is a bit mask of great interest—the mask used to set properties for accounts, such as whether the account is disabled.

Solution

This will involve writing some VB or C#, like the script for advanced attribute flow covered in Recipe 21.9, but we must set up flow rule names for the code in this section (refer to (8) in Figure 21-7):

1. Open Identity Manager.
2. Click the Management Agents button on the toolbar.
3. In the Management Agents pane, double-click the ADMA.
4. In the Management Agent Designer pane on the lefthand side, select Configure Attribute Flow.
5. Ensure "user" is selected in the data source object type drop-down list.
6. Ensure "person" is selected in the metaverse object type drop-down list.
7. In the Mapping Type section of the dialog, select Advanced.
8. In the Flow Direction section of the dialog, select Export.
9. Select userAccountControl from the Data Source attributes list.
10. Click New.
11. In the Advanced Attribute Flow Options dialog, select Constant.
12. Type 512 into the Value text box, and then click OK.
13. Notice in the Type column in the upper pane, the newly created attribute mapping is detailed as Constant, with an arrow indicating export attribute flow.
14. Click OK to close the Management Agent Designer.

Discussion

Active Directory requires a minimal set of attributes in order to create normal, usable, enabled accounts. In this recipe we have set the required attributes. We set the *user-AccountControl* flag to *512* (bit 9 set), which indicates that this account is a normal account. In other cases we might use a rules extension and set bit 1 to disable the account, e.g., if there was an employee status field in the HR Database that indicated the employee was inactive.

See Also

Recipe 21.1, Recipe 21.9, and Recipe 21.14 for writing a rules extension to provision user objects to the ADMA from objects in the HR Database MA, and the code examples in the "Simple Account Provisioning" walkthrough (*Scenarios* URL mentioned in Recipe 21.0) that show how to take an existing userAccountControl flag and set the additional bits you require—for example, if the account is already disabled, it will remain disabled

21.9 Configuring a Run Profile to Do an Initial Load of Data from the HR Database MA

Problem

You need to get the data from the HR Database to its connector space.

Solution

Before you can run a management agent, you must create a *run profile* for it (refer to (9) in Figure 21-7, which shows data being loaded from AD to the AD connector space):

1. Open Identity Manager.
2. Click the Management Agents button on the toolbar.
3. In the Management Agents pane, click the HR Database MA.
4. In the Actions pane on the far right side, click Configure Run Profiles.
5. In the Configure Run Profiles for HR Database, click New Profile.
6. In the Name text box, type Full Import (Stage Only), then click Next.
7. Ensure Full Import (Stage Only) is selected in the Type drop-down list, then click Next.
8. Ensure "default" is showing in the Partition drop-down list, then click Finish.
9. Ensure the details in the Step Details field looks like Figure 21-9.

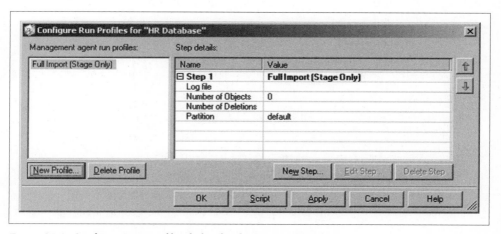

Figure 21-9. Configure Run Profiles dialog for the HR Database MA

10. Click OK to create the run profile.

Discussion

There are three steps required to get data into the HR Database MA connector space:

1. Create the MA.
2. Create a run profile to run the MA.
3. Execute the run profile. In this recipe you have created the run profile.

It is generally a good idea to give the run profiles exactly the same names as the step-type they represent. You will later create scripts that call run profiles. It is possible to give a run profile a name such as "Complete Cycle" and combine many steps in the run profile. However, when calling such entities from scripts, the calling script isn't self-documenting, in that it hides what it is doing. It is also much easier to debug scripts when you know exactly what step is being called. Hence, you have created a run profile called Full Import (Stage Only), which consists of a single step of type Full Import (Stage Only). The one exception to this general rule is discussed in Recipe 21.17.

See Also

Recipe 21.10 for more on how to use the run profile to load data and Recipe 21.17

21.10 Loading Initial HR Database Data into ILM Using a Run Profile

Problem

With the MA and run profile created, you now want to load the data into ILM.

Solution

You need to execute the run profile to load the data. Refer to (1) in Figure 21-7, which shows data being loaded from the HR Database to the HR Database connector space:

1. Open Identity Manager.
2. Click the Management Agents button on the toolbar.
3. In the Management Agents pane, click the HR Database MA.
4. In the Actions pane on the far right side, click Run.
5. In the Run Management Agent dialog, select Full Import (Stage Only) and click OK.
6. You'll have to be quick if there is only a small amount of data in the database. Notice the MA says "Running" in the State column of the Management Agents pane.

7. In the Synchronization Statistics pane in the bottom lefthand corner, statistics showing the number of adds are displayed. If you click the hyperlink, you can navigate the information that was loaded.

> The HR Database you are importing from must have records in it before ILM can import any data.

Discussion

When designing a large system, work with a very small, representative set of data during development (maybe 10 records). This is because you will frequently find errors in your rules, and set about deleting everything in ILM, reconfiguring your rules, and starting again. It is much better to do these initial data loads with 10 or so records rather than 100,000 records, which will take a long time to load. When you are convinced your rules are good, start working with larger datasets.

See Also

Recipe 21.1 and Recipe 21.9 for how this run profile was configured

21.11 Configuring a Run Profile to Load the Container Structure from AD

Problem

Before you can provision and synchronize data in the AD connector space, you need to build the container structure in the connector space to reflect the container structure of Active Directory.

Solution

To do this, you have to create an appropriate run profile for the ADMA and import the AD container structure into the connector space.

> The fact that you have to separately import the container structure from AD into the MA's connector space is not obvious, and is frequently overlooked by even the most experienced ILM developers. If you fail to perform this step, the synchronization process will fail when it tries to provision new objects into the AD connector space.

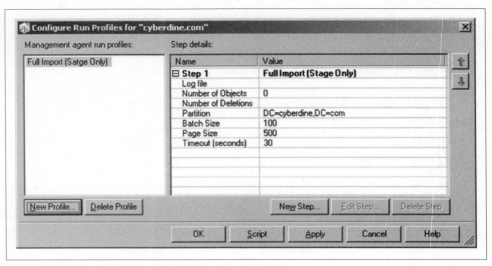

Figure 21-10. Configure Run Profiles dialog for the ADMA

Refer to (9) in Figure 21-7, which shows data being loaded from AD to the AD connector space:

1. Open Identity Manager.
2. Click the Management Agents button on the toolbar
3. In the Management Agents pane, click the ADMA.
4. In the Actions pane on the far right side, click Configure Run Profiles.
5. In the Configure Run Profiles dialog click New Profile.
6. In the Name text box, type Full Import (Stage Only), then click Next.
7. Ensure Full Import (Stage Only) is selected in the Type drop-down list, then click Next.
8. Ensure the correct domain partition is showing in the Partition drop-down list, then click Finish.
9. Ensure the details in the Step Details field looks like Figure 21-10 (note: your partition name may be different).
10. Click OK.

Discussion

There are three steps required to get data into the ADMA connector space:

1. Create the MA.
2. Create the run profile.
3. Execute the run profile. In this recipe you create the run profile.

When you create an ADMA, you specify which partitions (naming contexts) you wish to synchronize. When creating a run profile, you must be careful to select the correct partition (Naming Context in AD terms, but you will usually be after the domain NC) from which to load the container structure.

A common mistake among ILM novices is to get "object does not have a parent" errors when running a synchronization step. This is because the container structure for Active Directory isn't loaded into the ADMA's connector space.

ILM can create missing containers based on rules, but you need to configure and write those rules. That is beyond the scope of this book.

See Also

Recipe 21.1, Recipe 21.12 for more on how to use the run profile that was configured in this recipe, and the TechNet ILM Forum for many discussion threads on programming techniques for the creation of missing containers (search for "OU creation" after you have joined the forum at *http://forums.microsoft.com/TechNet/ShowForum.aspx ?ForumID=540&SiteID=17*)

21.12 Loading the Initial AD Container Structure into ILM Using a Run Profile

Problem

With the ADMA and run profile created, you need to get the data into ILM.

Solution

You now need to run the ADMA run profile to import the AD container structure (refer to (9) in Figure 21-7, which shows the data being loaded from AD into the AD connector space):

1. Open Identity Manager.
2. Click the Management Agents button on the toolbar.
3. In the Management Agents pane, click the ADMA.
4. In the Actions pane on the far right side, click Run.
5. In the Run Management Agent dialog, select Full Import (Stage Only) and click OK.
6. You'll have to be quick if there is only a small amount of data in AD. Notice the MA briefly says "Running" in the State column of the Management Agents pane.
7. Notice in the Synchronization Statistics pane in the bottom lefthand corner, where statistics showing the number of adds are displayed. If you click the hyperlink, you can navigate the information that was loaded.

Discussion

The first time you load the container structure into ILM, you need to use a full import step. Once the container structure is loaded, subsequent imports can use delta import steps, which in normal daily operations will be considerably faster to execute, and will consume less resources on the ILM server, the AD domain controller, and the network.

See Also

Recipe 21.1 and Recipe 21.11 for more on how to configure the run profile that was used in this recipe

21.13 Setting Up the HR Database MA to Project Objects to the Metaverse

Problem

The objects in the HR Database connector space now need to be projected into the metaverse. There are three steps:

1. Configuring the MA for projection.
2. Creating a synchronization run profile.
3. Executing the synchronization run profile.

Solution

Refer to (3) in Figure 21-7, which shows objects being provisioned from the HR Database MA's connector space to the metaverse:

1. Open Identity Manager.
2. Click the Management Agents button on the toolbar.
3. In the Management Agents pane, double-click the HR Database MA.
4. In the Management Agent Designer pane on the lefthand side, select Configure Join and Projection Rules.
5. Click the New Projection Rule... button.
6. In the Projection dialog, ensure Declared is selected and that the drop-down list shows "person," and then click OK.
7. Notice in the "Join and Projection Rules for person" frame, the columns are detailed thus:
   - Mapping Group: 1
   - Action: Project
   - Metaverse Object Type: person

---

8. Click OK.

Discussion

The synchronization process *projects* (or creates) metaverse objects that are *joined* to objects in the HR Database MA connector space. When projected, ILM can *provision* new objects to the ADMA's connector space. Hence, in our demonstration it is *projection* that initiates *provisioning*; however, it is perfectly legal for changes in attribute states to trigger provisioning if you have written your provisioning extensions to observe such workflows. The most common example would be looking for a change in an HR employee status attribute to trigger creation of a new account in AD. While novices often use the terms *project* and *provision* interchangeably, they mean quite different things.

From the ILM perspective, *provision* means "to create a new CS object in a CS where there was no object previously." From an AD administrator's perspective, provision generally means creation of an AD account complete with all of the standard accoutrements (home directory, terminal server profile, and so on) so it is important to be clear, depending on your audience.

Table 21-1 clarifies this and introduces some new terminology: `csentry` for connector space objects and `mventry` for metaverse objects.

Table 21-1. Synchronization process

HR Database con	Action	Metaverse	Action	AD connector space
csentry objects →	Project to metaverse →	mventry objects →	Provision to connector space →	csentry objects

See Also

Recipe 21.1 and Recipe 21.14 for more on provisioning

21.14 Writing a Rules Extension to Provision User Objects

Problem

This recipe specifically covers writing a rules extension to provision user objects to the ADMA from Objects in the HR Database MA. You want ILM to provision objects to the ADMA's connector space based on objects in the HR Database MA.

Solution

There are three steps to *provisioning*:

1. Write a rules extension.

2. Configure a run profile.

3. Execute the run profile.

In this recipe, you will write a Provisioning-Rules-Extension. ILM will help you with
the initial project creation. Refer to (6) in Figure 21-7, which shows objects being provisioned from the metaverse to the AD connector space:

1. Open Identity Manager.

2. From the menu select Tools→Options.

3. In the Options dialog click the Create Rules Extension Project button.

4. Ensure the Create Extension Project dialog looks like Figure 21-11.

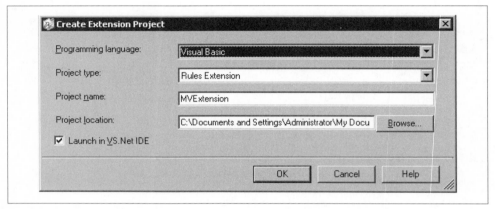

Figure 21-11. Dialog for creating the metaverse Provisioning-Rules-Extension

5. Click OK.

6. In Visual Studio, double-click *MVExtension* in the Solution Explorer.

7. The first few lines of the code pane should look like this:

```
Imports Microsoft.MetadirectoryServices

Public Class MVExtensionObject
    Implements IMVSynchronization
```

8. Navigate to the section that looks like this:

```
Public Sub Provision(ByVal mventry As MVEntry) Implements
IMVSynchronization.Provision
        ' TODO: Remove this throw statement if you implement this method
        Throw New EntryPointNotImplementedException()
    End Sub
```

9. Modify it to contain the following code:

```
Public Sub Provision(ByVal mventry As MVEntry) Implements _
IMVSynchronization.Provision
```

```
Dim container As String
Dim rdn As String
Dim ADMA As ConnectedMA
Dim numConnectors As Integer

Dim myConnector As CSEntry
Dim csentry As CSEntry
Dim dn As ReferenceValue

' Ensure that the cn attribute is present.
If Not mventry("cn").IsPresent Then
    Throw New UnexpectedDataException("cn attribute is not present.")
End If
' Calculate the container and RDN.
container = "CN=users,DC=rallencorp,DC=com"
rdn = "CN=" & mventry("cn").Value

ADMA = mventry.ConnectedMAs("rallencorp.com")
dn = ADMA.EscapeDNComponent(rdn).Concat(container)

numConnectors = ADMA.Connectors.Count

' create a new connector.
If numConnectors = 0 Then
    csentry = ADMA.Connectors.StartNewConnector("user")
    csentry.DN = dn
    csentry("unicodePwd").Value = "Password1"
    csentry.CommitNewConnector()

ElseIf numConnectors = 1 Then
    ' If the connector has a different DN rename it.
    myConnector = ADMA.Connectors.ByIndex(0)
    myConnector.DN = dn
Else
    Throw New UnexpectedDataException("Error: There are" + _
    numConnectors.ToString + " connectors")
End If
    End Sub
```

10. Notice the highlighted entries "CN=users,DC=rallencorp,DC=com". You will need to enter your own domain and container information here.

11. Notice the highlighted entry mventry.ConnectedMAs("rallencorp.com"). You will need to modify this to your own ADMA name.

12. From the file menu select Build→Build Solution.

13. Open Identity Manager.

14. From the menu select Tools→Options.

15. In the Options dialog, click Browse.

16. Select *MVExtension.dll*, and click OK to close the Options dialog.

Discussion

Because you can use any .NET programming language, ILM is very flexible in a multiteam environment. Like with many modern systems, it is not great programming skills that help you build good rules extensions with ILM: it is experience and familiarity with the object model. It is well worth getting to know the ILM object model. Many novices spend hours or days coding a function only to find there is already a method on the object that does the thing they have spent all their time on.

If you are working on distributing the workload for provisioning to multiple systems (e.g., each MA is assigned to a developer or team), consider adopting the MV Router model whereby each MA is compartmentalized into its own project DLL and controlled by a single "router" DLL. In this manner, you reduce the amount of testing involved whenever code for a single MA is changed since you are not affecting code in other projects. For more information, refer to the ILM 2007 Technical Reference "Example: Creating a Rules Extension from Multiple Sources, located at *http://msdn2.microsoft .com/en-us/library/ms696018.aspx*.

See Also

Recipe 21.1, Recipe 21.4 for a description of how the code in this recipe is triggered, and Recipe 21.13 for setting up the HR Database MA to project objects to the metaverse (remember, in this demonstration it is *projection* that triggers *provisioning*)

21.15 Creating a Run Profile for Provisioning

Problem

You need to synchronize data using the management agent to provision new accounts in the AD connector space. Before you can run the MA, you have to create a run profile that will synchronize the MA's connector space with the metaverse.

Solution

You now need to create a provisioning run profile for the HR Database MA to synchronize user objects from it to the ADMA's connector space. The run profile step is of type *synchronization*:

1. Open Identity Manager.
2. Click the Management Agents button on the toolbar.
3. In the Management Agents pane, click the HR Database MA.
4. In the Actions pane on the far right side, click Configure Run Profiles.
5. In the Configure Run Profiles dialog, click New Profile.
6. In the Name text box, type Full Synchronization, then click Next.

7. Ensure Full Synchronization is selected in the Type drop-down list, then click Next.

8. Ensure "default" is showing in the Partition drop-down list, then click Finish.

9. Ensure the details in the Step Details field looks like Figure 21-12.

10. Notice in the Management Agent run profiles list, the Full Import (Stage Only) profile you created earlier is still there.

11. Click OK.

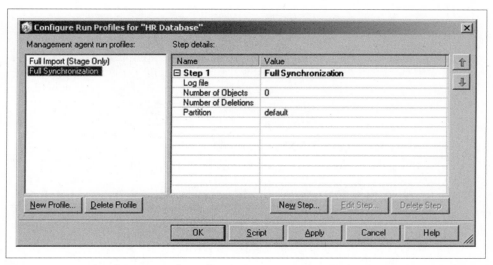

Figure 21-12. Dialog showing a Full Synchronization run profile added to the HR Database MA

Discussion

There are two types of synchronization run profiles: full and delta. A *full synchronization* will process every object in the connector space. This is obviously necessary when it is the very first synchronization on the data. But in normal daily operations, you only want to perform *delta synchronization* steps because they only process objects that have changed since the last synchronization.

Full synchronization is also used when you have made a change to management agent configuration, e.g., you have added a new attribute flow. Usually you will want to run the reconfigured MA against all of the objects in the connector space. A delta synchronization would only apply the rule to objects that had changed since the last synchronization.

See Also

Recipe 21.13 for setting up the HR Database MA to project objects to the metaverse, Recipe 21.14 for writing a rules extension to provision user objects to the ADMA from objects in the HR Database MA, and Recipe 21.16 for executing the run profile created in this recipe

21.16 Executing the Provisioning Rule

Problem

You need to *provision* new objects to the AD connector space.

Solution

You need to run the provisioning run profile. The provisioning run profile triggers projection ((3) in Figure 21-7). The arrival of new objects in the metaverse ((4) in Figure 21-7) in turn triggers provisioning ((6) in Figure 21-7) and creates new objects ((7) in Figure 21-7) in the AD connector space. Follow these steps:

1. Open Identity Manager.
2. Click the Management Agents button on the toolbar.
3. In the Management Agents pane, click the HR Database MA.
4. In the Actions pane on the far right side, click Run.
5. In the Run Management Agent dialog, select Full Synchronization, and click OK.
6. Notice the MA says "Running" in the State column of the Management Agents pane, and then says "Idle."
7. Notice in the Synchronization Statistics pane in the bottom lefthand corner, statistics showing the number of projections and provisioned entries are displayed. If you click one of the hyperlinks, you can navigate the information that was projected and provisioned.

Discussion

Inbound attribute flow is only processed on the MA that the run profile is executed against. That includes joins and projections, and since we have to have an MV object from which to provision, we will need to run a synchronization run profile against the HR MA in order to trigger provisioning to create the objects in the ADMA. If you were to run a synchronization run profile against the ADMA at this stage, nothing would be provisioned.

See Also

Recipe 21.1, Recipe 21.13 for setting up the HR Database MA to project objects to the metaverse, Recipe 21.14 for writing a rules extension to provision user objects to the ADMA from objects in the HR Database MA, and Recipe 21.15 for creating the run profile that was executed in this recipe

---

21.17 Creating a Run Profile to Export Objects from the ADMA to Active Directory

Problem

You want to create the new accounts in Active Directory.

Solution

There are two steps to get the data from an MA to a connected system: creating an *export* run profile and executing the profile. This is the first step (the second step is in Recipe 21.18):

1. Open Identity Manager.
2. Click the Management Agents button on the toolbar.
3. In the Management Agents pane, click the ADMA.
4. In the Actions pane on the far right side, click Configure Run Profiles.
5. In the "Configure Run Profiles for..." pane, click New Profile.
6. In the Name text box, type Export, then click Next.
7. Ensure Export is selected in the Type drop-down list, then click Next.
8. Ensure the correct domain partition is showing in the Partition drop-down list, then click Finish.
9. Click New Step.
10. In the Configure Step dialog, ensure Delta Import (Stage Only) is selected in the Type drop-down list, then click Next.
11. Ensure the correct domain is selected in the Partition drop-down list, then click Finish.
12. Ensure the details in the Step Details field look like Figure 21-13 (note: your partition name may be different).
13. Click OK.

Discussion

It was mentioned earlier that it is a good idea to name the run profiles you create exactly the same as the run profile steps; i.e., a run profile of type Full Import (Stage Only) is named Full Import (Stage Only). The one exception to this general rule applies to export run profiles. When an export is completed, the only way the MA can truly know the data was successfully written to the target data store is to reimport the changes and compare them with what it believes was written out. This is known as a *confirming import*. In AD, for example, if we programmatically create a user account without a password, AD will automatically disable the user account by setting a flag in the

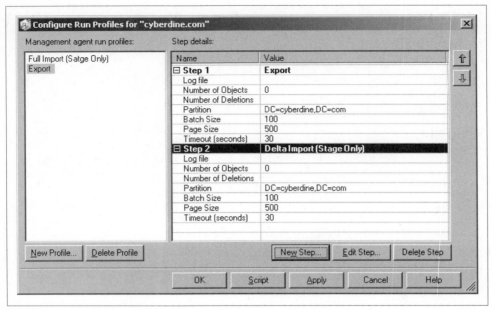

Figure 21-13. ADMA Export run profile showing an Export step followed by a Delta Import (Stage Only) step

`userAccountControl` attribute. For ILM to maintain knowledge of this state, the confirming import brings this knowledge back into ILM. Therefore, exports need to include a confirming import stage. If the system we are exporting to supports some form of change logging (as AD does through USNs), then the type of confirming import can be a delta import (stage only). If the system doesn't expose any form of change logging (e.g., Novell eDirectory and NT4), a full import (stage only) step will be necessary.

ILM's sync engine performs delta imports using the Active Directory DirSync control. You need to assign the "Replicate Directory Changes" right to the user associated with the ADMA for delta imports to work (see MS KB 303972 for instructions).

See Also

Recipe 21.18 for more on how to use this run profile to export objects to AD, and MS KB 303972 (How to Grant the "Replicating Directory Changes" Permission for the Microsoft Metadirectory Services ADMA Service Account)

21.18 Exporting Objects to AD Using an Export Run Profile

Problem

You need to execute the export run profile.

Solution

The second step is executing the export run profile to get the data into AD (the first step is in Recipe 21.17). Refer to (9) in Figure 21-7, which shows the objects being exported to AD; (10) in the same figure shows the objects created in AD. Follow these steps:

1. Open Identity Manager.
2. Click the Management Agents button on the toolbar.
3. In the Management Agents pane, click the ADMA.
4. In the Actions pane on the far right side, click Run.
5. In the Run Management Agent dialog, select Export and click OK.
6. You'll have to be quick if there is only a small amount of data in the ADMA. Notice the MA says "Running" in the State column of the Management Agents pane.
7. Notice in the Synchronization Statistics pane in the bottom lefthand corner, statistics showing the number of adds are displayed. If you click a hyperlink, you can navigate the information that was written to AD.
8. Open Active Directory Users and Computers.
9. Navigate to the Users container.
10. Ensure the user objects have been created.

Discussion

User accounts in Active Directory may be flagged as disabled even though you think they should be active. Assuming you set the `userAccountControl` attribute correctly, the usual reason for this is that some other attribute has not been set correctly and Active Directory has disabled the account. For example, if you do not set a password on an account, or the password you set does not meet the domain password requirements, Active Directory will disable the account.

 If you do not set a password on a user object using the Active Directory Users and Computers MMC snap-in, you will receive a warning. If you do it programmatically, as ILM does, the account will be disabled.

By performing all the previous recipes successfully, you have provisioned user accounts from employee records in the HR Database to AD.

See Also

Recipe 21.1 and Recipe 21.17 for how to configure the run profile that was used in this recipe

21.19 Testing Provisioning and Deprovisioning of User Accounts in AD

Problem

You want to test that new and deleted employee records in the HR Database propagate correctly to Active Directory.

Solution

You will add a new employee record and delete an existing employee record from the HR Database. You will then execute a series of run profiles that will perform the necessary operations:

1. Add and delete records from the HR Database (using SQL Server Management Studio).

   a. Open SQL Server Management Studio.

   b. When prompted with the Connect to Server dialog, ensure that Database Engine is selected for Server type and then enter the name of the SQL Server your ILM database resides on. Then click the Connect button.

   c. In the Object Explorer pane, expand the Databases folder by clicking the plus sign.

   d. Navigate down to the HR database and expand the entry by clicking the plus sign.

   e. Expand the Tables folder by clicking the plus sign and then select the Employees table in Object Explorer.

   f. Right-click the Employees table and select Open Table.

   g. Add a new row (you can type directly into the table at the marker in the extreme lefthand edge of the column labeled *). Make sure you create a unique number in the Badge Number column and when you have completed the data for the column, ensure that you select another row to save the new row into the table.

   h. Delete a row by clicking one of the gray unlabeled buttons on the extreme lefthand edge of the table contents to select the row, and then press the Delete key. Note the name of the employee you deleted.

2. Add and delete records from the HR Database.

   a. Open SQL Server Enterprise Manager.

   b. In the lefthand pane, drill down in to *Console Root\Microsoft SQL Servers\SQL Server\SQL Server Group\(local)(Windows NT)\Databases\HR\Tables*.

The same operation can be accomplished with SQL Server 2005 Server Management Studio by expanding the *Root Node* *Databases\HR\Tables*.

c. Right-click the Employees table in the righthand pane, and select Open Table→Return all rows.

d. Add a new row (you can type directly in to the table at the marker in the extreme lefthand column labeled *). Make sure you create a unique number in the Badge Number column.

e. Delete a row by clicking one of the gray unlabeled buttons on the extreme lefthand edge of the table contents to select the row, and then press the Delete key. Note the name of the employee you deleted.

3. Execute the following run profiles in this order:

a. HR Database MA's Full Import (Stage Only) run profile (for details on how to execute this run profile, see Recipe 21.10)

b. The HR Database's Full Synchronization run profile (see Recipe 21.16 on executing the provisioning run profile)

c. AD's Export run profile (see Recipe 21.18 on exporting objects using an export run profile)

4. To check if the add and remove were successful, open Active Directory Users and Computers.

5. Navigate to the Users container.

6. Ensure the user objects you modified in the HR Database have been created and deleted correctly.

Discussion

As the HR Database is modified, ILM makes corresponding modifications to Active Directory. The order in which the MAs are run is important: import, synchronization, export. Inbound synchronization is executed only on the MA that imported data, while export attribute flows are executed on all other connectors.

Delta imports are lightweight operations because ILM requests only changes since the last time it connected to the data source (when the MA supports it). Delta synchronization only processes changed objects. Export run profiles only export changes.

Performing full imports and full synchronizations places a significant processing requirement on ILM and its connected systems. If the system you are connecting to exposes a delta mechanism, you should use delta import and delta synchronization steps in normal daily operations. Database MAs connect to a delta-view or delta-table on the database server, which you will need to create before you can perform delta imports.

See Also

Recipes 21.10, 21.16, 21.18, and the Design and Planning Collection (*http://www.microsoft.com/downloads/details.aspx?familyid=DADC5021-222B-4AF7-8C58-2227C358756F&displaylang=en*)

21.20 Creating a Run Profile Script

Problem

It is impractical to continually use the UI every time you wish to execute a run profile. You want to automate the process by calling ILM run profiles to perform the required actions.

Solution

You need to create a run profile script:

1. Open Identity Manager.
2. Click the Management Agents button on the toolbar.
3. In the Management Agents pane, click the HR Database MA.
4. In the Actions pane on the far right side, click Configure Run Profiles.
5. In the Configure Run Profiles dialog, select the Export run profile.
6. Click the Script button.
7. In the "File name" text box, type HR Database MA Export.
8. In the "Save as type" text box, select VB Script.
9. Click the Save button.
10. Repeat Steps 3–9 for the other run profiles in the HR Database MA and the ADMA. Follow the same file-naming convention.

Discussion

The scripts free you from the UI and can also form the building blocks of an ILM implementation that runs unattended. You have several options, including:

1. Submit the scripts to the Windows Task Scheduler Service to run on a specified daily schedule. To do this, open the Task Scheduler, double-click Add Scheduled Task, and follow the steps in the wizard.
2. Create a Windows service that calls the scripts according to your own criteria, perhaps by submitting them to the task scheduler using its APIs.
3. Use the SQL Server Agent process to invoke run profiles on the ILM server. This approach is especially useful if you are using a SQL Server cluster and need your profiles to follow the active node in case of a failure condition.

4. If you already have a script execution environment, incorporate the new scripts.

See Also

Recipe 21.21 to create a controlling script, the MSDN walkthrough about creating a Windows Service Application (*http://msdn.microsoft.com/library/en-us/vbcon/html/ vbwlkwalkthroughcreatingwindowsserviceapplication.asp*), and the Task Scheduler API reference (*http://msdn.microsoft.com/library/en-us/taskschd/taskschd/task_scheduler _reference.asp*)

21.21 Creating a Controlling Script

Problem

You want a self-contained script that controls an entire sequence of operations, e.g., import the HR Database, synchronize, and then export to AD.

Solution

1. Open Notepad.

2. Type this script (or copy and paste the contents of the *GroupPopulatorSync.cmd* file from the MIIS Scenarios, referenced in the section called "See Also"):

```
@echo off
rem
rem Copyright (c) Microsoft Corporation. All rights reserved.
rem

setlocal
set zworkdir=%~dp0
pushd %zworkdir%

set madata="C:\Program Files\Microsoft Identity Integration Server\MaData"

rem Full Import of HR Dzatabase Employee Records
rem ------------------------------------------
cscript runMA.vbs /m:"HR Database" /p:"Full Import (Stage Only)"
if {%errorlevel%} NEQ {0} (echo Error[%errorlevel%]: command file failed) _
& (goto exit_script)

rem Full Sync of HR Database Employee Records
rem ----------------------------------------
cscript runMA.vbs /m:"HR Database" /p:"Full Sync"
if {%errorlevel%} NEQ {0} (echo Error[%errorlevel%]: command file failed) _
& (goto exit_script)

rem Export users in to AD
rem --------------------
cscript runMA.vbs /m:"rallencorp.com" /p:"Export"
if {%errorlevel%} NEQ {0} (echo Error[%errorlevel%]: command file failed) _
```

```
& (goto exit_script)

:exit_script
popd
endlocal
```

3. In this case, HR Database is the name of the MA and Full Import (Stage Only) is the name of the run profile.

4. It is the same for the highlighted entries on the other two lines.

5. Save the file with a *.cmd* file extension.

6. Close Notepad.

7. Open Notepad.

8. Type the following script (or copy and paste the contents of the *RunMA.vbs* file in the ILM scenarios, referenced in the section called "See Also"):

```
option explicit
on error resume next


'=-=-=-=-=-=-=-=-=-=-=-=-=-=-=-=-=-=-=-=-=-=-=-=-=-=-=-=-=-=-=-=-=-=-=
'SCRIPT:         runMA.vbs
'DATE:           2003-02-05
'=-=-=-=-=-=-=-=-=-=-=-=-=-=-=-=-=-=-=-=-=-=-=-=-=-=-=-=-=-=-=-=-=-=-=
'= Copyright (C) 2003 Microsoft Corporation. All rights reserved.
'=
'*************************************************************************
'* Function: DisplayUsage
'*
'* Purpose:  Displays the usage of the script and exits the script
'*
'*************************************************************************
Sub DisplayUsage()
        WScript.Echo ""
        WScript.Echo "Usage: runMa </m:ma-name> </p:profile-name>"

        WScript.Echo "                        [/s:mms-server-name]"
        WScript.Echo "                        [/u:user-name]"
        WScript.Echo "                        [/a:password]"
        WScript.Echo "                        [/v] Switch on Verbose mode"
        WScript.Echo "                        [/?] Show the Usage of the script"
        WScript.Echo ""
        WScript.Echo "Example 1: runMa /m:adma1 /p:fullimport"
        WScript.Echo "Example 2: runMa /m:adma1 /p:fullimport /u:domain\user
/a:mysecret /v"
            WScript.Quit (-1)
End Sub


'*************************************************************************
' Script Main Execution Starts Here
'*************************************************************************
'--Used Variables------------------------
dim s
dim runResult
```

```
dim rescode
dim managementagentName
dim profile
dim verbosemode
dim wmiLocator
dim wmiService
dim managementagent
dim server
dim username
dim password
'----------------------------------------

rescode = ParamExists("/?")
if rescode = true then call DisplayUsage
verbosemode = ParamExists("/v")

managementagentName = ParamValue("/m")
if managementagentName = "" then call DisplayUsage

profile = ParamValue("/p")
if profile = "" then call DisplayUsage

if verbosemode then wscript.echo "%Info: Management Agent and Profile is _
<"& managementagentName &":"& profile &">"
if verbosemode then wscript.Echo "%Info: Getting WMI Locator object"

set wmiLocator = CreateObject("WbemScripting.SWbemLocator")
if err.number <> 0 then
        wscript.echo "%Error: Cannot get WMI Locator object"
        wscript.quit(-1)
end if

server = ParamValue("/s")
password = ParamValue("/a")
username = ParamValue("/u")

if server = "" then server = "." ' connect to WMI on local machine

if verbosemode then

        wscript.Echo "%Info: Connecting to MMS WMI Service on <" & server &">"
        if username <> "" then wscript.Echo _
        "%Info: Accessing MMS WMI Service as <"& username &">"
end if

if username = "" then
        set wmiService = wmiLocator.ConnectServer _
        (server, "root/MicrosoftIdentityIntegrationServer")
else
        set wmiService = wmiLocator.ConnectServer_
        (server, "root/MicrosoftIdentityIntegrationServer", username, password)
end if

if err.number <> 0 then
        wscript.echo "%Error: Cannot connect to MMS WMI Service <" _
```

```
        & err.Description & ">"
        wscript.quit(-1)
end if

if verbosemode then wscript.Echo "%Info: Getting MMS Management Agent via WMI"

Set managementagent = wmiService.Get( "
MIIS_ManagementAgent.Name='" & _
managementagentName & "'")
if err.number <> 0 then
        wscript.echo _
        "%Error: Cannot get Management Agent with specified WMI Service <" & _
        err.Description & ">"
        wscript.quit(-1)
end if

wscript.echo "%Info: Starting Management Agent with Profile <"& _
managementagent.name &":"& profile &">"
runResult = managementagent.Execute(profile)
if err.number <> 0 then
        wscript.Echo "%Error: Running MA <"& err.Description & _
        ">. Make sure the correct profile name is specified."
        wscript.quit(-1)
end if

wscript.Echo "%Info: Finish Running Management Agent"
wscript.Echo "%Result: <" & CStr(runResult) & ">"
wscript.quit(0)

'*****************************************************************************
'* Function: ParamValue
'*
'* Purpose: Parses the command line for an argument and
'*          returns the value of the argument to the caller
'*          Argument and value must be seperated by a colon
'*
'* Arguments:

'* [in]        parametername        name of the parameter
'*
'* Returns:
'*          STRING      Parameter found in commandline
'*          ""          Parameter NOT found in commandline
'*
'*****************************************************************************
Function ParamValue(ParameterName)

        Dim i                      '* Counter
        Dim Arguments              '* Arguments from the command-line command
        Dim NumberofArguments      '* Number of arguments from the command-line
        Dim ArgumentArray          '* Array to store arguments from command-line
        Dim TemporaryString        '* Utility string

        '* Initialize Return Value to e the Empty String
        ParamValue = ""
```

```
        '* If no ParameterName is passed into the function exit
        if ParameterName = "" then exit function

        '* Check if Parameter is in the Arguments and return the value

    Set Arguments = WScript.Arguments
        NumberofArguments = Arguments.Count - 1

        For i=0 to NumberofArguments
                TemporaryString = Arguments(i)
                ArgumentArray = Split(TemporaryString,":",-1,vbTextCompare)

                If ArgumentArray(0) = ParameterName Then
                    ParamValue = ArgumentArray(1)
                    exit function
                End If
        Next
end Function

'*****************************************************************************
'* Function: ParamExists
'*
'* Purpose:  Parses the command line for an argument and
'*           returns the true if argument is present
'*
'* Arguments:
'* [in]      parametername      name of the paramenter
'*
'* Returns:
'*           true       Parameter found in commandline
'*           false      Parameter NOT found in commandline
'*
'*****************************************************************************

Function ParamExists(ParameterName)

        Dim i                   '* Counter

        Dim Arguments           '* Arguments from the command-line command
        Dim NumberofArguments   '* Number of arguments from the command-line
        Dim ArgumentArray       '* Array to store arguments from command-line
        Dim TemporaryString     '* Utility string

        '* Initialize Return Value to e the Empty String
        ParamExists = false

        '* If no ParameterName is passed into the function exit
        if ParameterName = "" then exit function

        '* Check if Parameter is in the Arguments and return the value
        Set Arguments = WScript.Arguments
        NumberofArguments = Arguments.Count - 1

        For i=0 to NumberofArguments
```

```
                    TemporaryString = Arguments(i)
                    If TemporaryString = ParameterName Then
                           ParamExists = true
                           exit function
                    End If
             Next
      end Function
```

9. Save the file in the same folder as the previous script we created and name it *runMA.vbs*.

10. Close Notepad.

Discussion

A script to control these operations, known as a *controlling script*, is required. You could simply create a script that called each of your other scripts in turn, but managing large numbers of scripts as the solution gets more complex becomes a problem. Before you start this recipe, you may want to make sure you have the *GroupPopulatorSync.cmd* and *RunMA.vbs* files available. Refer to the "See Also" section for the URLs.

Using the *RunMA.vbs* script inside of a batch file to create a wrapper around your run profile execution is a common way to control when profiles get called. In a majority of solutions, you will find yourself needing to halt the processing of one run profile should a preceding run profile end in an error condition. By using this process, you ensure that any `errorlevel` other than 0 is an error, and you can either choose to halt processing altogether or branch accordingly.

See Also

In Developer Help, navigate to *Microsoft Identity Lifecycle Manager 2007 Developer Reference/WMI Provider/Using the WMI Provider/Creating Scripts*; the *runMA.vbs* and *GroupPopulatorSync.cmd* script files can be obtained from the Group Management folder in the ILM scenarios: *http://www.microsoft.com/downloads/details.aspx?Family ID=15032653-d78e-4d9d-9e48-6cf0ae0c369c&DisplayLang=en*

21.22 Enabling Directory Synchronization from AD to the HR Database

Problem

You want AD to become the authoritative source for the `telephoneNumber` attribute of Active Directory users.

Solution

You need to configure both the import attribute flow from the ADMA connector space to the metaverse, as well as the export attribute flow from the metaverse to the HR Database MA connector space (refer to (5) and (8) in Figure 21-7, which show where the rules will be configured):

1. Open Identity Manager.
2. Click the Management Agents button on the toolbar.
3. In the Management Agents pane, double-click the ADMA.
4. In the Management Agent Designer pane on the lefthand side, highlight Select Attributes.
5. In the Attributes pane on the right side, select "telephoneNumber."
6. In the Management Agent Designer pane on the lefthand side, highlight Configure Attribute Flow.
7. In the Mapping Type section of the dialog, select Direct.
8. In the Flow Direction section of the dialog, select Import.
9. Ensure "user" is selected in the data source object type drop-down list.
10. Ensure "person" is selected in the metaverse object type drop-down list.
11. In the data source object type drop-down list, select "telephoneNumber."
12. In the metaverse object type drop-down list, select "telephoneNumber."
13. Click New.
14. Notice that in the Attribute Flow pane, the arrow for this mapping indicates an import attribute flow. Click OK.
15. In the Management Agents pane, double-click the HR Database MA.
16. In the Management Agent Designer pane on the lefthand side, highlight Configure Attribute Flow.
17. In the Mapping Type section of the dialog, select Direct.
18. In the Flow Direction section of the dialog, select Export.
19. Ensure "person" is selected in the data source object type drop-down list.
20. Ensure "person" is selected in the metaverse object type drop-down list.
21. In the data source object type drop-down list, select "telephoneNumber."
22. In the metaverse object type drop-down list, select "telephoneNumber."
23. Click New.
24. Notice in the Attribute Flow pane, the arrow for this mapping indicates an export attribute flow. Click OK.

Discussion

You configured import attribute flow (IAF) from the ADMA to the metaverse and export attribute flow (EAF) to the HR Database MA. Notice these flows only dealt with attribute data. The object-level operations of projection and provisioning were not required because the objects already exist.

To put the new configuration to work, you will need to configure run profiles to import, synchronize, and export the data. These steps are covered in Recipe 21.23.

See Also

Recipes 21.1, 21.23, and MIIS 2003 Design Concepts for Correlating Digital Identities, which is found in the MIIS 2003 Design Concepts download documents (*http://www .microsoft.com/downloads/details.aspx?familyid=40A52201-A297-4C35-82E9 -F0B4CA05DAEB&displaylang=en*)

21.23 Configuring a Run Profile to Load the telephoneNumber from AD

Problem

You need to get the AD `telephoneNumber` attribute into ILM and synchronize it.

Solution

Configure a run profile that combines import and synchronization as demonstrated in this recipe, then execute it (see Recipe 21.24):

1. Open Identity Manager.
2. Click the Management Agents button on the toolbar.
3. In the Management Agents pane, click the ADMA.
4. In the Actions pane on the far right side, click Configure Run Profiles.
5. In the Configure Run Profiles for "rallencorp.com" (the name in quotes will reflect the name you chose when creating the ADMA), click New Profile.
6. In the Name text box, type Delta Import and Delta Synchronization, then click Next.
7. Ensure Delta Import and Delta Synchronization is selected in the Type drop-down list and then click Next.
8. Ensure the correct domain partition is showing in the Partition drop-down list, and then click Finish.

9. Ensure the details in the Step Details field look like Figure 21-14 (note: your partition name may be different and the assumption is that you have completed the previous recipes).

10. Click OK.

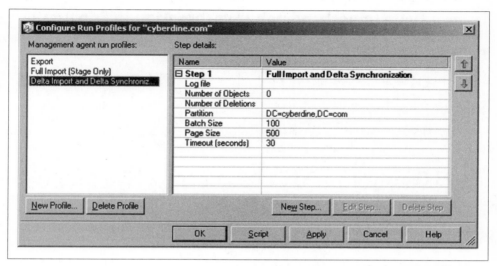

Figure 21-14. Dialog showing Delta Import and Delta Synchronization run profile added to the existing ADMA run profiles

Discussion

Because a previous import step was completed in an earlier recipe, you can use the combined Delta Import and Delta Synchronization step so that ILM imports and synchronizes changes that have occurred in AD since the last time it connected. You can use this run profile from now on since it keeps track of changes internally using the DirSync control.

The Delta Import (Stage Only) step in the AD Export run profile (the confirming import from Recipe 21.17) also imports changes, which suggests you could simply configure a delta synchronization run profile to process those changes in this recipe. Such an approach will work. The decision about which approach to use will depend on the service-level agreements you make. If it is two hours since the last AD import, your service-level agreement might force you to import and synchronize the changes that have occurred over the last two hours and feed them to the HR Database; however, you may only need to export to AD every four hours. If you only rely on the changes detected in the confirming import step, you will only be able to update the HR Database with changes every four hours.

See Also

Recipe 21.17 and Recipe 21.24 for how to use the run profile configured in this recipe

21.24 Loading telephoneNumber Changes from AD into ILM Using a Delta Import and Delta Synchronization Run Profile

Problem

You need to pull the data from AD into ILM.

Solution

With the MA and run profile created, you can now load `telephoneNumber` attribute data into ILM by executing the run profile.

In Recipe 21.1, (11) in Figure 21-7 shows the `telephoneNumber` data being loaded into the AD connector space. The synchronization process then flows the data to the metaverse ((6) in Figure 21-7) and from there to the AD connector space ((3) in Figure 21-7).

1. Open Active Directory Users and Computers.
2. Navigate to a user in the container you are managing with ILM.
3. Double-click the user object.
4. Ensure the General tab is selected and then type a telephone number into the Telephone Number text box and click OK.
5. Open Identity Manager.
6. Click the Management Agents button on the toolbar.
7. In the Management Agents pane, click the ADMA.
8. In the Actions pane on the far right side, click Run.
9. In the Run Management Agent dialog, select Delta Import and Delta Synchronization and click OK.
10. Because you have changed the rules but not yet run a full synchronization on all the existing objects, a Run Step Warning dialog appears, as shown in Figure 21-15. Click No.
11. Notice the MA briefly says "Running" in the State column of the Management Agents pane.

Notice the Synchronization Statistics pane in the bottom lefthand corner displays statistics showing the number of updates and connectors with flow updates. If you click one of the hyperlinks, you can navigate the information that was loaded.

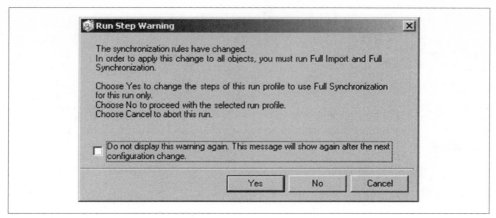

Figure 21-15. Run Step Warning dialog box

Discussion

The Run Step Warning dialog will pop up to annoy you anytime you change any of the ILM rules or configuration settings. Even changing (adding, updating, or deleting) files in the *Extensions* directory will cause this warning to pop up on all run profile executions until every MA undergoes a full synchronization. This is done to force you into reconciling the state of every connector whenever there is a policy change. In this manner, ILM is one of the few Identity Management products that place such a serious emphasis on complete reconciliation and convergence of identity—often at the cost of some performance.

If you ignore the warning, the updates will only apply to connectors processed by the run profile (in our case, only the records we changed). However, the warning will continue to generate MIIServer Event ID 6127 Warning messages in the Application Event log until you do so. This is also a cheap but effective method of monitoring for unscheduled changes to your ILM server.

With respect to the `telephoneNumber` data that already exists in the connector space, that data won't be subjected to those new rules. The warning is asking if you'd like to apply the new rules to the existing objects. Essentially, you ignored the warning because if you have followed these recipes exactly, you should have only one new object in the ADMA's connector space with a telephone number, and that is the only one that will be synchronized.

See Also

Recipe 21.1 and Recipe 21.18 for exporting objects to AD using an export run profile, which contains information about the confirming import (a Delta Import [Stage Only] step type)

21.25 Exporting telephoneNumber Data to the HR Database

Problem

You need to export the data from the HR Database MA connector space into the HR Database.

Solution

You need to configure and execute an export run profile. First, create the run profile:

1. Open Identity Manager.
2. Click the Management Agents button on the toolbar.
3. In the Management Agents pane, click the HR Database MA.
4. In the Actions pane on the far right side, click Configure Run Profiles.
5. In the Configure Run Profiles for HR Database pane, click New Profile.
6. In the Name text box, type Export and then click Next.
7. Ensure Export is selected in the Type drop-down list and then click Next.
8. Ensure default is showing in the Partition drop-down list and then click Finish.
9. Click New Step.
10. In the Configure Step dialog, ensure Full Import (Stage Only) is selected in the Type drop-down list and then click Next.
11. Ensure default is selected in the Partition drop-down list and then click Finish.
12. Ensure the details in the Step Details field look like Figure 21-16.

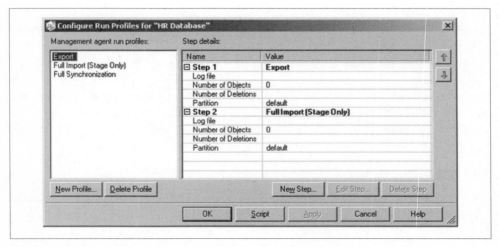

Figure 21-16. Export Run Profile added to the existing HR Database MA run profiles

13. Click OK

Discussion

You had to select Full Import (Stage Only) for the confirming import step in this run profile because the HR Database hasn't been configured to provide deltas.

See Also

Recipe 21.17 for similarities in how a run profile is configured to export objects to AD

21.26 Using the HR Database MA Export Run Profile to Export the Telephone Number to the HR Database

Problem

The run profile is configured, but you need to actually move the data from ILM to the HR Database.

Solution

You need to execute the run profile (refer to (12) in Figure 21-7, which shows the `telephoneNumber` data being exported to the HR Database):

1. Open Identity Manager.
2. Click the Management Agents button on the toolbar.
3. In the Management Agents pane, click the HR Database MA.
4. In the Actions pane on the far right side, click Run.
5. In the Run Management Agent dialog, select Export and click OK.
6. Notice the MA briefly says "Running" in the State column of the Management Agents pane.
7. Notice that in the Synchronization Statistics pane in the bottom lefthand corner, statistics showing the number of updates are displayed. If you click the hyperlink, you can navigate the information that was written to the HR Database.
8. Edit the Employees table in SQL:
    a. Open SQL Enterprise Manager.
    b. In the lefthand pane, drill down to *Console Root\Microsoft SQL Servers\SQL Server\SQL Server Group\(local)(Windows NT)\Databases\HR\Tables*.

 The same operation can be accomplished with SQL Server 2005 Server Management Studio by expanding *Root Node \Databases\HR\Tables*.

c. Right-click the Employees table in the righthand pane, and select Open Table→Return all rows.

d. Find the record of the user you added the telephoneNumber to in AD and ensure the [telephoneNumber] column has been updated.

Discussion

Now is a good time to add the last two run profiles you created to the controlling script in Recipe 21.21. Then we can make multiple changes to AD and the HR Database and watch the effects by simply running the script. We could even put a simple loop into the script so that it is executing continuously and watch new users, deleted users, and telephoneNumber change as they propagate around the systems.

See Also

Recipe 21.1, Recipe 21.18 for similarities in how a run profile is used to export objects to AD, and Recipe 21.21

21.27 Searching Data in the Connector Space

Problem

You have started to use ILM, but things aren't going according to plan. You want to see if the changes you made to either the HR Database or AD have made it into the associated connector space.

Solution

1. Open Identity Manager.
2. Click the Management Agents button on the toolbar.
3. In the Management Agents pane, click the MA you wish to search.
4. In the Actions pane on the far right side, click Search Connector Space.
5. In the Search Connector Space dialog, click the Search button.
6. You will notice records returned in the main search pane.
7. If this is the HR Database MA, the DN of each record will be the Badge Number —the primary key in the database that ensures uniqueness in the recordset. If this is the ADMA, the DN will be the object's DN in LDAP format (e.g., CN=Steve Plank,OU=oreilly,DC=rallencorp,DC=com).
8. Record the RDN of a record from the step above. If it's the HR Database MA, the RDN is the same as the DN. If it's the ADMA, it's the element that contains the least-significant object in the DN (e.g., CN=Steve Plank).
9. Select RDN in the Scope drop-down list.

10. Type the RDN you have recorded into the text box (e.g., `CN=Steve Plank`).

11. Click Search.

12. You will notice a single record returned, which matches the RDN you have specified.

13. If you double-click any of the returned records, you can examine the object in detail.

Discussion

You will see in the Scope drop-down list that there are more entries than just Subtree and RDN. The error collections are useful when trying to debug records that give errors from a large connector space with many thousands of objects in it. We find it particularly useful to use the Pending Export scope to look at outbound changes whenever performing a change to a production system. The Pending Export scope allows you to filter additionally by selecting Add, Modify, or Delete to include in the result set. It's very reassuring to verify that there are no delete operations pending when you make a new change.

Also, once you have double-clicked a record and are viewing its properties, you will notice a Lineage tab at the top of the page. On it, there is a Metaverse Object Properties button. This will show you the properties held on the related metaverse object as well as when the last change was imported from the connected directory. Validating when the last change was seen by ILM can be extremely helpful when troubleshooting why ILM didn't process a change.

See Also

Recipe 21.28 for searching data in the metaverse and the ILM 2007 help file section *Microsoft Identity Lifecycle Manager 2007/How To…/Manage a Connector Space/ Search a Connector Space*

21.28 Searching Data in the Metaverse

Problem

You are troubleshooting and want to view a metaverse object.

Solution

You need to search the metaverse:

1. Open Identity Manager.

2. Click the Metaverse Search button on the toolbar.

3. Click the Search button.

4. Records from the metaverse are returned in the Search Results pane.

5. Double-click a record in the Search Results pane.

6. You can see which MA contributed data to this metaverse object. If you double-click the object that you added a `telephoneNumber` to in AD, you should see its attributes detailed in the pane below the Attributes tab.

7. Click the Connectors tab.

8. You can see which MAs this metaverse object is joined to.

Discussion

The Connectors tab highlights the difference between projection and provisioning. You should see that the link between the metaverse object and the connector space entries was created because of projection rules for the HR Database MA and provisioning rules for the ADMA. That is because you configure the HR Database MA to project objects to the metaverse, and then you wrote a rules extension to provision objects from the metaverse to the AD connector space.

See Also

Recipe 21.27 for searching data in the connector space and the ILM 2007 help file section *Microsoft Identity Lifecycle Manager 2007/Concepts/Using Microsoft Identity Lifecycle Manager 2007/Using Management Agents/Using Metaverse Search*

21.29 Deleting Data in the Connector Space and Metaverse

Problem

You want to clear out the connector space or the metaverse, perhaps so you can perform another complete run-through of all these recipes to consolidate learning.

Solution

1. Open Identity Manager.

2. Click the Metaverse Designer button on the toolbar.

3. In the Actions pane on the far right side, click Configure Object Deletion Rule.

4. Ensure the "Delete metaverse object when connector from this management agent is disconnected" radio button is selected.

5. Select the HR Database MA from the drop-down list, then click OK.

6. Click the Management Agents button on the toolbar.

7. In the Management Agents pane, click the MA you wish to delete objects from—do the ADMA first.

8. In the Actions pane on the far right side, click Delete.

This is important: you risk deleting the whole MA if you do not perform the following step correctly.

9. Ensure the "Delete connector space only" radio button is selected.

10. When prompted that you are sure you want to delete the connector space, click Yes.

11. A message box appears with details of how many records were deleted. Click OK.

12. Perform steps 7–11 again on the HR Database MA.

Discussion

You configured the metaverse object deletion rule so that when objects from the HR Database MA were deleted, the related metaverse objects would also be deleted. That is why you deleted objects from the ADMA first. When you performed steps 7–11 the second time, the metaverse objects were also deleted. You can prove this by searching the metaverse in between delete operations.

There is no metaverse delete; ILM ensures that objects in the metaverse *always* have a join to at least one object in a connector space from at least one MA. The object deletion rule is the configuration that tells ILM what to do with metaverse objects when connector space objects get deleted.

For more control, you can specify that a rules extension should be used to make the decision for you.

It is impossible to end up in the situation where ILM has an object in the metaverse, but no corresponding object in any connector space.

See Also

Navigate the ILM 2007 help file to *Microsoft Identity Integration Server 2003/How To…/ Work with Management Agents/Create and Edit Management Agent Run Profiles/Delete a Management Agent and Connector Space* to delete both the connector space and the MA, and open the MIIS 2003 Developer Reference help and navigate to *Microsoft Identity Lifecycle Manager 2007 Developer Reference/Microsoft Identity Lifecycle Manager 2007 Reference/Microsoft.MetadirectoryServices Namespace/Interfaces/IMVSynchronization/IMVSynchronization.ShouldDeleteFromMV* and to *Microsoft Identity Lifecycle Manager 2007 Develeoper Reference/Microsoft Identity Lifecycle Manager 2007 Reference/Microsoft.MetadirectoryServices Namespace/Interfaces/IMASynchronization/ IMASynchronization.Deprovision* to understand more about writing rules extensions to make deletion decisions

21.30 Extending Object Types to Include a New Attribute

Problem

You want to add a new attribute to an existing object type in the metaverse so you can hold data specific to your implementation.

Solution

1. Open Identity Manager.
2. Click the Metaverse Designer button on the toolbar.
3. In the "Object type" pane, select the object type you wish to modify (e.g., Person).
4. In the lower Actions pane, click the Add Attribute listing.
5. In the Add Attribute To Object Type dialog box, click the "New attribute" button.
6. In the New Attribute dialog box, fill in the following properties:

   a. Attribute name (the name of the attribute as you will see it in the metaverse attributes list)

    Choosing a nonindexed value will let you store a much larger value here but it cannot be indexed and should never be used for purposes of a join.

   b. Attribute type (the type of attribute data you can store; it defaults to String (indexable))

   c. Multi-values (check this if you intend this attribute to be multivalued)

   d. Indexed (check this if you intend the value to be used during join operations)

7. Click the OK button twice to accept the changes.

Discussion

Once an attribute is created and attached to an object type, it can be linked to any other object type by following steps 1–4 and then checking off the attribute(s) that you wish to add.

21.31 Previewing Changes to the ILM Configuration

Problem

You want to make changes to one or more flows and you would like to confirm the exact effect the change will have before you roll it out.

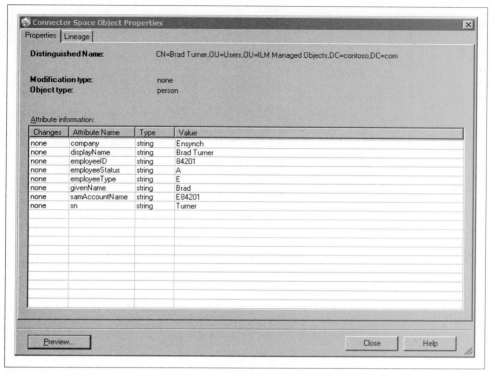

Figure 21-17. Connector Space Object Properties dialog—Preview

Solution

The solution involves the use of the *Preview* function, which is accessed as a property of an individual connector space object:

1. Open Identity Manager.

2. Locate the connector space object you would like to preview changes against by using the recipe for searching the connector space—you need to pick the connector in the MA that you would run the full or delta synchronization against.

3. On the Connector Space Object Properties dialog, click the Preview button (see Figure 21-17).

4. On the Preview dialog, under the "Select preview mode" section, select between a Full Synchronization or a Delta Synchronization; select the radio button accordingly and then click the Generate Preview button (see Figure 21-18).

5. In the contents pane, you can now browse each step and follow from Source Object Details all the way through, provisioning to Export Attribute flow on individual connectors.

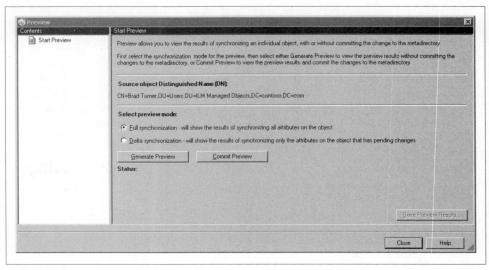

Figure 21-18. Preview dialog—Select preview mode

Discussion

Preview is one of the most useful aspects of the ILM product; it allows you to do *what if* scenarios and ascertain the exact effect any configuration change will have on the state of all identities. Incidentally, the Preview function is actually a side effect of basing ILM on SQL Server. Under normal circumstances, any given run profile step is wrapped in a SQL transaction (one transaction for every connector space object in the MA of the run profile), and as each identity is converged across all connectors, that transaction is committed to the database. In the event of an exception, only that transaction is rolled back and the next identity is processed. Given this feature, the Preview ability simply rolls back the transaction for the given object. This means that ILM is not simply simulating what a run would look like; it's actually executing the process exactly as it would be under normal circumstances, with the exception that the changes are not committed.

 Since Preview is executing every step and rolling back the transaction, be extremely careful in your rules extensions that you are not performing actions that can't be undone. Anything you do through a rules extension to any source outside of ILM *will not be rolled back* because it is outside of the scope of the SQL transaction. You should use the `Utils.InPreviewMode()` property to determine when you are in Preview mode, and gate certain functions of your flow.

See Also

The ILM 2007 Feature Pack 1 Developer Reference section *Identity Lifecycle Manager 2007, Feature Pack 1 Reference/Microsoft.MetadirectoryServices Namespace/Classes/ Utils/Properties/Utils.InPreviewMode* for more information on the *Utils.InPreviewMode* property, Recipe 21.27 for searching data in the connector space, and the ILM 2007 help file section *Microsoft Identity Lifecycle Manager 2007 Feature Pack1/Concepts/Using Microsoft Identity Lifecycle Manager 2007/Using Management Agents/Using Metaverse Search*

21.32 Committing Changes to Individual Identities Using the Commit Preview Feature

Problem

You want to make changes to a rules extension or flow but you would like to confirm the exact effect the change will have before you roll it out. In addition, you want to commit the changes to only a handful of records that need the changes to go into effect right away and you can't afford to run a full synchronization to get them.

Solution

1. Open Identity Manager.
2. Locate the connector space object you would like to preview changes against by using the recipe for searching the connector space—you need to pick the connector in the MA that you would run the full or delta synchronization against.
3. On the Connector Space Object Properties dialog, click the Commit Preview button (see Figure 21-17).
4. On the Preview dialog, under the Select preview mode section, select between a Full Synchronization or a Delta Synchronization; select the radio button accordingly and then click the Commit Preview button (see Figure 21-18).
5. In the contents pane, you can now browse each step and follow from Source Object Details all the way through provisioning to Export Attribute flow on individual connectors!

Discussion

Commit Preview functions like the Preview button; however, it actually commits the transaction at the end for the given connector. This allows you to atomically apply new policies to specific connectors; you should only used this strategy when you absolutely cannot afford (from a time perspective) to run a full sync. Using Commit Preview during testing and certification is recommended when you want to follow a change across data sources.

See Also

Recipe 21.27 for searching data in the connector space, Recipe 21.31, and the ILM 2007 help file section *Microsoft Identity Lifecycle Manager 2007 Feature Pack1/Concepts/ Using Microsoft Identity Lifecycle Manager 2007/Using Management Agents/Using Metaverse Search*

21.33 Passing Data Between Rules Extensions Using Transaction Properties

Problem

You are tracking an event that occurs in an authoritative data source and want to pass a message or a data element to one of the other extensions.

Solution

1. Open Visual Studio and open your rules extension project solution.

2. You first need to set a transaction property, and while these properties can be set anywhere, you will most likely set them in ShouldProjectToMV, MapAttributesFor Join, ResolveJoinSearch, MapAttributesForImport, MapAttributesForExport, and Deprovision, or within the Provisioning rules extensions. The following example shows two ways of setting different types of Transaction Properties:

   ```
   ' String
   Dim strWF As String = "foobar"
   Utils.TransactionProperties.Add("WORKFLOW", strWF)

   ' Boolean
   Utils.TransactionProperties.Add("DELETE", True)
   ```

3. Once you have one or more properties set, you can query for them elsewhere:

   ```
   If (Utils.TransactionProperties.Contains("DELETE") AndAlso
   Utils.TransactionProperties("DELETE").Equals(True)) Then
       ' This allows for a typesafe way to query for the existence of a property
   End If

   If (Utils.TransactionProperties.Contains("WORKFLOW") AndAlso
   Utils.TransactionProperties("WORKFLOW").ToString.Contains("foo")) Then
       ' This allows you to search the contents of a string property
       ' You can then do an assignment
       Dim strWFResponse As String = Utils.TransactionProperties("WORKFLOW").ToString
   End If

   If (Utils.TransactionProperties.Contains("WORKFLOW") AndAlso
   Utils.TransactionProperties("WORKFLOW").Equals("foobar")) Then
       ' This allows you to do a simple comparison
   End If
   ```

Discussion

A Transaction Property is only good for as long as the current ILM transaction is running. This makes it relevant only to the identity you are processing and is available across all extensions that are touched as part of the synchronization of that identity; when the next identity is loaded for processing, all Transaction Properties are destroyed.

See Also

Recipes 21.31 and 21.32

21.34 Using a Single Rules Extension to Affect Multiple Attribute Flows

Problem

You have several attributes that you would like to apply the same block of code to and you don't want to duplicate the same block of code or call the same function from multiple `case` statements.

Solution

1. Open Visual Studio and open your rules extension project solution.

2. Add a code block like this (before your main `select case FlowRuleName` statement):

```
If FlowRuleName.StartsWith("Trim:") Then
    ' Trim String
    '
    ' Reusable code to convert an attribute to its string format
    ' FlowRuleName will be passed as "Trim:srcAttribute,destAttribute"
    '
    Dim strAttributeName, strSrcAttribute, strDestAttribute, arrAttribs()
    As String

    ' Replace the beginning of the flowrulename with nothing
    strAttributeName = FlowRuleName.Replace("Trim:", "")
    arrAttribs = strAttributeName.Split(",","c)   ' Splits the string
                                                  ' on a comma
    trSrcAttribute = arrAttribs(0)                ' Assigns the first value
    strDestAttribute = arrAttribs(1)              ' Assigns the second value

    ' Now we can assign the value and trim any whitespace at the front and back
    mventry(strDestAttribute).Value =
    csentry(strSrcAttribute).Value.ToString.Trim

Else If FlowRuleName.StartsWith("MyFunction:") Then
    ' Apply custom function
    '
```

```
      ' Reusable code to apply a custom function to an attribute
      ' FlowRuleName will be passed as
"MyFunction:sourceAttribute,destinationAttribute"
      '
      Dim strAttributeName, strSrcAttribute, strDestAttribute, arrAttribs()
      As String

      ' Replace the beginning of the flowrulename with nothing
      strAttributeName = FlowRuleName.Replace("MyFunction:", "")
      arrAttribs = strAttributeName.Split(","c)   ' Splits the string on a comma
      strSrcAttribute = arrAttribs(0)             ' Assigns the first value
      strDestAttribute = arrAttribs(1)            ' Assigns the second value

      ' Now we can apply your custom function prior to the assignment
      Dim strSrcAttributeValue As String
      strSrcAttributeValue =
MySharedCodeLib.MyFunction(csentry(strSrcAttribute).Value)
      mventry(strDestAttribute).Value = strSrcAttributeValue

Else
      ' Continue on as you normally do
      Select case FlowRuleName
```

3. Open Identity Manager.

4. Apply the rule.

Discussion

Using this approach allows you to create several reusable code sections and apply them to new advanced flows without the need for code changes or recompiles. This approach is valid in both the import and export flow sections.

21.35 Flowing a Null Value to a Data Source

Problem

You need to delete or "flow a null" to an attribute in another data source.

Solution

1. Open Identity Manager.

2. Click the Management Agents button on the toolbar.

3. In the Management Agents pane, double-click the ADMA.

4. In the Management Agent Designer pane on the lefthand side, select Configure Attribute Flow.

5. Ensure "user" is selected in the data source object type drop-down list.

6. Ensure "person" is selected in the metaverse object type drop-down list.

7. In the Mapping Type section of the dialog, select Advanced.

8. In the Flow Direction section of the dialog, select Export, and then check the box to Allow Nulls.

 If you don't check the box to Allow Nulls, the rule value will never be contributed.

9. Select `telephoneNumber` from the data source attributes list.

10. Select `<object-id>` from the Metaverse attributes list.

    Selecting `<object-id>` here ensures that the source value will always be present; otherwise the rule will not fire if the source value in the metaverse is `null`.

11. Click New.

12. In the Advanced Attribute Flow Options dialog, type "Delete:telephoneNumber".

13. Open Visual Studio and open your rules extension project solution.

14. If you are using the recipe from Recipe 21.34, insert the following before the final `Else`; otherwise, only the final line is needed in a standard `Case` block:

```
Else If FlowRuleName.StartsWith("Delete") Then
    '
    ' Reusable code to delete the referenced attribute
    ' FlowRuleName will be passed as "Delete:Attribute"
    '
    Dim strAttributeName As String

    ' Replace the beginning of the flowrulename with nothing
    ' to find the attribute to be deleted
    strAttributeName = FlowRuleName.Replace("Delete:", "")

    ' This is whre we delete the value
    csentry(strAttributeName).Delete()
```

Discussion

You never have to actually set a "null value" to contribute a delete to another data source. This is partially due to the fact that different systems handle null values differently and in order to contribute the proper value, the `Delete()` property is used to handle that translation for you.

To process any Advanced Rules extension, you need to have a value in the source attribute. A common problem occurs when the source attribute is null in the metaverse, preventing the rule from firing on that identity. An advanced flow will fire if an existing value is deleted (by contributing a null), but it will never fire if the value is null to begin with. In addition, while using a fixed value like `<object-id>` ensures that the value will never be null, this value will never change and therefore you will require a full synchronization run to trigger this rule; however, you can use Recipe 21.32 to force a full synchronization on an individual identity and commit the changes.

See Also

Recipes 21.8, 21.32, and 21.34

21.36 Contributing a UTCCodedTime Attribute in Active Directory

Problem

You need to contribute a date/time value to Active Directory and the attribute type in AD is *UTC coded time* syntax. You have likely extended the schema, or are working with a product that has extended the schema, and need to contribute this value.

Solution

1. Open Identity Manager.
2. Click the Management Agents button on the toolbar.
3. In the Management Agents pane, double-click the ADMA.
4. In the Management Agent Designer pane on the lefthand side, select Configure Attribute Flow.
5. Ensure "user" is selected in the data source object type drop-down list.
6. Ensure "person" is selected in the metaverse object type drop-down list.
7. In the Mapping Type section of the dialog, select Advanced.
8. In the Flow Direction section of the dialog, select Export.
9. Select the UTC Coded Time attribute to contribute to from the data source attributes list.
10. Select the string-formatted date attribute from the Metaverse attributes list.
11. Click New.
12. In the Advanced Attribute Flow Options dialog, type the name of your rules extension: "UTCCodedTime".
13. Open Visual Studio and open your rules extension project solution.

```
Case "UTCCodedTime"
    ' Formatting strings for writing UTC Coded Time to Active Directory
    ' For use with AD Attributes of the String(Generalized Time)/UTC Coded Time
syntax (2.5.5.11)

    Dim strDate As String
    Dim strUTC As String

    ' data source records midnight local time
    strDate = mventry("StartDate").Value      ' Look like "2007-08-28 00:00:00"
    strUTC =
```

```
System.DateTime.Parse(strDate).ToUniversalTime.ToString("yyyyMMddHHmmss.0Z")

    csentry("UTCAttribute").Value = strUTC
```

Discussion

UTC coded time allows you to store a date/time value in the directory in universal time format also known as Zulu time (GMT 0:00). Storing the date and time in this format allows the user interface to interpret the time relative to the time zone configured in the local operating system.

See Also

Visit *http://www.identitychaos.com/2007/08/writing-utc-coded-time-to-ad.html* for more information on writing to UTCCodedTime, and visit *http://www.identitychaos.com/2008/02/toutccodedtime-extension-method.html* for information on how to leverage extensions like this as an *extension method* in Visual Studio 2008

21.37 Importing and Decoding the accountExpires Attribute

Problem

You want to import the accountExpires attribute into the metaverse as a string formatted date/time value. This could be any of the Large Integer/Interval syntax attributes, such as accountExpires, badPasswordTime, lastLogoff, lastLogon, lastLogonTimestamp, lockoutTime, or pwdLastSet.

Solution

1. Open Identity Manager.
2. See Recipe 21.30 to add a new metaverse attribute if necessary.
3. Click the Management Agents button on the toolbar.
4. In the Management Agents pane, double-click the ADMA.
5. In the Management Agent Designer pane on the lefthand side, select Configure Attribute Flow.
6. Ensure "user" is selected in the data source object type drop-down list.
7. Ensure "person" is selected in the metaverse object type drop-down list.
8. In the Mapping Type section of the dialog, select Advanced.
9. In the Flow Direction section of the dialog, select Import.
10. Select accountExpires from the data source attributes list.
11. Select the attribute created in step 2 or an existing String attribute from the Metaverse attributes list (e.g., AccountExpirationDate).

12. Click New.

13. In the Advanced Attribute Flow Options dialog, type "ConvertFileTime:accountExpires,AccountExpirationDate".

14. Open Visual Studio and open your rules extension project solution.

15. If you are using the recipe from Recipe 21.34 insert the following before the final Else; otherwise, only the final line is needed in a standard Case block:

```
ElseIf FlowRuleName.StartsWith("ConvertFileTime:") Then
    '
    ' Reusable code to convert generalized time into string format
    ' FlowRuleName will be passed as
"ConvertFileTime:sourceAttribute,destinationAttribute"
    '
    Dim strAttributeName, strSourceAttribute, strDestinationAttribute, arrAttribs()
As String

    ' Replace the beginning of the flowrulename with nothing to find the attribute
to be deleted
    strAttributeName = FlowRuleName.Replace("ConvertFileTime:", "")
    arrAttribs = strAttributeName.Split(","c)
    strSourceAttribute = arrAttribs(0)
    strDestinationAttribute = arrAttribs(1)

    ' NOTE: The value will be invalid if it was never set
    ' (9223372036854775807 (0x7FFFFFFFFFFFFFFF))
    ' or 0 if it was set and then later cleared

    Const AD_ACCOUNT_NO_EXPIRATION As Long = 9223372036854775807

    If (strSourceAttribute = "accountExpires") Then
        If (csentry(strSourceAttribute).Value = 0 OrElse
csentry(strSourceAttribute).Value = AD_ACCOUNT_NO_EXPIRATION) Then
            ' The value was cleared or never set
            mventry(strDestinationAttribute).Value = "Never"
    Else
            ' The value has been set
            Dim dtFileTime As DateTime =
DateTime.FromFileTime(DateTime.Parse(csentry(strSourceAttribute).Value).ToFileTme)

            mventry(strDestinationAttribute).Value = Format(dtFileTime, "yyyy-MM-
dd")
        End If
    Else
        ' We are not dealing with the accountExpires attribute, just decode it
        Dim dtFileTime As DateTime =
DateTime.FromFileTime(DateTime.Parse(csentry(strSourceAttribute).Value).ToFileTime)

        mventry(strDestinationAttribute).Value = Format(dtFileTime, "yyyy-MM-dd")
    End If
```

Discussion

The Large Integer/Interval syntax in Active Directory can be decoded by using the `DateTime.FromFileTime()` function in the .NET Framework. By using the `DateTime.Parse().ToFileTime` property, you are ensuring that the value you are getting is a valid date/time.

 If you are concerned with data integrity here, consider wrapping this in a `Try/Catch` block.

See Also

Recipes 21.30 and 21.34

21.38 Exporting and Encoding the accountExpires Attribute

Problem

You want to export to the `accountExpires` attribute from a string-formatted date/time value in the metaverse. This could be any of the Large Integer/Interval syntax attributes, such as `accountExpires`, `badPasswordTime`, `lastLogoff`, `lastLogon`, `lastLogonTimestamp`, `lockoutTime`, or `pwdLastSet`.

Solution

1. Open Identity Manager.
2. Click the Management Agents button on the toolbar.
3. In the Management Agents pane, double-click the ADMA.
4. In the Management Agent Designer pane on the lefthand side, select Configure Attribute Flow.
5. Ensure "user" is selected in the data source object type drop-down list.
6. Ensure "person" is selected in the metaverse object type drop-down list.
7. In the Mapping Type section of the dialog, select Advanced.
8. In the Flow Direction section of the dialog, select Export.
9. Select `accountExpires` from the data source attributes list.
10. Select an existing String attribute from the Metaverse attributes list (e.g., `AccountExpirationDate`).
11. Click New.

12. In the Advanced Attribute Flow Options dialog, type "ConvertFileTime:accountExpires,AccountExpirationDate".

13. Open Visual Studio and open your rules extension project solution.

14. If you are using the recipe from Recipe 21.34, insert the following before the final `Else`; otherwise, only the final line is needed in a standard `Case` block:

```
ElseIf FlowRuleName.StartsWith("ConvertFileTime:") Then
    '
    ' Reusable code to convert generalized time into string format
    ' FlowRuleName will be passed as
"ConvertFileTime:sourceAttribute,destinationAttribute"
    '
    Dim strAttributeName, strSourceAttribute, strDestinationAttribute, arrAttribs()
As String

    ' Replace the beginning of the flowrulename with nothing to find the attribute
to be deleted
    strAttributeName = FlowRuleName.Replace("ConvertFileTime:", "")
    arrAttribs = strAttributeName.Split(","c)
    strSourceAttribute = arrAttribs(0)
    strDestinationAttribute = arrAttribs(1)

    ' NOTE: The value will be invalid if it was never set
    ' (9223372036854775807 (0x7FFFFFFFFFFFFFFF))
    ' or 0 if it was set and then later cleared

    Const AD_ACCOUNT_NO_EXPIRATION As Long = 9223372036854775807

    If (strDestinationAttribute = "accountExpires") Then
        If (mventry(strSourceAttribute).IsPresent = False) Then
            ' The value in the metaverse is empty so remove the account
expiration
            csentry(strDestinationAttribute).IntegerValue = 0
        Else
            ' We should have a date value present to enforce
            Dim dtFileTime As DateTime =
DateTime.Parse(mventry(strSourceAttribute).Value)

            csentry(strDestinationAttribute).IntegerValue =
dtFileTime.ToFileTimeUtc()
        End If
    Else
        ' We are not dealing with the accountExpires attribute, just encode it
        Dim dtFileTime As DateTime =
DateTime.Parse(mventry(strSourceAttribute).Value)

        csentry(strDestinationAttribute).IntegerValue = dtFileTime.ToFileTimeUtc()
    End If
```

Discussion

The Large Integer/Interval syntax in Active Directory can be encoded by using the `DateTime.ToFileTime()` function in the .NET Framework. By using the `Date Time.Parse()` property, you are ensuring that the value you are getting is a valid date/time.

 If you are concerned with data integrity here, consider wrapping this in a `Try/Catch` block.

See Also

Recipes 21.30, 21.34, and 21.37

Index

Symbols

32-bit systems, converting 64-bit numbers for, 275

A

account lockout policy
    parameters controlling, 273
    viewing for a domain, 271
account partners, 839, 846
    creating, 851
account store
    configuring Active Directory account store, 847
    configuring ADAM or AD LDS account store, 848
accountExpires attribute
    exporting from string formatted datetime value in metaverse, 1013
    importing and decoding in ILM, 1011
    user object, 303
ACL Editor, 674
    configuring permission inheritance, 678
    customizing, 676
    defining auditing in SACL of objects, 724
    modifying ACL of an object, 680
    viewing effective permissions on an object, 677
acldiag utility, 682
    listing effective permissions on an object, 678
ACLs (access control lists), 659
    ACEs for computer object manged by user or group, 358
    ADAM/AD LDS permissions, 834
    changing ACL of an object, 680
    comparing ACL of object to default defined in schema, 682
    DACLs and SACLs, 322
    deny Change Password ACEs on user object, 293
    group ACL for delegated OU administration, 233
    modifying ACL on administrator accounts, 688
    modifying default ACL for object class in schema, 681
    resetting object's ACL to default defined in schema, 683
    retrieving and revoking delegated permissions, 674
    viewing for an object, 674
Active Directory
    Exchange Server and, 864
    nomenclature changes in Windows Server 2008, 22
    preparing for Exchange, 868
    versions, 3
Active Directory Application Mode (see ADAM; ADAM/AD LDS)
Active Directory Domains and Trusts MMC snap-in
    changing domain mode for Windows 2000 AD domain, 34
    configuring alternate UPN suffix, 857
    configuring forest trust for ADFS, 856
    creating an external trust, 48
    creating shortcut trust between AD domains, 52

We'd like to hear your suggestions for improving our indexes. Send email to *index@oreilly.com*.

creating transitive trust between AD forests, 50

creating trust to a Kerberos realm, 54

creating UPN suffix for a forest, 311

finding domain controllers acting as Domain Naming Master, 126

finding NetBIOS name of domain, 30

listing domains in a forest, 28

raising domain functional level, 36

raising forest functional level, 39

removing trusts, 63

selective authentication for trusts, 67

verifying trusts, 58

viewing trusts for a domain, 55

Active Directory Federation Services (see AD FS)

Active Directory Lightweight Directory Service (see AD LDS; ADAM/AD LDS)

Active Directory Migration Tool (ADMT) MMC snap-in

migrating group to another domain, 330

moving computer into new domain, 365

moving objects, 191

Active Directory Schema MMC snap-in

finding domain controllers acting as Schema Master, 126

modifying default ACL for object class in schema, 681

registering, 459

Active Directory Services Interface (see ADSI)

Active Directory Sites and Services MMC snap-in

configuring universal group caching for site, 526

creating a subnet, 529

deleting a site, 522

enabling caching of universal group membership, 345

enabling or disabling global catalog, 113

finding domain controllers or GC servers in a site, 119

foring replication between domain controllers, 586

linking sites in a forest, 519

listing replication partners for domain controller, 604

listing subnets, 530

managing AD LDS replication, 831

modifying inter-site replication interval, 593

moving domain controller to different site, 101

renaming a site, 521

Active Directory Users and Computers MMC snap-in

ACL Editor (see ACL Editor)

adding additional fields to users and computers, 70

adding and removing group members, 326

adding or removing computer account from a group, 370

assigning or removing manager for OU, 234

changing group scope or type, 332

changing user's primary group, 285

copying existing user account, 265

copying user's group membership to another user, 287

creating a computer object, 352

creating a group, 316

creating an OU, 212

creating computer account for a user or group, 354

creating inetOrgPerson user, 250

creating users, 246

delegating control of OU, 233

delegating management of group membership, 340

delegation of control over objects, 669

deleting a computer account, 360

deleting a user, 256

deleting a user's mailbox, 903

deleting all child objects in an OU, 221

deleting OU and all objects within, 222

determining user's last logon time, 303

enabling and disabling user account, 278

enumerating objects in an OU, 218

enumerating OUs in a domain, 214

Exchange version, 865

finding an OU in a domain, 217

finding computer object OS, 380

finding disabled users, 280

finding domain controllers for a domain, 95

finding orphaned objects, 602

finding PDC Emulator, RID Master, and Infrastructure Master, 126

finding users with no recent logons, 306
finding user's primary group ID, 342
identifying a computer's role, 389
listing all computer objects in a domain, 387
mail-disabling a user, 895
mail-enabling a user, 889
mailbox-enabling a user, 898
modifying attribute for several users at once, 255
modifying default display name for users created in ADUC, 244
modifying PRP (Password Replication Policy), 81
modifying user's logon hours, 307
moving a computer within a domain, 364
moving a mailbox, 905
moving objects in an OU to another OU, 223
moving OU and all its child objects, 226
moving user to different container or OU, 260
preventing expiration of user password, 295
preventing user from changing a password, 291
protecting computer against deletion, 390
protecting group against accidental deletion, 348
protecting OU against accidental deletion, 238
removing all group memberships from a user, 284
renaming an OU, 228
renaming users, 263
requiring user to change password at next logon, 293
resetting a computer account, 372
restricting anonymous access, 667
restricting DHCP administrators, 655
revoking delegated permissions, 673
setting expiration of user account, 302
setting password for a user, 290
setting user's account options, 299
setting user's profile attributes, 258
unlocking a user, 268
viewing direct group members, 323
viewing FGPP for user account, 277
viewing group membership of a user, 281
viewing group permissions, 319
viewing nested members of a group, 324
viewing RODCs that cached user password, 298
AD DS (Active Directory Domain Services), 22
    adding binaries to server, 76
    stopping during maintenance operations, 738
AD FS (Active Directory Federation Services), 839–862
    configuring AD account store, 847
    configuring AD FS Web Agent, 859
    configuring ADAM or AD LDS account store, 848
    configuring alternate UPN suffix, 857
    configuring an application, 854
    configuring resource partner, 853
    creating account partner, 851
    creating organizational claims, 849
    enabling logging for AD FS Web Agent, 861
    installing Federation Service on Windows Server 2003 R2, 844
    installing Federation Service on Windows Server 2008, 846
    installing prerequisites for Windows Server 2003 R2, 840
    installing prerequisites for Windows Server 2008, 842
AD FS MMC snap-in, 840
    configuring a resource partner, 853
    configuring AD account store, 847
    configuring ADAM or AD LDS account store, 848
    configuring an application, 855
    creating account partner, 851
AD FS Web Agent, 855
    configuring, 859
    enabling logging for, 861
AD LDS (Active Directory Lightweight Directory Service), 801
    (see also ADAM/AD LDS)
ADAM (Active Directory Application Mode), 801
    versions and features, 801
ADAM ADSI Edit, 825
    (see also ADSI Edit MMC snap-in)
    configuring intrasite replication, 831

managing ADAM/AD LDS organizational units, 816

viewing and modifying ADAM object attributes, 827

ADAM/AD LDS

changing password for user, 819

changing port used by instance, 810

configuring account store, 848

configuring intrasite replication, 831

creating groups, 823

creating new instance of, 804

creating new replica of configuration set, 806

enabling auditing of AD LDS access, 836

enabling or disabling ADAM user, 821

features in Windows Server 2008, 802

forcing replication of application partition, 831

importing data into an instance, 829

installing, 803

listing instances installed on computer, 810

managing AD LDS replication authentication, 832

msDS-ReplAuthenticationMode values, 833

managing ADAM users, 817

managing application partitions, 813

managing group memberships, 825

managing organizational units, 815

managing permissions, 834

stopping and starting an instance, 808

viewing and modifying ADAM object attributes, 827

add-QADPermission cmdlet, 626

address list, creating, 917–921

addressBookContainer class, 920

AdFind utility

binding to object using its GUID, 152

checking if application partition is instantiated on DC, 791

configuring mailbox storage limits, 914

connecting to well-known GUIDs in Domain NC, 154

determining number of child objects for an OU, 232

displaying efficiency statistics for LDAP queries, 713

displaying RootDSE of domain controller, 137

enabling LDAP controls, 147

enumerating direct members of a group, 323

environment variables to specify long or often used switches, 816

exporting objects to CSV file, 208

finding account lockout and password properties of a domain, 271

finding ADAM object attributes, 827

finding all domains in a forest, 28

finding an OU in a domain, 217

finding application partitions hosted by server, 788

finding application partitions in forest, 781

finding computer object OS, 380

finding conflict objects from replication collisions, 600

finding current domain functional level, 36

finding deleted objects, 770

finding disabled users, 280

finding domain controllers for a domain, 95

finding domain controllers or CG servers in a site, 119

finding domain controller's site, 99

finding global catalog servers in forest, 118

finding NetBIOS name of a domain, 31

finding object metadata, 606

finding orphaned objects, 602

finding replica server for application partitions, 786

finding replication partners of domain controller, 604

finding RODCs that cached computer's password, 392

finding RODCs that cached user's password, 298

finding user's last logon, 304

listing all computer objects in a domain, 387

listing all GPOs in a domain, 396

listing objects in an OU, 219

listing sites or site properties, 520

listing subnets, 530

message tracking on Exchange Server, 930

obtaining FSMO information, 127

obtaining group permissions, 319

piping query results into AdMod to delete object in OU, 221

querying for an object, 140
querying the global catalog, 159
removing trusts, 63
retrieving count of object matching a query, 145
retrieving current forest functional level, 39
retrieving OUs in a domain, 215
searches using attribute-scoped queries, 164
searches using bitwise filter, 167
searching for objects in a domain, 156
top-quota usage output, 735
using with AdMod to add fields to users and computers, 71
using with AdMod to copy user's group membership to another user, 288
using with AdMod to disable compression on inter-site replication, 595
using with AdMod to move objects from one OU to another, 224
using with AdMod to remove group memberships from user, 284
using with AdMod to undelete deleted objects, 772
viewing created and modified timestamps, 202
ADFS MMC snap-in
creating organizational claims, 850
ADM files, 412
Admin Role Separation feature, 80
Administration Tools Pack (adminpak.msi), 274, 882
installer, schmmgmt.dll file, 460
administrator accounts
modifying ACL on, 688
AdminSDHolder object, 679
AdminSDHolder process, 688
ADML files, 414
admod utility
adding or modifying UPN suffixes, 857
converting user objects to and from inetOrgPerson, 253
creating a subnet, 529
creating inetOrgPerson object, 251
creating many users, 249
creating UPN suffix for a forest, 311
creating user accounts, 246
deleting a computer, 360
deleting a user, 257

deleting an object, 198
enabling or disabling global catalog, 114
modifying default ADUC display name for users, 244
moving a user object, 261
moving domain controller to different site, 102
raising domain functional level, 37
raising forest functional level, 40
removing all group memberships from user, 284
removing trusts, 63
renaming a user, 264
requiring user to change password on next logon, 294
setting user's password, 290
setting user's profile attributes, 259
updating domain mode from mixed to native mode, 34
AdMod utility
adding and removing group members, 326
adding or deleting ADAM/AD LDS organizational units, 816
adding or removing ADAM or AD LDS group memberships, 825
adding or removing computer account for a group, 370
adding replica server to application partition, 783
assigning or removing manager for an OU, 234
changing group scope or type, 332
changing machine account quota for a domain, 376
configuring mailbox storage limits, 914
creating a computer object, 353
creating a site, 517
creating ADAM/AD LDS groups, 823
creating crossRef object, 194
creating dynamic group, 338
creating group object, 317
creating objects, 171
creating organizational units, 212
deleting a site, 522
deleting container and its child objects, 200
deleting OU and all objects within, 222
dynamically linking auxiliary class to an object, 181

enabling group caching, 345
enabling LDAP controls, 147
enabling universal group caching for site, 526
environment variables to specify long or often used switches, 816
managing AD LDS replication authentication, 832
managing ADAM/AD LDS users, 818
message tracking enabled on Exchange, 930
modifying ADAM object attributes, 828
modifying ADAM/AD LDS user's password, 821
modifying allowed DNS suffixes, 650
modifying an OU, 230
modifying attributes on objects, 174, 175
modifying computer object attributes, 378
modifying garbage collection period, 765
modifying group attributes, 334
modifying group membership to restrict anonymous access, 668
modifying inter-site replication interval, 594
modifying intra-site replication interval, 591
modifying PRP (Password Replication Policy) on an RODC, 81
modifying reference domain for application partition, 795
modifying replication notification delay for application partition, 793
modifying tombstone lifetime, 774
modifying tombstone weight in quota calculation, 731
moving a computer within a domain, 364
moving a group within a domain, 328
moving an OU, 227
moving object to different OU or container, 189
online defrag of DIT file, 758
refreshing dynamic objects, 185
renaming a site, 521
renaming an object, 196
renaming an OU, 228
setting default quotas, 733
using with AdFind to delete objects in OU, 221

using with AdFind to move objects from one OU to another, 224
ADMT (see Active Directory Migration Tool MMC snap-in)
ADMX files, 413
ADO (ActiveX Data Objects)
searching with, 158
paged searching, 163
using for authentication, 8
adprep utility, 42–46
determining whether process is completed, 44
preparing AD forest for Windows upgrade, 464
preparing Windows 2000 forest or domain for Windows Server 2003 upgrade, 42
adrestore utility, 770
ADSI (Active Directory Services Interface), 2
adding and removing group members in PowerShell, 327
creating computer object with PowerShell, 354
enabling SSL and secure authentication, 663
fast binds, 151
modifying group information, 333
native methods in PowerShell for attribute-scoped queries, 165
use with Exchange Server 2003, 865
using to create group in PowerShell, 318
ADSI Edit MMC snap-in
ACL Editor (see ACL Editor)
applying FGPP to group object, 350
applying FGPP to user object, 275
changing computer's allowed DNS suffix, 649
changing intra-site notification delay, 591
changing maximum number of computers user can join to domain, 376
converting user objects to and from inetOrgPerson objects, 253
creating ADAM/AD LDS groups, 823
creating FGPP, 449
creating objects, 170
delegating control of application partition, 796
delegating control of DHCP server administration, 653

deleting an object, 198
dynamically linking auxiliary class to an
  object, 180
editing a FGPP, 452
enabling anonymous LDAP access, 665
enabling List Object Access mode, 686
enabling or disabling ADAM user, 821
encryption and signing of traffic between
  client and server, 662
finding replica servers for application
  partition, 786
garbage collection interval, changing, 764
mailbox-enabled user, viewing attributes
  for, 901
managing AD LDS replication
  authentication, 832
managing ADAM or AD LDS group
  memberships, 825
managing ADAM/AD LDS application
  partitions, 814
managing ADAM/AD LDS users, 817
modifying an OU, 229
modifying computer object attributes, 377
modifying default display name for users
  created in ADUC, 244
modifying default LDAP query policy, 203
modifying default TTL settings for dynamic
  objects, 186
modifying group attributes, 334
modifying objects, 173
modifying tombstone lifetime for a domain,
  774
moving group within a domain, 328
moving object to different OU or container,
  189
referencing external AD domain, 193
renaming objects, 195
setting default quota for security principals
  in partition, 732
setting reference domain for application
  partition, 794
setting replication notification delay for
  application partition, 792
tombstone objects, relative weight in quota
  calculation, 730
viewing user's manged objects, 310
ADsPath
  specifying domain name in, 7
  specifying server name to target DC, 7

ADSTYPEENUM enumeration, 144
ADS_GROUP_TYPE_ENUM, 333
ADS_PROPERTY_OPERATION_ENUM,
  176
ADS_USER_FLAG_ENUM values,
  userAccountControl, 301
ADUC (see Active Directory Users and
  Computers MMC snap-in)
ADUC MMC snap-in (see Active Directory
  Users and Computers MMC snap-in)
aging configuration for DNS records, 635
alerts
  creating performance alert for
    administration, 720
  emailing administrator on performance
    alert, 721
Ambiguous Name Resolution (ANR), 168
anonymous access
  enabling for LDAP, 665
  restricting for AD, 667
ANR (Ambiguous Name Resolution), example
  search, 714
anti-spam agents, installing on hub transport
  servers, 928
application partitions, 18, 777–800
  adding or removing replica server, 782
  creating and deleting, 779
  delegating management of, 796
  domainDNS and crossRef objects, 778
  finding in a forest, 780
  finding replica servers for, 786
  finding those hosted by a server, 787
  managing for ADAM/AD LDS, 813
  moving AD-integrated zones into, 618
  setting reference domain for, 794
  setting replication notification delay for,
    792
  verifying correct installation on server, 790
attribute flow rules, 948
  advanced import attribute flow, 960
  configuring both import and export
    attribure flows, 991
  implementing advanced attribute flow rules
    extension, 962–965
  setting up advanced export attribute flow in
    AD, 966
  simple export attribute flow to AD, 959
  simple import attribute flow, 957
attribute flows

contributing UTCCodedTime attribute to Active Directory, 1010
exporting accountExpires attribute, 1013
flowing null value to a data source, 1008
importing accountExpires attribute into metaverse, 1011
single rules extension affecting multiple flows, 1007
attribute-scoped queries, 164
attributeDisplayNames attribute, 72
attributes
    containing bit flags, modifying, 177
    modifying on an object, 173–177
    viewing and modifying on ADAM objects, 827
    viewing for an object, 140–145
attributeSchema objects, 458
    searchFlags and systemFlags attributes, 168
auditing
    changes to Registry keys, 726
    enabling for AD LDS access, 836
    enabling for directory access, 723
    enabling for Windows NT token-based applications, 861
auditpol utility, 837
Authenticated Users group, 668
authentication, 659
    (see also security and authentication)
    Selective Authentication for trusts, 66
authoritative restore, 106
    performing complete authoritative restore, 752
    performing for object or subtree, 750
Authorization Manager MMC snap-in
    creating dynamic group, 337
    new features in Windows Server 2008, 338
auxiliary classes, dynamically linking to objects, 180
AzMan (see Authorization Manager MMC snap-in)

B

backupgpo.wsf script, 440
backups, 738
    deleted objects and, 738
    GPOs, 439
    Windows 2000 and Windows Server 2003 AD backups, 740

Windows Server 2008 AD backup, 742
bcdedit utility, 746
    increasing LSASS cache on domain controller, 111
bit flag attributes
    modifying, 177–180
        options attribute, site-link objects, 595
        sample bit flat attribute values, 178
    options attribute, site-link objects, 595
    userAccountControl, 301
bitwise filter, searching with, 166–170
books and magazines about Active Directory, 14
boot.ini file, editing, 111
bootcfg utility, 110
BOR operator, 296
brute force method of removing a forest, 23
BXOR operator, 296

C

caching
    clearing DNS cache, 636
    finding RODCs that cached a computer's password, 391
    universal group, 344
CD (connected directory), 939
CDO (Collaborative Data Objects), 722
CDOEXM (Collaboration Data Objects for Exchange Management), 865
certificate installation
    on Windows Server 2003 R2, 842
    using certreq on Windows Server 2008, 844
Certificate Lifecycle Manager (CLM), 935
certificate requests
    generating in Windows Server 2003 R2, 840
    generating via command line in Windows Server 2008, 843
certreq utility, 844
circular logging, 737
claims, AD FS
    creating organizational claim, 849
    processing by web application hosted by resource partner, 861
    types of, 850
claims-aware applications, 855
classes, 671
    (see also objects)

delegation of, 671
classSchema objects, 458
CLM (Certificate Lifecycle Manager), 935
cmdlets, 2, 3
  (see also PowerShell)
  listing all EMS cmdlets, using Get-
    ExCommand, 867
  Quest PowerShell Commands for Active
    Directory, 30
  SDM AD Tombstone Reanimation cmdlets,
    770
  SDM Group Policy cmdlets, 396
  SDM Software GPMC cmdlets, 237
code examples from this book, xxi
Collaborative Data Objects (CDO), 722
collisions, replication, 599
comma-separated variable files (see CSV files)
command prompt, opening using alternate
    credentials, 4
command-line interface (CLI), 2
  help information for tools, 11
  modifying Active Directory data, 5
  producing compatibility report from, 47
  third-party command-line tools, 4
Commit Preview feature (ILM), 1005
Compare-Object cmdlet, 283
compression of inter-site replication traffic,
    595
Computer Management MMC snap-in
  stopping and starting Exchange Server, 884
computer objects, 351–392
  adding additional fields to, 70
  adding or removing computer account for a
    group, 370
  allowing DNS suffixes different from their
    domain, 649
  attributes of, 74, 351
  attributes specific to, 379
  binding to default container for computers,
    382
  changing default container for, 385
  changing machine account quota for a
    domain, 375
  creating, 352
  creating computer account for a user or
    group, 354–359
  deleting a computer account, 360
  deleting on removal of domain controllers,
    92

enabling or disabling computer settings of a
    GPO, 417
finding by OS, 379–382
finding inactive or unused, 374
finding RODCs that cached computer's
    password, 391
GPO application to, 439
identifying a computer role, 388
joining a computer to a domain, 361
listing all in a domain, 387
modifying attributes of, 377
moving a computer into new domain, 365
moving a computer within same domain,
    364
operating system attributes, 381
protecting against accidental deletion, 390
refreshing GPO settings on, 447
renaming, 367
resetting a computer account, 372
RODC, interesting attributes of, 76
testing secure channel for, 371
userAccountControl attribute, 168
Computers container, 351
  reasons not to use, 387
concurrent binds, 150
conditional forwarding, 624
Configuration NC, 17, 777
  Deleted Objects WKGUID, 384
  Partitions container, 32
  Sites container, 513
  well-known GUIDs (WKGUIDs), 155
configuration set, creating for ADAM/AD LDS,
    806
conflict objects from replication collisions,
    599
connected directory (see CD)
connector space (see CS)
connectors, 936, 943
containers, 211
  binding to default container for computers,
    382
  changing default container for computers,
    385
  deleting container and its child objects,
    200
  moving objects to different container, 188
  moving user object to different container,
    260
  undeleting container objects, 773

well-known GUIDs corresponding to, 154
control access rights, 673
control, delegating (see delegation of control)
copygpo.wsf script, 399
createDialog attribute, 245
creategpo.wsf script, 398
CreateMailbox method, 901
createmigrationtable.wsf script, 411
createTimestamp attribute, 202
Cross Domain Move LDAP control, 367
cross-forest trust, 16
crossRef objects
    application partition, delegating control
            over, 799
    attributes of, 19
    creating, 193
    creating and removing, 780
    interesting attributes applying to
            application partitions, 778
    msDS-NC-Replica-Locations attribute, 785,
            787, 790
    msDS-SDReferenceDomain attribute, 794
    NetBIOS name of a domain, 32
    querying to find application partitions in
            forest, 782
    removing for orphaned domains, 27
    replication notification delay attributes,
            794
CS (connector space), 941
    connector space object properties dialog,
            Preview, 1003
    deleting data in, 1000
    flowing attribue from HR database MA's CS
            into metaverse, 958
    MA (management agent) versus, 947
    projection and joins, 942
    searching data in, 998
cscript utility, 395
CSV (comma-separated variable) files
    exporting objects to, 208
    importing objects using, 209
csvde utility
    exporting objects to CSV file, 208
    importing objects, 209
custom claims, 851

D

DACLs (Discretionary Access Control Lists),
        322, 834

data binding
    binding to default container for computers,
            382
    binding to object GUID, 152
    using fast or concurrent bind, 150
DC locator process, 97, 122
dcdiag utility, 89
    checking for replication problems, 597
    CheckSDRefDom, VerifyReplicas, and
            CrossRefValidation tests, 791
    listing services advertised by domain
            controller, 104
    RegisterInDNS switch, 638
    testing application partition installation on
            server, 790
    tests performed by, 90
    verifying DC registration of resource
            records, 637
dcgpofix utility, 448
DCInstall settings, Windows Server 2003, 88
dcpromo utility, 21
    creating a domain, 24
    extended logging for, 697
    /forceremoval switch, 93
    installation of RODCs, 79
    promoting a server to domain controller,
            76
    promoting RODCs, 77
    removing a domain, 25
    removing a forest, 22
    unattended DC promotion or demotion,
            87
Dcpromo.log and Dcpromoui.log files, 88
DCs (see domain controllers)
DDNS (dynamic DNS), 23
    registrations of resource records, 643
default aging configuration setting, 635
defaultSecurityDescriptor attribute, 682
defragmentation of DIT file, 112
    offline defrag to reclaim space, 762
    online, performing manually, 757
delegation of control
    AD-integrated DNS zone, 625
    administration of GPOs, 431
    application partition management, 796
    DHCP server administration, 653
    effects of moving objects to different OU,
            225
    managing group membership, 339

1026 | Index

revoking delegated permissions, 673
sites, 523
using Delegation of Control Wizard, 669
Delegation of Control Wizard, 669
    customizing, 671
deleted objects, 738
    attributes of, 739
    searching for, 769
    undeleting container object, 773
    undeleting single object, 771
Deleted Objects container, 738
deletegpo.wsf script, 402
DeleteMailbox method, 904
DeleteObject method, 199, 258
delta import run profile, 992
delta imports, 940
delta synchronization, 945
    run profile, 977, 992
deprovisioning, 957
    testing for user accounts in AD, 982
deregistration, WINS, 23
DFS (Distributed File System), replication of,
        708
DHCP, 651–657
    authorizing a DHCP server, 652
    locating unauthorized DHCP servers, 654
    restricting DHCP administrators, 655
DHCP MMC snap-in, authorizing DHCP
        server, 652
dhcpClass object class, 653
dhcploc utility, 654
diagnostics logging, 698
    Garbage Collection diagnostics logging
        option, 766
    inefficient or expensive LDAP queries, 710
    listing of settings for Windows Server 2003
        and Windows Server 2008, 699
    setting Garbage Collection diagnostics
        logging option, 761
Dim keyword (VBScript), 10
directory information tree (DIT), 211
Directory Services Event Viewer, 725
Directory Services Restore Mode (see DSRM)
DirectoryContext objects, contexts created by
        constructor, 101
DirectoryEntry class, 3
    creating objects, 172
DirectorySearcher class
    finding application partitions in forest, 781

finding conflict objects from replication
        collisions, 601
finding orphaned objects, 603
PageSize property, 163
properties related to directory search, 158
properties related to LDAP controls, 148
searches for objects in a domain, 157
DirectoryServices namespace, 3
    creating AD users, 247
    creating an OU, 817, 824
    creating inetOrgPerson object, 252
    creating new AD user, 818
    disabling a user, 279
    finding all GCs in domain or forest, 118
    finding domain controller or global catalog
        servers in a site, 121
    finding FSMO role holders, 128
    group membership, copying from one user
        to another, 289
    listing of computer accounts, 388
    modifying machine account quota, 377
    modifying user display name, 245
    modifying user profile attributes, 259
    moving a user, 261
    moving group within a domain, 329
    preventing user password from expiring,
        295
    renaming a PSO, 453
    renaming a user, 264
    requiring user to change password, 294
    searching for computers, 381
    setting user password, 291
disconnectors, 943
Discretionary Access Control Lists (see DACLs)
display names of users, changing, 244
DisplayAttributes function, 144
DisplayMembers function, 325
distinguished name (see DN)
distinguishedName attribute, 96
Distributed File System (DFS), replication of,
        708
Distributed Link Tracking (DLT) objects,
        cleaning up, 112
distribution groups, 315
DIT (Directory Information Tree), 737
DIT file, 737
    checking integrity of, 753
    creating reserve file for, 760
    database write transactions, 737

defragmentation of, 112
deleted objects in, 772
determining size of, 767
finding amount of whitespace in, 761
moving, 754
performing offline defrag to reclaim space,
    762
performing online defrag manually, 757
recovering when other methods have failed,
    759
repairing or recovering, 755
dltpurge.vbs script, 112
DN (distinguished name), 18
attribute flows, 949
DN with Binary attributes, 791
nTDSDSA object of domain controller, 100
original, of renamed object, 197
RootDSE mechanism for naming contexts,
    138
DNS (Domain Name System), 609–651
ADM file disabling dynamic DNS
            registration for Windows 2000
            clients, 412
clearing DNS cache, 636
configuring forwarding, 622
configuring zone transfers, 620
converting zone to AD-integrated zone,
    617
creating and deleting resource records, 627
creating forward lookup zone, 611
creating reverse lookup zone, 613
delegating control of AD-integrated zone,
    625
deleting resource records on removal of
            domain controllers, 92
deregistering DC's resource records, 642
dnsZone and dnsNode objects, attributes of,
    610
enabling DNS srver debug logging, 639
finding domain controllers and GCs via,
    121
finding PDC Emulator FSMO role owner,
    132
modifying allowed DNS suffixes for domain,
    649
modifying server configuration, 631
moving AD-integrated zones into
            application partition, 618
namespaces, 15

preventing DC from dynamically registering
            resource records, 643
querying resource records, 630
registering DC resource records, 642
removing all entries for demoted domain
            controllers, 23
scavenging old resource records, 633
server performance statistics, 705
storage of DNS data in AD-integrated zone,
    610
verifying registration of resource records by
            DC, 637
viewing server's zones, 614
DNS Management MMC snap-in
configuring forwarding, 622
configuring zone transfers, 620
converting zone to AD-integrated zone,
    617
creating and deleting resource records, 627
creating forward lookup zone, 611
creating reverse lookup zone, 613
delegating control of AD-integrated zone,
    625
deregistering DC's DNS records, 643
enabling DNS server debug logging, 639
flushing DNS cache, 636
modifying DNS server configuration, 632
moving AD-integrated zones into
            application partition, 618
scavenging stale resource records, 633
viewing zones on a server, 615
DNS WMI provider, 612
DnsAvoidRegisterRecords setting, 648
dnscmd utility
/clearcache switch, 636
/config switch settings, 632
configuring forwarding, 623
configuring zone transfers, 620
creating AD-integrated reverse zone, 614
creating AD-integrated zone, 612
creating and deleting resource records, 627
enabling DNS server debug logging, 639
enumerating zones on a server, 615
/enumzones switch, filters for, 616
scavenging stale resource records, 634
/statistics option, 706
    statids for, 707
/zonechangeddirectorypartiton switch, 619
/zoneresettype switch, 617

dNSHostName attribute, computer objects, 650

dnsNode objects, 610

dnsRoot attribute
    application partitions, 782
    crossRef objects, 32

dnsZone objects, 610

Domain class, FindAllDomainControllers( ) method, 119

Domain Controller Security Policy MMC snap-in, 723

domain controllers, 73–133
    application partition on, 779
    attributes of RODCs, 75
    automating promotion or demotion of, 87
    changing preference for, 122
    checking for upgrade readiness, 47
    cleaning up Distributed Link Tracking (DLT) objects, 112
    computer objects, attributes of, 74
    configuring to use external time source, 107
    demoting, 86
    deregistering DNS resource records, 642
    determining if GC promotion is complete, 115
    DNS resource record registration
        forcing, 642
        verifying for, 637
    DNS server responsibilities, 609
    dynamic registration of resource records, preventing, 643–649
    enabling /3GB switch to increase LSASS cache, 110
    finding closest in a domain, 96
    finding for a domain, 95
    finding FSMO role holders, 126–129
    finding in a site, 119
    finding number of logon requests, 110
    finding services advertised by, 104
    finding site for, 98
    finding via DNS lookups, 121
    forcibly removing for an orphaned domain, 28
    ignoring GC lookup failures, 125
    moving to different site, 101
    nTDSDSA objects, 75
    performing nonauthoritative restore, 749
    promoting, 76

    promoting RODCs, 77
    promoting Windows Server 2003 DC from media, 82
    querying RootDSE in domain of currently logged-in user, 7
    removing unsuccessfully demoted DC, 90
    renaming, 93
    replication
        determining if domain controllers in sync, 579
        enabling and disabling, 588
        forcing between partners, 586
        listing replication partners for DC, 604
        viewing status of several, 582
        viewing unreplicated changes between domain controllers, 583
    resetting TCP/IP stack, 106
    restarting in DS Restore Mode, 746
    restoring deleted domain controller, 105
    System State backups, 741
    targeting specific, 5
    transferring FSMO roles, 129–131
    troubleshooting promotion or demotion problems, 88
    two-stage RODC installation, 78
    verifying promotion of, 89
    viewing RootDSE, 137

domain functional levels, 36
    summary of, 38

domain local groups, 316

domain mode, changing, 34

Domain Naming FSMO role, 27, 128

Domain NC, 17, 777
    domainDNS objects and crossRef objects, 778
    LostAndFound container, 603
    well-known GUIDs (WKGUIDs), 384
    well-known GUIDs corresponding to containers, 154

Domain Security Policy MMC snap-in, 271

DomainControllers class, IsGlobalCatalog( ) method, 119

domainDNS objects
    attributes of, 18
    creating and deleting, 780
    interesting attributes applying to application partitions, 778
    ms-DS-MachineAccountQuota attribute, 377

msDS-Behavior-Version attribute, 36, 38
wellKnownObjects attribute, 384
domainFunctionality attribute, RootDSE
    object, 38
DomainPrep
    running in AD to prepare for Exchange
        Server, 872
DomainPrep containers, 45
DomainPrep process
    installing in AD and running, 869
domains, 15
    adding RODCs, 78
    creating, 24
    creating external trust for, 48
    creating shortcut trust between AD
        domains, 52
    DNS suffixes for, 649
    enumerating OUs in, 214
    finding a specific OU, 216
    finding all in a forest, 0
    finding domain controllers in, 95
    finding duplicate SIDs in, 69
    finding NetBIOS name for, 30
    joining a computer to a domain, 361
    listing all computer accounts in, 387
    login attempts, GC requirement for, 124
    moving a computer into another domain,
        365
    moving a computer within a domain, 364
    moving group to another domain, 330
    moving groups within a domain, 328
    moving object to different domain, 191
    moving objects between, guidelines for,
        367
    preparation for Exchange Server, 871
    referencing external AD domain, 193
    removing, 25
    removing an orphaned domain, 27
    renaming, 32
    searching for objects in, 155
    structure and contents, 18
    viewing trusts for, 55–58
    Windows 2000, preparing for Windows
        Server 2003 upgrade, 42
DOMAIN_CONTROLLER_INFO flags, 105
DS command-line tools supporting LDAP
        signing and encryption, 663
dsacls utility
    configuring permission inheritance, 678

creating computer account for user or
    group, 355
delegating control of a site, 524
delegating control of application partition,
    797
delegating group membership management,
    340
granting and delegating permissions, 670
granting control over AD-integrated zone,
    625
managing ADAM/AD LDS permissions,
    835
modifying ACL of an object, 680
protecting computer against accidental
    deletion, 390
protecting group against deletion, 349
protecting OU against accidental deletion,
    238
protecting user against deletion, 314
resetting object's ACL to default defined in
    schema, 683
setting ACLs, 233
viewing group permissions, 319
DSAdd utility
    creating a computer object, 353
    creating groups, 317
    creating objects, 171
    creating organizational units, 212
    creating users, 246
    using with for-do loop to create many users,
        249
dsadd utility
    creating quotas, 728
dsamain utility, 743
    exposing snapshot as LDAP server, 744
dsdbutil
    changing port used by ADAM/AD LDS
        instance, 810
    listing ADAM/AD LDS instances installed
        on computer, 810
DSGet utility
    displaying user's group membership, 282
    enumerating direct members of a group,
        323
    enumerating nested members of a group,
        324
    finding quota usage for security principal,
        734
    listing subnets, 530

viewing site properties, 520
DsGetDcName method, 97
dSHeuristics attribute, 667
    List Object Access mode, 686
dsmgmt utility, creating and deleting ADAM application partition, 814
dsmod utility, 5
DSMod utility
    adding and removing group members, 326
    adding and removing members from a group, 655
    changing group scope or type of group, 332
    dsmod user options for setting userAccountControl, 299
    enabling and disabling user account, 278
    enabling or disabling global catalog, 114
    modifying group attributes, 335
    modifying group membership to restrict anonymous access, 668
    modifying objects, 174
    modifying tombstone weight in quota calculation, 731
    moving a group within a domain, 328
    preventing user from changing password, 292
    preventing user password expiration, 295
    renaming a user, 264
    requiring user to change password on next logon, 293
    setting default quotas, 733
    setting user account expiration, 302
    setting user's password, 290
    updating user's profile attributes, 259
DSMove utility
    moving a computer within a domain, 364
    moving a user object, 261
    moving domain controller to different site, 102
    moving object to different OU or container, 189
    renaming a site, 521
    renaming a user, 263
    renaming an object, 196
    renaming an OU, 228
    using with DSQuery to move domain controller to another site, 103
DSQuery utility
    combining with DSGet to find if site enables group caching, 345
    determining number of child object of OU, 232
    enumerating GCs in a forest, 117
    enumerating OUs in a domain, 215
    finding all domains in a forest, 28
    finding application partitions hosted by a server, 788
    finding application partitions in forest, 781
    finding computer object OS, 380
    finding conflict objects from replication collisions, 600
    finding disabled users, 280
    finding inactive computers, 374
    finding orphaned objects, 602
    finding user passwords nearing expiration, 296
    finding users with no recent logons, 306
    listing all GPOs in a domain, 396
    listing attributes for an object, 140
    listing contents of an OU, 219
    listing sites in a forest, 520
    listing subnets, 530
    modifying attribute for several users at once, 255
    moving objects from one OU to another, 224
    querying for replication partners of domain controller, 604
    querying owner of individual FSMO role, 127
    querying the global catalog, 159
    quota command, 729
    retrieving current domain functional level, 36
    retrieving current forest functional level, 39
    searches using bitwise AND filter, 167
    searching for large number of objects, 162
    searching for objects in a domain, 156
    using with DSMove to move domain controller to another site, 103
    viewing created and modified timestamps, 202
DsReplicaGetInfo method, 607
dsrevoke utility, 674
DSRM (Directory Services Restore Mode), 347, 738
    deleting a computer, 360

deleting a site, 522

deleting a user, 257

deleting all child objects in an OU, 221

deleting an object, 198

deleting container and its child objects, 200

deleting OU and all objects within, 222

resetting administrator password for, 747

restarting domain controller in, 746

dumpgpoinfo.wsf script, 420

dynamic DNS (see DDNS)

dynamic groups, 337

dynamic objects

creating, 182

modifying default TTL settings, 186

refreshing, 184

special properties, 184

E

edb.logfile, 737

Edge Transport Server role, 864

effective permissions of an object, 678

EMC (Exchange Management Console), 865, 866

configuring mailbox storage limits, 915

creating a mailbox store, 926

creating address list, 918

creating storage group, 923

deleting user's mailbox, 903

enabling message tracking, 931

mail-disabling a user, 896

mail-enabling a user, 893

mailbox-enabling a user, 899

moving a mailbox, 906

EMS (Exchange Management Shell), 865

moving mailboxes, 908

EMS Snap-in for Power Shell, 866

encryption (LDAP traffic), 659

disabling, 664

enabling SSL or TLS for, 660

using SSL, TLS, or signing, 662

enumprop command, 140

running with alternate credentials, 4

Err object, 9

error checking, using VBScript, 9

esentutl utility, recovery or repair of AD database, 759

ESM (Exchange System Manager), 865

configuring mailbox limits, 913

creating a mailbox store, 925

creating address list, 917

creating storage group, 922

enabling message tracking, 929

viewing mailbox sizes and message counts, 910

event codes, DNS debug logging, 641

Event Viewer MMC

checking Directory Services Event Log for completeness of GC promotion, 116

Exchange Management Console (see EMC)

Exchange Management Shell (see EMS)

Exchange Server, 863–933

Active Directory and, 864

administration tools, 864

Exchange 2003, 865

Exchange 2007, 865

configuring mailbox limits, 913–917

Exchange 2003, 913

Exchange 2007, 915

creating a mailbox store, 925–928

Exchange 2003, 925

Exchange 2007, 926

creating a storage group, 921–925

Exchange 2003, 922

Exchange 2007, 923

creating address list, 917–921

Exchange 2003, 917

Exchange 2007, 918

creating unattended installation files for, 879

Exchange 2003, 879

Exchange 2007, 880

deleting a user's mailbox, 902

Exchange 2003, 903

Exchange 2007, 904

enabling message tracking, 929–933

Exchange 2003, 929

Exchange 2007, 931

Exchange Server 2007 architecture, 864

installing anti-spam agents on hub transport servers, 928

installing Exchange Management tools, 881

Exchange 2003, 881

Exchange 2007, 883

installing first in an organization, 873

Exchange 2003, 873

Exchange 2007, 875
mail-disabling a user, 894–897
    Exchange 2003, 895
    Exchange 2007, 896
mail-enabling a user, 888–894
    attributes changed on user object, 891
    Exchange 2003, 889
    Exchange 2007, 893
    internetEncoding attribute values, 891
mailbox-enabling a user, 898–902
    Exchange 2007, 899
    Exchange Server 2003, 898
moving a mailbox, 905–910
    Exchange 2003, 905
    Exchange 2007, 906
preparing Active Directory for, 868
    Exchange 2007 solution, 870
starting and stopping
    listing of Exchange services, 886
stopping and starting, 884
    Exchange 2003, 884
    Exchange 2007, 885
viewing mailbox sizes and message counts, 910–913
    Exchange 2003, 910
    Exchange 2007, 911
Exchange System Manager (ESM), 865
exchmbx utility
    mail-disabling a user, 895
    mail-enabling a user, 889
    mailbox-enabling a user, 898
    moving a mailbox, 905
expensive searches, 710
explicit connectors and disconnectors, 943
export attribute flow, 992
export run profile
    creating for HR database MA, 996
    executing for HR database MA, 997
Extensible MA for Connectivity (XMA or ECMA), 936

F

fast binds, 151
federated trust, 839
Federated Web SSO, 839
    account partner configuration as, 852
Federated Web SSO with Forest Trust, 839
    account partner configuration as, 852
    configuring forest trust for, 856

federation servers, 845
FGPP (Fine-Grained Password Policies), 274
    applying to group object, 349
    applying to user object, 275
    creating in Windows Server 2008 domain, 449
    editing, 452
    viewing FGPP for user account, 276
File Replication Service (FRS), monitoring, 708
FindExpAcc joeware tool, 296
Flexible Single Master Operations (see FSMO roles)
forceful removal of a forest, 23
ForceGuest security policy setting, 363
ForeignSecurityPrincipal objects, 827
forest trust, 51
    creating for AD FS, 856
forestFunctionality attribute, RootDSE object, 41
ForestPrep containers, 46
ForestPrep process
    installing in AD and running, 868
    running in AD to prepare for Exchange Server, 871
forests, 16
    brute force method of removal, 23
    creating, 21
    creating transitive trust between AD forests, 50
    creating UPN siffix for, 311
    finding all domains in, 0
    finding application partitions in, 780
    finding global catalog servers in, 117
    linking sites in forest, 519
    preparation for Exchange Server, 871
    preparing for Windows upgrade, 464
    raising functional level, 39–42
    removing, 22
    structure and contents, 17
    Windows 2000, preparing for Windows Server 2003 upgrade, 42
forwarders, 624
fowarding, configuring, 622
FQDNs (fully qualified domain names)
    deregistration of domain controller resource records, 642
    mapping to IP addresses in forward lookup zone, 611

FRS (File Replication Service), monitoring, 708
FRS Member object, deleting on removal of domain controller, 92
frsdiag utility, 708
FSMO (Flexible Single Master Operations) roles, 73
    Domain Naming Master, 27
    finding role holders, 126–129
    identifying for a computer, 388
    listed, 128
    seizing a role, 131
    transferring to different domain controller, 129–131
    transferring when demoting domain controllers, 86
fSMORoleOwner attribute, 128
fsutil utility, creating reserve DIT file, 760
full imports, 940
full synchronization, 945
    run profile for HR database MA, 976
functional levels
    domain, 36–39
    forest, 33, 39–42

G

Garbage Collection diagnostics logging option, 761, 766
garbage collection interval, changing, 764
GCs (global catalogs)
    determining if GC promotion is complete, 115
    disabling GC requirement during domain login, 124
    disabling GC requirement for Windows Server 2003 or Windows Server 2008, 125
    enabling and disabling, 113
    finding GC servers in a site, 119
    finding GC servers in forest, 117
    finding via DNS lookups, 121
    forest-wide search using the GC, 158
    searching user's memberOf attribute, 290
Get-ExCommand cmdlet, 867
Get-MailboxStatistics cmdlet, 911, 913
get-QADGroupMember cmdlet, 283
get-QADObject cmdlet, 29, 157
Get-WMIObject cmdlet, 865
getreportsforgpo.wsf script, 404

GetUserInfo tool, 282
global catalogs (see GCs)
global groups, 316
Globally Unique Identifiers (see GUIDs)
GlobalNamesZone (see GNZ)
GNZ (GlobalNamesZone), 609
GPInventory tool, 395
gpLink attribute of OUs, 237
GPM.GetBackupDir method, 444
GPM.GetDomain method, 399
GPMBackup objects, 409, 444
GPMBackupDir.GetBackup method, 444
GPMC (Group Policy Management Console) MMC snap-in, 394
    applying security filter to GPO, 429
    assigning logon or logoff script, 415
    backing up GPOs, 440
    blocking GPO inheritance on an OU, 424
    configuring loopback processing for, 439
    copying GPOs, 399
    creating a migration table, 410
    creating GPOs, 398
    creating WMI filter, 434
    delegating GPO administration, 432
    deleting a GPO, 402
    disabling user or computer settings, 417
    enabling strong domain authentication, 685
    enforcing GPO link settings, 426
    finding GPOs in domain, 396
    importing custom ADM settings into GPOE, 412
    importing security template, 433
    importing settings into a GPO, 407
    installing application with a GPO, 416
    linking GPO to an OU, 235, 422
    listing GPO links, 420
    modifying Kerberos settings, 692
    preventing dynamic registration of certain resource records, 645
    preventing LM hash of password from being stored, 684
    restoring a GPO, 442
    simulating RSoP, 445
    using GPOE to modify GPO settings, 406
    viewing GPO settings, 404
GPMDomain objects, 399
GPMDomain.GetSOM method, 424
GPMDomain.GetWMIFilter method, 438

GPMDomain.RestoreGPO method, 445
GPMDomain.SearchGPOs method, 397
GPMDomain.SearchSOMs method, 421
GPMGPO objects, 397
GPMGPO.Backup method, 442
GPMGPO.CopyTo method, 401
GPMGPO.Delete method, 403
GPMGPO.GenerateReportToFile method, 405
GPMGPO.GetSecurityInfo method, 431
GPMGPO.Import method, 409
GPMGPO.SetComputerEnable method, 419
GPMGPO.SetUserEnable method, 419
GPMGPO.SetWMIFilter method, 438
GPMSearchCriteria object, 401
GPMSitesContainer.SearchSites method, 421
GPMSOM.CreateGPOLink method, 424
GPMWMIFilter objects, 438
GPOE (Group Policy Object Editor), 394, 406
  importing custom ADM settings into, 412
GPOs (Group Policy Objects), 393–455
  applying security filter to, 428
  applying WMI filter to, 436
  assigning logon/logoff or startup/shutdown scripts, 415
  backing up, 439
  blocking inheritance of GPOs on an OU, 424
  configuring loopback processing for, 438
  copying, 399
  creating, 397
  creating custom GPO settings, 412
  creating FGPP, 449
  creating GPO link to OU, 422
  creating migration table, 410
  creating WMI filter for, 434
  delegating administration of, 431
  deleting a GPO, 402
  disabling user or computer settings, 417
  editing a FGPP, 452
  enabling auditing of AD LDS access, 837
  enabling auditing of Registry keys, 726
  enforcing GPO link settings, 426
  finding in a domain, 396
  GPO client logging, 701
  importing security template, 433
  importing settings into, 407
  inability to apply to Computers container, 387

inheritance of, objects moved from one OU to another, 225
installing applications with, 416
linking GPO to an OU, 235
listing links for, 419
managing, 394
modifying settings, 406
refreshing GPO settings on a computer, 447
restoring, 442
restoring default GPO, 448
simulating RSoP (Resultant Set of Policies), 445
viewing effective PSO for user, 454
viewing RSoP, 446
viewing settings of, 403
gpotool utility, 396
GPP (Group Policy Preferences), 394, 436
gpresult utility, 447
GPSOM.GPOInheritanceBlocked method, 426
gpupdate utility, 447
group claims, 850
group objects
  applying FGPP to, 349
  attribute-scoped queries against, 165
  attributes of, 316
Group Policy Management Console MMC snap-in (see GPMC MMC snap-in)
Group Policy Modeling, 445
Group Policy Objects (see GPOs)
groups, 315–350
  adding and removing members, 326
  adding or removing computer account, 370
  changing scope or type of group, 332
  changing user's primary group, 285
  copying user's group membership to another user, 287
  creating, 316
  creating ADAM/AD LDS groups, 823
  creating computer account for a group, 354–359
  creating dynamic group, 337
  delegation of membership management, 339
  enabling universal group membership caching, 344
  group objects, attributes of, 316

included in AdminSDHolder processing, 689

managing ADAM or AD LDS group memberships, 825

modifying attributes of, 334

moving to a different domain, 330

moving within a domain, 328

protecting against accidental deletion, 348

removing all group memberships from user object, 284

resolving primary group ID for a user, 342

restoring deleted group, 347

user membership in many, Kerberos authentication and, 694

viewing direct members of, 322

viewing group membership of a user, 281

viewing group permissions, 319

viewing nested members, 324

groupType attribute, 319, 333

GUI-based tools, signing and encrypting LDAP traffic, 662

GUIDs (Globally Unique Identifiers)

connecting to object GUID, 152

connecting to well-known GUID, 153

object renaming and, 196

well-known GUIDs mapping to container objects, 384

GUIs (graphical user interfaces), 2

H

homeDirectory attribute, 260

homeMDB attribute, 902

homeMDBBL attribute, 927

hostname, renaming, 369

hub transport servers, installing anti-spam agents on, 928

I

IADs::GetInfo method, 144

IADsAccessControlEntry interface, 359

IADsContainer::Delete method, 200, 258

IADsContainer::GetObject method, 151

IADsLargeInteger object, 275

IADsOpenDSObject::OpenDSObject method, 8, 151

IADsPropertyEntry object, 144

IADsPropertyList object, 144

IADsTools interface, 96

comparing up-to-dateness for domain controllers, 580

GetMetaData method, 607

listing unreplicated changes between domain controllers, 584

wrapper for DsGetDcName method, 97

IADsUser::AccountDisabled property method, 279

IADsUser::ChangePassword method, 291

IADsUser::IsAccountLocked method, 269

IADsUser::SetPassword method, 291

identity claims, 850

account partner, 851

resource partner, 853

Identity Integration Feature Pack (IIFP), 937

Identity Lifecycle Manager (see ILM)

IFM feature, Windows Server 2008, 85

IGPMSearchCriteria interface, 428

IIFP (Identity Integration Feature Pack), 937

IIS (Internet Information Services)

installing on Windows Server 2003 R2 server, 840

installing on Windows Server 2008, 842

performing unattended install of, 841

ILM (Identity Lifecycle Manager), 935–1015

advanced import attribute flow, 960

architecture, 939

committing changes to individual identities using Commit Preview feature, 1005

configuring HR database MA for projection, 972

configuring run profile for HR database MA, 967

configuring run profile to load container structure from AD, 969

configuring run profile to load telephoneNumber from AD, 992

connector space (CS), 941

connectors, 943

contributing UTCCodedTime attribute to Active Directory, 1010

creating Active Directory MA, 954

creating controlling script, 985–990

creating HR database MA, 952

creating run profile script, 984

creating run profile to export objects from AD MA to Active Directory, 979 deleting data in connector space and metaverse, 1000

enabling directory synchronization from AD to HR database, 990

executing provisioning rule, 978

exporting and encoding accountExpires attribute, 1013

exporting data to HR database, 997

exporting objects to Active Directory using export run profile, 980

exporting telephoneNumber data to HR database, 996

extending object types to include new attribute, 1002

Feature Pack 1, ILM 2007, 937

flowing null value to a data source, 1008

implementing advanced attribute flow rules extension, 962–965

importing and decoding accountExpires attribute, 1011

importing data, 939

loading AD data using delta import and delta synchronization run profile, 994

loading initial AD container structure into, 971

loading initial HR database data into, using run profile, 968

management agents (MAs), 946

MAs (Management Agents), 936

metaverse (MV), 942

metaverse object deletion rule, 956

metaverse Provisioning-Rules-Extension, 973

passing data between rules extensions using transaction properties, 1006

previewing changes to configuration, 1002

projection and join, 942

requirements for, 937

rule profile for provisioning, 976

searching data in connector space, 998

searching data in metaverse, 999

setting up advanced export attribute flow in AD, 966

simple export attribute flow to AD, 959

simple import attribute flow, 957

single rules extension affecting multiple attribute flows, 1007

state-based synchronization, 944

synchronizing AD from an HR database, 949

testing provisioning and deprovisioning of user accounts in AD, 982

import attribute flow, 992

importgpo.wsf script, 407

inefficient searches, 710

inetOrgPerson object class, 252

inetOrgPerson objects, 247

converting between user objects, 253

creating, 250

delegating control over, 672

Infrastructure FSMO role, 128

inheritance

Active Directory hierarchy of classes, 135

configuring for permissions, 678

GPO, blocking on an OU, 424

interfaces, objects retrieved with fast binds, 151

Interim functional level, 38

Internet Service Manager MMC snap-in

configuring website to use Windows NT token-based authentication, 860

Internet Services Manager MMC snap-in, 840

enabling SSL for Default Web Site, 840

internetEncoding attribute, 893

values of, 891

Intersite Topology Generator (see ISTG)

ipconfig utility

/flushdns switch, 636

ISTG (Intersite Topology Generator), 103

I_NetLogonControl2 method, 110

J

joeware utilities

support of SSL, 663

website, 12

joins, 942

K

KCC (Knowledge Consistency Checker), 103

creation of replication topology, 605

diagnostis logging for, 699

KDC (Kerberos Key Distribution Center), 690

Kerberos, 660

access tokens, 693

enabling Kerberos logging, 704

forcing to use TCP, 691

modifying default settings, 692
policy settings, listed, 693
viewing and purging tickets, 689
Kerberos realm, creating a trust to, 53
kerbtray utility, 689
klist utility, 689
Knowledge Consistency Checker (see KCC)

L

lastKnownParent attribute, 603
lastLogon attribute, 305
lastLogonTimestamp attribute, 304
LDAP (Lightweight Directory Access Protocol)
    connecting to well-known GUID, 153
    creating group based on LDAP query, 337
    Cross Domain Move LDAP control, 192,
        367
    disabling LDAP signing or encryption, 664
    enabling anonymous access, 665
    encrypting traffic with SSL, TLS, or signing,
        662
    LDAP controls supported by Active
        Directory, 148
    modifying default query policy, 203
    over SSL/TLS, 660
    query policy settings, 204
    referrals, 194
    searches using Attribute Scoped Query
        control, 164
    searches using base DN search scope and
        search filter, 157
    Tree Delete LDAP control, 201, 223
    using LDAP controls in an LDAP operation,
        147
    version 3 specification, 135
LDAP Data Interchange Format (see LDIF)
LDAP Data Interchange Format files (see LDIF
    files)
LDAP queries
    inefficient and expensive, logging of, 710
    using STATS control to view query statistics,
        712
LDIF (LDAP Data Interchange Format), 5
LDIF files, 6
    exporting objects to, 206
    importing objects using, 207
    predefined, for ADAM/AD LDS, 813
ldifde utility, 6
    adding DNS suffix, 649

adding fields to users and computers, 71
bulk import of unique user names, 249
changing computer quota for a user, 376
changing domain mode, 34
changing tombstone lifetime, 774
changing tombstone weight in quota
    calculation, 730
creating a subnet, 529
creating address list, 917
creating crossRef, 193
creating dynamic objects, 183
creating inetOrgPerson user, 251
creating objects, 171
creating storage group, 922
dynamically linking auxiliary class to an
    object, 181
enabling group caching, 345
enabling universal group caching for a site,
    526
exporting objects to LDIF files, 206
extending ADAM/AD LDS schema, 812
forest functional level, changing, 40
garbage collection interval, changing, 764
importing data into an ADAM or AD LDS
    instance, 830
importing objects with, 207
mail-disabling a user, 895
mail-enabling a user, 889
modifying computer object attributes, 378
modifying group attributes, 334
modifying inter-site replication interval,
    594
modifying intra-site replication interval,
    591
modifying objects, 174
online defrag of DIT file, 758
raising domain functional level, 37
refreshing dynamic objects, 185
setting default quotas, 732
LDP
    binding to container using its GUID, 152
    binding to default container for computers,
        382
    changing default container for computers,
        385
    changing password for ADAM/AD LDS
        user, 819
    connecting to well-known GUID, 153
    counting objects in Active Directory, 145

creating dynamic objects, 182
creating objects, 170
deleting a user, 257
deleting an object, 198
determining number of child objects of an OU, 231
fast or concurrent bind, 150
finding application partitions hosted by server, 787
finding application partitions in a forest, 780
finding computer objects with particular OS, 379
finding conflict objects resulting from replication collisions, 600
finding domain controller's site, 98
managing ADAM/AD LDS application partitions, 813
managing ADAM/AD LDS permissions, 834
modifying objects, 173
online manual defrag of DIT file, 757
redirecting users to alternative OU, 262
refreshing dynamic objects, 184
renaming leaf object, 195
retrieving NetBIOS name of a domain, 31
searching for deleted objects, 769
searching for large number of objects, 161
searching for objects in a domain, 155
searching the global catalog, 158
searching with bitwise filter, 166
suport for encryption, 662
undeleting a single object, 771
using LDAP controls, 147
using STATS control to test efficiency of LDAP queries, 712
viewing attributes of an object, 140
viewing object metadata, 606
viewing RootDSE, 136
leaf nodes, 211
legacyExchangeDN attribute, 892
licensingSiteSettings objects, 513, 519
lingering objects, 599, 739
linking a GPO to an OU, 422
links to files on NTFS partitions, tracking by DLT service, 112
List Object Access mode, 686
listastallgpos.wsf script, 396
LM (LAN Manager) authentication, 686

LM hash of password, preventing storage of, 684
locked-out users
    finding, 267
    unlocking, 268
lockout policy, viewing for a domain, 271
lockout problems with accounts, troubleshooting, 270
lockoutDuration attribute, 268
LockoutStatus program, 270
lockoutstatus.exe tool, 270
lockoutTime attribute, 267
logging
    audit events for directory access, to Security event log, 723
    database write transactions into edb.logfile, 737
    Dcpromo.log and Dcpromoui.log files, 88
    diagnostics logging, 698
    DIT whitespace information, 761
    DNS debug logging event codes, 641
    DNS server debug logging, 639
    enabling for AD FS Web Agent, 861
    enabling GPO client logging, 701
    enabling Kerberos logging, 704
    enabling NetLogon logging, 700
    enhanced logging of replication events, 597
    extended dcpromo logging, 697
    inefficient and expensive LDAP queries, 710
    message tracking logs on Exchange Server, 929–933
    number of expired tombstone objects, 766
    Performance Monitor Trace Logs, 717
logical AND operator, 168
logical OR operator, 168
logon requests processed by domain controller, 110
logon/logoff scripts in GPO, 415
logonHours attribute, 309
loopback processing of GPOs, 438
loose replication consistency, 597
LostAndFound container, 603
LSASS cache, increasing on domain controller, 110

M

machine account quota, 375
mail attribute, changing for renamed user, 265

mailbox databases, 927

mailbox stores, creating, 925–928

mailboxes

    configuring storage limits on Exchange Server, 913–917

    moving, 905–910

    viewing sizes and message counts, 910–913

MailDisable method, 897

MailEnable method, attributes changed on user object, 891

mailing lists, 13

mailNickname attribute, 892

managedBy attribute, 235, 311

    site objects, 523

managedObjects attribute, 235, 310, 311

management agents (see MAs)

MAP (MS Assessment and Planning) tools, 48

MAs (management agents), 936, 946

    attribute flow rules, 948

    configuring HR database MA for projection, 972

    configuring run profile for HR database MA, 967

    creating Active Directory MA, 954

    creating export run profile for HR database MA, 996

    creating HR database MA, 953

    creating run profile for AD MA, 969

    delta import and delta synchronization run profiles for AD MA, 992

    example scenario, synchronizing AD from HR database, 949

    executing HR database MA's provisioning run profile, 978

    import attribute flow from HR database, 957

    Metaverse Designer, 948

    provisioning user objects to AD MA from HR database MA, 973

    run profile for HR database MA to provision accounts in AD CS, 976

    run profile to export objects from AD MA to Active Directory, 979

    run profiles, 947

masteredBy attrubute, domain object, 96

MaxTokenSize value, modifying, 694

member attribute, group object, 324, 325

    write property (WP) permission, 340

memberOf attribute, 283, 289

group membership of user, 343

group object, 324

MemberOf joeware utility, 282

    enumerating nested members of a group, 324

message tracking on Exchange Server, 929–932

metadata

    removal of all metadata for removed domains, 26

    removal with ntdsutil, 91

    viewing object metadata, 605

metadirectory synchronization tools, 936

metaverse (MV), 942

    adding new attribute to existing object type in, 1002

    configuring HR database MA for projection into, 972

    deleting data in, 1000

    flowing attribute from HR database MA's connector space into, 958

    flowing attributes in metaverse to attributes in AD, 959

    projection and joins, 942

    searching data in, 999

Metaverse Designer, 948

metaverse object deletion rule, 956

metaverse Provisioning-Rules-Extension, 974

Microsoft Assessment and Planning Solution Accelerator, 47

Microsoft Developers Network (see MSDN)

Microsoft Exchange Server (see Exchange Server)

Microsoft Identity Integration Server (see MIIS)

Microsoft Identity Lifecycle Manager (see ILM)

Microsoft Knowledge Base (see MS KB articles)

Microsoft Management Console (see MMC)

MicrosoftDNS container, 610

MicrosoftDNS_ResourceRecord class, 629

    query of resource records, 631

MicrosoftDNS_Server class, 633

    clearing DNS cache, 637

    DNS debug logging, 640

    scavenging of stale resource records, 635

MicrosoftDNS_Statistic object, 706

MicrosoftDNS_Zone class

    ChangeZoneType method, 618

    CreateZone method, 612

migration tables, creating, 410

MIIS (Microsoft Identity Integration Server), 935
    documentation on Microsoft website, 951
    versions of, 937
mixed mode Windows 2000 AD domain, 34
MMC (Microsoft Management Console)
    running snap-ins with alternate credentials, 5
    running with alternate credentials, 4
mode of a domain (see domain mode)
modifyTimestamp attribute, 202
monitoring
    creating administrative performance alert, 720
    enabling auditing for AD LDS access, 836
    enabling auditing of directory access, 723
    enabling auditing of Registry keys, 726
    File Replication Service (FRS), 708
    performance alert, emailing to administrator, 721
    performance of AD, 715
    using Perfmon trace logs for AD monitoring, 717
    using STATS control to view LDAP query statistics, 712
    viewing DNS server performance statistics, 705
    Windows Time Service, 709
MoveHere method, 190
    using to rename an object, 197
movetree utility, 191
MS Assessment and Planning (MAP) tools, 48
MS KB (Microsoft Knowledge Base) articles, 1, 11
ms-DS-MachineAccountQuota attribute, 377
MSDN (Microsoft Developers Network), 1
    information on Active Directory and programmatic interfaces, 12
msDS-AllowedDNSSuffixes attribute, 650
msDS-Approx-Imed-Subordinates attributes, 232
msDS-Behavior-Version attribute
    domainDNS object, 36, 38
    Partitions container, 41
msDS-DefaultQuota attribute, 734
msDS-HasInstantiatedNCs attribute, server nTDSDSA object, 791
msDS-NC-Replica-Locations attribute, crossRef objects, 785, 787, 790

msDS-NeverRevealGroup attribute, 82
msDS-PasswordSettingsObject, 451
msDS-QuotaContainer objects, 696
msDS-QuotaControl objects, 696
msDS-QuotaEffective attribute, 734
msDS-QuotaUsed attribute, 734
msDS-ReplAttributeMetaData attribute, 608
msDS-ReplAuthenticationMode attribute, 833
msDS-Replication-Notify-First-DSA-Delay attribute, crossRef objects, 794
msDS-Replication-Notify-Subsequent-DSA-Delay attribute, crossRef objects, 794
msDS-ReplValueMetaData attribute, 608
msDS-RevealedDSAs attribute, 299
msDS-RevealedUsers attribute, 299
msDS-RevealOnDemanGroup attribute, 82
msDS-SDReferenceDomain attribute, crossRef objects, 794
msDs-TombstoneQuotaFactor attribute, 732
msDS-TopQuotaUsage attribute, 734
msDS-UserAccountDisabled attribute, 823
msExchangeStorageGroup class, 924
msExchPrivateMDB class, 927
multimaster domain controllers, 73
multimaster replication in ADAM and AD LDS, 808

N

name resolution, DNS and NetBIOS, 30
namespaces, DNS, 15
naming contexts, 777 (see NCs)
    DN (distinguished name) of, 138
    referrals to, 32
native mode, Windows 2000 AD domain, 34
nCName attribute, application partitions, 782
NCs (naming contexts), 17
.NET, PowerShell interfacing with, 3
net localgroup command, 668
net start utility
    starting ADAM/AD LDS instance, 809
    starting Exchange Server 2003, 884
    starting W32 time service, 108
net stop utility, 738, 768
    stopping ADAM/AD LDS instance, 809
    stopping Exchange Server 2003, 884
    stopping W32 time service, 108
NetBIOS name of a domain, 19
    finding, 30–32

netdiag utility
    testing for Kerberos problems, 692
    verifying domain controller promotion, 89
netdom utility, 363
    configuring forest trust for AD FS, 856
    creating external trust for a domain, 49
    creating shortcut trust between AD
        domains, 53
    creating transitive trust between AD forests,
        51
    creating trust to Kerberos realm, 54
    enabling quarantine for a trust, 66
    enabling selective authentication for trusts,
        67
    enabling SID filtering for trusts, 64
    enumerating trusts for a domain, 55
    finding FSMO role holders, 126
    joining computer to a domain, 361
    removing trusts, 63
    renaming a computer, 368
    renaming domain controllers, 94
    resetting a computer account, 373
    resetting trusts, 61
    verifying trusts, 59
NetLogon service, 645
    enabling logging for, 700
netmon program, 89
netsh utility
    authorizing DHCP server, 652
    finding PDC Emulator FSMO role owner,
        133
    resetting TCP/IP stack on domain
        controller, 106
newsgroups, 13
nlparse utility, 701
nltest utility
    confirming domain controller functioning
        as GC server, 116
    /dsderegdns switch, 642
    /dsregdns switch, 642
    enabling NetLogon logging, 700
    enumerating domain trusts, 55, 56
    finding closest domain controller, 96
    finding domain controller's site, 99
    listing services advertised by domain
        controller, 104
    number of logon requests processed by
        domain controller, 110
    resetting secure channel, 373

testing secure channel for a computer, 372
no-refresh interval for DNS records, 635
nonauthoritative restore, 106
    performing, 749
nontransitive trusts, 20
normal connectors and disconnectors, 943
notifications (replication), changing intra-site
        delay, 590–593
nslookup utility
    examining SRV record weights, 123
    finding domain controllers and GCs, 121
    finding PDC Emulator FSMO role owner,
        132
    querying resource records, 630
    zone transfers in Windows 2000, 622
NT LAN Manager (NTLM) authentication,
        686
NTBackup utility, 740
NTDS performance object counters, 715
NTDS.DIT file
    promotion of domain controllers and, 83
nTDSConnection objects
    attributes of, 516
    listing within Sites container, 604
nTDSDSA objects, 74, 514
    attributes of, 75, 516
    differentiation of domain controllers from
        other servers, 100
    options attribute, enabling or disabling GC,
        115
    queryPolicyObject attribute, 205
nTDSSiteSettings objects, 513, 519
    attributes of, 515
    universal group caching, 528
ntdsutil
    application partition, creating and deleting,
        779
    authoritative restore of object or subtree,
        751
    complete authoritative restore of AD
        database, 752
    creating snapshot of database, 743
    determining size of DIT file, 767
    finding all domains in a forest, 28
    finding and cleaning duplicate SIDs in a
        domain, 69
    finding replica servers for application
        partition, 786

forcibly removing domain controllers for orphaned domain, 28
integrity check of DIT file, 753
modifying default LDAP query policy, 203
modifying default TTL settings of dynamic objects, 187
mounting Active Directory snapshot, 744
moving DIT file, 755
offline defrag of DIT file, 763
recovering or repairing DIT file, 756
removal of unsuccessfully demoted DC, 91
removing all metadata associated with a removed domain, 26
removing orphaned domains, 27
replica server, adding or removing from application partition, 782
resetting DSRM password, 748
restoring deleted domain controller, 106
restoring deleted group, 347
seizing a FSMO role, 131
setting reference domain for application partition, 795
transferring FSMO roles, 130
ntfrsutl utility, 708
nTMixedDomain attribute, 35

O

objectClass attribute, 151
adding inetOrgPerson value to, 254
dymanicObject value, 184
objectGUID attribute, 153
objects, 135
ADAM, viewing and modifying attributes of, 827
commom attributes of, 135
conflict objects resulting from replication collisions, 599
connecting to object GUID, 152
counting in Active Directory, 145–147
creating, 170
creating dynamic object, 182
creation of, quotas on, 695
data binding using fast or concurrent bind, 150
deleted, 738
deleting a single object, 197
deleting an OU and all objects within, 222
deleting container and its child objects, 200

deleting objects in an OU, 221
dynamically linking auxiliary class, 180
enumerating in an OU, 218
exporting to CSV file, 208
exporting to LDIF files, 206
importing using CSV file, 209
importing using LDIF file, 207
lingering objects, 599
metadata, viewing, 605
modifying attributes of, 173–177
modifying bit flag attribute, 177
modifying default LDAP query policy, 203
modifying default TTL settings for dynamic objects, 186
moving from one OU to another, 223
moving to different domain, 191
moving to different OU or container, 188
orphaned objects within Active Directory, 602
reference to external AD domain, 193
refreshing a dynamic object, 184
renaming, 195
restoring, 750
searching for large number of, 161
searching for objects in a domain, 155
searching the global catalog, 158
searching with attribute-scoped query, 164
searching with bitwise filter, 166–170
using LDAP controls in an LDAP operation, 147
viewing attributes of, 140–145
viewing created and last modified timestamps, 202
viewing RootDSE, 136–140
OIDs (Object Identifiers), 147
generating for schema extensions, 462
LDAP controls, 148
use with bitwise search filters, 168
OldCmp joeware utility
finding, disabling, and deleting inactive computer accounts, 374
report on user objects, 306
OpenDSObject method, 8
operating system (OS), finding for computer objects, 379–382
operating system attributes, computer objects, 381
options attribute, site-link objects, 595
organizationalUnit objects, attributes of, 211

orphaned domains, removing, 27
OUs (organizational units), 211–239
   assigning or removing a manager, 234
   blocking inheritance of GPOs, 424
   creating, 212
     reasons for, 213
   creating GPO link to an OU, 422
   creating with DirectoryServices in
     PowerShell, 824
   delegating control of, 233
   deleting all objects in, 221
   deleting OU and all objects within, 222
   determining number of child objects, 231
   enumerating objects in, 218
   enumerating OUs in a domain, 214
   finding a specific OU in a domain, 216
   linking a GPO to, 235
   managing ADAM/AD LDS OUs, 815
   modifying, 229
   moving an OU and all its child objects, 226
   moving object to different OU, 188
   moving objects from one OU to another,
     223
   moving user object to different OU, 260
   organizationalUnit objects, attributes of,
     211
   protecting against accidental deletion, 238
   redirecting users to alternative OU, 261
   renaming, 227
Outlook
   Exchange tools installation on machine
     running Outlook, 882

P

PAC (Privilege Attribute Certificate), 694
paged searching, 161
partitions, 777
   (see also application partitions)
   application, 18
   created by ADAM or AD LDS installation,
     815
   predefined (naming contexts), 777
Partitions container, 18
   crossRef objects, 32, 778
   uPNSuffixes attribute, 312, 859
password policies
   applying FGPP to user object, 275
   Fine-Grained Password Policies (FGPP),
     274

properties that can be set, 273
   viewing for a domain, 271
Password Replication Policy (see PRP)
passwords
   applying FGPP to group object, 349
   finding user passwords nearing expiration,
     296
   preventing expiration of user password,
     294
   preventing user from changing, 291
   requiring user to change password at next
     logon, 293
   setting user's password, 290
   viewing RODCs that cached user's
     password, 297
PasswordSettingsObject (see PSOs)
PDC Emulator FSMO role, 128
   configuring to sync with external time
     provider, 107
   finding owner via DNS, 132
   finding owner via WINS, 133
   reducing traffic on, 124
Performance Monitor
   creating administrative alert, 720
   enabling Trace Logs for AD monitoring,
     717
   monitoring performance of AD, 715
   NTDS counters, listing of, 715
   viewing DNS server performance statistics,
     705
PermissionByte values, description of, 835
permissions, 659
   (see also security and authentication)
   and abbreviated codes, Delegation of
     Control Wizard, 672
   configuring inheritance of, 678
   effective permissions on an object, 677
   viewing group permissions, 319
policy boundary, domains as, 18
PowerShell, 2
   AD FS
     adding or modifying UPN suffixes, 858
     configuring forest trust, 856
   ADAM/AD LDS
     changing user password, 821
     creating groups, 824
     enabling or disabling ADAM user, 822
     listing ADAM object attributes, 833
     managing group membership, 826

managing organizational units, 817, 818

stopping or starting an instance, 809, 811

viewing and modifying object attributes, 829

address list, creating and updating, 919

application partitions

    adding or removing replica server, 784

    finding in forest, 781

    finding replica servers for, 787

    finding those hosted by a server, 790

    setting replication notification delay, 793

    setting SD reference domain for, 796

cmdlets, 3

computer objects

    adding or removing from a group, 371

    binding to default container, 384

    changing machine account quota, 376

    creating, 353

    deleting, 360

    finding OS or service pack, 381

    finding RODCs caching computer's password, 392

    listing all in a domain, 388

    modifying attributes, 379

    moving computer within a domain, 365

    protecting against deletion, 391

    renaming, 369

deleted objects, finding using SDM AD Tombstone Reanimation cmdlets, 770

deleting user mailboxes, 904

DHCP Administrators group, adding or removing members, 656

DNS

    clearing DNS cache, 637

    configuring forwarding, 624

    configuring zone transfers, 621

    creating AD-integrated forward zone, 612

    creating AD-integrated reverse zone, 614

    creating and deleting resource records, 629

    delegating control of AD-integrated zone, 626

    enabling DNS debug logging, 640

    listing zones on a server, 615

    modifying allowed DNS suffixes for domain, 650

    modifying server configuration, 633

    preventing DC's dynamic registration of records, 645

    preventing DC's registration of certain resource records, 648

    querying resource records, 631

    scavenging stale resource records, 635

domain controllers

    finding closest in a domain, 97

    finding DC or GC servers in a site, 120

    finding for a domain, 96

    finding site for, 100

    moving to different site, 103

EMS cmdlets, listing with Get-ExCommand, 867

Exchange Server 2007, starting and stopping, 885

extension in Exchange Management Shell, Exchange Server 2007, 865

forests, domains, and trusts

    changing domain mode from mixed to native, 35

    creating external trust for a domain, 49

    creating transitive trust between forests, 51

    enabling SID filtering for trusts, 64

    finding all domains in a forest, 29

    finding NetBIOS name of a domain, 32

    listing domain trusts, 56

    raising domain functional level, 38

    raising forest functional level, 41

    removing trusts, 64

    resetting trusts, 62

    verifying trusts, 60

FSMO role holders, finding, 128

FSMO role holders, retrieving, 128

FSMO roles, transferring, 130

Garbage Collection diagnostics logging option, setting, 762

Garbage Collection diagnostics logging, enabling, 767

garbage collection interval, changing, 765

GCs

    confirming GC promotion is complete, 117

enabling or disabling GC on domain
    controller, 114
finding all GCs in domain or forest, 118
GPOs
    add-SDMgplink cmdlet, 423
    add-SDMgposecurity cmdlet, 430
    add-SDMWMIFilterLink cmdlet, 438
    blocking GPO inheritance on an OU,
        425
    enabling or disabling GPO user or
        computer settings, 419
    export-SDMgpo cmdlet, 441
    get-QADUser cmdlet, 454
    Get-SDMGPLink cmdlet, 421
    get-SDMgpo cmdlet, 397
    Import-SDMGPO cmdlet, 409
    import-SDMgpo cmdlet, 444
    modifying PSOs, 453
    New-QADPasswordSettingsObject, 451
    new-SDMgpo cmdlet, 398
    out-SDMgpsettingsreport cmdlet, 405
    preconfigured permissions in SDM
        cmdlets, 431
    remove-SDMgpo cmdlet, 403
    SDM Group Policy cmdlets, 396
    update-SDMgp cmdlet, 448
groups
    adding and removing members, 327
    changing scope or type of group, 333
    creating a group, 318
    delegating membership management,
        341
    enabling universal group caching, 346
    enumerating direct members of a group,
        323
    enumerating nested members, 325
    finding group permissions, 322
    finding primary group of a user, 343
    modifying group attributes, 335
    moving within a domain, 329
    protecting against deletion, 349
    set-QADGroup cmdlet, switches for
        group attributes, 336
LDAP controls, 148
logging
    dcpromo extended logging, 698
    enabling diagnostics logging, 699
    enabling Kerberos logging, 705
mail-disabling a user, 896

mail-enabling a user in Exchange 2007,
    894
mailbox database, creating, 927
mailbox reporting, Get-MailboxStatistics
    cmdlet, 911, 912
mailbox storage limits, configuring, 916
mailbox-enabling users, 900
message tracking, enabling in Exchange
    2007, 931
monitoring
    displaying DNS server statistics, 706
    emailing performance alert to
        administrator, 722
moving a mailbox, 907
objects
    binding to object GUID, 153
    connecting to LDAP using well-known
        GUIDs, 154
    counting in Active Directory, 146
    created and last modified timestamps,
        202
    creating crossRef objects, 194
    creating dynamic objects, 183
    creating objects, 171
    deleting, 199
    deleting container and its child objects,
        201
    displaying attributes of, 143
    displaying RootDSE, 138
    dynamically linking auxiliary class to an
        object, 181
    exporting to CSV file, 208
    modifying attributes on, 174, 177
    modifying bit flag attributes, 178
    modifying multivalued attributes, 177
    moving object to different OU or
        container, 189
    paged searching, 162
    refreshing dynamic objects, 185
    renaming, 196
    searches using attribute-scoped queries,
        165
    searching for objects in a domain, 157
    searching the global catalog, 159
    searching using bitwise filter, 168
online defrag of DIT file, 758
OUs (organizational units)
    assigning or removing manager, 235
    creating, 213

deleting objects in, 221
deleting OU and all objects within, 223
enumerating contents of, 219
enumerating OUs in a domain, 215
finding specific OU in a domain, 217
linking GPO to an OU, 237
modifying an OU, 230
moving, 227
moving objects from one OU to another,
224
protecting against accidental deletion,
238
renaming an OU, 228
piping results of Get-QADObject query into
Add-QADPermisson cmdlet, 239
Quest AD cmdlets, switches available to
create user accounts, 248
Quest PowerShell Commands for Active
Directory, 30
quotas, setting default, 733
replication
changing inter-site interval, 594
comparing up-to-dateness for domain
controllers, 581
compression of inter-site traffic, setting
options bit value, 596
displaying object metadata, 607
finding conflict objects from, 601
finding orphaned objects, 603
finding replication partners of domain
controller, 605
forcing between domain controllers,
587
modifying inter-site replication interval,
595
modifying intra-site replication interval,
592
setting intra-site interval, 590
strict or loose consistency, 599
security and authentication
configuring permission inheritance, 679
delegating control, 670
disabling LDAP signing or encryption,
665
enabling anonymous LDAP access, 667
modifying ACL of an object, 681
revoking delegated permissions, 674
viewing ACL for an object, 675
selective authentication for trusts, 68

site topology
creating a site, 518
creating a subnet, 529
delegating control of a site, 525
deleting a site, 523
enabling universal group caching for site,
528
listing sites in a forest, 520
listing subnets, 531
renaming a site, 521
snapshot data, accessing, 745
Stop-Service cmdlet, 738
Storage Group, creating, 923
tombstone lifetime, modifying, 775
tombstone quota factor, modifying, 731
use in Exchange Server 2007 installation,
878
users
applying FGPP to, 276
changing user's primary group, 286
converting user objects to inetOrgPerson
objects, 254
copying existing user account, 266
copying group membership to another
user, 289
creating inetOrgPerson object, 252
creating large number of, 250
creating users, 247
deleting a user, 257
enabling or disabling user account, 279
finding disabled users in a domain, 281
finding group membership of a user,
283
finding locked-out users, 267
finding RODCs caching user password,
298
modifying default ADUC display name,
245
modifying profile attributes, 259
moving user to different container or
OU, 261
preventing password from expiring, 295
protecting against deletion, 314
removing all group memberhsips from,
285
renaming a user, 264
requiring to change password, 294
retrieving domain password and account
lockout policies, 272

setting account expiration, 303
setting attribute for several users at once, 256
setting user account options, 300
setting user's password, 291
unlocking a locked user, 269
viewing and modifying permitted logon hours, 309
viewing FGPP for user account, 277
viewing objects managed by a user, 310
using with Exchange 2003, 865
Pre-Windows 2000 Compatible Access group, 668
Preview function (ILM), 1003
primaryGroupID attribute, 287, 343
primaryGroupToken attribute, 287, 343
Privilege Attribute Certificate (PAC), 694
profile attributes for a user
listed, 259
setting, 258
programmatic solutions, 2
projection, 942
configuring HR database MA for, 972
provisioning, 973
creating run profile for HR database MA, 976
metaverse Provisioning-Rules-Extension, 974
running provisioning run profile, 978
testing provisioning of user accounts in AD, 982
user objects to AD MA from objects in HR database MA, 973
PRP (Password Replication Policy), 75
modifying, 80
psbase keyword, 191
psomgr utility, 452
applying FGPP to group object, 350
applying FGPP to user object, 276
creating starter PSOs, 453
modifying PSOs, 452
viewing effective PSO for user, 454
viewing FGPP for user account, 277
PSOs (PasswordSettingsObjects), 276
creating, 451
creating starter PSOs, 453
modifying, 452
modifying account settings, 350
precedence rules for, 277

viewing effective PSO for user, 454
purportedSearch attribute, 921
PutEx method, 175, 336
PowerShell bug using PutEx to clear attribute value, 177
pwdLastSet attribute, 294, 297

Q

Quarantine, enabling for a trust, 66
query policy, LDAP, 203
querybackuplocation.wsf script, 442
Quest AD cmdlets, 29
-argumentList Append and -argumentList Delete options, 785
quotas, 695
changing relative weight of tombstone objects in calculation of, 730
creating, 727
finding quotas assigned to security principal, 729
finding usage for security principal, 734
machine account quota, 375
msDS-QuotaContainer objects, 696
msDS-QuotaControl objects, 696
setting default for all security principals in partition, 732

R

RDN
changing to rename a user, 264
renaming a user, 263
setting for subnet, 530
Read-Only Domain Controllers (see RODCs)
realm trust, 53
reanimating objects
container object, 773
single object, 771
Recordset, RecordCount property, 146
recovery (see restores)
reference domain for application partition, 794
referrals, 194
referrals to other naming contexts, 32
refresh interval for DNS records, 635
regedit utility
changing preference for a domain controller, 123

disabling GC requirement for domain logins, 124

Registry keys, enabling auditing of, 726

Registry settings
adding IgnoreGCFailures key, 125
changing intra-site replication interval, 589
configuring W32Time Service, 107
confirming complete GC promotion, 116
dcpromo logging, 697
diagnostics logging, 698
dynamic registration of DNS resource records, 643, 646
enabling auditing for Windows NT token-based application, 861
enabling GPO client logging, 701
enabling Kerberos logging, 704
enabling or disabling schema modifications, 461
expensive and inefficient searches, 711
Garbage Collection diagnostics logging option, 761, 766
Kerberos, 691
LDAP signing or encryption, 664
LM hash of password, storage of, 684
message tracking on Exchange Server, 930
mnemonics for resource records, 648
modifying intra-site replication delay in Windows 2000, 592
NetLogon logging, 701
strict or loose replication consistency, 598
viewing GPOs applied to computer, 447

regsvr32 utility, 459

Reliability and Performance Monitor, 715
(see also Performance Monitor)
creating administrative alert, 721
enabling Trace Logs for AD monitoring, 718

Remote Server Administration Tools (RSAT), 274

repadmin utility
checking for replication problems, 597
enabling and disabling replication, 588
enabling strict or loose replication consistency, 598
finding differences between domain controllers, 583
forcing ADAM/AD LDS replication, 832
forcing replication between domain controllers, 586

setting replication notification delay for application partition, 792
viewing object metadata, 606
viewing replication status of domain controllers, 582
Windows 2000 syntax to compare domain controllers, 580

replaceable text in examples, 10

replica servers
adding or removing in application partition, 782
finding for application partition, 786

replicas, ADAM/AD LDS, 808

replication, 579–608
application partitions and, 779
changing inter-site interval for, 593
changing intra-site interval, 589
changing intra-site notification delay, 590–593
checking for potential problems, 597
conflict objects resulting from replication collisions, 599
determining if two domain controllers are in sync, 579
disabling inter-site compression for, 595
DNS zone data, 609
enabling and disabling, 588
enhanced logging of events, 597
File Replication Service (FRS), monitoring, 708
finding orphaned objects, 602
forcing ADAM/AD LDS replication, 831
forcing between domain controllers, 586
intrasite, configuring for ADAM or AD LDS application partition, 831
listing replication partners for domain controller, 604
managing AD LDS replication authentication, 832
setting notification delay for application partition, 792
strict or loose replication consistency, 597
viewing object metadata, 605
viewing status of several domain controllers, 582
viewing unreplicated changes between domain controllers, 583

replInterval attribute, 595

replPropertyMetaData attribute, 605

reserve file, creating for DIT file, 760
resource partners, 839, 846
    configuring, 853
resource records, DNS, 609
    creating and deleting, 627
    deregistering DC's resource records, 642
    dynamic registration by DC, preventing,
        643–649
    forcing DC registration of, 642
    querying, 630
    scavenging old records, 633
    SRV records, 121
    verifying DC registration of, 637
resources for further information, 11
restoregpo.wsf script, 443
restores
    accidentally deleted group, 347
    authoritative restore of object or subtree,
        750
    complete authoritative restore of AD
        database, 752
    default GPO, 448
    deleted domain controller, 105
    GPO, 442
    performing database recovery, 759
    performing nonauthoritative restore, 749
    restarting domain controller in DS Restore
        Mode, 746
    restoring deleted domain controller, 106
    restoring deleted user account, 312
    restoring single deleted object, 772
    soft recovery of DIT file, 756
    undeleting a container object, 773
    undeleting a single object, 771
Richards, Joe, 12
Richards, joe, 867
RID FSMO role, 69, 128
RIDs, 69
RODCs (Read-Only Domain Controllers), 74
    attributes of, 75
    finding RODCs that cached a computer's
        password, 391
    modifying PRP (Password Replication
        Policy), 80
    performing two-stage installation, 78
    promoting, 77
    viewing RODCs that cached a user's
        password, 297
roles, Exchange 2007, 864

installing with setup.com switches, 878
selecting during installation of Exchange
    Management tools, 883
root domain, creating for a forest, 21
RootDSE objects
    attributes for transfer of FSMO roles, 131
    domainFunctionality attribute, 38
    DoOnlineDefrag attribute, 759
    dsServiceName attribute, 100
    forestFunctionality attribute, 41
    isGlobalCatalogReady attribute, 116
    viewing, 136–140
RRs (see resource records, DNS)
RSAT (Remote Server Administration Tools),
    274
RSoP (Resultant Set of Policies) MMC snap-in,
    446
RSoP (Resultant Set of Policies), simulating,
    445
rules extensions
    passing data between using transaction
        properties, 1006
    single rules extension affecting multiple
        attribute flows, 1007
Run Deleted Objects LDAP control, 770
run profiles, 947
    configuring delta import and delta
        synchronization run profile for AD
        MA, 992
    configuring for HR database MA, 967
    configuring to load container structure from
        AD, 969
    creating export run profile for AD MA, 979
    creating export run profile for HR database
        MA, 996
    creating run profile script, 984
    executing export run profile, 980
    executing export run profile for HR database
        MA, 997
    loading initial HR database into ILM using,
        968
    using AD MA run profile to import AD
        container structure into ILM, 971
runas command, 4

S

SACLs (System Access Control Lists), 322,
    834
sAMAccountName attribute, 247

ADAM or AD LDS users and, 819
computer objects, 354
scavenging interval, 635
schema, 457–511
classSchema objects and attributeSchema
objects, 458
classSchema objects, attributes of, 457
default ACL for object class
changing, 681
comparing ACL of an object to, 682
resetting object's ACL to, 683
enabling updates, 460
extending, 463
extending ADAM/AD LDS schema, 812
generating OID for new class or attribute,
462
preparing for AD upgrade, 464
registering Active Directory Schema MMC
snap-in, 459
schema objects, anatomy of, 457
Schema FSMO role, 128
running ForestPrep on DC that owns, 868
Windows 2000, enabling schema updates,
460
Schema NC, 17, 777
scope of management (SOM), 426
scopes
changing group scope, 332
group, 316
scriptable API for GPMC, 394
scripts folder, Exchange 2007, 866
scripts, assigning in a GPO, 415
SDM AD Tombstone Reanimation cmdlets,
770
SDM Software GPMC cmdlets, 237
search-filter expansion
ANR search example, 714
LDAP query example, 714
secedit utility, 448
secure channel for a computer
resetting, 372
testing, 371
Secure Sockets Layer (see SSL)
security and authentication, 659–694
AD LDS replication authentication, 832
changing ACL of an object, 680
changing password for ADAM/AD LDS
user, 819
configuring permission inheritance, 678

customizing ACL Editor in ADUC, 676
customizing Delegation of Control Wizard,
671
disabling LDAP signing or encryption, 664
enabling anonymous LDAP access, 665
enabling List Object Access mode, 686
enabling SSL/TLS, 660
enabling strong domain authentication,
685
forcing Kerberos to use TCP, 691
Kerberos logging, 704
managing ADAM/AD LDS permissions,
834
modifying ACL on administrator accounts,
688
modifying default ACL for object class in
schema, 681
modifying default Kerberos settings, 692
NetLogon logging, 701
preventing storage of LM hash of password,
684
resetting object's ACL to default defined in
schema, 683
restricting anonymous access to AD, 667
revoking delegated permissions, 673
using Delegation of Control Wizard, 669
viewing access tokens, 693
viewing ACL for an object, 674
viewing and purging Kerberos tickets, 689
viewing effective permissions on an object,
677
security boundary, forest as, 16
security descriptors
reference domain
determining default for application
partition, 796
setting for application partitions, 794
single instance storage of, 764
Security event log
directory access audit events logged to, 723
sample event logged to, 724
security filter, applying to a GPO, 428
security groups, 315
Security Identifiers (see SIDs)
security principals
in ADAM/AD LDS groups, 826
creating quotas for, 727
finding quota usage for, 734
finding quotas assigned to, 729

protected by AdminSDHolder process, 679

setting default quota for all in partition, 732

security template, importing into a GPO, 433

Selective Authentication for trusts, 66

Server Manager MMC snap-in, 76

    configuring AD FS Web Agent, 859

    enabling SSL/TLS, 661

    installing AD FS on Windows Server 2008, 846

    installing IIS on Windows Server 2008, 842

server objects, 100, 121, 514

    attributes of, 515

    moving to different site, 103

serverless binds, 5

    example for RootDSE in VBScript, 7

servermanagercmd utility, 77

    installing AD FS on Windows Server 2008, 847

    installing AD FS Web Agent in Windows Server 2008, 860

    installing ADAM/AD LDS, 803

    installing Web Server (IIS) role and necessary subcomponents, 843

servers

    application partitions hosted by, 787

    DNS, modifying configuration of, 631

    federation servers, 845

    viewing DNS zones on, 614

Servers container, 121, 514

serversContainer objects, 519

servicePrincipalName attribute, computer objects, 650

services

    finding advertised services for domain controller, 104

set-QADObject cmdlet, 35

SetDsGetDcNameFlags method, 98

setgpopermissions.wsf script, 429

setpwd utility, 748

setup command

    /createunattend switch, 880

    installing first Exchange 2003 Server, 873

Setup.com

    switches for Exchange 2007 installation, 876

    switches preparing AD for Exchange 2007 installation, 870

Setup.com utility

referencing the answer file, 880

switch selecting roles to install, ManagementTools option, 883

switches residing in unattended answer file, 880

shortcut trusts, 52

showInAddressBook attribute, 920

SIDs (Security Identifiers), 69

    enabling SID filtering for trusts, 64

    finding duplicate SIDs in a domain, 69

    restricting domain SIDs in a trust relationship, 66

    well-known SIDs, 669

signing

    disabling LDAP signing, 664

    encrypting LDAP traffic with, 662

single instance storage for security descriptors, 764

site objects, 514

site topology, 513–578, 595

    (see also replication)

    attributes of site toplogy objects, 514

    configuring universal group caching for site, 526

    creating a site, 517

    creating a subnet, 528

    delegating control of a site, 523

    deleting a site, 522

    linking sites in a forest, 519

    listing subnets, 530

    renaming a site, 521

site-link objects

    changing replication interval, 593

    disabling compression of replication traffic, 595

siteLink objects, 519

    attributes of, 515

siteObject attribute, subnet objects, 530, 531

sites

    finding a domain controller's site, 98

    finding domain controllers or GC servers in a site, 119

    moving domain controller to different site, 101

Sites container, 513

sn attribute, changing for renamed user, 265

snapshots

    accessing Active Directory snapshot data, 744

creating snapshot of Active Directory database, 742

mounting Active Directory snapshot, 743

SOM (scope of management), 426

SQL Server, 935

location on same server as ILM server, 938

SRV resource records, 121

Priority or Weight fields, modifying, 123

SSL (Secure Sockets Layer), 659

enabling on IIS Default Web Site on Windows Server 2003 R2, 840

enabling on IIS Default Web Site on Windows Server 2008, 842

encrypting LDAP traffic, 662

SSL/TLS, enabling, 660

SSO (Single Sign-On) web-based solutions, 841

Federated Web SSO, 839

startup/shutdown scripts in GPO, 415

state-based identity management products, 944

STATS LDAP control, 712

sample output on LDAP query, 713

storage group, creating, 921–925

strict replication consistency, 597

stub zones, 609

subnet object matching domain controller subnet, 103

subnet objects, 515

subnets

creating, 528

listing subnets in AD, 530

subtree, nonauthoritative restore, 750

synchronization of data, 945

summary of process, 973

synchronization run profiles, 977

sysocmgr utility, 841

saving AD FS Web Agent unattended file, 860

System Access Control Lists (see SACLs)

System container, trustedDomain object, 64

System State

backing up in Windows Server 2008, 742

backing up using NTBackup utility, 740

System State backup of domain controllers, 83

System.DirectoryServices namespace, 3, 39

systemFlags attribute, crossRef objects, 782

SYSVOL folder, replication of, 708

T

TCP/IP stack, resetting on domain controller, 106

templates

default, defining GPO settings, 412

security template for GPOs, 433

text, replaceable text in examples, 10

third-party PowerShell cmdlets, 3

third-party tools

cmdlets, 3

command-line utilities, 4

Exchange management, 867

tickets, Kerberos, 690

time provider (external), configuring domain controller to use, 107

time service, monitoring of Windows Time Service, 709

timestamps, created and last modified, 202

TLS (Transport Layer Security), 659

(see also SSL/TLS)

encrypting LDAP traffic, 662

token-based applications (see Windows NT token-based applications)

tokenGroups attribute, user object, 730

tokensz utility, 693

tombstone lifetime, 739

modifying for a domain, 774

tombstone objects, 738

attributes of, 739

backup strategy and, 739

expired, logging number of, 766

reanimating, 771

relative weight in quota calculation, 730

searching for, 769

tombStoneLifetime attribute, 599

tools

running with alternate credentials, 4

where to find them, 4

Trace Logs, 717

example summary.txt file for domain controller, 718

tracedmp utility, 718

tracerpt command, 718

Transaction Properties (ILM), 1006

transitive trusts, 16

Transport Layer Security (see TLS)

Tree Delete LDAP control, 223

trustedDomain objects, 64

attributes of, 20

TrustMon WMI provider, 57, 60
trusts
    anatomy of, 20
    configuring forest trust for AD FS to use
            Web SSO with Forest Trust
            configuration, 856
    creating an external trust, 48
    creating shortcut trust between AD
            domains, 52
    creating to a Kerberos realm, 53
    creating transitive trust between AD forests,
            50
    cross-forest trust, 16
    enabling quarantine for, 66
    Federated Web SSO with Forest Trust, 839
    managing selective authentication for, 66
    removing, 62
    resetting, 60
    SID (Security Identifier) filtering for, 64
    transitive trust relationship between
            domains in a forest, 17
    verifying, 58–60
    viewing for a domain, 55–58
TTL settings for dynamic objects, 186

U

UDP fragmentation of Kerberos packets, 692
unattended installation
    creating files for Exchange Server, 879
    Exchange Management tools in Exchange
            Server 2003, 882
unattended promotion or demotion of DCs,
            87
unicodepwd attribute, 291
universal group caching, 344
    enabling for a site, 526
universal groups, 316
unlock utility, 267, 268
up-to-dateness vector, comparing for two
            domain controllers, 579
update command
    /createunattend switch, 880
UPN (userPrincipalName) attribute
    AD logon request in UPN format, 847
    modifying for user, 264
    use in ADAM or AD LDS logon requests,
            848
    using with ADSI and ADO, 9
UPN suffixes, 852, 854

creating for a forest, 311
    modifying or adding new for users in AD
            forest, 857
uPNSuffixes attribute, Partitions container,
            312, 859
user objects, 241
    (see also users)
    applying fine-grained password policy to,
            275
    attributes changed by mailbox-enabling,
            901
    attributes of, 241
    converting between inetOrgPerson objects,
            253
    creating, 245
    tokenGroups attribute, 730
    for trusts, 21, 64
    userAccountControl attribute, 168
userAccountControl attribute, 168
    account status, 279
    ADS_USER_FLAG_ENUM values, 300
    bit flag for disabled account, 281
    disabling password expiration, 296
    making user account immediately available,
            247
    viewing or setting for user account, 299
userProxy objects, 827
users, 241–314
    ADAM/AD LDS
        changing password for, 819
        enabling or disabling ADAM user, 821
        managing ADAM users, 817
        managing group memberships, 825
    adding additional fields to, 70
    changing user's primary group, 285
    copying existing user account, 265
    copying user's group membership to
            another user, 287
    creating computer account for a user, 354–
            359
    creating inetOrgPerson user, 250
    creating larg number of user objects, 248
    delegating control over, 672
    deleting a user, 256
    deleting user's mailbox, 902
    determining last logon time, 303
    effective PSO for, 454
    enabling and disabling user account, 278

enabling or disabling user settings of a GPO, 417

finding disabled users, 279

finding locked-out users, 267

finding passwords nearing expiration, 296

finding users with no recent logons, 306

GPO application to, 439

group membership for, Kerberos authentication and, 694

mail-disabling, 894–897

mail-enabling a user, 888–894

mailbox-enabling a user, 898–902

modifying attribute for several users at once, 255

modifying default display names for users created in ADUC, 244

moving user object to different container or OU, 260

preventing from changing a password, 291

preventing password from expiring, 294

primary group ID, finding for user, 342

protecting user object against accidental deletion, 313

redirecting to alternative OU, 261

removing all group memberships from user, 284

renaming, 263

requiring to change password at next logon, 293

restoring deleted user object and its members, 312

setting account options (userAccountControl), 299

setting password for a user, 290

setting profile attributes, 258

setting user account expiration, 302

troubleshooting account lockout problems, 270

unlocking locked-out user, 268

viewing and modifying permitted logon hours for, 307

viewing domain-wide account lockout and password policies, 271

viewing FGPP in effect for user account, 276

viewing group membership of, 281

viewing objects managed by a user, 309

viewing RODCs caching user's password, 297

Users container, redirection of default OU for new user creation, 263

UTCCodedTime attribute, contributing to Active Directory, 1010

V

variables, defining in VBScript, 9

VBScript, 2

  AD FS

    adding new UPN suffix, 857

    configuring logging for token-based application, 861

  ADAM/AD LDS

    changing user password, 820

    creating groups, 823

    enabling or disabling ADAM user, 822

    listing ADAM object attributes, 828

    listing instances installed on computer, 811

    managing AD LDS replication authentication, 833

    managing ADAM users, 818

    managing application partitions, 814

    managing group membership, 825

    managing organizational units, 816

    stopping or starting an instance, 809

  application partitions

    adding or removing replica server, 783

    delegating control over, 797

    finding in forest, 781

    finding replica servers for, 786

    finding those hosted by a server, 788

    setting replication notification delay, 793

    setting SD reference domain for, 795

  computer objects

    adding or removing for a group, 370

    binding to default container, 383

    changing default computers container, 386

    changing machine account quota, 376

    creating, 353

    creating account for user or group, 355

    deleting, 360

    finding OS of, 380

    finding RODCs caching computer's password, 392

    identifying computer role, 389

    joining to a domain, 361

listing all computer accounts in a
        domain, 387
    modifying attributes, 378
    moving between domains, 366
    moving computer within a domain, 364
    renaming, 368
    resetting, 373
defining variables, 9
DHCP Administrators group, adding
        member to, 656
DIT whitespace information, logging of,
        761
DNS
    adding domain DNS suffix, 650
    clearing DNS cache, 636
    configuring zone transfers, 620
    converting zone to AD-integrated, 617
    creating AD-integrated forward zone,
        612
    creating AD-integrated reverse zone,
        614
    creating and deleting resource records,
        627
    delegating control over AD-integrated
        zone, 625
    enabling DNS debug logging, 640
    enumerating and configuring
        forwarders, 623
    listing zones on a server, 615
    modifying server configuration, 632
    preventing DC from registering certain
        resource records, 646
    preventing DC from registering resource
        records dynamically, 643
    querying resource records, 630
    scavenging, enabling for AD-integrated
        zones, 634
domain controllers
    configuring to use external time service,
        108
    finding closest in a domain, 96
    finding DC or GC servers in a site, 119
    finding for a domain, 95
    finding site for a domain controller, 99
    moving to different site, 102
error checking, 9
Exchange Server
    creating a storage group, 922
    creating address list, 918

creating mailbox store, 925
    listing mailboxes and their sizes, 911
    mail-disabling a user, 895, 903
    mail-enabling a user, 890
    mailbox storage limits, 914
    mailbox-enabling a user, 899
    message tracking, enabling, 930
    moving a mailbox, 906
    starting and stopping Exchange 2003,
        884
forests, domains, and trusts
    adding fields to AD users and computers,
        71
    enumerating domain trusts, 55, 57
    finding all domains in a forest, 29
    finding NetBIOS name of a domain, 31
    raising domain functional level, 37
    raising domain mode to native, 34
    raising forest functional level, 40
    removing trusts, 63
    resetting trusts, 61
    verifying trusts, 59
FSMO role holders, finding, 127, 128
FSMO roles, transferring, 129
Garbage Collection diagnostics logging,
        enabling, 766
garbage collection interval, changing, 765
GCs
    disabling GC requirement for domain
        logon, 125
    enabling or disabling GC for domain
        controller, 114
    finding GC servers in forest, 118
GPOs
    applying security group filter to, 429
    applying WMI filter to, 436
    backing up, 440
    blocking GPO inheritance on an OU,
        424
    copying source GPO into new GPO,
        399
    creating, 398
    deleting, 402
    enabling or disabling user or computer
        settings, 418
    enforcing link settings, 426
    importing settings into, 407
    linking GPO to an OU, 422
    listing GPOs in a domain, 396

listing links for a GPO, 420
restoring from backup, 443
viewing settings of, 404
groups
    adding and removing members, 327
    changing scope or type of group, 332
    creating dynamic group, 338
    creating global security group, 317
    enabling universal group caching, 345
    enumerating direct members, 323
    enumerating nested members, 324
    finding group permissions, 319
    finding user's primary group ID, 342
    granting write access to member
        attribute of, 340
    modifying group attributes, 335
    moving to another domain, 331
    moving within a domain, 328
issues with solutions, 7
LDAP controls and, 148
logging
    dcpromo extended logging, 697
    enabling diagnostics logging, 698
    enabling GPO logging, 701
    enabling Kerberos logging, 704
monitoring
    displaying DNS server statistics, 706
    emailing performance alert to
        administrator, 721
objects
    binding to object GUID, 152
    binding to well-known GUID, 154
    created and modified timestamps, 202
    creating crossRef, 194
    creating dynamic objects, 183
    creating objects, 171
    deleting, 198
    displaying attributes of, 141, 142
    displaying RootDSE attributes, 138
    dynamically linking auxiliary class to an
        object, 181
    listing number of objects matching
        specific criteria, 146
    modifying attributes on, 174, 175
    modifying bit flag attribute, 177
    modifying default LDAP query policy,
        204
    modifying TTL settings of dynamic
        objects, 187

moving to different container or OU,
    189
moving to different domain, 192
paged searching, 162
refreshing dynamic objects, 185
renaming, 196
searching for objects in a domain, 156
searching the global catalog, 159
searching using bitwise filter, 167
online defrag of DIT file, 758
OUs (organizational units)
    assigning or removing manager, 234
    creating, 213
    deleting objects in, 221
    determining number of child objects,
        232
    enumerating contents of, 219
    enumerating OUs in a domain, 215
    finding an OU in a domain, 217
    linking GPO to an OU, 235
    modifying an OU, 230
    moving an OU, 227
    moving objects between OUs, 224
    renaming an OU, 228
    viewing and clearing properties, 230
PRP (Password Replication Policy),
    modifying, 81
quotas, setting default for partition, 733
replication
    comparing up-to-dateness vector for
        domain controllers, 580
    compression on inter-site traffic, 595
    finding conflict objects from, 600
    finding orphaned objects, 602
    forcing between domain controllers,
        586
    listing replication partners of domain
        controller, 604
    listing unreplicated changes between
        domain controllers, 584
    modifying inter-site replication interval,
        594
    modifying intra-site replication delay,
        591
    setting intra-site interval, 589
    strict or loose replication consistency,
        598
    viewing object metadata, 606

running scripts using alternate credentials, 8

schema, enabling or disabling modifications, 461

security and authentication
    configuring permission inheritance, 678
    enabling anonymous LDAP access, 665
    enabling List Object Access mode, 686
    enabling SSL and secure authentication using ADSI, 663
    forcing Kerberos to use TCP, 691
    restricting anonymous access, 668
    viewing ACEs in an ACL, 675

serverless binds, 7

site topology
    creating a site, 517
    creating a subnet, 529
    delegating control of a site, 524
    deleting a site, 522
    enabling universal group caching for site, 526
    listing sites in a forest, 520
    listing subnets, 531
    renaming a site, 521

snapshot data, accessing, 744

tombstone lifetime, modifying for a domain, 774

tombstone quota factor, modifying, 731

users
    changing primary group, 286
    converting user object to inetOrgPerson, 253
    copying existing user account, 265
    copying group membership to another user, 288
    creating inetOrgPerson object, 251
    creating large number of users, 249
    creating UPN suffix for a forest, 311
    creating user accounts, 246
    deleting a user, 257
    displaying group membership of, 282
    displaying password and account lockout policies, 271
    enabling or disabling user account, 278
    finding disabled users in a domain, 280
    finding RODCs caching user password, 298
    last logon time for, 304
    modifying default ADUC display name, 244
    moving user to different container, 261
    preventing from changing a password, 292
    preventing password from expiring, 295
    removing all group memberships from, 284
    renaming a user, 264
    requiring to change password, 294
    setting account expiration, 302
    setting attribute for several users at once, 255
    setting profile attributes, 259
    setting user account options, 299
    setting user's password, 290
    unlocking a locked user, 269
    viewing and modifying permitted logon hours, 307
    viewing user's managed objects, 310

W

W32time service, 107
W32Time Service registry key, 109
w32tm utility, 709
wbadmin utility, 742
    performing nonauthoritative restore, 749
web page for this book, xxii
websites for information and code for this book, 12
well-known GUIDs, 153
    defined by Domain NC, 384
wellKnownObjects attribute, 154
    domainDNS object, 384
whitespace in DIT file, 759, 761
whoami tool, displaying user's group membership, 282
Win32_ComputerSystem::JoinDomainOrWorkGroup method, 363
Win32_ComputerSystem::Rename method, 369
Win32_UserAccount WMI namespace, 344
Windows 2000, 3
    creating a domain, 24
    default GPO restore tool, 449
    preparing domain or forest for Windows Server 2003 upgrade, 42
    renaming of domains, 33
Windows 2000 functional level, 38

Windows command prompt, opening using alternate credentials, 4
Windows NT token-based applications, 855
  configuring AD FS Web Agent for, 860
  enabling auditing for, 861
Windows Script Host (see WSH)
Windows Server 2003, 3
  Administration Tools Pack (adminpak.msi), 882
  checking domain controller readiness for update to, 47
  preparing Windows 2000 domains or forests for upgrade to, 42
  promoting a domain controller, 76
  promoting domain controller from media, 82
  raising functional level of a forest, 39
Windows Server 2003 functional level, 38
Windows Server 2003 R2
  installing AD FS Federation Service, 844
  prerequisites for installing AD FS, 840
Windows Server 2008, 3
  checking domain controller readiness for update to, 47
  fully removing Active Directory forests, 23
  implementing prerequisites for Exchange 2007 SP1 installation, 879
  installing AD FS Federation Service, 846
  installing AD FS prerequisites, 842
  nomenclature changes for Active Directory, 22
  preparing Windows 2000 forests or domains for upgrade to, 42
  promoting a domain controller, 76
  promoting domain controller from media, 84
  raising functional level of a forest, 39
  Server Manager MMC, 77
  servermanagercmd.exe command-line tool, 77
Windows Server 2008 functional level, 38
Windows Support Tools package, 4
Windows Time Service, monitoring, 709
winnt32 utility, checking domain controllers for upgrade readiness, 47
WINS
  finding PDC Emulator FSMO role owner via, 133
  removing all entries for demoted domain controllers, 23
WINS deregistration, 23
Winsock, resetting, 107
WMI (Windows Management Instrumentation)
  applying WMI filter to GPO, 436
  creating a filter, 434
  DNS provider, 612
    WQL query of resource records, 631
  filters, 393
  use with Exchange 2003, 865
  Win32_UserAccount namespace, 344
WMI TrustMon provider, 57, 60
wmic utility, 389, 390
WMIPolicy container, 435
WQL (Windows Query Language), 435
WQL queries
  finding all MicrosoftDNS_Zone objects, 617
  finding matching resource records, 631
WSH (Windows Script Host), 2
  trusts for a domain, 55

X

XMA (Extensible MA for Connectivity), 936

Z

zombie objects, 739
zone files, 610
zone transfers, configuring, 620
zones, DNS, 609, 619
  (see also DNS)

About the Authors

Laura E. Hunter is an architect with the Oxford Computer Group, specializing in Microsoft Identity and Access Management technologies, including Active Directory design and implementation, troubleshooting, and security topics. Laura is a Microsoft MVP for Windows Server-Networking.

Laura's previous experience includes positions as an AD architect for a global engineering firm, IT project leader with the University of Pennsylvania, and the director of computer services for the Salvation Army. She also operates as an independent technical speaker and writer. Laura has a B.A. in American history and an M.A. in computer science from the University of Pennsylvania.

Robbie Allen is an author, entrepreneur, and web industry veteran. He's worked in IT for the last 12 years and runs the popular sports website *http://statsheet.com*. He has authored or coauthored 10 books.

Colophon

The animal on the cover of *Active Directory Cookbook*, Third Edition, is a bluefin tuna (*Thunnus thynnus*), also known as a horse mackerel. It inhabits both the Atlantic and Pacific Oceans in temperate and subtropical waters. The body of a bluefin tuna is a metallic, deep blue on top, while the undersides and belly are silvery white. The first dorsal fin is yellow or blue; the second is red or brown. The rear fin and finlets are yellow, edged with black. The central caudal keel is black.

The bluefin tuna is one of the largest and fastest species of marine fish. An adult can weigh as much as 1,500 pounds (680 kilograms) and can swim up to speeds of 55 miles per hour (88.5 kilometers per hour). A bluefin tuna can swim across the Atlantic Ocean in 40 days. Recent pop-up satellite tracking has revealed that the bluefin tuna can dive to depths greater than 3,000 feet in a matter of minutes and still maintain a body temperature of 77 degrees Fahrenheit (25 degrees Celsius), even in near-freezing water.

Commercial fishing has reduced the stock of bluefin tuna to the extent that a single fish, once caught, can be worth up to $40,000. However, the situation is reversible, and the numbers of tuna could increase if the guidelines of the International Commission for the Conservation of Atlantic Tuna (ICCAT), an intergovernmental fishing organization that oversees tuna, are followed.

The cover image is from the *Dover Pictorial Archive*. The cover font is Adobe ITC Garamond. The text font is Linotype Birka; the heading font is Adobe Myriad Condensed; and the code font is LucasFont's TheSansMonoCondensed.

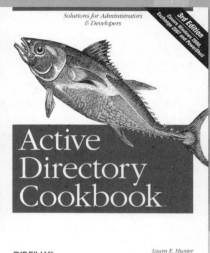